ALEXANDER WATSON

Ring of Steel

Germany and Austria-Hungary at War,
1914–1918

PENGUIN BOOKS

PENGUIN BOOKS

UK I USA I Canada I Ireland I Australia
India I New Zealand I South Africa

Penguin Books is part of the Penguin Random House group of companies
whose addresses can be found at global.penguinrandomhouse.com.

First published by Allen Lane 2014
Published in Penguin Books 2015
004

Set in 8.98/12.17 pt Sabon LT Std
Typeset by Jouve (UK) Milton Keynes
Printed in Great Britain by Clays Ltd, St Ives plc

A CIP catalogue record for this book is available from the British Library

ISBN: 978-0-141-04203-9

www.greenpenguin.co.uk

MIX
Paper from
responsible sources
FSC
www.fsc.org   FSC® C018179

Penguin Random House is committed to a
sustainable future for our business, our readers
and our planet. This book is made from Forest
Stewardship Council® certified paper.

For Ania

Contents

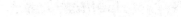

List of Illustrations

List of Maps

Acknowledgements

While writing this book, I have been the beneficiary of many acts of great kindness. My first thanks are to David Stevenson for recommending me to Penguin to write the book, and to Niall Ferguson, who taught me a good deal of what I know about writing history. I am extremely grateful to my editors, Simon Winder and Lara Heimert. Simon approached me with the exciting idea of a history of the war from the Central Powers' perspectives, and ever since my first book proposal he has been a source of inspiration and uplift. From Lara, I received immensely valuable feedback, which greatly improved my manuscript. Both have shown superhuman levels of patience and understanding.

Over the past six years, I have been fortunate to work at three excellent institutions, the University of Cambridge, the University of Warsaw and Goldsmiths, University of London. My colleagues there and in other places have been extremely supportive. I am especially grateful to Bernhard Fulda for many thought-provoking conversations, for his hospitality in Berlin, and above all for reading and giving detailed feedback on the bulk of the manuscript at very short notice. Other friends and colleagues were also generous with their time. Jonathan Gumz, Stephan Lehnstaedt and Richard Grayson all read and provided incisive comments on individual chapters. I owe thanks to Piotr Szlanta for helping me integrate into Warsaw academic life, and to Philipp Stiasny for providing material on films and for always being such a generous and exuberant host whenever I visit Berlin. Anatol Schmied-Kowarzik also kindly sent me material. John Deak taught me how to find my way through the maze of files in the Österreichisches Staatsarchiv, and Tim Buchen pointed me in the direction of valuable sources from Jerusalem. At Goldsmiths, I am extremely grateful to Jan Plamper, Richard Grayson and Stephen Pigney for rescheduling teaching and putting themselves to inconvenience so that I could finish my manuscript. More generally, I wish to thank Heather Jones, Holger Afflerbach, Peter Holquist, Nathaniel Wood, Alan Kramer, John Horne, Jens Boysen, Julia Eichenberg,

Jonathan Boff, Jarosław Centek, Brian Feltman, Tom Weber and Hugo Service for conversations that have helped shape my view of the First World War, and especially the experience of it in east-central Europe. Lastly, I am grateful to those senior colleagues who have supported me at critical moments during the last decade, most especially Sir Hew Strachan, Christopher Clark, Sir Richard Evans, Richard Bessel and Tomasz Kizwalter.

The research for this book could not have been undertaken without support and opportunities offered by funding bodies. A British Academy Postdoctoral Fellowship supported me at Cambridge University between 2008 and 2011, an experience that I value as one of the most exciting and intellectually stimulating of my life. The research funds that came with the Fellowship permitted visits to archives in Poland, Austria and Germany. In 2011–13, I held a 7th European Community Framework Programme Marie Curie Intra-European Fellowship (No. PIEF-GA-2010-274914). The work that I undertook was for a different project, but I still owe the European Commission thanks here. There are few other opportunities for a British academic to spend two years on the other side of Europe, and without this grant it would have been far more difficult to improve my Polish language skills and impossible to gain the same familiarity with Poland's excellent libraries and superlatively organized and stocked archives. I also would not have had the chance to work at Warsaw University's Institute of History, an experience that taught me much and made me a better historian. I am sincerely grateful. Lastly, I thank the Institute of Historical Research in London for a Scouloudi Historical Award. This funded preliminary archival research in 2008.

There are two groups of professionals to whom I owe thanks. The first are archivists. To write this book I used material from archives in five countries. I am extremely grateful to the staff of the Bibliothek für Zeitgeschichte, Stuttgart; the Bundesarchiv Berlin-Lichterfelde; the Bundesarchiv-Militärarchiv Freiburg; the Deutsches Tagebucharchiv, Emmendingen; the Geheimes Staatsarchiv Preußischer Kulturbesitz, Berlin; the Generallandesarchiv Karlsruhe; the Hauptstaatsarchiv Dresden; the Hauptstaatsarchiv Stuttgart; the Hessisches Hauptstaatsarchiv, Wiesbaden; the Österreichisches Staatsarchiv; the Central Archives for the History of the Jewish People, Jerusalem; the Archiwum Archidiecezjalne w Poznaniu; the Archiwum Narodowe w Krakowie; the Archiwum

Państwowe w Katowicach: Oddział w Raciborzu; the Archiwum Państwowe w Olsztynie; the Archiwum Państwowe w Poznaniu; the Archiwum Państwowe w Toruniu; the Biblioteka Narodowa, Warsaw; and the Imperial War Museum and the National Archives in London. Additionally, I would like to thank the ever-friendly and helpful staff of the Archive of Modern Conflict, London; the Museum Historyczne Miasta Krakowa; the Muzeul National Brukenthal, Sibiu; and the Bildarchiv der Österreichischen Nationalbibliothek, Vienna, for providing many of the photographs in this book.

The second group are those people who helped prepare and who produced the book. Rumen Cholakov found and translated Bulgarian source material for me. My agent, Andrew Kidd, was on hand to guide me through the publishing world. At Penguin, Richard Duguid oversaw the production process. I thank the teams at Penguin and Basic Books, especially Marina Kemp and Leah Stecher. I am also very grateful to my copy-editor, Richard Mason, for being so exacting in his corrections of my text.

One of the points this book makes is the importance of family, and I know how lucky I am with my family. My mother and father, Susan and Henry, and my brother Tim have always been an immense support, and I am very grateful for their love and encouragement during the writing of this book. They and the others close to us, Aunt Judy, Peter and Jana, bore with patience and humour the long period in which I was 'finishing' this book. I owe Lindsey and Caley special thanks for their understanding. I am also grateful to my relatives in Poland. Alfred and Wiesia Czogała followed the book's progress with enthusiasm and offered a loving home from home in the south. Wojtek and Marysia Burkiewicz and their sons Mateusz, Michał and Marcin all looked after me during my time in Warsaw.

The last thanks, to my wife and daughter, are most important. My daughter, Maria, arrived in the final months of the writing of this book, and every day of her life brings immense joy and new meaning to mine. To my wife, Ania – I simply could not have written this without you. Thank you for your love, your understanding and your patience, and thank you for keeping a sense of perspective when I was losing mine.

Ania, this book is dedicated with all my love to you.

1. Europe

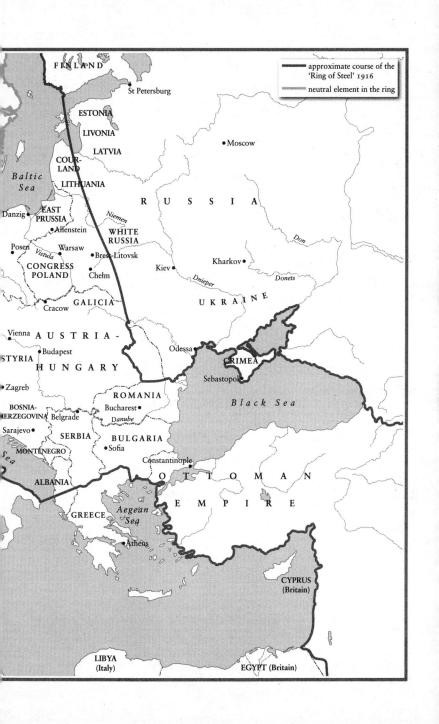

FINLAND

St Petersburg

ESTONIA

LIVONIA

•Moscow

LATVIA

COUR-
LAND

*Baltic
Sea*

LITHUANIA

Danzig•

EAST
PRUSSIA

Niemen

R U S S I A

•Allenstein

WHITE
RUSSIA

Don

Posen
•

Warsaw
•

Vistula

•Brest-Litovsk

Kharkov•

CONGRESS
POLAND

Chełm

Kiev•

Dnieper

Donets

GALICIA

U K R A I N E

•Cracow

Vienna•

A U S T R I A -

Odessa•

CRIMEA

STYRIA

•Budapest

H U N G A R Y

Sebastopol•

Black   Sea

•Zagreb

ROMANIA

BOSNIA-
HERZEGOVINA

Bucharest•

Belgrade

Danube

Sarajevo•

SERBIA

BULGARIA

MONTENEGRO

•Sofia

Sea

Constantinople

O   T   T   O   M   A   N

ALBANIA

E   M   P   I   R   E

GREECE

*Aegean
Sea*

•Athens

CYPRUS
(Britain)

LIBYA
(Italy)

EGYPT (Britain)

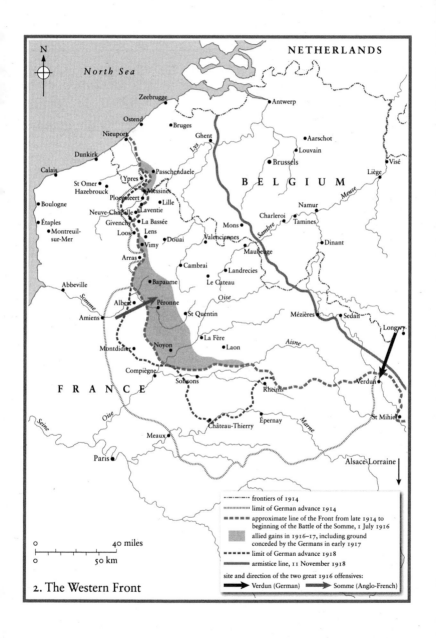

N

North Sea

NETHERLANDS

Zeebrugge

Antwerp

Ostend
Bruges
Aarschot
Louvain

Nieuport
Ghent
Lys
Dunkirk
Visé

Calais
Brussels
Liège

St Omer
Ypres
Passchendaele
BELGIUM

Hazebrouck
Messines
Meuse

Boulogne
Ploegsteert
Lille

Neuve-Chapelle
Laventie
Namur

Étaples
Givenchy
La Bassée
Charleroi

Montreuil-
Loos
Lens
Mons
Tamines

sur-Mer
Vimy
Douai
Valenciennes
Dinant

Arras
Sambre
Maubeuge

Abbeville
Cambrai
Landrecies

Somme
Bapaume
Le Cateau

Albert
Péronne
Oise

Amiens
St Quentin
Mézières
Sedan

Montdidier
La Fère
Longwy

Noyon
Laon
Aisne

Compiègne
Soissons
Rheims
Verdun

FRANCE
Oise
St Mihiel

Seine
Château-Thierry
Épernay
Marne

Meaux

Paris
Alsace-Lorraine

·–··–··–·	frontiers of 1914
··············	limit of German advance 1914
▬ ▬ ▬	approximate line of the Front from late 1914 to beginning of the Battle of the Somme, 1 July 1916
(shaded)	allied gains in 1916–17, including ground conceded by the Germans in early 1917
- - - - -	limit of German advance 1918
▬▬▬▬	armistice line, 11 November 1918

site and direction of the two great 1916 offensives:

→ Verdun (German)   → Somme (Anglo-French)

0 ———————— 40 miles

0 ———————— 50 km

2. The Western Front

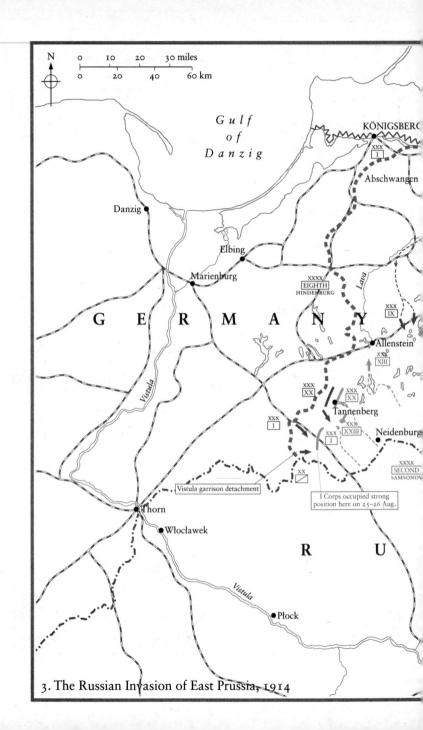

N

| 0 | 10 | 20 | 30 miles |

| 0 | 20 | 40 | 60 km |

*Gulf
o f
D a n z i g*

KÖNIGSBERG

XXX
I

Abschwangen

Danzig

Elbing

Marienburg

XXXX
EIGHTH
HINDENBURG

Lava

XXX
IX

G   E   R   M   A   N   Y

Allenstein

XXX
XIII

XXX
XX

XXX
XX

Vistula

Tannenberg

XXX
I

XXX
XXIII

Neidenburg

XXX
I

XX

Vistula garrison detachment

I Corps occupied strong
position here on 25–26 Aug.

XXXX
SECOND
SAMSONOV

R   U

Thorn

Włocławek

Vistula

Płock

3. The Russian Invasion of East Prussia, 1914

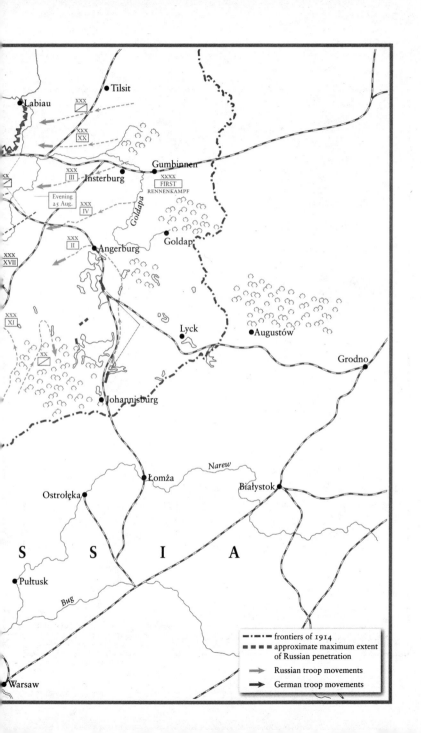

Tilsit

Labiau

XXX

XXX
XX

Gumbinnen

XXX
III

Insterburg

XXXX
FIRST
RENNENKAMPF

XX

Evening
25 Aug.

XXX
IV

Goldapa

Goldap

XXX
II

Angerburg

XXX
XVII

XXX
XI

Lyck

Augustów

XX

Grodno

Johannisburg

Narew

Łomża

Białystok

Ostrołęka

S   S   I   A

Pułtusk

Bug

Warsaw

—·—·— frontiers of 1914
▪ ▪ ▪ approximate maximum extent
        of Russian penetration

→ Russian troop movements
→ German troop movements

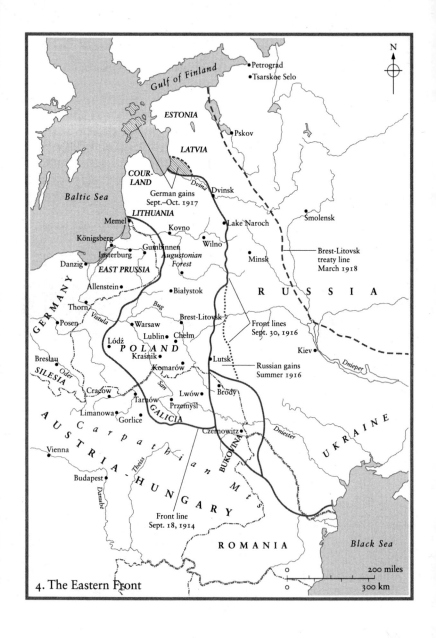

4. The Eastern Front

5. The Balkans

Salonika front line, November 1914
Salonika front line, August–September 1918

6. Ober Ost and Poland

Introduction

*The World War of 1914–18 was utterly unlike most former
wars ... it was a war for existence, a war of the people in the
fullest sense.*

Erich Ludendorff[1]

The First World War has long been recognized as the twentieth century's
'great seminal catastrophe'.[2] Seventy million men were mobilized to
fight over the four years and four months that it raged. Nearly ten
million people were killed. Communities were destroyed, populations
displaced. Hatred, bitterness and grief consumed the belligerents. East-
central Europe was the epicentre of this disaster. Germany and
Austria-Hungary, the two states spread across the region, were the conflict's instigators and its losers. Together, they suffered one-third of all
the war's dead.[3] No other societies sacrificed more or lost so much. If
the 1914–18 conflict was indeed the cause of the evils that would later
beset Europe, totalitarian dictatorship, another world war and genocide, this was first of all because it so profoundly changed the societies
of central Europe. The key to the tragic course of the continent's modern history lies in this region, and in the extraordinary exertion,
unredeemed sacrifices and physical and moral displacement undergone
by its peoples in 1914–18.

This book is the first modern history to narrate the Great War from
the perspectives of the two major Central Powers, Germany and
Austria-Hungary. It seeks to understand the conflict through their
statesmen's eyes. Above all, however, it is the story of their peoples.
Whether civilians standing in the food queues of Vienna and Berlin,

soldiers embroiled in the bloody fighting on the Somme or at the Brusilov offensive, or sailors engaged in tense underwater warfare, their fears, desires and ordeals lie at the heart of this account. The peoples were central to this conflict. The First World War's dynamism and transformative potential derived in large part from its nature as a *Volkskrieg* – a 'People's War'. For conservative statesmen like the German Chancellor Theobald von Bethmann Hollweg, perturbed by the demise of the old cabinet wars with limited goals and casualties, what defined this new and frightening struggle, its 'most miraculous feature', was 'the immense power of the people'.[4] Popular commitment fuelled the war's violence and determined its duration. The Central Powers mobilized their populations on a scale unrivalled in Europe. In Germany, 13,387,000 men, an astonishing 86 per cent of the country's entire male population between eighteen and fifty years old, passed through the armed forces between 1914 and 1918. Austria-Hungary stood only a little behind with eight million soldiers, around 78 per cent of its military-aged manpower.[5]

The war experience of the Central Powers was determined by their strategic situation. Germany and Austria-Hungary, together with their allies, Bulgaria and the Ottoman Empire, were trapped during hostilities within a ring of steel. Encircling them was a vastly superior enemy coalition. To the east lay Russia. In the north, west and south were Britain, France, Italy, later the United States, and a host of smaller nations. By war's end, these enemies controlled 61 per cent of the globe's territory, 64 per cent of its pre-war gross domestic product, and comprised 70 per cent of its population.[6] The Central Powers were isolated from neutral trade. A British naval blockade, tightened ever more ruthlessly as the war continued, closed the ring. Central Europeans imagined themselves as barricaded and besieged within a great fortress. The millions of men called up were needed to keep out the enemy. Yet this siege warfare on a massive scale drew in entire societies. Total mobilization and blockade blurred the distinction between combatant and non-combatant. Not only the young, fit and single, but husbands, fathers, the middle-aged and frequently even the infirm fought this war. At home, women took over their conscripted men's jobs or migrated into the booming armaments factories. Children were mobilized to help with the harvest and collect valuables for the war effort. These civilians, far from being mere auxiliaries, became targets, and were ravaged by deprivation, malnutrition, sickness and exhaustion. Not just soldiers fighting on the battlefields but also their families struggling to survive at home found that war soon permeated every aspect of their daily lives. To contemporaries, whether in Europe's major metropolises or its under-modernized rural backwaters, the conflagration appeared terrifyingly all-encompassing, unceasing, expansive. Eight months into hostilities, a Pole living on the Austrian side of the Eastern Front succinctly captured the ubiquity of the horror that had spread across the continent: 'war on land, in the ground, on water, under water and in the air; war encompassing ever greater circles of Humanity.'[7]

Why did the peoples of Austria-Hungary and Germany hold out for so long in the face of terrible hardship and against dreadful odds? Their determination is all the more baffling as few historians today doubt the great culpability borne by their leaders in starting the conflagration or in pursuing aggressive war aims. In part, the peoples had no choice. At the outbreak of war armies in central Europe were granted extraordinary powers over domestic society. States and militaries had effective tools of repression with which they imposed censorship, restrictions on public gatherings and in some places martial law to enforce compliance.[8] Yet as an explanation for the long duration of peoples' readiness to fight, endure and sacrifice, coercion is far from satisfactory. Both Austria-Hungary and Germany were *Rechtsstaaten*, 'states of law', which during the half century before the First World War had guaranteed their subjects' basic freedoms and fostered educated civil societies.[9] While rights were suspended at the outset of hostilities, civil society's mentalities and institutions persisted, and proved indispensable in underpinning a successful mobilization. In Germany, it was recognized early that a European conflict involving mass conscript armies and requiring the near-total mobilization of industry and agriculture could not be conducted against the will of the people. Austrian leaders who at first attempted to suppress public opinion had found to their cost by the end of 1916 that authoritarianism merely increased resentment and resistance. Both of the major Central Powers granted more, not less, space for public expression in the last two years of hostilities, even as discontent mounted. Persuasion was at a premium, and propaganda, the dark art of guiding opinion, became ever more important. Ideas able to inspire the masses were turned into powerful weapons of war.[10]

This book's central argument is that popular consent was

indispensable in fighting the twentieth century's first 'total war'. It recounts how the German and Austro-Hungarian peoples supported, tolerated or submitted to the conflict, and how participation changed them and their societies. Three themes run through the pages of this book. First, it explores how consent for war was won and maintained in Austria-Hungary and Germany. It shows that mobilization was never simply an order from state to subject. Rather, the institutions of civil society, local officials, political activists, the Church, trade unions and charities mediated and managed an astounding self-mobilization, taking their communities to war in 1914–15. The account explores how, when popular commitment to victory sagged in 1916–18, increasingly sophisticated propaganda was used to underpin resilience by shaping soldiers' and civilians' understandings of the war. It also scrutinizes for the first time the fears, ambitions, prejudices and grievances of Germans and Austro-Hungarians, and seeks to explain what they saw to be at stake in the conflict. The book demonstrates that the war's hardships and horrors not only undermined but could also strengthen resolve to fight on and endure. Fear and anger, both justified and exaggerated, towards enemy belligerents proved to be powerful mobilizing emotions, lasting up to and well beyond 1918.

Second, the book explains how extreme and escalating violence during 1914–18 radicalized German and Austro-Hungarian war aims and actions, and it explores the consequences of this radicalization for those societies and their war efforts. At the outbreak of hostilities, both the populations and – notwithstanding their aggressive actions – governments were united in a defensive consensus. However, initial expectations that the conflict would be brief and purely military in nature were thwarted by the failure of any belligerent to win a decisive victory in the opening campaigns. The onset of a British naval blockade of doubtful legality under international law, which defined food as 'contraband', threatened the civilian populations of the Central Powers with starvation and exposed their extreme vulnerability to economic attack. The book shows how, a quarter of a century before Hitler's slave empire, Germany and Austria-Hungary responded with a ruthless exploitation of the food and human labour in the territories they had occupied in the east and west. The new economic warfare encouraged German and Austro-Hungarian governing elites, parts of which had already harboured imperialist aspirations, to see their states' future security and stability as dependent on maintaining permanent control of these foreign resources. Official war aims expanded greatly, as German military and business elites in particular developed ambitions to build an empire in the east. These aspirations clashed with the wider population's commitment to defend only pre-war borders and its hopes for a quick peace that would end the hardship. A crisis of state legitimacy resulted, and ultimately the people withdrew their consent, precipitating political collapse and the war's end.

The book's third theme is the tragic societal fragmentation caused by the First World War, a break-up which not only preceded and precipitated political collapse, but persisted even after state order had been resurrected in central Europe. This fragmentation took different forms in Germany and Austria-Hungary, for whereas the former was a nation state, the latter was a multinational empire. In Austria-Hungary, policy-makers had commenced hostilities in 1914 in part as a desperate remedy for endemic peacetime nationality disputes which they feared might tear the Empire apart. Initially, their gamble appeared effective, as the peoples rallied to the flag. However, already at its opening the conflict exacerbated national feelings and enmities, which were further inflamed by the military persecution of 'suspicious' ethnic groups, floods of unwelcome refugees from the eastern and southern borderlands, food shortages, and nationalist propaganda by exiles allied to the enemy powers. As the Habsburg state increasingly lost its legitimacy and wartime hardship worsened, people retreated into their national communities. Even before the state was formally dissolved, its multi-ethnic societies had already collapsed into violence, with Jews becoming a particular target. In Germany too, wartime shortages exacerbated anti-Semitism and in the ethnically mixed eastern borderlands, racial conflict. However, as a largely homogeneous nation state, its society fragmented principally along lines of class. These class tensions were supercharged from 1917 by growing calls for annexation from the right and, on the left, the ideology of the two Russian revolutions. The divisions widened further after defeat, spawning civil war and new parties of the far left and radical right.

General Erich Ludendorff, the man who managed Germany's war effort in 1916–18, was right to characterize the struggle as 'a war of the people in the fullest sense'. The great emotional and material investment of the German and Austro-Hungarian peoples not only made possible the sustained struggle of the Central Powers, but also ensured that defeat, when it came, would have a catastrophic impact on their societies. The internal divisions that had developed during the war shaped the chaos at its end: in Germany, left-wing revolution brought down the government. In Austria-Hungary, defeat was accompanied by ethnic violence and fragmentation into new, national states. Peace brought only a fragile respite. Across the region, war had impoverished the people, torn apart multi-ethnic communities and destroyed faith in state structures. Bitterness at unredeemed sacrifice, stark ideological divisions, racial hatreds and a new readiness to exert violence remained. A dark future awaited central Europe.

I

Decisions for War

THE CONSPIRATORS

'We began the war, not the Germans and still less the Entente – that I know.' With this admission, Baron Leopold von Andrian-Werburg, a member of the tight-knit group of young diplomats influential in shaping Austria-Hungary's foreign policy in the last years of peace, began his memoir of July 1914. Andrian, at the time the Habsburg Consul-General in Warsaw, had been on leave in Vienna during the tense weeks after the assassination on 28 June 1914 in Sarajevo of Austria-Hungary's heir to the throne, Archduke Franz Ferdinand, and his wife, Sophie, Duchess of Hohenberg, by Bosnian Serb terrorists. He was called into the Habsburg Foreign Ministry on 9 July to advise on Russia's probable reaction to aggressive action against Serbia, the country that government circles believed was behind the crime. Looking back four years later, a chastened but unrepentant man, Andrian described the strange, conspiratorial euphoria he encountered at the Ministry. Count Alek Hoyos, the thirty-six-year-old *chef de cabinet* at the centre of the group, who was later driven almost to suicide by the thought that he was, as he told a confidante guiltily in 1916, 'the real initiator of the war', had greeted him jovially.[1] 'We must let Andrian in on the secret,' he had exclaimed. 'A totally new epoch' was being prepared. Serbia was 'to eat humble pie'. After years of isolation, provocation and humiliation, the venerable Habsburg Empire would no longer stand by passively as predators encircled it. All the young diplomats agreed, and their political masters also believed, that the threat was mortal and time was short. Fear and desperation paved the way for a reckless elation as Habsburg leaders resolved finally to lash out decisively and violently by initiating war in the Balkans.[2]

The First World War was begun by small ruling elites. Their peoples were not consulted. Mutual suspicion, brinkmanship, arrogance, belligerence and, above all, fear were rife in the halls of power across Europe in the summer of 1914. Yet Austria-Hungary's leaders were exceptional, for they alone actively planned from early July 1914 to take their country to war. The conflict that they wanted in the aftermath of the Sarajevo assassinations was a Balkan rather than a world war, and they went about provoking it with startlingly single-minded determination. The Austro-Hungarian Foreign Minister, Count Leopold von Berchtold, a sensitive man whose true passions were for art and horses rather than politics and who had not previously been known for forcefulness, was the prime mover in these machinations. The aggressive young diplomats under him and the Habsburg military urged him on. On the afternoon of 30 June, two days after the murders, he visited Emperor Franz Joseph. The eighty-three-year-old monarch had not been close to his murdered nephew, but Berchtold found him shocked and grieving. Together, they agreed that the time for a 'policy of patience' was past. A tougher approach towards Serbia was now needed.[3]

The network of alliances and balance of power in Europe in 1914 made any Austro-Hungarian attack on Serbia, diplomatic or military, fraught with peril. Habsburg relations with Serbia had in fact been hostile since a nationalist military coup had placed the Karadjordjević dynasty on its throne in 1903. The new government and its officials had not only shaken the country free of its status as a Habsburg satellite but had gone on to support, sometimes covertly and at other times more overtly, Greater Serbia agitation intended to tear from the multi-ethnic Empire its South Slav provinces. Colonel Dragutin Dimitrijević, the powerful head of military intelligence and founder of the secret revolutionary society Ujedinjenje ili smrt! (Union or Death!), sponsored terrorism in Habsburg Bosnia and Croatia, and although Austro-Hungarian investigators did not know it, he was the organizer of the plot to murder Archduke Franz Ferdinand in 1914.[4] However, the small kingdom of Serbia was backed by the might of Russia, the Habsburg Empire's main competitor in the Balkans. Russia was tightly tied by alliance to France and, since 1907, more loosely to Great Britain in a 'Triple Entente'. Any dispute between the Empire and Serbia would quickly draw in these great powers. Berchtold knew that to have a free hand against the country he believed – firm proof was still lacking – had plotted the Austrian heir's death, he needed to bring in the Germans, the Habsburg Empire's sole reliable ally and Europe's premier military power, as co-conspirators. Alek Hoyos was sent to Berlin on 5 July to seek their support, carrying two documents. The first was a letter from Franz Joseph addressed to Kaiser Wilhelm II. Composed in the Habsburg Foreign Office, it warned that Serbia's 'criminal agitation' must not go 'unpunished'. The second was a memorandum offering a gloomy assessment of the Central Powers' strategic situation. Written by a senior Foreign Office section chief, Baron Franz Matscheko, at Berchtold's order just before the Sarajevo assassinations, it had been hurriedly redrafted in their aftermath with a more belligerent tone and reframed to appeal to German anxieties. The slipping Habsburg influence in the Balkans and the need to align more closely with Bulgaria instead of the Central Powers' secret and unreliable ally, Romania, were stressed. So too was the Franco-Russian alliance's growing assertiveness; a cause of acute worry to Berlin. A postscript warned of the intense danger of a 'greater Serbian agitation that will stop short of nothing' and, hinting at violence, advocated strong action. Neither document mentioned war overtly, because although Berchtold was determined, the Emperor was not yet irrevocably fixed on this course and Count Tisza, the powerful Minister President of Hungary, whose views could not be ignored, was opposed. The choice of Hoyos, an outspoken advocate of war with excellent connections in Berlin, was Berchtold's means of circumventing their doubts. The hawkish *chef de cabinet* would ensure the Germans understood that the Habsburg administration was set on war.[5]

The Germans received Hoyos's message positively. Kaiser Wilhelm had been a close friend of Franz Ferdinand and was outraged by his death. The Kaiser's view, scribbled furiously on a report filed by his ambassador in Vienna two days after the murders, was that 'the Serbs must be disposed of, and that right soon!'[6] On 5 July he lunched with the Habsburg ambassador, Count Szögyényi, who had been briefed by Hoyos, and was given the letter and memorandum. After reading the documents, the Kaiser offered his 'full support', although with the reservation that he must also talk to his Chancellor, Theobald von Bethmann Hollweg.[7] The next day, Szögyényi and Hoyos met Bethmann and were told, as the diplomats reported to Vienna, 'whatever way we decide, we may always be certain that we will find Germany at our side'.[8] With this infamous 'blank cheque', Germany's leaders had offered the diplomatic support essential to permit a Habsburg attack on Serbia, and opened the way for the international crisis at the end of the month. Crucially, they did so in the full knowledge that it could provoke, as Wilhelm II remarked after reading Franz Joseph's letter, 'a serious European complication'. The German Undersecretary for Foreign Affairs, Arthur Zimmermann, with whom Hoyos had lunched on 5 July, even estimated the risk at '90 per cent for a European war, if you undertake something against Serbia'.[9] However, once Wilhelm met with the Chancellor, Zimmermann and his military advisers later that afternoon, these concerns faded. Both the Chancellor and the War Minister, Erich von Falkenhayn, doubted that the Austro-Hungarians were in reality serious and the leaders agreed that even if their ally did act decisively, Russia would not intervene.[10] The Germans now simply handed all initiative to Vienna. The Chancellor emphasized in his meeting with Hoyos and Szögyényi on 6 July that the decision on how to proceed lay entirely with Austria-Hungary. The only preference he expressed was that if military action were considered necessary, it should be initiated sooner rather than later.[11]

The Germans' response strengthened Berchtold's hand when the Common Ministerial Council, the closest thing Austria-Hungary had to a cabinet, met on 7 July. Berchtold, who chaired the session, pushed from the beginning for 'a show of force [that] might put an end to Serbia's intrigues once and for all'. The Austrian Minister President Count Stürgkh and the Empire's finance and war ministers, Leon Biliński and Alexander von Krobatin, all favoured war with Serbia. The sole dissenter remained the Hungarian Minister President. While Tisza was able to veto an immediate strike on Serbia, this was a hollow victory, for the Habsburg army had granted so many soldiers harvest leave that summer that such an attack was anyway an impossibility. He suggested an ultimatum be sent instead, and conceded that the demands 'should be hard'. Berchtold, however, in summing up the meeting, put his own belligerent spin on what had been agreed. While acknowledging 'the differences of opinion', he insisted that 'still an agreement had been arrived at, since the propositions of the Hungarian Premier would in all probability lead to a war with Serbia, the necessity of which he and all the other members of the Council had understood and admitted'.[12] The Habsburg Foreign Minister could be certain that war would result, for the task of drawing up the ultimatum lay with his ministry, even if the Council would afterwards check it. Berchtold was quite open about his intention to phrase the ultimatum so as to incite a war: he told the German ambassador frankly on 10 July that he was 'considering what demands could be put that would be wholly impossible for the Serbs to accept'. His instructions to the Empire's ambassador to Serbia, Baron von Giesl, who was in Vienna on the day of the Council and came to him after it ended, had been even blunter: 'however the Serbs react – you must break off relations and leave. It must come to war.'[13]

The most disconcerting characteristic of Habsburg leaders' decision-making process is the ease with which they contemplated war. Just a week and a half after Franz Ferdinand's assassination, the military and all the civilian ministers except Tisza were advocating the invasion of Serbia; indeed, most had already decided in favour of it on hearing of the murders.[14] Disregard the fact that not until 13 July, six days after the key Common Ministerial Council meeting, did the investigator tasked with establishing Belgrade's involvement in the plot report, and that he could show at most a vague 'moral culpability', not complicity or responsibility on the part of the Serbian government.[15] Put aside too the doubtful ethics of launching a war, even a short one, with all its attendant suffering and loss of innocent lives in response to the murder of one royal couple. Purely in terms of power politics, an invasion of Serbia was an extraordinarily dangerous decision because it risked provoking Russia, whose standing army was three times the size of that maintained by Austria-Hungary.[16] Berchtold knew that Serbia's humiliation would matter deeply to the eastern colossus, for he told Franz Joseph gleefully on 14 July that it would strike 'a blow to Russian prestige in the Balkans'.[17] The ministers too were aware of the risks, for they had invited Franz Conrad von Hötzendorf, Chief of the General Staff, to discuss his war plans at their meeting a week earlier. Conrad had told them that if Russia intervened after war with Serbia had begun, he could switch the Habsburg army's deployment to counter it providing that he knew no later than the fifth day of mobilization. He was confident, although it is unclear whether he stated this explicitly at the meeting, that with Germany's help he could beat Serbia and Russia. Yet much of what he did say should have concerned the ministers. He dispelled the delusion that the Habsburg Empire's north-eastern frontier could be protected by Germany alone, while its own army fought the Serbs in the south. He warned that parts of the Empire's border province of Galicia might be invaded in the initial stages of the campaign. In the worst, although fortunately unlikely, scenario that the Empire had to face Romania and Montenegro, as well as Serbia and Russia, the chance of victory was, the Chief of the General Staff judged, 'not favourable'.[18]

Disregarding the great risk, Habsburg leaders now advanced their preparations for war in great secrecy. They were driven by a fearful urgency; as Berchtold told his colleagues on 7 July, the Empire had 'no time'. Inaction, not armed conflict, appeared to pose the greatest existential threat. Even Tisza, who came round to advocating war on 14 July, admitted that 'the noose has already been placed around our neck and if we do not cut it away now, it would have strangled us at a more appropriate time'.[19] Yet although Austria-Hungary's ministers, soldiers and Emperor had reached consensus, they could not confront Serbia immediately. Two issues forced a delay. First, the army was not ready. This was ironic, for Conrad had long been the most belligerent of Habsburg leaders. Since becoming Chief of Staff in 1906, he had called repeatedly for preventative war against Serbia, Montenegro, Russia and even Romania and Italy, which were allies of the Empire. Berchtold wryly paraphrased his advice after the Sarajevo murders as 'War! War! War!'[20] However, the Habsburg army, as already noted, had allowed its men home on harvest leave during the summer, and although Conrad had stopped further leave being granted just before the 7 July meeting, he could not recall the thousands of soldiers already released without alerting Europe to the Empire's belligerent intentions. Thus, no military action could start before 25 July, the date on which the men were scheduled to return. The second reason to delay was the state visit to St Petersburg, the Russian capital, of French President Raymond Poincaré and Prime Minister René Viviani between 20 and 23 July. For reasons of diplomatic etiquette and on the Machiavellian rationale that it would be advantageous if the two allies had no opportunity to coordinate a response, Habsburg leaders decided to wait until the French leaders departed before presenting their ultimatum to Serbia.[21]

The last Common Ministerial Council of peace met discreetly at Berchtold's home on 19 July. The ministers came in unmarked vehicles, just one of many precautions they had taken to preserve secrecy. Already five days earlier, Conrad and War Minister Krobatin had ostentatiously taken leave in order to present the impression that no military action was planned. The Viennese and Budapest press, whose sharp exchanges with Serbian papers gloating over the royal murders had increased tension, had been asked to avoid discussion of Serbia. The ministers wanted to take Europe by surprise and forestall any attempt at mediation or deterrence.[22] At this meeting, the ministers approved the ultimatum, which had been painstakingly drafted by Berchtold's young advisers in the Foreign Ministry. The tone of this document was dignified but wrathful, its demands were firm. The preamble gravely accused the Serbian state of tolerating 'a subversive movement ... whose ultimate aim is to disjoin certain portions from the territory of Austria-Hungary'. The state thus bore moral guilt, for its inaction had permitted 'a series of attempts at murder and ... murders', culminating in the assassinations of 28 June. The ultimatum demanded that the Serb government should publish in the official press verbatim a humiliating repudiation of all strivings aimed at the separation of territory from Austria-Hungary, and a warning that officials and others who persisted with this policy would be punished with 'great severity.' It then elaborated ten further points on which action was required. The first four ordered the suppression of purveyors of propaganda against the Empire, including the Serb nationalist society Narodna Odbrana (Serbian National Defence) to which the assassins were linked. Points 7 and 8 insisted on the arrest of Serbian officials who had aided them and point 9 insisted that the Serb government explain why some of its functionaries had spoken 'in hostile terms' about Austria-Hungary after the murders of 28 June. Point 10 was merely a command that Serbia confirm promptly that all the other demands had been met. The most controversial points were 5 and 6, which broke a taboo by impinging on Serb sovereignty. Point 5 wanted consent for Austrian officials to participate in the suppression of Serbian conspiratorial movements. Point 6, which had been added specifically to make the memorandum unacceptable, insisted that Austrian officials would take part in a judicial inquiry on Serbian territory against all the co-conspirators of the assassins. The Serbs were permitted just forty-eight hours to respond, and Ambassador Giesl was instructed verbally to demand unconditional acceptance, with the threat that any other answer would lead to an immediate break in relations.[23]

The ultimatum was a tool designed solely to provoke war. True, it can be argued that Austria-Hungary could ensure Serbia's full compliance only by imposing its own officials and that there were good reasons not to trust the troublesome Balkan state.[24] Yet Berchtold had repeatedly made clear during July that the ultimatum was written to be rejected.

Giesl in Belgrade was sent strict instructions on how to break off relations. In an attempt to localize the coming conflict, an official explanation of the Habsburg standpoint was drawn up for the other great powers.[25] How effective this would be, however, was already cast into doubt on 21 July, the day that the Emperor approved the ultimatum, the last step needed before its delivery. Despite all precautions, rumour that a harsh note was in preparation had leaked and reached first the Russians and through them French statesmen's ears. That evening, the Austro-Hungarian ambassador in St Petersburg telegrammed Berchtold that France's President Poincaré had asked what Austria-Hungary's demands to Serbia would be and warned that a government could be held responsible for an action only if hard proof could be provided. If Austria-Hungary had no such proof, he had admonished menacingly, it should remember that Serbia 'has friends' and that 'through this would arise a dangerous situation for peace'.[26] The information was of no consequence; the Habsburg Foreign Minister was not to be intimidated or diverted from his course. Yet at 6 p.m. on 23 July 1914, when the Serb government was finally confronted with the ultimatum, it was already likely that Austria-Hungary would get a war, but one much larger than that for which its leaders had hoped or planned.

WAR OF EXISTENCE

The actions of Austro-Hungarian rulers in the summer of 1914, although secretive and aggressive, were motivated less by belligerence than a profound sense of weakness, fear and even despair. Their multi-ethnic Empire had a history stretching over nearly four hundred years. It had seen off the Ottoman Sultan, outlasted Napoleon and survived religious struggle and revolution, but by the early twentieth century it appeared to many statesmen both inside and beyond that its days were numbered. Even Germany's Foreign Secretary, Gottlieb von Jagow, a man representing the only solid friend that the Empire had in the world, referred to it unflatteringly in July 1914 as 'that ever increasingly disintegrating composition of nations beside the Danube'.[27] As Habsburg leaders well knew, others were much less kind. A strong warning about the sort of comments being passed in diplomatic circles had been sent to them by their ambassador in their ally Romania, Count Ottokar Czernin, just six days before Franz Ferdinand's assassination. 'The firm conviction has grown here, as in many other parts of Europe, that the Monarchy is an entity doomed to downfall and dissolution,' the ambassador observed. The chatter was that 'in the near future the Habsburg Monarchy will be put up to European auction'.[28]

Why did Austria-Hungary's situation appear so grim in 1914? And why were Habsburg leaders so determined to cow their small, troublesome neighbour Serbia, even at the cost of unleashing a disastrous European conflagration? The Empire's domestic troubles provide part of the answer. Franz Joseph's multi-ethnic realm, home to eleven recognized nationalities, had last undergone major reorganization in 1867, when in the aftermath of the 1848 revolutions and two lost wars in 1859 and 1866 the Emperor had finally succumbed to pressure and agreed a new 'Dualist' system. Under what became known as the 'Compromise' between the Crown, Austrian German and Hungarian Liberals, the Empire had been divided into two largely autonomous states, Austria in the west and Hungary in the east, held together both constitutionally and in personal union through Franz Joseph, who was King of Hungary and Emperor of Austria. The Monarch appointed three Common Ministers, one for War, another for Foreign Affairs and the third for Finance, to manage areas of joint interest. The separate Austrian and Hungarian governments were each headed by a Minister President, who was also named by the Monarch but could rule only with the cooperation of the states' elected legislative assemblies, the Austrian Reichsrat and the Hungarian House of Representatives. Once a year, the assemblies sent executive committees, the Delegations, to confer with each other and with the Common Ministers. Every ten years, major negotiations took place to set the 'quota', the percentage that each state would pay towards common expenses, to agree on economic matters of shared interest, such as tariffs and some indirect taxes, and to settle on the percentage of recruits that each would provide to the Common Army. The three Common Ministers and two Minister Presidents, as well as the heir to the throne before his assassination, all had seats in the Common Ministerial Council, which met periodically to discuss important issues pertaining to the whole Empire and which had plotted war in July 1914.[29]

This structure was designed to keep Crown control in the key areas of foreign policy and the army while satisfying the political aspirations of the two most influential and assertive peoples in the Empire, the

Austrian Germans and the Magyars. Both had become the largest groups in their respective halves through the reorganization (see Table 1).

In addition, an Ottoman territory, Bosnia-Herzegovina, had fallen under Habsburg administration in 1878 and had been permanently annexed in 1908. In order not to upset the delicate ethnic balance, it was kept outside the main Dualist structure of the Empire and run by the Common Finance Minister. It was effectively a colony, in which the Habsburgs pursued what they regarded as a cultural mission. By introducing professional administration, education and improvements

Table 1. Peoples in the Habsburg Empire (by territory), 1910

Ethnicity	Percentage of Population in Territory
Cisleithanian Austria (territory):	
Germans	35.6
Czechs (including Slovaks)	23.0
Poles	17.8
Ruthenes	12.6
Serbo-Croats	2.8
Italians	2.8
Romanians	1.0
Hungarian Crown Lands (territory):	
Magyars (i.e. Hungarians)	48.1
Romanians	14.1
Germans	9.8
Slovaks	9.4
Croats	8.8
Serbs	5.3
Ruthenes	2.3
Bosnia-Herzegovina (territory):	
Serbs	42.0
Muslims	34.0
Croats	21.0

Source: A. Sked, *The Decline and Fall of the Habsburg Empire, 1815–1918*, 2nd edn (Harlow and London, 2001), pp. 278–9, and A. Wandruszka and P. Urbanitsch (eds.), *Die Habsburgermonarchie 1848–1918. Die Völker des Reiches* (Vienna, 1980), iii.1, insert between pp 38–9.

in the land and infrastructure, they intended not only to civilize and modernize the region but also to absorb it into the core of the Empire.[30]

By 1914 the state structure brokered in the 1867 'Compromise' was coming under severe strain. German and Hungarian nationalists felt that it failed to meet their aspirations, while the peoples cut out of the deal, mostly Slavs but also Italians and Romanians, resented its manifest unfairness. By the last decade of peace, the representative institutions on both sides of the Empire had become dysfunctional or ceased to work altogether. In Hungary, the Liberals who dominated the House of Representatives had only ever considered the Compromise to be a starting point for the acquisition of new national powers, while the opposition revered the memory of the revolution of 1848–49 against the Habsburgs and desired independence. A highly restrictive franchise encompassing just 6 per cent of the population excluded workers and most non-Magyars, leaving the Hungarian gentry, who alone could satisfy its property qualifications, in charge. A particular bugbear of this group, which spanned both sides of the House of Representatives, was Franz Joseph's refusal to permit a Hungarian national army, or at least the use of the Hungarian language in the Empire's Common Army, and in 1903 this issue sparked a decade-long parliamentary crisis. The tension became acute after the 1905 election returned a pro-independence 'Coalition of National Parties', breaking the Liberals' long hold on political power. A standoff with the Monarch, whose prerogative it was to appoint the government, ensued. The parliament was at first dissolved and only in 1906, after the Crown had threatened the pro-independence nationalists with the introduction of universal suffrage, and through this extorted a secret promise not to challenge the Dualist arrangement, were they permitted to rule. Unable to fulfil the manifesto of nationally advantageous reform of the Habsburg state and army on which it had been elected, the new government instead played to its constituents' chauvinism and provoked resentment in the peripheries by harrying Hungary's Slav and Romanian minorities. In May 1910 elections were rigged to return the Liberals, now renamed the Party of Work, under Count István Tisza. It was Tisza, at that time the parliamentary speaker, who finally imposed order upon Hungary. By overawing the unruly parliament with troops in 1912, he forced through a ban on filibustering and passed a much-needed army bill. However, his unconstitutional methods were greatly resented. One enraged deputy took out a gun in

17

one session and fired three shots at Tisza, which missed, before then turning the weapon on himself.[31]

The Hungarian parliament may have been full of rancour and drama, but it appeared a model of order compared with the lower house of the other half of the Empire, the Austrian Reichsrat. Here, the German Liberals had lost their dominance in 1879, when the Czechs, the real losers of the 1867 system, had ended a self-defeating boycott and started to attend. From the 1890s, bitter disputes about language rights in ethnically mixed areas increasingly paralyzed the institution. A crisis erupted in 1897, when Minister President Count Badeni decreed that officials in Bohemia and Moravia should learn both Czech and German within three years, so they could communicate with all the peoples of these lands. Parliamentary sessions descended into farce as in protest German deputies obstructed legislation with speeches that lasted hours while the Czechs, who favoured the measure, tried to drown them out by shouting, banging on desks or playing musical instruments. When, by sleight of hand, the rowdiest behaviour was banned and the police ejected ten deputies, there was rioting in the German-populated cities of the Empire. The protests forced the withdrawal of the measure and the dismissal of the Minister President. Thereafter, however, there was no stopping the Czechs from using the same methods to halt any legislation of which they disapproved. The government resorted to forcing through laws by decree under the emergency Article 14 of Austria's Basic Law: this had been invoked on average once per year before 1897, but in the seven subsequent years it was used seventy-five times. Even the introduction of universal suffrage in 1907, a measure implemented not out of any democratic idealism but in the hope that social allegiances would replace the national obstruction blocking parliament's work, failed. In March 1914 Minister President Stürgkh finally closed the Reichsrat – an explicit acknowledgement of Austrian parliamentarianism's bankruptcy.[32]

In the Empire's localities, as well as at its centre, disgruntled nationalism was proving troublesome. Nationalist activists eyed each other suspiciously, squabbled over rights and jealously guarded their privileges. Petty issues provoked violent reaction. The opening of an Italian-language Law Faculty at Innsbruck University in 1904, for example, prompted riots by German students which forced its closure.[33] In Trieste, political competition between Italians clinging onto their traditional dominance of local governing institutions and Slovenes, whose numbers in the city had expanded rapidly in the early twentieth century, frequently spilled over into street clashes.[34] In Bohemia, another centre of national conflict, political tensions prompted Czechs and Germans to boycott each other's shops and businesses in 1898, 1908 and 1910. The extreme Czech National Socialist Party organized the Czech boycotters, nationalist newspapers stirred up ill will, and in German areas even town councils intervened, posting placards admonishing 'Buy only from Germans!'[35] Protests by Czech troops about the army's use of German as its language of command in 1898, after the Badeni crisis, and the mutiny of some Bohemian units during mobilizations in 1908 and 1912, raised fears that the nationality disputes were affecting the army and undermining its reliability.[36]

In the last years before the war, there was also particular concern about conditions in Galicia, in the north-east of the Empire. This Crownland (as the Austrians called their provinces) was run by the Polish nobility, and it had exceptional autonomy. Its administrative language had been Polish since 1869, not German as in the rest of Austria, and a Polish Minister without Portfolio sat in the Austrian cabinet to guard Polish Galician interests. Poles also dominated the provincial parliament, the Sejm, as a result of a suffrage that covered just 10 per cent of the population. Poles numbered only 3.8 million of 8 million inhabitants, however. There were also 3.2 million Ruthenes (who today would be called Ukrainians) concentrated in the east of the Crownland, as well as 872,000 Jews and 90,000 Germans.[37] Among the Ruthenes, Ukrainian nationalists comprised the most powerful political force, with twenty-eight deputies in the Vienna Reichsrat in 1911. They were loyal to the Habsburgs but intensely hostile towards the Polish administration, which discriminated against them in education and political representation. Tensions peaked in April 1908 when Count Alfred Potocki, the Polish Statthalter, head of the Galician administration, was killed by a Ukrainian nationalist student.

The other important group among Galicia's Ukrainian speakers were the Russophiles, who were identified as 'Little Russians'. They had less popular support, attracting around one-third of the votes of the nationalists and winning just two Reichsrat seats in 1911. However, they were prominent, not only because they received funding from Russia but also because the Polish administration saw them as the lesser threat to its own interests and tended to support them over their nationalist competitors.

Their leaders had carried out subversive and disloyal activities in the last years of peace. The conversion of hundreds of Ruthenes from the pro-Habsburg Catholic Uniate Church to Russian Orthodoxy caused great concern in Vienna and exacerbated tensions with St Petersburg. So too did the Russophiles' spying on behalf of the Tsarist state: the Austro-Hungarian General Staff estimated that between 1907 and 1913 spies operating in the Crownland multiplied more than tenfold. On the eve of the war, the Emperor and the Austrian government had prevailed upon the Poles to concede a limited reform of the Sejm and the promise of a Ukrainian-language university in order to avoid alienating the Ruthenes yet further.[38]

The South Slavs, and above all the Empire's Serbs, provided the other major source of anxiety for the Habsburg administration. In the Kingdom of Croatia, a semi-autonomous region that lay within Hungary, Magyar leaders were deeply perturbed when in 1905 Serb and Croatian opposition deputies in the Croatian parliament, the *Sabor*, overcame their traditional hostility and declared themselves one nation. Two years later, their coalition won power in Agram (now Zagreb). The National Parties' government in Budapest, frustrated in its programme by the deal with the Crown, quickly provoked a clash with them by ruling in May 1907 that all Croatian railway officials must learn Hungarian. In 1909, during the heightened political tension after the annexation of Bosnia-Herzegovina, relations reached a new low when the Hungarians put the Serb leaders of the *Sabor* coalition on trial for high treason, claiming that they had received funds for agitation from Serbia and had conspired to separate Habsburg South Slav lands and join them to Serbia. The charges were proved to be based on fraudulent evidence and the trial was so manifestly unfairly conducted that its sentences were quashed. Austria-Hungary's international reputation was severely damaged.[39] Meanwhile, in Budapest's House of Representatives, Croatian deputies retaliated for the railway language law by obstructing all business there with long speeches given in their own language. When the *Ban*, the Viceroy in Croatia, suspended its constitution in the *Sabor* as punishment, someone threw a bomb at him, injuring him badly.[40]

The Habsburg 'cultural mission' in Bosnia had also turned sour. At the Common Ministerial Council on 7 July 1914, Biliński, the Common Finance Minister responsible for Bosnia, observed that the military chief in the region, General Potiorek, had been arguing for a couple of years that a 'trial of strength with Serbia' would be needed to hold Bosnia and Herzegovina.[41] There was anxiety about Pan-Serb agitation in the province. Narodna Odbrana, the Serb nationalist society whose abolition was demanded by Austria-Hungary's ultimatum of July 1914, had an extensive network there. To the despair of Bosnia's rulers, their own schools also appeared to be fostering Serb nationalism over Habsburg dynasticism. The education system built by the Empire had difficulty in ridding itself of Serb nationalist teachers, who taught their pupils with maps that showed Bosnia tied to Serbia. Students were the most radical part of the population. The 'Young Bosnia' milieu, pan-Serb, progressive, literary and romantic, was a breeding ground for violent conspiracy. It produced Gavrilo Princip, the nineteen-year-old terrorist who killed the Habsburg heir on 28 June 1914. He was preceded, however, by Bogdan Žerajić, a would-be assassin, who in 1910 narrowly failed in an attempt to murder the Bosnian Governor-General.[42]

The chaos in and closure of parliaments, the street fighting between neighbours of different ethnicities, and the attempted or successful assassinations of the Emperor's ministers and officials all suggested a state in crisis and fuelled talk of disintegration. This greatly concerned the diplomats and soldiers who pushed hardest for war. Their conversations in July 1914 reveal a striking distrust of their own peoples. Berchtold's response when Conrad had told him on 29 June, the day after the Sarajevo murders, that Austria-Hungary must mobilize, is telling: he immediately objected that this would surely trigger revolution in Bohemia.[43] Just three weeks earlier, Berchtold had proposed to both Minister Presidents the establishment of a new inter-ministerial agency to coordinate policy towards all irredentist movements in both parts of the Empire.[44] Conrad shared some of his anxieties. Although he dismissed concerns about a Czech revolution, he did fear further acts of terrorism and pleaded unsuccessfully with the Emperor on 5 July for martial law to be declared throughout Austria-Hungary.[45] The fact that the assassins were Habsburg subjects is significant. Berchtold and Conrad advocated war in part because they believed that nationalist ideals needed to be violently crushed. Serbia, with a population less than one-tenth of the Habsburg Empire's 50,800,000, posed little military threat, but its very existence and the activities of some of its officials offered inspiration and support for South Slav irredentists. Both men feared that to leave the heir's spectacular murder unpunished would start a domino effect, encouraging other irredentists in their efforts to join with nation states on the Empire's borders. At the meeting of 7 July, Berchtold warned Tisza and the other ministers of the bad example that inaction would give to Transylvanian Romanian nationalists. Conrad's view was that Austria-Hungary had to wage war if it did not want to 'open all barriers to the internal fighting which would inevitably result in the disintegration of the polyglot Monarchy'.[46]

The tragedy is that these assessments, which contributed significantly to the disastrous decision to provoke a war, were almost certainly far too gloomy. Habsburg diplomats and soldiers worried about the Empire's internal problems because they were conscious of how these problems diminished Austria-Hungary's international prestige and also because they were anxious about an army whose funding and manpower increases were blocked by obstreperous nationally minded parliamentarians. The group of diplomats around Hoyos and Andrian were, moreover, conditioned to think of foreign policy as a means to resolving domestic discontent. They had been trained under and revered Berchtold's predecessor, Count Alois Lexa von Aehrenthal, who had sought through his foreign policy, albeit peaceably, to bring constitutional reform to the Empire.[47] However, neither the Empire's soldiers nor its diplomats were engaged with its daily governance, and they possessed no real insight into the mood and loyalties of its population. Newspaper headlines which screamed murder or political crisis obscured a strange durability and quiet permanence. Mark Twain, always an astute observer, remarked on this while reporting on the Badeni crisis: 'Things have happened here recently which would set any country but Austria on fire from end to end, and upset the government to a certainty; but no one feels confident that such results will follow here.' Indeed, Twain found that the only issue on which all Austrians could agree was that 'there will be no revolution'.[48]

One pillar of the Empire's legitimacy was the centuries-old Habsburg dynasty, which could scarcely have had a better representative than Franz Joseph. Remote but grandfatherly, with six decades of rule behind him, he embodied the ideal of a paternalistic monarch standing above the rough and tumble of nationalist politics. His age, a venerable eighty-three when the war broke out, was an incalculable advantage. It made him a rare point of constancy in a rapidly modernizing world and yet reminded those frustrated with the status quo that a change of ruler, and thus also reform to the state's creaking Dualist structure, could not be too long in coming.[49] The dynastic cult had valuable publicity agents in the Catholic Church and the army. Prayers for the Emperor and parades preserved the sacred mystique and promoted the secular might of the Habsburg dynasty.[50] Peacetime military service, for which all healthy men were eligible even if only a portion were actually conscripted, also cultivated imperial allegiances. In 1909, 200,000 ex-soldiers were members of one of the 1,400 local associations within Austria's veterans' organization, the *Österreichische Militärveteranen-Reichsbund*. Some joined just for the mutual insurance that was offered, but for many lower- and lower-middle-class men, participating in the associations and their patriotic activities was an important means of expressing both regional and heartfelt imperial allegiances.[51]

Less well recognized, both by diplomats and soldiers at the time and, until recently, by most historians, is that the Empire's governmental system also provided some degree of satisfaction to the peoples. First, it perpetuated and drew some legitimacy from historical entities such as the Lands of St Stephen, the lands of the Bohemian Crown and (more arguably) the Kingdom of Croatia, whose borders it preserved as internal administrative divisions.[52] These often still held great emotional significance in 1914: Czech activists, to take one example, thought increasingly in terms of ethnicity by the early twentieth century yet their most potent call remained for historic Bohemian 'state right' to be respected by the Emperor.[53] Second, although the Dualist structure was widely regarded with dissatisfaction, in the Austrian half of the Empire the large measure of local self-government permitted was some compensation. It gave the energies of nationalist activists an outlet and enabled them to satisfy their ambitions in key areas, such as schooling. It also created a very odd and, for outsiders such as soldiers and diplomats, misleadingly alarming style of politics. In public, parties and deputies courted their disgruntled and nationalist electorates with vociferous language against the government. Behind closed doors, however, the same firebrands affably cut deals, made compromises and haggled over money for their constituencies with state officials.[54] Finally, in practice in Austria, although more notionally in Hungary where Magyarization prevailed, constitutional guarantees of equality at the local level in language and religion protected most minorities from too blatant discrimination.[55] The broad success of these arrangements accounts for why nationality disputes were so often over relatively petty issues. It also offers the best explanation for why hardly anybody, outside small extremist groups such as Young Bosnia, spoke of leaving the Empire. Reform, not revolution, was what the mass of Habsburg subjects urgently desired, and few before 1914 could imagine a national existence that did not in some way feature the dynasty.[56]

Habsburg military and diplomatic leaders in July 1914 were, however, not only anxious about the internal condition of their Empire. They were also preoccupied by the growing danger of its international position. The decisive region was the Balkans, which had become increasingly unstable as the Ottoman Empire weakened and nationalism surged. The first major blow was the army-led coup and brutal assassination of the pro-Austrian King Alexander of Serbia and his queen in June 1903, and the instalment of Petar Karadjordjević on the throne. Literally overnight, the Serbian state shifted from a Habsburg satellite to an assertive adversary driven by pan-Serb ideology to strive for possession of Bosnia-Herzegovina. The Austro-Hungarians' aggressive attempt to subdue its neighbour by imposing punitive tariffs on its products, the so-called 'pig war' of 1906–9, was disastrously counterproductive, sharpening antagonism and prompting the Serbs to search out new markets and new allies.[57]

The Habsburg position was further threatened by Russian engagement in the Balkans after 1907. Russia had been preoccupied at the start of the twentieth century with furthering its interests in the Far East, but a calamitous defeat at Japanese hands in the 1904–5 war followed by revolution had quashed its ambitions. A second area of Russian imperialist interest, Persia, was also closed off once an entente was reached with Britain in 1907, its main rival in the area. Russian leaders seeking to soothe belligerent nationalist opinion at home and restore damaged prestige were therefore redirected by default to the Balkans.[58] The year 1908 brought a major international crisis. Austria-Hungary's occupation of Bosnia-Herzegovina had been limited by the 1878 Treaty of Berlin to thirty years, and so a declaration of formal annexation, long foreseen, was necessary if the provinces were to remain under its control. The Young Turk revolution in the summer of 1908 gave the measure even greater urgency, as rumours circulated that the new Ottoman rulers were planning elections throughout the Empire, including in Bosnia-Herzegovina, which could be used to bring the territories back under their control. The Habsburg Foreign Minister at the time, Count Aehrenthal, was keen to resuscitate a ten-year-old understanding with Russia to pre-serve the Balkan status quo, and so attempted to make a deal. In return for accepting formal Habsburg sovereignty over Bosnia-Herzegovina, hardly a major blow to any great power as Austria-Hungary had already ruled the region for three decades, it was agreed that the Russians would receive Habsburg support for their long-held aspiration of greater access to the Turkish Straits, which would allow their warships to pass from the Black Sea to the Mediterranean. However, when the annexa-tion was declared on 5 October, far from bringing great-power détente in the Balkans, it triggered bitter confrontation. The Austro-Hungarians established their permanent hold over the region, but the Russians were thwarted and embarrassed by what proved to be a lack of international support for their own ambitions in the Straits. The Serbian and Monte-negrin governments were livid about the annexation and mobilized. In response, the Habsburg army reinforced its south-eastern frontier, resulting in an armed stand-off which lasted over the winter and into the following spring. Finally, in March 1909, Germany threatened the Russians that it would support Austria-Hungary's right to use force in the Balkans unless they joined the other European powers in compelling Serbia to accept Bosnia-Herzegovina's new status, and this ended the dispute. Antagonism continued, however. The Russians had been publicly humiliated and Serb nationalists were irreconcilably bitter. Austria-Hungary's prestige also suffered, for it had forced through the annexation only with the decisive German intervention, making it appear as a satel-lite of its more powerful ally.[59]

The greatest damage to Austria-Hungary's international position fol-lowed with the Balkan Wars of 1912–13. These two conflicts upturned the order in the region, ending over half a millennium of Ottoman rule in south-east Europe. The first war opened in October 1912, when a coali-tion of Serbia, Bulgaria, Greece and Montenegro attacked the Ottoman Empire's European possessions. Ottoman weakness had been exposed by an Italian invasion of Libya that had started in September 1911, and the Balkan League's hopes of success were soon stunningly vindicated. The Serb army advanced to the shores of the Adriatic, Greece captured Salonika (Thessaloniki) and the Bulgarians came within thirty kilome-tres of Constantinople. The fighting was ended by the Treaty of London on 30 May 1913. In the second conflict, which broke out just a month later, the victors, along with Romania and the Ottomans, turned on

Bulgaria, the major beneficiary of the first war, and divided most of its gains among themselves at the Peace of Bucharest on 10 August 1913.[60] For Austro-Hungarian leaders, the wars not only turned the power constellation in the Balkans against them but also revealed that they were encircled. Russia behaved malevolently. First, it had been instrumental in bringing together Serbia and Bulgaria, the core of the Balkan League, which, even worse, had initially been conceived against Austria-Hungary, albeit as a defensive alliance. Second, Russia, encouraged by France, had implemented highly provocative military measures as the fighting further south had begun. A week and a half before the start of the First Balkan War it had announced a trial mobilization in four of its military districts and then, rather than release conscripts who had completed their peacetime service as usual in October 1912, had retained them until January 1913. As new recruits were still called up, this measure increased the army's strength by 350,000 men and raised many frontier units almost to their wartime establishment. Its purpose was to intimidate Austria-Hungary into accepting the gains made by the Russians' client states. At first, there was no Habsburg response but in November and December 1912 reservists were drafted to strengthen the army in Galicia, opposite the Russians, and in Bosnia and Herzegovina. Only in March 1913, after Austro-Hungarian finances had been strained to the limit, was a disengagement agreement reached between the two powers.[61]

The Austro-Hungarians nearly went to war on four occasions during this tense time, for regardless of the Russian military measures in the north the Balkan League's gains threatened key Habsburg interests. Most of the friction was over Albania, the Muslim client state that Austria-Hungary wished to set up opposite the entrance to the Adriatic; this was a crucial strategic point, for through it passed all the Empire's maritime traffic. Serbian and Montenegrin troops had occupied much of northern Albania by mid-November 1912, and in the following month, with tensions peaking, not only the Habsburg military but even briefly Franz Ferdinand, who was usually an advocate of peace, was recommending war. When Scutari (today Shkodra), a major city necessary for a viable, independent Albania, fell to the Montenegrins, the Empire again came close to war, a stance supported by the Germans. However, the Montenegrins yielded to the verdict of Europe's great powers, who in May 1913 awarded the city to the new Albanian state. Greater difficulty was experienced in forcing the Serbs, who hankered after a port, to withdraw their troops from other territory allocated to Albania. Only after Habsburg requests, demands and then an ultimatum threatening military action did Serbia finally yield in October 1913. Even despite this retreat, it had doubled in size and its population had jumped from 2.9 million to 4.4 million as a result of conquests made during the year's fighting.[62]

The Balkan Wars left Habsburg leaders deeply fearful and, in consequence, more belligerent. The spectacle of a coalition of small Balkan countries brought together by Russia eviscerating another venerable but ailing multi-ethnic empire made a powerful impression. So too did the Russians' attempt to prevent Habsburg military action in the south through a mobilization opposite Galicia. 'After Turkey comes Austria; that was the catchphrase', remembered the diplomat Baron von Andrian-Werburg.[63] The sound of swords being sharpened in the east was unmistakable. In April 1914 St Petersburg's most influential newspaper *Novoe Vremya*, on whose board the Tsarist Finance Minister sat, was agitating openly for the destruction and division of the Habsburg Empire. The following month, another Russian minister informed the French ambassador that if Franz Joseph ever abdicated, 'we would be obliged to annex Galicia', a territory that he claimed was 'basically Russian'.[64] While there was in fact no Russian master plan, such statements make entirely comprehensible Berchtold's warning to the ministers on 7 July 1914 that 'a decisive conflict with the Monarchy' was being prepared.[65] Within the Habsburg Foreign Ministry, dark talk circulated of a 'conspiracy' directed by Russia 'against the integrity and autonomy of Austria-Hungary'.[66] The Tsar and Tsarina's visit that June to Romania fuelled these suspicions and raised the fear that Austria-Hungary's sole ally in the Balkans was about to defect. Austro-Hungarian leaders were convinced that Serbian provocations were already guided from St Petersburg.[67] The Habsburg heir's murder by a hit squad of his own Bosnian Serb subjects, turned assassins by Greater Serbia agitation, was understood as evidence that no moral or political restraints remained. The nightmare scenario envisaged by Berchtold's advisers was of a concentric attack, launched once Russia's 'Great Programme' of rearmament was completed in 1916. With her forces pinned in the north by Tsarist military action, or even as in 1912–13 just a hostile Russian mobilization, Austria-Hungary would be rendered impotent against invasion and dismemberment by a new Balkan League.[68]

Rather than wait, as the Hungarian Minister President Tisza put it, for the Entente to forge 'an iron ring around us' in the Balkans as a prelude to 'world war', Habsburg leaders chose to act.[69] An immediate, decisive attack on Serbia ironically appeared in the summer of 1914 to offer the best chance to avoid disaster. If Russia did not intervene while its client-state was crushed, its prestige in the Balkans would be destroyed and the encirclement that it planned broken. At worst, in Habsburg leaders' eyes, the move against Serbia would simply bring forward an inevitable war with the great eastern enemy, at a time when he was not fully prepared. Russian rearmament plans were still incomplete and Romania remained in the Central Powers' camp; as the Habsburg Chief of Staff told the ministers, the future military balance could only change 'to our disadvantage'.[70] Moreover, there were warnings from within the Ballhausplatz that the speed with which Yugoslav ideals were spreading could make this 'the last moment at which the Slavic parts of the Monarchy, especially the Croatians, could be dragged along for the war against Serbia'.[71] Now was the time to strike, to prove the Empire's vitality and to smash its enemies before they coalesced into an invincible coalition. In July 1914 Habsburg leaders were desperate men. They were ruthless because they felt they had nothing to lose.

THE MISCALCULATED RISK

The German leadership played a secondary yet crucial role in preparing war in July 1914. Habsburg rulers would not have dared provoke a Balkan conflict without the promises of unconditional support given to Szögyényi and Hoyos by the Kaiser and his Chancellor on 5 and 6 July.[72] The German leaders recognized, even if they underestimated its likelihood, that Russia might intervene if Austria-Hungary moved against Serbia, and that this could result in a European cataclysm. Why take that chance? In the meeting on the afternoon of 5 July at which the German response to Austria-Hungary's appeal for support was discussed, the three most important figures – Kaiser Wilhelm, War Minister Falkenhayn and Chancellor Bethmann Hollweg – together exemplified the indecision, fatalism, aggression and fearful calculation that shaped the Reich's foreign policy. The Kaiser, an inveterate but erratic sabre-rattler, was angry about the death of his friend the Archduke, and wanted to be a good ally.

He possessed sufficient insight to appreciate the considerable risk of backing strong Habsburg action against Serbia but let his advisers convince him of the improbability of European war and departed as planned for his annual North Sea cruise on 6 July. In the longer term, however, he believed in the inevitability of what he had referred to a year and a half earlier as a 'final struggle between the Slavs and the Teutons'.[73] War Minister Erich von Falkenhayn was a very different personality, a cold and self-confident professional soldier. Cynical towards humanitarian considerations, a Social Darwinist who believed in the national necessity of war, he was eager to see how the painstakingly drilled and prepared German army would meet the supreme test, but doubted that the Austro-Hungarians possessed the stomach for firm action against Serbia.[74] The most complex personality, and the man who guided German policy up to the last days of July, was Chancellor Bethmann Hollweg. He had been in his post since July 1909. A moderate conservative, convinced monarchist and accomplished political tactician, he was deeply concerned about what he perceived, with much justice, to be the Reich's encirclement by hostile powers. In offering unconditional support to Austria-Hungary, Bethmann implemented what he later conceded was 'a *policy of utmost risk*' intended through diplomatic victory or continental war to overturn the existing constellation of power in Europe.[75]

Germany was a strong power in 1914. It was a state that had been forged in war, the fruit of the three spectacular victories of the Prussian army and its allies over Denmark, Austria and France in 1864, 1866 and 1870–71 respectively. Since its creation was proclaimed in the Hall of Mirrors at the Palace of Versailles on 18 January 1871, this new superpower at the heart of Europe had only become more intimidating. In terms of population, one index of military might in an age of conscript armies, France's 36.2 million people had lagged only a little way behind the 40 million in the new German state in 1871. On the eve of the First World War, however, the Republic's citizens had increased only slightly to 39.7 million whereas the Reich's subjects had multiplied to 67.8 million. Further, late nineteenth-century Germans were not only rather good at making both love and war; they also demonstrated a talent for making money. The Reich industrialized with startling speed at the end of the nineteenth century, competing with Britain to be Europe's workshop. Between 1880 and 1913, Germany's share of world manufacturing moved from being little more than a third of Britain's share to overtaking it.[76] The Reich's pig-iron production came to exceed Britain's by a third (15.6 million as against 10 million in 1911) and its steel production on the eve of war was more than double that of the United Kingdom (13.7 million against 6.6 million). In new industries such as chemicals, optics and electrics it led the world. This achievement was in part built on unparalleled research universities and pioneering technical high schools specializing in applied science and engineering. The banker Max Warburg was right when he told the Kaiser in June 1914 that Germany would be wiser simply to wait rather than consider war: 'We are growing stronger every year.'[77]

Nonetheless, Bethmann Hollweg and the rest of the German ruling elite had good reason to be anxious in 1914, for Germany was surrounded by unfriendly powers in an increasingly unstable world. It did have allies, but hardly the sort for which one would wish. Austria-Hungary, to which it had been tied since 1879, was militarily weak and becoming a basket case. Italy, an ally since 1882, was barely a great power and certainly not to be trusted. It hankered after Habsburg Italian-speaking lands and Albania, and had signed secret agreements with France in 1900 and 1902 nullifying most of its commitments to the other Central Powers. When war came in 1914, it would indeed declare neutrality on the grounds that as its allies had not been attacked, its treaty obligations remained inactive.[78] The fourth, secret member of the Triple Alliance, Romania, was tacking towards Russia. By contrast, the Triple Entente was hardening, strengthening, and relations with it had become increasingly antagonistic over the past decade. Germany itself, as historians since Fritz Fischer have rightly stressed, bore a large part of the blame. The ascent of twenty-nine-year-old Wilhelm II to the throne in 1888 and the forced resignation in the spring of 1890 of the long-serving Chancellor who had engineered German unification, Otto von Bismarck, were important caesuras. The Germans shortly after dropped their defensive 'Reinsurance Treaty' with Russia, leaving her free to ally with France in the Double Entente in 1894.[79] However, a more significant change came in 1897, when Bethmann's predecessor as Chancellor, Bernhard von Bülow, had inaugurated a new 'World Policy'. This was not the start of the Reich's efforts to win what Bülow called 'a place in the sun', as Germany had already acquired in the 1880s a couple of African territories. It was certainly no well-thought-out imperialist doctrine. Rather, it signalled a new, more assertive stance primarily

intended to unite behind the government the fractious right-wing constituency in Germany's parliament, the Reichstag, who wished to see
their country's new economic power translated into global influence.
Expectations, once having been raised, had to be satisfied, but this
proved difficult in the face of solid opposition from established colonial
powers. German imperial ambitions were unexceptional in the context
of the time, but the government's need to demonstrate to a frustrated
middle-class audience at home that it was being proactive stamped its
actions with unusually aggressive rhetoric and some bizarre showman-
ship. Wilhelm II's exploits, landing on the Moroccan coast in 1905 to
announce his personal support for its Sultan or, still worse, in 1898
unilaterally declaring himself protector of 300 million Muslims, made
him look faintly ridiculous. Yet in the context of Germany's real economic competitiveness, its expanding population, military prowess
and determined naval expansion, other powers could not help feeling
menaced and affronted.[80]

Still, Germany was not, as Fischer and his disciples have claimed, on
an aggressive drive for world power before 1914. Had Reich leaders
wished to advance expansionist aims through war, the military weakness of the Entente in the years immediately after the 1905 Russian
revolution offered ideal yet unused opportunities.[81] Nor did they create
the major international crises that stamped the decade before 1914,
although their cack-handed and greedy diplomacy certainly exacerbated
them. French aggression, much more than German, destabilized Europe
in these years. The French, in their bid to take control of Morocco in
1905, not only contravened an 1881 agreement making alterations in
the country's status subject to multilateral consent, but also at first provocatively tried to exclude and override German interests. While the
Germans succeeded through diplomatic pressure in forcing the resignation of the French Foreign Minister, they subsequently overreached
themselves in rejecting a reasonable offer of bilateral negotiations and
demanding a multinational conference. Their purpose was to undermine
the new Entente Cordiale formed the previous year between Britain
and France, but when representatives of the great powers gathered at
Algeçiras in January 1906 no country except for Austria-Hungary
backed the German efforts to rein in French ambitions.[82]

British support for France at Algeçiras and the tightening bonds within
the Triple Entente during the following years were primarily motivated

by London's wish to reduce imperial overstretch after the Boer War of 1899–1902. The Entente with France ended decades of tension over the British occupation of Egypt, and Britain's understanding with Russia in 1907 was intended to limit conflict in Persia, thus bringing a considerable degree of imperial security. The Central Powers simply had nothing to offer the British that could compete with these attractions; this was a problem, for as Algeçiras showed, it meant that any great-power conventions called to solve international disputes would almost inevitably decide against the Central Powers.[83] However, the Germans' own actions pushed Britain further into Franco-Russian arms. Their naval building programme, the brainchild of the Chief of the Reich Navy Office, Admiral Alfred von Tirpitz, greatly increased antagonism from 1898 both because the British government rightly understood it as a direct challenge and because popular passions were inflamed. In each country pressure groups formed and propaganda campaigns were run in order to encourage public emotional investment in the fleets and push parliaments to fund these expensive warships and symbols of national power, prestige and unity. More emotionally involved than anybody was the Kaiser, who told the permanent secretary at the British Foreign Office in August 1908 that he would rather 'go to war' than discuss naval limitations. Bethmann Hollweg, by contrast, regarded an understanding between Germany and Great Britain as his primary foreign policy goal, but he was consistently hindered by the Kaiser and navalists; and when he was permitted to make an offer in 1912 his demand for a treaty promising 'benevolent neutrality' in the event of a war with other powers was unsurprisingly far too much for the British.[84] Tirpitz's strategy aimed not to match the Royal Navy's strength but to have a fleet so large that the British would not dare cross the Reich for fear that a maritime battle would leave their force too weak to secure their Empire. Sixty capital ships by 1920 were thought likely to suffice. The balance of dreadnoughts and battlecruisers, the super-battleships introduced by the British in 1905, was 18:30 in Britain's favour in 1914.[85] Yet far from deterring a confrontation, Germany's naval building ironically increased its likelihood. In order to ensure that enough battleships remained in home waters to counter the *Kriegsmarine*, the Royal Navy arranged with the French in 1912 that it would concentrate in northern waters while their fleet covered the Mediterranean. When on 1 August 1914 it appeared that the United Kingdom might not enter the war, the

French ambassador to London could appeal to this agreement as imposing a moral obligation on Britain to provide support, as through it his country had denuded its northern coast of protection.[86]

The Germans eventually abandoned the naval race themselves in 1912, as their attention and finances were diverted towards the army. Two new army bills raised the annual intake of conscripts. Some 287,770 men had been called up for military training in 1911. A bill passed in 1912 added 38,890 recruits and a 1913 bill swelled the annual contingent by a further 63,000 soldiers.[87] The increases were a defensive response to an ever more unstable international environment. After the tension caused by Austria-Hungary's Bosnian annexation in 1908–9, another crisis centring on Morocco began, again precipitated by French expansionism. In the summer of 1911, having undermined economic agreements that had formed the basis of a minor détente with Germany in 1909–10, the French set 15,000 troops marching on Fez. The Germans reacted crudely by sending a gunboat, SMS *Panther*, and belligerently demanding the whole French Congo in compensation. British leaders, through a speech by the Chancellor of the Exchequer, David Lloyd George, forcefully warned off the Germans, threatening intervention in the event of war.[88] Not even the Austro-Hungarian government was prepared to support their claims. This experience reinforced for German rulers the lesson of Algeçiras five years earlier, that the international system was now irrevocably biased against their interests. Concerned at their obvious isolation, they resolved to expand their army.

Unfortunately, far from providing security, Germany's army increases sparked a land arms race against France and Russia much more dangerous than the naval race against Britain. Worse still, it was a race that Germany was doomed to lose. The Reich faced two insurmountable disadvantages. The first was that its only trustworthy ally, Austria-Hungary, had neglected its army for far too long to be able to repair its deficiencies quickly. Austria-Hungary's annual recruit contingent had not kept pace with the rise in its population and was, by international standards, small. It trained 0.29 per cent of its people annually, less than Russia with 0.35 per cent and Italy with 0.37 per cent, and much less than Germany with 0.47 per cent and France with 0.75 per cent. The Habsburg force's soldiers in 1912 numbered 391,297, not even a quarter of the Tsar's 1,332,000-strong standing army. Habsburg military spending also lagged behind that of all other great powers except Italy.

The belated passing of an army bill in 1912 raising peacetime man-power to 450,000 and providing extra funds for equipment helped, but the main burden of the Central Powers' collective security still fell on Germany.[89]

Second, while the Germans had the men and potentially the finances to match French and Russian military expansion, there were political constraints on the army's size. Even within the officer corps, there were reservations: while the General Staff was keen fully to exploit national manpower and put forward a proposal in December 1912 for an increase in strength by 300,000 soldiers, the War Ministry worried about the impact of so great and sudden an enlargement on military quality and political reliability and instead proposed a lesser, but still very large, rise of 117,000 men.[90] A more serious check on expansion, however, were parliamentary constraints on military spending. The Kaiser was a constitutional monarch, and although he appointed his own Chancellor and formally had the right to determine the strength and structure of the army, military expenditure had to be agreed by Germany's parliament, the Reichstag. This was elected on the basis of universal male suffrage, giving it one of the most democratic franchises in Europe.[91] In 1912, after elections which had made the Social Democrats the largest party, their deputies and those of the second largest group, the Catholic Centre Party, dominated the assembly and were critical of using the socially regressive indirect taxation at the assembly's disposal to fund military expenditure. Direct taxation such as income and property tax was the preserve of the twenty-five states within the Reich's federal system. The largest state, Prussia, covered two-thirds of Germany and had a regional diet elected with a restrictive and, among the working classes, much hated three-class franchise which weighted voters by the tax that they paid. Highly conservative Prussia controlled the Bundesrat, the federal council in which the states were represented, and for a decade this fought off central government's attempts to gain a share of direct tax revenue. In 1913 Bethmann Hollweg managed to push the Army Law through the Reichstag only by proposing a tax on property and dividing this law from its funding bill. The left and centre parties voted through the funding to establish the precedent for Reichstag power over direct taxation, while a national coalition of centre and right combined to pass the increase in numbers of recruits.[92] Even after the two major army bills, however, the Reich spent 3.5 per cent of its GNP on defence, a higher proportion than Austria-Hungary (2.8 per cent) but lower than France (3.9 per cent) and much less than Russia (4.6 per cent).[93]

The Chief of the German General Staff, Helmuth von Moltke, became increasingly pessimistic and anxious at this time. The manpower gap between the Central Powers and Entente widened in consequence of Russian rearmament and France's replacement of two- with three-year conscript service. In 1912 the Germans calculated that their adversaries' standing armies already outnumbered German and Austro-Hungarian forces by 827,000 men. By 1914 the difference was reckoned to exceed one million soldiers.[94] Railway building by the Entente, a highly sensitive subject as German security against these superior numbers rested to a great extent on their army's speed advantage in mobilization, also proceeded apace. In the winter of 1911–12, German intelligence believed that over the past five years new railways financed by French loans had halved the time needed by the Russian army to concentrate its units on the Tsarist Empire's western border. In 1913 another French loan for railway-building caused panic in the German General Staff, who calculated that it would permit the Russians to speed their deployment so that instead of half, two-thirds of the army would be at the Reich's frontier by day thirteen of mobilization.[95] In the context of the upheaval brought by the First Balkan War, the tightness of the Entente alliance exacerbated German leaders' anxiety and sense of encirclement. A turning point came in December 1912 when, with Russian troops menacingly concentrated on the Austro-Hungarian border, a discreet warning was given to the German ambassador in London, Prince Karl von Lichnowsky, that Britain valued the continental balance and could not stay out of a European conflict sparked by a Habsburg attack on Serbia. The Kaiser, in a rage at what he condemned as a 'moral declaration of war', called his three chief naval advisers and Moltke together in the infamous 'War Council' of 8 December.[96] Insisting that Austria-Hungary 'must deal energetically' with the Serbs, and foreseeing that this would lead Russia to attack Galicia, drawing in Germany, Wilhelm II ordered – in light of the recent warning from London – that the fleet must be prepared to fight the British. Tirpitz wanted a postponement of war for a year and a half, but Moltke argued that even then the navy would not be ready and delay would be unfavourable to the army because shortage of funds meant Germany could not keep up with the armament programmes of its prospective adversaries. His message was 'war, the sooner the better'.[97] Little definitive emerged from the meeting. The participants' single decision, that a press campaign to prepare the German people for war against Russia should be organized, was never implemented. Nonetheless, the episode had significance. The Kaiser, as he made clear in a letter written to his Foreign Secretary on the same day, felt existentially threatened by a circle of hostile powers: 'The question at stake,' he wrote, 'is whether Germany is to be or not to be.'[98] The conviction he expressed at the meeting in the necessity for aggressive Habsburg action against Serbia, and his readiness to support it even at the cost of drawing the Reich into war with the Triple Entente, proved fateful. Moltke's call for preventative war, although not his first and at that point not acted upon, only underlined the peril that was understood to confront Germany.[99]

The key figure shaping German foreign policy in July 1914 was, however, Bethmann Hollweg, who had not been invited to what he himself had sardonically christened the 'War Council'. He regarded the Kaiser's behaviour as hysterical. In his view, the British warning was not threatening: 'It only affirmed what we have long known: *now as before England follows a policy of balance of power and therefore will stand up for France if the latter is in danger of being annihilated by us.*' He quashed an attempt to introduce another naval funding increase and instead emphasized multilateralism and worked to restrain Austria-Hungary from violent action. Germany and Britain cooperated effectively to ensure that the Balkan Wars sparked no European conflagration.[100] The difference between Bethmann's policy in early 1913 and his actions in the summer of 1914, when he sanctioned a Habsburg attack on Serbia and sabotaged British efforts to mediate jointly, is thus striking. What changed in the interim? First, the Chancellor re-evaluated the threat posed by Russia to the Reich. In early July 1914, he described the Tsarist Empire as 'looming above us as an increasingly terrifying nightmare'.[101] Officially inspired, belligerent newspaper articles in both countries and tension about the German military mission to Constantinople, which the Tsar's government feared could lead to German control of the Turkish Straits and the ability to choke Russian maritime trade from the Black Sea, further soured the countries' relations.[102] Above all, however, the 'Great Programme' of rearmament passed by Russia's Duma in June 1914, which would add 500,000 men and more artillery to the Russian army, unnerved German decision-makers. By

1917, the Russian military was projected to be, at over two million men, three times the size of Germany's conscript force.[103] Falkenhayn and Moltke both believed war inevitable and saw the Reich's situation deteriorating with time. The Chief of the General Staff even appealed to the Foreign Secretary, Jagow, in the early summer of 1914, before the assassinations in Sarajevo, to engineer a preventative war. Although this was refused, the German military leaders' anxiety and pressure influenced Bethmann. A preventative war had appeared ever more attractive, he later confessed, through 'the constant threat of attack, the greater likelihood of its inevitability in the future, and by the military's claim: today war is still possible without defeat, but not in two years!'[104]

Bethmann Hollweg was influenced not only by the German army's fear of Russia but also by his own assessment of the Reich's deteriorating relations with Britain and Austria-Hungary. After fruitful cooperation during the Balkan Wars, Anglo-German relations had become more distant. While an agreement over the future partition of the ailing Portuguese Empire was reached in April 1913, subsequent negotiations over the extension of Germany's Berlin–Baghdad railway to the Persian Gulf proved dishearteningly difficult. In the end though, what destroyed Bethmann's faith in Britain's readiness to act multilaterally and continue restraining Russia was intelligence, lifted by a German agent in Russia's London embassy, of secret Anglo-Russian naval discussions in May 1914. Among the subjects discussed was a joint landing in Pomerania, an invasion of Germany. This was, the Chancellor told his assistant in early July, 'the last link in the chain'. Yet if Britain had finally committed itself unconditionally to the Franco-Russian alliance, this had implications for Germany's relations with Austria-Hungary. These had cooled during the Balkan Wars due to German unwillingness to support aggressive Habsburg action against Serbia. Now, however, with trust in Britain's pacific intentions and readiness to restrain Russia undermined, the Reich's security rested more than ever on preserving and supporting its one solid ally.[105]

When Hoyos and Szögyényi arrived in Potsdam on 5 and 6 July 1914 bearing Emperor Franz Joseph's plea for support, Bethmann Hollweg and the Kaiser thus had no hesitation in assenting. The Chancellor is often characterized as being fatalistic and resigned at this time due to the death of his wife two months earlier, but this hardly fits with the purposefulness that he displayed.[106] He and Wilhelm II had met after news of the Sarajevo assassination reached Berlin. His admonition to the Habsburg emissaries on 6 July that any action should be executed quickly betrays a strategy already conceived. Bethmann's plan was to exploit the crisis to strengthen the Central Powers' alliance and break the coalition surrounding Germany. As he explained a few days later to his assistant, what was needed was 'a rapid *fait accompli* and afterwards friendliness towards the Entente'. Bethmann recognized and feared that 'an attack on Serbia can lead to world war'. Indeed, the British had warned the Germans of this explicitly in December 1912. The Chancellor's complete surrender of the decision on how to proceed against the Balkan state to Austria-Hungary was perhaps a subconscious attempt to avoid responsibility for so monstrous an outcome, which he rightly foresaw would be cataclysmic. By contrast, Bethmann was prepared to accept a continental conflict against Russia and France. Moltke was confident that the army could win such a struggle, and if the two powers did intervene on Serbia's behalf, German leaders considered that this would merely prove they had always intended to attack.[107] The Chancellor's preferred outcome, however, was a diplomatic victory. If Russia failed to support Serbia, he calculated, its prestige would be shattered in the Balkans, easing the pressure on Austria-Hungary. French or British refusal to back Russia would plausibly result in a crisis of trust, bringing the break-up of the Entente and a resulting German hegemony in Europe. Central to the hope that a conflict could be localized were the assumptions that the Tsar's army was not yet ready to fight and that the Habsburgs would eliminate Serbia quickly, while international sympathy was still on their side and before surprised governments could respond. Both assumptions were wrong. As events in the last week of July were to prove, Bethmann had made a terrible miscalculation.[108]

WORLD WAR

When, on 24 July 1914, the great powers received copies of the Austro-Hungarian ultimatum handed to Serbia one day earlier, reactions ranged from concerned to angry. Sir Edward Grey, the British Foreign Secretary, famously called it 'the most formidable document I have ever seen addressed by one State to another'.[109] His Russian counterpart, Sergei

Sazonov, ruled the document's demands 'simply unacceptable'. Entreaties to monarchical solidarity had left him unmoved. 'I see what is going on,' he had raged. 'You are setting fire to Europe.'[110] Lest these men's views be dismissed as coloured by their indifference or hostility towards Austria-Hungary, the experienced and trusted Viennese politician Joseph Maria Baernreither, who had previously served as the Habsburg Trade Minister, similarly thought the demands 'totally impossible'.[111] No one among the Vienna and Berlin decision-makers could be surprised that an ultimatum written deliberately to be rejected should elicit such reactions. Bethmann Hollweg was satisfied by the Entente's responses. The Russian Foreign Minister, although angry, had avoided stating a firm commitment to intervene militarily for Serbia, and Britain's attitude was understood as worried but disinterested. On 25 July it still seemed feasible to localize an Austro-Serbian conflict.[112]

The only opportunity to avoid any sort of war was if the Serbs unconditionally capitulated to Habsburg demands. This turned out to be more likely than most of Europe's diplomats had predicted. Prime Minister Nikola Pašić had been away from Belgrade campaigning for re-election when the ultimatum was received by his deputy Lazar Paču, the Serbian Finance Minister, and Pašić only returned at 5 a.m. on 24 July. At first he hoped to procrastinate but he soon came around to the view that without Russian support, Serbia would have to offer 'full satisfaction'. However, on the morning of 25 July, news arrived from Serbia's ambassador in St Petersburg, that 'energetic measures, even mobilization' on Serbia's behalf were promised. The small Balkan state was officially to be taken under Russia's protection. This information stiffened the Serbian government's resolve. The reply to the Habsburg ultimatum drafted that afternoon was couched in conciliatory language but was careful to accept no culpability and conceded the Austro-Hungarians very little. In particular, it agreed only with reservation to point 5, the demand that Habsburg officials be allowed to participate in suppressing anti-Austrian movements on Serbian soil, and it rejected point 6, which had ordered the Serbs to permit the involvement of Habsburg officials in the prosecution of the conspirators. Pašić had reason to resist this last demand, for there is good evidence that he had known of the plot, tried to stop it, but was unable to control the soldiers. Serbia's military intelligence service was heavily implicated. The Austro-Hungarians could not know that the idea to kill

Franz Ferdinand had come from within its ranks or that the plot was organized by its head, Colonel Dimitrijević. However, as a note accompanying the ultimatum made clear, they had established already that the assassins had been assisted by an army major, Dimitrijević's right-hand man Voja Tankosić, that they had received weapons training in Belgrade and bombs and guns supplied from a Serbian arsenal, and that Serb customs officers had helped to smuggle them across the border.[113]

Even before the Austro-Hungarian ambassador, Baron Wladimir Giesl, read the Serbian reply and, as instructed, broke off relations and left Belgrade, moves had already begun to localize the coming conflict. On 24 July, Berchtold had called the Russian chargé d'affaires into the Habsburg Foreign Ministry to insist that nothing could be further from his mind than the humiliation of Serbia. 'It had been my particular care to eliminate from the Note everything which could have been interpreted in this sense,' he claimed disingenuously. He appealed to the Russians as another dynastic power, explained the danger of the irredentist agitation to the Habsburg Empire, and assured him that 'we had no intention of increasing the size of our territory'.[114] This last point was superficially true, for Tisza, Minister President of Hungary, had made it a condition of his agreement to go to war. Nonetheless, the Habsburg ministers had agreed that 'strategically necessary corrections of the frontier lines' might be made, a formula that during hostilities came frequently to be used as code for very extensive annexations, and they certainly intended to reduce Serbia and distribute its territory to client states, cementing the Habsburg hold over the Balkans.[115]

The Germans too worked hard at localizing the conflict. As early as 21 July, Bethmann Hollweg had ordered the Reich's ambassadors in Entente capitals to stress that Austria-Hungary and Serbia should be left to resolve their disputes alone. Once the Habsburg ultimatum had been delivered, he sabotaged all attempts at restraint. A proposal by Sir Edward Grey for mediation by Germany, Italy, France and Britain on 24 July was deliberately forwarded late by Jagow, the Reich's Foreign Secretary, so that it reached Vienna only after the ultimatum had expired. Over the following days, Bethmann continued firmly to insist that international adjudication should be directed solely towards Austria-Hungary and Russia, not Serbia; a stance designed to enable the Balkan conflict to go ahead without triggering a continental war. When another British proposal for mediation was made to Berlin on 27 July, it was again passed on late to Austria-Hungary, and only after the Habsburg ambassador had first secretly been instructed that the German government advised that it be disregarded.[116] So determined was the Chancellor to push through his strategy of risk that he even attempted to exclude the Kaiser, whom he feared might weaken as danger approached, by urging him to stay on his North Sea cruise. This proved prescient. Wilhelm II disregarded his Chancellor's advice and returned to Potsdam on 27 July. When, on the following morning, his officials belatedly gave him the Serbian answer, he judged it a 'capitulation of the most humiliating kind' and pronounced (with underlining to show how strongly he felt) that 'every cause for war has vanished'. He advocated mediation after the Habsburgs had taken Belgrade, just across their southern border, as a sop to their honour and a guarantee that the Serbs would meet their demands. The Kaiser's new pacifism was never permitted to influence the Austro-Hungarians, however, for while Bethmann's next instructions to the German ambassador in Vienna incorporated Wilhelm's idea that Belgrade might be occupied as a guarantee of good Serbian behaviour, they crucially omitted any indication that war was no longer necessary. Instead, Bethmann warned that no impression should be given 'that we wish to hold Austria back'. The Germans' repeated urging during the past days had in fact left the Habsburgs in no doubt that their allies wanted them 'to press forward immediately and to confront the world with a *fait accompli*'.[117]

Bethmann Hollweg was, however, already at this point losing grip on his deadly diplomatic game of risk. From the German perspective, there were two problems. The first was the excruciating slowness of Austria-Hungary's move to war. Although Emperor Franz Joseph ordered mobilization on 25 July, the first day was set for 28 July, and only on the following day did troops start to arrive at their units. Moreover, it was solely at Berchtold's insistence that war was declared at noon on that day; Conrad von Hötzendorf, Chief of the General Staff, who earlier had been so full of belligerence and talk of immediate strikes on the Balkan enemy, now wanted the declaration to be delayed until 12 August, the first day on which his forces would be fully ready for operations. Even had Habsburg leaders been so inclined, no lightning strike and a halt in Belgrade as the Kaiser suggested were possible, for their army's units were scheduled in two waves: the first deployment was opposite Serbia's western border, and only later was a contingent scheduled to arrive against its capital in the north.[118] The second problem was that, in stark contrast to the Austro-Hungarians, the Russians reached for arms extraordinarily quickly. In this, they were urged on by the French, whose President and Prime Minister had made clear during their visit in St Petersburg – and thus, even before they had seen the Habsburg ultimatum – that no demands on Serbia should be tolerated.[119] Already on the weekend of 24–25 July, before the Serbs had answered the ultimatum, the Tsar and his ministers resolved to impose the 'Period Preparatory to War' on four western military districts, Odessa, Kiev, Kazan and Moscow. The first orders to prepare for mobilization were sent to these areas on 24 July, that is, even before the Serbs or Austro-Hungarians, the principal protagonists in the dispute, had made any military moves.[120] The Tsar's ministers and diplomats knew they were playing for high stakes. Even with Habsburg promises that no Serbian territory would be annexed by the Empire, it was obvious to Russia that an Austro-Hungarian victory over Serbia would totally undermine its position in the Balkans. A senior Russian diplomat, Prince Troubetzkoi, spelled out most clearly the Russian government's justified scepticism to the Italian ambassador on 29 July 1914: 'Austrian assurances regarding annexation of Serbian territory were worth little because the results of the Austrian policy would be to isolate and bring Montenegro under its dominance, to place Albania under its protection, to reward Bulgaria with Serbian Macedonia, and to make Romania an appendage of the Triple Alliance. The Austrian plan was to secure the supremacism of Germanism in the Balkans at the expense of Slavism.'[121]

For Russia's leaders, however, Germany, not Austria-Hungary, was the central problem. Foreign Minister Sazonov was convinced that the Reich lay behind the Habsburg ultimatum and argued that Russia's past diplomatic retreats and concessions had merely encouraged aggression. Using the messianic racial language so common among Russian leaders, he warned his colleagues that the Tsarist Empire's 'historic mission' of leading the Slav peoples should not be abandoned. Backing down would lead to the loss of Russia's great-power status: 'she would be considered a decadent state and would henceforth have to take second place among the powers'.[122]

Sazonov's belief, which was accepted by the other ministers, that German aggression was behind the crisis meant that from the very beginning the Russians considered it to be not merely a Balkan but a European issue. This, combined with their rush to military action, was fateful. The Tsar and his ministers briefly attempted to avoid provoking the Germans by keeping the Warsaw district that faced both Germany and Austria on a peacetime footing. However, in the early hours of 26 July, the Russian Chief of Staff, General Nikolai Ianushkevich, who had already instructed his officers to act energetically and permitted them to go beyond the regulations in their preparations, extended the 'Period Preparatory to War' to cover all of Russian Europe. Military technical considerations justified this extension: the Russian General Staff had no plan for a partial mobilization against Austria-Hungary. Denying itself the use of the important rail hub at Warsaw would cause chaos. Moreover, as its regiments did not draw their reserves from a single military district, it was inevitable that manpower in areas beyond the four districts mobilized would be drawn in.[123] Nevertheless, it meant effectively that the first stages of a mobilization directed not only at Austria-Hungary but, critically, also at Germany had begun. From the early hours of that morning, the military railway department and personnel essential for running the troop transports were brought up to a full state of readiness, magazines, supply depots and fortresses were put on alert, screening troops took up position near the border and reservists were drafted to frontier divisions. The training of officer cadets was abruptly terminated, they received commissions and were sent to fill vacant command posts. Under no circumstances can these measures be interpreted as deterrence, for they were carried out in strict secrecy. When, on the night of 26 July, the German ambassador and military attaché in St Petersburg confronted Sazonov and accused the Russians of moving troops to the western border 'in accordance with a mobilization directive', he denied that any 'mobilization order' had been issued. Nor were the Russians naive; they had long understood the likely consequence of a move to arms. At the height of the tensions caused by the First Balkan War in November 1912, the then Prime Minister Count Vladimir Kokovtsev had pointed out that Russian mobilization would be countered by the Germans with war.[124]

The German military, so often portrayed as the instigators of the First World War, was thus unequivocally reacting to, rather than leading the armed escalation in the last days of July 1914. In particular, Helmuth von Moltke, the Chief of the General Staff responsible for the Reich's Field Army, exhibited behaviour that was far more anxious and restrained than either his German civilian colleagues or his Tsarist counterpart. Moltke had been away from Berlin on a rest cure in early July but had been kept abreast of decisions in the Central Powers' capitals. The War Minister Falkenhayn had advised the Kaiser on 5 July but a few days later had departed for an official trip and then a fortnight's holiday. Neither man had thought war likely and neither had given much (or in Moltke's case, any) input into policy. No military precautions were taken up to 16 July, and even then all that was done was to suggest that eastern intelligence posts observe Russian activities with a little greater vigilance.[125] The situation changed with the Austro-Hungarian ultimatum. Falkenhayn was back at his desk on the morning of 25 July, while Moltke returned to Berlin that evening. Yet late next day when they spoke, the Chief of Staff was still confident that military measures would be 'premature'.[126] Moltke's opinion was not the product of complacency. Intelligence posts had been at a heightened state of alert since the Habsburgs issued their ultimatum on 23 July, and on 25 July the Chief of German Military Intelligence, Major Walter Nicolai, had been recalled from holiday to Berlin. He had ordered the dispatch of so-called 'tension travellers', civilians or military men who undertook short round trips across the border pretending to be tourists or business travellers in order to look out for signs of military preparations. A report from the German military plenipotentiary at the Tsar's court, supported on 27 July by news from these travellers, quickly alerted the General Staff to the Russian military preparations under the 'Period Preparatory to War'.[127]

On 28 July, as Austria-Hungary at last declared war on Serbia and the Tsar responded by ordering the partial mobilization of the four military districts where preparations had begun, Moltke composed an 'Assessment of the Political Situation' for the Chancellor. This has since often been interpreted as an unacceptable encroachment by the military into the civilian government's prerogatives.[128] In fact, it is far better understood as an early indication of a problem that would wrack the German and Austro-Hungarian war efforts throughout 1914–18. Whereas western states like Britain and France had a clear governmental hierarchy in which civilian control was established over the military, in central Europe ruling structures attempted to maintain a strict parity and separation between civilian (or 'political') and military spheres. Constitutionally, the Kaiser or Emperor was responsible for their coordination but neither Franz Joseph nor Wilhelm II proved capable of this task. More fundamentally, 'total war' by its nature blurred the boundaries between the military and political spheres. The poor coordination and clashes between soldiers and civil servants that characterized the war efforts of both Central Powers stemmed to a great extent from their insistence on a separation that grew ever more fictitious throughout hostilities. Moltke's intervention was simply an indication that already in July 1914 the military and political situations were tightly intertwined. The tone that he adopted in the memorandum was surprisingly moderate for a man who during the last eighteen months had pushed for a preventative war. The text was both fatalistic about the likelihood of war (avoidable, he thought, only through a 'miracle') and peppered with warnings about the horror it would entail. Its purpose was to warn Germany's civilian leaders, whose primacy in directing policy Moltke implicitly acknowledged in submitting the memorandum to Bethmann Hollweg, that Russian mobilization by stealth threatened to place the Central Powers not only at a military but also a political disadvantage. At this point, he rightly saw the preparations as still aimed principally at Austria-Hungary, but he alerted the Chancellor to the real danger that they threatened to trigger a chain reaction, activating alliance obligations which would spread war across Europe. Worse still, the Russians' covert military measures had political and diplomatic implications, for they would permit the eastern enemy publicly to shift the blame for escalation onto the Central Powers, whose security depended on a quick armed response to any sign that overwhelming forces were concentrating against them. Moltke needed the Chancellor to establish whether Russia and France, which had also begun preparing for mobilization, were serious about war with Germany. If the Entente did have belligerent intentions, delay could be fatal; already, the Chief of Staff warned grimly, 'the military situation is becoming from day to day more unfavourable'.[129]

What Moltke was emphatically not doing was clamouring for a war which, his memorandum foresaw, 'will annihilate for decades the civilisation of almost all Europe'.[130] His conduct was defensive and reactive, determined not even by alliance obligations to Austria-Hungary but by his assessment of the military threat to Germany. This grew frighteningly over the following days. The Russian Chief of Staff Ianushkevich had no intention of accepting a partial mobilization, which his subordinates agreed was nonsensical and even harmful, for just hours after its announcement, on the night of 28 July, he had wired the commanding officers of the Tsarist Empire's twelve military districts stating that the first day of the general mobilization would be 30 July.[131] Squeezing permission out of the Tsar in fact proved more difficult than he clearly had anticipated. Moltke inadvertently helped him; his call to establish whether Russia was serious about war had spurred Bethmann to instruct Germany's ambassador in St Petersburg to give notice that unless Russia ceased military preparations, the Reich would mobilize and fight. The Tsar's Foreign Minister Sazonov may well have interpreted this warning, which was communicated to him on the afternoon of 29 July, as further confirmation that German rather than Habsburg aggression lay behind the crisis, and that mobilizing against Austria-Hungary alone was pointless.[132] Together, he and Ianushkevich extracted an order from the Tsar that evening for general mobilization, but it was countermanded almost immediately when a telegram from Wilhelm II arrived promising to urge the Austro-Hungarians to parley with the Russians. Only on the afternoon of 30 July, still before the Germans had taken any significant military measures, did the Tsar authorize general mobilization. An hour later, at 6 p.m. local time, the order went out to Russian units.[133]

These days brought a confused turn in attitudes in Berlin. Throughout 29 July, Moltke was restrained. Falkenhayn had been pushing since the day before for the 'State of Imminent War', Germany's much shorter equivalent of Russia's 'Period Preparatory to War', to be declared, and with the Kaiser's permission had recalled troops on manoeuvre to barracks. To the War Minister's frustration, however, the Chief of the General Staff asked that morning only for permission to station sentries to protect key transport infrastructure and in the evening offered only tepid support for his unsuccessful pleas to the Chancellor and Kaiser for the 'State of Imminent War' to be announced.[134] The first major change was rather in Bethmann's stance, and it came as a result of British, not Russian developments. Although signals from Britain about how she would act in a continental war had been contradictory, the Chancellor's assumption up to the morning of 29 July, was that she would stay neutral. News from the Kaiser's brother, which arrived the day before, of a conversation with George V of England in which the King had said Britain would 'try all we can to keep out of this' bolstered this belief.[135]

Nonetheless, Falkenhayn's frantic urging and the warnings in Moltke's memorandum of a likely continental war caused Bethmann to conclude that the time had come to confirm and cement it. Late in the night of 29–30 July, in discussion with the British ambassador Sir Edward Goschen, he clumsily tried to do a deal. In return for British neutrality, he offered assurances that the Reich would annex no territory from mainland France and, implicitly betraying the German army's plan to advance through Belgium, would preserve Belgium's integrity, providing that she did not join Germany's enemies.[136] Yet no sooner had the meeting ended than Bethmann received a telegram from his own ambassador in London, Prince Lichnowsky, sent earlier but only now decoded, which revealed how misguided had been not only his proposal but his whole calculated risk. The ambassador reported that the British Foreign Secretary, Sir Edward Grey, continued to desire a four-power conference but now warned privately that Britain would not stand aside if France were drawn into the conflict. For Bethmann, this was a disaster: while Germany could beat the continental powers Russia and France, he had little faith in prevailing against the world might of Britain. Within two hours he was telegramming, for the first time sincerely, to Germany's ambassador in Vienna, Baron Heinrich von Tschirschky, and to the Habsburg Foreign Ministry the urgent need for Austria-Hungary to accept great-power mediation. His readiness to support his ally's Balkan attack and his hopes of benefiting from it were now abandoned, while his error in surrendering the initiative at the start of July was regretted. The tone of this message, sent too late, was suddenly stern and hypocritical: Germany would do its duty as an ally 'but must refuse to allow Vienna to draw us into a world conflagration frivolously and without regard to our advice'.[137]

Bethmann's abrupt change of tack found little understanding among Habsburg leaders, who predicted humiliation in any great-power mediation and decided to continue their war with Serbia; to preserve peace was no longer in the German Chancellor's hands.[138] Compounding his problems, on the evening of 30 July Moltke began for the first time in the crisis to press seriously for military measures. Unlike Bethmann, whose eyes were firmly fixed on Britain, the Chief of the General Staff's gaze was riveted on Germany's continental opponents. The day had not been a good one. Although Moltke did not yet know that the Russians had just ordered general mobilization, the news was still extremely grim.

Military intelligence was warning that the 'Period Preparatory to War' measures were 'far advanced' in the 'German-Russian frontier region'. In the west, France remained relatively calm, but Belgium had started to call up reserves and prepare the fortifications around the city and rail hub of Liège for action. Moltke's plan of campaign for a two-front war, the only plan that the German army possessed, was imperilled by these measures, for no attack on France through Belgium could be undertaken without first subduing this city-fortress and seizing intact its railways to supply Germany's advancing armies [139] Thus, there was a furious argument when, at the end of the day, he and Falkenhayn met with Bethmann and advocated war. Eventually, the Chancellor, still thinking of British opinion but now above all concerned to ensure that the German people should consider Russia as the aggressor, persuaded the two soldiers to postpone until noon the next day a declaration of the 'State of Imminent War'.[140]

The postponement was not purely a political tactic but also a reflection of Moltke's tendency, noted with irritation by the hawkish Falkenhayn, still to swing from belligerence to caution. What made the 'State of Imminent War' inevitable was the news of Russia's general mobilization, which began to trickle in overnight from 'tension travellers' and border intelligence posts. Moltke, according to his personal adjutant Major Hans von Haeften, spent the night in 'serious psychological turmoil'. On one hand, he had displayed more insight than most decision-makers into the suffering that would come with what his memorandum to Bethmann had termed 'the mutual butchery of the civilised nations of Europe'.[141] Yet the policy of his own government, which over the longer term he had helped to prepare, Habsburg desperation and Russian belligerence had created a situation of critical danger. As the evidence of the Tsarist army's general mobilization mounted, he fired off a telegram to Conrad, telling him to concentrate his troops against Russia and promising German mobilization, and sent a message through the Habsburg military attaché in Berlin admonishing that war alone could save Austria-Hungary.[142] Yet neither concern for the Habsburgs nor formal alliance obligations pushed Moltke to war; had they been a real cause, then Germany, as the terms of the Central Powers' agreement demanded, would have had to act already in response to the Russian partial mobilization. Instead, what motivated the general was, as he told his adjutant, the fear that after five days of restraint while

Tsarist forces undertook covert and extensive military preparations, delay now would 'allow our opponents to carry the war into German territory'.[143] On the morning of 31 July, the reports from intelligence posts all along the eastern frontier of red Russian mobilization posters, one of which Moltke insisted be taken and read out to him over the telephone, finally settled the matter. With a deep breath, he concluded, 'It can't be helped then; we'll have to mobilise too.'[144]

From this moment, as leaders in all the powers could have predicted, the shift to continental war was terrifyingly rapid. At 1 p.m. on 31 July the 'State of Imminent War' was proclaimed in Berlin and that afternoon Russia was threatened with a German mobilization unless it ceased hostile action against Austria-Hungary within twelve hours. France was given eighteen hours to affirm its neutrality. The following day, 1 August, first France at 3.45 p.m. and then Germany at 5 p.m. mobilized, and at 7 p.m. the Kaiser, having received no answer to his ultimatum, declared war on Russia. A German declaration of war against France followed exactly forty-eight hours later, justified by false claims of French aircraft bombing railway lines and incursions by French troops onto Reich territory.[145] Italy, whose monarch had as recently as February 1914 promised the Germans to send an army to protect Alsace in the event of war, wriggled out of its alliance obligations on the grounds that the Habsburgs had provoked the conflict after Sarajevo. Almost as an afterthought, Austria-Hungary and Russia finally went to war on 6 August.[146]

The only real question at the start of August was whether the global superpower Britain too would intervene and turn the conflict into a world war. Division at the top of the British Liberal government had been responsible for the mixed messages on intervention or neutrality coming out of London. Grey's warning on 29 July to Lichnowsky that Britain could not stand aside if France were drawn into the fighting had been 'private' precisely because Grey did not yet have sufficient support for such a policy in the British cabinet. Yet on 1 August, with most ministers opposed to intervention, he told the French ambassador not to reckon on British military support. At the same time, he began to explore whether it might be possible to limit the war to the east. A telegram sent from Lichnowsky with news that Grey planned to parley caused considerable excitement in Berlin when it arrived shortly after 5 p.m., when the Reich's order to mobilize had just been sent out. From what

Lichnowsky could gather, Grey intended to propose that if Germany refrained from attacking westward, Britain would guarantee her own and France's neutrality. A second telegram from the ambassador suggested that Britain might stay neutral even if France went to war. The Kaiser called for champagne. His civilian and naval advisers were astonished but delighted.[147] Only the military was unimpressed. Falkenhayn, ever cool and doubting the veracity of the messages, bided his time and stayed silent. Moltke, by contrast, mounted hysterical resistance. The army's plan for a campaign solely against Russia had been abandoned in 1913. If the Kaiser tried to lead the troops eastwards he would have, explained the Chief of the General Staff, 'no combat ready army but a chaotic mass of disorganised armed men without supplies'.[148] German vanguard patrols had already invaded Luxembourg in order to secure railways crucial to the campaign, and the 16th Trier Division was not far behind. After heated argument, the leaders settled on continuing the deployment but halting troops before they crossed the border. Moltke returned to the General Staff building to weep tears of despair; 'I felt as if my heart would break,' he later remembered. The strain of the experience may have triggered a light stroke. His wife recalled that 'he was purple in the face, his pulse hardly countable. I had a desperate man in front of me.'[149]

Moltke's reaction, sometimes understood as the quintessential expression of German militarism, merely reflected his realistic appraisal of Germany's strategic situation. The military technical problems of shifting the deployment of millions of men from west to east were overwhelming. More importantly, the British offer lacked credibility: as the general pointed out, France had already mobilized and Britain with the best will in the world could not guarantee French neutrality. Within hours, Grey had anyway withdrawn from the offer, claiming a 'misunderstanding'. By the evening of 2 August, Britain had already made significant moves towards intervention. The fleet was mobilized and the cabinet, which only three days earlier had decided that alone Britain had no obligation to defend Belgium's neutrality under the 1839 treaty signed by all great powers, had altered its view to regard a 'substantial violation' of Belgian territory as a sufficient trigger for war. In all likelihood, the British would have joined the war on the side of the Entente even without Moltke's invasion of Germany's small, neutral neighbour. Grey considered that Britain had a moral obligation to France and both he and the Prime

Minister, Herbert Asquith, were prepared to resign over the issue. Less emotionally committed Liberal colleagues were thus aware that if they did not opt for war, their government would fall, and in all probability be replaced by pro-intervention Conservatives, who themselves would declare hostilities. Strategic calculations too militated for war: neutrality would leave Britain dangerously isolated, regardless of which continental bloc ended victorious. What Moltke's invasion of Belgium did ensure was that Britain would enter the war earlier rather than later and united in moral fervour. How far this mattered would depend on whether Moltke could win a quick victory in the west.[150]

Fear, not aggression or unrestrained militarism, propelled the Central Powers to war in the summer of 1914. Rulers in both countries believed that they faced an imminent existential threat. Defensive motives stood behind belligerent actions. At the centre of the crisis was Europe's weakest and most under-armed great power, Austria-Hungary. Guided decisively by Berchtold and the young hawks in the Foreign Ministry, its leaders feared internal subversion and were convinced of their neighbours' hostile intentions. Alienated from the international order and overwhelmed by a sense of dire threat and the conviction that war alone offered an escape, these men were intensely dangerous. Alek Hoyos, the *chef de cabinet* at the heart of decision-making, expressed the attitude most clearly when, after letting slip to an acquaintance in mid-July that 'the war was as good as agreed', he added, 'if the world war comes out of it, it makes no difference to us'.[151] In Germany, Chancellor Bethmann Hollweg, who guided Reich policy in July 1914, was also disillusioned with multilateralism and sufficiently ruthless to consider a 'preventative war', but he did care deeply about avoiding global conflagration. He disastrously miscalculated the risk he faced. Despite their warnings, he underestimated Russian and British willingness to fight. Yet his greatest mistake was to place Germany's fate unconditionally in the hands of the desperate and despairing men in Vienna. At the end of July it was this, not military urging for mobilization, which made retreat impossible.

Despite all the blame subsequently heaped upon them, the Central Powers' soldiers played only an indirect, albeit important, role in bringing about the conflagration. Both Conrad and Moltke, through their urgent calls for preventative war, prepared the path to the catastrophe by impressing on the civilian officials who guided policy in the July crisis the need for aggressive action as the only escape from a nightmare strategic situation. Yet, once faced by the reality of war, both proved hesitant. Conrad was indecisive. Moltke was clearly scared. Falkenhayn was more aggressive, as were his underlings: the mood in the Prussian War Ministry when the 'State of Imminent War' was declared was euphoric: 'everywhere beaming faces, handshakes in the corridors, each congratulates the other'.[152] Yet between them, Bethmann and Moltke delayed mobilization to the point at which the Russian military's premature, aggressive and secret preparations made invasion appear imminent. For public opinion, this was crucial. The leaders of Austria-Hungary and Germany, having failed in their bid for localized war and triggered instead a general conflagration, were beholden to their peoples. Bethmann at least was hopeful: 'if war comes and the veils fall, the whole nation will follow, driven by necessity and peril'.[153]

2

Mobilizing the People

ASSASSINATION

On Monday, 29 June 1914, Vienna's morning newspapers carried doleful reports of the previous day's assassination of the imperial heir and his wife. Their front pages were edged with thick black borders, and the tone was one of shock and deep bereavement. 'One simply cannot grasp the monstrousness of it,' lamented the *Reichspost*. 'Our heir to the throne, the man on whom the peoples of the Habsburg Monarchy had placed all their hopes, their entire future, is no longer.'[1] The gutter press thought the murder 'an appalling calamity', and the Christian Socialist workers' *Arbeiter-Zeitung* considered it a 'breathtakingly hard misfortune'.[2] To any foreigner unfamiliar with the Empire's internal condition, sipping his Melange and flicking through the eulogies that morning, it must have appeared that Franz Ferdinand had been universally loved and admired. He was, gushed the metropolitan elite's paper, the *Neue Freie Presse*, an 'exceptional figure', whose demise was to be lamented: 'The Monarchy has lost something great.'[3]

The uniformly glowing newspaper obituaries to the archduke belied a complex popular reaction to news of the assassination. Franz Ferdinand's demise elicited a very wide range of emotional responses in Austria-Hungary. Significantly, however, belligerence was not generally among them. The desire of the Habsburg Foreign Ministry and military hawks for war was not widely shared. Central to understanding how the war could take place and why it was subsequently fought with such tenacity is a shift in popular opinion in July and early August 1914. The Austro-Hungarian and German peoples underwent a remarkable but rarely recounted emotional journey during that summer of crisis, culminating in acceptance and even belief in the necessity of conflict. The Habsburg heir's violent death was the starting point. Its ability to incite popular passions has long been dismissed, for, notwithstanding the obligatory panegyrics of the Viennese press, Franz Ferdinand had not been popular in the capital. He was known as crass and boorish, and people had worried what he might do when he finally grasped the levers of power. German nationalists feared his reputed pro-Slav tendencies; others believed (probably more accurately) that he would cause upheaval by attempting to recentralize authority. His insistence on the divine right of kings did little to recommend him to the capital's Socialist workers.[4] Yet contrary to what has often been claimed, citizens were anything but indifferent. When, five days after the murder, the bodies of the archducal couple passed through Vienna, people did turn out in large numbers. Journalists recounted how they crammed into the *Hofburgpfarrkirche* (the Church of the Imperial Court) to see the funeral bier in the morning and, late in the evening, tens of thousands lined the route to the city's western rail station, whence the bodies were to be transported to their final resting place at Artstetten Castle.[5] The majority came out of curiosity, rather than from any real sense of loss. One onlooker from out of town found to his surprise that 'no-one in the masses of people packed solid around me expressed any special signs of grief or sorrow, and, indeed, there was much laughter and telling of jokes'.[6]

This curiosity, morbid fascination with a celebrity death, and not belligerence, was what really defined Vienna's mood in the first week of July. The same observer was right on the mark when he described a city 'agog with excitement' at news of the assassination.[7] The pictures that came out of Sarajevo made for compulsive viewing. Readers of popular illustrated journals could ghoulishly follow the final hours of the archducal couple, from the scene of the first, failed bomb attack, through their fateful departure down the steps of Sarajevo's city hall (a photograph, it was stressed, taken just 'minutes before the catastrophe'), to the dramatic apprehension of the killer Gavrilo Princip (or someone thought to be him) by gendarmes and exotic-looking Bosnians in fezzes, just after he had fired the fatal shots.[8] Newspapers drew in even those unsympathetic to the monarchy by playing up the human tragedy. The heir and his wife were a little too middle-aged to move many hearts, but they left behind them three young and photogenic children. First to recognize this lucrative angle was Prague's *Národní Listy*, which needed to catch the attention of a Czech nationalist audience unlikely to weep many tears over a dead Habsburg. Already on 30 June, it carried on its front page a large sketch of twelve-year-old Princess Sophie and her brothers, Princes Maximilian and Ernst, eleven and ten respectively, underneath the headline 'Sarajevo Tragedy'.[9] The Viennese press soon caught on, however, and devoted much space to the orphans' plight. The imperial house's care for them and their distraught reactions on learning of their parents' deaths were earnestly discussed. The morbid pathos reached excruciating levels when it was put about that Franz Ferdinand's last words to his mortally injured wife were 'Sophie, stay living for our children . . .'[10]

The other major topic of conversation was, of course, who was behind the assassinations. Right from the start, the newspapers suspected a plot with origins in Serbia. Although investigations had only just begun, already on 30 June, the *Reichspost*, a paper close to Franz Ferdinand, published a report claiming Serbian involvement to have been officially proven. That same evening, angry demonstrators gathered outside the Serbian embassy singing and shouting 'Down with Serbia!' They burned a Serbian flag before being moved on by police.[11] Several nights of patriotic and anti-Serb protests followed. On 1 July a patriotic crowd marched to the Hofburg, the imperial residence, singing and shouting 'Up Austria!' before trying and failing to get close enough to the Serbian embassy to protest. On the next evening, when the bodies of the arch-ducal couple arrived in Vienna, the protestors were more determined and the mood was uglier. A whistling and boisterous crowd several thousand strong faced off police near the embassy, and a few even succeeded briefly, at around half past nine in the evening, in breaking through the cordon surrounding it. Although they were eventually persuaded to depart, more demonstrators arrived a couple of hours later and fighting broke out. Street cobbles were prised up and hurled at the patrolmen; one police horse lost an eye. The cordon had, however, been reinforced, and the crowd was unable to penetrate it. Eventually, the protestors gave up and marched instead to the Bulgarian embassy to cheer Bulgaria and shout 'Down with Serbia!' A small number headed for the Russian embassy, around which the police had, with foresight, already placed a guard. Only at one in the morning were the streets again quiet. This was not the last of the trouble, however. Only on the following evening did violence reach its peak when demonstrators returned, singing patriotic songs and armed with sticks, stones and fireworks. They confronted 500 patrolmen and 200 mounted police. The fighting was bitter. The police launched mounted charges in order to clear the streets, but again only at one in the morning did this 'patriotic' riot finally end.[12]

The aggression of these crowds was not representative of public opinion in Vienna. The people taking part in the protests came from various walks of life, but they were all young men. While the *Neue Freie Presse* noticed some workers and apprentices, and blamed much of the rioting vaguely on 'half-grown boys', the core of the demonstrations was in fact, as another of Vienna's papers observed, made up of 'numerous students, office workers and members of the educated classes'.[13] The singing of the patriotic hymn 'The Watch on the Rhine' alongside the imperial anthem may also suggest that hard-line German nationalists were among them. The numbers actively involved were relatively small, usually from 600 to 1,000 people. This was true even at the last major demonstration outside the Serbian embassy on 3 July. Then, although tens of thousands were passing through the streets near the embassy and one paper estimated the crowd at 15,000, those actually participating in the rioting totalled perhaps 800 people.[14] Nonetheless, their violence was to some extent the prelude to a wider shift in mood, reflected in newspaper commentary, which took place in the second and third weeks of July. Public anger grew, fuelled by the Serbian press's arguments that Austria-Hungary, through its misguided policies in the Balkans, had only itself to blame for Franz Ferdinand's assassination, and by the release of evidence uncovered by the official investigation implicating the Serbian authorities in the murder. Hostilities did not yet appear likely; the Habsburg Foreign Ministry encouraged newspapers not to unsettle people with this possibility prematurely, and as late as 15 July the Hungarian Minister President, Count Tisza, told the Magyar parliament that although war with Serbia was possible, it was neither desirable nor probable.[15] In upper- and middle-class circles, however, a wish for some sort of decisive response, even if not necessarily armed conflict, increased. By 19 July, as the government was preparing its ultimatum, even the formerly moderate *Neue Freie Presse* was demanding ominously that 'relations with Serbia must be clarified'.[16]

Beyond the Habsburg metropolis, Franz Ferdinand's murder caused disquiet. The archduke was certainly not short of enemies among nationalists and Socialists in the Crownlands. The Polish Socialist Ignacy Daszyński, for example, later described him vitriolically as 'in our circles the most disliked, bah, the most hateful personage. A clericalist, fierce reactionary, enemy of the Poles . . . the archduke personified for us the threat for the future.'[17] Yet in the far-flung corners of the realm, where people had seen little of the heir and were less conscious of his faults, his violent death frequently came as a shock. *Czas*, the Polish conservatives' paper, was probably more sincere than its Viennese counterparts when it started its first report on the assassination 'Tragic news stuns the state and its population.'[18] In Lwów's public parks, unlike in Vienna's Prater, the music did stop when accounts of the murder reached the city, and in Prague the Czech National Theatre broke off a performance, announced the news from the stage and sent its audience home.[19] In Carniola, loyal Slovene subjects lined the track when the train carrying the couple's bodies to Vienna passed through on 2 July. At stations, the train was mobbed by tearful crowds.[20] Everywhere, there were Habsburg subjects who, like the Czech Jan Vit, at least rued the archducal couple's 'tragic death'.[21] Some were seriously shaken. Aleksandra Czechówna, for instance, a good Catholic and patriotic Pole who moved in Cracow's theatrical circles, had met the archduke once a few years previously when he visited her home town, and admired his deep religious faith and the sacrifices that he had made for his wife. She was horrified by the 'terrible crime'. He had been, she confided to her diary, 'the nicest and, one can say, ideal man whom one couldn't help but adore'.[22] Others in the Monarchy's borderlands had justified worries about the murder's political consequences. Mieczysław Schwestek, the Polish stationmaster of Zbaraż, a small town in the north-eastern corner of Galicia, remembered that 'the news of the tragic death of the archducal couple made a frankly dreadful impression on us'. Living just half an hour from the Russian frontier, he had every reason to keep an eye on international events, and knew how strained relations between Austria-Hungary and Serbia had become. 'Supposing that the initiative for the assassination came from Serbia, we predicted the outbreak of war between these states and feared that this entanglement might trigger the outbreak of a world war.'[23]

Above all, the assassination markedly increased racial tensions right across the Habsburg Empire. This began, unsurprisingly, in Sarajevo, which was rocked on the day after the murder by anti-Serb riots. Shops, private residences and Orthodox Church buildings were all attacked. During the following twenty-four hours, unrest spread to other towns in the region, and on 1 July martial law was declared across Bosnia-Herzegovina.[24] It also jumped to nearby Dalmatia and Croatia, which had their own Serb minorities. In Agram (now Zagreb), there were protests over several days, similar in some ways to the Vienna riots but with the significant difference that they were directed not only against a foreign power, but above all against Habsburg Serb subjects. Thus on 1 July around 500 people, many of them students, carried a Croatian flag and a huge portrait of Franz Ferdinand through the city's streets. When they became bored of chanting 'Down with King Peter!' (the Serbian monarch) and 'Down with the murderers!', they wrecked a café and threw stones at Serb property. In Ragusa (today Dubrovnik), disturbances on 4 and 5 July were similar in sentiment but were caused mainly by peasants from outside the city. Some forced the mayor to take down the Serbian flag flying at half mast next to the Croatian tricolour on the town hall, while others stampeded through the premises of Serb nationalist associations, broke into a Serbian school and destroyed signs with Cyrillic writing. Troops only restored peace with difficulty on the second day, when two people were injured and fifteen arrested. By 8 July, such violence was so widespread that the Emperor's representative in the neighbouring Kingdom of Croatia, the *Ban*, authorized his officials to use all necessary means to enforce public order.[25]

It was not only Serb minorities that were affected, however; other Habsburg South Slavs faced discrimination and persecution. For people across the Empire, it seemed scarcely credible that a gang of teenage students armed with nothing more than a few hand grenades and Browning pistols could alone have murdered the heir to the throne, the second most important man in the realm. Conspiracy theories swept the land. The Habsburg authorities, unable to believe their own incompetence, were no less gripped. The Austrian Interior Ministry sent a coded telegram to all Crownland heads on 2 July warning that more Serb assassins had entered the Monarchy. There were house searches in Prague and arrests of Serb students, alleged spies and sympathizers all across the Empire, from Ljubljana to Lwów.[26] In ethnically mixed areas in the centre and south, Habsburg South Slavs found their neighbours eyeing them nervously. We know most about Styria, a Crownland which lay 400 kilometres from Sarajevo and was inhabited by Germans and

Slovenes, not Serbs. Here, the reporting of the local German press on the assassination was from the start hysterical. Newspapers, regardless of their political affiliation, surmised that a network of spies and activists buried deep in Habsburg society and controlled from Belgrade was at work. Nationalist agitators were alleged to have led astray the Slovenian population. Its clergy was regarded with particular suspicion. So too were Slovenian 'Sokol' gymnastic clubs, which were accused, no less unjustly, of having celebrated the heir to the throne's demise. One paper even reported completely mendaciously that on the same day as the Sarajevo assassinations, South Slav activists had attacked another archduke in the Styrian town of Marburg as part of a devious plot to extinguish at one stroke the entire Habsburg dynasty.

The German populace reading these reports naturally panicked. People saw threats where there were none. A wave of denunciations flooded local authorities. Police were ordered to conduct searches. There was an atmosphere of emergency which demanded they show results, and the pressure was further heightened by another warning, sent from the Interior Ministry on 20 July, that the Serbs might carry out terrorist attacks beyond Bosnia-Herzegovina. Lacking firm leads, the police substituted action for thought and arrested anyone whom they or their informers considered suspicious. As early as 29 June, a female 'spy' was stopped on the railways, and, as war came closer and tensions escalated, increasing numbers of the Crownland's loyal Habsburg Slovene subjects were taken into custody. Foreigners were also targets of distrust; one Reich German, arrested at the end of July, was held for seven weeks until he was proven to be totally harmless. A vicious circle began, in which arrests prompted by rumours and suspicions appeared to confirm an anxious public's fears, leading to more denunciations and yet more arrests.[27]

Ethnic groups with no sympathy for Serbia but who were suspected of harbouring their own irredentist ambitions also fell victim to the spiralling fear and paranoia. In the western corner of the Monarchy, Habsburg Italians in Trient were falsely rumoured to be engaged in treasonous conspiracy.[28] At its eastern extreme, in Hungary, the Romanian minority could, one of its members later complained, 'hardly move for gendarmes and police spies' in the month after Franz Ferdinand's murder. 'All kinds of rumours flourished,' he remembered. 'Every man spied on his neighbour, no matter how placid and peace-loving.'[29] Nor did the north of the Empire, a region not short of long-standing ethnic enmities, go untouched by the fear and heightened racial antagonisms of July 1914. In Vienna, the schools of Czech immigrants had their windows broken by Germans wishing to avenge the archduke's murder by a Slav.[30] The same thing took place in Troppau, the German-dominated capital of Austrian Silesia, where, at least according to the Polish press, German professors led their students in the vandalism. Other brutal clashes between Czech and German crowds, and between demonstrators and police, were reported too from Moravia.[31] The first weeks of the month also witnessed a wave of riots and demonstrations in Galicia, although there, unlike elsewhere, Germans were the victims. These were not directly related to events in Sarajevo; a clash between German and Polish youths, in which the latter had come off worst, had taken place in the town of Biała on the day before Franz Ferdinand's assassination and was the cause of widespread Polish indignation. Nonetheless, the backdrop of acute tension in the rest of the Monarchy helps to account for the unusually tumultuous response. In the Crownland's major cities, as well as in smaller communities, violent protests took place. Students in Lwów smashed the windows of the clubhouse of the 'German Association in Galicia' and then destroyed German shop signs and displays in the city's main streets on the evening of 29 June. At the start of the following month, there were further anti-German riots in Przemyśl and, just over a week later, in nearby Tarnów. The violence in turn outraged Germans beyond Galicia. In the middle of July, the German population of Czernowitz, the capital of the neighbouring Crownland Bukovina, gathered in order to protest.[32]

As the Habsburg Common Ministerial Council gathered on 19 July to discuss for a final time its ultimatum to Serbia, the Empire's peoples were already in a state of acute anxiety, in some areas even upheaval. While opprobrium towards the Serbs had grown in some quarters and there was even growing support in the capital for harsh measures, the fact that most of the tension and aggression was directed inwards should have acted as a warning to the leaders plotting war. The protests and anti-Serb pogroms in Bosnia-Herzegovina, Dalmatia and Croatia laid bare the illusory nature of the government's fears that the South Slav lands were seriously tempted by a greater Serbia. The ethnic tensions and suspicions inflamed by the assassination across the Habsburg Empire should have cast doubt on the unreasoned faith that armed conflict would somehow bring greater unity to a divided realm. The Ministerial Council, set on its course, ignored such considerations. Instead, the ultimatum was approved, and four days later placed before the Serb government. With it, a drastic step had been taken towards war.

THE JULY CRISIS

The Austro-Hungarian ultimatum issued to Serbia on the evening of 23 July made newspaper headlines across Europe. In Germany, the assassination of the Habsburg heir and his wife had dominated front pages at the end of June, but interest had soon waned. It was far from the only news that summer; there was war in Albania, a French state visit to Russia and, at home, by-elections and the condemnation of the well-known Alsatian artist 'Hansi' for inciting class hatred. The sensational murder trial of Madame Caillaux, the French cabinet minister's wife who had shot and killed the editor of Paris's foremost conservative newspaper *Le Figaro*, also made absorbing reading for the holiday season. The Habsburg note, however, wrenched German attention back to the Balkans dispute. Its harshness startled the public, for there had been widespread predictions of a relatively moderate response. For all that the bourgeois press, in accordance with the wishes of the Reich government, insisted that Austria-Hungary's terms were justified, the danger of the move quickly became apparent. Russia's warning on the following day that it could not remain indifferent in any Austro-Serbian conflict raised the possibility of a major international crisis.[33]

In Austria-Hungary, the ultimatum turned the attention of the Empire's already agitated peoples back outwards. The press had received official instructions on how to portray the note. The demands were, it was acknowledged, 'severe' but also 'completely justifiable and necessary, left no room for discussion and did not exclude the hope of maintaining peace'.[34] Newspapers presented the population as entirely behind the initiative: the Viennese were characterized as 'calm and serious' yet relieved that decisive action was being taken against Belgrade. In Hungary, representatives at a parliamentary sitting on Friday, 24 July, were said to be at one with their people when they agreed that Serbia's provocations could not go on: 'Clarification,' it was insisted, 'with all means and at any price is an unavoidable necessity.' Entente intervention was dismissed in the parliament as 'inconceivable'. If it did happen, not the Empire but 'Europe' would 'bear the responsibility' for a world war.[35]

On the evening of Saturday, 25 July, after forty-eight hours of waiting and mistaken reports that Serbia would accept the Habsburg demands, news of the 'unsatisfactory' response arrived at 7.45 p.m. in Vienna and at around 9.30 p.m. in Berlin. The capitals were packed full of people, on the main squares, around newspaper buildings, and in cafes and beer halls; if one wanted news in an age before radio, one went out and looked for it. A particularly large crowd of over ten thousand had gathered outside the Habsburg War Ministry, anticipating that an announcement would be made here. When the ultimatum's rejection and the break in diplomatic relations became known, first through newspaper extras but then spread quickly by word of mouth, most people went home. Those who stayed, however, created one of the most enduring and powerful memories of the First World War's outbreak. Outside the War Ministry in Vienna, a mood of infectious patriotism prevailed. The crowd cheered the Habsburgs, Austria, the army and the now inevitable war. Stirring patriotic refrains lifted to the sky: 'The Watch on the Rhine', 'Hail to Thee in Victor's Garland' and, most fittingly, the old Austrian song about the siege of Belgrade in 1717, 'Prince Eugen, the Noble Knight', adapted to the crowd's expectations of the coming campaign:

> Archduke Eugen the noble knight,
> Will battle the Serbs brave and well
> He will a bridge erect
> We'll go across direct
> And we'll occupy Belgrade!

From the mass of people, a student – we do not know his name – climbed onto the plinth of the Radetzky Monument and gave a speech calling on those gathered to sacrifice 'possessions and blood for Kaiser and Fatherland!' Somebody unfurled an imperial black-gold flag and, under this standard, around a thousand cheering people marched together down the middle of the Ringstrasse. Similar scenes played out that evening across the centre of Vienna, at monuments, outside friendly embassies and in front of the imperial residence. The whole city was, wrote one resident, 'seething with excitement'.[36]

In Berlin, the press wrote more frankly of the tension felt among the waiting people. Horror was the most obvious first reaction to news of the Habsburg ultimatum's rejection. Nonetheless, here too, in the city centre, spontaneous patriotic demonstrations quickly formed. These began already at 8 p.m., when the first rumours of Serbia's refusal started to circulate. Groups of people, some carrying German or Austro-Hungarian flags, gathered, cheered the German and Austrian Kaisers, and sang patriotic songs. Witnesses tell of demonstrations of 2,000, some of even 10,000, people. They paraded arm in arm up and down Berlin's main street, Unter den Linden, being applauded by spectators in the cafes on either side. Patriotic landmarks, as in Vienna, formed the focal points of the demonstrations: there were impromptu speeches and there was singing outside the Kaiser's palace (unoccupied, as he was on his annual North Sea cruise) and, on the other side of the Brandenburg Gate, at Bismarck's statue. The crowd marched to the Habsburg embassy, where they were thanked by the ambassador. Some gathered outside the offices of the Reich's Chancellor, and were greeted by him. A noisy protest, later criticized in the press, was also held at around midnight in front of the Russian embassy. Only at 3.45 a.m. were the streets quiet.[37]

These first patriotic demonstrations were repeated in the following days, as Austria-Hungary and then Germany went to war. In Berlin, a few thousand people marched on the 26 July. Although thereafter the demonstrations waned and then disappeared in the midweek, the proclamation of the 'State of Siege' on 31 July and mobilization on 1 August brought out crowds of unprecedented size. On the latter date, between 40,000 and 50,000 people gathered around the Kaiser's palace. Moreover, the patriotic manifestations were replicated, albeit on a smaller scale, across the Reich. Already on 25 July there were processions in major cities such as Hamburg, Munich and Stuttgart, and in university towns like Freiburg and Jena, and others followed on subsequent days.[38] The Habsburg Empire's capital, where partial mobilization against Serbia had been ordered as early as 25 July, was the scene of huge but organized patriotic demonstrations in the following week. On 26 July the city's tram workers, along with veterans' and apprentices' associations, together around 15,000 people, marched to join a crowd of 25,000 outside the City Hall. Three days later, after war with Serbia had begun on 28 July, a parade by Vienna's veterans' associations was watched, it was estimated, by over 100,000 people, many probably relatives of those marching.[39] The city's newspapers reported excitedly that similar demonstrations were taking place across the Empire. All divisions appeared miraculously to have been overcome. 'Everywhere,' wrote the *Reichspost*, 'in Tyrol and Silesia, in the Carpathians, the Hungarian Puszta, on the shores of the Adriatic, no less than in the imperial city Vienna, the population is rising in passionate approval of the decision to fight.'[40]

Was it true, as both countries' bourgeois press insisted, that these demonstrations expressed a united enthusiasm for war among Germans and Austro-Hungarians? There are good reasons to think not. For a start, the genuinely spontaneous early patriotic actions attracted only modest numbers of participants. The groups parading in Vienna on 25 July were each mostly between 600 and 1,000 strong; altogether, probably between 5,000 and 15,000 people took part.[41] Together with the at most 30,000 who marched in Berlin that evening, they were a tiny minority among the more than two million inhabitants of each capital. The marchers also represented a very select demographic. Wandering through the centre of Vienna late on the evening of 28 July, the day war was declared on Serbia, the Austrian politician Joseph Maria Baernreither was struck that 'the enthusiastic crowd was very young'. Commentators said the same in Germany: those singing and shouting patriotic slogans were youthful, upper middle class and mostly, although not exclusively, male. From the start students, later joined by youth organizations, played a leading role.[42]

These young demonstrators should not be lightly dismissed as aggressive chauvinists. They were moved by multifarious motives to take to the streets. Certainly, many were ardent patriots, some belligerent, but plenty supported the war with reason. Especially among Vienna's upper classes, there was a strand of opinion which considered that Serb provocations had gone far enough and that decisive action was necessary. Many young men parading on 25 July were thus, as in the violent protests earlier in the month and as one upper-middle-class woman remembered of her sons, 'filled with thoughts of revenge against Serbia'.[43] In Berlin on the same night, however, the intention of demonstrators was to express support for Austria-Hungary, not to demand violent intervention by Germany. For all the positive associations of adventure and heroism which war had for many in that generation of bourgeois youth, the rowdiness accompanying some of the parades betrays young people taking advantage of a once in a lifetime chance briefly to overturn social norms; opportunities to stomp, shout and cheer through main streets, while knocking off the hats of passers-by who failed to show respect for the patriotic anthems being sung, were naturally rare in imperial cities.[44] For those who felt anxious, and privately very many did, the demonstrations provided a welcome chance to release tension, and a comforting act of solidarity. Students' motivations have been particularly misunderstood. For the fraternities, infamous for their duelling and drinking (although while the latter was universal, the former was not), the mark of a man was his readiness to sacrifice himself for the greater national good. Students identified themselves as stalwart patriots; most were neither naive nor stupid. Their demonstrations expressed a readiness to face, not a desire for, the horrors of armed conflict.[45]

The larger crowds which gathered in German and Austro-Hungarian cities during that last week of July 1914 were certainly not demanding war. Most were awaiting news, some excitedly, many with great anxiety. 'Strange, feverish gestures, excited faces, whispers' all betrayed the nervousness that these people felt as conflagration threatened.[46] So awful was the thought that many refused to accept it could come to a European conflict. After Austria-Hungary rejected Serbia's answer to its ultimatum as insufficient, one shop owner in the city of Freiburg, not far from the Franco-German border, observed ruefully that 'no one yet wanted to believe in a general war, no one wanted to presume that Russia, on whom alone war or peace depended, would really take its role as protector of Serbia so far as to unleash a world war'.[47] At the start of the week there were still grounds for optimism. Although Austro-Hungarians recognized that a Balkan conflict was inevitable, both they and the German public were led by the press, which reported on British proposals for mediation, to hope for its 'localization'.[48] Many nonetheless took precautions. When city banks opened on Monday morning, 27 July, queues of people, mostly small savers, among whom women were especially prominent, were waiting to close their accounts. Small change ran short as people hung on to silver and gold coinage, and tradesmen had to be warned that they faced a legal obligation to accept paper money. As the crisis worsened, people also began to buy up and hoard food, which in consequence suddenly became very expensive. This began earlier in Austria than in Germany: already by 30 July, the day that the cost of food started to become a serious problem in the Reich, maximum prices had been introduced and officials were ordered to combat war profiteering in Bohemia.[49]

In both Austria-Hungary and Germany it could be expected that, far from being enthused by such a conflict, a significant part of the populations would actively resist going to war. The Habsburg government particularly feared the Czechs' reaction; Foreign Minister Berchtold, as we have seen, thought on 29 June that revolution could break out in Bohemia if the Monarchy attempted to mobilize against Serbia.[50] Special precautions were taken in Prague on 15 July, the day that the ultimatum expired, to prevent pro-Russian demonstrations. In the event, however, the Crownland's governor was able to report to his superiors in Vienna that 'everywhere calm' had prevailed.[51] There was also no open resistance from Austrian Social Democrats, although on 25 July they published in the party newspaper a manifesto against war. The explanation for the lack of resistance is straightforward: on the same day, the government issued in conjunction with the order for partial mobilization a set of 'Emergency Laws' suspending Habsburg subjects' constitutional rights, including their rights of free speech and assembly. Civilians in the Austrian half of the Monarchy became subject to military courts for a range of 'political' offences, such as, but not limited to, disturbances of the public peace, rioting and insurrection, lese-majesty, high treason and interference with the railways or army. Anyone trying to hinder mobilization would also be put before a court martial.[52] Victor Adler, the Social Democrats' leader, was cowed by this new regime. 'The party is helpless,' he told fellow Socialists on 29 July. 'We cannot stave off the danger. Demonstrations have become impossible ... Our entire organization and our press are at stake.'[53]

The German Social Democrats (SPD) were far more formidable than their Austrian counterparts. With 1.1 million members, they were ten times the size of the Austrian party and the largest organization in the Reich, excepting the war veterans' umbrella association, the Kyffhäuserbund. The so-called 'Free Unions', with which the SPD possessed a close relationship, together numbered more than 2.5 million workers; there was an obvious potential here for massive disruption.[54] Moreover, at the International Socialist Congress of 1907 the SPD had committed itself to hinder the outbreak of any war or, if unsuccessful, strive to hasten its end while exploiting the inevitable accompanying economic and political crisis to accelerate the capitalist class system's demise. The fiery rhetoric, influenced by French and Russian Socialists, in fact belied the party's reformist instincts. By 1914, its leadership was dominated by men who wished not for a violent break, but rather a legal transition to real democracy. They were also, despite being tarred by their enemies as 'comrades with no Fatherland', patriots who had frequently stated their readiness to defend the Reich. Still, there could be no doubt that an aggressive action in the sphere of foreign policy would meet with firm resistance. Already at the time of the second Morocco crisis in 1911 and during the Balkan Wars in 1912–13, the SPD had demonstrated its ability to call out mass peace demonstrations.[55]

The ultimatum issued by Austria-Hungary to Serbia had not been viewed favourably in the SPD. The *Hamburger Echo*, one of the local party newspapers, spoke for most German Socialists when it observed that the Habsburg note looked 'very similar to an intentional provocation for war'.[56] Unlike Socialists in Austria, where the immediate partial mobilization and imposition of emergency laws ruled out organized opposition, the SPD did have a little time to react. On 25 July the party's executive committee appealed for mass meetings 'to express the unshakeable desire for peace of the class-conscious proletariat'.[57] The German government permitted these to go ahead, on condition that they were held in closed rooms, not on the streets. The response was impressive. In Berlin alone, thirty-two meetings were held, with over 100,000 attendees. Across the Reich, at least 288 anti-war gatherings took place in 163 towns and cities, mostly between 28 and 30 July. Three-quarters of a million Germans participated. The Socialist press wrote of halls so full that crowds were left standing outside, unable to enter. In a few places after the meetings, the ban on street protests was disregarded, and spontaneous marches began into city centres. In Berlin on the evening of 28 July, between 1,000 and 2,000 anti-war demonstrators made their way to Unter den Linden and confronted patriots in a 'singing war'. The workers' 'Marseillaise' briefly drowned out 'The Watch on the Rhine' before they were dispersed by mounted police. Stuttgart and Düsseldorf saw particularly violent clashes with security services. Generally, however, the meetings were quiet, even subdued. The SPD's principal hope was that Germany's leaders could still restrain their warmongering Habsburg ally. Speakers rarely criticized the government. No advice was proffered to listeners on how to resist if hostilities did break out; the party itself had no plan for protests or strikes. Some on the right of the party, such as Mannheim's Reichstag deputy Ludwig Frank, told their audiences that if it did come to war, they would have to fight.[58]

The countryside, where around a third of Germans, over half of Austrians and three-fifths of Hungarians were employed in agriculture, saw less public drama than the cities in the last week of July.[59] There were no crowds here, no marchers, no patriotic songs or anti-war speeches. It was harvest time and people were busy. In some remote and poorly connected parts of the Habsburg Empire, there was even surprise at the mobilization. In Tyrol, far from Serbia and Russia, villagers working in the fields were sometimes astonished when summoned by church bells. They rushed back expecting a fire, and instead were dismayed to be told of mobilization.[60] Such parochialism was probably exceptional, however. There had, after all, been high tension across the Empire in the weeks following Franz Ferdinand's death. What was common to the rural communities of this diverse land was the despair and fear felt at news that their men and horses would be called up for war. When a trumpeter shattered the peace of the Sabbath in Zabłotów, an east Galician shtetl of 4,775 souls that was the childhood home of Manès Sperber, the news that he brought was generally considered disastrous. Some young men were gung-ho, but the women wept and rushed to the community cemetery, where, Sperber remembered, they 'begged the dead for help, asking them to intercede with the Almighty'.[61] The reaction was hardly better hundreds of kilometres to the west in Austrian Silesian Jabłonków, a market town of just under 4,000 people, mostly Polish but with a German minority and a smattering of Czechs and Jews. As Father Dominik Ściskała, one of the town's Catholic priests, recorded vividly in his diary:

> For us in Jabłonków, the first visible sign of the serious situation was news of the announcement of general mobilization, put up in the window of the post office at 3.30 p.m. on 31 July. The marketplace immediately teemed with people. Groups formed, animatedly discussing the significance of the moment. Men predominated. Everyone realized that the situation was dangerous. All were seized by a strange fear of the unknown, great and threatening. Enthusiasm, which newspapers from a few towns are reporting, was not and is not present here.[62]

In Germany, most of the rural population was similarly depressed and frightened. There, as in the towns, the anxiety had begun with the issuing of the Habsburg ultimatum on 23 July and climbed in the subsequent week. Ruth Höfner, from the village of Sakrau in Upper Silesia, recalled how during the last days of July, 'great disquiet ruled, the people stood in the street and didn't want to work'.[63] The signs that war was imminent multiplied rapidly from 31 July, as first the 'State of Imminent War' was proclaimed and then, a few hours later at 4 p.m., the 'State of Siege' regime was imposed, which enabled the suspension of constitutional rights and permitted the military to issue orders to local civilian administrations. The announcement of mobilization, issued at 5 p.m. on the following day and reaching most rural communities that same evening, was seen as a catastrophe. Karol Małłek, a farmhand from the Masurian village of Brodowen, described how 'everybody cried and wailed'.[64] That the coming of war should cause particular upset in communities like Sakrau and Brodowen, both close to the Russian frontier, should come as no surprise. Both Höfner and Małłek fled their homes; Höfner had left, with her weeping mother, in an overcrowded train early on the morning of 31 July. Yet reactions to mobilization were not much less anxious in relatively safe regions. 'Hearts were filled with dismay and horror,' wrote one policeman in Ering, a village situated well out of harm's way in the south of Bavaria. 'All merrymaking was ended at a stroke. People spoke from this time only about the war and about how now to organize domestic and family matters.'[65]

While the coming of a European conflagration was seen almost universally as a catastrophe, with few exceptions the German and Austro-Hungarian peoples, like those within the Triple Entente, did not regard it as the fault of their own governments. Emperor Franz Joseph, in his appeal 'To my People', explained the war with Serbia in fundamentally defensive terms: 'After long years of peace, the intrigues of a hate-filled opponent force me, for the preservation of my Monarchy's honour, in defence of its reputation and political power, and in order to secure its rights, to grasp for the sword.' The old Emperor reminded his subjects that it had taken far more than one murdered archduke to provoke this war. 'A criminal activity reaches across the border to undermine the foundations of public order in the south-east of the Monarchy,' he warned them. The Serbs had long sought 'to shake the people ... in its loyalty to dynasty and Fatherland, to mislead the rising generation of youth and to incite wicked acts of madness and high treason'. Franz Ferdinand's assassination, a result of a 'methodically prepared and executed conspiracy', was only the latest 'visible bloody trace of those secret intrigues'. The time had now come for action. Austria-Hungary's 'moderate and just demands' had been rejected by the Serbian government. 'Thus,' explained Franz Joseph, 'I must intervene to win through force of arms the guarantees that are essential to secure for my states internal tranquillity and a lasting external peace.'[66]

Awkward debate about whether Serbia's response to the Habsburg ultimatum had in fact been sufficient to make war unnecessary was avoided by delaying the text's publication. It appeared in newspapers only on Tuesday, 28 July, the day of the Monarchy's declaration of hostilities.[67] For good measure, fabricated news of a Serb attack on Habsburg forces a day earlier at Temes Kubin was also publicized, although contrary to what is sometimes assumed, this was never a central plank in the Austro-Hungarian justification for war; Minister President Tisza publicly dismissed it on the day that it was supposed to have taken place as 'an incident of no significance at all'.[68] There was very little time for people to question the only partially justified official interpretation of events, as already on 28 July reservists began hurrying to their units. The partial mobilization against Serbia, designed to raise two-fifths of Habsburg military strength for an invasion, embraced corps based in Bohemia, Dalmatia, Croatia, Bosnia-Herzegovina and parts of Hungary including Budapest.[69]

For other Austro-Hungarians and for the German public, the focus now shifted to Russia. The governments and bourgeois press of both Central Powers stressed the desire for 'localization'. Whether war would spread across Europe, people were told, 'depends on decisions in St Petersburg'.[70] Reich Germans' accounts testify to the overwhelming stress felt during the second half of the week as reports of Tsarist military preparations mounted. These were, as one Berlin student later put it, 'tense days, the worst that I experienced'.[71] On Thursday, 30 July, Germans awoke to news of Russian partial mobilization against Austria-Hungary. In the early afternoon, there was a scare when one of the capital's newspapers, the *Berliner Lokal-Anzeiger*, keen to get a scoop, erroneously announced German general mobilization. The report was rapidly withdrawn but other unsubstantiated rumours of assassination, military preparations, even of a German ultimatum to Russia, were quickly passed from mouth to mouth. People waited nervously.

Most hoped that a diplomatic solution might still be found; it was common knowledge that the Kaiser was in contact with the Tsar. There was also anger. A sailor, Wilhelm Wagner, travelling that day by rail for a last visit to his parents, noted in his diary how his carriage was full of 'lively discussion, in which Russia was dealt with harshly'.[72] As evening drew in, the newspapers were reporting: 'Still No Decision'.[73]

The following two days, the final forty-eight hours before the cataclysm, were decisive for the internal state in which Germany entered the First World War. On the afternoon of Friday, 31 July, rumours, this time accurate, of Russian general mobilization signalled that the country was under threat of invasion. The mood in Berlin that day was different from previously – still very nervous, serious, but as the announcement of the 'State of Imminent War' became known, now demonstratively patriotic. Wilhelm II had cut short his North Sea cruise and returned to the capital at around 3 p.m. After the 'State of Siege' was declared an hour later, a large crowd of between 10,000 and 40,000, consisting mostly of middle-class Berliners of all ages, gathered before the imperial palace. At 6.30 p.m. the Kaiser came out onto a second-floor balcony, to tell his people why Germany may have to fight: 'envious rivals everywhere drive us to legitimate defence. The sword has been forced into our hand.'[74] His message of a conflict imposed on a reluctant Reich resonated with the popular mood and was reinforced by newspapers that evening, which damned the Tsar and his general mobilization for destroying all efforts at mediation. The ultimatum sent to Russia ordering that it cease all military preparations within twelve hours was not looked upon hopefully. The *Kölnische Zeitung*, one of the country's foremost newspapers on foreign policy, pithily summed up the situation in its headline: 'The Russians Want War'.[75]

This understanding of the coming conflict as fundamentally defensive was the precondition for a solidarity that became manifest on 1 August 1914. The crowds gathered early that day in cities across Germany, waiting, mostly sombrely, to hear whether Russia had backed down. For a long time no news came. Finally, shortly after 5 p.m., the mass of people gathered around Berlin's imperial palace were told by an officer that the Kaiser had ordered the mobilization. There was a momentary silence. Some then cheered, others started to sing 'The Watch on the Rhine'. It was no coincidence, however, that at this point of crisis most in the crowd sung not a patriotic refrain, but instead took up a Lutheran hymn:

> A mighty fortress is our God,
> A trusty shield and weapon;
> He helps us free from every need
> That hath us now overtaken.

In other towns and cities, Germans overwhelmingly reacted to the news of mobilization, at least in public, calmly and seriously. Many, after the tension of recent days, even experienced it as 'a deliverance from the terrible pressure'.[76] There was some loud patriotism expressed in pubs, cafes and on the streets. Cheering marchers again circulated in the centres of big cities like Hamburg and Frankfurt am Main. In Berlin a noisy patriotic procession wound its way to the Chancellor's offices. People, particularly middle-class people, spoke of 'enthusiasm'. Yet what really impressed that evening was the solidarity that they sensed. 'Poor and rich shake hands, speak together in the streets,' observed one woman in the university town of Heidelberg. 'All are unified in the thought: hold together, come what may.'[77] Exactly this idea was expressed most famously by the Kaiser, when he stood on the balcony again at 7.30 p.m. before the crowds surrounding his palace and, thanking them for their affection and loyalty, said:

> In the battle now lying ahead of us, I see no more parties in my *Volk*. Among us there are only Germans, and if some of the parties in the course of past differences turned against me, I forgive them all. All that now matters is that we stand together like brothers, and then God will help the German sword to victory.[78]

There were clear limits to this unity. The Kaiser's talk of forgiveness betrayed his determination to maintain his position of power within the Reich; even if Germans were to become brothers, he still saw his role as the imperial father figure. The Social Democrats had their own reservations. Bourgeois press attempts to frame the nation as united in 'war enthusiasm' were categorically rejected; the mass attendance of anti-war demonstrations earlier in the week proved their point. Yet the middle classes themselves were less enthused than anxious, serious and ready to uphold the national interest, which on 1 August meant protecting home territory from Russian invasion. This was an idea around which Germans of all classes could unite; as the Ruhr workers' paper *Volksblatt* declared on that day, 'the German Social Democrats are ready to the last man to repel an attack'.[79] War enthusiasm, had it been the main drive, would probably not have carried the German war effort beyond August 1914. The desire to defend the homeland, on the other hand, proved a remarkably stable base on which to mobilize a people.

MOBILIZATION

Military mobilization changed the face of central European societies with bewildering speed. Millions of men were immediately drafted. The Habsburg army expanded from a peacetime strength of 450,000 to 1,687,000 troops in three and a half weeks. Its German ally achieved in just twelve days an even more dramatic increase, from 808,280 to 3,502,700 soldiers. Already by the middle of August 1914, around a quarter of Austro-Hungarian men aged nineteen to forty-two and one in every three German men aged seventeen to forty-five were with the colours.[80] Reservists often had only a few days, in Germany sometimes no more than twenty-four hours, to set their affairs in order and say goodbyes before leaving for barracks. Younger men hurried to see parents, bid farewell to work colleagues, perhaps, once in uniform, had a snapshot taken with a sweetheart as a keepsake for the front. The happily married couple spent a final, precious evening together. There were practicalities to organize: farmers issued last-minute instructions to their wives, men rushed to purchase essentials for active service. Officers, in particular, had much to do to put their kit in order. Departure was never easy. As Major Artur Hausner, who had served since 1897 in the Habsburg army, confessed in his diary on 27 July 1914, even for professional soldiers who had spent their lives training for this moment, 'the possibility that one will never again see those he most loves constrains the feelings of enthusiasm'.[81]

The mood in Austria-Hungary and Germany at war's outbreak was defined by two intertwined emotions. Fear was the first, and it was endemic. The second, which developed to a great extent in reaction, was a feeling of communal solidarity. Fear is the more straightforward to explain, for its causes and the ways in which it was expressed were similar in both countries. Above all, as Hausner hinted, people were afraid of the loss of their own or close relatives' lives. Although only the old could remember the last European wars fought by these states, the Franco-Prussian War of 1870–71 and the Habsburg anti-insurgency campaign in Bosnia-Herzegovina in 1878–82, there was little naivety in either society about the coming conflagration. Men and their families prepared for the worst. Church attendance surged, especially in Catholic regions. In Jabłonków, Father Ściskała reported a 'remarkable crowd' in his church on 1 August, the day after general mobilization was ordered in Austria-Hungary. 'Whole packs of men departing for the army come to confession. And in the evening till late into the night prayers and singing reach the town from roadside crosses and chapels. War teaches people to pray.'[82] The Socialist workers who populated Germany's major cities were less likely to turn for comfort to religion, but they too held few illusions about modern battle's lethality. 'All have the feeling of heading straight for a slaughter house,' wrote one Social Democrat after he observed reservists departing in Bremen.[83] Whether in town or countryside, Monarchy or Reich, contemporaries everywhere agreed that this was a time of tears. 'Little could be heard but shouting, sighs and weeping' when men left Sibiu, in Transylvania. As middle-aged reservists gathered with their families south of Cracow, there was 'a good deal of crying and whimpering'.[84] Deep sadness and fear was also on display at German railway stations. 'Seeing the men depart is quite awful,' wrote one girl helping out at a refreshment stand on Cassel station during mobilization. 'Some have tears in their eyes when they look at their women and children staying behind, and to see all the tearful faces of those staying behind is too terribly sad!'[85]

While apprehension about separation and fears for the safety of sons and husbands account for much of the anxiety, there were also other good reasons to be tearful in August 1914. The start of war precipitated an economic crisis threatening many families' material existence. In the countryside, farmers' wives wondered in despair how they could bring in the harvest when their husbands, workers and horses had been taken by the army. In the cities, by contrast, there was sudden mass unemployment. Around 5 per cent of the workforce in Austria and a mere 2.7 per cent of that in Germany had been without a job in July 1914, but in the following month the proportions jumped respectively to 18.3 and 22.7 per cent.[86] Small businesses closed down as owners were called up, leaving workers on the streets. Larger firms, expecting war to suppress demand, downsized, put employees on short time, or abruptly cut wages by, on average, 10 per cent for men and up to 25 per cent for women.[87] Domestic trade was disrupted by military takeover of the railways, export industry laid low as customers became enemies and contracts were cancelled; Siemens, for example, lost foreign orders for 5.8 million light bulbs.[88] The dismissals and wage reductions caused very severe hardship for working-class families. So too did conscription itself. Even once so-called 'Family Aid', a benefit given to German soldiers' families, was added, the drafting of a husband decreased income to a third of its pre-war level for the wife and child of an unskilled labourer, and to less than a quarter for those of a skilled worker.[89] The difficulty many families had in paying their landlords explains why a rumour that rents could not legally be demanded for the war's duration, although false, spread like wildfire. In Berlin, police were already reporting in late August material misery and growing desperation among the proletariat.[90] The same was true elsewhere. A secret report on Austrian Galicia at the start of September described 'the pauperization of our society' and warned that official aid was urgently needed. 'Hunger,' it warned menacingly, 'can be a bad adviser.'[91]

Beyond these individual worries, there was a pervasive sense of threat; a fear, frequently refracted inwards, that the community was under attack. In Austria-Hungary that feeling had, as we have seen, developed in many of the Crownlands immediately after Franz Ferdinand's assassination. It was heightened further by the war's outbreak. The newly established 'War Supervision Office' complained already on 8 August about the 'avalanche-like spread' of 'all manner of totally uncontrollable rumours' unsettling the Austrian population.[92] Similar panic gripped Germany once hostilities began. There, fears were inflamed by a government warning on 2 August that 'Russian officers and agents are underway across the land.' The warning implicitly appealed for vigilantism: 'the safety of the German Reich requires that . . . the entire people cooperate without fail to neutralize such dangerous persons'.[93] Stories circulated of enemy attempts to poison the water supply and of attacks on railways and telegraph lines. There were fears of air raids; phantom flyers were reported over Berlin. The country was seized by 'spy hysteria'. The Reichstag deputy Hans Peter Hanssen described how on the capital's Potsdamer Platz on 3 August he saw an enraged mob beat a man 'unmercifully with clubs and umbrellas'. This, he was told, was the fourth 'spy' that they had caught in the last half hour.[94]

The anxiety was greatest in places close to frontiers and with ethnically mixed populations. The fortress city of Posen, fifty-five kilometres inside Germany's eastern border, offers a good example. There, the outbreak of war was exceptionally fraught. As their city was situated within a ring of forts guarding one of the key approaches into the Reich, the Polish and German inhabitants were warned already on 1 August that if the Russian army approached, any people without sufficient provisions to withstand a siege would be evacuated. All households were ordered to register with the police and state their preferred destination.[95] Nervous about the external threat, the German minority quickly came to regard their Polish neighbours, with whom peacetime relations had not been warm, with similar trepidation. Terrorism was feared. Already on 3 August, there was a bomb scare and the military was called after somebody left a travel hamper in a bank.[96] Some even imagined that local Poles were planning insurrection. One zealous non-commissioned officer sent the police a letter, bizarre even for those anxious times, cataloguing a list of suspicious incidents which, he argued, indicated that preparations for a Polish uprising were well underway. Women were, he claimed, pushing prams containing child-sized dolls through the city, always along the same route. Waiting at a tailor's workshop, he had seen six civilians come in, all of whom had ordered tunics in the rank of *Feldwebelleutnant* (a junior officer rank) and then argued with the tailor over the price. Girls, the soldier worried, were entering the barracks and leaving with packages; he was sure that they must contain rifle cartridges. Perhaps what most concerned him was the last point in the letter: 'I am often asked by Polish girls whether I am Polish. I request urgently that measures be taken.'[97]

Among the many fearful fantasies that swept through central European populations in that first week of August 1914, the most disruptive was the myth of the 'gold cars'. This began on 3 August with two separate but simultaneous reports of enemy automobiles driving through the Central Powers' territory. The first, originating with the Prague gendarmerie and referring to forty Russian cars attempting to enter Bohemia via field tracks, quickly dissipated. The second, which claimed that a convoy of French cars was attempting to bring gold for the Tsarist Empire's war effort across Germany, spread far more widely. It started with a story told by an officer – killed shortly afterwards – which reached second hand the Administrator of Geldern, a Prussian district bordering the Netherlands. He notified his superior, the County President in Düsseldorf, who in turn informed the Prussian Interior Minister. Warnings were issued to other government offices and published in newspapers. The German public, already alarmed by alerts over the previous days about spies and agents, responded with alacrity. Civilians armed themselves and set up roadblocks. By 6 August frustrated officials were complaining that 'it has already gone so far that every village considers itself obliged to halt every automobile at two or three places. Every farmer takes part in the search and criticizes the identity papers presented – in short it is now utterly impossible to travel through the country with a car.'[98] The French convoy was first numbered at twelve, later eighteen, twenty or twenty-five cars, and was said to be carrying Frenchmen dressed as Prussian officers or impersonating women. After a day of fruitless hunting, it was suggested, on 5 August, that the personnel had changed their disguises to labourers and unloaded their 80 million gold francs onto bicycles. At this point, some did pause; one newspaper calculated that this amount of money would weigh around 26,666 kilograms, and needed at least 1,066 cyclists to transport it. The people at the barricades were, however, unfazed. The searches were extended to anyone riding a bike.[99]

The delusion did not remain within the confines of the Reich. It also jumped across the border via the German District Administrator at Ratibor, as well as other German authorities, to Bohemia, Austrian Silesia and Galicia, prompting frantic searches by police, false sightings and general chaos. There was even a report that one of the imaginary cars had been stopped after a fire-fight at Cracow, its occupants, French officers dressed as women, arrested, and 30 million (or, in one telegram, 60 million) francs captured. Sentries in Austria not only halted cars and bicycles but also farm carts and even, in some areas, river rafts. If vehicles failed to stop at a challenge, they were shot at; a particular problem for the rafts because, as was eventually pointed out, they were dragged along by currents. Trigger-happy sentries killed at least twenty-eight people in the Reich and many others in Austria. Already by 7 August, the German military, whom some suspected of planting the story in the first place with the intention of whipping up patriotic fervour, began trying to de-escalate the mood, and the following day the command went out to dismantle roadblocks. Austrian authorities too ordered that traffic controls be relaxed. Anxious communities and local police proved resistant, however. Only gradually during August did the barricades disappear from central Europe's roads.[100]

The public reaction to the 'gold car' fantasy, the willingness to suspend disbelief even as the stories became ever more absurd, might now seem amusing, but it reflected the extraordinary stresses of the time. These people, and indeed their police, soldiers and civil authorities, were living through an event for which no experience in the past half-century of peace had prepared them; the stuff of fiction could seem possible when set within the disorientating, terrifying context of the outbreak of a European war. The response to the 'gold cars' was revealing in other ways too. It demonstrated how people sought to cope with the new situation. The frantic activity offered both a diversion from more personal worries and an apparent means of taking control and contributing to warding off the danger. Above all, it showed a natural instinct to seek safety through solidarity with the community. The ability of governments to guide and cement this solidarity would be critical in determining the durability of the Austro-Hungarian and German war efforts.

The German people entered the First World War remarkably united. Differences of class and confession, region and race, seemed to many who lived through these times suddenly to melt away in the national emergency. The Russian general mobilization decisively shifted popular opinion, turning war from an unthinkable horror into a defensive necessity. The fear at the outbreak of hostilities was important in promoting readiness to suspend domestic quarrels and seek safety in solidarity. The Reich government also acted skilfully, however, in building consensus and cultivating unity. The distrust between Germany's conservative authorities and its largest political party, the Social Democrats, should not be underestimated; on 30 July, after German mobilization was mistakenly reported in the *Berliner Lokal-Anzeiger*, Friedrich Ebert, one of the party's two chairmen, and Otto Bauer, its treasurer, fled with the party finances to safety in Switzerland. As late as 31 July its leaders reckoned that if war broke out, they would be arrested.[101] It was thus little short of astounding and of immense importance for Germany's war effort that less than a week later, the party would vote unanimously for war credits, and its other chairman, Hugo Haase, announce to the

Reichstag that 'in the hour of danger we do not leave the Fatherland in the lurch'.[102]

The government, and above all Chancellor Bethmann Hollweg, had worked hard to make this possible. From the start of the crisis, it had shown respect for the Social Democrats. On 26 July, Haase had been called to the Prussian Interior Ministry and told that the SPD's anti-war protests would not be suppressed. An invitation from the Chancellor had followed three days later, but as neither Haase nor other SPD leaders were in Berlin another Socialist, Albert Südekum, attended. Bethmann stressed to him the peaceful intentions of the Kaiser's government, and was assured by Südekum that the party had no intention of initiating strikes or sabotage. The Chancellor reported the following day to the Prussian Ministry of State that there was 'nothing particular to fear' from the SPD. The government was also sufficiently confident of the Socialist unions' patriotism once war broke out that on 2 August their leader Carl Legien was informed that there was no intention to repress his organization.[103]

The Prussian military, belying its reputation as reactionary and politically unsavvy, also played its part. This was crucially important. Once the 'State of Siege' was declared late on the afternoon of 31 July, wide-ranging powers had passed, under the provisions of Prussia's 1851 'Law on the State of Siege', to the generals who headed the twenty-four Army Corps Districts that covered the Reich. They or, once they had mobilized their units and left for the battlefield, their deputies were responsible for the maintenance of public security during the emergency. They could suspend constitutional rights and had the authority to issue orders to the civilian administration within their Corps Districts. The army's view in peacetime, based on studies of insurgencies, had been that early and decisive action was the key to maintaining internal order in a crisis. Yet the soldiers also understood that repressing organizations which possessed the loyalty not only of many reservists but also of the railway workers essential for a successful mobilization would be both risky and damaging for national morale. As early as 25 July, after discussion with the civilian government, the Prussian War Minister, General Erich von Falkenhayn, issued Army Corps District generals with guidelines recommending vigilance, but warning against overly hasty or strict action: 'It is not desirable,' the generals were admonished, 'for political parties, through the suppression of their press and arrest of their leaders, to be pushed from the beginning into sharp opposition to the government.'[104]

The Army Corps District generals could be given orders only by the Kaiser. Yet although under no obligation, they did follow the War Minister's guidelines towards the Social Democrats and unions. Interestingly, however, this was less true of their treatment of the other major suspect groups in Germany, its minorities. Even in 1914, race posed a greater barrier than class to entry into the national community. In West Prussia and Upper Silesia, Polish-language newspapers were temporarily banned, although admittedly in the former so was the SPD press. Many Poles, including some minor community leaders, were arrested. So great was the suspicion that there were even searches of Catholic churches for weapons or for the entrances to tunnels leading to Russia. Local military commanders were responsible for these actions. Disgruntled provincial civil authorities, who generally had not been consulted, later pointed out that the arrests did not result in even a single prosecution.[105] Unsurprisingly, the measures were demoralizing for a community that was overwhelmingly obedient in August 1914; they signalled clearly, as one disgruntled Polish-speaker noted in his diary, 'you are the enemy'.[106] In the west of Germany, Alsace-Lorrainers were treated even more harshly. Civil-military relations in this area had been poisonous before the war, and the army, which suspected the population of French sympathies, did not hesitate to take around 400 people into custody, including nineteen clergymen and two deputies from the regional parliament. As with the Polish minority, the soldiers were unfamiliar with local conditions and, relying on denunciations, ended up unjustly detaining many loyal subjects.[107] These peoples lived on enemy frontiers, which goes some way to explaining the nervousness and repression. This was not true of Germany's Danish minority, however, whose press was also closed and its leaders arrested. Some 172 people associated with the Danish national movement, including Reichstag deputy Hans Peter Hanssen, were imprisoned. A further 118 German Danes were deprived of their freedom solely because of their knowledge of the coastal waters; it was feared that they might help men not wishing to be drafted flee across the Danish border or even assist in a British naval attack.[108]

The SPD's leaders were brought to support the war not by persecution, which was never likely to give satisfactory results, but by persuasion. As late as 31 July, most of the party's Reichstag deputies had been unwilling to vote in favour of war credits, but thereafter a shift in opinion rapidly took place. This was influenced in part by the government's new readiness to enter a dialogue, albeit on unequal terms, and still more by the implicit promise of political reform and a better future contained in the Kaiser's declaration of 1 August that he saw 'no more parties ... only Germans'. The shift was also a response to the war's outbreak. While plenty of Social Democrats considered the Reich government at least partially responsible for hostilities, it was clear to most that opposition at this point would be not only senseless but potentially catastrophic for party and country. At best, it would likely lead to the suppression of the SPD. At worst, it would facilitate an invasion of Germany by the Tsarist army, a force that served Europe's most reactionary and brutal regime. Modern historians tend to underestimate just how realistic and frightening this prospect was, dismissing the fear as primarily a product of German Socialists' deeply ingrained Russophobia. Ludwig Frank, who was convinced already from 25 July of war's unavoidability, succeeded in gaining from at least twenty-five other deputies, around a quarter of the Reichstag fraction, an undertaking that they were prepared to defy party discipline and vote for war credits. In the event, such drastic action proved unnecessary, as by the afternoon of 3 August, when the SPD's deputies gathered to decide their stance in the following day's parliamentary session, most wanted to support the government. In a vote, seventy-eight declared themselves in favour, and only fourteen were opposed to passing the war credits motion.[109]

The Reichstag session of 4 August 1914 was in consequence an immensely powerful piece of political theatre. It was carefully choreographed in order to project a message of German unity. The Chancellor met all party leaders, including Haase and his colleague Philipp Scheidemann, at midday on 3 August in order to prepare and, although their deputies had not yet settled on their stance, the Social Democrats agreed several symbolic compromises that assumed a unanimous acceptance of war credits. The day of the vote began with a Mass in Berlin Cathedral, followed in the early afternoon by the Reichstag opening ceremony at the imperial palace. Although, as was usual, SPD deputies attended neither, in both the theme of unity was stressed. The Kaiser spontaneously repeated his celebrated promise: 'I no longer recognize any parties. I know only Germans.' An amnesty for those convicted of political crimes such as lese-majesty, which above all benefited Social Democrats, was announced on the same day. The Reichstag session, the day's centre-piece, was attended by all the parties, the democratically elected representatives of the German people. The first speech was given by Chancellor Bethmann Hollweg and outlined the official explanation of the war's causes. Russia had acted duplicitously and aggressively, and France was accused of having attacked without warning. 'The great hour of trial has struck for our people,' he ended. 'Our army is in the field, our navy is ready for battle – behind them stands the entire German nation, the entire German nation', and here he turned pointedly to the Socialists, 'united to the last man.'[110]

Even Social Democratic deputies, in a spontaneous show of patriot-ism, cheered the Chancellor's speech; a first for the Reichstag, where no Socialist had ever applauded a government official. The Reichstag Presi-dent, Dr Johannes Kaempf, a member of the bourgeois Progressive People's Party, echoed the Chancellor in stressing both that this was a 'war for the defence of our country' and that 'never before have the people been more united than they are today'.[111] After an intermission, it was Haase's turn to get up and speak for the SPD. He had not wanted to do this. It was Haase who had composed the SPD's appeal of 25 July for mass peace demonstrations, and he had remained true to his anti-war convictions to the end, voting in the party's own discussions a day earlier as one of the fourteen deputies opposed to passing the war cred-its motion. Socialist discipline, however, demanded not only unanimity but also a display of party unity, and for this reason members of all opin-ions had wished Haase to make the agreed statement. In this statement, a compromise between the different party factions, he condemned past imperialist policies, emphasized how the SPD had striven for peace 'in cordial agreement with our brothers in France', and expressed the hope that the horrors of war would 'awaken in millions . . . abhorrence . . . and win them over to the ideal of socialism and of peace among nations'. The statement also, however, warned against the danger posed by Tsarist Russia 'for our people and its freedom', insisted on 'the right of every people to national independence and self-defence' and, crucially, agreed to the requested war credits.[112] The speech met with frosty silence from the right-wing parties, but the centrist Progressives along with SPD dep-uties applauded, and that was sufficient for newspapers to report general acclaim. There was another small hint of divisions to come during the voting, when two minor SPD deputies left the chamber unnoticed in order to avoid having to vote. Nonetheless, the war credits were passed unanimously, and the *Burgfrieden*, the 'fortress peace' in which all internal quarrels were suspended for the duration of hostilities, was thus very publicly demonstrated. The session closed with another, and again unprecedented, display of unity when the house, including reformist Socialists, gave three cheers for 'Kaiser, *Volk* and Fatherland'.[113]

The Reichstag session of 4 August strengthened and institutionalized at a national level the solidarity that had started to develop within German society once Russian general mobilization became known. Hanssen, after being released from his brief imprisonment, noted already on 2 August, the first day of German mobilization, that reservists' 'grave anxiety' was accompanied by 'a determination to do one's duty'.[114] Others made similar observations. A doctor inspecting draftees in Weiden, a Bavarian town not far from the Austrian border, was impressed: 'from the reserve year groups all appear,' he jotted in his diary on 4 August. 'No man missing. None is ill or wants to be ill. From the *Landwehr* group [of older reservists between twenty-eight and thirty-eight years old], all come. Some are seriously ill (lung and heart complaints), but no one wants to shirk.'[115] Everywhere, men obeyed their call-up orders conscientiously. Moreover, as the first weeks of war passed, an overt patriotism became more prominent, especially where troops were departing. On their trains, the soldiers scrawled self-confident, aggressive ditties. There was the ubiquitous promise 'Every shot a Russian, Every punch a Frenchman, Every kick a Brit.' More imaginative was a rhyme addressed to the Russian Tsar which went 'Nikolaus, be afraid, / From you liver sausage will be made.' Food was, apparently, very much on the minds of the departing soldiers. 'Menu' stated another piece of troop-train graffiti: 'French Goulash with Tsar Compote' or 'Poincaré Soup, Russian Salad, English Sauce'. Another morbid humourist chalked a mock advertisement on the side of his wagon for 'Quarter litre of Russian blood – 30 Pfennigs'.[116] The crowds seeing off soldiers also became more festive and patriotic by the middle of August. 'The Watch on the Rhine' frequently rose up across station platforms in these days, although nostalgic songs for home, 'Home, Oh Home, I Must Leave You', 'Tomorrow I Must Leave, Lovely Berlin', or 'Cologne on the Rhine, You Pretty Little City' were also often heard, and it was these that men sung themselves once on their journey to the front.[117]

There was no contradiction between these public displays of patriotism and bravado and private fear and sorrow; they went hand in hand. Cheering and singing were means for soldiers and civilians, however upset, to express solidarity, temporarily quash anxiety, and cope with the painful emotions of departure. They did indeed help. One man described how the 'enthusiasm on the railway stations . . . literally swept us along, so that soon the somewhat depressed mood to be seen on several faces on our transport made way for an enthused and confident atmosphere'.[118] Some, deeply moved by the scenes, believed themselves to be living through a national rebirth. Middle-class men like Eugen Mortler, a bank trainee, grasped for the Kaiser's rhetoric to explain what they saw: 'no differences, no parties, everyone helps, Germany is united'.[119] While the hope of many intellectuals – that the sense of community they later mythologized and venerated as the 'spirit of 1914' would be made permanent – was illusory, that sense itself was widely felt and expressed in the first weeks of the war; and not merely as a strategy for suppressing anxiety.[120] There was a widespread unity of purpose and identification with Germany's cause which, especially after the SPD voted for war credits, extended even to the working classes. The Chief of the Berlin Police remarked with surprise a month after the mobilization that his men 'who through their job have much to do with the worker milieu can scarcely believe that these are the same people who just recently cheered the Internationale in protest gatherings and now bubble over with patriotism'.[121]

The most spectacular manifestation of patriotic unity was the flood of volunteers rushing to serve in the German army. Newspapers reported excitedly that over a million men had joined from 'all levels of society and age groups, all occupations and classes'.[122] The true figure was smaller but still highly impressive: 250,000 men volunteered for military service in August 1914, and in total around half a million came forward during the course of the war. Prussian units alone accepted 143,922 volunteers in the first ten days of hostilities; by comparison, only 40,000 Frenchmen volunteered for their national army during the whole of 1914. Not only was the German volunteering movement's speed and size remarkable but so too was its spontaneity. These men acted on their own initiative; the government issued no appeal, and the army was unprepared for the queues that suddenly appeared outside its barracks. They had to go to considerable effort to be accepted for service, as most regiments met all their manpower needs from the draft. Many volunteers travelled long distances, some visiting as many as six or seven depots before finding a unit willing to recruit them.[123]

The volunteers were not, contrary to the claims of the papers, representative of German society. They were young; over half were under twenty, the age of conscription, and almost 90 per cent were less than twenty-five years old. The majority, around two-thirds, came from a broad urban middle-class background. Students, secondary-school pupils and academics, the types of people who had participated in the 'war enthused' processions at the end of July were particularly well represented, but just as many lower-middle-class men, such as craftsmen, tradesmen and office workers, came forward. Industrial workers, although a little under-represented in terms of their share of society, still accounted for around three-tenths of the volunteers. Some joined up to escape unemployment, but others had impeccably patriotic motives. The SPD set an example: 783 of its youth group leaders volunteered as, most famously, did the forty-year-old Reichstag deputy Ludwig Frank, who was killed fighting on the Western Front on 3 September 1914. He saw the conflict as a chance to prove the SPD's loyalty to Germany, and thereby hasten political reform; 'we are undertaking a war for the Prussian franchise,' he once wrote. However, he was insistent that his enlistment was not a political tactic but, like the vote of 4 August, 'arose from an inner necessity'; an act undertaken because he and his fellow Socialists 'take the duty of defending the homeland bitterly seriously'.[124] The only groups largely absent from the volunteers' ranks were farmers and rural workers. Such men were particularly favoured by the army as deferential soldiers, and therefore were over-represented among conscripts. The dire labour shortages in the countryside and the urgent need to bring in the harvest go far to explain why few of the remainder volunteered (see Table 2).[125]

The middle-class Germans who volunteered, although not summoned by any call to arms, were following a deeply embedded cultural script. The memory of the 1813 Wars of Liberation against Napoleon, in which urban middle-class volunteer *Freikorps*, or 'Free Corps', had played an important role, was venerated in imperial Germany, and above all in its Prussian heartlands.[126] At a time of national emergency, when the Reich's cause appeared so obviously just, and when much of the language used to explain the war self-consciously echoed the idealism of 1813, it was

Table 2. Social composition of German volunteers, 1914–18
(sample size: 2,576)

Background	Numbers	Percentage
Tradesmen and craftsmen	435	16.89
Skilled urban manual workers	429	16.65
Businessmen and property owners	342	13.28
Unskilled urban manual workers	330	12.81
Students	321	12.46
White-collar workers	306	11.88
Pupils (and school leavers)	189	7.34
Professionals and academics	126	4.89
Farmers	59	2.29
Waged agricultural workers	35	1.36
Without occupation	4	0.16

The figures in this table diverge slightly from those in the source. The original table mis-classified 59 students as professionals and academics (48), white-collar workers (7) or farmers (4). This error is corrected here.

Source: A. Watson, 'Voluntary Enlistment in the Great War: A European Phenomenon?', in C. Krüger and S. Levsen (eds.), *War Volunteering in Modern Times: From the French Revolution to the Second World War* (Basingstoke and New York, 2011), p. 170.

only natural that middle-class men should instinctively follow their forebears' example and volunteer for military service. For southern German Catholics, who possessed different historical traditions, volunteering could be a demonstration of regional loyalty or, conversely, understood as an act of national solidarity, symbolizing the healing of rifts left by the 'Culture War' between the state and the Catholic Church in the 1870s. Jews volunteered in particularly large numbers; a postwar investigation calculated that over 10,000 came forward, meaning that a community which made up less than 1 per cent of the Reich's inhabitants supplied around 2 per cent of its war volunteers. They enlisted to express their close identification with the German Fatherland, and often in the hope that by visibly participating in its defence, they would end the informal discrimination that they had suffered in peace.[127]

Prussian Poles, who volunteered in far smaller, but not negligible numbers, may have had similar considerations, although Russophobia and the immediate danger posed by the Tsarist army to their own homes were probably more important factors.[128] Not all middle-class volunteers were influenced by higher ideals. Some young men were swept up in the excitement of the war's outbreak, attracted by the soldierly ideal of manliness and motivated by 'thirst for adventure'; others went because their peers were going, and they felt that they could not stay at home. However, contrary to the patronizing assumptions sometimes voiced later that educated men in their teens or early twenties were too naive or stupid to recognize that armed conflict was likely to involve hardship, suffering and death, very few expressed 'war enthusiasm'. Volunteers insisted that they had 'known from the beginning that a modern war is an unparalleled tragedy and a crime against humanity'. The overriding point for the majority, and the single most important cause of the volunteering movement's speed and spontaneity, was that as soon as war broke out, the homeland with which they identified and to which they felt an obligation was under threat of invasion. This was the conclusion reached by a survey of volunteers' motivations undertaken by psychologists at the beginning of hostilities. 'Patriotic feeling,' it argued, 'was there to a great degree – as an impulsive, categorical imperative: we have a duty to protect the Fatherland. War has been declared, weapons are our only remaining resort.'[129]

The urge to participate in the nation's defence, to be, as contemporaries put it, 'allowed to take part' in the momentous events of August 1914, was not confined to male youth. Older men served as sentries in their community's home guards (*Bürgerwehren*), guarding railway lines and bridges.[130] Women too felt the need to contribute. Some thought that the national emergency demanded a rethinking of rigid gender roles. One Berlin girl, Margarete Bäckmann, wrote to the Kaiser on 6 August 1914, entreating him 'from the bottom of my heart' to allow her to join the army: 'Should a German girl not be permitted to give her blood?', she appealed. 'Should I not be allowed to fight for the homeland?'[131] Most, however, were content to accept the more traditional auxiliary tasks permitted to them; their mission was not to arm themselves but rather, as the Kaiserin framed it in an appeal to the womanhood of the Reich, perform a 'holy work of love'.[132] In the war's first months, middle-class girls, usually supervised by an older lady both for the sake of organizational efficiency and to hinder 'immoral' activities, could be seen on every station serving refreshments to troops passing through. Others assisted in charitable efforts to alleviate the economic distress suffered by soldiers' families and unemployed working-class women. For many bourgeois girls, however, the ideal was nursing, which seemed to epitomize 'feminine strengths' of love and care. One of the earliest wartime first-aid training courses, intended for 3,000 participants, attracted 40,000 applications.[133] Those who did get work in hospitals were very quickly confronted by war's horror. Wounded were streaming back from the front already in late August. In Freiburg, one volunteer, Elisabeth Stempfle, reported that schools had been converted to field hospitals and that all were already nearly full. The girls were thrown into the daily drudgery of cleaning and caring for ill soldiers. They saw awful wounds and amputations. The job also made immense emotional demands. One friend, she recorded in her diary, had been alone all night comforting a dying reservist. For such women, the switch from peace to war was sudden and shocking.[134]

A vast network of women's organizations underpinned this activity. The 'Patriotic Women's Association' (*Vaterländischer Frauenverein*), along with other women's groups affiliated to the Red Cross, had half a million members already trained in first aid by 1914. Other organizations offered their services to the authorities. Already on 1 August, Gertrud Bäumer, chairwoman of the 300,000-strong League of German Women's Associations' (*Bund Deutscher Frauenvereine*), which in peacetime had campaigned for the extension of female rights in education and the professions, female suffrage and the banning of prostitution, offered to take some of the burden of war welfare from the Prussian Interior Ministry. The initiative was followed by a *Burgfrieden* among women's organizations. The League joined with Protestant and Catholic groups and with Socialist women to form the National Women's Service (*Nationaler Frauendienst*). At the local level, this resulted in sudden cooperation between groups that had been either in competition or, in the case of bourgeois and Socialist women, in milieus which had previously been almost totally apart. Needless to say, their members had very different expectations of what might come out of the war. Many of Bäumer's women hoped that their patriotic efforts would be rewarded with an extension of women's rights, while Catholic and Socialist female activists shared their menfolk's aspirations for the full political integration of their communities into the Reich. Women from circles of Protestant intelligentsia, like their male counterparts, sometimes wished for the moral renewal of society. For most, however, the experience of unity at the war's opening was heady. As Bäumer herself declared, 'today we are not individuals, today we are solely a people'.[135]

General Helmuth von Moltke had predicted in 1911 that 'the German people would take up arms unitedly and enthusiastically in a war that was forced upon them'.[136] In the summer of 1914 the Reich's population proved him right. The abrupt change from the anxiety, depression and dread of July to the solidarity of August nonetheless requires some explaining. The first step was the Russian general mobilization, which was intended, and understood, as a threat. From this point, Germans saw the coming war as defensive, and feared Tsarist invasion. In reaction, a panicked solidarity asserted itself. The government's skilful harnessing of this mood was the second step. The Kaiser's promise of 'no more parties' and the unanimous Reichstag vote for war credits on 4 August 1914 were immensely influential. The political *Burgfrieden* resonated widely. It was repeated at the level of local government, and in society, as the women's groups demonstrated.[137] The SPD's cooperation cemented workers' support for the war. Across society, a cult of unity was embraced, which took different expression in different milieus. Rural people expressed it when they tried to stop 'gold cars', workers did so when they hung out imperial flags or cheered at train stations. The middle classes were its greatest advocates; possessing the financial security and time, as well as the greatest stake in imperial society, bourgeois men and women volunteered for the army or for patriotic work in large numbers. These August days did not, as some middle-class people like Bäumer believed, change Germans. They remained individuals with personal fears and private lives, and they continued to be part of sub-national communities, class-conscious, religious, regional, with their own particular aspirations. Yet crucially, all parts of the Reich's society were sufficiently integrated and felt enough self-interest not to make such change, the dropping of all other identities, necessary in August 1914. Fear of invasion and communal solidarity in the face of threat, channelled and cultivated capably by their rulers, brought Germans together to defend their country. This struggle was to be a people's war.

*

Mobilizing a multi-ethnic empire like Austria-Hungary was a much more complicated matter than bringing a nation state into war, even one as imperfect as the German Reich. Unity was no less important, yet the Habsburg peoples' immense diversity made this difficult to achieve. It was not simply that mobilization posters had to be issued in fifteen languages. Rather, Habsburg subjects lacked a common identity. Each nationality had its own history and traditions, a state of affairs that peacetime Habsburg education had perpetuated and accentuated, rather than challenged.[138] For all the 'national indifference' felt by many individuals in 1914, cultural specificity mattered, as did varying attitudes towards the state and its enemies.[139] In a polity in which national ideology divided rather than unified peoples, the horizontal links binding society were fragile; Bohemians serving on the South-Eastern Front hardly felt more affinity to their fellow Habsburg subjects in Bosnia, whether Muslim, Croatian or Serb, than to the Serbs whom they marched against. Tyroleans sent to the east could not distinguish between Russian-subject Slavs and those of their own Emperor.[140] Still, Austria-Hungary was not without ideological appeal. Vertical bonds with the state, above all, in the form of loyalty to the Emperor, were strong. The dynasty's centuries of rule and, especially in Austria, readiness to treat with national aspirations lent it great legitimacy. Moreover, Habsburg subjects were, if divided by ethnicity and language, united to a great degree by religion. The Catholic Church had long been a stalwart and influential supporter of the Monarchy, almost four-fifths of whose population was Catholic. The principal Habsburg enemies in 1914, Serbia and Russia, were Orthodox. The Empire's loyal clergy thus had no difficulty in presenting the struggle as 'a just, a holy war' and a fight 'to preserve Christian culture and the Catholic belief'.[141]

The Habsburg authorities also made explicit from the start that they would brook no opposition. In both halves of the Empire, emergency legislation suspending basic rights and increasing state control over society and economy was activated. In Hungary, it was the civilian administration that under Law LXIII of 1912 accrued new coercive powers.[142] In Austria, by contrast, civil officialdom subordinated itself, and the population, to the military. The new responsibility of the army's courts to try civilians for political offences, a measure supposed to ensure rapid punishment and deter disloyal action, was just one of the earliest extensions of the soldiers' influence over the workings of the state. At the end of July, a military-headed War Supervision Office (*Kriegsüberwachungsamt*) was established in the Habsburg War Ministry and tasked with overseeing and coordinating the use of the emergency laws to suppress dissent. So secret was this agency that newspapers were permitted only to mention its name, not explain its function. Moreover, on 31 July, the day on which general mobilization was ordered, large parts of Austria were designated as the 'Area of the Army in the Field'. Galicia, Bukovina, eastern Silesia and north-eastern Moravia in the north, and Dalmatia in the south, all fell into this area. Later, when Italy declared war on the Monarchy in May 1915, not only the Crownlands abutting the south-western border, Tyrol, Carinthia, Gorizia, Gradisca, Trieste and Istria, but also those behind them, Salzburg, Carniola, Styria, Vorarlberg, were drawn in. Here, unlike in the rump hinterland, army commanders-in-chief had the power to issue orders to the local civil administration and imposed very harsh martial law. While pre-war planning had envisaged that the extraordinary measures could be rolled back, at least partially, once the army had successfully mobilized and departed for the front, this did not take place. The emergency laws remained in force and were even extended up to the recall of the Austrian parliament, the Reichsrat, in 1917. Only then were some of the more repressive measures lifted, and the army command lost its authority in the wide areas behind the front.[143]

The tight control over Habsburg society from the end of July 1914 proved, against expectations, to be largely unnecessary. Conrad von Hötzendorf, Chief of the General Staff, who distrusted the nationalities and had called already at the start of July for martial law to be imposed across the Empire, confessed the following month that 'the enthusiasm of the people for the war was ... a great surprise to him'.[144] Reports from the time testify to widespread support for the imperial cause. In Vienna, citizens were characterized as 'steady and resolute' after general mobilization was ordered. 'In all classes,' noted officials, 'a deep sympathy for the honour of the Monarchy and conviction in the necessity of what has happened is perceptible.'[145] In Hungary too, at least among the Magyars, Minister President Tisza testified at the start of August to a 'very good' atmosphere. Soldiers passing through the Kingdom were greeted everywhere with 'frenetic rejoicing, with music and song'.[146] More remarkable was the reaction of the once squabbling peoples in the Austrian Crownlands. In Carniola, home to a predominantly Slovene population, the regional president described how men obeyed the summons to arms 'with enthusiasm, thoroughly convinced of the necessity and justice of the warlike action forced upon the Empire'.[147] In Bohemia, the Military Command in Prague recorded that after partial mobilization against Serbia was ordered, 'against expectations, the reservists reported for duty punctually and in large numbers; even a certain enthusiasm was noticeable.'[148] Railway officials watching departing draftees and their families were still more upbeat: Bohemia was calm, Moravia and Lower Austria were enthusiastic.[149] Similar goodwill and obedience were observed on the Empire's peripheries. In the Trentino, Italian irredentists conceded that the rural population was loyal to the Habsburg dynasty.[150] Far to the east in Bukovina, Ruthenes were characterized as 'with few exceptions very ready to make sacrifices and patriotically minded'.[151] Military units in Galicia were, as elsewhere, overwhelmed when far more men than expected reported for duty. Some of those arriving at barracks were under no obligation to serve. Those who were superfluous were transferred to the north of Hungary, to fill the ranks of new formations.[152]

The Habsburg Empire demonstrated over the summer that, for all the troubles of peacetime politics, it still possessed great legitimacy among its peoples. The nationalities' politicians and Church leaders were unstinting in their declarations of loyalty to Franz Joseph, conscripts everywhere obeyed the call to arms, and officials were emphatic, though amazed, that loyalty, not fear, lay behind the impressive popular response. There were even war volunteers. Vienna's *Reichspost* described men 'storming the war administration in person, by telegraph or by letter to get enlisted'. Already before the end of the first week of August, 'many thousands' were said to have come forward.[153] Still, despite the pride with which such enlistments were reported, the volunteers were revealing of the limits of dynastic patriotism's mobilizing potential. To judge from newspaper descriptions, these men were not from the broad, urban middle-class volunteering movement seen in the German Reich but instead came predominantly from a narrower circle of cosmopolitan elites. Aristocrats, parliamentary deputies and retired soldiers were reported to have offered their services. Many state officials were among the volunteers; they requested release from the civil service to enlist in sufficiently large numbers to necessitate discussion in the Austrian ministerial council about whether this should be permitted.[154] Students also joined their ranks, although numbers were paltry compared with the thousands enlisting in Germany; 184 from Vienna, 38 from Graz and a mere 14 from Prague had joined the Habsburg army by the end of September 1914.[155] There were also some men of lesser social standing among the volunteers, but they were not necessarily all keen to die for the Emperor. Sigmund Sperber, for example, a thirty-nine-year-old pharmacist, worried that a draft order would carry him away from his frail mother and force his shop into bankruptcy. Volunteering seemed to offer a solution. In early August he wrote to the War Ministry offering his immediate services, but only on condition that he be given a posting in Vienna. That way, he earnestly informed the Ministry, he would, in his free time, 'alongside the true fulfilment of duty for our much loved Emperor and my dear Fatherland, also be able to discharge the responsibilities of a son'.[156]

The Habsburg mobilization, while revealing strong vertical bonds between peoples and Emperor, never achieved the horizontal social solidarity or depth of commitment seen in Germany. Partly this was simply a function of the greater distance between peoples of different language and cultures living in a multi-ethnic empire than between members of a unitary nation state. Still, Germany's divisions, particularly of class, were stark before the war. Equally influential, therefore, were the actions of government. Austro-Hungarian leaders were focused on compliance not unity in the summer of 1914; the strenuous efforts made in the Reich to reconcile, or at least suspend, peacetime disputes had no real equivalent in Franz Joseph's lands. Hungary did, it is true, benefit from a political truce, the *Treuga Dei*, from the end of July. In November, when parliament met for its first wartime session, Tisza eulogized the conflict as a unifying force: it 'has put a stop to party strife, it has put a stop to the class struggle, relegated the nationality conflicts into the background, and given rise to splendid manifestations of unity and mutual love both at home and on the battlefield'.[157] Nonetheless, this demonstration of unity could not exert so powerful an impact on public opinion as the German Reichstag's war-credit vote of 4 August. The Hungarian parliament lacked the same legitimacy and representativeness; its small franchise, rigged elections and discrimination against non-Magyars meant that it spoke only for the elite.

The Hungarians did, nonetheless, at least attempt to create a semblance of political unity. In Austria, by contrast, the Reichsrat, which had been closed in March 1914, was not recalled. The building was instead ostentatiously converted into a military hospital. Minister President Stürgkh may have been correct to fear that assembling unruly deputies would result in a damaging public relations debacle. However, the readiness of the Monarchy's peoples to heed its call in the crisis indicates that the government underestimated their loyalty, and the penalties of not reconvening parliament were very great.[158] First, a chance was missed to reinforce the conflict's legitimacy by gaining the sanction of the nationalities' democratically elected representatives. Crucially, it also denied the peoples a forum in which to bury past quarrels publicly and declare Austrian solidarity. The decision to run the war effort through decree, rather than parliamentary consent, additionally left the government highly vulnerable to criticism; should the war go badly, it would be clear that the regime alone was at fault. More dangerous still, Stürgkh's administration not only failed to recognize the importance of cementing broad political consent for war, but actually abandoned the strategy of negotiating with and conciliating nationalist interests which in peace had helped to keep the Austrian half of the Monarchy functioning. A demand for unconditional obedience, backed by the threat of military repression, took its place. The Minister President laid out the new attitude in a circular to Crownland heads at the end of July: 'considerations of administrative procedure, regard for the mood of the parties, calculations about the present or future circumstances of domestic politics; all this has stopped. There is only one thing now: the orientation of all forces in the state towards the certain, speedy and complete attainment of the purposes of war.'[159]

In the absence of any Austria-wide *Burgfrieden*, the Habsburg Empire's success in bringing its peoples to war was underpinned by what can be described as a double mobilization. First, there was the official patriotic mobilization, comprising the call up of the army and the appeal to the population as loyal imperial subjects. In tandem, however, there was a semi-official national mobilization, varying in strength in different regions, and which at this early stage supported the state's own efforts. Elected local politicians such as town mayors and also clergy were important figures in this second mobilization. Although many were nationalists, they combined ethnic with imperial loyalty and drummed up support for the Habsburg cause in their communities.[160] People were appealed to not just as imperial subjects but often and emotively as members of a national group. In western Galicia, for example, reservists were reminded that they belonged to a Polish nation whose historic role was to be a bulwark defending 'western Europe against the barbaric Asiatic deluge'.[161] Similarly, in Ljubljana, Mayor Dr Ivan Tavčar told mobilized men from the town hall's balcony that they 'go to fight for the Slovenian nation, since every stone of this house speaks loudly that the Slovenians would have long been vanquished, had the majestic House of Habsburg not taken them under protection'.[162] The military bands circulating the streets of the Empire's cities in the first days of hostilities, drawing the crowds that Vienna's bourgeois press interpreted as proof of universal war enthusiasm, attracted a following by playing not just imperial marches but also national songs.[163] Men mustered to the army might choose to wear imperial symbols, such as medallions showing the Emperor, to express Habsburg patriotism. Equally, however, they often left for war waving Bohemian, Slovenian or Croatian flags or, in the case of Poles, singing the national refrain 'Boże coś Polskę'.[164]

The Empire's more than two million Jews stand out as a special case, for they were mobilized on the basis of three identities. They were among the most loyal of Habsburg subjects. Many revered Froyim Yossel, as Yiddish speakers' communities affectionately called Franz Joseph, as the ruler who had granted them emancipation. Feelings of civic pride in Austria too were well developed among both more traditional shtetl communities and the modernizing Jews in major cities. A second identity that propelled Jews to war was consciousness of their membership as a religious group and people. The fight against Tsarist Russia, which cruelly suppressed its Jews, was understood as a war of liberation, even a 'holy war'.[165] Finally, modernizing Jews, due to their identification with one or other of the Monarchy's peoples – most frequently German, but also sometimes Hungarian, Czech or Polish – often underwent a triple mobilization. In the days following the outbreak of war, for example, a placard was posted on the streets of Cracow addressed to the town's Jewish population. Characterizing the war as a 'blood feud between civilization and barbarism, between freedom and despotism', the anonymous authors urged their fellow believers to do their duty, not just as Jews but as Austrians and also as Poles: 'In this historical moment, we, the Jews of the Polish lands – full of unwavering civic fidelity towards the Austrian constitutional state – are paying homage to the still relevant laws and ideals of Poland. We ardently desire that these ideals will be fulfilled as quickly as possible, we wish fervently for the victory of the right and just cause.'[166]

The appeals to national sensibilities, though a crucial element in mobilizing the peoples, were not without drawbacks. As was familiar from peacetime, any incitement of national feelings could rapidly provoke clashes between rival ethnic groups, fracturing wider imperial unity. This was exactly what happened in Fiume (today Rijeka), where already from August 1914 soldiers raised from the city's Croatian-populated surroundings and proudly displaying Croatian colours were repeatedly attacked on their way to the main railway station by Italian-speaking residents and police. In one typical case, recruits who had pinned Croatian cockades and tricolours to their uniforms and were shouting 'Up Austria!', 'Up Croatia!', 'Down with Serbia!' were stopped on the bridge into the city by Fiume policemen, who demanded that they remove their insignia. When they refused, a constable with drawn sword lunged at one of the soldiers, ripped the colours from his chest and trampled them in the dirt. Other incidents involved gangs of Italian-speaking youths, who, sometimes with the police's help, beat up Croatian soldiers and forced them to remove their national badges. The attacks continued into the autumn, despite the army's protests. Needless to say, they were not conducive to building a feeling of Habsburg solidarity among either the mixed local populations or Croatian soldiers setting off for the front.[167]

The lack of an Austria-wide *Burgfrieden* also meant that bonds of solidarity strengthened within, rather than between, ethnicities. Political truces were called by rival factions in some national groupings. Thus, in Galicia, Polish parties came to agreement and on 16 August jointly established in Cracow a Supreme National Committee (*Naczelne Komitet Narodowy*). This was an impeccably loyalist organization, but it sought to advance Polish interests within the Empire, hoping in particular to reform the Dualist Austro-Hungarian structure into a Trialist system, with Galicia joined to annexed Russian-held Congress Poland as a third Habsburg state.[168] National interest groups also manoeuvred to improve their negotiating positions for the expected post-war reordering of the Empire by setting up legions to fight alongside the Common Army. An attempt by Josip Frank's Serbophobe Pure Party of the Right to start a special Croatian volunteer formation was quashed by Tisza, who saw it as the first step in a plan to separate Croatia from Hungary and realize another trialist vision, different from that of the Poles, involving the creation of a new South Slav state within the Habsburg Empire. However, small units of Ukrainian- and Romanian-speaking volunteers were formed in Bukovina, and a Ruthenian nationalist unit, the Sič riflemen, operated in Galicia from the autumn of 1914. This latter was 2,000-men strong, mostly intelligentsia but with a smattering of peasants and workers.[169]

The Polish Legion was by far the most impressive of the nationalities' volunteer forces, and also best illustrative of the Pandora's box opened by the national mobilization at the war's start. The formation of the Legion had its roots in the pre-war intrigues of Polish exiles from Russia, foremost among whom was the nationalist, Socialist, freedom fighter and revolutionary, later Marshal of independent Poland, Józef Piłsudski. In 1906, Piłsudski had offered the services of his conspiratorial group, the Polish Socialist Party-Revolutionary Fraction (*Polska Partia Socjalistyczna-Frakcja Rewolucyjna*), to Habsburg military intelligence, promising to supply information on Russian forces in Congress Poland in return for a secure base in Galicia from which to carry on the struggle for Polish independence against the Tsarist Empire. Then, the offer was rejected, but two years later, after the Bosnian annexation crisis had soured Austria-Hungary's relations with its eastern neighbour, a deal was reached. The PPS-FR, now combined with other Polish independence groups to form the dramatically named Union of Active Struggle (*Związek Walki Czynnej*), was permitted by the Habsburg army and Cracow police, without the knowledge of the Galician *Statthalter* or the government in Vienna, to prepare for insurrection in Tsarist Poland. Funded from the proceeds of a mail-train robbery carried out by Piłsudski in Russia in September 1908, the group at first set up terrorist schools, which trained activists in skills such as bomb-making. In 1910, when rifle clubs were made legal in Austria, thinly disguised paramilitary formations were also quickly founded across Galicia. Their membership was modest: by 1914, the two organizations sponsored by the ZWC and secretly armed by the Habsburg army, *Strzelec* in Cracow and *Związek Strzelecki* in Lwów, counted at a generous estimate around 8,290 men, while rival groups like the National Democrats' *Polskie Drużyny Strzeleckie* together had a further 5,000.[170]

When war broke out, Piłsudski ordered his men to mobilize and distributed flyers around Cracow claiming, not very convincingly, that a national government had formed in Warsaw and named him commander of Polish armed forces. The ZWC's riflemen combined with their National Democrat competitors under his leadership, and on 6 August the first mixed company crossed the border. The men in it were, as other volunteers in 1914, mostly young, between nineteen and twenty-four years old. Gentry and students predominated. The vast majority were not Habsburg subjects but – a term they would have hated – Russian Poles.[171] Their mission was a total failure. The Habsburg army had hoped that they would at least cause disruption in its enemy's rear areas and, at best, trigger insurrection in Tsarist Poland. Instead, the unit, and others that followed it, was shunned by the local populace; 'no one gives us a glass of water, no one gives us a piece of bread,' complained one of Piłsudski's men later.[172] The volunteers briefly took the capital of the Kielce region, but within days were forced to retreat. The Austro-Hungarian army, disappointed with the riflemen's performance, was at this point inclined to disband their units. Instead, however, an agreement was brokered by the Mayor of Cracow and head of the Reichsrat's Polish 'Circle', Dr Juliusz Leo, to incorporate them into new Polish Legions – the name was an inspired reference to the Dąbrowski Legions that fought with Napoleon and were venerated in Polish national mythology – under the supervision of the cross-party Supreme National Committee. Recruitment started immediately and, as in Germany, it was a broad range of young middle-class men brought up on the tales of national heroes like Dąbrowski who were most responsive. In two and a half months, more than 10,000 recruits, many of them members of the nationalist rifle associations so popular in Galicia, had enlisted (see Table 3).

It must have seemed to Habsburg leaders like a good outcome: the units remained as a symbol of Austro-Hungarian benevolence towards Polish national aspirations, but their extremist leader was neutralized by being granted the relatively lowly post of regimental commander, and the potentially dangerous nationalist project transferred into the hands of a committee dominated by Austro-Polish conservative loyalists. The Legionaries swore an oath to the Emperor, and were placed within the Habsburg military command structure. Conversely, however, the agreement also had the effect of rooting that project much more

Table 3. Social composition of 11,480 Polish Legion volunteers,
up to 7 November 1914

Background	Number	Percentage
Craftsmen	2,642	23.0
Workers	2,128	18.5
Students/Academics	1,884	16.4
Pupils	1,645	14.3
Professionals	1,040	9.0
Farmers/Peasants	825	7.2
White-Collar Workers	420	3.7
Tradesmen	386	3.4
State Officials	282	2.5
Primary School Teachers	169	1.5
Journalists/Writers	47	0.4
Clergymen	12	0.1

Source: J. Mleczak, *Akcja werbunkowa Naczelnego Komitetu Narodowego w Galicji i
Królestwie Polskim w latach 1914–1916* (Przemyśl, 1988), p. 150.

deeply in Galician society. The Legions became a popular *cause célèbre*,
reaching a strength of over 21,000 men by 1917, and raising Piłsudski's
public profile. This was storing up trouble for the future.[173]

The upsurge of both imperial loyalty and nationalism facilitating the
Habsburg mobilization was accompanied by another distinctive, and
countervailing, manifestation: the fierce suppression by the state of any
sign, real or imagined, of disaffection. Civil and military authorities'
intense nervousness at war's outbreak was in part incited by the conspiracy theories, spy scares and denunciations that during the whole of
the past month had gripped the Empire's multi-ethnic communities and
bureaucracy. However, it also had deeper roots in the leaders' inherent
distrust of their peoples. In Hungary, secret instructions dating from
1912 ordered the gendarmerie that 'persons under acute suspicion of
espionage should be detained on the day of mobilization'.[174] In Austria,
Minister President Stürgkh demanded an extraordinarily high level of
compliance from the population. Crownland heads were told at the
end of July 1914 that not only 'hostile' elements but even those who

displayed an 'indifferent' attitude to army and state were to be persecuted 'with unyielding energy and implacable severity'.[175]

The result was a massive wave of arrests across the Empire immediately after mobilization was declared. Even in Vienna, where in 1913
just eighteen arrests were made for so-called 'political crimes' like high
treason, lese-majesty and disturbing the peace, twelve times this number
were detained on suspicion of these offences in 1914.[176] In Austrian
Crownlands inhabited by Slavs and the non-Magyar populated
regions of Hungary, the net was cast much wider. In Styria, for example,
the gendarmerie arrested 800 people, mostly Slovenes, up to mid-
September 1914.[177] Doubtless this neutralized some dissidents, but the
majority of those swept up in the paranoid crackdown were individuals
from the lowest rung of society whose offences were trivial. A drunken
cry of 'Up Serbia!' or a disparaging comment about the Emperor, best
understood as expressions of frustration and unhappiness by the powerless, not dangerous attempts to undermine the state, frequently landed
individuals in jail. Statements of reluctance to fight, occasionally accompanied by insults against other Habsburg nationalities, were prosecuted
as disturbances of the public peace. One Moravian mill hand, for
example, was sent to prison after he mused 'I'd instantly go and shoot
the Germans, but against the Serbs; with them I'd wait and think about
it.'[178] Absurdities were also punished. An itinerant worker who, after
hearing of medallions showing the Emperor, had pointed to his genitals
and remarked 'I have such things hanging from there' was sentenced to
six months' hard labour. The military courts tasked with trying such
offences, far from being efficient, were overwhelmed. They lacked
the personnel to handle the overnight expansion of their jurisdiction from a few hundred thousand soldiers to millions of civilians.
Although employing their own procedures, they were obliged to pass
sentence using the unfamiliar civil code. Moreover, there was immense
confusion about where civilians were to be tried; criminal as well as
political offences could, in certain circumstances, fall within the remit
of the army courts, and in all cases the illegal action had to have been
committed on or after 26 July. Considerable time was wasted as
papers were shuffled back and forth between military and civil courts.
Instead of the eight days legally permitted, suspects spent weeks or even
months in detention while investigations were ongoing. Ultimately,
most ended in acquittals due to the poor quality of supporting evidence;

anonymous denunciations, gendarmes' suspicions and drunken witnesses' statements were all sufficient to prompt an arrest, but not to bring a prosecution.[179]

The persecution was really damaging, however, not when it targeted people at society's margins but when it embraced the nationalities' community leaders. In the Slovene-inhabited lands of the Monarchy alone 117 priests were arrested. Teachers too were detained, as were several of the minority's Reichsrat deputies, none of whom had previously been considered untrustworthy by the authorities. As these were precisely the people needed to mobilize national sentiment in the Monarchy's support, this harassment jeopardized the success in these areas of the Habsburg war effort. In the traditionally loyalist Slovene population, the unjust removal of prominent figures and closure of nationalist, but largely loyal associations left, as Styria's *Statthalter* himself acknowledged in mid-September, 'resentment and ill-feeling'.[180] It was civil authorities, not as is usually assumed the military, who implemented the excessive security measures in Styria, Carniola and Carinthia. In these regions designated as the hinterland, the gendarmerie, prompted initially by its civilian superiors and then sometimes on its own initiative, was the principal tool of repression. The army's main role was to try the suspects delivered to it. In Hungary, where on 25 July Tisza ordered a show of strength against the minorities, civil authorities were even more aggressive. The gendarmes arrested so many non-Magyars there after mobilization was declared that already on 2 August the Interior Minister had to clarify that only the really dangerous should be detained. One month later, however, the Minister President was still demanding in relation to Hungary's Serb minority 'relentless severity against the criminals'.[181] Slovaks too were caught up in the sweeps despite neither living near a border nor having kinship to any nation that the Empire was fighting. By the start of October 1914, 600 languished in prison.[182]

Nonetheless, the military made matters much worse. Its malign influence was manifested in two ways. First, while it quickly dawned on the civil administration in the Austrian hinterland that the repression was exaggerated and counter-productive, many soldiers, and particularly the Army High Command (AOK), remained convinced of its necessity. The view of Conrad, Chief of the General Staff, was 'better lock up one hundred people than one too few'.[183] The War Supervision Office, deeply suspicious of the Slavic population, promoted harsh and arbitrary measures. Only in the autumn did the Emperor finally order it to cease detaining people on the basis of anonymous denunciations.[184] Individual commanders, even when unfamiliar with local circumstances, were also not shy of exceeding their authority; already on 27 July, the day before war began, Tisza protested to the Emperor that the officer commanding the Hungarian VII Corps district, the south of which was home to Serbs, had illegally launched mass arrests. Other military abuses, including the arrest of diet deputies, officials and clergy, and the taking of hostages, were committed in Croatia and, in its east, Slavonia.[185] On a higher level, the AOK's obsession with disloyalty in the population and its efforts to intervene in political matters would in the coming years cause constant tension with the Austrian government.

Second, the AOK and the Balkan Force Commander exercised untrammelled power in the wide territories designated as their areas of operations. In Dalmatia, which had been a focus of South Slav agitation in the years before the war, hundreds, including some prominent politicians, were interned. Military conduct deeper in the war zone, in Bosnia-Herzegovina and Galicia, was, as we shall see, vicious, far exceeding any violence against civilians in western Europe. Suffice it now to note that already, by the early autumn, there was serious alarm in the highest Habsburg circles at the effect of the repression on public mood across the Monarchy. On 24 August the head of the Emperor's military chancery wrote to Conrad, complaining that many of the measures against inhabitants were 'positively ludicrous' and warning that 'much lamentable ill-feeling is being stirred up'. 'The baby is being thrown out with the bathwater,' he wrote. 'We cannot harass the population, which has shown itself beyond all expectation loyal and willing to make sacrifices, unnecessarily.'[186] After a second wave of arrests by military authorities under the AOK in mid-September, the War Minister, Alexander von Krobatin, also intervened, appealing successfully to the Emperor to issue an order urging commanders to detain people only if they had serious grounds for suspicion, as unjustified arrests were 'capable of driving even loyal elements into the camp of our enemies'.[187] By then, however, it was very late. Military units had begun also to behave arbitrarily in northern Hungary, harassing officials and arresting and mistreating Uniate priests. The disastrous consequences of the army's intervention in delicately balanced multi-ethnic communities had already been foreseen by Tisza in his complaint of 27 July against VII

Corps' mass arrests. 'Such measures,' he had warned, 'if not undertaken after careful consideration by qualified and responsible authorities, provoke the population, alienate peaceful, loyal elements, spread far-flung anxiety and panic and thus can instantaneously have the most damaging consequences and would, in the long term, have disastrous repercussions for the peaceful coexistence and loyal, contented disposition of the nationalities.'[188]

The Habsburg Monarchy mobilized far more successfully than any of its leaders had dared hope. Everywhere there was obedience, and in many communities despite intense anxiety triggered by Franz Ferdinand's murder and raised still further by war's outbreak, there was a determination to fulfil patriotic duty. As Major Artur Hausner, gratified by what he called the 'enthusiasm' of the Hungarians, concluded with satisfaction in his diary, 'it is a genuine people's war into which we go.'[189] Still, while superficially the mobilization was a demonstration of Habsburg patriotism and unity, a more complex picture is revealed on closer inspection. The state effort was in part successful in 1914 because it was underpinned by national mobilizations, varying in strength in different parts of the Empire, but almost universally loyalist. Yet there were problems. First, this loyalty was not unconditional, and conflict and the sacrifices it entailed could only raise nationalist hopes and expectations. Second, even as national communities drew closer together in the crisis, the government did little to reinforce imperial solidarity. Hungary remained an oligarchy with no promise of change. In Austria, parliament stayed shut, rule continued by decree, and it was made clear that compliance rather than consensus was sought. The heavy-handedness of the gendarmerie and military at the opening of hostilities risked discrediting the regime in loyalist areas and often removed precisely those mediating figures, nationalist clergy and politicians, with the influence to bring their peoples wholeheartedly behind the Emperor's cause. Impressive though the popular response was in 1914, reflective of state legitimacy to a great degree, it nonetheless obscured unnecessarily weak foundations beneath the Habsburg war effort. These would be exposed by the stresses of the coming conflict.

3

War of Illusions

WAR PLANS

The German and Habsburg General Staffs confronted a strategic night-mare in the summer of 1914. Each faced war on two fronts. To Germany's west stood the modern French, Belgian and British armies; opposite Austria-Hungary's south-eastern border were battle-hardened Serbian and Montenegrin troops; and in the east over both loomed the mighty Russian military. Together these enemies fielded 5,726,000 soldiers organized into 218 infantry and 49 cavalry divisions. Against them, the Central Powers had just 3,485,000 men in 137 infantry and 22 cavalry divisions.[1] German and Austro-Hungarian generals knew that if victory were to be won despite their forces' numerical inferiority, it would have to be quickly, for the odds against them would only lengthen in a prolonged conflict. France and Russia's combined gross domestic product exceeded that of the Central Powers by one-fifth, and the Tsarist Empire's population alone outnumbered their inhabitants by one-third. Moreover, German military planners had assumed since 1908 that Britain would inevitably, if not immediately, enter hostilities and place its enormous financial and naval resources at the Entente's disposal.[2] There were sound domestic reasons too to fear a long conflict. Habsburg leaders, already anxious about their peoples' loyalties in peace, could scarcely welcome the destabilizing hardship and discontents that would accompany extended hostilities. Alfred Graf von Schlieffen, the Chief of the Prussian General Staff from 1891 to 1905, had predicted that any drawn-out war would bring economic ruin and quite probably revolution.[3] The Central Powers' armies thus developed high-risk schemes predicated on the need to crush their opponents rapidly and decisively. Ruthless and peremptory action would characterize their conduct on the battlefield against both enemy military forces and any sign of popular uprising.

Surprisingly, given how tightly their fates were bound and the difficulty of the task that they faced, the German and Habsburg armies had cooperated only loosely in planning their wars. Under Schlieffen, who was intensely secretive about his plans and contemptuous of Austro-Hungarian military capabilities, contacts between the Chiefs of the General Staff were by 1905 limited to an annual exchange of Christmas cards. The rise of Helmuth von Moltke and Franz Conrad von Hötzendorf to the top of the armies in January and November 1906 respectively, and the international tensions sparked by the Bosnian crisis in 1908, brought more cordial relations and some greater openness about what the allies hoped from each other. To his credit, Conrad pressed for more detailed discussions in the years directly before the First World War, but neither Emperor Franz Joseph and his government nor the Germans were keen. Instead, the agreements reached were personal undertakings between the two Chiefs of Staff.[4] In 1909 the Austro-Hungarians were told that in a two-front war, the Germans planned first to deploy the overwhelming majority of their forces in the west. Moltke needed an early Habsburg offensive to distract the Russians from the Reich's weakly defended eastern border while his army quickly defeated the French; as a sop and reassurance, he promised Conrad that the small forces left there would attack in order to draw off as much enemy strength from the south as possible. For the Habsburg Chief of the General Staff, the prospect of taking on almost the full might of the Tsarist army alone was daunting already in 1909. Moltke's promise appeared increasingly unrealistic in the years afterwards, as the eastern enemy rearmed and updated its deployment plans. However, Conrad did not press him hard for any more detailed commitment. After a German victory in the west and a successful Habsburg holding action, the Reich's army would be transferred eastwards, enabling the Central Powers to overwhelm their Russian enemy. With this assurance, Conrad could risk a confrontation with Serbia, an operation that he passionately wished to undertake.[5]

The German campaign plan for the Western Front was the keystone of the Central Powers' strategy in 1914. Moltke was broadly correct when he told Conrad in February 1913 that 'Austria's fate will not be definitively decided along the Bug but rather along the Seine.'[6] His aim was to turn encirclement to advantage, concentrate his forces over- whelmingly against France and then, once that enemy was eliminated, use the Reich's efficient railway system to transport them eastwards. Time was critical: if the western campaign took longer than six weeks, the slow but powerful Russian army would be able to mobilize fully, giving it the opportunity to overwhelm the Austro-Hungarians in Gal- icia and the weak German force left in East Prussia. The German Chief of Staff's key challenge was thus to defeat France quickly. German offi- cers in the war's aftermath claimed that the answer to this problem was bequeathed to Moltke in a memorandum written in 1905–6 by his illus- trious predecessor: the infamous 'Schlieffen Plan'. This plan envisaged an army of ninety-six infantry divisions, eighty-two of which, later joined by five others from the south, were to be deployed as a strong right wing between Metz and Aachen and tasked with sweeping through the Benelux countries in order to bypass France's chain of border for- tresses and break into its north-east. The point of Schlieffen's plan was not, contrary to an oft repeated claim, to capture Paris. The encirclement of the French capital that it proposed was merely a highly undesirable last resort, necessary only if the enemy retreated so far that his left flank rested on the fortified city. Instead, the plan's primary objective was the envelopment, wherever that might prove possible, and through it the annihilation, of France's army.[7]

Moltke was heavily influenced by Schlieffen's memorandum.[8] Like his predecessor, he envisaged a strong right wing conducting a decisive offensive through Belgium, outflanking the French fortress belt and enveloping the enemy army. However, Schlieffen's plan had been com- pleted while Russia was incapacitated by revolution. Moltke worked in far less favourable circumstances: he was confronted not only with a two-front war, which necessitated leaving nine divisions in the east, but also with a western enemy likely to fight more aggressively than ten years earlier. He was also pessimistic, or rather more realistic, about many of the assumptions built into the Schlieffen Plan. Consequently, he introduced important modifications. Most notably, and against his pre- decessor's legendary deathbed exhortation to keep the right wing strong, he weakened it; whereas Schlieffen placed eighty-seven divisions there, Moltke had only fifty-four. The ratio of forces between the left and right wings was also changed, from one-to-seven in the original 1905–6 plan to one-to-three in 1914. To Moltke's post-war denigrators, this was a disastrous decision that cost Germany its chance of an early victory. In actuality, it made a lot of sense. Moltke needed fewer divisions on the right because unlike Schlieffen, he neither intended his troops to march through Dutch, as well as Belgian, territory nor in any circumstances to march around Paris. Taking on Holland, he recognized, would absorb considerable strength better deployed against Germany's real enemies. Moreover, Moltke knew his plan was already a high-risk enterprise; he wanted insurance and hoped that if the initial offensive failed and static war developed, a neutral Holland might act as a 'wind pipe', through which the blockaded Reich could funnel goods and raw materials.[9]

Moltke's decision to allocate more troops than Schlieffen had planned to the left wing, south-east of Metz, was in part a product of the same calculation. It helped to protect the Saar, an industrial region that would be crucial if the initial gamble failed, leading to a long war. More importantly, however, Moltke envisaged this wing's sixteen divisions playing a significant, if subordinate role in the coming campaign. He foresaw correctly the likelihood of a limited French offensive into Lorraine and wanted his left wing to fix or, better still, draw in the enemy's strength, which would then be counter-attacked from the flanks, enveloped and annihilated. The strong right wing, meanwhile, would not advance around Paris; it had neither the requisite men nor any need to do so. Instead, the wing's task was remorselessly to push the rest of the French army, its numbers reduced by the commitment to its own offensive, to the south-east, bringing about a second, much larger encirclement. With the German left wing to its front and the right wing, after an anticlockwise concentric sweep through Belgium, attacking over the river Oise in its rear, the French army's capitulation would be all but assured.[10]

If Moltke's plan in 1914 was somewhat better grounded in reality than its precursor, it was still reckless. To crush the French army, one of Europe's most modern, best-equipped and largest armed forces, in less than a month and a half was a breathtakingly audacious and, as it turned out, foolhardy aspiration. How could the Chief of Staff possibly think that it could work? Moltke had no numerical advantage. Even with almost his entire force deployed in the west, seventy-three and a half German divisions still had to beat eighty French, six Belgian and six British divisions. His edge in armaments was slight. The single real advantage was in heavy artillery. The French could field only 308 heavy guns against the German army's 848 and they had nothing to match its medium and heavy howitzers, weapons which thanks to their high angle of fire were to prove invaluable in trench warfare. The best German units outgunned their French counterparts. The twenty-three German active corps deployed in the west, formations of two divisions containing the youngest, fittest and most recently trained soldiers, were each supported by 160 artillery pieces (fifty-four 77mm field guns and eighteen 105mm howitzers per division and sixteen heavy 150mm howitzers per corps), between twenty-four and twenty-eight more than their French equivalents. However, the French partly compensated with superior field artillery: their superb Soixante-Quinze ('75'), of which there were 4,780 in service, could outrange the 5,068 German 77mm guns and gave a higher rate of fire with a heavier shell.[11] The French army had a slight lead in aerial technology. The Germans' railway troops, engineers and other technical units were marginally better trained. Otherwise in materiel, there was little to separate the two enemies.[12]

For Moltke, however, as for other contemporary military professionals, a war's outcome was not reducible to big battalions or the size of gun calibres. There were, as he explained in 1911, far more important determinants of defeat and victory: 'The number of military units is not by itself decisive in a war. Forces come to play that . . . lie in the realm not of mathematics but of morale. A whole nation's ability to fight, its readiness for war, bravery, the will to make sacrifices, discipline, talent of its leadership, are to be valued more highly than mere numbers.'[13] The Germany army's real advantage, and the reason for Moltke's readiness to put his faith in such an audacious plan, lay not in its materiel or technology but in the quality of its personnel: its upper leadership, officer corps and manpower. The Great General Staff, the army's centre for operational planning, was Prussia's characteristic contribution to what contemporaries praised as Europe's five 'perfect' institutions; the others being the Roman Curia, Russian Ballet, French Opera and British Parliament. It had acquired its reputation as the architect of Prussia's series of stunning victories in the 1860s, culminating with its triumph over France in 1870–71. The Great General Staff made two key contributions to the German army's fighting effectiveness. First, it was responsible for formulating the annual mobilization and deployment plans; these tasks included drawing up the intricate railway schedules for troop transports, assigning concentration areas and developing operational strategy. It also identified weapons and manpower needs, and observed other forces, especially potential enemies. The Great General Staff owed its legendary efficiency in these tasks to a gruelling and highly competitive selection process and an institutional culture that prized intellectualism, technical mastery and a formidable work ethic. Its great defect, however, was its narrow vision: its distance from diplomacy, exclusive focus on operational excellence and obsession with detail were all reflected in the desperate risks run in Moltke's campaign plan.[14]

Second, the Great General Staff instilled in its officers, and through them the German army, a shared understanding of battle which made possible an enviable unity of action that other forces found difficult to emulate. The Chief of the General Staff trained his officers personally, inculcating through staff rides and tactical-strategic exercises a set of basic principles of how to behave in different combat situations. While 113 General Staff officers worked in the planning and analytical departments in Berlin, more than double this number were posted to divisional and corps staff. This small group of elite officers used their key positions to spread the doctrine throughout the army. The German military's infamous and highly effective *Auftragstaktik*, or 'mission tactics', was built upon this system: senior commanders, confident that their officers would behave similarly in any given tactical situations, could simply set operational goals. Their subordinates, better placed to judge conditions on the ground, would through their shared training naturally coordinate in choosing the tactics to fulfil their missions.[15]

The German officer corps considered itself the guarantor and repository of the army's 'spirit', the moral and psychological quality revered by early twentieth-century militaries. Numbering 33,036 professional and 40,000 reserve officers at war's outbreak, its values were influenced less by its technocratic General Staff elite than an older, aristocratic martial culture. The nobility accounted for nearly a third of professional officers and predominated in its upper ranks, where a little over half of men from colonel (*Oberst*) to general came from the traditional warrior caste. The bourgeoisie supplied the remainder of active officers as well as almost all the reserve officers. High educational barriers and, for prospective reserve officers, the need to pay for a year of training, shut out the proletariat.[16] Curious to modern eyes, the army's leadership was utterly convinced that this social exclusivity was indispensable in its ability to carry out its martial function. The corps wanted men who through upbringing and education had internalized the code of honour that it embraced, would conform to its high moral expectations and would offer unfailing loyalty to the monarch, to whom it owed fealty. Wilhelmine officers pointed to the French corps, which recruited over half of its men from the ranks, as a warning of the dangers of surrendering to more socially progressive fads. They regarded it with some justice as politicized, divided and demoralized, and doubted that its moral authority would suffice to hold men to discipline under the immense strains of combat.[17]

The German corps' aristocratic conception of leadership, although in part a matter of snobbery, did indeed contribute in two ways to its performance. First, it promoted a conscientious paternalism. The corps insisted that 'never resting care for the welfare of his men is the good and rewarding privilege of the officer'.[18] Upper-class officers were thought best suited for this responsibility because they had been taught from an early age the precepts of *noblesse oblige*, the aristocratic doctrine that privilege carried with it responsibility to social inferiors. While this assumption was not always borne out, as Socialists' peacetime complaints about officers' mishandling of men testify, in 1914 and 1915 this model of command worked well in oiling inter-rank relations, protecting troops from hardship and increasing their resilience.[19] Second, men who possessed a strong code of personal honour, and were prepared in peace to duel to defend it, were believed to be more ready to lay down their lives to defend the honour of their corps, regiment, Kaiser and Fatherland. Officership was conceived less as a management role than as a moral and didactic calling: 'The officer is the model of his men; his example pulls them forward with him.' 'Strength of character' and 'moral seriousness', qualities cultivated in German cadet institutes and *Gymnasien* no less assiduously than in British public schools, were essential if officers were to win their men's respect and provide the inspirational examples of courage and self-sacrifice necessary to lead them forward across the fire-swept battlefield.[20] The German officer corps' death rate suggests that it vindicated these expectations during the war. Whereas 13.3 per cent of German soldiers were killed, 15.7 per cent of reserve officers and a horrifying 24.7 per cent of professional officers died in the course of duty.[21]

The German army's other ranks were also confidently regarded as a match for those of its enemies. The force's backbone was its 107,794 professional non-commissioned officers.[22] These men were highly capable, the most senior among them carrying out tasks which in other forces were the responsibility of subalterns. The German army had, thanks to its relatively generous conditions of service, been able to retain eighteen to twenty career NCOs in each of its peacetime companies, more than double those of French companies and ten times those in Russian companies. Their fund of experience proved invaluable in war, permitting the devolution of command responsibilities.[23] The army's conscripts, who in peace served for two years, were also thought to be better than those fielded by the French. Germany, with a youthful population totalling 67 million, drafted between 51 and 53 per cent of each male year group to maintain an army of 800,000 men in the last years of peace. Its recruiters could pick their manpower discriminatingly. France, with a population of 39 million, had to conscript 83 per cent to keep up, and so accepted all but the lame or seriously ill. Its inferior demography, with a relatively low birth rate which ensured that its population size continued to fall behind, was frequently cited in Social Darwinist terms as evidence that the Republic had passed the high point of its development. Militarily, this demography was understood to be significant not only because of its effect on the overall fitness of the French army's recruits but also because it left the force with only a small pool of reserves. Conscious of the extreme risks of their campaign plan, German military commanders could comfort themselves with the thought that even if it failed, France could not sustain a long war.[24]

German troops' morale, discipline and training were also believed superior to those of their French counterparts. Conservative Prussian officers tended to misinterpret French republican ideals as undermining rather than, as proved during the war, forming the basis of French conscripts' loyalty and obedience.[25] Racial stereotypes too informed their assessments. Moltke hoped that the 'nervous' character of the Gallic race would contribute to a quick collapse of morale in defeat.[26] The Kaiser's officers were on safer ground in their confident estimations of their own soldiers. The army enjoyed immense social prestige in Germany. Particularly in the countryside, from which it had drawn a disproportionate number of recruits in peacetime, the two-year period of military service was widely seen as a rite of passage to manhood. In the cities, the army was, despite its officers' hostility towards Social Democracy, a force for national integration. Many workers welcomed the break from industrial life's monotony offered by peacetime conscription. They made well-disciplined soldiers and during the war proved better prepared than rural folk to master technical weaponry such as machine guns.[27] The German army provided a thorough course of training for these men. Its facilities were unrivalled: France simply had nothing to compare with the Reich's twenty-six manoeuvre grounds of at least 5,625 hectares each.[28] The doctrine taught was generally sensible too, although not flawless. Crucially, the Prussian drill regulations of 1906, unlike those issued in the French army in 1913, recognized the need to gain fire superiority before any attack. The importance of cooperation between the infantry and artillery was acknowledged, even if its difficulties were not fully understood. However, the army remained conservative in its attitude towards the open tactical formations that were necessary to minimize the effect of fire but were difficult to control. Loose skirmisher lines were favoured in the attack, but officers were encouraged to deploy late and as a result in 1914 German soldiers were caught in dense tactical formations and suffered heavy casualties. The army's training was nonetheless sufficiently good to enable it successfully to field thirty-one reserve divisions, composed of men who had completed their peacetime training up to a decade earlier. While the German army had not found a solution for the age's key dilemma of how to move forward under lethal modern firepower, its training was sufficiently grounded in the new reality to produce an impressive battlefield performance in 1914.[29]

The Austro-Hungarian army's task in a European war was at first glance straightforward: during the six weeks in which its ally defeated France, it was to bear the main burden of holding the Russians in the east. However, Conrad, unlike Moltke, could not simply plan for one major conflict. The predators that surrounded the Empire could plausibly attack in a number of combinations, and so unlike their German allies, with their obsessive focus on one single scheme, the Austro-Hungarians had stacks of war plans. There were plans for conflict with Russia (War Case 'R'), in the Balkans (War Case 'B') and, although formally an ally, with Italy (War Case 'I'). The army also prepared to deploy against combinations of these enemies and, a case considered hopeless even by the optimists in the Habsburg General Staff, against all three in alliance.[30] In order to meet all eventualities, Conrad divided his operational force into three groups. A-Echelon, the strongest group with nine corps containing twenty-seven of the army's forty-eight infantry divisions, was intended to provide protection against Russia. The Balkan Minimal Group of three corps (with nine divisions) had the task of defending against Serbia and Montenegro. Finally, there was a swing group, B-Echelon, which comprised twelve divisions that could be sent wherever needed. The circumstances of July 1914 presented two possibilities for this echelon. Habsburg leaders had to decide whether they faced 'War Case B', a conflict solely against Serbia, or whether Russia would intervene, bringing about 'War Case B+R'. In the former case, B-Echelon was to be sent to the southern border for an offensive. In the latter, it would urgently be required in Galicia, where, with the units of A-Echelon, it would take part in an attack intended to disrupt the Tsarist Empire's mobilization.

Conrad's plans comfortingly appeared to deal with all eventualities. Yet there were fatal flaws which, combined with indecision and wishful thinking on the part of the Chief of the General Staff, disrupted mobilization and severely damaged Habsburg hopes of any early victory. First, the railway plan was geared to flexibility, when what was really needed was speed. The four corps allocated to the swing B-Echelon all lay far from Galicia but had access to good railways. The Budapest IV Corps could travel to the eastern fortress-city of Przemyśl on a double-tracked line. The Prague VIII and Leitmeritz IX Corps were on the Monarchy's most modern rail artery, the *Nordbahn*. If speed had been the priority, then it would have been optimal to transport these distant units first and then start moving the divisions of A-Echelon, most of which were based closer to the battlefront. However, Conrad's demand for flexibility meant that the army's rail experts did the opposite. B-Echelon was to be held stationary, while A-Echelon was loaded into the first transports. Worse still, the delay was compounded by the military rail technicians' ridiculously cautious timetabling. The regulation speed for Habsburg military transports on single tracks was just 11 kilometres per hour. On double-tracked lines they were expected to reach a heady 18 kilometres per hour. The trains themselves were permitted to be no more than forty-nine wagons' long, comparable to other armies' transports but just half the length of the civilian trains that usually travelled the *Nordbahn*. Stops of six in every twenty-four hours for fuel and feeding were calculated into the deployment programme. How slow all this was is clear from comparison with the French and German armies, which assumed basic speeds of 30 kilometres per hour for their mobilization transports. The result was that even under the best circumstances, a Habsburg general mobilization against the Tsarist Empire would be tardy. The Russians expected their enemy to complete concentration against them in fifteen days. However, under the Austro-Hungarian military rail plan the final units of B-Echelon deployed only on the twenty-fourth day of mobilization.[31] The prioritization of flexibility over speed in Conrad's plans therefore negated the one real advantage that the Habsburg army possessed. The Russians planned by the twenty-fourth day of their mobilization to have thirty-seven and a half infantry divisions on the Galician Front, just two fewer than their enemy. By the thirtieth day, they would enjoy a significant numerical superiority, with forty-five infantry and more than eighteen cavalry divisions.[32]

The Austro-Hungarian army could ill afford to sacrifice this single advantage, for its multinational character made it difficult to command and the Hungarian parliament's obstreperousness had left it under-manned and underfunded. It exhibited the structural complexity typical of Habsburg institutions. The Common Army was the main force with two-thirds of the Empire's infantry and nearly all its artillery and cavalry. Alongside it were the Hungarian *Honvéd* and Austrian *Landwehr*, formations originally intended as second-line national guards but which through decades of Magyar parliamentary pressure had developed into first-line forces. A small Croatian-Slavonian force, the *Domobran*, served within the *Honvéd*, reflecting the autonomous position of Croatia within the Lands of St Stephen. The Common Army recruited from all parts of the Empire, while the other formations drew their soldiers exclusively from Hungary, Austria or Croatia respectively. The army was a dynastic force; all its parts owed allegiance solely to Franz Joseph as Austrian Emperor or King of Hungary and Croatia.[33]

While the German and French conscript forces were, in the jargon of the time, 'people's armies', composed of each nation's manhood, the Austro-Hungarians fielded, as its history proudly asserted, 'an army of peoples'.[34] The ethnic composition of the force's rank and file closely mirrored that of the Empire which it served and from which it was drawn (see Table 4).

The Habsburg army had followed other European forces and switched to territorial recruitment in 1882, raising units within sixteen corps districts, a measure that accelerated mobilization and limited the

Table 4. The ethnic composition of the Austro-Hungarian army, 1910 (by language)

Nationality	Percentages			
	of Population	of all Ranks	of Professional Officers	of Reserve Officers
Germans	24	25.2	78.7	60.2
Magyars	20	23.1	9.3	23.7
Czechs	13	12.9	4.8	9.7
Slovaks	4	3.6	-	0.1
Ruthenes	8	7.6	0.2	0.3
Poles	10	7.9	2.5	2.8
Slovenes	2	2.4	0.4	0.5
Serbo-Croats	11	9.0	2.4	1.6
Romanians	6	7.0	0.9	0.6
Italians	2	1.3	0.7	0.5

Source: N. Stone, 'Army and Society in the Habsburg Monarchy, 1900–1914', *Past and Present* 33 (April 1966), p. 99.

mixing of the nationalities.[35] Even so, the force still had to overcome considerable communication challenges. These were resolved in the first instance by designating one tongue as a 'language of command' and 'language of service'. This was German in the Common Army and *Landwehr*, Hungarian in the *Honvéd* and Croatian in the *Domobran*. Each soldier learned eighty words in this language so that he understood basic commands like 'Attention!', 'At Ease!' or 'Fire!' The men also memorized around a thousand technical terms, including the names for the parts of their weaponry; conversation might not be possible, but soldiers from different corners of the empire should be able to strip their rifles or service a field gun together. Additionally, to facilitate everyday communication at lower levels of the military organization, any tongue spoken by at least 20 per cent of the soldiers in a regiment (a unit of around 3,000 men) was designated a 'regimental language'. In 1914, even though the army was territorially raised, only 142 regiments, fewer than half the total, were sufficiently ethnically homogeneous to be considered monolingual. Some 162 regiments officially had two languages, twenty-four used three, and there were even a few regiments raised from areas so mixed that four languages had to be recognized. Any new officer arriving at a regiment had three years to learn its languages. The duty was taken seriously, for the men had the right to speak in their own tongues to their superiors up to company commander, and failure meant delayed promotion or even dismissal. Most Habsburg professional officers were therefore proficient in at least two tongues. The corps' high-flyers usually spoke more: Conrad, for example, had mastered seven.[36]

The officer corps, which numbered 18,506 professionals and 13,293 reserve officers, was the army's greatest asset. The corps shared its Prussian ally's aristocratic ethos and honour credo, but its social profile was less exalted: two decades before the war, the share of nobles among career officers had been 28.6 per cent, but it had fallen by 1914.[37] Most professional officers were of Austrian German stock, although the four-fifths suggested in the official figures (see Table 4) is probably an exaggeration.[38] Perhaps one-sixth were from Slavic backgrounds. Whatever their origins, the vast majority were anational, identifying only with the Austrian state idea and their feudal lord, the Emperor. Recruitment for both the professional and reserve corps was blind to ethnicity and confession. One of the consequences was that Jews, who were informally but totally barred from commissions in the pre-war Prussian army, were four times over-represented in the Habsburg reserve corps, making up no less than 17 per cent of its officers.[39] Although the Common Army was a conscript force, its professional officers held aloof from civilian society. The corps resented its lack of prestige in that society and was hostile to the rising nationalism. These attitudes, combined with Habsburg officers' lesser social status, and education and pay comparing poorly with those of their German counterparts, influenced its command style and performance. Inter-rank relations in the Habsburg army were indifferent; better than those in its Russian enemy, for sure, but not so trusting as in Germany's military, even though its officers had to spend more time than German officers instructing their men because their companies usually had only between one and three professional NCOs. This was not merely a matter of communication difficulties. Whereas the liberal reform of Prussian discipline had taken place at the start of the nineteenth century, not until 1873 had the more socially detached Habsburg force finally instructed its commanders to 'show sympathy' and 'get to know and understand' their subordinates.[40] On the other hand, the corps' self-isolation and rejection of civil society probably reinforced its intense devotion to the Emperor. The sacrifice that it made during the war was astonishingly high: 31.3 per cent of professional officers and 16.5 per cent of reserve officers fell in imperial service.[41]

The Common Army's biggest problem with its men was that it simply did not have enough. Its 1,687,000-strong Field Army was dwarfed by the 3,400,000 soldiers of the mobilized Russian force. Additionally, the low proportion of the male population drafted in peace meant there was a relatively small pool of trained reserves to act as casualty replacements in war.[42] The manpower pool from which the army recruited was very mixed. In the west of the Empire, educational standards and the acceptance of state power were little different from that of western nations.[43] In peacetime, just 3 per cent of German-speaking Austrians had attempted to dodge the three-year (from 1912 two-year) military conscription. In the disgruntled but well-educated Czech lands, 6–7.3 per cent of men ignored the summons to the colours. By contrast Hungarians, who still bore a grudge for Habsburg soldiers' brutal suppression of their 1848 revolution and disliked the Common Army, had an absentee rate before the war of a little over 25 per cent. Worst of all were Galicia and the South Slav lands, areas with much illiteracy and irredentist movements as well as high emigration, where resistance in the last decade of peace had risen to the point that over one-third of those mustered failed to present themselves.[44] Of course, war was a very different situation. Punishment for disobedience was more severe and a wave of patriotism did sweep the Empire as hostilities broke out. Nonetheless, it was inevitable that units raised in different parts of the Empire would in war display wildly differing capabilities and performance. Scepticism about the loyalty of some peoples also prevailed. As the Habsburg War Minister's aide-de-camp remarked of South Slav reservists on the eve of war, 'they will arrive at the depots all confident, but they'll already be less willing when the time comes to march. Whether they attack over the last 1,000 metres, no one can give any sure guarantee.'[45]

The army's main deficiencies in 1914 nonetheless lay not, contrary to what is often claimed, in the loyalty or willingness of its Slav soldiers, but rather in inadequate support, poor training and, as the campaigns would reveal, spectacularly incompetent higher leadership. Its gravest materiel shortage was in modern artillery, a consequence both of inadequate funding and indecision and infighting about the specifications for the new weaponry among the army's senior commanders. Habsburg Common Army divisions had forty-two field artillery pieces; eight to ten more than first-line Serbian divisions but far fewer than the sixty supporting Russian divisions.[46] Worse still, only two-thirds of these guns were modern 05/08 80mm cannon. The others were obsolete 100mm field howitzers without recoil mechanisms for quick aiming and firing or armoured shields for the gun teams' protection. The heavy artillery, which comprised eight 99/04 150mm howitzers in each corps, was similarly old-fashioned. All Habsburg gun barrels were cast of bronze, rather than stronger steel, which made them heavy and limited their range. Even in Serbia, the 150mm howitzers, which could fire 5,000 metres, found that the enemy's heavy artillery could outrange them by no less than 3,000 metres. The Common Army had some excellent specialist artillery. The force had designed a superb mountain artillery gun, although only four of fifty-two mountain batteries had received it by 1914. The army was also equipped with some state-of-the-art fortress-busting 305mm Skoda super-heavy mortars. Neither weapon compensated for deficiencies elsewhere, however, nor for the army's inadequate ammunition stocks. Just 330 rounds per howitzer and 550 rounds per field gun were available, around half that stockpiled by the other great powers.[47]

The tactical skill of the Habsburg infantry was unlikely to compensate for this deficiency in materiel. The army not only lacked professional NCOs; it also relied more on reservists, whose martial skills were rusty, than was wise. The German army kept its peacetime units at two-thirds strength, so that on mobilization only the two youngest and most recently trained classes of reservists needed to be called to bring them to their full complement.[48] In Habsburg infantry companies after mobilization, by contrast, only 20–25 per cent of the complement were active soldiers undergoing peacetime military training. To fill the ranks, men who had not seen service for a decade had to be drafted. So great was the army's need that even *Ersatzreservisten*, men who had received no more than an annual eight-week military training, were called up. The army, denied funding through Hungarian intransigence in the last decade of peace, also lacked the equipment and infrastructure needed for an orderly expansion on mobilization. Most continental conscript armies followed the Prussian model of organizing three main lines. The 'active' units that composed the standing army and had the best equipment were filled with men undergoing their peacetime service and topped up with the youngest classes of reservists. The depots also kept sufficient equipment, NCOs and officers to permit the building of a second line: reserve regiments containing trained men aged between twenty-three and thirty-two. A third line of less well-equipped *Landwehr* or territorial units, intended principally for rear-area duties, was formed from reservists aged twenty-eight to thirty-eight. Additionally, older men up to forty-five years of age might be allocated to *Landsturm* police or labour units.[49] The Habsburg Common Army, by contrast, treated its *Landwehr* and *Honvéd* regiments as first-line by 1914 and lacked the surplus equipment and officers needed to form extra second-line reserve units on mobilization. To supplement its weak front-line strength, it instead relied upon *Landsturminfanteriebrigaden*, scratch-built militia composed of men aged between thirty-two and forty-two issued with obsolete rifles and easily visible peacetime uniforms or even just arm-bands in imperial black-yellow colours. Their artillery support amounted to no more than one gun per battalion. During 1914 and 1915, similarly poorly equipped 'march battalions', whose purpose was to bring drafts to front-line units, were frequently also thrown into combat. Lacking training, equipment, cohesion and leadership, the march battalions and *Landsturm* brigades predictably achieved little and suffered horrendous casualties.[50]

These deficiencies were multiplied by a misguided tactical doctrine. The 'cult of the offensive', an overestimation of the superiority of the attack and a conviction that raw will could beat firepower, was embraced by all armies in 1914, but those that felt themselves to be behind in the technological and material race extolled it most. The French army, with its faith in the *offensive à outrance*, is remembered as the most fervent advocate of these attitudes, but the Austro-Hungarian military leadership was no less fanatical in its belief.[51] This was in large measure due to Conrad, who was considered in the army to be a tactical genius. His key work 'On the Study of Tactics' had appeared in 1890, and a quarter of a century later he clung to the same principles. Energy, decisiveness and action were his answers to firepower. 'The attack,' he insisted, 'is the action most suited to the spirit of war.'[52] To prepare his men for the war of manoeuvre that he expected, he put them through ferocious route marches. Disastrously, unlike his German ally, he denied the necessity for combined arms tactics. His infantry regulations of October 1911, the last issued before the outbreak of war, insisted that foot soldiers could 'win the victor's laurels even without support from other weapons and against enemy numerical superiority if imbued with confidence and aggression, if equipped with unbendable steadfastness of will and the greatest physical toughness'.[53] The only concession to the destructive effects of firepower was to recommend that troops be deployed in loose skirmishing lines, and in practice even this was frequently disregarded. Time and again after pre-war manoeuvres, foreign observers criticized Habsburg troops' slow movement in closed formations. Officers stood up behind their firing lines or even stayed on their horses, offering ideal targets. The obliviousness towards terrain, failure to reconnoitre and lack of cooperation with artillery made these soldiers, in the German military attaché's view, mere 'cannon fodder'.[54]

The Central Powers' campaign in the summer of 1914 was unrealistic in the demands that it placed on both armies. Capable though it was, the German military was asked to achieve the impossible: a victory over France in just six weeks. Even Moltke lacked confidence in the chances of success. He hoped against reason for a quick victory, yet foresaw a horrendous conflict lasting up to two years. He had even, albeit half-heartedly, pushed civil authorities to prepare financially and secure the Reich's food supply.[55] The Austro-Hungarian army led by Conrad, an even more vociferous advocate of preventative war, was grievously unprepared to face Serbia and Russia combined. The decade-long funding freeze imposed by the Hungarian parliament must certainly bear much responsibility. Yet Conrad and his generals were reckless in accepting the task of holding the Russian army, contributed to the delay in their force's re-equipment with modern artillery, and imposed a tactical doctrine divorced from the reality of the twentieth-century battlefield. Fatally, neither German nor Austro-Hungarian military leaders were willing to acknowledge their forces' limitations in their operational planning. Their soldiers would pay for these illusions.

THE WESTERN FRONT

The German army's mobilization was everything for which its General Staff could have hoped. When the 'State of Imminent War' was declared on 31 July, the active soldiers in barracks had changed into wartime field-grey uniforms and border regiments had issued ammunition and sent contingents to guard the frontiers. From 2 August, the first day of mobilization, reservists began to flood into the depots. There was, recorded one regiment's historian, 'no sign of exuberance, either from hatred of the enemy or celebratory enthusiasm, no hysterical shouting, no bluster'. Instead, the men were sober, purposeful and knew what was expected of them.[56] Most active units reached full strength within four or five days and frantically practised route marches to harden their new arrivals. The transport of the entire Field Army, excepting just nine divisions earmarked for the Eastern Front, to westerly concentration areas began on 4 August. An enormous technical ballet lasting twenty days and choreographed down to the minute by the General Staff now played out across the Reich, as 20,800 rail transports carried 2,070,000 men, 118,000 horses and 400,000 tons of material smoothly to their jump-off points. Soldiers were brought across the country from as far afield as Breslau and Posen. Behind the deployment area of Moltke's strong right wing, one train clattered across Cologne's Hohenzollern Bridge over the Rhine every ten minutes from 2 until 18 August. When the concentration was complete, seven armies were stretched along the length of the western border. The First, Second and Third Armies, with 164, 159 and 104 battalions respectively, composed the right wing and were arrayed against Belgium. Below them opposite Luxemburg and in northern Lorraine stood the 123 and 147 battalions of the Fourth and Fifth Armies. The Sixth and Seventh Armies with 131 and 108 battalions were the southernmost forces, guarding Lorraine and Alsace.[57]

Even before concentration was underway, the campaign started. On the night of 1–2 August the 16th Division had bloodlessly secured Luxembourg's railways. The first combat operation then began early on 4 August, when after an ultimatum demanding free passage an assault force of 39,000 men crossed into Belgium, violating the Kingdom's neutrality, and marched towards the fortified city of Liège.[58] The city's rapid capture was vital, for as a fortress it blocked any German advance into Belgium and as a key rail hub it was essential for the supply of troops passing through the country. The invaders had hoped to find just 6,000 soldiers, supported by 3,000 members of Belgium's home guard, the *Garde Civique*. Instead, they were confronted by 32,000 men with thirty machine guns and 150 artillery pieces garrisoning the twelve forts encircling the city or manning hastily dug earthworks outside. This first operation set the tone for much of the ensuing campaign. First, it was costly. The initial attempts to storm the forts, each furnished with modern armaments and able to withstand calibres of up to 210mm, were repulsed with heavy casualties. Some units lost over half their men. On 8 August the German High Command (*Oberste Heeresleitung* – OHL) abandoned the assaults and ordered in another 60,000 troops and siege artillery. In a rare case of harmonious and decisive allied cooperation, the Habsburg army loaned four batteries of super-heavy Skoda 305mm howitzers to the German army, and it was these, along with the force's five 420mm Krupp mortars, which battered the fortresses into submission.

Second, the operation was intensely frustrating. Commanders, conscious of racing against the clock, fumed at the delays: 'We're still sitting here in front of this damned fortress,' fulminated General von Einem, commander of the second, larger force sent to take Liège, on 11 August. 'If only we could advance!'[59] The Habsburg guns could not be brought up until the next day, and it was thus only on 16 August, already two days behind the schedule set out in Schlieffen's 1905–6 plan, that the last of Liège's forts capitulated. The bloodiness of the fighting and frustration at the delay both contributed to the third feature that would mark this operation and the rest of the campaign: violence by German troops against civilians. Already on 4 August, the first day of invasion, civilians were shot down. When heavy fighting began the following day, executions and massacres mounted. German soldiers, shocked and disorientated by their first experience of modern war, became convinced that they were being ambushed by inhabitants. 'One cannot grasp the havoc wreaked by the bestial mob in Liège,' recounted one soldier who was probably part of a force that had infiltrated between the forts and entered the city on the morning of 6 August:

> When we forced an entry into the city after a brief fight outside it, we were at first greeted with cheers by women. At the same time, the sly population hung white flags, white dresses, teacloths etc. out of the windows ... However, that was just a malicious trick ... Scarcely had we passed the houses when rifle barrels were poked out of the windows and we were shot in the back. There were also shots aimed at our legs fired from cellar coal holes.[60]

The city's population, as later investigation discovered, had indeed at first greeted the advancing troops, mistaking them for British soldiers.

The fierce fire that the Germans had faced soon after came, however, not from civilians but from Belgian troops, whose use of cover and smokeless munitions made them hard to see. The sudden shift from an initial, apparently friendly reception to a lethal hail of bullets understandably led the Germans to conclude that they were victims of civilian treachery. Similar reports of inhabitants' aggression, some also prompted by confusion at the rudimentary, civilian character of the *Garde Civique*'s uniforms, but almost none of which were true, flooded in from other units engaged around the city. By 8 August von Einem rued what he called the 'terrible character' of the hostilities: 'the population is energetically taking part in the war'.[61] In just five days, his troops massacred 850 Belgian civilians and burned down around 1,300 buildings in retaliation. Moltke, believing that his worst fears of the 1871 *'franc tireur'* war repeating itself were being realized, issued a 'Solemn Warning' on 12 August. Condemning the Belgian population for illegally joining the fighting and committing 'atrocities' against his men, he threatened dire punishment. Any individual who behaved in this way would, he promised, be 'immediately shot according to martial law'.[62]

While this heavy fighting was going on around Liège, the French opened their campaign in the south. On 7 August one corps raided over the German frontier into Upper Alsace, captured the region's major city of Mülhausen on the following day, but after twenty-four hours was thrown out. The main French offensive, the first stage of which was an assault by two armies into Alsace-Lorraine, opened on 14 August. The attack was intended to pin down as much enemy strength as possible so that other troops could manoeuvre further north against the centre of the German line. By 19 August the Republic's tricolour again flew over Mülhausen.[63] This defence of German territory, not Moltke's more famous attack through Belgium and north-west France, produced the bitterest fighting seen in August. The German Seventh Army lost nearly 18,000 men to wounds alone, an extraordinary 12 per cent of its strength, in repelling the French invasion of Alsace and then going over to the offensive. The Sixth Army, covering Lorraine, lost 7.6 per cent of its strength to wounds that month, the two German armies in the centre suffered 7 per cent casualties, and the German First, Second and Third Armies a relatively light 4 per cent as they charged through central Belgium.[64]

For Alsatian civilians, caught between two groups of nervous, heavily armed soldiers, these were nightmarish days. Border villages were fought over and bombarded, the men forced by one side or the other to dig trenches and bury dead, sometimes under fire. Agricultural work stopped as it was unsafe to venture into the fields.[65] The Germans distrusted the population, especially after some of Mülhausen's citizens greeted the first invaders. Commanders complained of the 'extremely hostile attitude' that their soldiers encountered. Rumours of treason circulated and combat officers raged that 'inhabitants . . . are shooting with small calibre pieces at our men'. As at Liège, the German army reacted violently, with summary executions.[66] The French invaders sometimes behaved no better, despite their pretensions to be the liberators of an oppressed 'French' population. Already during the first raid on 7–10 August, French troops shot labourers whom they imagined were disguised German soldiers and burned down the farms of inhabitants believed to be aiding the defenders.[67]

What made the invasions so awful, however, was not just the killing but also the extensive arrests and deportations carried out by the French army. The French War Ministry ordered its troops on 22 August, near the end of the second, larger offensive, to hold hostage officials and teachers in Alsace-Lorraine. Hundreds of harmless lower state, community and Church officials, as well as some quite important ones like the Mayor of Mülhausen, were taken and imprisoned in France. Eight thousand military-aged Alsatian men were also rounded up and interned; an extraordinarily high number given the short duration of the campaign and the small area overrun. Most officials were German, and so not only security fears but also French desire to exclude malign influences from the population may have motivated the order to remove them. The deportations of military-aged men were excused as a measure to protect them from German reprisals, although probably equally if not more important was the wish to deny the enemy army new recruits once it reoccupied the province. The French authorities' intense suspicion of the deportees, who were all carefully interrogated to assess their national loyalties, certainly testifies to motives beyond concern for their welfare.[68] More difficult to explain is the forced removal of over 3,000 women, children, youths and pensioners. Some were evacuated later for their own safety from a small, 8,000-square kilometre border strip that the French managed to retain throughout the war. However, and not implausibly given both the arrests of German officials in 1914 and the exclusionary policies and expulsions that followed the French annexation of the province at the conflict's end, the Germans complained of what amounted to wartime ethnic cleansing; a campaign to weed out pro-Reich elements from an indigenous population assumed to be naturally Francophile.[69]

Throughout mid-August, the French fought to seize control of the campaign. The second stage of their offensive, intended to be decisive, opened on 21 August with the Third and Fourth Armies advancing north-east against the German centre in the Ardennes. General Joseph Joffre, the Chief of the French General Staff, had failed to recognize that the Germans were committing reserve divisions immediately to combat and consequently underestimated their total strength and assumed this part of the line to be weak. A breakthrough here would have permitted him to outflank his enemy's right wing, halting its manoeuvre in Belgium. In fact, the nine corps that attacked were faced by ten corps of the German Fourth and Fifth Armies, and French plans quickly unravelled. Rather than smashing through a weak German centre and cutting off enemy troops advancing further north, Joffre's offensive instead broke against fierce resistance from the hub of Moltke's swing through Belgium. French units were outfought. Their reconnaissance was sloppy, leading to infantry and even artillery being surprised and destroyed. Coordination between units was poor, a problem exacerbated by regimental commanders' frequent failure to keep higher commands in touch with their situation. In the hilly terrain, the Germans' high-angle howitzers offered a distinct advantage over their opponents' 75mm cannon. Worse still, the French infantry often lacked any fire support at all when it went forward. The commander of Joffre's Third Army, General Ruffey, saw this as decisive for his troops' defeat. Their attacks, he warned on 23 August, had 'failed solely because they were not prepared by artillery, or even by the fire of infantry'.[70] The Germans also made errors. Units were devastated by shrapnel when, in trying to follow their pre-war training, they waited too long to deploy from close formations into skirmisher lines. Nonetheless, by the end of the three-day battle, German troops had inflicted 40,000 fatalities on the French and forced their enemies into headlong retreat.[71]

Further north, the German swing through central and southern Belgium, the defining manoeuvre of the August battles, had begun on 18 August. For the troops of the right wing, the month was dominated by frantic, strenuous marching as they attempted to get around the French army's left flank. The men of the northernmost First Army, who had furthest to travel, typically notched up 30 or 40 kilometres per day.[72] This was an extraordinary performance, especially as so many were reservists ripped out of civilian life just a fortnight earlier and now in uniform, armed and heavily laden. Each carried an eleven-kilo pack stuffed with underwear, a spare pair of boots, sewing and washing kit, cap, two iron rations, tent pegs, rope and thirty rounds of ammunition. With coat and poncho, mess kit, rifle and multifarious accoutrements, including a bayonet, shovel, another ninety rounds of ammunition and water bottle, hung around his body on leather strapping, each soldier's load totalled around thirty kilos.[73] Topping it all off was the *Pickelhaube*, the infamous spiked helmet of the Prussian infantryman. It may have symbolized Prussia's martial spirit, but few items of headgear less practical have been fashioned. Made of leather, heavy and sweaty, it gave little protection from the sun and none at all from enemy projectiles. Unsurprisingly, not everyone was able to endure the strain of marching with this kit in blazing heat and clouds of dust. Exhausted soldiers littered the roadsides, marking the path of rapidly advancing units. Two-fifths of all cases of heatstroke in the German army over the four and a quarter years of war were treated that first month.[74] Discipline also began to fray. Ernst Baier, a Sergeant Major in Grenadier Regiment 2, described how during rest stops the men plundered cafes and restaurants while their captain looked on. The artillery and cavalry were worse, he insisted, but infantry too were guilty of 'all sorts of heroics of the genre of wine cellar-smashing and house-burning'.[75]

While the soldiers of the right wing did not lack opportunities for genuine heroics, they faced less danger than their comrades further south. Battle casualties (killed, wounded and missing) in the three northernmost German armies totalled 5 per cent of strength in the last ten days of August; bloody, to be sure, but still about half the rate in the southernmost Sixth and Seventh Armies and just a third of that suffered by Fourth Army in the Ardennes.[76] Among the three armies, Second Army saw the toughest fighting, clearing the way to the Meuse River at the start of the campaign and fighting off the French Fifth Army on the Sambre River on 21–23 August. The First and Third Armies on either side faced little significant opposition before the last days of the month. The bulk of the Belgian army had retreated to the northern fortress of

Antwerp and even the arrival of the much-vaunted British Expedition-ary Force directly ahead of the First Army at Mons on 23 August posed few problems; the Germans simply knocked it back with their weight of numbers. Nonetheless, throughout the advance, these same German troops felt themselves to be in great danger. They feared less the enemy military than the Belgian population. As at Liège and in Alsace, the soldiers lashed out. Their progress was marked by executions, hostage-taking, some of whom were used as human shields, massacres and destruction. The German right wing was the epicentre of violence in which other armies further south also participated, and which resulted that summer and autumn in the murder of 5,521 Belgian and 906 French civilians, and the deliberate demolition of between 15,000 and 20,000 buildings.[77]

These 'atrocities', taking place in an invasion that the Reich's Chan-cellor himself had publicly conceded was illegal, dealt a reputational blow from which imperial Germany never recovered. Entente govern-ments were quick to protest against the violence and their countries' newspapers cast the German advance through Belgium and north-eastern France emotively as the 'march of the barbarians'.[78] The German army's destruction of world-famous cultural treasures appeared to vin-dicate the description. Neutral opinion was particularly shocked by the force's bombardment of Rheims Cathedral on 17–19 September, a measure undertaken because, it was claimed, the French were directing their artillery fire from its towers. There was also great international horror at a rampage by troops in Louvain in the last week of August that destroyed a sixth of the city, including the university library with its priceless collection of medieval manuscripts, and cost 248 citizens their lives.[79] Elsewhere too, the invaders were vicious: Visé, the first Belgian town to face systematic destruction with 23 civilian dead; Aarschot, where 156 inhabitants were killed; Tamines, with 383 massacred; and Dinant, which suffered 674 killed, almost 10 per cent of its population; these quickly became notorious as sites of German brutality.[80] British and French propaganda interpreted the violence not just as military excesses or even war crimes but as more fundamental manifestations of a perverse and savage German 'Kultur', the polar opposite of their own 'civilization'. Their press's outraged rhetoric was highly gendered and sexualized. Bel-gium's invasion and the atrocities perpetrated there were portrayed as literal violations of the country and its people. Sadistic Prussian officers

and brutish soldiers were accused of raping Belgian and French innocents. Fantasies, ironically adapted from Belgian colonial misdeeds in
the Congo earlier in the century, of the invaders mutilating and cutting
off (usually female) children's hands also came to define German barbarity for peoples in the Entente countries.[81]

The German soldiers were not monsters. Nor, despite the absurd
stereotypes of Entente propaganda, and the occasional historian who
has uncritically echoed them, was German culture at fault.[82] Even anti-
Catholicism and racism, which were embraced by some parts of the
Reich's population, lack conviction as primary explanations for the violence, as Catholic Germans served in large numbers in the invasion
force and ethnicity divided rather than united civilian victims: French,
Belgians and Alsace-Lorrainers in the west and Poles and Jews living in
the city of Kalisz in the east were all subjected to German military violence in August 1914.[83] War atrocities, as research on the later twentieth
century has demonstrated, are not the preserve of psychopaths or ideo-
logues. Put them with comrades in a military environment under
discipline and 'ordinary men' too will kill.[84] Moreover, German soldiers
had good, if misguided, reasons to fear civilian attack in 1914. The last
major war in which Germans had fought, the 1870–71 conflict, had
been characterized by quick victories over the French army followed by
a protracted campaign against an estimated 57,000 guerrillas. *Francs
tireurs* – the contemporary name for these irregular combatants – had
killed some 1,000 German soldiers and forced the General Staff to allocate another 120,000, around a quarter of the army, to guard the lines
of communication.[85]

As important in alerting troops to the probability of a 'people's war'
were their own mobilization experiences. These men had, after all, just
left a country whose population was busily engaged in setting up home
guards and blocking roads in order to catch the mythical 'gold cars'.
Troops rolling west across Germany were also struck by the sight of
civilian volunteers armed with hunting rifles or shotguns standing
beside the railway embankments and guarding every bridge. Ernst Baier,
who had travelled with his regiment from Stettin, was not the only
soldier who thought 'they looked like guerrilla fighters'.[86] These sights
prepared the way for the uncritical acceptance of stories of civilian
aggression at Liège, which were passed by word of mouth and disseminated by newspapers among the waiting soldiers of the main invasion

force in early August. They had become better in the telling. The Belgian population was accused not just of illegally taking up arms but of violating all rules of civilized warfare. Not only men but women too were said to have participated in the fighting, launching fanatical attacks with revolvers, kitchen knives and even boiling water. Wounded Germans' hands and feet had been cut off and children were said to have poked their eyes out.[87] When the main invasion began on 18 August, troops were thus already scared, angry and deeply suspicious of the enemy's civilians. Baier, for example, was pondering female Belgians' 'atrocities' already on 13 August, while his regiment was still on German soil. In any attack, he had told his parents grimly, 'no quarter will be given'.[88]

A good description of how decent individuals could become killers under wartime conditions has been left by Wilhelm Schweiger, a thirty-year-old rifleman serving in *Reserve Jäger Bataillon Nr. 7*, formed in the town of Bückeburg, north-western Germany. Schweiger, from his writing, seems to have been a gentle man, keen to get on with the soldiers around him, shocked by war's destruction but determined to do his bit to save the Fatherland. He was clearly very much in love with his fiancée, Erna, for whom he wrote a diary detailing his short service. He was killed in France on 20 September 1914. Schweiger's unit crossed into Belgium on 15 August, and on the morning of 17 August arrived at Liège, a day after its last fort had capitulated. Schweiger's diary had at first expressed understanding rather than enmity towards the Belgian population. However, after they entered Liège, he and his comrades were told that their sister battalion, the active *Jäger Bataillon Nr. 7*, which had been part of the initial assault on the city, had been treacherously attacked by the population. The troops were ordered to search the houses, find food and billets, and, as Schweiger's diary explains, 'simply throw the residents onto the street. Anyone, whether man, woman or child, who in any way resisted should without more ado be shot.'[89]

Living alongside a population said to have wiped out half of a battalion was inevitably going to be tense, and the men's anxiety increased when, on their first night in Liège, an infantryman on watch was shot. Two nights later, Schweiger himself came under what he believed to be *franc-tireur* fire. His unit had posted sentries around the town, and he and ten other men were escorting their Second Lieutenant back to his quarters. They were walking down a quiet leafy street when suddenly from behind them three shots rang out. The German soldiers scrambled behind the trees and began to return fire. Schweiger was certain that he saw the muzzle flash of rifles from the second storey of houses fifty metres away, and he and his comrades shot frantically at the windows and then charged. They battered down one of the front doors and were ordered by an infantry colonel, who along with some General Staff officers had been attracted to the scene by the heavy firing, 'immediately to set the house alight and to shoot any living being who came out'. The command, wrote Schweiger, 'had to be carried out and was carried out':

> The rage among us riflemen, who had been so treacherously shot at, was boundless. To my great relief and joy, however, the people fleeing from the neighbouring houses, and women and children, got away without being shot. A Bückeburger rifleman cannot shoot women and children, thank God! Still, it was terrible, quite terrible. That is war in all its horror.

Schweiger did not say how many men he and his comrades executed that night. Significantly, he also did not mention finding any weapons; his diary dwells only on the fine furniture that the soldiers found in the house, which they first dowsed with petrol and then set alight. Whether Schweiger later had doubts about the source of the firing is impossible to know, but his conscience was clearly troubled. That night, although exhausted, he could not sleep. 'The excitement, the awful impressions weighed too heavily on us,' he explained. 'I only did my duty and obeyed orders, but it is dreadful. If only this horrible war were at an end.'[90]

The harshness of the orders that Schweiger received from his officers is perhaps the most striking aspect of his account. Commanders' decisions were highly influential in determining the level of violence. They were shaped by the German army's own culture, which ruthlessly prioritized 'military necessity' and was characterized by deep scepticism towards international law.[91] The officer corps had been traumatized by its experience in 1870–71, when French *francs tireurs* had perverted a miraculously rapid military victory into a gruelling and bloody purgatory. Its conservative leadership was deeply concerned that civilians should not intervene in 1914, for embroiled in a two-front war against materially superior enemies it could afford neither the time nor the troops for a prolonged pacification operation. The force's abhorrence of irregular fighters was motivated by an old-fashioned humanitarianism, as well as pragmatic self-interest. German officers agreed that one could do no more for humanity than to keep fighting as brief as necessary. To this end, participation should be limited to the professionals. Irregular combatants were seen as an abomination, for they fought covertly, and thus without honour, and increased bloodshed without offering a realistic chance of victory. In meetings convened to draw up international laws of war, German representatives, supported by the Russians and opposed vociferously by the Belgians and the western Entente, had fought largely successfully to restrict civilians' right of resistance. The 1907 Hague Convention all but banned guerrilla warfare. Civilians were permitted to rise up spontaneously only if not already under occupation and, a clause totally at odds with the reality of twentieth-century combat, 'if they carry arms openly'.[92]

The focus of German commanders in planning and fighting the 1914 campaign was on annihilating the enemy's army, not the population.[93] The first impetus for repression came from below, from combatants like Schweiger who honestly but erroneously believed themselves to be under attack by Belgian civilians.[94] Commanders, drawing on the experience of suppressing *francs tireurs* in 1870–71 and the precepts of 'military necessity', quickly legitimized and expanded their men's violent and often panicked response. Under international law, they were entirely within their rights to try and execute any civilian found bearing arms illegally.[95] The repression they instituted, however, went well beyond all legal limits. First, suspected *francs tireurs* were usually summarily shot, not tried. Second, higher commands, including corps and army commanders, ordered mass reprisals; a practice specifically forbidden by the Hague Convention.[96] General von Einem, for example, told his troops as early as 8 August that villages where ambushes had taken place should be burned and all inhabitants shot. Mass arrests were also carried out. Some 10,000 French and 13,000 Belgian civilians, including women and children, were deported to Germany. Fines too were levied on communities accused of resistance. These measures were intended to instil in the Belgian population what the Commander of 10th Division, Major General Kosch, called a 'healthy terror'.[97] They were supported by pre-emptive actions such as hostage-taking, arms searches and the posting of placards warning inhabitants of the dire penalties of resistance. Moltke himself, albeit very late, on 27 August, advocated 'energetic' deterrence.[98]

The draconian measures of German commanders against the illusory popular resistance were shocking and traumatic for the invasion zone's inhabitants. Nearly 1.5 million Belgians fled their homes.[99] However, it might well be asked why the repression was not much worse. Intense fear and belief in the *franc-tireur* attacks were ubiquitous among all ranks of the German army, yet the ensuing panic, reprisals and what the atrocities' foremost experts have called a 'deliberate strategy of deterrence by terror' prompted this force of 2 million soldiers to kill just 6,427 civilians; less than 0.1 per cent of the 7.8 million inhabitants of the territory overrun in August and early September 1914.[100] By historical standards too this was negligible; Napoleon's troops fighting guerrillas in Spain just a century earlier had routinely torched villages and sacked towns, massacring whole communities. Recent attempts by historians to present the atrocities as a prelude or pointer to Nazi genocide and annihilation warfare in eastern Europe three decades later lack credibility, for these slaughtered millions and were driven principally by a racial ideology absent in the imperial army's violence of 1914. Nor, as will be seen, were Germans' delusions of civilian resistance unusual or their conduct outside other contemporary armies' norms of violence; if anything, they were milder.[101] Most astonishing is how abruptly the atrocities ceased. After a first wave during the Liège siege and in the south before 12 August, the major surge of killing took place in the week after the main invasion of Belgium began on 18 August. Thereafter, the violence plummeted and by the end of the first week of September, excepting a few outliers, it was ended (see Fig. 1). The troops' discipline must generally have held, for the incidence of atrocities did not correlate with the force's growing supply problems nor, unlike in other armies, did its retreat in the middle of that month inflame new bloodshed.[102]

Commanders not only expanded the violence first perpetrated by their scared and angry soldiers but were even more crucial in restraining and quickly halting it. German officers, while placing the blame firmly on a 'fanaticized' enemy population, often expressed horror at the brutality of insurrectionary war.[103] The corps' aristocratic honour culture was a strong, if not fail-safe, brake on harsh reprisals: the massacre of civilians, especially women and children, and the destruction of towns sat poorly with the chivalrous self-image of professional officers. There were also sound military reasons to limit violence: any orgy of killing

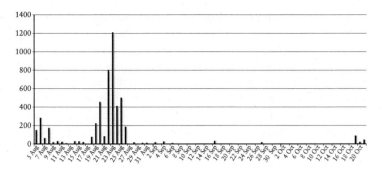

Figure 1. The pattern of German military 'atrocities': Belgian and French civilians killed by the German army, August–October 1914 (incidents with ten or more civilian deaths only).

Source: J. Horne and A. Kramer, *German Atrocities 1914: A History of Denial* (New Haven, CT, and London, 2001), Appendix I.

and arson, along with the pillage and rape that might accompany it, undermined troops' discipline. Finally, doubts about the extent of the popular insurrection soon emerged, along with concern that arbitrary brutality might provoke even greater resistance. Major General Kosch, whose division had killed over 200 Belgian civilians and hundreds of wounded French soldiers between 21 and 24 August, provides an illustration of how these considerations rapidly converged to prompt at least partial reassessment and restraint. His tone was notably defensive when he wrote to his wife on 26 August: 'We are not Huns and do not want to sully the honour of the German name.' He insisted that 'the bloody events in Belgium, where treacherous shooting came from every house, and even clergy and women took part, made necessary a merciless burning of villages and shooting of guilty inhabitants'. Nonetheless, with his soldiers now plundering and vandalizing the region, he was concerned about order. His unit's departure from Belgian territory and entry into France offered a face-saving excuse to halt the violence. 'The Frenchman,' he argued, 'is showing himself to be more peaceful and accommodating.' Repression there was 'stupidity, for we rob ourselves of the aid of the land, undermine discipline and provoke the population to a dreadful people's war'.[104]

The German army's *franc-tireur* delusion had already passed its climax before hopes for a rapid victory over France were definitively thwarted in early September at the Battle of the Marne. The seeds of this battle were laid a fortnight before it opened, when Joffre had finally recognized the true path of the German advance. On 25 August he outlined a new strategy that envisaged a concentration of force at Amiens for an encirclement of his enemy's right wing. Troops were rapidly moved north-west by rail to build a new Sixth Army, comprising nine infantry and two cavalry divisions, outside the German envelopment. An offensive by the German Sixth and Seventh Armies in the south failed even to pin down French strength, let alone break through the fortified front to achieve a double encirclement. Although Joffre's Amiens attack was not launched because the British commander, Sir John French, considered his troops too exhausted to participate, growing Entente strength in the north offered other possibilities. By 6 September, the German First, Second and Third Armies, which on 23 August had outnumbered their enemies by 25½ against 17½ divisions, faced 41 divisions. The French had made a remarkable recovery since their early shattering defeats. Fifty-four incompetent commanders had been fired and brutal discipline, including summary execution, had been used to enforce order among demoralized troops. Over 100,000 men had been taken from depots to restore units to strength. Far from being beaten, as German leaders thought, by the start of September their opponent was more capable than ever of offensive action.[105]

By contrast, the Germans' operational situation worsened as they advanced. The first problem was command: Moltke, based first at Coblenz and then Luxembourg, was hundreds of kilometres from the battle and had only intermittent radio contact with the three armies on the right. This hindered his ability to coordinate them. Second, even as Entente forces swelled in the north, the strength of the German right wing was rapidly dissipating. Two corps were detached to guard against a sortie by the Belgian army from Antwerp and another was held outside the French fortress at Maubeuge. Moltke transferred two others from the Second Army on 25 August to assist defenders hard-pressed by the Russians in East Prussia. Only eleven corps continued to advance south-west through France. Third, the further these troops marched, the more difficult it became to keep them supplied. The 80 kilometres from a railway reckoned to be the outer limit at which early twentieth-century armies could operate effectively had been greatly exceeded: First Army was nearly 140 kilometres and Second Army 170 kilometres from their railheads on 4 September. The horse-drawn wagons tasked with taking supplies from the stations to the troops could not keep up with the advance and the army had only 4,000 motor lorries, of which three-fifths had broken down by the Battle of the Marne.[106] While prodigious effort kept the troops supplied with ammunition, everything else ran short. Sergeant Major Baier, whose Grenadier Regiment 2 was at the head of First Army, complained on 30 August that his unit had no bread. The first soldiers to arrive at a village picked it bare, leaving those behind hungry. After covering 600 kilometres on foot with scant chance to bathe or change, the men, he wrote, 'look the pits'. They and the units around them had also started to take heavy casualties. Baier had fought a fierce but phoney war against enemy stragglers and imaginary *francs tireurs* since crossing into Belgium on 14 August, but on 28 August he had his real baptism of fire in battle against French troops. The Germans won, capturing two gun batteries with munitions wagons, but the encounter cost Baier's company a quarter of its strength.[107]

Nonetheless, despite the hardships, all still appeared to be going well. On 29 August, Moltke had shifted the right and centre's line of march from south-west to south, so that the whole force passed east of Paris. On 2 September he directed them as in his plan to push the French to the south-east. Yet at this moment, just as the German encirclement was starting to close, there was a failure of coordination. The First Army, which was on the edge of the right wing, now had to guard the flank against Paris, but it was a day's march ahead of the neighbouring Second Army. The commander of First Army, General Alexander von Kluck, believed that if he pressed on he could take the rear of the French Fifth Army and destroy it. Instead of withdrawing and facing west, he pushed his men south over the Marne. Joffre grasped his chance. On 5 September the Sixth Army smashed eastwards north of the river into the single reserve corps that Kluck had left to protect his flank. In the following days, the German general was forced hurriedly to move two corps from his front to help fend off this assault 100 kilometres to the north, but in so doing he created a 40-kilometre gap between his army and Second Army. Entente forces in the south-east and south had gone on the offensive on 6 September, and the British Expeditionary Force marched into this gap, menacing the right and rear of the German Second Army. Its commander, General Karl von Bülow, pulled back his exposed right wing, widening the hole. Neither general informed the other of his actions, and Moltke only discovered through intelligence intercepts that the British were between his two armies. A staff officer was dispatched to find out what was happening and on 9 September, the fortieth day of mobilization and the point at which by German planning France should have been beaten, he told both armies to retreat. Moltke confirmed the order two days later.[108]

The Germans never had much chance of completing their scheme once French forces moved north. Their troops were exhausted, their supply stretched to the limit, and the numbers arrayed against them too great. Baier, whose corps was one of those quickly sent north to help repel the French Sixth Army's attack, described the fighting with horror. 'I looked death in the eye a hundred times yesterday,' he told his parents on 8 September. 'We are lying opposite an enemy with superior artillery, whom it is impossible to approach as he simply shoots our infantry to pieces.'[109] The Marne battle was conceived and decided by manoeuvre, but the fighting itself pointed towards the static, artillery-dominated future. By mid-September, if figures collected by the Medical Officer of III/Infantry Regiment 52, a battalion in First Army, are typical, shellfire had caused three-quarters of the German infantry's casualties.[110] Baier's experience of being trapped during the battle 'in the most terrible artillery fire, against which we were powerless' would characterize warfare on the Western Front. From 9 September the German army retreated 60 kilometres in good order, reaching new positions behind the river Aisne five days later. The armies dug trenches, stabilizing the front. Men too found ways of fortifying themselves for further struggle: 'It is terrible how the nerves become dulled. One lies in battle as if in a dream, afterwards everything appears as if in a novel, not a reality. The groans of the wounded and the often horrible sight also hardly move one any longer. We live as if outside of reality.'[111]

THE HABSBURG WAR

The Habsburg army fought a vicious and unusually unsuccessful war in the summer of 1914. Its leadership, which for so long had demanded hostilities and pushed strongly for them again after the Sarajevo assassinations, proved curiously unsure and irresolute when war finally came. The Chief of the General Staff, Conrad von Hötzendorf, who organized the military deployment and, under his titular superior the Archduke Friedrich, led the army against the Russians in Galicia, and the commander of the Balkan forces, General Oskar Potiorek, displayed unrealism, incompetence, callousness and selfish ambition. For years after, Habsburg staff officers would insist that their Empire's early defeats were the fault of anybody but themselves: the Austrian and Hungarian parliaments, the peoples, diplomats, railway experts and their German allies. Yet ironically, it was these men, the Empire's most loyal defenders, who brought catastrophe upon it.[112]

Conrad bore the greatest responsibility of all, for not only had he pushed for war, produced an ill-conceived mobilization plan and bestowed on his army a tactical doctrine unfit for purpose, but he also bungled the force's deployment in July 1914. His worst mistake was to persist for too long in prioritizing the Balkan deployment, 'War Case B'. When deployment only against Serbia was ordered on 25 July, with the first day of mobilization designated for 28 July, it made sense as immediate general mobilization would have been a clear provocation towards Russia. Yet Conrad received numerous warnings of Russia's war preparations from 26 July onwards, and he later admitted having 'full clarity' about its intentions when news of its partial mobilization arrived shortly after midday on 30 July.[113] Nonetheless, rather than respond by implementing 'War Case B+R', he ordered against the advice of his rail staff, who had not planned for this scenario, that transports heading towards the Balkans should be prioritized, but that A-Echelon should immediately begin to concentrate in Galicia. On the following day, however, a chorus of disapproval rose from the Central Powers' political leaders. Emperor Franz Joseph's admonition that Habsburg strength should be deployed against Russia was supported by Minister President Tisza and Austria-Hungary's alarmed German allies. Accordingly, late on the evening of 31 July, Conrad tried to revert to the planned deployment for 'War Case B+R'.

The Habsburg Chief of Staff's strange decision to prioritize the attack on Serbia while a mortal threat gathered in the east was, like the German gamble against France, the product of a short-war illusion. However, whereas Moltke succumbed to but never wholly believed in the mirage of a six-week victory in the west, and planned obsessively to make it possible, Conrad's focus on Serbia was wholly emotional. The desire to fight the war he wanted against an enemy he hated was overwhelming. The fruits of victory too were alluring: the destruction of Serbia, immediate diplomatic realignment in the Balkans, the entry of Bulgaria and Romania into the war, and (so the theory went) renewed inner vitality for the Empire. More personally, Conrad hoped that coming back a war hero would at last let him marry his mistress Gina von Reininghaus, the wife of a Viennese industrialist whom he had obsessively pursued for seven years.[114] Of course, these were all dreams, yet dangerous ones when the lives of men and an empire were at stake. For the Emperor and Tisza, it was clear that Russian troops would flood the naked Galician front long before their army could disengage from Serbia. Even so, Conrad probably believed that he still had time to make his decision. The former head of the Railway Bureau had told him in November 1913, and Conrad had repeated to the Common Ministerial Council on 7 July, that the mobilization plan could be switched up to the fifth day of mobilization. In the summer of 1914, this was 1 August.[115]

Conrad's shock is thus easy to imagine when, on the evening of 31 July, his attempt to change the deployment to 'War Case B+R' was firmly rejected by the War Ministry's new Transport Chief, General Staff Colonel Johann Straub, who warned that any such attempt would cause 'chaos on the railway lines'.[116] The most that could be done, Conrad was told, was to return the transports destined for the Balkans to their bases, and restart the whole deployment. Even the Chief of Staff, who was notoriously obtuse about public opinion, could see how silly the army would look if soldiers who had just departed with great fanfare were to steam back to their stations. For the sake of home morale and the glory of the army, it was therefore decided instead to allow the troops to proceed on a 1,000-kilometre diversion through the Balkans and up to Galicia. Conrad should have pressed his Transport Chief. On 31 July only vanguard traffic had departed; most trains were still in sidings. With a little imagination, it should have been possible to send the troops directly to the east.[117] Yet Conrad did not contest his railway experts' judgement. His acceptance was probably made easier by their assurance, which itself was a testimony to how mad peacetime planning had been, that B-Echelon's joyride to the Balkans should not matter. If the pre-war plan had been followed, it would anyway be sitting in barracks while 'A-Echelon' concentrated in Galicia. General mobilization would not be delayed.[118]

In fact, this mistake mattered a great deal. Austria-Hungary did not have sufficient locomotives to carry B-Echelon to the Balkans and A-Echelon to Galicia simultaneously, so general mobilization, although announced on 31 July, could begin only on 4 August. Time, and with it any hope that the Habsburg army might achieve even parity on the Eastern Front, was thus squandered. Already on the eighteenth day of its mobilization, 17 August 1914, the Russian army had gathered thirty-five infantry and twelve and a half cavalry divisions on the Galician front, whereas the Austro-Hungarians had fewer than thirty divisions. A fortnight later, the Russians had fifty-three and a half infantry and eighteen cavalry divisions against thirty-seven Habsburg infantry and ten cavalry divisions.[119] Worse still, B-Echelon, once dispatched to the Balkans, was subsequently not all released to the Galician Front. Already on 31 July, Conrad had decided to detach the Prague VIII Corps and leave it in the Balkans. He also allowed Potiorek to use B-Echelon, now renamed Second Army, during its ten-day sojourn on Serbia's northern border for a 'demonstration'; a limited action aimed at distracting enemy forces from the offensive to their west, which was scheduled to begin on 12 August. However, Potiorek was determined to keep as much of the army as possible, and embroiled the Budapest IV Corps in fighting. In consequence, only two of Second Army's four corps left as intended on 18 August for Galicia, the IV Corps departed on 24 August and the VIII Corps remained in the Balkans. Conrad's indecision and Potiorek's selfishness brought about the worst result possible, for the forces kept in the Balkans were insufficient to swing the balance against the Serbs, but their removal from Conrad's order of battle, along with the lateness of Second Army's arrival, left the eastern wing of the Habsburg armies in Galicia fatally weak.[120]

Conrad, with assistance from his military rail experts in Vienna and Potiorek in Bosnia, had thus squandered any opportunity to keep pace with the Russian mobilization and, without gaining any advantage elsewhere, had weakened his already inadequate force in Galicia, the Empire's most important theatre of war. As if to guarantee catastrophe, he made one other calamitous change in that theatre. In March 1914 it had been discovered that a homosexual Habsburg General Staff officer, Colonel Alfred Redl, had been blackmailed into betraying the Empire's offensive mobilization scheme. Conrad had therefore altered the plan, choosing a defensive deployment along the San and Dneister Rivers, which cut diagonally through Galicia. The north-eastern third of the Crownland, including its capital Lwów, was to be left to the Russians. In mid-July, as war approached, he had told the railway staff that the troops should be concentrated for this defensive stance, and rail schedules had therefore been hurriedly altered. However, when Conrad decided on 31 July to transport units from the swing 'B-Echelon' to Galicia, he returned to an offensive conception. Yet it was then too late to move the unloading points back to the border, so troops who would otherwise have journeyed by rail to their concentration points disembarked in the middle of the Crownland and then marched hundreds of kilometres to the borders. This not only wasted more precious time. It also meant that the Habsburg army was exhausted even before it entered battle.[121]

The Habsburg army's two opening campaigns, although thousands of kilometres apart, led by different generals, and fought in dissimilar terrain against two distinct enemies, nonetheless shared two defining characteristics. First was extraordinarily poor higher leadership. Neither in Serbia nor in Galicia did Habsburg senior commanders prove capable of matching the limited resources at their disposal to their ambitious goals. Operational planning was also extremely poor. The aims of both offensives were ill-defined, logistical constraints were ignored and the expectations about what the troops could achieve proved wildly optimistic. The result was military disaster. Against Serbia, an opponent that the Habsburg force felt confident of beating, it experienced humiliating defeat. In Galicia, a bungled mobilization, poor planning and numerical inferiority led to an early catastrophic rout. Second, the Habsburg army proved exceptionally murderous in both campaigns. The history of east-central Europe and the Balkans as the continent's 'bloodlands' did not begin with Fascist and Communist regimes later in the twentieth century. Already in 1914, decades before the advent of genocidal totalitarian states, military action, racial ideology and ethnic conflict turned them into killing grounds, broke taboos and sowed the seeds of later exterminatory warfare.[122]

The Habsburg commander in the Balkans, General Oskar Potiorek, was one of the most respected, if not well-liked, soldiers in the Common Army. His life had been dedicated to the military. He had grown up in a cadet institute, came top of his class during general staff training at the Habsburg War School, and was only narrowly beaten by Conrad to the position of Chief of the General Staff in 1906.[123] As Governor of Bosnia-Herzegovina, he had also been to blame for the lax security arrangements on the day of Archduke Franz Ferdinand's assassination. Potiorek thus had much to prove in July 1914. His minimum goal, as laid down by Habsburg military headquarters, was to defend home territory against Serb incursions. However, this fitted neither his ambition nor the offensive drive of a Habsburg General Staff officer. Instead, encouraged by Conrad, Potiorek favoured an ambitious plan for the invasion of Serbia. 'I am fully aware that the operation appears risky,' he told Conrad in a letter of 12 August, 'but nothing else is possible given the general situation.'[124]

Potiorek's invasion scheme envisaged an assault by three armies on Serbia. The Habsburg Fifth Army would advance from Bosnia into the north-west of Serbia, while the Second, composed of three corps from the B-Echelon, would attack from Croatia in the north. As these forces drew in Serb strength, the Sixth Army would launch a decisive blow in the south-west from Herzegovina, taking the enemy in the flank.[125] On paper, this looked brilliant. Closer examination, however, reveals it less as 'risky' than reckless. Potiorek's forces lacked the strength for the scheme. The army he fielded in August 1914 totalled 282,000 infantrymen, 10,000 cavalry and 744 guns. He thus had a small but significant numerical advantage over the Serbs' 250,000 soldiers and 528 guns supported by militia. The problem was, however, that this superiority would exist only for the first week of operations. With the departure of Second Army on 18 August, Potiorek would lose 60,000 infantry, nearly half his cavalry and around a third of his guns. The urgent need for these troops in Galicia prevented the attack from the north, so Potiorek instead had to hope that a weak 'demonstration' here would suffice to distract the Serbs from the main threat in the west. There too, however, flawed thinking prevailed. The Fifth and Sixth Armies not only had to cross extremely difficult mountainous and marshy terrain but they were also deployed too far apart to enable mutual support. The lack of roads in the area of operations would hamper the resupply of food and munitions to the advancing units. What made Potiorek's scheme so irresponsible was that all these problems had been identified in war games, the latest of which he had organized in April 1914. The exercises had consistently ended in victory for the side playing the Serbs, yet astoundingly, no adjustment had been made to the campaign plan.[126]

The invasion began on 12 August with Fifth Army fording the Drina, the river that marked the border between Bosnia and Serbia. For the troops, their commanders' detachment from reality was obvious from the start: Alfred Fiedler, a howitzer battery officer serving with the 42 *Honvéd* Infantry Division (HITD) on the army's south wing, recorded how he and his comrades gaped with 'despairing feelings' at the 'steep, for the most part wooded mountains' rising behind the Serb bank.[127] The initial assault was given a slightly surreal air by the sight of columns of armed men in their underpants wading across the river – a measure necessitated by the army's lack of bridging equipment. Even once trousers had been pulled back on, belts buckled, and platoon officers had pointed the way, progress was predictably difficult due to the lack of roads, glowering heat and resistance by Serb irregulars, the *Komitadjis*. Supply lines collapsed within days, forcing men to live off what they could requisition or steal. The Sixth Army began its attack further south two days later. Its Bosnians and Dalmatians were, unlike the Croats, Czechs and Germans of Fifth Army, trained for mountain warfare, but they were nonetheless soon slowed by similar problems. Only Second Army in the north had a little success. Its 'demonstration' began with artillery fire on the afternoon of 11 August, which was followed the next day with an infantry advance a short way into Serb territory. The operation captured the towns of Šabac, Mitrovica and Jarak, but failed in its primary object of distracting Serb attention.[128]

The advance was accompanied immediately by violence against the Serbian population. Fiedler saw columns of smoke rising 'everywhere' on the Serb side of the Drina on 14 August, as attacking Habsburg troops burned haystacks and peasant huts. 'A senseless beginning,' he remarked.[129] Worse was to follow. During the thirteen-day invasion, Habsburg troops massacred between 3,500 and 4,000 Serb civilians. Given that the operation was so brief and the armies advanced not much more than 20 or 30 kilometres into Serb territory, this was an extraordinary level of civilian bloodshed. We know something of what happened from an investigation carried out in the months directly after the invasion by a professor at the Swiss University of Lausanne, Archibald Reiss.[130] His report was commissioned by the Serb government. It was propaganda intended to influence world opinion in favour of a Balkan state that to a great degree had brought its own fate upon itself. Nonetheless, Reiss was conscientious in gathering evidence. He interviewed Serb eyewitnesses and victims, and personally inspected and photographed sites of massacre and even excavated mass graves. He also talked with Habsburg prisoners of war in order to establish the motives for the violence. The atrocities he uncovered included a wide range of killings. Men had usually been shot, bayoneted or beaten to death. Women, who accounted for around a quarter of fatalities in the districts that Reiss investigated, most often had died by being shut in houses burned by Habsburg troops. The professor believed a 'very great' number of rapes to have been perpetrated. 'In many of the invaded villages,' he asserted, 'almost all the women from the very youngest to the very oldest have been violated.' He also advanced other evidence of sadism and brutality, including accounts of corpses with limbs broken, mutilated faces or genitals cut off. Many of these claims should be treated with scepticism. Similar tales of severed children's hands and women's breasts, which circulated on both the Western and Eastern Fronts, were false. Where corpses revealed severe injury, it was often caused by rifle fire or shellfire.[131] Nonetheless, a few of Reiss's more disturbing stories do ring true. The seventy-five-year-old man, for example, found shot with his penis stuffed into his mouth in the village of Tchokeshina, does not fit easily with the usual atrocity fantasies on all sides of females and youthful innocents as mutilation victims.[132]

The most awful massacres that Reiss recorded have also been confirmed from Austro-Hungarian documentation.[133] The town of Šabac, a trading centre on the south bank of the Danube with a population of 14,000, was the site of a catalogue of atrocities. The town was taken on 12 August after Habsburg troops had overcome light resistance from soldiers of the Serb army's Third Levy, who were older reservists with no uniforms. On the first day, the invaders used Šabac's women as a human shield to help them suppress resistance in the surrounding area. All afternoon, Habsburg troops marched the women in front of them around the town, ordering them to lie down and returning fire when Serb defenders were encountered. Many of the women were imprisoned for five days in a hotel, given only water, and interrogated on the whereabouts of their soldier husbands and the Serb army's positions. There were beatings and rapes. The men still in Šabac were imprisoned in a church. In the following days, Serb counter-attacks mounted and

Habsburg discipline started to fail. Houses and shops were plundered. On the night of 16–17 August, Habsburg units accidentally attacked each other, causing panic and colossal casualties.[134] The next morning, with tension at its height and Serbs outside the city, a general ordered that the male captives in the church should be inspected, any Bulgars removed, and the rest killed. The deaths numbered at least 60 but most contemporaries put them higher, at between 100 and 200 killed. Another 1,500 of the town's residents were interned.[135]

The bloodshed in the Balkans, although it shared some causes with the German atrocities, sprang from a different military culture and different battlefield conditions. The Habsburg officer corps' central trauma had taken place in 1848, when revolutions in Vienna and Prague and secessionist wars in northern Italy and Hungary had almost ripped apart the Empire. The experience stamped this highly conservative force with an abiding distrust of civil society and an aversion to any armed action by civilians. Habsburg officers despised Serbia not only as an upstart parvenu but as a pirate state that was democratizing and nationalizing violence against international law. Its king, Petar Karadjordjević, had come to power in 1903 through a regicide, and its officials armed civilians as assassins and spread a creed of revolt among their compatriots on Austro-Hungarian territory. Habsburg officers had also observed with disapproval Serbian deployment of civilian paramilitaries during the Balkan wars. In a report issued in July 1914, the chief of Habsburg military intelligence, Colonel Oskar von Hranilović-Czvetassin, had outlined the fighting methods of the *Komitadjis* and advocated harsh countermeasures. 'The most effective protection against [these] bands is,' he argued, 'to regard them as standing outside international law.' The bands should be entirely eliminated and, he advised, 'punitive expeditions' should be undertaken 'in the most energetic and harshest manner against places which in any way support the bands. Great care should be taken to ensure that knowledge of such ruthlessly executed actions is widely disseminated.'[136]

The year 1914 was not the first time the Habsburg army had faced guerrillas. Counter-insurgency operations had been conducted in Bosnia-Herzegovina in 1882 when the army had hunted rebels mercilessly but abstained from retributive measures against civilians.[137] Hranilović's exhortation to employ terror against the wider population was thus new. In part, the change may have been a product of the officer corps' growing aggression, as it tried to compensate for its army's material inadequacies through ruthless willpower and the 'most energetic' actionism.[138] However, and in this regard it differed from its German ally, it was also a reflection of a growing tendency to think of enemies as racial collectives. In 1914 the army felt itself to be in what historian Oscar Jászi termed a 'double war', waged not only against external states but also ethnic groups inside the Empire's boundaries.[139] In the Balkans, the army attacked not only the Serbian kingdom's military and population but also the Serb population on its own side of the border, who it believed was participating in hostilities. 'The entire population in the areas of deployment was unreliable because they were Serb' was the revealing opinion of Brigadier General Aurel le Beau, commander of the 61st Infantry Brigade, a Second Army formation.[140] As already recounted, arrests had begun in Serb communities in south Hungary even before war broke out. This repression expanded when the invasion began. To deter insurgent attacks, Habsburg Serb community leaders were held as human shields at railway stations, gendarmerie buildings and military headquarters. Some were even tied to stakes next to government offices or reservoirs.[141] Once no longer needed, they were not released. Instead, by the middle of September 1914, 2,584 'politically suspicious' Habsburg subjects from these areas had been interned in eastern Hungary.[142]

Habsburg officers considered such measures wholly legal. The Austro-Hungarian army's service regulations, laid down long before the war, ordered that civilian uprisings should be met 'with the greatest severity'. The measures for constraining 'an enemy or unreliable population' included summary justice and the taking of hostages.[143] Under *Kriegsnotwehrrecht*, best translated as 'The Right of Defence in a War Emergency', officers were permitted to order executions without trial when their units were threatened. The War Supervision Office and AOK (the Army High Command) encouraged the use of this procedure.[144] Formation commanders also regarded the situation as justifying its wide employment. The Commander of IX Corps, a formation operating around Šabac, warned his men that the Serb population was 'inspired by fanatical hatred' and admonished them to observe 'an attitude of extreme severity, extreme harshness and extreme distrust ... towards everybody'. Non-uniformed combatants were to be 'unconditionally executed' and hostages killed if shooting broke out in their localities. An assumption of guilt prevailed: 'every inhabitant encountered in the open, and especially in the woods, is to be considered the member of a band which has concealed its weapons', the general ordered. 'These people are to be executed if they appear even slightly suspicious.'[145]

These orders, and Habsburg troops' bloody conduct, have to be seen in the context of both the army's expectations and the actuality of combat in Serbia. Even before the campaign started, senior officers, as Hranilović's report makes clear, expected to face a vicious people's uprising. Before departing for the war theatre, reservists' training included lessons on how to distinguish clean from poisoned wells and warnings about *Komitadjis*. The description they were given was worryingly vague: men in peasant clothing and cartridge belts.[146] Once combat was joined, the Serbs lived up to some of these expectations. Most obviously, and in contravention of the Hague Convention, to which it was not a signatory, the Serb state deployed many soldiers with no uniforms. While most, although not all, of the first levy, the youngest troops aged twenty-one to thirty-one, had uniforms, many of the men in the second levy, aged thirty-one to thirty-eight, and all the even older third-levy troops went to war in peasant clothing.[147] Habsburg soldiers' confusion about who exactly was the enemy is thus entirely explicable. Civilians and military genuinely blurred in Serbia, to produce a more 'total' war than was waged in the west. This combat was extremely stressful. As one Habsburg combatant explained:

> Here, every peasant carried a rifle and the soldiers (presumably slyly) wore peasant clothes and there were stories that even women and children perpetrated hostile and cruel acts against our wounded lying on the battlefield. In every operation surprise blended with betrayal, one had always to expect fire, ambush and assault. There was never a quiet night. This mental tension was more difficult to endure than hunger and thirst.[148]

The harsh orders for repression, which in targeting whole communities and dispensing with trials also contravened international and sometimes Habsburg military law, were a primary cause of what one officer termed the theatre's 'exorbitant' cruelty and bitterness.[149] The admonitions and warnings from on high, which included unlikely bans on drinking or bathing in the Drina as the Serbs were supposed somehow to have poisoned the entire river, combined with the chaos of combat and shortage of supplies, also fostered a mass hysteria among the troops. From the soldiers' perspective, fuelled by their own operational plan's total failure, there appeared no limit to Serbs' cunning and barbarity. Serb civilians were firmly believed to be signalling to their own side with lights and smoke. One particularly imaginative fantasy had it that geese herders were betraying Habsburg strength, each goose herded to a river representing one Austro-Hungarian battalion.[150] Officers' brutal orders and troops' readiness to kill may also have prompted a Serb reaction and spiralling violence. Stories, some possibly truthful, others clearly exaggerated, abounded in Habsburg ranks of Serb soldiers castrating and disembowelling prisoners and corpses, cutting out their eyes and skinning them.[151]

The invasion lasted less than two weeks because, unlike the Habsburg forces, the Serbs had a sensible leadership. They also demonstrated considerable skill, endurance and ruthlessness that more than compensated for their poor equipment. Their commander, Vojvoda Radomir Putnik, had at first adopted a defensive stance, leaving only light forces along the frontier. His three armies were mobilized in the central north of Serbia. Once he recognized the direction of attack, he marched them to the border, concentrating particularly on the Habsburg Fifth Army, the key point in the invasion, against which he achieved a 3:2 superiority.[152] The decisive battle took place on the night of 16 August, when divisions of the Serb Second Army ambushed the 21 *Landwehr* Division (LITD) on the Cer Plateau. The Serb veterans fought dirty, placing Czech sentries off guard by claiming to be Croatian *Honvéd* and then opening fire at point-blank range. In the ensuing melee, the Habsburg unit lost nearly one-third of its infantry and half of its field artillery. A chaotic retreat ensued. Not just the 21 LITD but also the 9 Infantry Division (ITD), its sister unit in the VIII Corps, vacated their positions. The Fifth Army's other Corps, the XIII, also withdrew. An attempted intervention by Second Army's IV Corps served only to delay its departure for Galicia. The Sixth Army, whose advance in the south had stalled, was withdrawn. By the night of 24 August, no Habsburg units remained in Serbia. In thirteen days, Potiorek had lost 28,000 men, thirty machine guns and forty-six artillery pieces. Serb military losses came to 16,000.[153]

The defeat was a spectacular humiliation for the Austro-Hungarian army. Any possibility that Romania or Bulgaria might enter the war early on the side of the Central Powers was dashed. A second invasion in

November, which briefly captured Belgrade but ended in mid-December with another retreat simply underlined Habsburg shame.[154] For the soldiers, the defeat was deeply demoralizing. In Fiedler's unit, back behind the Drina, rumours of winter quarters circulated already at the end of August. Other officers prayed 'Please God let us have a better leadership at the top or more luck!' Starting a trend that would continue through the war and prove deeply divisive at home, the command unfairly shifted the blame for the disaster onto Czech troops.[155] The best that could be said of the operation was that it was brief. As it ended, an even worse disaster was just starting to unfold for the main Habsburg force in Galicia.

While failure in Serbia was humiliating, Habsburg defeat in Galicia was a catastrophe. The bulk of the Empire's army, 1,200,000 troops, including most of the cavalry and around 2,000 guns, was deployed in this theatre.[156] It was arrayed against Russian armies that were a third larger. Conrad's indecision and errors during mobilization, which had unnecessarily weakened his force, were compounded by an unrealistic and ill-conceived battle plan. His army was routed within a month. For Galicia's inhabitants too the campaign was a tragedy. Habsburg officers' fears and prejudices, and the strain and confusion of a traumatic retreat, combined with a bitter nationality struggle in the multi-ethnic area of operations to produce the bloodiest massacre of civilians perpetrated within Europe during 1914.

Galicia, the territory in which the army was to operate, was a centre of seething national ambition and conflict. The struggle for power between the Polish-dominated administration and Ruthenian nationalist intelligentsia was, despite recent concessions, still fresh and bitter in 1914. The stakes in the political competition had in fact become even higher once war broke out, and both peoples' representatives tried to curry favour with the Emperor and win political leverage by raising armed forces, the Polish Legions and Sič riflemen. Both peoples were mostly loyal to the Habsburg state, in good part because they needed its support in their conflict. Among the Poles, even Ignacy Daszyński and his Socialist comrades had approached the government in Vienna at the start of August and optimistically promised an uprising in Russian-held Congress Poland, claiming to have tens of thousands of revolutionaries prepared and waiting for the moment to attack the Tsarist oppressor.[157] Only the National Democrats, who had their base in eastern Galicia, were tactically pro-Russian, but even they were quiescent in the summer of 1914. The Ruthenes, as the weaker people, were even more reliant than the Poles on Vienna's support. The majority Ukrainophiles – the nationalists – fervently proclaimed their allegiance to the Empire's war effort in 1914. However, this people's public image had been tarnished by the pre-war spy scandals and accusations, unjust for all but a small part of the population, of Russophilia.[158] The Polish civil administration introduced repressive measures as war with Russia neared. At the beginning of August, the *Statthalter*, the chief of the Galician administration, had warned police and district administrators that as the Russophile movement could 'have a disastrous influence in a serious situation on the action of our armed forces', they must 'crush this movement energetically with all means available'. The language was violent: officials were ordered 'to act ruthlessly against the guilty'.[159] By the middle of the month, 147 'politically suspicious' people had been arrested and the administration intended to transport a further 800 Russophile political prisoners from the Crownland.[160]

The Habsburg army completed its concentration in Galicia between 19 and 23 August. Conrad planned to attack from the Crownland north-east with two armies. The First Army, covered by a small 'army group' on its left, was stationed to the west, at the confluence of the Vistula and San rivers, and Fourth Army gathered in the centre of Galicia, at the fortress city of Przemyśl. These armies, with three and four corps respectively, were smaller than expected but faced an enemy of similar strength. Covering their eastern flank were Third Army and, below it, the core of what would become Second Army when B-Echelon arrived from the Balkans, Army Group Kövess. Together, this eastern guard comprised four corps. Conrad's scheme was ill-conceived and failure virtually guaranteed. Two key problems doomed the plan. First, Conrad simply did not have the troops to cover a frontier extending 280 kilometres. In the absence of the B-Echelon units, his eastern guard was confronted by Russian forces nearly double its strength. Second, it was entirely unclear what the thrust of First and Fourth Armies north-east was supposed to achieve. In pre-war years, there had been vague talk of a joint concentric offensive, in which German troops attacking south-east from East Prussia and Habsburg forces advancing from Galicia would cut off Russian Poland. However, German weakness in the east had always made this implausible and it had been firmly ruled out by Moltke on 3 August 1914. Conrad's decision to go ahead nonetheless meant that the Habsburg offensive was a strike into thin air.[161]

The plan's chances were further diminished even before the main operation began. Conrad spent his cavalry at the outset by sending all ten divisions on a reconnaissance mission 100 kilometres into Russian territory. Some units made round trips of 400 kilometres, as due to the premature unloading of troops in the centre of Galicia they had first to ride great distances in order just to reach the frontier. The mission failed totally. The cavalrymen were unable to penetrate behind Russian screening troops. Even worse, a new, ill-fitting saddle designed to give troopers a stiff posture on parade turned out to rub the skin off the horses' backs, and by the third week of August half of the animals were out of action.[162] When the main offensive opened on 22 August, Habsburg forces thus stumbled blindly forwards. The First and Fourth Armies committed themselves well, and at the end of the month the latter almost succeeded in encircling the Russian Fifth Army at Komarów and took 20,000 prisoners and nearly 100 guns. Yet the advance north-east extended Conrad's eastern flank, making the task of his weak Third Army, which temporarily gave up three divisions to assist Fourth Army, even more impossible. Once the vastly superior Russian forces opposite began to move westwards, Third Army lacked the strength to stop them. By 30 August it had been routed.[163]

These early clashes exposed the over-ambition of Conrad's plan but also the flaws in the tactical doctrine in which he had trained his army. The greatest deficiency was in combined arms tactics: the commander of 32nd Lwów Field Artillery Regiment was not unusual in conceding that 'the cooperation of the artillery with the infantry was weak on our side'. Officers at all levels failed to coordinate, different arms did not communicate, and the gunners selected their own targets.[164] The infantry, although its intensive training in route marching paid off, was also often outclassed by the Russians, who had learned much from their defeat nine years earlier in the Russo-Japanese War. By the end of September, the AOK was urging its soldiers to imitate the enemy's trench-building and stressing the need to reconnoitre before attacking and to deploy into 'very loose skirmisher lines' in the advance in order to limit losses from shellfire.[165] The diary of Josef Gamst, a platoon commander in Moravian *Landwehr* Regiment 9, a unit in Fourth Army, gives a good sense of how chaotic and frightening was this early combat. Gamst's regiment came into action in a potato field around 50 kilometres south of Komarów on 29 August. The Russians had positioned themselves 800 paces away on the edge of a wood and were difficult to see, let alone kill. Shells flew over the soldiers' heads and, once an enemy battery on the right opened up, in their midst too. Small arms fire crescendoed: 'particularly unpleasant is the machine-gun fire'. Bullets whistled in from behind, as Austro-Hungarian reserves in the rear, unaware of the *Landwehr* men hidden among the potato plants, began shooting. The unit took casualties: 'The cries of those hit and the groaning and whimpering of the wounded are nerve-shattering.' Gamst was one of the unlucky ones. A bullet grazed him, ripping his cap from his head. Blood ran down his face and he lost consciousness. Several hours later, he awoke to find his unit gone, a dead man slumped over him, and a Russian patrol pointing their rifles at him.[166]

Fantasies of civilian resistance were no less pronounced in this eastern theatre than on any other front. There was a grain of truth in the Habsburg army's conviction that it faced treachery and hostility. The Russians had built up a small spy network in the province.[167] Even their defenders admitted that in the Russophile north-east of Galicia, some Ruthenian peasants may have shot at Habsburg troops.[168] Nonetheless, the fears were overblown for the Russians had no history of organizing units like the Serb *Komitadjis*, and the mass of the minority peoples on either side of the border had no wish to risk themselves for the oppressive Tsarist regime. Ruthenes, who were the subjects of most suspicion, were found by investigations after the Russian occupation to have been overwhelmingly loyal to the Habsburg dynasty and state.[169] Austro-Hungarian rules of engagement when facing a population believed to be hostile were, however, extraordinarily harsh. On 19 August, Army Group Kövess operating in the south-east of Galicia issued a typical warning to its soldiers:

> In our troops' operations up to now, it has been repeatedly the case that they have been shot at by the population or also by Russian soldiers in male or female civilian clothing . . . It has also been ascertained that the Russophile population of various places in our own land is working in cooperation with the enemy and by informing the enemy (frequently through signals) is betraying its own troops.

Such illegal conduct, stressed Kövess, demanded that officers and men respond 'most energetically'. Any individual found carrying a weapon, or even keeping one at home, was to be immediately shot if on enemy territory or court-martialled and condemned if on Habsburg land. Villages and farms from where shots were fired were to be surrounded, set ablaze, and the guilty executed. When troops were to be quartered in a village inhabited by suspected 'Russophile elements', their advance guard should take the most influential inhabitants hostage and announce that 'the slightest hostile act' would result in them being 'publicly and immediately executed'. Villages were also to be held responsible for the telegraph lines in their vicinity. The hostages would also be executed if these were cut. It was not enough for Kövess that this order should be read to the troops. Rather, the men were 'to be told most forcefully to shed the habits of peace as soon as possible and to realize that we are dealing with a cruel and treacherous enemy, against whom careful and ruthless action is urgently necessary'.[170]

Civilians of all ethnicities living in both the Austrian and Russian borderlands fell victim to Habsburg violence. In predominantly Polish western Galicia, at least a peremptory legality was usually observed. Offenders, if they were lucky, might get a trial at one of the permanent, professionally staffed *Landwehr* divisional courts. The sentences handed down were extremely harsh because the Crownland was part of the 'Area of the Army in the Field' and therefore subject to martial law. How hard these courts could be is illustrated by the case of Michał Św., a decorator from the mountain village of Lachowice who in September 1914 was condemned to death for making insulting remarks about the Emperor. He was executed within two hours and posters announcing his fate were put up in nearby Cracow as a public warning.[171] Front units, however, conducted short trials at best and could skip troublesome lengthy investigations to prove guilt. They also took hostages in the border areas of western Galicia. Jan Słomka, the long-serving Polish mayor of Dzików, a village in First Army's concentration area, was arrested after a soldier's cigarette started a fire in nearby stables, killing two army horses. Officers immediately assumed deliberate sabotage, rather than accept that one of their men was to blame, and they held seventy-two-year-old Słomka and four others hostage for eight days, promising in the event of a repetition to shoot them and burn the village. Other Polish mayors were arbitrarily interned or condemned to be hanged.[172]

In Russian territory, legal niceties were, as Kövess's order indicated, considered less necessary. The Habsburg army's innate suspicion of civilians, its harsh procedures for responding to non-military resistance, and the shock of battle, rather than racism, were sufficient to drive much of the violence. The 12 ITD demonstrates this well. This division was stationed in Cracow in peacetime and Poles formed the largest single contingent in its regiments, yet at the opening of the war it murdered and burned its way through Congress Poland.[173] The First Army, the force to which the division belonged, was gripped by a belief that signals and even secret telephones were being used to inform on Habsburg troop movements – highly improbable in economically backward Poland. Orders were issued that civilians who cooperated with the enemy or even just tolerated enemy observation points or telephone lines in their homes were to be 'ruthlessly killed on the spot'.[174] The 12 ITD, despite its Polish composition, had no scruples in so acting. When people in Kłodnica, a small village about 60 kilometres west of Lublin, were suspected of guiding enemy artillery by fire signals, Major General Paul Kestřanek, the 12 ITD's commander, ordered that the mayor and another community official be arrested and, if they could not identify the fire-raiser, shot.[175] A report that the population of nearby Chodel had ambushed troops provoked a similarly brutal response: 'Pull out the mayor, priest, assistant priest [all of who would have been Catholics] and a few others, principally Jews, and shoot them immediately. Then burn the place and try to knock down the church steeple.' While the mayor and priest had sensibly already fled before the 12 ITD's troops attempted to carry out this order, they did catch and hang the parish assistant and selected five Jews for execution. Only three houses in the village were spared, on the grounds that they were sheltering Habsburg wounded.[176] Other formations even turned their men's shared ethnicity with enemy civilians to their advantage. One unit equipped a soldier, presumably a Pole, with peasant clothes and roubles and sent him out among the population as an agent provocateur.[177]

Racism nonetheless did play a role in exacerbating some of the violence. First, the most brutal part of the Habsburg army was, significantly, also its most nationalistic: the Hungarian Honvéd. Within days of its arrival in Galicia, the force acquired an ugly reputation. Peasants complained that 'the Russians are bad, the Germans are bad, but Honvéd soldiers are the worst beasts'.[178] The Magyars came from a society that had long regarded Slavs with contempt and pursued obtrusive assimilationist policies. Anti-Semitism was on the rise and the political disputes in the decade before hostilities had sharpened Hungarian nationalism.[179] Honvéd troops were thus likely to look down on Poles, Ruthenes and Jews. Exacerbating the violence was the force's poor discipline. Regular Habsburg officers in Galicia condemned the Magyars as 'cowardly and without discipline' and cursed the Honvéd, especially its cavalry, as 'the greatest evil of all'.[180] There was also a third factor making Magyar troops especially likely to attack civilians. Modern neuroscientific research stresses the importance of 'otherization' in the perpetration of atrocities. Stereotyping, ingroup and outgroup dynamics, a sense of threat and disorientation in a new environment all contribute to producing crucial distance between the perpetrator and his victim.[181] Magyar troops were particularly likely to be reliant on prejudices and stereotypes and to misinterpret their environment because they were so ill-equipped to communicate with the population. Slavic troops had at least a chance of understanding something of what local Poles or Ruthenes were saying. German could also act as a lingua franca; it was the Common Army's language of command and was sufficiently widely known in towns linked by rail to the outside world to ensure that someone able to translate could usually be found. Beyond the railways, Yiddish-speaking Jews might act as intermediaries. By contrast, nobody spoke Magyar in Galicia. Once Hungarians decided or were told that inhabitants were hostile, their linguistic isolation limited their ability better to understand their environment and revise the opinion.[182]

The other way in which race was important was in the particularly vicious targeting of one group, Galicia's Ruthenian population. The conviction that the whole people, not merely individuals within it, were traitorous was fixed at all levels within the Habsburg army. Conrad was open about the killing that resulted: 'we fight on our own territory as in hostile land,' he told the politician and jurist Josef Redlich. 'Everywhere Ruthenes are being executed under martial law.'[183] The small intelligentsia, including many Uniate priests, suffered especially badly. As one outraged parliamentarian complained: 'The most loyal people, respected, worthy persons, were put in chains and mishandled on the streets and in railway stations, beaten with rifle butts, truncheons and sticks until they bled, held for days without food in rain, cold and filth, cursed and spat at, threatened with revolvers and with the noose, treated like the most despicable spy.'[184] Peasants and priests were strung up at the side of the road on the orders of Habsburg officers keen, as ever, to produce a visible deterrent against disloyalty. The full extent of death and suffering will never be wholly clear. By November 1914 over 7,000 Ruthenes had been confined in grim conditions in Thalerhof and Theresienstadt internment camps within the interior of the Habsburg Empire. Many others, members of villages condemned as unreliable by army officers, had been forcibly evacuated.[185] A large number of Ruthenes were simply executed on the spot. The most plausible estimates give a total of 25,000–30,000 Galician Ruthenes slaughtered.[186]

Galicia's Ruthenes became the focus of military violence for three reasons, two of which had a racial or racist component. First, spy trials and conversion scandals had already tarred the entire people with the suspicion of treason and Russophilia, even though the numbers involved were tiny and the support at elections for pro-Austrian Ukrainian nationalist parties overwhelming.[187] This ethnic group was thus prejudged: on their arrival, one officer recalled, troops were warned to be 'extremely careful and uncommunicative, as the population of Galicia was not friendly and spies swarmed everywhere'.[188] Second, the pre-war nationality struggle between Polish Crownland authorities and Ukrainian nationalist intellectuals played a part in raising the body count. Polish civilian officials were responsible for drawing up lists of unreliable people to be interned, and subsequent investigation by the army and Foreign Ministry found that many used the opportunity to rid themselves of rivals. Baron Leopold von Andrian-Werburg, the Habsburg Foreign Office's expert on the Polish-Ukrainian territories, stressed the part played by 'personal motives, and above all the rancour of influential local Polish agents' in the deportation of loyal Uniate priests.[189] Ruthenian representatives too blamed the 'extremely partisan Galician civil authorities' for duping officers into believing that all Ruthenes were traitors. All too often, they claimed, dangerous Russophiles had been ignored while Ukrainian nationalists loyal to the Empire but opposed to Polish control of Galicia had been denounced or deported.[190]

The third factor making Ruthenian civilians' experiences of invasion particularly bloody was the Habsburg army's retreat, which began among them in eastern Galicia. On 26 August, Third Army guarding Conrad's right flank had clumsily attacked Tsarist forces double its size and was driven back. Although new defensive positions were prepared on the next river, the Gniła Lipa, Russian forces routed the army on 30 August and on 3 September captured Galicia's unfortified capital, Lwów. The Second Army arrived from the Balkans just in time to participate in but not avert the disaster. Conrad's response to the threat in the east, an attempted encirclement of the Russian attackers, demonstrated his total detachment from reality. His soldiers were exhausted after weeks of marching, and having frittered away his cavalry at the start of the campaign he had only a hazy notion of Russian movements.[191] At the front, there was chaos. Captain Karl Lauer, a General Staff officer with the 17 ITD, Second Army, described how already since 26 August an 'indescribable and incomprehensible' fear of the Russians had gripped the troops. He heard of officers jumping out of first-floor windows to escape imaginary Tsarist attackers and on the Gniła Lipa saw Habsburg cavalry assaulting their own panicking transport units in an attempt to stop them fleeing rearwards.[192] 'There is a great lack of discipline', worried another Second Army officer, Major Artur Hausner, at the start of September. 'Officers and men return to Stryj [a city south of Lwów], supposedly separated from their units, all very run down and wretched and telling terrible stories about the fighting. The town is crawling with marauders ... Every wagon brings fleeing inhabitants mixed with soldiers without weapons, without equipment.'[193] In the disorder, looting increased. Outrages against Ruthenes were exacerbated by indiscipline and defeat, as officers and soldiers concluded that inhabitants' treachery had brought about the catastrophe. The violence against civilians peaked during the retreat that autumn, but lasted up until the early summer of 1915.[194]

On 11 September, Conrad ordered a general retreat, first to the Dniester River, which divided the north and south of eastern Galicia, and then to the San River, which separated the west from the east of the Crownland. In the event, the Russians pushed his forces back much further, to the gates of Cracow in the west and the Carpathians in the south. His opening campaign had nearly destroyed the Habsburg army. The losses of professional officers were so heavy that in October those retired or unfit had to be re-examined and certified for service at the front.[195] Some 100,000 soldiers and officers had been killed, 220,000 wounded, 100,000 lost as prisoners and 216 artillery pieces abandoned; all told, about one-third of the force.[196] A cholera epidemic that accompanied the Russians added to the horror and loss of the retreat; from the second half of September, the sight of cramped-up soldiers dying in ditches along the roadside was common.[197] No less serious was the shattered morale left by the calamity. As the front crumbled in September, healthy troops deserted on hospital and postal trains.[198] There was a rash of self-inflicted wounds, especially among Romanian troops.[199] A 'remarkable number of units' had simply fled, conceded the Austro-Hungarian army's official history of the war, a volume written specifically to glorify its exploits.[200] Total dissolution was staved off by draconian discipline. Officers were reminded of their duty to shoot shirking or deserting soldiers immediately.[201] The mood, however, was miserable. With what Captain Lauer called a 'bleeding heart', the Emperor's troops started a long march westwards.[202]

The Central Powers' offensive plans failed in 1914. There would be no short war. For each General Staff Chief the campaign was a personal tragedy. Moltke had a nervous breakdown and lost his job. Conrad lost his officer son Herbert, killed in September on the Eastern Front. For the states that they served, the failure had far-reaching consequences. General Erich von Falkenhayn, Moltke's successor as Chief of Staff de facto from 14 September (but, in order to hide the defeat on the Marne and avoid unsettling the public, only officially from 1 November), attempted to redeem the situation. A series of battles, shifting ever northwards, began on the Western Front, as both sides tried in vain to outflank the other before the sea was reached. This ended with a German offensive at Ypres in October and November 1914, in which many of the volunteers who had come forward in August were committed. The German army suffered a further 80,000 casualties for no real gain before exhaustion and shell shortage forced an end to the battle. With trench lines hardening along the entire front, it was now impossible to ignore the fact that the Central Powers were committed to a very long war against enemies whose will and morale had been underestimated and who were materially far superior. Falkenhayn doubted that the war could be won against all three Entente powers and wanted a separate peace with France or Russia by promising no annexations. As he astutely told the Chancellor, 'if Russia, France, and England hold together, we cannot defeat them in such a way as to achieve acceptable peace terms. We are more likely to be slowly exhausted.'[203]

The campaigns of 1914 not only led into a long war of exhaustion but also set the conditions under which this gruelling struggle was to be fought. Austria-Hungary's defeats weakened its international prestige, denied it for the following year potential Balkan allies, and were ruinous for its army. The Empire's slide under German domination, which became ever clearer during hostilities, had begun. Domestically too, the campaign heralded the rising ethnic conflict and disillusionment with the state that would gradually come to dominate the wartime home front. The army alienated the Ruthenes through its brutal treatment. Conrad also aggrieved Polish elites by insisting on the replacement, in July 1915, of the traditionally Polish *Statthalter* of Galicia with a 'neutral' general. In Galicia, relations between the two ethnicities and the Jews were further soured.[204] Nonetheless, although the campaign had suffered a major and mostly unnecessary blow caused by Conrad's odd mix of indecision and unrealistic ambition, it revealed, like the popular response to the outbreak of war, the venerable Empire's reserves of strength. Despite disastrous leadership and horrendous casualties, the army did not collapse. Instead, it went on to fight a determined retreat and then endure awful winter battles in western Galicia and the Carpathians, sustaining total losses of 189,000 dead, 490,000 wounded and 278,000 prisoners of war by the end of 1914.[205]

For the Germans, the balance of the opening campaign in the west was more favourable. Moltke had not won his short war, but his army had succeeded in ensuring that for the next four years it would be French and Belgian territory, not German, which would be devastated by the fighting. In the south, the army notched up a usually forgotten achievement in fighting off a French invasion. Quite what would have happened if the Republic's army had invaded with greater success is unclear. Certainly, once regained, Alsace-Lorraine would not have been relinquished. Some in the French military set their war aims higher by the autumn of 1914, demanding that the Reich be pushed back to its 'natural frontiers' east of the Rhine and the left bank placed under French military control.[206] Even more importantly, in the north the Germans' own invasion had dealt a catastrophic blow to France's ability to wage a total war. The country's heavy industrial heartland, as well as some very fertile agricultural land, had fallen under German control. At a stroke, France's capacity to produce cast steel fell to 42 per cent and cast iron to 36 per cent of what they had been in peacetime. A sixth of the entire manufacturing industry was forfeit.[207] The agricultural losses were also not negligible. Some 8,239,000 acres had been captured by the Germans, three-quarters of which had been under cultivation and contained some of the most fertile soil in France, supplying in 1913 more than a tenth of the Republic's potatoes, a fifth of its wheat, a quarter of all oats and half the national sugar-beet crop.[208]

Whether German conquest and Habsburg resilience would be enough to triumph in the coming war of exhaustion was, however, far from clear. The German opening campaign, as well as the 'race to the sea' and the fighting at Ypres, had cost 500,000 officers and men dead or permanently wounded.[209] The invasion and atrocities in Belgium had severely damaged the Reich's reputation among neutrals. It had also fatefully ensured Britain's early entry into hostilities. In the longer term, this would pose the most serious threat to both Central Powers. In 1914, however, there was an even more pressing menace. The German failure to grasp decisive victory in the west and the disaster suffered by the Habsburg army in Galicia left both powers very vulnerable. In 1914 and well into 1915, Austria-Hungary and Germany faced a Russian invasion in the east.

4

The War of Defence

INVASION

'The German people may honestly say once more in this hour that it did not want this war . . . But it will not allow the soil of the Fatherland to be overrun and devastated by Russian regiments.'[1] With these defiant words, the Reich's foremost liberal newspaper, the *Berliner Tageblatt*, had explained on the outbreak of hostilities why so many ordinary Germans believed that they had no option but to fight. In the last years of peace, the conviction of an inevitable clash with the despotic empire to the east had grown within both Austria-Hungary and Germany. Russia's frantic rearmament, her belligerence in the Balkans, the forceful assertion of semi-official claims to eastern Galicia in her pan-Slavic press, Orthodox proselytizing in the Crownland, and a surge of enemy spies all raised fears of her hostile intent. In August 1914 the nightmare of invasion became reality. Tsarist troops charged over the Central Powers' frontiers, bringing mayhem and panic to the invaded provinces, the Reich's East Prussia and Habsburg Galicia. The first year of Germany's and Austria-Hungary's war on the Eastern Front would be dominated by invasion, atrocities and a desperate struggle to liberate lost territories and repel a mortal threat.[2]

The Tsar's army deployed at the start of the First World War according to 'Plan 19', a scheme conceived in 1910 as defensive but which by war's outbreak had developed into an ambitious plan of attack. Russia's forces in Europe were divided into two 'Fronts'. The North-West Front, composed of the First and Second Armies with 16 infantry divisions, 8½ cavalry divisions and 1,230 guns, was tasked with breaking into East Prussia. Its offensive was to begin early, by the fifteenth day after mobilization, in order to draw German units away from the western campaign quickly, and thus alleviate pressure on Russia's ally France. The South-West Front, comprising the Third, Fourth, Fifth, and Eighth Armies, which by the end of August fielded 45 infantry and 18½ cavalry divisions, was charged with the annihilation of Habsburg forces in the Austrian Crownland of Galicia. The capture of East Prussia and Galicia, both of which jutted into Tsarist territory, sandwiching Russian Poland between them, would secure the Russian army's right and left flanks, preparing the way for an invasion into the heart of Germany. Once war began, the Russian High Command, Stavka, discovered that its enemies had sent more units to other theatres than predicted, unexpectedly leaving their eastern borders weakly defended. A further change was therefore made to the deployment. Confident of their superiority in both north and south, and acting on anguished French demands for urgent aid, the Russians formed a new force, the Ninth Army, in their centre. With this, they would be immediately ready, once the North-West and South-West Fronts fulfilled their missions, to outflank the Germans' formidable Vistula River defences and attack Posen, opening, the Tsar himself said, 'as quickly as possible the road to Berlin'.[3]

Few historians today recognize the danger posed by the Russians to the Central Powers in 1914. The Tsarist army's first assault on East Prussia in August and September, although poorly executed and quickly repelled, briefly overran two-thirds of the province and was intended as the preliminary step for an invasion deep into Germany. In Galicia, the Russians won spectacular early victories, capturing the Crownland's capital, Lwów, forcing the Habsburg army into general retreat, and encircling Austria-Hungary's defensive keystone, the fortress of Przemyśl. At the start of November, when Russian forces advanced to the outskirts of Cracow and a new army, the Tenth under General Sievers, launched a second invasion of East Prussia, German commanders briefly panicked. For a short time, before the Russians were halted in the north and pushed back in Galicia, it appeared that Posen, the gateway of the main invasion route into the Reich, faced imminent siege.[4] The stakes were high, for Russia's rulers and army quickly developed extensive territorial ambitions. Influential voices in St Petersburg were pressing for the permanent annexation of at least the northerly parts of East Prussia by the autumn of 1914. For Galicia, Russian plans extended far beyond mere conquest. The Tsarist army regarded this campaign as a war for racial unity, and it formulated radical plans to remake the east of the territory into what would be not only politically but also ethnically Russian land; this dream looked forward to the bloody racial design, the Generalplan Ost, which the Nazis would embark upon in the same region only a quarter of a century later. While Tsarist plans did not share the Nazis' genocidal intent, they placed racial considerations at the centre of the region's future, contravened international law, and caused tremendous suffering to hundreds of thousands of people in 1914–15.[5]

The ordeals of the Central Powers' peoples in the eastern invasions at the beginning of the First World War are today forgotten, obliterated by memories of the far greater horrors perpetrated in the same lands in the mid-twentieth century. Yet at the time, the invasions were recognized as a defining experience; no other event did more to shape central Europeans' understanding of what was at stake in this war, or the ability of their states to fight it. The shock of invasion reverberated far beyond the battlefield. News of the Russian attack and atrocities in East Prussia horrified and mobilized the population of the whole Reich. Both Central Powers, but most acutely Austria-Hungary, faced humanitarian crises as floods of refugees swept westwards. Yet the people who remained in the invaded areas suffered most. The Tsarist army's jarringly modern ambition not merely to conquer but to remould the population of Galicia impacted in ways ranging from obtrusive cultural assimilation to mass deportation. Its spy fear and security paranoia generated a brutality towards civilians which, in contrast to the very rapid dissipation of German violence in the west, radicalized throughout the campaign, producing ever more violent actions and suffering. Moreover, invasion was always traumatic, even under the best of circumstances where it was brief and the invaders behaved well. Long after occupying troops had departed, powerful emotions of fear, anger and humiliation lingered. A close look at one East Prussian city, Allenstein, during the Russians' August invasion illustrates how deep these scars could run.

ALLENSTEIN

The city of Allenstein, with 33,000 inhabitants, was what passed in agricultural East Prussia for a major conurbation. Founded by the Teutonic Knights in the mid-fourteenth century, it had a long history of sieges, sackings and occupation. The town's most famous resident, the astronomer Nicolaus Copernicus, had taken time away from his studies to organize its defence during the Polish-Teutonic War of 1519–21. Allenstein had been captured and half burned to the ground by marauding Swedes at the start of the eighteenth century and occupied by Russian troops during the Seven Years War of 1756–63. The French too had taken the town, mercilessly plundering it in 1807. Napoleon narrowly escaped assassination in its marketplace.[6] Yet for the remainder of the nineteenth century, Allenstein had experienced an unaccustomedly long period of peace and, in its final decades, rapid development. The town became a busy rail junction and its population expanded quickly, quadrupling from 4,800 in 1864 to 19,136 in 1890 and then nearly doubling again over the following twenty years. By the early twentieth century, there could be no doubt that Allenstein was on the rise. In 1905 it became a regional capital, it was designated a self-governing city in 1910, and the Prussian military chose it as the base of the newly established XX Army Corps in 1912. When war broke out two years later, the city was engaged in the building of a grand town hall, designed appropriately in the architectural style of the German Renaissance, to symbolize its new importance.[7]

Lying only 50 kilometres from East Prussia's south-eastern border, Allenstein was certain to be an early victim in any Russian invasion of Germany. Its citizens, aware of their vulnerability, had followed the international crisis in July with deep apprehension, and news of hostilities between Austria-Hungary and Serbia prompted a few of the most cautious to leave.[8] Once Germany declared war against Russia on 1 August, others also decided to seek safety. The rich, with the funds to travel and social connections beyond East Prussia, were the first to go. A rumour invented and spread by the wife of a Second Lieutenant in the garrison, that officers of the XX Army Corps had been ordered to send their families into the interior as the army was to withdraw behind the Vistula River, well to Allenstein's west, hastened their departure. The majority of the city's population, the working and middle classes, stayed put, however, until in the middle of the month traumatized refugees arrived from the border districts with stories of terrifying Russian atrocities. Farms and villages had been burned by rampaging Cossacks, towns laid waste by rapidly approaching Tsarist armies. There was talk of murder, rape and sadistic brutality: women, for example, were supposed to have been nailed to barn doors or forced to watch as their children were crucified.[9] The population's uncertainty and anxiety increased. Many more Allensteiners now packed their bags and headed west by rail, on horse-drawn buggies, with bicycles or even on foot. Concerned at the swelling exodus, the city's mayor issued a poster on 22 August dismissing the 'foolish rumours' and appealing for calm. 'As I have ascertained from the responsible authorities, our situation is entirely favourable,' he reassured citizens. 'There is no cause for alarm.'[10]

The shock was therefore all the greater when, during the night of Sunday, 23 August, civilian state officials suddenly left Allenstein. For the population, this act of betrayal both signalled that the Russians were close and lent further credence to the stories of their barbarity. Panic broke out as people scrambled to leave. 'Thousands of families are storming with their belongings to the railway station,' recorded a local teacher, Herr Rittel, in his diary. 'Very many stand day and night on the overcrowded platforms without managing to depart.'[11] His neighbours were so anxious to get away that they abandoned their frail ninety-four-year-old grandmother locked in their apartment. Early on the morning of Tuesday, 25 August, the military too announced its intention to leave the city. It warned residents not to shoot at the enemy and comfortingly claimed that its withdrawal would avoid any risk of a fire-fight and allow them to remain at home, where they were 'best off'.[12] Hardly anyone was prepared to believe it. When, a few hours later, at 10.45 a.m., the final evacuation train provided for the public departed Allenstein, it was a disturbing sight: 'an immensely long train composed of coaches, cattle trucks and goods wagons, crammed full with people who even stood on the sideboards, wagon roofs and in the brake houses'. The passengers thought themselves lucky, but false reports of a victory led to their train being stopped 90 kilometres down the line and ordered to turn back. The exhausted refugees were decanted in Allenstein on Wednesday morning, just in time to witness the first Russian troops enter the city.[13]

By this point, Allenstein had almost emptied. No more than 3,000 people, fewer than a tenth of the residents, remained.[14] Among them were some of the poorest, who, once the station had been evacuated on the Tuesday, grasped the opportunity to pillage first its refreshment rooms and goods shed, then nearby shops and apartments.[15] The remainder waited tensely in their homes; 'an eerie stillness' ruled in the city centre that evening.[16] Yet still the city's fate remained unclear. Optimists were encouraged on Wednesday morning by rumours of great Russian defeats and by the return of the refugees to the railway station. The city's trams resumed service, contributing to an air of normality.[17] Many residents nonetheless prepared for the worst. Paul Hirschberg, a well-off hotelier and city councillor, buried his account books and insurance policies in his wine cellar.[18] Rittel's wife, who, unwilling to expose her children to the hardships of flight, had decided to remain with her husband, bought two bottles of cheap sparkling wine, sausage and ham, and laid this food and drink out in her front room in the hope of pacifying rampaging Russian soldiers.[19] The senior municipal officials who had chosen not to evacuate also planned for the enemy's arrival. In the best Prussian tradition of public-spiritedness and paternalism, Mayor Zülch and his deputy, Herr Schwarz, the senior Catholic and Protestant clergymen, Father Weichsel and Superintendent Hassenstein, and the police chief had all resolved to stay with their beleaguered citizens. These men would play a critical role in ensuring that Allenstein and its inhabitants passed through the coming forty-eight hours of danger largely unscathed.

The first Russians to enter Allenstein were a cavalry patrol of three men and an officer who rode into the city at around five o'clock on the afternoon of Wednesday, 26 August. They were nervous. One of them called out in Polish that nobody should do anything to them; they would not harm anyone. After looking around the centre for any sign of German soldiers, the riders turned back but were then surrounded by a crowd of civilians, some of whom were drunk. Stones were thrown at the patrol and one of the troopers raised his rifle, but he was stopped from firing by his officer. The confrontation was diffused by the city police chief, who fortunately had seen the horsemen ride past his window and rushed after them with some of his men. They cleared the crowd quickly and the Russians departed, only to be followed on their way out of the city by a roving force of German *Uhlans*, who shot the officer off his horse and took him prisoner.[20] This first contact could have been disastrous for Allenstein. Had the Russians concluded that *francs tireurs* were present, or even just that the city possessed an alert defence, reprisals or bombardment could have followed. Yet both sides acted sensibly and with moderation. Unsure of how strongly garrisoned the city was, the Russians waited until morning before sending out further patrols. Meanwhile, the municipal authorities strove to avoid any further confrontation. Stray German soldiers, who had resolved individually or in small groups to undertake a hopeless defence of the city, were rounded up that evening by Allenstein's police chief and set marching westwards. Citizens were reminded to surrender any pieces of military uniform or firearms in their possession and were ordered under no circumstances to shoot at or otherwise harass enemy troops. Early on Thursday, when Russian horsemen returned, police in plain clothes were posted on the bridge to the south to tell them that no single German soldier remained in the city.[21]

At half past ten that morning, the Russian XIII Corps, part of General Samsonov's Second Army, began its entry into Allenstein.[22] This was no victory parade but rather a cautious advance into territory clearly perceived as potentially hostile. Horsemen spread out and moved towards the city centre, keeping each other in sight. The advance guard, a troop of thirty cavalrymen, arrived in the marketplace around noon, and its captain demanded to see the mayor. Negotiations ensued, during which the city's representatives were assured that international law would be obeyed. This promise was later publicly repeated by a staff officer, along with the admonition that civilians must not shoot. At three o'clock that afternoon, the main Russian force, perhaps 40,000 men in total, marched through Allenstein. The infantry came first, 'sturdy, stalwart figures wearing yellow-grey uniforms mostly completely soaked through with sweat and dirt', followed by cavalrymen riding on powerful horses, and then artillery and supply columns.[23] German onlookers were impressed with their discipline. Outside almost every shop, sentries were posted in order to prevent plundering, and alcohol was placed off-limits to the army. When soldiers wanted something, they were polite and paid in cash. The reception they received from the population was also not unfriendly. Eager to pacify their conquerors, residents made gifts of food, tea and cigarettes, and brought out stools for the sentries to sit on. Much to the police's disapproval, some women even flirted with the soldiers. Nonetheless, tension and suspicion persisted. Paul Hirschberg, who served lunch in his hotel to Russian General Staff officers, was repeatedly ordered to drink the refreshments he had prepared for them in order to prove that they were not poisoned.[24]

That afternoon, Mayor Zülch, his deputy and six other city worthies were called to the central hotel, where the Russian commanding general

Major General Kluyev and his staff had established their headquarters. After introductions, a Russian colonel explained in broken German that the troops urgently required supplies. The city was ordered to deliver, by eight o'clock on the following morning, 120,000 kilograms of bread, 6,000 kilograms of sugar, 5,000 kilograms of salt, 3,000 kilograms of tea, 15,000 kilograms of grits or rice and 160 kilograms of pepper.[25] Failure to meet this demand would result in punishment.[26] For the mayor and his companions, gathering this enormous quantity of food was a daunting prospect. The city itself had only flour and salt in its stores, so the other goods would have to be taken from shops and warehouses abandoned by their owners. Hirschberg was put in charge of the task, and the mayor appealed for volunteers to help him, warning them of the Russians' threat of reprisals: 'my dear fellow citizens,' he pleaded, 'help me in the most difficult hour of my life'.[27] It quickly proved to be a hazardous endeavour. Russian sentries had orders to stop plundering, and intervened when they saw goods being removed from shuttered shops by German civilians. One policeman had a bayonet pointed at his chest by soldiers who thought that he was looting. Other helpers were taken by the Russians to supplement their transport as wagon drivers; two municipal workers who assisted Hirschberg that evening were commandeered and never seen again. Yet with the fear of requisitions or reprisals hanging over their city, the volunteers had little choice but to continue the search until at half past two in the morning word unexpectedly came through that the Russians had decided enough had been collected.[28]

It was the demand for bread that caused the city the greatest difficulty. The weight laid down by the Russians was equivalent to around 60,000 loaves, an extraordinary amount to have to find in under twenty-four hours. Moreover, unlike the other goods, they insisted that the full quota be delivered. Some was taken from shops. People were sent door to door, pleading with residents to give up what they had. Private apartments were even broken into and searched. The shortfall nonetheless remained enormous. To satisfy the Russians, citizens therefore had to bake. Locked-up bakeries were forced open and volunteers found to staff them. Herr Rittel participated in this civic effort, running two bakeries near his home with the help of other locals, his wife and daughter among them, and four soldiers sent by the Russians. As most of Allenstein's bakers had fled, it took time to find someone who knew how to

switch on the steam ovens. Finally, around midnight both were in operation, but their first loaves proved to be, in Rittel's words, 'scarcely
edible' due to lack of yeast or sourdough. With the assistance of an
armed Russian escort, some was found in a station goods shed, and,
now with all the necessary ingredients, production could move into
full swing. Through the night, Allenstein's girls and women kneaded
dough, relieving each other at hourly intervals. Others baked in their
own ovens at home. The fresh bread was then piled high alongside the
other goods at the city's fire brigade depot, where the mayor awaited
the Russians.[29]

In the small hours of Friday morning, 28 August, well before the
agreed deadline, a Russian captain appeared with carts at the depot.
The main Russian force had already pulled out, leaving behind only a
couple of battalions, and the food was urgently needed. Yet in spite of
the night's tremendous exertions, Allenstein was still well short of its
targets. Little more than half of the sugar and salt demanded had been
gathered, less than a third of the grits and rice, and only a small amount
of tea and no pepper. Instead of the 120,000 kilos of bread that the officer had come to collect, the city had only 25,096 kilos.[30] There therefore
followed some anxious hours for Mayor Zülch. The captain disputed
the weight of the bread delivered by the city, and it was only after fierce
argument that he relented and issued a receipt. Shortly after, a general
arrived, complaining about the bread's quality and threatening retribution for the shortfall. Again, Zülch stood his ground, explained that the
city had done everything possible to cooperate, and succeeded in convincing the Russian that punitive action would be unjust.[31] After the
general finally departed, the weary mayor returned home to sleep, but
as he arrived back was recalled to settle payment for the supplies. This
entailed yet another argument about the amount and value of the goods,
which lasted for several hours. At midday, just as a compromise had
been found, the sound of gunfire was heard and the meeting was inter-
rupted by the Russian city commandant who stormed in, waved a
bandaged hand at the mayor and cried 'your people have shot at me'.[32]

In fact, the shot that wounded the officer had not been fired by a
civilian *franc tireur* but by German troops from the Eighth Army who
were quickly closing in on the city. Standing on the roof of their bakery,
Rittel and his helpers saw grey-clad soldiers in skirmishing order coming from the east. From the edge of the city, startled Russians came

running back. Others took up positions in gardens and on crossroads, but were soon forced to flee by advancing German infantry. The fighting, although brief, was punctuated by moments of brutality; General Paul von Hindenburg's troops, many of whom were from Prussia's eastern borderlands, wanted to exact retribution from the invaders of their homeland.[33] In the bakery, Rittel's daughter was confronted by two German riflemen who smashed through the locked doors and, weapons at the ready, demanded to know the whereabouts of the Russians who had helped with the baking. When the frightened girl was unable to tell them, they conducted a frantic search, discovered their enemies cowering in the coal cellar, and beat them with rifle butts before bundling them outside. Elsewhere, the liberators were even more vicious: three Russian prisoners were put up against the wall of Hirschberg's hotel by German troops and, in sight of his family, shot. By half past three that afternoon, Russian resistance in Allenstein had been broken. A few hours later, the former city commandant lay dead on a battlefield 10 kilometres to the south, and the officer who had negotiated payment with Mayor Zülch yet had never handed over any money had been captured along with many men. Liberating soldiers were received jubilantly by the population, who thrust flowers, cigarettes and their remaining food at them. Although fire-fights with isolated Russian stragglers continued until Sunday and caused some alarm, news of the great German victory won by the Eighth Army soon spread, bringing confidence that the Tsarist army would not return. Allenstein's ordeal was over.[34]

Undoubtedly, Allenstein came away lightly from occupation. There were no atrocities against its population, the Russians were thrown out so quickly and unexpectedly that they had no opportunity to destroy any major infrastructure, and the liberation itself cost the lives of only three German soldiers, an officer and one female civilian, the last hit by a bullet in the fighting.[35] Yet it would be wrong to conclude that the city was never in any danger. The Russians were nervous of civilian resistance, and the occupation took place at a particularly tense time, during the Battle of Tannenberg. Although Russian commanders acted with moderation and their troops were well-disciplined in Allenstein, on the day the city was liberated there were massacres in two small towns nearby, Soldau and Ortelsburg.[36] The municipal officials who bravely remained in Allenstein when other authorities had evacuated deserve much credit for the absence of bloodshed: the police chief, who defused tension between the crowd and the first Russian patrol, sensibly cleared the city of German soldiers and posted men at its entrances to tell the invader that it was undefended; Hirschberg and lesser functionaries such as Rittel who collected the supplies demanded by the occupying force; and above all Mayor Zülch, who negotiated with Russian senior officers, organized citizens to comply with their orders, and received a well-earned Iron Cross for his efforts.[37]

Invasion, even though brief and bloodless, profoundly affected the city's inhabitants. As their local newspaper observed, 'anyone who didn't go through these Allenstein "Russian days" cannot grasp how deeply we who stayed behind felt the ignominy of Russian rule in our German city'.[38] The occupation was extremely frightening. Rittel's daughter, for example, was very shaken by her experiences. In November 1914, when German troops pulled back again on the Eastern Front and evacuated supplies and wounded from Allenstein, she forced the family to flee. Many who had been through the first invasion clearly felt similarly, for the exodus from the city was even greater than in August.[39] The intense emotions which invasion had elicited, fear, humiliation, and also pride at the civic solidarity that had been displayed under occupation, not only stamped the city's collective psyche but were also literally built into its physiognomy. Once the danger had passed, the plans for Allenstein's new town hall were altered. Scenes from the invasion, including 'the negotiation with the enemy general about the fate of the city' and the 'baking of bread during the tyranny' were sculpted on a bay jutting out from the main building. The city's rancour towards its foes was also lastingly inscribed in stone. Long after the war's end, on each of the seven keystones in the frames of the hall's lower windows, could be seen gargoyles, representing an Englishman, a Frenchman, a Russian, an Italian, a Serb, a Japanese and an Indian.[40]

RUSSIAN ATROCITIES

Not everywhere in East Prussia was invasion so brief and bloodless as in Allenstein. The stories brought by the panicked refugees who had arrived in the city at the beginning of August had a firm basis in truth. From the first days of the war, raiding Tsarist troops had shot inhabitants and burned hamlets and farmsteads along the border. Once the

Russian First Army under General Paul Rennenkampf invaded the east of the province on 15 August, followed five days later in the south by General Aleksandr Samsonov's Second Army, the violence became much worse.[41] Even the German military was shocked. Lieutenant Colonel Max Hoffmann, the First General Staff officer of the defending Eighth Army, exclaimed with horror on 23 August that 'there has never been such a war as this, and never will be again – waged with such bestial fury. The Russians are burning everything down.'[42] Indeed, the destruction was immense. While East Prussia's few cities escaped largely unscathed, three-fifths of its small towns and more than a quarter of its villages and farms were scarred or ruined. 100,000 buildings were damaged or destroyed. Worst of all was the loss of civilian life. Some 1,491 East Prussians died at the hands of Russian troops, most during the first invasion in August and September 1914. Some were executed, others were the victims of plunder-related killing, and still others died in massacres induced by panic or perpetrated as officially sanctioned reprisals. The scale of the violence was, proportional to East Prussia's much smaller population, no different than that of the more famous contemporaneous German atrocities in Belgium and France.[43]

The Russian army invaded East Prussia primed to meet civilian resistance. The force had long experience of counter-insurgency warfare, but unlike for its German enemy past trauma with *francs tireurs* did not shape its suspicion of enemy subjects. Instead, its distrust stemmed from its use of ethnic profiling. Tsarist commanders had prepared for the coming conflict by commissioning ethnographic studies of the populations in the lands over which they would fight, linking race explicitly to political reliability. Germans were identified as the most dangerous among the border peoples. East Prussia, where four-fifths of the 2,064,175 inhabitants were German and the remainder Polish-speaking Masurians loyal to the Prussian Crown and Lithuanians, could thus only be regarded as extremely hostile territory.[44] As soon as the Russian First Army crossed into the province, General Rennenkampf attempted to deter the expected opposition through a blunt warning. Promising not to harm peaceful civilians, he laid out draconian penalties for those who attacked his troops. 'Any resistance carried out by the inhabitants against the imperial Russian army will be ruthlessly punished, regardless of gender or age,' he admonished. Disregarding international law, he also threatened collective punishment, promising that 'places in which even the smallest attack on the Russian army is perpetrated . . . will be immediately burned to the ground'.[45]

The Russian army's violence during the invasion was motivated in large part by the belief that this warning had been widely flouted by civilians. As Quartermaster General Iurii N. Danilov, the Tsarist military's third-in-command, later recalled, officers who had served in East Prussia 'unanimously' testified 'to the excellent organization of the support given to [enemy] troops by the German population'. A spy fear gripped the army. Units reported that windmills were being turned to track their progress as they marched. The people were said to be betraying troop movements with light signals and by ringing church bells. Inhabitants were even thought sufficiently fanatical that they would set their own homes alight to produce a smoke signal for their own side; a curious case of Russians' anxieties being projected onto the victims of their own violence. There were also paranoid accusations of armed resistance. *Francs tireurs* were rumoured to rove the countryside on motorcycles and bicycles, German soldiers in mufti to be mingling among the population, and seemingly innocuous civilians to be plotting to poison unsuspecting Tsarist soldiers.[46]

Like the stories that were simultaneously gripping the Kaiser's army in Belgium and France, all this was fantasy. Later German investigation uncovered only isolated cases of shooting by foolhardy individuals in East Prussia; the mass of the population followed the admonitions of their own authorities not to antagonize the invader.[47] The Russians' greatest fear, spying, was also rare. At the start of the invasion, brave telegraph and postal officials did take great risks to get word to the German army of the enemy's arrival. In one celebrated incident, the postal director in the border village of Eydtkuhnen kept the Russians talking on the ground floor of his building while upstairs his staff hurriedly telegraphed Prussian military and civil authorities to warn of their arrival and then smashed the equipment. Elsewhere, courageous female telephone operators ensured the news reached the German army. Fräulein Moritz of the Memel postal service was one such example, hopping on her bike when the Russians came and riding under rifle fire to the nearest German watch to warn it of the danger. Seldom, however, did spying extend any further than these spontaneous acts of heroism. There were no spy rings, no intricate plots. The postmaster of the village of Kolletzischken, who found himself with a working telephone and heroically transmitted reports of Russian troop movements to the other side of the front until his line was discovered in early September, was probably unique.[48]

As in the west, the initial, highly disorientating mobile combat fuelled the invaders' fears and presumptions of civilian resistance. Skirmishes with small well-camouflaged German patrols easily prompted jittery Russians to jump to the conclusion that they were being attacked by the population and to exact retribution. On some fifty separate occasions, after coming under fire from German troops in or near a village, Tsarist soldiers undertook no investigation but simply burned down some or all of the surrounding houses.[49] The violence was at its most intense at, although certainly not limited to, crisis points. In the south of East Prussia, the bloodiest period was during the last, confused days of Samsonov's advance, when his Second Army was being encircled by German defenders. In the east, killings spiked in September, as Rennenkampf's army hurriedly retreated. Its logistics and discipline partially collapsed and its scared, frustrated and hungry soldiers were gripped ever more tightly by delusions of spies and *francs tireurs* and vented their rage on civilians.[50] The bloodshed was also exacerbated by the Tsarist military's patchy discipline. This made some units prone to panic and violence. It also meant that plunder, often accompanied by assaults and murder, was a ubiquitous feature of this campaign. While some Russian combat units were praised for the strict control in which their officers held them, supply columns were condemned as bands of thieves. Small fast-moving cavalry patrols without officer oversight were also reported to have behaved particularly atrociously. As the Evangelical Church in East Prussia observed pithily after interviewing its clergy, they 'stole, robbed, murdered to their hearts' content'. Cossacks, the army's elite but unruly light horsemen, were especially feared.[51]

The Russians' racialized preconceptions, mixed discipline and disorientation in fluid fighting combined to turn the East Prussian countryside into an extremely dangerous place in August and September 1914. Men were most at risk. Many victims had inadvertently attracted the invader's attention. Putting on or even possessing any item of military clothing was a major error, for the Russians were convinced troops in mufti were hiding among the local population. Unfortunately, German reservists had often taken hard-wearing army footwear, a cap or jacket back with them to civilian life after their peacetime conscript service as a souvenir or for use in the fields. The scope for confusion was large. Possession of a pair of army boots or a military pass could cost a man his life in 1914.[52] The hypersensitivity of the Russians to spying made other articles dangerous too. Farmers in breeches and gaiters were assumed to be Prussian officers, telescopes, whistles and even notebooks were considered evidence of treacherous activity. For one individual, possession of a school atlas was sufficient to be landed in trouble. Cyclists were among the greatest victims of the invasion. One in twenty of all those killed by the Russians was on a bike. In the poverty-ridden Tsarist Empire, privately owned bicycles were a rarity, and so soldiers and officers tended to regard them as military machines and to assume that their riders were disguised combatants. Trials were generally seen as superfluous. As one East Prussian gendarme reported, 'cyclists [whom the Russians] met on the street had their bicycles broken up without ceremony and they themselves were also for the most part shot'.[53]

The Russians not only executed individuals but also mercilessly punished whole communities for perceived resistance. On 2 September, Grand Duke Nikolai Nikolaevich, the Tsarist army's commander-in-chief, ordered that places whose inhabitants fired upon troops should suffer 'complete destruction'.[54] This, however, merely legitimized a practice that had already been going on for weeks. The small town of Neidenburg was subjected to a punitive artillery bombardment on 22 August after an erroneous report that its citizens had shot at reconnoitring Cossacks. Villages became sites of massacres in similar circumstances. Among the long list of obscure habitations which experienced bloodshed, a few that suffered most deserve mention. In the village of Santoppen, twenty-one people were killed on 28 August, among them two women and a Catholic priest. The bloodshed may have been intended as a reprisal for shooting, as two Cossacks had been fired on near the village earlier in the day, probably by a German patrol. Alternatively, signalling may have been uppermost in the Russians' minds, for the village's church bells had been rung that afternoon, ironically sounding death knells for a man shot by the Russians on the previous day.[55] In Bischofstein on 29 August, after a fire-fight with a six-man German patrol that had then hurriedly dispersed, the Russians executed thirty-six men in the town and the surrounding area.[56] The bloodiest massacre of the invasion was perpetrated on the same day in

Abschwangen. After German cavalrymen had shot a senior Russian officer travelling in a car through this village, Tsarist troops stormed in, killed some of its male inhabitants, and set the place alight. The men who remained were gathered in two groups at either end of the village. One group was executed, but the other was pardoned after a local councillor named Graap stepped forward and presented a note that he had been left by a Tsarist officer quartered in the village, which testified to his good conduct. The massacre, arson and mass execution cost sixty-one lives.[57]

For East Prussians, this was a terrifying period. The case of Anna S., the wife of a wealthy farmer in the southern district of Rössel, illustrates the awful abruptness with which a family's fortunes could change under invasion. We have her story because in mid-September she told it at the Allenstein County offices, where she had gone to plead for help. 'On 31 August, a Cossack patrol rode by our farm,' she recounted. The Cossacks had skirmished with German troops who, outnumbered, had withdrawn. There then arrived Russian infantry, who apparently had not seen the patrol fight but had heard the shots and were convinced that they had come from the farm. They threatened all present with bayonets and demanded to know 'where the German soldiers are hidden'. Tragedy followed, as Anna explained:

> My husband had hidden himself in the haystacks. These were set alight by the Russian soldiers. When my husband rushed out, he was asked by the soldiers to hand over all his cash. My husband gave them 200 marks and pleaded for his life, for the sake of his eight children. The Russians said to him, after they had the money, he need not worry and could go; they wouldn't do anything to him. Scarcely had my husband taken a few steps, when he was shot down by them.

After mortally wounding the farmer, the Russians burned down the whole farm, with the exception of a single cottage. Anna S.'s six-year-old son, Josef, perished in the flames, along with a nanny, a female farm labourer and all of the cattle. Her fourteen-year-old son was shot and wounded, and one of the family's male labourers was killed. She had fled barefoot with her remaining seven children.[58]

Executions and massacres were condoned and carried out at the order of Tsarist commanders. This was not true of either plunder-related violence or rape. Where sexual assault was reported, thorough investigations were launched and, if the perpetrator could be identified, severe punishment was meted out.[59] Nonetheless, women were intensely vulnerable in the war zone. Requisitions and house searches offered troops ample opportunity to enter dwellings, and even if the victim reported rape, attackers were difficult to track down in the chaos of the battlefield. The number of sexual assaults that took place during the invasions was never firmly established. East Prussian officials recorded 338 cases, but as not all districts reported and as the victims of sex attacks were notoriously unwilling to come forward, this figure is certainly far too low.[60] A more reliable estimate might be reached by extrapolating from pregnancies resulting from rape. Two and a half years after the invasions, thirty-seven 'Russian children' were in receipt of state support and the provincial authorities knew of another eleven who had been stillborn or since died. If modern obstetric research's findings that 5 per cent of rapes lead to pregnancy are also applicable to the early twentieth century, this would suggest that the invaders committed nearly 1,000 sexual assaults in the province.[61]

Horrendous human suffering lies within these statistics. A single testimony, by Anna N., a twenty-year-old who was seven months pregnant when she was attacked in October 1914, might serve as representative of the ordeal. Her account of what was done to her was neither sensational nor even emotional but is all the more powerful for being delivered in the matter-of-fact tone that rape victims of all nationalities typically adopted before authority:

> Three Russian soldiers came on foot into our village in Wysockem, Lyck district, and searched our house. They searched all rooms for men, but found nobody. My mother and I stayed in the hall while this went on. One of the Russian soldiers pushed me violently from the hall into the room and demanded that I give myself to him. I resisted and was then violently thrown to the floor by the soldier. After he had finished with me, a second Russian soldier, who had waited in front of the door and refused my mother entry, came in. This one threw me on the bed and also forced me to surrender myself to him. After this one too had finished with me, the two soldiers left the house and departed. The third soldier had already earlier gone away. He had obviously been against entering, for he said to his comrades that they should leave me in peace.

The whole awful episode took just ten minutes but its effects were enduring. Anna N.'s child was stillborn, and she was still sickly from the attack in January 1915.[62]

The Russian army's most distinctive and extensively used tool of oppression was deportation. New Field Regulations issued at the end of July 1914 granted the Tsarist army unlimited authority over the population in war zones, including this power of removal. Whether in international law it was legal was more ambiguous, for its use had not been foreseen. During the first invasion of East Prussia, thousands of men were arrested and taken. Most were of military age, and were removed to stop them from joining the German army, a measure that Prussian authorities accepted as legitimate.[63] Others were press ganged with their farm wagons to serve in the Tsarist military's supply column, a clear violation of the 1907 Hague Convention. Whether legal or not, the arrests and deportations caused anguish to the men and their families. One father expressed his raw pain in a letter to Prussian authorities in which he pleaded for help to recover his seventeen-year-old son, dead or alive. On 29 August, he told officials, forty Cossacks had suddenly descended on his farm, firing their carbines. The family had been terrified:

> My wife, my only child, my 17-year-old sturdy son Josef, and I fled from one room to the other, and finally in the furthermost chamber fell together on our knees and jointly prayed. The savages fell upon us like a cat or a wild beast falls on a bird family in its nest. We were mercilessly punched, pushed, thrown about. My wife screamed, was punched half to death, body searched. They pushed me to and fro with their rifles and mercilessly carried away my only son. The boy cried . . . 'Father, save me, father save me.' I pleaded, implored, cried as only a father can for his only child. Nothing helped.

The father followed the soldiers and his son to the edge of the nearby town, despite being threatened and beaten back. Eventually, he wrote, 'I had to return; my child was stolen. It was in broad daylight. My God, my God!'[64]

After the Russians broke into East Prussia for a second time in November 1914, occupying the province's eastern districts, deportation practices radicalized drastically. The army's spy mania did not disappear quickly like the Germans' *franc tireur* delusion but instead spiralled to new heights that autumn. The Chief of the Russian General Staff, Nikolai Ianushkevich, decided in October to make full use of his power to deport, commanding that front areas should be emptied of all enemy subjects in order to maintain operational secrecy and protect the troops from spying or ambushes.[65] First enemy subjects and then, over the winter of 1914–15, hundreds of thousands of ethnic German Russian subjects were cleansed from the Tsarist Empire's western regions. East Prussians were caught up in these vast movements. The static front in the province assisted this new Russian project, permitting the consolidation of supply lines that in turn facilitated the removal of large numbers of people, and also loot from systematically organized plundering. Not only men as earlier but also women and children, among a total of 13,000 East Prussians, were forcibly transported to the Russian interior.[66]

The numbers of deported would have been far higher had the head of the East Prussian civil administration, Adolf von Batocki, along with the provincial authorities and army, not organized an evacuation as the Russians advanced. Some 200,000 people from endangered areas were assisted to safety at the start of November and mostly billeted across northern and central Germany. About 50,000 made their own arrangements to escape to the hinterland, and 100,000 refugees travelled across to the western districts of East Prussia.[67] For those who refused evacuation and took a great risk in remaining, Russian confusion and poor coordination sometimes proved their salvation. Despite the Chief of Staff's order, the Tsarist commander in East Prussia, General Sievers, initially told his units to sweep German men towards enemy lines. Lower-ranked officers also had their own security concerns and solutions with the consequence that deportations were haphazard. In some places, everybody was taken, elsewhere only military-aged men, and in other areas people were left undisturbed.[68] Still, according to the head of Gumbinnen County, in his invaded eastern districts over 30 per cent of the inhabitants who had not evacuated were deported.[69] Desperate East Prussians fled into the province's thick forest for protection. One man who ran off when the Russians came to his village in mid-December dug a hole in the side of an isolated gully and stayed there through the winter, living off flour mixed with cold water and unthreshed rye. He had no knowledge of the liberation in February 1915 and was discovered only at the beginning of April when, weak from hunger, he decided to give himself up and returned home.[70]

Those people who neither evacuated nor escaped underwent a miserable and dangerous odyssey.[71] Most were transported with great inefficiency and in appalling conditions across thousands of kilometres. Infants and old people, who were numerous among the deportees, perished on the journey. The majority were dumped either on the Volga River or between it and the Ural Mountains. The US embassy in Russia, the neutral representatives tasked with checking on their welfare, was by the autumn of 1915 expressing alarm about their condition. Nowhere did Russian civil authorities have much idea of who the deportees were or feel responsible for their well-being. There was no official financial support and, to make matters worse, some authorities had banned the prisoners from paid work. In some areas, they therefore sat in compulsory idleness and penury. Elsewhere they were put to hard forced labour. American officials visiting the Volga observed 'very real suffering' and a 'lack of sufficient nourishment'. Unsurprisingly given the harsh conditions in which the deportees were transported and the deprivation they faced in internment, many died. Almost one-third of the deportees, over 4,000 people, did not survive to see their homeland again.[72]

The invasions and the violence that accompanied them inflicted great suffering on East Prussia's inhabitants but, rather counter-intuitively, strengthened the wider German war effort. The Reich lost little of economic value, for the province was by national standards poor, agricultural and sparsely populated. Only its capital, the port city of Königsberg, was of significance and fortunately it was never captured. Instead, the invasions gave two major psychological boosts to the Reich's mobilization. First and most famously, the victory over the Russian Second Army at Tannenberg in the last days of August 1914 provided a powerful morale uplift for an anxious public. In Berlin, the arrival of refugees from the eastern border earlier in the month had caused great unease. News of the victorious battle, in which 92,000 prisoners and 400 guns were taken, was greeted with what the editor of the *Berliner Tageblatt* described as 'unbelievable enthusiasm'.[73] The commander of the defending Eighth Army, Paul von Hindenburg, became a household name overnight. The Kaiser, aware of the immense political capital that came with being seen as the liberator of East Prussia, would hurry to the province the second time it was freed, in mid-February 1915, but by then it was too late. Hindenburg's reputation as the country's 'Saviour' was already firmly fixed. The fame and popularity that he and his Chief of Staff, Erich Ludendorff, won from their defence of the province set them on a meteoric rise that would culminate two years later in appointment to the command of the German army and, ultimately, to the duo becoming Germany's de facto wartime leadership.[74]

Second, less well recognized but even more significant, the Russian invasions provided the German public at the very start of hostilities with a terrifying warning of the consequences of defeat. The invasions were a formative trauma undergone not only by East Prussians but vicariously by the entire German nation. Germans hundreds of kilometres from the fighting read in their newspapers vivid, frightening and largely accurate reports of Tsarist atrocities. Troops fighting in the province, a good number of whom hailed from other parts of the Reich, added credibility to the journalism with their own, often exaggerated stories of the enemy's brutality. Most important in transmitting East Prussia's trauma to the rest of the country were the floods of refugees. During the Russians' summer attack, 800,000 refugees, more than a third of East Prussia's population, left their homes and headed westwards. The second invasion in the autumn produced fewer refugees, but thanks to the better organized official evacuation they travelled much further. Chartered trains took 34,000 to Pomerania, 21,000 to Schleswig, 20,000 to Lüneburg, 12,000 to Potsdam, and many others to different destinations across the Reich. Another 80,000 East Prussians went to relatives, mostly in Berlin and Westphalia. These people brought Germans in the centre and west of the country face to face with the consequences of invasion. Their numbers were swelled by military evacuees, as in November, fearing a deep invasion of the Reich, the army removed thousands of young men from other eastern frontier provinces. The purpose of the measure was to protect them from deportation, but according to the popular rumour mill it was necessary because the Russians routinely cut off the hands of fit German males. The measure and the myths that accompanied it underlined for all Germans the great danger faced by the Reich.[75]

The invasions not only inflamed widespread feelings of fear but thus quite literally brought together the German people, cementing the national solidarity that had formed at the start of hostilities. In the face of the destruction and atrocities, both true and exaggerated, it could hardly be questioned that the conflict was being fought for a good and just cause. Even the Social Democrats, the most sceptical of all Germany's political groupings, regarded the Tsarist campaign in East Prussia to be 'a flaming symbol of a thoroughly barbaric method of warfare'.[76] Regardless of the fact that many East Prussian refugees were Polish-speaking Masurians or Lithuanians, all were feted as German brothers and what was widely presented as their 'sacrifice for our holy cause' was publicly honoured.[77] The most powerful sign of the solidarity felt across the country, and a mark of how much other Germans identified with the beleaguered people in the invasion zone, was the spectacular success of the national fund-raising campaign to alleviate their suffering and repair the damage. Donations flooded in from all parts of the Reich, and by May 1916 had reached the impressive sum of twelve million marks.[78] The trauma inflicted by this vicarious invasion, and the intense emotions of fear, anxiety and anger that had accompanied it, were not quickly forgotten. For the rest of the conflict, East Prussia would stand as an awful warning of the consequences of allowing enemy troops onto German soil. The memory and myths of the invasions would retain their ability to mobilize and unify the German people long after all danger from the Russians had passed.

RACE WAR

In Galicia, the Russian campaign of 1914–15 had a very different course and outcomes from the attacks further north. The Habsburg Crownland was, at 77,300 square kilometres, more than twice the size of East Prussia. With 8,025,675 inhabitants, 15 per cent of Austria-Hungary's population, and a large if poor agricultural sector, it was economically a much more significant territory. Although Galicia and East Prussia were both multi-ethnic places, competition and conflict were far more marked among the peoples of the Habsburg territory. Polish aspirations for greater autonomy or independence clashed with Ukrainophiles' hopes for a separate Crownland. The Viennese bureaucracy wished in vain that all peoples might invest more in the Austrian state idea. The Russians too had their own vision for the land. Galicia's annexation was one of their primary war aims and there an idealistic rhetoric absent in East Prussia marked the Tsar's campaign. The chaos of the Habsburg army's deployment in August 1914 combined with its inferiority in numbers and equipment to give the Russians an excellent chance of success.

The Russians' ambition and ideological aims in Galicia were manifest from the very start of the invasion. The Tsar's army, the instrument of Europe's most autocratic state, considered itself to be fighting a war of liberation. It regarded Ukrainian speakers as a 'Russian people' and aspired to unite their home, Eastern Galicia, to the Russian Motherland. The commander-in-chief, Grand Duke Nikolai Nikolaevich, issued an appeal to Galicia's inhabitants on 16 September 1914 couched in idealistic language:

> In the name of the great Russian Tsar I declare to you that Russia, which has more than once shed her blood for the emancipation of peoples from foreign yokes, seeks nothing but the restoration of right and justice. To you, peoples of Austria-Hungary, she will now bring freedom and the realization of your national aspirations.[79]

The contrast with Rennenkampf's nervous warning not to resist on his entry into East Prussia could hardly have been greater. The army's ethnographers and officers had high hopes of a friendly reception from the Crownland's 3.2 million Ruthenes, or 'little Russians' as they thought of them. They were less confident about its 3.8 million Poles. Not only was the Galician Polish elite largely content with its autonomy under the Habsburgs but the brutality with which the Tsarist regime had suppressed the 1863 uprising in Congress Poland and the 1905–6 revolution still rankled. Confessional differences also mattered. Russian military ethnographers blamed Poles' hostility on 'Catholic fanaticism'.[80] In an attempt to win over this people, Grand Duke Nikolai addressed a public manifesto to them on 14 August 1914, promising a reunification of the Polish nation, 'joined in one under the sceptre of the Russian Emperor'.[81] The Tsarist High Command's conciliatory stance shaped its soldiers' conduct. Jan Słomka, mayor of the Galician village of Dzików, found for example that, just so long as they were sober, Russian troops were polite and friendly when they arrived in September 1914.[82]

The Russian army's invasion of Galicia was thus not at first so dominated by the delusions of civilian resistance and by the military punishments and reprisals that marked its conduct in East Prussia. Nonetheless, there was violence. This was aimed at the Crownland's two smallest peoples, its 872,000 Jews and 90,000 Germans. The Tsarist officer corps regarded both ethnic groups as malign alien influences within a Slavic land. While the Germans were objects of fear, the Jews were targeted due to what one observant contemporary – the Jewish aid worker Shloyme Rappaport-Ansky, who travelled widely in Galicia during the occupation – called 'the bestial anti-Semitism permeating the entire army'.[83] Pre-war military ethnographic studies had portrayed Jews as untrustworthy rather than threatening: the materialistic 'kikes', officers agreed, were too selfish, cowardly and busy making money to put up resistance. At most, they might become paid spies for both sides.[84] Once the campaign began, Russian units did sometimes convince themselves that Jews had ambushed them and reacted violently. On 29 August, in the north-eastern border village of Liwcze, for example, seventeen men and one woman, among them some Jews, were shut in a house and massacred by Tsarist troops as reprisal for shots said to have come from the settlement.[85] Generally, however, Russian assaults on Galicia's Jewish population took the form of unruly pogroms motivated by prejudice and poor discipline. These were generally less lethal than the military punishments in East Prussia, for the primary intention was not to kill but rather to humiliate, rob and rape. The deaths that did take place were more usually the result of vicious sexual assault or brutal handling than of officially sanctioned execution.[86]

The Russian army's earliest pogrom on Galician soil took place in mid-August 1914 at Brody, a town on the north-eastern border in which Jews composed over two-thirds of the 18,000 residents. Cossacks, who were the most anti-Semitic troops in the army and perpetrated many of the worst outrages, rode in, looted homes and shops and burned down 162 Jewish houses, factories and mills. The unlikely claim that a Jewish girl had shot at Russian troops was used to excuse the destruction; an insult, for the implication was that Jewish men were not manly enough to protect their own homes. Three Jewish men, two women and a Christian woman were killed.[87] As Tsarist forces advanced deeper into the Crownland they perpetrated similar outrages. Robbery and rape were integral to the violence. Jews in the small town of Jaryczów Nowy, situated just east of Lwów, testified that they 'did not stop for a full three months'. In Zabłotów, 200 kilometres south of Brody, Russian troops robbed townspeople and raped three Jewish women on 29 September.

At Nadwórna, 60 kilometres to the west, six other Jewish women died through sexual assault and one later killed herself. The international law expert stationed at Russian military headquarters confirmed the existence of many other similar cases, some in which young girls were the victims.[88] Murders were also committed. In the town of Głogów, in western Galicia, for example, a Jewish family of four was massacred after the father tried to protect his daughter from attack. Other people died from beatings or arson.[89] The bloodiest and most notorious of the Russians' atrocities took place in Galicia's capital, Lwów, on 27 September, three weeks after they entered the city. After shots were heard and blamed on Jews, Cossacks rode through the Jewish quarter shooting. Subsequently, no one was sure of how many people were killed, but the most plausible estimates suggest that around forty-seven died. About 300 Jews were arrested.[90]

Despite the half-hearted orders of some senior Tsarist commanders to stop the pogroms, troops who perpetrated outrages could be confident that they would not face punishment. There were officers who even welcomed the violence, for besides inflicting pain on the despised Jews it also served the pragmatic function of winning over Polish or Ruthenian peasants, who were often encouraged to participate in the looting. Many Jews were beaten up and robbed by their neighbours.[91] Not everywhere was this the case, however. Joachim Schoenfeld recalled that in his shtetl, Śniatyn, many Jews found safety with Christian families when Cossacks rampaged through in August 1914.[92] Much depended on the example set by community leaders. In Jesierna, a town of 7,000 souls in Zborów district, the priests, one Polish and the other Ruthenian, helped the Jewish mayor to protect his fellow believers. Both warned their flocks against harming Jewish townspeople. The Catholic priest sheltered Jews in distress in his own lodgings and distributed material aid. When Russian troops broke into Jewish shops and threw their wares onto the streets, the Uniate cleric chased off a crowd hoping for a share of the loot, gathered up the goods, and took them for safekeeping to the town council's office.[93]

The Galician Jewish population had received some warning of the danger, for before heavy fighting began in the second half of August, Russian-subject Jews started to pour across the border, running from violence meted out by the Tsar's army as it concentrated in preparation for the campaign. As in East Prussia, the wealthy were first to leave, but once the Russians invaded poorer Galicians also departed, blocking the roads as they struggled westwards. Terror of the Russians was such that half of Galicia's Jewish population, around 400,000 people, fled.[94] Germans, the other group most in danger, also set out on the road. Often, whole communities travelled together. Georg Faust, the pastor of Dornfeld, a German village situated 6 kilometres south of Lwów, described his flock's surprise and alarm at the speed of the Russian advance. They had thought their region would be staunchly defended, given the proximity of the Crownland capital in the north and the Mikołajów bridgehead over the Dniester River to the south, but when Habsburg troops fell back through their village shouting at them to get out, they suddenly realized how little time they had:

> What to do now? . . . Anyone who went through the last hours of tormenting uncertainty will never forget them. What it means to abandon house and farm, to relinquish to the enemy the harvest just brought in, to give up one's home patch – that's difficult to understand . . . At eight in the morning on 1 September, a long procession moved out of the village. The old people, weak from age, the ill, [and] women with infants on their breasts [sat] on the farm wagons, which were loaded with food, fodder and bedding. Between them was driven the bleating cattle.

Altogether, there were 1,000 people, 500 head of cattle, 200 horses and 80 wagons in the column. The Dornfelders travelled for weeks, but in adverse weather 'already after a few days several infants died, the old followed them gradually'.[95]

The Habsburg army's unwillingness to warn civilian authorities of its withdrawals was not unique; German commanders embraced the same misguided secrecy during East Prussia's first invasion, making civil-military coordination impossible and causing much unnecessary panic among the population. Galician civilians' plight was worse, however, due to a lack of civil leadership. In Germany, *Landräte*, the district administrators who were the key figures in local government, and civil servants below them were obliged by instructions issued in 1891 to stay at their posts in an invasion. Although this rule was made less stringent during the 1914 invasions and some officials caused scandal by fleeing prematurely, the emphasis remained very much on staying with and guiding the unfortunate population.[96] In Austria-Hungary, possibly reflecting the greater distance of imperial authorities from their peoples, very different rules applied. Instructions to the *Bezirk-shauptleute*, the district administrators in Galicia, and to other civil servants ordered them to evacuate just before enemy troops arrived. Cooperation with an invader would be contrary to the oath of officials to Kaiser and state, the instructions stressed, and the benefits of a functioning administration to civilians must 'yield in the face of these considerations'.[97]

The result of the Habsburg instructions to civil authorities was predictable: officials fled, leaving the population without guidance. Some abandoned communities panicked and, like the Dornfelders, set out on the road without making adequate preparations. Those people who remained lost all respect for the Habsburg administration. Dr Alfons Regius, a court official in the city of Czernowitz, expressed the disgust and bitterness felt by many in the invaded Crownlands of Galicia and Bukovina at the start of September. 'The postal directorate, the Land President, but also the police directorate, the parliamentary representatives, most councillors, the rector (of Czernowitz University) with almost all professors and naturally all rich Jews have fled,' he fulminated in his diary. All these authority figures, Regius noted with disgust, had apparently departed without 'even only for a moment considering that it might be their duty to hold out with the citizenry'.[98]

Swelling the flood of refugees fleeing eastern Galicia and Bukovina were people forced to evacuate the great fortress cities of Przemyśl and Cracow. The Habsburg army evicted residents for their own safety, in the case of Ruthenes for its own security, and above all to preserve garrisons' food stocks. It also made many inhabitants of the surrounding countryside homeless, as it demolished villages in order to allow unobstructed fields of fire for the forts. Przemyśl's evacuation began on 4 September 1914, when all but 18,000 of its 57,000 citizens were removed. Around the city, twenty-one villages were cleared against the protests of their inhabitants.[99] Cracow presented greater difficulty, for although its fortress girdle, at 50 kilometres, was only slightly longer than that of Przemyśl, the population of the city and its suburbs numbered 183,000 people.[100] The first evacuation took place in mid-September, just after the Habsburg army sounded its general retreat. Initially, only enemy civilians were obliged to leave, while Austrian subjects not engaged in essential tasks were merely encouraged to depart. Those determined to stay were told to stockpile supplies for three months and warned that if before a siege it was discovered that they were inadequately provisioned, they would be 'forcibly expelled'.[101] The mood in the city darkened as rumours of military catastrophe circulated in early September and it worsened considerably when residents realized that Tsarist forces were approaching. Jan Dąbrowski, a historian living in the city, observed 'an ever greater greater pessimism' taking hold of his neighbours. 'People are already counting on the possibility of a Russian government.'[102] By 18 September, 50,000 people had left, around a third of Cracow's population. To municipal authorities' dismay, many leaders of the city's large Jewish community were among those who departed. The President, Vice-President and numerous members of the local Jewish Council, as well as the administrators of the Jewish hospital and shelter for the terminally ill, all evacuated, leaving no funds to help their poorer and more vulnerable co-believers. When the respected Liberal Rabbi and head of the city's Temple Synagogue, Dr Osias Thon, abandoned the city too, outrage gripped the Jewish quarter of Kazimierz.[103]

The Austro-Hungarian army's advance and the relief of besieged Przemyśl on 9 October ended the emergency, but only temporarily. At the start of November, the Russians again pushed forward, this time to within just 12 kilometres of Cracow.[104] Panic gripped the city: 'people are anxious about a siege,' Dąbrowski recorded in the middle of the month. 'It is possible to see even the most esteemed men fearful.' Defensive preparations added to the unease. Seemingly never-ending columns of soldiers marched grimly through Cracow and, as at Przemyśl, new emplacements were dug in front of the forts and villages on the perimeter were burned.[105] Cracow's fortress commander, General Karl Kuk, pressed citizens to depart. The poor, among whom rumours were circulating of horrendous refugee camps, steadily resisted. Appeals were ignored and most free evacuation trains departed empty.[106] This time, therefore, evacuation was made compulsory. The military planned to move 80,000 to 90,000 people out of the city.[107]

On 6 November posters appeared on Cracow's streets warning that residents without three months of provisions had five days to leave. Twenty commissions circulated houses to check citizens' stocks of food. Evacuation trains, each capable of carrying 1,500 people, were organized.[108] Already three days later, soldiers started to herd poor people to the railway station. Yet ensuring that they departed proved impossible. Once their military escort had left them on the platform, those designated for compulsory evacuation turned around and scurried home. Some hid or locked themselves in their apartments. Others fooled the commissions tasked with checking their supplies. Barrels, chests and sacks containing a sprinkling of sugar, flour or potatoes on top and padded underneath with cardboard were presented for inspection.[109] Neighbours pooled their resources; supplies were borrowed, shown as evidence that the 'owners' could feed themselves for three months and, once permission had been granted to remain, those same supplies were passed to another family to put before the commissions.[110] Desperate to reduce the city's population to just 40,000, Kuk resorted to violence. On 12 November town officials, police and six companies of soldiers were gathered to drive out the poor 'with armed force'. The troops were instructed to 'proceed ruthlessly' and ensure that those without permission to stay were left beyond the fortress defences.[111] Even this failed, however. The fortress commander admitted despairingly that 'whole regiments would have to be used' in order to clear the city. Most evacuees would have to walk and, he fatalistically predicted, the operation would 'doubtless be the most serious calamity'.[112]

Fortunately, the Russian army's advance ended outside Cracow. Residents listened anxiously to the thunder of artillery throughout the second half of November, but at the start of the following month a Habsburg offensive south of the city forced a Russian withdrawal. By the end of 1914, the front stretched along the Dunajec River 70 kilometres to the east and along the Carpathians bordering Hungary.[113] Cracovians could breathe a sigh of relief. Despite another scare in March 1915, when the fortress of Przemyśl fell to the Russians, their city would not be threatened again during the First World War. However, for their fellow Habsburg subjects languishing under Tsarist occupation further east, the ordeal was anything but over. Indeed, for Galician Jews, life was about to become much, much worse.

LIFE IN GREAT RUSSIA

In April 1915 on a visit to subjugated Lwów, the Russian Tsar Nikolai II made a proclamation which, though for him an incontestable truth, was in reality a radical vision of a new order: 'there is no Galicia, rather a

Great Russia to the Carpathians'.[114] Governor General Count Georgii Bobrinskii and the military occupation regime installed under him in September 1914 had the task of bridging the gap between the multi-ethnic Habsburg reality and the Tsar's imagined Russian future for the Crownland. The Governor General was a moderate, at least by the extreme standards of pan-Slavic imperial Russian officialdom. His first speech eight days after taking office promised religious tolerance to Galicia's population and he showed himself willing to cooperate with local elites, if only to ensure smooth administration. Nonetheless, Bobrinskii's regime was anything but benign. Ominously for its inhabitants, the occupied territory was reorganized on the administrative model used within the Tsarist Empire, with three provinces established around Lwów, Tarnopol and Czernowitz, along with a fourth around Przemyśl after its capture in March 1915. From the start, the Governor General made clear that eastern Galicia and the Lemko region were 'native Russian lands and should be ruled according to Russian principles'.[115]

Bobrinskii favoured a course of cautious state-building in Galicia. Russian control was to be established but inhabitants should not be antagonized in wartime with more drastic initiatives. Government ministers, fearful of attracting negative press in the liberal western European allies on whom their empire was dependent for financial support, agreed. However, military commanders, above all the army's anti-Semitic Chief of Staff, General Nikolai Ianushkevich, were much more radical. At Stavka, the Russian High Command, war was regarded as a unique opportunity to implement dramatic change under martial law, before peace returned civilian oversight and greater international scrutiny. The generals' views mattered, as they retained considerable power in Galicia. The South-West Front's Quartermaster General, Lieutenant General A. Zabelin, was Bobrinskii's superior. Moreover, the Governor General's authority in the occupied territory was not absolute, for the Third and Eighth Army commanders controlled their own rear areas, possessed independent hierarchies answering only to them, and frequently issued orders affecting the civilian population. Hyper-patriotic activists of the Galician-Russian Benevolent Society with connections at the Tsar's court and in Stavka agitated tirelessly for radical assimilationist measures. Lower officials transferred to help administer the occupied territory also often shared army officers' Greater Russian chauvinism and anti-Semitism. Consequently, even when Bobrinskii sought to avoid or curb abrasive treatment of civilians, his orders were not necessarily followed.[116]

The Russians embarked with alacrity on the project of remaking, or as their officials preferred to present it, restoring eastern Galicia to its 'primordial' Russian state. When Lwów fell on 3 September, the occupiers set about erasing all awkward evidence of its Habsburg past or inconvenient multiculturalism. The city hall's clock was reset to St Petersburg time and the Julian calendar introduced to mark the end of the Austro-Polish era. Habsburg eagles were torn from public buildings and shopkeepers were ordered to display Cyrillic signs. Lwów's Polish street signs were eventually covered over by new Russian ones, although the Polish municipal authorities stalled on this for many months. Russian festivals were also imposed. On 19 December 1914, the Tsar's name day, military police went from house to house to ensure that all displayed suitably coloured decoration.[117] Bobrinskii did make some concessions. Lwów's Polish-dominated municipal council was permitted to continue functioning under its Vice President Tadeusz Rutowski. In accordance with international law, the Austro-Polish civil administration, including the courts and police, was kept in operation and Austrian law continued to be dispensed, although now 'in the name of the Russian emperor'.[118] State offices were permitted to continue using the Polish language, as under the Habsburgs, but 'only temporarily', and Catholic clergy were permitted to devote public prayers for 'the Emperor', without specifying whether the Habsburg Monarch or Romanov Tsar was meant. Some among the Polish elites sought to ingratiate themselves with the occupier. A few nobles fearful of losing their property became friendly once the Russians started to sequester the estates of absent aristocrats. Polish National Democrat leaders also offered support, although in their case on ideological grounds: they believed the promises of a united and autonomous Poland in the event of Tsarist victory. Few among their followers were convinced, however, and the party newspaper's circulation plummeted from 13,000 to 3,000 during the occupation. For most educated Poles, it was clear that the Russians posed a mortal threat to their political hegemony in eastern Galicia.[119]

The stakes were still higher for Ruthenes, who under Russian rule faced the prospect of cultural annihilation. The Tsarist regime denied the existence of any such entity as the Ukrainian people, and had long striven ruthlessly to suppress all nationalist stirrings within its own Ukrainian minority. In eastern Galicia, it began the occupation by imprisoning Ukrainophile leaders, whose numbers had already been decimated through internment by Polish Galician authorities and misguided persecution by the treason-obsessed Habsburg army at the war's outbreak. Some 173 were taken as hostages to Russia, among them forty-five Uniate priests as well as directors of Ruthenian schools and economic institutions. The most prominent prisoner was the respected and influential Greek-Catholic Metropolitan of Lwów, Archbishop Andrei Sheptits'kyi, whose combating of Russophile Orthodox missionizing in Galicia and secret proselytizing in Russian Ukraine before the war had made him a marked man for the Tsarist army. The Chief of Staff, Ianushkevich, had promised to bring him in 'dead or alive'. In September 1914 he was personally arrested by General Brusilov, commander of the Eighth Army, and deported across the border to Kiev.[120]

With the deportation of nationalist intellectuals and hostile priests, Bobrinskii's regime could embark on remoulding Ruthenes into Russians. It received some support for this project from Galician Russophile intellectuals and Orthodox priests, a minority which, in this land of still fluid national identities, regarded itself as part of the Russian people.[121] Two key sources of identity were attacked. The first was the Ukrainian language, which as in Russia was banished from public life. Ukrainian bookshops were closed and books and newspapers in the language banned from publication. The Polish press were forbidden by the censor from even printing the word 'Ruthenian'; 'Russian' had to be used instead.[122] Most importantly, educational reform was introduced. All schools in Galicia were shut down after the invasion, and although at the end of 1914 some Polish ones were permitted to reopen, Ruthenian schools remained permanently closed. The occupation authorities, taking a long view, plotted to turn Galicia into an organic part of Great Russia by educating Ruthenian children in Russian. Over the winter of 1914–15, special courses were organized in both Galicia and St Petersburg to train teachers in the conqueror's language. Take-up was disappointing, however, for only around 250 Ruthenian teachers, one-tenth of the total, agreed to attend. While fighting continued and the region's fate remained undecided, there were limits to the ability of the military occupation regime to implement its Russification programme.[123]

The second pillar of Ruthenes' identity, their Uniate Church and faith, was also attacked. Unlike the campaign against the Ukrainian language, this proved not merely ineffective but actually counter-productive. Initially, the Tsarist military had been successful in courting Ruthenian peasants. For them, life during the occupation was better than in peace under their Polish noble landlords. The Russians encouraged Ruthenians to loot estates and settle scores with Jewish neighbours. The occupiers offered seed, food and other goods, often plundered from Jews, at bargain prices. Their popularity rose further when the rumour spread that the Tsar wished to take the land from nobles and Jews and distribute it to the peasantry.[124] However, much of the goodwill evaporated once the Russians began to interfere in peasants' confessional lives. The Tsar was personally to blame for this misstep, for it was he who appointed Archbishop Evlogii, a militant cleric who had made his reputation fighting tooth and nail to rein in Catholic influence in Russia's western borderlands, to further the interests of the Orthodox Church in Galicia. From his arrival in December 1914, Evlogii's conduct was insulting. His first act was to celebrate the Tsar's name day by holding Masses, against the wishes of their clergy, in two of Lwów's Uniate cathedrals. He gave a provocative sermon, calling on the priests of 'Galician Rus' to lead their people into 'organic unity with Great Russia' and to bring about a 'historic union with the Orthodox Russian Church'.[125]

Bobrinskii and Ianushkevich were usually at loggerheads, but Evlogii succeeded in bringing them together with his proselytizing zeal, which both feared would inflame resistance in the army's rear areas. In the spring of 1915 these concerns brought about his recall. Nonetheless, ruthless missionizing continued. Bobrinskii's stricture that Orthodox priests should not be sent to replace Uniate incumbents unless three-quarters of the people in any parish had first voted in support was frequently disregarded. Uniate priests were forced to share or even surrender their churches to Russian Orthodox clergy. Some saw parts of their land, on which they depended for their livelihood, transferred to their rivals. A few were murdered. Their parishioners were also coerced. Peasants were threatened with the confiscation of their land or told that their children would be taken from them if they did not convert to Orthodoxy.[126] More subtle methods were also employed; by holding Orthodox Masses in Uniate churches, some of Evlogii's clergy sought to convert by stealth. Nonetheless, their success was very limited. Time was short, peasants' loyalties to their Church were strong and the incumbent clergy resisted, advising flocks to take Mass in a Roman Catholic church when no Uniate priest was available. By the occupation's end, despite the pressure exerted by Tsarist officials, only between fifty and a hundred of the Uniate Church's approximately 1,500 Galician parishes had opted for Russian Orthodoxy.[127]

The greatest victims of Russian occupation were Galicia's Jews. Their treatment was, as an official Habsburg report written in the aftermath of the invasion discovered, 'much more severe than that of the rest of other classes in the population, in places truly inhuman'.[128] Tsarist officers soon came to believe that, as the ethnographic studies had predicted, Jews were spying and working to undermine the Russian occupation, and so singled them out for harsh treatment. Hostages, whose numbers increased rapidly from October 1914, were drawn disproportionately from the Jewish population: although Jews made up only an eighth of eastern Galicia's inhabitants, they were more than half – 1,160 – of the 2,130 hostages deported by the Russian army up to mid-1915.[129] Financial penalties too were levied primarily against them. When Stanisławów, a city in the south-east of the Crownland, was fined 50,000 crowns as a punishment for alleged sabotage, it was stipulated that Jewish residents were to pay 36,000. To rub in the unfairness, the sum was collected in full, while the city's Poles and Ruthenes were forgiven the remaining 14,000 crowns. Similarly, when telephone lines in the surroundings of Kołomyja were damaged, Jews were blamed and warned either to pay a heavy fine or face expulsion from the city.[130]

Tsarist civilian officials appointed to oversee the localities were even worse than the army officers. The dregs of the imperial bureaucracy, poorly educated, anti-Semitic and venal, they abused Jews mercilessly. The City Governor of Lwów, Yevstafiy Nikolaiyevich Skalon, is a good example. As the well-informed Rappaport-Ansky recounted, he had already become notorious for his corruption as Police Commissioner of Kiev. In Galicia, he 'openly took bribes, fleeced the living and the dead, and victimized both individuals and the whole community'. With house searches, arrests and threats 'to string up every tenth Jew', he extorted a thousand roubles of protection money from the Jews of the city.[131] Disturbingly for Austrian leaders, many Habsburg police and justice officials collaborated with the Russians, and some took advantage of the occupation regime's anti-Semitism to vent their own hatred of Jews.

These Polish civil servants, it was claimed, had 'made their business the systematic persecution of the Jews, their suppression, pauperization and humiliation in front of the authorities and population'.[132] The Chief of Police in Przemyśl, Eugen Wierzbowski, who was subsequently sentenced to a year and ten months' hard labour for collaboration, was singled out for particular criticism. Jews were convinced, against the denials of Galician officials, that Wierzbowski had directed Russian officers seeking billets to wealthy Jews' apartments, singled out the most respected Jews for hard and demeaning street cleaning and fortress-building work, and betrayed Jewish men of military age, who were then deported.[133]

Persecuted, unprotected by law, and at the mercy of prejudiced Tsarist town commandants and greedy civil officials, hate-filled collaborators and violent soldiers, the Jews found themselves in a form of purgatory due to the occupation. Accentuating their suffering were epidemics brought by Russian troops into Galicia. Typhoid, smallpox and above all cholera ravaged the whole population. The damage to housing and infrastructure – 188,981 buildings were destroyed during the invasions – made all vulnerable, but Jews, whose shtetls had often been singled out for arson by Russian troops, were probably particularly exposed.[134] Some 200 Jews died in the town of Zaleszczyki and 300 each in Nadwórna and Horodenka. In Jaryczow Nowy, the 140 people killed by epidemic diseases represented about a sixth of the town's Jewish population.[135] To Manès Sperber, a child at the time in the shtetl of Zabłotów, it seemed that the end of the night was the peak time for deaths, for it was then that the weeping of the bereaved frequently awoke him. 'In the nocturnal stillness' one could hear 'the cries of the family trying to hold back the dying person.' The corpses of the dead were terrible to behold, their faces distorted. 'Some lay there as if their terrible cramp had only relaxed that very instant.'[136]

The Tsarist High Command, and especially the virulently anti-Semitic Chief of Staff, Nikolai Ianushkevich, foresaw no place for Jews in Galicia's Russian future. Meals at headquarters were enlivened by animated debate among officers on how best to go about 'exterminating' them.[137] However, in practice, Stavka had no genocidal intentions but instead proposed to uproot Galicia's Jews by destroying their livelihoods. The first step was to demand the confiscation of the 8 per cent of Galician land in Jewish ownership. Against objections from both Bobrinskii and the government, Ianushkevich argued cynically that if the victims were to have Russian citizenship imposed on them, the plan would not contravene international law. A census of Jewish land ownership was taken over the winter of 1914–15, and in February 1915 the Tsar signed a 'Liquidation Law' permitting land owned by Austro-Hungarian and German Jewish subjects within 160 kilometres of the front to be expropriated. Other, even more damaging measures aimed against Jews were the restrictions placed by the military on their freedom of movement in February 1915 and, after Ianushkevich's complaints, in March the dismissal of nearly all Jewish Galician court employees. The limitations on movement were a particularly heavy blow, for although motivated principally by security concerns, their primary effect was economic. Jews were forbidden to enter Galicia or to move between its districts, and as Bobrinskii had rightly predicted, this cut off Jewish traders from their markets and hindered the army from buying the goods it needed. That, in turn, led commanders to claim that Jews were sabotaging the war effort by denying the wares they now did not have to the Russian military.[138]

The Tsarist army's security paranoia, which spiralled over the autumn of 1914, ultimately prompted it to turn in Galicia, as elsewhere, to mass deportation. Jews were late victims of this measure. First to be affected in the summer had been enemy subjects in Russia's western borderlands and military-aged men in conquered territories. In the winter of 1914–15, the practice had radicalized when the army started targeting Germans as an ethnic group. The thousands of East Prussians deported to the Volga were dwarfed by the hundreds of thousands of people from Russia's own German minority cleared from western regions. Only from January 1915 were Jews, still considered a less dangerous collective than the Germans, subject to major centrally organized deportations. Interestingly, the measure was conceived at first in reaction to Habsburg atrocities, an early case of racial stereotyping by the region's autocratic regimes interacting to produce escalating suffering and bloodshed for its ethnically mixed population.[139] After the Habsburg army recaptured Czernowitz, the capital of Bukovina, in October 1914, disturbing reports of its brutal punishments, including the hanging of Russophile peasants, reached Russian military commanders. Local Jews were blamed for identifying Russian sympathizers to the Austrians. When, after being retaken by the Russians, Czernowitz appeared again to be about to fall to Habsburg forces in late January 1915, Ianushkevich ordered hostage-taking and deportations 'in order to prevent atrocities against the population which is devoted to us'.[140]

Ianushkevich's obsession with spies bred collective hysteria throughout the army and soon led to the extension of deportations across the Galician front.[141] Embracing an idea first suggested for use against German men, the commander-in-chief Grand Duke Nikolai ordered on 12 March 1915 that Jews be pushed towards Austro-Hungarian positions. Within a week the order had been carried out, although, as in East Prussia, patchily. The town of Tyśmienica was one place affected. On 17 March, Russian troops herded around 2,000 Jews towards the firing line. As a means of expulsion, the measure was totally ineffective; eventually the unfortunate people were allowed to return. Their absence did, however, allow local officials and soldiers the opportunity to plunder their homes. In other areas, Jews were sent east rather than west. The Jewish population of Mościska was driven, regardless of age or health, 35 kilometres eastwards to Gródek and some people were made to trek 65 kilometres to Lwów. The Russians claimed that spying by these people had prevented their troops from capturing the nearby besieged fortress of Przemyśl.[142] Around 10,000 people were caught up in similar expulsions. When, a fortnight later, the fortress city did capitulate to Tsarist forces, more deportations followed. From late March, 17,000 Jews were expelled from Przemyśl, many of whom crowded into Lwów. Bobrinskii, who disapproved of the measures, faced a humanitarian crisis. The old, infirm and infants were among the people forced out of their homes, with no thought given as to how they could be provisioned and sheltered. Many died from hunger, exhaustion and exposure. When Bobrinskii's military superiors ordered him to transfer the deported Jews to Russian governorships further east, the horrified imperial government belatedly became aware of Stavka's actions and began to protest vociferously. Regardless, the deportations continued in April.[143]

At the start of the following month, the strategic balance on the Eastern Front was overturned when the Central Powers launched a successful offensive at Gorlice-Tarnów. In the following chaotic Russian retreat through Galicia, attacks on Jews escalated dramatically. Shloyme Rappaport-Ansky observed how 'fiery rings', the sign of villages and towns burning, were clearly visible at night along the routes taken by withdrawing troops. Jewish quarters were plundered and people beaten, murdered and executed. Again, there were many rapes. Community leaders were taken as hostages to Russia.[144] Jews were the principal victims, but Galicia's Gentile population also now found itself in danger. Jan Słomka, the Polish mayor of the village of Dzików, described how during this period his district 'was stripped cleanest of everything'. Germans and Poles were, after Jews, targeted as hostages. They were taken as insurance that Russophiles would not be punished by the advancing Habsburg army.[145] As Stavka's desperation grew, its orders became more ruthless. First, units were commanded to arrest all men aged between eighteen and fifty. Then, on 12 June, ten days before the fall of Lwów, a new instruction was issued to evacuate the entire population from the front zone. As a concession to the Russian government, Jews were excluded from the measure; instead, they were to be forced towards the enemy. Some Galicians managed to flee when the Russians came. Others bribed corrupt commanders to overlook them. Nonetheless, the number of people moved was staggering. Some 50,000 Jews were shifted pointlessly and painfully around Galicia and between 20,000 and 50,000 were forced into Russia, many ending up in Siberia or Turkestan. About 50,000 Gentiles were also deported or evacuated under wretched conditions in the summer of 1915.[146]

The Tsarist army's attempt to remake Galicia as a Russian land was a disaster. People who had once sympathized with the Tsar's pan-Slavic aims were alienated by his army's brutality and religious intolerance. Astonishingly, however, Habsburg rulers failed to benefit, for on reconquering the Crownland, they themselves promptly set about alienating every section of the population. Emperor Franz Joseph made a grave error in listening to the advice of his General Staff Chief, Conrad von Hötzendorf, and replacing the Polish *Statthalter*, the head of the Crownland's administration, with a soldier, General Hermann von Colard. Conrad blamed the Polish establishment as the cause of what he still believed had been ubiquitous Ruthenian treason in the autumn of 1914. The Poles, he argued, had pushed Ruthenes into the Russian camp in peacetime by repressing Ukrainophile nationalists and promoting Russophiles who had appeared to pose less of a threat to their local political hegemony. While this argument had some merit, the removal of the Crownland from Polish conservatives' control inevitably perturbed and alienated these traditionally loyal elites.[147] That the appointment of a general found much favour with Ruthenes is also unlikely. They were still traumatized by the Habsburg army's autumn bloodletting. Fearful of another encounter with the force, many thousands fled with the retreating Russians. As one refugee told Rappaport-Ansky, they were still afraid of the Magyars: 'Wherever they arrive, they take along the healthy young men and slaughter everyone else!'[148]

The initial joy at liberation felt by much of the rest of the population also did not last long. The Habsburg military administration foisted on Lwów was incompetent and repressive, and the city suffered a severe food supply crisis in the months after it was freed. By the end of 1915, there were complaints that only smuggling from Hungary, to which the authorities turned a blind eye, was keeping the population alive.[149] Worse still, the army launched a witch hunt for collaborators, demonstrating how little it had learned since the autumn. Hundreds were arrested in Lwów alone. In villages in western Galicia, Polish peasants accused of cooperating with the enemy were strung up.[150] The military caused further antagonism with the predatory way that it went about seizing recruits to replace the soldiers frittered away in the war's first campaigns and in fruitless winter offensives in the Carpathians. Dawn house searches and flying checkpoints were used to trap new cannon fodder. More generally, Habsburg troops' cruel and contemptuous treatment of the Galician population, which they clearly regarded as universally Russophile, was alienating. Lwów illustrates the hostility that developed among Galician civilians for the Habsburg military. There, relations descended to the point at which citizens rioted against the garrison. Detested Hungarian soldiers were withdrawn but the Czechs who replaced them were no better. 'Seldom was an administration so hated,' observed one contemporary. Pro-Austrians joked bitterly that the Russians should award the Habsburg army a medal: 'it has understood perfectly how to alienate the Lwów population'.[151]

'UNWELCOME CO-EATERS'

The Russian invasion of Galicia had a profound impact on Austria-Hungary. Not only did the Habsburg and Tsarist armies' brutality undermine the credibility of both imperial regimes among peoples in the Crownland but, as with East Prussia, the effects of invasion reverberated over much greater distances. Unlike in the Reich, however, these effects were wholly negative. The seeds of the Habsburg Empire's collapse were sown by the invasion. Economically, Galicia was, in contrast to the Reich's invaded province, a crucial region. It was indispensable for Austria's food supply, containing about one-third of the western half of the Empire's arable land. The invasion disrupted its agriculture, destroyed infrastructure and depleted cattle. In the Crownland's east, the number of horses and cows dropped by over 40 per cent and that of pigs by a catastrophic 70 per cent.[152] This damage to farming would soon be rued in kitchens across Austria and be a key cause of the shortage and starvation that brought social and political turmoil in later war years. Additionally, Galicia was the Central Powers' main source of petroleum. Its oil industry suffered significant damage: two-thirds of its derricks were burned down, some wells set on fire, and around a million tons of oil were lost through damage to reservoirs and production stoppage. Here, however, the retreating Tsarist army missed a potentially decisive opportunity. Too intent on beating up Jews to recognize the strategic importance of oil fields, it undertook no systematic sabotage and even left 480,000 tons of oil in storage tanks. Galicia went on to supply three-fifths of the Central Powers' wartime petrol and diesel. Germany's notorious U-boat campaigns later in the conflict would not have been possible without it.[153]

The invasion of Galicia not only damaged Austria-Hungary economically but also tore apart its fragile society. As in East Prussia, waves of refugees rippled from the Crownland spreading the shock and trauma to distant parts of the Empire. The humanitarian disaster was even greater than in the Reich because the Russians penetrated much deeper and several major cities had to be evacuated. Over a million people fled their homes and sought shelter in the Austrian heartlands to the west in 1914–15.[154] They imposed an immense financial burden on the Habsburg state. In total, 2,243.1 million crowns were spent on war relief for refugees, which was 2.36 per cent of Austria-Hungary's direct war expenditure.[155] More damaging, however, was the social cost. The Empire had just about coped in peacetime with internal disputes between neighbouring peoples over local power and resources. When hundreds of thousands of Galicians suddenly arrived in the west of the Empire, placing huge strains on infrastructure, they exposed the weakness of a vast multi-ethnic empire at war. The solidarity felt across the

German nation state towards East Prussian refugees was not seen in Austria, where Germans, Czechs, Slovenes and Hungarians regarded the impoverished Jewish, Polish and Ruthenian arrivals as unwelcome foreigners. The large population movements soon inflamed racial strife and, due to the great number of Jews among the refugees, a virulent anti-Semitism.

Refugees' woes had already begun in Galicia, where official hostility added to the hardships of flight. The Habsburg army had not foreseen that masses of people would flee westwards and evinced little sympathy for them. At best, refugees were regarded as an unpatriotic nuisance, selfishly obstructing roads urgently needed for military transport. At worst, gripped like its opponent by spy paranoia, the army treated them as objects of fear and suspicion. Commanders warned hysterically that disguised Tsarist officers were mixed in among the refugees. Some were said to be reconnoitring behind Austrian lines, others to be heading to the Empire's major cities in order to make contact with Russian prisoners of war.[156] More justifiably, refugees were also feared as disease-carriers who might spread a cholera or typhus epidemic into Austria-Hungary's heartlands. The civil bureaucracy, although also initially surprised by the mass exodus, acted ruthlessly. The Austrian Interior Minister, Baron Karl Heinold von Udyński, deliberately attempted in early October to reduce the speed at which the wretched people could escape the Crownland. The number of special evacuation trains was decreased and Galician authorities were ordered to cease issuing free rail passes to refugees.[157]

As well as attempting to slow the flood, Habsburg authorities took measures to direct and control it. An early intention to treat evacuees who left on military orders differently from refugees departing of their own volition proved impracticable, as both groups mixed on trains out of Galicia.[158] Instead, refugees' experiences were shaped by other criteria. Wealth and social standing were extremely important. Those capable of supporting themselves could go where they wished. The impoverished majority, however, were caught up in the workings of a huge bureaucracy. They were, so far as possible, stopped from travelling on ordinary trains and collected for dispatch in special refugee transports. To supervise them, police boarded the transports at three so-called 'embarkation stations', Wadowice, Ujzsolna and Oświęcim; many of the wretched Jewish refugees who passed through the last of these locked in cattle wagons in 1914 and 1915 would return in similar transport three decades later when, under its German name, Auschwitz, it was the most infamous killing centre of the Holocaust. The transports then steamed to 'Inspection Stations', the two largest of which were situated at Prerau and Ungarisch-Hradisch (today Přerov and Uherské Hradiště in the Czech Republic). Here the refugees were disembarked, registered and divided according to ethnicity and religion. They then passed through a minimum two-week quarantine period. The accommodation was poor and overcrowded, the food bad, and compulsory baths in cold water made many of the people ill. These places consequently bred rather than isolated epidemic disease. If the refugees survived this period, they were distributed to the camps or communities earmarked to house them. Ruthenes were sent to Carinthia, while Poles were divided in a rough ratio of three to one between Bohemia and Carniola (a region today in Slovenia). Jewish refugees were transported to Moravia.[159]

Instead of fleeing westwards, some Galician refugees chose to head south, into Hungary. Yet in an early demonstration of the lack of solidarity that was to plague the Habsburg war effort until 1918, the Magyar government took the view that the refugees were a purely Austrian problem and refused to assist. Many were stopped at border posts, although often they simply crossed at other points. Tens of thousands were ejected from Magyar lands. Others stayed but were not made welcome. An appeal sent to the Austrian Ministry of the Interior by some of these impoverished people in November 1914 explained their tragic situation:

> It is already four months since we Galician refugees were thrown out of our homeland, where we left behind all our goods and possessions – [We are] in a land (Hungary) where no one understands us and we don't understand them[.] There is no mercy[,] we are considered to be animals . . . We remain poor and naked, our elder sons are on the field of battle, our small children cry for bread, we are numb with cold and no one cares for us.

Begging for help, the refugees asked the Minister 'either to take pity with bread in order to keep us alive, or to have all of us shot, as starvation is much worse than death'.[160]

The plight of refugees in Austria was, however, often little better. Those sent to barrack camps, around 200,000 people by mid-1915, suffered most. The camps had been built hastily in the first months of war with the intention of both housing the refugees and, no less import-ant, isolating them from the Austrian hinterland's population. They were prisons. Even under Austria's unusually draconian emergency laws, the indefinite incarceration of subjects not accused of any crime was illegal. The Interior Minister acknowledged this but consciously prioritized what he termed 'important state interests' above the law, lamely hoping that the measure might, at some later point, be justified. Perhaps no more could be expected of a government which, since the closure of the Reichsrat in March 1914, had ruled unconstitutionally. Living conditions in the camps were awful. The camp at Chotzen in Bohemia, built to hold 22,000 Polish refugees, offers a typically miser-able example. Each of its thirty-seven barracks of 878 square metres was supposed to hold 530 people. Every family was allocated a small room with wooden walls on three sides and a canvas screen on the fourth. Rooms that backed onto an exterior wall had access to light but were too far from the two stoves in the middle of the barracks to be warm. Rooms on the inside were warm but had no light. A journalist who visited the camp condemned the conditions as 'horrendous'. The air, he wrote, 'is putrid, stinking and damp'. There was hardly any priv-acy: 'The crying of ill children, boys playing on mouth harmonicas and the noise made by several arguing women ... as well as the loud and threatening orders of the barrack commandant fill the air here and unite in a symphony of such discord that any person would seek to exit this terrible place of refugee misery as quickly as possible'. As a result of the unsanitary living conditions and lack of medical care, there were numer-ous epidemics. A third of the Polish refugees incarcerated in Chotzen perished.[161]

Despite early intentions to house all refugees in camps, the flood of people from Galicia and, later, from the border with Italy was so large that no more than a fifth could be accommodated.[162] Most were either billeted on smaller communities across the land or managed to make their own way to one of the Empire's great western cities. Few corners of Austria were left untouched by the waves of refugees. In November 1914 there were 90,000 refugees in Bohemia, 6,000 in Carinthia and 4,000 in Upper Austria. Moravia and Styria had 25,000 each, and Salzburg and Carniola 5,000 each. In spite of belated attempts to bar entry, Vienna was, with 140,000 refugees, a particularly important destination.[163]

These large numbers did not reflect any enthusiasm in the Crownlands to take in Galician refugees. Although Austria's Interior Ministry ruled that refugees might constitute no more than 2 per cent of a community's inhabitants, thus limiting the burden of helping these people, only areas with labour shortages expressed any interest in taking them in.[164] The hostility that Galicians met from bureaucrats and public alike contrasted strikingly with the great public sympathy that East Prussian refugees attracted in Germany. To a large degree, this reflected the more tenuous ties between peoples in a multi-ethnic empire compared with the solid 'imagined community' of a modern nation state. East Prussia, with its past of Teutonic Knights, castles and border skirmishes, occupied a central position in German national mythology and was imagined as an integral part of the Reich. Austrians, by contrast, felt no such affinity to Galicia. The land was a peripheral imperial possession. No romantic history linked its peoples to the rest of Franz Joseph's realm. To his subjects in the more developed west, Galicia's conservatism and poverty were more resonant of barbaric Asia than Austria or Europe.[165]

The lack of a strong bond between the disparate Habsburg lands was accentuated by three further circumstantial factors generating hostility towards refugees. First, the narratives disseminated by governments and newspapers to explain the unfortunate people's plight encouraged fear and distrust. In sharp contrast to Germany, where public praise of East Prussians was fulsome, in Austria Galicians were scapegoated for the Habsburg army's first catastrophic defeats. The stories of Ruthenes' treachery that gripped the front were spread by newspapers throughout the Empire, and the segregation of so many refugees in camps, the like of which was not seen in the Reich, also sent a strong signal that the new arrivals were criminal. Suspicion and fear prevailed. Miecisław Schwestek, one of 3,000 Galician and Bukovinian railway employees evacuated to Tyrol, found the people there hostile even at the end of September 1914. They made no distinction between Poles and Ukrainians and, he complained, were 'suspecting us of treason'.[166]

Second, in the autumn of 1914, just as the refugees arrived en masse in the west, the first food shortages and price inflation were starting to be felt across Austria. The newcomers were naturally blamed and resented, in the words of one Crownland head, as 'unwelcome co-eaters'. By April 1915 the Viennese Police were warning presciently that unless food shortages eased, attacks on refugees by the population were to be expected.[167] Above all in the capital, although also in Bohemia and elsewhere, these economic grievances were closely tied to a third factor: anti-Semitism. Jews made up two-fifths of the refugees in Austria, but they were the vast majority of the 200,000 sheltering in Vienna. Many had gone to the capital in the hope of staying with family or friends. Others had been directed there by authorities who hoped that the city's large Jewish community would help to support its impoverished Galician co-believers. Hostility was immediate: complaints that Vienna was 'overfilled' with refugees were already heard in mid-September, when fewer than 50,000 had arrived in this metropolis of one million souls. A month later, signs were posted around the city, telling the refugees to go home.[168]

Jewish refugees were special targets of hatred in Vienna in part because of their numbers and also because the city had a history of anti-Semitism, formed during earlier waves of Orthodox Jewish immigration. Since the stock market crash of 1873 middle-class Viennese had tended to regard Jews as practitioners of a particularly selfish and ruthless brand of capitalism, and this prejudice dovetailed very neatly with new wartime economic grievances.[169] Accusations that Jewish refugees were spongers and spivs were soon voiced out loud and grew more numerous as supplies of food and household items diminished. Wild rumours were widely believed. One typical story claimed that a single Jew had managed to corner the supply of matches in Budapest, raising prices sky high. In fact, contrary to the implication of such stories that Jewish refugees had immense wealth at their disposal, most lived in conditions of abject penury. Municipal authorities, terrified that the refugees might stay, strove to make life unbearable for these unwelcome guests, denying them work permits and repeatedly urging them to return home at the earliest opportunity. The state support for refugees, at 70 hellers, covered only a third of minimum living costs. To make ends meet, refugee families crowded into rooms together, contributing to a rise in epidemic disease during the first half of 1915. Both the Interior and Finance Ministers recognized the patent inadequacy of the support, yet straitened state finances ruled out any increase to a realistic level. Refugees who complained risked having even this slender allowance cut.[170]

Austrian attitudes towards refugees were, in fairness, not characterized solely by indifference and hostility. There were individuals and private organizations who worked tirelessly to alleviate suffering and intervene with government on behalf of refugees. Foremost among them was the Vienna-based Central Welfare Bureau for Refugees from Galicia and Bukovina. This body, which was funded by the Interior Ministry, paid out support and distributed warm clothing, helped refugees to find accommodation, employment and medical aid, and managed nurseries, schools and even a library. Charities too chipped in to help. Zionist and assimilationist Jewish organizations vied to assist and gain adherents among the refugees.[171] Nonetheless, the assistance had limited impact. The refugees were too numerous and the state's generosity and competence severely limited. Civil society urgently needed to be engaged, yet there was little public understanding of the suffering endured by refugees, a situation not improved by extremely tight Austrian censorship that suppressed all suggestion of state weakness. Reports on the hardship of refugees were banned. The tenuous bond between the Empire's peoples was implicitly acknowledged in the division of the refugees by nationality and faith. Military disaster in Galicia did not bring them together. Instead, the flood of people from periphery to centre greatly exacerbated social tensions and racial antagonism, and had highly negative consequences for the state and its war effort. The head of the Central Welfare Bureau summed up the disappointing result incisively. 'Instead of the expected deepening of the common thought of the Great Austria and Whole Austria idea, the conflicts have become greater,' he observed, 'bitterness grows daily.'[172]

The invasions of Germany and Austria by Russia do not receive much mention in history books today. The victims have been forgotten, their suffering and the wrongs inflicted upon them disregarded. Yet the importance of the Russian attacks cannot be overstated. The Tsarist army's invasions in the east, far more than the contemporaneous German attack and 'atrocities' in the west, offer the closest link between the campaigns of 1914 and the genocidal horrors of the mid-twentieth century. Racial ideology, anti-Semitism and ambitious plans to remould and exclude populations, all hallmarks of later Nazi actions in the same region, characterized these operations. The army's embrace of ethnicity as a marker of political loyalty and its radical readiness forcibly to move whole communities would be seen again under Joseph Stalin on an even greater scale. The loss of life among Habsburg and Hohenzollern subjects in 1914 was still relatively modest. Yet the Russian violence, and the motives behind it, heralded the descent of east-central Europe into the century's 'Bloodlands'.

The invasions had inverse outcomes for Austria-Hungary and Germany. The loss of Galicia was a catastrophe for the Habsburg state. The Russians destroyed infrastructure and dislocated the people. It soon became clear that without the agriculture of this undervalued Crownland, Austrians would suffer terrible hunger. No less disastrous, the flood of refugees fleeing the war zone exposed how tenuous was the solidarity between the peoples of the multi-ethnic Empire. The arrival in the interior of hundreds of thousands of desperate Poles, Ukrainians and above all Jews provoked racial conflict and anti-Semitism. By contrast, the Russian attack on East Prussia actually increased Germany's ability to wage war. Outrage at the violation of national territory and Tsarist atrocities strengthened German solidarity, cemented conviction in the righteousness of the national cause, and acted as a terrible and lasting warning of the penalties of defeat. The victories over the Russians produced new saviour-heroes, Hindenburg and Ludendorff, and lifted public morale. This boost to popular confidence and the strengthening of solidarity would be much needed. With the opening offensives and desperate defensive battles at an end, and the outcome still in the balance, a new, very different type of conflict, a struggle of endurance that they were ill-equipped to win, now confronted the Central Powers.

5

Encirclement

THE LONG WAR

By the turn of 1914–15, it had become clear to leaders and peoples alike that the war had entered a new phase. Major Artur Hausner, still serving on the Eastern Front in mid-December 1914, reflected with surprise on its unexpected duration. When he had left his wife at home at the end of July, nobody, he remembered, was 'expecting so long a separation. The war was after all only against Serbia, and we hoped to make short work of that murderous riff-raff. Yet in the meantime, out of that small war in the Balkans has come a world war of incalculable duration.' In the west, the German gamble on rapid victory had failed, and Erich von Falkenhayn's autumn offensive in Flanders had been unable to renew the advance. From the Swiss border to the Belgian coast, a line 750 kilometres long, troops had dug in and deadlock prevailed. On other fronts, the first months of fighting had also brought no decision. Serbia remained unbeaten to the shame of Habsburg commanders. Yet in the east, Tsarist armies' deep penetration into Galicia had failed to knock Austria-Hungary out of the hostilities, and defeats in the summer and early autumn at the hands of Paul von Hindenburg had thwarted the Russians' best chance of invading the Reich. The Central Powers had also been strengthened by the Ottoman Empire's entry into the war in November 1914. In this context of growing numbers of belligerents, huge armies and military indecision, Hausner was right to gaze with worry into the future. 'It is actually not impossible,' he realized, 'that it will still be very long before we once again have peace.'[1]

The nature of the war had changed too, adversely for the Central Powers. It was Britain's entry that made the difference. With an empire covering one-fifth of the earth's surface, it brought immense financial and industrial resources to the Entente alliance. Britain not only made a long war possible by helping France to survive the loss of its industrial heartland to German occupation, but it provided the coalition with a huge advantage; the Triple Entente had at its disposal three times the output as well as five times the population of Austria-Hungary and Germany, enabling it to absorb even severe military setbacks and making victory highly probable in a long conflict.[2] Moreover, Britain radicalized the war, for it fought differently from the continental belligerents. As the world's premier naval power with control over sea lanes, coaling stations and underwater telegraph cables, it used economic warfare proactively, as a means to strangle its enemies. With Britain's involvement, the conflict ceased to be a purely military affair. Instead, it became a grinding attritional contest that assailed whole communities and turned civilians into targets. Helmuth von Moltke had foreseen and greatly feared this new model of hostilities, even before his appointment as Chief of the Prussian General Staff. The next war, he wrote in 1905, will be 'a long arduous struggle'. No state would capitulate 'until its entire national strength is broken' and the victor too 'utterly exhausted'. This new nightmare conflict would be, he predicted, 'a people's war'.[3]

The Central Powers responded to the novel threat by gradually improvising siege economies. In cooperation with big business, measures were taken to control and direct economic resources towards war efforts. As early as 13 August 1914, at the urging of two industrialists from the electrics firm AEG, the Prussian War Ministry established the War Raw Materials Department (*Kriegsrohstoffabteilung*), which was given the task of registering essential raw materials. In Germany 'War Raw Materials Corporations' (*Kriegsrohstoff-Gesellschaften*) and in Austria so-called 'Centrals' (*Zentralen*) were also founded from the autumn of 1914, each of which was entrusted with the acquisition and efficient allocation of a particular commodity. Run by businessmen, they initially dealt only with metal, wool and chemicals in the Reich, and cotton, wool and metal in Austria, but others were set up during the war so that by its end ninety-one Centrals and nearly two hundred Corporations existed.[4] From the autumn of 1914, the War Ministries in both countries were prompted by shell shortages to seek out new manufacturers for army contracts, and industry gradually switched to war production. Labour was also mobilized. The unemployment crisis precipitated by the outbreak of hostilities, whose potential to cause internal unrest had so worried military commanders, receded from the late autumn of 1914, and by the spring of 1915 both economies were suffering severe manpower shortages.[5] The most significant mark of shifting priorities was the release of skilled workers drafted as soldiers; a quarter of Austria-Hungary's miners had been conscripted in 1914, and some German firms crucial to the war effort, such as Bosch electrics and the Bayer chemicals company, had lost half of their workforce to the army. Henceforth, a new system of exemptions was introduced to take into account industry's manpower needs, as well as those of the military.[6]

The war's turn into an economic struggle against better-financed, more populous opponents both increased the importance of civilians to the Central Powers' war efforts and exposed them to new and worsening hardships. The outbreak of hostilities had already caused severe strains at home. Beyond the splitting of families as men went to war, the closure of businesses and the sudden wave of unemployment, the cost of food and basic necessities had spiralled due to the disruption of supply by military purchases and troop movements, the collapse of imports from countries that were now enemies, and hoarding by civilians. Comfort-eating, one of the ways in which people coped with the upheaval, had also played a part.[7] Even agricultural areas were affected. In rural Thorn, a district in the east of Germany, the cost of a pound of barley groats rose by more than a quarter, that of bacon by a fifth, and potatoes, the staple food, by an eighth between the end of August and December 1914.[8] In urban and industrial regions, price inflation was still greater and the stocks of some basic foodstuffs ran low. Berlin and Vienna were both already suffering from bread shortages by the autumn of 1914, and potatoes became scarce in early 1915.[9] The British naval embargo on food imports into Germany, announced just three weeks after the country entered the war, and, for Austria, the Russian invasion of its Galician agricultural heartland, ensured not only that the Central Powers never recovered but greatly exacerbated these supply difficulties. Civilian livelihoods were now under attack; non-combatants were subjected to ever worsening material hardship, hunger and exhaustion. This suffering was accompanied by prolonged anxiety about loved ones at the front and bereavement, as ever more soldiers were killed. Mourners were already numerous by the end of 1914, for by this point 189,000 Austro-Hungarian and 250,000 German soldiers had fallen.[10]

The German and Austro-Hungarian war efforts rested on the ability of their societies to adapt to and cope with the new conditions. The new mode of conflict was characterized by the ever greater needs of mass armies for weapons and supplies and by efforts to strangle economies of both food and industrial goods. It turned homelands into besieged 'home fronts', essential for supporting soldiers in the theatre of operations both materially and emotionally. This was not a 'people's war' in the old sense, in which civilians rose up under arms, but in a new way, where whole societies contributed less violently yet indispensably to deciding the outcome. Public support and consent were crucial. Pre-war military plans had focused on shifting bodies, on concentrating soldiers at the front; now, however, it was hearts and minds at home that had to be moved. States gave some guidance, but societies proved to an extraordinary extent to be self-mobilizing. Intellectuals, journalists, clergy and politicians, with marginal prompting from governments, interpreted the long war for the public. Community organizations and Churches arranged voluntary actions to aid the war effort. The new conditions and hardships of war sparked a process of adaptation in the way people thought and acted. 'War cultures', formulated in the middle and lower levels of the community and placing a premium on sacrifice and unity, underpinned resilience in these societies under siege.

A WAR OF LOVE

On the home fronts, a mix of calculations and emotions motivated civilians' readiness to strive for the war efforts of their state. Russia's warmongering had promoted outrage and indignation, and there was also a good deal of fearful self-interest; the dangers of invasion had, after all, been chillingly demonstrated by the devastation of East Prussia and Galicia. Hatred of the enemy too was felt, although it was far from universal and, especially in the Reich, proved a double-edged sword. Hatred is often assumed to be at the core of 'war cultures'.[11] Yet strange to say, in Austria-Hungary and Germany, far more central in mobilizing and sustaining people was love.[12] Love dominated the rhetoric of war. Its purest expression was found in the horror of the battlefields. The soldier's readiness to fight and die was understood idealistically as an act of higher love. As one priest told his flock in October 1914: 'Love is the main thing in everything; without it one can do nothing. If our courageous brothers who fight for us in east and west were not fired with a higher love for our Fatherland, out of the war would come murder and flames.'[13] The soldiers were seen to be offering a 'sacrifice', an instantly familiar and highly emotive ideal to these Christian societies. Those who fell were venerated as martyrs, who had 'died the hero's death for the Fatherland on the Field of Honour'. In the war's early years some men, especially those with a middle-class upbringing, expressed their trials and suffering in similar elevated terms.[14]

Home communities reciprocated with acts that were also understood as expressions of love, but of a gentler, healing kind which contemporaries associated with ideals of nurturing womanhood. Germany's Kaiserin set the tone in the war's first days when she appealed to her female subjects to embrace the 'holy work of love' necessary to support husbands, fathers and sons in the army and aid the Fatherland in its 'decisive struggle'.[15] Her call was quickly echoed at lower levels of society. The mayor of the southern German town of Heilbronn, for example, neatly captured a highly gendered image of an entire community at war when he declared that 'behind the army of weapons, the army of love must now array'.[16] In Germany and Austria, voluntary work for the community at war became known as *Liebestätigkeiten* – 'activities of love' – while parcels sent by civilians to their soldiers at the front were christened *Liebesgaben*, literally 'gifts of love'.[17]

The wide appeal of this rhetoric is easy to understand, for the message of love was one that resonated with anybody who had a relative at the front. Families were the basic building blocks of the community at war, and they went to great lengths to support their soldiers. The efforts of one Hamburg woman, Anna Kohnstern, assisted by her four daughters, to care for her son Albert who was serving in the locally raised Infantry Regiment 76, illustrate just how apt was the term 'gifts of love'. Like hundreds of thousands of other families, they scrimped, saved, stood for hours in queues, begged and bartered in order to collect treats or the ingredients to bake a cake that they could send to him on the Western Front. When eggs and butter became too expensive, Anna instead experimented with a recipe for honey cake needing neither. Sometimes the family added newspaper cuttings to Albert's parcels so he would know what was going on at home. Their letters, and the gifts that accompanied them, were material expressions of deep affection, constant worry and intense longing for Albert's safe return home. Any delay in an answer, either because Albert was too tired or busy to write or because there were stoppages in the delivery of field post, caused intense anxiety; one of his sisters warned him to be punctual in replying to 'save us the terrible waiting from one postal delivery to the next'. The fear was even worse at times when the family knew that Albert's regiment was in action. After the unit had taken part in an attack along the Côtes de Meuse in April 1915, his mother's relief on receiving news from him was palpable:

> My dear Albert!
> I have received both of your cards from 26/4 and 30/4. I can hardly tell you how happy we all were when your first card arrived, for I knew that you were in the attack and when the dispatch to the H[amburg] Senate arrived confirming that the Hamburg regiment had greatly distinguished itself, I had no peace until at last your card came. I prayed many times to the dear God, that he might protect you.

After reminding her son that she had sent him chocolate and another cake, Anna signed off with a final wish that 'the dear God continue to watch over you, so that you come back healthy to us. Your mother – who is always with you.'[18]

War culture spread this love beyond the bounds of the biological family to promote solidarity within wider circles. Albert did not receive *Liebesgaben* solely from his family. At Christmas 1914 he was also sent a parcel by the management of the Comerz- und Disconto-Bank in Hamburg, where in peacetime he had worked as a clerk, 'as a sign of our remembrance'.[19] Such gestures were common in the war's first years. Associations too, whether Socialist, religious or hobbyist, sent gifts and newsletters to their members in the army. Parishes, especially in rural areas, were central networks of care and support for soldiers and their families. Priests organized community prayers for troops and meetings in which the letters of local men at the front were read out. They informed their congregations of the latest war news and advertised appeals for money or presents for soldiers and the war wounded. Some intervened with authorities to request home leave for individuals. When men were reported missing, priests helped the families to seek information about their fates. Naturally, clergy were key figures in helping society to cope with mass bereavement.[20] Less personally but influentially, care also took place at the level of the municipality and region. Local identities were strong in both Germany and Austria-Hungary, and towns made strenuous efforts to look after their own. In Hamburg, thirty-four cars carrying gifts departed the city's main marketplace for the front in October 1914; Anna Kohnstern, ever mindful of her son's welfare, wrote to check that Albert had received something. Municipal councillors, keen to express the gratitude of their communities, often accompanied such convoys and personally distributed the presents to their cities' regiments.[21]

The German and Austro-Hungarian states sought both to guide and be a part of these networks of love. Centralized welfare bodies were established. The Habsburg War Ministry was home to a 'War Welfare Office' (*Kriegsfürsorgeamt*), while in Germany a similar 'War Welfare' (*Kriegsfürsorge*) organization assisted in the support of soldiers' families. Semi-official charities also played a major welfare role. The Red Cross and Austria-Hungary's Imperial Widow and Orphan Aid Fund were the most important. Other specific causes won royal patronage. In Germany, for example, a 'War Committee for Warm Underwear' was formed at the Kaiserin's wish and based in the Reichstag.[22] Still, despite the high connections and official oversight, all these organizations were dependent on networks of local activists and the support of regional or municipal elites. German and Austrian officials quickly recognized too that people were more willing to donate for local and regional rather than national or imperial causes: close identification with the wider polity was not so far advanced as in older and more ethnically homogeneous states. Consequently, in Austria, the state tried to extend and exploit the 'double mobilization' that had been so successful at the start of hostilities, and placed the running of its war welfare organizations in nationalists' hands. In Bohemia, German and Czech welfare activists were given control as early as June 1915, and in the following year the policy was extended to nationalist organizations in other parts of the western half of the Empire. This had profound consequences for the Habsburg war effort. For fund-raising, it was undoubtedly a good move. Well-organized national activists were co-opted for the state. The female middle-class volunteers who did much of the work were happier, especially in Bohemia, offering their time and labour for national rather than imperial causes. However, from a longer-term perspective the delegation was problematical. Dividing war welfare between the nationalities was an implicit acknowledgement of the frailty of imperial solidarity. The state was encouraging its people not to support each other but rather to retreat into the protection of their own national groupings.[23]

All these initiatives were immensely successful in mobilizing female populations to support not only their own blood relatives but also local regiments and even the national and imperial efforts. The Chief of Police in Berlin noted with wonder in October 1914 that 'almost all of womanhood is busy with the production of socks, wristlets, vests, waist-warmers and other woollen things for our troops'.[24] The words were echoed a couple of months later and hundreds of kilometres to the south-west, in Austrian Salzburg, where the local War Assistance Bureau observed with pride that 'in all the schools, nunneries, houses, farms and huts of the land, the needs of our warriors are being seen to industriously by the female part of our population'.[25] Figures from Vienna give some indication of the extraordinary extent of the voluntary effort. By March 1917 the city's War Welfare Office had sent 257,972 pairs of gloves, 636,388 woolly hats and 2,708,180 pairs of socks as *Liebesgaben* to the troops. The other more than thirty branches of the office scattered across Austria had undertaken similar work, as had the Red Cross and various women's organizations.[26]

Nonetheless, so great was the debt civilians felt they owed the troops that even this huge material support appeared to some inadequate as recognition of their sacrifices. The German bourgeoisie in particular decided early in hostilities that they must also offer spiritual solidarity. Seriousness was their watchword; frivolity appeared morally reprehensible when men were dying at the front. Theatres consequently took light comedies off the stage and ran classics with martial themes, like Schiller's *Wallenstein's Camp*, or hurriedly written war plays. Some cities banned live music and dancing in pubs and coffee houses.[27] New wartime forms of entertainment were devised. Popular in the first months were 'Patriotic Evenings' in which locally written war poetry was recited and songs fit for the 'holy war' were performed. The cultural, Church and women's associations that organized them donated proceeds to war causes like the Red Cross.[28] 'War lectures' by academics also attracted mass followings in this period: around 10,000 people attended a series run in the city of Münster between September 1914 and February 1915.[29] A high-profile set of lectures in Berlin even made it into print, disseminating university professors' views on Entente war guilt and German virtue to people far beyond the capital. At stake, readers were told, was 'a question of our national existence, of our entire freedom and development'.[30]

Even the earnest and patriotic German middle classes could stomach this dour intellectual diet for only a limited time; by the end of 1914, many of them had decided after all that laughter could be a virtue in coping with war's hardship, and lighter fare began appearing again on theatre stages.[31] For the working classes, who had always been hostile to the middle class's seriousness campaign, and whose entertainments had been its primary targets, this brought only limited relief. 'Trashy' books, 'cinematic smut' and festivities like *Fastnacht*, the spring carnival beloved of south-western Germans, continued to attract disapproval from clergy and middle-class moralists.[32] In Austria, some found ways to resist and subvert bourgeois patriotic earnestness. Drunk punters derived considerable amusement from repeatedly demanding that establishments play the imperial anthem. No one could demur without risking at best insult, or at worst a charge of lese-majesty. In one case that reached the courts, a guest who had risen from his chair four times as the anthem was played in quick succession, had enough on the fifth occasion and refused to stand. He was joyfully cursed by those present and then handed over to the police. Similar cases were still clogging up Habsburg military courts in 1916.[33]

A less exalted but highly revealing aspect of 'war culture' was its commercial manifestations. Firms and manufacturers attuned to the *Zeitgeist* recognized that patriotism sold, used it to advance their interests but thereby also contributed to the mood of unity. Foreign-owned multinationals were gleefully castigated by competitors as corporations 'founded with English money, working with English capital and managed mainly by native Englishmen' whose 'profit flows to England'.[34] In Germany, with official encouragement, they dropped foreign words to emphasize the Germanness of their products. In the heated patriotic mood of 1914 and 1915, 'Keks' were sure to sell better than 'cakes' and an international 'Cigarette' could never be as satisfying as a more German-looking 'Zigarette'.[35] The goods themselves were adapted to meet wartime patriotic and militaristic tastes. Why buy an alarm clock when one could have a 'War Alarm Clock', complete with a mortar battery mounted on top, the faces of Kaisers Wilhelm and Franz Joseph painted on its dial, and a guarantee to make a 'frightful noise'? Harmonicas were manufactured in the shape of famous navy vessels like the *U9* or the *Emden* and found their way into soldiers' gift parcels.[36] Another effective sales strategy was to name products after the hero of the hour, Hindenburg; no fewer than 150 firms marketed a 'Hindenburg Cigar'.[37] The same strategy was tried in different parts of the Habsburg Empire, although the hero naturally varied; in Galicia, for example, it was Józef Piłsudski who appeared on chocolate wrappers.[38] Toy firms excelled above all others in imaginatively adapting and promoting 'war culture'. Steiff, the teddy-bear company, produced cuddly goose-stepping Prussian soldiers for those middle-class parents looking for something more exciting for their offspring than the ubiquitous sailor suits and tin soldiers. A very few lucky children with wealthy and loving fathers received the Steiff prisoner transport set, which came with French prisoners of war, German guards and a hospital. The toy firms, until prevented by material shortages, also proved quick at keeping up to date with wartime conditions. After food rationing was introduced, dolls came with a ration card accessory.[39]

Wartime patriotic entertainments and kitsch were predominantly bourgeois expressions of a war culture with deeper, more universal values. Its core dogma was *Burgfrieden* solidarity, a virtue embraced even by workers: in 1915, despite the return of full employment, only 14,000 German workers downed tools, causing the loss of a mere 42,000 working days.[40] Beyond general compliance, two forms of behaviour defined central European 'war culture'. The first was sparing and saving. This was encouraged by government propaganda. Britain's naval blockade, the public was warned, was intended to cause starvation but could be thwarted if food was treated carefully: 'we have enough corn in the land to feed our population until the next harvest. *Only nothing must be wasted.*' In order to encourage frugality, civilians were admonished to 'think always on our soldiers in the field, who in forward positions would often be happy if they had the bread that you waste'.[41] As a persuasive technique, this was highly effective. It not only played on the consciences of those at home, but also offered them an opportunity to show that they too could make sacrifices, even if these ranked far below the suffering and martyrdom of the soldiers. Anna Kohnstern offered a good illustration of this mentality. Writing to her son Albert to tell him about the price rises and growing food shortages in Hamburg at the beginning of 1915, she employed the rhetoric of steadfast but

1. 'I DID NOT WANT THIS!' Kaiser Wilhelm II denies responsibility for the war. Wilhelm was fond of belligerent rhetoric in peace and bore ultimate responsibility for his government's disastrous decision-making in July 1914, but the world conflagration frightened him and he blamed Russian aggression for forcing his hand.

„ICH HABE ES NICHT GEWOLLT!"

2. A PEOPLE'S WAR. Old Civil Railway Watchmen and young war volunteers in the German city of Göttingen, 5 September 1914. The old men, who had come forward to protect the railway from spies and saboteurs, are equipped with armlets and obsolete rifles. For the war volunteers, bayonets appear to be the only weapons left.

3. ATROCITIES (1). 'Campaign of 1914. Marianne's Punishment'. This German propaganda is supposed to be a humorous comment on the ability of the Kaiser's army to beat the French Republic (personified by a wanton Marianne) but comes uncomfortably close to portraying the sexual rapacity of conquering soldiers.

4. ATROCITIES (2). 'Beginning of August 1914. Deportation of *francs tireurs*' (original caption). The Belgian or French women's defencelessness contrasts strikingly with the powerful build and fixed bayonets of the German soldiers escorting them.

5. ATROCITIES (3). Austro-Hungarian troops hang a civilian in Galicia, 1914. Franz Joseph's army far exceeded its German ally and enemies in murderousness, massacring between 25,000 and 30,000 of its own Ruthenian (Ukrainian) population for largely imaginary acts of treason in 1914–15.

6. ATROCITIES (4). Other Ruthenes suspected of treachery were forcibly deported westwards. Note the soldiers around this group, probably autumn 1914 or early 1915.

7. THE INVASION OF GERMANY (1). The Russian army parades
in the German city of Insterburg, East Prussia, 3 September 1914.
General Rennenkampf, commander of the First Army, and Grand Duke
Nikolai, commander-in-chief of the Tsar's army, are the figures
marked 1 and 2.

8. THE INVASION OF GERMANY (2). Refugees hurry to Allenstein's railway station, summer 1914. Some 800,000 people fled their homes during the first and 350,000 during the second Russian invasions of East Prussia.

9. THE INVASION OF GERMANY (3). German civilians, alongside some military dead, massacred by the Russian army during its bloody raid on the East Prussian town of Memel, March 1915.

10. NAIL FIGURES (1): 'The Iron Hindenburg of Berlin'. Nail figures
were the most striking material expression of Austrian- and Reich-German war
culture, representing and reinforcing communal pride, solidarity and patriotism.
None was more imposing than Berlin's 'Iron Hindenburg'. Constructed out
of Russian alder wood and iron, the figure was 12 metres tall and weighed
33,300 kilograms. Around 20,000 people hammered in nails on the
day of its unveiling, 4 September 1915.

11. NAIL FIGURES (2): 'The Iron Knight' in Hermannstadt (Sibiu). German communities as far east as Transylvania erected nail figures.

12. NAIL FIGURES (3): 'The Column of the Legions' in Cracow. Galician Poles eagerly imitated Germans' nail figures, but used them to further their own nationalist aims. While in German parts of the Habsburg Empire money from nailing went to imperial causes, the funds raised by Cracow's column were given to the families of Piłsudski's national-minded Polish Legions.

13. 'GOD PUNISH ENGLAND'. Hatred as one motivation to fight. Children were the most ardent 'haters'. They were also among the most dedicated members of the war community, helping with the harvest, collecting valuables for war causes and acting as a conduit by which state propaganda could reach their parents.

14. 'GIFTS OF LOVE'. Love, not hate, was the emotion that really underpinned popular support for the war: love for the Fatherland, love for one's local community and, above all, love for the husbands, fathers and sons in the army. Here, German soldiers on their way to the front are receiving sustenance from Red Cross helpers, 1914.

Transit items (s)

Current time: 23/09/2021,
17:04
Item ID: C901729748
Title: Ring of steel :
Germany and Austria-
Hungary at wa
Transit to: Ballyhackamore
Library
Transit to group: Full
access to all libraries,
Belfast Group, FLOATING
Exceptions

Libraries NI

subordinate sacrifice. 'Don't worry about it, for we're still not starved out,' she reassured him. 'We at home will certainly get through it, for we must, after all, stand <u>worthily</u> at your side. You and all of you who are in the field have much more to endure.'[42]

The British 'starvation war' worried the German government sufficiently to prompt it to launch its first organized propaganda campaign. On 24 January 1915, Prussia's Interior Minister announced that several hundred public speakers would be trained to 'enlighten' the people on 'British starvation policy'. Not only teachers and clergy, the traditional community elites on whom the government relied, but also, reflecting the *Burgfrieden*, female and working-class union activists participated in the courses. These people were crucial in giving a credibility to the message that government lacked when communicating directly with the population, especially Socialist labourers.[43] Not only admonishment but also practical advice on saving food and cooking with wartime ingredients was provided. Towns in Germany and Austria-Hungary ran cookery courses and set up nutritional advice bureaus.[44] These efforts were supported by the National Women's Service, whose personnel toured the Reich educating women in home economics. Considerable ingenuity was displayed in inventing new recipes to circumvent fat shortages, although some of the dishes were very strange indeed. The cookery classes held in the town of Thorn in March 1915 taught citizens to make 'Quark Dumplings', 'Artificial Honey' and 'Fake Chocolate Soup'. Ominously, 'Turnip Mash' was also among the culinary innovations. As an aide-memoire and for those unable to attend the courses, war cookbooks were available; no fewer than sixty-nine different editions were published in Germany in 1915.[45] Some of these made good use of recent advances in nutritional science; while experts did not yet understand the importance of vitamins and minerals, the energy requirements of the human body were known. The meal plans that the cookbooks suggested illustrate the modest, repetitive yet calorie-rich diet which middle-class activists and officials thought was still realistic in the first year of war:

The First Day ,
Morning: Gruel with skimmed milk and sugar
Breakfast: For each, one slice of bread with butter or jam
Midday: Barley broth with beef and potatoes

Afternoon: For each, one slice of bread with butter or jam

Evening: Coffee with milk and sugar, bread (for each two pieces) with sausage

(9,665 calories [for four people, so 2,416.25 per adult])

The Second Day

Morning: Milk coffee with sugar, for each two pieces of bread with jam

Breakfast: For each, one slice of bread with butter or jam

Midday: Macaroni with dried fruit

Afternoon: For each, one slice of bread with butter or jam

Evening: Potato salad and smoked herring

(10,227 calories [for four people, so 2,556.75 per adult])

The Third Day – 'Bread Saving Day'

Morning: Porridge with milk and sugar

Breakfast: For each, one slice of bread with butter or jam

Midday: Potatoes with carrots and meat

Afternoon: For each, one slice of bread with jam

Evening: Potatoes boiled in their jackets, herring, butter and onions

(9,920 calories [for four people, so 2,480 per adult])[46]

The diet may not have looked particularly appetising, the advice on chewing longer and keeping heated food in insulated containers was sensible but mundane, yet the need to preserve food was framed as a sacred duty. Ten 'War Commandments' were formulated for German housewives, including such wisdom as 'eat nothing more than necessary', 'regard bread as holy', 'eat a lot of vegetables and fruit' and 'collect all kitchen waste unsuitable for human consumption as cattle fodder'. With these means, German women were armed for the 'rescue of our Fatherland'.[47]

Collecting was the second behaviour at the heart of war culture. The gathering of food and warm clothing by civilians to send to troops was just one, albeit important, part of a much larger sphere of activity. The core values of 'unity' and 'sacrifice' meant also helping the war's victims on the home front such as refugees or those whose economic livelihood had been destroyed by war. Collecting could be combined with other motifs of war culture in order to maximize its attraction. The most dramatic campaign to help the home front's war victims was the 'I Gave Gold for Iron' appeal, launched in both Austria and Germany in 1914. The idea, which took its inspiration from a similar collection in the

1813 German Wars of Liberation, was that people should donate gold jewellery for the good of the war community, and in exchange receive a clasp or ring of iron. The campaign captured the public imagination. Already by September 1914, 90,000 Austrians had surrendered precious metal, often their wedding rings.[48] In Germany too it was popular. The citizens of Frankfurt am Main alone donated silver, gold and platinum to the value of 303,403 marks in 1914. The success of the appeal was undoubtedly thanks in large part to the material proof of patriotism given to those who sacrificed. For many people, it was the act of giving (and being seen to give) that mattered; the cause itself was less important. Newspapers noted the 'frequent uncertainty' encountered among the public about what cause donations for the 'Gold for Iron' campaign actually supported. In Frankfurt, just under a tenth of the proceeds were used to cover the cost of the iron jewellery, 10,000 marks were given to the 'Committee for Supporting Needy Artists', around a third went to supplement the income of families already in receipt of the government's 'Family Help', a war entitlement for soldiers' dependants, and the remainder went to those who were in straitened circumstances and ineligible for official aid.[49]

Children were the most numerous, enthusiastic and successful collectors. While a few hundred thousand women engaged in voluntary war activity, between six and seven million German schoolchildren were mobilized to help with the various appeals. The readiness of Austrian youths to do war work was no less impressive: those volunteering 'substantially exceeded demand', observed one official in Carinthia.[50] The earliest 'collecting' to which children were put was agricultural: already in 1914, school pupils were taken from class to bring in the harvest. Soon they were sent on scavenging trips to the countryside to gather kindling, mushrooms, berries, and leaves for fruit tea. Later, as the blockade tightened, they collected kitchen waste, paper, metals, bottles and even human hair from cities for recycling for the war effort. The well-known ability of nagging offspring to squeeze money from their elders was also put to the use of the warring states. From the late autumn of 1914, German pupils were set to work bolstering the Reichsbank's bullion reserves by persuading people to exchange 10- and 20-mark gold coins for paper notes.[51] Austrian schools followed the example. The tactic won considerable praise, for over 150 million marks in specie were collected by schools across Germany alone in 1915. 'Children are the best agitators for gold purchase,' observed one trade official in the east of the country in 1918. They 'won't leave their parents in peace, and in cases where every advertisement and all publicity work is useless, children achieve what appears to be the impossible'.[52]

The most crucial role that children performed was as collectors and agitators for the public War Loans on which both Germany and Austria-Hungary relied to fund much of their war efforts. This work quickly became highly organized to ensure that even the happily childless could not rest easy. Each school was allocated a collecting area. The children were marshalled, equipped with collection books and sent systematically around the block, until all households had been visited. Pupils' enthusiasm for the task rested not solely on love of the Fatherland or Emperor. Anna Kohnstern's daughter Julia – known in the family as 'Lulu' – informed her soldier brother Albert that each time she persuaded somebody to donate a gold item she received ten pfennigs from her school. Her older siblings were granted a day's holiday for every fifty marks that they collected. Teachers promoted competition between classes, again with the promise of reward. The most diligent and successful collectors, as well as those from the wealthiest families, received medals, plaques, and even had their names published in the local press. So important was the role of children in attracting public subscriptions to the Third War Loan in the autumn of 1915 that the Kaiser himself decreed a school holiday in thanks.[53]

Even if children's strivings were far from wholly altruistic, boys and girls were most committed to the war effort. Admonitions to be 'soldiers of the home front' and help shorten the conflict resonated especially with those who had older brothers and fathers in combat. Girls obsessively knitted socks, gloves and scarves for *Liebesgaben* packets, not only in knitting classes but even in lunch breaks and at home. Hermine Gerstl, a twelve-year-old living in Lower Austria in 1915, recalled how 'we girls were so enthusiastic about knitting for the poor soldiers that on school-free days we did without any games – each wanted to produce as much as possible'.[54] Collecting, knitting and packing *Liebesgaben* could all help cope with anxiety about family members in the army. These activities also permitted children to feel part of a war community defining itself through love, unity and sacrifice.[55] They themselves did much to strengthen that community. Younger children still in school acted as conduits through which official propaganda could reach unsuspecting parents. They were also employed very effectively to reinforce the connection between home and front. Their 'gifts of love' to soldiers were not dispatched anonymously; enclosed was also a postcard or letter from the boy or girl who had made the knitwear or packed the present. Particular emphasis was placed on ensuring that soldiers with no families of their own would receive such parcels.[56] In this way, the nation or Empire itself became a substitute family for these men. A child's letter could have a powerful emotional impact at the front; it was a moving reminder to combatants of the people they were defending, reinforcing their willingness to endure the risk and hardship of active service. Many children, to their pride and delight, received letters of gratitude, from which a regular correspondence sometimes developed. This encouraged the children further to invest emotionally in events on the battlefield. They worried for 'their' soldiers. Thirteen-year-old Piete Kuhr, for example, was 'overcome with fear' when she learned that 'my gift parcel soldier Emil', as she called him, had been stabbed in the chest at the front.[57]

The most dramatic and symbolic expression of war culture, revealing all its tropes and virtues, were the 'nail figures' erected across central Europe in 1915–16. These were statues or shields, usually carved in soft lime wood and set up in public places. People paid to hammer nails into them. The proceeds from the nails' sale, as well as from spin-off merchandise like postcards and albums, went to support the families of fallen soldiers, and the figures gradually became coated in an iron 'armour', making them symbols of and shrines to the unity, sacrifice and steadfastness of communities. The trend began in Vienna, inspired by local tradition: the imperial capital was home to the medieval 'stave of iron' (*Stock im Eisen*), a tree trunk studded with centuries-old nails which, legend had it, itinerant craftsmen had hammered in to banish the devil. In 1915, Vienna's Central Committee for the 'Widow and Orphan Aid Fund' decided to mobilize the custom for the fight against new evils. On 6 March, at a ceremony attended by members of the imperial house as well as the Austrian Minister President, Count Stürgkh, his entire cabinet, Vienna's mayor, and the German and Ottoman ambassadors, it unveiled the war's first nail figure: the 'Warrior in Iron' (*Wehrmann in Eisen*). A knight in armour, standing a man and a half tall, it gripped a drawn sword and gazed resolutely ahead. The mayor opened the nailing ceremony with a speech stressing that from the unity of the people came the will for victory. The first nail, a golden one, was then hammered in, in the name of Emperor Franz Joseph; the second and third were knocked in by the German and Ottoman ambassadors representing their monarchs. When the worthies had finished, the figure was opened to the capital's inhabitants. By the war's end, they had coated it with half a million nails.[58]

The 'Warrior in Iron' aroused widespread admiration and inspired imitation by German communities across the Habsburg Empire, as far east as Sibiu, Transylvania. Reich Germans also enthusiastically adopted the idea. They took the form to its extreme in their capital, where a 12-metre tall 'Iron Hindenburg' was erected directly under the *Siegessäule*, Berlin's monument to the victory of 1870–71, and opened on 4 September 1915. Art critics castigated the huge statue as 'distasteful' and 'barbaric', but it proved a hit with the public. On the first day alone, 20,000 people climbed the gantry surrounding it to hammer in nails. The figure was too large, even for a city as populous as Berlin, to be completely covered – like other German endeavours, ambition proved greater than available reserves of material or, in this case, resolution – but the response was nonetheless impressive; ultimately, around thirty tons of nails were bashed into the sculpture, more than doubling its weight.[59] Moreover, it was only the largest of more than 700 nail figures set up across the Reich, which together raised over 10 million marks for war widows and their children. These were powerful reflections of local communities' importance to and investment in the national war effort. While a central committee within the 'National Foundation for the Surviving Dependants of Fallen Soldiers' advertised and offered advice on the erection of nail figures, the decision on whether to commission one and the form that it should take belonged to communal authorities. Patriotic symbols such as the Iron Cross were popular, as were knights, soldiers and German mythological heroes. Some cities, like Dresden and Zwickau, followed Berlin in dedicating their nail figures to the new saviour Hindenburg. Very often, however, the imagery chosen was resonant of an explicitly local pride and identity. Düsseldorf, seat of the Grand Duke of Berg, was inspired by the Duchy's heraldic arms to erect a wooden lion. Altona's 'Isern Hinnerk' commemorated the warrior count who in the fourteenth century had ruled the surrounding region of Holstein. In the industrial Ruhr region, figures frequently reflected the connection of towns with the coal or metal industries. Recklinghausen boasted a

'Miner's Column', Essen, Hagen and Bochum all put up 'Iron Black-smiths', and several other towns in the area chose 'Iron Swords'.[60] Local craftsmen were generally commissioned to design the figures and, against the central committee's wishes, the revenues from the nailing were not pooled nationally but went to communities' own bereaved families.[61]

The rituals choreographed around the nail figures celebrated and reinforced a conservative vision of a united but hierarchical society. City mayors and senior provincial officials usually hosted unveiling ceremonies, while local dignitaries, and in larger cities regional royalty, were always first with the hammer. The nails were not all alike: the hoi polloi generally had the satisfaction of armouring the figure with an iron nail for as little as 50 pfennigs or one mark. Wealthier citizens showed off their status and patriotism by buying silver-coloured nails for two or five marks. For elites, the nails were golden and cost 50 or 100 marks. The ceremonies affirmed communities' ties both with the nation and the front: Wiesbaden's mayor, for example, addressed the audience at the opening of his city's 4.2-metre-high 'Iron Siegfried' on 26 September 1915 as 'German women and men!' 'Every nail in the armour of Siegfried,' he told the gathered citizens, 'is . . . a greeting to the lonely graves of our heroes in the land of the enemy and a means of assuaging the distress of their wives, their fathers and mothers.'[62] At the centre of the ceremonies, however, remained the local community itself. Craft and professional associations, religious groups, women's organizations and hobbyists expressed their unity and identification with municipality and nation by taking part or even holding their own ceremonies.[63]

Youth were also mobilized to pay homage at these altars of communal solidarity. In Wiesbaden, a city of 109,000 people, 12,000 children were marched down to Siegfried in October 1915, where they listened to the municipal school inspector hold forth on the German virtues of truth and loyalty and the bond between the people and the Kaiser. Not only was a golden nail bought on behalf of all the children, but donations ensured that each child, however poor, had the chance to bang his or her own iron nail into the statue.[64] Of course, these minors had no choice but to attend. The crowds that thronged around these statues in the weeks and months after their unveiling, and the large sums of money that were collected testify, however, that they did satisfy a psychological need. Nailing allowed civilians partially to repay the debt that many felt was owed to the front by demonstrating love for the relatives of fallen soldiers. It enabled them to feel they could contribute, at least symbolically, to 'steeling' their society against shared adversity. The spread of metal 'armour' across the wooden surfaces of the statues also provided reassuring evidence of a wider unity and readiness to sacrifice, and could be understood as a metaphor for communal resilience. There is every reason to conclude that the nail figures were highly successful in strengthening popular readiness to endure, in raising community solidarity and in further binding local societies to the German national war effort.[65]

The popularity of nail figures was not confined to the German-speaking world. Austrian Poles also adopted the new custom enthusiastically. Some seventy-seven towns in Galicia set up a nail monument, although, as these communities were on average smaller and poorer than those in Germany, modest shields were generally preferred over grandiose sculptures. There were some exceptions, however. The first and most important of the Polish 'nail figures' was Cracow's 5.5-metre-high 'Column of the Legions' (*Kolumna Legionów*), unveiled on 16 August 1915. This bore much in common with Vienna's nail figure and with those in Germany. It expressed a similar municipal pride and inclusivity: its plinth displayed the arms of Cracow, and those of the important districts of Podgórze and Kleparz and the city's Jewish quarter Kazimierz. Like its German cousins, the column stood at the heart of the community. It was erected on Cracow's main marketplace, opposite the famous landmark of St Mary's Church (the *Kościół Mariacki*). The city authorities publicly supported the initiative. They did not lead the unveiling ceremony, but the vice-mayor attended along with much of the city council and many officials. At a second major celebration on 29 November, the mayor himself, Dr Juliusz Leo, hammered two nails into the column, one worth 50 crowns as a personal donation and another on the city's behalf with a value of 1,000 crowns. The educational, professional and social networks and institutions that belonged to the municipality also participated: representatives of Cracow's university, societies, financial institutions, women's associations, guilds and veterans of the 1863 uprising, all bearing their standards, were at the Mass that opened the festivities and gave generously. Thousands of private citizens were also present. So many wanted to attend the service before the nailing that St Mary's became filled to capacity, and crowds were left standing outside in the marketplace.[66]

The meaning of Cracow's nail celebrations in 1915 was, however, radically different to that of the German ceremonies. Rituals in the Reich stressed the unity of local communities behind their nation state's armed struggle. Galicia's nail figures, in contrast, embodied the disconnect between local and imperial war efforts in Austria. The Polish Supreme National Committee, the political union that stood behind the Polish Legions, was responsible for erecting Cracow's column and the smaller shields favoured by other towns in the Crownland. Surmounted by a 90-centimetre-high silver Polish eagle, the 'Column of the Legions' was an explicitly national symbol; it proclaimed Cracow's belonging to a Polish nation, not the Habsburg Empire. The unveiling ceremony successfully reinforced the column's national message, despite a police ban on speeches. The guest list alone was telling: Polish towns in Galicia, Austrian Silesia and Congress Poland, newly freed from Russian rule, were all invited to send representatives. The date of the unveiling was the first anniversary of the Supreme National Committee's foundation and the column, and later the shields, were all dedicated to the Polish Legions. The communities that hosted them had far more men serving in the Habsburg Common Army than in the Legions; Cracow itself was a garrison city, home to the Austro-Hungarian I Corps, in which many of its citizens fought.[67] Regardless, the money raised from the nailings was, unlike that collected by Vienna's *Wehrmann*, intended not for the bereaved relatives of Habsburg soldiers killed in action but to help support the families of fallen Polish Legionnaires. This donation campaign was not anti-dynasty – the majority of functionaries in the Supreme National Committee would have been quite content with a united Poland in a Trialist Empire – but its indifference to the Austro-Hungarian state was striking and ominous. Elected municipal officials who enthusiastically supported the initiative across the Crownland were prioritizing their national identity over imperial allegiances. Clearly, the appeal to a specifically and exclusively Polish solidarity also resonated with much of western Galicia's population. Newspapers observed with pride that peasants came with their families to participate in the nailings. Smaller communities, although still recovering from invasion, usually raised thousands of crowns through their shields. The column in Cracow attracted the impressive sum of 115,047 crowns, 53 hellers.[68]

The 'war cultures' that developed in central Europe in the first year of hostilities were a source of great strength to its peoples. All could identify with a creed based on love. The cultures established a hierarchy of sacrifice, at the apex of which stood soldiers, yet they were also highly inclusive, encouraging women and children to collect, save and strive for victory. They valued unity and patriotism. As at mobilization in the summer of 1914, local community leaders played a key role. In lands in which municipal and regional identities were far stronger than any central allegiance, these elites rallied local loyalties and channelled them in the service of wider state war efforts. This worked well in the young German nation state. It was less successful in Austria-Hungary, where the dangers of relying on these often nationalist figures were apparent already in 1915. Nonetheless, there was no alternative. Love within families, broadened to encompass local communities, formed the necessary basis for a wider solidarity and armoured the state and its people for a long war.

GERMANY VERSUS BRITAIN

Central European war culture had two faces. While internally it preached love, fear and hatred contorted its face to the outside world. Social scientists interested in propaganda and wartime mobilization have emphasized since the First World War the importance of cultivating animosity: 'There must be no ambiguity about whom the public is to hate.'[69] Yet in Germany and Austria-Hungary, hatred proved a highly problematical emotion. At first, it may have contributed to promoting wartime solidarity in the face of threat. However, in both states, it ultimately turned inwards to consume the very national or imperial communities that it was supposed to mobilize. This process played out differently in each of the Central Powers. Germans focused their hatred on one enemy. They began the conflict directing their anger at Russia. Most blamed the Tsar for turning the Balkan dispute into a European conflagration and for mobilizing early, and the Russian army's invasion of East Prussia and its atrocities there had shocked the country at large, summoned powerful feelings of solidarity, unified the people, and cemented the *Burgfrieden*. However, even as Hindenburg cleared East Prussian territory of Russian invaders for the first time, the attention of the German public had begun to shift towards an even more dangerous adversary. Already by the middle of September, a majority of opinion in the Reich's newspaper columns had begun to consider 'England' as 'our most brutal opponent'.[70]

The German government, though it played a part in promoting this shift, was not solely responsible. Indeed, its ability and ambition to direct and manipulate public discourse were decidedly limited in 1914. The leadership certainly recognized at the outbreak of war the importance of public opinion, but the first priority was on maintaining inner peace, not provoking hatred. Moltke set the tone when he acknowledged as early as 13 August 1914 the essential role played by the 'united attitude of the parties and the up to now unanimous stance of the press in favour of the war' in creating 'the spirit of devotion and unity for Germany's great mission'. He warned that 'come what may, this must continue for the whole duration of the war'.[71] A press service was established under Major Walter Nicolai, Moltke's Chief of Intelligence, and daily briefings with Berlin newspaper representatives began immediately, eventually developing into twice- or thrice-weekly press conferences, attended as needed by officials from civilian ministries. The formulation of a coordinated press strategy was hindered by two factors, however. First, at this early stage of the war, the primary concern was not to guide public opinion but merely to prevent the publication of any information that could harm military interests or the *Burgfrieden*. Already on 31 July 1914, the day on which the State of Siege was announced, the Chancellor issued a list of twenty-six topics, all related to military or naval mobilization and technical matters, banned from mention in print. It was also telling that the army, an institution with limited experience of managing journalists, was given responsibility for censorship. Second, the fragmented nature of Wilhelmine government was a major obstacle to any unified press strategy. The Foreign Office, Naval Ministry and Postal Ministry all pursued separate policies through their own press departments, while the Chancellor, the most important civilian official, possessed no press representative until August 1917. Censorship was divided between the military's twenty-four regional Deputy Commands. A Supreme Censorship Office tasked with coordination began working in February 1915. However, not until the following October was a dedicated War Press Office, responsible for coordinating censorship, supplying the press with controlled information, and facilitating cooperation between the civilian and military leadership, set up within Nicolai's department. Moreover, only in February 1918 were the influential posts of Director of the Press Department of the Foreign Office and Press Chief with the Chancellor finally merged into a 'United Press Department of the Reich Government'.[72]

The vehemence and rapidity of the public's shift of focus to Britain as their main enemy was thus not the work of a skilful state propaganda apparatus, for such machinery did not exist in 1914. Moreover, the shift was surprising for another reason: in peacetime, despite the countries' commercial rivalry and the antagonism caused by the pre-war naval race, educated Germans had, as a rule, respected and often rather liked the British. There was much that they shared. At the top of the social hierarchy, the monarchs may have hated each other, but they were still family, and many of Germany's highest government officials, including Chancellor Bethmann Hollweg, had children who had studied at Oxford. Britain also provided inspiration to a remarkably wide and diverse range of German society. At one end of the Wilhelmine political spectrum, imperialists envied her navy and colonies, while at the other, Left Liberals admired her parliamentary system and Social Democrats praised the recognition that trade unions were accorded in Britain, unlike in Germany. Culturally, the Germans felt vastly superior in their nation's musical achievements, and confident too of their own literary heritage. Yet outside the United Kingdom, it was the Reich that was home to Shakespeare's most adoring fan base. The two nations also shared some recent glorious history; it was, after all, only a century earlier that Marshal Blücher's Prussians had saved the British at Waterloo, and the powers had together rescued Europe from Napoleon's French tyranny.[73]

The vitriol aimed at Britain was thus at first motivated mostly not by any ingrained hatred, but rather by a deeply felt sense of hurt and betrayal. Particularly among German scholars, important shapers of public opinion in 1914, there was intense disappointment that 'England' had, as the internationally respected philosophers Ernst Haeckel and Rudolf Eucken put it, declared itself for a 'Slavic half-Asiatic power against German culture', and shock that it had chosen to fight 'not only on the side of barbarism, but also of moral wrong'.[74] Further aggrieved by accusations, especially those made by their peers across the Channel, of German aggression and brutality in Belgium, intellectuals of all political colours mobilized themselves in defence of the Reich. Academics organized appeals denying the charges, including one in the name of 'the Universities of the German Reich' and another, the 'Declaration of the German University Teachers of the German Reich', which was signed by over three thousand lecturers.[75] The most famous, the 'Appeal to the Civilized World!' of 4 October, was drawn up at the suggestion of the Reich's Navy Office, one of the more publicity-savvy government ministries, but was written by two celebrated authors and attracted the support of ninety-three top scholars, artists and writers. Although clumsy and politically naive, it expressed the intellectuals' strong emotions. Indignantly decrying the charges of barbarism levelled at Germany, the signatories insisted that the real atrocities had been committed in East Prussia, where 'the earth is drenched with the blood of women and children slaughtered by the Russian hordes'. 'Believe us!' exhorted the men of letters. 'Believe that we shall fight this fight to the bitter end as a civilized people.'[76]

German intellectuals were overwhelmingly united in attributing Britain's enmity to unscrupulous economic self-interest. Germany's rise on the world market, it was argued, was perceived by the mercantile kingdom as a threat to its own domination of global trade. Britain's diplomacy over the past decade was interpreted as a return to traditional 'balance of power' politics; just as Spain and France had found themselves facing hostile coalitions organized by the British when they strove in past centuries for continental hegemony, so now Germany, as Europe's strongest and most dynamic land power, was the strangled victim of British-inspired 'encirclement'.[77] The suspicion that British leaders had welcomed the trouble in the Balkans as an opportunity to eliminate their dangerous competitor grew after the release of Anglo-German official correspondence in August, which showed that on the brink of war the Kaiser's government had been ready to refrain from fighting in the west if Britain stayed out and guaranteed France's neutrality. Further evidence of British hypocrisy and ill-will against the Reich was found in reports of pre-war Anglo-Russian naval discussions; and, in October, the publication of captured, slightly doctored documents suggesting that Anglo-Belgian talks for action against the Reich in the event of a Franco-German conflict had taken place as early as 1906.[78] Some intellectuals saw Britain's cynicism and duplicity not merely as a matter of recent policy but deeply rooted in its people's utilitarian and materialist character. Most notoriously and, even in Germany, controversially, the economist Werner Sombart framed the conflict as a struggle between two peoples with fundamentally opposed ideologies: money-grabbing mercantilist Anglo-Saxon 'traders' faced idealistic and altruistic German 'heroes' in a 'war of belief'.[79]

The shift in the attention of the German public from Russia to Britain was also a symptom of fear; the imperial superpower was, quite simply, by far the most frightening of the Reich's opponents. The threat that Britain posed was regarded as qualitatively different and far more difficult to overcome than the military challenge from Germany's continental neighbours. Anxious newspaper columnists, as well as intellectuals, saw the British not as fighters, but rather master puppeteers able to manipulate the European peoples for a quick profit. As the conservative *Kölnische Zeitung* argued on 30 October, not only was it 'England' that had 'from sheer selfishness stirred up the peoples of the continent into this terrible war', but Germans, French and Russians had been duped into 'tearing each other to pieces so that England can rob and steal undisturbed'.[80] Moreover, Britons were soon seen to be using their vast empire and international standing to turn the rest of the world against Germany. When Japan declared war on the Reich on 23 August, Britain was widely blamed, and the fall of the Reich's naval base at Tsingtao in China to Japanese forces at the beginning of November sparked indignation, particularly on the political right. One outraged official publicly suggested that, in protest, newspapers should for a fortnight substitute the words 'Englishman' or 'Japanese' for 'murderer' and 'murderous bandit' in their columns.[81] While the general public did not participate in such hysteria, events in this hemisphere did not pass unnoticed. The exploits of the German commerce raider, the *Emden*, which had been stationed at Tsingtao, were followed with enthusiasm. The story of the plucky cruiser, which sank one Russian and one French warship and sixteen British steamers before being hunted down by vastly superior Entente forces, resonated with a public that saw itself as the underdog in the struggle with the global hegemon.[82]

The German public's particular animus against Britain was ensured by the Royal Navy's long-range, ever-tightening and, by contemporary international law, illegal trade blockade. On its entry into the war, Britain restricted access to the North Sea, instituting checks on shipping passing through the English Channel and posting a force, the X Cruiser Squadron, to patrol between the Shetland islands and Norway. German maritime trade was confined to the Baltic. On 20 August 1914 the

British additionally warned that they would stop not only vessels destined for German ports but also any neutral ship carrying so-called 'conditional contraband', including food, which was suspected of being ultimately intended for the Reich. This was highly threatening to Germany, for in peacetime its population had been reliant on imports for 19 per cent of the calories it consumed. The country had an even greater need for external sources of protein and fats, 27 per cent and 42 per cent of which respectively came from abroad.[83] Two and a half months later, on 5 November, an even more radical step was taken when the British Admiralty attempted to force all commerce through the Straits of Dover, where it could easily be controlled, by declaring the entire North Sea a war zone. When the Germans foolishly attempted to respond in February 1915 by announcing that their U-boats would sink shipping in the seas around the British Isles, they simply antagonized neutrals and gave their enemy a justification for further tightening the blockade. On 11 March all German goods, regardless of whether or not they were classed as contraband and including exports that had previously been exempt, became liable for seizure.[84]

The British blockade was legally dubious for two reasons. First, the 1856 Declaration of Paris, still in force in 1914, had permitted blockades but only with the proviso that 'to be binding, [they] must be effective'. This was generally understood to mean that they should take the form of a cordon of ships off an enemy port or coast; distant blockades like that of the British during the war, which attempted to close an entire sea, were inadmissible. Second, more recent rules on the types of item that could be confiscated, and the circumstances in which this was allowed, were also violated. The 1909 London Declaration, the result of negotiations called by the British, had divided goods into three categories: unambiguously militarily useful 'absolute contraband', mixed-purpose 'conditional contraband', including food, and a free list. Britain had long held to a doctrine of continuous voyage, which had insisted on the right of belligerents to stop ships carrying goods to a neutral port when those goods were then to be re-exported to the enemy, but under the London agreement this was abandoned for 'conditional contraband'. The Royal Navy was never bound by these 1909 rules, as Britain's Parliament had refused to ratify the Declaration. Still, the decision, made less than three weeks into the war, to reinstate the doctrine of continuous voyage looked hypocritical and placed Britain outside the pre-war moral consensus on how naval warfare should be conducted. The Germans can, in this light, be forgiven a certain amount of scepticism towards their enemy's much-vaunted concern for international law.[85]

The blockade did more than any other action to radicalize the conflict. While the act of restricting access to the entire North Sea, and therefore to both enemy and neutral ports across northern Europe, was drastic, most damaging was the blockade's erosion of the distinction between combatants and non-combatants. At first, the British did attempt to limit such erosion. The London Declaration's prescriptions about handling goods differently, depending on their military or civil use, were largely followed. Nonetheless, already on 26 August 1914, the Royal Navy was ordered to halt all ships taking food to Rotterdam, continental Europe's premier port, on the assumption that unless guaranteed by the Dutch government, their cargo was destined for Germany. When unrestricted blockade was imposed in March 1915, distinctions of 'absolute' and 'conditional contraband' were abandoned. New mechanisms for tightening the stranglehold on German soldiers and civilians alike were also introduced. The continental neutrals were pressured to accept import quotas sufficient for their own needs but not for re-export to the Central Powers. Later, they were blackmailed into selling part of their own surplus produce to the Entente at prices lower than those offered by starving Germany. The British also exploited their control of the world's coaling stations to deny fuel to ships trading with the Reich. In 1916 a new 'navicert' system streamlined cargo inspection and blacklists of firms regarded as agents of the Central Powers were drawn up. Those on the lists were unable to do business with British companies and their ships were subject to immediate detention.[86]

The German reaction to these measures was apoplectic. The British were denounced for waging a 'starvation war'. A hugely influential study undertaken by a group of scientists headed by the nutrition expert Professor Paul Eltzbacher, and published at the beginning of 1915 under the eye-catching title *The German People's Food Supply and the English Starvation Plan*, portrayed in dire terms the threat faced by Germany's population. The enemy's intention, readers were told, was to 'seal [the Reich] hermetically from the rest of the world and ... vanquish our people through hunger'. The eminent professor did not mince his words: 'The concentration camps of the Boer War were final evidence that the English gentleman does not disdain a fight against women and children.

Now he wants to use the tested means of fighting in the absolute greatest measure and ideally make of all Germany a single concentration camp.'[87] Even in a world before 'concentration camp' had acquired its association with Nazi genocide, this was explosive stuff. Fourteen years earlier, 28,000 Boer women and children had perished from malnutrition, neglect and epidemics in British South African camps. The British army's strategy of suppressing guerrillas by burning their farms and herding their families into holding centres, where callousness and administrative incompetence rather than genocidal intentions caused mass death, had deeply shocked continental Europe. In Germany, the press had condemned the brutality, thousands had attended protest meetings, and flyers publicizing 'the hell' in South Africa had circulated. Eltzbacher's suggestion that the Reich could now suffer similarly was terrifying.[88]

This was all the more the case because the alarming rise in the cost of food and the disappearance of basic items from shops in big cities gave credibility to the propaganda. In actuality, the blockade was at first ineffective in stopping the import of goods into Germany. The British Foreign Office was anxious not to alienate neutrals with measures too draconian, the navy found it difficult to ascertain the final destination of ships' cargos, and while neutral governments did issue guarantees that goods were solely for domestic consumption, re-export to Germany was often unpreventable. Denmark's import figures give some indication of the extent to which this was practised: the country's imports, worth 178 million Danish kroner in the last year of peace, had rocketed to 487 million by the end of 1915.[89] In fact, the Reich's initial food supply difficulties owed more to the war's outbreak and mobilization, the absence of any peacetime stockpiling and official mismanagement. The Interior Ministry had received warnings about Germany's inadequate agricultural base and the risk of a naval blockade, but had dismissed them as scaremongering. Failing to recognize the country's heavy reliance on imported fertilizers, it had argued complacently that cereal yields could easily be increased in wartime. Fodder requirements had been overlooked and the Ministry had little understanding that as domestic stocks diminished and foreign imports declined, humans and animals would be competing for nutrition.[90]

After war broke out, the interventions of German authorities into the market were reluctant, halting, and reflected a total lack of understanding about the complexity of the domestic economy. At first, the Deputy Generals commanding the Reich's twenty-four army corps districts, or the civilian officials under them, imposed price controls locally. The regional price variations that resulted prompted farmers to shift their produce to wherever they were permitted to charge most, leading to dearth elsewhere. In October 1914 general price controls were therefore introduced to overcome this, first on bread cereals, but later that year on potatoes, sugar and cattle feed, and, in 1915, on butter, fish, milk, pork, fruit and vegetables. However, the gradual manner in which these controls were implemented inadvertently added perverse incentives to agricultural production, worsening the shortages. Farmers used grain urgently needed for bread to feed their livestock, as selling it to mills or wholesalers at fixed prices was less profitable than dealing in pork, on which for most of 1915 there was no maximum price enforced. The notorious *Schweinemord*, the slaughter of nine million pigs, a third of Germany's porcine population – ordered by the government on the advice of Eltzbacher's experts in the spring of 1915 in order to try to divert grain consumption from animals to humans – only encouraged this behaviour as, after a brief glut, meat became even scarcer and more expensive. When pork did finally become subject to centrally set maximum prices in November 1915, producers withdrew their pigs from the official market, and sold them instead through illegal channels. False steps and a lack of coordination bedevilled German food administration throughout the war, even after attempts were made to impose unity and order, first with the establishment of price supervisory boards in September 1915 and subsequently with the setting up on 22 May 1916 of a War Food Office (*Kriegsernährungsamt*).[91]

The 'starvation war' rhetoric helped to hide the authorities' inefficiency and prepare the public to accept some necessary but literally unpalatable measures to stretch Germany's diminishing food stocks. Eltzbacher's experts had argued that Britain's threat to the food supply, although serious, could be overcome if Germans economized. Bread and flour rationing, entitling each adult to a daily 250-gram portion, was introduced first in Berlin in January 1915 and then extended across the Reich. In the spring, cake baking was forbidden and Tuesdays and Fridays were declared 'meatless days'.[92] As well as bans and controls, there was also innovation, of a sort. In October 1914 one of the war's iconic foodstuffs, *K-Brot*, was launched on the German public. It was never openly stated whether the 'K' stood for 'Krieg' (war) or 'Kartoffel' (potato), but this bread, in its first incarnation at the end of October 1914, was rye or 'grey' (rye and wheat) bread with 5 per cent potato flour. The proportion of potato was soon raised to 10 per cent due to the growing scarcity of grains and, in January 1915, so-called *KK-Brot* containing 20 per cent potato flour was introduced.[93] The attack on an item so fundamental to normal life as bread was a daily reminder to Germans that, as sixteen-year-old Hilde Götting wrote in her diary in February 1915, 'England's greatest and most fervent wish is to starve us out!'[94]

The land war also contributed to the particular animosity against the British. This was surprising, as the British army was, for all the importance of its contribution on the Marne in September and defence of Ypres in October and November 1914, still tiny compared to the great conscript armies of France and Russia. Even in 1915, just 20,090 German soldiers, less than 10 per cent of the fatalities suffered that year by their entire army, were killed facing the British on the Western Front.[95] Yet from early in the war, partly in response to British accusations of German barbarism in Belgium, the British were presented to the Reich's public as dishonourable adversaries. First, reports were issued of British troops using explosive or dumdum bullets, cut across the nose so that they shattered on impact, causing horrendous injuries. The story may have originated from shock at the awful damage inflicted on the human body by ordinary modern high-velocity bullets. However, the Prussian General Staff promoted it, informing the press in early September that troops 'constantly' found such bullets on British and French prisoners of war, allegedly still in their 'factory wrapping'. There was no truth to this claim, but it was widely believed in 1914.[96] In the autumn the deployment of Indian army units on the Western Front caused further anger among the German population. Ironically, given conditions already prevailing there, brown-skinned colonials were accused of having brought savagery to Europe's battlefields. The German government issued an official protest against their participation as a crime against civilization.[97]

The German authorities naturally also made much of the genuine contraventions of international law by British forces. The Briton's most notorious crime, which at the time caused international scandal, the sinking of the German submarine *U27* and murder of its crew by HMS

Baralong. On 19 August 1915 the *U27* had stopped a British steamer, the *Nicosian*, carrying American mules for the British army, 70 nautical miles south of Ireland. The submarine had let the *Nicosian*'s crew evacuate in their lifeboats and was shooting at the abandoned freighter when the Q-Ship *Baralong*, a heavily armed submarine trap disguised to look like an American cargo ship, approached under the Star-Spangled Banner and signalled for permission to pick up the forlorn seamen. The British warship was allowed to approach and, when directly in front of the U-boat, dropped the screens hiding its weaponry, opened fire, and ran up the Royal Navy's ensign. All but eleven of the crew of *U27* went down with their vessel. Six of the survivors were immediately shot dead in the water. The remainder managed to swim to the *Nicosian*, where they were ruthlessly hunted down by *Baralong*'s marines, who had orders from their captain to 'take no prisoners'. One of the five, *U27*'s Lieutenant Commander Bernd Wegener, dived back into the sea and, according to American crew members of the *Nicosian* who spoke out on their return to the United States, was killed while raising his hands in surrender.[98] Germany's government issued an official complaint based on the Americans' sworn testimony, and its newspapers indignantly condemned the enemy's 'bestial viciousness'. The Britons had 'placed themselves outside of civilized humanity ... with the Indians, the savages, the Huns', went typical press commentary. The point was clear: 'Their actions prove who the Huns really are.'[99]

Accusations that 'England' had planned the Reich's encirclement, accounts of the unfair and brutal fighting methods of its forces, and the 'starvation war' that it conducted against civilians, all gave rise to a very public hatred within Germany. Already before August 1914 was out, ardent patriots were offering bounties for successful strikes against the British. Particularly desired was the capture or sinking of a large British warship. Private individuals and businesses offered bounties worth thousands of marks for such a triumph. One anonymous German-American put up as much as 6,000 marks.[100] Such gestures were obviously confined to the very rich. A manifestation among the broad middle classes was the slogan 'Gott strafe England!', which briefly even became a form of address. As Hilde Götting explained in her diary in February 1915: 'one is terribly bloodthirsty – the favourite greeting is: "God punish the English!" – Answer: "and soon!"'[101] That it should have achieved particular popularity among children like Hilde is unsurprising, for the hatred was cultivated fervently in schools. Teachers, ordered at the outbreak of war by Prussia's education minister 'to make room everywhere to exploit the great events of the times for education and instruction', embraced new methods of war pedagogy and set their pupils essays like 'Why Do We Hate England?' or 'England's Jealousy'.[102] Still, adults shared in the loathing. Over-zealous patriots stuck labels printed with 'Gott strafe England' on their envelopes, prompting Swiss postal authorities to warn that letters bearing such marks would not be handled. Soldiers, even those heading to the Eastern Front, chalked the slogan on their railway wagons.[103] Plays and poems too were published, the most notorious of which was Ernst Lissauer's 'Hymn of Hatred':

> French and Russian they matter not,
> A blow for a blow and a shot for a shot . . .
>
> We have but one and only hate,
> We love as one, we hate as one,
> We have one foe and one alone:
> England![104]

Even at the time, much of this was recognized as deeply silly. The British satirical magazine *Punch* ridiculed it with a cartoon of a scowling family, complete with bad-tempered dachshund, at the breakfast table entitled 'Study of a Prussian Household Having its Morning Hate'. There were occasions, however, on which the opprobrium turned genuinely nasty. When prisoners of war, and especially British captives, were unloaded at German railway stations in the autumn of 1914, they were often confronted with agitated and angry civilians who taunted, spat, and even threw water or urine over them. A few were assaulted. How far these incidents reflected societal hatred against the enemy is debatable. Crowds at railway stations in the conflict's first months were likely to be particularly emotional; they had often just bid goodbye to mobilized family members or were there to meet injured sons, husbands and fathers returning from the front. The presence of heavily wounded German soldiers on the trains along with prisoners may also have spurred civilians' aggression.[105] Nonetheless, underlying the hostility was a desire, widespread in German society in 1914–15, to find some way of retaliating against an enemy that was ruthlessly laying siege to the Reich yet was itself removed from any of the horrors of war. As Berlin's Chief of Police reported at the beginning of October 1914, there was 'a general demand for a German attack against the English on England's soil'.[106]

The Reich's armed forces did partially satisfy this popular wish. In the last months of 1914 the navy bombarded Great Yarmouth, Hartlepool and Scarborough, killing and injuring hundreds of civilians. The attacks had the strategic objective of luring the British fleet out into newly laid minefields, but for some Germans at home it was their retributive function that was important. 'I'd have loved to have seen the horror and rage of the English!' gloated the auxiliary nurse Elisabeth Stempfle when news of the Yarmouth raid was circulated.[107] In the New Year, the first Zeppelin attacks on the east coast of England were also applauded, although not by everyone. The clear-thinking editor of the Left Liberal *Berliner Tageblatt*, Theodor Wolff, rightly recognized that the killing of children and other civilians could only reinforce Germany's international reputation for barbarity. The raids were, he thought, 'senseless'.[108] For those who yearned for the fight to be taken to British shores, however, it was the U-boat that offered the most exciting prospects. This was a new weapon in 1914 – the first submarine had been launched only at the turn of the century – yet within two months of the outbreak of war, *U9* had sunk three British cruisers in little over an hour, and suddenly the public was fixated. The army had failed to deliver on expectations of a quick victory, but no matter; Germans had discovered a wonder weapon.[109]

The German public's exaggerated hopes about what U-boats could achieve were matched by the navy's hubris, and the issue of how to deploy the submarines soon became a source of acrimony that undermined both the government and *Burgfrieden*. The debate began when Admiral Alfred von Tirpitz, the State Secretary of the Imperial Navy Office and, against stiff competition, probably the most divisive figure in Imperial Germany's history, mused about the possibility of a U-boat campaign against commerce in an interview with an American journalist at the end of 1914. 'England wants to starve us,' he told the representative of United Press International. 'We can play the same game, bottle her up and destroy any ship trying to run the blockade.'[110] He had no authorization to bring up the topic. The Chancellor was horrified, the navy's operational commanders were livid that strategy had been betrayed to the Entente, but the public, especially on the political right, greeted the suggestion with elation. Conservative, National Liberal and Centre Party politicians quickly became vocal in demanding the unrestricted use of the U-boats against British trade. This wish was ill-considered for two reasons. First, the Reich simply did not have the strength to break Britain's sea lifelines. A German naval study undertaken in the spring of 1914 had concluded that 222 U-boats would be necessary for an effective campaign against British commerce. When the first submarine offensive began in February 1915, Germany possessed just thirty-seven U-boats, and many of these were in repair, completing trials, or needed for training. Naval commanders swung over to advocating a U-boat campaign largely because the inability of the High Seas Fleet to wrest maritime control from the British had been demonstrated in the course of 1914. Their recommendations were based not on any clear analysis of the probability of naval success, political risk and national interest, but, as repeatedly and disastrously throughout the war, merely to justify their service's existence.[111]

The second reason why a U-boat offensive against commerce was a bad idea in early 1915 was that it would inevitably strain relations with neutral powers. With no movement on the Western Front, part of East Prussia as well as much of Galicia still under occupation, growing economic difficulties, and an increasing likelihood of hostilities with the erstwhile ally, Italy, this was not the time to make new enemies. Bethmann Hollweg had recognized the diplomatic and strategic dangers immediately and, in the coming years, it was these rather than humanitarian or legal scruples that motivated his resistance to the introduction of unrestricted submarine warfare. When, at the start of February 1915, the new Commander of the High Seas Fleet, Admiral Hugo von Pohl, prevailed upon the Kaiser to declare the seas around Great Britain a war zone in which neutral ships were at risk of being attacked, the Chancellor was quickly proven correct. The United States reacted to the declaration by warning the German government that it would be held to 'a strict accountability' for the actions of its submarines. Once the campaign began, there were clashes with neutral ships already in the spring, but ironically the major diplomatic crisis was triggered by the sinking of a British vessel, the passenger liner *Lusitania*, on 7 May 1915. The *Lusitania* was an enemy ship, it was certainly carrying a cargo of small-arms munitions and possibly also high explosives, but

1,198 civilians, including 128 American citizens, drowned when it went down, causing a public outcry across the Atlantic. The United States' government protested and a diplomatic break appeared to be a real possibility. The Germans sought at first to avoid halting submarine warfare, but when another British passenger ship, the *Arabic*, was torpedoed on 27 August with the loss of more American lives among the forty-four drowned, Bethmann, with the army's backing, insisted that U-boats be forbidden from further attacks on liners without warning. On 18 September the newly appointed Chief of Admiralty Staff, Henning von Holtzendorff, effectively suspended the campaign, ending U-boat action against merchant shipping in the English Channel and west of the British Isles, and he ordered that in the North Sea stop-and-search 'prize law' procedures rather than indiscriminate surprise attacks should be adopted against all vessels.[112]

However, once whetted, it was difficult to set to rest the public's appetite for a method of warfare widely understood to be capable of punishing the English and bringing hostilities rapidly to a victorious end. The Chancellor, supported by the Social Democrats in the Reichstag, rightly feared provoking the United States into hostilities with what he termed a 'game of *va banque* whose stakes will be our existence as a Great Power and our entire national future'.[113] Yet he could not publicly admit to the submarine force's actual weakness. Nor were arguments about the need to respect neutral rights likely to be well received. Germans were fully aware that factories in the United States were manufacturing huge quantities of weaponry for the Entente. Their newspapers reported on the artillery pieces, small arms and explosive being produced in this neutral land, ready to be shipped to Europe where they would kill and maim the fathers, sons and brothers of their readers.[114] The fragmented nature of the official publicity machine and, above all, the Wilhelmine elite's inability to agree on and pursue one policy, also prevented the dissemination of any clear message advocating caution in U-boat warfare. Tirpitz, who until March 1916 controlled the propaganda apparatus of the Imperial Navy Office, agitated with the support of naval officers, right-wing politicians and pressure groups for the resumption of a ruthless U-boat offensive. Fantastical claims circulated: it was even rumoured that just six weeks of unrestricted submarine action would suffice to bring England to her knees.

The result was that the campaign of hatred towards England, initially an effective tool of mobilization particularly for the middle class, was disastrously refracted inwards. The increasingly acrimonious public debate about how to deploy the U-boats shifted focus away from the enemy against whom they were to fight, Britain, and instead led to the vilification of those identified by Tirpitz and his allies as obstacles to the most ruthless prosecution of the war – above all the Chancellor. Public confidence in the government was seriously shaken. By March 1916 police were characterizing the mood in the Reich's capital as 'extremely ugly'. Above all the educated classes, but also even some workers, held 'the view that England remains our most dangerous enemy and that it can only be defeated through the ruthless deployment of all the means of war at our disposal, especially the U-boats and the Zeppelins'. Those so minded, it was reported, 'do not shy away from voicing the most vigorous criticism of the Reich leadership'.[115]

AUSTRIA-HUNGARY'S LOCAL WARS

The Habsburg Empire never achieved Germany's unity of purpose or single-minded hatred of one enemy. The Empire's peoples were too diverse, their histories too different, and their homes too distant to share a single understanding of the war. The nationalist politicians and clergy so crucial in endorsing the Habsburg cause to their peoples during the 'double mobilization' of August 1914 and shaping public opinion afterwards all promoted their own conflicting war aims. Hopes that a strong, centralized German-run Empire would emerge from the trial by fire were dominant among the Austro-German intelligentsia. Their Magyar counterparts, by contrast, saw themselves in a war to preserve their privileged position within the Dual Monarchy, the integrity of their lands and access to the sea. Croatian and Polish nationalist politicians and clergy had other, totally incompatible visions. For them, the war derived much of its meaning as a quest to establish a new Trialist state, in which the united South Slav lands or Galicia joined to Congress Poland would be raised to a third entity on an equal footing with Austria and Hungary.[116] The Habsburg official narrative of how the small war in the Balkans had avalanched into a European conflict, in which Austria-Hungary faced not only Serbia but also Montenegro, Russia, France and Britain, remained underdeveloped. As a consequence, Franz Joseph's subjects fought many local conflicts, not one great imperial war.

The Habsburg government's own disunity was much to blame for the absence of a clear imperial war narrative. The great autonomy possessed by the two halves of the Empire, Austria and Hungary, excluded any possibility of a unified press policy. Further complicating coordination was the fact that many parts of the administration – including the War Ministry, the Foreign Ministry, the offices of the Hungarian and Austrian Minister Presidents, and regional and district governments – managed their own press sections. Yet neither Austria-Hungary's civilian leadership nor its military leaders evinced much interest anyway in courting public support in 1914. Conrad von Hötzendorf, Chief of the General Staff, in striking contrast to Moltke, was oblivious of the need to preserve unity. 'Public opinion, the idea of the people, all immaterial problems of modern politics are unknown to him', criticized one astute contemporary.[117] Austria's public relations strategy, far more than Germany's, was centred on suppression rather than management of information and debate at the opening of hostilities. The War Surveillance Office (*Kriegsüberwachungsamt*) oversaw censorship in the parts of Austria designated as the 'hinterland', including Vienna. A parallel organization, the *Hadifelügyeleti Bizottság*, performed the same function in Hungary. Habsburg military censors, unlike the German army with its regular press conferences, initially displayed little willingness to discuss events with newspapers. Complaint about overly stringent or capricious censorship met in 1914 with the arrogant response that 'the people's job in wartime is to shut up and obey'.[118] In the front zone, the *Kriegspressequartier*, a 'War Press Office', managed war correspondents. While later in hostilities this office would be heavily involved in efforts to raise troop and civilian morale, at this early stage its main duty was to control, rather than assist, journalists seeking war news. The office was consequently located at a distance from the High Command and, as there was little good to report from the front during the first year of fighting, the military preferred to restrict access rather than gamble that knowledge of the defeats would strengthen and not undermine the Habsburg peoples' resolve.[119]

The Empire's multinational subjects were not wholly disparate. The Habsburg dynasty had ruled most of its territories for centuries, acquiring much legitimacy through longevity. Especially in rural areas, people were united by affection for the venerable Franz Joseph. The Catholic Church also provided a further important point of imperial unity, for almost four-fifths of the population belonged to it.[120] The bishops were fervent supporters of the Monarchy, and were at the peak of their influence after war broke out, preaching to packed pews on the righteousness of its struggle. As Vienna's Cardinal Pfiffl proudly proclaimed to his flock in October 1914, 'We fight for truth and justice, we fight for God and our sacred faith, we fight for our Emperor and our home soil. In this struggle for what is most holy to us, God is with us!'[121] Yet while clergy across Austria-Hungary echoed these sentiments, the message varied slightly but significantly in every region. Priests and bishops had regional and often national identities alongside their imperial and confessional allegiances, and they tailored their message to the loyalties of their congregations. Like elected politicians, they thus contributed to the Monarchy's national and imperial dual mobilization. The Polish Bishop of Przemyśl, for example, reminded his clergy in February 1915 that at stake in the war was 'not only the integrity and honour of the Austro-Hungarian Monarchy but also the future of Poland and Catholic interests, threatened by the Orthodox Church and Freemasonry'.[122]

In the absence of much government guidance, the Habsburg peoples directed their enmity towards different foes, their choice being determined by war experience, national priorities and, very often, historical animosities. At the Empire's centre, the Viennese intelligentsia and bourgeois press were initially obsessed by the 'punishment expedition' against Serbia and the battles with Russia. Yet already in October 1914, the capital's newspapers followed the Reich's German media in refocusing their ire on the western Entente.[123] This had some parochial logic. Vienna was far from any battle front and, as the fighting was not going well in any theatre, censorship was tight. Food shortages were growing, and thus were likely to attract a readership in the capital. Moreover, providing that an officially approved angle was taken on the story, the censor was content to approve articles on the shortages, limiting the number of disconcerting white spaces left where copy had been removed at short notice. As in Germany, the shortages were initially the result of the disruption to trade and transport from mobilization, and also of irresponsibly large military food purchases undertaken with no thought to civilian needs. The shortages were worsened by the Habsburg army's woeful performance in Galicia, which resulted in the loss of Austria's bread-basket region to the Russians. Hungarian obstinacy was also partly to blame for Vienna's especially dire situation. The Empire did not lift customs duties on food in the first months of war, consequently missing a crucial opportunity to attract large imports, because the Hungarian government feared for the profits of its gentry supporters and blocked the measure. Adding to the Austrian capital's plight, from January 1915 the Magyars limited their own exports to Austria.[124] Naturally none of this could be stated in print. More open to attack was Austrian bureaucracy's lackadaisical and unimaginative reaction to the shortages. Only in April 1915 were ration cards issued in Vienna, and then solely for flour and bread. Sugar, milk, coffee and lard were rationed from 1916, potatoes and jam in 1917 and meat only in 1918. Nonetheless, the favoured explanation of the shortages for most newspapers in 1915, as well as for the Austrian government, was the British blockade. This useful scapegoat offered a compelling story of enemy inhumanity while avoiding the broadcasting of military defeat in the east, internal disunity and administrative incompetence. Newspaper headlines screamed 'Starvation War!'[125]

For peoples further east, the arch-enemy was Russia. The attitudes of Hungarian and Polish intellectuals to the war was a strange combination of romanticism and grudge match. Both peoples nurtured a national mission as historic defenders of European civilization against tyranny. As the novelist Zsigmond Móricz proclaimed lyrically in December 1915, the 'thousand-year-old task' of the Magyars was to be 'the first reef against all storms of the frightful East'.[126] Much of the Magyar gentry was also itching to have a go at the Russians. One officer expressed the thoughts of many when he remarked that he would be 'glad to pay back the Russians for '48', the year in which Tsarist forces had crushed Hungarian rebels fighting for independence. Yet as the 1848 uprising had been against the Habsburgs, this was not an unproblematic basis on which to mobilize: 'the next war,' the same officer insisted, 'into which he would go with even greater enthusiasm, would be a war with the Austrians.'[127] Polish loyalties were less complicated. The fiftieth anniversary of the 'January Insurrection', when Polish nobles in Russian-held Congress Poland had risen up and been brutally suppressed, had fallen in 1913 and had been enthusiastically and militantly celebrated across Galicia.[128] The Russian suppression of Polish revolutionaries in 1905–6 was a fresh grievance. As if any further proof were needed, the occupation and attempted Russification of Galicia in 1914–15 had illustrated the threat posed by Russian ambitions to what Polish elites considered to be their lands. Yet fear alone did not drive Poles. Many of the educated were also inspired by liberationist ideals. Brigadier Jan Edward Romer, commander of an Austrian artillery regiment stationed in Lwów, was a typical example. He yearned that the war might lead to 'the breaking of the Moscovite manacles pressing heavily on the major part of the [Polish] nation'.[129] When the armies of the Central Powers advanced in the summer of 1915 and, on 5 August, captured Warsaw, tremendous excitement spread across Galicia. The Supreme National Committee immediately issued a proclamation, which strangely the censor allowed to pass, demanding that Congress Poland and Galicia be reunited and the Polish state resurrected. Ordinary Poles too rejoiced: 'I am very happy,' wrote Aleksandra Czechówna in Cracow. 'I thank the Lord God as for a great favour.'[130]

Habsburg Jews shared Poles' liberationist ideals. Their co-religionists had suffered more than most under Tsarist oppression. In the Pale of Settlement, Jews had been impoverished by legal discrimination and subjected to bouts of extreme violence. There had been pogroms in the south of the Pale in 1881 and across the Russian Empire's western regions in 1903–6. The most famous, at Kishinev, had resulted in 47 Jews murdered and 424 wounded, attracting international condemnation.[131] The Russian army's anti-Semitism in Galicia in 1914–15 reinforced hatred, although whether that emotion made Jews more willing to fight was controversial. Austrian anti-Semites insisted that, as in peacetime, Jews were avoiding service.[132] Senior army officers also suspected that Jewish men were using falsified medical papers, deliberate self-starvation, and even altering their birth dates in locally kept records to dodge the draft. The Chief of Staff in I Corps, Brigadier General Demus-Moran, advocated, fortunately without result, singling out Galician Jews, forcing them to undergo medical checks regardless of their paperwork, and impressing those too weak for combat into new 'Galician Jewish Civil Worker Battalions'.[133] On the other hand, many Jews clearly served with distinction on all fronts. Loyalty to Franz Joseph, gratefully misremembered as the cause of their emancipation, or a vain desire to shut the anti-Semites up with a display of loyalty and bravery, motivated Jewish soldiers. So too did an understanding of the conflict in the east as nothing less than a struggle between good and evil. Rabbis elevated it to a 'holy war'.[134]

The Habsburg Empire came closest to a genuinely imperial war, attracting the commitment of all its peoples, in its conflict with Italy. The former ally's declaration of war on 23 May 1915 was condemned by Franz Joseph in widely publicized words as a 'perfidy of which history knows not the like'. It is difficult not to sympathize, for the Italian government's cynicism and aggression were breathtaking. The Prime Minister, Antonio Salandra, was frank about a policy he called 'sacred egoism'. He had sold his country's services to the Entente. By the Treaty of London, signed on 26 April 1915, the Italians agreed to open hostilities within a month, and in return were secretly promised the lands of South Tyrol, Trieste and its hinterland, Gorizia, the northern half of Dalmatia, islands in the Adriatic, northern Albania and Valona. Some of these territories had been Habsburg for over half a millennium. By annexing them, the Italians would not only complete the *Risorgimento*, the unification of Italian speakers into a single nation state, but would also absorb lands with an overwhelmingly South Slav population and achieve Italian hegemony over the Adriatic.[135]

No one beyond Entente leaders was privy to this agreement in 1915, but Habsburg commentators had justified suspicions about Italian greed. The Emperor's indignation at what was a blatant land-grab by a country that for thirty-three years had been an ally reverberated across his realms. Vienna's *Neue Freie Presse* condemned the Italian attacker as 'worse than a thief'.[136] As far away as Cracow, the reaction was aggrieved. How could it be, the city's leading liberal paper *Nowa Reforma* wondered, that 'Italy and France stand shoulder to shoulder with the ancient enemy of Poland and western European civilization; with that Russia which has still not washed itself of the fresh blood of its own sons.' Italy was sacred ground for Poles, for it was where Dąbrowski's Legions had fought a hundred years earlier. The Italian unification struggle had also inspired Liberals hoping to resurrect independent Poland. To find this much-admired country in the enemy camp was thus disillusioning: 'We Poles, whose state lost its political independence through the greed and avarice of its neighbours, in spite of all the services that we did for western European culture and for the idea of freedom, must feel this insidious coup more deeply than anyone.'[137]

Predictably, however, the strongest reaction was among peoples directly exposed to Italian attack. Slovenes and German- and Italian-speaking Tyroleans had already fought on the Serbian and Galician fronts. The majority being conservative Catholic peasants, they had gone obediently to defend the Emperor's honour, but neither people had really felt that these were their fights.[138] The conflict with Italy was different. The Slovenian Catholic weekly *Domoljub* caught the popular mood with its headline 'Our War' and called for the defence of 'Slovenian soil and faith' against the 'avaricious hand' of the liberal and anti-Catholic Italian state. Prince-Bishop Jeglič, the Slovenes' foremost spiritual leader, also grasped for the language of holy war to mobilize fellow believers. Austria, he asserted, had won Liberal and godless Italy's enmity as 'the only still strong defence of the Holy Father and of the holy Catholic Church'.[139] The response to Italian hostilities was even more impressive in Tyrol, where local and imperial loyalties combined in a remarkable defensive effort. The southern frontier was virtually defenceless in May 1915. With the Habsburg army heavily committed in Galicia, all that could be spared to defend Tyrol's 350-kilometre border were a measly twenty-one battalions. In desperation, the Emperor summoned to protect their homeland the *Schießstände*, the venerable shooting associations of Tyrol and neighbouring Vorarlberg, some of which could trace their roots back to medieval militia.

Most youthful *Standschützen*, as *Schießstände* members were known, had been drafted into the regular army. The heavy casualties in Galicia had necessitated a rise in the age of service to fifty, which meant that many older men had also left for the Eastern Front. What remained to answer the Emperor's anguished call in May 1915 were thus 18,000 riflemen, many positively geriatric and with barely any combat training. Uniforms and military rifles had been delivered only in April. The units the *Standschützen* formed were highly unorthodox. Everyone knew each other, and their officers, two-thirds of whom were over forty, were elected. This was less progressive than it appears, for the region's strong conservatism ensured that local notables were generally chosen to occupy the leadership positions. Still, it meant that the units genuinely embodied communities at war, and the transference of peacetime hierarchies into their structure ensured the instant authority of their commanders. The men were highly motivated, knew the border areas intimately and were practised shots. Their units comprised more than half of the manpower initially available to defend the frontier. Regular army formations took over the more dangerous sectors, while the *Standschützen* gave invaluable service guarding the mountain peaks. Many patrolled at altitudes of 3,000 metres or more, enduring extreme cold, rain and snow, and, lacking artillery, engaged in pushing rocks onto Italian troops below.[140]

In 1915, Austria-Hungary had so many enemies that for most peoples and regions in the Empire it was easy to find some self-interest in fighting, whether from national idealism, parochial loyalties or historic enmities, as well as allegiance to Emperor or faith. Nonetheless, the absence of a dominant and universally accepted imperial war narrative mattered. First, as Galician and later Italian and Slovene refugees found, it exacerbated the lack of common feeling among the Empire's peoples. It was partially responsible for the hostility they encountered in distant lands from populations who, although of a different ethnicity, were also Habsburg subjects like them. Second, the peoples' greater commitment to local wars rather than the overall imperial conflict affected military operations. The AOK, unlike other High Commands, had to consider ethnicity alongside military needs when deploying its soldiers. Although Poles and Jews fought best on the Eastern Front, Croats and Bosnian Muslims were motivated by long historical enmities to fight hardest against Serbia. Slovenes and Dalmatians, intent on defending their homelands, were most effective on the Italian Front. Conversely, Italian-speaking Habsburg troops attracted suspicion, often unjustly, when serving in their own locality, but when transferred en masse to the Eastern Front they were praised as 'brave and reliable'.[141] A few minorities were not trusted anywhere. Habsburg Serbs were usually formed into labour battalions. Regional, not merely ethnic, identity was also recognized as important, however. Serbs from the Upper Danube, who were considered loyal, were posted to Bosnian combat units.[142]

Third, and most importantly, failure to inspire commitment to the greater imperial war effort and hatred of its enemies hamstrung the Habsburg authorities in dealing with nationalities that had no 'local war' to fight. Among Hungary's Transylvanian Romanian minority, there was little interest in the Habsburg cause: a report found that, instead, 'aspiration to a Greater Romania is very strong among the population, and especially among the intelligentsia'. Draft dodging and desertion were mounting already from the start of 1915.[143] In Austria, the prime example of a people without a cause was the Czechs. This nationality was far from the alienation of Transylvanian Romanians, but many felt with justice that the Empire's dualist structure discriminated against them, and in influential parts of the population pan-Slavic feeling produced some sympathy for the Russians. In wartime, the distance of the Czech homeland from any battlefield made it difficult to feel that the fate of the nation was at stake. In July 1914, Czech men had responded obediently to the call to arms against Serbia, taking the Habsburg army by surprise, but they were never mobilized effectively to fight a long conflict for the Monarchy. The mood in Bohemia began to sour in the second half of September 1914, when wounded soldiers, a source of information against which the military censor was impotent, returned home with stories of the fiascos on the Serbian and Galician fronts. Soon, men were scrambling to avoid service. Doctors complained that in some towns three-quarters of Czechs mustered suddenly developed debilitating ailments.[144]

Even more worrying for the military was the rise of insubordination and protest in Bohemian units leaving for the front. The first incident took place on 22 and 23 September 1914, when battalions of Infantry Regiments 8 and 28 departed wearing national colours in their caps and carrying three flags in the red-white-blue of pan-Slavism and a red flag on which was written 'We are marching against the Russians and we do not know why.'[145] The slogan was repeated by soldiers of other regiments in the following month. Drunk Czech soldiers of the 60th *Landsturm* from Písek chanted it when they marched to the town's railway station on 20 October.[146] Troops belonging to Infantry Regiments 21, 36 and 98 travelling to Galicia at around the same time daubed their railway wagons with 'Meat Export Abroad' and, once again, 'I'm going against the Russians and don't know why.'[147] These signs of discontent were soon followed by military collapse at the front. In the autumn of 1914, Czech soldiers from Königgratz's Infantry Regiment 36 and Jungbunzlau's *Landwehr* Infantry Regiment 30 were accused of going over to the enemy in Galicia. In April 1915 the most notorious military disaster of the war took place, when Infantry Regiment 28, the unit that had caused the first trouble in Prague in September, capitulated to the Russians in the Carpathians.[148]

The AOK, already distrustful of Czech troops after their language protests and strikes in 1898, 1908 and 1912, was encouraged by home army district commanders to see the roots of the indiscipline in political agitation.[149] A small but well-known group of Czech politicians were indeed seeking to bring down the Empire. Václav Klofáč, the leader of the radically anti-Habsburg Czech National Socialists, had already in peacetime offered his services to the Tsarist General Staff. He had been thrown into jail in September 1914, but other anti-Habsburg politicians remained at large. The most important were Tomáš G. Masaryk, leader and sole Reichsrat deputy of the Realist Party, and Karel Kramář, head of the far more influential Young Czechs. Masaryk is one of the most attractive early twentieth-century figures from central Europe. A professor of philosophy at Charles University in Prague and later the first president of independent Czechoslovakia, he had been on the Bohemian political scene since his election to the Austrian Reichsrat in 1891. He was a man of conviction: he prized tolerance, freedom of conscience and civic education, and he saw democracy as the best way to institutionalize these qualities in a society. His despair at Habsburg inertia and refusal to recognize Czech sovereignty had moved him to advocate an independent Czechoslovak monarchy, a form of government that he thought would receive the widest support. However, he lacked any mass following, and went into exile in December 1914 with the purpose of convincing the western Entente to support his plans.[150] Kramář, a committed Russophile, stayed on, convinced that at any moment the Tsar's army might break through and end the war victoriously in Prague. His vision of the Czech future was very different: he wished naively for a Slav confederation under Tsarist leadership. In early 1915 he and several other Young Czechs joined a conspiratorial group, known to the initiated as the *Maffie* (Mafia), established by Masaryk's successor as chairman of the Realists, Přemysl Šámal, and his associate Eduard Beneš. The tiny cell, comprising at its core just five activists, possessed neither the resources nor the support to incite resistance in the army or revolution at home. Even in its primary aim, the support of exiles trying to influence foreign opinion for the Czech national cause, it was of doubtful effectiveness.[151]

Czech politicians and parties in fact were united, with only these exceptions, in their attitude to independence plans as lunatic schemes likely to provoke repression. The approaches of the *Maffie* were everywhere rebuffed. Political agitation played no part in turning troops into traitors. Habsburg military ineptitude in fact bore much of the blame for the collapse of the Czech units. In the case of the notorious surrender by Infantry Regiment 28 in April 1915, poor training, exhaustion, a supply shortage, and attack in indefensible positions by a greatly superior Russian force all offer sufficient explanation for its capitulation.[152] Nonetheless, even if political disaffection was not a problem, the protests and riots in regiments departing for the front indicate incomprehension among Czech soldiers about why fighting was necessary. The troops were quite open about this: repeatedly in their protests they appealed 'We are marching against the Russians and we do not know why.' That they should wonder is not surprising, for wider Czech society had begun to ask the same question as news of defeats and heavy casualties had spread. As a children's nursery rhyme circulating in Bohemia in early 1915 put it:

> Little red apple
> Round and round you go
> The Emperor fights
> Why? He doesn't know
> Maria Theresia staked Silesia and lost
> The Emperor stakes everything, oh that's going to cost![153]

In these circumstances, where a deficit in ideological motivation rather than outright disaffection was responsible for the protests, a propaganda campaign might have raised support for the Empire's cause. Yet neither the Habsburg high command nor the Austrian Minister President Stürgkh considered persuasion. The state and army's knee-jerk response, as at the start of the war in South Slav lands, was repression. In Bohemia, 950 people were arrested, and eighteen who had voiced sympathy for Russia were condemned to death by the end of 1914. In neighbouring Moravia, a further 500 people were tried for so-called political crimes and seven sentenced to death by the summer of 1915.[154] In a Czech population numbering six and a half million, these figures were small, but they had a disproportionate impact. In part, this was because anybody, even minors, could be punished for trivialities: seventy-five Czech-speaking children between six and sixteen years old were among those who had been arrested for treason, lese-majesty, or unpatriotic conduct in Bohemia by mid-1917, some for just singing nursery rhymes like 'Little Red Apple'.[155] Above all, it was because political elites were targeted. In the small Czech town of Radnice, sixteen members of the local council were taken into investigative military custody simply because they missed Masses celebrating Franz Joseph's birthday or name day in August and October 1914.[156] Thanks to the military's readiness to exceed its authority and disregard more politically attuned civil authorities, national figures were also imprisoned. The army arrested Kramář in March 1915 on suspicion of high treason. He was found guilty and condemned to death in June 1916 but was later granted an amnesty. The charge was justified, as Kramář had been plotting with the Russians, but the long legal process and draconian sentence turned him into a martyr. After the persecution of Slovene and Croat representatives in 1914 and later Italian-speaking deputies, Kramář's arrest, wrote one astute political observer, exerted a negative impact 'impossible to exaggerate'.[157]

The slights, humiliations and obvious distrust in which authorities held the Czechs prompted their attitude to shift from doubt to anger. The army's treatment of Czech soldiers was characterized by a distinct lack of even-handedness: while other nationalities were permitted to march to war waving national flags, a Czech carrying Bohemia's standard was regarded as traitorous.[158] Even a very dubious denunciation could prompt commanders to search through the personal belongings of Czech troops for evidence of treason.[159] The 60th *Landsturm* illustrates well the alienation provoked by the mistrust of their superiors. The soldiers' protest was provoked when gendarmes were sent to escort them to Písek's railway station. To this point they had been obedient, but they regarded the gendarmerie's presence as unwarranted, demeaning and provocative. When the gendarmerie officer who defused the tension asked them to raise a cheer for the Kaiser, they and the family members alongside them responded enthusiastically.[160] Czech civil society was also humiliated. Already by the end of 1914, forty-six newspapers had been closed down in Bohemia and many Sokol branches, feared by the army as centres of nationalism, had been forcibly dissolved. Symbolic, yet hurtful, measures were also imposed. Prague's street signs were repainted, for example, because their red-white-blue colours carried associations of pan-Slavism. Czech-speaking bureaucrats suffered more tangible discrimination, when moves were made by local officials, with some support from the Bohemian *Statthalter*, to insist on a policy of the German language only being used in the workplace. Rather than attempt to invest the war with meaning for the Czechs, the army and administration made them pariahs, attacked their cultural symbols, and in consequence refocused the population's discontent as resentment against the state.[161]

The AOK was responsible for much of this damaging repression, even though Bohemia lay outside its jurisdiction in the 'hinterland'. Its misguided assumption that political agitation was undermining the discipline of Czech units caused the AOK to petition for ever harsher measures: it wanted more house searches, a ban on all but explicitly patriotic organizations, and an order forcing civilians to hand in their letters open at post offices so as to facilitate censorship. The AOK also had little faith in Bohemia's civil administration, regarding it as infiltrated and corrupted by national interests. It therefore appealed to the Emperor to extend its powers into the Crownland. Initially Conrad von Hötzendorf, the moving force in the AOK, wanted direct authority over Bohemia's military courts and administration. By the beginning of December 1914, however, he was demanding nothing less than a purge of its bureaucracy and the replacement of the *Statthalter*, Prince Thun, widely regarded as Czechophile, with a general. This power grab failed. The AOK was denied the authority that it desired and although Thun was removed in March 1915, a civilian was appointed as his successor. Austrian Minister President Stürgkh rightly objected to military encroachment, believing its reforms would provoke unrest in Bohemia.[162]

The AOK's intervention in Bohemia was just one aspect of the most damaging of all Austria-Hungary's 'local wars': the Habsburg army's war on its own peoples and civil administration. During the first half of hostilities, the military made a sustained although uncoordinated effort to excise hated national sentiment and disloyalty among the non-German and Magyar peoples. The repression began with mass arrests by individual military commanders and gendarmerie in South Slav lands during July and August 1914. This was followed in the autumn by the extraordinarily bloody reprisals against supposedly traitorous Ruthenes. The AOK's pressure for harsh measures against Czechs in Bohemia and its later discrimination against Italian speakers in the Monarchy's south were motivated by the same paranoia about nationalist agitation. Conrad believed the expansion of military control to be the most effective means to fight the apparently ubiquitous treason. He asked the Emperor to install military men as Crownland heads not only repeatedly for Bohemia but also for Galicia, Bukovina, Croatia,

Slavonia and Dalmatia. He requested too that martial law be applied across the Austrian half of the Empire. The High Command was even prepared to support an intrigue to unseat Minister President Stürgkh in the autumn of 1915. Stürgkh was, with some justice, considered ineffective in running the war effort, but his success in thwarting almost all the military's demands for extra powers may also have earned him its enmity.

The army's encroachment into the government's sphere in part reflected the dissolution of boundaries between military and civil affairs in a period of total war; domestic agitation, if it undermined the citizen army's combat performance, was naturally of concern to the High Command. However, already in 1914, the AOK's agenda went well beyond ensuring the efficient management of the war effort; it aimed at a drastic reform of the Habsburg state. Conrad's vision of change was less a master plan than an evolving wish list. In November 1914 he primarily wanted to use the state of war to force through measures enabling national interests to be overridden in favour of the military. His demands included a larger and better-paid officer corps, more recruits in peacetime and, bound to provoke a strong reaction in Hungary, the incorporation of the *Honvéd* and *Landwehr* into one united army. There was a hint of what was to come in Conrad's wish for the 'ruthless combating' of anti-state and anti-military agitation and the 'regeneration of the nationally fragmented state civil service'.[163] Ten months later, after convincing itself of 'the unreliability and antipatriotic cast of mind of a large part of the population', the AOK's reforms were further reaching. As a note to the Emperor signed by Conrad's superior, Archduke Friedrich, explained, an 'inner consolidation' of the Monarchy was necessary. Schools must be used to inculcate loyalty to Austria, the bureaucracy reconstructed so that nationalist influences were excluded, and all movements hostile to the state were to be crushed. Dynamic government would be needed to break through the peoples' resistance and impose a new constitution.[164]

The army was right to see the prioritization of national over imperial interests and the Empire's fragmented structure as impediments to waging total war. In everything else, however, it was wrong. The Emperor was wise to grant the military few of the extra powers that it sought over the domestic administration and not to attempt to implement most of its reforms, for they would have alienated large swathes of his subjects. The Austrian government also recognized this and resisted; Stürgkh criticized the AOK's 'distance from reality' ('Weltfremdheit').[165] Even so, its actions seriously harmed the Empire's war effort. Mutual suspicion and acrimony were the inevitable results of Conrad's incessant assaults on the civil administration. Moreover, the army anyway wielded sufficient power in the war zones and exceeded its authority in the hinterland to inflict real damage on the population's commitment to the Austrian state and war. The AOK completely failed to understand the 'double mobilization' underpinning the Habsburg peoples' will to fight. Certainly, the national loyalties and interests that it attacked sometimes took treasonous form, and more often weakened inter-ethnic solidarity and encouraged parochial concerns with local wars rather than the greater imperial conflict. Nonetheless, when correctly channelled, national allegiances complemented rather than contradicted imperial loyalties, as the successful call to arms in 1914 had revealed. The army's narrow conception of national and imperial interests as inevitably in opposition only became true when its disproportionate and inept repression started to drive them apart. Military paranoia and hatred of national interests disregarded the realities of waging conflict with a multi-ethnic society, damaged the state's legitimacy and undermined one of the dual pillars supporting the Habsburg war effort.

The war culture that grew up across central Europe in 1914 and 1915 was a highly adaptive response to the conflict's mutation into a long attritional struggle. It developed from within societies rather than being imposed by governments. Love was at its core, manifested through family support, community solidarity and a hierarchy of sacrifice, at the top of which stood the front-line soldiers. The culture was inclusive: children and women could participate by sparing and saving, sacrificing and collecting for troops and for the community's war victims. Regional or, most effectively, municipal loyalties were crucial, for they permitted local elites to bridge the distance between individual and state. In Germany, mayors, teachers, priests and journalists in cities or parishes were key figures in mediating the mobilization, harnessing more parochial loyalties for the national cause. In Austria-Hungary, these same figures frequently had national sympathies but continued to underpin a dual national and imperial mobilization in 1915. However dangerous this was in the long term for the multi-ethnic state, it was unavoidable: on family love and thousands of local mobilizations rested national and imperial resilience in the uniquely gruelling and all-embracing conflict.

Hatred, the emotion more usually associated with war culture, proved destructive. A clear view of who was the enemy certainly helped warring states mobilize their populations. The Habsburg Empire's failure to provide an imperial war narrative adversely affected its peoples' commitment and unity, and the strength and purpose of its war effort. Nonetheless, at best hatred was a double-edged sword. It turned inwards and attacked the solidarity within the societies of both Central Powers. In Germany, the hatred of Britain inflamed by encirclement and blockade evolved, thanks to the immoderation of annexationist conservative elites and the unrealism of the navy, into a rancorous internal dispute about U-boats that undermined trust in the national government and the *Burgfrieden*. In Austria, the army's pathological hatred of nationalists and fear of political subversion led it to launch wars against distrusted ethnic groups among its own peoples, South Slavs, Ruthenes, Italians and Czechs, stoking animosity and damaging the Empire's stability and reputation. The divisions that had been opened would only become wider and the questions of why the war was being fought and how victory could be won more pressing as 1916 brought a new intensity of combat and, for civilians, unimaginable hardship.

6

Security for All Time

MITTELEUROPA

When the First World War began, idealistic slogans had rung out across Hohenzollern and Habsburg lands. Leaders, politicians, clergymen, academics and newspapers had mobilized their peoples for a struggle against criminal regicide and a perfidious international conspiracy. Great principles were at stake. The Austro-Hungarian Monarchy had taken up arms to preserve its 'honour' and 'rights'. Germans were fighting 'for the fruits of our peaceful industry, for the inheritance of a great past, and for our future'.[1] In East Prussia and Galicia, the brutality and barbarism of Cossack hordes had exposed the bloody threat posed to European civilization by the Tsar's 'Asiatic' Empire. In the west, selfish English materialism and perverse French individualism challenged what German intellectuals claimed to be the purer, heroic communality of their own culture. Above all, leaders in Germany and Austria-Hungary were careful to emphasize that the war was 'purely defensive'. 'We are not incited by lust for conquest,' the Kaiser had proclaimed. 'We are inspired by the unyielding determination to keep for ourselves and all future generations the place which God has given us.'[2]

How far did the Central Powers' official aims fit this rhetoric of an honourable and defensive war in 1914–16? For what were their men actually fighting and dying? German leaders entered the conflict with no firm goals, but their army's rapid advance through Belgium and into northern France soon focused minds on the fruits of victory. Already on 9 September 1914, Chancellor Bethmann Hollweg approved the first highly secret but still provisional war aims programme. Written by his principal assistant, Kurt Riezler, this document stated boldly that 'the general aim of the war' was 'security for the German Reich in west and east for all imaginable time'. This disarmingly simple aim was to be the basis of German policy throughout hostilities. While it was defensive in conception, the intention to achieve everlasting security was extraordinarily ambitious. When combined with a world view that regarded security as a zero-sum game to be won through domination not cooperation, it soon slid into aggression. To secure Germany 'for all imaginable time' could not, even in Bethmann's mind and certainly not for the more hawkish elites around him, mean merely a return to the unstable status quo of the last peacetime years. Instead it required permanent control of invasion routes and the subjection of dangerous neighbours: 'France must be so weakened as to make her revival as a great power impossible for all time. Russia must be thrust as far as possible from Germany's eastern frontier and her domination over the non-Russian vassal peoples broken.'[3]

The September memorandum was a list of maximum demands to be imposed if the German army succeeded decisively in beating the French in the west. Two broad themes ran through it. First was security. France was to be eternally exposed to the threat of invasion through possible border adjustments in the Vosges, the seizure of the Belfort fortress in that region, and the razing of other frontier defences. Her military potential would be eliminated by a war indemnity 'high enough to prevent [her] from spending any considerable sums on armaments in the next 15–20 years'. Belgium was to be 'reduced to a vassal state' and like France made vulnerable by the confiscation of the fortress and city of Liège that the German army had found so difficult to defeat one month earlier. The memorandum was intent on establishing, along with the enduring security of the Reich's western border, a base for continuing war against its most formidable enemy, Britain. The maritime power's perfidious influence on the continent would be negated through the occupation of Belgium's naval ports. The taking of the French coast from Dunkirk to Boulogne, possibly joined to the new submissive Belgian state, would enable the Kaiser to station his navy opposite Dover, permanently threatening the United Kingdom's southern coast.

The second preoccupation in the September memorandum was economic. It emphasized and furthered German peacetime imperial goals in seeking 'a continuous Central African colonial empire'. However, the document mostly broke with the past in focusing less on overseas possessions than on formal and informal economic expansion in Europe. The Germans planned to grab some valuable economic assets from their enemies. The Longwy-Briey mines, which yielded 81 per cent of French iron ore and were already in German hands, were to be permanently annexed. Avariciously, the Chancellor's memorandum also envisaged taking the premier commercial entrepôt of Antwerp. A German-owned corridor would run from the city south-east to Liège, which would become German Lüttich. However, the keystone of the new economic order envisaged in the September programme was a more subtle 'central European economic association through common customs treaties, to include France, Belgium, Holland, Denmark, Austria-Hungary, Poland, and perhaps Italy, Sweden and Norway'. Here lay the beginnings of Bethmann Hollweg's infamous *Mitteleuropa* project. It was not a new idea. Proposals for closer European economic integration had circulated for decades. Walther Rathenau, the director of the big electrics firm AEG, had suggested as recently as 1913 that an economic association might calm western European antagonism and counter US competition.[4] However, the wartime scheme was much more ruthless, informed not by pan-European idealism but rather nationalist ideology: the association would be 'under German leadership and must stabilize Germany's economic dominance over *Mitteleuropa*'. It would guarantee German goods European markets in any future peace, regardless of residual war antagonism. The project was also envisaged as a weapon against Britain. As Riezler explained, the association would establish a 'European blockade', gaining time for the Germans (rather optimistically) to stoke revolution in British India and Afghanistan.[5]

While the September programme enunciated overarching German aspirations for security and economic hegemony, and while a Belgian vassal state continued to occupy a central role in both, official war aims evolved throughout hostilities. Bethmann's priorities shifted with the fortunes of war and he was far from the sole arbiter of aims within the government: the Kaiser, for example, had wanted in early September to annex Belgium, whereas the Foreign Secretary, Gottlieb von Jagow, wished to see it partitioned.[6] The public too had their own ideas. Although discussion of war aims was banned from mid-October 1914 on the grounds that it could upset the *Burgfrieden*, conservatives pressured the government for extensive annexations. Bethmann was barely exaggerating when he complained of 'a greedy nationalism that wants to annex half the world'.[7] The Reich's most extreme nationalists, the tiny but influential Pan German Association, as well as its industrialists and intellectual elite, demanded huge swathes of territory. The 'Petition of the Six Economic Associations', submitted by middle-class, agricultural and industrial clubs on 20 May 1915, was only the most notorious of numerous appeals for conquest. It advocated in the west the total subordination of Belgium, the annexation of the French coast as far as the Somme, extensive border adjustments, the Briey iron ore mines and the coal mines in the Nord and Pas-de-Calais departments. Economic assets were to be transferred to German hands. Similarly ambitious aims were formulated for the east, along with a demand for a large colonial empire. Placing a fig leaf over its naked greed, the petition argued that only the weakening of the Reich's enemies, not treaties, could secure a permanent peace. It also justified its demands by making a connection that was to become increasingly important in driving expansionist goals in an ever more total war. 'Our actual experiences in this war prove,' it argued, 'that our military successes, particularly in a long war, and their further exploitation depend to a large extent upon the economic strength and ability of our people.' Economic demands, the six associations insisted, 'must be viewed in the light of the urgent necessity for the greatest possible increase of our national strength, and also from a military standpoint'.[8]

Germany's intellectuals, as well as businessmen and landowners, overwhelmingly supported large-scale annexation. Seven weeks after the six economic associations submitted their petition, a similar appeal signed by 1,347 learned men, including many of the country's most highly respected professors, was submitted to the Chancellor. A counter-petition organized by the historian Hans Delbrück, which wisely warned against the annexation of independent peoples, was supported by only 141 liberals.[9] A War Aims Majority desirous of expansion also dominated the Reichstag, although the bourgeois parties of which it was composed differed in their views of how much should be taken: the Progressives sought territorial additions to strengthen Germany's security, but most deputies in parties further to the right wished for extensive economic gains.[10] Only the Social Democrats (SPD) stood outside this consensus. The party remained officially committed to an interpretation of the war as a struggle for narrow defensive goals.

Bethmann's recognition that working-class Germans would not

willingly die or labour for a war of conquest did act as a major deterrence from open commitment to annexationist aims. The SPD's deputies, despite the official party line, were a less effective check. The dominant centre and right of the party prioritized preserving the *Burgfrieden* and during the first year of war avoided confronting annexationist propagandists. Only in August 1915 did the SPD agree on its own list of war aims. These rejected annexations and demanded the restoration of Belgium, but they also displayed an unsocialist preoccupation with the preservation of national territory, categorically opposing French claims to Alsace-Lorraine. The patriotic, moderate attitude of the SPD was summarized by its Reichstag faction chairman, Philipp Scheidemann, in October 1916: 'what is French should stay French, what is Belgian should stay Belgian and what is German should stay German'. Yet while most SPD parliamentarians firmly advocated the status quo in the west, they were eager to see radical change in the east, in what they regarded as a war to liberate subject peoples and working-class Russians from Tsarist oppression. In the SPD's leftist minority, there was mounting frustration and alienation at the refusal of the party leadership to demand from the government an explicit promise of no annexation as a precondition of support. In December 1914, Karl Liebknecht was the first Reichstag deputy to vote against further war credits. Over the course of 1915 almost a third of party deputies, including one of the SPD's chairmen, Hugo Haase, followed him. In a vote at the end of that year, 22 of the party's 110 deputies abstained and another 20 opposed granting further war credits. Disagreement over war aims and over relations with the government grew increasingly bitter, and in 1917 it split the SPD.[11]

Along with very limited Socialist parliamentary pressure, strategic considerations also acted as some small restraint on official German war aims. Leftist Social Democrats would have been surprised, given the antagonistic relationship between the army and the SPD before the war, that their greatest ally against annexations was the Chief of the General Staff, General Erich von Falkenhayn. In November 1914, after Moltke's defeat on the Marne and his own failure to restore the situation with a breakthrough in Flanders, a worried Falkenhayn had warned Bethmann that the army could not beat the whole Entente. He advised that a separate peace be concluded with France or, preferably, Russia, so that resources could be focused on defeating Britain. To tempt Russia to parley, Falkenhayn was willing to relinquish hopes of annexation and ask only for reparations. From France, he wished for no more than compensation and the destruction of its Belfort fortress. These were the most moderate aims advocated by the military during the war. However, they led nowhere for two reasons. First, Britain, France and Russia had agreed at the start of September 1914 not to conclude peace separately and, as neutral attempts to mediate the following year revealed, they were no less determined than Germany to continue hostilities. Second, Bethmann considered Falkenhayn's strategic assessment too negative and politically impossible. Popular passions were inflamed. Bethmann understood that any separate peace in the east or west would be difficult to justify to a public that had not and, without risking a total collapse in morale, could not be told about the seriousness of the defeat on the Marne. He was also reluctant to abandon the prospect of winning extensive continental gains.[12]

Bethmann was, by contemporary standards, a moderate annexationist. To keep the Socialists on side, he continually stressed the defensive purpose of the war, while insisting that 'defence is no feeble goal exhausting itself in the maintenance of the status quo'. He was determined to create 'a strong and untouchable Germany'.[13] The retention of the valuable mines at Briey, possibly in exchange for some worthless Alsatian villages as a sop to French pride, was a constant on his war aims wish lists. However, the core of his vision, and the only point in the September programme that he considered non-negotiable, was the Mitteleuropa project of an economic association in central Europe.[14] Informal domination was to be achieved through customs treaties and, in some cases, military pacts. A 'United States of Europe' under German control would, in the longer term, offer the opportunity to compete with the world's other great economic blocs: the United States and the British and Russian Empires. Moreover, it would permit the neutralization of Belgium as an invasion channel, without having to annex the country and dilute the ethnic homogeneity of the German nation state. This was a major preoccupation, even though the Kaiser's army, not the French, had used Belgium as a channel in 1914. The Mitteleuropa strategy was one of the 'diagonal' paths so favoured by Bethmann between the polarized aims of the German right and left, offering substantial national economic and political gain to satisfy the former while superficially avoiding the war of conquest that the latter found unacceptable.

Finally, *Mitteleuropa* was attractive as a means to suborn not only the Reich's continental opponents but also her allies. The customs federation with Austria-Hungary mentioned in September eventually became the plan's centrepiece.[15]

Although developed behind the Reich Chancery's closed doors, the *Mitteleuropa* ideal received considerable publicity. In Germany, the Progressive Liberal Friedrich Naumann attracted interest in the concept with his best-seller *Mitteleuropa*, which sold over 100,000 copies after its release in October 1915.[16] However, it was among Austrian German nationalists that the idea won greatest support. For them, the attraction of a closer bond with the Reich was that it would improve their position against Austria's other nationalities and strengthen the Habsburg Empire. The historian Heinrich Friedjung, who formulated the most influential Austrian version of the plan, envisaged Germany acting 'like a heavy stone holding together the centrifugal elements in our Monarchy'. A customs union with the northern ally would abolish tiresome decennial negotiations with Hungary. Military agreements would halt the Magyars' undermining of the Common Army. The scheme would be complemented with a reorganization of the Empire, enlarged through the annexation of Serbia and formerly Russian-ruled Poland. The newly expanded Habsburg Polish territory would be given its own parliament for internal affairs, leaving the Germans to rule over Czechs and South Slavs in the rest of Austria.[17] Bethmann was impressed by Friedjung's ideas. They appeared to present a solution to the dilemma of what to do with the Polish territories captured that summer and seemed to have popular backing in Austria, for the Chancellor's office had been inundated by suggestions from Austrian German organizations and private individuals for closer economic union. Bethmann's vision of *Mitteleuropa*, which had been conceived in September 1914 as a means of dominating western Europe and combating Britain, developed into an even more ambitious scheme, the centre point of which was further east, in an Austro-German customs union. On 10 and 11 November 1915, Bethmann put before Baron István Burián, Berchtold's successor as Austro-Hungarian Foreign Minister, a thirty-year customs alliance resting on preferential tariffs as a precondition for allowing the Tsar's Polish territories to come under Habsburg control.[18]

The *Mitteleuropa* plan helped Bethmann to manoeuvre between Germany's conquest-hungry elites and defence-minded working classes, but for all the effort invested it yielded no concrete result. Within the German government, there were doubts about the economics of what was first and foremost a political project. The Reich's Interior Minister, Clemens Delbrück, believed it unlikely that the Reichstag would support a customs union. There were concerns that German agriculture could not compete without tariffs against cheap Habsburg produce and worries that the signing of even a diluted version, in the form of a most preferential trade agreement, would provoke retaliatory measures from other powers.[19] Austro-Hungarian leaders were reluctant to commit. In particular Tisza, Minister President of Hungary, was rightly suspicious of *Mitteleuropa* schemes and condemned Naumann's book as 'a cleverly concealed vassal state offer'. The Emperor also refused any limitation on his power. Burián's response to Bethmann's proposal in November 1915 was superficially positive, but careful to stress that closer economic ties should not impinge on sovereignty, it warned of likely problems and was studiously vague about when negotiations might begin. Austria and Hungary's own decennial economic agreement was in any case nearly due for renewal, and the Hungarians' insistence on a reduction in their contribution to the Empire's common budget caused long argument and delayed a return to talks with the Germans. Only in October 1918 were the outlines of a tariff and trade deal agreed, but the war ended before it could be put before the German, Austrian and Hungarian parliaments.[20]

Germany's war aims in western and central Europe were thus extensive but not limitless. The Reich government coveted France's Longwy-Briey mines. After any German victory, Belgium would have lost much of its independence. Nonetheless, Bethmann, who in the war's early years was the figure with most influence over the Reich's war aims policy, favoured a path of indirect domination. *Mitteleuropa* lay at the centre of his vision for German hegemony in Europe. It was a compromise policy. It tempered the desire of Reich elites for absolute security and economic gain with recognition that Austria-Hungary must agree to an alliance and that the absorption of large numbers of resentful foreigners into Germany was undesirable. Domestically, it permitted the Reich government to balance precariously between the rabid demands of the political right for extensive conquest and the willingness of the left and wider public to fight only a war of defence. However, in the east different calculations prevailed. There, German strategists, like other belligerents, imagined much more radical plans. Annexation, settlement and population movements were all part of visions for eastern multi-ethnic borderlands.

EASTERN UTOPIAS

The land to the east was not a natural site for German expansion in 1914. Imperialist energies in the pre-war period had been directed towards Africa and China. In their own eastern borderlands, a region that today is in Poland, German officials had felt themselves on the defensive. In Posen and West Prussia, two provinces in which Poles were a majority, the state had spent 400 million marks since the mid-1880s settling Germans and had also introduced obtrusive assimilationist measures, all in the cause of strengthening Germandom. Yet despite the enormous expense and effort, this had achieved little except sharpen racial antagonism. The prospect of expanding eastwards into Russian-ruled Congress Poland and bringing yet more Poles, as well as another detested group, Orthodox Jews, into the Reich would make anyone in government blanch.[21] At the outset of war, the Kaiser had hoped that these Poles might liberate themselves by rising up against the Tsar and had vaguely pondered the establishment of a satellite Polish state.[22] However, there was no Polish revolution and German decision-makers remained indecisive. It would be war itself that pushed policy in radically new directions.

Initially, not only the negative experience of Germany in its own eastern borderlands but also international factors prompted its leaders to take a moderate attitude to the east. The Habsburg Foreign Minister in 1914, Count Leopold von Berchtold, had strong views on Poland's future and acted early to stake out the territory for his monarch. On 12 August, just three and a half weeks after he and other Habsburg leaders had promised Tisza there would be no substantial annexations, Berchtold began lobbying for the attachment of Congress Poland to Galicia. Neither Berchtold's Austro-Polish solution nor a satellite state were especially attractive options to German decision-makers, but they offered the most plausible means to realize the September programme's aim of 'thrusting Russia back as far as possible'. However, everything remained in flux and in the autumn of 1914, after Falkenhayn privately announced that the combined Entente powers could not be beaten, the option of returning any land won to Russia in return for a separate peace gained in appeal. It was entirely plausible that Germany might end the war against Russia empty-handed.[23]

In the event, German war planning in the east did come to embrace radical ideas of annexation and settlement. This was not because, as the historian Fritz Fischer famously argued, there was an ingrained aggression built into the fabric of Reich state and society; nor, as more recent scholars have assumed, was it a result of conquest and occupation. The radicalization began before Russia's Polish and Baltic borderlands were overrun in the summer of 1915. The initial drive was instead defensive: the radicalization of eastern plans came about in reaction to the traumatic defensive experience of beating off Russian invasion.[24] The attack on East Prussia in the summer of 1914 prompted calls from right-wing intellectuals for annexations in the east. However, it was only at the start of December that the government began seriously to consider the question. On 6 December, Bethmann asked Hindenburg to propose adjustments to the frontier in order better to protect the Reich's eastern provinces. This request was made in the immediate aftermath of military crisis, after the Tsarist army had launched its second invasion of the province and further south briefly reached the outskirts of Cracow. The possibility of attack on the Reich's key industrial region of Silesia and an advance on Posen, the gateway to Berlin, had been real and frightening. This narrowly averted mortal peril was what focused minds on how Germany's eastern border could in the future be secured.[25]

In this context, it was only natural that the first detailed, official scheme for a border strip should be drawn up by the President of beleaguered East Prussia, Adolf von Batocki. His memorandum, 'On World Peace 1915. From an East Prussian', completed on 20 December 1914 and sent to the Reich Chancery, illustrates how defensive fears rather than aggressive ambitions could drive radical actions. Batocki was convinced that the recent invasion had proven the need for a stronger frontier. His solution was to shift the border eastwards onto easily fortified river lines. The defensive glacis that he envisaged was not large: at around 36,000 square kilometres, it was in fact only two-thirds the area of the eastern territories that Germany would forfeit to Poland, Lithuania and the League of Nations at the war's end.[26] Rather, Batocki's plan was radical because of what it proposed to do with the 2.4 million inhabitants of the annexed territory. The majority, 1.3 million, were Poles, while the remainder comprised 300,000 Lithuanians, 230,000 Jews, 130,000 Germans and 40,000 Russians. For Batocki, none of these people, except the small German minority, would be welcome additions to the Reich. Instead, he advocated a population exchange as the best means of ensuring regional stability. Chillingly, he argued that peoples of undesirable race should be expelled and their land resettled with Russia's own ethnic German subjects, who at the time were being forcibly deported by the Tsar's army from the sensitive western provinces deep into the Russian Empire.[27] The racialized solution had an alluring symmetry about it that obscured the immense individual suffering it would have caused. Batocki forestalled moral objections by insisting that the transfer could be carried out humanely. 'Man,' he speciously argued, 'even at his most home-loving, is attached less to the place than to the community of people.' Providing that villages and districts could be kept together, he was sure that transfer need entail no hardship. Indeed, the people themselves might actually benefit if they were sent to more fertile regions.

It was no coincidence that this proposal originated with the President of East Prussia. Batocki not only felt vulnerable as a result of Russian attacks, but the experience of the invasions directly inspired the idea of moving populations that would finally be realized brutally by Hitler and Stalin in this very region thirty years later. Batocki argued that the mass flight of East Prussians from the Russian army demonstrated that whole communities could be quickly shifted with little damage: 'If in East Prussia in August 1914 far more than 100,000 inhabitants on wagons with horses and cattle could travel over land, with no possibility of any official organization, thirty to forty miles in one direction and just as much during the six-week-long return with no substantial damage to persons or livestock, that is proof that with the correct preparation large-scale resettlement is possible without harming the rural population.' The urban population, Batocki wrote with confidence, would be even easier to move. His certainty was doubtless grounded on his own administrative experience. In November he had organized a successful evacuation of 200,000 East Prussian civilians from the borders hundreds of kilometres into the interior of Germany. The fact that these people had been desperate to leave, whereas the population of the border strip would likely resist being forced out of their homes to unknown destinations, was passed over in Batocki's plan.[28]

If the defence of East Prussia against Tsarist invasion in the summer and autumn of 1914 was the first impetus to new, extreme and racialized action, advance and conquest in the east from the early summer of 1915 acted as a second impetus and swelled the ambitions of both Central Powers. The joint offensive at Gorlice-Tarnów at the beginning of May not only caused a Russian military collapse in the south, liberating most of Galicia, but forced a general retreat of between 250 and 400 kilometres from the Russian-ruled territory known as Congress Poland. On 5 August, Warsaw fell to German troops. Further north, Lithuania and Courland were in German hands by the autumn. The invaders' arrival probably came as a relief to much of the population, especially Jews. The Russians had conducted a vicious scorched-earth retreat, callously celebrated in the western Entente press as 'a masterpiece of strategy'. Cattle was taken, cities were stripped of all valuables and burned. In Poland, nearly 20 per cent of all war damage was inflicted by the Tsar's army in this short period.[29] Worst of all was the rounding up of the population, especially military-aged men and people of ethnicities condemned as unreliable, who were forced into a miserable march eastwards with the retreating army. In total, 3.3 million civilians were brought back in the catastrophic withdrawal, in which no preparations had been made to feed or quarter them. Advancing into the deliberately devastated landscape, encountering scattered, desperate and dispossessed inhabitants, German soldiers could be left in no doubt that they faced an evil empire.[30]

The imaginations of German and Habsburg leaders were excited by the capture of this eastern territory. For Austria-Hungary, the conquest of Congress Poland offered its best chance finally to implement long-delayed and much-needed structural reform. In August 1915, as Warsaw fell, the Germans appeared to be leaning towards conceding the territory to their ally, albeit at the price of economic concessions and a border strip.[31] Habsburg leaders were keen. While the problem of how to deal with Serbia once it was vanquished had prompted acrimonious debate, all had agreed as soon as Russia entered the war that Congress Poland must be annexed. The question was how? Even more than other aspects of the Empire's foreign policy, war aims were defined by the need to maintain a fragile domestic balance within the realm. Schemes for replacing the Habsburg Dualist structure with a Trialist one were proposed. The Finance Minister, Leon Biliński, and the Polish Supreme National Committee wanted Galicia and Congress Poland to be fused as a new Habsburg state. Conrad von Hötzendorf, who was less enthused by annexation in the north, envisaged a different third state, this one constructed from Habsburg South Slav possessions tied to a newly annexed Serbia.

Both schemes were blocked by Minister President Tisza, whose priority was to preserve Hungary's influence in a Dualist system. Instead, in August 1914, a classic Habsburg contortion was adopted. In the spirit of Count Taaffe, a former Austrian Minister President who had described his job as keeping Franz Joseph's fractious peoples in a state of 'well-tempered discontent', a solution was agreed that would only partially satisfy everybody.[32] Austrian Poles would be united with their compatriots further north, but at the cost of predominantly Ruthenian eastern Galicia, which would be removed from their control and joined with Bukovina and some Ukrainian territories annexed from Russia, satisfying Ruthenes' aspirations for their own Crownland. The Austrian Germans, including Minister President Stürgkh, welcomed the idea, for under cover of giving Poles complete autonomy over domestic affairs in their new, more ethnically homogeneous Crownland, Polish deputies could be removed from Austria's Reichsrat, leaving Germans to overawe the troublesome Czechs. The Hungarians could also live with the new structure. An enlarged but divided Galicia would have no claim to be a Trialist state, and instead would occupy a sub-Dualist position within Austria. To maintain balance between the two halves of the Monarchy, Hungary would also grow, absorbing Bosnia-Herzegovina, thus resolving the long-standing dilemma of what to do with this orphan territory, along with Austrian Dalmatia.[33]

The disastrous performance of Habsburg military commanders in Galicia and Serbia during 1914 made these ambitions moot. Far from carving up conquered territories, Franz Joseph's ministers and diplomats spent the first months of 1915 fending off German calls to purchase Italian and Romanian neutrality by relinquishing the Austrian Trentino or part of Hungarian Transylvania.[34] However, the eastern victories in the summer of 1915 upturned the strategic situation, placing territorial gain and reform back on the agenda. This was true not only in Austria, but also in Hungary, where the calls of the restless Croatian parliament, the *Sabor*, for Croatia to be joined with Dalmatia and Bosnia-Herzegovina added urgency. Tisza, despite his Magyar imperialist instincts, understood South Slav aspirations must be partially met if they were to be neutralized and he gradually developed a dual strategy. The first arm of this strategy was to continue to oppose Serbia's annexation, which he feared would lead to a South Slav bloc threatening Hungary's privileged position within the Empire. After Serbia was finally conquered with German and Bulgarian help in the autumn of 1915, Tisza advocated Austria-Hungary's own border strip, in which the populace of northwest Serbia, including Belgrade, would be replaced with loyal Magyars and Germans. Like the strip planned by the Germans in the north, which was intended for defence but had a secondary purpose of cutting Prussian Poles off from their eastern compatriots, Tisza's strip was intended to quash irredentism by dividing Habsburg South Slavs from the remnants of Serbia.

Tisza also recognized that the advances in the east offered an opportunity to please the *Sabor*. The second part of his strategy built on this insight and was intended to give some satisfaction to South Slav ambitions. In October 1915 he proposed in Vienna the transfer of Bosnia-Herzegovina and Dalmatia to Hungary. His suggestion, and with it some lessening of South Slav discontent, failed to make headway for two reasons. First, Stürgkh was reluctant to hand over Dalmatia. Second, the deal would have been contingent on the Austro-Polish solution being implemented, and by the time Tisza made his move the Germans were already having second thoughts about the wisdom of relinquishing the conquered Polish territory on the relatively generous terms discussed in August. In November, determined to cement Austrian German political control inside the Empire and Reich German economic dominance over it, Bethmann broke to István Burián, the Austro-Hungarian Foreign Minister, the unwelcome news that the issue of Poland was still on the table only if Vienna first agreed to join his *Mitteleuropa* project.[35]

Further north on the Eastern Front, Lithuania and Courland were marked from their occupation in the summer of 1915 as areas of unequivocally German expansion. The plans for these regions bore similarity to the population transfers and annexation envisaged for the neighbouring Polish border strip, but on a much larger scale; Ober Ost, as the militarized state set up in this region during the war was known, covered 108,808 square kilometres.[36] The project could also be presented in humanitarian terms, thanks to the Tsarist regime's brutal deportation of hundreds of thousands of Russian-subject ethnic Germans from the region over the winter of 1914–15. While the Reich government had never regarded the so-called *Volksdeutsche* with much interest before the war, it now asserted a right, ominously on the basis of shared ethnicity, to protect these 'tortured and persecuted countrymen', and they immediately became central to Baltic colonization schemes.[37] The Berlin University Professor of Agronomics and Germany's foremost expert on settlement, Max Sering, set out in an influential report in the autumn of 1915 proposals for annexing and Germanizing the territory. Courland, today in western Latvia, was judged easily assimilable because its land-owning barons and small urban bourgeoisie were ethnic Germans. The other 90 per cent of inhabitants were mostly illiterate Lett peasants. With the right education and an influx of settlers, who would be drawn from Russia's 1.8 million German subjects, it was thought possible to Germanize them within a couple of generations. Lithuania, which was more densely populated, was regarded by Sering as a greater challenge. Nonetheless, if the native Polish aristocracy were deported, and with exemplary administration, he thought optimistically that Lithuanians might be won over to German rule.[38]

Major General Erich Ludendorff, the Chief of Staff on the Eastern Front, ruled Ober Ost as his own personal fiefdom. He shared Sering's conviction that the Baltic lands must be retained, and at the end of April 1916 began to prepare for colonization by ordering reports on the ethnicity and religion of the indigenous population, land ownership and soil quality.[39] His Social Darwinism and German supremacism, beliefs he shared with the Reich's rabid political right, account in part for his actions. However, in the spring of 1915 Ludendorff had rejected what he condemned as the 'exaggerated demands' circulating at home. Besides the Briey mines, Liège and a border strip, an annexation of the Congo and reparations, which combined was a far more modest set of aims than those laid out in Bethmann's September programme, he wanted 'only minor border corrections' in the east. Not until October did he advocate the annexation and colonization of Courland and Lithuania. His change of opinion owed much to opportunism: with the Baltic now in German hands and Russia beaten back along the entire Eastern Front, plans, not only dreams, of conquest were possible. Yet, although not generally recognized, the shift was also motivated by Ludendorff's appreciation of the changing nature of war. Already in April 1915 his letters to Moltke, now Chief of the Deputy General Staff in Berlin, responsible for the army at home, evince a preoccupation with the Reich's food supply. During 1915, as shortages drastically worsened, recognition dawned that the conflict was no traditional battlefield contest but a new struggle for resources. Ludendorff was focused not only on winning total victory in this new type of conflict but he also had an eye on the next war. He drew two conclusions. First, he saw control and the ruthless extraction of resources as means to compete with the material superiority of the Entente. Ober Ost became a brutal experiment in extreme exploitation. Second, in order for Germany to survive over the long term, Ludendorff regarded conquest as indispensable. The country must expand or perish. As he warned at the end of 1915, 'we shall be reliant only on ourselves and on our power. Nothing else matters!'[40]

German plans for conquest and settlement advanced in subsequent years. The border strip soon acquired rationale beyond the initial defensive considerations. Friedrich von Schwerin, a Pan-German official who was founder of the Society for the Furtherance of Inner Colonization and was brought in by the government to work on the project, considered it a panacea for the Reich's domestic problems. The settlement of ethnic Germans from Russia would resolve once and for all the competition between Poles and Germans for possession of the eastern marches. It would offer an agricultural counterweight to the growing industry of the Reich, and deferential peasants' votes would slow the rise of the Social Democrats so disturbing to Prussian conservatives like Schwerin. The new territories, he argued, could even provide a stable base for the fulfilment of German ambitions to be a world power. By 13 July 1915, when a meeting was held at the Reich Chancery, the government was clearly set on annexation, and the occupation administration in Poland received an oral order to begin discreetly settling Russian Germans in the designated area and, where possible, move Jews and Poles out. Wholesale forced expulsion was not agreed, however, and in the war's middle years the civilian administration backed away from this idea, although military circles, led by Ludendorff, continued to plan for deportations and colonization in the Baltic.[41]

These plans pointed the way towards the Nazi future. The new wartime focus of Germans' most ambitious expansionist aims away from overseas towards eastern Europe, the preoccupation with racial reliability, the use of population statistics, and the readiness to consider radical options like forced expulsion and resettlement, all were ominous precursors of Hitler's 'Generalplan Ost'. This Nazi plan of 1941 intended to cleanse Poland, the Baltic and the western Soviet Union of 45 million Slavs and replace them with German soldier-peasants.[42] Nonetheless, two provisos should be stressed. First, Imperial German designs for expansion in the east were not, unlike Generalplan Ost, genocidal. Indeed, as the war continued, civilian decision-makers' doubts about expulsion grew and even the more ruthless military pronounced as unnecessary wholesale deportation.[43] Second, the German plans appear unexceptional in the context of equally or often more radical and advanced projects in contested borderlands by other imperial powers. Hungary's leader, Tisza, also wanted a resettled border strip in northern Serbia. More significantly, France had already begun to remove suspect people from the thin strip of Alsace-Lorraine that it captured. Even worse, in the conflict's immediate aftermath, France expelled 200,000 inhabitants who lacked at least one French grandparent.[44] Probably the best subjects of comparison are Germany's foe, Russia, and its ally, Ottoman Turkey. The Russian army's schemes for the ethnic reorganization of Galicia may not have been so carefully planned as German designs for the Baltics and the Polish border strip, but they were no less radical. Moreover, while German decision-makers, as historians have noted, 'could never resolve on an open break with international law through annexation during the war', the Tsar unhesitatingly declared his intention to retain eastern Galicia, and his army was already deporting Jews and Germans and launching its campaign to assimilate Ruthenes during the first year of the conflict.[45]

While the actions of the Russian army in Galicia, its empire's western regions and the Caucasus were brutal, the Ottoman state's treatment of its Armenian minority was genocidal. Over the previous two decades, the Muslim state had sanctioned bloody pogroms against this Christian minority, which numbered around 1.3 million people in 1914 and had most of its lands in eastern Anatolia. After the nationalist, modernizing Young Turks seized power in 1908, the minority became even more imperilled. The following year, between 15,000 and 20,000 were massacred. The new Ottoman leaders' distrust of Armenians grew first with the Balkan Wars of 1912–13 and reached fever pitch during the First World War. Like Ruthenes in the Habsburg borderlands, the whole community was suspected of collaborating with the Russians, yet the fact that the state, not just the army, regarded the minority as traitors allowed local measures and massacres to radicalize into the extermination of a whole people. In February 1915, Armenian units in the Ottoman army were disarmed and the following month the decision was taken to deport the minority. The official excuse later given was that this was a security measure, and the main deportations from 23 May did indeed begin after an uprising in the city of Van on the Caucasus Front. However, as Armenian leaders in distant Constantinople were first arrested and other communities far from the war zone deported, this was clearly not a complete explanation. The deportations were designed to kill. Some Armenians, after being forced to leave most of their possessions, travelled in crammed and sealed cattle wagons on the Ottomans' German-built railway. Most, however, were set walking on a circuitous route to nowhere. Often, their guards shot or hacked them to death after a few days, stealing what belongings the wretched people had taken with them. Others were led many hundreds of kilometres on death marches towards the Euphrates River, and across to the Syrian desert. Foreign missionaries were forbidden from helping them and German soldiers and diplomatic staff, who might possibly have halted the violence, refused to intervene. The brutality of guards, the absence of preparations to receive the deportees, and the frequent refusal to provide food, water or shelter for them when it was available, testify that the purpose of the action was not to deport but to kill. Some women did escape by converting to Islam, some through forced marriage to Muslim men. The Ottoman state took some Armenian orphans into homes and gave them new Turkish identities. These were a small minority, however. A million people perished through thirst, hunger, disease, exhaustion and execution.[46]

German plans to reorganize populations – and unlike the schemes of other continental states, they remained only plans – were thus not unique but situated somewhere in the middle of a continuum of continental European barbarity. Nor were the Reich's more conventional schemes for annexation as irrational or inflexible as has been claimed. For Bethmann, no less than other German leaders, perpetual security meant continental hegemony, and the German government was under considerable pressure from conservatives, whom it regarded as its natural supporters, to make extensive gains. The Chancellor's readiness to pursue large maximum aims was the source of much righteous moral outrage among German historians in the 1960s, yet in the strategic context of 1915 this was only realistic policy, for return to the status quo was unacceptable to all major belligerents. The Russians were approached with proposals for a separate peace three times during the first eight months of 1915, yet although Bethmann was able to offer military and economic use of the Turkish Straits, Russia's main war aim, each time the Tsar refused.[47] The western Entente was no less uncompromising. The French were interested only in victory.[48] British leaders in contrast did consider an American-mediated compromise peace in early 1916, as they struggled to readjust to reality their expectations of a short war and limited participation. Yet even then, they still envisaged emerging as overall winners. A memorandum drawn up between Colonel Edward House, the policy adviser to US President Woodrow Wilson, and the British Foreign Secretary, Sir Edward Grey, conspired to bring about a peace comprising not only the restoration of Belgium, but also the ceding of Alsace-Lorraine to France and an outlet to the sea for Russia. Germany would be offered the sop of compensation from France's colonial holdings and threatened with American intervention if it refused.[49] The agreement, had it ever been implemented, would have stood little chance of winning the acceptance of the Central Powers, for it disregarded both enemy sentiments and strategic reality. For German leaders, the surrender of any national territory would clearly have been an admission of defeat. At a point where their armies stood on French and Belgian soil and had just conquered vast tracts of Russian territory, conceding so much would have been not only unacceptable but also inexplicable to a German public still largely supportive of the war. It would inevitably have destabilized the imperial regime.

German and Habsburg leaders' pursuit of maximum war aims in 1915 may not have won them the moral high ground, but in the absence of any possibility of a separate peace or an acceptable general peace it cannot be dismissed as irrational. Both governments regarded territorial gain as essential to shore up their domestic positions. Moreover, in Germany especially, collective security was rejected; Bethmann and the military agreed that after what they considered to be the deliberate encirclement of the pre-war years, safety could be guaranteed only by overwhelming strength. Defence and aggression blurred as they sought to win continental hegemony. Nonetheless, this course inevitably led to problems. The large advances, ambiguous official statements and agitation by annexationists, which was less heavily censored by sympathetic military officials than left-wing opinion, all raised Socialist fears that the people had been duped. The radical firebrand Karl Liebknecht had accused the government of a 'capitalist war of expansion' as early as September 1914, and in December 1915 he and the nineteen other SPD deputies who voted against further war credits justified their action as a rejection of plans of conquest.[50] The growing antagonism between the annexationist right and the more cautious left was by this time undermining the political *Burgfrieden*. Suspicion that a war of conquest was being fought also grew among the peoples. In Austria, the Czech population had become increasingly disgruntled. By early 1916, even some German troops had taken to calling the war a 'swindle'.[51] This was ominous, for civilians and soldiers were about to face new, unprecedented hardships and sacrifice. The middle war years would be defined at the front by a new, intense and terrifying type of battle, the *Materialschlacht*, and at home by extraordinary hunger peaking in the awful misery and deprivation of the 'turnip winter'.

7

Crisis at the Front

BLOOD

The year 1916 brought the Central Powers new crises. German and Habsburg leaders had long known that in any extended conflict their forces risked being crushed under the weight of larger armies. After a year and a half of fighting, despite the vast conquests in the east, there were plenty of signs that this time was approaching. British and Russian recruitment had proceeded apace, the Central Powers' fickle former ally Italy had thrown in its million-strong army against them, and as a result the Entente outnumbered its enemies by 356 to 289 divisions.[1] The Entente had also made great progress in ending the material shortages that from late 1914 had hampered its campaigns. By the autumn of 1915, French factories were daily assembling 100,000 shells for their army's feared 75mm guns. The Russians had simultaneously mobilized their smaller industrial base, expanding production of field artillery munitions fourfold to an output of 50,000 per day. To the outrage of the German public, who read about the deliveries in their newspapers, neutral America was supplying millions of pounds worth of arms and equipment for Britain's New Armies, recruited in wartime to deliver the final blow for victory.

Entente generals were not just accumulating massive material superiority; they were also learning how to employ it effectively. Germany had profited throughout 1915 from the failure of its western and eastern enemies to coordinate their offensives. The French commander-in-chief, General Joffre, was determined not to repeat this mistake. At his headquarters in the town of Chantilly on 6–8 December 1915 he prevailed upon British, Russian, Italian, Belgian and Serbian military representatives to agree for the coming year a 'simultaneous and combined offensive'. The German and Austro-Hungarian armies would be overwhelmed by assaults on all fronts, forcing peace by the close of 1916.[2]

German leaders too wished to end the war, although where the Entente was hopeful, they were pessimistic. Erich von Falkenhayn, the man appointed as Chief of the General Staff after Moltke's failure on the Marne, estimated gloomily that Germany's allies would not survive past the autumn and, as he told Bethmann Hollweg in January 1916, the Reich's own 'economic and internal political conditions' also made a speedy conclusion to the conflict 'extremely desirable'.[3] However, while it was easy to assert that the war must be ended rapidly, it was far more difficult to know how this could be achieved. The Western Front, the war's decisive theatre, was heavily fortified. Since the autumn of 1914, armies had entrenched all along the 750 kilometres from the Swiss border to the Flanders coast. The Germans had learned at Ypres in October and November 1914, and again in the spring of 1915, how hard it was to break through even rudimentary earthworks. The failure of repeated French attacks in Artois and Champagne, despite the expenditure of millions of shells and hundreds of thousands of lives, had offered further bloody confirmation. Some generals had concluded it was useless even to try to break through. 'There will be no decisive battle as in other times', the future French commander-in-chief, General Philippe Pétain, had argued in June 1915, when he was leading the Second Army in Artois. 'Success will come eventually to the side that has the last man. The only objective we should seek is to kill as many Germans as we can while suffering a minimum of losses.'[4]

The new difficulties posed by trench warfare had prompted commanders on both sides to shift their attention from territory to body counts. Yet Pétain's pessimism about the possibility of breaking through remained a minority view. The fighting in 1915 had also shown that with enough heavy artillery even strong and well-defended trenches could be penetrated. The problem for Entente leaders at Chantilly was how to convert such tactical success into a decisive operational victory. By the year's end, the Germans had laid out second and third lines behind their front defences. After any break-in, an unequal race to bring up reinforcements began. The defence had a natural advantage, for having been pushed closer to its railheads it could usually add troops quickly to plug the gap or retake lost positions. By contrast, reinforcements for

the attackers were slowed by the need to carry up supplies and munitions across broken land, in which they were vulnerable to enemy
shellfire. At Chantilly the Entente resolved not to try to win this race but
to abolish it by eliminating the enemy's reserves. A 'wearing out' phase,
a euphemism for a period of preparatory killing, would be necessary
to make possible a genuine breakthrough. The British had started seriously to analyse German manpower and casualties over the summer.
In December 1915 the Entente's military leaders settled on a monthly
quota of 200,000 German soldiers killed, maimed or otherwise disabled. Only once this bloodshed had been completed was the great
combined offensive to be launched.[5]

Falkenhayn also embraced a strategy of attrition, but his version was
more cunning and complex than that of the Entente. Unlike his Habsburg
counterpart Conrad von Hötzendorf, Falkenhayn no longer believed in
a decisive breakthrough or total victory. He saw attrition not as a prelude to an offensive that would return movement to the battlefield but as
a strategic tool, capable of bringing at least one of Germany's opponents to the negotiating table. He judged Britain too strong to be defeated.
Russia also appeared unpromising: despite over two million casualties
and the loss of Congress Poland in 1915, the Tsar had proved frustratingly unreceptive to any separate peace deal. Falkenhayn's gaze therefore
focused on France as both the most vulnerable Entente power and 'England's best sword' on the continent. The plan that he formulated at
the end of 1915 to force France out of the war was no less cynical than
his enemies' ambitions to 'wear out' German reserves but tactically far
cleverer. The German army would exploit the defensive advantage
offered by the Western Front. It would choose a point that the French
could not surrender – the fortresses of Belfort and Verdun were both
considered – and through massive artillery superiority and limited use
of infantry, advance at little cost to tactically advantageous positions.
It would then halt and permit the enemy to counter-attack in highly
unfavourable conditions. The French, as Falkenhayn explained, would
'thereby bleed themselves white'. The inevitable catastrophe might,
it was hoped, prompt the British to launch a premature offensive with
their untried New Armies to relieve their ally, which would grind
down their strength against the well-fortified German line. If the calamitous losses and British failure did not force France out of the war, then
Falkenhayn's army would go over to the attack, delivering the final

blow to the already exhausted French and driving the British from the continent.[6]

These intentions shaped the war on both sides of Europe in 1916. Three great battles defined the year: the German offensive at Verdun and the two major Entente campaigns in east and west, the Brusilov offensive and the Somme. The Germans attacked first. Falkenhayn regarded his Habsburg allies with contempt and did not inform them of, let alone request support for, his plan. In consequence the Central Powers dissipated their strength just as their enemies were beginning to move in lockstep. Conrad's own 'Punishment Expedition' out of the Trentino against the Italians began a full three months after Verdun, and within weeks was overtaken by the start of the Entente's combined offensive. The Russian Brusilov offensive opened this drive in June and was followed by the Anglo-French offensive on the Somme from July. Subsidiary attacks by the French at Verdun and, in August, by Italy and another of their former allies, Romania, stretched the Central Powers' manpower and material resources between distant fronts. In the summer and autumn of 1916 the survival of Germany and Austria-Hungary hung in the balance.

THE GROGNARDS

At the start of 1916, the Central Powers' armies were no longer the forces that had gone to war in 1914. They were far larger. The Habsburg army had not merely replaced the horrific losses of the conflict's first years but had nearly tripled its manpower to reach an average strength of 4,880,000 men in 1916. Its German ally had doubled its complement to 6,791,733 soldiers by the start of the year.[7] Both armies were also far less professional than ever before. Career soldiers had been diluted in the expansion and their numbers depleted by heavy casualties. Most personnel were civilians in uniform, some with peacetime military experience but ever more of whom had been hastily trained during hostilities. Contrary to the assertion often made with regard to the German army by historians seeking to excuse woeful British and French performance on the Somme, neither the Habsburg nor German force was 'at the height of its morale and physical effectiveness'. In fact, the armies' casualties, the need to absorb millions of new men and the strain of two years' intensive warfare had made their adaptation to the unfamiliar conditions of combat more challenging, heavily diluted their expertise, and brought new and unexpected problems.[8]

The fighting effectiveness of the German and Habsburg forces had suffered its most damaging blow through the losses inflicted on their professional officer corps in the early campaigns. These tend to be glossed over by British historians, but they were staggering. Nearly one in eight Habsburg and one in six German active officers had been killed by the end of 1915.[9] Many more – German medical statistics suggest nearly twice the number – had been wounded. Numerous junior leaders had also been lost by the Austro-Hungarian army as prisoners during its defeats in Serbia and Galicia. Some 30 per cent of its officer casualties were missing or captured; the equivalent proportion of the German officer corps' casualties was 5.2 per cent.[10] The creation of new units, a measure necessitated by the exponential growth of enemy forces, had raised the demands on a shrinking pool of career officers. The German army had gone to war with ninety-two infantry divisions but by the end of 1915 it had created another seventy. All needed professionals to fill senior command positions.[11] Many career officers were withdrawn from front-line posts to take up staff work in the rear. Peacetime-trained reserve officers had also suffered heavy casualties and were too few to replace them; even on mobilization in August 1914, neither army had sufficient peacetime-trained reserve officers, and retired officers, cadets and NCOs raised to 'Deputy Officers' (Offizierstellvertreter) had been used to fill gaps in the command structure.[12] In order to provide leadership for the expanded armies and substitutes for fallen, wounded and captured peacetime-trained officers, the German army thus commissioned 220,000 and the Austro-Hungarians nearly 200,000 so-called 'War Officers' (Kriegsoffiziere). Frequently young and hailing from lower sections of the middle class than their socially elite forebears, these hurriedly trained wartime leaders shouldered the burden of front-line command in 1916.[13]

Professional non-commissioned officers had undergone a similar but less drastic cycle of loss and replacement. The 148,229 regular and peacetime-trained reserve NCOs in the German Field Army after mobilization in August 1914 had given it an edge over its enemies, as they were better trained and more numerous than non-commissioned ranks in other forces. The German military's innate conservatism had helped to maintain their quality. Most German NCOs were blocked from rising to the officer corps by its high educational requirements; an important distinction from French practice in which efficient NCOs were generally commissioned, leaving the less competent carrying stripes on their sleeves. Some long-serving soldiers resented this, especially when they were placed under young and less capable War Officers, but the practice did preserve the prestige and efficiency of the German NCO corps.[14] With 362,304 NCOs deployed in the Field Army in January 1916, and heavy casualties in earlier fighting, the professionals' influence was nonetheless reduced, if still less than in most other forces. The Habsburg army was in a far worse position. Its peacetime professional NCO corps had numbered just 18,000 men and, although the force was smaller than its ally, casualties had been far greater. Permanent losses during the first twelve months of hostilities, swollen by epidemics and frostbite, amounted to 2,738,500 soldiers, NCOs and officers.[15]

The Central Powers' rank and file had also dropped in quality. Men trained in peace had been quickly expended. Already by the end of 1914, the 1.3 million men needed by the German army for casualty replacement and for building new units nearly equalled the 1,398,000 trained reserves that had not been immediately mobilized in August. The Habsburg force was again at a disadvantage, for the low rate of conscription in peacetime meant that nearly all trained reservists had already been used to fill units on mobilization, and when these were squandered during Conrad's botched summer campaigns in Galicia and Serbia the pre-war expertise was largely lost.[16] The soldiers recruited in wartime were on average less effective than their predecessors for three reasons. First, they were often less fit. To meet urgent manpower needs, the German army had lowered its medical requirements drastically at the end of 1914, drafting even the partially disabled, mentally ill and deaf. Predictably, these proved poor soldiers, and in the spring of 1915 medical entry standards were again raised and a new gradation system dividing men as fit for front, garrison or labour service was introduced. Second, the wartime replacements were often a little too young or too old than was optimal for soldiering. The Habsburg and German armies both lowered their drafting age to eighteen in 1915. The Austro-Hungarians also raised the upper limit for military service from forty-two to fifty years old.[17] The changing age composition of the forces' combat units was reflected in fatality statistics. The contingent in their twenties who had borne the brunt of the fighting in the opening campaigns had been squeezed by 1916 between older and, especially in the Habsburg force, very young soldiers (see Fig. 2). These age groups found the physical hardship and sleep deprivation at the front difficult to endure. Psychiatrists reported that both were especially prone to collapse with hysteria, a contemporary diagnosis that covered states of extreme nervous agitation and somatic manifestations of mental anguish such as compulsive shivering, cramps, strange gaits, paralysis, deafness and loss of speech.[18]

Finally, these new soldiers had passed through only brief military training. In peacetime, drafted men served for two years. In war, recruits in the German army received eight weeks of basic instruction in home camps plus another four in field recruit depots, where veterans taught them the latest lessons from the front.[19] In the Habsburg army, regiments were filled with so-called *Ersatzreservisten* and recruits who had passed through crash courses in rudimentary soldiering of just six or eight weeks.[20]

The changes in the armies' composition, combined with the onset of material shortages and the peculiar circumstances of static warfare,

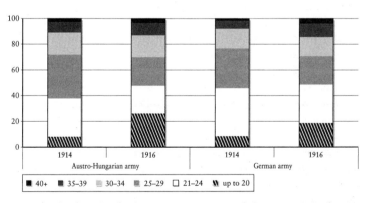

Figure 2. Fatalities in the Austro-Hungarian and German armies by age, 1914 and 1916 (per cent)

Sources: Germany: R. Bessel, *Germany After the First World War* (Oxford, 1993), p. 9. Austria-Hungary: Percentages have been calculated from statistics in W. Winkler, *Die Totenverluste der öst.-ung. Monarchie nach Nationalitäten. Die Altersgliederung der Toten. Ausblicke in die Zukunft* (Vienna, 1919), pp. 47–54.

brought new disciplinary and morale problems. In the German army, the relations of officers with their soldiers had generally been harmonious in the first two years of hostilities, but from early in 1916 these began to deteriorate: one critic even wrote with hyperbole of infantrymen's 'irreconcilable hatred' for their officers.[21] Left Liberals and Socialists interpreted the discontent as a manifestation of class: the army, with its officer corps barred to working men due to its high formal education standards, operated on an 'obsolete military model'. This argument made little sense, however, for inter-rank animosity came about just as the army's leadership was becoming less elite, with increasingly lower-middle-class officers replacing the socially superior and, as was universally acknowledged, popular professionals.[22] The 'Officer Hate', as contemporaries called it, was in fact an amalgam of two different grievances. The first was growing front-line antagonism towards the staff; a phenomenon not unique to the Germans but faced by all armies embroiled in static warfare. German critics stressed that the primary targets of troops' animosity were middle-ranking staff officers down to battalion commander, not junior officers.[23] The staff who planned operations and placed troops in extreme danger lived safe beyond the range of most artillery and all small-arms fire. Combat soldiers accused them of being out of touch with battlefield conditions and resented their better pay, quarters and more generous leave allowances. Their superior rations and the preference given to them in the distribution of medals were felt to be especially unjust.[24]

Nonetheless, in the German army, junior War Officers also became a second target of criticism. In part, this was a result of overly heavy demands placed on these new leaders. Many soon found themselves at the head of companies of 150 men, and not all coped with the responsibility. Ironically, given the Socialist interpretation of the army's social shortcomings, the fact that these officers were of more modest background than the pre-war professionals may also have exacerbated the disgruntlement of troops, for the new men lacked their predecessors' paternalistic instincts and upbringing. Yet crucially, they also worked in far more difficult circumstances. The food shortages that the German army began to suffer in the spring of 1916 were especially damaging, causing the once unquestioningly accepted privileges of officers to become objects of bitter jealousy. The army's tardy response did little to allay the anger. Only at the end of the year were commissions comprising men of all ranks set up to ensure the fair distribution of rations. The only effective solution, an order to officers to eat with their men, was ruled out on the grounds that discipline depended on keeping the ranks separate.[25]

The criticism of the War Officers was also a product of the generational shift within the army. Older men were particularly averse to being placed under young, newly minted War Officers. These 'boys of 19 years,' they complained, 'understand nothing of the world, already have big mouths and pocket large salaries'.[26] The 'boys' sometimes inflamed the antagonism by acting crassly to assert their authority. Complaints that officers yelled at and, in the home army, even physically manhandled soldiers flooded into the High Command.[27] Yet fortunately for the army, the tensions were far more pronounced in rear-line than in combat formations. Older men were concentrated in rear-line security, logistical and labour units, and the rations they were allocated were less than for front-line troops, inevitably exacerbating envy of their officers' privileges. In the crucial combat units, soldiers were generally younger, rations higher and the shared danger reduced the distance between the ranks. Additionally, the casualty rates of officers in these units were much higher than those of their men, making their material privileges appear more justified. Letters sent home from the front showed that even at the war's end, when the relations between officer and ordinary soldier had broken down completely in the rear, at the front they often remained good.[28]

The Habsburg army experienced some of the same problems. Youthful War Officers and older men in the ranks also came into conflict.[29] However, the force's prime concern was national disloyalty. The educated classes from which officers could be drawn were most likely to harbour the nationalist allegiances that were anathema to the Empire's army. Major General Alfred Krauß, the Chief of Staff of the Southwestern Front up to 1917, explained the extreme danger posed by disloyal officers: 'The men were everywhere superb – even the Czechs who fell into such disrepute – if they were in the right hands, if the officers were on the spot. However, where elements disloyal to the state came into leadership positions as reserve officers and where active officers were infected with national sentiment or neutralized, these conditions led to the sorriest manifestations of the war.'[30] The Habsburg army was consequently cautious in selecting whom to promote. The influx of War Officers did dilute the German-dominated leadership, but at first only marginally. Germans continued to be the majority in the reserve corps, their share falling only modestly from 60.2 per cent before the war to 56.8 per cent in 1915. Hungarians and Poles, two nationalities regarded as loyal to the Empire, were beneficiaries, increasing their shares respectively from 23.7 per cent to 24.5 per cent and 2.8 per cent to 3.3 percent. The Czechs also became more numerous among reserve officers, for although regarded with suspicion they had, by Habsburg standards, a large and educated middle class. Czech speakers' share of the reserve corps rose from 9.7 to 10.6 per cent (see Table 5).

The force's conservatism in its recruitment of reserve officers meant that in the first half of the war, incomprehension, far more than nationalist subversion, was a serious impediment to its performance. Unlike the pre-war polyglot professionals, reserve officers often spoke just one language. The great difference between the reserve officer corps' ethnic background and that of the rank and file meant that many found

Table 5. Ethnic composition of the Austro-Hungarian army, 1915 (by language)

Nationality	Percentages		
	of Active Officers	of Reserve Officers	of Other Ranks
Germans	76.1	56.8	24.8
Hungarians	10.7	24.5	23.3
Czechs	5.2	10.6	12.6
Slovaks	0.1	0.1	3.6
Ruthenes	0.2	0.5	7.8
Poles	2.7	3.3	7.9
Slovenes	0.5	0.8	2.5
Serbo-Croats	2.7	1.9	9.2
Romanians	1.0	0.7	7.0
Italians	0.8	0.8	1.3

Source: R. G. Plaschka, H. Haselsteiner and A. Suppan, *Innere Front: Militärassistenz, Widerstand und Umsturz in der Donaumonarchie 1918. Erster Band. Zwischen Streik und Meuterei* (Munich, 1974), i, p. 35.

themselves at the head of troops with whom they could barely communicate, never mind subvert. The corps itself also became less homogeneous and united. Where a regiment's officers were of mixed ethnicity, there could be tensions. One peacetime-trained captain discovered the problem when in April 1916 he lunched with the multi-ethnic officers of the 20th Jäger. Dismayed by the political debate in the regiment's mess, he gloomily concluded that 'after the coming peace it will not be a jot better in the Austrian parliament'.[31]

The disappearance of professional officers from the front, the influx of new men, including many older ones who had wives and children, and the strain of heavy fighting and worsening shortages, all stamped the Central Powers' forces with a more makeshift and less martial feel than at the outbreak of war. The civilians in uniform who filled German ranks groused about their unappetizing rations, knew they were vastly outnumbered, but fought on regardless. They sung of themselves as 'the darling, darling jam army'. Irony was far more important than militarism in their mental armoury. The proud refrains of army anthems like 'The soldier, the soldier, / He's the best man in all the state' were parodied by wartime troops as 'Marmalade, marmalade, / That's the only chow in all the state.'[32] Civilian values and identities underpinned their resilience. When a wartime psychologist asked a sample of troops from the south-west of Germany what thoughts they found useful in coping with danger at the front, few mentioned discipline or patriotism. Humour and fatalism came higher up the list, and social emotions, the comfort of knowing trusted comrades were nearby, were the third most frequently named as helpful. However, the two most popular responses were 'memories of home' and, above all, 'religious feelings'.[33]

The same sentiments were expressed in troops' diaries and letters. In the face of all-pervasive death, they turned for reassurance to the faith in which they had been raised. Gratitude to God for survival so far, the hope or belief that He would continue to act as a protector in the future, and a fatalism or calm certainty that a loving God 'guides everything for the best' permeated soldiers' writings.[34] Religion was most important for the predominantly Catholic Austro-Hungarian army. The multi-ethnic force could not exploit nationalist ideology to motivate its troops and so invested heavily instead in encouraging and supporting their faith. Habsburg divisions were allocated up to twenty-four chaplains, four times the number serving in German divisions. Most of the army's manpower was rural, conservative and pious. Many Slovenian troops, for example, carried rosaries and prayer books, fervently embraced a Marian cult, and were, so one military chaplain claimed, 'keen to say prayers . . . as often as they possibly can'.[35] Piety could motivate some behaviour at odds with military effectiveness: 'I've already got used to the shooting,' one Czech soldier at the front informed his family, 'but up to now I have not fired a shot from my rifle as I do not want to break the Fifth Commandment and have a murder on my conscience.'[36] Nonetheless, faith was a powerful factor in sustaining troops through the hardship of life at the front. In German formations, the depth of belief was more variable. Men from the pious south often drew much strength from Christian faith, whereas Berlin's atheistic industrial proletariat was indifferent. Nonetheless, even relieved non-believers were often observed after a bloody action joining in with the hymn 'Nun danket alle Gott' ('Now Thank We All our God').[37]

The desire to protect their homes and families also underpinned the resilience and motivation of German and Austro-Hungarian citizen-soldiers. '"Patria" is no longer the great wide German homeland with her 70 million souls', another psychological study argued. 'Patria is the home of each individual; it is Prussia, Bavaria, Saxony, Baden, etc.; in fact it is no longer even that, but less: . . . "Patria" is the home, is the family of each individual, is the wife and the children, father and mother and siblings.'[38] The central place of German troops' relatives and homes in their combat motivation revealed itself in many ways. One expression was in the songs that they sung. 'Argonnerwald' ('The Argonne Forest'), one of the most popular in the war's middle years, resonated with so many men because it combined sentimentality towards loved ones at home with a determination to hold back the enemy whatever the cost. The ballad told the story of a soldier during a night attack in one of the most bloodily contested sectors of 1915:

> Argonne Forest at midnight,
> A Pioneer stands on watch.
> A little star high in the heavens,
> Brings him a greeting from distant home.

He has his spade in his hand,
The way of things demands it.
With longing he thinks of his love,
Will he see her still one more time?

From the rear shoots the Artillery,
We stand before the Infantry;
Shells smash down around us,
The Frenchies want to take our trench.

Let the enemy attack us hard,
We Germans are no more afeared.
It does not matter what his strength,
He will not break into our trench![39]

Sometimes men voiced their motivation openly to their families: 'I live and fight for you,' wrote one soldier passionately to his wife.[40] Yet even when troops were more reticent, the eagerness with which they looked forward to the arrival of post betrayed the importance of home to them. The German Field Postal Service carried 28.7 billion postcards, letters and parcels between the front and home during the First World War. The times when letters were distributed were, another man explained to his family, 'the best moments in the field . . . you should see how everyone listens intently for whether their names won't be read'.[41] The men's concern to defend their families tied them to wider national or imperial war efforts. The sight of the front's smashed trees and pocked earth only reinforced their determination. As one soldier concluded after surveying the devastation at Verdun, 'We can be very glad not to have the enemy in our own land!'[42]

Nonetheless, men's capacity to endure was eroded as war dragged on interminably. Whether wallowing in Flanders mud, shivering on an Alpine mountain top or languishing in the wide spaces of the east, men hoped for an end to the ordeal. The news from home in 1916, where civilians were struggling with food shortages far more serious than those in the armies, also worsened, and families became a source not just of strength but of worry. The admonitions of authorities to civilians to write cheerfully to soldiers at the front, and make every letter a 'talisman' radiating 'strength and determination', were in vain.[43] With most troops permitted only one annual leave of a fortnight, relationships became strained and sometimes broke down. One can imagine the misery of the Austrian soldier who received the following letter while fighting in the mountains on the Italian Front:

My dear, good Josef,
I am writing to tell you that I have made a mistake. I can't do anything about it now. Forgive me for all that I tell you. I was caught up by another . . . He talked me around and said you're not going to come back from the front. And he used my hours of weakness. You're aware of feminine weakness and can do nothing better than forgive me. It's already done and I thought that something must have happened to you, as for three weeks you hadn't written. I was very shocked when I received your letter and [found that] you're still alive. Perhaps the child will die, then everything will be good again. I don't like the fellow any more, as you are still alive. Here everything is very expensive and it's good that you're away at the front. There at least the food costs nothing. The money that you send me is very much needed. Now I shall close my letter as there's no more space. With sincere greetings, your Frieda.[44]

Infidelity was of course not limited to women. In fact, soldiers had more opportunity and were threatened with much less societal disapproval if they slept around. Some formed relations with enemy civilians in the rear. When Otto Steinhilber, an NCO in Bavarian Infantry Regiment 12 on the Western Front, feared that his wife Lina was getting rather too friendly with their local blacksmith, he warned her that he might retaliate by finding himself 'a strapping French girl'. The threat in his case was empty, but not outlandish: 'some women here have a soldier with whom they live as with their husbands,' he told her. 'Several of them are also already pregnant.' Whether through stable relationships or, more commonly, casual liaisons, some 10,000 children were born in occupied France to German soldier-fathers.[45]

Sex was a commodity in the war zone. Women sold themselves to feed themselves in the occupied territories, especially in Russian Poland and the Baltic which, unlike Belgium and north-eastern France, received no food aid from neutral powers. Fearing an epidemic of venereal disease, the armies attempted to force the trade into officially sanctioned brothels, where prostitutes underwent regular gynaecological checks. These were strange and disturbing places. Disciplinary considerations (no officer wanted to be caught by his men with his pants down) dictated that there must be a strict separation between brothels for officers only and those for the rank and file. For soldiers, the girls in the officers' houses were yet another privilege contributing to the 'Officer Hate'. The rumour was that they were the most attractive and they certainly earned far more; up to twenty times as much as workers in the regular military brothels. These latter were squalid. The women received little, often just a couple of marks per client, had to pay their madam sometimes as much as twenty marks per day for food and lodging, and were not permitted to leave the premises. The men queued up, watched by sentries tasked with keeping order, outside the house. A medic was sometimes stationed on the ground floor to check the troops for VD and hand out protective ointment or gut and rubber condoms. A soldier gave a description of what typically followed:

> We had expected to find a brothel here like in the big cities, where one chooses the girl, who then assents, in a salon. But there was nothing like that here. After we had received instructions that no woman might be detained for longer than ten minutes, we had to wait in a room and from time to time came the cry: 'next!'
>
> After three-quarters of an hour waiting it was my turn.
>
> 'Room number six!' shouted the corporal after me and I stumbled up the steps. Half shaking with conflicted feelings I opened the door.
>
> A nasty smell of mercuric chloride and patchouli hit me. I saw from the outline of the body under the black negligee that a woman stood in the half darkness of the room with her face to the window. With a composed movement she turned around and simply let herself fall onto the edge of the bed, the negligee gathered up . . .[46]

Despite issuing prophylactics, ordering men to disinfect their genitals after intercourse, lecturing them on the perils of venereal disease and attempting to control prostitution, armies were unable to stamp out venereal infections. German military doctors treated 713,491 cases; a little over 5 per cent of the force's soldiers. The highest rates were registered in home units, however, rather than those at the front. The Habsburg military had even greater problems, registering 1,275,885 cases in the first three years of war. Hungarian troops were twice as likely as Austrians to be infected. Lax preventative measures partly account for the

Habsburg army's high rate. So too do the territories in which it fought, for venereal disease was rife on the Balkan and Eastern Fronts.[47]

While the Central Powers' armies had been buffeted by wartime strains, they had also acquired from their experiences valuable new lessons for combat. Since 1914, the crucial importance of firepower had been recognized and weaponry upgraded. The Germans had greatly expanded their heavy artillery, which had proved itself a battle-winning weapon, from 148 batteries at the outbreak of war to 1,380 in August 1916. The Habsburg artillery had almost tripled from 2,790 to 8,300 guns. Both armies had also invested heavily in machine guns. Every German infantry battalion had its own machine-gun company in 1916, and the Austrians had increased production by one-third over the course of 1915 to a monthly output of 400 automatic weapons.[48] New weapons, such as gas, and some older reinvented ones, such as mortars and hand grenades, had become important in the Central Powers' armouries. There was also tactical progress. The Germans and, by the start of 1916, Habsburg forces had finessed the art of siege warfare, using well-prepared fortifications as a strength-multiplier. Three lines of defences, deep dugouts and a conviction that the front line should at all costs be held characterized both armies' tactical ideal. More radical experimentation was underway in the German army. During 1915 the storm troop had evolved; a new type of soldier who instead of fighting in line under supervision operated in small self-supporting squads equipped with a mix of weaponry and trained in tactics centred on individual initiative, flexibility and close teamwork. In 1916 these new combat methods were still confined to a small group of specialists and some units that had developed similar tactics independently. The experience of facing the might of the Entente's combined great offensive would hasten their dissemination and acceptance as official doctrine. The German army and at least parts of its Austro-Hungarian ally would be transformed by a tactical revolution.[49]

The Central Powers' armies were still solid at the beginning of 1916. The German force, despite the devastation of its professional officer corps and the depletion of its career NCOs, remained a formidable opponent. The Habsburg military had undergone a remarkable regeneration after its early defeats. Both armies were larger and better equipped than in 1914. Nonetheless, they were also showing the strain of one and a half years of hard fighting. The manpower of both forces had changed, raising new problems and tying morale more closely than ever before to the suffering home fronts. Their combat formations, which had the greatest turnover, were more hastily trained than at the outbreak of war. Neither force had yet fully adapted to the new, challenging conditions of the modern battlefield. Their ability to endure, let alone win, the intense 'material battles' planned for the coming year was far from a certainty. In 1916, German and Habsburg survival would hang in the balance, dependent on the skills of their armies' remaining professionals and the resilience and resolution of their vastly outnumbered citizen-soldiers.

VERDUN

The start of 1916 offered the Central Powers a chance to grasp the initiative, and Falkenhayn did so by settling on the French city and fortress complex of Verdun as the site of his gambit to bring a quick and favourable end to the war. The place was well chosen. For two and a half centuries Verdun, situated in the Meuse department in the north-east, had been a bastion guaranteeing France against invasion. It had been besieged in the Thirty Years War, again a hundred years later during the Revolutionary Wars, and in 1870 it had been the last of the great French fortresses to capitulate. In 1914 it was one of the most modern and formidable defensive complexes in Europe. With twenty major and forty smaller forts arranged in concentric belts and built on the crests of the undulating ground, it presented a frightening obstacle. Yet, although Verdun was essential early in hostilities as a pivot for the Entente counter-offensive on the Marne, the French High Command had subsequently condemned the concrete defences as obsolete and had stripped them of all moveable armaments. In 1915 the equivalent of forty-three heavy and eleven field artillery batteries, along with 128,000 rounds, had been transferred to the Field Army. None of this was made public, however, and the complex remained a powerful symbol of French national security. To lose it when the north-east of the country was already under German occupation would have been a devastating blow to state prestige and public morale.[50]

Falkenhayn selected Verdun not just because no French government could afford to abandon it. Operationally, the area was well suited for his 'bleeding to death battle' (*Ausblutungsschlacht*). The plan was not to take Verdun, merely to threaten it. If the German infantry could capture the high ground to the east of the city, it would be perfectly positioned, with a mass of artillery behind it, to eviscerate the inevitable French counter-attacks. Verdun's location in a salient would help the initial advance and subsequent slaughter, for it meant that the sector could be fired upon from three sides. The sector's extensive rail network also made it attractive, for Falkenhayn envisaged an artillery battle and therefore needed the infrastructure to keep his guns fed with enormous quantities of ammunition.[51] The German artillery concentrated in the area comprised three 38cm naval guns, twenty-six super-heavy 42cm howitzers, 416 heavy howitzers, 209 heavy cannon and 550 field guns. They were supplemented by 202 trench mortars to blast a way for the infantry through to the high ground. To make possible an initial heavy bombardment, 213 trains brought up munitions. Thereafter an average of 33¾ munitions trains arrived daily throughout the offensive. Other German preparations for the attack were no less thorough; the General Staff, the only part of the army largely protected from casualties, had preserved its operational prowess. Aircraft carefully reconnoitred French defences. The nine crack infantry divisions designated for the offensive marched to the sector by night in order to maintain secrecy. The attack was rehearsed using mock-up trenches. Some units formed storm-troop detachments armed with hand grenades and trained in the new tactics. Shelters called *Stollen*, together capable of accommodating 10,000 men, were dug into the front line to hold the assault troops.[52]

However, these painstaking preparations could not compensate for some serious flaws in the attack's planning. Falkenhayn's preoccupation with limiting losses, and his determination to hold back a strategic reserve to fight the British, motivated him to restrict the offensive to a narrow 14-kilometre front on the east bank of the Meuse, the river that ran through Verdun. The Chief of Staff of the Fifth Army, General von Knobelsdorf, who had responsibility for drawing up a detailed operational scheme and whose troops would carry it out, was dismayed. He rightly recognized that attacking in the east alone would expose his men to enfilade fire from French artillery on the west bank, but his protests were overridden. Falkenhayn did provide two extra corps in order eventually to widen the attack, but he refused to release them immediately.[53]

Two other factors detracted from the likelihood of the offensive's success. One was that the Fifth Army's command did not itself share Falkenhayn's concept and prioritized actually seizing Verdun's fortress complex rather than inflicting losses on the French army. The conceptual confusion would cause doubt lower down the chain of command about what the offensive aimed to achieve, and which tactics should be used. The other big problem was the weather. The offensive was scheduled for 12 February, but on that day snow fell in sheets. As the gunners could not see, the attack was postponed. It was hoped at first that the delay would be just twenty-four hours, but rain and snow fell for a full nine days. The French, who had known that an assault was in preparation but had been unable to work out exactly from where it would be launched, were alerted by Alsatian deserters. By the time the weather cleared, the French front had been reinforced and much of the element of surprise had been lost.[54]

At last, on 21 February at 8.12 a.m., the German guns opened up, bombarding French lines for a full nine hours. To an officer in the German trenches opposite, it sounded 'as if the horsemen of the apocalypse were riding by'. There was not one continuous roar but a cacophony, as one calibre crescendoed only then to be drowned out by other guns: at times it sounded 'like an express train, then like a waterfall, then it warbled into high, then into deep tones'. Mine-throwers, which joined the bombardment at 10 a.m. with 'a terrible crash that rocked the shelter at its joints', smashed the French earthworks.[55] Gas shells were used to suppress enemy artillery; gunners whose breathing was hampered by gas masks were unable to load their guns quickly. At 5 p.m. German infantry patrols and pioneers armed with flame-throwers climbed into no-man's-land and captured much of the enemy's first line. Where woods had hidden the French defences from observation the attackers had to overcome stiff resistance. Elsewhere, however, the positions had been effectively pounded and shaken defenders were relieved to surrender.[56]

The first week of the German offensive was a stunning success. The main attack began on 22 February, with troops of the VII Reserve Corps on the right advancing particularly rapidly along the Meuse River. By the end of the third day, the whole of the French first position had fallen and the Germans started to drag their artillery forward for the next assault. Their most spectacular triumph was the capture of Fort

Douaumont, which at a third of a kilometre in width, was the largest and most modern of Verdun's fortresses. Under most circumstances, it should have been impregnable. Its two and a half metre-thick reinforced concrete roof was constructed ingeniously with a metre layer of sand in the middle and up to five metres of earth atop. The sand acted as a cushion and made the fort capable of withstanding blows from even the Germans' heaviest shells. Retractable artillery and machine-gun turrets, flanking galleries with light artillery and searchlights, two fields of barbed wire, spiked railings, and a moat eight metres deep combined to turn any infantry assault into a forlorn hope. Yet in common with the other forts, most of the guns at Douaumont had been removed in 1915. This was bad enough; even worse was that commanders in February 1916 neglected even to garrison the fortress. An order to man the defences was never sent. In consequence, a pioneer sergeant and two small groups of soldiers under officers from the 24th Brandenburgers were able to carry out one of the most remarkable coups of the entire war. They entered the fort unopposed and took the fifty-seven-strong caretaker garrison prisoner without loss. The fortress became a key shelter, logistical and medical point for the German attackers for the rest of the battle. The effort to retake it, which was only managed in October, cost the French army an estimated 100,000 casualties.[57]

The victories lulled Falkenhayn into believing that all was going according to plan. Yet, in fact, even at this early stage there were problems. As the Fifth Army command had foreseen, enfilade fire from the untouched west bank of the Meuse was already causing severe casualties from the second day of the offensive. Additionally, French resistance on the eastern bank was stiffening. Pétain was given command of the Fortified Region of Verdun on 25 February. His first order to his troops to 'retake immediately any piece of land' played into German hands, but he was effective in stiffening the defence. Moreover, by the following day, nine French corps were either in or on their way to the sector. On 27 February the offensive ground to a halt. The attackers had advanced up to 8 kilometres and had captured 216 French officers and 14,534 men, but they had lost 25,000 men themselves. To push towards the safety of the Meuse heights, the capture of which was so critical to his attritional plan, Falkenhayn conceded that an attack would also have to be made on the river's west bank, and on 6 March this began against fully prepared French troops. This time there would be no quick victories. The battle descended into a mutual annihilation. The Germans had not reached the high ground, so their troops lay in positions exposed to heavy bombardment from the flanks and even in some cases from the rear. By the end of March, their losses had risen to 81,607 men.[58]

The German army's performance at Verdun shook the French. Major Raynal, the commandant who led the defence of Fort Vaux, in whose unlit underground corridors some of the most vicious fighting of the battle took place at the start of June 1916, wondered at the enemy soldiers' courage, discipline and tenacity. 'Whatever the content of the order, the German carries it out, even if in doing so, it is certain that he will fall,' he remarked in his diary.[59] Yet the Kaiser's troops were only human, and the heavy shellfire, the difficulty of getting food and water up to the front and the weeks of living in mud among corpses tested their resilience. Psychiatric casualties rose rapidly from the start of the battle, and in May they reached an incidence a third above those of the Field Army on the Western Front. Medical officers reported anxiously on an epidemic of nervous digestive disorders (see Fig. 3).[60] Nor were German

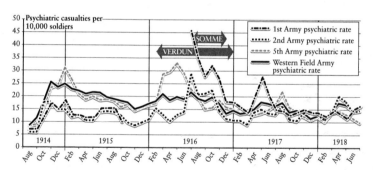

Figure 3. German psychiatric casualties in the Second and First Armies (which fought on the Somme in the second half of 1916), in the Fifth Army (which fought at Verdun in 1916) and in the entire Western Field Army, 1914–1918

Source: Heeres-Sanitätsinspektion des Reichskriegsministeriums (ed.), *Sanitätsbericht über das Deutsche Heer (Deutsches Feld- und Besatzungsheer) im Weltkriege 1914/1918 (Deutscher Kriegssanitätsbericht 1914/18). Die Krankenbewegung bei dem deutschen Feld- und Besatzungsheer im Weltkriege 1914/1918* (3 vols., Berlin, 1934), iii, pp. 6* and 42*.

citizen-soldiers as selfless or lemming-like as Raynal's description implies. The diary of Max Wittmann, a soldier in Reserve Infantry Regiment 207, offers a vivid corrective with its honest description of the chaos, confusion and compromises that actually defined combat.

On 24 May 1916, Wittmann's battalion was ordered into the attack on the notorious Le Mort Homme hill on the west bank of the Meuse. The artillery had hammered French lines since midday and he spent an anxious few hours crouched at the bottom of a trench, hardly daring to peek over the parapet. All the soldiers were deafened by the shellfire. They awaited the command to go over the top. At 6 p.m. the assault began. The 8th company, Wittmann's outfit, was designated as the reserve while the rest of the battalion attacked. The company was told to shift to the right but instantly came under heavy fire when it tried, so Wittmann and some of his comrades moved away without orders. 'Just as well,' he jotted in his notebook, 'for after ten minutes everybody dashed back because there had been direct hits on the trenches, with several men buried and dead.' The attacking companies did no better. The assault was delayed because the battalion's commander was heavily wounded and its adjutant killed as they went forward to the advance sap, where the operation was supposed to begin. The soldiers, in terror or relief, had 'skedaddled back as there was no leadership'. After the first squads to be sent over were mown down by machine-gun fire, no one else was willing to go forward.

This first debacle and refusal to be uselessly slaughtered defined the rest of the tour. After 'two tough days' at the front, Wittmann recorded that 'many in our company have hidden themselves and done a bunk so that we now number around 45–50 out of 170 men'. After a night spent cowering in a shell hole in no-man's-land under artillery fire, he too decided that discretion was the better part of valour and headed back to German lines in search of deeper shelter. When he rejoined his company as it withdrew the following day, there was no rebuke, just joy that 'one after the other' the soldiers were returning. The relief at leaving the battlefield, even though the respite would be only temporary, was overwhelming. 'God be praised,' wrote Wittmann when he arrived at his rest quarters and was able to eat, sleep, wash and shave, 'at least a place where one can say that one is human.' He counted himself lucky to have survived. 'My whole squad has disappeared,' he recorded in his diary, 'two of them dead, six wounded, I alone remain.'[61]

The Verdun offensive raged on even though the rapid capture of the heights, the precondition for the success of the original plan, had failed. Falkenhayn, although anxious about the offensive's progress, persisted in part because he overestimated the kill ratio: 'the enemy's losses were carefully noted and compared with our own . . . for every two Germans put out of action five Frenchmen had to shed their blood'.[62] In fact, his information was incorrect. Pétain's *noria* system, named after the irrigation wheels whose buckets sweep through water, raising and then depositing their load in an unbroken sequence, rotated 259 of France's 330 infantry battalions through the front. The Germans misinterpreted this as evidence that enemy troops were being rapidly annihilated. In fact, the French were withdrawing units for rest and refit once their casualties reached 50 per cent.[63] This was good practice, for it preserved veteran cadres on which to rebuild and gave the soldiers at the front some hope of getting out of the battle alive. German troops, by contrast, were condemned to stay in the line until so depleted that they could no longer hold. The policy was determined by Falkenhayn's desire to keep a fresh reserve for a decisive counter-attack once Entente forces had worn themselves out. For the men of the forty-eight German divisions that fought at Verdun, this was terribly hard. As the army's official history rued, it also ruined their units: 'some German divisions were so burned out in the battle on the Meuse that only after many months did they again become just about capable of combat'.[64]

The offensive was also continued because, with awful irony, as ever more blood was spilt, the Germans, like the French, came to value Verdun as a prestige object. To disengage without shaking public morale meant being able to demonstrate some tangible achievement. For Falkenhayn personally, the outcome of the battle became tied to his reputation and authority. Furthermore, the Fifth Army, which had embraced Falkenhayn's aim to bleed the French dry, advised that the attack be continued. As troops' positions were so exposed by the summer, stopping would be suicidal, and the only alternative, returning to the offensive's start lines, was unthinkable after so many casualties. Only in mid-July, after the onset of the Somme offensive, did the OHL (Oberste Heeresleitung), the German Army High Command, halt attacks at Verdun. Even so, fighting continued at a lower pitch as the French strove to regain lost ground. Eventually, in October and November, the two forts taken by the Germans, Douaumont and Vaux, were recaptured.[65] In terms of kill ratios, Falkenhayn's priority at the opening of the offensive, the campaign was also a total failure. The Germans, far from suffering light battle casualties, had lost 310,231 men between 21 February and 9 September. Some 241,860 of these troops were wounded, 41,632 killed and 26,739 missing. French losses at Verdun are usually stated to be higher, at 377,231, but this figure includes casualties up to December 1916. The losses of the French Second Army, which faced the German Fifth in the battle, totalled 309,998 soldiers to the end of August, making the blood count on both sides near identical.[66]

BRUSILOV'S OFFENSIVE

The AOK, the Habsburg Army High Command, began 1916 in high spirits. Since the previous summer, Galicia had been liberated, Russian Poland conquered and Serbia finally crushed. These achievements had only been possible through combined operations with allies. Nonetheless, the Austro-Hungarian army had not only recovered from its heavy losses but at last appeared to have worked out how to stand against the Russians. The turn of the New Year had seen a mighty Tsarist offensive in Bukovina smashed. For the loss of 20,000 of its own troops, the Habsburg Seventh Army had inflicted 70,000 casualties on attackers amply supported with artillery and double its strength, all without any assistance from the Germans.[67] With such a performance, Conrad von Hötzendorf could be heartened about the prospects of an offensive in Italy. True, Falkenhayn had reacted negatively when the possibility was raised with him in December 1915. He had been busy with the preparations for his own attack on Verdun and saw little advantage to a hammer blow in the south; the enemies who would decide the war were on the Western Front. Yet German support was not considered a precondition for the operation. With Russia in abeyance and Conrad's units filled up with replacements, the Chief of the Habsburg General Staff optimistically believed his own armies to be capable of a great victory.

Any account of the catastrophe on the Eastern Front that befell Austria-Hungary in the summer of 1916 must start with Conrad's Italian offensive, because the operation was so fundamental in weakening the Empire's strategic position. Falkenhayn and Conrad's failure to agree was spectacularly irresponsible, for the Central Powers' fates were bound together and their enemies were gathering overwhelming strength against them. With their attention focused on the Western and South-Western Fronts, the eastern theatre was disastrously neglected. Falkenhayn bears much of the blame, being insultingly secretive about his plans and contemptuous of his ally. Yet his Verdun battle was at least the product of a reasoned strategy for ending the war. Conrad's campaign was, by contrast, self-indulgent. He thought not with his head but with his heart. The offensive he planned to launch from the Trentino could scarcely have been more different from Verdun. Where Falkenhayn's attack was a new approach to overcome static warfare, Conrad behaved as if it were still 1914 and prepared an old-fashioned encirclement. Verdun was the product of cold calculation, statistical analysis and corpse counting. The Trentino 'Punishment Expedition' was fuelled by emotion. Conrad had long nurtured a pathological hatred of Italy, made more intense by the former ally's 'treason' in 1915. Romantically, he imagined his troops sweeping out of the Trentino, over the mountain ranges to the sea, cutting the Italian army's supply lines and winning a famous victory.[68]

The planning of the Trentino campaign also owed much to fantasy. Conrad never visited the front; he issued his orders from his headquarters in Teschen more than 1,200 kilometres away on the Empire's northern border. His imagination, although vivid, did not extend to predictable problems of terrain and weather. The offensive had to be postponed three times because the mountains over which the troops were expected to advance had been covered in a four-metre thick blanket of snow. Nor did he think much of the Eastern Front, and the possible consequences of withdrawing troops. Falkenhayn had already taken eight divisions for Verdun. Conrad transferred away another four, along with fifteen batteries with nearly all the Habsburg army's heavy guns. Overcoming all logistical obstacles, a force of 157,000 soldiers well supported with artillery was concentrated in the Trentino. On 15 May, after a two-hour bombardment, the troops charged forward. The success of the assault surprised allies and enemies alike; Habsburg troops took the Italian First Army's front lines along a 20-kilometre front. In the next weeks they pressed forward, but already by the end of May the conditions of static warfare favouring the defender had asserted themselves.

Habsburg supply lines became dangerously overstretched. The Italians poured in reserves at an unmatchable rate and when they counter-attacked on 6 June, Austro-Hungarian forces had to relinquish most of their hard-won territory.[69]

The Italians were not only energetic in defending themselves but added their voices to those of the French screaming to the Eastern Front for relief. The Russians had already tried an offensive, at Lake Narotch against the Germans in March 1916. They had fielded more than four times the men and three times the guns of their enemy, but the oper-ation had still been a bloody and embarrassing failure, with 100,000 casualties against the 20,000 of the defenders.[70] In mid-April, when Stavka convened the army staffs to discuss another attack, few were therefore enthused. Only General Aleksei A. Brusilov, the commander of the South-West Front, offered to attack in the summer, striking the first blow for the Entente's combined counter-offensive. He was warned by the Russian Chief of the General Staff, Mikhail Alekseev, and accepted, that he must use what men and guns he had; large re-inforcements would not be granted. To most of his colleagues, he appeared to be setting himself up for failure. Where they had failed to penetrate the Central Powers' lines with concentrated artillery fire and massed infantry even on narrow fronts, Brusilov was proposing to attack a well-fortified line over 300 kilometres long at the south end of the Eastern Front with scarcely any material advantage. Brusilov had just 132,000 more men than the 500,000 predominantly Habsburg soldiers opposing him. With 1,770 light and 168 heavy guns against the Central Powers' 1,301 light and 545 medium and heavy pieces, he had no artil-lery superiority.[71] Brusilov could not even count on surprise to carry his men through. The five Austro-Hungarian armies targeted knew months in advance that an attack was planned. Aerial reconnaissance had detected the Russians' construction of new trenches and large dugouts to hold their reserves. Front-line units had observed enemy guns regis-tering and infantry digging saps to within seventy-five paces of their front line, both obvious preludes to assault. By mid-May, their com-mands could accurately predict where the focus of the attack would be. When, in early June, Russian deserters spoke of having been issued with wire cutters and fresh underwear, it was understood that an assault was imminent.[72]

On 4 June 1916 at the ungodly hour of four o'clock in the morning, the Russians' bombardment began. Their first major attack was launched in the northernmost sector, against the 117,800-strong Habsburg Fourth Army. The defence here, as elsewhere along this front, was designed to thwart familiar ponderous Russian tactics that eschewed surprise in favour of a very heavy artillery bombardment followed by unskilled mass infantry assault. Habsburg 'best practice' was to dig a front line with a second line ten metres behind well connected to the first with defensible communication trenches. A third reserve line was then sometimes set out 100 metres to the rear. Great effort had been made to make the front line impregnable. Barbed-wire obstructions had been erected in front of it, and in the line concrete machine-gun emplacements, mortar and flame-thrower positions had been built. In some places, field artillery had been dug in for direct fire support. A key feature were shelters, known in the Habsburg army as 'fox holes' (*Fuchslöcher*), three or four metres underground and capable of withstanding a direct hit from a 15cm shell.[73] The Prussian General Alexander von Linsingen, who was responsible for the Habsburg Fourth Army and the Army of the Bug to the north, had a fortnight before the attack personally inspected the positions of 2 Infantry Division (ITD), a unit filled with Poles and Ruthenes that was to be at the centre of the Russian bombardment and initial breakthrough. To the divisional commander's obvious relief (all Habsburg officers were scared of Linsingen), even the pernickety Prussian pronounced himself 'convinced that [they] would defy any attack'.[74]

On the first day of Brusilov's offensive, albeit only on that day, this confidence was fully vindicated. While the Russian bombardment did cause damage, the 2 ITD and its neighbouring formations fought off enemy patrols and probing attacks. The division's regiments reported proudly in the late afternoon that not only had all attacks been repelled but even Russian attempts to confuse the defence by sending forward German speakers in their assault waves had failed. Habsburg troops remained in good spirits and while most reserves were already in place directly behind the first position, they had not been needed.[75] Night attacks were easily thrown back. Only the next morning did the Austro-Hungarian defence lose control over the battle. At dawn on 5 June the Russian artillery opened up again and at around 9 a.m. built up to drumfire. The men of 2 ITD took cover in their fox holes, as they had been taught. They remained there too long. The Russians suddenly shifted their fire onto the line immediately behind the front and unleashed their storm troops, who, thanks to saps dug across no-man's-land, did not have far to run. The defenders lost the race to the parapet. As two 2 ITD officers explained:

> In the shelters of the first trench, in Infantry Regiment 82, the men still had the roar of the barrage ringing in their ears, even though for five seconds it had no longer been directed against the trench. In the sixth second some quick-witted person perhaps cried: 'Out into the trenches!' In the seventh second, he collided with someone in the stairwell, who between mangled and splintered low-hanging beams flung a hand grenade after him. And in the eighth second, a voice from above called to the people in the shelter that they could give themselves up. All resistance would be useless.[76]

The reserves, in accordance with the Habsburg army's defensive doctrine, were positioned just behind the front, with the unintended result that they were embroiled in the battle too soon to be organized for a counter-attack. The 13 *Landwehr* Division (LITD), the Fourth Army's reserve held further back, should have intervened, but the order was not delivered because its commander and his staff had been displaced by Russian artillery fire and could not be found. What remained of 2 ITD, fewer than 100 of its 3,500 men, was told to withdraw to the rudimentary third position, along with 13 LITD. Further down the line, the 70 *Honvéd* Division (HITD) had also lost the centre of its first position, and with little chance of restoring the situation due to the loss of 40–50 per cent of its men, it too retreated.[77]

These retreats started a spectacular collapse that overtook the whole Fourth Army on the next day. The infantry at the front were under constant Russian pressure and their artillery spent more time galloping rearwards than giving fire support. The gunners claimed that they lacked shells. In fact, there were plenty of shells but all too often panicking batteries abandoned their stocks and the munitions columns ordered to replenish them found their positions deserted. Worse still, after all but two of the eight divisions in the army reserve had been committed, there were insufficient spare troops to stem the attack and an utter failure of coordination at all levels of command. X Corps, the formation to which the 2 ITD belonged, made an independent decision to pull its troops back shortly before midday on 6 June. Fourth Army command failed promptly to countermand the order and as a result was left with no choice by the early afternoon but to sound a retreat along its whole 81-kilometre front. By mid-afternoon, what was left of the 70 HITD had broken and was streaming back to the Styr River. Units became mixed up, panic spread and exhausted troops ceased to obey orders to form defensive lines and instead flooded rearwards. The army's main supply base, the town of Lutsk, was abandoned on 7 June. Such was the state of dissolution that it was not possible even to re-form the line along the defensible Styr River. Already that night, the Russians began to cross to the west bank, in many places without opposition, and kept going until they had advanced 75 kilometres from their jumping-off points. The Habsburg Fourth Army was broken. In just four days its strength plummeted from 117,800 to only 35,000 men, a fall of almost 70 per cent.[78]

As the Fourth Army collapsed, the Habsburg Seventh Army at the southern end of the line also crumbled. This force, composed of reliable Hungarian and Croatian troops under a proven commander, General Karl von Pflanzer-Baltin, was bombarded south of the Dniester River by 200 guns firing 100,000 shells. 'Our brave *Honvéd* troops were literally buried,' recalled its Chief of Staff, Colonel Theodor von Zeynek. The Russians, as a result of their diligent sapping, had no more than forty and in some places just twenty paces to run in order to reach Habsburg trenches. In consequence, as against the Fourth Army, they were able to move into their enemy's positions with startling speed and, 'as the drum-fire ceased and the curtain fire [aimed behind the lines to stop Habsburg reserves coming up] began, one saw whole columns marching into Russian captivity'.[79] To stem the main Russian success near the village of Okna, Pflanzer-Baltin then made the error of committing all his reserves, with the result that when, on 7 June, the Tsarist Ninth Army launched a sudden assault to the north of the Dniester River and broke through the line, he was rendered helpless. He ordered a retreat south-west into Bukovina two days later, but German protests that this would expose the flank of the *Südarmee* on the Seventh Army's left forced him to switch to a westerly withdrawal. The change in the direction, combined with continued Russian pressure, broke the army. By 8 June it had lost 76,200 of its 194,200 soldiers. Four days later, after just a week of action, Brusilov's forces had captured one-third of the Habsburg army's personnel on the Eastern Front, namely 2,992 officers and 190,000 soldiers, along with 216 artillery pieces. Taking account of the killed and wounded, the total Habsburg loss came to around half the army's complement.[80]

Why had the opening stages of the battle gone so disastrously wrong for the Austro-Hungarian army? Brusilov, the man who conceived and led the offensive, deserves much of the credit for bringing a unique system and effectiveness to Russian offensive planning.[81] He had studied recent Tsarist assaults to understand why they had failed. He ordered his four armies to attack on a front of at least 30 kilometres each, recognizing that any less would leave advancing troops vulnerable to flanking fire. His offensive preparations were characterized by a thoroughness unprecedented on the Eastern Front. At his order, aircraft photographed Habsburg positions, artillery firing programmes were painstakingly drawn up, munitions stockpiled, and dugouts for holding the storm infantry and saps for taking them safely across no-man's-land were constructed. Most importantly, Brusilov did not, in part because he could not, rely on the weight of materiel or men to advance. Instead, he exploited his troops' intelligence and inculcated in them his own clarity of thought to enable speed of action. The general allocated his artillery clearly defined tasks suited to its capabilities: while the heavy guns were ordered to bombard rear lines and lay a curtain of fire after the first break-in, the light guns were set to counter-battery work. The infantry too had its mission carefully explained. Behind the lines, copies of the Habsburg trench systems were laid out on which troops could train for the attack. Brusilov was determined that in the confusion of combat, his soldiers would know their objectives and know how to achieve them.[82]

In contrast, the Habsburg army's preparations for the coming attack were misguided. To a great degree this was a product of the force's perennial problem of incompetent senior leadership. Fourth Army, which alone was to face nearly half of Brusilov's amply supplied light artillery, was particularly unfortunate in its command. Archduke Joseph Ferdinand, its commander, ran a thoroughly dysfunctional staff operation. He had no time for his Chief of Staff, General Otto Berndt, who had been imposed on him after an earlier defeat, was generally intolerant of criticism, and hated the fact that a Prussian officer had been appointed over him to command the Army Group. The Seventh Army had a little more luck with Pflanzer-Baltin and his Chief of Staff Zeynek, who had won laurels repelling a Russian offensive at the start of the year. However, the victory had hardened their tactical and operational convictions, leading to disastrous dispositions in June 1916 when two-thirds of their troops were deployed in or just behind a supposedly impregnable front line, and as a result were immediately lost when the Russians attacked. It also did not help that when the offensive began, Pflanzer-Baltin was bedridden with influenza.[83]

The Habsburg leadership's problems went deeper, however. As one German general observed after extensive service alongside Habsburg staff officers, their key deficiency was their distance, psychological as well as physical, from the men. Conrad and his staff officers, safely ensconced with their wives at the AOK in Teschen, nearly 500 kilometres from the Eastern Front, is the exemplar, but the same mentality was also seen among other General Staff officers. Zeynek, for example, revealingly complained that commanders at the front had built up their positions incompetently; the thought that someone from Seventh Army headquarters should have inspected the works before they were completed evidently never crossed his mind.[84] This detachment, along with the ample evidence of incompetence provided by two years of fighting, had cost commanders the respect of their subordinates. Troops' disgust with their leaders was reflected in slang used at the front, which dubbed General Staff officers' distinctive caps 'prosthetic brains'. So far had the collapse of authority progressed that neither the Fourth nor Seventh Army command proved able to get troops to act against the Russians' sapping. Both recognized the obvious danger posed by the enemy tentacles unfurling towards their lines, yet their orders to stop it prompted little response. Some half-hearted raids over no-man's-land were launched; most ended badly. A few units suggested that it might be preferable to move their lines back, rather than provoke an ugly confrontation with the Russians about their saps. The 2 ITD met an attempt to get it to attack first with procrastination and then, among its junior officers, resistance. The division's parent X Corps, unimpressed when an assault on a dangerous sap was aborted on the lame excuse that dawn had been approaching, ordered another attempt to be made, and added a warning that company commanders who had shirked the operation claiming ill health, and platoon commanders who had thought they could escape through suicide attempts, would all face courts martial.[85]

The scramble by junior officers to avoid the 2 ITD's raid was symptomatic of a wider lack of fighting spirit among the Habsburg army's lower ranks by mid-1916. Even as the debacle unfolded in June, rumours blaming Slavic disloyalty circulated. Already by the middle of the month, Vienna's chattering classes were spreading the story, probably inspired by the 2 ITD's disintegration, that Ruthenian and Polish troops had surrendered unnecessarily to the Russians.[86] Others begged to differ, claiming that it was mass desertion by the Czechs of Moravian Infantry Regiment 8 which had triggered Fourth Army's collapse.[87] In July, when the crisis worsened, Jewish men also came under scrutiny. The General Staff's Intelligence Bureau warned of 'mass desertion' by German, Polish and Hungarian Jews. This was blamed not solely on what it called Jews' 'inherent fear of the strain of war' but also on systematic agitation by mysterious Zionist forces in England.[88] In reality, nationality was a poor predictor of the resistance put up by Habsburg units in the summer of 1916. Seventh Army, for example, had five Slavic divisions, one Polish-Ruthenian, one Ruthenian, one Croatian and two Czech, in late June. The worst relative losses, including in prisoners, had been inflicted on the Croatian and part-Polish divisions, whose peoples were generally regarded as loyal, while the Czech units, the usual scapegoats in any defeat, had shed the fewest soldiers. Ethnically German units also lost large numbers of prisoners. Most of 13 LITD's 13,000 Viennese officers and men surrendered when their positions were overrun by the Russians in the first week of June. Only 1,714 soldiers escaped to fight on.[89]

The Habsburg army's hypersensitivity to disloyalty from the Empire's subordinate peoples, a trait that had cost many civilians their lives in Galicia and Serbia and inflicted much damage on the regime's reputation in 1914 and 1915, undermined its fighting performance in 1916. First, it distracted from the real causes of poor performance. By scapegoating their men, Habsburg commanders right up to Conrad successfully avoided the self-criticism that might have fostered a learning process and improvement. Second, it encouraged the adoption of poor tactics. An investigation after the debacle of summer 1916 was correct to conclude that troops 'had dug too much and exercised too little', yet missed the key point: an army that distrusted half of its soldiers naturally had little interest in training them in initiative or independence. Far better, it seemed, to seek security in reassuringly solid earthworks where troops might easily be supervised.[90] In actuality, these only exacerbated the force's weakness. Officers and soldiers, whose self-confidence could scarcely be high given their hasty training and the suspicion of their commanders, drew a similar comforting but highly dangerous illusion of security from their 'impregnable' fortifications. They consequently preferred not to leave the apparent safety of their earthworks to contest no-man's-land and suppress Russian sapping. Worse still, when that strong front line failed in June 1916, these troops lacked the skills, cohesion and independence to react effectively. Chaos and collapse thus inevitably engulfed the army.[91]

The collapse of the Habsburg Fourth and Seventh Armies in the first half of June was followed by heavy fighting, panic and retreat. The entire front pulled back. The Russians pursued, but overextended supply lines and a lack of cavalry hindered their pursuit. Brusilov turned against the German Army of the Bug on his right flank, though neither his attacks, nor a much larger offensive 260 kilometres to the north near Baranovitchi by massive Tsarist forces under General Everth at the start of July, were successful. The pressure on the defence nonetheless did not ease. Habsburg troops found the Russian soldier, contrary to his image as a stolid peasant, to be an imaginative adversary in the fluid fighting further south. One ambush on a Habsburg cavalry squadron, for example, was carried out by 300 Russians who approached at night by ringing cow bells, a deception that really could only have worked on the Eastern Front. When the sun rose, the 'cows' gave a 'wild roar' and attacked from three sides. Half the Austrians ran, the rest were taken prisoner or killed.[92] Conrad, who had first dismissed the offensive as no real threat, panicked and absurdly tried to evacuate his wife, Gina, from the distant Teschen headquarters. More rationally, he also swallowed his pride and on 8 June travelled to Berlin to beg an unimpressed Falkenhayn for reinforcements. Falkenhayn initially dispatched four divisions, the first on 6 June, but he made Conrad close down his offensive in Italy to free up strength for the Eastern Front. By 20 June ten and a half divisions had been sent to help stem the break-in. However, these troops could only prevent total collapse, not reverse the situation. They arrived gradually and were fed into the battle piecemeal. Moreover, casualties in the demoralized Habsburg army continued to mount. By the end of June, the force had lost 6,740 officers and 319,500 men, of whom 186,850 were 'missing'. A month later, total losses had reached 475,138, of whom 265,931 were missing or captured.[93]

Austro-Hungarian soldiers were not alone in their despair. Habsburg civilians in the battle zone were also terrified by the Tsarist army's advance. In Galicia, Russian gains were modest, for the line advanced only 20 or 30 kilometres. In neighbouring Bukovina, into which the broken remnants of Seventh Army flooded in mid-June, the consequences were more serious. Dr Alfons Regius, a court official in the Crownland's capital, Czernowitz (today Chernivtsi in south-western Ukraine), who had lived through the Russian occupation of 1914–15, spoke for many when, already on 6 June, he declared himself 'VERY worried'. He had learned to read between the lines of official dispatches and found the telegram reporting the battle 'so ambiguously framed that one could assume we had taken back our line along the entire front around five to six kilometres up to the Styr'. In the following days, anxious silence in the streets of Czernowitz was replaced first by the clatter of people rushing to leave and then by the crash of shellfire, as Habsburg batteries took up position in the city. On 17 June, Regius was able to watch through opera glasses Russian infantry storming forwards outside the city. At this point, the inevitability of a renewed occupation became obvious: 'I felt as if a cold hand grasped my heart,' he wrote, 'and the realization dawned on me that our poor soldiers, already partly rendered *hors de combat* by the artillery fire's destructiveness would not WITHOUT machine guns be able to repel this enemy flooding onwards in dispersed masses.' There was not long to wait. That night, at quarter to two, four drunken Russian soldiers armed with rifles and bayonets kicked down his door and looted the house. In spite of this beginning, the Tsarist army behaved more humanely than during its previous sojourn. The atrocities perpetrated in 1914 and 1915, above all against the Jewish population, were not repeated. The occupation was long, however: Czernowitz was finally liberated on 3 August 1917. Its loss was yet another blow to the sinking prestige of the Habsburg Monarchy.[94]

THE SOMME

The Central Powers' acute crisis in the summer of 1916 started in the east but spread to other fronts as the western Entente implemented its plan for simultaneous offensives. The idea of launching an attack on the

Somme River in north-western France had first been raised by the French in December 1915, and in the early months of 1916 generals Haig and Joffre had agreed on the region as the site of a combined Anglo-French offensive. Initially, the area was earmarked as the location for a mid-April preparatory assault to wear down German reserves. By mid-February, this idea had been abandoned in favour of a much larger operation with twenty-five British and no fewer than forty French divisions operating north and south of the river. The jump-off date was set for 1 July. However, soon after this decision, Falkenhayn opened his attritional battle at Verdun and Joffre's army lost so heavily that he was compelled to reduce its contribution to the Entente's offensive.[95] In consequence, the Somme became a British-led campaign. In the context of the concurrent Russian victories over Habsburg forces in the east, the French army's successful though costly defence of Verdun, and in August the opening of an Italian offensive and the entry of Romania into the war on the Allied side, an Anglo-French victory on the Somme offered a chance to deal a death blow to the now vastly outnumbered and overstrained Central Powers.

The Somme offensive's failure to meet its potential was to a great degree the fault of the British Expeditionary Force's commander, General Sir Douglas Haig. The first plan of attack was drawn up by General Sir Henry Rawlinson, the officer Haig appointed to command the Fourth Army, the formation that would conduct the offensive, and the plan was admirably realistic in setting limited objectives. By preparing smaller attacks during 1915, Rawlinson had gained insight into operational dynamics on the Western Front. After the Battle of Neuve Chapelle in March, he had recognized 'that it is always possible by careful preparation and adequate Art[iller]y support by heavy Howitzers to pierce the enemy's line', providing also that field guns could cut the enemy wire. At Neuve Chapelle he had deployed one gun for every six yards of enemy trench and won an initial success. Experiments in later battles with weaker artillery support had failed.[96] His plan for the Somme drew on this lesson, for the offensive's scale and objectives were calibrated according to the guns and men available. The Fourth Army's ten divisions and 200 howitzers were reckoned to be sufficient for a 20,000-yard (18-kilometre) front. Rawlinson's preferred option was a two-stage advance. After a bombardment of between fifty and sixty hours, troops would initially capture only the Germans' forward position and key tactical points. Thinking in somewhat similar terms to Falkenhayn, Rawlinson conceived this 'bite and hold' method as a means 'to kill as many Germans as possible with the least loss to ourselves'.[97]

Haig was shown the plan at the beginning of April and immediately extended the offensive's objectives. In so doing, he disregarded not only Rawlinson's advice but also the views of all of his corps commanders. The commander-in-chief insisted in his response to the draft that Fourth Army should capture the entire German second line above Pozières, in the north of the battlefield, in a single bound, and also push further in the south. He doubled the average advance of around 2,500 yards (2 kilometres) envisaged by Rawlinson. Later, Haig's imagination swelled further. He spoke of distant objectives; Douai, 110 kilometres ahead of Fourth Army, was mentioned. By June, the attack's aim had become 'to break the enemy's defensive system'.[98] Although his later self-exculpatory talk of the offensive as a 'wearing-out battle' disguised it, the British commander was seeking a decisive breakthrough. Yet to sweep into open territory, it was first necessary to break into German lines, and by pushing back the objectives, Haig was ignoring the key lesson of 1915, that defences must be saturated with high explosive. The number of heavy guns and amount of ammunition available were simply inadequate to bombard thoroughly the territory Haig wished to conquer. By one calculation, under his modified plan each 10 square yards of German line would receive just a single pound of high explosive from the offensive's preparatory bombardment.[99]

However, any claim about the inadequacy of the British army's resources in 1916 can be made only in the context of its commander's surfeit of ambition. The well-established portrayal of the British and their ally as underdogs on the Somme, a narrative of victimhood that still crops up in history books today, has little basis in fact. A glance at the figures for opposing forces at the start of the offensive illustrates in just how much trouble German defenders were on the 40-kilometre Anglo-French front (see Table 6).

The material superiority available to the Entente should have been overwhelming. That it was not is often attributed to two causes, beyond the flawed plan. The first was the German defences. General Fritz von Below's Second Army had spent twenty-one months fortifying the area on either side of the Somme River. By the end of June 1916, it had two defensive positions plus a third that had only been sketched out, but

Table 6. The strength of opposing forces on the Somme, 1 July 1916

	Entente	German
Infantry Divisions	19 (+ 10 in reserve)	7
Aircraft	386	129
Heavy Guns	393	18
Medium Guns	933	372
Light Guns	1,655	454

Source: H. H. Herwig, *The First World War: Germany and Austria-Hungary, 1914–1918* (London, 1997), p. 199.

not actually built. The first line was formidable. Before it were two belts of barbed wire, each between 4.5 and 9 metres wide. Defended villages, Beaumont Hamel, Thiepval, Ovillers, La Boiselle and Fricourt, all with solid stone houses, had been built into the fortifications and wired. In the trenches, the chalky soil of the region had permitted the excavation of shelters to a depth of 12 metres. These were often connected, with multiple exits, in order to prevent soldiers from becoming trapped. They were equipped with beds, stoves and kitchens. Stocks of boots, socks, shirts and rations were kept in some large shelters for the garrisons. Some had rails fitted to their staircases, up which a heavy machine gun could be hauled in an emergency.[100] The second line, which ran 2–3.5 kilometres behind the first, was weaker, had fewer dugouts, but still featured intimidating strongpoints capable of all-round defence.[101]

These positions were well built but not impregnable. Mistakes had been made. Most seriously, when the front had been chosen in 1914, tactical thinking had not yet recognized the value of reverse slopes. The Germans' front line was positioned in full view of the enemy on forward slopes, giving an excellent field of fire over no-man's-land but making these trenches easy to shell accurately. Rawlinson had been heartened when he had first visited the sector in February 1916. It was, he had commented, 'capital country in which to undertake an offensive . . . for the observation is excellent and with plenty of guns and ammunition we ought to be able to avoid the heavy losses which the infantry have always suffered on previous occasions'.[102] However, the Germans' second line lay hidden from view behind the hills, which reinforced the argument for a step-by-step assault. On the south of the attack front, the French General Marie-Émile Fayolle leading the Republic's Sixth Army in support of the British, adopted just such a systematic approach. The first line was his primary objective, but preparations were made to bring the artillery forward rapidly to completed emplacements for a speedy assault on the second line while defenders were still disorientated. The British, although less well supported by heavy guns than their allies further south, were prompted by Haig, in turn under pressure from Joffre to try for a deep penetration, to overreach themselves. Had the planning been more realistic and the advance limited but systematic as in the south, the German front defences should have imposed no insuperable obstacle.[103]

The second factor often cited to explain the disappointing results of the Entente's initial assault was the British Expeditionary Force's inexperience. To a far greater degree than either the French or German armies, this was a scratch-built wartime army, for Britain had no peacetime conscription. In just two years the British military had expanded from a 247,432-strong professional force backed by 245,779 part-time Territorials to a mass army of 1.25 million soldiers.[104] Although the army's senior ranks are generally now remembered with least sympathy, these large numbers confronted them with a daunting prospect. In 1916 the five British armies on the Western Front, each fielding hundreds of thousands of soldiers, were led by men who in 1914 had directed divisions of 20,000. Corps commanders with 40,000 men had headed brigades of just 4,000. Learning how to manage such large numbers of men while simultaneously coming to grips with the unexpected and difficult conditions of modern static war was an immense challenge. The fact that all corps commanders supported Rawlinson's initial plan for limited objectives testifies to a realistic awareness of their limitations. Yet this did not equate with a lack of imagination or ambition. Considerable innovation was ongoing at all levels of the army's command. The care with which British battalion commanders selected their tactics for the attack on the Somme on 1 July 1916, and the diversity of methods chosen, offer a good illustration. Stories of overladen men walking slowly towards German trenches, only to be mowed down by machine-gun fire, are largely the stuff of legend. Fifty-three of eighty battalions in the first assault crept into no-man's-land in order to rush enemy positions, and another ten stormed forward from their own parapet. Among the twelve battalions that marched slowly, several did so because they were following creeping barrages intended to keep defenders' heads down, and they proved highly successful.[105]

The focus of most accounts of the Somme has always been on the British infantry. The fact that the men were nearly all wartime volunteers, the sentimental association of their units' names with the English shires or Scottish Highlands, and the charming naivety of the titles of 'Pals Battalions' like The Post Office Rifles, North Eastern Railway Pioneers or Grimsby Chums, have inspired accounts filled with pathos. Landmark works have long portrayed them as 'uniformed innocents' entering battle against a well-entrenched, battle-hardened opponent.[106] Yet this is hyperbole dressed up as fact. The Britons who attacked that summer on the Somme were, as one of them later reminisced, 'very different from the greenhorns who had landed in France a year earlier'.[107] The men had already completed more than nine months of home training and then had spent at least six months, and more often nine or twelve, hardening and learning field craft on the Western Front. Their units had conducted raids and taken casualties. By May 1916 their opponents were observing with surprise how adept the British infantry, mortars, machine guns, artillery and aerial reconnaissance had become at combined operations.[108] In fact, if anybody on the Somme battlefield is overdue to be treated with a little pathos it is not the attackers, with their threefold artillery superiority, total control of the air and copious reserves of manpower, but rather the German defenders opposite. The men who met the British attack on 1 July were mostly from the south of the country, and as likely to curse in sing-song accents 'the damned Prussians' as 'Tommy' or the 'Franzmann'. By no stretch of the imagination can they be described as professional. Many were wartime-trained soldiers like their opponents, and their units were mostly reserve regiments, which from mobilization at the outbreak of war had only ever had a smattering of career officers. They were the sorts of soldiers who defined the German army of the middle war years, grumbling about the rations, praying to God to protect them just that little bit longer, and yearning for Maria, Ursel or Greta. It was their bad fortune to be in the path of a juggernaut determined, as they saw it, to carry the devastation around them into their homeland.[109]

Signs of a brewing military storm had been mounting on the Somme front for months. From April, the Württembergers of 26 Reserve

Division in the north of the sector had heard at night snatches of the rumble of traffic and supplies being unloaded behind British lines. Enemy aerial activity had suspiciously increased. In the middle of June the aeroplanes became even busier, constantly circling overhead, and the Württembergers' patrols stumbled across so-called Russian saps, like the ones Brusilov's soldiers had dug, stretching from British lines 90 metres into no-man's-land. The first day of the Somme battle, 24 June 1916, was heralded at 5 a.m. by shellfire peppering along the line. In the following hours, 3,000 heavy and field guns and more than 1,400 mortars began to bombard the whole 40-kilometre attack front. Among the intended victims of this attack, there was at first some wishful thinking. Lieutenant Adolf Spemann, for example, the adjutant of the II Section, Württemberg Reserve Field Artillery 27, stationed north of the village of Ovillers, initially hoped that it was no more than a demonstration. The shelling was continuous but appeared uncoordinated. However, once it increased in intensity that afternoon, with 900 shells dropping over his sector in a single hour, he accepted 'that in fact it will be something big'.[110]

No one on the German side of the lines quite foresaw just how 'big'. The Entente had planned a bombardment of six days, but poor weather on 26 and 27 June meant that it was extended to a full week, in which 2.5 million shells were fired into the defenders' positions. Gas was also released at irregular intervals, day and night. The bombardment was most intense and effective in the French Sixth Army's sector south of the Somme River. In the British Fourth Army's area of attack, especially in the north, its results were generally more disappointing. There were a number of reasons for the difference. First, the three French corps were simply better supported. They had nearly 100 more heavy guns than the five British corps on their left. Second, their ammunition worked much better. German experts praised French shells' sensitive fuses, which triggered the explosive before the projectile could bury itself too deep in the ground and muffle the blast. By contrast, three-quarters of the shells fired by British artillery were of shoddy North American manufacture. According to German observations made just before the battle, three-fifths of British medium calibre and nearly all shrapnel shells did not explode. This high proportion of duds exacerbated the problem, built into the offensive's planning, that insufficient guns and ammunition were available to cover all targets in Haig's extended area of attack. The

British could devote only 180 guns for crucial counter-battery work. Their 188,500 heavy shells, the only projectiles capable of caving in deep German shelters, were too few. Moreover, around two-thirds of available munitions were not fired at the enemy trenches at all but were needed to clear the thick wire belts in front of them.[111]

Despite all these deficiencies, the sheer weight of metal thrown into German lines wreaked considerable destruction. Even in the north, where the bombardment was least effective, the Württembergers reported heavily damaged trenches, munitions stores hit and barbed wire largely shot away already after three days. Crucially, however, almost all shelters survived and that meant the positions remained defensible.[112] It also protected the Second Army from heavy casualties. In the last ten days of June, the force registered just 2,478 killed and missing and 4,482 wounded. Two-fifths of the killed and missing were suffered by 121 Division opposite the well-armed French.[113] Yet even if the troops were relatively safe, sheltering under a seven-day bombardment was exhausting and, as one frankly put it, 'extraordinarily frightening'.[114] Lieutenant Adolf Spemann's diary for the period described the ordeal. Tension rose as already on 25 June his artillery regiment was blinded by the shooting down of its observation balloons and next day it suffered its first officer casualties. By 27 June, he wrote worriedly, if not wholly accurately, that 'the infantry positions have been completely filled in, the obstacles totally wiped away, the shelters collapsed . . . Mayday calls from [Infantry Regiment] 99 from Thiepval are perpetually despaired.'[115]

Spemann was not a man easily perturbed; he had fought on the Western Front since August 1914 and would end the war with an Iron Cross 1st and 2nd Class and a Knight's Cross.[116] Nonetheless, by the fifth day of the British bombardment, panic was creeping into his diary. 'The superiority [of the enemy] is immense,' he confided. He had good reason to feel even more nervous on the next day, when a shell slammed into the air duct of his dugout. There was 'a horrible jolt and bang', the candles went out and the shelter was filled with smoke, dust and the odour of hydrogen cyanide from the explosive gases, which forced occupants to put on their gas masks. There had been a partial roof collapse, the entrance was blocked, but a faint ray of light seemed to be coming from above. The dugout had been built underneath a latrine, and the shell had opened up a channel. Fearing asphyxiation or the rest of the roof collapsing, with no helmet and only one boot, Spemann crawled through shit to the surface and then, to escape observation from the all-seeing flyers above, he and his comrades scattered for cover.[117]

The long bombardment tested men's endurance. Commanders did what they could to keep their men in condition to fight. Food was critical. Under stress, soldiers ate more. Units were told that every lull in the shelling must be used to bring forward warm food to the front garrisons, not merely to maintain their physical strength but also because 'the nerves of the troops will hold longer, the more food is brought to them'.[118] The continual need to stay alert for gas attacks and, in the front line, for a sudden shift in the shellfire that might herald the start of an assault was very wearing. So long did the ordeal last that some came to believe that the bombardment was an end in itself. 'The buggers want to wear us down and smoke us out using only their technical means,' raged Spemann. A story circulated, almost certainly apocryphal but illustrative of the defenders' mindset: 'an English officer at Beaumont [Hamel, a village through which the German front line passed] jumped out of his trench and shouted across: "Do you swine think we'll attack? We'll shoot you dead with artillery!"' After five days under siege, this seemed entirely plausible to German troops. Spemann rued his participation in a new 'lunatic' way of war, 'which money and America have created, simply to destroy everything and not to advance with a single man'.[119] The idea frightened the defenders more than any assault. At the end of June, infantry units were reporting that their men 'All had just one hope: let the endless shelling finally stop and the enemy attack.'[120]

The wish was granted when, at 8.30 a.m. on 1 July, 55,000 Entente assault troops climbed over their parapets to storm German lines.[121] The defenders were ready. Four hours earlier, Reserve Infantry Regiment 110, stationed in front of La Boiselle, had intercepted a British wireless message telling enemy soldiers to defend all gains stubbornly. Although no time of attack was given, the intelligence was rightly interpreted as implying that one was imminent, and news of it was quickly flashed to all other German units at the front. At 6.30 a.m. the Entente bombardment, which had pounded away all night, reached a new intensity and twenty minutes later sentries reported that the trenches opposite were filling with men.[122] Unnoticed by the Germans, the British had tunnelled under no-man's-land over the past months and packed 40,000 pounds of high explosive below a particularly strong position guarded by Reserve Infantry Regiment 119. At 8.20 a.m., ten minutes before the attack, this was detonated. The earth suddenly erupted, the whole of the 26 Reserve Division's sector seemed to rock and a crater 50 metres wide and 15 metres deep was carved into the ground. One and a half platoons were buried. Yet despite their shock, the Württembergers reacted quickly. Two companies raced from the second and third lines to the shattered position. They reached the crater before the British assault troops rushing from the opposite direction, and were able to mow down most of the attackers. The enemy artillery in this sector had lifted to allow the assault to go ahead, permitting the rest of the men in Reserve Infantry Regiment 119 to exit their shelters unimpeded and take up battle positions. When the British 29 Division launched its main assault ten minutes later, it was met by a hail of fire. The 29 Division lost 5,000 men in this first attack and the subsequent failed attacks on 1 July. The casualties of Reserve Infantry Regiment 119 on this day and during the week-long bombardment that preceded it came to 144 men and 7 officers killed and 274 wounded.[123]

The story was similar across most of the north of the battlefield. German defenders avoided the error of their allies at Lutsk a month earlier, climbing the steps of their dugouts in time and warning their artillery, if not through telephone then with red flares or prearranged messages with machine-gun bursts, to lay down a protective barrage. Very often, the wire in front of the German positions had not been well cut and, regardless of whatever innovative tactical formation they had adopted at the start of their advance, British troops bunched together, offering ideal targets for German gunners. On the occasions when the assaulting troops did manage to penetrate the forward line, they were so reduced in number and the difficulty of reinforcing them was so great that sooner or later they were overwhelmed by counter-attacks.[124] However, further south the Germans' defensive system worked less well. The Badisch 28 Reserve Division, the 26 Reserve's neighbour, suffered a partial defeat. The artillery arrayed against it was more fearsome as British guns had been supported by those in the adjacent French sector. The shelters were less robust than in the north and largely confined to the first line. The infantry was severed from its artillery support, which was anyway devastated by counter-battery fire. With help from three small mines the British captured the fortified village of Fricourt from Reserve Infantry Regiment 111. Within twenty minutes of the attack going forward, the regiment had relinquished parts of its front line. To the east, its sister unit, Reserve Infantry Regiment 109, was also pushed out of its first line, and by the evening had conceded the village of Mametz. Having lost 1,200 of its 2,592 men and expended most of its ammunition and hand grenades in vicious hand-to-hand fighting, and after appealing for reinforcements, Reserve Infantry Regiment 111 also retreated under cover of darkness.[125]

The Badeners were on the edge of a larger emergency that was developing in the south. The Silesian 12 Division, reinforced by Bavarians sandwiched between them and the Somme, lost its first line to British and French assault troops. South of the river the attack by the French Sixth Army, which began two hours after the start of the assault in the north, was also tremendously successful. By 12.30 p.m., French colonial troops had taken the whole of the German first line and 2,000 prisoners for minimal casualties. Their victory owed much to the superior artillery support received by the *poilus* compared with British troops further north. Whether, as was proudly claimed by Joffre then and repeated more recently, it reflected a significantly higher level of tactical skill among the French infantry is more debatable.[126] Fayolle's men on the south bank of the Somme were in fact lucky to face a far weaker enemy than that in the north. Falkenhayn, believing the French to be pinned at Verdun and denying they had forces to spare for an offensive, left just three divisions facing them, while double this number were stationed north of the river.[127] Moreover, the 121 Division on which the French blow was focused was a much more fragile unit than any opposing the British. Unlike the formations in the north, the division was a veteran and victim of Verdun. A six-week tour in the 'Mill on the Meuse' in March and April had cost it around a third of its complement: 5,690 men and 96 officers. Some of its infantry regiments had lost nearly half of their strength. The unit was still recovering from this trauma and, as it had only arrived in its defensive positions in the second half of May, it knew its terrain far less well than did the Württembergers and Badeners on the other side of the Somme.[128] When attacked by overwhelming forces, it quickly lost over 5,000 men and fell back. Only by hastily throwing in reserves did the Germans halt French troops in front of the second position.[129]

The first day of the western Entente's combined offensive was a clear victory for the Germans. Despite a massive commitment of men and materiel, the Entente missed its opportunity to precipitate a real crisis for the defenders. Only in the south, where the bombardment had been most effective and their troops were weakest, had German commanders feared a breakthrough. The French had moved forward everywhere on their 15-kilometre front, advancing around 3 kilometres by the evening. The British had success just north of the Somme River, where along a 6-kilometre front they advanced 1.5 kilometres, taking the German first line. However, beyond this point, the malign effects of Haig's ambition and the dilution of artillery resources were felt. British attacks in the north were repelled with very heavy casualties. In total, the Fourth Army lost a staggering 57,470 men that day. Some 19,240 soldiers were killed or had died of their wounds, 35,493 were wounded, 2,152 missing and 585 captured. No firm figure exists for French losses, although one estimate puts them as low as 1,590 men. Around 13,000 German defenders had been lost. About 8,000 of their casualties had been inflicted north of the Somme, 2,200 of whom were prisoners in British hands.[130] The sacrifice had not been in vain. Though parts of the front line had been lost, German troops' bravery and steadfastness had protected their vastly outnumbered army from catastrophe, thwarted the Entente's best chance of a major break-in, and disorganized the great combined western offensive.

The Entente did not immediately press the limited gains made on 1 July. On the main northern attack front, the British needed time to reorganize after their heavy losses. The more successful French operation in the south had been intended to be merely auxiliary, and so the reserves necessary to follow it up were not immediately available. Meanwhile, the Germans reinforced their hard-pressed defence. Eleven divisions, twenty-seven heavy and fifteen light artillery batteries, and thirty aeroplanes had been brought into the sector by 5 July.[131] With the first danger contained, they prepared to wage a bitter defence. On 3 July the commander of Second Army, General von Below, warned his tired troops what was at stake: 'On the victory of Second Army on the Somme hangs the outcome of the war. The battle must be won by us, despite the momentary superiority of the enemy in artillery and infantry ... For now, everything depends on holding onto our current positions at all costs and on improving them with small counter-attacks. I forbid the voluntary evacuation of positions ... Only over corpses may the enemy find his way forward.'[132]

Thus was the battle fought. Constant small-scale, wasteful attacks by the British in the first half of July were followed by a larger, better-planned assault along a 5,500-metre front on 14 July. The provision of ample artillery allowed a bombardment five times the intensity of that fired before 1 July and the British infantry demonstrated their skill, crawling into no-man's-land under cover of darkness and then surprising the defenders in the early hours of the morning. By midday, the entire second German line between Ovillers and Hardecourt, roughly the area that the Badeners had defended at the start of the month, had been captured and an awkward salient eliminated.[133] Yet thereafter the fighting settled back into an attritional grind. Second Lieutenant Ernst Klasen, a company commander in the elite Grenadier Regiment 12, left a good description of the defenders' ordeal. In late July he found himself stationed in Delville Wood, the furthest point reached by the 14 July attack and a key position where the line shifted direction from west to south. The Tommies who fought there nicknamed the place 'Devil's Wood', but the wordplay does not work so well in German; to Klasen, it was simply 'hell'. He had been through the hectic advance of August 1914, taken part in the fierce position warfare of 1915, and survived the opening phase of Verdun, where he had seen 'much horrific' that had temporarily left his 'nerves ... somewhat broken', but those five days and nights at the front on the Somme, he told his family, 'were the worst days of the whole war'.[134]

To reach their exposed front line, Klasen and his men had to hop from shell hole to shell hole. The air, he wrote, had been 'full of iron'. Once they arrived, the enemy immediately bombarded and assaulted them. This first experience set the tone for the next days. Klasen's unit was under a constant 'murderous drumfire' from heavy guns, which was then followed by infantry attacks. Only once could ration carriers get through with food and drink. What provisions the men had, they shared. 'On such occasions,' observed Klasen, 'one meets true comradeship.' The last day was the worst. A three-hour barrage of extraordinary violence filled in their trenches and almost everybody in the company was buried or lightly wounded. Klasen himself was hit twice by shell fragments, which fortunately just ripped his uniform and left bruises. Suddenly the fire stopped and British troops stormed forwards. The Germans opened up with machine guns and rifles, but the attackers were only finally repelled after a vicious fight with hand grenades. The position held, but at a terrible cost. Only Klasen, who was awarded an

Iron Cross 1st Class, and two others among his battalion's officers, returned unscathed. As company commander, his duties when he reached the rest areas included writing condolence letters to the families of 130 dead, wounded and missing men.[135]

The Entente deployed unmatchable resources throughout the Somme battle. The alliance had far more manpower than its enemy: by mid-August, 106 British and French divisions had fought 57½ German ones. The British alone fired off 7.8 million shells in the sector in the two months after mid-July. New technology was eagerly embraced. At the Battle of Flers–Courcelette in September, for example, they deployed the first ever tanks; lumbering twenty-eight-ton monsters spitting fire from sponson-mounted cannon and machine guns. The British also used aircraft innovatively and extensively for reconnaissance missions, directing artillery fire and even bombing and machine-gunning defenders' positions.[136] German divisional commanders in desperation appealed for more guns, much more ammunition, aircraft, signalling equipment, labourers for fortification-building and more training time for their troops. 'Where to get it all from?' wondered General Max von Gallwitz, the head of the new Second Army formed south of the river when the old Second Army was divided into this and a new First Army in the north.[137] Yet thanks to poor planning and coordination, as well as the sacrifices of men like Klasen, the vast Entente resources produced remarkably modest results, right up to November when the battle was finally halted. The breakthrough for which Haig hankered never happened. The territory captured was very limited, covering an area no more than 8 kilometres deep and 25 kilometres wide by the end of August. Given the restraints imposed by the Western Front battlefield, that was not surprising, but a command which had concentrated its forces instead of frittering them away in disjointed battalion-strength attacks could have gained the territory at a lower cost in blood.[138] More seriously, and contrary to Haig's subsequent exculpatory dispatch on the battle, the Entente failed even to pin German forces to the Somme Front. Fifteen German divisions were transferred away from the west during the campaign to meet more urgent threats on other fronts. Intense though the pressure was, the Central Powers retained sufficient reserves to fire-fight emergencies and survive.[139]

The most common argument put forward to justify the Entente's effort on the Somme is that it inflicted lethal damage on the German army. Haig argued in retrospect that the fighting had served its function as the first stage of an extended 'wearing-out battle', and in the aftermath of the war a heated debate took place, with strangely little reference to German sources, about which side had lost more men. The British and French officially acknowledged losses of 419,654 and 204,253 respectively at the Somme: 623,907 Entente soldiers altogether. The German army in its official history stated that its casualties reached nearly 500,000.[140] Deliberate confusion about whether this figure was complete was spread by the authors of the official British military history to cast Haig and his army in a better light. However, the figure was not just comprehensive, but cautious and even conservative. German units submitted returns every ten days, reporting permanent casualties (killed, missing and wounded), and sick and lightly wounded who could be expected to return. Those compiled for the Second and First Armies on the Somme recorded a casualty rate of 416,802 killed, wounded (including lightly wounded) and missing. If gas casualties (3,053 for both armies) and psychiatric disorders (officially 9,354 men, although the Germans, as other armies of the period, misdiagnosed and underestimated these ailments) are added, total recorded German battle casualties reach 429,209.[141]

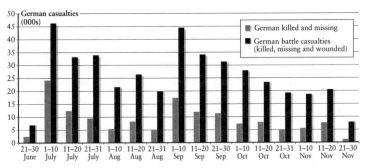

Figure 4. Battle casualties sustained by German First and Second Armies on the Somme, ten-day periods from June to November 1916

Source: Heeres-Sanitätsinspektion des Reichskriegsministeriums (ed.), *Sanitätsbericht über das Deutsche Heer (Deutsches Feld- und Besatzungsheer) im Weltkriege 1914/1918 (Deutscher Kriegssanitätsbericht 1914/18). Die Krankenbewegung bei dem deutschen Feld- und Besatzungsheer im Weltkriege 1914/1918* (3 vols., Berlin, 1934), iii, pp. 52–3.

The Entente thus certainly inflicted grievous losses on the 103 German divisions that fought in the battle, but it failed to deal a death blow to the German army. This continued to rise in strength: in June 1917 at its peak, it had three-quarters of a million men more than a year earlier, at the start of the Franco-British attack.[142] The impression that the Entente failed in what was supposed to be its year of attrition in 1916 is borne out by casualty statistics. Despite the vast numerical and material superiority of its enemies, and the fact that at least notionally they were following a deliberate attritional strategy, the German army's 1,393,000 killed, wounded, missing and prisoners (336,000 of them dead) in 1916 were 311,000 fewer than its casualties in 1915.[143] Even if reframed in retrospect as an attritional battle, the Somme battle was clearly badly managed. The first ten days of July 1916, justly remembered as a catastrophe for the British, were also the period of greatest loss to the Germans (see Fig. 4). Never again in the course of the battle did the attackers inflict such casualties on their enemy. If placed in proportion to overall strength, only once, at the opening of September, were casualty rates heavier. Fierce British and French attacks launched on 3 and 4 September eliminated 13 per cent of the First and Second Army's strength, in contrast to around 10 per cent in the first ten days of July or between 6 and 8 per cent in a normal week and a half of disjointed small-scale attacks on the Somme.[144]

The Somme battle's most damaging impact on the German army was in fact not material but psychological. An early sign that this battle was different from previous clashes, more intense and awful, was the sudden tripling of psychiatric casualties among troops stationed opposite the British in July 1916 (see Fig. 3). The combat may have been less bloody than more mobile fighting but it was far more stressful. As Prince Rupprecht of Bavaria, a thoughtful soldier who from 28 August led the Army Group overseeing the Somme battle, discovered, 'the effect of overwhelming enemy artillery fire, existing in the shell holes, not enough rations, the stench of corpses, and all the other difficulties of a lengthy battle quickly consume the nerves of leaders and men'.[145] The unpredictability of death by shellfire and the helplessness felt by soldiers under the battle's extraordinarily heavy bombardments were deeply disturbing. Some lost their religion: belief in the guiding hand of a loving God could be simply too difficult in this suffering and chaos. Field chaplains reported that attendance at services had dropped.[146] By the autumn, the strain had begun to damage some units' combat performance. General Gallwitz recorded in mid-September that more men were reporting sick, and desertion and self-inflicted wounding were on the increase.[147] Rumours circulated of Rhinelanders, men whom the army worried about due to their proletarian background and often strong Socialist sympathies, fragging their officers.[148] More substantively, the ratio of captured and missing to killed increased as the Somme dragged on, an indication that troops were becoming more inclined to surrender. By October on the Somme and also at Verdun where the French recaptured the fortresses of Douaumont and Vaux, panicked German units were reported to have fled wholesale or capitulated.[149]

The Entente missed an opportunity on the Somme in 1916. An initial break-in all along a 40-kilometre front was not only in the bounds of possibility but, even if shallow, would have been extremely difficult to seal for an army already heavily committed at Verdun and forced to shore up its ally on the other side of Europe. The subsequent British failure to concentrate force and, with only a few exceptions, plan large, systematic assaults, wasted an unprecedented material superiority and permitted the Germans to transfer strength elsewhere. The offensive's success as an attritional battle has been vastly overstated. Although it became famous as a *Materialschlacht* – a battle of material – its main impact was psychological. The horrendous combat conditions and the obviously great material inferiority of their own side shook German troops. Gallwitz maintained that the majority of soldiers continued to recognize the 'necessity of holding out'.[150] The duty to defend hearth and home remained strong: 'In der Heimat, In der Heimat' – 'At home, at home, / We'll see each other again' – was sung by men coming out of combat on the Somme.[151] Nonetheless, not just the generals but their soldiers too now knew how powerful their enemies were and how close they had come to being overwhelmed. For the first time, there was doubt about whether Germany would win this war.

OUTCOMES

All fronts were calm by December 1916. The Entente had little to show for all its planning and exertions. The British on the Somme had finally taken Beaumont Hamel, an objective laid down for the offensive's first day, in November. The French had recaptured most of the land lost in the first half of the year at Verdun. The Italians had achieved somewhat more, taking the prestige objectives of Gorizia and Monte San Michele in their August offensive. However, they had then exhausted their troops in three poorly prepared and executed battles of the Isonzo (the Seventh, Eighth and Ninth). Brusilov's offensive had, after a period of attritional warfare, ground to a halt in November. Much more significant than these 'bloody victories' was the Central Powers' occupation of most of Romania after a rapid campaign that ended with the capture of Bucharest at the start of December.[152]

Nonetheless, belying the modest changes to Europe's map, the fighting of 1916 had a profound effect on both Central Powers. Austria-Hungary's year had been especially disastrous. The Brusilov offensive not only cost the Habsburg army nearly 500,000 casualties but also had a much wider impact on the Empire. The territory overrun by the Russians was valuable. The loss of Czernowitz was a major blow to prestige and the surrender of the Jakobeny mine in Bukovina, the Empire's main source of manganese, had serious implications for its war effort. Although Bosnian mines could partially compensate, the loss forced Austria-Hungary to lower the percentage of manganese in its steel.[153] Even more significant, in appealing for help to fight off Russian attack, Habsburg leaders suborned their empire to Germany, relinquishing military and much foreign policy independence. On 6 September a 'United Supreme Command' in the east was organized under Wilhelm II, after at the end of July most of the Eastern Front had already been placed under German command. German power was cemented by changes further down the Habsburg military hierarchy. Key Habsburg command positions were taken by German generals, and German officers were even inserted as battalion or company commanders into Habsburg units, while their opposite numbers were transferred to German formations to learn the art of war. The Central Powers' alliance was tightened through these measures, but with Austria-Hungary now bound in explicitly as the junior partner.[154]

In Germany, the crises of 1916 precipitated a change of army command. Field Marshal Paul von Hindenburg, the hero of Tannenberg, was appointed on 29 August 1916 to Chief of the General Staff, with Erich Ludendorff as his First Quartermaster General. Falkenhayn's star had waned with the failure of his Verdun strategy, his relations with the

Chancellor were bad, and the Kaiser lost confidence in him once Romania declared war. The new army commanders, the Third OHL, worked from the basis, as Ludendorff later put it, that 'men, war material and moral resolution were matters of life and death to the Army'.[155] Steps were immediately taken to conserve manpower. A methodical system of fortnightly rotation was introduced on the Somme to spare troops. The orders not to relinquish territory were condemned as needlessly wasteful of men's lives and rescinded. A flexible 'elastic' defence was instead ordered.[156] Later, more radical measures were introduced. At the end of the Somme battle, Hindenburg and Ludendorff settled on a strategic withdrawal. In the rear of the battlefield 65,000 labourers, many of them unwilling French and Belgian civilians or prisoners of war, were set to work constructing the immensely strong Siegfried Line. The German front was strengthened and shortened by 50 kilometres, releasing ten divisions. Drawing inspiration from the destruction they had seen during the Russian Great Retreat of 1915 but adding German system and planning, the new commanders ordered a methodical devastation, codenamed Operation Alberich, of the land relinquished. When four German armies withdrew 20–40 kilometres to their new positions in conditions of highest secrecy in mid-March 1917, they left behind 1,500 square kilometres of depopulated wasteland.[157]

The Third OHL brought a new radicalism and ruthlessness to how Germany waged war. Society was to be remobilized for the army. Hindenburg and Ludendorff recognized the urgent need for new weapons and war machines from the home front; the Somme had demonstrated just how far the Reich lagged behind. Yet the prime lesson that the new German High Command drew from the fighting was that although materiel was important, human factors, the skill and motivation of soldiers, trumped it. 'In this war,' observed one army analysis of the Somme battle, 'which technology and numbers appear to dominate, the strength of will of the individual personality is in fact decisive.'[158] Small groups of soldiers, protected only by shell holes and their own wits in the later stages of the campaign, had successfully fought to a standstill the British and French armies. The Somme provided both wide experience of a new type of fighting, previously associated with the elite storm troops, and the spur to institutionalize its methods across the army. Under Hindenburg and Ludendorff, the German military embraced 'elastic defence', reformed its command structure, delegated authority downward and replaced the 200-strong company with eight-man squads as its basic tactical unit. In training, teamwork, initiative and independence were its watchwords: 'soldiers in the ranks with nerves as hard as steel' were, manuals explained, now 'the main bearer of the fight'. Here lay the paradox of the Somme: the German army bled heavily and was deeply shaken in the battle. The force that emerged was more brittle, as a jump in indiscipline and desertions revealed the following year. Yet through the ordeal, it adapted and underwent tactical revolution. The Entente in 1917 would find it a more flexible, skilled and dangerous opponent.[159]

8

Deprivation

SUFFERING AND SHORTAGE

For central European civilians, no less than for their soldiers, the year 1916 was grim. Home and front were intimately connected and the impact of the bloody struggles in east and west inevitably reverberated well beyond the battlefield. With seven million German and almost five million Austro-Hungarian men in garrisons or at the front, nearly every family had somebody to fret about. As casualties mounted – the total military dead of Germany and Austria-Hungary since the start of the war each exceeded one million during the course of 1916 – so too did the mourners in the homeland.[1] Moreover, these societies were not only desperately sad, anxious and stressed, but they were also becoming ever more exhausted and impoverished. The channelling of resources to the military, the ever tightening Entente blockade, soil exhaustion and bureaucratic bungling brought terrible hardship. Above all, the home front's year was defined by food shortage.

People living in German and Austro-Hungarian towns, and above all in the major metropolises, faced a miserable struggle to find food from the war's middle years. Anna Kohnstern's letters to her soldier-son Albert offer a window into the troubles that she and other citizens of Hamburg, Germany's second-largest city, endured. In March 1916 she told him how queues of 600 or 800 people formed outside shops whenever consignments of butter were delivered. Her April letters made clear that the home front was becoming a consumer battlefield: in a scramble to buy meat, she recounted, two women had been killed and sixteen hospitalized. Both butter and meat had been scarce and expensive for much of the previous year. What made 1916 worse was that grain from the last harvest had been consumed already before the year began and potatoes started to run out in the spring. The family lost weight; Anna especially, as she continually skimmed off part of her inadequate ration so as to send extra food to her son in the field. The summer brought Hamburg's first major hunger riots, in which thousands of working-class women and youths shouted for bread, looted bakeries and fought police. When a cold, wet autumn created the conditions for a fungus to destroy half of the annual potato crop, a terribly difficult winter, the worst in nutritional terms that Germany experienced during the war, was unavoidable. As Anna told Albert despairingly in November, 'shopping for food is becoming ever worse. One is underway the entire day and still gets nothing.' She and her five daughters closed off most of their lodgings and huddled in one room in order to save on heating fuel, which was also scarce and expensive. Like other families across central Europe, the Kohnsterns subsisted that winter on turnips, cattle fodder which the state had forced farmers to surrender. Anna's letters became openly desperate. 'It isn't going to be possible to get through winter,' she wrote on the first day of December, with the worst of the ordeal still before her. 'It is highest time that the war was ended.'[2]

Millions in towns and cities across Germany and Austria-Hungary shared the Kohnsterns' plight. The search for scarce essentials such as soap, fuel, clothing and, above all, food increasingly dominated civilians' lives. The *Berliner Tageblatt* reported as early as May 1916 on how cityscapes had altered as shopping, once so simple, had now become a cut-throat competition with one's neighbours:

> Whoever in these cool spring nights is willing to take a walk through the streets of the city will, already before midnight, see figures loaded up with all sorts of household equipment creeping here and there in front of the market halls, at times also in front of the various warehouses and grocery stores. At first there are only a few but with the chime of midnight the groups swell to crowds. Women form the majority. At first, they huddle on the steps of the surrounding shops and on iron park railings. Soon however one of them comes and puts down a straw sack next to the entrance, on which she makes herself comfortable. That is the signal for a general movement. Behind the lucky owner of the straw sack, a second woman sets up a deckchair. Close next to her a less demanding lady takes up position on a simple wickerwork chair, which she has brought – God

knows how far – from her apartment ... Between and behind the lucky
ones line up in ever extending rows with five to eight people next to each
other women, in modest numbers also men, and indeed even children.
Through the rows spreads a lively chatter.

In time, the conversations cease. The woman with the straw sack lies
down for a short nap. The woman with the deckchair follows her example.
The others stand there apathetically, some sleep standing and the moon-
light makes their pale faces appear even sallower. Police appear and walk
up and down morosely.

The morning dawns. New crowds arrive ... At last the selling begins.
And the result: to each a pitiful half or, if one has especial luck, a whole
pound of meat, lard or butter for half of the buyers, while the others must
leave with nothing.[3]

Berliners were not alone in dancing the 'Polonaise' – the wartime slang
for queuing because one stood in line and shivered. The same dance of
deprivation played out day and night in cities across central Europe.
The Viennese suffered more than most. In the spring of 1917, a quarter
of a million people, approximately 12 per cent of the city's population,
daily stood in one of almost 800 queues around the city. More than one-
fifth of these shoppers departed empty-handed, their strength wasted.
In some working-class districts, lines formed outside bakeries already
shortly after 10 p.m. Anyone who arrived after 3 a.m. was unlikely to
get to the front before the flour on sale was exhausted.[4]

The successful shopper needed not only to know where the next
irregular food delivery would arrive and come early enough to reach the
front of the queue before the limited supplies gave out. She (for those
queuing were largely female, as so many men were in either the army or
war industry and therefore had access to separate food provision) also
had to be able to afford the goods. Although official controls kept down
the price of some staple products, this nonetheless proved a challenge
due to rapid inflation. Food prices in Germany's cities were already one
and a half times their peacetime level at the end of 1915. The new shortages prompted a sudden spurt of further inflation, bringing prices in the
spring of 1916 to double the pre-war level, where they remained for the
rest of the year. In Austria, which lacked the financial means to sustain
a great war, inflation spiralled: the cost of living was two and a half
times its pre-war level already by the end of 1915, and it was over six

times greater by December 1916.[5] Earnings increased too, but failed to keep up with the rapidly rising costs. In Germany, the real wages of most male and female manual workers were worth 75 per cent of their peacetime value by March, and only around 60 per cent by September 1916. Even in war industries like munitions, metal-production, chemicals and electrics, where pay was much better than the average, workers' real wages fell by 8 per cent for women and over 20 per cent for men.[6] Workers in Austria fared worse, not only due to higher price inflation but also because they were subject to more compulsion than the proletariat in wartime Germany. Austrian factories producing for the army operated under the 'War Performance Law' (*Kriegsleistungsgesetz*) of 1912, which suspended employees' rights to resign or collectively protest. So in the metals industry, which in the Reich offered some of the highest and most durable wages, all but the most skilled Austrian workers saw their real earnings drop below half of the pre-war levels already by March 1916. In Bohemia, the Empire's core industrial region, workers' real wages would by 1918 be just 35 per cent of their pre-war value.[7]

White-collar workers were in even greater trouble. German salaries had been cut during the war's first eighteen months. Subsequently, office workers accrued rises and more allowances, yet at the end of 1917 their nominal earnings were only 18 per cent higher than at the outbreak of hostilities, whereas manual workers in factories not producing for the war had been given rises of 40 per cent, and many of those in war industries had increased their takings by 100 per cent. Civil servants were no more protected than desk-bound administrators in private businesses; by 1917 their salaries had lost around half of their value. Many white-collar employees now earned less than munitions workers, a change experienced as a deep humiliation.[8] In Austria too, bureaucrats watched their salaries inflated away. Their discontent was especially threatening, for the administration was the loyal, nationally indifferent 'glue' that held together the Habsburg Empire.[9] The bourgeoisie reliant on a fixed income such as a pension, or who lived off savings, also suffered severe hardship both in Vienna and in the Empire's peripheries. Aleksandra Czechówna, by no means one of Cracow's worst-off citizens, rued in September 1916 what she called 'expensive money' and regretted having 'to do without many things to which one was accustomed' and even 'now and then to starve'.[10]

As if the increasing scarcity and cost of food were not bad enough, it also declined in quality. The rye and potatoes used since 1914 to cut wheat flour ran short, forcing their substitution with less appetizing alternatives. Ground maize, lentils, peas, chestnuts, soya beans, clover and bran were all used to 'stretch' bread. So too were sand and sawdust, although this was illegal. Legitimate grains were milled less finely than in peacetime, allowing husk to enter the bread, which made it difficult to digest. The taste of war bread had generally not been too bad in 1914, when rye and potato were used; the worst gripe was that it lacked the crispiness of a white loaf. Later, however, war bread became vile: 'you couldn't slice it,' remembered one Cracovian with disgust decades later, 'you broke it up with your hands. It was yellow, sticky, not good.'[11] Some loaves made with rotten flour and poor ingredients had alarming effects on the body. 'I have been vomiting,' one woman told relatives in April 1918, when she was living off the poor-quality bread available on Bulgaria's ration. 'I feel burning from my mouth to my chest as if there is a fire and I feel heaviness as if there is a stone inside.'[12]

As familiar foods vanished from shops, a hunt began to find replacements. Historians scoured books for evidence of what their ancestors had eaten in times of dearth. Chemists attempted to extract oils from mustard, grape and poppy seeds.[13] Private enterprise participated eagerly. By the war's end, more than 11,000 ersatz (substitute) products were on sale in Germany, including thirty-three egg substitutes and 837 different types of substitute sausage. Before mid-1916 there was no official regulation, so manufacturers shamelessly cheated hungry customers. Some 'egg substitutes' were nothing more than coloured maize or potato flour. One 'substitute pepper' was 85 per cent ash. In Austria, an item marketed as 'coffee with sugar' turned out to have sand as one of its main ingredients. Some ersatz products were dangerous. 'Flour' made up of gypsum was among the lethal concoctions sold.[14] Even where an honest attempt to simulate the original product was made, the result was often unpleasant. Ersatz sausages, for example, were little tubes of slime. They could legally have up to 70 per cent water content, as not only meat but also the flour needed to pad them had run short. Central Europeans' beverage of choice, coffee, also deteriorated drastically. Even before 1914, only the rich had consumed expensive pure-bean coffee; the less wealthy had drunk it adulterated with chicory, grain or ground acorns. War shortages, however, prompted producers to experiment with other ingredients. By 1918, walnut shells, plum stones, even turnip heads and bark were all used to manufacture Coffee-Ersatz.[15]

Individuals fought against deprivation. Upping earnings was one obvious strategy, for food was always available outside official channels to those who could pay cash. In Germany, contrary to what has long been assumed, there was no sudden rush of women taking their first job, and with it their first step towards emancipation, during hostilities. Overall female employment remained at a level similar to that in peacetime. What changed, however, was *where* women worked. Hundreds of thousands left low-paid jobs in the textile industry, domestic service and, despite official attempts to hold them there, agriculture, for the better wages offered by war industries. This was also true in Austria-Hungary, albeit to a lesser extent due to the land's smaller industrial base. In the west of the Empire, around 40 per cent of the war industries' workforce was female by 1916. In the Magyar half, the number of women working in manufacturing industries increased by 65 per cent, from 137,075 to 209,833 between December 1914 and May 1916. Other women took over their conscripted husbands' positions. By the autumn of 1915, a fifth of the 14,000 female employees working for German tram companies, for example, were the spouses of drafted tram workers. For soldiers' wives with small children, home work, like sewing sandbags or assembling gas masks, could provide a small but useful supplement to state support.[16]

Family members worked together for survival. In the war's early years, food had flowed from home to front, but this partially reversed in 1916 as worried soldiers bought up foodstuffs in the occupied territories and sent them to their families. Anna Kohnstern was fortunate to have a brother serving in the military staging areas in Belgium who, after he came home on leave and saw how she was living, began to send her beans, butter and meat. Combat soldiers like her son, Albert, had less opportunity to buy food, but many sent money.[17] Adolescent daughters and sons also contributed to families' shared income. Girls had few opportunities for high wages, and so took over household tasks like cooking, cleaning, looking after younger siblings and queuing while their brothers or mothers went to work. For teenage boys, by contrast, war work became attractive and, for those over sixteen once the Auxiliary Service Law was passed in December 1916, compulsory. The proportion of industrial positions occupied by youth rose from its pre-war level of 16 per cent to over 25 per cent in 1916. Adolescents exploited the wartime economy's manpower shortages, switching jobs on average three or four times per year in order to get the highest possible earnings. In the munitions factories, their wages not only rose quicker than those of their mothers, but actually exceeded them by 1918.[18] Men, women and children in the factories worked extremely long hours. In peacetime, a 57-hour week, comprising six 11½-hour days, inclusive of two hours compulsory but unpaid rest, had been the norm for men in metalworking factories. These long days became still longer in wartime; some male workers were at their benches for 15 or even 18 hours per day, while women in the munitions industry worked 54–60 hour weeks. Unskilled workers were especially prone to work long hours in order to compensate for their low standard rate of pay with overtime supplements. Labour at night, on Sundays or holidays could attract bonuses of 40 or 50 per cent.[19]

Their weekly wages in their hands, workers hurried from work in search of food. In the cities, the front line of this hunger war, shops were bare and queues long, so people headed to the countryside to bypass the official supply system and buy direct from farmers. 'Hamstering' (*Hamstern*), as these illegal foraging trips were known, took place on a huge scale during the second half of the conflict. Travellers on rural railways on Sundays, the one day of rest, were so numerous by 1917 that in some areas police intervention had become impossible. Security personnel were posted at stations and bans issued on carrying rucksacks into the countryside, but the 'hamsters' resolutely worked around all obstacles. Field tracks were used to avoid police posts on the main roads, and journeys were made under cover of darkness. Women sowed pockets into their undergarments, thwarting the police, who lacked the female staff needed for body searches. Other women simply posted the food to themselves, until the authorities realized what was happening and started checking packages. Some women used ingenious disguises. There were some who feigned pregnancy, strapping cheese and butter to their bellies. In a strange twist on the fear at war's outbreak that enemy agents were disguising themselves as nuns, some 'hamsters' donned robes and wimples in the hope of passing untouched through the food checks.[20]

'Hamstering' marked the limits of Germans' and Austrians' wartime solidarity. The switch to individual (or familial) self-preservation as hunger increased was understandable, but it undermined the official supply system, and with it the *Burgfrieden*. Stuttgart's milk deliveries offer one striking illustration of how detrimental smuggling was for the official food supply. As a result of weekend 'hamstering', the city received just one-sixth the quantity of milk on Sundays and Mondays compared with what it received on other days. When the railway timetable was altered, making it impossible to reach a nearby farming region after work hours, the city's official supply system immediately received an additional 500 litres from that area.[21] In fairness, hungry foragers were not solely to blame. Smuggling was big business, carried out by chains of professional criminals. Black-market food in relatively well-off southern Germany cost at least twice as much as its official price and four to five times as much as what the item would have been sold at in peacetime. In Austria where food shortages were extreme, the differences were even greater: white flour, for example, was selling in 1917 on the black market in western Galicia at nearly six times the official price, and more than fifteen times its peacetime price.[22] The authorities, although they prosecuted hungry 'hamsters' and professional smugglers, were just as guilty of disregarding official prices. The Habsburg War Ministry and other central offices paid premiums already in 1916, simply because there was no other way to obtain certain foods in anything like sufficient quantities. Some municipalities bought foodstuffs at illegal prices.[23] Big armaments firms like Thyssen and Krupp undertook huge illegal food purchases with the connivance of military officials. The nutrition was distributed in factory canteens or given to employer-owned 'yellow unions' to keep workers fit and compliant, and was therefore doubtless beneficial for munitions production. Yet its removal meant hardship for everybody else.[24] The black market blossomed after 1916, and by 1918 between a third and a fifth of Germany's agricultural produce was sold through illegal channels, including between one-eighth and one-seventh of potatoes and bread, one-quarter to one-third of butter, milk and cheese, and one-third to half of all meat and eggs.[25]

Germans and Austrians did not just look to farmers for additional nutrition; they also grew their own food. Food shortages sponsored an enthusiasm for urban gardening in both countries. Some 200,000 square metres of land was turned over for allotments in Vienna's Prater district and by the autumn of 1918, 157,300 of the city's residents were cultivating their own 'war gardens'.[26] The rearing of small animals also captured the interest of desperate people. Cats and dogs were abandoned in favour of edible pets like rabbits, ducks, hens and geese. Goats in particular became very popular. While other cattle stocks plummeted during hostilities, the numbers of goats grew by nearly a million in Germany over the four war years. They were a source of scarce milk, easy to look after and required so little pasturage that apocryphal stories circulated of goats being kept on apartment balconies.[27] While some people gardened, others sought to increase their purchasing power by joining in food-purchasing cooperatives. Often these were organized through work, and many built on initiatives already begun in peacetime. Galician railway workers, who were especially active in this field, gave their food-purchasing associations worthy names like 'Solidarity' and 'Thrift'. Hard-pressed middle-class groups like teachers set up similar organizations. There were also informal and smaller-scale initiatives: Prague University's Law Faculty, for example, split a calf, acquired through official connections, between the staff every week in 1917.[28] Other cooperation was more exploitative. Anna Kohnstern, for example, unable to afford the meat to which she was entitled under the ration system, swopped her coupons with another woman, who gave her sweets in return. The woman could use the coupons to supplement her own diet or sell the meat that they brought her for a large profit. Still, from Anna's perspective, the otherwise useless coupons gave her 'something', as she said, 'with which one can drive away the hunger'.[29]

Regardless of what they did, be it gardening, 'hamstering' or working long hours of overtime for the money to buy food on the black market, central European civilians suffered terribly from the food shortages. They lost weight and became weak, exhausted and more vulnerable to illness. The extent of Germany's problem is illustrated by the fact that even soldiers, the best (or least worst) supplied section of the populace, were affected. A medical inspection of recruits at Infantry Regiment 46's depot in rural Posen found at the end of 1916 that after one month of training 15 per cent had lost weight, a few by as much as seven kilos. The cause was found to be underfeeding: the troops were getting four-fifths of their carbohydrate, half the protein and about a quarter of their fat entitlement. The army doctor who carried out the investigation warned of damage to the young soldiers' bodies and military performance if rations were not increased.[30] Civilians, who underwent exactly the prolonged undernourishment feared by the doctor, vindicated his warning. The food shortages wreaked terrible damage, especially on vulnerable groups like children and adolescents. Doctors in Munich found in 1916–17 that, compared with heights and weights before the war, children were 2–3 centimetres shorter and 2–3.5 kilograms lighter.[31] In Austria too, deprivation marked the young. Six- to thirteen-year-olds simply stopped growing during the last year of hostilities, and twelve- to fourteen-year-olds in Vienna looked like sickly eight- to ten-year-olds. In the barren Alpine lands, some children were so malnourished that they lacked the strength to walk.[32]

Whether civilians actually starved was, and remains, highly controversial. In the aftermath of the war, German authorities claimed that there had been 763,000 excess civilian deaths. Recent work by the historian Avner Offer has called that figure into doubt. Food was adequate, he argues, apart from during the 'turnip winter' of 1916–17 and the summer of 1918. It helped that people's need for calories declined as they lost weight. Supporting his point, infant mortality in the Reich barely budged, and in fact was slightly lower for much of the war than it had been in peacetime (see Table 7).

However, the poorest and hungriest are not well represented in the wartime studies on which Offer's work leans. All investigations also agree that even if people were not actually starving, they were dangerously malnourished, exposing them to disease. As a result, civilian deaths rose by one-third, and much more if those killed by the influenza epidemic of 1918 are counted. Significantly, the upward trend in German female deaths started in 1916, just as the food crisis became serious. The old as well as the young were very vulnerable. Tuberculosis, pneumonia and other lung diseases were major killers. Consequently, a somewhat revised excess fatality figure of 424,000, with another 209,000 deaths from the influenza of 1918, appears entirely plausible.[33]

Austria-Hungary's wartime public-health crisis was even worse. However, whereas after the war German civilian casualties prompted passionate debate and symbolized the wrongs inflicted by the Allies, the Habsburg Empire's non-combatant dead attracted little discussion – one mark of the greater value set on western than eastern European life throughout the twentieth century. Estimates extrapolated from deaths in Bohemia put the Empire's civilian war losses at 467,000.[34] The Habsburg population was three-quarters that of its ally, so this figure implies approximately equivalent civilian death rates in both Central Powers. There are, however, good reasons to believe that it understates overall civilian mortality. First, Bohemia was Austria's most fertile region and, along with Galicia, one of its most important agricultural centres. Together with its neighbours, Silesia and Moravia, it grew over

Table 7. Infant mortality, 1914–18 (per cent of live births)

	Germany	Austria*
1913	15.1	18.0
1914	16.4	16.9
1915	14.8	21.1
1916	14.0	19.8
1917	14.9	18.8
1918	15.8	19.5

* Refers only to the area that later became the Austrian Republic.

Sources: R. Meerwarth, 'Die Entwicklung der Bevölkerung in Deutschland während der Kriegs- und Nachkriegszeit', in R. Meerwarth, A. Günther and W. Zimmermann, *Die Einwirkung des Krieges auf Bevölkerungsbewegung, Einkommen und Lebenshaltung in Deutschland* (Stuttgart, Berlin, Leipzig and New Haven, CT, 1932), p. 65, and K. Helly, 'Statistik der Gesundheitsverhältnisse der Bevölkerung der Republic Österreich in und nach dem Kriege', in C. Pirquet (ed.), *Volksgesundheit im Kriege* (2 vols., Vienna and New Haven, CT, 1926), i, p. 20.

three-fifths of the western half of the Empire's barley and more than a third of its potatoes and wheat before the war. Supply was thus likely to be better here than elsewhere. Second, and supporting this point, there was clearly much variation among different Crownlands. The estimate can make no allowance for the invasion-related mortality in Galicia, where in 1915 the underfed and poorly sheltered population was ravaged by epidemics of cholera, typhus and dysentery.[35] Although their accuracy is questionable, there were also later reports of famine in South Styria and starvation in Croatia.[36]

Ration allowances also indicate that life was harder even in the relatively well-supplied east of the Habsburg Empire. In April 1917, German daily rations of meat, fat, flour and potatoes totalled 615 grams per head. Hungarian potato-producing regions received 595 grams, other Magyar districts 331 grams, and even less went to people in the Austrian half of the Empire.[37] The patchy statistics available for Austrian lands imply a crisis of unrivalled proportion. German infants in their first year of life, unlike young children, generally escaped the worst of the deprivation because they were breast fed and because birth rates dropped drastically. However, in the Austrian part of the Empire infant mortality rose during the war (see Table 7). For other age groups, the upward trend in civilian deaths began earlier than in the Reich, already in 1915.[38] The worst conditions were to be found in Vienna. There, starvation, not mere malnutrition, did kill. Doctors estimated lack of food to be the direct cause of around 10 per cent of wartime deaths and a contributory factor to 20–30 per cent of deaths. Germany teetered on the brink of starvation during the second half of the war. In the Habsburg lands, parts of Austria went over the brink.[39]

THE CAUSES OF SHORTAGE

Nothing, not even high casualties, the intervention of new enemies or annexationist war aims, did more to destabilize central European societies than food shortages. The 'turnip winter' of 1916–17 was the turning point; it was then that the peoples' patience snapped. Discontent and protests before the winter were but a prelude to the ubiquitous, more violent and increasingly politicized street and industrial unrest that defined urban life in 1917. Their importance makes it worthwhile to delve deeper into the causes of these shortages and the authorities' response. How was it that living conditions became so bad? Did the Central Powers' rulers recognize the threat that nutritional shortages posed, not just to the lives of their subjects, but to the very existence of their states? How effective were their countermeasures?

The Germans' basic problem was that their country, even in peacetime, had not been self-sufficient in agricultural produce. A quarter of the grain and two-fifths of the fats consumed by its people and animals had been imported before 1914.[40] War damaged this inadequate agricultural base. Food production, which already in 1914 and 1915 fell by 11 and 15 per cent from its 1913 levels, plummeted by 35 per cent in 1916 and by 40 per cent in 1918.[41] There were two causes. First was a shortage of labour. The army conscripted farmers and workers, removing the most skilled managers and fittest men from the country's farms. By 1916, over a quarter of German male rural labourers were under sixteen and nearly a sixth over sixty. One-third of the nation's farm horses were also drafted. These animals, inured to hard labour, were ideal for pulling the army's guns and supplies, but their absence hindered farms from sowing and harvesting all the land cultivated in peacetime. Second and even more important was the fertilizer shortage.

The artificial fertilizers available to farmers, most especially the nitrates that in peacetime had been mostly imported from abroad, fell by around two-thirds. Farmers also had only half the natural dung available in peace because their livestock catastrophically declined both in numbers and weight. Germany's cattle declined by over a tenth, from 11,320,000 in 1913 to 9,528,000 in 1918, and its pigs by more than half, from 25,659,000 to 10,270,000.[42] Poor feeding meant that these animals weighed just half the mass normal in peacetime, and produced less dung for the fields. This in turn meant fewer crops, and a vicious circle of ever diminishing supplies. Adolf von Batocki, President of the War Food Office established in May 1916, was not wholly wrong to complain that 'it is the shortages of supplies, not the system, that is to blame for our present situation'.[43]

Austria-Hungary, a much less industrialized society, had by contrast been self-sufficient in the major foodstuffs before 1914. The fact that wartime deprivation was greater than in Germany, and that the Austrian half of the Monarchy was at times reliant on Reich food aid, thus requires some explanation. Three factors were responsible for negating the initial Habsburg advantage. First, the foundations of disaster were laid already in 1914, with the Russian invasion of Galicia and Bukovina. These Crownlands were extraordinarily important for the Austrian half of the Empire's food supply, rearing almost a third of its cattle and growing over a third of its wheat and around half of its potatoes in peacetime. Both were devastated by the invasions. The population was displaced, draught animals were taken and farm infrastructure was destroyed. In 1915 the area sown with rye fell to 35.3 per cent, wheat to 18.4 per cent and barley and oats to just 5 per cent of that cultivated in the last pre-war years. The land never recovered during the conflict. In 1917 yields for these crops were just 25 per cent, or in the case of rye, 35 per cent of those in peacetime.[44]

Second, agriculture in the rest of the Empire suffered similar problems to those experienced by farmers in Germany, not only making it impossible to replace Galician production, but actually resulting in an even larger food deficit. There was the same shortage of animal and human labour: the Habsburg army took 814,000 horses, about a fifth of all those in the country, on mobilization. Millions of men were conscripted. The dung and fertilizer needed to regenerate the soil were also in short supply.[45] Statistics for food production in the region that at the war's end became the Austrian Republic illustrate how severely war affected even land untouched by military action (see Table 8).

Hungary's agriculture was less badly damaged, ironically because it was so underdeveloped. Artificial fertilizers had received only limited use there in peacetime, and so their disappearance from the market in wartime impacted on its yields less than those of the more modern, intensive methods of farming used in much of Austria and Germany. Nonetheless, by 1916, many crop harvests had fallen to three-quarters or less of the 1913 level and by the conflict's final year, most crop yields were little more than half of those in the last full year of peace (see Table 9).

The third factor, which explains why the deprivation in Austria was particularly severe, was the lack of solidarity between the two halves of the Empire. Even in peacetime, Austria could cover only two-thirds of its population's flour, one-third of its beef and just under half its pork consumption. Hungary, which had produced large agricultural surpluses despite the backwardness of its farms, had supplied over 90 per cent of the necessary imports. Vienna had been especially dependent on Magyar trade, most of the meat consumed in the city before 1914 having come from across the nearby border.[46] For the Austrian population, it was therefore a catastrophe that, by 1916, Hungarian imports had dropped to around half of the milk and meat, less than a third of the fat

Table 8. Austrian crop yields, 1913–17
(area of post-1918 Austrian Republic only)

Crop	1913 (in Kg.)	1914	1915	1916	1917
			(Index Numbers: 1913 = 100)		
Wheat	1,089,600,000	95	71	54	47
Rye	2,087,300,000	91	62	46	43
Barley	1,351,100,000	94	48	52	29
Oats	1,907,200,000	101	44	54	25
Potatoes	7,697,100,000	101	82	51	-
Sugar beet	6,780,800,000	100	68	66	43

Source: L. Grebler and W. Winkler, *The Cost of the World War to Germany and to Austria-Hungary* (New Haven, CT, 1940), p. 151.

Table 9. Hungarian crop yields, 1913–18

Crop	1913	1914	1915	1916	1917	1918
	(in Kg.)	(Index Numbers: 1913 = 100)				
Wheat	4,119,100,000	70	98	74	81	63
Rye	1,274,400,000	85	91	75	80	65
Barley	1,738,000,000	82	73	65	46	51
Oats	1,448,700,000	87	81	85	53	46
Potatoes	4,875,300,000	109	119	89	61	64
Sugar beet	4,775,800,000	84	53	42	33	45
Maize	4,624,800,000	95	88	51	57	52
Rutabagas	5,984,700,000	101	92	68	49	64

Source: L. Grebler and W. Winkler, *The Cost of the World War to Germany and to Austria-Hungary* (New Haven, CT, 1940), p. 153.

and just 3 per cent of the cereals that had been supplied in peacetime (see Table 10).

Hungary took sole responsibility for military provisioning from mid-1916, which partly explains the collapse of its exports to Austria. The 500 million kilograms of flour and grain that were delivered to the army during the following year approximated the amount sent to the western half of the Empire during 1915. However, as already in 1915 the cereal exported to Austria had been a mere 37 per cent of what it had received in 1913, this was not much of a justification. Moreover, Austrian civilians did not benefit from the new arrangement as, despite Hungarian promises, the soldiers' needs were not met and the army consequently requisitioned 290 million kilograms of Romanian grain marked for the Austrian population's consumption. Austria, in spite of its straitened circumstances, also supplied most of the military's sugar and 4,100,000 head of cattle, well over half of all provided.[47]

Hungary, as Austria's politicians and public were well aware, did not contribute its fair share to the Habsburg war effort. The Dualist system rendered Austria powerless to insist, however. Minister President Tisza not only refused to equalize rations across the Empire but also used Hungary's unusually strong position to advantage in the decennial negotiations to renew the Compromise in 1917. His pursuit of narrow

Table 10. Food imports into Austria from Hungary, 1914–17

Foodstuffs	Average of 1909–13 (in Kg.)	1914	1915	1916	1917
		(Index Numbers: 1913 = 100)			
Cereals	1,392,810,000	73	37	3	2
Flour	731,610,000	77	29	8	3
Legumes	14,710,000	197	162	48	4
Vegetables	151,970,000	68	106	81	37
Cattle (head of)	327,000	108	43	13	29
Milk	70,450,000	93	66	45	17
Butter	3,280,000	66	32	23	14
Bacon and fat	19,270,000	104	80	31	32
Meat	15,290,000	112	79	57	52

Source: H. Loewenfeld-Russ, *Die Regelung der Volksernährung im Kriege* (Vienna and New Haven, CT, 1926), p. 61.

Magyar interests was obtuse, for it fatefully disregarded the fact that Hungary's fate was bound to the survival of its starving Austrian neighbour. Yet it was also the product of a deeper problem: the rottenness of the Hungarian state. Tisza's government lacked strong legitimacy due both to the highly restrictive franchise of the House of Representatives and to the fact that it had won its majority there in 1910 only through corruption and intimidation. Wartime appeals to the people to accept greater sacrifices inevitably provoked scepticism and unwelcome demands for a reciprocal increase in democracy. Already in the 1915 spring session of parliament, Tisza had needed to slap down a proposal to enfranchise all front veterans over twenty years old, which he had feared could open the door to universal suffrage. Maintaining the food supply in Hungary, at least at a level above that of Austria, was essential for avoiding both popular unrest and calls for political reform.[48]

Even more important, any tampering with agriculture or the food supply risked antagonizing the landed aristocracy and gentry who dominated Hungarian politics. Tisza, who was himself a large landowner, thus made strenuous efforts to avoid damaging their material interests in the first years of hostilities, even at the expense of the wider imperial war effort. The Habsburg War Ministry had already recommended suspending import tariffs on grain at the beginning of August 1914, but Tisza, fearing that this could lower food prices, blocked the measure until October, losing the Empire the opportunity to import stocks from Romania and Italy before those countries imposed export restrictions. The Hungarian government refused in subsequent years to follow Austria in setting maximum prices on agricultural goods, and thus diminish the profits of its most important constituency. Moreover, it even insisted that deliveries should be of perishable flour rather than more robust grain in order to ensure that Hungarian, rather than Austrian, mills were kept in business. When Tisza's Austrian counterpart Stürgkh appealed for stricter Magyar measures to control food in December 1915, conjecturing that they could not be more difficult to introduce than the recent and successful decree to raise the age of military service to forty-two, he was missing the point. Whereas the latter affected a disenfranchised overwhelmingly rural populace, the former would damage crucial gentry support, much of which in any case was unsympathetic or actually hostile to Habsburg Austria. For Stürgkh, it was a straightforward contest between Hungarian 'fodder interest' or Austrian 'human nourishment'. The Magyar Agriculture Minister, Count Hadik, made his government's position on this question quite clear when he informed Austrian negotiators that 'Hungarian cattle and pig breeding must come out of the war unscathed.'[49]

While the Central Powers' propaganda blamed the deprivation on a ruthless British 'starvation war', the causes were thus more complex. Britain's naval blockade did not cause the shortages so much as force Germans and Austro-Hungarians back on their own ever shrinking resource base. The seal was far from hermetic at first but it gradually strengthened, especially once a new Ministry of Blockade was established by the British in February 1916. Strangling Germany and the Habsburg Empire of supplies was not merely a matter of sending naval patrols into the English Channel and North Sea or stationing ships off the Dalmatian coast. Ruthless coercion and imaginative diplomacy were equally important in stopping the flow of goods through neutral countries to the Central Powers. 'Black lists' of firms known to trade with the enemy were issued in February. British companies were banned from doing business with these firms, their vessels were denied fuel – a measure possible due to Britain's monopoly over coaling stations – and, if they somehow made it to European waters, they were subject to being detained by Royal Navy patrols. The measure was a powerful deterrent for businessmen tempted by trade with the Central Powers. Even more intrusively, Britain replaced a failed voluntary rationing scheme with forcible rationing for neutral countries from June 1916. Seaborne goods in excess of the neutrals' peacetime needs were now halted, in order to stem the massive re-export of goods from across the world by neutrals to Germany and Austria-Hungary that had taken place in the war's first year. Attention was also given to limiting the flow of the neutrals' own domestically produced goods to Britain's enemies. A solution was found in the imposition of purchasing agreements on neutral powers, guaranteeing the Entente the right to buy a share of their produce. Often, these agreements were less lucrative for neutral powers than selling to Germans desperate for supplies. However, Britain's threats to exploit its control over shipping lanes to reduce the rations or detain the ships of continental neutral countries usually sufficed to enforce compliance. From a humanitarian perspective it had highly perverse outcomes. As central European civilians became malnourished, Norwegian herring purchased by the British solely to stop their sale to the enemy were left to rot.[50]

The Central Powers' options to import food narrowed as their enemies multiplied. Italy's declaration of war on Austria-Hungary in May 1915 closed off another market. Fertile Romania's entry into hostilities on the side of the Entente in August 1916 was an even bigger blow. The defeat of Serbia in the autumn of 1915 had reopened the Danube waterways for half a year, enabling Germany and Austria-Hungary to import 2.5 million tons of cereal from Romania. The Central Powers did, at least in comparison to the Entente, develop an efficient purchase system. The first year of war brought chaos, as not only German and Habsburg state representatives but also those of their big cities, firms, communes and other private buyers bid up food prices on the open market. In September 1915, however, over two years before their enemies adopted similar measures, the states together centralized their foreign purchases by granting a monopoly to Germany's Central Purchasing Corporation (*Zentral-Einkaufs-Gesellschaft*).[51] Although not comprehensive – in the last years of the war, other state authorities took more responsibility for food imports – import statistics from this agency illustrate the dire effect of Britain's tightening blockade, Romania's entry into the war and finally the start of hostilities with the United States in April 1917 on the Central Powers' ability to find external sources of supply (see Table 11).

Table 11. German imports through the Central Purchasing
Corporation (1000s of tons)

Foodstuffs	1916	1917	1918
Grain and Fodder	1,040.93	9.03	45.04
Legumes	75.23	0.08	0.64
Fruit, Vegetables, Jam	82.35	82.20	88.89
Sugar	18.98	29.59	41.09
Eggs	40.40	37.19	16.39
Milk	10.12	23.17	16.82
Cheese	48.78	36.29	11.81
Butter	73.85	36.32	7.40
Fat	6.61	1.78	0.06
Meat	102.89	115.41	50.77
Fish	12.35	54.81	22.16

Source: A. Skalweit, *Die deutsche Kriegsernährungswirtschaft* (Stuttgart, Berlin and Leipzig, 1927), p. 24.

The decline of the Central Powers' domestic production and the closing off of external sources of supply through encirclement and naval blockade placed a premium on efficient management. The German and Habsburg peoples had been assured in the war's early years that food would suffice, if consumed sparingly, and from this sprung the expectation, reasonable but wrong, that their leaders would ensure the provision of adequate sustenance. In accordance with the central values of 'war culture', not only should all have enough but distribution of scarce resources should also be equitable. The ability of governments to meet these expectations had become by 1916 a key test of their legitimacy.

(MIS)MANAGING SHORTAGE

Attempts at food management by German and Austro-Hungarian officials in the first eighteen months of war had been a disaster. Uncoordinated local controls, a focus on ensuring that food was affordable for consumers rather than on incentivizing production, and a total failure to understand the complex system of agriculture had damaged output and created new shortages. With food becoming scarcer and public anger growing, the Central Powers' leaders were spurred to reform. Germany acted first by establishing a War Food Office (*Kriegsernäherungsamt*) under the War Ministry on 22 May 1916. The new office projected an image of a dynamic, impartial directorate run not only for but also by the people. Its council was composed in the best traditions of the *Burgfrieden*, with representatives of the Social Democrats, trade unions, cities and bourgeois women's groups. The man picked to lead it was the former President of East Prussia, Adolf von Batocki. Having faced off Russian invasion in 1914–15, he would, it was hoped, now overcome this latest existential threat against Germany.

Batocki was greeted excitedly by the press as a 'Food Dictator', fuelling vastly inflated public expectations. His War Food Office in fact did not have centralized control over provisioning. The army's supply remained outside the remit of the War Food Office and its authority was confined to Prussia, not the whole of Germany. Worse still, the Prussian Agriculture and Interior Ministries continued to exercise influence over food questions, leading to jurisdictional wrangling. The War Food Office did notch up some achievements. It imposed better coordination on the lower sections of the bureaucracy and introduced much needed tighter regulation on more foods. It also helped that a belated decision was made to forbid the deputy commanding generals in the regions from issuing orders affecting the food supply and prices without prior consultation with the War Ministry. Nonetheless, the War Food Office did not have the power to coordinate supply in Germany. Even had it been given such authority, the reduction of yields, the British blockade and the serious errors of earlier food policy were already insuperable obstacles to feeding the Reich's population.[52]

The War Food Office may have fallen far short of the hopes that Germans invested in it, but to Habsburg subjects despairing at their own leaders' fumbled attempts to manage supply, it appeared a model of efficiency. Given Austria's dire food situation after the invasion of Galicia and the reluctance of the Hungarian government to help, the listlessness of Stürgkh's government was scandalous. Bread rationing was adopted in Austria only in April 1915, two months after the Germans set an example. As foodstuffs grew scarcer, criticism of government inaction became louder. In comparison with the Reich's impressive sounding 'Food Dictator', the Inter-Ministerial Commission set up in Austria a week later, on 30 May 1916, to better coordinate supply policy looked feeble; it was merely another layer of bureaucracy on top of an indolent administration. A 'Food Office' was founded within the Interior Ministry at the start of October, but it was merely the product of an internal rejigging of responsibilities rather than a radical overhaul of provisioning. Three weeks later, on 26 October, the Hungarians upstaged Stürgkh's administration by establishing in their half of the empire a People's Food Office with responsibility for centralizing and managing public supply. Finally, with the people crying out not just for a food dictator but, as one report put it, for 'a Messiah', the Austrian government was moved to more decisive action. A new Office of the People's Food Supply (*Amt für Volksernährung*), with a chief reporting directly to the Minister President, began work after just three weeks of rushed preparation on 1 December 1916. Like the German War Food Office, it incorporated a council. The seven members included agricultural, industrial and military representatives and politicians, among whom was the Social Democrat Karl Renner. Attention was also given to ensuring the appointees had a mixed ethnic composition, in the hope that by involving all interest groups the Empire's damaged legitimacy might be restored.

Rebuilding legitimacy ultimately depended on the new organization's success in putting food in Austrian bellies, and that was determined above all by whether Hungary could be prevailed upon to release more supplies. By the end of 1916, two fairly centralized but independent food administrations existed in each half of the Empire. Cooperation between them remained weak. The AOK, which took hypocritical care to preserve the independence of the military food supply while anxiously carping about the looming catastrophe in civil provisioning, as ever thought that it could do better and proposed a united food authority led by a general. Tisza categorically refused. When a Common Food Committee (*Gemeinsamer Ernäherungsausschuß*) was eventually set up under General Ottokar Landwehr von Pragenau on 27 February 1917, it was a vehicle facilitating communication between the two governments, not the executive organ that Conrad von Hötzendorf had imagined, with the power to shift food around the Empire. A second attempt made at the end of the year to coordinate military and civilian needs more effectively in both parts of the Empire suffered from the same problem. Hungary would remain better provisioned than Austria throughout the war.[53]

To fulfil popular expectations of an equitable distribution of adequate food, the primary tool to which states turned was rationing. In Germany, this began in Berlin with flour in January 1915, and was rolled out across the country from the following month. Ominously, already in March, the initial daily allocation of 225 grams per person was reduced to 200 grams. The Austrians issued ration coupons for flour and bread in April 1915. The Hungarians, thanks to their greater agricultural wealth, avoided this measure until January 1916. As items ran short, the list of rationed goods lengthened. In the Reich, potatoes were rationed from the spring of 1916, and local rationing of meat began around the same time, although only in the autumn were coupons issued nationally. Fats were rationed from July and milk from late August. All major foodstuffs were obtainable legally only with ration cards by the winter of 1916. The Austrians took longer to organize themselves. Sugar was put on the ration almost a year after bread and flour cards were issued, in March 1916. Thereafter, further controls followed quickly. Milk cards were introduced in May, coffee cards in June and cards for fats in September. Only in October 1917 was a potato card introduced.[54]

Rationing appeared to be a food-saving device tailored for the *Burgfrieden* ideal. Theoretically, it spread sacrifice evenly and ensured the well-being of even the lowliest subject. In practice, getting rationing right proved extraordinarily difficult. Ration coupons were most effective when applied to scarce goods such as butter, sugar, flour or soup which required salespeople merely to act as distributors. Items that needed processing at the shop level before being handed over to the public, however, offered plentiful opportunity for abuses, personal jealousy and animosities. Meat is a good example. Butchers received carcasses, which they then trimmed, divided up and sold to consumers possessing ration cards. If the central authorities were too generous in their allocation, the butcher would have meat left over, which would be sold to favoured customers under the counter for prices above the legal maximum. If too little was supplied, the meat would run out before the needs of all customers entitled to buy had been satisfied. A further complication was that not all meat was of the same quality. The best cuts were likely to be saved for favoured customers or held back for illegal private sale.[55]

Public faith in the rationing system was undermined by two integral problems. The first was the frequent unavailability of the goods that the ration cards promised. This was why queuing was so ubiquitous. If shops ran out of food, then, as a satirical postcard of 1917 suggested with heavy sarcasm, people had nothing to eat but the cards themselves:

Sunday Roast 1917

Take the meat ration card, coat it in the egg card and fry until nicely brown with the butter card. Steam the potato and vegetable card until pleasantly soft and thicken them with the flour card. – As dessert brew the coffee card, add the milk and sugar card and use the bread card for dunking. – After the meal wash your hands with the soap card and dry them on the ration coupon.

But we Germans see it through!
We do it gladly![56]

Most depressingly, even if people had the money and were successful in collecting all the food to which they were entitled, this exercise in survival was in vain as the ration was set so low. Contemporary nutritionists reckoned on a grown man needing 3,000 calories per day (modern estimates suggest 2,500). Theoretically, the Reich's basic daily ration at first offered 1,985 calories, but this quickly dropped to 1,336 and then, in the summer of 1917, to 1,100 calories. Hungarians received 1,273 calories, which was less, as a contemporary expert pointed out, than a sleeping person needs for life.[57] Austrians, and especially the Viennese, were even worse fed. The basic ration in the Habsburg capital started at 1,300 calories and had fallen to 830.9 by the Armistice.[58] A nutritionist who attempted to live solely off the Reich's ration lost a quarter of his body weight in seven months. The public did not need such experiments to tell them the obvious: one woman in Upper Silesia wryly summed up Germans' dilemma when she complained that the official ration was 'too little to live on and too much to die'.[59]

The ration also failed to guarantee that hunger was spread equitably. Even agreeing on what was fair and equal proved difficult. From the first, it was clear that allocating the same amount of food to each individual was not the answer; when German Imperial Grain officials set rations for children aged between one and eight years old at half the adult level, some in the public were aghast at what was perceived to be official profligacy. Public jealousy focused on mothers, who were accused of unfairly benefiting from the oversized rations of their offspring.[60] The population was instead categorized according to the perceived needs of the individual and her or his service to the state. At least initially, there was broad consensus that some people had special needs. When milk went on the ration in the summer of 1916, breast-feeding mothers, invalids and infants were designated highest priority in both Austria and Germany. Especially in large cities, the supply of milk fell catastrophically; in Vienna it plummeted over the course of 1916 to half its peacetime level. In Berlin, already early in the year supply had dropped to just 20 per cent. Only the privileged had a chance of getting hold of what became known as 'white gold'.[61]

Much more controversial was the division of the population according to occupation. The basic split was between producers and consumers. Farmers were designated as *Selbstversorger*, or 'self-feeders', and in order to encourage them to deliver, their rations were set much higher than that of the ordinary city dweller: in Germany, they were permitted more bread and double the normal meat ration. A substantial section of the population fell into this category: in Austria, they accounted for over one-third of the population. Great variations existed, however, between different regions: whereas over half of people in rural Bukovina and Galicia were 'self-feeders', only 12 per cent of ethnically German Lower Austria was so designated, and less than 10 per cent of the inhabitants of Dalmatia and Istria.[62]

Wartime administrators also divided consumers, creating a new, heterogeneous mix of interest groups whose loyalties and membership shifted with changes in the distribution systems. The most important division was between recipients of the standard ration and the 'heavy worker' undertaking hard and critical labour for the war effort, who was allocated a supplement. This distinction was introduced in some Austrian and German cities during 1915. In June 1916 the practice was nationalized in Germany, and a new category, the 'heaviest worker', was introduced. Substantial supplements accrued to these people. 'Heavy workers' received 100 grams of bread daily on top of the usual ration of 200 grams, whereas the 'heaviest workers' received 600 grams and were entitled to a double ration of potatoes. Initially, only positions occupied by men were placed in these coveted categories, but in late

October 1916, just as the Third OHL's new armaments drive began, the list was widened to include women war workers. Simultaneously, the ration for all other people was cut. Mounting complaints that the system was unfair prompted German and Austrian authorities to reduce these workers' privileges in early 1917 and institute new supplements to help the worst off.[63] Nonetheless, being designated a 'heavy worker' or 'munitions worker' continued to offer nutritional advantages for large sections of the population. In Düsseldorf, one of Germany's most important industrial centres, around one-third of the population qualified by 1918. In Austria, although less industrialized than its ally, five million people, around a third of all non-self-feeders, were also eventually given 'heavy worker' privileges. In addition, there were other favoured groups. From November 1916, German police were designated among the 'heaviest workers'; by this point, the necessity of keeping security forces loyal was daily demonstrated, as markets filled with hungry shoppers and city centres became increasingly unruly places. In Vienna, unlike in Berlin, the civil service privileged itself by opening food outlets exclusively for its staff in 1916. As the hungry public blamed the administration's incompetence for the food shortages, this move was not calculated to increase its authority nor the regime's legitimacy.[64]

The failure of rationing to guarantee a constant or equitable food supply encouraged officials to seek other solutions. Their efforts resulted in one of central Europe's most distinctive wartime institutions: the public war kitchen, known also in Germany as 'People's Kitchens'. These used and expanded the soup kitchens of peacetime municipal poor relief, but were inspired by very different ideals. They were intended to cater for the entire national (or, in Austria-Hungary's case, multinational) community. They offered a new model of mass eating for the *Burgfrieden* age. Great efficiencies were expected. Supply would be streamlined: it was easier to guarantee regular deliveries to a limited number of large feeding centres than to thousands of competing shops and outlets. Precious fuel would be saved, for cooking in bulk consumed less coal or gas than if millions of portions were heated up by individual households. The new centres would also eliminate the need for queues, as diners would sign on and surrender their ration coupons a week in advance, so the caterers would know how many portions to cook. The risk of rioting by empty-handed and disgruntled shoppers would be eliminated. The civilian population, spared of the need to stand in line overnight, would be better fed and less exhausted, which would impact positively on war production. A single masterly policy appeared to offer the solution to all supply, health and public order problems, while simultaneously reaffirming the commitment of governments to the *Burgfrieden*. Prussian authorities acted with alacrity. In mid-April 1916 the Interior Minister ordered all large cities to integrate and expand their network of kitchens. By October, 1,457 public kitchens together capable of cooking nearly two million portions daily were operating across Germany.[65]

Advocates of wartime mass catering were disappointed when it became clear the people had little appetite for it. The problem was not that the 'People's Kitchens' served bad food. Especially in Austria, some of the early descriptions of the meals on offer are mouth-watering. Prague's first dining hall sold meatloaf, pork belly and potatoes, and, for dessert, apple strudel. Salzburg's hall, which opened in November 1916, was probably more typical in offering more modest but cheap and nutritious fare. For 60 hellers, diners there received three-quarters of a litre of soup and half a litre of vegetables and potatoes. On Sundays, holidays and whenever else available, a small portion of blood sausage or meatloaf was added.[66] Even in Germany, where complaints were heard about repetitive servings of gloppy stew, known in wartime slang as 'mass cow', the public kitchens were at least a source of cow in a land otherwise short of meat, dairy products and, ultimately, every other form of nourishment. The 'People's Kitchens' were instead rejected by anyone with other dining options simply because they were too reminiscent of poor relief. The lower middle classes had earned scarcely more than skilled workers in peacetime, and during the war their salaries were frequently less than the wages of war workers. Class identities thus depended to a great extent on maintaining the appearance of a bourgeois lifestyle. Eating in the mass halls or queuing in the street to buy a portion of stew from one of the roving army-style 'goulash guns' was a sure way of losing face in the neighbourhood; one sacrifice too far to the *Burgfrieden*. To overcome this resistance, separate 'middle-class' kitchens with food costing twice as much were established. This response not only was unsuccessful, but undermined the egalitarian ideal supposed to underpin the scheme and damned the kitchens for workers too, who also had their pride and objected to any implication, however inaccurate, that they were living off charity. In Berlin, where resistance to use of the halls was strongest, many had closed by August 1917.[67]

The 'People's Kitchens' nonetheless provided an indispensable safety net for the impoverished, whose numbers swelled the longer hostilities lasted. In Germany, the use of 'People's Kitchens' peaked during the terrible winter months at the start of 1917, but even two years later, as the war reached its end, almost 9 per cent of the inhabitants of German metropolises were eating in them regularly. Outside Berlin, the number of halls actually doubled between 1916 and the war's end. In the Habsburg capital, where food shortages were far worse, mass catering played an even more important role in keeping the population alive. In 1916, Vienna had twenty-eight war kitchens to accompany an already extensive network of poor relief dining halls. By the last year of hostilities, sixty-eight war kitchens were feeding an average of 150,000 people per day. Dining halls fed an additional 134,000 daily and private charitable institutions handed out bread, warm soup or hot drinks to another 120,000, in total 404,000 residents, around one-fifth of the city's population.[68] The number of meals dispensed free of charge offers an index of the growing impoverishment of citizens during the war (see Table 12). In cities in war-ravaged Galicia, the deprivation reached extraordinary levels. In Lwów, which never recovered from the damage to its transport links and supply caused by invasion, over 70 per cent of citizens needed some sort of food aid by January 1918.[69]

If central governments were unable to realize visions of equitable and adequate eating, this was not their fault alone. The task was made more difficult by the competition that grew at lower levels of administration. Provincial and municipal officials who recognized themselves to be in a

Table 12. Free meals dispensed at Viennese soup kitchens, 1914–18

Period	Free Meals
October 1914–December 1915	15,500,000
1916	20,000,000
1917	33,000,000
1918	41,000,000

Source: H. Loewenfeld-Russ, *Die Regelung der Volksernährung im Kriege* (Vienna and New Haven, CT, 1926), p. 354.

zero-sum game in which somebody would go short formed alliances and lobbied frantically. The *Städtetag*, the assembly of Germany's major municipalities, was so successful in defending its access to food (a fact that many citizens would admittedly have found difficult to believe) that in May 1916, Germany's rural districts similarly banded together in order to protect their interests. Regional and municipal officials travelled to Berlin or Vienna and circulated the many food offices, pestering the staff to increase their town or city's rations.[70] In Austria, they even cheated to improve their supply situation. Local authorities' false reporting of stocks and obstruction of attempts to remove food from their areas hamstrung any attempt to centralize the allocation system in the west of the Empire. A report of November 1916 presented a disturbing picture of how far the strain of shortages and public pressure had fragmented the imperial administration. 'Mutual distrust and underhandedness' were encountered 'all along the line', it complained. 'One state does not trust the other [meaning Austria and Hungary], inside the states neither do the Crownlands and committees, inside these nor do the districts and municipalities, and so on. Each tries thus to secure its own food supply, conceals its stocks and shuts itself off, in order not to lose anything.'[71]

Nonetheless, without the work of local officials, many of whom were tireless and imaginative in seeking remedies, shortages would have been much worse. Surplus land was put to the plough as municipalities turned to self-help in order to solve their supply problems. The star performer was Ulm, in the south of Germany, where with impressive foresight the city fathers as early as 1914 had ordered potatoes to be planted on municipal grounds. The measure cushioned its residents from the worst of the shortages two years later. Other cities made bulk purchases to supplement the diets of their poorer citizens. Berlin, for example, spent over 14 million marks accumulating a store of smoked and salted meat.[72] Councils intervened in distribution, a step unimaginable before the war. In Lwów, for example, half of all sugar sold in 1916 passed through municipal sales outlets. The German city of Freiburg adopted even more innovative and interventionist local policies. When its council suspected milk dealers of exploiting dearth to raise prices, it acted to ensure a supply of reasonably priced milk for residents by buying a controlling interest in the largest local milk cooperative. To raise production, it also opened a sewage drainage field for grazing. Almost 4 per cent of the city's milk came from 177 cows fed on its grass.[73] A good head for business, imagination and the self-assurance to act beyond the normal bounds of peacetime local governance were all qualities needed by wartime administrators. So too was tact and a little flexibility in dealing with merchants who knew their scarce goods gave them unmatched bargaining power. A good example is offered by Thorn, a city on Germany's eastern border 170 kilometres from the sea, whose council did a deal with a Hamburg fish merchant to set up shop and sell cut-price salted herring, a nutritious alternative to scarce pork, to its citizens. When, after six weeks of successful sales, the female proprietor announced that labour costs would necessitate a jump in the price of the fish, there was despair. A discussion soon clarified what the proprietor was really after. Her husband was, as luck would have it, a soldier in Thorn's fortress garrison. The city council arranged for him to be furloughed from the army. Frau Frisch, the clever proprietor, duly announced her labour problems solved, and the good citizens of Thorn could continue to fill themselves with cheap salted fish.[74]

The most imaginative response to the shortages, albeit one that smacked of desperation, was the introduction of rural holidays for urban youth. Just as one generation later children would be evacuated from the major conurbations in order to avoid Allied bombing, so in the second half of the First World War young Germans and Austrians were put on trains to the countryside in order to escape hunger. In both countries, the initiative at first came from private charity. In Austria, Styrian charities sent more than a thousand children to the countryside in 1917. The action drew the state's interest and at the end of March 1918 the *Kaiser Karl-Wohlfahrtswerk*, the Emperor's charity, established the 'Kinder aufs Land' ('Children in the Countryside') and 'Kinder zu Gast' ('Children as Guests') programmes. In 1918 these organized 64,805 malnourished children to be sent from Austria to Hungary. The Austrian countryside also played its part: 26,542 city children from Bohemia went to farms in Bohemia, Moravia and Upper Austria in order to be fed.[75] The German programme, run by the charity *Landaufenthalt für Stadtkinder* (Countryside Stays for Urban Children) was earlier and bigger; the fact that it was managed by a private organization again testifies to the strength of German civil society. The programme began in 1916 by sending 60,000 undernourished children to recover in the countryside. In 1917 schools and Church authorities were also mobilized, resulting in no fewer than 575,000 children in 1917 and another 300,000 in 1918 going on feeding holidays of one to five months. Hosts received nominal monetary compensation and the children were expected to carry out 'light' work in the fields. The scheme was a complete success. It not only helped to mitigate the impact of shortages and blockade on society's most vulnerable group, the children, but it also helped to repair some of the growing acrimony between town and countryside.[76]

Few, either during the war or afterwards, have found much to praise about German or Habsburg food administration. Austrians were doomed, especially after the loss of Galicia, by the Dualist system and Hungarian intransigence. However, their government also bore responsibility for its slow response to a clearly looming crisis. Few initiatives came from Austrian administrators; instead, they looked north and copied the Germans when pressured by outraged public opinion. The Reich's food administrators deserve a little more credit. Centralization was incomplete and belated, there was huge inefficiency and disastrous errors were made through ignorance and poorly thought-out measures. Public pressure rather than planning drove bureaucratic reforms. Yet the fact that throughout the war Germany's official ration was, in spite of a less favourable initial food base, higher than that in Austria and, still more significantly, Hungary, does speak in the administrators' favour. If mass starvation was avoided, this was also due in no small part to initiatives by local officials. Nonetheless, this was not enough. In both powers, food was distributed neither equally nor in adequate quantities. Malnutrition, exhaustion and illness still broke human bodies, and the consequent public rage and disillusionment eroded the legitimacy of governments and shattered societies.

SHATTERED SOCIETIES

Nothing did more than the food shortages to undermine the solidarity so carefully nurtured in 1914 and 1915. Hunger made people irritable, jealous, and prone to the nervousness and easy lapses into delusion so characteristic of wartime mentality. The fact that food had become the most prized commodity upturned the peacetime social order. Especially for the middle classes, this was traumatic. An education, cultivation or profession brought few rewards in wartime. A good desk job was a burden when competing for food against social inferiors in armament factories. Sophisticated city types now kowtowed to rustics, who before the war would have been ignored or mocked. The food shortages spectacularly undermined the *Burgfrieden*. In stark contrast to the cohesive communities portrayed by early propaganda, Germans and Austro-Hungarians divided into competing interest groups, all seeking to allay their hunger.

The earliest and deepest division was that between food producers in the countryside and urban consumers. By the end of 1916, German Home Military Commands were warning of 'the sharpening of the conflict between city and countryside', calling it 'one of the most noticeable and distressing manifestations of the war'.[77] Farmers were better fed than anybody, yet still had good reason to feel aggrieved. In peacetime, German and Hungarian economic policies had favoured agricultural producers. Wartime provisioning turned state priorities on their head. Faced with the need to feed large armies and a frustrated urban population, the focus switched to protecting consumers. In the first two years of war, maximum prices were imposed in order to achieve this objective. These had a further major advantage in that they suppressed inflation, but they offered no incentive to farmers to produce more and they rarely took account of rising production costs. The patchy and uncoordinated way in which controls were introduced led to a battle of wits between farmers and officials in which the loser was the urban consumer. Producers, confronted in 1915 by expensive fodder, much of which had been imported before the war, low official prices for cereals and potatoes and an absence of controls on meat, responded by withdrawing cereals and potatoes from the market and using them to feed livestock. Officials attempted to rebalance production by ordering pig culls, imposing controls on meat and tinkering with other maximum prices. Delivery quotas were gradually introduced and in 1917 and 1918 farms were searched for undeclared livestock and produce. Only in the second half of the war did the authorities reach for incentives, but by this time the economy had shifted to full-scale war production, there was little peasants could buy with the extra cash, and so their effect was limited. Instead, official measures inadvertently promoted a thriving black market, especially in meat and dairy products. Although farmers generally stayed one step ahead, they resented a system that they regarded as arbitrary and fixed against them.[78] A sense of persecution grew, inflaming both a desire for peace and distrust of the authorities. When, in the autumn of 1916, the Reich advertised its Fifth War Loan, farmers withdrew their money from savings accounts, as rumours circulated that the government might confiscate it in order to fund the war effort.[79]

The German government recognized the immense danger of an alienated countryside. As the Ministry of Agriculture warned on 22 February 1917, 'a firm influence over the rural population appears ... so much the more necessary as Germany's final victory depends just as much on the ... nourishment of our people as on the defeat of our enemy by the army and the fleet'.[80] A propaganda offensive opened to encourage farmers to release food onto the market at official prices. The War Press Office imaginatively arranged excursions to enable them to see for themselves the deprivation in the cities.[81] In the winter of 1916, Field Marshal Paul von Hindenburg personally called for extra food and especially for fats for the 'heavy workers' in munitions factories. Yet even the people's hero failed to move the hard hearts of farmers: in Bavaria, his appeal raised just an extra quarter pound's worth of meat for each industrial worker.[82]

The agricultural population's refusal to cooperate was a reflection not only of its anger towards the authorities but also of its alienation from city dwellers. Tales of urban suffering elicited limited sympathy, for farmers' lives were also difficult. By 1916 nearly half of Germany's farms were run by women, who had of necessity not only continued with their own tasks but also taken over the physically demanding responsibilities of their conscripted husbands and labourers. At the busiest period of the year, harvest time, it was common for the women to be out in the fields from three in the morning until nine at night. The plague of city 'hamsters' who descended on the countryside every weekend, stampeding across land and damaging or stealing crops, did not encourage pity. Black-market transactions also soured relations on both sides. To city dwellers, they proved that their rural compatriots were cheating the system. Farmers, by contrast, concluded from the high prices they were offered that the urban population was not so hard up as it claimed. Sometimes there were confrontations. Farmers who did not wish to sell might be threatened or assaulted. On other occasions, the rural populace resorted to violence to rid themselves of hungry city pests. Inhabitants of Austria's capital looking for food in the countryside had stones thrown at them and were chased away with shouts of 'Viennese riff-raff! Go home, you're eating us all out of house and home!'[83]

Urban consumers were one in their agreement that farmers' avarice and profiteering were ruining the country. In Germany, people blamed the absence of potatoes at the end of 1916 on producers hoarding them until the spring, when they would get better prices. In Austria, the Viennese nurtured similar suspicions. Stories circulated of pigs being fed on prime barley while the urban population was left with husks and fodder.[84] However, this was about all that united city dwellers. Food shortages inflamed urban class antagonisms. The middle classes justly complained about bearing an unfair share of wartime hardship. The anger and frustration felt by white-collar workers across the Reich and in Austria-Hungary were well expressed in a resolution passed unanimously in August 1916 by the Wiesbaden branch of the 'Middle-Class Association for Central Germany' (*Mittelstandsvereinigung für Mitteldeutschland*), an organization boasting 700,000 members nationwide. 'We are still very far removed from the genuinely equal people's food supply about which one hears so much praise and bragging,' members lamented. The state organized its price setting, they wrongly asserted, solely for the benefit of farmers and landowners. The white-collar workers observed bitterly that while 'very poor women and members of the working and middle classes' stood for hours in all weathers waiting to buy food, the 'upper ten thousand' apparently found queuing unnecessary. The real enemy was obviously domestic: 'Not the English, but the profiteers, producers and traitors to the Fatherland starve out our people.'[85]

The working classes were similarly antagonized, but far less united than the bourgeoisie. Older divisions of gender and skill differentials remained, but workers were further divided by new wartime distinctions, most especially between industrial sectors and the official ration categories. The high earnings of armaments workers could cause resentment among both the middle classes and labourers in other industries. What really rankled, however, were their large rations. Initially, Germany's 'heaviest workers' were granted supplements far in excess of what was actually necessary to compensate for their exertion: they were reckoned to burn almost 800 calories more than other workers, yet they daily received up to 2,000 calories extra. Widespread anger, not least among female munitions workers who were employed alongside male 'heaviest worker' colleagues but ineligible for their supplements, prompted the authorities in 1917 to flatten the differentials nationally and grant whole factories, rather than just certain workers, a new, less generous supplement.[86] German armaments workers, with their higher rations and access to factory canteens well stocked with illegal food, were privileged compared with the rest of the Reich's population and with their impoverished and tightly controlled colleagues in Austria. However, this did not deter them too from cursing a class of wealthy war profiteers. To a great extent this group was imaginary. Firms in the metals, machinery and chemicals sectors did substantially increase profits in the second half of the war, as a result of Hindenburg's rearmament drive. Yet overall, the war industries' profits sank to 82 per cent of their peacetime level. Mining did especially badly, with profits declining to just 39 per cent of their pre-war level in 1917. Despite the suspicions of German industrial workers, the war was not fought just at the expense of the poor. Wealth was not redistributed to the rich. Instead, the whole population paid.[87]

German and Austro-Hungarian societies did not simply split along class lines; instead they fragmented in much more chaotic and fundamental ways. At the level of everyday interaction, basic sociability was lost. Hunger brought out the worst in people, encouraging irritability, impatience, paranoia and envy. In marketplaces, growing antagonism between shoppers and salespeople was one manifestation. Consumers suspected merchants, just as they did farmers, of creating artificial shortages by hoarding supplies until prices increased. They believed, often correctly, that they were being cheated: milk was diluted with water, the best cuts of meat were reserved for favoured customers. In Vienna, around 320 traders were charged every week with exceeding official prices. The press stoked the anger, publishing reports of the latest tricks of tradesmen to rob the consumer:

> A typical case of the chain selling scam has been . . . discovered in Frankfurt am Main. An out-of-town factory delivered a large quantity of artificial honey for 38 pfennigs per pound to a wholesaler there. The agent passed them onto another agent for 58 pfennigs, and he sold it on for 75 pfennigs to a travelling salesman. He charged a small dealer 80 pfennigs, while the consumer finally got the article for 1 mark. The filing of charges has ensured that the work of these gentlemen, who have made the Fatherland into a den of thieves, has been halted.[88]

There were also bitter complaints about the rudeness of shopkeepers. With so many people wanting to buy, good customer service became superfluous. Dealing daily with tired, hungry and unruly shoppers constantly complaining about the cost and inferiority of the goods on sale also required a saintly level of patience that not everybody possessed. Some vendors lost their tempers: 'you should spread shit on your bread' one Berlin butcher screamed at a crowd criticizing the high price of his lard. With frayed nerves and short tempers on all sides, such abuse risked provoking violence. Already in October 1915, Berlin's first butter riots were attributed by police in part to curt and insulting behaviour by salespeople towards their clientele.[89]

Crime rates offer an index of societal cohesion. In the war's first two years, crime dropped (see Fig. 5). German police statistics (Austrian ones are patchy and less reliable) record that it had almost halved from its pre-war rate by 1915. While the drafting of millions of men into the army was the main cause of the fall, the wave of communal solidarity that swept the country in these years probably also contributed, for female rates dropped 12 per cent in 1914 despite the hardship at war's outbreak and in 1915 reached their lowest rate since records began. However, crime rose in the second half of the conflict, as deprivation and desperation grew and people became increasingly disillusioned with a state that neither kept up its side of the *Burgfrieden* contract nor obeyed its own laws. Fraud became endemic: checks in December 1916 found that the people registered to draw rations in Germany actually

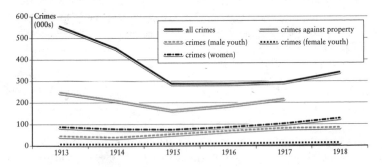

Figure 5. Crime in Germany, 1913–18

Source: M. Liepmann, *Krieg und Kriminalität in Deutschland* (Stuttgart, Berlin, Leipzig and New Haven, CT, 1930), pp. 15, 56, 98 and 134.

outnumbered the country's population. There was a brisk trade in forged coupons. Men committed the majority of crimes, even though so many had left for army service. However, the female crime rate increased rapidly from 1916, peaking at a third above its peacetime level in 1918. Crimes against property accounted for most of the rise, and, with 72,974 women convicted, made up nearly a quarter of all female offences by 1917. Also notable was an increase in threats and assaults on officials. Some 1,224 women, most married and between thirty and sixty years old, were found guilty of this offence in 1916. While male criminologists, in line with fashionable theories of the day, worried earnestly that wartime disturbances in the female sex drive might be contributing to this theft and disorder, even they were ready to admit that women's frustrations might also be a consequence of immense hardship and the greater but ineffectual interventions of officialdom into wartime life.[90]

The rise in youth crime was even more spectacular. Convictions of those under eighteen doubled in Germany between 1914 and 1918. The same was true in Austria's capital. The increase was not simply a consequence of the shortages, for after a drop in 1914, German juvenile convictions rose around 7,000 over the last full year of peace to 63,126 in 1915. The following year, there were an additional 17,000 extra cases, and then a further 15,000, making a total of 95,651 youth convictions in 1917.[91] The crime rate of boys was consistently six or seven times greater than that of girls, in part because the older ones went out to work while their female peers were stuck at home. Inadequate adult oversight encouraged delinquency among younger children. The call-up of over a third of German fathers, and probably a similar proportion in Austria-Hungary, removed strict paternal influence from households. Many mothers, working long hours in factories or fields or struggling to locate food, had little time and energy to watch over their offspring. Even after some armaments factories introduced limited day-care provision in 1918, one in seven mothers working in the south German war industry still had no choice but to leave her children home alone. Schools also provided less and less help. From the spring of 1915, they were open only for half or a third of the day because conscripted teachers could not be replaced and classrooms had been requisitioned by the military. In winter, they frequently closed completely due to a lack of heating fuel. Children thus had opportunities to steal or make nuisances of themselves and, especially once the severe shortages set in from 1916, a very strong motive. Truancy snowballed from the turnip winter, in part encouraged by stressed parents who now needed their children at home to cook or look after younger siblings while they queued or worked for food. Others, abandoned by the adult world, formed gangs with fantasy names like 'The Black Hand' or 'The Apaches' and thieved from bread wagons or coal yards to survive.[92]

Adults were unnerved not just by the unruliness of youth or its greater public visibility but also because they sensed a power shift taking place. The high wages that older male adolescents could earn in war industries made them families' primary breadwinners and the way in which these male teenagers used their new income added to adult anxieties. They drank in bars, went to the cinema to see trashy films, bought penny dreadfuls and rowdily caroused with female youths in public. In the minds of officials and many grown-ups, this 'immorality' merged with the crime wave to produce a general impression of an epidemic of youth delinquency. In Germany from the autumn of 1915 and in Austria, where the public debate about delinquency started later and was to an extent imported from the north, from the summer of 1916 decrees were issued banning adolescents from visiting bars or coffee houses in the evenings, smoking in public, gambling or watching films not approved for children. In Berlin, Cassel and, briefly, Hannover, mandatory savings decrees were issued by district military commanders, restricting the spending of those under eighteen. Their wages were paid into special accounts and if they wished to spend more than eighteen marks in a week, they or their families had to apply to the community administration for permission. In Berlin, the measure resulted in a huge sum, 8¾ million marks, being forcibly deposited in 104,000 savings accounts. Some 3½ million marks were paid out during the war. The remainder was released to its unhappy owners only after the Armistice.[93]

The crime wave reflected a breakdown not only in central European societies' food supply but also of trust. This had many other manifestations. One of the most prominent, stemming from hunger, fatigue and the fact one had to cheat the system to survive, was paranoid 'food fantasies'. People imagined their neighbours hoarding fantastical quantities of food, and denunciations swamped police desks. By popular demand, police in Vienna began carrying out house searches. Spot checks were also made to ensure that residents were observing legally imposed 'meatless days'.

Other Habsburg cities instituted similar practices, which in the minds of some residents amounted to not local but rather centrally imposed arbitrariness. Aleksandra Czechówna in Cracow, for example, anxiously noted in her diary in March 1917 the arrival of 'a commission from Vienna which goes around the houses and takes private supplies, leaving only a very small amount'.[94] If the neighbours were dishonest, then citizens were certain that people elsewhere were even worse. Newspapers stirred up resentment. Five months before Czechówna wrote her diary entry, the Viennese *Welt-Blatt*, part of the city's gutter press, reported on exactly the sort of inspections that so worried her, although carried out not by a Viennese Commission but by the Cracow police. 'The checks', the paper reported in an article provocatively entitled 'How one lives in Cracow on meatless days', yielded 'a very interesting result':

> It turns out that in the middle, apparently less affluent layers of the population even on the 'forbidden days' (Mondays, Wednesdays and Fridays) meat is consumed – and what is more, in very large quantities ... The police checks, which will be continued, have also proven that the richer parts of the population ... dispose of considerable supplies and not only lack nothing but currently, regardless of the prices of food, lead a significantly better life than in peace.[95]

Communal identities, which had been crucial in supporting the national and imperial war efforts in 1915, were now subverted to promote regional jealousies. In Germany, Hamburgers were convinced that Berliners were given first pick of available food. Wiesbadeners considered it 'a fact that Wiesbaden has the worst and lightest bread'.[96] All north Germans eyed the south with envy. It was common knowledge that cattle-rich Bavaria had banned the private export of food across its borders to the rest of the Reich and that it issued its people double or even triple the meat ration usual elsewhere. Bavarian particularism also flared. The flow of visitors into the state intent on sharing in its bounty, and the removal of foodstuffs by hamsters and smugglers to other parts of the country, caused resentment. Grumbling about having to fight 'Prussia's war' grew from 1916. These tensions were further fuelled by the fact that rations genuinely did become more differentiated the longer the war lasted. Implicitly acknowledging that 'hamstering' could not be stopped, the authorities made individual rations dependent on the size of communities. Residents of large cities were given a relatively large meat allowance, as their inhabitants had little access to farmers. Cities of between 50,000 to 100,000 people were given less and towns that were smaller were allocated the least. Yet the efforts of the War Food Office were in vain, merely creating the illusion that large cities were privileged when in fact they remained poorly provisioned. The worst sufferers were industrial communities full of fractious Social Democrats in the Rhineland, Westphalia and Saxony.[97]

The Austro-Hungarian Empire also started to fragment through even starker regional tensions. The earliest division was between Austrians, regardless of ethnicity, and Hungarians. The former were livid at being cut off by their neighbour and by the reports, some true, others exaggerated, of better Magyar rations. Local politicians whipped up this anger to deflect blame for miserly rations from themselves. Mayor Weiskirchner of Vienna provocatively compared 'chubby' Johann Hadik, the Hungarian Minister of Food Supply, with the 'withered almond' who performed the same role in Austria. Hungarians, he told his citizenry, are 'out of spite . . . more interested in seeing us starve to death than the English are'.[98] Hatred mounted. Agitated rumours soon circulated widely that the Hungarians preferred to sell their potatoes to Prussian Silesia than to their fellow Habsburg subjects in Austria. Some wished for just retribution: 'the Russians should just come to Hungary,' yearned one Austrian German in 1916. 'If they would only come in and eat all the miserable Hungarians' pork[!]'[99]

Yet anti-Magyar sentiment produced no pan-Austrian solidarity. On the contrary, food shortages reopened and exacerbated the national enmities of peace. In Bohemia, Germans held Czech farmers responsible for the dearth. Czechs, by contrast, were certain that shortfalls were caused by the export of Bohemian crops to the German Reich. Hate mail was sent to the German consulate in Prague, and already by the spring of 1916 rumours circulated that the Central Powers would lose the war and that an independent Bohemian Kingdom would be established under Russian or British protection.[100] Similar resentments were expressed elsewhere. In Tyrol, for example, Habsburg Italian speakers complained that their German neighbours were better provisioned. Nationalist activists worked hard to exploit the discontents and show the people that these social problems had only national solutions. The Habsburg state's war was blamed as the root cause of the deprivation.

Nationalist-dominated charities and voluntary welfare organizations offered material help and with it won recruits for their ideological aspirations.[101]

The fracturing of German and Austro-Hungarian society was also marked by an upsurge of anti-Semitism. In the Reich this had a primarily political character; in Austria, it was more of a social phenomenon. The accusations were identical in both states, however. Jews were presented as arch violators of a war culture based around sacrifice and community. They were accused of the two cardinal sins of this culture, war profiteering and draft dodging. Often these went together: an early public rebuke of Jews by a Catholic Centre Party deputy in the Reichstag in August 1915 claimed, for example, that they dominated the Reich Cereals Board and were using their positions to shirk active service. In Germany, anti-Semitism was at first unrelated to deprivation. Rather, it was, and remained, a tool of the far right, which worried that Bethmann Hollweg's conciliatory *Burgfrieden* policies would bring democracy and a diminution of conservative power in Prussia. Already in 1915 the far right sought to tar prospective reform by condemning it as intended for the benefit of Jews. However, as sacrifices mounted and scrutiny of compatriots' conduct became more paranoid, others joined the racists in demanding checks on whether Jews were fulfilling their national duty. In October 1916, Matthias Erzberger, the influential Centre Party deputy, called in the Reichstag's Budget Committee for Food Supply Issues for a survey of the War Corporations' personnel to determine gender, income, religion and how many were of military age. The purpose of the measure was to ascertain whether rumours of Jewish over-representation in these key wartime economic institutions were true, but it met resistance from both Socialist deputies and imperial officials.[102]

Erzberger's initiative was probably inspired by a notorious census ordered earlier in the month by the Prussian War Ministry, aiming to count how many Jews were serving at the front, in the rear and at home, how many had volunteered, been killed and won distinctions. Whether this census was a purely anti-Semitic measure or the product also of other efficiency-related issues is disputed.[103] The anti-Semitic attitudes within the military leadership are undeniable: the Prussian officer corps had refused before 1914 to commission Jews and the rise of the Third OHL in August 1916 had brought some radical anti-Semites, notably

Erich Ludendorff's right-hand man, Colonel Max Bauer, close to the centre of power.[104] On the other hand, the autumn of 1916 was a period of intense manpower strain. Not only was the army suffering heavy casualties on the Somme but the Third OHL was planning an economic remobilization requiring large numbers of new workers, and it was not clear from where they would come. Denunciations of Jewish draft dodging, officers' traditional anti-Semitic prejudices, and an efficiency drive combined to motivate the census. Careful statistical investigation by Jewish organizations proved after the war that claims of Jewish draft dodging were groundless. They also demonstrated that in the army under the Third OHL, pragmatism trumped ideological racism. Whereas there had been no Jewish officers before the war, the urgent need for educated men to serve in leadership positions meant that by its end, the army had commissioned 2,022, making Jews slightly over-represented in the wartime officer corps.[105] However, the leaked news of the census and the War Ministry's subsequent refusal to publish its results gave ammunition to the anti-Semites and raised public suspicions of Jewish shirking; this was disastrous as, with deprivation worsening, dark rumours were already circulating of Jewish food wholesalers and businessmen pushing up food prices. Given the signals from the centre, it was unsurprising that some Home Military Commands were reporting rising anti-Semitism within the German population by the end of 1916.[106]

In Austria, unlike in Germany, neither the government nor the military succumbed to pressure to discriminate against Jews. Yet within society anti-Semitism had long been stronger and more widespread than in the Reich. Whereas German Jew-haters had never enjoyed much electoral success, in Vienna the Christian Social Party under its anti-Semitic leader, Karl Lueger, had dominated municipal politics for two decades.[107] Jews were both more numerous in Austria (4.6 per cent in contrast to less than 1 per cent of Germany's population) and more visible, for many, Galician and Bukovinan Orthodox Jews in particular, remained unassimilated.[108] Moreover, during the war anti-Semitism had radicalized in reaction to the flood of dirty, diseased and desperate Jews from the east into the Empire's major western cities in 1914. Vienna was the reluctant home to 185,000 refugees in early 1915. Other cities faced smaller deluges: 20,000 Galician Jews sheltered in Budapest and around 15,000 in Prague.[109] These refugees quickly became firmly associated with profiteering and smuggling. Not only the press but also Mayor Weiskirchner of Vienna in February 1915 publicly rebuked them for raising prices.[110] The accusations had some basis of truth, not because Jewish refugees were, as anti-Semites claimed, naturally materialistic and unprincipled, but because the authorities had left refugees with few other options. State support had been sufficient to cover only one-third of living costs in 1914, and by the summer of 1917 galloping inflation had reduced this proportion to one-eighth. Worse still, Vienna's municipal authorities, fearing that these eastern European Jews might settle and stay, illegally obstructed their efforts to work. Receipt of a work book, which was a prerequisite for legal employment, was deliberately made conditional on presentation of full documentation, which municipal authorities and police knew would be impossible for most refugees. Only in November 1916 did manpower shortages force an end to this policy. By that time, however, the work-shy criminal Jewish refugee was a fixed stereotype attracting intense popular resentment. The prediction, made two years earlier by Viennese police, that refugees would be subject to violence if the food supply did not improve, came true in 1917, when in Vienna and Bohemia Jewish traders were beaten and shops plundered.[111]

The deprivation not only rent society, but also undermined two other key relationships on which rested the war efforts of the Central Powers. First, the hierarchy of sacrifice universally accepted in the war's first years came to be challenged as civilians began to wonder whether their own suffering was not, after all, worse than that of better-fed soldiers. By October 1917, the Association for the Protection of Mothers and Infants in the Kingdom of Bohemia could warn the Austrian Interior Ministry starkly that 'the conditions brought about by the war weigh on the population so heavily that victims in the rear threaten to exceed the bloody sacrifices'.[112] Such direct contestation of the relative value of home and front sacrifice was rare, yet reading between the lines in letters, there are hints that civilians had started to believe that at the very least some thanks should be flowing from front to home. In the Kohnstern family, Anna repeatedly assured Albert that however bad life was in Germany, his ordeal was worst. His siblings were less certain, however. In January 1917, for example, his sister, Gerda, wrote him a letter, which she began with the news that the family had sent off a parcel for him that morning, containing a home-made cake and 'a few blocks of

Gartmann chocolate'. Tracking down even this modest quantity of chocolate and the ingredients for a cake at the beginning of 1917 was a Herculean task, doubtless involving many hours of queuing, considerable self-denial, and possibly haggling with black marketers. Gerda did not go into details. Instead, she signalled to her brother how grateful he should be more subtly, yet devastatingly effectively, by making just a passing mention of the family's own diet: 'Every day now bring turnips, turnips and still more turnips.'[113]

The second relationship to be undermined, in this case much more threateningly and decisively, was that between civil society and the state. By the winter of 1916–17, popular blame for the shortages had shifted decisively from the British blockade towards the Central Powers' own governments. Their inability to organize sensible, adequate and fair food distribution was vociferously criticized. Their peoples were frustrated by queuing and the impossible maze of regulations, and infuriated by rumours of official waste, incompetence and corruption. The sanctity of their laws, and with it state legitimacy, was undermined, for to attempt to obey meant starvation. It infuriated citizens that although both regimes had introduced anti-profiteering measures, they appeared incapable of suppressing the 'real' criminals: supposed domestic 'traitors' like large landowners, avaricious farmers, cheating food traders and, in Austria, Jewish refugees. Desire for peace grew. So too did bitterness. As one Czech put it dramatically, 'the state is murdering our children'.[114]

The consequence of desperation and alienation was growing unrest. Strikes increased. In Germany, from a mere 14,000 strikers and 42,000 days lost in 1915, the figures rose the following year to 129,000 strikers and 245,000 days lost.[115] In large cities, disorders also mounted as food queues dissolved into protests and hungry demonstrators marched to town halls to demand that local officials provide higher rations. The hunger riots in the suburbs of Hamburg in August 1916 exemplify the tensions. Disorder began in the working-class district of Barmbek on the evening of 18 August, when crowds of women, teenagers and children surrounded bakeries and tried without coupons to get bread. It was no wonder that they felt entitled to a ration supplement, for the previous months had been inordinately tough. Throughout June and July, there had been no potatoes. Suddenly, at the end of July, so many had arrived at once that not all could be delivered to the shops, and many had rotted. The elusive tuber had then once again vanished from Hamburg's sales outlets. The accumulated frustration manifested itself that night in violence: bakeries' windows were smashed and their contents looted. The following day saw further disorder not only in Barmbek but also in another suburb, Hammerbrook. Police with sabres clashed with looters and military units were called in to restore peace. Sixty shops were plundered, thirteen people seriously wounded and thirty-seven arrested. The local Deputy Commanding General, reacting to the part played by minors in the disturbances, banned children under fourteen from appearing on the street after 8 p.m. without an accompanying adult.[116]

Similar scenes were seen with increasing regularity not just in Germany but also across the Habsburg Empire. In Bohemia, for example, food riots doubled from thirty-five in 1915 to seventy in 1916. They would expand even more in the following years, reaching 252 and 235 public demonstrations respectively in 1917 and 1918. They also became larger: forty had over 1,000 participants and some, such as one that took place in Königgratz, had over 10,000.[117] Yet the fact that deprivation was worse, the wartime regime more repressive, and there was no safety valve due to the continued closure of parliament and strict press censorship, gave Austrian fury more explicitly political expression as well. The build-up of anger among opponents of the war was dramatically revealed on 21 October 1916, when Friedrich Adler, the radical pacifist and Socialist son of the venerable Social Democrat leader Viktor Adler, publicly shot Minister President Stürgkh in a hotel restaurant in central Vienna. The assassin was a lone wolf. Within his party, he was a bitter but isolated critic of Socialist collaboration with a warmongering regime. Friedrich Adler was frustrated that his anti-war writings were suppressed by the censor and that like-minded comrades had been conscripted by the army. His violent protest was an act of depression and desperation. Nonetheless, his speech during his trial damningly and accurately indicted the Empire's leaders and their decision to wage the war not with the peoples' consent but by repression. He had, Friedrich argued, committed the same crime as the government: killing without the assent of the people. His act was legitimated by Stürgkh's unconstitutional means of rule and the lack of any other way to protest:

> The ministry has torn the constitution apart; the ministry has given up its legality; the ministry has given up its job of concerning itself with the laws

of Austria ... Everyone is justified to use force when the laws are destroyed ... where all constitutional approaches fail – where there is no parliament, where there is no guarantee of justice, where all these have been taken away.[118]

Ominously for the Habsburg regime, there was a striking absence of public sympathy for the victim. Friedrich Adler was condemned to death but, through the Emperor's intervention, was then reprieved and his sentence commuted to eighteen years' hard labour. The decision not to make him a martyr was wise, for he was soon feted in and beyond the Viennese working classes as a hero. A year after the murder, even the once conservative students of Vienna University marched for peace and clemency for the assassin.[119]

The food shortages were, as home military commanders confirmed, the decisive influence on the popular mood by the end of 1916.[120] Weakness and hunger sapped strength and support for the war. The solidarity on which war efforts were based eroded as competition for food splintered society. New, transitory interest groups competed with each other. The state lost legitimacy as its tangle of laws became impossible to follow, and as its attempts to supply an adequate and equitable ration floundered. It was no coincidence that in December 1916 the German Chancellor made the Reich's most sincere offer of peace yet to the Entente. With the armies of both Central Powers badly damaged after a year of intense fighting and their civilians hungry and exhausted, it appeared highly questionable how long their war efforts would endure. Hindenburg and Ludendorff, the new leaders who had risen first to command Germany's and then, de facto, the Central Powers' armies, were, however, set on a course of total and absolute victory. Even as the turnip winter closed in, a new remobilization drive had begun.

9

Remobilization

THE THIRD OHL

The appointments of Field Marshal Paul von Hindenburg to command of the German army and his Chief of Staff, Erich Ludendorff, as the force's First Quartermaster General on 29 August 1916 opened a new phase of the Central Powers' war. The two soldiers had reached the apex of their profession through martial skill, a fair bit of luck and a large dose of intrigue. Thanks to their victories on the Eastern Front and a carefully cultivated public image, they enjoyed the faith of the people. At a time when Kaiser Wilhelm II had receded from public view and most Reich institutions were losing credibility, this gave them immense influence. The duo's programme was victory, no matter what the cost. Germany's war effort under them was stamped by a new ruthlessness. For both men, military necessity trumped any humanitarian scruple. As Ludendorff frankly admitted looking back at the period of the Third OHL (Oberste Heeresleitung), the German Army High Command, 'in all the measures we took, the exigencies of war alone proved the decisive factor'.[1]

Field Marshal Paul von Hindenburg, aged sixty-eight when he became Chief of the General Staff, was the most revered personality in the German-speaking world by 1916. For most of the Reich's inhabitants, he was the man who single-handedly had saved the country from the ravages of the Tsar's hordes in August 1914. With the victory at Tannenberg, he had become a national treasure overnight. The immortalization of his person in Berlin's enormous nail figure in 1915 was an imposing mark of how completely he had usurped the Kaiser as the symbol of Germany's war effort. Tremendous faith was placed in the man: 'Our Hindenburg,' the German public repeated to itself at times of crisis, 'will sort it out.' His name, which summoned up visions of a medieval castle, its sturdy walls standing immovable against all assaults, suited his physical bulk. At six foot five inches, he was a very tall man, with a square head like a block of masonry mounted on broad shoulders. He looked like nothing could shake him, an impression amplified by his legendary calm and resolution. It was also exaggerated by propaganda; Hindenburg took great pains about his public image. Renowned artists and sculptors were invited to his headquarters to promote his fame and he maintained close relations with the press. He was undoubtedly vain, yet he was also acutely aware of the power conferred by his popular following. He was no mere symbol or cipher but a highly political general, sure of what he wished to achieve but content to leave the details to competent subordinates. The political capital gained from his personality cult gave him a unique chance to impose radical change on how not just Germany's army but the whole society waged war.[2]

Erich Ludendorff, Hindenburg's First Quartermaster General and right-hand man, was a very different personality. He was a master of minutiae, and a compulsive workaholic. Whereas his chief could be good company, charming visitors to the Field Army's headquarters with a relaxed manner and dry wit, Ludendorff was cold, highly strung and utterly humourless. Since joining a cadet institution at the tender age of thirteen in 1877, he had made the army his life, and had struggled against the disadvantages of his bourgeois roots to become one of the force's most respected, if not liked, General Staff officers. His concern to harness Germany's manpower for military needs had found early expression in 1912–13, when with Moltke (the then Chief of the General Staff) he had pressed for a vast increase in the size of the army. At that time under Ludendorff's influence, Moltke had insisted that 'our political and geographical position makes it necessary to ready all available strength for a fight which will determine the existence or nonexistence of the German Reich'. In the summer of 1916, as battle raged on all fronts, the same thought obsessed Ludendorff. The Entente's vast outlay of men and materiel during the Somme offensive had impressed on him with 'pitiless clarity' the urgent need for a drastic remobilization. The new First Quartermaster General had no respect for the customary division between 'political' and 'military' spheres within the Reich's government, which was hopelessly ill-suited to the all-embracing conditions of a gruelling war of endurance. With the Kaiser incapable of coordination and the civilian government under attack from the right and increasingly discredited by the food shortages, the army, its prestige still intact, was the institution with the best chance of providing some unity to a fragmented war effort.[3] However, Ludendorff's narrow military expertise and arch-conservative instincts had failed to equip him with an understanding of the complexity of German society or to negotiate its competing interests. What emerges from his memoirs, besides arrogance, patent exculpation and obdurate blindness to the great responsibility that he bore for his nation's defeat, is not a sense of power, but rather uncomprehending frustration at how the plans of the Third OHL were thwarted at every turn by political realities.[4]

Characteristically, the new OHL's programme for German remobilization had, as its starting point, the army. To counter enemy material superiority, the force would need to be upgraded. Ludendorff had encountered the elite storm troops in September 1916. Impressed, a month later he ordered the establishment of similar battalions within each army, and in December new tactical instructions for defensive warfare were issued based on their techniques and on analysis of the recent campaigns. To veterans of the Somme and Verdun, there was little novel in these instructions; lessons learned had been circulated throughout the force during the fighting, and many units had already embraced small-group fighting techniques through necessity, as by the end of the battles sturdy purpose-built lines had been lost or destroyed, leaving troops dispersed in shell-hole defences.[5] Yet to meet the new challenges, the force required not just the institutionalization of the growing emphasis on teamwork and individual initiative but also extensive rearmament. The Third OHL wanted to treble artillery and machine-gun production. The numbers of trench mortars, weapons that gave the combat groups their own close support, were to be doubled. With the memory still fresh of the anguished cries for more shells from front-line formations on the Somme, it was also decided to double munitions output. All this was to be achieved by May 1917, when a new Entente offensive could be expected. To realize these targets, and their military vision, Germany's new army leaders had to intervene heavily in their country's industry and society. The ensuing industrial and propaganda drive was christened the 'Hindenburg Programme'.[6]

THE HINDENBURG PROGRAMME

The Third OHL wasted no time in pushing for the total mobilization of German strength for the war effort. Already on 31 August 1916, Colonel Max Bauer, the arms procurement expert who worked closely with Ludendorff, had completed a memorandum for the War Ministry outlining the disadvantageous material and manpower position of the Reich's army and stressing that 'men . . . must be more and more substituted for by machines.'[7] Two weeks later, the Third OHL sent concrete proposals to Chancellor Bethmann Hollweg. To accelerate production, Ludendorff and Hindenburg regarded administrative reform as essential: the management of the war economy would have to be centralized. More fundamentally, as industrialists had stressed to the new leaders, any rise in the output of armaments would depend on bringing workers into the weapons factories. The army was prepared to furlough skilled workers to help with the armaments drive. Yet new sources of labour would also have to be found and mobilized.[8]

The prime administrative innovation introduced by the Third OHL for the purposes of economic remobilization was the Supreme War Office (*Kriegsamt*), at the head of which was installed the personable south German railway expert, General Wilhelm Groener. The new body came into existence on 1 November 1916. In part, it was a product of bureaucratic infighting. Ludendorff and Hindenburg regarded the War Ministry, whose agencies had been responsible for weapons and munitions procurement, with disdain. Although the Supreme War Office was situated within the War Ministry, Groener in practice answered to Ludendorff. Nonetheless, the reorganization was also a genuine attempt to move closer to a functioning command economy. The new office was, at its upper levels, organized on military lines for decisive decision-making, while a more conventional bureaucratic structure, with six major departments, operated below. The War Ministry's responsibilities for labour, arms and clothing procurement, as well as for the War Raw Materials Section, the Food Section and imports and exports, all passed into its remit. Eminent scientists, economic experts and industrialists filled its technical staff, who were tasked with planning and advising its chief. The ability of the Supreme War Office to coordinate the Reich's economy was greatly facilitated by the new right to issue orders to

Prussian deputy commanding generals in the home military districts. This right was conferred on the War Ministry and devolved by a new War Minister, installed at the behest of the Third OHL, to the Supreme War Office. The allocation of manpower and material to the army and industry could finally be rationally planned and centralized, instead of being at the whim of regional military commanders with no economic training and subject to local pressures.[9]

The Supreme War Office was, nonetheless, not the coordinating institution for which Ludendorff and Groener had wished. The new War Minister, Hermann von Stein, was Ludendorff's man, but when faced by Groener's over-mighty office within his own Ministry, his bureaucratic territorial instincts were kindled and he resisted all attempts to rein in the powers of the deputy commanding generals. There were conflicts too with civil authorities, most notably the Prussian Interior Office, which defended their own administrative jurisdictions. Bavaria, Saxony and Württemberg refused to subordinate their institutions to any Prussian administrative body, and accordingly set up their own parallel war offices within their war ministries. Moreover, the Supreme War Office was itself no paragon of efficiency. Its weird half-military, half-bureaucratic structure led to much duplication of effort and confusion. So great was the flood of competing directives issued by his staff chiefs and departmental heads that Groener found it necessary at one point to impose a two-week hiatus. Yet even had the War Office been rationally organized and not at the centre of bureaucratic infighting, it could never have sponsored an industrial resurgence capable of meeting the fantastical aims of the Third OHL.[10]

The Hindenburg Programme was doomed by the entirely arbitrary nature of its targets. Ludendorff and others would later stress the partly propagandistic motivation for the plan; the order to double or, in some cases, triple weapons production certainly added drama to the inception of the Third OHL. Yet, as Groener reflected, it was no way to run a war economy.[11] The War Ministry, whose efforts to procure munitions were disdained by the Third OHL, had sensibly used the production of explosive powder as a basis for its armaments planning. After the first shortages of autumn 1914, it had established an incremental programme to increase powder manufacture, in the first instance to 3,500 tons. The target had been raised in February 1915 to 6,000 tons per month, an output finally reached in July 1916. The Somme battle prompted the

War Ministry to increase its target further, to a monthly quantity of 10,000 tons of powder, to be achieved by May 1917. For the sake of an extra 2,000 tons and some striking press headlines, the Third OHL tore up these carefully calibrated plans. The result was, predictably, a disaster. The Hindenburg Programme, unlike the War Ministry's scheme, needed to create new capacity to fulfil its goals, and consequently diverted scarce materials and manpower to constructing factories, some of which could not be completed. The programme overstrained both the Reich's railways and its coal supply. Combined with freezing weather that iced up the canals, the programme thus contributed substantially to the shortages and misery of the German population during the 'turnip winter'. It also added to civilians' woes by fuelling inflation: the Third OHL cut back on foreign-currency-earning steel exports and, in attempting to incentivize greater output, abandoned the War Ministry's careful housekeeping and offered armaments manufacturers generous profits. Paper currency in circulation proliferated.[12] Remarkably, powder and guns were not linked in its programme, so if the targets had been achieved, there would have been a mismatch. However, the disruption meant that output never came close to being realized. Steel production was actually lower in February 1917 than six months earlier. Powder manufacture also suffered. Not until October 1917 did Germany produce 10,000 tons of powder in a month. The OHL would have been better off sticking to the War Ministry's paced plan.[13]

The Hindenburg Programme's most significant feature was undoubtedly its aspiration to change the moral basis of Germany's war effort. Labour was desperately needed. Even under the War Ministry's armaments plan, there was a shortfall of between 300,000 and 400,000 workers. The Third OHL's drive raised the need to between two and three million extra men.[14] The army released 125,000 skilled workers from the front. A ruthless cull of industries not producing directly for the war effort was undertaken, diverting their manpower into the armaments sector. Small, less efficient factories were closed on a large scale in 1917, to redirect both manpower and scarce resources. In Prussia, the 75,012 plants registered in 1913 had shrunk to 53,583 by 1918.[15] However, at the core of Ludendorff and Bauer's scheme was a desire to gain total control over the labour force. Hitherto, the *Burgfrieden* had informed the home authorities' policy towards labour. The government and deputy commanding generals had, for minor concessions, gained the voluntary cooperation of Socialists and trade unions. Now, much more coercive methods were to be adopted. In a letter to the Chancellor on 13 September, the Third OHL proposed among other measures that the upper limit for military service should be extended from forty-five to fifty years of age (a rise implemented by the Austro-Hungarians already in early 1915), and that a new war performance law should be introduced permitting workers to be transferred to armaments factories and making war work compulsory, even for women. All university departments except medicine should, it was argued, be shut down. The extent of the new army leaders' radicalism was best encapsulated by Hindenburg's chilling admonition to organize on the basis that 'he who does not work shall not eat'.[16]

There is little evidence that, had the Third OHL had its way, Germany's economic performance would have been improved. Austria was also inducted into the Hindenburg Programme; Article 4 of its 1912 War Law had permitted the conscription of all able-bodied individuals not in the army, and Article 6 held labourers at their place of work. Yet in spite of this coercive legislation and although 454 million crowns were paid out to build or expand factories, Austrian arms production actually declined in the second half of 1917.[17] In the Reich, civilian leaders were totally opposed to the OHL's plans for compulsory civilian mobilization. The State Secretary of the Interior, Karl Helfferich, objected that attempts to force women to work were superfluous, as more women were already seeking employment than were offered positions. Any attempt to introduce compulsion, he rightly feared, would be ruinous to the 'willing and enthusiastic collaboration' that workers had largely displayed during the *Burgfrieden*. The War Ministry too was hostile, doubted that raising the age of military service to fifty would make much difference and stressed that inner conviction, not coercion, must motivate workers. Ludendorff's response was simply to raise his demands and argue that all men from fifteen to sixty years old be given a military obligation. Most notable, and problematic, was the Third OHL's insistence that the measures should be passed as a law and thus legitimized by the Reichstag. The Prussian government, well aware that deputies were fractious as a result of the ineptitude of the official food management and abuses by deputy commanding generals of the Law of Siege, and aware of how controversial the law's provisions would be, regarded this as a grave error. Yet Hindenburg and Ludendorff brushed all reservations aside blindly. 'The Reichstag,' they asserted, 'will not deny passage to this bill when it is made clear that the war cannot be won without the help of such a law.'[18]

What became the Patriotic Auxiliary Service Bill was drawn up by Groener, whose Supreme War Office would control and allocate the nation's captive manpower. Groener was a reasonable man. Unlike Hindenburg and Ludendorff he had worked on the home front and knew the dire conditions there. He was prepared to compromise with the proletariat's representatives, recognizing that 'we can never win this war by fighting against the workers'.[19] His draft took account of civilian criticism. The extension of military service for fifteen to sixty year olds had mutated into a new obligation, Patriotic Auxiliary Service, which comprised war work of all sorts, in government offices and agriculture as well as in war industry. Only men were subject to this new duty; Hindenburg's demand for women too to be obligated was abandoned. In keeping with the Third OHL's wishes, the draft bill was short and general, but implicit in its statement that 'at the command of the War Minister' males of fifteen to sixty could 'be called upon to perform Patriotic Auxiliary Service' was the radical new power to transfer labour and restrict its free movement. Although Ludendorff pushed for immediate implementation, passing such a change through the Reichstag required extensive consultation. The civil authorities were not prepared to relinquish all control and added clauses granting the Bundesrat, the house representing the federal states of Germany, oversight of the decrees issued by the Supreme War Office in implementing the law and the right to revoke it. Ministers also rejected a provision for compulsory military training for adolescents over fifteen and they raised the lower boundary of obligation for Patriotic Auxiliary Service to seventeen years old. After meetings with industrialists and trade union representatives, guidelines were also added detailing how the bill should be implemented. To reassure the left, these included provision for arbitration committees with worker representation, which would mediate when an employee wished to leave his job but his employer would not grant a 'leaving certificate'. The intention was to pass the bill through the Bundesrat, and then take it to the Reichstag Steering Committee, where party representatives would haggle with Groener and Helfferich over its contents behind closed doors. Once agreement was reached, it was hoped the bill would in short order receive thunderous acceptance in the Reichstag, sending a powerful message of unity and will to continue the struggle and placing Germany's war effort on a new, more efficient and controlled basis.[20]

Hindenburg and Ludendorff were in for a rude shock. Social Democratic, Centre and Progressive deputies in the Reichstag and its Steering Committee did not share the Third OHL's vision of a suborned command economy and were unwilling to place unconditional trust in the hands of the military or government. The heavily revised bill accepted by the parliament on 2 December and signed into law by the Kaiser three days later was very different from the generals' intentions. In contrast to Groener's concise and general early draft, the long text was filled with concessions to the workers and their institutions; Ludendorff later denounced 'the form in which the Bill was passed' as 'equivalent to a failure'. The disgruntled Helfferich complained similarly that 'one could almost say the Social Democrats, Poles, Alsatians and the trade union secretaries made the law.'[21] For the conservative soldiers and statesmen, it was deeply worrying that the Reichstag had forced through a demand to set up a special committee of fifteen of its members to supervise the implementation of the Auxiliary Service Law, and even more so that general regulations would need their consent. Many industrialists, looking forward to having a captive workforce at their disposal, making planning easier and undermining employees' ability to bargain for higher wages, were dismayed to find workers' committees and conciliation agencies foisted on any factory with over fifty personnel. The trade unions had come closer to achieving a long-standing aim of forcing employers to recognize and parley with them. Perhaps worst of all, the primary objective of reducing worker mobility, a precondition for the central management of manpower resources, had to a large degree been thwarted. The left had spotted the potential for huge profits for industrialists, and had insisted that workers too should have the opportunity to better their lot. In consequence, although theoretically war workers were fixed to their employment, the prospect of 'a suitable improvement of working conditions' was explicitly acknowledged to be a valid justification to switch jobs.[22]

The Third OHL's attempt to remobilize Germany on a new basis of compulsion and control was thus a resounding failure. Ludendorff showed great naivety in imagining that a law limiting labour's freedoms would be accepted without demand for compensation. He disowned the final Patriotic Auxiliary Service Law as 'not merely insufficient, but positively harmful'; it was, he self-servingly argued, a manifestation of the weakness of civil authorities and avarice of the political left that ultimately cost the Reich victory.[23] Yet the real issue for Ludendorff was that he had been thwarted and the forces of democracy and Socialism had received a boost. The Reichstag committee's oversight of the law, the cooperation between the SPD and centrist bourgeois parties and the imposition of arbitration committees in which workers sat in judgement alongside employers were deeply disturbing for conservatives. Their claims, backed by some historians, that the Auxiliary Service Law undermined the war effort generally lack a firm basis in evidence. The increase in strikes in 1917 was a response to deteriorating social circumstances rather than the altered employment conditions under the new law, and the complaint that the law increased labour turnover appears doubtful. By contrast, the law was extremely successful in freeing up military manpower by substituting fit workers with men liable for auxiliary service. Crucially, the concessions made also kept the trade unions invested in the imperial regime and assured their cooperation; an invaluable achievement, especially given the tumultuousness of 1917. Attempting to militarize the workforce regardless of all other interests would inevitably have led to disaster. In a war that could only be fought with the consent of the people, the compromise and concessions of the Patriotic Auxiliary Service Law were Germany's best hope of holding out.[24]

FORCED LABOUR

The Third OHL failed in 1916 to shift the basis of Germany's war effort from consent to control, but coercion nonetheless remained an important tool in economic mobilization. German workers might be intimidated into compliance by police, employers or the generals in charge of the country's home districts. However, the harshest and most blatant compulsion on Reich soil targeted enemy subjects. It is rarely remembered today just how dependent Germany was on foreign labour during the First World War. By 1918, around a seventh of its labour force, 2.5 million people in total, came from abroad. Most were, in some sense, forced labourers. Some 1.5 million military prisoners of war made up the majority and could legally be put to non-war-related tasks. However, there were also very many civilians: hundreds of thousands of Russian-subject Polish seasonal labourers were detained on large agricultural estates; tens of thousands of Belgian civilians were forcibly brought to Germany to labour in its industry; and even among the many foreigners who did sign an employment contract, compulsion had often played some part in their decision. Yet strikingly and perhaps counter-intuitively given the Nazis' extensive use of slave labour in the Second World War, the primary lesson of the 1914–18 conflict was that forced labour did not work terribly well. The more violent the compulsion, the more miserable and recalcitrant workers became, and the less was achieved.[25]

Before the war, the booming German economy had attracted much immigrant labour. There had been half a million foreigners working in agriculture and a further 700,000 in industry. When hostilities broke out, 350,000 Russian-subject Polish seasonal workers were caught on the wrong side of the border. At first, the priority was to keep those of military age from joining the Tsar's army. All others were to be retained only for the root-crop harvest and then expelled. However, by October 1914, it had dawned on the Prussian Secretaries of the Interior and Agriculture that these people would be crucial to the Reich's farming and food supply in a long war, and they were consequently forbidden from returning home or leaving their jobs. Russian-subject Poles working in German industry were soon placed under similar restrictions. The home district generals accepted responsibility for enforcing discipline among these Poles. They were banned from striking or acting insubordinately and travel beyond their assigned locality was forbidden without prior permission from the general. To provide a semblance of legality for detaining people ineligible for military service, intense pressure was placed upon them to sign employment contracts 'voluntarily'.[26] Two points should be noted. First, in detaining these people, the German state demonstrated right from the start of hostilities that it was prepared to act ruthlessly and against the spirit of international law to benefit its war effort. Second, its treatment of what were regarded as uncultured easterners was different from citizens of 'civilized' western states. British women, for example, were permitted to return home at the start of the war, while their 4,000 military-aged men were first forbidden exit and in November interned in a relatively comfortable camp, Ruhleben, just outside Berlin. In contrast to the Russian Poles, they were never made to work for Germany's war effort. French and Belgian male civilians were mostly forced to labour only from 1916.[27]

The Third OHL thus did not pioneer forced labour in Germany, but its urgent need for workers for the Hindenburg Programme prompted it to extend the practice in a new and harsher direction. With German manpower nearly at full stretch, the High Command cast covetous eyes towards occupied Belgium, an industrialized land with a skilled but largely unemployed workforce. The idea of recruiting these workers had been in circulation for a while. Big manufacturers in the Reich had already approached the Prussian War Ministry before Hindenburg and Ludendorff's rise, and it in turn had urged General Moritz von Bissing, the head of the administration in the General Government Belgium (GGB), first in March 1916 and then again in the summer, to mobilize Belgian manpower for the German war effort. Voluntary recruitment had little success: fewer than 30,000 workers had come forward, and as the War Ministry needed at least ten times that number for its armaments programme, forced labour had been proposed. The Governor General blocked the suggestion. Even under pressure, he would compromise no further than a decree, issued in mid-May 1916, permitting workers who were unemployed or had refused to labour for German interests in Belgium to be deported over the border. Bissing's objections were in part motivated by pragmatism. He rightly doubted the economic effectiveness of forced labour and feared it would cause unrest in Belgium and provoke a negative international reaction. Bissing was also thinking strategically: he hoped Belgium would ultimately be attached to the Reich, and therefore wished to treat its population 'reasonably'. Finally, something of the paternalism inherent in the old Prussian officer corps played into his actions. He understood his role as 'administrator of the land', and felt a responsibility to oppose the more rapacious forms of exploitation. 'I am of the opinion that a pressed lemon has no value, and that a dead cow gives no more milk,' he had observed a year earlier, in June 1915. 'For this reason, it is so important and necessary that a land which economically and also in other respects has such significance for Germany is kept viable and that the wounds of war are, as far as possible, again healed.'[28]

In the end, Bissing's resistance was broken by Ludendorff and Hindenburg, who regarded the introduction of forced labour as a greater priority. Just a week and a half after their appointment to head the

German army, they met the Governor General to discuss Belgian resources. Five days later, on 13 September, they ordered him to provide labour for German needs, regardless of social or legal scruples. Bissing resisted. He consulted with the Chancellor and then travelled to Pleß, more than 1,000 kilometres from his seat in Brussels, to reason with the High Command. On 19 September he personally refused Ludendorff's demand for any general use of Belgian forced labour in Germany. It was only on 6 October, after a conference in which the GGB's representatives were isolated among both military and civil representatives in their categorical rejection of forced labour, and after an unsuccessful appeal to the Chancellor, that Bissing reluctantly agreed to organize deportations of Belgian industrial workers for Germany.[29]

It would have been difficult to make a worse decision, for on every level the deportations were a fiasco. Once Bissing had relented, the first group of unemployed and so-called 'work-shy', 729 all told, were rounded up and transported on 26 October 1916. A total of 115 such actions would take place before the deportations were halted on 10 February 1917. Initially, the OHL hoped for 20,000 workers to be transported weekly, but in the face of considerable problems, above all an overstrained rail system and lack of suitable accommodation in Germany, this figure was revised downwards, first to 12,000–13,000 and then 8,000. By 10 December the army intended to deport 2,000 Belgian workers weekly, but in practice, although 10,000 or even 12,000 had been transported during some weeks in November, even this number proved impossible to reach by the year's end. In total, 60,847 Belgians were deported. The army's crude strategy was to bring them to camps in Germany, where through deliberately harsh treatment, inadequate nutrition and poor sanitation they were to be coerced into bettering their lot by signing employment contracts in German war industry, thereby becoming 'voluntary' workers. A measure of how bad these holding camps were is the mortality in them: in a matter of months, 1,316 inmates died. Regardless, only 13,376 Belgian deportees, less than a quarter of the total, succumbed and signed a contract. Callous treatment encouraged bitterness and hatred, not submissiveness.[30]

The deportation of a few thousand wretched workers had no bearing on Hindenburg's armaments drive but it did unleash an international public relations disaster rivalled only by the massacres and destruction of the *franc-tireur* delusion of August 1914. The Belgian Catholic clergy and government in exile issued protests. So too did the Entente. The Germans' reputation for barbarity was cemented. In neutral lands there was public outrage. The Pope condemned the practice of mass deportation. Most damaging was the reaction in the United States. There was a flurry of condemnation by intellectuals, in the press and at mass rallies in the country's major cities. The popular outrage, stoked by America's pro-war faction, undermined President Wilson's efforts to engineer an American-made negotiated peace. In the winter of 1916–17, as a consequence of the deportations, Germany finally conclusively lost what its ambassador in Washington termed 'the struggle for the American soul'.[31]

The Germans, along with their Habsburg allies, had more success in the use of military prisoners for labour. As Ludendorff later observed, these were 'of the utmost importance' to the Reich's war economy.[32] Their numbers far exceeded the civilians who were forced to work. By the end of 1914, the Germans had captured 219,364 French, 19,316 British and around 300,000 Russian soldiers. Their captives swelled to 1.5 million in 1915 and to 2,415,043 by war's end. The Austro-Hungarians held around two million enemy soldiers.[33] At first, these men's labour was not called upon. They languished in overcrowded prison camps, where in the first half of 1915 a typhus epidemic raged, necessitating strict isolation from the civilian populations.[34] Nonetheless, plans were soon formulated to exploit prisoners' labour and from the middle of the year in Austria and Germany they were sent out en masse in work details. There was nothing illegal about this deployment. International law proscribed only activities connected 'with the operations of the war' for military captives.[35] Initially, the Austrians proposed to employ the prisoners on ambitious state land reclamation and railway projects. In Germany, they were first put to similar work but soon after began to be allocated to the iron industry or mines, where they quickly became a large section of the labour force. By August 1916, the month of Hindenburg and Ludendorff's rise, they accounted for around 14 per cent of workers in the Ruhr coal industry.[36]

It was in agriculture that military prisoners were most numerous and proved invaluable. Around two-thirds of Germany's prisoners were set to agricultural tasks. In Austria too, their deployment to farms was ruled 'a state necessity of the first rank'.[37] At first they worked only on large estates, because the Central Powers' armies, preoccupied with security concerns, insisted that private enterprises wishing to use the labour of captives take a minimum of thirty. It was uneconomical to guard any fewer. However, as economic priorities became more pressing, the military adopted a more flexible attitude and from October 1915 permitted individual POWs to be accommodated permanently on farms. Thereafter it was quite common for prisoners to be distributed singly or in pairs. At war's end, 1.5 million prisoners were spread across 750,000 German farms and firms.[38] The men allocated to peasant farmers could count themselves fortunate. Captives sent to work in industrial areas were poorly paid, badly fed and at risk of epidemic disease. An even worse fate befell those, 16 per cent of all Germany's and over 20 per cent of Austria-Hungary's prisoners, who were retained by the armies for labour directly behind the lines. Criminally inadequate rations, beatings and overwork stamped life in their prisoner labour companies. They accounted for many of the perhaps 140,000 and 230,000 men who died respectively in German and Austro-Hungarian captivity.[39] By contrast, prisoners allocated to small farmers in the countryside were often treated well. The female proprietors valued the scarce labour, food was available and, as the prisoners often lived in the farmhouse, barriers of language and national enmity broke down and many came to be treated as part of the family. This form of forced labour, a model far removed from the brutal servitude usually associated with the term, was the great foreign labour success of Germany and Austria-Hungary during the war. The men, mostly Russians with farming backgrounds, knew they were lucky and, in contrast to prisoners in industry or the front prisoner companies, they offered a high level of productivity.[40]

The success of farms in employing just one or two prisoners did not escape the notice of hard-pressed small entrepreneurs. To businesses struggling in a land where the best and brightest men had been called to the army, prisoners appeared to offer salvation. Helene Grus, the proprietor of a hairdressing salon in Posen, wrote for example to her local military commander in April 1918, hopefully requesting that she be allocated a prisoner skilled with scissors. Her husband had been called up in September 1916, and it had been a nightmare to find replacement staff. Her only German assistant, she complained, was 'so mentally substandard and so deficient in professional training that he not only does not serve the current clientele properly but through his behaviour and disorderliness diminishes and drives away this clientele from the business'.[41] Whether her request was granted is unknown, but it does illustrate the degree to which prisoners at work became a normal part of the fabric of wartime society.

Yet the use of forced labour was never unproblematic, even in this most benevolent guise. The presence of Russian soldiers within German society during the war had two negative consequences. The first was that it caused considerable social angst. Some women formed relationships with prisoners, and a few hundred became pregnant. The press exaggerated these cases into a national moral crisis. Anxieties about female sexuality combined with wartime xenophobia. Home district generals banned relations with the enemy. Women who dared defy their strictures were pilloried in the press as traitors and punished, sometimes with months in prison; to right-wingers, the relationships were further evidence of a selfish home front letting down the supposedly selfless heroes in the trenches.[42]

More seriously, the presence of hundreds of thousands of barely supervised enemy soldiers in the German society and economy inflamed official paranoia. In the cities they were seen as a threat to public order. Obsessive fears peaked in the summer of 1917, when the Prussian War Ministry warned that British and French agents were coordinating preparations for a mass prisoner revolt, the signal for which would supposedly be contained in weather reports sent from Switzerland. To thwart the imagined threat, censorship was tightened, police were put on high alert and guards were instructed to use their weapons at the first sign of a prisoner mutiny.[43] While the feared mass uprising never materialized, there was also a constant and more justified anxiety about prisoner sabotage of war production. The suspicions of home district commanders were fuelled by fires, explosions and apparent accidents in factories producing for the war effort. The default position came to be to assume prisoners working there were guilty. As the general in command of the XVII Army Corps district warned in mid-1917, 'the suspicion of sabotage by war prisoners may only be regarded as ruled out if another perpetrator or another cause is conclusively identified'.[44]

Most frightening to officials, however, was the knowledge that Germany was, ironically, totally dependent for its survival on hundreds of thousands of unsupervised enemy soldiers on its farms. On their labour rested the country's fragile food supply. No wonder then that the discovery that French intelligence was exhorting its countrymen in captivity to commit acts of sabotage caused German authorities to panic. Prisoners were being sent instructions and equipment for harming potatoes and livestock. So-called 'extirpators', instruments designed for poking out potatoes' eyes, as well as ingeniously disguised delayed-action incendiary devices, were discovered hidden in cakes, toothpaste tubes and tins with false bottoms in captives' Red Cross parcels. According to German intelligence, the French even experimented with biological warfare, supplying pastilles to prisoners that would infect German cattle with anthrax.[45] The danger, which was greatly overestimated, prompted the home district generals to issue hysterical proclamations. The captives, the rural population was told, were working to a devilish enemy design: 'According to a large-scale, calculated plan, our next harvest will be destroyed by the prisoners of war.' People were commanded to be 'mistrustful and watchful towards every prisoner of war ... even if he appears to you to be friendly to Germans'. Clergy, teachers and mayors were asked to alert the public to the French sabotage operation, and farmers were told to keep a close watch on their prisoners and ordered not to arrange letters or packages for them, or else they might themselves have to answer for treason.[46] The conspiracy theory took root at the highest levels that prisoners were already responsible for the country's suffering. The Deputy General Staff in charge of the army on the Reich's home front spread the fantastical but frightening story among officials that by destroying the country's seed potatoes, prisoners had caused the 'turnip winter' of 1916–17.[47]

The Germans' use of forced labour at home demonstrated the difficulty and costs of compulsion. The Third OHL's harshest use of coercion, its attempt forcibly to transport reluctant Belgian workers to the Reich, failed totally and attracted heavy international condemnation. The Polish civilians illegally detained at the war's outbreak and exploited on large eastern estates were of more yet still limited value. They were poorly motivated workers with high absconding rates.[48] Strikingly more successful was the legal use of military prisoners in agriculture. These men were generally treated well and proved indispensable to the Reich war effort. Yet even in this case, there was a heavy societal and moral price to pay for forced labour, for the use of these prisoners encouraged spiralling paranoia, mistrust and racism. These experiences did not wholly discredit the economic possibilities of harsh coercion, but they did demonstrate that it was ill-suited to a relatively free society, complete with press and parliament and under international scrutiny. In the Central Powers' occupied territories, where such conditions did not exist, there was more scope for ruthlessness and brutality. Even there, however, the coercive exploitation of human and material resources proved to have serious costs.

THE OCCUPIED TERRITORIES

The Central Powers had conquered extensive enemy territories in the first half of the war. By the end of 1916, they had overrun an area of 525,500 square kilometres, which, if its resources could be mobilized, could help to alleviate their siege and bolster their war economies significantly.[49] Twenty-one million foreign subjects, equivalent to around a third of the Reich's population, lived under German domination. There were around six million people in occupied Belgium, 300,000 in Luxembourg, two and a half million in north-eastern France, six million in the north of Congress Poland, known under the Germans as the General Government Warsaw, and nearly three million in so-called Ober Ost, which comprised Courland, Lithuania and Białystock-Grodno. Some 3.4 million Romanians, conquered at the year's end, were ruled by a regime run by the Germans, but in which the other Central Powers retained influence. Austria-Hungary too had occupied territories, more modest than those of its ally yet still extensive. The Habsburg military controlled 45,000 square kilometres in the south of Congress Poland, covering the districts of Piotrków, Kielce, Radom and Lublin, which were home to around four and a half million people, and Serbia, whose war-ravaged population numbered 1.4 million. Montenegro and Albania also lay under Austro-Hungarian rule.[50]

The Central Powers imposed a variety of occupation regimes on these territories. Belgium and Poland had one of the Germans' typically confused chains of command with a military Governor General answering solely to the Kaiser supported by a civilian bureaucracy under the purview of the Reich Chancellor. Most other areas were placed under exclusive army control. When territory on the Baltic was overrun in 1915, Ludendorff and Hindenburg, at that time commanding Germany's armies on the Eastern Front, determinedly resisted civilian interference and created their own military state, Ober Ost. Occupied north-eastern France, an area of 21,000 square kilometres, along with the western corner of Belgium was designated as a rear-line area and carved into six regions run by armies operating on the Western Front.[51] By the time half of Romania was conquered, a shortage of suitable personnel meant that installing a civilian administration was not feasible, and so the military also ran this territory in combination with allies and local elites willing to collaborate. The Habsburg conquered territories all had the Austro-Hungarian Army High Command (AOK) as their ultimate authority. Larger territories like southern Poland, Serbia and Montenegro were ruled by a military governor. Smaller regions, like Albania or later captured Italian lands, were placed under corps commands. All these administrations had similar tasks. The first priority for any occupation regime was pacification. This was a precondition for a second, central objective, economic exploitation. The antagonism that this provoked among inhabitants undermined a third, longer-term aim pursued in many territories, namely to cement permanent German or Habsburg domination through suborning the population or winning over local elites.[52]

The defining feature of the Central Powers' occupation regimes was their exploitative nature. Administrators were quite frank about their goal; as Major von Kessler, the head of the German Economic Staff in Romania, put it, the occupation authorities' most pressing task was 'to get out of the land what can be gotten out'.[53] Experts in the 1940s looking back on 1914–18 doubted that the Central Powers had been very successful. They assessed Germany's gross profits from its conquered lands at 5,700 million gold marks, covering little more than 5 per cent of its total direct war expenditure. Once the expenses of occupation were subtracted, these lands appeared of even less value.[54]

However, contemporary figures point to a different conclusion. Large quantities of diverse resources were extracted from the occupied territories (see Table 13). Moreover, the Central Powers' leaders, especially their military men, attributed an importance to them belying these modest figures. Above all, the food produced there, while not worth much in

Table 13. Selected items extracted by Germany from the occupied
territories, 1914–18

	Belgium	Ober Ost	Poland	Romania
Grain (tons)	-	-	1,228,200	711,157
Horses (head)	150,000	90,000	-	-
Cattle (head)	900,000	140,000	1,816,000	9,877
Pigs (head)	-	767,000	1,363,000	29,337
Sheep/goats (head)	-	-	1,520,000	1,208
Coal (tons)	59,900,000*	-	14,500,000*†	-
Oil (tons)	-	-	-	803,218
Salvaged metal (tons)	376,000	-	153,000	4,550
Wood (m³)	-	3,850,000*	7,300,000*	c. 44,030

* Total mined (not only for German use)   † Germany and Austria-Hungary

Sources: Belgium: P. Liberman, *Does Conquest Pay? The Exploitation of Occupied Industrial Societies* (Princeton, NJ, 1996), pp. 75 and 77, A. Henry, *Études sur l'occupation
allemande en Belgique* (Brussels, 1920), p. 194, and A. Solanský, 'German Administration
in Belgium', unpublished PhD thesis, Columbia University (1928), p. 115. Poland and
Ober Ost: V. G. Liulevičius, *War Land on the Eastern Front: Culture, National Identity,
and German Occupation in World War I* (Cambridge, New York and Melbourne, 2000),
p. 73, I. Ihnatowicz, 'Gospodarka na ziemiach polskich w okresie I Wojny Światowej', in
B. Zientara, A. Mączak, I. Ihnatowicz and Z. Landau, *Dzieje Gospodarcze Polski do
1939 r.* (Warsaw, 1965), p. 457, J. Molenda, 'Social Changes in Poland during World War
I', in B. K. Király and N. F. Dreisziger (eds.), *East European Society in World War I* (Boulder, CO, and Highland Lakes, NJ, 1985), pp. 189–90, S. Czerep, 'Straty polskie podczas
I wojny światowej', in D. Grinberg, J. Snopko and G. Zackiewicz (eds.), *Lata wielkiej
wojny. Dojrzewanie do niepodległości, 1914–1918* (Białystok, 2007), p. 188 and
M. Bemann, '"... kann von einer schonenden Behandlung keine Rede sein". Zur forst-
und landwirtschaftlichen Ausnutzung des Generalgouvernements Warschau durch die
deutsche Besatzungsmacht, 1915–1918', *Jahrbücher für Osteuropas, Neue Folge* 55(1)
(2007), pp. 10 and 24. Romania: Abteilung V. des Wirtschaftsstabes des O.K.M., 'Ausfuhr
aus Rumänien und Bessarabien bis zum 20. September 1918'. AVA Vienna: MdI, Präsidium 22/Bukowina 1900–1918 (Karton 2096): Akte 37818.

monetary terms, was invaluable in sustaining Germany and Austria-
Hungary under siege. Ludendorff stressed in his memoirs how 'the
occupied territories helped us with food supplies' and even asserted that
after 1916 'we should not have been able to exist, much less carry on
the war, without Rumania's corn and oil'.[55] Major General Franz von

Wandel, Prussia's Deputy War Minister, also rated their enforced contribution highly when he told the Reichstag in March 1916 that it was thanks to the economic committees tasked with resource extraction in conquered regions that 'our men in the field are so well fed' and that 'large supplies [can be] conveyed from the occupied territories into the home country'.[56] Habsburg commanders were no less convinced of the value of the far smaller foreign territories under their control. For the Deputy Chief of the Habsburg General Staff, Major General von Höfer, they were 'the anchor of hope' in the desperate days at the end of 1916. Without them, he thought, 'holding out until the beginning of the new harvest is impossible'.[57] To Colonel von Zeynek, the Chief of the AOK's Quartermaster Section, they 'offered us a very important means to keep the army alive'.[58]

Close examination indicates that the agricultural resources of occupied territories did help to alleviate the food shortages of the besieged Central Powers. Germany's population had consumed 13.3 million tons of grain annually in peacetime. Taking into account animals' consumption, its needs were over 25 million tons, one-fifth of which had been imported. The 500,000 tons that were taken on average yearly from occupied lands in wartime thus compensated for between one-tenth and one-sixth of the lost imports. Animal-rearing in the occupied lands was even more important to the Central Powers. As the Reich's own pig stock plummeted from over 25 million to around 10 million, the more than two million taken from the east provided a substantial contribution to alleviating Germans' hunger.[59] The conquest of Romania was especially significant. Ludendorff exaggerated when he claimed that 'in the year 1917 only Romania enabled Germany, Austria-Hungary and Constantinople to keep their heads above water'.[60] Peaceful trade, which between the autumn of 1915 and August 1916 had permitted the Central Powers to import 2.5 million tons of grain, was much more effective than military domination in securing food supplies.[61] Nonetheless, the capture of Romania's full granaries in December 1916, in the midst of the acute shortages of the 'turnip winter', was timely, and through rigorous exploitation Germany, Austria-Hungary, Bulgaria and the Ottomans were also able in subsequent years to exchange very extensive resources for the worthless, unbacked currency they introduced into the occupied country (see Table 14).

Table 14. Selected items exported from Romania by the Central
Powers, 1916–18

Product	Quantity
Grain (tons)*	1,871,546
Oats (tons)	21,093
Straw (tons)	72,276
Fresh vegetables (tons)	4,580
Fresh fruit (tons)	15,712
Eggs/egg powder (tons)	2,074
Cattle (tons)	91,387
Pigs (head)	105,347
Sheep/goats (head)	488,168
Metal (tons)	53,129
Oil (tons)	1,036,595

*Wheat, rye, corn, barley, flour and corn flour

Source: Abteilung V. des Wirtschaftsstabes des O.K.M., 'Ausfuhr aus Rumänien und
Bessarabien bis zum 20. September 1918'. AVA Vienna: MdI, Präsidium 22/Bukowina
1900–1918 (Karton 2096): Akte 37818.

Moreover, official export figures do not tell the full story. Armies
lived partly off the land. German forces in Romania, for example, themselves consumed 267,879 tons of food and fodder from the occupation
zone between 1916 and 1918.[62] Consumption by the Habsburg military
was even more significant, for the force was distinctly reluctant to share
captured bounty with their own population. The German and Austro-
Hungarian armies had very different conceptions of the war they fought
and their relations to their homelands. Especially under Ludendorff
after 1916, the German military recognized that the new industrial warfare demanded the fusion of state, society and the army. By contrast,
Habsburg officers steadfastly persisted in their outmoded view of themselves and the army as separate and superior to civilians, and acted as if
the home front barely mattered. They evinced none of their German
counterparts' urgent concern to help the suffering homeland with food.
Instead, they vigorously defended their exclusive access to the agriculture of occupied lands. Civilian purchasing agents were forbidden from

entering conquered territories and, if discovered, they were arrested and deported. The AOK's monopoly on food from the occupied territories enabled its officers to maintain an extravagant lifestyle in 1917 and 1918, indifferent to the desperate hunger of their own people. Other ranks also derived some benefit: Habsburg training units were transferred to Serbia and Poland for the sole purpose of feeding them. The army estimated that 15 per cent of its total cereal needs were met by resources from the occupied territories.[63]

On top of official exports and military consumption, significant amounts of food were dispatched privately to the homeland, ensuring that the armies' statistics never fully represented the extent of resources removed from conquered territories. Within the German occupying forces, soldiers were permitted to send 5-kilogram food parcels to friends and relatives; extensive use was made of this privilege. In just eight months in 1916–17, troops in Romania sent home enough foodstuffs to fill 1,002 wagons. A further 18,000 tons were brought back by men on leave. Similar arrangements were in place for the Habsburg army, where furloughed men were allowed to bring 25 kilograms of provisions home with them from the occupied lands.[64] For soldiers' beleaguered families, the periodic supplements to their inadequate official ration were welcome. Anna Kohnstern in Hamburg rejoiced whenever the family's Uncle Friedrich arrived from the Belgian rear areas 'overloaded' with butter, bacon, fat, beans and even live rabbits.[65] However, the mass purchases of food by the Central Powers' troops did not endear them or their regimes to occupied civilians. German soldiers flooded the conquered territories like a swarm of locusts. The purchasing power of the German mark made these troops the favoured customers of farmers but ensured that for everyone else prices rose to abominably high levels. Already in 1915, disgruntled city dwellers in both enemy and allied countries were blaming German troops bitterly for rapid inflation and hunger. Even in the countryside, peasants also eventually became disgusted with visits from foreign soldiers looking to buy items for themselves or on official requisitioning missions. They started to hide their grain. As the demands became greater, the ruses adopted to keep food out of the hands of occupying forces became more elaborate. In Romania, some peasants even hid stores of food in coffins and held fake funerals.[66]

*

The Central Powers' occupation regimes may all have had economic exploitation as their most pressing goal but the means adopted and the style of rule varied among the conquered territories. Regions run purely by the military were treated differently from those managed by army–civilian hybrid authorities. The culture, prejudices and procedures that administrators brought with them shaped how they governed and treated inhabitants. What they encountered when they arrived in the occupied regions also mattered. Contemporary international law envisaged local authorities continuing their functions under occupation, but in the east invading armies found that Tsarist officials had retreated, leaving lawless and devastated territories. Local elites might be negotiated with or ignored, and the occupying forces also had to decide how to balance competing multi-ethnic interests. The Central Powers' long-term plans for conquered territories influenced these decisions. Germanization schemes in the Baltic or the strip of Polish land to be annexed to the Reich appear to point towards the larger, genocidal racial reorganization of the east desired a quarter of a century later by the Nazis. However, large, utopian schemes were generally not a feature of German or Austrian occupation practices in the First World War. There was some limited state-building but much more confusion and chaos, which, along with the overriding need to plunder resources for the war effort, hindered the formulation and implementation of grand new designs.[67]

The First World War's most notorious occupation regime, and the clearest antecedent for Nazi methods of domination in eastern Europe, was Ober Ost in the Baltic. Ludendorff founded this military state in 1915, and his domineering personality and the martial culture of its soldier-administrators stamped the state's character. Ober Ost was a testing ground for a new form of more total mobilization; it was here that the future First Quartermaster General developed and practised his ideas for a centralized war effort run by command. It was also the prime object of the general's longer-term colonizing ambition. Its rule was marked by idealism – of a sort; Ludendorff described the occupation as 'a work for civilization' which 'benefited the army and Germany as well as the country and its inhabitants'.[68]

Ober Ost's rulers saw themselves as conveyors of culture. 'German Work', labour imbued with the highest moral motives, would tame the wild land and raise its peoples from sloth and ignorance. The military authorities' press section trumpeted their achievements. Not only was the infrastructure damaged by the Russians in their 'scorched earth' retreat repaired, but new roads, railways and telegraph lines were built with remarkable speed; already by the end of 1915, 434 bridges had been erected, including one spanning the great Bug River, alone in what would become Ober Ost's southernmost Białystok province. Officers intervened in agriculture, taking over the management of abandoned estates, and brought new industry to the region: jam factories, dairies, and potato and mushroom drying facilities were all constructed. Twelve million marks were invested in setting up saw mills, wood-processing plants and carpentry workshops in order to capitalize on the dense forest that covered the south of the territory. The army promoted not only what it regarded as a much needed work ethic among the inhabitants but also hygiene and education; under its watch the number of schools doubled to more than 1,350. Ludendorff and his subordinates dreamed of turning this neglected backwater into a productive region capable of contributing to German security. Ober Ost could become a granary, protecting the Reich in future wars from the deprivation its people were now facing. Moreover, the work undertaken would, it was hoped, prepare the way for settlement by ethnic Germans who would form for the Reich a living barrier against the barbarous east.[69]

In reality, behind this utopianism lay an extremely oppressive military regime. Ludendorff staffed its bureaucracy with officers and experts in uniform, and shut out all civilian influence. The principle on which the occupation was built, laid down explicitly in the closest thing that this military state had to a constitution, the 'Order of Rule' of 7 June 1916, was that 'the interests of the army and the German Reich always supersede the interests of the occupied territory'.[70] The military rulers imposed a repressive and obsessive system of control. Inhabitants over ten years of age were registered, photographed and issued with an identity card, for which each was compelled to pay one mark. During 1915–17, 1.8 million people, nearly two-thirds of the scattered population, were put through this compulsory procedure. A survey of possessions was undertaken, which covered everything from land ownership and cattle to household utensils. Fearing the spread of disease and espionage, the occupation authorities restricted people's freedom of movement: not only was Ober Ost sealed off from the outside world by chains of border posts but the new state was itself divided arbitrarily into districts between which inhabitants were not allowed to move without the permission of local commanders. Even in their own areas, travel by horse, wagon and boat or on skis also required a pass. The documentation of the local population, census of their goods and restrictions on their movement, as well as the 'German Work' of road and railway building, laid the foundation for highly effective exploitation. Contrary to the assumptions of the experts who tried in the 1940s to calculate the profits of occupation, the initial, large expenditures on infrastructure and administration were more than recouped: while materials imported into Ober Ost were valued at 77,308,000 marks, those removed were worth nearly five times more, at 338,606,000 marks. The population was taxed heavily, not only through a graded head tax and duties on land, housing and profits, but also indirectly through the imposition of state monopolies on cigarettes, liquor, beer, salt, sugar, saccharin and matches. Fishing licences raised extra revenue, as did a bitterly resented charge imposed on dog owners. These levies placed a disproportionately heavy burden on the poor.[71]

The occupation authorities were above all focused on harnessing Ober Ost's agricultural and human resources. Initially, the Russian army's earlier depredations meant that there was little food to be had. Ludendorff, who was otherwise dismissive of what he termed 'false humanitarian reasons', admitted in his memoirs that to ward off starvation his army had shared its provisions with Ober Ost's urban population during the winter of 1915–16; clearly, despite the parallels highlighted by recent historiography, there remained some considerable distance between Imperial German occupation practices and the genocidal 'hunger plan' that the Nazis intended to apply to the same region a quarter of a century later.[72] However, once the new harvest was ready in 1916, requisitions became ever more systematic and extreme. The quotas imposed on farmers were extraordinarily high. Although only yields for hay, clover, rape-seed and flax were adequate, the army took grain, tubers and vegetables not solely for its own use but also to feed the German homeland (see Table 15). The military was especially ruthless in tapping the territory for meat supplies. One-third of all meat eaten by the 1–2 million German troops on the Eastern Front came from Ober Ost.[73]

The other commodity of major value to the military occupation authorities was manpower. The railway and road building, farming and logging praised by propaganda as 'German Work' were in fact to a very

Table 15. Selected foods taken from the 1916 harvest in
Lithuania* by the German army (tons)

	Wheat	Rye	Barley	Potatoes
For the Army	2,965	5,630	3,231	32,801
For Germany	22	61	3,160	149

*Lithuania was initially one province of six within Ober Ost. In July 1916 the Vilna province was merged into it, making Lithuania around one-third of the total land area ruled by the military state.

Source: A. Strazhas, *Deutsche Ostpolitik im Ersten Weltkrieg. Der Fall Ober Ost, 1915–1917* (Wiesbaden, 1993), p. 47, n. 203.

great extent the products of the forced labour of Lithuanians, Latvians, Belarusians, Poles and Jews. The military administrators who ran the Ober Ost state easily applied their habits of command and expectations of unconditional obedience to the helpless civilians under their control. Compulsory labour was patronizingly justified as a moral lesson to teach work-shy easterners the value of honest graft. Local measures, such as setting the unemployed to repair roads or ordering peasants to work on abandoned estates, began immediately, in the autumn of 1915. In January 1916 the central authorities, unable to attract sufficient manpower at miserly rates of pay for their ambitious projects, pondered a more systematic organization of compulsory work. Soon after, worker columns appeared, into which inhabitants were temporarily conscripted to carry out specific tasks near their homes. The 'Order of Rule' published in the summer laid down the tasks that inhabitants of both genders could be compelled to undertake and set stiff penalties of 10,000-mark fines or five years' imprisonment for refusal.[74]

In October 1916, with Ludendorff now at the OHL demanding the extension of compulsory labour everywhere to assist in the new industrial drive, Ober Ost's administration took a final step: it decreed that workers pressed into forced labour could be deployed outside their places of habitation. This opened the way for Civil Worker Battalions (ZABs), the harshest manifestation of forced work practised by Germany in the First World War. The life of those enslaved in these units was truly miserable. The pay was a tenth of that earned by free unskilled labourers; rations, at 250 grams of bread per day, were inadequate for heavy labour; and accommodation was in draughty barrack camps surrounded by barbed wire. Beatings were frequent, illness was endemic and the prisoners – for that is what they were – had little or no contact, written or otherwise, with their families. The battalions were officially disbanded in September 1917; in practice, however, they continued in existence under different titles and their personnel, after being intimidated into signing contracts, were recategorized as 'volunteers'. Exactly how many people were subjected to compulsory labour is unknown. There were five ZABs in Ober Ost, each notionally containing 2,000 men, although escapes, death and disease eroded their numbers. Those conscripted temporarily to work in labour columns, which contained women as well as men, were much more numerous. Jews, who were particularly vulnerable to both the unemployment that was used to justify and excuse the columns and to officials' prejudices, were disproportionately affected. In the Lithuanian province of Ober Ost alone, a credible estimate is that 130,000 inhabitants were so misused.[75]

The coercion of the Ober Ost regime was effective in the short term at thoroughly plundering the land's material and human resources. However, it also had severe costs: it was wasteful and highly counterproductive for the realization of goals in the medium and longer term. The frantic efforts to gather as much food as possible in 1916 disastrously depleted the animal stocks on Lithuanian and Latvian farms and left insufficient seed for the 1917 harvest.[76] Above all, the state's reliance on intimidation and naked violence to underpin its authority was not only immoral and illegal but also no way to promote production. The population was alienated, not motivated: the frequent beatings and humiliation at the hands of gendarmes, punitive fines for misunderstanding decrees that were poorly translated or posted only in German, sudden and indiscriminate manhunts for work details, and payment in worthless 'East Marks' gave no reason for the people to strive for Ober Ost. Forced labour was carried out slowly and reluctantly. Open defiance was dangerous: when villagers in the Girkalnis district, for example, refused to surrender goods on demand, their houses were burned down and they were bloodily beaten up, placed in chains and marched around the area as a warning to others. Over 1,000 people were executed alone in the Lithuanian province of Ober Ost.[77]

Nonetheless, far from cowing inhabitants, the repression provoked resistance that ultimately destabilized the state. German officials and police were murdered in growing numbers and magazines filled with confiscated goods were set alight. Men who had fled to the forests to escape compulsory labour turned to banditry and partisan warfare, both terrorizing the population and undermining the occupiers' grip on the land. The half-hearted efforts of military rulers in 1917, after the Russian revolution, to co-opt local elites fooled nobody into thinking that inhabitants' wishes would now be seriously considered. In Courland, in the north of Ober Ost, other peoples were ignored and only the Baltic German barons were called to a new Land Assembly. In the south, a Lithuanian council, the Taryba, was allowed to convene in the autumn; a foolish act, as German leaders were unwilling to make any real concessions to Lithuanian nationalist aspirations and arrogantly overestimated their ability to coerce it. The Taryba in fact refused to confer greater legitimacy on the occupation, worked to thwart hardening German plans for permanent control and then declared Lithuanian independence on 16 February 1918. Despite intense pressure, it held steadfastly to this position over the summer months and, when the German war effort collapsed in the autumn, was instrumental in forming a Lithuanian national government.[78]

The warped utopianism of the German regime in Ober Ost was driven by Ludendorff's nationalism and militarist ambitions, but the extreme brutality and control mania exercised there were not due to him alone; they had deeper roots in German military culture. In north-eastern France, the occupation regimes of the Western Front armies bore some striking similarities to the one in Ober Ost. Most obviously, these occupations shared that regime's obsession with control and utilized many of the same tools to achieve it. The German military photographed all French citizens and issued identity cards that had to be carried at all times. People were not permitted to travel outside their own communes without applying for a pass, and having good reason. Privacy was eliminated: every house had to display a list of its residents, and periodic spot parades were held by the Germans to ensure that everyone was present. All residents were ordered to keep their doors unlocked. The male population, suspected as being most likely to resist, was controlled particularly carefully. In January 1915 all military-aged men living in Lille, the major city in the zone of occupation, were ordered to register, under threat of imprisonment. Some were interned in Germany. The military-aged men who remained in the occupation zone received a red (presumably for danger) identity card, instead of the white one issued to other civilians, and were obliged to gather once a month in order to be counted.[79] In fairness, these French areas directly behind their lines were highly sensitive for the German armies. Resistance, unlikely though it was, had the potential to cause dangerous disruption to the forces' supply lines, and hostile acts such as espionage and the assistance of escaped Entente prisoners were undertaken by French agents or civilians. The armies here had valid security concerns, but their reaction was very heavy-handed.[80]

More difficult to justify, but indicative of mentalities similar to those in Ober Ost, was the occupiers' control of the French population. Civilians could be moved around based on the needs of the military. The most shocking example took place in April 1916, when to solve an agricultural labour shortage and ease food supply problems in the cities, the Sixth Army's Quartermaster General simply removed between 24,000 and 30,000 people, mostly women, from Lille, Roubaix and Tourcoing to the countryside. As in Ober Ost, forced labour was a feature of the occupation. Temporary local work columns for field labour or fortification building had been formed as early as 1914. The further radicalization of these practices was not a local initiative but a result of Hindenburg and Ludendorff's appointment to head the German army. The Third OHL, drawing on its experiences in the east, ordered the introduction of ZABs. Twenty-five battalions were established in the rear areas between October 1916 and the spring of 1918. Around 30,000 French civilians were enslaved at any one time in these labour units, but exhaustion, illness and deaths induced by the hard work, inadequate food and beatings by guards ensured that many more men passed through them.[81]

The major difference between the German regime in Ober Ost and those in occupied France was that the latter lacked the brutal idealism of the former. There were no plans for German settlement in occupied France. Nor was there a desire to spread a mantra of 'German Work'. The so-called 'Economic Committees' of the German armies were only organizations of plunder, not production. The armies' rear areas contained a third of France's metallurgical industry and mines that had produced half of its pre-war coal output, but the damage to these installations, the displacement of their workforce and the front's proximity meant that they could not be put to work for the Reich. Instead, the military occupiers looted the facilities, de-industrializing the region by scrapping or transferring its machinery to Germany. The devastation that they left was crushing. All twenty-four large metallurgical plants and ten car, cycle and arms factories, 205 of 209 steel mills, rolling mills and foundries, 106 of 110 engineering factories and 492 of 500 smaller metallurgical establishments were damaged or destroyed.[82] The land too was ravaged rather than improved. Four-fifths of occupied France's grain harvest was sent to Germany and its pig herd had fallen from 356,000 in 1914 to just 25,000 by 1919.[83]

Not all German occupation regimes had the hard-wired brutality of Ober Ost and the armies in north-eastern France. The Governor Generals, General Bissing in Belgium and General Hans Hartwig von Beseler in Poland, who ran two other important occupied regions, were well disposed to their territories and prepared to act with moderation, stances that cast doubt on whether German military culture was so deterministically violent as sometimes claimed. Their attitudes were reinforced, rather than determined, by their civil administrations, which were generally more alert to the costs of flouting international law than were soldiers. Longer-term hopes of tying Poland and Belgium to the Reich, most likely as satellite states with restricted sovereignty, also militated in favour of conciliatory conduct. Nonetheless, moderation proved a difficult line to hold under wartime pressures. The overriding need to extract resources, demands from authorities beyond the occupation zones and the difficulty of motivating indifferent or even hostile populations to work for Germany's war effort all pushed the regimes towards an extensive use of coercion. The large-scale plunder carried out by the Central Powers to satisfy immediate wartime needs inevitably had costs for their longer-term objectives.

Bissing's Belgium offers a good illustration of some of the problems. The Governor General wished that Belgium would eventually fall under the permanent control of the Reich, he was keen not to alienate Belgians totally, and he was even prepared to use local Flemish separatists as a means to reduce French influence and tie the state closer to Germany. He wished not to ruin Belgian industry but rather set it to work for the German war effort.[84] However, his plan was thwarted from two sides.

First, German military, political and economic elites opposed it. The Prussian War Ministry was reluctant to grant contracts to Belgian firms, and German industrialists, who were well connected with the military and with the civilian administrators in the General Government Belgium, also lobbied against a programme that aimed to revive a major competitor. Both they and the Reich government preferred to use the opportunity proffered by war to eliminate competition and infiltrate Belgian industry with German capital. Second, Belgian civilians ruined Bissing's design by their unwillingness to collaborate. Although half a million Belgian workers, half of the country's workforce, were unemployed as a result of the war, there was widespread passive resistance against contributing to the German war effort. Quarries refused to supply crushed stone to the military administration and factories rejected orders that they knew came from German sources. The personnel of the Belgian railways, from navvies to managers, refused to work for the occupiers.[85] Belgians also at first displayed little willingness to work in Germany. Recruitment only picked up in 1917, in part from fear induced by the forced deportations over the winter of 1916–17, but, more importantly, due to greater incentives, including bonuses, family benefits and formal equality between Belgian and German workers. Some 160,000 Belgians signed contracts for employment in the Reich.[86]

Belgians were exceptional in their sustained passive resistance to German occupation. This was possible only because they could rely for sustenance on the Commission for Relief in Belgium (CRB). Organized by the millionaire mining engineer and future American president Herbert Hoover, the CRB supplied more than five million tons of food to Belgium and north-eastern France during the First World War.[87] The British allowed the food to pass through the blockade on condition that the Germans abstained from requisitioning it or the equivalent home produce. A further convention in July 1915 reserved all Belgium's bread grains for domestic consumption, and in April 1916, German purchases and requisitions of all foodstuffs in the territory were halted completely. The agreements came too late to stop the country's agriculture from being destroyed; in 1919, Belgium had just 327,332 pigs, compared with 1.5 million before the war.[88] Nonetheless, the CRB's food aid kept Belgians alive and, by relieving them of the need to earn, made possible a four-year strike that effectively sabotaged Bissing's hopes of industrial mobilization. In contrast to the 1,500,000 tons of pig iron and 900,000 tons of steel manufactured in Belgium before the war, the occupiers managed to coax only an annual 100,000 tons in 1915 and 1916. In February 1917 the Third OHL ordered all 'non-essential' plant to be closed. Some 151 Belgian factories were decommissioned, 24,000 machines transported to the Reich and another 12,000 machines put into storage.[89] The sole industry to maintain significant production was coal mining; the CRB did not provide this essential fuel and, with no other source of supply, the Belgians had to dig it out or freeze. While the mines never yielded as much as their annual peacetime 22.8 million tons, 16.9 million tons were dug out in 1916 and 13.9 million in 1918. Up to half of this coal was sold in Belgium, a tiny amount was exported and the rest went to the German army and railways. It proved a useful but not critical supplement to a nation that in peacetime had produced 277.2 million tons of coal annually.[90]

The occupation of the northern half of Congress Poland under Governor General von Beseler was another regime that ought to have been moderate. The General Government Warsaw (GGW), as this area was known, was saved from Ludendorff's grip by Bethmann Hollweg and Falkenhayn in 1915 and organized on the Belgian model. Beseler, the conqueror of the fortresses of Antwerp and Novogeorgievsk, was appointed despite having little political experience and no familiarity with the complex politics surrounding Europe's Polish question. Nonetheless, proving that the Prussian officer corps was not wholly incapable of empathy and open-mindedness, he prepared for his new responsibilities by reading Polish history, consulting with both Poles and Germans, and travelling widely around his area of rule. In stark contrast to Ludendorff, whose interests in the population of Ober Ost did not extend beyond what it could contribute to the German war effort, Beseler's studies gave him some sympathy for the Poles. The population, he thought, 'is certainly gifted and has good qualities'. His attitude mirrored that of the more benevolent among contemporary colonists, who justified domination of foreign peoples as a pedagogic exercise in self-government. German rule in the GGW took the form of a balancing act, in which imperial authorities sought to ensure permanent control over Poland, while simultaneously granting increasing powers of self-government to the local Polish elites.[91]

Two factors besides Beseler's initial goodwill set limits on the harshness of occupation practices in the GGW. First, as in Belgium a civilian administration answering to the Chancellor worked below the Governor General. This had been established at Bethmann's behest and against Hindenburg's and Ludendorff's wishes already in January 1915 in what was then a thin strip of occupied territory, and its jurisdiction was expanded once the GGW was established in August.[92] The other factor that should have restrained excesses against the GGW's population was the Poles' importance for Germany and Austria-Hungary domestically and on the international stage. The Central Powers' large Polish minorities maintained a fervent interest in the welfare of their compatriots across the border; Prussian officialdom noted, for example, the large sums that Poles in Germany's eastern marches donated to a 'Committee for the Suffering in the Parts of Russian Poland Occupied by German Troops'. Abuses were reported and redress demanded by the minority's representatives, supported by at least some German Socialists, in the Reichstag.[93] Moreover, the exercise in Polish state-building undertaken by the Germans in the GGW required the collaboration of local elites and thus also served to restrain overtly brutal behaviour. The high point of these efforts was the proclamation made by the German and Austrian monarchs on 5 November 1916 promising the creation after the war of an independent Poland.[94]

Nonetheless, the exigencies of blockade and war against superior powers meant that the immediate priorities of the GGW regime were the same as those of other German occupiers. The head of its civil administration, Wolfgang von Kries, defined his mission as 'to maintain peace and order in the area of administration, to secure the homeland's connection with the fighting front and, through the area of administration's economic assistance, to support the [Reich's] war economy, above all with food'.[95] The last goal, economic exploitation, was the most important. Even though the GGW contained two major cities, Warsaw and Łódź, and its cereal harvest plummeted to a mere 35 per cent of the peacetime level, huge quantities of food were taken. Northern Polish farms yielded not only 1.2 million tons of grain but also 220,000 tons of potatoes, 26,000 tons of oats and 40,000 tons of sugarbeet for the Reich or its soldiers. Millions of animals were bought or requisitioned.[96] The GGW's civilian occupiers exceeded their military counterparts in Ober Ost in their reckless exploitation of the land's forests, felling nearly 8,000 hectares. Already in 1917, officials conceded that as a result, 'the future

Polish state will have difficulties in covering its wood needs'.[97] Taxes were heavy. As in Ober Ost, the state asserted profitable monopolies over all manner of goods, from grain, salt, sugar and meat to matches, cigarettes and petroleum. Only one-third of these funds were reinvested in the territory, while the rest went to the German war effort.[98]

The burdens imposed by the occupiers eased Germany's own supply problems at the expense of the lives of the GGW's Polish and Jewish population, especially in the cities. In Warsaw, the official ration was set in mid-1916 at just two-thirds of the already utterly inadequate levels current in the Reich. By the spring of 1918 it was, at 891 calories, only about half the size. Worse still, impoverished and frequently unemployed residents of Warsaw were less able than Germans, for whom such supplements became extremely important, to afford extra nutrition on the black market. The Polish Socialist Party estimated plausibly that the population of Warsaw ate just 39 per cent of the food consumed by Germans. How many died of starvation is unknown, but weakened by malnutrition and cold due to severe fuel and clothing shortages, and lacking the soap essential for hygiene, the vulnerability of residents to disease certainly increased. Overall, the city's death rate doubled between 1914 and 1917. Old people and children were especially numerous among the victims.[99]

The GGW regime thus proved hardly less callous and exploitative than Ober Ost. It was also oppressive: thousands of people were interned and, as in the west, cities were forced to pay heavy 'contributions', in Poland's case totalling six million roubles.[100] The regime's main claim to humanity lay in the lesser use of coercion within its borders. Forced labour was introduced by the Governor General only very briefly in October 1916, principally at Ludendorff's urging. The legislative foundation was provided by a 'decree for the combating of idleness' issued on 4 October, and shortly afterwards mayors were ordered to submit lists of unemployed. Around 5,000 workers, half from Łódź, were dragooned into ZABs and sent to Ober Ost, while a larger number were made to accept temporary work in their home areas. The overwhelming majority of the people taken were Jews, a hamfisted and unsuccessful attempt by Beseler to limit Polish outrage. The policy was halted immediately after the Central Powers' proclamation on 5 November promising an autonomous Poland.[101]

The harnessing of Poland's manpower for the German war effort was central to the GGW regime, but persuasion and, sometimes, trickery rather than force were the principal tools used, with considerable success. Poland was an indispensable source of immigrant labour. Already in March 1915, even before the great advances in the east, German authorities began to recruit workers from Polish territory to replace conscripted German men.[102] Commercial agents were active from the start of 1915, but in the summer occupation authorities granted the 'German Worker Central' (*Deutsche Arbeiterzentrale* – DAZ), an organization set up in peacetime to place Polish seasonal workers with employers, a near monopoly. The offers of work in Germany were not unwelcome to Poles: as a result of wartime economic disruption, fighting and damage to factories and infrastructure by the retreating Russian army, there were 200,000 unemployed in the GGW. However, men and women who signed up frequently found that the pay and conditions they were promised either failed to materialize or were soon reduced. Worst of all, the DAZ did its best to obscure the fact that agreeing to employment in Germany was a one-way ticket; workers had no right of return. When knowledge of this fact spread among Poles, their readiness to contract themselves to Reich employers waned.[103]

The GGW administration played an iniquitous role in ensuring the continued flow of workers to Germany. Forced labour was held over the population's head as a threat. In October 1916, when it was briefly introduced, the German Chief of Police in Warsaw, Ernst Reinhard von Glasenapp, informed citizens that the measure could be halted only if sufficient volunteers for work came forward.[104] More important was ruthless economic pressure. The GGW's economy was plundered by the War Raw Materials Agencies working under the Reich Ministry of the Interior, lowering living standards and leaving the unemployed little option but to emigrate or starve. Congress Poland's industry was destroyed. Textile manufacture collapsed: the 39,000 looms of 1914 declined to 33,000 in 1916 and then, as the occupying authorities stepped up their requisition of machines for use in Germany or as scrap, to just 12,000 by 1918.[105] Polish milling also suffered, as the Germans did not permit grain to be milled locally but sent it to the Reich. Other industries fared no better: one Polish contemporary described with horror how 'factories were dismantled, copper boilers, driving belts and machines removed'. The measures benefited German industrialists, who not only saw prospective competitors eliminated but also gained their equipment at little or no cost. The GGW authorities, although initially opposed to the depredation, strove to ensure that the industrialists received the workers too. Warsaw and Łódź, the main industrial centres, were ordered to suspend all emergency works and free meals for the unemployed, with the clear intention of forcing the desperate to emigrate. These efforts were, from a German perspective, highly successful. By the spring of 1916, there were barely any skilled labourers left in the GGW. Overall, between 200,000 and 240,000 Poles were recruited for work in Germany during the war, which, taken with the 300,000 Poles trapped in the country in August 1914, made them far and away the most numerous of the Reich's foreign civilian labourers.[106]

The Germans may have been successful in mobilizing labour and ruthlessly extracting resources from Poland, but the overt economic exploitation and thinly veiled desire for political domination hobbled their ambition to reshape eastern Europe. Reich leaders competed with their Habsburg ally to determine the future of Poland. Bethmann had soon regretted his offer of November 1915 to cede it to Austria in exchange for participation in the Mitteleuropa project, and at a second meeting with Habsburg Foreign Minister István Burián in April 1916 he had withdrawn from the tentative agreement and instead had demanded a buffer state attached to Germany. He was encouraged by Governor General Beseler, who was already engaged in limited state-building, intervening in municipal government and schooling. The German administration's most symbolically powerful act was to authorize the re-establishment of Warsaw University in the autumn of 1915. The Tsarist regime had Russified the institution, and its return as a seat of Polish learning was enthusiastically welcomed by local elites. The Germans' support could be understood as a mark of their cultural superiority over the Russians and a willingness to permit the training of a Polish leadership capable, within limits, of managing its own national affairs.[107]

Burián still wished to acquire the whole of Congress Poland for the Habsburgs and was dismayed by Bethmann's reversal. The deadlock between the two Central Powers might have continued indefinitely had it not been for the combined Entente offensive that summer. First, the Brusilov offensive so damaged the Habsburg Empire militarily and politically that the Germans were able to impose their vision of a Polish buffer state. In August, Burián assented reluctantly to an independent Kingdom of Poland with a hereditary monarchy and constitution. The state was not to be established until the war's end and no firm decision was made about its size. However, the Germans would get their border strip, and it was agreed that the new state's foreign policy and army would remain in the hands of the Central Powers, although in the latter case a primary role was given to the Germans.[108]

Second, the heavy fighting in the summer of 1916 prompted a frantic search for new sources of military manpower. Poles had been considered as possible soldiers before; Falkenhayn had raised the possibility of recruiting in Congress Poland as early as September 1915, but Bethmann had at that time questioned the legality and practicality of such action. In mid-July, Falkenhayn and Ludendorff, concerned at the Austro-Hungarian military collapse during the Brusilov offensive but impressed by the Polish Legion, one of the few formations to emerge with credit from the debacle, urgently clamoured for replacement manpower to be drawn from Poland. This brought the dilemma about the country's future to a head. As Governor General Beseler pointed out, recruitment was hardly likely to succeed while no decision on Polish independence had yet been reached. He estimated optimistically that if Poles were offered a modicum of freedom, at first three divisions of 30,000 men and later an army of 100,000 soldiers might be raised. Bethmann was inclined to stall, for he was aware of the drawbacks of establishing a new Polish state and did not wish to close off a separate peace with Russia. Yet even once the Brusilov offensive was fading, the appointment of the radical Third OHL ensured that there was no slackening of the pressure on him. Ludendorff's calculation was simple: 'Everything comes down to power, and we need men.'[109]

The Central Powers' manifesto of 5 November 1916 was undermined by the differences in German and Habsburg political visions for Congress Poland and the secret intention among Reich leaders to annex a large border strip, and it was stamped by the military priorities that had called it into existence. The manifesto offered no immediate change and, as the Central Powers did not agree, only vague commitments for the future. It held out an 'autonomous state with hereditary monarchy and constitutional regime', yet without any indication of who that monarch might be or where the borders of this state would lie. What it did make clear was that a Polish army should be the new kingdom's priority. To underline this central message, the German and Austro-Hungarian Governor Generals published a second proclamation just four days later opening recruitment. 'The struggle with Russia is still going on and is not yet completed,' the generals observed, 'so stand by our side as volunteers and help us complete our victory over your persecutor.' To Poles, the self-serving motives behind the offer could scarcely have been more obvious, and its political cynicism increased the distrust already instilled by the occupiers' economic rapacity. In under twenty-four hours most of the appeals in Warsaw had pasted next to them posters with the slogan 'No Polish Army without the Polish Government!' Recruitment was a total failure: even before the year's end, Beseler rued the entire endeavour as a 'great disappointment'. In contrast to the expected minimum of three divisions, a mere 3,200 men had come forward by February 1917.[110]

The Germans overreached themselves in Poland. The November proclamation was a historic moment, for it was the first concrete promise made by heads of state to restore the country after more than 120 years of partition. Bethmann was able to talk the talk of freedom. In April 1916 he had vowed before the Reichstag that Germany and Austria-Hungary would 'solve' the Polish question. The Reich, he had pledged, would never 'voluntarily surrender to the rule of reactionary Russia the peoples . . . between the Baltic and the marshes of Volhynia whom she and her ally have liberated'.[111] Yet the Germans' desire for political control was too naked and their economic exploitation had gone too far in alienating Poles, and the proclamation consequently won them few friends.[112] Instead, the Third OHL, Bethmann and Beseler soon found that they had fashioned a rod to beat themselves. The 5 November proclamation opened an international bidding war for the hearts and minds of east-central Europeans. Once President Wilson of the United States began to take part in January 1917, and especially after the Russian revolution the following spring, the Central Powers had no hope of winning this ideological contest. The proclamation also undermined the stability of the GGW's occupation regime. The Germans had hurriedly conceded a Provisional Council of State once they had recognized the patent inadequacy of the 5 November offer. Although this was powerless and failed to satisfy Polish national aspirations, it and its successor, a Regency Council formed in the autumn of 1917, provided weak but alternative sources of authority to the Governor

General. Józef Piłsudski, the founder of the Polish Legions, sat as chairman of its Military Commission and used his position to agitate for a national government and army. The Third OHL learned nothing from the fiasco. Ludendorff's insistence that the Polish Legions, transferred to the GGW as the basis of a Polish army, swear an oath to the German Kaiser, destroyed what little remained of the Central Powers' credibility and the plans to create a military ally from occupied Poland.[113]

The Third OHL brought a new ruthlessness but not efficiency to the Central Powers' war efforts. Ludendorff and Hindenburg sought to impose centralization, control and rationalization, yet they pursued goals that were complete fantasies: their rearmament plan was an emotional and propaganda response to Entente material might, not the product of a reasoned assessment of the Reich's capabilities. Most profoundly, they tried to change the basis on which their country's war effort rested. Compulsion was to replace the consent that for the first half of the war had stood Germany in good stead. The best expression of how totally the duo wished to subordinate society and economy to their war effort was Hindenburg's demand that 'he who does not work shall not eat'. The inspiration for this model of waging conflict came from their own creation in the east, the military state of Ober Ost. There, humans were enslaved and the land pillaged of its wealth, all for the German military machine.

The Germans were not unique in their ruthless exploitation and programmes of forced labour for enemy subjects. Habsburg military authorities liked to present themselves as the benevolent occupier, in contrast to brutal Teutons or rapacious Bulgarians, but in practice they were similarly single-minded about extracting resources from their occupied territories. Requisitioning *Honvéd* troops, villagers in Congress Poland discovered, 'were not open to negotiation. At even the weakest protest or pleading, they reached for sabre or revolver.' In Poland, the Austro-Hungarian army introduced civilian forced labour before its German ally. Some 122 civilian worker divisions, into which around 30,000 men were impressed, were formed to mend roads and work on rivers. However, the village riots that this provoked halted the practice by July 1916.[114] The Germans, by contrast, expanded their reliance on forced labour, culminating in the terrifying ZAB battalions that circulated in Ober Ost and the area behind the Western Front. The urgent need for resources tended even in the Germans' more moderate occupation regimes to encourage compulsion, which, regardless of human suffering, proved effective for short-term plunder. Yet even abroad, it was a miserable way to run a war effort. Ruthless and coercive exploitation could not mobilize production and, as the Central Powers found in Poland in 1916, could also have significant political and strategic costs.

The Third OHL's vision for Germany was certainly less violent and coercive than that in the occupied territories but the level of compulsion it envisaged would have been enough to shatter the fragile *Burgfrieden* consensus. Despite Ludendorff's disgust, the hijacking of the Auxiliary Service Bill by the Social Democrats and unions was thus probably the best outcome for the Reich's war effort. Yet even if the OHL's bid to control labour was thwarted, its attempted armament drive put severe strains on German and, as the Habsburgs also took part, Austro-Hungarian society. New exertion was demanded of people: for a time at least, scarce food was made available to armaments workers rather than the vulnerable, and overtime was enforced. Remaining stocks of metals were requisitioned: even church bells were sacrificed to Mars, contributing over three-quarters of the copper alloy at the disposal of the Habsburg war effort in 1917.[115] Yet despite all the extra hardship, the Hindenburg Programme brought no increase in weapons production. With deprivation on the home front, rapidly increasing levels of exhaustion in the army and no sign of the demanded jump in armaments production, the OHL grasped other means to intensify violence. To end the war, it placed all bets on Germany's most popular, controversial and riskiest weapon: the U-boat.

IO

U-Boats

THE WORST DECISION OF THE WAR

A material and morale crisis seized the Central Powers at the turn of 1916–17. Their populations were shivering through a miserable winter of deprivation and their armies were exhausted by the summer's heavy fighting. A negotiated peace ending the war on favourable terms appeared very distant; the Entente categorically rejected as 'empty and insincere' the December Peace Proposal of German Chancellor Bethmann Hollweg.[1] The Third OHL, although shaken by the summer battles, was resolved to continue the fight, yet its massive rearmament drive was not only failing to produce the expected results but actually worsening conditions, overstraining the railways and consequently disrupting rhythms of production and the urban food supply. With the army adopting a defensive stance in the west, there was no prospect of relief through a land victory, merely more gruelling static combat. In a mix of desperation and determination, Germany's rulers turned to their navy. The possibility of flouting international law and unleashing its submarines in a ruthless 'unrestricted' campaign to starve the British Isles into submission had been widely discussed since the end of 1914. Only fear of America, which insisted on the right of its ships and citizens to travel unharmed where they wished, had deterred German leaders. On 9 January 1917 what the Chancellor called 'the last card' was finally played: legal and diplomatic reservations were cast aside and the leadership resolved to launch an unrestricted U-boat campaign.[2]

This was the worst decision of the war. Unbeknown to the Germans, the exertions of the past year had almost bankrupted the British. Paying for food and raw materials such as steel, as well as semi-finished or finished armaments, was costing the Treasury two million pounds a day, and British gold reserves and securities were on course to be exhausted by March 1917.[3] Meanwhile the French army, even more than its German opponent, was demoralized after the bloodletting at Verdun and on the Somme. Its disillusionment with its commanders would break out in a mass strike in the spring and summer of 1917. Most ominous, the Russian Empire was on the edge of revolution. Little over a month after the unrestricted submarine campaign started on 1 February, the Tsar was overthrown by a popular uprising, an event that could have upturned the strategic situation and gifted the Central Powers a real chance of triumph. Instead, as one great enemy gradually collapsed, another, thanks to the U-boat campaign, entered hostilities. Entirely predictably, the United States broke off diplomatic relations in response to the campaign. On 6 April, a couple of weeks after the first American ships had been sunk, the mighty power across the Atlantic placed its formidable wealth and resources in the service of the Entente and declared war on the Reich.

How could Germany's leaders have been so extraordinarily stupid? Was their decision a result of militarism run wild? Did it reflect a parochial, nationalist arrogance towards the new power over the seas? Or was it a logical response to a strategic situation that appeared near hopeless? The Chief of the Admiralty Staff, Henning von Holtzendorff, was certainly audacious in his claims for what the U-boats could achieve. 'I do not hesitate to declare,' he had written in a memorandum dated 22 December 1916 and circulated among decision-makers before the key Crown Council on 9 January 1917, 'that we can, in the current circumstances, force England through unrestricted submarine war to make peace in five months.'[4] This was no impulsive boast. To research how Britain could be defeated, the Admiralty Staff's Department B-1 had recruited an impressive group of financial, industrial, commercial and agrarian experts. Nemesis takes strange forms in a people's war, and the two figures central to plotting Britain's demise in Department B-1 were an ex-bank manager, Dr Richard Fuss, and a Heidelberg professor of economics, Dr Hermann Levy. Fuss had been responsible since March 1915 for collecting data on British trade. As early as August 1915, Levy had identified Britain's wheat supply as a point of vulnerability. He noticed that unlike continental powers, Britain neither grew nor stored large stocks of wheat, but instead fed its population through constant imports. A determined attack on this maritime supply thus had excellent chances of forcing Germany's most dangerous enemy to sue for peace. Department B-1 produced a series of Admiralty Staff memoranda over the following sixteen months that developed and added to this argument. Supplying copious statistics, charts and graphs, their papers 'proved' that unrestricted submarine warfare would inevitably lead to a German victory.[5]

Holtzendorff's memorandum of 22 December 1916 was the culmination of this Admiralty Staff series of papers. Following the earlier research, it analysed Britain's shipping and economy in order to support its primary claim that the world's greatest maritime power could be vanquished by 1 August 1917. The paper estimated that the British had access to 10.75 million tons of cargo space, after deducting roughly 10 million tons dedicated to military supply, under repair, in the service of other Entente powers or employed solely on coastal trade. Some 6.75 million tons of this shipping was British, a little under a million belonged to other Entente powers and the remaining three million tons was owned by neutral countries. Extrapolating from experience, the memorandum argued that an unrestricted submarine campaign could sink 600,000 tons of merchant shipping per month and scare from the seas another 1.2 million tons of neutral freighters, around 40 per cent of the total. After five months, the tonnage on which Britain's supply rested would thus be reduced by 39 per cent, to little over 6.5 million tons. 'England would not be able to bear this,' Holtzendorff insisted. She would be unwilling to lose the merchant fleet on which her peacetime prosperity depended and so would be incapable of continuing to wage war.

In the memorandum Britain's defeat was projected to happen primarily because of the interruption for five months of her wheat supply. She was ill-equipped, judged Germany's naval experts, to overcome a sudden stoppage of deliveries of this crucial commodity. Unlike the Reich, Britain had no other grains with which to 'stretch' her flour, and would have no time to gather them. She possessed neither the administrative machinery nor, it was thought, the popular consent needed to introduce food-conservation measures. The timing was auspicious, for a poor harvest in North America in 1916 meant that British grain ships would have to travel further, to India, Argentina and Australia, increasing the strain on precious tonnage. To add to Britons' misery, other key imports would also be diminished. Cutting Britain off from Holland and Denmark would cause fats to run short. Breaking her links with Scandinavia would reduce stocks of wood, crucial for pit props, and ore, which would reduce coal, steel and munitions production. The U-boat campaign had to begin no later than 1 February in order to take effect before the next harvest in August, but then Britain would be starved out, its people panicked by shortages and spiralling prices, its exchequer emptied and its war industries crippled by strikes and a lack of key raw materials.[6]

The precondition for realizing this apocalyptic scenario, the German navy insisted, was the introduction of U-boat warfare unfettered by international law. The submarines' rules of engagement had been altered repeatedly during the war, as the navy's desire for greater aggression was balanced by diplomatic scruples. There were debates within the Reich's leadership about whether passenger liners could be attacked and when merchantmen might be sunk on sight. During a period of 'sharpened' warfare in March and April 1916, armed enemy merchant ships had been destroyed without warning everywhere and unarmed freighters had met the same fate if they were encountered within a designated war zone. For much of the war, however, the U-boats had fought under something approximating traditional 'prize rules'. The standard procedure for submarines was to halt a merchant ship and permit the crew to disembark. If the vessel belonged to an enemy nation, it was then sunk. If it were neutral, its papers would be checked to establish whether it was taking 'contraband' to an enemy port, and if so, it too would be sunk. This practice was more abrupt and destructive than that of surface ships, which took enemy or suspicious merchant vessels back to their home station to have their fates decided by a prize court.[7] However, it was widely, albeit reluctantly, understood that submarines had little space for prize crews and no easy way of bringing a ship back across open sea, the surface of which at least was still ruled by Britannia. The last U-boat campaign conducted under these rules was extremely successful, sinking an average of 326,000 tons per month between October 1916 and the end of January 1917, and, no less crucially, not unduly provoking the Americans.[8]

Nonetheless, Holtzendorff and his experts considered these results inadequate. Submarine warfare conducted along lines tolerated by the international community, they estimated, could destroy at most 18 per cent of British shipping over five months; a painful blow, to be sure, yet not nearly enough to force Germany's arch-enemy to the peace table. An illegal sink-on-sight campaign, by contrast, would enable submarines to avoid risky attacks on the surface, where they might be hit by the guns of armed merchantmen or surprised by a Q-Ship (a British warship disguised as a merchant vessel), and allow commanders to throw caution to the wind, thus raising the kill rate. The prospect of being sunk without warning by a torpedo strike was also intended to inspire terror in British and, still more importantly, neutral sailors. Holtzendorff's unrestricted submarine warfare was another innovation of total war; it was conceived as a campaign of terror and its ability to provoke 'panic and fear' was explicitly regarded as an 'indispensable precondition of success'. Of course, the admiral recognized that this ruthless way of fighting was certain to provoke the Americans to declare war. However, while paying lip service to 'so serious a matter', he did not regard the United States as a major threat. It could provide the Entente with little extra tonnage and without ships no American troops could intervene on Europe's battlefields. Most likely, he predicted, once Britain sued for peace, the US would quickly also parley.[9]

Unfortunately for Germany's leaders, the memorandum's ambitious claims, forceful language and intimidating statistics disguised considerable wishful thinking. Holtzendorff and the staff of Department B-1 underestimated the robustness of modern economies: 'the economy of a country resembles a masterpiece of precision mechanics', their December memorandum insisted. 'Once it falls into disorder, interference, frictions and breakages continue incessantly.' The view was understandable, for it reflected the German economy's own war experience. Official intervention had proven powerless to solve food shortages, and dabbling with the market had frustratingly resulted in unforeseen distortions in production and the disappearance of goods from legal sales outlets. To the Reich's leaders and bureaucrats, suffering under fierce public criticism, it did indeed seem that Britain's 'hunger blockade' had thrown their country's economy into a cycle of 'disorder, interference, frictions and breakages'. Still, the planners' strenuous denial that Britain could counter the U-boat threat was clearly exaggerated. Their bald assertion that it was incapable of 'stretching' food or implementing conservation measures was a reckless underestimation of a formidable enemy.[10]

Holtzendorff and the specialists of Department B-1 also made other unwarranted assumptions. The admiral's dismissal of convoys as 'a great boon for our U-boats', because their length and slowness would make the ships sitting ducks, would later prove to be disastrously misguided.[11] Despite their confident tone, the planners did not in fact know how much British shipping was devoted to the transport of grain. They were also guessing about how much more destructive unrestricted submarine warfare would be: an initial estimate in February 1916 posited it to be three times as effective as operations conducted under prize rules, but ten months later their estimate had mysteriously dropped to around twice as effective.[12] In fairness, the British Admiralty shared the Germans' doubts about convoys, and the estimates of how much the U-boats could sink monthly proved remarkably accurate. Nevertheless, there were too many unknowns and too much poor or biased judgement to justify the German navy's confidence and ambition. The memorandum was an extremely dangerous document, for under a comforting veneer of scientific certainty it pushed a high-risk strategy, whose failure guaranteed devastating consequences. Bethmann accurately characterized unrestricted submarine warfare as a 'game of *va banque* whose stakes will be our existence as a Great Power and our entire national future'.[13]

The siren call of the imperial navy's experts to gamble everything on unrestricted U-boat warfare was consistently opposed by the Reich's Chancellor. Bethmann had no humanitarian scruples about torpedoing merchant ships; he simply doubted that it would defeat Britain and he greatly feared provoking the United States. In his reading, which admittedly looked less convincing after the Entente had strongly rejected the German peace offer in December 1916, mutual exhaustion offered the most likely opportunity for a satisfactory settlement. American belligerence would be disastrous, as it would stiffen Entente resolve for total victory. In 1915, Bethmann had succeeded in response to neutral pressure in forcing the navy to modify aggressive rules of engagement so that neutrals and all passenger liners were not attacked. Throughout 1916, he had successfully opposed the navy's constant urgings for unrestricted submarine warfare. Here, he was aided by other civilian ministers, who also harboured grave misgivings about the navy's plans. When an unlimited submarine campaign was mooted in August, the Vice Chancellor, Karl Helfferich, had disputed Holtzendorff's figures and warned that such a campaign would bring 'catastrophe'. The

Foreign Secretary, Gottlieb von Jagow, agreed, stressing that it would turn the whole international community against the Reich.[14] Even on 9 January 1917, when Bethmann met Hindenburg and Ludendorff before the Crown Council, he had argued for over an hour against unrestricted submarine warfare. This time, however, he failed to halt the campaign. The Third OHL and the Admiralty united behind it, and the Kaiser, in whose hands the decision ultimately lay, had according to the Chief of his Naval Cabinet, Admiral Georg von Müller, already decided the evening before that he was 'definitely in favour of it'.[15]

Bethmann's final failure in January 1917 to stop unrestricted submarine warfare from going ahead was a consequence of power shifts that had taken place late during the preceding summer and autumn. The right had long clamoured for unrestricted U-boat warfare, but by this point even centrists wanted it, and Bethmann found himself under strong pressure to submit. In August 1916 he had felt obliged to conjecture openly in the Bundesrat – the parliamentary house containing the states' representatives – about when such a campaign could be launched, and had named February 1917. Even more threatening to the Chancellor's position was the formation in October of a Reichstag majority in favour of unrestricted submarine warfare. The Catholic Centre Party, whose best-known member Matthias Erzberger had to this point been opposed, now joined right-wing parties in demanding that the submarines be unleashed. 'Should the decision fall in favour of undertaking unrestricted U-boat war, the Chancellor may be certain of the agreement of the Reichstag,' Erzberger had assured him. Bethmann was urged to defer to the rising power of the Third OHL.[16]

Hindenburg and Ludendorff had refused to support the Admiralty at the end of August 1916. With heavy fighting on the Somme and at Verdun, a frail ally in the east and the new need to defend against Romania, the army's manpower was totally committed. The Field Marshal and his First Quartermaster General feared no soldiers would be left to defend the borders if the submarines provoked Denmark or Holland into war against the Reich. However, German leaders had not rejected unconditional U-boat warfare outright; rather, a firm decision on the submarine campaign had been postponed until the Romanian threat was eliminated. Bethmann had also come out of these discussions with his authority weakened. He had explicitly conceded that the decisive voice on whether to launch unrestricted submarine warfare should be that of the Third

OHL. Tactically, he had been extremely clever, for he was able to defuse some of the pressure from parliament and heavy industry for unrestricted U-boat warfare by sheltering behind the refusal to countenance it of the wildly popular Hindenburg. Had Bethmann stepped back, however, he would have seen that this same popular pressure had pushed him into the arms of the military. When Hindenburg and Ludendorff turned in favour of an unrestricted campaign, the Chancellor was in no position to refuse.[17]

The Third OHL's opposition to unrestricted U-boat warfare was always temporary. Hindenburg had judged the future to be 'darker than ever' at the end of August 1916, but already in September he and his Quartermaster General gave conditional support to Holtzendorff's urging to launch a campaign from mid-October. The OHL's complete conversion to unrestricted submarine warfare came as a result of the crushing of Romania in December. The strategic situation was still worrying, but the victory had released the men needed to secure Germany against war with irate neutrals and U-boat warfare seemed worth trying. The reasons listed by Ludendorff to Bethmann on 9 January 1917 for supporting Holtzendorff's plan testify to grave concern rather than aggression. Above all, his priority was to relieve pressure on the army: 'We must spare the troops a second Somme battle.' Ludendorff counted on the submarines to damage Entente munitions production. Hindenburg was more gung-ho, claiming that Germany, although not its allies, could hold out for much longer, but he agreed that 'the war must be brought to an end faster'.[18]

One other factor, more emotional than reasoned, also influenced the decision of German leaders to launch unrestricted submarine warfare. Whether they feared or dismissed the United States, the Reich's leaders harboured bitter and largely justified resentment against the country. President Woodrow Wilson, son of a Presbyterian minister and a man who had devoted his political life to progressive causes, usually adopted a tone of moralistic condescension when addressing warring Europeans. His sanctimonious preaching on 'behalf of humanity' rankled with German leaders, who were well aware that the ships passing from America to Britain carried US-produced weapons and munitions intended to kill their subjects.[19] Ludendorff was, for once, justified in complaining that 'The attitude of the United States in regard to the question of the supply of munitions left no doubt about their one-sided conception of neutrality.'[20] Hindenburg too brought up the problem of American munitions in the Crown Council on 9 January, hoping that the submarines might reduce the deliveries.[21] The United States was raking in immense profits from helping Europe tear itself apart; its net gain in foreign trade during the period of neutrality totalled between 4.5 and 5 billion dollars.[22] This exploitation of the old world's misery activated the inherent animosity towards all things commercial harboured by the Kaiserreich's aristocratic ruling classes. Above all, this was true for the Kaiser, in whose hands rested the ultimate power to launch the submarines. For him, as he explained in January 1917, 'the war is the struggle between two world views: the Teutonic-German for morality, right, loyalty and faith, genuine humanity, truth and real freedom, against the Anglo-Saxon [world view], the worship of Mammon, the power of money, pleasure, land-hunger, lies, betrayal, deceit and – last but not least – treacherous assassination!'[23]

THE UNRESTRICTED SUBMARINE CAMPAIGN

The German navy had been the Kaiser's pet project and a source of intense national pride before the First World War. In a country united for only a few decades in a federal structure, where the army still comprised four distinct, if closely linked, forces – the Prussian, Bavarian, Saxon and that of Württemberg – the navy was a rare, genuinely German institution. Its expansion, and particularly its growing number of dreadnoughts, had been seen domestically and internationally as a mark of the Reich's aspiration to world power. However, in war the performance of the vaunted surface ships of the High Seas Fleet had been uninspiring. The fleet had launched a few raids in 1914, and in the summer of 1916 at Jutland it had finally fought a battle with the force it had been constructed to beat, the much larger British Grand Fleet. It had acquitted itself well, sinking fourteen British ships for the loss of eleven of its own vessels, but the battle had not changed the overall strategic balance. The fleet remained bottled up in its own ports and the Baltic, stopped by its superior enemy from sallying out to cut British supply lines or smash the blockade against Germany.[24]

The dramatic escapades of Germany's submarines had contrasted sharply with the surface fleet's apparent inactivity already in 1914. Over the course of subsequent years, they had not only become the public's darlings but had also acquired a much more important position in the navy's order of battle and operational planning. German U-boat strength had risen from a paltry thirty-seven, at the start of the first abortive attempt to conduct unrestricted warfare in February 1915, to 105 submarines two years later. Forty-six U-boats were in the High Seas Fleet and twenty-three smaller vessels served with the Flanders Flotilla. All these operated around the United Kingdom and off the coast of France. Another twenty-three U-boats were stationed at the Austro-Hungarian Pola and Cattaro bases in the Mediterranean, three worked out of Constantinople in the Black Sea and the remaining ten patrolled in the Baltic.[25] These vessels would permit the navy to step out from the army's shadow and at last prove its value for the German war effort. As Admiral Reinhard Scheer, Chief of the High Seas Fleet, informed his men proudly on 31 January 1917, a day before the new rules of engagement went into force, 'the trust of the nation' and 'responsibility for exerting the decisive pressure on our main enemy has been placed on the navy'.[26]

The U-boats were unquestionably formidable weapons. The modern vessels that were the mainstay of the force could reach speeds of over sixteen knots with their diesel engines on the surface, nine or ten knots running off batteries under water, and had a range of at least 7,500 and in some cases 11,500 nautical miles. Most had six torpedo tubes, four up front in the bow and another two in the stern, and two deck-mounted 8.8cm and 10.5cm cannon. The smaller U-boats deployed by the Flanders Flotilla and in the Mediterranean were less powerful, but still dangerous. Some, the so-called UC boats, were mine-layers for whom a relatively low surface speed of twelve knots was not a major disadvantage. UB boats, which carried torpedoes as their primary armament, were faster, reaching eight knots under water and fourteen on the surface. From May 1917, the navy also deployed large U-cruisers, whose displacement of 1,510 tons was nearly double that of ordinary U-boats and three times that of the biggest and most modern UB and UC submarines. U-cruisers had originally been developed as submersible cargo vessels capable of evading the British blockade, and one, the 'Deutschland', had made two trips in this role to the United States in 1916, causing a huge public stir on its arrival in Baltimore. When re-equipped for fighting, they mounted two 15cm guns, as well as torpedo tubes. They were extremely unwieldy, but their tremendous range of up to 13,500 naut-ical miles and ability to remain at sea for three and a half months allowed the navy to project force into hitherto unreachable waters.[27]

From the outset of the unrestricted submarine campaign, German naval commanders stressed the overriding need for speed and ruthless-ness. The Leader of Submarines of the High Seas Fleet, Commander Hermann Bauer, resolved to work his forces at a frenetic pace in the bid for final victory. Submarine commanders were ordered to keep cruises short and violent. operations were ideally to last just fourteen days, in which all torpedoes should be expended. 'No vessel must remain afloat the sinking of which is authorized,' warned Bauer. To maximize the time in the main hunting grounds in the Atlantic, U-boats were ordered to cease travelling around the coast of Scotland. Instead, commanders were to take the more direct, and dangerous, route through the English Channel. Maintenance on the submarines was to be reduced to a bare minimum, so as to waste no time in dock. The men's leave was also to be restricted and, this being the navy, warnings to sailors about the per-ils of venereal disease were redoubled. The commanders were told to stress to their crews that the campaign was 'to decide the whole war'.[28] These instructions, along with the new rules of engagement, clearly made an impression, for in February 1917 sinkings rose by 50 per cent over those of the previous month, to nearly 500,000 tons. This was short of what Holtzendorff had promised, but was excusable because the first half of the month had seen some restraint so as to allow neutral ships at sea when the blockade zone was declared to return home. The Flanders Flotilla was upbeat at the beginning of March. Neutral ships were staying in port and, it reported, the enemy's counter-measures were ineffective. The submariners felt invincible.[29]

The operations of the following months bore out this optimism. Sinkings by U-boats rose to nearly 550,000 tons in March and to a spectacular 841,118 tons in April. The Admiralty was also encouraged by intelligence reports stressing the dire impact of the campaign on the enemy's war effort. Supplies for the French and Italian armies were said to be badly disrupted and British sailors, livid at their own fleet's failure to protect them, on the brink of revolt.[30] The navy's insistence on unre-stricted warfare appeared to be vindicated. In fact, a close look at the figures shows precisely the opposite.[31] Had the new ruthless 'sink on sight' tactics been the cause of success, each U-boat would have been recording a much higher average daily rate of sinkings. However, in the campaign's first five, most successful months, this rate rose by a measly average of 54 tons per day. In the Mediterranean, the average sinkings per U-boat actually dropped. The German success was due not to the new tactics but to the much larger number of U-boats on patrol at any one time. The navy not only had more and better submarines than previously, as those ordered in 1915 came into service, but it also used them much more intensively. The order to navigate the English Channel paid dividends, for British defences proved to be largely ineffectual and the shorter route shaved six days off each mission. Less sustainably, the tempo of operations, with little time permitted for rest and repair, also increased the kill rate. The April sinkings were achieved in good part by pushing the officers and men of the submarine arm to the limits of their endurance. The success of that month was never again equalled, neither in the First World War nor, despite considerably more submarines and sophisticated equipment, in the Second World War.[32]

The sleek shark-like U-boats, a triumph of early twentieth-century technology, have captured many a writer's imagination. Yet all too often the officers and men who operated them are forgotten; the submarines are pictured coursing through the water dealing death and destruction almost of their own volition. In reality, a U-boat was only ever as good as its crew and commander. These sailors endured extremely tough conditions. One captured submariner who spent three years in the marine infantry on the Western Front before joining the Submarine Section told British interrogators that he preferred the trenches to life on the U-boats.[33] Submarine service entailed an absence not so much of personal privacy as of any personal space at all. The typical U-boat of the High Seas Fleet was around 70 metres in length and just 6.5 metres at its widest point. Into these claustrophobic confines were crammed a crew of around forty and everything that they needed for a month-long cruise. The commander had a tiny cabin, while other officers shared small quarters with each other, as did warrant officers and petty officers. The men slept on bunks in the torpedo rooms, their space often restricted by extra torpedoes supplementing the U-boats' limited standard stock of ten, twelve or at most sixteen. Equipment typically included a machine gun, searchlight and hundreds of rounds of ammunition for the deck artillery. Seven to twelve tons of drinking water were stowed.[34]

Food for the voyage filled any empty nook or cranny. 'Every available corner and space is filled with provisions,' wrote one U-boat commander. 'The cook . . . must hunt below in every conceivable place for his vegetables and meats. The latter are stored in the coolest quarters, next to the munitions. The sausages are put close to the red grenades, the butter lies beneath one of the sailor's bunks, and the salt and spice have been known to stray into the commander's cabin.'[35]

It was not easy to bear such living conditions, especially as the discomfort was exacerbated by the other hardships of active service. Heavy seas would cause submarines to roll violently, with ill-effects on their crews' digestive systems. Martin Niemöller recalled how on his maiden voyage as Second Watchkeeper in *U73*, half the sailors were permanently seasick while the other half cleaned up after them. The buffeting might be escaped by submerging, but this brought its own problems. Ideally, the U-boat would be ventilated before diving, but often there was no time and so sailors had to work in a choking atmosphere of machine oil, cooking and sweat. Although crews were equipped with potassium compounds to soak up carbon dioxide, after several hours underwater the air became 'very thick and foul'. Temperatures rose to an unpleasant 30°C, and to an almost unbearable 40°C in the engine room.[36] The longer a voyage lasted, the greater the stink. To save water, sailors were allowed to wash only once per week, and pumice and sand made inadequate substitutes for the soap that was lacking everywhere in Germany. Many suffered from a skin complaint known as 'petroleum disease', which caused small sores to appear all over the body and was widely blamed on the low-quality Galician diesel used to power the vessels.[37]

Above all, life on the U-boats was perilous. The seas were treacherous. Niemöller had joined *U73* after its entire bridge complement was swept overboard by high waves in the North Sea, and on his own first voyage the submarine lost another man to the deep. The enemy too was dangerous. To fight in a U-boat was not just to hunt but to be hunted. To submariners, the whole sea appeared to be 'a powder keg'. 'Mines, nets, explosive devices, shells and sharp ship's keels are our enemies,' wrote one U-boat commander in 1916. 'Any minute we could be thrown a hundred metres up in the air or a hundred metres under the water.'[38] Losses can only be described as horrendous: 5,132 men, half of all who served on the U-boats, were killed during the war. The year 1916 was comparatively safe, with twenty-three U-boats sunk from a force whose monthly strength averaged sixty-seven vessels. In 1918, the most costly year, 102 were destroyed from an average monthly strength of 124 submarines. The pattern of casualties was quite distinct from that of land forces. Whereas infantry units suffered a trickle of losses punctuated by devastation in the periodic offensives, casualties in submarines were either very light or total. When a vessel sunk, its whole crew almost invariably perished.[39]

Nonetheless, chances of survival were not equal for all submarine crew members. Men stationed in the conning tower had a slight advantage over their comrades trapped in the boat's confines. The commander of *UC65*, Lieutenant Commander Claus Lafrenz, escaped death when his vessel was torpedoed by a British submarine because the explosion threw him out of the tower high into the air. Similarly, the three survivors from *UB72*, a coastal boat sunk in May 1918 by another torpedo strike, were two look-outs and an extremely lucky seaman who had come up to the conning tower to throw potato peelings overboard and had lingered for a cigarette. This man, not the watch, noticed the torpedo's wake and jumped into the sea just before it hit. The two look-outs went down with the U-boat but were blown back to the surface in an air bubble. A bubble also saved Engine-room Petty Officer Karl Eschenberg, the sole survivor of *U104*, in April 1918. He wrested open a torpedo hatch as his depth-charged vessel slid into the deep and was pushed up the tube by escaping air. As his ordeal illustrates, even if sailors made it to the surface, survival was far from guaranteed. Eschenberg kicked off his clothes and had to tread water for three hours before he was picked up by a British warship. He was fortunate that it was spring, for in autumn or winter sailors pitched into the Atlantic soon succumbed to exposure and drowned.[40]

The war's most remarkable escape was probably that from *UB81*, which struck a mine in the English Channel on 2 December 1917. Survivors recounted how there was an explosion, the boat shook and then two sailors rushed forward shouting that the stern was flooding. The watertight doors separating the compartments were quickly shut, but the weight of the water dragged the submarine down onto the seabed. The crew tried to surface, but the aft ballast tanks were damaged, so only the bow lifted. With the stern resting on the seabed, the boat was suspended in the water diagonally, powerless to right itself. The woes of the men wedged uncomfortably inside increased as the second compartment began leaking ice-cold water, raising the air pressure and making breathing difficult.

There was one very slim chance of escape. *UB81* had been operating in shallow waters, and its commander, the popular and successful Lieutenant Reinhold Saltzwedel, reckoned that the bow might be poking above the surface. With the boat stuck at a 53° angle, the crew laboured for hours to remove a live torpedo from one of the forward tubes and, once this had been achieved, three sailors were pushed inside, one on top of the other and the tube was cautiously opened. Miraculously, they found to their delight that the bow lay a foot above the water, making it possible for those inside the tube to crawl to freedom and pull comrades out to join them. Even then, however, their problems were not over. The icy cold forced some to return to the U-boat, saying, according to one of the survivors, that 'they would rather die down below than up above'. Those sailors who remained fired flares to attract attention, but when, finally, a British patrol boat did arrive, waves knocked it against the stricken submarine, sending the wreck to the bottom, this time permanently. Of the thirty-five-man crew, only the seven who had gone up the torpedo tube and chosen to brave the weather were rescued and one of them died of exposure before reaching port. Saltzwedel, whose idea it had been to escape through the tube and who refused to leave until all his men were off the U-boat, perished with them.[41]

To cope with the high risk of an unpleasant death, submariners developed a rich fund of superstitions. The first cardinal rule of the service was that a commander should never switch U-boats. This belief had some logic, as no two submarines handled alike and a commander could get more out of a vessel whose quirks he knew than one with which he was unfamiliar. The second rule, more difficult to rationalize but firmly insisted upon throughout the Submarine Section, was that it was terribly bad luck to begin a mission on a Friday. The commander who was ordered to take out *U93* for its maiden voyage on Friday, 13 April 1917, had to reassure his anxious crew that the Friday and the thirteenth cancelled each other out.[42] Other superstitions were specific to particular formations. The crews of the Flanders Flotilla developed a curious belief about the commander of *UB40*, Lieutenant Emsmann, who, although widely considered a 'gentleman', was also thought to bring misfortune. Any boat that left harbour on the same day as Emsmann's vessel was believed to be doomed. To raise their chances of survival, the sailors of this flotilla took to painting eyes on their U-boats, which they convinced themselves was an oriental charm bringing good luck.[43]

Whether submariners worried about the moral dilemmas of sinking merchant shipping is difficult to know. A sailor from *U48* captured in November 1917 claimed that 'a large majority of the men . . . do not like torpedoing Merchant ships', but as he was under interrogation and may just have wanted to pacify his interviewers, his opinion should be treated with caution. Disaffected minorities may have been more likely to be genuinely critical. A Polish machine-gunner on *U55* was heard by a British merchant captain held prisoner on the U-boat to condemn the campaign as 'nothing but murder' and whispered 'Thank God' when a torpedo missed its intended victim.[44] Later in the campaign, men were more likely to condemn it on pragmatic grounds than from moral scruples. Sailors on *UB124* criticized the campaign in July 1918 as 'doomed to failure' because Germany did not have sufficient U-boats.[45] Commanders probably devoted more thought to moral issues; after all, it was they who ordered torpedoes to be fired into civilian vessels. Many excused their ruthless means of warfare as a response to the British blockade, a way, as one put it, 'simply [to] pay off our account against their criminal wish to starve all our people, our women, and our children'.[46]

Nonetheless, to assume commanders were all alike and morally indifferent would be wrong. Senior officers on shore urged ruthlessness. The Leader of Submarines, fearing that the terror effect on which the campaign partially depended might be undermined, strongly condemned and forbade all mercy, warning that it 'deludes steamer crews about the seriousness of the U-boat war'.[47] Some commanders took note. Lieutenant Commander Gerlach on *U93*, for example, refused to take prisoners on board his submarine, as they were 'useless eaters' who reduced the time he could spend out on operations. However, many commanders chose to ignore their leaders' admonitions. They continued to stop neutral ships and permitted crews to disembark even after the new sink-on-sight orders of unrestricted warfare had come into force. There were cases of commanders halting their submarines in order to tell neutral sailors in lifeboats how far they were from land or even picking up men for whom there was no room in the lifeboats. Baron Edgar von Spiegel, Gerlach's predecessor as commander of *U93*, stands out as positively gentlemanly by the brutal standards of twentieth-century warfare. After sinking the Danish schooner *Diana* on 28 April 1917, he took the crew's lifeboat in tow to bring it closer to land. He even displayed an unusual care for the welfare of enemy sailors. When, a little later in the cruise, *U93* sunk the British steamer *Horsa*, pity was taken on the fourteen survivors, some of whom were unclothed or badly wounded. They were brought into the cramped confines of the submarine, given medical care, and later in the day handed over to a Finnish bark.[48]

In view of the hardship, danger and doubtful morality of the war they waged, why did submariners not only endure but also fight so dedicatedly? Few were volunteers; the navy found it more efficient to allocate men with proven technical skills to the Submarine Section. To judge from their conduct during prisoner interrogations, the submariners were also not overly patriotic. Many talked freely to their captors. Petty Officer Fritz Marsal, the sole survivor of *UC63*, sunk in October 1917, was noted as extremely unusual in having 'expressed regret at being unable to continue to fight for his country'.[49] The resilience of the U-boat crews instead rested on military factors. First, the men were very thoroughly trained, at least until 1918. In contrast to the miserable twelve weeks' training given to infantrymen, submariners could count on at least sixteen and often as many as twenty-six weeks of instruction in seamanship, signalling, torpedoes, or electrical engineering and U-boat courses. The training of petty officers was even more thorough, lasting eight or nine months. Once these courses were completed, the new submariners were allocated as supernumerary personnel for three months to a veteran U-boat, participating in an operational cruise and in the preparatory and subsequent refits. When new U-boats were commissioned, a core of veterans was always provided in order to keep up morale and skill levels, and time was allocated to permit the new crew to train together. This considerable investment of time and resources ensured that submariners, all selected men under thirty-two years old, knew their jobs intimately and could be confident in their ability to get the best out of their U-boats on active service.[50]

Second, the submariners' treatment helped to instil in them the sense of being an elite. The men were not only thoroughly trained but also very well looked after. The rations they received were far better than those of soldiers and, even more so, of sailors on the battleships, whom they looked down upon as 'swabbing coolies'.[51] By the end of 1917, they were almost uniquely privileged in still receiving an issue of real coffee. Leave too was relatively generous. Even after the unrestricted campaign began, with all its attendant pressures, submariners generally managed to get away once every six to eight months. The men also appreciated their good wages, which were swollen by numerous allowances. On top of specialist bonuses, there were supplements for price inflation and for constricted living conditions. In harbour, the sailors were given extra for carrying out work on their vessel and at sea they earned 'diving pay' of 1.50 marks for each day that the U-boat submerged.[52] No less valuable was the prestige of service on a submarine. Decorations were lavished on the crews. Every man on U58, for example, possessed the Iron Cross First or Second Class.[53] The personnel were also wildly popular among the public. The so-called *U-Boot-Spende* – an appeal for submariners and their families issued in February 1917 – raised over 20 million marks by the war's end.[54] The most successful commanders stood on a par with flying aces as hero-celebrities who, like their counterparts in the air, wore the Reich's highest distinction, the *Pour le Mérite*. Lothar von Arnauld de la Perière, the war's highest scorer with 453,716 tons of shipping sunk, was no less famous at the time than the better remembered fighter pilots Oswald Boelcke or Manfred von Richthofen. He and his submarine, the *U35*, even starred in a feature film, *The Magic Girdle*, which followed their exploits in the Mediterranean.[55]

A final key reason for the resilience of the U-boat service was its crews' tight cohesion. Submarine complements enjoyed a high degree of stability; the nature of the fighting meant that there was less of the gradual erosion or need to rebuild after heavy casualties so typical in military units. The long periods spent together in training, boat maintenance and operations fostered mutual trust and confidence among the crews, which in turn promoted individual motivation and harmonious teamwork. Moreover, in stark contrast to the antagonistic relations between ranks prevailing on the big surface ships of the German navy by 1917, U-boat men and their officers were generally on good terms. It was a mark of the section's *esprit* that many commanders were known by affectionate nicknames: 'The Kid' in *U34*, 'Sea Boot' in *UB103* and 'Hein Schniefelig', a moniker suggesting dubious personal hygiene, in *UC77*. Submariners frequently praised their officers as friendly and caring. The commander of *U104*, for example, was characterized as 'a man of feeling', while his counterpart on *UB72*, Lieutenant Traeger, was said to be 'very popular with his men, as he treated them with consideration and kindness and did not stand upon his dignity'.[56] As befitted an elite arm, crews judged their leaders not only on their paternalistic care but also on their skill and aggression in battle. As the crew of *U103* put it, a 'Draufgänger' – an aggressive and spirited leader – was much preferred over a nervous or mediocre commander. Traeger's popularity on *UB72* was not harmed by his overconfidence, although it ultimately played a part in the loss of his boat and life. Sailors from *U48* and *UB85*, by contrast, expressed frustration at their commanders' poor aim with torpedoes. The navy too placed a premium on skill and aggression among its submarine commanders, who if they failed to notch up sufficient sinkings could expect to lose their positions. In the competitive culture of the Submarine Section, where U-boats vied in the amount of tonnage they destroyed, the thorough training of its sailors, the prestige and privileges that they garnered, and the good officer–men relations, which in part rested on the close contact and teamwork demanded by their working conditions, all contributed to its success and endurance.[57]

Even as the U-boats achieved their highest rate of sinking in April 1917, parts of the German naval hierarchy began to harbour doubts about the unrestricted campaign. The Marine Corps, the parent formation of the Flanders Submarine Flotilla, warned at the end of the month that despite the successes, there was no evidence that Britain would be defeated by August. Crews and boats were already being pushed to the limit and only the transfer of new vessels could bring greater destruction of shipping.[58] The Marine Corps was clearly not alone in its scepticism, for in May the Leader of the High Sea Fleet's U-boat forces, Commander Hermann Bauer, issued an order condemning all who expressed misgivings. The campaign's feasibility was already statistically proven, he asserted. Intelligence reports all indicated that Britain was headed for catastrophe. What was needed now, he stressed, shifting from the material to the mystical, was 'belief'. All faint-hearted thoughts should be quashed. 'Only if we . . . carry within us and spread unshakeable belief in the natural necessity and, under the blessing of a higher power, the continuing decisive effect of our weapon can we achieve the goal that we have been set – the greatest ever demanded from a single arm – the saving of our Fatherland.'[59]

The British were indeed in trouble; three months of unrestricted submarine warfare had cost them 1.9 million tons of shipping. They nonetheless proved adaptive and resilient. Their response to the U-boat threat was threefold. First, the Ministry of Food and the Food Production Department under the Board of Agriculture, both established at the turn of 1916–17, sought to reduce reliance on imports through cultivating and better managing domestic resources. Over 1916–18, strenuous efforts were made to raise home cereal production by turning 7.5 million acres of pasture over to arable farming. This led to a reduction in meat production, and so had only a limited impact on overall calories, but it was spectacularly successful in increasing the crucial staple foods: potato and wheat yields came to exceed those of 1904–13 by 40 per cent. Even more importantly, the British, like the Germans two years previously, stretched their flour stocks with husk and by mixing in other cereals, principally barley. The quality of British loaves never descended to the depths reached by German 'War Bread', however. Bread, despite the best efforts of the U-boats, was never rationed in the United Kingdom. Meat ration cards were issued only in February 1918.[60] Captured German submariners observed the comparative abundance of food possessed by their enemy despondently. 'One hardly notices anything of the war here, no cards of any kind, not even for bread,' remarked the commander of *U93*, Edgar von Spiegel, in a letter to his wife after being taken prisoner by the British at the end of April 1917. 'It is very sad, but it is true.'[61]

Second, the British were ruthless in ensuring that merchant shipping remained available to them. The calculations underlying the unrestricted submarine campaign had been predicated in large part on its ability to scare neutral vessels from the high seas. The British countered with a little terrorism of their own: continental neutrals were warned that if they did prevent their ships from sailing, their own supplies would be cut. This was a wholly credible threat due to Britain's control of coaling stations and access to the English Channel and North Sea. It was reinforced by the introduction of a 'ship for ship' policy: Dutch and Scandinavian ships were held hostage – to all intents and purposes – in British ports and were permitted to return home only when similar sized vessels trading under the same flag arrived to replace them. Other neutral vessels were released only if their captains promised to head to an Entente port or return with an approved cargo.[62] Ship-building was also given new priority. The 53,000 tons that Britain produced each month in 1916 doubled to 102,000 tons in 1917. Its effort was dwarfed by that of the United States, which more than tripled the merchant tonnage at its disposal from 2.75 million tons in April 1917 to a colossal 9.5 million tons by September 1918. Even so, the Allies did suffer a shipping crisis in the war's last year. Ironically, however, the cause was far less the U-boats than the new demand placed on the merchant fleets to convey to Europe and keep supplied millions of US soldiers. This was emphatically not the crisis that Henning von Holtzendorff had wanted or expected.[63]

The third and, for the U-boat crews, most ominous response of the British to the unrestricted submarine campaign, and specifically to its initial success, was the introduction of convoys. Troopships and supplies had always been escorted across the Channel, and the tactic had also earlier been used successfully to protect merchant shipping on certain routes to Holland, Scandinavia and, in the case of the coal trade, France, but British admirals had baulked at any general introduction. A large convoy, they reasoned, would attract attention to itself by the smoke it produced and offer the U-boats more targets. Freighters could not be expected to keep formation. Moreover, the quantity of shipping that would need to be protected appeared so large as to make convoys unfeasible: statistics on arrivals and departures at British ports suggested that more than 300 ships would need escorting daily.[64] In fact, these port statistics double-counted vessels by recording both arrivals and departures and also made no distinction between coastal traffic and large ocean-going freighters. When the U-boats' successes forced a closer analysis, it turned out that rarely more than twenty cargo ships from across the Atlantic arrived daily at British ports. This was a far more manageable number, although the destroyers needed for the escorts were still in short supply. The Royal Navy estimated that it had forty available for convoy work, but required seventy-two. The ships were gradually provided by its US ally, the first six arriving in British waters in early May. By this point, the merchantmen's horrendous losses the previous month had prompted the British War Cabinet to intervene and force a rethink in the Admiralty. The Prime Minister, David Lloyd George, pushed at the end of April for convoys to be trialled and on

10 May, the first group of sixteen ships under armed escort left Gibraltar. It proved a complete success.[65]

The U-boat campaign was not instantly broken by the introduction of convoying. Indeed, as the figures for merchant tonnage sunk reveal (see Fig. 6), in June 1917 the submarine crews achieved their second highest score of the war, sinking nearly 670,000 tons of enemy and neutral merchant shipping. The Allies (as the Entente became with the entry of the United States into the war) needed time to implement the new system, and the US Navy Department was at first reluctant to commit large forces to the protection of merchantmen. While regular convoys sailed from Hampton Roads, Virginia, across the Atlantic from mid-June and were extended to other North American ports in the following weeks, only at the end of July did regular convoys begin leaving Gibraltar; and although some local escorting was introduced, not until mid-October was an organized convoy system developed in the Mediterranean.[66] The U-boats also proved adept at locating chinks in the Allies' new armour. The proportion of ships sunk on return voyages to America, which travelled unescorted until August 1917, rose over the summer. The U-cruisers attacked the weakly protected shipping around Madeira, the Azores and the Cape Verde islands, where another exclusion zone was declared in November. U-boats in the Mediterranean, helped by the sea's narrowness and also by poor Allied coordination, remained more dangerous than those in northern waters.[67] Most

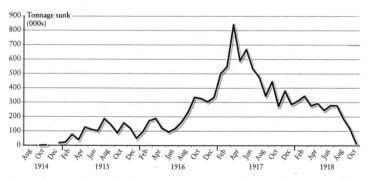

Figure 6. Merchant shipping sunk by German U-boats (tonnage)

Source: J. Schröder, *Die U-Boote des Kaisers. Die Geschichte des deutschen U-Boot-Krieges gegen Großbritannien im Ersten Weltkrieg* (Lauf a. d. Pegnitz, 2000), p. 430

importantly, U-boats in the north switched from deep-sea operations to patrolling Britain's coast, where there were still plenty of freighters steaming unprotected to the point at which a convoy was scheduled to gather or to a port for unloading, their convoys having dispersed. Whereas from February to July 1917 just 20 per cent of ships sunk were attacked within ten nautical miles of the coast, the proportion nearly tripled to 58 per cent in the second half of the year. Monthly sinkings, after falling precipitously from the heights recorded in spring, fluctuated between 270,000 and 450,000 tons in the autumn and winter, and from the start of 1918 until the war's final months they stabilized at around 300,000 tons. While no longer sufficient to pose a mortal threat to Britain, this was far greater than at any point before October 1916 and a severe drain on Allied shipping.[68]

Nonetheless, if convoys did not eliminate the U-boat threat, they were the key factor in retarding it so significantly. The convoys not only emptied the seas of easy targets by concentrating and protecting shipping but they themselves proved unexpectedly difficult for submarines to locate. Between October and December 1917 just 39 of the 219 Atlantic convoys that sailed were even sighted by submarines. Their low detection rate was a consequence not just of the vastness of the seas but also of the British Admiralty's ability to reroute the ships around danger. Warships, unlike most merchantmen, had powerful wirelesses, which could receive messages from London about the location of U-boats based on sightings or the interception of their radio communications. The Germans found no answer to this problem. The tactic used in the Second World War to intercept on land the wireless messages of Allied convoys and then direct boats onto targets was not practicable in 1917 and 1918 because the radios of U-boats were too primitive. A plan to equip one of the big U-cruisers with wireless and decryption personnel, and station it off the west coast of England to identify convoys' locations and coordinate U-boat attacks, was rejected. Moreover, even when submarines spotted convoys, attacking them was difficult. A single U-boat lost the advantage of surprise already after its first shot and was not superior to heavily armed escorts. The tactic of grouping submarines into pairs or even packs was suggested, among others by the Kaiser, but an experiment in May 1918 showed that U-boat numbers were too few to allow for both cooperation and the guarding of all seaways. While the Allies had to put up with delays caused by collecting ships together and longer unloading times at ports, as groups of twenty, thirty or in one case even forty-seven ships arrived, the safety offered by the convoys outweighed all their disadvantages. Between August and October 1917 ships still sailing independently had a loss rate of 7.37 per cent; the rate in the convoys was just 0.58 per cent. The escorts also proved their value in protecting the liners and converted freighters carrying US troops across the Atlantic. Some 2,078,880 American soldiers were safely transported to Europe, mostly in 1918. Just 314 were lost at sea through U-boat action.[69]

The convoys not only impeded the efforts of U-boats to sink ships but also forced them to fight under very unfavourable conditions. The offensive sweeps by warships, which had previously been the Royal Navy's prime anti-submarine tactic, and which were still continued in the last years of the war, were highly ineffective because U-boats had no reason to engage and detection equipment was still in its infancy.[70] Once convoys were introduced, however, the submarines had no choice but to confront escorting sloops and heavily armed destroyers: as the commander of *UB52* observed ruefully, the patrols had been easy to evade, but with convoys 'now every target met with has an attendant defender'.[71] Improvements in Allied weaponry further increased the danger to submarines. The depth charges carried by escorts, dismissed by U-boat crews in 1916 as 'firecrackers', had just a year later been developed into powerful devices capable of sinking or forcing to the surface a submarine if they exploded within 30 metres. To be depth-charged was the naval equivalent of sheltering under an artillery bombardment; captured submariners described how sitting helplessly under depth-charge attack summoned a 'feeling of oppression . . . very difficult to overcome'.[72] When the U-boats turned increasingly to coastal traffic in order to find unescorted targets, this made them more vulnerable to interception, for once near land they came in range of aerial reconnaisance. As early as June 1917, submarines off England's east coast were being gravely hampered by airship activity. By 1 January 1918 the British were deploying 100 airships, 23 aeroplanes and 291 seaplanes on anti-submarine duties. Aircraft destroyed at most four U-boats, but they provoked nervousness disproportionate to this success and by the summer of 1918 many submarines had returned to hunting further out to sea in order to avoid them.[73] The new danger posed by convoy tactics and improved weaponry was reflected in the submarines' loss rates: in 1917 twenty were sunk by enemy action during the first six months, but more than double that number, forty-three in total, during the second half of the year. Losses were even worse in 1918, amounting to 102 from all causes.[74]

Mine-laying also made a significant but late contribution to the fight against German submarines. British mines were, for most of the war, extremely unreliable. One UC-boat commander, confident they would not explode, even scooped two up on a mission in October 1917 and had them made into punch bowls on his return home. Only when the British gave up trying to design their own contact mine and copied a proven German pattern did they begin to have success. By the turn of 1917–18, their new H2 mines were being laid in such numbers and proving so lethal that submarine crews had lost their nonchalance and were becoming very frightened.[75] Thirty-four of the 178 U-boats sunk through enemy action during the war were accounted for by mines or combinations of mines and underwater nets. The ambition of British naval planners went far beyond destruction, however; they hoped to use mines to box in or at least impede the movement of the submarines. Efforts to confine German and Habsburg U-boats to their Adriatic bases by placing mines, nets and drifters in the Strait of Otranto, between the heel of Italy and Albania, failed. A megalomaniac US plan to block the entrance to the North Sea resulted in 70,263 mines being sown along a stretch of water 400 kilometres in length in the war's last months. At a cost of 40 million dollars, this 'Northern Barrage' sunk at most seven submarines. However, the more manageable goal of closing off the Dover Strait was achieved. The first British attempt in December 1916 comprised an intricate combination of nets and minefields between Goodwin Sands and Dunkirk. It was quickly damaged by the Channel's strong currents and proved totally useless: as many as thirty German U-boats crossed over it monthly to and from their hunting grounds further west. At the end of 1917 the British had a second try, this time laying a deeper minefield and posting trawlers with flares and searchlights to illuminate the surface of the water at night. The hope that U-boats attempting to creep across would be forced by the glare to dive into the minefield beneath was vindicated. On the very first night that the new system was trialled, UB56 was caught in the searchlights, dived, and was destroyed by a mine. Over the next five months, the new barrage accounted for a submarine on average every three weeks. Consequently, the U-boats again began to travel around Scotland to reach their hunting grounds, losing valuable time that in turn reduced the rate of merchant sinkings.[76]

One of the gravest consequences of the drawn-out and increasingly unfavourable fighting was the dissipation of the 'unshakeable belief' that Hermann Bauer, Leader of Submarines, had urged upon his crews in May 1917. The sailors became exhausted: in the first seven months of the unrestricted campaign most spent over one-third of their time at sea and those in the Flanders Flotilla over 40 per cent.[77] By November, men from U48 captured by the British were reportedly attributing 'the recent increase in the number of losses . . . mainly to this system of "driving" the submarines all the time at top pressure'.[78] The force also deskilled. Much has been made of the German navy's complacency in not constructing sufficient submarines: none were ordered between September 1915 and May 1916, and those started afterwards were still being built when the war ended. Nonetheless, enough were completed in 1918 to keep the numbers reasonably stable, despite severe losses, at about 128 U-boats, the German force's strength in March 1917.[79] The real problem was finding and training crews and competent commanders for these new submarines. Reserve crews were said to be 'nothing more than untrained recruits' and veteran petty officers were increasingly scarce.[80] Exhaustion, rising casualties and the influx of new, inexperienced sailors into the service lowered morale. In April 1918 British intelligence observed that 'the recent heavy losses in submarines have made the crews extremely nervous'.[81] Officers of the Flanders Flotilla started to consume noticeably more alcohol onshore and the formation was sardonically dubbed the 'Drowning Command for ex-Merchant Service Officers' – a reference to the merchant-fleet background of many of the reserve officers now commanding smaller German submarines.[82]

The intense exhaustion, falling morale and declining quality of submarine crews inevitably impacted negatively on fighting performance. Lack of skill or nervousness and misjudgement started to cause U-boat losses. The sinking of U110 in March 1918, for example, was blamed partly on the 'striking . . . youth and inexperience' of its crew, among whom were just four veteran petty officers.[83] The next month, UB85, whose crew were also novices, surrendered after a disastrous cruise in which every torpedo fired had missed its target. When the U-boat had dived, the conning tower hatch had been left open or malfunctioned and fifteen tons of water had poured in, short-circuiting a motor and reacting with the acid in the boat's batteries to produce poisonous fumes. Frightening as this was, the submarine could still have escaped over open water with its diesel engines, and British interrogators considered the commander to have acted 'somewhat prematurely' in bringing his crew up on deck and having them shout 'We surrender' in unison at a nearby Royal Navy patrol ship.[84] At the other extreme, exhausted veteran commanders also became nervous and started to make unforced errors. Lieutenant Commander Robert Moraht, a professional officer who had served in submarines since 1915 and had won the *Pour le Mérite*, frankly admitted that faulty judgement, stemming from his poor mental health, had cost him his boat, the *U64*, in June 1918. He knew that after two years in the service 'his nerves had begun to suffer', but had resisted transferral to an appointment onshore. He had lost his ability accurately to assess risk, attacked a well-protected convoy, and was sunk by its escorts. All but himself and four others of *U64*'s forty-one-strong crew had gone down with the boat.[85]

The U-boat war was not, as it is often presented, solely a matter of numbers, technology or tactics. As in land fighting, the skill, resilience and determination of men played a key part in its outcome. The increase in sinkings after February 1917 was due not only to more numerous and efficient deployment of U-boats but also to the pushing of their crews to the limits of endurance. Human psychology was always central to unrestricted submarine warfare. The campaign's success hinged in good part on its ability to spread terror, yet Holtzendorff and his experts overestimated their own commanders' ruthlessness and underrated their enemy's courage and resilience. The submarines drove neither British nor neutral merchant shipping from the seas. Instead, as their opponents' tactics and weaponry improved, as losses increased and as the high tempo of operations exhausted them, it was the will of German U-boat commanders and crews that waned. The U-boats never realized their aim of inflicting panic and collapse on British society. Instead, through its failure the submarine campaign's greatest impact would be felt in Germany.

WONDER WEAPON BLUES

The mass of the German people had placed great emotional investment in the U-boats to end the war quickly and victoriously. True, in February 1917, there had been voices urging caution. Moderate intellectuals including the military historian Hans Delbrück and, in Austria, the jurist and politican Josef Redlich saw through the Admiralty's overly rosy predictions and rightly feared provoking the United States.[86] Yet these people were a minority. Most of the population greeted the unrestricted campaign with a hope that even the immediate diplomatic break with the United States did not suppress. The newspaper editor of the liberal *Berliner Tageblatt*, Theodor Wolff, no friend of the annexationists calling most insistently for the submarines' ruthless deployment, punned in February about the 'unrestricted U-boat optimism' sweeping the country.[87] The generals in charge of the home districts made similar observations in their monthly morale reports. The commander of IV district, which covered Prussian Saxony in the middle of Germany, caught the nation's mood best when he wrote that 'scarcely has any step of the Reich leadership been greeted with such approval and such striking unanimity, right down to the parts of the population furthest to the left, as the decision to undertake the submarine war without restrictions'.[88]

The enthusiasm is not difficult to understand. After a cold and hungry winter, many Germans felt a certain *Schadenfreude* at the thought of the British being starved out by the submarines. Their animosity towards America too should not be underestimated. For years, they had read press reports detailing the huge quantities of armaments manufactured in the neutral United States for the Entente. Publicists spread news of how millionaires were being created across the Atlantic by the flood of war orders. German Americans had tried hard to have an embargo imposed on weapons exports, but commercial interests and the government's growing sympathy for the Entente took precedence. Woodrow Wilson's administration insisted disingenuously that it could not interfere with free trade.[89] The weapons shipments provoked much anger in the German public. One of the more imaginative responses took place within the army, where in 1915 troops vented their irritation with a satirical art exhibition held behind the Somme lines. The first piece on display, entitled with heavy irony 'Wilson, the neutral', was a chalk bust of the American president wearing a supercilious smile set over a rostrum of unexploded shells, all made in the USA.[90] German military home commands referred to the ingrained resentment from the arms deliveries to explain the population's 'calm composure' when on 3 February 1917 America broke diplomatic relations. Nonetheless, by far the most important reason why the Reich's weary populace supported the unrestricted submarine campaign was that it promised a rapid end to the conflict. Few, unlike the conservatives who had been the primary agitators for unrestricted U-boat warfare, were in favour of annexations. Yet whether wishing for a speedy end or total victory, there was widespread confidence in February that the campaign would succeed. Most Germans firmly believed, noted the home generals, 'that the year 1917 will bring the Fatherland the hoped for victorious peace'.[91]

The German people remained, as the Reich Navy Office remarked with satisfaction, 'under the spell of the unrestricted submarine war' through the spring of 1917.[92] The high rate of sinkings encouraged public optimism that within half a year peace might be restored. The true figures were impressive enough, but those released by the naval authorities to the press and Germany's allies tended, whether by accident or design, to inflate them by a third. The people read that the U-boats had sunk 781,500 tons (instead of the genuine figure of 499,430) in February and a colossal 861,000 tons (rather than 548,817) in March.[93] Newspapers were kept under tight censorship. All articles referring to the U-boats had to be submitted for inspection before publication, and the rhetoric surrounding the campaign was shaped skilfully to appeal to the Socialist working classes. Portrayals of it as revenge or as a starvation war were banned. Instead, it was stressed that the campaign was a means for ending hostilities quickly.[94] Private publishers, recognizing that patriotism could be profitable even in the war's third year, exploited and fuelled the excitement with hurriedly written, cheap and sensational accounts by submariners of their war experiences. The Berlin publisher Ullstein was the leader in a market that printed no fewer than nine 'penny dreadful' U-boat novels in 1917. They provided a human angle to the submarine campaign, portraying a face of masculine toughness and heroism that neatly complemented the navy's impressive statistics.[95]

While commerce thus continued to play a role in popular mobilization, it along with other private initiatives had receded in importance from the heady days of 1914–15 due to war-weariness and material shortage. Instead, official propaganda, which also made imaginative use of the U-boats, was now becoming much more organized and influential. The centrepieces of civil and military efforts were the biannual War Loan appeals. The Sixth War Loan advertised in the spring of 1917, just after the unrestricted campaign began, attracted 7,063,347 subscribers, nearly double those who had signed the preceding loan six months earlier.[96] Its unprecedented success at attracting large numbers of small sums, making it a genuinely popular exercise, rested in part on its appropriation of commercial methods of advertising. Nearly 1,500,000 posters designed by professional artists were hung up across the Reich on advertising boards and in stations, offices, and on public transport. Twelve million flyers were distributed explaining why people should contribute and millions of attractive, illustrated postcards were issued with the intention of keeping public attention focused on the war loan.[97] The submarines featured in the propaganda, with Germans urged to 'sign war loans for the U-boats against England'. One poster aimed at the army featured a submarine commander with his arm on a soldier's shoulder and pointing in the distance to a sinking ship. 'That's the way your money helps you to fight!', read the caption. 'Turned into U-boats, it keeps enemy shells from your body! Therefore: sign the War Loan!'[98] Above all, the remarkable readiness of people to buy war loans after so demoralizing a winter can be explained only with reference to the popularity of the submariners and the great expectations raised by the unrestricted U-boat campaign. With victory apparently close, buying into the state's Sixth War Loan not only was a patriotic act but also appeared to be a safe investment.

In spite of this success, popular confidence had already taken its first serious knock at the start of March due to a piece of extraordinary stupidity by the new German Foreign Secretary since November 1916, Arthur Zimmermann. On 1 March, American newspapers published a highly sensitive telegram that Zimmermann had sent to the German ambassador in Mexico, but that the British had intercepted, decrypted and passed onto the US government. In it, Zimmermann had proposed an alliance with Mexico in the event of war with the United States, promising German financial aid as well as Texas, New Mexico and Arizona. This was explosive, and the publication caused outrage across America.

In Germany, the public could barely comprehend their government's incompetence. Theodor Wolff of the *Berliner Tageblatt* was disgusted at Zimmermann's recklessness and right in describing the telegram as 'boundlessly naive'. One of his business associates joked that after it a sure way to get rich would be to build a spittoon factory: 'thirty million spittoons – that would satisfy an urgent need, for the entire people would like to spit!'[99] For thinking Germans, the news cast doubt upon the reports of tremendous success at sea. 'If we are so sure of defeating England in a few months,' mused one front-line officer in his diary, 'then surely we don't need an ally like Mexico!!'[100]

Few were surprised when little over a month later, on 6 April 1917, the United States declared war on Germany. Some people took the news badly. Ruth Höfner in Silesia wrote in her diary a cry of despair: 'What crime has our people committed that it must suffer so terribly?!'[101] The effect on the army of acquiring yet another enemy to fight was, as one nationalist commentator conceded grudgingly after the war, 'not exactly encouraging'.[102] The middle of the month also witnessed the Reich's first major political strike, with 217,000 workers downing tools in Berlin. Stoppages also took place in other centres, above all in Leipzig. The protests suggest that some on the left had little faith in the U-boat campaign to end the war quickly and many more distrusted its most fervent supporters' domestic plans for Germany's future after victory: among the workers' demands were a non-annexationist peace, the annulment of wartime restrictions on political rights, and the introduction of universal and equal suffrage.[103] Nonetheless, if the news of US animosity lay in the background, it was not a major factor in inciting the stoppages. Berlin's Police Chief reported that the capital's inhabitants had in fact responded calmly to the start of hostilities with the US, as well as to the subsequent declarations of war by South American states. The generals in the home districts agreed: the population beyond the metropolis reacted 'with complete composure'. The middle classes were grimly resolute. Elisabeth Stempfle was probably representative of the bourgeoisie when she adamantly promised in her journal 'we will hold out!'[104]

It was only in the summer that morale really crumbled. The German home front itself entered a new supply crisis, as both food and coal ran out, and with Britain still showing no sign of being on the verge of capitulation despite the submarines' best efforts, the population stopped believing. 'On what should we now set our hopes?' appealed Anna

Kohnstern in Hamburg to her soldier son Albert at the end of June. 'Everything looks so wretched. At first they say here that the war will be finished in August and then it's said again that it will last another year.'[105] As despair gripped the people, democratic politicians took note. The Social Democrats' leadership warned the Reich government that the failure to realize promises of a rapid U-boat victory had left workers at the end of their endurance.[106] The Catholic Centre Party representative Matthias Erzberger also realized that unrestricted submarine warfare had failed, and the conclusions that he drew from this precipitated a major political crisis. On 6 July in the Reichstag Steering Committee, Erzberger questioned official figures on tonnage available to Britain and argued rightly that the enemy's ability to counter the U-boat threat had been underestimated. He accused the government of erring in its promise to deliver victory within six months. Moreover, he pointed out, 'the wonderful work of our U-boats cannot make it possible for a single ship to reach us, while 90 per cent of ships arrive in England'.[107]

The Centre Party's scepticism towards the submarine war was particularly significant, for its conversion in favour of an unrestricted campaign in the autumn of 1916 had been crucial in urging upon the Chancellor naval and military demands to release the U-boats. Erzberger's recognition that the gamble had failed now prompted him to demand an intervention by the Reichstag to set Germany on a new path. The ensuing political crisis pushed Bethmann Hollweg from office and on 19 July 1917, barely a fortnight after Erzberger had proposed it in his speech, a Reichstag majority of Centre, Social Democrat and Progressive deputies voted through a Peace Resolution. It rejected the 'acquisition of territories by force' – the policy favoured by those conservatives who had most fervently agitated for unrestricted U-boat warfare – and instead advocated 'a peace of understanding'.[108]

Both the war and the submarine campaign continued, but the hope of politicians and the public that the U-boats could bring a quick end to the fighting was replaced with apathy or even anger. After briefly uniting the population in the hope of some sort of victory – for most, above all, quick, and for a small minority, total – the submarines again became a source of discord. The Admiralty was not forgiven for its claim that it would deliver victory in five months. Moreover, as the United States mobilized, criticism mounted about the underestimation of this new enemy. By October there were loud complaints that, contrary to the promise made in the Reichstag by the Secretary of State for the Navy, Admiral Eduard von Capelle, troop transports had not proven at all easy to sink.[109] The official claim that the number of US troops arriving in France was being overstated failed to mollify the population.[110] Indeed, rumours circulated in the German army that the US was deliberately being treated leniently. These had a slight basis in truth: the Kaiser had initially forbidden US warships or shipping in the blockade zone around Britain to be attacked and, fearing that it would later make a negotiated peace more difficult to achieve, had banned the navy from large-scale submarine operations off the American coast. US ships were also spared in the Mediterranean during the first eleven months of the campaign, as Austria-Hungary and the US were not at war until December 1917.[111] None of this, however, accounted for the navy's failure to destroy more than three loaded Allied troop transports. Instead, as an official response to the rumours lamely explained, 'the ocean is really big and . . . it therefore remains a matter of chance if a U-boat . . . comes across an American steamer carrying troops'.[112] The submarines, which had once made such good press, were by 1918 something of an embarrassment to the Reich government. A British intelligence analysis of German propaganda found a decrease in reports about the U-boat war. By the spring, they were in 'total eclipse'.[113]

Germany's U-boats inflicted tremendous damage to Allied shipping during the course of the war. Over a total of 3,274 operations, they sunk 6,394 ships with a cumulative weight of 11,948,702 tons. In 1917 the U-boats' most successful year, they reduced British imports to 37 million tons, two-thirds of the pre-war level.[114] Yet although at its height in the spring and summer of 1917 unrestricted submarine warfare appeared briefly to pose a mortal threat, ultimately the destruction was not sufficient to bring Britain to her knees, either in the promised five-month window or afterwards. The Germans' campaign was another illustration that ruthlessness and flouting international law brought worse than nothing. As with the Third OHL's attempted use of Belgian forced labour, the returns were negligible; most of the rise in sinkings was due to an increase in submarine numbers and efficiency improvements that could have been implemented while continuing to use cruiser rules. The reputational cost was similarly huge, and this time had a decisive impact. The disastrous decision to open unrestricted submarine warfare and the consequent and inevitable declaration of war by the United States cost the Reich victory in the First World War.

The decisive impact of the United States on the war was in large part due to the immense resources it added to the Entente's war effort. The Americans spent 42.8 million dollars a day from mid-1917, dwarfing British, French and German daily expenditure of just over 32 million dollars each. They provided naval reinforcement to assist with convoying and to tighten the blockade against Germany. Their contribution to replacing sunk merchant shipping was especially large: in 1918 alone, the US constructed 2.6 million tons, nearly half of the 5.4 million tons built in total by the Allies. Although the US was no military power – a key reason why the OHL tended to dismiss it – it quickly set about expanding its small professional army of 128,000 men and was ultimately able to send over two million soldiers across the Atlantic.[115] Yet no less important than the material contribution made by America, and much more immediate, was the idealism and moral weight that it brought to the Entente cause. President Wilson in the west, together with Russian revolutionaries in the east, would in 1917 confront the Central Powers with a new and very dangerous ideological challenge.

II

Dangerous Ideas

REACTIONARY REGIMES

In the spring of 1917 the nature of the war changed fundamentally. The outbreak of revolution in Russia and the entry of the United States into hostilities brought a new, ideological edge to the conflict. In President Wilson's words to Congress on 2 April, 'democracy' and 'the rights and liberties of small nations' were the causes for which the war was now to be fought.[1] He echoed the new revolutionary regime in Russia, which already at the end of March – although nobody had voted – proudly declared itself a 'Russian democracy' whose war aim was the 'establishment of stable peace on the basis of the self-determination of peoples'.[2] These were not just powerful slogans intended to please domestic audiences. They had a universal appeal and struck deep at divisions inside Germany and Austria-Hungary. From being the norm in Europe in 1914, monarchical rule suddenly began to look dated. The timing was dangerous, for these ideas of popular governance would resonate with populations increasingly angry and disillusioned with their unelected leaders' wartime errors, and above all their inability to provide and fairly distribute food. The Russian revolution was particularly frightening for the Central Powers' governments and inspiring for their dissidents, as it revealed that violent, popular regime change was no chimera but a very real possibility in these extraordinary times.

The year 1917 was defined in central Europe by deepening division between peoples and their governments. Political reform was one key area of contention. In 1914 large marginalized groups had mobilized hoping for reform as a reward for their service and sacrifices: the Social Democrats (SPD) and Poles in Germany and those nationalities in

Austria-Hungary who felt short-changed by the 1867 Compromise, most vocally the Czechs and South Slavs. The calls became louder due both to the extreme hardship at home and to the ideals issuing from abroad; Wilson's call for 'government by the consent of the governed' appealed to democrats and nationalists alike.[3] The autocratic governments' efforts in 1917 to conform to the *Zeitgeist* and implement change were, however, half-hearted, ill-organized, and frequently met insurmountable opposition from groups that refused to surrender their privileged positions.

A second cause of the widening division between peoples and rulers was controversy over war aims. The prohibition on public discussion of war aims had been lifted in Germany at Ludendorff's insistence in November 1916, and both there and in Hungary arguments became increasingly vitriolic in response to the Russian revolution and America's declaration of war. With deprivation and misery endemic, many Austro-Hungarians and Germans found attractive the call made by the revolutionary Petrograd Soviet at the start of April 1917 for international peace through a democratic settlement 'without annexations or indemnities'.[4] Yet far from the war ending, enemies multiplied, food shortages worsened and the suspicion grew that rulers were deliberately prolonging the war to win vast conquests. While annexationist conservatives and nationalists welcomed this, wider sections of the population came to fear, as the Social Democrats' newspaper *Vorwärts* observed in November 1917, 'that the real and most profound reason making it so enormously difficult to get peace lies in the *military successes of Germany*'.[5] Toxically, both causes of anger and disillusionment were intertwined. The Central Powers' governments, through their refusal to raise their peoples' stake in the state and its war effort, failed to underpin their waning legitimacy. They, and the reactionary elites supporting them, staked their existence on the fallacy that popular commitment won by reforms, rather than being a precondition, could be replaced by total victory.

In Austria-Hungary the year 1917 began with the promise of change. The venerable Emperor Franz Joseph had passed away the previous November and his successor was a very different persona. Emperor Karl was just twenty-nine years old when he ascended the throne, but he and his young family symbolized hope to an Empire in distress, and the press greeted him optimistically as a man of exceptional character: a benevolent and humane war hero who had spent time at (or, more accurately, near) the front and knew the travails of his soldiers. As with all tributes to royalty, the praise was exaggerated. In Vienna the new Emperor's critics quipped that 'you hope to meet a 30-year-old there, but you find a man with the appearance of a 20-year-old youth, who thinks, speaks and acts like a 10-year-old boy'.[6] Karl unquestionably had faults. He was a man who managed to combine obstinacy with irresolution, insisting on a hard and sometimes courageous course, yet lacking the will or boldness to push it through. His sense of honour and his loyalty to his oaths and allies, qualities that should have been virtues, prevented him from acting decisively for the greater needs of his peoples. He was well educated but insufficiently prepared for the immense responsibilities that he had inherited. What Karl did have was good intentions. He recognized the need for internal reform and was prepared to work in order to set his stamp on government. Moreover, he desired an end to hostilities. The new Emperor's manifesto on taking the throne greatly raised the hopes of the war-weary, for among the customary platitudes was a promise that Karl himself had insisted should be included: 'I want to do everything to banish the horrors and sacrifices of the war as soon as possible and to win back for my peoples the sorely missed blessings of peace.'[7]

The new Emperor's first task, however, was to take control of his realm. The first six months of his reign saw the wholesale replacement of Franz Joseph's advisers with a younger team. A new Austrian Minister President, Count Heinrich Clam-Martinic, and a Common Foreign Minister, Count Ottokar Czernin, were appointed on 20 and 23 December 1916 respectively. These choices signalled that far-reaching reform was intended, for both men had belonged before the war to Archduke Franz Ferdinand's Belvedere Circle, and had contributed to planning the heir to the throne's intended restructuring of the Habsburg Empire. Reform was now more urgent than ever, for the Dualist system's unwieldiness had inhibited the Monarchy's war effort, not least in the effective and equitable distribution of food supplies; change was in any case almost inevitable, as any gain or exchange of territories would upset the delicate balance between the two halves of the Empire. Most significantly, Karl reined in the military's independence and malign influence on Austrian politics. He personally took over the Supreme Command in early

December, relieving Franz Joseph's appointee, Archduke Friedrich. A month later, he annulled powers sanctioning military rule and encroachment in areas well behind the battlefront. Conrad von Hötzendorf, the Chief of the General Staff whose battlefield failures and interventions in the interior of the Monarchy had so damaged its legitimacy, was dismissed at the end of February 1917. The overhaul of personnel was completed in April when the War Minister, Baron Alexander von Krobatin, was sent instead to the Italian Front. General Arthur Arz von Straussenburg, the new Chief of the General Staff, and the replacement War Minister, General Rudolf Stöger-Steiner, were soldiers without political ambition.[8]

Karl's endeavour to reform the Dualist system was nonetheless hamstrung from the beginning by a lack of planning and poor decision-making. He made his biggest mistake on his first day as Emperor, when he agreed on an early coronation as King of Hungary, instead of waiting the six months that was legally permitted. Count Tisza, Minister President of Hungary, had acted with speed, visiting Karl on the morning after Franz Joseph's death and impressing on him that the best way to peace was through coronation. In fact, the Machiavellian Minister President's real concern was to secure Hungary's territorial integrity and privileged position. By 1917 pressure was building for fundamental reform of the Empire, to turn it from a land based on historic territories to one with a new legitimacy derived from organization into national and possibly federal territories. In particular, South Slav (and above all Croatian) nationalists wished for the unification of the Kingdom of Croatia, one of the historic lands of St Stephen that constituted Habsburg Hungary, with Austrian Dalmatia and Bosnia-Herzegovina. Earlier in the war this might have been achieved within Dualist Hungary. However, the only circumstance that could have made this politically feasible, the compensation and expansion of Austria through the addition of formerly Russian-ruled Congress Poland, had by 1917 been all but ruled out by Germany's ambitions and the Central Powers' proclamation of an independent Polish state. Similarly threatening to Magyar elites in 1917 was a new fad among Czech nationalists to demand unification with Hungarian-ruled Slovaks, whose realization would also force a drastic revision of Dualism and historic borders. Persuading Karl quickly to take the Hungarian coronation oath was Tisza's means of quashing these schemes, for it obliged the new king to pledge to maintain the integrity of the lands of the Crown of St Stephen. The scheduling of the ceremony for 30 December 1916 left no time to force a reorganization of the Dualist system before this oath was given. Afterwards, reform became all but impossible, for the reactionary Hungarian government's opposition could not be overridden without reneging on this promise.[9]

With imperial reorganization blocked, Karl could only try to restructure Austria. However, his government's initial plan was ill-considered. His key ministers were all Austrian Germans (only one Czech was appointed, as the unimportant Minister of Public Works) and their programme corresponded to their nationalist compatriots' vision for Austria's future. German was to be the sole language of administration and the historic Czech lands were to be divided for the benefit of their German minority along ethnic lines into self-governing districts. German domination in the Reichsrat was to be assured by removing Polish deputies, a measure justified by increasing Galicia's autonomy, and by the introduction of new rules banning obstruction. The Czechs were to be a powerless minority. These measures, which would have been anathema to most Austrian Slav representatives, were to be imposed through imperial decree, the *Oktroi*. It was predictable that measures so partial, forced on a land already resentful after three years of oppressive, unrepresentative government, would incite considerable discontent and further undermine the Monarchy's standing among its Slav subjects.[10]

The Russian revolution halted Karl's move along this disastrous course. The new Emperor was very frightened by the upheaval in the east. As he wrote to his ally, Kaiser Wilhelm, on 14 April, 'We are fighting against a new enemy, more dangerous than the Entente: against the international revolution.'[11] Fearing revolt among his own hungry and increasingly turbulent people, Karl attempted to give them a greater stake in the war effort, a move that led to significant change in both halves of the Empire. In Hungary he pressed Tisza at the end of April to use his party majority to pass social measures and extend the suffrage. Opposition politicians had recognized the seething mood in the country and already in February had reintroduced to the parliament 'the heroes' right to vote' bill that had been quashed two years earlier. The urgency of extending the franchise was underlined by a wave of strikes, which started among miners, metalworkers and railway staff that month and continued through the spring. On May Day 1917 widespread worker demonstrations and demands by union leaders for universal suffrage made manifest that

Hungary's war effort would not last much longer without some concession to the will of the people. With Tisza refusing to countenance any significant dilution of the Magyar gentry's power through real democracy, the King-Emperor decided that the desperately unpopular Minister President, who for nearly a decade and a half had dominated Magyar politics, would have to go. On 23 May, at Karl's request, Tisza submitted his resignation.[12] Austria's political system underwent an even more fundamental transformation one week later. In April, impressed by Russia's revolution and food riots in Bohemia, Karl had abandoned the plan to restructure the western half of the Empire by decree. Instead, he broke dramatically with the autocratic past and tried to restore waning Habsburg legitimacy by convening Austria's parliamentary representatives. On 30 May 1917, for the first time in over three years, the Reichsrat reopened.[13]

In Germany too, pressure for political reform was growing. Chancellor Bethmann Hollweg's decision at the outbreak of war to co-opt the Social Democrats into the national effort and fight with consent rather than simply coercion had worked far better than Austria's oppressive bureaucratic-military dictatorship, but there was a price to pay. The Kaiser's pronouncement at the start of the *Burgfrieden* that he saw 'no more parties . . . only Germans', and the Chancellor's promise of a 'new orientation of internal policy', inflamed hope for the abolition of Prussia's bitterly resented three-class franchise, which had made the votes of the rich disproportionately influential in elections to the lower house of the state parliament.[14] While the SPD and unions had cooperated closely with Reich authorities, the latter had still made no real concessions by the spring of 1917. Patience, like everything else in Germany, was running short. The popular mood, which was already fragile after the hardship of the winter, turned uglier as news arrived of revolution in Russia. As Theodor Wolff, the perceptive editor of the liberal *Berliner Tageblatt*, observed in late March, there was a seething resentment 'directed against the government, against the estate owners who hoard food and don't give it out, against the war, against the entire regime'.[15]

Even the Kaiser, who possessed a remarkable ability to see only what he wished, recognized that the people's mood was 'dangerous'.[16] The authorities at first stuck to the view that any reform must be left to the war's end and they settled on a press campaign to counter the dangerous ideas coming from the revolutionary east. Yet it quickly became clear that this would be inadequate. The SPD's moderate and patriotic leadership was embroiled in acrimonious conflict with a minority on the left, which fiercely criticized cooperation with Reich authorities, regarded the war as one of aggression and resented that its views and influence were being overridden. The party was on the verge of schism. The leadership urgently needed some concession to demonstrate to its increasingly uneasy members that the *Burgfrieden* policy was beneficial to proletarian interests. To exert pressure on the government, on 19 March Philipp Scheidemann, the SPD's parliamentary co-chair, published an article in *Vorwärts* that pointed menacingly to Russia as an illustration of what could happen when reforms were delayed.[17] Officials were concerned and the moderate middle-class parties, the Progressives and some National Liberals, were sufficiently frightened by the thought of revolution in Germany that they joined with the SPD in the Reichstag to press for greater democracy.[18]

Throughout March, the Chancellor tried to tread a middle way between castigating conservatives who denied the need for political change while delaying any concrete commitment until the war's end. However, at the start of April, the United States' imminent declaration of war changed his view abruptly. With President Wilson declaring America's enemy to be not the German people but its autocratic rulers, it was essential to demonstrate at home and abroad that such distinction was fantasy, that the ruling system had popular legitimacy and that the country was engaged in a war supported by the people. Bethmann now prescribed a dramatic gesture: the immediate introduction of direct and secret voting under equal suffrage for Prussia's parliament. His more reactionary colleagues in the Prussian Ministry of State disagreed and diluted his proposal. Consequently, the Kaiser's 'Easter Message' to his people on 7 April 1917 announced reforms that worried conservatives but were too weak to win over sceptical Social Democrats. It pledged to broaden the membership of the Prussian House of Lords and, for the lower house, to abolish the three-class franchise and introduce direct and secret elections. Crucially, however, there was no promise of universal suffrage and the reforms were only to be enacted 'immediately upon the successful end of the war'.[19] Neither a committee created by the Reichstag on 30 March to consider constitutional reform, nor even a promise made by the Kaiser at Bethmann's urging in July

1917, ever succeeded in imposing equal franchise on the Prussian parliament.[20]

Regardless, the German political system was rapidly evolving. In peacetime, the Kaiser and the Chancellor whom he appointed had been the centre of power. However, the overwhelming need to assure the cooperation of the population in a 'people's war' meant that leaders with a popular mandate came to the fore. German politics was pushed in two opposite directions. On one side were Hindenburg and Ludendorff, proponents of autocracy and total victory. They had already demonstrated their readiness to intervene in society and the economy and were well aware of the power that their popularity gave them. On several occasions, Hindenburg had used the threat to resign to try to get his own way, knowing that a public outcry would follow were it accepted. The duo were not shy either about intruding on the Kaiser's prerogative to determine military and political appointments. While at Ober Ost they had intrigued against Falkenhayn, and at the Third OHL they showed no hesitation in attempting to depose Bethmann Hollweg too, once they had decided that 'lack of resolution' made him unsuitable to lead. The soldiers first demanded Bethmann's dismissal by the Kaiser on the day after the unrestricted U-boat campaign had been decided against his opposition. Although initially thwarted, together with conservative allies grouped around the alienated former head of the Imperial Navy Office, Admiral Tirpitz, they persisted throughout the spring and contributed to the Chancellor's fall in the summer. Reactionaries anxious about the reformist drives in the Reich hoped for a military dictatorship. They saw in Hindenburg and Ludendorff the 'strong men' for whom they yearned, capable of not only bringing total victory but also halting the rise of the political left.[21]

The second, contrary trend, and a prime cause of conservative fears, was the increased influence and assertiveness of Germany's most important representative institution, the Reichstag, and particularly the unprecedented cooperation between its left and centre parties. The power of Reichstag deputies to vote through war credits raised the parliament's importance. In peacetime it had scrutinized and voted on budgets, but war credits were different because they were requested so often – no fewer than sixteen times up to February 1919 – and because the votes were invested with great symbolism.[22] The *Burgfrieden* had first been sealed on 4 August 1914 with effectively a unanimous vote for war credits, and thereafter the readiness of the Social Democrats, who had always abstained as a party in peacetime budget votes, to support the credits was seen as proof of the continuance of German unity. From the third war credit in March 1915, almost a third of the SPD's 110 deputies abstained. At the fifth vote in December, twenty, including one of its chairmen, Hugo Haase, opposed the credits and a further twenty-two abstained.[23] However, the fact that the majority of the party continued to support them helped to maintain the *Burgfrieden* and keep the Reich's working classes acquiescent. As a result, even though Socialist deputies, who occupied about one-third of the 397 seats in the Reichstag, were not numerous enough to block the credit, the Chancellor was committed to maintain the SPD's cooperation and unusually willing to hear, if not act upon, its views.[24]

The Reichstag's bourgeois majority wished at heart for a total victory and hoped for some gains for their country once it was won. It had exerted its influence in the autumn of 1916, when its deputies had followed their constituents' enthusiasm and severely restricted Bethmann's freedom of action by urging him to heed the advice of the Third OHL to launch the U-boat campaign. After the spring of 1917, however, majority opinion in the house began to move leftwards. Partly, the Russian revolution encouraged greater sympathy among the moderate middle-class parties for immediate democratic reform. The really big shift, however, came with the realization of Matthias Erzberger, the influential Centre Party deputy, in the summer that the U-boat campaign would not defeat Britain. His speech in the Reichstag Steering Committee on 6 July 1917 smashed the navy's argument that ruthless submarine warfare could work and radically proposed that the Reichstag take the initiative in preparing the groundwork for a peace of understanding with Russia: 'If in the Reichstag an enormous majority or possibly even all deputies could bring themselves to agree on the idea of 1 August 1914 – we stand for a war of defence ... we strive for a peace of reconciliation, which recognizes the power constellation that has come about through the war, a peace which brings no forcible oppression of peoples or border areas – if the Reichstag could say this to the Reich government, this would be the best way to bring about peace.'[25]

Erzberger's speech cemented the shift to the left in the Reichstag that had begun with the reform question and triggered the most acute political crisis experienced to this point in the war by Germany. On the same day, deputies of the Centre, Progressives, National Liberals and Social

Democrats established an Inter-Party Committee, which agreed on the need for universal suffrage in Prussia and a parliamentary government formed from party representatives, and decided to issue a declaration for 'no annexations, no reparations' in the Reichstag.[26] This was a historic moment; the coming together of the Centre, Progressives and Social Democrats in the Inter-Party Committee lasted throughout the war and helped to provide the Reich with an alternative basis of authority in late 1918, once the advocates of total war had failed and destroyed the old regime's legitimacy. Scheidemann, the SPD leader, was right to see it as 'the first step of a parliament that was taking independence'.[27]

However, in the shorter term the initiative backfired very badly for parliamentary moderates. The main victim of their manoeuvre was Bethmann, a man who, while no dove, opposed the unlimited annexationist ambitions of the Reich's military and conservative elites. His contortions to maintain his 'politics of the diagonal' between left-wing demands for domestic change and right-wingers' desire for conquest had by this point made him the subject of hostility from all sides of the political spectrum. While the National Liberals, who shortly after left the Inter-Party Committee, favoured a total victory and disliked the Chancellor's ambiguity, the Centre and their allies on the left considered him an obstacle to reform and peace. Bethmann reacted to the parliamentarians' manoeuvres by urging reform on the Kaiser. He again demanded the immediate adoption of universal suffrage and, in a drastic break with the past, was prepared to invite Reichstag party representatives into his government. Nonetheless, he failed to stop the peace resolution. The clear evidence that he could no longer guide moderate and left-wing opinion in the country and Reichstag enabled his conservative and military enemies to give him the final push. Hindenburg and Ludendorff threatened the Kaiser with their resignation unless Bethmann were dismissed, and he went on 13 July. Subsequent chancellors were creatures of the OHL; little more, in the words of one left-wing deputy, than an 'advertisement for the omnipotent military clique' with no interest in either reform or a negotiated peace.[28]

The peace resolution that was passed in the Reichstag on 19 July by 212 against 126 votes, with 17 abstentions, was also not all that its name implied or for which Socialists wished. Erzberger's call for 'a peace of reconciliation, which recognizes the power constellation that has come about through the war' was as revealing as it was unrealistic;

he hoped that somehow Germany's enemies could be persuaded to accept her wartime gains, and he intended that the vote stiffen, not undermine, the people's will to hold out. Within twenty-four hours of the vote he was advising the Reich's new Chancellor, the former Prussian Food Controller Georg Michaelis, that the Longwy-Briey ore fields might be won through exchange and that Lithuania should become a duchy with Wilhelm II at its head. The SPD, which in April had accepted the Petrograd formula of a peace 'without annexations or reparations', and committed itself 'to press the government for a clear rejection of any policy of conquest', tried to present the resolution as a German equivalent to the programme of the Russian Workers' and Soldiers' Council. Yet as Haase was quick to point out in a critical speech, the resolution contained nothing about the right of national self-determination and twisted or diluted the Russian revolutionaries' progressive demands. Only 'territorial acquisitions achieved by force and violations of political, economic, or financial integrity' were excluded, not the subjugated satellite states and informal empire imagined by Erzberger. The resolution's tone was angry and nationalistic: it criticized the enemy for threatening 'Germany and its allies with territorial conquests and violations' and ended by defiantly asserting that 'the German people are unconquerable'.[29] Its total meaninglessness was assured by the new Chancellor, who accepted it ambiguously 'as I interpret it'. This, however, was sufficient for all parties involved in the drafting of the resolution to vote in favour of 15,000 million marks in new war credits.[30]

GOING FOR BROKE

The German government had, from the outbreak of the First World War, sought to gain advantage. Bethmann Hollweg's primary objective, as laid down in the programme of September 1914, 'security for the German Reich in west and east for all imaginable time', remained the guiding aim of foreign policy, even in very dark days. Plans to secure economic hegemony or political domination had been a means to achieve this, as well as to hide or justify much more explicitly aggressive aspirations. The rise of the Third OHL brought a new inflexibility and even greater megalomania to the Reich's war aims. Hindenburg and Ludendorff were interested in power, not rights. Their enemies' blockade and methods of industrial combat had taught them the importance of securing an extensive resource base. Rule in Ober Ost had provided them with the experience of how to harness people and materials ruthlessly. The duo were focused not merely on winning the present conflict. Like Bethmann, their gaze extended into the future, although the world they inhabited was much darker than his, defined by a perpetual, violent Social Darwinist struggle between states. The OHL's prime purpose, as Ludendorff explained in September 1917, was to achieve 'an economic and military position which allows us to face another war of defence without anxiety'.[31]

Even in the dark days of December 1916, when Hindenburg and Ludendorff had used the dire strategic situation to justify the desperate gamble of unrestricted submarine warfare, their wish list of annexations had been formidable.[32] As the OHL asserted the primacy of military aims over politics, and as the Russian revolution presented new strategic alternatives, its ambition became problematic. Bethmann was keen for a separate peace with Russia, but also opportunistic and deeply averse to being pinned down by any inflexible war-aims programme. He told Czernin in March 1917 that he envisaged large annexations from Russia in the event of total victory, but would reduce these substantially – probably to frontier adjustments in the Reich's favour – to secure the end of hostilities in the east.[33] For Hindenburg and Ludendorff, such vagueness and moderation were unacceptable. In April 1917 they not only pressed the Chancellor to lay out official aims and wrung from him a concession to prioritize military above political and economic considerations, but also prevailed upon the Kaiser to order Bethmann to draw up maximum and minimum war-aims programmes as preparation for possible peace with revolutionary Russia and negotiations with Austria-Hungary over how to divide the spoils of victory.[34]

On 23 April 1917 a meeting between Hindenburg and Ludendorff, the Chancellor, the Foreign Secretary, Arthur Zimmermann, and the Head of the Political Section of the Government General in Belgium was convened at Kreuznach, in the Rhineland, to discuss war aims. The OHL, confident at this time that the U-boat campaign would bring Britain to her knees 'in at latest 2–3 months', forced through its conception of a peace of extensive conquest.[35] In the west, as the September 1914 Programme had demanded, the valuable French mining region of Longwy-Briey was to be won for the Reich. Elsewhere, however, the demands of 1914 had expanded. Belgium was to remain 'in German military control until it is politically and economically ready for a defensive and offensive alliance with Germany'. Liège and the Flemish coast were to be either permanently occupied or held on a ninety-nine-year lease, a demand about which, it was stressed, that there could be no compromise. Belgium was to lose its south-east corner to the Reich, Luxembourg would become a German federal state, and the possibility of compensating France with a small part of Belgium or a worthless strip of German Alsace was also mooted. In the east, Germany was to acquire Courland and Lithuania, Hindenburg and Ludendorff's own military colony. Buffer zones were to be carved out of the newly established Poland to protect key German territories, most notably heavily industrialized German Silesia. German oil interests in Romania were also to be secured. Austria-Hungary was to be handed parts of Serbia, Montenegro and Albania, as well as territory in Romania's western Walachia. While Bethmann added a confidential minute refusing to be bound by these aims in any negotiations, they nonetheless thwarted his hopes of offering Russia an easy separate peace.[36]

Hindenburg and Ludendorff were playing for high stakes. They wanted to dictate peace to a defeated Russia, not parley, and they adopted a strategy to destabilize the new Russian regime and precipitate total chaos. Civilian officials made the fateful decision to allow Vladimir Ilyich Lenin, the Bolshevik revolutionary firebrand then in exile in Switzerland, passage through the Reich to Petrograd in April 1917.[37] The military concentrated on breaking Russian forces with a pioneering campaign of psychological warfare on the Eastern Front. Both sides had dropped leaflets over enemy lines earlier in hostilities, but no one had ever attempted anything like the Germans' carefully planned and coordinated propaganda offensive. The Foreign Ministry chose the themes to be used: Germany wished for but did not need peace. The new Russian government was a puppet of England, prolonging the people's suffering for the benefit of western imperialists. The German army and its Habsburg ally developed innovative new methods to disseminate this message. Russian-speaking intelligence officers were posted in the front line and made contact with units stationed opposite. At Easter, commanders permitted ceasefires and fraternization along the front in order to give the impression of German goodwill. Later, more subtle techniques were introduced. Among the most effective was the distribution of newspapers filled with apparently authoritative but carefully selected information intended to demoralize.[38]

To Russian soldiers already disorientated by the upheaval in the rear, starved and desperate for information, and distrustful of their officers, the Central Powers' propaganda only added to uncertainty and the hope of peace. Prussian units on the Eastern Front were enthusiastic about the impact of psychological warfare. The 12 Infantry Division, for example, reported in mid-April that 'the disintegration of the Russian army through the revolution is becoming widespread'. Enemy troops were moving freely in the open, welcomed the propaganda flyers fired in their direction, and were happy to take part in live-and-let-live truces or even to fraternize.[39] The Central Powers' propaganda chimed with the message of Bolshevik agitation in the hinterland, and thereby helped not only to erode the Russian army's combat motivation over the summer but also to pave the way for regime change. On 7 November, Lenin seized power in Petrograd, and when two weeks later he sent a wireless order to all units, over the heads of military commanders, instructing troops to elect representatives for armistice talks, the Germans intercepted and also transmitted it in order to ensure that it reached as many front-line units as possible. In the short term, the Central Powers' strategy was spectacularly successful: on 3 December 1917 armistice talks opened with the now impotent opponent.[40]

The Third OHL's push for maximum war aims have with much justice been characterized as militarism run amok, yet behind it stood more logic than Ludendorff's critics then or now have been ready to concede. Nobody thought the outcome of the war was settled in 1917. The Central Powers' chance of total victory was greatly improved by Russia's impending collapse, and although the longer term looked bleak thanks to the entry of the United States into hostilities, the new belligerent was without a large army and would be unable for some time to affect the decisive war on land.[41] Ludendorff's strenuous insistence after the war that no peace of understanding had been possible in 1917 was, at least for the west, probably correct, even if the OHL's uncompromising stance contributed to the deadlock.[42] The Americans before they joined hostilities, the Austrians, Socialists and the Pope all failed to broker peace during 1917 due to the distance between the belligerents' war aims and the firmness with which they held to them. Even aside from German aims – and even Bethmann, a moderate by comparison with the other members of the Reich's elite, was not willing entirely to sur-render Belgium and wanted the annexation of Longwy-Briey – peace was scarcely possible when the French insisted inflexibly on regaining Alsace-Lorraine, a territory that for four decades had been integral to the Reich and whose population's identity was by no means so un-ambiguously French as the Entente claimed.[43]

Moreover, apparently moderate French wishes disguised aggressive intent, for French leaders coveted Alsace-Lorraine with the borders not of 1870, but of 1814 or even 1790, encompassing the unambiguously ethnically German but extremely valuable industrial and coal-mining Saar region, and they also planned a long-term military occupation of the left bank of the Rhine. These highly secret aspirations were compar-able to Bethmann's intention to grab Longwy-Briey. The Germans certainly knew about them, for, along with French consent to Russian annexation of the Reich's eastern borderlands, they were leaked to the public in 1917.[44] No less ominous were French calls to their allies to establish a self-sufficient economic bloc and the Entente's reply to US mediation attempts in January 1917, which demanded 'the liberation of Italians, of Slavs, of Roumanians and of Tscheco Slovaques from for-eign domination'.[45] Clearly, Germany's enemies intended to return her to what her statesmen regarded as the pre-war 'encirclement', weak-ened, economically isolated and either with no allies or at best an enfeebled and reduced Austria-Hungary. No Reich minister or even the parliamentarians who voted for the 'Peace Resolution' could find any of this acceptable. Even negotiating the return of Alsace-Lorraine would have been understood at home and abroad as an admission of defeat, with destabilizing consequences for the country's government.[46]

The Third OHL's territorial aims were on a totally different scale from the French government's demands, but as the deliberations at the 1919 Paris peace conference and the Versailles Treaty revealed, both shared something of the same zero-sum view of international relations: both sought security at their enemy's expense.[47] As Germany had so many bitter enemies, and as war had exposed her great economic vul-nerability, her gains, so Ludendorff's reasoning went, would have to be large to guarantee her safety. To understand his motives one has to look beyond tired stereotypes of Prussian militarism or the general's person-ality; Ludendorff had, after all, been against large-scale annexations in early 1915 and the east was not a natural place for Germany to exercise its expansionist ambitions. The decisive recalculation had clearly come about in wartime, in response to the failure of the offensive bid for a quick victory in 1914 and the new economic conflict introduced by the British. Shocked German military leaders had been forced to re-evaluate the acquisition of raw materials as a military necessity. 'The importance in war of coal, iron and food was known before the war,' Ludendorff affirmed in his memoirs, 'but how absolutely decisive they would actually become was only demonstrated to all the world as hostilities proceeded.'[48]

Other wartime developments had also informed the expansion of German military aims. To protect the Reich's precious industrialized border regions of Silesia, Lorraine, Westphalia and the Rhineland from the long-range artillery and aircraft that had developed so quickly during the war, protective barriers formed from enemy territory would be needed. At Kreuznach in the spring and again at a Crown Council in the autumn of 1917, Ludendorff demanded Belgium's subjugation into economic and political dependence and the acquisition of Liège on the grounds that this would block an invasion route into the Rhenish-Westphalian industrial region.[49] For the imperial navy, the retention of the Flanders coast was even more essential in light of the war experience, in order to counter future British blockades better and to facilitate access to the Atlantic, which in turn would enable contact to be maintained with the vast colonial territories it hoped Germany would also acquire.[50]

Most important, Ludendorff understood after three years of total war that 'corn and potatoes are power, just like coal and iron'.[51] The 'turnip winter' of 1916–17 had revealed that the Reich's own farmland was insufficient to feed its population. Ludendorff's answer to this problem was to seize an eastern empire, a solution Hitler would also hit on a quarter of a century later for making German-dominated Europe what he termed 'the most blockade-proof place in the world'.[52] Ludendorff's experience of exploiting Ober Ost convinced him that the territory must be permanently retained as a granary.[53] Like the Polish border strip intended to protect the Reich's eastern frontier, it would be secured by displacing the native population and settling German soldier-farmers. The Reich's civil authorities proposed that 20,000 German refugees from the Volhynia region of Russian-controlled Ukraine who had fled the fighting and were living in the Reich would make ideal colonists. The racial thinking behind these schemes was similarly a harbinger of Nazi plans. The German settlers were to act as a 'human wall' protecting the Reich and the occupied land would serve, Ludendorff hoped, as 'breeding grounds for people, who will be necessary for further fights' in the barbarous, threatening east.[54]

The Austro-Hungarians were dragged along in Germany's wake only very reluctantly. Emperor Karl was sincere in his manifesto: he and his new Foreign Minister, Ottokar von Czernin, were intensely anxious about what would befall the Monarchy should hostilities not be concluded quickly. Unbeknown to the Germans, Karl had begun to put out peace feelers to the western Entente already in December 1916, using as an intermediary his wife's brother, Prince Sixtus de Bourbon-Parma, an officer of the Belgian army. By February 1917, Karl was in indirect contact with leading French statesmen and had been made to understand that no peace in the west would be possible unless Germany surrendered Alsace-Lorraine and restored Belgium's independence. In great secrecy, without informing even his own Foreign Minister, he wrote a letter on 24 March, addressed to Sixtus but intended for the French President, Raymond Poincaré, in which he pledged to support 'by every means' France's 'just claims' to the German region, agreed that Belgium 'must be re-established as a sovereign state', and even offered Serbia access to the sea, if it promised to drop its Great Serb propaganda. A second letter in May conceded that Italian claims to the Trentino might be met through an exchange of territory.[55]

Karl's peace feeler was doomed for the same reasons that blighted other approaches: the gulf between the two sides' interests and the strength of the alliances. The Emperor himself, despite his reputation as a man of peace, was little less opportunistic than other statesmen of the First World War. He stated his chief war aim in January 1917 as simply 'the preservation of the Monarchy's integrity', yet he also embraced a maximum programme encompassing the annexation of Congress Poland, Montenegro and Serbian Mačva, some territory on the Transylvanian border, and the replacement of Serbia's Karadjordjević dynasty.[56] The Sixtus initiative in no way compromised Karl's minimum objective: it was intended to extract the Empire from a debilitating war through a general peace paid for not by Karl but by the Germans. The Empire urgently needed a quick, compromise peace, not only because of its dire internal state but also because its weakness was such that a German total victory would leave it effectively as a satellite state of its much more powerful ally. Czernin attempted to speed up peace in the east by publicly renouncing on 26 April any ambition to annex Russian territory. Both he and the Emperor urged the Germans to moderate their war aims in the hope of enabling a separate peace with Russia or, better still, an end to the world war. Yet they simultaneously continued to haggle with their ally over any prospective spoils. At a meeting on 17 and 18 May 1917, Czernin not only received a German guarantee of the Habsburg Empire's integrity but also, in exchange for giving over Poland after the war, acquired rights to Romania and a sphere of influence in the Balkans.[57]

Karl had no leverage with which to bring his ally to surrender Alsace-Lorraine and he had no wish to seal a separate peace with his western enemies. The Sixtus approach demonstrated his impotence. Significantly, it also showed that the Entente's intransigence left no scope for any sort of compromise peace in 1917. Karl's approach was extremely enticing: he conceded France and Britain's primary war aims, and although he stated that he was not seeking a separate peace, his interlocutors still hoped that after minor compromise Austria-Hungary might be torn from Germany. The French were very excited; President Poincaré was even ready to sweeten the deal by offering Karl Silesia and Bavaria from a defeated Germany. British Prime Minister David Lloyd George too was interested. However, when they approached their Italian ally, Foreign Minister Sidney Sonnino categorically refused to negotiate on the enormous gains his country had been promised as a reward for entering the war in 1915. Without Italian consent, negotiations were stuck, for Karl was unwilling to cede south Tyrol or any part of Istria and Dalmatia to an enemy whose war effort and army he and his generals held in contempt. Britain and France feared that abandoning their greedy ally would undermine their claim to be fighting to uphold international treaties and would shake the confidence of Serbia, Romania and possibly Russia in the alliance. This too was a reason why the Sixtus approach led nowhere.[58]

The Central Powers chose to go for broke in 1917. The rise of the Third OHL hardened and expanded Germany's official war aims. Hindenburg and Ludendorff, although anyway never interested in negotiation, were more realistic than many about the Entente's readiness to offer a compromise peace. With Russia tottering and the US lacking any significant army, they thought that they had a window of opportunity to win total victory. The Austro-Hungarians trailed reluctantly behind their allies, largely due to an absence of any real strategic alternative. However, Ludendorff had miscalculated. He not only underestimated his enemies, especially the United States, but also ignored the German people. They had been mobilized in 1914 to fight a war of defence, to protect what Bethmann had described in the Reichstag as 'the inheritance that we won in 1870'.[59] Ludendorff may have regarded his demands as the bare minimum for perpetual German security, but they went far beyond this inheritance. While the Reich government had the sense to keep them secret, officials' euphemistic talk of 'safeguards', 'frontier rectifications' and 'an honourable peace for the Fatherland' all excited widespread fear that rulers were shedding the people's blood in a needless war of conquest.[60] At a time when public exhaustion, the regimes' waning legitimacy and ideological challenge from overseas all sponsored a great and growing popular desire for some way out of the suffering, this was intensely dangerous. Czernin recognized the likely consequence: 'If *the monarchs* of the Central Powers are unable to conclude peace *within the next months*,' he warned in a memorandum of 12 April 1917 drawn up for Karl and sent to Wilhelm II, 'then the peoples will make it over their heads, and then the waves of revolution will sweep away everything for which our brothers and sons are still fighting and dying today.'[61]

OPPOSITION

'A terrible time we live through at the moment,' confided the Cracovian Aleksandra Czechówna glumly to her diary at the start of March 1917. 'We hear absolutely nothing about the end of the war but instead they speak ever more often about the hunger threatening us.'[62] Across central Europe, the public mood was subdued. The food shortages had not eased. Exhaustion, despair and anger were growing. During April reductions in the bread and flour ration sparked a rash of riots in Austria and Germany. Strikes also multiplied as everybody grappled with inflation. In the Reich, the number of workers downing tools was up by over half a million on the previous twelve months, reaching 650,000 by the end of 1917.[63] So bitter was the atmosphere in Vienna that Amalie Seidel, the leader of the Socialist women's movement in the Habsburg capital, felt 'that we are sitting on a volcano'.[64] Above all, there was a growing wish for peace. In Germany, people hoped at first that the U-boats might bring a rapid end to the war, but there, and even earlier in Austria, the ideas from abroad, President Wilson's 'peace without victory' and the Petrograd formula of a settlement 'without annexations or indemnities', captured the public imagination. Radical Socialists and nationalists, who offered ways out of the horror and new visions of the future, capitalized on popular distrust of governments and began to gain adherents.[65]

In Austria, Emperor Karl's recall of the Reichsrat was a brave attempt to shore up the state and restore the dynasty's waning legitimacy. The parliament's reopening on 30 May 1917 was supposed to mark the start of a new relationship between the Habsburg peoples and their Emperor. The monarch hoped for reconciliation and public support. More cynically, a return to a legal and more representative system of rule also offered the opportunity to spread the blame more widely for the realm's continuing woes. The summons to the deputies betrayed this prime purpose of the recall, as well as the limited political concessions on offer, when it began by declaring that the Reichsrat would 'deal with the food question, as well as economic, social, and financial matters arising out of the War'.[66] The idea was good, but its execution revealed just how out of touch Karl's government was. Three years of repressive bureaucratic-military dictatorship had left deep psychological scars, distrust and bitterness, represented at the Reichsrat's opening by the absence of 40 of its 516 members due either to exile or imprisonment.[67] Moreover, Minister President Clam-Martinic had alienated most Slav deputies with his first plan to implement pro-Austrian German reforms of the Empire by decree. His belated attempt at reconciliation by organizing meetings with parliamentarians barely a week before the Reichsrat reopening was utterly inadequate to win their goodwill. Astoundingly, Karl and his government, in recalling the peoples' representatives, were permitting a forum for long-suppressed grievances to be expressed, without any plan for how to manage or resolve them.[68]

The Reichsrat opening was dominated by statements from national groups that illustrated how tenuous loyalty to the Habsburg order had become. The Czech Union, a body of all but two of the Czech parties, formed in November 1916 at the initiative of the chairman of the powerful Czech Agrarian Party, Antonín Švehla, to defend national interests, made the greatest impact. Most politicians had expected the Czechs to read out the statement that they had delivered at every Reichsrat opening since 1879, which asserted Bohemia's historic rights that had been disregarded under the Dualist system. Instead, the message that František Staněk, the Czech Union's chairman, read to the assembled members was new and shocking, for it was manifestly inspired by the dangerous ideas that the Russian revolution and America's entry into the war had unleashed:

> The representatives of the Czech nation are deeply convinced that the present Dualist system has led to the emergence of ruling and subject nationalities which is detrimental to the interest of all of them, and that in order to remove every national injustice and assure the general development of each nation in the interest of the empire and dynasty as a whole it is necessary to transform the Habsburg-Lorraine monarchy into a federal union of free and equal national states.
>
> Basing ourselves at this historic moment on the natural right of nations to self-determination and free development, reinforced moreover in our case by inalienable historic rights, we shall demand the unification of all branches of the Czechoslovak nation in one democratic state, including the Slovak branch living in a unit contiguous to its Czech motherland.[69]

From the perspective of Habsburg officials, the best that could be said for the statement was that it at least advocated reform within the bounds of the Monarchy. This had been by no means assured; when the statement was drawn up, there had been heated argument within the Czech Union about whether the Monarchy should be mentioned at all.[70] In all other respects, however, it was decidedly menacing. The call to the 'natural right of nations to self-determination' echoed both Wilsonian idealism and Russian revolutionary rhetoric, and showed how radical Czech political aspirations had become. The hope in 1914–15 of the Young Czech leader Karel Kramář to resurrect a Czech kingdom under the pan-Slavic protection of the Russian Tsar – a hope embraced by only a tiny band of conspirators – was now seriously outdated. Instead, freedom, democracy and self-determination, the ideals of 1917 embraced by the Czech Union's statement, were attracting a far wider following by challenging the monarchical ideology and historical legitimacy that underpinned the Habsburg Monarchy. The Czechs, while not entirely abandoning historical 'state rights', were now prioritizing a more modern conception of the nation based on popular will and national self-determination. By laying claim not only to the traditional Czech lands in Austria but also to Slovak-inhabited territories that by historical state right lay under the Hungarian Crown of St Stephen, they were demanding that the entire Empire be reconstructed. No longer would its legitimacy rest on history, venerable law and the divine rights of kings. If Czech politicians had their way, it should instead reflect an alleged 'natural right of nations' and its structure should be defined by race.

There was also no good news for the Empire from the political groupings of the other nationalities. The South Slavs, who two months earlier had formed an alliance with the Czech Union, echoed its demands. In their vision of the future, Slovenes, Croats and Serbs would be united 'in one autonomous state . . . ruled in a democratic manner and under the sceptre of the Habsburg dynasty'. Other national groups advanced conflicting demands. The Poles, once firm supporters of the Monarchy but now aggrieved by the government's failure to realize its promises to them of November 1916, wished for an independent Poland with access to the sea. Their aspirations clashed with those of the Ruthenian deputies, who wanted Galicia to be broken up into Polish and Ruthenian Crownlands. The united German parties were horrified by the implication for their co-nationals in Bohemia of Czech demands and promised to oppose the federalizing ambitions of both the Czech Union and the South Slavs. The deputies' division into unified national groups, the antagonism between them, and the contradictory nature of the programmes that they put forward on that first day, exposed the naivety of hopes that the Reichsrat's return might bring reconciliation and stability to the beleaguered Monarchy. The speech by Emperor Karl the following day was too vague on how governance of his realms might be reformed. His refusal to take an oath to the Austrian constitution, an attempt not to reprise the mistake he had made in Hungary, merely increased the unease of deputies. His Minister President was also unhelpful. Although the paralysis between the nationalities was entirely foreseeable, Clam-Martinic was not ready to respond to the deputies' speeches for two weeks. When he did reply in the Reichsrat on 12 June, he dismissed the nationalities' plans as irreconcilable and therefore unrealizable and instead vacuously proclaimed that 'the programme of my government is Austria'.[71]

The Reichsrat's reopening was only the most important of an array of measures that changed how wartime Austria was ruled. The government, belatedly recognizing that the Habsburg war effort stood or fell on the will of its peoples, attempted to co-opt them and their representatives. At the very highest level, this strategy failed. When Ernst von Seidler, successor to the woeful Clam-Martinic as Minister President, attempted to reconstruct the Austrian cabinet in August from one of officials to one representing the nationalities, no Czech parliamentarian accepted the invitation. Other Slav politicians and Social Democrats also refused to form so close a link to the regime without political reforms.[72] However, further down the hierarchy there was some double-edged success. Two new ministries, a Ministry for Social Welfare and a Ministry of Food, were established. The Ministry of Social Welfare was particularly significant, for it drew into its service the expertise of nationalist activists and the extensive welfare organizations that these activists had created for their own peoples. The state hoped to bolster its legitimacy through association with these popular organizations, as well as to alleviate more effectively the hardship of its peoples. Nonetheless, this was no reprise of the 'double mobilization' of 1914 and 1915, for whereas then national feeling had been channelled towards an imperial war, now nationalists marked out their own turf. The nationalist-run orphanages and welfare centres absorbed under the Ministry of Social Welfare in 1917 were strictly segregated. Nationalists' participation in imperial welfare converted social problems into national issues, accelerating the dissolution of the already frail bonds between peoples even as they combated the deprivation and misery.[73]

The new spirit of governance was also manifested in a reduction in repression and an attempt at conciliation by the Emperor. The army's conduct at home had been very divisive, and in the summer of 1917 its powers there were curtailed. The government revoked emergency legislation permitting the military to issue orders to Crownland civilian officials, and the Reichsrat abolished the jurisdiction of military courts over civilians in the hinterland. In September, at the Reichsrat's urging, the secretive War Supervision Office, tasked with overseeing censorship and maintaining order, was disbanded. The War Ministry took on its responsibilities, but pressure from parliamentarians ensured that information flowed much more freely than earlier in the war.[74] The most controversial measure was Emperor Karl's amnesty for all political crimes, declared on 2 July. Karel Kramář, Václav Klofáč and around a thousand other Czech prisoners were released. As with the Reichsrat opening, the impact of the measures was not all that Karl or his government wished. Limiting the state's repressive capabilities at a time of popular discontent was perilous, especially as the amnesty failed to elicit the expected goodwill from Czech nationalists. Embittered enemies of the dynasty as well as innocents were released into society. Austrian German opinion was horrified. Additionally, the state's authority suffered. The amnesty was an implicit admission of the injustice of much of the past repression, and the parliamentary debates that accompanied the judicial reforms publicly revealed just how vicious the army's conduct had been in Galicia and on the Serbian Front in 1914 and 1915.[75]

The politicians of the Empire's various nationalities were wary of associating themselves with the Habsburg regime by 1917, but how alienated were the peoples? The Czech case is the most interesting. The Czechs, well educated, industrialized, with energetic, nationalist politicians both at home and in exile, had often been accused of treason and scapegoated for military debacles during the war, yet they were essential for the continued existence of the Habsburg state. Ominously, their intelligentsia was well along the road to divorcing that state. Thanks to the playwright and director of the Prague National Theatre, Jaroslav Kvapil, it took a lead part in emboldening Czech politicians to issue their forceful declaration at the opening of the Reichsrat. Kvapil was in cahoots with the exiles working in the west to promote support for the Czech national cause and bring down the Monarchy, and, with an actor's timing, he sensed that Russia's revolution and America's entry into war had created a moment ripe for dramatic gesture. He thus organized a 'Manifesto of Czech Authors', ultimately acquiring the signatures of 222 prominent men of letters, the first of whom was the immensely popular historical novelist Alois Jirásek. The military authorities completely missed the significance of the move and, to the amazement of all involved, permitted its publication in the Agrarian paper *Večer* on 17 May. It instantly caused a stir. Warning that 'a democratic Europe, consisting of autonomous and free states, is the Europe of the future', it urged the deputies to demand an end to the government's repressive policies and admonished them to advance 'Czech rights and Czech *desiderata*' at a time when the 'Czech fate was being sealed for centuries'.[76]

The loyalties of the wider Czech-speaking population in the nation's Bohemian heartlands are more difficult to pin down. Private correspondence collected by the Empire's censors testifies to a high state of national consciousness within the community at the start of 1917. Ideas of Czech autonomy were popular but only a small minority, mostly from the middle class or intelligentsia, actively pursued full-scale independence.[77] Nonetheless, anger and bitterness were widespread and rising. Bohemia was in tumult in the spring of 1917. There was not enough food or, partly in consequence, coal. Miners in the north-west of the Crownland were so underfed and exhausted by March that production had dropped to just 75 per cent of the norm and some pits had to close. Inhabitants responded with riots and strikes. In Prague, these began as early as February, but soon other cities were also rocked by demonstrations, especially once potatoes disappeared from the market and the bread ration was cut in mid-April.[78] Dissidents did their best to channel the anger from mundane concerns about survival into political demands. Police reported graffiti demanding an independent Bohemian state.[79] Treasonous posters were put up in towns. One placard that appeared in working-class Uhříněves, on the outskirts of Prague, offered readers the following detailed instructions:

> To the Czech people! One of the main tasks of the Entente states is the liberation of the Czechs and Slovaks from foreign rule. Nine-tenths of Czechs long for this. After the victory of the Entente states the Bohemian lands will leave the union of Austria and from them a Czech state will be formed ... Thus, keep in mind: 1. Not a single heller for the war loan or other imperial collections. 2. Do not support the war. 3. Don't believe the newspapers; they lie ... 4. Call out 'Up the Entente states' and 'Down with Austria'.[80]

This sort of propaganda by disaffected individuals made little difference. Nonetheless, in the context of the Russian revolution, the American entry into the war and the Reichsrat's recall, the demonstrations did quickly acquire overtly political goals. On 30 May, the day parliament reopened, a strike was staged by 6,000 industrial workers in Prague. The authorities referred to it as a 'peace demonstration', but the younger workers in particular had other aims. Their first demand was for the release of the treasonous chairman of the Czech National Socialists,

Václav Klofáč. In peace, the National Socialists had attracted barely 7 per cent of the Czech vote, but this mass of workers acted in ways that left little doubt they shared the party's rabidly anti-Habsburg stance. Many loudly denounced the monarchy and cheered both the most prominent wartime Czech exile, the Realist Party's Tomáš Masaryk, and Czech independence. Other workers sung the pan-Slavic anthem 'Hej Slované' with an altered line: 'The Russians are with us and France helps us.'[81]

Hungry and angry Czech industrial workers had no monopoly on contempt for the Habsburg government. Extreme deprivation and total lack of faith in the leadership were in fact pretty universal not just in Bohemia but throughout the Empire. At its centre, Vienna, a wry joke playing on the weather vane of the city's famous cathedral captured the disenchanted mood:

> A German soldier walking around St Stephen's Cathedral asks a policeman 'Is that a Catholic Church?' On receiving an affirmative answer, he expresses surprise that on the tower instead of a cross there is a cockerel. The policeman replies: 'That's how it is with us. We always have a dumb animal at the top, and that is our cross'![82]

Demands for independence did not inevitably follow from disgust with rulers, however. Even in the Czech lands, wistful rumours that the Emperor would soon come to Prague and let himself be crowned King of Bohemia, a long-standing Czech demand, or that he would reside in Prague Castle until his wife gave birth to a son, testify to a latent affection for the dynasty.[83] Some Czechs may have embraced a belief popular among Austrian Germans that Karl was unaware of the abuses in his realm. More significantly, hatred of the Reich Germans deflected some vitriol from the Habsburgs. The Germans' aggression seemed unbounded. They were blamed for preventing peace and some Czechs were convinced that they were planning an invasion of Bohemia. Kaiser Wilhelm was considered a madman. One of the more bizarre stories that circulated around Prague in the summer of 1917 was that worker unrest had forced the Kaiser to flee the Reich and he was now hiding in a Bohemian lunatic asylum, where his post was delivered to him by Zeppelin.[84]

The material hardship continued over the summer and autumn. At the start of August, the food supply in Bohemia completely collapsed. Not only was there not enough bread or meat but there were also no potatoes, fruit or vegetables for sale. The gathering-in of the harvest brought temporary relief, but in October the supply fell back into crisis. Ironically, the cause was the Habsburg army's greatest victory of the war, the Caporetto offensive, in which over 250,000 Italian soldiers were captured. The logistics of this Austro-German operation required over half of the Empire's rolling stock, leaving insufficient wagons to supply its cities with food.[85] As morale reports confirmed, nobody cared about the victory; the difficulty of surviving was much more pressing. Large strikes took place. The authorities' attempt to impose discipline on the arms factories by placing their workers under military law at first worsened the upheaval, as 30,000 workers in the important Škoda arms factory in Plzeň (known also by its German name Pilsen) downed tools at the end of June. Order was restored but the Czech population had become irretrievably alienated. The Czech Social Democrat leader Bohumír Šmeral, one of the few who still believed in reform within the Empire, knew he had lost the argument by August. The people, he observed, had embraced a 'religious-mystical enthusiasm for independence'. Some 95 per cent approved of Masaryk's efforts to persuade the Entente to support openly the creation of a Czechoslovak state.[86] Habsburg security services agreed. By December, the Military Command in Prague was reporting anxiously that 'national antagonism . . . has climbed alarmingly, the greater Austrian allegiance has sunk to minimum and the mood is correspondingly miserable'.[87]

Other nationalities in the Empire were similarly separating from the Habsburg state. A survey of letters by soldiers and civilians at the end of 1917 found in them a revolutionary mood and deep alienation. Among those writers who discussed nationality issues, a minority of 40 per cent, or just 28 per cent if Hungarians and Austrian Germans were excluded, still expressed loyalty to the monarchy.[88] However, it was Czech popular opinion that most clearly and quickly translated into political actions. The people's representatives in the Czech Union felt the rebellious mood on the streets and, in stark contrast to the start of the year when at Czernin's insistence they had denounced Entente pretensions to be liberators of 'Tscheco Slovaques', they now distanced themselves from the Habsburg regime. The declaration at the opening of the Reichsrat in May was only the first step. Over the summer, power within the Union shifted towards radical Czech nationalists, who with the aid of Masaryk's conspiratorial *Maffie* were able to prevent the group from participating in the Reichsrat subcommittee formed to advise on constitutional reform. Finally, a new level of defiance, and an important move in the struggle to win Entente recognition of Czech national aspirations, was reached with the Union's Epiphany Declaration of 6 January 1918. Unlike the statement of May 1917 in the Reichsrat, this made no mention of a future under the Habsburgs. Instead, the Czech deputies even more explicitly echoed President Wilson's language. Numbering themselves among the 'democratic nations of the world', they asserted their people's 'right of a free national life and of the self-determination of nations'. These ideals, they emphasized, 'must be the basis of future international law'. When the Austrian Minister President heard of the proclamation, he angrily dismissed it as 'war psychosis'. In reality, these dangerous ideas were already shaping central Europe's future.[89]

In Germany, the public mood in the first half of 1917 was a little less depressed than in Austria. The shortages were catastrophic but never so severe as across the border. The Western Front remained solid. In the spring, a British operation at Arras had been halted after a bloody struggle, and on the Chemin des Dames a supposedly decisive offensive by a new French commander, General Robert Nivelle, had been quashed in short order. The U-boats still seemed to offer the promise of a quick victory. Nonetheless, the German people were burdened with sacrifice. The army had lost 1.6 million men killed or missing and another 2.8 million had been wounded.[90] At home, the food supply reached its nadir in the summer, with an official ration of just 1,100 calories. Any material of value, from rags to lubricating grease, was being requisitioned for Hindenburg's rearmament drive. From the middle of the year, this would even extend to the removal of church bells, a measure that caused sadness everywhere and some violent resistance in the Reich's pious eastern borderlands.[91] The majority of Germans may still not have been willing to end the war at any price, but morale was very fragile and the atmosphere fractious. The home district commanders warned 'that the longing for peace is widespread in general and in all classes of the population'.[92] The Third OHL ignored public opinion at its peril. The people, explained another military report astutely, had 'no desire to continue the war in order to achieve exaggerated war aims. The lower classes right up to deep into the bourgeoisie especially reject such war aims.'[93]

Discontent about material hardship, controversy over political reform and disputes about war aims, all inflamed by the Russian revolution, fuelled leftist opposition and radicalism. The SPD leadership's policy of support for the war and cooperation with the government had already faced growing internal challenge in 1916. The minority who were prepared to defy it were made even angrier by the attempts to suppress their voice. The leadership, or Socialists close to it, had connived with the military to have its anti-war opponents drafted and had wrested control of party newspapers, including the leading Berlin title *Vorwärts*, from the minority's control. At the start of 1917, after bitter mutual recrimination, the minority was expelled and in April founded its own party, pointedly named the Independent Social Democratic Party (USPD). Hugo Haase and Georg Ledebour became its chairmen. The new organization took with it 17 Socialist Reichstag representatives and 57 of the majority SPD's 357 local election district organizations. Its members were highly diverse, united only by opposition to the war and to the government. The central management was dominated by men such as Haase, who opposed the war, were committed to international Socialism and thought the SPD had sold out. There were old Socialists like Eduard Bernstein and Karl Kautsky who would have preferred to have remained as oppositional voices within the main party. Then, on the USPD's far left were the Spartakists, genuine revolutionaries who took their name from the slave who led the famous revolt against the Romans. Their best-known leaders, Karl Liebknecht (the first Socialist deputy to vote against war credits) and Rosa Luxemburg, were in jail. They were only a very small group, but they had been almost alone in their readiness to oppose the war and government openly, and consequently they had acquired a notoriety that belied their weakness.[94]

Many in Germany's proletariat were excited by the Russian revolution. Wartime changes to the national economy had hastened the process of alienation. The Hindenburg Programme had closed many smaller firms in the name of efficiency, leaving large, impersonal enterprises with distant or adversarial employee–management relations. An influx of male youth, who became highly skilled workers, accentuated the shift towards militancy. These new labourers were often employed far from the stabilizing influence of their families and like the mass of unskilled workers who entered the armaments factories, they lacked their older peers' ingrained discipline and respect for the SPD and its unions. In Berlin's metal industry, a new power, Richard Müller's revolutionary shop stewards, had risen. These informally organized radicals with influence over thousands of highly skilled and, for the war economy, indispensable lathe operators and other metalworkers stood on the far left wing of the USPD. While the new party attracted only a minority of its parent party's parliamentary deputies, thanks to these structural changes its membership was nearly equal: 120,000 members, as against the SPD's 150,000 by the autumn of 1917. Along with the continued deprivation after the 'turnip winter' and the impact of the Russian revolution, the new labour force's more militant composition and leaders also accounts for the growth of strikes in the last two years of war. The two largest and most politicized were those in Berlin and Leipzig in April 1917 and the January 1918 peace strikes, which rocked Austria and Germany.[95]

The April 1917 strikes, in which 300,000 workers participated, were sparked by the reduction in the bread ration. In Berlin, the orderly demonstrations that took place on 16 April under union oversight were solely about food, although the release of Richard Müller, arrested a few days earlier, was also successfully demanded. However, in the stoppage that broke out simultaneously in Leipzig the strikers advanced overtly political demands, which over the following days disgruntled workers in Berlin also adopted. They wanted not just higher rations but also the introduction of equal and universal suffrage, a government undertaking that it was ready to seal a non-annexationist peace, and annulment of the Law of Siege, the Auxiliary Service Law and all restrictions on gatherings and the press. Political prisoners were also to be released. The inspiration taken from the uprising to the east was clear from the revolutionary leaflets circulating:

> <u>Workers!</u> Our brothers, the Russian proletariat were in the same situation 4 weeks ago. We know what occurred in Russia: the working people rose there and did not just force the regulation of the food question. <u>It also at the same time – much more importantly – won freedom for itself; something of which the German worker does not yet dare to dream.</u>
>
> Should we patiently continue to put up with the old misery, the

exploitation, the hunger and the mass murder – the cause of all our agony and suffering? No! A thousand times no! Leave the workshops and factories! ... And recognize your power! ... <u>Down with the war! Down with the government! Peace! Freedom! Bread!</u>[96]

The appearance in Leipzig of a workers' council to manage the strike was also inspired by the Russian example. The scale of the strikes was menacing, as was the role of USPD deputies in persuading the Berliners to adopt the politicized demands of their Saxon comrades. Nonetheless, the revolutionary potential of the strikes should not be overstated. They were of brief duration, lasting just three days in Leipzig and a week in Berlin. For most participants, the primary grievances were economic. In Leipzig, where the strike at first appeared most radical, workers were easily pacified by a cut in the working week to fifty-two hours and a wage hike.[97]

Even so, General Groener at the Supreme War Office was livid. He was determined not to permit military authority to be challenged and wanted to draft 4,000 strikers as punishment, but he was thwarted by factory owners who feared losing their skilled workforce. The general recognized the need to maintain good relations with the SPD and unions, who were crucial in restraining worker unrest.[98] He built on the reputation he had won among them as fair-minded and criticized industrialists who disregarded the aspects of the Auxiliary Service Law that they disliked, as well as striking workers. Wisely, he advised the generals in charge of the home military districts to make a sharp distinction between the majority SPD and the independent Socialists, whom he blamed for the politicization. In Berlin, some factories whose workforce had been particularly recalcitrant were militarized and workers were warned that if they did not return to their jobs, they would be drafted, placed under military discipline and forced to work for much lower soldiers' pay. A private discussion with Haase, in which Groener threatened to suppress demonstrations on the coming May Day with troops, ended with the Independent Socialist agreeing to restrain the more radical members of his party. Along with coercion, the authorities also tried to touch workers' patriotism and social conscience. An appeal by Hindenburg warned them that any drop in the production of war materiel through strikes was 'an irresponsible weakening of our defensive strength and ... an unforgivable sin against the army and particularly against the man in the trenches, who would have to bleed for it'.[99]

Despite these attempts to pacify the workforce, the summer of 1917 was very turbulent. Strikes broke out in the Ruhr industrial region and in the coal mines of Upper Silesia. In Cologne at the start of July, 30,000 metalworkers walked out, demanding a fifty-one-hour week and higher wages. The OHL became increasingly unnerved. In mid-August, Groener was dismissed. Ludendorff had looked on his conciliation of the unions with disfavour, and Groener had made many enemies in big business, which had the ear of the High Command, for trying to rein in profits.[100] Ludendorff, along with the Prussian government and many home military commanders, interpreted the unrest not as an index of the rising distress within German society. Instead, they deluded themselves that it was the fruit of agitation by traitors and enemy agents. A circular sent by the Prussian Ministry of the Interior in July 1917 set out this argument:

> Various recent disturbances caused by the shortage of food follow much the same pattern. Simultaneous downing of tools in industrial complexes far removed from each other, sometimes on a particular signal, streams of demonstrators coming together at a clearly pre-arranged point, the putting forward almost everywhere of identical demands, in the case of threatened police intervention almost everywhere women, youths and children to the fore, obviously in the hope that in this way the police or military can be prevented from using the sharpest measures . . . The speed with which the crowd in most places rushes through the streets and the fact that plundering of grocery and other shops takes place also points to uniform intentions.
>
> All these circumstances leave little doubt that we have faced demonstrations and riots painstakingly spread through arrangement passed from mouth to mouth. They were not simply spontaneous expressions of uproar about the worsening food crisis but in part are to be attributed to the secret agitation of unscrupulous rabble-rousers, possibly to be sought in the ranks of the supporters of radical Social Democracy, or possibly agents in the pay of our enemy or their henchmen.[101]

Intensely anxious officials were seized by fantasies similar to those at the start of the war. Edgy German commanders at home imagined a host of adversaries. Ludendorff, possibly thinking of the Reich's sponsorship of Lenin, feared that enemy agents had enlisted radical Socialists and pacifists within Germany: 'Especially since the entry of the United States into the war,' he claimed, 'an ambitious coordinated action has been observable.'[102] Mormons and Seventh Day Adventists attracted particular suspicion. However, subversive agents could in the minds of officials take any form: as one home commander warned, 'They carry out their highly treasonous activity in the garb of bourgeois citizens, political agitators, yes, even under the mask of the field grey soldier.'[103] This mindset was dangerous, for it widened the gulf between leaders and people. Paranoid higher-ranking military and civilian officials came to regard their fellow citizens as potential agitators. Moreover, their interpretation of strikes and protests as products of subversion misguidedly encouraged them to dismiss real grievances and cast those who uttered them as willing or naive traitors to the Fatherland.

The OHL not only feared politically motivated disorder on the home front but was even more acutely concerned that similar agitation might undermine the army's discipline and performance. An order issued on 25 July 1917 warned hysterically that political propaganda was entering the force 'from the most diverse sides'. Independent Socialists were singled out as 'conducting . . . subversive activity most damaging for the men's discipline'. Commanders also feared dangerous ideas from the west. Conscious of the damage that its own propaganda was wreaking on the Russians on the Eastern Front, the OHL attempted in April to prevent any comparable Allied campaign in the west by announcing that enemy pilots shot down after dropping propaganda flyers would be court-martialled as acting against the laws of war.[104] These anxieties were exacerbated by the knowledge that since the Somme, the army's morale had become more brittle. Desertion had tripled over the rate of 1916, reaching around 20,000 men by the year's end. From the summer, a catalogue of small mutinies, indiscipline and panics had hampered units fighting on the Western Front.[105] There was some evidence of a leftist political edge to men's discontent. Letter censors reported complaints that 'the whole state is only a tool of capitalism and the profiteers'.[106] One bitter ditty became ubiquitous across the front:

> We do not fight for Fatherland
> We do not fight for God
> We're fighting for the rich people
> The poor are getting shot.[107]

It was even rumoured that men on leave and the hospitalized wounded were discussing 'revolution', albeit only once they had beaten the enemy.[108] Their attitude was revealing: a readiness to defend hearth and home against the external foe still trumped class antagonism and limited the appeal of revolutionary Socialist propaganda for the western Field Army. Growing exhaustion and the strain of fighting a materially superior enemy, not political disaffection, were the causes of lowered morale and indiscipline.[109]

There was more evidence of political subversion in the navy. A mutiny on 2 August 1917, most seriously affecting the battleships *Prinzregent Luitpold* and *Friedrich der Grosse*, was treated by the *Reichsmarine*'s leaders as a revolutionary insurrection. In the aftermath, courts martial handed down ten death sentences, two of which were carried out, and terms of imprisonment totalling over 360 years. The two conspirators who were executed, Stoker Albin Köbis and Sailor Max Reichpietsch, had hoped to spark a strike demanding peace across the battle fleet. Reichpietsch, a USPD member, was a fantasist who deluded himself that he had been tasked by the party to build up a subversive movement within the navy. He had distributed and encouraged discussion of USPD newspapers and pamphlets among the men on the *Friedrich der Grosse*. He had also organized a list of signatures supporting the USPD's efforts to promote a peace without annexations or indemnities at the international Socialist conference in Stockholm. Around 5,000 sailors had signed.

Nonetheless, the revolutionary potential of the fleet in the summer of 1917 should not be exaggerated. As one sailor noted at the time in his diary, while his comrades' rebellious spirit owed something to 'events in Russia ... much has yet to be done to merit such a comparison'.[110] Anger about service conditions rather than political alienation motivated insubordination in the fleet. Sailors on the battleships were more distant from their officers than both U-boat personnel and front-line soldiers. Their service seemed pointless, for the clash with the British at Jutland had changed nothing and the High Sea Fleet had not been out on an operation since October 1916. Above all, food was a flashpoint of inter-rank conflict far worse than any in the army. The rations of battleship crews were miserable, while their superiors still ate well. The navy had prevaricated for six months before following the army's example and introducing food-checking commissions, and even then many captains had disregarded the order. The summer of 1917 had seen repeated strikes on several battleships, as sailors had tested the limits of authority and tried, mostly successfully, to assert their rights. The 'mutiny' of 2 August that finally unleashed the navy's wrath was a limited affair not so different from these earlier strikes. Six hundred men from the *Prinzregent Luitpold* had left their ship, and planned to spend three hours in the tavern as a minor protest against the imprisonment of some of their comrades for skipping duty the day before when an excursion was cancelled. Nonetheless, despite the strikes' modest aims, they were not without political impact. An attempt in the Reichstag by Chancellor Michaelis to censure the USPD for the strikes met strong opposition from a Reichstag left and centre majority, which saw the move as an assault on deputies' immunity. In another illustration of parliament's power, its hostility forced Michaelis to resign on 31 October 1917. The seventy-four-year-old Bavarian Centre Party politician Georg von Hertling was appointed to replace him. His long career in the Reichstag and in Bavaria's government, and the decision to consult party leaders before his appointment, appeared to point towards another step on the way to a true German democracy. But his conservatism and age meant in practice that he was no counterweight to the power of the Third OHL.[111]

There were powerful forces in Germany that feared the Reichstag's new assertiveness and the left's appeal for a peace 'without annexations or indemnities'. The right's response to the July peace resolution came in September 1917 with the foundation of a new movement, the German Fatherland Party. With the former State Secretary of the Imperial Naval Office, Alfred von Tirpitz, as its figurehead and donations from heavy industry funding its activities, the new party set itself the task of unifying 'all patriotic forces' to resist democratization and proselytize for a 'strong German peace' with very extensive gains in the west and east, and beyond Europe. Tirpitz's leadership was a huge draw for the right. By February 1918 it had attracted nearly 300,000 members and by the autumn, after the German army's advances on the Western Front in the first half of the year, its membership had risen to 800,000. Around half were members of other nationalist organizations that were affiliated to the party, but the remainder were still more numerous than the combined membership of Germany's Socialist parties. However, the Fatherland Party appealed only to a very specific section of society. Its strength lay above all in the Prussian east, the old Kingdom's conservative heartlands and the ethnically mixed region whose German inhabitants had most to lose from a national defeat. In southern Germany, by contrast, the Fatherland Party was extremely weak. Higher officials, professionals, academics and estate owners were all present in the party in large numbers. Pastors and teachers played a key role in its decentralized organization. The party was thus a bastion of the respectable and wealthy middle class. Tradesmen and workers stayed well away.[112] The organization was also unpopular with the troops. Many wondered why the government did not take steps to rein it in. While the Fatherland Party claimed that the army would not stand a moderate peace, men at the front shared the defensive conception of their home compatriots.[113]

The Third OHL was also spurred into action by the Reichstag's peace resolution, as well as fears about leftist agitation and falling morale in the army's ranks. Ludendorff, having experienced success with propaganda in Russia, now focused on influencing his own men's hearts and minds. 'Patriotic Instruction', as his programme became known, was introduced two days before the resolution passed, on 17 July 1917. As he explained, it was intended to rejuvenate troops' 'combat effectiveness and with it confidence in victory' and to 'counter the agitators, skivers and weaklings at home and in the army'.[114] The army commands at the front and the home military district commands were tasked with running the programme. Each combat division ultimately appointed a dedicated 'Instruction Officer' who guided officers at the front in disseminating the propaganda. The programme also embraced entertainment and welfare, for example new infrastructure such as field libraries and soldiers' rest homes. It was a pioneering attempt both to raise morale and to indoctrinate troops; a product of the OHL's insight, so different from its attempts to impose compulsion on despised civilians, that its citizen-soldiers could not merely be ordered but must be inspired to fight. The methods that the programme adopted were also innovative. Care was taken to identify soldiers' anxieties and grievances and to assess their reactions to the propaganda. Postal censorship reports, discussions with company officers, regimental doctors and chaplains, and information from *Vertrauensleute*, troops tasked with reporting on their comrades' moods, enabled Instruction Officers to adapt their material to their audience's concerns. The feedback also allowed these officers to improve their communication. When lectures proved unpopular and ineffective, more imaginative techniques were adopted. Some Instruction Officers won an audience by squeezing in talks during company evenings with free beer or before cinema outings. It soon dawned on military propagandists that the entertainment itself could be used to strengthen soldiers' combat motivation: plays were picked that would not only entertain but also educate. Films showing cities and landscapes in Germany were especially popular, and reminded troops why they should hold out.[115]

The programme was opposed by Socialists as disseminating a political message of total victory. The OHL attempted to persuade its men of the necessity of annexations. Under the slogan 'More land!' soldiers learned why a peace without annexation was impracticable. The blockade showed that, without more territory for food, Germany would remain vulnerable to British naval power.[116] However, here, as in its other propaganda, the military took care to stress Entente aggression. Soldiers were warned about the enemy's aims: 'the Rhine should be French, the Oder Russian and the North Sea English'. In defeat, Germans would be enslaved and suppressed.[117] The success of Patriotic Instruction in steeling the will of its troops to hold out – and despite limited resources, some reluctance among officers to take on the new propaganda duties, and apathy among soldiers, there is good evidence indicating that it did have an effect – was down to the army's recognition of the fundamentally defensive combat motivation of its rank and file. Guidelines stressed that 'everyone must hear time and again that in the case of an enemy victory not only the farther and nearer homeland but he himself and his relatives are lost'.[118]

Propaganda also did much to sustain civilian readiness to hold out in 1917. The activism and energy of 1914 and 1915, when local elites had led the public mobilization, had withered under the hardship, war weariness and food shortages. The state had stepped into the gap to provide motivation. The propaganda organization was, as in 1914, still splintered. Ludendorff's appeal for a centralized agency to formulate press strategy and synchronize the fragmented ministerial publicity agencies fell on deaf ears in 1916.[119] Nonetheless, the War Press Office under the OHL did provide some coordination through its monthly meetings with the Supreme War Office, the War Food Office and the Ministries of War, Public Works and Culture. It guided the press and supplied most of the material for the army's Patriotic Instruction programme.

It also engaged with crucial local community elites and opinion formers: its *Deutsche Kriegswochenschau*, a weekly newssheet with facts and figures useful for shaping the popular view of recent war activities, was sent to clergy, teachers, youth workers, railway and postal officials, as well as farmers' and middle-class organizations. The initial issue of 80,000 soon expanded and at the most intense periods of propaganda ran to 175,000 copies. The new medium of film was also embraced. The Third OHL established the Photographic and Film Office in January 1917 to produce propaganda pictures. With a library of over 200,000 photographs, it supplied the War Press Office and other official bureaus with movies and illustrations for their campaigns.[120]

At the regional level – always important in the federalized Reich – another propaganda organization had been developed. Civil authorities had been spurred by the food crisis to intervene in public opinion, rather than simply rely on the military censor to suppress negative views. The Bavarians were the first to take the decisive step towards actively shaping public opinion in February 1916, but others soon followed, using clergy and schools to track and influence the people's mood. The major change in 1917 was that due to the Third OHL's regard for morale as the war's decisive factor, the home military commands also became active in propaganda, working closely with local civil authorities. Principal themes included questions of food supply, military issues, citizenship and the economy. The propagandists did not confine themselves to direct appeals but, like the War Press Office, sought the cooperation of court organizations and key opinion-formers whose support would give their message greater weight. Middle-class organizations, unions and workers' committees and, for women, the Church were all co-opted. Propaganda was skilfully packaged depending on its intended audience. Thus, the middle class, regarded by the Reich's authorities as the backbone of the people but suffering more than any other section of society from price inflation, was bombarded with material on the consequences of defeat, the war economy and, particularly frightening for anyone with property or a business, the dangers of Bolshevism. In contrast, when addressing workers, the language of the labour movement was adopted to persuade them of their interest in a German victory. The war against mercantile England was twisted into a crusade against Anglo-Saxon world capitalism.[121]

The campaign for the Seventh War Loan in the autumn of 1917 illustrates how effective German propaganda had become, as well as the themes it employed. The biannual war loans advertised in the spring and autumn of each year were the high points of the propagandists' calendar. The Reichsbank's Information Bureau led the campaign, but it was supported by the War Press Office, the civil authorities, army commands and home district commands. The campaign was no mere fund-raising exercise; while the war loan helped to cover the German government's immense war expenditure, its symbolic value as a plebiscite on popular determination to continue the war was even more significant. Moreover, the impact of the loan campaigns on the national willingness to hold out was achieved not merely by persuasion. War loans gave each subscriber a material interest in victory, as it was inconceivable that the Reich's government would be able to repay its immense debts unless it could force an indemnity on its enemies. The Sixth War Loan campaign had been the first to employ modern advertising techniques. It had a signature picture by the respected artist Fritz Erler, depicting a hardened front-line soldier in a steel helmet and with a gas mask slung around his neck, that carried the message 'Help us triumph! Sign the War Loan', which was reproduced on nearly 1.5 million posters and 11 million postcards. Two flyers, each with a run of 12 million copies, three short publicity films and a specially composed theme tune entitled 'Help us triumph!' all assisted in ensuring that no one in Germany could ignore the appeal.[122] The campaign, launched when the people's optimism about a rapid victory through the U-boats was still fresh, was a tremendous success. The loan mobilized small savers, attracting over seven million signatures, nearly twice the number of the Fifth War Loan, and raised 13,122 million marks.[123]

The Sixth War Loan was always going to be difficult to follow, but the circumstances in which the Seventh was advertised were especially discouraging for anyone considering investing in German victory. The U-boats had disappointed, Russia continued to fight, and the food supply was in crisis. Morale had plummeted to a new low.[124] All the more impressive then that the campaign collected 5,530,285 signatures and raised 12,626 million marks; although somewhat less than its predecessor, these were still more subscribers and, in nominal terms, more money than for any of the other five previous war loans. The loan's success in extremely adverse conditions owed much to the message that accompanied it. Hindenburg, the people's hero and 'saviour', featured heavily.

A pamphlet released by the Reichsbank illustrated to potential investors how in every way – land, industry, resources and people – Germany was superior to its arch-enemy, 'England'.[125] However, the campaign literature was above all stamped by a propaganda of fear. With defeat looming, the propagandists drew a nightmare vision of how peace might look. Germans were reminded of the official view that envious Britain had incited the war to crush competition from their commerce and industry. It wanted, they were told, 'to annihilate us so we never recover!'[126] 'World history' had 'proven again and again that England takes everything from her vanquished and treats the poor, robbed people just as slaves.'[127] Ragged Germans were shown being put to the plough or forced to labour in Entente colonies under brutal black guards. The suffering of Ireland under British rule was held up as a terrible warning of what the future would hold for a defeated Reich. The story of the Irish famine in the 1840s, closer to contemporaries than the First World War is to us, could be expected to resonate with malnourished, blockaded Germans. The British had turned Ireland, a 'once so blooming land', into a 'hunger state', and had 'taken around half of its inhabitants through murder, hunger and forced deportation'.[128]

Most emotively, the propaganda sought to reactivate the feelings of the national trauma of invasion in 1914. 'German land should, as once in East Prussia, be laid waste and destroyed' if the war effort slackened, the population was informed. The publicists called on the 'robbery, murder, arson and rape' that the north-easterly province had suffered to illustrate the consequences for the Reich if the enemy broke through.[129] A short film was also shot that drew on this recent history in order to advertise the Seventh War Loan. The drama showed a wealthy and contented farmer's family in East Prussia suddenly disturbed by the cry 'the Russians are coming'. As the staging directions explained:

> Cossacks and Russians rush like animals into the village, burning and laying waste to everything in their path – the terrified inhabitants want to save themselves from the sea of flames – but mercilessly the Cossacks throw them back into the blazing fire, pull women and children onto the road and pitilessly knock down all who approach them to plead . . . They pay

no attention to the whimpering women – the screams for help of following children echo unceasingly in the ears.

If Germans did not wish to see these scenes repeated in 1917, there was only one course of action: 'Yes, we must support our Fatherland with money!'[130]

By the autumn of 1917, the German and Habsburg regimes were in a deep crisis of legitimacy. The half-hearted attempts at constitutional reform during the first part of the year had failed, sabotaged by their leaders' reluctance, by entrenched interests in the Prussian *Landtag* and Hungarian parliament and by the tangle of conflicting ambitions nurtured by Austria's nationalities. Peace, the peoples' other demand, was also no closer to being realized. German leaders were set on an all-or-nothing gamble. The Third OHL's rise and Bethmann's dismissal had made their war aims even more expansive and inflexible. Austria-Hungary was dragged along in its ally's wake. Emperor Karl lacked the courage to try for a separate peace, and the Entente powers, as their response to his approach showed, were anyway no more interested than their opponents in a negotiated settlement. Yet even if the idea of a compromise peace was a chimera in 1917, the failure of the Central Powers' governments to respond adequately to popular desire for reform and relief jarred with the new *Zeitgeist* of Russian revolutionary fervour and Wilsonian idealism. The ideas from east and west of 'self-determination of peoples' and a 'peace without victory' were dangerously alluring. Against them, the Central Powers' barren cry of 'hold out!' could only provoke the question 'for what?'

For Germany's military leaders, there was no choice except to continue the war. In the generals' zero-sum view of international politics expansive gains were essential; the conflict itself had taught them that not only favourable frontiers but above all food security were necessary to defend the Reich in perpetuity. Internally, the Reichstag's growing power and the ever louder calls for greater democracy also encouraged expansionary aims. Germany's conservative elites saw their salvation from reform in, and staked their whole legitimacy on, achieving that victory. In Austria-Hungary, where material conditions were worse, society angrier and the crisis of legitimacy more acute, the regime failed to find an exit from the war, and its fate remained bound to that of

Germany. The Central Powers' decision to continue the fight despite the doubts, disappointment and even disaffection of a growing proportion of their peoples placed them on a course of almost inevitable disaster. Yet, at the end of 1917, when Lenin and his Bolshevik followers seized control in Russia and shortly afterwards took the country out of the war, it suddenly appeared that this high-risk strategy might just succeed.

12

The Bread Peace

BREST-LITOVSK

The war efforts of the Central Powers were reinvigorated when, in November 1917, the Bolsheviks launched their *coup d'état* in Russia and a few weeks later sued for an armistice. For German leaders, it was a triumph. The Reich had gone to war in 1914 in large part through fear of Russian rearmament and aggression. The country's earliest war-aims programme had stated that the behemoth to the east 'must be thrust back as far possible . . . and her domination over the non-Russian vassal peoples broken'.[1] The turmoil in Russia's interior and the dissolution of her army after its last failed offensive in Galicia in the summer of 1917 now made this almost utopian objective appear achievable. For Austria-Hungary, the Bolsheviks' peace request came as a lifeline. Emperor Karl and his Foreign Minister, Ottokar von Czernin, hoped that the cessation of hostilities in the east might lead to general peace. At the very least, they thought the resumption of trade might bring relief from the Empire's catastrophic food shortages and permit their regime to survive. However, the peace they negotiated in practice accelerated their Empire's demise. The Treaties of Brest-Litovsk with Ukraine and Russia brought political disaffection and social disaster to Galicia and by opening a way for revolutionary propaganda and new discontents also undermined the Habsburg army.

The armistice on the Eastern Front began on 15 December 1917 and one week later a peace conference between all four Central Powers, Germany, Austria-Hungary, Bulgaria and the Ottoman Empire, and the Bolsheviks opened in the town of Brest-Litovsk (today in Belarus), at the German Eastern Field Army's headquarters. For opinion at home and abroad, the Reich's Foreign Minister, Richard von Kühlmann, and his Habsburg counterpart, Czernin, at first assented to Bolshevik proposals for peace without annexations or indemnities, but only with reservations, the most important of which was that the western Allies must participate in negotiations. Kühlmann in particular was playing a clever game. He planned to subvert the right of national self-determination and, as he later explained, through it 'get for ourselves . . . whatever territorial concessions we absolutely needed'. The Germans had set up national councils in Poland, Courland, Lithuania and parts of Estonia. By strong-arming these councils to issue declarations seceding from Russia and either inviting German troops or proclaiming a wish for a close connection with the Reich, they were able with a veneer of legitimacy to prise these territories from Russia and draw them into Germany's orbit.[2]

The strategy was too subtle for the OHL. Ludendorff and Hindenburg were outraged, fearing that by conditionally agreeing to Bolshevik proposals, Kühlmann had renounced the chance to dictate peace. The Bolsheviks too did not get it, thinking they had won a diplomatic victory until General Hoffmann, the OHL's representative at the conference, explained to them that Russia was about to lose a lot of territory. What Kühlmann regarded as 'absolutely needed' filled a very long list. He himself wrote of 'detaching huge areas from the present Russia and building up those districts into effective bulwarks on our frontier', and the OHL was certainly not going to permit him to come away from the talks with anything less than their own objectives. In December 1917, Ludendorff wanted Lithuania, Courland, Riga and the nearby islands for the Reich 'so that we can feed our people'. Poland was to be tied to the Central Powers. Russia was to evacuate Finland, Estonia, Livonia, Bessarabia, Armenia and the eastern tip of Galicia still under its control. Her economy would be opened to Reich influence, she would pay compensation for her prisoners held in Germany, and would deliver grain, oil and other materials at favourable prices.[3]

The Germans forced through their demands. When, after an eleven-day intermission, the peace conference resumed on 9 January 1918, the western Allies had, as Kühlmann had foreseen, not replied, so he could argue that his conditional agreement in December to a peace with no annexations or indemnities was no longer binding. Leon Trotsky, who had come to lead the Bolshevik delegation, had no army capable of resisting the Germans. His only hope of staving off a humiliation was that revolution might break out in the Reich. The onset on 28 January of a huge peace strike in Berlin, organized by the new force in the labour movement, the revolutionary shop stewards under Richard Müller, and attracting 400,000 workers in the capital and tens of thousands more in Hamburg, Kiel and other industrial centres, stoked optimism. However, these strikes were quickly stamped out.[4] There was also no chance that the Reich's politicians would restrain its military; when an expansive treaty with Bolshevik Russia was eventually put before the Reichstag in March, the bourgeois parties that had supported the peace resolution eight months earlier all voted unhesitatingly for it, and even the SPD abstained.[5]

Trotsky played into Ludendorff and Hindenburg's hands by declaring 'no war, no peace' and storming out of the conference. The Third OHL wanted a firm finish to the war in the east, and had been itching to unleash the army again. Kühlmann had resisted, hoping rather wistfully that an agreement, however harsh, might avoid totally alienating Russia and permit future cooperation, but he was overruled by the Kaiser. German forces began rolling forward on 18 February, covering 240 kilometres in five days. On 3 March, Lenin and his colleagues in the Bolshevik Central Committee capitulated and signed a treaty even worse than the one they had earlier rejected. Ever since, its terms have been recounted with breathless horror. The Russian Empire lost around 2.5 million square kilometres of territory with 50 million inhabitants, 90 per cent of its coal mines, 54 per cent of its industry, and a third of its agriculture and railways.[6] However, these losses need to be put in context. The Treaty of Brest-Litovsk, had it stood, would have left Russia somewhat larger than it is today. The Bolsheviks deserve little sympathy, for they had insisted on national self-determination in the hope of destabilizing the Central Powers but ironically had instead themselves become the first to lose from the ideal: the treaty detached minority peoples, not ethnic Russians.[7]

The bulk of the wealth lost by the Russian Empire was in Poland and Ukraine, lands to which Russia's rulers, regardless of ideological persuasion, had no moral claim and whose peoples, especially the Poles, had suffered more than a century of Tsarist religious and political persecution.[8] The Germans were in no way idealistic or altruistic; pure self-interest and a desire for European hegemony shaped their policy at Brest-Litovsk. Nonetheless, for the populations of these territories, the power shift was an improvement on their previous plight. What was created was not a precursor to Hitler's empire of 1941, but instead was similar to the Soviet reorganization of east-central Europe into satellite states in 1945. Unlike Tsarist Russia, Germany was at least prepared to allow these peoples to build some of their own institutions, and already during the war was finding these a struggle to control, especially in Poland and Lithuania. Moreover, however exploitative and intrusive a Germany that emerged victorious from the First World War may have been, for Ukraine, falling into its orbit could scarcely have been worse than the future that awaited. Ukrainians under the Bolsheviks in the interwar period would suffer conflict, brutal collectivization and 3.3 million deaths from man-made famine.[9]

While the Germans had a good peace conference, the Austro-Hungarians were much less successful. Karl stressed to his Foreign Minister during negotiations that 'the whole fate of the Monarchy and dynasty depends on peace being concluded as quickly as possible'.[10] Czernin needed to secure food from the east for the starving Empire. He hoped to rein in German expansionism, fearing that it would prolong the war. He also wished to secure Poland for the Habsburgs, although this objective was less important than stopping hostilities. Czernin and his master's desperation for peace constricted the Habsburg room for negotiation. 'The peace with Russia *must* come about,' the Foreign Minister admonished his deputy at the start of the conference. '*Any eventuality is acceptable save the breaking off of the negotiations by the Central Powers.*' This stance was reinforced by subsequent events. The head of the Common Food Committee, General Ottokar Landwehr von Pragenau, warned at the start of January 1918 of the impending collapse of the food supply. What reserves were available in Hungary could not be transported to Austria because coal deliveries from German Silesia had dropped sharply. When on 14 January it was announced that the flour ration was to be halved, strikes broke out. They first flared just outside Vienna but then quickly spread across both halves of the Empire, encompassed 700,000 workers of all nationalities and lasted a full ten days. At the start of February, a mutiny broke out on ships at the naval base of Cattaro (Kotor, now in Montenegro). For three days, sailors had flown the red flag, demanded a peace without annexations and in the course of the mutiny killed an officer. To Habsburg leaders, it appeared the realm was on the brink of revolution.[11]

The Germans, who had judged the Bolsheviks' weakness correctly, were not going to budge from their expansive demands. Even Czernin's bluff of a separate peace failed to push them into a hasty and more moderate settlement. Hoffmann was unfazed, replying that it would permit the welcome release of twenty-five German divisions from the Habsburg sector of the Eastern Front. However, Czernin had another option. On 16 December 1917 a delegation from the Ukrainian People's Council, a nationalist government established after the March revolution smashed Tsarist authority, had arrived at Brest-Litovsk and asked to participate in the conference. For the Germans, this was good news as the group offered a publicity-friendly opportunity to detach Ukraine from Russia. For Austria-Hungary, the admission of the delegates to the talks was more double-edged. The Poles in the Warsaw Regency Council, established by the Central Powers in October 1917 to help govern the putative Polish state and provide legitimacy to its occupiers, feared their competing claims in the region would be disregarded and demanded representation. Habsburg Czech and South Slav representatives, testing the Central Powers' commitment to national self-determination, also unsuccessfully demanded entry to the talks. However, although it was ideologically problematic, Czernin grasped the chance of parleying with Ukrainians while Germans and Russians were at loggerheads. Ukraine, the breadbasket of the east, appeared to hold the key to the Empire's near fatal food supply problems.[12]

There is no more telling a mark of how far the Habsburg Empire had fallen than Czernin's readiness to appease the Ukrainians. The Ukrainian People's Council were upstarts, 'boys, scarcely more than twenty years old, people without experience, without property, without reputation, driven by adventure, perhaps megalomania'.[13] They were members of the country's tiny intelligentsia possessing no sway with the still mostly nationally indifferent peasantry in the countryside. It was not clear that the Council would be able to keep any promises it made or even whether it would be around long enough to try: the Bolsheviks had their own 'Workers' and Peasants' Government of the Ukrainian Republic' and in February their army briefly pushed into Kiev, assisted by the city's workers, before being thrown out by the Germans.[14] The Council's representatives were thus breathtakingly arrogant in demanding from the Habsburg great power eastern Galicia and Bukovina, and also the Chełm region, which until 1912 had been a part of Congress Poland. Remarkably, Czernin listened. He parried the claim on Habsburg territory, but he made humiliating concessions. He signed Chełm over to the National Council, and he even permitted interference in the Empire's own internal affairs, promising secretly that the Ruthenes' prewar demand for Galicia to be split into a western Polish and eastern Ukrainian Crownland would be realized. Both concessions, once they became public, would clearly alienate the Galician Poles, historically the most loyal of all the Empire's Slavic peoples, and destroy any lingering possibility of tying Congress Poland to the Habsburg Crown. For this immense cost, Czernin won a secret undertaking from the Ukrainians to supply at least one million metric tons of grain by 1 August. The treaty was signed on 9 February.[15]

Czernin's folly soon became apparent. The Germans quickly muscled in, established themselves at the centre of power in Kiev and confined Habsburg troops to just three of the land's nine provinces. The National Council predictably proved incapable of delivering what it had promised. Even after the Germans deposed it and set in place a leader who had the support of most Ukrainian landowners, the *Hetman* Pavlo Skoropadskyi, little was extracted. In the end, only 42,000 railway wagons carrying food, 18,000 of which went to Austria-Hungary, rolled westward. The grain delivered to all Central Powers totalled just 113,400 tons, just over half of which went to the Habsburg Empire and most of the rest to Bulgaria and the Ottoman Empire.[16] One of the German units tasked with extraction, the 224 Division, outlined the problems it faced. First, it asserted testily the food was 'simply not there'. The Central Powers had fallen victim to Ukrainian trickery and their own wishful thinking at Brest-Litovsk. Moreover, what food was available, reported the division, was not easy to get. The Ukrainian government was impotent and the Germans lacked the troops to organize a thorough extraction, and could not persuade the peasants to sell. A particular gripe with the division was the need to be friendly. 'With strictness, certainly by using weapons, really significant supplies might have been retrieved,' it argued. However, after the peace treaty this type of conduct was no longer practicable.[17] The German army was in fact fairly civilized in its dealings with Ukrainians, working with local authorities and, unlike its conduct at the outbreak of war, restraining itself from violence against civilians. Its Habsburg ally, by contrast, had learned nothing. Karl ordered his army to 'requisition with no remorse, even with violence'. Unlike the Germans, it saw no need for judicial process and in the early summer swift executions of people labelled as 'suspected robbers' or 'Bolshevik murderers' multiplied. Moreover, by setting up its own purchasing agencies in the territory, the Habsburg army also impeded the civil authorities tasked with food purchases.[18]

The Habsburg Empire had never ratified the Treaty of Brest-Litovsk with the Ukrainians, for to have tried to pass it through the Reichsrat would have meant revealing the secret clause promising a Ukrainian Crownland in eastern Galicia. The failure of the Ukrainian National Council to keep up its end of the bargain with food deliveries, and its replacement by the *Hetman*, enabled Austria-Hungary quietly to drop this clause. However, by this point the ill-effects of the peace made at Brest-Litovsk were already being felt. The March treaty with Russia ended the hard fighting on the Eastern Front but fatefully opened the way for the return of prisoners, who brought the soft poison of Bolshevism into the army. The February treaty with Ukraine provoked immediate and dramatic reactions. After the Germans published the treaty, the entire Regency Council in Warsaw immediately resigned in protest, as did the Habsburg military governor in Lublin, Count Szeptycki. On 15 February the Polish Auxiliary Corps, the remnants of the Polish Legions that had gone to war with Piłsudski in 1914, mutinied. A battle with Austro-Hungarian troops left many dead, but 1,600, including their commander, General Józef Haller, managed to defect to Russian lines. They would later form a core part of a new Polish army being prepared to fight with the western Allies in France.[19] Worst of all, however, was the reaction in Habsburg Galicia. Foreign Minister Czernin's disregard for Polish national interests at Brest-Litovsk finally divorced Polish society from the Habsburg cause.

GOODBYE GALICIA

The commitment of Galicia's Polish population to the Habsburg cause had waned since the heady days of 1914 and 1915, when the Polish political parties had established their Supreme National Committee and society had rallied around the Polish Legions. The Emperors' declaration of an independent Kingdom of Poland in November 1916 had been well received.[20] Thereafter, however, the mood had soured. There had been a political crisis in the summer of 1917 when two-thirds of the Polish Legionaries, by this point transferred to German control in occupied Congress Poland, had refused to swear an oath of loyalty set by the Central Powers to an as yet unknown future king of Poland and to promise 'loyal comradeship in arms with the armies of Germany and Austria-Hungary'. Piłsudski, whom the Germans rightly regarded as being behind the refusal, was imprisoned and the recalcitrant Legionaries interned.[21] In Galicia, the shabby treatment of a formation in which large swathes of Polish society had invested so publicly was bound to demoralize people, although few came out to protest against Piłsudski's arrest.[22] According to the Habsburg censor, social concerns were most pressing for the majority. By the autumn of 1917, letters were full of complaints about the 'unbearable conditions of living' and expressed 'increasing impatience' for 'speedy relief from the misery of the war'. Galicia was gripped by strikes in January 1918. When, in the spring, the authorities diverted food from Galicia to starving Vienna, they clumsily ensured that economic grievances in Galicia would peak simultaneously with the political shock from the treaty with Ukraine.[23]

The news that Chełm would go to Ukraine caused outrage in Galician society. The politicians of the Reichsrat's Polish Circle bitterly denounced the treaty. National Democrats and Socialists were especially scathing. Ignacy Daszyński, the leading Socialist light, declared 'the star of the Habsburgs [to have] gone out in the Polish sky'. The conservatives were at first more hesitant about a total break with the Monarchy, but the later revelation of the secret agreement to divide Galicia administratively between Ruthenes and Poles alienated them too. After fifty years of loyalism, Polish politicians had been pushed into opposition by Czernin's catastrophic diplomacy.[24] In sharp contrast to what was perceived as Habsburg betrayal, the Allies had raised their ideological bid for the Poles' support. The US President, Woodrow Wilson, had demanded a month earlier in his influential manifesto for a post-war world, the 'Fourteen Points', that 'an independent Poland should be erected which should include the territories inhabited by indisputably Polish populations, which should be assured a free and secure access to the sea, and whose political and economic independence and territorial integrity should be guaranteed by international covenant'.[25]

Among the Polish people of Galicia, there was also anger and a feeling of betrayal. 'For the blood and toil of our soldiers, for the despair and tears of our sisters and mothers, for agony, torment, for hunger and impoverishment, for the death of our best youth in the Legions they pay us with a *Fourth Partition of Poland*' raged one protest appeal. It caught the general feeling of disgust well.[26] A general strike was called by a united front of all Polish parties. The Polish peasant leader, Wincenty Witos, was still impressed with the public response when he recalled it two decades later. 'On this day, everything stopped completely all across Galicia,' he wrote in his memoirs. 'Work stopped in offices, factories, workshops . . . while in every city, town, village mass protest rallies took place.'[27] In Lwów, the day began with a Mass. The city's Progressive Jewish community showed solidarity, holding services in their synagogues. At the city's central symbolic points, the town hall and the statue of Poland's national poet, Adam Mickiewicz, stages had been erected and patriots harangued a 20,000-strong crowd. The release of Piłsudski and the interned Legionaries, the end of Prussian militarism, and separation from Austria were all demanded. The associations so important in Polish Galician civic society, the scouts, schools, *Sokół* gymnasts and elderly veterans of the 1863 uprising against Russia were all out in force. Senior officials and university professors also took part. The participation of peasants from the surrounding region was enthusiastically taken as proof of the unity of the entire Polish nation.[28]

Particularly ominous for Emperor Karl and his regime was the widespread participation of officials in the demonstrations. In the fortress town of Przemyśl, the district chief and his staff attended, while the city's bishop supported the protests with a sermon. In Cracow too, officials took part and in many smaller towns they helped to organize the protest. Ever since Galicia had received de facto autonomy in 1869, its Polish administration had been nationally minded, but before the war this had not been incompatible with dynastic loyalty. Now, however, the presence of officials at protests so explicitly anti-Habsburg and pro-independence was a sign that these allegiances were in opposition and that the Crownland's administration was separating from the state. The removal of Habsburg symbols and their replacement with Polish eagles was also a sign of a political shift at the grassroots level. Railway officials filed off the dynasty's crown on their cap badges. The public unscrewed Habsburg eagles from official buildings and symbolically hanged or burned them. In schools too a new age was starting. In class-rooms, the obligatory portraits of the Emperor were thrown out and replaced with pictures of Piłsudski, the man who represented the ideal of an independent and united Poland.[29]

Nowhere were protests against Brest-Litovsk more dramatic, violent or filled with symbolism than in Cracow. As the traditional heartland of loyalist conservatism and home to the Supreme National Committee, which from 1914 had attempted to realize the Austro-Polish solution desired by the dynasty, the city had particular reason to feel betrayed. News of the treaty reached Cracow on the day it was signed, 9 February 1918. The city's students already had a demonstration planned for 10 February in the marketplace in protest at the shooting of a school pupil in riots at Lwów at the beginning of the month. The reports from Brest-Litovsk turned this into a major event, with 10,000 people attending.[30] Thousands gathered in the following two days and attacked the city's German consulate. On 11 February around 500 people, about one-third of whom were students and schoolchildren, also attempted to rescue Polish Legionaries under Prussian escort at the city's railway station.[31] On 12 February the crowds confronted troops from a Ruthenian unit sent to pacify the city, and shots were fired in the main square, although nobody was injured.[32] With passions riding high, the protests in Cracow peaked on 13 and 14 February, when the crowds became so large and so violent that the police were forced to withdraw. Signs marked with the double-headed Habsburg eagle were defaced, removed or replaced with Polish eagles. Austrian medals were nailed to trees for people to spit at or hung around dogs' necks, and obscene caricatures were posted up in public depicting Kaiser Wilhelm II being hanged or wearing noth-ing but a spiked helmet.[33] The protest's focal point was in the main market. Up to October 1917, the Column of the Legions had stood here, testimony both to the Polish nationalism and Habsburg loyalism of the community. In February 1918 the marketplace became the site of a very different symbolism. A display of three paintings was set up. In the middle was a crucified Christ, and flanking him were pictures of Kaiser Wilhelm and Emperor Karl. Below was written 'Jesus Christ, never on the Cross were you in the company of such rascals.'[34]

Brest-Litovsk did not just snap the last threads of allegiance felt by Galician Poles for their monarch. Its failure to bring the promised flow of Ukrainian food also meant the continuation of a supply crisis that broke multi-ethnic central European society. National conflict and above all virulent anti-Semitism would stamp the region in the war's aftermath. While in many places this had roots in the pre-war period, its intensification and brutalization was a wartime product. In large part at the political level it stemmed from the new legitimacy conferred on 'national self-determination', and the expectations and disappointments this fuelled, from 1917. However, at the societal level, massive wartime deprivation, the result of total mobilization and British blockade, had a lasting and decisive impact on the ethnically mixed communities of east-central Europe. People withdrew for protection into their own ethnic groups, and as communities nationalized, Jews in particular came to be regarded less as unwanted neighbours than as malign foreign objects with no right to belong. Even in places where ethnic relations had been relatively harmonious in peacetime, understanding between different peoples collapsed.

The city of Cracow provides an excellent illustration of how twentieth-century conflict destroyed once thriving multi-ethnic communities. On the eve of war, Jews had made up one-fifth of its 183,000 inhabitants. The people had lived in the city since the thirteenth century. This long history contained episodes of discrimination and persecution. In 1495 they had been forced out of the city to Kazimierz, a place just south of the city's castle that became known as Cracow's Jewish district. There had been growing religious intolerance in the seventeenth century, and one Jew had been burned at the stake for blasphemy in 1663. Yet there had also been moments of unity, as in 1846 when revolution took hold of Cracow and the community sent 500 'Israelite Brothers' to the insurrectionists' army. By the early twentieth century, Cracow Jews were more likely than their co-religionists elsewhere to use Polish, and their political leadership was firmly integrationist and pro-Polish. They remained distinct, yet not separate citizens; while intermarriage between Jews and Gentiles was almost unheard of, they rubbed shoulders, traded and shared the municipality's lively popular press. As an indication of these harmonious relations, when anti-Semitic riots rocked western Galicia in 1898, Cracow had stood aloof. Jews had a special place in their hearts for the city. They identified closely with it and, although they possessed their own communal council, actively participated in the city's governance. In 1914 no fewer than twenty of the eighty-seven city councillors were Jewish.[35]

In the first years of the war, Cracow's Jews had participated in its Polish national and Habsburg loyalist 'double mobilization'. Several hundred had joined the Polish Legion. The unity of Cracow's citizens, regardless of faith, and the contribution of its Jews were symbolized by the inclusion of the arms of Kazimierz, the historic Jewish quarter, on the base of its Column of the Legions in 1915.[36] However, as food shortages and hardship gripped the city, the mood became less inclusive. Food prices spiralled; potatoes sold at five and flour at over fifteen times their pre-war prices at the end of the 'turnip winter' in February 1917. Jews, who were greatly over-represented among small traders and dominated key food industries in Galicia, above all milling, were widely suspected of hoarding and profiteering.[37] The city's first major hunger demonstration took place in March 1917. Although this and subsequent protests were directed at city authorities, the burgeoning anti-Semitic feeling was sufficiently obvious by May to prompt a suggestion that the Jewish community should set up a home guard to protect itself.[38] At the end of the year, there was a warning of what was to come when hunger demonstrators in the centre of town decided to march south on Kazimierz. They were stopped by police.[39]

It was in April 1918 that resentment finally broke out into open racial violence. Cracow was already in a state of militant turbulence. The January strikes and riots had caused 140,000 crowns of damage and ended with twenty-six policemen injured and sixty-three people arrested.[40] The protests over Brest-Litovsk in February had further stoked the inflammatory mood. Positive, violent action had replaced legality, and all faith in the authorities was gone. Class and ethnic grudges prevailed. An eavesdropped conversation between two women on a tram was indicative of people's attitudes. If the bread shortage continued, the women decided, 'we won't go to the town council or governor, we'll just demolish the shops where they sell cakes and rolls'. They resented Jewish neighbours for monopolizing black-market food supplies. Flour from Congress Poland was not to be had because 'the Jews ... buy it up for any price'.[41] The final collapse of Cracovian society, and of its relationship with political authority, fittingly came at a food market in the north of the city. Christian shoppers, bitter at the high prices and accusing Jews at the market of attempting to outbid them for the scarce goods, set off five days of anarchy in which the two communities clashed with each other and with the security services. The

Viennese press characterized the Christians' attack more or less accurately as 'a proper pogrom'.[42] On 16 April, the first day of clashes, several hundred protesting youths took the trouble to walk the twenty-five minutes from the north of Cracow to Kazimierz, plundering Jewish shops along the way while the police stood by. Attacks on Jewish property continued on the following day, and soldiers were ordered onto the streets. This calmed the city on 18 April, but there was further violence against the Jewish population on 20 April.[43]

The Cracow violence made a powerful impression well beyond the boundaries of Galicia, for the Austrian capital's newspapers quickly picked up on the story, which shocked and outraged Vienna's large and influential Jewish community. It was among the earliest in a series of pogroms that rippled across Galicia in the summer and would peak during the collapse of the Central Powers in the autumn of 1918.[44] It was also notable for other reasons, however. First, it was not only Christian resentments that translated into racial violence. On 19 April, when the north of the city was quiet, Jews in Kazimierz, enraged by the previous days' plundering and rumours that one of their own had been killed by Christian rioters, rose up. Christian traders at a flea market were attacked by over one hundred Jewish youths armed with sticks and iron bars.[45] Second, despite the animosity between Cracow's two communities at this stage of the war, they were united in their hatred of municipal and state security forces. Both Christian and Jewish crowds fought with soldiers: one reserve officer was chased around the city's main marketplace by youths on their way to Kazimierz on 16 April. Soldiers who attempted to help him were restrained by rioters.[46] On the next day, Habsburg soldiers opened fire on a crowd pelting them with stones, killing a fourteen-year-old boy and wounding three others.[47] In the Jewish quarter on 19 April, police and troops were also attacked by large crowds; one account even suggests that civilians there fired shots.[48]

The demise of Cracow's once thriving multi-ethnic community under the pressures of war was only the saddest example of collapse sponsored by the unmitigated hardship. By the summer Galicia was becoming ungovernable. The Cracow Military Command was spot on when it warned in May 1918 that 'it cannot be discounted that the masses, discontented by the long deprivation, viewing the flawed social and national structure of the state as the cause of the situation in which they find themselves, reject the state with these foundations and yearn for a social and national reform or revolution'.[49] In the cities, the mood was reported to be 'very excitable ... anti-dynastic and anti-Austrian'. Respect for the Monarchy had plummeted to the point where it was widely rumoured that Emperor Karl was a drunk, whose addiction was being exploited by his advisers to enact measures against the Poles.[50] The Galician countryside swarmed with tens of thousands of army deserters. These formed dangerous armed robber bands, contemptuous of the weak security services arrayed against them. They intimidated the gendarmerie. One post stationed near the town of Jarosław was left a note in Polish on the door of its headquarters warning 'Give us peace, and we'll also leave you in peace. Otherwise your life will be forfeit.' Anxiously, police authorities begged for help in fighting this 'deserter plague'.[51]

Galicia's torn multi-ethnic social fabric and anger at the regime were especially dramatic and violent, but they were not unique. Conditions in Croatia and Slavonia, another multi-ethnic shatter zone, were similar: armed bands stalked the countryside and within influential parts of the population ideas of separation and a universal wish for peace had become overwhelming during the spring and summer of 1918. Even in Bohemia and the Austrian heartlands, there were plentiful, if somewhat less totally anarchic, signs of social and political disintegration.[52] The Empire's major cities were again shaken by protests against food shortages and spiralling prices. Anti-Semitism was widespread, both because of the shortages and because many associated traditionally pro-Habsburg Jews with the now hated regime. In Bohemia, all that still united Czechs and Germans was what one report termed the 'anti-Jewish attitude in all classes'. Prague had a small anti-Semitic demonstration in May 1918.[53] In the Empire's capital, Vienna, anti-Semitic agitation by German nationalists and the Christian Social Party in parliament, public meetings and newspapers had been on the rise since the relaxation of censorship in mid-1917 and reached its peak in the summer of 1918. Not only the Galician refugees but all Jews had become their target. So bloodcurdling and frequent were the pogrom threats that at the end of July 1918 the city's Jewish representative body together with another 439 Jewish community councils from across the western half of the Empire finally broke their long silence and publicly protested. It made no difference. In Vienna, and across east-central Europe, the broken ethnic relations and virulent anti-Semitism that had formed through hunger and suffering would outlast the wartime ordeal and become more intense and radicalized in defeat.[54]

THE HABSBURG MILITARY

On the face of it, the Treaties of Brest-Litovsk should have been good for the Habsburg army. The force had sixty-three divisions at the start of 1918. Thirty-two infantry and twelve cavalry divisions were stationed on the Russian Front. Although mostly set marching eastward to secure Ukraine rather than being relieved and transferred, they were finished with heavy fighting. Whether the cessation of hostilities did much to raise morale is uncertain; Czechs at least feared that their soldier relatives would simply be sent to the Italian Front.[55] However, it did hold out the welcome chance to solve at a stroke the force's manpower problems, which had grown acute by the end of 1917. Some 2.1 million Austro-Hungarian prisoners of war in Russian hands would now be released and returned to their homeland. Conrad von Hötzendorf, who since his dismissal as Chief of the General Staff had been serving as Commander of the South Tyrol Army Group, now bombarded Habsburg military headquarters in Baden with new, grandiose schemes to vanquish the Italians.[56]

General Arthur Arz von Straussenburg, the man who replaced Conrad as Chief of the Habsburg General Staff in February 1917, had worked hard to renew the army since its catastrophe in the summer of 1916. The force's organization had been standardized, so that each infantry division had four regiments, each of three battalions. The regiments had been restructured to be more ethnically mixed, a measure intended to obstruct mass desertions. New equipment had become available. Each division now had twenty-four heavy and seventy-two light artillery pieces. Mortar and anti-aircraft batteries had been added. Infantry companies had received light machine guns and grenades.[57] Attention had also been given to morale and training. The army had sent officers to the Western Front to learn the new combined arms and initiative-led way of warfare. In March 1918 it had also emulated Ludendorff in establishing a propaganda organization, the Enemy Propaganda Defence Agency (*Feindespropaganda-Abwehrstelle*). The new organization was intended to combat war-weariness and Bolshevik and Western efforts to undermine troops' loyalty and performance. As in the German army, each division was ordered to appoint an education officer. The message was to be positive. Troops were encouraged to be grateful for the 'freedom and equality' guaranteed under the Habsburgs. The nationality disputes that the government in Vienna was incapable of solving were not to be mentioned. Instead, discipline, duty, and a vague state patriotism and dynastic loyalty were to be cultivated.[58]

While the Enemy Propaganda Defence Agency was set up too late and lacked personnel, funding and the genuine ideological appeal necessary to guide minds successfully, not all the army's efforts to reform were in vain. There were Habsburg formations in which 'best practice' in training and troop management equated to that found in their German ally. The 9th Mountain Brigade offers a good example. Its commander, the Pole Jan Romer, found a general malaise when he arrived at the unit in March 1918. In one regiment, Infantry Regiment 104, many of the soldiers were stunted products of starving Vienna. The other regiment, Infantry Regiment 117, was composed of Slovenes who were fitter but included in their ranks disaffected men and officers. All personnel were in urgent need of rest and many had developed frostbite or bronchitis from service in the Italian Alps. Romer set about raising their military value through a mix of traditional paternalism and a thoroughly modern training regime. He set for his officers a personal example of paternalistic care by inspecting the men's facilities and getting to know their wishes and problems, organizing extra food for them and improving their rest areas. Singing, games, pep talks and close attention by leaders to their troops' needs were all encouraged in order 'to awake in the soldier contentment and self-confidence'. The field instruction that Romer organized for his men was a world away from the clumsy, unsupported charges of the war's opening months or the misguided reliance on static fortifications found in 1916. The soldiers of 9th Mountain Brigade undertook combined-arms exercises with mortars, artillery and even aeroplanes. Romer, like Ludendorff, focused on developing the individual's fieldcraft and self-confidence. Tactical training was 'based as far as possible on concrete combat experiences', and live ammunition was used. Troops practised shooting, grenade throwing, bayonet fighting and negotiating obstacle courses.[59]

Even if the Habsburg army, or at least parts of it, was more capable of learning than has been recognized, it still faced very serious problems. As on the home front, there were materiel shortages. Munitions and arms production were plummeting. The attempt to participate in the Hindenburg Programme at the start of 1917 proved a huge error, for to meet the targets, steel and iron had to be diverted from maintaining the transport system. This exacerbated an already severe shortage of rolling stock and led to lowered train speeds and haulage capacity and congestion. Coal could not be delivered to the armaments factories. Added to this, the efficiency of exhausted and starving blast-furnace workers had dropped by a third. Building up ammunition stocks was therefore an impossibility.[60] Clothing troops was also becoming more difficult. The practice of giving soldiers a spare pair of boots had to be stopped. Tunics, trousers and greatcoats were all in short supply. As for troops' rations, the best that could be said was that they were only marginally less meagre than those of civilians. The army's daily individual flour ration stood at 283 grams in April 1918, down from 500 grams a year earlier. While the supply system would totally break down only in the second half of the year, the troops were already threadbare and hungry.[61]

In part as a consequence of these miserable conditions, the army had been battling a desertion epidemic since the autumn of 1917. Conrad, who reported in September that desertions to the enemy had nearly tripled, blamed agitation on the home front and the poor example for discipline set by Emperor Karl's amnesty for political prisoners of July 1917. Conrad also regarded military reforms in discipline and organization as part of the problem. Harsh discipline had always been a key pillar supporting the motivation of Habsburg troops. The force executed 754 of its own soldiers during the war, more than the French (600 executions), the British (346 executions), and far more than the Germans, who enacted the death penalty on a mere forty-eight men.[62] Moreover, the Habsburg army not only punished minor crimes by leaving men tied for hours to a tree or post – like the British and, up to 1917, the Germans – but also went a step further in manacling petty offenders hand and foot. However, in July 1917, Habsburg military courts and commanders had lost their right to confirm death sentences.[63] Tying up and manacling had also been abandoned at Karl's express order, withdrawing, in Conrad's somewhat exaggerated phrasing, 'every reliably effective means of punishment'. The former Chief of the

General Staff was on firmer ground when he complained about the counter-productive consequences of mixing men from unreliable ethnicities into loyal regiments. While this strategy permitted the close supervision by loyal troops of distrusted Czechs, Serbs, Ruthenes and Romanians, it risked worsening their alienation: 'In the midst of foreign-speaking soldiers, where in many cases the officer is also not capable of speaking their language, such elements naturally soon feel isolated, embittered and flee at the first opportunity to the enemy.'[64] Conrad's deep concern was entirely justified. In the first quarter of 1918, the Hungarians alone were searching for 200,000 absconded soldiers.[65]

The return of Austro-Hungarian prisoners from Russian captivity further damaged the army's discipline. These men had been exposed to extensive propaganda throughout their captivity. The Tsarist regime had resolved in August 1914 to separate prisoners by ethnicity, keeping Slavs, who were regarded as potentially friendly, in European Russia while banishing irredeemably hostile Germans and Hungarians to Siberia. Later years saw illegal and largely ineffectual attempts to recruit national units from prisoners or, in the case of Serbs and Italians, to transfer them abroad for service in 'their' national armies. Only in the case of the Czechs was there some success; the Tsarist army had used a small number of Czech prisoners of war for intelligence tasks, and after the first revolution the Russian Provisional Government had expanded recruitment, fielding in July 1917 a three-regiment Czech Legion in eastern Galicia. This ultimately reached a strength of 40,000 men, and deepened the distrust of Habsburg authorities for their Czech population and soldiers.[66]

However, in early 1918 what preoccupied the Habsburg military was the fear that returning prisoners might bring back with them not national ideals (of which plenty were already circulating in the Empire) but Bolshevism. Lenin had the same expectation: 'Hundreds of thousands of prisoners of war,' he later gloated, 'returned to Hungary, Germany and Austria, and made it possible for the bacilli of Bolshevism to deeply penetrate into these countries.'[67] The Bolsheviks had been agitating among foreign prisoners of war since the second half of 1916. Worryingly for the Habsburg army, Hungarian and German prisoners, ethnic groups it usually regarded as dependable, had proven to be particularly receptive, in part because the miserable conditions in which the Tsarist army kept them spawned resentment. The propaganda had become especially intense once the Bolsheviks seized power. Leaflets and journals published in their own languages introduced prisoners to Lenin's ideas. Leftist captives collaborated in the agitation, and formed in January 1918 the All-Russian Prisoners of War Committee. The Hungarian Béla Kun, who would lead a short-lived Communist regime in Hungary in 1919, was one of the leading prisoner-agitators, urging each comrade returning home to 'be the master teacher of revolution in your divisions. Tell your brethren . . . that only the revolution can save us all from destruction.'[68]

Habsburg military commanders were determined to prevent this message from reaching their demoralized soldiers and weary and angry populations on the home front. The flow of returning prisoners began in December 1917, soon after the Bolshevik coup, and had already reached half a million by the time a final agreement on prisoner exchange had been signed at the end of June. To receive them, the Austro-Hungarian army established a quarantine system. After ex-prisoners were liberated in Ukraine, where a third were imprisoned, or met at the border, they were given a medical inspection and deloused. They were then held in a camp for between ten days and three weeks, where they restarted drill and military training. Ideally, they would have been fed well and issued new uniforms, but dearth meant that rations were poor and the ambition to give each returnee a new tunic was soon lowered to a new cap and then dropped further to the point where military authorities were issuing an armband or cockade on civilian clothing. Once confirmed to be physically and ideologically sound, prisoners were transferred to training units, where the circumstances surrounding their captivity were checked and deserters filtered out. Only after the men had passed through this ordeal were they finally given what all longed for after often years away: four weeks of home leave.[69]

The army's fear of Bolshevism was understandable but its reaction was counter-productive; as with its arrests and imprisonments without trial across the Empire in 1914, unjustified blanket suspicion led to coercion that alienated previously loyal men. Letter censorship reports had in fact uncovered little radical socialism. Czech and Polish prisoners were most disgruntled with the Empire, but they tended to express their grievances in national terms. Most other captives just felt miserable and abandoned.[70] The army's treatment of them accentuated these feelings. There was no welcome home; instead, the men found themselves thrown into an impersonal and mechanistic processing procedure. The army disregarded their suffering and, by incarcerating them once again in camps, did nothing to help them adjust. Some had developed what contemporaries called 'Barbed Wire Disease' during their long years of imprisonment, a psychiatric illness whose symptoms included irritability and problems with concentration.[71] Others had been through extraordinarily traumatic experiences. Returnees captured in 1914 had been fortunate to survive a typhus epidemic that had raged through Russian camps in the war's first winter. Others, mostly Hungarians and Austrian Germans, had been set to work on the Tsar's own death railway, built to carry Entente supplies from Murmansk to the interior. Around 25,000 prisoners, 40 per cent of the men who laboured on this project, had died through exposure and exhaustion in temperatures as low as −35°C.[72] Finally, former prisoners were not prepared for the deprivation in Austria-Hungary. With dreams of home fixed in the pre-war world, many were shocked and demoralized by the impoverishment and exhaustion of their families. The intense suspicion and blithe expectation that they would soon return to combat also alienated the returnees. To be so 'distrusted, bullied and scoffed at' was, observed one ex-prisoner angrily, a 'disappointment and bitter awakening'.[73]

The trouble that swept through the Habsburg training units in the first half of 1918 actually owed far more to the army's insensitivity and the unwillingness of exhausted ex-prisoners to be sent back into combat than to Bolshevik indoctrination. Between the end of April and mid-June, there were thirty mutinies by returning prisoners.[74] Mostly, these were small spontaneous actions provoked by poor food, grievances over leave, or reluctance to join march battalions destined for the front. However, there were also larger-scale incidents, starting with complaints about the army but soon manifesting national or social grievances and racial antagonisms. Slovenian soldiers, long regarded as the most loyal of all the Empire's South Slavs, were responsible for three major outbreaks of violence. Among the most violent was that which took place in Judenburg, Styria, where returned prisoners led 1,200 men in the draft battalion of Infantry Regiment 17 on a night of plunder and destruction. The officers' mess and local barracks were vandalized, shops looted, and the town's railway station was attacked and its priest intimidated. Two mutineers, four other soldiers and a female civilian were killed. Hunger, anger towards officers and drunkenness all contributed to the disorder. The men also had poorly thought-out but genuine political wishes. One of the ringleaders articulated their motivations at the start of the mutiny. 'Come on lads, get dressed,' he had appealed to his comrades in barracks. 'We're going home. We're doing it not just for us but as a favour to the comrades at the front. The war has to be ended now . . . Whoever's a Slovene should come with.'[75]

The Habsburg Empire should have stood triumphant in the early summer of 1918. It had outlasted the autocratic regime of the Tsar that in peacetime had so publicly hoped for its collapse and dismemberment. Moreover, the external irredentist threats that had so frightened Austro-Hungarian leaders before the war had been eliminated. Serbia and the south of Poland were under occupation, a favourable treaty had been signed with Romania in May 1918 and the Italians were in abeyance after their heavy losses the previous autumn in their rout at Caporetto. There was no reason to continue fighting. Yet neither Emperor Karl nor Czernin ever considered a separate peace. The Habsburg Foreign Minister argued later that any such action would have led to German troops in Tyrol turning on the Empire and civil war at home.[76] Whether the Germans could really have afforded the men in 1918 for an occupation of Austria-Hungary is doubtful. However, by sticking to their ally, Habsburg leaders guaranteed that any victory by the Central Powers would leave their Empire as nothing more than a German satellite. Another step along this course was taken in May when, after the French publicly revealed his secret peace approach through Prince Sixtus a year earlier, Karl had to pacify his angry allies and indignant Austrian German elites. A humiliating trip to prostrate himself at German army headquarters at Spa and the signing of a provisional agreement on a long-term military, economic and political alliance laid bare to the world the subjection of the Habsburg state.[77]

The war therefore continued, against the interests of the Empire and the will of the mass of its peoples. The Poles were irredeemably alienated by the Habsburg readiness to sacrifice the Chełm region to their Ukrainian rivals for a fantasy 'bread peace'. The Czechs had given up on the Empire's ability to reform itself. The strikes of January 1918 had demonstrated the deep desire for peace across all Emperor Karl's lands. Multi-ethnic society had already fragmented, and racial hatred divided its peoples. The army too was crumbling. Bolshevik ideals and, still more, the deep disgruntlement of ex-prisoners were undermining discipline, and the exodus of deserters had not been stemmed. The shifting of military bases, so that troops were stationed in areas foreign to them, cynically exploited the bitter animosities between the Empire's peoples to ensure temporarily that civilians and soldiers would not, as in Russia, unite in revolution.[78] Nonetheless, the end was coming, but its form and its horror were now no longer in the hands of the Habsburg Monarchy. These would depend on events further west, and on the Germans.

13

Collapse

LAST CHANCE

At the beginning of 1918, a Central Powers' victory still appeared to many contemporaries to be attainable. Colonel Albrecht von Thaer, a General Staff officer close to Ludendorff, summarized the reasons for optimism as he looked into the New Year. 'Since the start of the war,' he mused, 'our situation was really never so good. The military colossus Russia is totally finished and pleads for peace; the same with Romania. Serbia and Montenegro have simply gone. Italy is still supported only with difficulty by England and France and we stand in its best province. England and France are still ready for battle but already much exhausted (above all the French) and the English are very much under pressure from the U-boats.' The sole trump card in the Western Allies' hands was the United States, and Thaer seriously doubted the ability of this primarily maritime power to swing the balance on the crucial Western Front.[1] Nonetheless he disregarded the German army's own very serious problems. The force had passed the peak of its strength and in the previous year had shown signs of weariness and indiscipline. Above all, as the OHL was painfully aware, time was against it. Across the Atlantic, a mighty American army was in training and the U-boats' record gave little cause for hope that it might be stopped from crossing the ocean. The war had to be won before the Americans arrived in Europe. 'All that mattered,' Ludendorff recalled, 'was to get together enough troops for an attack in the West.'[2]

The stakes could not have been higher. After the failure of German and Austro-Hungarian leaders to push through half-hearted political reforms or make peace in 1917, the regimes' legitimacy now rested solely on their ability to win a quick and total victory. The defeat of Russia had bought them a little breathing space. To many Germans, fighting on now appeared to offer a real chance of a rapid and happy conclusion.[3] In Austria-Hungary, peoples watched and waited for what events in the west would bring. Yet although the German army could now transfer units from the defunct Eastern Front and build a numerical superiority in the west, forcing a military decision there would be difficult. Not only were the British and French formidable opponents but it was hard to know how to defeat them. The Social Democrat Philipp Scheidemann voiced the problem most perceptively in a speech to the Reichstag Steering Committee in January 1918. 'Suppose,' he argued, 'we were to take Calais and Paris ... suppose such a breakthrough was completely successful, would that mean peace?' On past experience, he doubted it very much. 'We have overrun entire states, we have chased hostile governments from the land and yet we still have no peace.'[4] Finding a solution to this conundrum was the pivotal task of the OHL. Failure would collapse the last prop supporting the Central Powers, making inevitable not only defeat but also revolution.

Ludendorff had already begun to ponder a western offensive in October 1917. The U-boats had not fulfilled the navy's promises and although the two most important army group commanders on the Western Front, German Crown Prince Wilhelm and Crown Prince Rupprecht of Bavaria, doubted that the German army could win a decisive operational victory, the training of a large American army overseas meant that inactivity was not an option. As the OHL's Chief of Operations, Major Wetzell, had stressed on 23 October, an offensive would have to be launched if the Germans were not to be crushed by sheer weight of numbers.[5] With the Russian army's collapse, the Bolshevik revolution and Lenin's armistice at the end of the year, troops could be transferred westwards and the possibility of securing a decisive victory in the west gained in plausibility. German commanders debated the merits of attacking the British or French and drew up detailed operational plans for offensives at different parts of the line. For the Chief of Staff of Crown Prince Wilhelm's army group on the Western Front, Colonel Count von der Schulenburg, an assault on the French offered the best prospect of victory. The Germans were aware of the demoralization and mutinies that had wracked the Republic's army the previous summer.

The French home front was also in a parlous state: inflation was higher than in the Reich and worker militancy rising.[6] Schulenburg doubted that France could survive another severe military defeat. However, for Ludendorff and other military commanders, the British appeared the more vulnerable. Their force was regarded as tactically clumsier than its ally. An intelligence assessment drawn up at the start of 1918 rated British units' level of training as inadequate for mobile warfare and observed that after their setbacks in 1917 much of the troops' confidence was gone: 'There is a great deal of war weariness.'[7]

Ludendorff chose the right enemy, but not wholly for the correct reasons. The British would indeed make disastrous tactical errors in the spring of 1918 and their command structure, hard-wired for static warfare, did break down in the rapidly changing environment produced by mobile war. However, the Germans underestimated the rank and file's toughness, which did much to compensate for the failure of leadership and tactical skill.[8] The real vulnerability of the British Expeditionary Force was logistical. All armies on the Western Front required extensive railway systems to keep them supplied, but the network behind British lines was barely adequate. It possessed two choke points, the forward marshalling and switching yards in the French towns of Hazebrouck and Amiens. Through each passed around half of the supplies dispatched from Britain: Hazebrouck, situated around 30 kilometres behind the line in the north, channelled materials that came through the ports of Boulogne, Dunkirk and Calais. Amiens, 60 kilometres behind the British southern sector's front, helped distribute goods from Rouen, Le Havre and Dieppe, and also handled 80 per cent of north–south traffic along the line. Any German advance would have had to be deep, but the reward for capturing these key rail nodes would have been immense. The loss of Amiens would have cut two of three double-tracked railways over the Somme, leaving the British a transport capacity of only ninety trains per day, fewer than half the total needed to sustain the heaviest fighting. Were Hazebrouck to fall too, the British position on the continent would be untenable. Their commanders were painfully aware of this danger. General Sir Henry Rawlinson, the co-planner of the 1916 Somme Offensive and commander of Fourth Army from July 1918, warned that Amiens was 'the only [place] in which the enemy can hope to gain such a success as to force the Allies to discuss terms of peace'.[9]

The OHL never recognized this potentially fatal vulnerability. Ludendorff's strategy focused on psychology rather than on territory. He refused to designate any final ground objectives. To subordinates who urged him to do so, and thereby clarify what the offensive was supposed to achieve, he retorted that 'In Russia we always merely set an intermediate objective, and then discovered where to go next.'[10] This was revealing: Russia had collapsed not in 1915, when it had lost large swathes of territory and prize towns like Warsaw and Łódź, but in 1917 through a crisis of morale. Ludendorff's intention was to break the British army's cohesion and will. The unwieldy enemy would be incapable of coping with the fast pace of mobile operations and would be torn apart by the constant pressure of the attack. What was important to Ludendorff was thus the initial breakthrough to restore movement rather than where the troops were headed. For this reason, the operation was constructed entirely around tactical needs. After considering many plans, the First Quartermaster General opted to attack south of the British line, on a front of 80 kilometres on either side of the Somme. The ground was firm here in the early spring, unlike further north in waterlogged Flanders, and the British had only recently taken over the lines on the left bank of the river, which the former French garrison had left weakly fortified. Manpower shortages had forced the BEF's High Command to make hard compromises. While the armies protecting the Channel ports were strong, the British Fifth Army guarding the south of the area that Ludendorff had designated for the attack had only twelve infantry and three cavalry divisions to cover 68 kilometres. Each division's front was a third longer than the norm for other British armies. The sector was ripe for a breakthrough, yet there was a catch: the British were weak here precisely because there were no key objectives to defend. Ludendorff might hope to tear them from the French, but his troops would be advancing into the desolation left by the Somme battle of 1916 and their own withdrawal in early 1917.[11]

The preparations for the great offensive were unprecedentedly thorough. Over the winter of 1917–18 the Germans transferred forty-eight divisions to the Western Front from other theatres, mainly Russia, raising their strength there to 191 against their enemies' 178 divisions.[12] The Seventeenth, Second and Eighteenth Armies, the forces tasked with executing what was codenamed Operation Michael, together had sixty-seven divisions. The artillery support for the attack was formidable:

6,473 guns and 3,532 trench mortars would lay down the initial bombardment. To serve them, huge munitions dumps were created. The Eighteenth Army alone stockpiled nearly three million shells. Naturally, given the central position of tactics in the offensive's design, great care was taken over training and the organization of manpower. Resources would not stretch to equipping all divisions equally, so the army was divided. Most divisions were classed as 'trench divisions', suitable for position warfare. However, fifty-six elite 'assault divisions' were tasked with spearheading the attacks, and were allocated the pick of weaponry, specialist units, horses and the youngest, fittest soldiers. Each of these divisions was taken out of the line and given four weeks of instruction. A new manual, *The Attack in Position Warfare*, was issued to explain to an army inured to fighting on the defensive how the cooperation between different arms, initiative and delegation promoted fervently for elastic defence since the Somme battle of 1916, could also be applied to offensive action.[13]

A great effort was made to surprise and deceive the enemy. The OHL permitted troops to march only at night to the attack sector. An elaborate and successful misinformation campaign was launched to trick the French into believing that the assault would be conducted against them north of Verdun or in the Champagne.[14] The Germans also made a start on demoralizing the British. One leaflet scattered across British lines bluntly asked the soldiers 'What are you fighting for?' The Tommies, it pointed out, had no interest in shedding blood to recapture 'foreign places of no earthly use to England'. The Russians, Romanians and Montenegrins had all quit, 'ingrate Belgians' expected others to liberate their country for them, and 'the Frenchies', claimed the German propagandists, continued solely in order to seize Alsace-Lorraine. Disingenuously, they insisted, 'all the world knows that the Germans never mean to keep any part of France'. No help could be expected from fickle Americans, who were now claiming that 'another year or two must pass before the big army they promised . . . can reach France'. At the current pace, it would be 'six months at least to reach Cambrai . . . eight years to Mons, sixteen years to Brussels, thirty-two years to Antwerp, sixty-four years to Cologne, and 132 years to Berlin. It was, mocked the propagandists, 'a far longer way to Berlin evidently than to Tipperary'.[15]

On the eve of the offensive the morale of German troops was high, yet fragile. After the tough fighting in the autumn of 1917, the Bolshevik revolution and armistice had raised spirits. By January 1918 there was consensus in the ranks that Russia was 'finished' and many soldiers began to hope for an end to hostilities. The strikes at home in that month were roundly condemned by most men at the front, who saw them as likely to prolong the war and steel the enemy. Instead, they saw their road home in front of them – leading through the British barbed wire. As the Fifth Army's postal censor observed, troops were ready 'to confront the enemy for the last great blow', but their willingness was highly conditional: the effort would be made 'if through it the longed for peace will be reached'.[16] What would happen if the attacks did not bring peace was barely considered, but in March 1918, on the eve of the offensive, few thought this likely. Troops were impressed with the sight of, in one diarist's words, '[supply] column after column, munitions deliveries day and night, deployment of guns, especially mine throwers, lorries . . . bringing all sorts of material'.[17] Better rations for the assault force in the final weeks before the offensive also raised morale. The atmosphere, one officer remembered, was one of 'firm confidence in a good success'.[18]

The offensive's preliminary bombardment opened at 4.20 a.m. on 21 March. For five hours the German guns threw 1,160,000 shells into the positions of the British Fifth and Third Armies, battering the front line and suppressing the opposing artillery with gas. At 9.40 a.m. the infantry of thirty-two German divisions charged forward in thick fog, following a creeping barrage that kept down the heads of any British troops still capable of resistance. While in the north the defenders resisted hard, the southern sector of the front quickly crumbled. The Fifth Army had organized its positions in what it believed to be a German-style elastic defence scheme. Outposts in a lightly held Forward Zone were supposed to inflict casualties and hold off attackers, winning time to man a strongly fortified Battle Zone in the rear, out of the range of any opening bombardment. However, on 21 March dense fog allowed German assault troops to infiltrate and surround the forward positions. The British had not gathered sufficient reserves and held what they had too far back, so with no hope of relief, positions that had been expected to hold for two days soon surrendered. On this first day alone the Germans took 21,000 men as prisoners, and inflicted 7,512 killed and 10,000 wounded. The three attacking armies overran 255 square kilometres of ground, forced the British from their Forward Zone and, in its weakly fortified south, also pushed the Fifth Army out of most of its Battle Zone.[19]

Nonetheless, the offensive had not gone as planned. Seventeenth Army, the northernmost of the German forces, was supposed to provide the main weight for the attack, punching towards Arras and Albert, and then with its neighbour, Second Army, separating British from French forces and rolling the former up in the direction of the Channel. It had committed sixteen of its eighteen divisions yet had advanced only four to five kilometres into well-defended territory and was stuck in front of the British Third Army's Battle Zone. The Eighteenth Army, whose task was to guard the assault forces' left flank on the Somme River, had attacked the weakest point and advanced the furthest. Ludendorff opted to build on its success and dispatched reinforcements. This was a fateful decision. At first, it appeared fully vindicated by the spectacular advances over the following days. By 23 March the Kaiser, who had been plunged into depression by the stoppages in the north, was exuberant. 'The battle is won,' he gloated, 'the English have been utterly defeated.'[20] In the ranks too the men were euphoric, boasting proudly to friends and family of having helped 'thrash Tommy's hide'.[21] When the offensive was closed down on 5 April, the troops of Eighteenth Army had advanced 60 kilometres from their jump-off points – an achievement greater than any seen in the west since 1914. The British Fifth Army had been shattered. Some 90,000 Allied troops had surrendered, among them 75,000 British, and 1,300 artillery pieces had been captured.[22]

Impressive though these figures were, they had only a marginal bearing on the strategic situation. The British replaced most of their losses: already by the end of Operation Michael, over 100,000 drafts had been sent across the Channel to refill the BEF's depleted ranks.[23] Critically, Ludendorff's earlier dismissal of calls to define a strategic objective cost the army, for it permitted damaging indecision and misguided opportunism. On 23 March as the Kaiser was toasting victory, Ludendorff dissipated his force's strength by ordering his three armies to attack north-west, west and south-west in an overambitious attempt to separate the French and British, destroy the British and eliminate the French reserves. He repeated the error on 26 March with an order for two new attacks further north. Amiens could have fallen had the Germans recognized its significance early and concentrated troops on it. When the city was belatedly designated an objective on this day, their advance guard came within just 11 kilometres, but French reinforcements and fierce British resistance thwarted attempts to seize it. The Germans thus won nothing of value from Operation Michael. British resistance had been supported by promptly dispatched French reinforcements and had not been broken. The 3,100 square kilometres overrun were worthless: the Seventeenth, Second and Eighteenth Armies sat in a wasteland with their supply lines grossly overextended.[24] Their casualties had been horrendous, totalling nearly 240,000 irreplaceable men killed, missing or wounded. Losses had been especially heavy among experienced officers and in the elite assault divisions. In some attacking units two-thirds of the infantry had been wiped out.[25]

Ludendorff retained the initiative and sought to keep the Allies off balance. An offensive in Flanders codenamed Operation George had been considered as an alternative to Michael, and although the region had been ruled unsuitable for an early attack owing to its waterlogged soil, preparations had continued through January. The First Quartermaster General now ordered that it go ahead. The heavy fighting in March forced its scale to be cut back, and to reflect this its name was changed to Georgette, but even so it remained dangerous. The two German armies ordered to attack, the Fourth and Sixth Armies, had twenty-eight divisions and were supported by 1,199 field guns, 971 heavy guns and forty super-heavy guns. Facing them were just eight British divisions and one tired and demoralized Portuguese division. In contrast to Michael, the operation was targeted at a worthwhile objective, the railway centre of Hazebrouck. When the offensive opened at 4.15 a.m. on 9 April, it at first achieved considerable success. After a heavy bombardment, German storm troops advanced in thick fog and immediately broke the Portuguese division. By the evening, they had gained 10 kilometres. The advance continued over the following days and on 12 April the Germans came within 6 kilometres of Hazebrouck, but could not capture it. Ludendorff bore much of the blame, for, as in March, he dissipated his force's strength by failing to stick to a single objective. On 12 April, when all effort should have been directed towards Hazebrouck, he ordered troops to take the town of Bailleul.[26]

The failure of Operation Georgette was not solely the result of mistakes made by the High Command. The troops were exhausted. Among the thirty-six divisions made available for the attack, twenty-seven had fought in the Michael offensive and the others were trench units.[27] Infantry strengths were low: the divisions each had around 6,000 men. Each was also at least 500 horses short, hampering mobility.[28] Most ominously, there were clear signs of burgeoning despair in the ranks. By the end of April, the optimism with which troops had started the offensive was gone and in exasperation they were wishing that this 'wretched war soon ends'.[29] Senior commanders recognized the shift in mood. General Hermann von Kuhl, the Chief of Staff of Army Group Crown Prince Rupprecht, worried on 18 April that 'the troops appear to be finished'.[30] Colonel Thaer, whose IX Reserve Corps had taken part in Georgette, was also disturbed. Soldiers' exaggerated expectations for the outcome of the spring offensive were, he thought, to blame for the depression. 'They had too much hope that this great blow in March would end the war,' he observed ruefully. 'Thereupon, they had once more summoned together all their courage and all their energy. Now the disappointment is here, and it is great. It is the main reason why even attacks well prepared with artillery fizzle out as soon as our infantry goes beyond the heavily bombarded zone.'[31]

With the failure of Operation Georgette to break the British, the German offensives passed into their final phase. Ludendorff hoped to attack again decisively in Flanders, but he first needed to draw off the Allied reserves there. To do so, he opted for a diversionary assault on the French army on the Chemin des Dames. The new offensive was the ultimate demonstration of both German tactical virtuosity and strategic bankruptcy. Guns, engineers and specialist units were moved secretly south from Flanders, marching at night to avoid detection from the air. The artillery, its 1,158 batteries almost four times as numerous as those pitched against them, registered without alerting the enemy. When it opened a barrage at 2 a.m. on 27 May, surprise was total. The infantry, men of the Seventh Army, going forward at daybreak quickly overwhelmed all defences and pushed as far as 22 kilometres in a single day; the largest advance of the war on the Western Front.[32] There was no way the Germans could win any decisive victory in this region, but Ludendorff again chose to expand the attack. His troops reached the Marne, raising anxious memories of 1914 for the Entente and causing panic in Paris, just 70 kilometres distant. Another offensive in June 1918 pushed out a little way the exposed salient the Germans had created. By now, however, the game was up. Not only were further advances strategically bereft, but at last the Allies also had the measure of their opponents tactically. The Germans' final offensive in the Champagne on 15 July was betrayed by prisoners and halted only days after its opening by an effective French elastic defence. On 18 July the first of the Allied counter-offensives was launched that over the autumn would push the Germans back almost to their own border. Two French armies of twenty-four divisions, backed by 2,000 guns and 750 tanks, suddenly advanced. Some 17,000 surprised and weary German soldiers had surrendered three days later and at the end of the month their army evacuated the indefensible salient. The tide had turned.

DEFEAT

The German army was doomed by the summer. More far-sighted commanders recognized the French counter-offensive on the Marne to be, as General Hermann von Kuhl put it, 'the turning-point of the war'.[33] Another great attack, this time launched by the British on 8 August outside Amiens, confirmed that the Allies now held the initiative. In one of the greatest set-piece battles of the war, ten infantry divisions and 552 tanks supported by 2,060 guns surprised and broke through the German Second Army outside Amiens. The attackers advanced nearly 13 kilometres and took 15,000 German prisoners and 450 guns. For the rest of August and the first half of September hammer blows coordinated by Marshal Ferdinand Foch, the Supreme Commander of the Allied Armies on the Western Front, rained down on different parts of the German line. On 26 September a general Allied offensive began along the entire Western Front. By the armistice on 11 November the Allied armies had advanced up to 160 kilometres.[34] Germany's army was a mere shadow of its former self at the war's end. Casualties since the start of the Allied counter-offensive in mid-July had totalled 800,000 soldiers. Just 750,000 infantrymen were still at the front, what one General Staff officer called 'a spider's web of fighters'.[35] While elite machine-gunners continued to inflict heavy losses on Allied attackers, German rifle units were universally reported to be depleted, half-trained, exhausted and despondent. Propelled inexorably towards the Reich's frontier, without hope of relief or reinforcement, these men had no chance of preventing an invasion of their homeland.[36]

The startling swing in the strategic situation owed much to the Allied forces' superior numbers. The German army's strength had gone into freefall during its offensives. Between March and the end of July it had suffered 977,555 casualties. Some had recovered from their wounds and returned to the front, but a lack of new recruits meant that many of the dead and severely wounded could not be replaced, and the western Field Army had shrunk by 300,000 men.[37] In the same period over a million American troops had arrived in Europe. Allied rifle strength exceeded that of the Germans for the first time that year in mid-June. By the start of August, the Allies fielded 1,672,000 infantrymen, 277,000 more than the Kaiser's army.[38] Still worse for the Germans, their enemies also enjoyed a considerable advantage in weaponry. Even at the start of the German offensives, the Allies had possessed 18,500 guns and 4,500 aircraft against the 14,000 and 3,760 of their adversaries. They enjoyed almost a monopoly on armoured vehicles. The French and British fielded hundreds of tanks in their opening attacks during the summer of 1918, whereas the Germans only ever built twenty of their own design, the unwieldy and underpowered A7V, and refurbished another seventy-five captured models.[39] Ludendorff blamed the Allied armour for his army's defeat. But tanks alone were no war-winning weapon. What made the French and British so formidable was their ability to combine these arms into a battle system. The Germans had no answer to the skilful coordination of aircraft, artillery and infantry. Fear of Allied armour prompted German commanders to position their field artillery far forward, but this weakened their counter-bombardment and made the guns vulnerable to being overrun. Their divisions, supposed to contain 6,750 infantrymen, often had fewer than 1,000 by the late autumn, making it impossible to organize a modern defence in depth.[40]

Even so, suggestions that the victory of the Allies rested solely on their industrial strength, materiel, logistical skill or martial prowess smack of triumphalism. At least as important was the morale of their German opponents: Ludendorff himself conceded that the 'spirit of the troops' was decisive in the defeat of the Kaiser's army.[41] The force's demise in 1918 is best understood as the product of a psychological collapse, which started with the rank and file but rapidly spread to junior officers and ultimately to the OHL itself. The malaise had begun to manifest itself already in the spring. The enthusiasm of German troops at the start of their offensive was predicated solely on a quick victory. As noted, already in April the absence of any such decisive outcome produced crushing disappointment, which combined with exhaustion to have a very adverse impact on the soldiers' combat motivation. Discipline too was shaky. German soldiers had delayed their advance during Operation Michael by stopping to plunder. The temptations of French wine cellars and British supply depots, well stocked with food-stuffs like white bread and bacon that they had seen little of for four years, were too much for the men to resist.[42] Ominously for the army, once the offensive slowed and chances for plundering enemy stores declined, troops turned on their own depots. From April, reports increased of attacks by hungry German soldiers on military supply trains. By May some divisions were equipping these trains with light machine guns. Fatigue, which reached unbearable levels in some units as they were thrown repeatedly into new attacks, sponsored even more serious military crime. Small-scale mutinies by exhausted troops multiplied during the early summer. In May the men of Infantry Regiment 74 mutinied and threatened to desert when they were ordered back to the front after suffering heavy casualties. The following month, a battalion in Infantry Regiment 419 similarly refused to march up the line. These were not isolated incidents, for on 12 June the commander of Second Army warned that 'cases of soldiers openly refusing to obey orders are increasing to an alarming extent'.[43]

The most widespread and dramatic indiscipline was perpetrated not by tired troops at the front but by fresh men travelling along its lines of communication. Reinforcements sent from Germany deserted in large numbers. In May 1918 it was common that a fifth of the soldiers who embarked were no longer on the trains when they reached the war zone. No comprehensive figures exist, but if desertion from such transports continued at this rate until the war's end, it cost the force 180,000 soldiers.[44] There were also loud and disruptive protests. Officers and NCOs tasked with maintaining discipline on the transports were assaulted and railway station commandants pelted with stones. In July orders had to be issued to confiscate all live ammunition from drafts leaving home depots for the front, in order to stop them shooting out of their railway wagons. Some had even thrown hand grenades.[45] Even where there was no violence, the troops' mood was sullen and rebellious. The Chief of

Staff in the Seventh (Westphalia) Military District described what typically followed whenever troop transports halted at a station:

> The train emptied quickly and about 500 people poured noisily into the
> waiting room. It soon became routine that in the darkness they raged and
> shouted. The provocative call [and threat to officers] 'Light out! Knife out!
> Let him have it!' soon became habit. If the signal to re-entrain was given,
> hardly anyone took any notice. Gradually the practice was developed
> whereby the train very slowly started up. Only then did the waiting rooms
> empty more or less quickly, and when everyone had climbed in, the train
> accelerated.[46]

Ludendorff self-servingly blamed the home front for corrupting the
army. Recruits of the 1919 class called up from mid-1917 had, he hinted
darkly, been turned by the radical left's 'secret agitation'.[47] Munitions
workers drafted in punishment for participating in the January strikes
were also singled out by senior officers as 'poison for the troops'.[48] Prisoners of war returned from Russia were another suspect group. Like
their Habsburg counterparts, they were thought to have been influenced
by the Bolsheviks and were extremely reluctant to return to active service. However, they were less disruptive, simply because their numbers
were smaller; a mere 26,000 by mid-May, in contrast to the 380,000
Habsburg ex-prisoners repatriated by the end of April.[49] The hunt for
malign external influences to explain the Field Army's demoralization
was an exculpatory attempt to preserve intact its reputation, and those
of its commanders. A great deal of the surviving evidence in fact shows
that much of the bad mood travelled in the other direction, from front
to home. Training units were often less concerned about young recruits
than about veterans returning to the front after recovering from wounds.
These old soldiers were reported increasingly to evince 'sullenness and
apathy'. The atmosphere in the units was also spoilt by the continual
stream of bad news from the front in the summer months. New troops
preparing for combat could hardly be expected to display anything but
foreboding, for across training camps it was widely known by September 1918 'that the Front itself no longer believes in success'.[50]

The apathy and exhaustion that gripped the rank and file revealed
itself most clearly from the start of the Allied offensives. Men had lost
the will to resist. On 8 August, 'the black day of the German army' in

Ludendorff's words, the First Quartermaster General was not only shocked by the British advance but particularly dismayed at his own soldiers' conduct:

> I was told of deeds of glorious valour but also of behaviour which, I openly confess, I should not have thought possible in the German Army; whole bodies of our men had surrendered to single troopers, or isolated squadrons. Retiring troops, meeting a fresh division going bravely into action, had shouted out things like 'Blackleg', and 'You're prolonging the war', expressions that were to be heard again later. The officers in many places had lost their influence and allowed themselves to be swept along with the rest.[51]

Plenty of evidence supports Ludendorff's recollection. British military intelligence officers who interrogated prisoners after the Amiens attack found a 'marked depreciation' in the enemy's morale, commenting that 'the belief is prevalent among officers and men that Germany cannot now win the war'.[52] The command of 41 Division, a formation at the centre of the defeat that had been routed and lost 1,700 prisoners to the British, also blamed its men for fighting badly. Thick fog, highly effective air cover and the deployment en masse of tanks had indeed all made the assault formidable, but, the formation commander complained, 'many of the division's soldiers did not fulfil their duty'. The formation had been splintered by the surprise attack, and some soldiers had ceased to resist and sought safety in the rear. The worst were those who 'threw away their weapons in order to get away quicker and so as not to be able to be led back into the fight'.[53]

The poor combat motivation of German troops was key to allowing the unprecedented Allied advances during the summer and autumn of 1918. However, the relationship was reciprocal, for morale in the Kaiser's army plunged further with every enemy success. The cohesion of German units was placed under strain by both fierce Allied attacks and the army's own retreat. Some infantry regiments disintegrated on the battlefield. Already after the first French-led counter-offensive in mid-July, disgruntled German artillerymen were complaining bitterly that their protective infantry had collapsed, leaving 'stragglers, shirkers, etc.' who 'swarmed immediately behind our front line'. The army responded by setting up an extensive network of patrols and straggler collection points to the rear of its battle positions.[54] With the outlook hopeless, increasing numbers of troops tried to shirk front-line duty altogether. At the beginning of August, Ludendorff criticized the increase in soldiers going absent without leave since the start of heavy fighting.[55] Other men and even officers used more subtle methods to escape service at the front. Some feigned sickness: one staff doctor claimed that four-fifths of the officer patients in a reserve hospital he inspected at the end of September were fit for front-line service.[56] The summer influenza, which temporarily robbed the army of half a million soldiers, offered a pretext for some to head for the rear. Others found ingenious methods to dupe suspicious battalion doctors. Kits designed to produce leg boils were doing a brisk trade among soldiers as early as May 1918. For the thrifty but desperate, the inhalation of a small amount of gas could provide a yearned-for relief from front-line service.[57]

Nonetheless, until the German government issued a 'peace note' on 3 October, the discipline of the Field Army largely held. The early summer mutinies by exhausted troops stopped once the Allied offensives began. Desertion and shirking were on the increase, but remained within manageable limits; the claim, put about by conservative officers in the war's aftermath and sometimes still repeated today, that up to a million deserters and shirkers had undermined the force was a lie intended to shift blame for defeat onto the rank and file.[58] Desertion statistics for the entire army do not survive, but detailed studies of divisions refute any notion of a mass exodus. In the 11 Bavarian Division, a formation containing 10,852 soldiers at the start of May 1918, cases of suspected absence without leave or desertion tripled in the second half of 1918 compared with the previous six months, yet still totalled just seventy-one men. Its sister 2 Bavarian Division registered similar numbers, while 4 Bavarian Division, with over 200 suspected cases of desertion or absence between July and December 1918, suffered greater yet still not crippling problems.[59] Records from straggler collection posts tell much the same story. The posts were kept busy during the retreat, but only in the last three weeks of war were they overwhelmed with tens of thousands of displaced or deserting soldiers. The number of absconders arrested on leave trains had actually dropped by late September.[60] There are simple reasons to explain why soldiers generally did not desert at the front, whereas the crime was much more common along the lines of communication. Desertion from a poorly policed transport still in Germany was far easier than absconding from a combat unit, evading the patrols and paper checks behind the lines, and struggling homeward through foreign territory. To desert at the front might mean abandoning trusted comrades and officers. The punishments were also much more severe, although right to the end of the war, army courts rarely used the death penalty. Years in a civilian prison or assignment to a military prisoner company for dangerous work in the line were generally the harshest sentences dispensed.[61]

After battle casualties and sickness, mass surrenders rather than desertion or shirking were in fact the major drain on the German army's manpower during the summer of 1918. Prisoner losses in this final phase of the war were shattering: in four months the Allies captured 385,500 German soldiers, a little more than half of the 712,000 German prisoners taken on the Western Front in the whole four and a half years of fighting.[62] Detailed figures for the British army, which took 186,053 prisoners in the months following its first counter-attack at Amiens on 8 August, illustrate the startlingly sudden rise in the propensity of German troops to surrender (Fig. 7). The sudden loss of so many men deeply unnerved commanders. General von Einem, the commander of Third Army, for example, was in despair at his heavy prisoner losses by mid-September. 'If this continues, the German army will die of

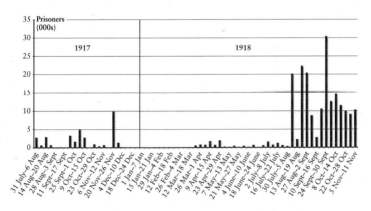

Figure 7. German prisoners captured weekly in the British sector of the Western Front, 31 July 1917–11 November 1918

Source: [British] War Office (ed.), *Statistics of the Military Effort of the British Empire during the Great War, 1914–1920* (London, 1922), p. 632.

exhaustion . . . no war can be won with men who give themselves up.'[63] His suspicion that troops were capitulating prematurely was borne out by prisoner interrogations on the British side of the lines. Bemused British intelligence officers reported in early September that prisoners 'expressed the wish that the whole German Army could be captured so that the war would be brought to a speedy end'. Men of 1 Guards Division 'not only exhibited every sign of pleasure at being taken prisoner, but actually urged our men to go on attacking, and to capture as many Germans as possible so that the war might quickly end. Each fresh batch of prisoners brought into the Cage was greeted with open delight at our success.'[64]

The huge increase in prisoners owed much to improvements in Allied tactics, which permitted them to break into enemy defences, take units in the flank or even encircle them, leading to mass capitulations. Allied propaganda also may have helped. The British alone had dropped four million leaflets over German lines between May and July 1918, and when the counter-offensives began, between four and five million leaflets were scattered by the Allies every month.[65] Some of this material sought to exacerbate the divisions that had grown between much of the German people and its leaders, questioning the sense of 'struggling for the Kaiser, the Junkers, and the militarists'. Other propaganda played on antagonism between southern and northern Germans. Bavarians were pitied as slaves of Prussia and told that they were bleeding disproportionately for its megalomaniacal ambitions. However, probably more effective than political exhortations were simple appeals to German troops' stomachs. The US army scattered over a million copies of a 'prisoner leaflet' that included a list of the ample rations served in its POW camps.[66] This propaganda hit its target. By the late summer of 1918, German soldiers on leave could be heard promising one another that 'as soon as [the attacks] again began [they] would desert to the enemy; then everything would be over and they would at least get something to eat.'[67]

Most important in enabling mass surrenders was, however, the conduct of German officers at the front. In the summer of 1918 the army's psychological crisis had embraced these junior leaders. The offensives of the first half of the year had exhausted them and depleted their numbers: casualties had been proportionately twice as heavy as those of their men.[68] Their quality was much reduced. The onset of the Allied offensives broke them: as one recalled, after it became clear that all sacrifices had been in vain, 'despair ate deep into the officer corps'.[69] By September most of the officers in Seventeenth Army believed the war could not last longer than the late autumn or winter.[70] Troops noted the change. As a soldier in Sixth Army wrote home, 'our officers have also had enough. They're not allowed to say it openly but now and again they let it be known.'[71] It was thus perhaps not surprising that officers were well represented in Allied prisoner cages. The British alone captured 4,727 during their counter-offensive. Some were there because they had lacked the will or authority to make their troops resist. Under Allied pressure, units could collapse startlingly suddenly. Reserve Second Lieutenant Mechow, an officer of Infantry Regiment 145, described this well. On 8 October 1918 his unit was attacked. The battalion on its right had been surprised by the British and his own company was suddenly assaulted from behind by French troops. Mechow explained what happened: 'My men in part still lay in their fox holes, some were already raising their hands, some fled! "Shoot, shoot!", I yelled and myself grabbed a machine gun. It was all in vain. A chaotic tangle arose; everything mixed up, friend and enemy. Where should I shoot? Ever more and more enemies arrive; there is no point any more, the mass overwhelms us. The men give up, no one fights any longer.'[72]

Nonetheless, more often than not German officers did maintain authority over their soldiers, and surrenders happened at their behest. Crown Prince Rupprecht, the head of the army group facing the British, confirmed as much when he complained in mid-October that officers and large units had repeatedly surrendered themselves.[73] Doubtless the Allies' rapid advance and encirclements placed many units in hopeless positions, permitting their commanders legitimately to capitulate. Yet jittery and despondent officers also surrendered prematurely. In one of the earliest and most celebrated cases at the Second Battle of the Marne in mid-July, a German major gave himself up and over a hundred troops to twelve Americans who had ambushed them.[74] He was far from exceptional. Other officers, certain the war was lost, frightened by the firepower of the Allies, and unwilling to sacrifice their men uselessly, 'advised' them, as one put it, 'to surrender ... if hard pressed'. Occasionally, the paternalistic concern of commanding officers for their soldiers' well-being motivated them to take extreme risks to negotiate the laying down of arms. One German officer in the autumn of 1918 displayed remarkable bravery when he crawled across no-man's-land, entered British trenches, surrendered himself to the surprised garrison and then asked permission to return to fetch his men as they too wished to capitulate. As troops' letters testified, at the front, unlike in rear-line formations, there was no sharp division between officers and men. British statistics show that the ratio of officers to men among German prisoners was the same as in the whole Field Army, confirmation that soldiers were generally not defying their leaders and giving up without them but were marching into captivity as cohesive units. The participation of officers was crucial in making surrender attractive. A collective surrender organized by an officer was more likely to be recognized by the enemy and provided some security against being killed by one's captors. It also removed any possibility of being accused by one's own side of being an *Überläufer* – a deserter to the enemy. This was important, for punishment for this crime was extremely severe: loss of citizenship, confiscation of property, and death on return to Germany.[75]

The entire German Field Army was diagnosed by one contemporary military psychiatrist as suffering in the last months of war from a state of 'neurasthenic exhaustion'.[76] This psychological crisis that had begun with the rank and file in the late spring and gripped combat officers by the summer of 1918, ultimately spread further, right up to the OHL. General Ludendorff was under no less stress than the soldiers he commanded. For two years he had struggled to run the entire German war effort. The failure of the offensives in the first half of 1918 was on his head, for he had insisted upon, personally planned and commanded the operations. They had also brought him personal tragedy. On the third day of Operation Michael his youngest stepson Erich, a fighter pilot, had been shot down over the Western Front. The deep emotional impact that the boy's death had on this highly strung, arrogant man was hinted at in his decision not to send the body back to Berlin but instead to organize a burial in the grounds of his headquarters. 'I wanted to keep him here,' Ludendorff explained to his wife. 'I go to him often.'[77] The general was thus in a poor psychological state to cope with a reversal of everything for which he had striven and sacrificed. The French counter-attack on the Marne in mid-July left him extremely nervous but unwilling to acknowledge the shift in the strategic balance. Only with the British offensive outside Amiens on 8 August did he accept that a catastrophe had taken place. A week after its start, Colonel Thaer found him serious and depressed. Ludendorff had recognized the wider loss of faith within his army: 'For sure, he now sees that our troops are more or less broken.'[78]

The sequenced Allied offensives against different parts of the line, the exhaustion of his army's reserves, and the steady retreat throughout August and September, placed further intense pressure on Ludendorff. To the Kaiser and the Reich's civilian government, he was bullish. When Wilhelm II, recognizing that 'the war must be ended', called a Crown Council on 14 August, Ludendorff assured his Monarch, the Crown Prince, Chancellor and Foreign Secretary that a 'strategic defensive with periodic offensive action' offered 'good prospects for finally crippling the enemy's will to war'. Until the end of August he persisted in the demand that Germany should retain Belgium in any peace settlement.[79] However, his staff were well aware of their leader's psychological turmoil. He was grappling with the reality that, as he conceded privately to Hindenburg and Wetzell at the start of September, 'we no longer have any prospect of still winning the war'.[80] His staff sought means of helping the defeated general. An officer was appointed to ease his workload and a Berlin psychologist was dispatched to the OHL to provide professional treatment. Dr Hochheimer, the man brought in to heal Ludendorff, found his patient overworked and exhausted. He had become almost a caricature of a Prussian militarist, with uniform, monocle and voice fixed permanently in the shrill tone used to give commands. 'Ludendorff,' the doctor wrote on 5 September, 'is after all the hard years of work and emotional turbulence of the immense responsibility and above all under the impression of the last eight weeks very mentally depressed.'[81]

Ludendorff's psychological treatment lasted through the following four weeks of crisis. Hochheimer ordered a strictly regulated de-stress regime of walks, regulated breathing, singing, massage and more sleep than the one to five hours the general was in the habit of taking. The doctor created a space of security and tranquillity to which Ludendorff could withdraw. Most striking about the psychologist's account is the general's submissiveness. Ludendorff clearly embraced the release from responsibility. He followed the doctor's instructions as if they were military orders and boasted of being his 'obedient patient'. On one occasion, Hochheimer wrote, the general fell asleep 'literally under my hands'. The treatment had some success. The doctor considered Ludendorff 'wonderfully recovered' by early October and staff officers too noticed improvement.[82] Nonetheless, outside the artificial security provided by Hochheimer, the general's world continued to collapse. The second half of September was a period of acute crisis. In the east, the Allies attacked on 14 September and routed Bulgaria's army, forcing her within a fortnight to seek an armistice. At the time this news arrived at the OHL, the German army's leaders were also facing disaster in the west. On 26 September, Foch opened his general offensive to end the war. The strongest position the Germans possessed, the Hindenburg Line, was under furious bombardment. The staff at the OHL had already circumvented Ludendorff to warn the Reich's Foreign Secretary, Admiral Paul von Hintze, of the desperate situation and to urge him to come to military headquarters. On the evening of 28 September, Ludendorff too surrendered to his fears and informed Hindenburg that an immediate armistice must be sought.[83]

The psychological crisis that had started with the German army's soldiers spread upward in the early summer to its officers and facilitated the Allied advances during the second half of 1918, culminating in the nervous exhaustion of the First Quartermaster General. Ludendorff may not, contrary to his enemies' suggestions, have suffered a total collapse on the evening of 28 September, but his fateful decision to demand an immediate armistice certainly smacked of blind panic.[84] Moreover, it was intimately related to his army's psychological crisis. Bulgaria's exit offered a convenient excuse to end the war without accruing personal blame. However, as a frank speech to his confidants at the OHL on 1 October revealed, the general's haste to close down hostilities was a response to the coming Allied onslaught in the west and the demoralization and poor combat performance of German soldiers. 'The OHL and the German army are finished,' he complained to the assembled staff officers. 'No more reliance could be placed on the troops. Since 8 August, it has rapidly gone downhill. Continually, units have proved themselves so unreliable that they have hurriedly had to be withdrawn from the front.' He 'could not operate with divisions which could no longer be trusted'.[85]

Ludendorff's belated admission that 'final defeat is unavoidably imminent' confronted Germany's elite with an existential problem.[86] The imperial regime's legitimacy by this point rested solely on its ability to deliver a quick and total victory. As Foreign Secretary Hintze worriedly told Hindenburg and Ludendorff when the news was broken to him on 29 September, the sudden admission of defeat 'must give the nation such a shock, that the Reich and dynasty would scarcely be able to survive'. The three men searched for a solution. None believed that the instalment of a dictator to mobilize the masses would work without any prospect of victory. Instead, all agreed, a 'revolution from above' must be initiated. President Wilson, the enemy leader most likely to offer lenient terms, would be tempted with the possibility of a peace based on his Fourteen Points. To shore up the thoroughly delegitimized imperial regime and seek a favourable end to hostilities, the 'broadest possible circles' would be called to government.[87]

REVOLUTION

The Central Powers' defeat took place on the Western Front, but the populations and politicians at home determined its consequences. The misery of civilians and their knowledge of what was taking place on the battlefield provided a crucial backdrop for state collapse. Austria-Hungary, not only Germany, was vulnerable to the irretrievable reverses a thousand kilometres away on the Western Front, because by 1918 Habsburg domestic politics were tied inextricably to the international balance. Both the Central Powers' regimes recognized that defeat made reform unstoppable, and both attempted to manage it by instituting revolutions from above. The failure of these last desperate efforts to stave off total collapse hastened the end of the fighting, which ceased on the Italian Front on 4 November and on the Western Front on 11 November 1918. Yet even before these armistices had been signed, the post-war world had started to take shape. Centuries-old dynasties had fallen. Revolution had taken hold in parts of central Europe and the old continent of empires was giving way to one of imperfect nation states.

The dramatic changes of 1918 cannot be explained without first confronting the despair felt by people across central Europe. The eighteen-year-old Upper Silesian Ruth Höfner described this movingly. 'This war, oh, this war! If only it would come to an end!' she cried in her diary at the beginning of April 1918:

> Four whole years we've had war. Some people will say we've got used to
> it. I have also perhaps sometimes so spoken; but no, it is not true! We who

once knew peace will never get used to it. We, who in war turned from
children to adults, will get used to hunger and poor clothing but never to
the sorrow of war, which destroys any budding happiness like frost with
the first tender flowers on a spring night. She is everywhere, this lingering
sorrow. Go where you will . . . God in heaven, when will it end![88]

The despair Ruth felt, although she expressed it unusually beautifully,
was familiar to people across central Europe. The majority lived in a
state of advanced misery by the spring of 1918 and conditions would
worsen, for the summer of 1918 saw both a drop in food supply to the
levels of the 'turnip winter' and the onset of an influenza pandemic that
would kill at least 20 million worldwide. Society was bereaved,
exhausted and yearned for peace.[89]

The peoples of the Central Powers were aware that the shape of the
peace – and, by this point more important to many, its imminence –
would be decided by the great battles in the west. The progress of their
armies was followed closely. The claim, often made, that civilians were
unaware of how dire Germany's plight was by the summer and autumn,
is a myth. After four years of war, the populations were skilled at reading between the lines of official dispatches. They were attuned to when
reports stopped discussing advances and could recognize a retreat in a
heroic withdrawal. The imperial government did not make the setbacks
difficult to spot. Richard von Kühlmann, Hintze's predecessor as Foreign Secretary, conceded in the Reichstag in late June that 'an absolute
end [to the war] through pure military decisions alone without any
diplomatic negotiations could scarcely be expected'.[90] From August, the
press belatedly started preparing the German public for retreat in the
west.[91] Most importantly, soldiers were far from reticent about the disasters at the front over the summer and autumn. Contrary to Ludendorff's
bitter accusation that the home front was demoralizing the army, very
much the reverse was the truth. Civilian officials were distressed that
men on leave were telling the population 'horror stories' about the
front. Rumours of men going over en masse to the enemy were circulated.[92] Troops were also frank in letters to their families about the
desperate conditions at the front. The letters of Private First Class Fritz
Schlamp, serving in 21st Bavarian Pioneer Company, offer a good illustration. He told his father in mid-September that he and his comrades
were sure that the war would be over that year. 'We win the battles and

England wins the war. I believe we can be glad if we get what we had and don't have to pay anything.' A friend taken prisoner had 'at least saved his neck'. As the end approached, Schlamp attempted to thwart the censor and give an explicit warning. At the bottom of an innocuous note thanking his parents for cigarettes, he wrote an odd-looking series of numbers; a simple code to get across a secret message: 'The situation is bad. Everyone is running away. If there is no armistice, make as much cash liquid as possible.'[93]

The Habsburg Empire had been frozen in a state of impending collapse during the 1918 German offensives. For its peoples, the alternatives had at least become clearer. German victory would mean a Dualist Empire, its western half centralized and dominated by Austrian Germans, and satellite status under its powerful northern neighbour. After the French had embarrassingly published the letter that the Emperor had sent during the Sixtus peace approach of a year earlier acknowledging France's 'just claims' to Alsace-Lorraine, Karl had tied his regime to this vision. In May he had made a humiliating trip to the OHL at Spa to assent to *Mitteleuropa* and with it sign away his Empire's independence. By the end of the summer the consequences of defeat for the Empire were equally clear. The Allied position had hardened. In January 1918 the American President had advocated in his Fourteen Points speech a federal Austria-Hungary, whose peoples 'should be accorded the freest opportunity to autonomous development'. In June, however, after Karl's commitment to the Reich's post-war Europe, Wilson had shifted to advocate that 'all branches of the Slav race [*sic*] should be completely free from German and Austrian rule'. His allies, now sure that there could be no separate peace with the Habsburgs, began working to destroy them. At the start of June, the British, French and Italians had echoed the support Wilson had given in January to a 'united and independent Poland with access to the sea'. More fatally, at the end of that month the French formally recognized Tomáš Masaryk's dissident Czechoslovak National Committee in Paris as the legal representatives of a Czechoslovak nation. The British granted their recognition on 9 August and the Americans on 3 September. By the autumn, as the German army was forced back on the Western Front, it was clear that the last days of the Habsburg Empire were approaching.[94]

The Habsburg army was powerless to shape events. In June it had tried to support the German offensives with one of its own on the Italian Front. Even had the attack been a success, it would have made no difference to the war's outcome, but in the event it turned out to be a bloody failure. The cause was in part the perennial Habsburg problem of poor leadership. Emperor Karl, who had taken over the Supreme Command shortly after his accession to the throne, had been presented with two equally bad plans by the commanders on the spot, the former Chief of the General Staff, Conrad von Hötzendorf, in Tyrol, and the commander on the Isonzo Front, General Svetozar Boroević. With typical indecisiveness, he had divided his forces equally between the pair, ensuring neither would have sufficient strength for success.[95] The material and psychological state of the army should have called into question the wisdom of launching any sort of attack, and certainly an ill-conceived one on an 80-kilometre front. The ammunition stockpiled for the assault, over six million shells, could not be brought up the mountains in time because the horses available were underfed, scraggy and simply too few. The force's soldiers were in a similar condition. Since 1917, Habsburg field strength had dropped by 550,000 men, in large part through endemic desertion and the diversion of seven divisions to security duties in the interior of the Empire.[96] Those troops who did remain on active service were on rations little more than half the size of those a year earlier, poorly clad and demoralized by Italian propaganda. When, on 15 June after a weak bombardment, the troops went forward, some units were stopped dead. Others used their German-style training to advance, but soon found themselves in an elastic defence system, where counter-attacks launched when they were exhausted and at their most vulnerable halted them. By the end of the second day, the attackers' supplies were running out and Conrad was in retreat. On 20 June the offensive was called off and those gains that had been made on the right bank of the Piave River were relinquished. This useless operation cost 142,550 men.[97]

The Emperor, as the army's commander, took a severe reputational blow from the June defeat. Deputies in both the Magyar parliament and the Austrian Reichsrat condemned the offensive as 'foolishness and irresponsibility'. Some even demanded that those who had authorized it be put on trial.[98] Wags in Vienna started referring to their monarch as Karl the Last.[99] The whispering campaign against Empress Zita, Karl's wife, was a sure sign of the peoples' distrust in their leadership, mirroring what had befallen Tsarina Aleksandra a year earlier in Russia. Zita was of French and Italian noble lineage and spoke with a foreign accent, enough evidence for wartime xenophobia to condemn her as a traitor. It was rumoured that she had betrayed the June offensive to the Allies. Some claimed that she had been locked up in a Hungarian castle to prevent her from doing any more damage.[100] Hunger-induced paranoia doubtless contributed to the popularity of these conspiracy theories. Vienna's food supply situation was particularly disastrous. In April, mass starvation had only narrowly been averted by the desperate expedient of confiscating barges carrying Romanian grain belonging to Germany up the Danube.[101] There was a severe bread shortage that summer throughout much of the Empire and although the gathering in of the harvest provided some relief, this was brief: Austria's plight by the beginning of October was summed up by the head of its Food Office, Hans Loewenfeld-Russ, as 'utterly desperate'.[102]

While the Emperor still stood precariously at the head of his realm, he had lost much of his power to rule it. Crownland officials, many of whom had been instrumental in the success of the double mobilization in 1914, were by this point prioritizing national allegiances and protecting local over imperial interests. It was especially unfortunate that the two peoples whom by 1918 the Empire had alienated more than any others, the Czechs and Poles, also happened to live in Austria's two most important food surplus regions, Bohemia and Galicia. In both Crownlands, district officials and railway employees, urged on by local newspapers and public opinion, obstructed the export of supplies to other regions.[103] Large tracts of countryside in these Crownlands and further south had anyway been wrested from state control by deserters formed into robber bands and Bolshevik 'Green Cadres'. The towns too were fractious and violent. On the Slav peripheries they were full of hatred towards Germans and Jews. Vienna was a centre of anti-Semitism. Everywhere there were food riots, protests and debilitating strikes.[104] Attempts to promote a multinational and dynastic 'Austrian state idea' were long abandoned. In a mark of its total bankruptcy, the Habsburg regime retained a modicum of control only by exploiting national enmities in their fragmented society. Security troops were deliberately garrisoned in areas foreign to them, where they could not communicate and where often they were actually hostile to the local populace. Magyar soldiers policed Czechs, and Czech military personnel kept order in Hungary.

Austrian Germans watched over Slovene and Polish civilians, Bosnians over Germans, and Poles over Ruthenes. The Empire had finally become what its enemies had long and unfairly criticized it as: 'a prison of peoples'.[105]

The first clear sign that the Habsburg government was cracking was Karl's appeal for peace on 14 September. His Foreign Minister, Count István Burián, had desired this since August, but the Germans had stalled and then instead advocated mediation by a neutral power. The note was therefore sent without their approval, an indication that in spite of Austria-Hungary's wartime decline, the Emperor still had scope for independent action. However, at this late stage it achieved nothing besides further sour relations with the Germans. French and British leaders regarded the call as a ploy to split their coalition, and the American answer sent three days later pointed out that as the United States had already stated its peace terms, talks were superfluous.[106] In spite of this negative response, Habsburg leaders were prompted to try again just a couple of weeks later. The catalyst was Bulgaria's military collapse. Far more than for Germany, this mattered to Austria-Hungary, for it opened the way to Habsburg-occupied Serbia. Even more important, as Burián warned in a Crown Council on 27 September, after news of Bulgaria's request for an armistice had arrived, was the 'impact upon the nerves of our population'. He predicted it would be 'the last straw'. 'We must make decisions,' he urged the assembled Austrian and Hungarian leaders, 'if we want to avoid the peoples themselves taking fate into their own hands and making decisions about their futures over the heads of the governments.'[107]

German and Habsburg elites adopted similar strategies at the start of October 1918 to end the conflict. Their appeals to President Wilson were issued in parallel on the night of 3 October. They proposed peace negotiations on the basis of the Fourteen Points and requested an immediate armistice. Both regimes also recognized that defeat made unavoidable long-delayed political reform. The 'revolutions from above' initiated in Germany and the Habsburg Empire were intended to pacify their resentful populations, and pre-empt violent upheaval. They were also undertaken in the hope of impressing the US President, who had made clear that he saw democracy as the bedrock of any lasting peace. In both aims they failed. There would be no easy peace and the central European monarchies would not outlast the defeat.

In Austria-Hungary, Emperor Karl's attempt to stave off revolution took the form of a roadmap for hasty reform, issued on 16 October while he waited for an American reply. The 'Peoples' Manifesto', as its sponsors hopefully named it, promised to reorganize the Empire on a federal basis 'as its people desire'. Karl envisaged German, Czech, South Slav and Ukrainian territories, each with their own institutions. The Habsburg Polish territories would be permitted to secede to the independent Polish state that Wilson's Fourteen Points had demanded 'should be erected'. As during consultations held four days before its release Czech and South Slav politicians had made clear that they would reject it, the manifesto was nothing more than a publicity exercise doomed to stillbirth. Moreover, instead of restoring faith in the Empire, it painfully exposed the inability of Habsburg leaders to offer any satisfactory reform. Strikingly, the only mention in the manifesto of the lands of the Hungarian Crown stressed that they lay outside its purview. The Magyar Minister President, Sándor Wekerle, had not only refused to permit any promise of federal reform in his land but had even threatened to halt food deliveries unless the manifesto explicitly excluded it. South Slav nationalist wishes for the unification of Croatia with Bosnia-Herzegovina, Dalmatia and Slovenia were thus not to be met. Appearing at the end of a lost war and issued by a broken, discredited monarch, the manifesto could not possibly compete with the full independence for the peoples offered by the Empire's enemies. Nonetheless, it mattered, if only as a public sign of weakness that accelerated Habsburg collapse.[100]

The Habsburg regime's doom was sealed when Wilson's response to the note sent two and a half weeks earlier arrived on 20 October. The Fourteen Points that Karl's government had proposed as a basis for negotiation had left open the possibility of a post-war future for Austria-Hungary by demanding the possibility of 'autonomous development'. However, any hope of survival was quashed by Wilson's answer, which stated that having recognized the Czechoslovak National Committee as a de facto government and the justice of South Slav national aspirations, autonomy for these peoples could now not be a basis for peace. This pronouncement provided the signal for dissolution.

National politicians were already waiting to take control. Already in July, Czech political factions had come together in a Czechoslovak National Committee, the *Národní výbor československý*.[109] In early October other peoples had taken similar steps. A National Council of Serbs, Croats and Slovenes had hurriedly been formed in Zagreb two days after the Central Powers issued their peace notes. On the following day, 7 October, the Polish Council of Regency, the advisory body set up by the Germans in Warsaw, had proclaimed a 'free and independent Poland' to which Galicia was to be attached.[110]

Ironically, the first acts of revolution were taken by the peoples most favoured by the Monarchy, the Germans and Hungarians. On the day after Wilson's reply, the Austrian German parties came together and formed a twenty-member National Committee to take over government.[111] In Hungary, where the suppression of opposition and resistance to reform had permitted greater pressure to build, the power shift was more turbulent. Wekerle's conservative government had attempted at first to isolate Hungary from Karl's federalist reforms by announcing on 16 October that it no longer considered itself bound by the 1867 Compromise. However, this could not stop the vocal demands for national self-determination crossing the border to Hungary's Slovaks and Romanians. Magyar opposition politicians led by the 'Red Count', Mihály Károlyi, also became assertive. On 26 October, after demands that power be transferred went unheeded and Karl refused to appoint him Magyar Minister President, Károlyi, the Hungarian Social Democrats and the Radicals founded a National Committee that claimed for itself the sole right 'to speak and act in the name of the Hungarian nation'. Its twelve-point programme demanded the abolition of the ruling system, universal male and female suffrage, independence, peace and the renunciation of the German alliance. By offering the national freedoms advocated by Wilson, it hoped naively that Hungary might retain all its territory and mixed peoples.[112]

The people, or at least highly visible and politically assertive groups within it, were decisive in enabling the National Committee to grasp power. On 24 October the revolution began when thousands of students went onto the streets of Budapest to demand peace, independence and a Károlyi government. The following day saw cries of 'Up the Republic!' – and the first clashes with security forces. With the formation of the National Committee, the demonstrations swelled. On 27 October a 30,000-strong crowd gathered in front of parliament in support of the Committee and the next day the revolution gained its martyrs, when police fired on protestors trying to break through their cordons onto the city's Chain Bridge across the Danube. Three died and fifty were wounded.[113]

The old order's days were already at this point numbered. Magyar officers loyal to the National Committee had formed a soldiers' council, which agitated in Budapest's garrison and prepared the overthrow of the city's military command. On 30 October revolutionary officers and soldiers publicly swore an oath of loyalty at the Committee's headquarters. The people too were on the streets, tearing Habsburg double-headed eagles from the buildings. Not the red flag but Hungary's red-white-green tricolour was the symbol of this national revolution. General Lukachich at the head of the local military command attempted to resist, but his ability to deploy troops around Budapest was undermined when the city's central telephone exchange defected to the revolution, and the soldiers anyway refused his orders to shoot at protestors. Even the once reliable Bosnians in the garrison mutinied and got drunk; their officers were eventually found cringing in a locked room for fear of being lynched. When Lukachich appealed to the Emperor for even just one reliable regiment to be sent, Karl quietly told him 'enough blood has already been spilt'. On the morning of 31 October, Károlyi was appointed Minister President and the executive of the National Committee became the government. Lukachich was held under arrest. A few soldiers decided that one last act must be undertaken to eliminate absolutely the old order: that afternoon, they broke into Tisza's villa on the outskirts of the city. The former Minister President was murdered in revenge for his part in starting the past four years of misery, hunger and death. Otherwise, the day was one of celebration. The national tricolour was hung out across Budapest, and hundreds of thousands rejoiced in the city's squares. The Hungarian Republic had been born.[114]

By this date, revolution had spread across the Empire, catalysed by a last Habsburg admission of defeat. On 24 October the Italians had launched a last-minute offensive on the South-Western Front in order to position themselves better for the coming peace negotiations. After three days, defending troops of all nationalities had refused to go into the line and on 28 October the imperial authorities had unconditionally requested an armistice.[115] In Prague, the news unleashed a genuinely popular revolution. People came out into the streets and gathered in Wenceslaus Square to celebrate. Cries of 'Long live Masaryk!' and 'Long live Wilson!' echoed through the city. There the tone was, as in Budapest and in most of the Empire's other major municipalities, national, rather than Socialist or Bolshevik. The bourgeois politicians who dominated the national committees ensured that their ideology prevailed. When Czech Socialists had called a general strike on 14 October, in the hope of creating an opportunity for the proclamation of a republic, it had failed in the face of military counter-measures and a lack of support from the Czechoslovak National Committee. In Ljubljana, the Russian revolution of the previous year was held up as a warning, not an exemplar. On the same day as the Prague revolution, the Slovenian revolutionaries there were admonished to respect property and demonstrate for Yugoslav liberty. In Zagreb too, from 21 October revolutionaries flew Croatian, Slovene and Serb flags, not the red flag of leftist struggle. Democracy too was celebrated. As one of the Croatian leaders, Stjepan Radić, joyfully proclaimed on the following day, 'The peoples rise in order to deliver freedom with their blood and over the whole world Wilson's principles enjoy victory.'[116]

A second characteristic of the Habsburg revolutions, contradicting Radić's assertion, was their relative bloodlessness. Emperor Karl deserves credit here for encouraging restraint, but it was also in part a consequence of the somewhat ambiguous status of the national committees. Karl's manifesto had promised that Austria was to be federalized on a national basis, which appeared to confer legitimacy on these organizations as prospective regional governments. The impression was reinforced on 25 October by the appointment of a new Minister President, the pacifist Professor Heinrich Lammasch, who hoped sincerely but futilely to lead not a cabinet but an 'Executive Committee of the united National Governments'. The Czechoslovak National Committee's way to power was certainly eased by this, for its members could claim to the local Habsburg military command that by taking control of the critical food supply they were merely acting according to the Emperor's design.[117] A further reason for the smooth transition was that the revolutions merely formalized the national fragmentation of the Empire that had already taken place during the war. In Bohemia and Moravia, Czech district officials had long prioritized their own people's food supply over pan-Austrian solidarity. It was only natural that after the independent Czechoslovak state was declared on 28 October, these officials should place themselves under the authority of its National Committee.[118]

Habsburg functionaries did not merely defect after the revolutions, but were instrumental in some places in bringing about regime change. The city of Cracow best illustrates how officials who had been central to the success of the 'double mobilization' in 1914 and 1915 had turned by 1918. Their Polish nationalism, which had been entirely compatible with imperial loyalty at the outset, had through the war experience turned to a stance of irreconcilable opposition. The city council first manifested open disloyalty on 28 October, when it confiscated food transports intended for the Habsburg army. On 30 October municipal officials gathered at the city's university and together decided that they owed their allegiance to the new Polish state forming to the north. On the following day, the revolution began. Polish troops of the garrison had been secretly alerted, and early in the morning they surprised and disarmed their German Moravian comrades. Arms were taken from the barracks' magazines and handed over to students. The city's police chief was in on the conspiracy and his men were already on the streets wearing Polish eagles and red-white cockades on their caps. At the city hall, the Polish Legionary Brigadier Bolesław Roja, whom the revolutionaries had appointed their military chief, negotiated the surrender of the city fortress with its disorientated Habsburg commander. Outside, soldiers unscrewed Habsburg eagles from the walls. The changeover was quick and orderly, 'without any revolution and riots', as the resident Aleksandra Czechówna remarked with astonishment.[119] Notices were pasted around the city to inform its people of the changed circumstances. A Polish guard relieved the Austrian watch in the old city hall tower overlooking Cracow's main marketplace.[120]

The Habsburg state, defeated and drained of legitimacy, fell with very little resistance. Yet this did not mean that the replacement of the multinational Empire with nation states was seamless and straightforward. In this land with such intermixed ethnicities, where racial enmities had been inflamed by war and where Wilson's organizing principle of national self-determination raised competition between peoples to a winner-takes-all struggle of national survival, such change inevitably brought bloodshed. Any place whose population was mixed and whose ownership was contested saw clashes or the suppression of the weaker group. The German-inhabited north and west of Bohemia briefly declared itself a part of German Austria but was overrun in early November by Czech troops. In Fiume, a 15,000-strong Italian mob gathered at the end of October to shout 'Down with the Croatians!' Some areas, such as the Romanian countryside around Czernowitz and parts of western Galicia, were sites of anti-Semitic outrages. One of the bloodiest inter-ethnic confrontations, the clashes and pogrom that took place in the former Galician capital of Lwów in early November, may stand both as an example and a conclusion illustrating the inter-ethnic animosities and new violence bequeathed to central Europe by the First World War.[121]

Lwów had suffered greatly during the war. Russian occupation, food shortages and maladroit Habsburg diplomacy had all heightened tensions between its three major ethnic groups, Poles, Ruthenes and Jews. By the war's end, the Poles who dominated the city council and accounted for just over half of its population were looking forward to joining the new independent Polish state. However, for Ukrainian nationalists the city was desirable as the capital of a new Ukrainian state that would stretch to the San River. They only made up a fifth of the population but could rely on two major advantages. First, the countryside around the city was overwhelmingly Ruthene. Second, thanks to Habsburg security policies, the majority of troops in Lwów that autumn were also Ruthenes. The coup launched with these soldiers on the night of 1 November 1918, which took the city centre and led to a yellow-blue flag being flown from the city hall, opened a period of bitter conflict. Polish residents resisted, soon helped by reinforcements from western Galicia. Polish fatalities amounted to 439 people; those of the Ukrainians are not known, but eventually, on 22 November, the Ukrainian troops were forced out of the city. As if this bloodletting was not sufficient, exultant Polish troops then turned on Lwów's Jews, who had set up their own militia for protection but had remained scrupulously neutral. In a three-day pogrom, shops and houses were plundered, women were raped, seventy-three Jews were killed and hundreds more injured. This violence between ethnic groups and vicious anti-Semitism in Lwów boded very ill for the new national order of east-central Europe. The wiser among the residents recognized this. 'You see those little holes?' asked one showing an American visitor around the city in 1919. 'We call them here "Wilson's Points". They have been made with machine guns; the big gaps have been made with hand grenades. We are now engaged in self-determination, and God knows what and when the end will be.'[122]

Germany's 'revolution from above' in the last month of war was not so abortive but no more successful than that of Austria-Hungary. In the hour of defeat, the Reich's rulers decided that it would be best to spread the blame. The decree issued by the Kaiser on 30 September at the behest of the OHL suddenly announced a wish 'that the German people would cooperate more actively than hitherto in the determination of the fate of the Fatherland'. Now, at a time when that fate was already sealed, 'men who have the confidence of the people should have a broad share in the rights and duties of government'.[123] Appointed to head the new administration was the fifty-one-year-old prince Max von Baden. Although a scion of southern German royalty, he had acquired a reputation as a liberal and it was believed that he could attract the confidence of a Reichstag majority. The government he formed was very different from any the Reich had ever seen. Among its ministers were Reichstag deputies from the Progressives, Centre and Social Democrat parties. These men could be expected to give the coming armistice credibility, for their parties had been behind the Reichstag peace resolution in July 1917.[124]

The new administration immediately came under immense pressure from Ludendorff to open negotiations with the Allies to halt the fighting. The First Quartermaster General was intensely fearful that his army would collapse totally without an armistice and had naively hoped a new government would be in place and a note sent to Wilson by 1 October. To Max's questioning about whether it was really necessary to appeal for an armistice so abruptly, leaving him in a very weak negotiating position with the Reich's enemies, Ludendorff insisted on the '*speediest possible* despatch' of a note and Hindenburg warned of a looming potential 'catastrophe'. The army unnerved the party leaders too with a speech approved by Ludendorff and delivered to them on 2 October. Its explanation for why an armistice was necessary differed markedly from what the First Quartermaster General had told his officers at general headquarters a day earlier. Blame was heaped on Bulgaria's military collapse, a misfortune for which conveniently nobody at the OHL could be held culpable. Where it was conceded that problems did exist on the Western Front, these were said to be of a purely material nature: the enemy had in the tank an invincible weapon and unmatchable reserves of manpower. Ludendorff clearly wished to preserve the army's prestige, for the stress he had placed on the troops' unreliability in the talk at general headquarters was not repeated. Indeed, the politicians were assured that 'the old spirit of heroism had not disappeared'. Officers and men, it was claimed, 'vied with one another'. Most revealing of military leaders' desire to shirk all blame were the blatant contradictions within the speech. 'The German Army,' the party leaders were assured, 'is still strong enough to hold out against the enemy for months', and yet simultaneously they were also admonished that 'no time should be lost. Every twenty-four hours can make the situation worse.'[125]

Prince Max and most Reichstag politicians were prepared to continue the fight. By uniting Germans in national defence, they hoped to stiffen resistance to win better peace terms.[126] Confronted by the panic of the military and warned by the Kaiser that he had 'not been brought ... to make difficulties for the Supreme Command', Max relented and on the evening of 3 October dispatched via Switzerland a note requesting President Wilson to 'take steps for the restoration of peace' and organize an immediate armistice.[127] The calculation of appealing directly to the American President instead of to the bloodied and bitter French and British at first appeared correct. When Wilson's reply of 8 October arrived, it was cautious but not hostile, seeking clarification on whether the German government was now representative of the people's will and whether it accepted the Fourteen Points. However, his tone hardened in a response sent six days later to a second German note. In part, this was a consequence of pressure from the President's disgruntled allies and American hardliners. It was also the result of a U-boat strike. With impeccably bad timing, *UB123* sunk the British passenger ship *Leinster* on 11 October, with the loss of 450 lives, including 135 women and children and some Americans. Wilson's second note shattered the illusions on which the German peace approach was founded. It emphasized that 'satisfactory safeguards and guarantees' would have to be conceded to preserve the Allied armies' current military advantage, it fulminated against the continuation of 'illegal and inhumane practices' by German forces and, most ominously, it sought to exploit and widen the already stark divisions between the Reich's people and its rulers. The 'arbitrary power' that Wilson still regarded as in control of Germany was condemned as an impediment to peace. The solution lay with the people: 'It is within the choice of the German Nation to alter it.'[128]

The clear evidence that Wilson would not permit Germany an easy armistice and was attempting to meddle with its internal politics inflamed resistance. Ironically, Ludendorff was one source of opposition. He had recovered from his panic at the end of September, and while he still hoped for an armistice, by mid-October he wanted just a temporary pause to permit his army to withdraw undisturbed and take up strong positions on the German frontier.[129] At a meeting with the government on 17 October, he told Prince Max that Wilson's conditions were 'too hard'. If Germany's enemies wanted to impose them, he declared defiantly, 'we should tell [them] that they must fight'. In contrast to the OHL's dire warnings earlier in the month, Ludendorff now estimated that the Germans would get better peace conditions if they fought into the following year. A military breakdown was 'possible but nor probable'. The key was just to get through one more month: if 'we get into winter,' he claimed, 'we shall be "out of the wood"'.[130] Quite what this new optimism was based upon is difficult to fathom. Ludendorff had started the meeting confident but he was certainly buoyed up during it when the new War Minister, General Heinrich Scheüch, offered him another 600,000 men. However, if he genuinely believed these were available, he was deluding himself. Only at the cost of stripping mining and the railways, and therefore crippling Germany's industrial capability to wage war, could they be conscripted.[131]

The situation at the front had not improved either. True, the Allies' general offensive that had so scared the OHL at the end of September had not precipitated the feared rout and was slowing.[132] However, the Hindenburg Line had been broken and, even worse, the armistice note that Ludendorff had insisted be sent had undermined what was left of his army's combat motivation and, still more disastrously, its discipline. By mid-October, field post censors were reporting that soldiers demanded 'peace at any price'.[133] Some had surrendered claiming that an armistice had already been signed. Even worse, the number of stragglers and deserters in the rear areas had swelled after the armistice note, widely taken to be an admission of defeat, had been issued. Commanders understood the reasoning behind this indiscipline well. The men had decided, one army commander reported in the middle of the month, that 'they would be stupid if they now still let themselves be shot dead'.[134]

Ludendorff's opposition sparked a power struggle between the OHL and the civilian government. A strange reversal of positions had taken place. Prince Max was now determined to pursue the approach to Wilson to the end. The first note of 3 October had raised popular expectations of peace that could not be disappointed without provoking a dangerous wave of anger and Ludendorff had been unable to justify why fighting on should secure a better peace. Deeply suspicious of the general, Max feared that his hubris and vanity would lead to a destructive invasion of the Reich.[135] Overcoming military opposition by threatening to resign, he forced the Kaiser to support his desire to accede to Wilson's demand to halt submarine warfare. However, tension peaked when the American President's third note arrived on 23 October, in which he judged the reforms in German government as insufficiently far-reaching and warned that 'the United States cannot deal with any but veritable representatives of the German people ... If it must deal with the military masters and the monarchical autocrats of Germany ... it must demand, not peace negotiations, but surrender.'[136]

The army High Command responded to Wilson's note by issuing an order to the troops stating that the American President had demanded a capitulation, an unacceptable demand for the armed forces. Contradicting the Chancellor's policy, it warned that there was no choice but to embrace a 'fight to the bloody end'. The following day, 25 October, Hindenburg and Ludendorff hurried to Berlin against Max's express wishes. Their intention was to have the Kaiser dismiss him, break off negotiations with Wilson and return the country to a total war footing. Earlier in the conflict, their threats of resignation had succeeded in intimidating Wilhelm II into following their policy. However, now circumstances had changed. The OHL's prestige was diminished. Hindenburg remained important as a figurehead but Ludendorff's reputation had been greatly damaged by the military defeats. No less importantly, the Kaiser feared for his throne. Wilson's notes had made clear his disdain for the Reich's rulers, and the latest message appeared to offer Germans easier terms in exchange for revolution. As the imperial authorities were only too aware, so low was Wilhelm II's stock that his people would willingly sacrifice him for a better peace. 'In German newspapers, the removal of the Hohenzollern dynasty and the abdication of the current Kaiser is quite bluntly demanded,' observed one official report from 22 October. Advocates of this course had ceased to be confined to the ranks of the Independent Socialists and now extended well into the middle classes.[137]

Faced with this desperate situation, the Kaiser was prepared to support his Chancellor. Adopting Ludendorff's methods, Max had threatened to resign should the First Quartermaster General not be removed from his post. Decisive in winning over the monarch was the hope, planted in his mind by the Chief of the Privy Cabinet, Clemens von Delbrück, that it was Ludendorff's head rather than his own which Wilson really wanted.[138] On the morning of 26 October, Ludendorff and Hindenburg were summoned to the Bellevue Palace in western Berlin for an imperial audience. The Kaiser's demeanour was gruff. He reproached the two soldiers for their recent conduct, and declared that he had lost confidence in the General Staff. They had brought him 'to a terrible situation'. He criticized how scarcely three weeks earlier the OHL had demanded an armistice, but now wished to fight on and reject Wilson's offer, and he condemned its unauthorized order to the army to continue the fight. The interview ended with Ludendorff's dismissal. Hindenburg, whose departure the government feared might further fatally demoralize the army, was ordered to remain.[139]

A second and more fateful source of opposition to Max's peace policy came from the navy. Admiral Reinhard Scheer, the Chief of the Admiralty, was particularly disgruntled about the move to terminate the war. He feared that Ludendorff would surrender the navy to get a land armistice and the turn towards peace stopped preparations for his own personal vanity project: a vast naval armaments drive, intended to produce 450 new U-boats, named the Scheer Programme.[140] The Admiral's discontent grew when, after Wilson's second note, the government ordered an end to unrestricted submarine warfare. The fleet command took a weirdly detached view of Germany's plight. 'The Navy does not need an armistice' asserted a strategy document of 16 October, as if the marine could go on fighting when the rest of the nation had stopped. Still, with the army having conceded inevitable defeat and the government determined not to break peace negotiations, the fleet command searched for an appropriate response. The cessation of U-boat warfare permitted the battleships of the High Seas Fleet once again to become operational, and the Naval Command decided to send it out on a last, desperate operation against its arch-enemy, Britain's Grand Fleet. 'Even if it is not to be expected that this will bring a decisive turn in the course of events,' observed a naval strategy document of 16 October, 'nonetheless it is from a moral perspective a question of the Navy's honour and existence that it does its utmost in the final battle.'[141]

The Naval Command kept its intentions secret. Beyond a brief and obscure mention that the fleet now had operational freedom, neither the Kaiser nor Chancellor were consulted about the coming mission. Only Ludendorff was informed, and he was told to keep it quiet. The Naval Command did not aim to sabotage the government's peace moves. Nor would a fleet action relieve any of the pressure on the German army. Rather, in a further example of the myopia that had pushed them to advocate unrestricted U-boat warfare, naval commanders were thinking only of their service's prestige and interests. Officers' honour demanded a show of force before national capitulation. They were also motivated by more pragmatic considerations. The peacetime justification for building a surface fleet, that it could deter Britain from entering hostilities against Germany, had been shown to be false in 1914. Worse, still, the expensive vessels had been of little use in wartime, proving too few to beat the stronger Royal Navy decisively and impotent against the British blockade.[142] To save the service's prestige and future funding, its commanders felt dramatic action was needed before the war's end. Scheer's Chief of Staff, Rear Admiral von Trotha, set to work in early October on a suitably desperate scheme. His Operation Plan No. 19 envisaged a night attack by the whole High Seas Fleet in the Hoofden, the water that lay between Britain and the Netherlands. Smaller vessels would first harass maritime traffic on the Flanders coast and in the mouth of the Thames. This would, it was hoped, provoke the British Grand Fleet to sally out. Newly laid minefields and submarines stationed along its path would erode the Grand Fleet's strength, and give the Germans, who had only half its numbers, a chance of inflicting more damage. That few, if any German ships would return did not bother officers determined to choose death over dishonour. To the men, however, it was a 'suicide sortie'.[143]

There was no way that sailors would participate in such an operation. Morale in the High Seas Fleet was at its nadir. Sailors were still bitter about the repression after the mutinies in the summer of 1917, relations with officers were at best distant and often hostile, and the

Der **Arbeitsmann** gibt **Herz** und **Hand** wenn in **Gefahr** das **Vaterland**!

Jch kenne keine Parteien mehr.

15. THE 'FORTRESS PEACE'. An idealized image of the proletariat stalwartly offering its services for Germania's protection. The slogan on the shield is the Kaiser's famous phrase 'I no longer recognize any parties.'

16. HUNGER. People queuing to buy food in Cracow in 1916. Two policemen escort away a queue-jumper, while others keep order in the crowd.

17. THE WAR ON LAND (1). Austro-Hungarian soldiers manning one of their elaborate trenches on the Eastern Front, June 1916. The trench's depth offers protection from shellfire, and staves and brushwood weatherproof its high walls. However, troops would need time to get from its 'fox hole' shelter to the upper firing platform; a weakness which would prove fatal during the Brusilov offensive.

Pe această carte nu este iertat a se face ⊙ alte împărtăşiri.

Na ovoj dopisnici ne-smije se inače ništa ⊙⊙ saopćiti.

Auf dieser Karte darf sonst ⊙ nichts mitgeteilt werden. ⊙

Ezen a levelezőlapon mást nem ⊙⊙⊙ szabad közölni. ⊙⊙⊙⊙

⊙⊙⊙ Ich bin gesund und es geht mir gut. ⊙⊙⊙
Egészséges vagyok és jól érzem magamat.
⊙⊙⊙ Jsem zdráv a daří se mně dobře. ⊙⊙⊙
⊙ Jestem zdrów i powodzi mi się dobrze. ⊙
⊙⊙⊙ Я є здоров і менї веде ся добре. ⊙⊙⊙
⊙⊙⊙⊙⊙⊙⊙⊙ Sono sano e sto bene. ⊙⊙⊙⊙⊙⊙⊙⊙
⊙⊙⊙ Jaz sem zdrav in se mi dobro godi. ⊙⊙⊙
⊙⊙⊙⊙⊙⊙⊙ Zdrav sam i dobro mi je. ⊙⊙⊙⊙⊙⊙⊙
⊙⊙⊙⊙ Sunt sănătos şi îmi merge bine. ⊙⊙⊙⊙

Na tomto lístku nesmí se nic jiného sděliti.

Na tej kartce nie wol-no nic więcej dopisać.

Na tej dopisnici se ne sme ničesar drugega prijavljati.

Su questa cartolina non si dovrà ⊙ fare ulteriori comunicazioni. ⊙

На сїй картцї не вільно нїчо ⊙⊙ більш повідомляти. ⊙⊙

18. THE WAR ON LAND (2). A standard Austro-Hungarian field service postcard. The soldier could choose from nine different languages but was permitted to send only one compulsorily optimistic message: 'I am healthy and doing well'.

19. THE WAR ON LAND (3). German troops carry out a realistic practice assault behind the Eastern Front, spring 1916. The German army's trust in its men's intelligence and readiness to use training to cultivate initiative set it apart from its ally and goes far to explain its impressive combat performance.

Wie verhängnissvoll die „Eisernen-Portionen" im Felde sind.

Du sollst deine eiserne Portion nicht unerlaubt auffressen!

Eine Portion Eisen!

3 Tage strengeren Arrest = 2 Stunden am Baum.

20. THE WAR ON LAND (4). 'How fateful "iron rations" are in the field'. A German military pun: the soldier on the right has been tied to a tree after eating his emergency 'iron rations' without permission; a punishment known as *Anbinden* that was practised until 1917. The soldier on the left is running from a very different 'iron ration' fired over by the enemy.

21. THE WAR AT SEA (1). A German U-boat crew on the High Seas.
A shell has exploded prematurely in their deck gun, destroying its barrel;
just one of many hazards faced by submariners.

22. THE WAR AT SEA (2). Allied merchant seamen surrender in their lifeboats.
Their fate now depended in part on the U-boat commander who had sunk their ship.
Some commanders left their enemies to drift, but others disobeyed orders to act
ruthlessly and helped the wounded or even gave victims a tow towards land.

23. THE WAR AT SEA (3). Direct hit. A U-boat torpedoes an
Allied merchant vessel. U-boat warfare was typically conducted at
such close quarters.

24. CONQUERORS (1). 'Who is the Victor?' A propaganda poster
illustrating the Central Powers' extensive conquests and contrasting
them with the measly Entente gains, end of 1917.

25. CONQUERORS (2). 'The little enemy eats and speaks, / You Germans, you're not
barbarians after all!' The Germans imagined themselves as kindly culture-bearers in the
occupied zones. Yet in stark contrast to this propaganda, they were ruthlessly extracting
and exporting homewards as much food as they could lay their hands on.

26. THE END (1).
German prisoners
taken at the Battle of
St Quentin Canal,
2 October 1918. In the
war's final four months
385,500 German
soldiers surrendered,
a devastating loss of
manpower which
unnerved Ludendorff
and crippled his army's
fighting power.

27. THE END (2). Corpses on the Italian Front.

28. THE END (3). Revolution! Insurgents loyal to the revolutionary workers' and soldiers' councils take control of the streets of Berlin, 9 or 10 November 1918.

Der letzte Gruss

29. 'THE LAST GREETING'. A woman mourns her fallen husband with two of his wounded comrades. There were 533,000 war widows and 1,192,000 orphans in Germany by the armistice in November 1918.

best personnel had long ago been transferred to the U-boats.[144] Those who remained were fractious and looking forward to peace. At the end of September 1918 a rumour had circulated that the men would leave their ships if no treaty were concluded by mid-October. When, on the evening of 29 October, word spread that the fleet's squadron chiefs had been called to the High Sea Command in order to be briefed for an operation scheduled for the following day, the reaction was immediate. At 10 p.m., sailors on three of the Third Squadron's five battleships announced that they would passively resist any operation. When insubordination spread to other ships, the mission was cancelled. Making a terrible error, the fleet's commander decided to disperse his rebellious squadrons, and divided the battleships between the Elbe, Kiel and Wilhelmshaven.[145]

The final collapse of imperial Germany began in Kiel. The Third Squadron steamed into the port on 31 October. The city's naval governor, Vice Admiral Wilhelm Souchon, had only just arrived at his post, and was totally unprepared for the arrival of thousands of mutinous sailors. The battleships' officers did nothing to help him, for, anxious to rid their vessels of rebellious personnel, they granted generous shore leave. At first, the men protested solely for the release of arrested comrades. However, once the authorities attempted to stop them meeting and refused any compromise, defiance spread. The port's dockyard workers and garrison went over to the sailors and Souchon suddenly found himself with hardly any reliable units to control ever larger crowds. On 3 November, 6,000 people demonstrated for the arrested sailors' release. Some had broken into army barracks and, without resistance from the sentries, armed themselves and freed the sailors. When the crowd was fired upon by a patrol of NCOs and officers, there was a brief fire-fight, with seven dead and twenty-nine people wounded. The bloodshed triggered revolution. On the following night, soldiers' and sailors' councils were formed in all barracks and on all the ships docked at Kiel. The revolt now became explicitly political. The sailors, continuing to follow the script of the Russian revolution, addressed each other as 'comrade Bolsheviks'. Demands for regime change were now loud. The revolutionaries wanted the abdication of the Hohenzollerns, universal suffrage for men and women, and a peace concluded on the basis of self-determination without annexations or indemnities.[146]

In the following days, the revolution spread as sailors left Kiel for other parts of Germany. The cities on the north coast were first to join. Five hundred red sailors took Lübeck bloodlessly on 5 November, and Hamburg, Bremen and Wilhelmshaven fell the next day. On 7 November the revolution moved inland, taking Hanover, Oldenburg and Cologne. In Munich, 50,000 people joined in a demonstration organized jointly by the SPD and USPD, which took the city's public buildings and barracks. In the early hours of 8 November the USPD's Kurt Eisner proclaimed a Socialist Republic of Bavaria.[147] The real prize and the key to the success of the revolution was, however, Germany's capital, Berlin. Prince Max's government learned of how serious the revolt in Kiel had been on 5 November, when Gustav Noske, the SPD deputy sent to the port to restore order, reported. On the same day Wilson had sent his final note informing the Germans that Marshal Foch, the Supreme Commander of the Allies on the Western Front, had been authorized to communicate armistice terms to their representatives. As the revolution's rapid spread became known, the new First Quartermaster General, Wilhelm Groener, advised that the Allies' terms must now be accepted immediately. Peace appeared to offer the Reich's sole chance of stopping the revolution.[148]

The government in the meantime attempted to slow the spread of the revolutionaries. The military did what it could to protect Berlin. The local military commander, General Alexander von Linsingen, banned USPD demonstrations and posted troops at the railway stations to catch revolutionary sailors.[149] However, the pressure from Wilson and the desire of a large section of the population for far-reaching reform was overwhelming. Friedrich Ebert, the SPD chairman, feared Bolshevik revolution no less than Prince Max, and was prepared to continue the party's wartime work of reining in the masses. However, as radicalization and anger had grown, the moderate Social Democrats could maintain credibility and appeal only by voicing popular demands. On 7 November, Ebert warned the Chancellor that 'if the Kaiser does not abdicate, the social revolution is inevitable'. Later that day, the SPD issued an ultimatum to the government stating that the Kaiser and Crown Prince must abdicate by noon on the morrow. The publication of the ultimatum helped win the SPD support in Berlin, stopping workers turning to more revolutionary groups to vent their discontent. Yet even on 8 November the Kaiser, who was at military headquarters at Spa, refused. In an evening telephone conversation with Max, he informed his frustrated Chancellor that he intended to restore order at the head of his armies.[150]

Time ran out for the Kaiser, Max and Imperial Germany on 9 November. The decisive pressure came from the two rival centres of power that had developed during the war: the army and the SPD. On the Western Front, Groener had called in thirty-nine middle-ranking commanders to canvass their views on the troops' readiness to fight for the Kaiser and against Bolshevism.[151] Just one thought that his men would follow their monarch, a damning indication of the disappearance of the regime's legitimacy among soldiers as well as civilians. The news jolted the Kaiser into tentatively accepting abdication, although he still tried to hang on, proposing that evening to relinquish the German but not the Prussian throne. By that time events had left him far behind. In Berlin, the Independent Socialists had called a mass demonstration for 9 a.m. in the morning. The SPD could now not afford to appear as a part of the old regime and abandoned the government. Max, believing that procrastination merely increased the danger, announced the Kaiser's abdication on his own authority at noon. He then passed his chancellorship to Ebert. On the streets were tens of thousands of factory workers urged on by the revolutionary shop stewards. Military units across the capital had mutinied. A soldiers' council occupied the War Ministry.[152] Pre-empting the Independent Socialists, at 2 p.m. the SPD leader Philipp Scheidemann stepped out onto the Reichstag's reading room balcony and proclaimed the creation of a republic. He assured the crowd that Wilhelm II had abdicated and that the new government would be made up of both the Reich's Socialist parties. With an eye to limiting popular radicalism, he made clear that this should be a very German revolution: 'Calm, order and security, that is what we now need!' Most poignantly, seeking to find some achievement from four years of horror, he presented the break between Germans and their defeated and delegitimized leaders as a victory of sorts. 'The German people has triumphed everywhere. The old rotten regime has collapsed. Militarism is finished!'[153]

An armistice delegation headed by the Centre Party deputy Matthias Erzberger had crossed the Western Front on the evening of 7 November 1918. On 11 November, at 5.20 a.m., its four members, together with the Allied Supreme Commander, Ferdinand Foch, and the British First Sea Lord, Admiral Sir Rosslyn Wemyss, signed an armistice agreement, which went into effect just under six hours later, at 11 a.m., at last ending the fighting. Perhaps justly, given the spirit in which the German military had started its move to peace, the conditions were hard. The German army was obliged to give up large stocks of weaponry, materiel and rail equipment, and was to undertake an immediate evacuation of all western invaded territory. The fleet would be interned. German territory on the left bank of the Rhine would be occupied and Alsace-Lorraine surrendered. Less fair, and certainly the harshest blow for the German delegates, was the continuation of the British naval blockade. Although some grudging help with provisioning was promised, the Reich was to be kept hungry and helpless. A formal protest read out by Erzberger at the signing warned that the terms would drive Germans into anarchy and famine. Although humiliated, he ended defiantly: 'A nation of seventy millions of people suffers, but it does not die.'[154]

For Germans, and indeed for most central Europeans, the armistice was not quite the caesura that is remembered further west. There was no return to 'peace' as in France or Britain. 'Normality' had become a permanent casualty of the war. True, the mass slaughter of the *Materialschlacht* was over, but misery, deprivation and shortages continued until, and even beyond, the summer of 1919 when the blockade was lifted. The violence was also not ended. Although smaller in scale, it had transferred into the homelands that men had sought to protect. The political and ethnic fault lines deepened by war were the new 'fronts' of the post-armistice period. Radical leftist revolutions and right-wing putsches would shake the weakened German state in the coming years. In the east, the Polish minority would rise up and fight for cession. Among the victims of this post-war bloodshed would be Erzberger himself, who was murdered while out for a walk in August 1921 by right-wing extremists – for signing the armistice agreement. The First World War had ended. Its legacy of suffering and violence proved far longer lasting.[155]

Epilogue

The brave new world that formed in the dying embers of the war was fixed and formalized in the months after the armistices of the autumn of 1918. While the leaders of the victorious Allied powers earnestly debated the continent's future in Paris, the new nation states of central Europe cemented control over their territory and secured with force contested land, most often at the expense of the German, Austrian and Hungarian republics. A treaty ending the war in the west was signed with Germany on 28 June 1919. To underline their enemy's humiliation, the French selected the Hall of Mirrors in the Palace of Versailles as the venue – the place where nearly half a century earlier a unified Germany had been proclaimed. Almost as an afterthought, a treaty with the new Austria was signed at Saint-Germain in September 1919. Due to Bolshevik revolution, and then a brutal counter-revolution, only in June 1920 was the Treaty of Trianon with Hungary sealed.[1]

The old order had long disappeared by this point. Most of its members did not suffer greatly. Kaiser Wilhelm II had crossed into Holland on 10 November 1918. He formally abdicated on 28 November. For sure the first eighteen months of exile were anxious. Money was tight, and his future uncertain. He grew a beard to make himself less recognizable and at the turn of 1918–19 was reduced to feigning madness in the hope of avoiding extradition. All ended happily, however. The Dutch reluctantly protected him. The international determination to try him for what Article 227 of the Versailles Treaty described vaguely as 'a supreme offence against international morality and the sanctity of treaties' eventually waned. Wilhelm bought a lovely moated villa outside the Dutch village of Doorn, from which he terrorized the neighbours with his imperial ways. His wife died in April 1921, but a year later, at the age of sixty-three, he married thirty-five-year-old Princess Hermine of Schönaich-Carolath. He passed away disgruntled but not discontented on 4 June 1941.[2] Emperor Karl's fate was stranger. Having dodged putting his name to the armistice with Italy by relinquishing control of his armies, he gave up all right to involvement in the governance of the Austrian state on 11 November 1918. However, he never formally abdicated. After he attempted twice in 1921 to reclaim the Hungarian Crown of St Stephen, the Allies decided he was a threat to European stability and moved him with his family from exile in Switzerland to distant Madeira. There on 1 April 1922, aged thirty-four, he died of influenza. Alone of the Central Powers' leaders, this weak and uncourageous man is remembered with some fondness – possibly helped by the fact that unlike most he never put pen to paper to give a painfully self-exculpating account of his war. Although he was incapable of working miracles during hostilities to release his peoples from misery and bloodshed, some claim that he managed one after the conflict: the lesser feat of curing after his death a Brazilian nun suffering from varicose veins. In October 2004, Pope John Paul II beatified this last Habsburg Emperor.[3]

The Central Powers' other wartime leaders did not suffer, despite the Allies' declared intention to punish those whom they regarded as responsible for the horrors of the conflict. Several of the men who had led them into hostilities were already dead by 1918. The Austrian and Hungarian Minister Presidents in 1914, Stürgkh and Tisza, had both been assassinated during the war. The Chief of the Prussian General Staff, Helmuth von Moltke, had died a broken man in 1916. Bethmann Hollweg, the former German Chancellor, survived and was unique among the leaders of any power in his readiness to answer for and defend his actions. On learning in June 1919 that the Allies intended to try the Kaiser, he honourably wrote to the French Premier Georges Clemenceau to ask that he stand trial in his imperial master's stead. 'According to the constitutional laws of the empire,' he had argued, 'I bear entire responsibility for the emperor's political actions during my tenure of office as Chancellor.' His offer went unanswered.[4] The Allies' conveniently simplistic understanding of the conflict as a German crime meant that surviving Habsburg leaders were ignored. Count Berchtold, the Austro-Hungarian Foreign Minister in 1914, a man who bore more guilt than most for the conflagration, was permitted to retire unmolested to his estates at Csepreg in Hungary, where he died in 1942. Leon Biliński, the Finance Minister who was far less culpable but had attended the conspiratorial Common Ministerial Councils in July 1914 where war with Serbia was planned, served in the same post in 1919 for France's new ally, independent Poland.[5]

Most importantly, no senior military figures ever stood trial. The Chief of the Habsburg General Staff until 1917, Franz Conrad von Hötzendorf, would today be a prime defendant at any war crimes tribunal, both for his part in starting the conflict and as the commander of an army that massacred tens of thousands of Ukrainian civilians in 1914. Yet the Allies had little interest in the Habsburg regime and still less in dead eastern European peasants. He was left to make a fortune on his memoirs and died at the pleasant south German spa of Bad Mergentheim in August 1925.[6] Paul von Hindenburg and Erich Ludendorff were very briefly placed on a list of suspected war criminals, before the Allies thought better of it. The military duo who had led Germany through the last two years of war had very different futures. Ludendorff cut a pathetic figure after his failure. In mid-November 1918 he had fled Berlin, fearing that if he stayed he would be lynched or tried. He lay low in Sweden, writing a set of self-pitying memoirs until the revolution abated. After his return to Germany, his paranoia grew and he settled on Jews as the scapegoat for his downfall. He participated in far-right politics and was a co-conspirator in the Nazis' 1923 Munich Putsch, but a run at the presidency in 1925 was an embarrassing failure.[7] By contrast, Hindenburg ended the war with his reputation intact. He marched back at the head of the German army in November 1918, successfully contriving to lay the blame for the Third OHL's military defeat on civilians and a government that supposedly had 'stabbed' the loyal soldiers 'in the back'. He was able to capitalize on his wartime popularity in order to return as Germany's figurehead. In 1925, after the death of its first incumbent, Friedrich Ebert, he ran for and won the presidency of the German republic. He was in his second term when in 1933, during acute economic and political crisis, he appointed as his Chancellor Adolf Hitler.[8]

The German and Austro-Hungarian states, it should by now be clear, had no monopoly on brutal and illegal conduct during the First World War. Nonetheless, even by the still poorly developed standards of contemporary international law, they had committed some heinous crimes. The German invasion of neutral Belgium and unrestricted submarine warfare, the ruthless exploitation of civilians as slave labour, above all in Ober Ost and with the 1916 Belgian deportations, and the killing of non-combatants in 1914, all constituted violations. However, the men responsible for these actions and for the far greater atrocity perpetrated by the Central Powers' ally Ottoman Turkey, the Armenian genocide, went largely unpunished. To be fair, after the Ottoman armistice of 30 October, the Sultanate installed by the British did investigate, at the urging of the Allies. Special Military Tribunals uncovered copious evidence of the intention to wipe out the Armenians and sentenced the Empire's wartime leaders to death, but as all were tried *in absentia* the rulings lacked impact.[9] The trials that the German state was forced by the Allies to hold at the High Court in Leipzig in 1921, after it refused to extradite war crimes suspects, were far less diligently pursued or inspiring. Forty-five cases were submitted, but just seventeen actually tried. The accused were small fry: army personnel, mostly officers, who had ordered military prisoners to be shot or had neglected them in camps, others who had attacked civilians, and submarine commanders accused of sinking hospital ships. Only four trials ended with convictions.[10] International law, which had already been undermined by both sides' naval blockades and brutal behaviour towards occupied enemy subjects, was further discredited by the failure to prosecute and punish major violations, if only those committed by the defeated. This mattered dreadfully. Hitler drew the appropriate lesson when in August 1939 he prepared to launch racial war against Poland. Urging his generals to undertake 'the physical destruction of the enemy', he quashed scruples with a nod to the past: 'Who, after all, speaks today of the annihilation of the Armenians?'[11]

The post-war order quickly turned out to please nobody in east-central Europe. The region's reorganization along national lines had already taken place on the ground before the leaders of the victorious powers began their peace deliberations in Paris in January 1919. In all likelihood this offered the only possibility of stability, but the chances of success were not good. The region was simply too ethnically mixed to permit strong homogeneous nation states. In Poland, Czechoslovakia and a new Romania swollen with ex-Hungarian territory, around a third of the populations were ethnic minorities. The Kingdom of Serbs, Croats and Slovenes was, as its name suggested, a mishmash of peoples, who below the elites often nurtured long-held historical grievances towards each other rather than embrace the new Yugoslav idealism.[12] In the post-war settlement's favour, it has been pointed out that Europe's political reorganization halved its minorities, from 60 million to 30 million. Treaties imposed on the new states were supposed to guarantee minority rights.[13] Yet this misses the crucial point that both Wilsonian propaganda's espousal of the 'self-determination of peoples' and the war itself had raised national aspirations to fever pitch. Minority status in a continent constructed upon the basis of nation states was far less attractive or acceptable than under the old empires. By one reckoning, even though minority numbers had declined, ethnic conflicts in the territory of what had been Austria-Hungary nearly doubled after 1918, from nine to at least seventeen. Older antagonisms, such as that between the Czechs and Germans of Bohemia, were joined by new national struggles as Czechs and Poles in Teschen, Germans and Croatians in Yugoslavia, and Romanians and Germans in Romania all squared up to each other.[14]

President Wilson made a fatal mistake in placing the 'self-determination of peoples' at the centre of his post-war vision. The slogan made effective wartime propaganda and contributed to his popularity and moral authority, but it also ensured that his post-war order would be immediately discredited in many eyes. The reason for this was simple: so mixed were the peoples of east-central Europe that not everyone could be permitted to exercise this new right. There would be winners and there would be losers, and *Realpolitik* dictated that the latter would be the two ethnic groups cowed by defeat, the Germans and the Magyars. Both peoples had just reason to feel deeply aggrieved with Wilson. The American President had indicated in speeches and in his responses to the Central Powers' peace notes in 1918 that his war was with autocrats, not their peoples. While 'surrender' would be demanded of the old imperial regimes, he had warned on 23 October, a genuinely representative government could expect 'peace negotiations' on the basis of the Fourteen Points. The Germans had duly revolted, but half a year later there had been no negotiations, just a 'Diktat', which their representatives had been permitted to comment upon before the victors' final ruling. The Hungarians' experience was more turbulent and less to Wilson's liking, comprising a moderate revolution, a Bolshevik takeover, and then a right-wing autocracy led by a former Habsburg admiral, but they received similar treatment at the Allies' hands. The terms imposed on both powers were, as even members of the Allied delegations recognized, devastating. Germany's Foreign Minister, Count Ulrich von

Brockdorff-Rantzau, said after he had read the voluminous list of demands, conditions and losses to which his country was expected to bow under threat of invasion that Wilson and his associates should have saved their time. A single clause would have sufficed: 'L'Allemagne renonce à son existence.'[15]

Versailles and Trianon constructed the post-war order at the expense of Germans and Hungarians, a fact that explains why neither country's government ever accepted it. The non-application of its central organizing principle, national self-determination, to the losers was later confirmed when German Austrians, who in October 1918 had assumed they would join Germany, were forbidden by the victors from doing so. At Versailles, Germany was refused access to the League of Nations, the international body supposed to bind the new post-war world, and it lost 13 per cent of its territory and 10 per cent of its population. Hungary did even worse, losing a staggering 67.3 per cent of its territory and 73.5 per cent of its inhabitants.[16] Of course, most of the subjects transferred were Romanians, Slovaks, Alsace-Lorrainers, Danes or Poles who could plausibly, if not always correctly, be presented as desirous of joining Romania, Czechoslovakia, France or Poland. In ambiguous areas like Masuria and Upper Silesia in Germany's east, plebiscites were held to determine the wishes of their inhabitants. Nonetheless, there were grievous injustices, most notably the transfer of unambiguously German Danzig to the League as a free state (a measure taken to give Poland access to the sea). The territory transfers and refusals to permit German Bohemians to 'self-determine' and join with Austria, or Austrians with Germany, left 13 million Germans outside the Reich's borders. Outside interwar Hungary were Magyar minorities totalling 3.23 million people.[17] The anger felt in the heartlands at the territorial loss was nothing compared with the intense bitterness of compatriots with property and livelihoods there who sold up or were forced out. From the Polish Corridor, the strip of formerly German land allocated to Poland that cut East Prussia from the rest of interwar Germany, 575,000 of the 1.1 million Germans who had resided there in 1919 had six years later moved to the new German Republic.[18] In the west, as many as 200,000 of the 300,000-strong German population left or were expelled from Alsace-Lorraine.[19] Some 426,000 Hungarians had also fled from territories taken by Czechoslovakia, Yugoslavia, Romania and Austria by 1924. The large numbers who departed underline that territorial loss brought by defeat and Wilson's new order were not merely smears on national honour; they destroyed many ordinary people's lives.[20]

In addition to the loss of territory imposed or confirmed by Versailles and Trianon, the treaties demanded reparations. Article 231 of Versailles, which set out the legal basis for this claim, asserted 'the responsibility of Germany and her allies for causing all the loss and damage to which the Allied and Associated Governments and their nationals have been subjected as a consequence of the war imposed upon them by the aggression of Germany and her allies'. Historians have pointed out that the figure of 132 billion gold marks that the Allies settled on for Germany in 1921 was largely notional and intended to satisfy vengeful domestic opinion. The sum that they really aimed at, 50 billion gold marks paid over thirty-six years, was entirely manageable.[21] However, the German public was shocked by the larger claim. Hyperinflation, which was caused by their government's economic mismanagement but blamed on reparations, wiped out the value of their savings and their war bonds and increased their anger. Reparations became a particular source of acrimony for two other reasons. First, the German delegation in Paris in 1919 tried to discredit the legal basis on which claims for payment rested by casting Article 231 as 'the war-guilt clause'. Although the Allies were not in fact demanding any admission of culpability, the term stuck and turned a financial transaction into an emotive moral issue. Second, in January 1923, after the German state had continually defaulted on payment, the French and Belgians, who together with the British were already in occupation of the left bank of the Rhine, invaded the industrial Ruhr region. The propaganda of fear spread by the imperial authorities in 1917 now appeared uncannily prescient. Enemy invasion, German workers coerced to labour for a hated oppressor, even the deliberately humiliating use of black French troops to oversee the loading of coal into wagons for dispatch to France, had all come about in the wake of defeat. There was violence. Some 132 German civilians were killed, 4,124 imprisoned and 172,000 expelled by French and Belgian forces. The Reich's army, reduced by Versailles to just 100,000 men, was impotent to react.[22]

All this broke on a people that, like all east-central European societies, was already deeply traumatized. Central European peoples had invested heavily in the war and its psychological impact was correspondingly enormous. Some have blamed the long years of mass killing for the brutalization of interwar society and politics.[23] Yet the paramilitary violence that wracked the region after the war was perpetrated by only a small minority of men. As the speed with which the German army demobilized at the end of 1918 testifies, most soldiers just wished to go home.[24] Instead, suffering was key to shaping the conflict's emotional legacy. Suffering was everywhere across east-central Europe. It was most visible in the human wreckage left by war – the millions of disabled veterans and the bereaved. In Germany, 533,000 war widows and 1,192,000 orphans survived their fallen soldiers.[25] Czechoslovakia, whose population was one-fifth of that of the Reich and whose soldiers were alleged not to have fought well, paid pensions for 121,215 war widows and 238,000 orphans.[26] However, war had brought a surfeit of suffering with many causes. Besides battle and bereavement, hunger and cold on the home fronts caused intense suffering. Invaded East Prussians and deported Galician Jews had suffered. So too did people who lost their homes after the war as borders moved.

This suffering, and the jealousies, prejudices and violence that it spawned or exacerbated, was highly and lastingly destructive. One specific and suggestive link between German suffering in the First World War and the crimes against humanity committed a quarter of a century later can be made. Germans who lived in ethnically mixed border areas, where war deprivation inflamed racial animosities, were disproportionately likely to take part in the Nazi genocide of the Jews. Those who in addition lost their homes as frontiers moved at the conflict's end were six times over-represented among Holocaust perpetrators.[27] More generally, wartime suffering at home fractured societies along class and racial fault lines. These would be torn open further by inter-ethnic paramilitary fighting, left-wing revolutions and bloody far-right reprisals in the aftermath of the conflict. Wartime suffering was at the root of what one left-wing intellectual described ominously in 1929 as 'the wild and brutal atmosphere of hatred and revenge which is still the dominating current of Eastern Europe'.[28]

The other important legacy of wartime suffering was a desperate search for meaning. At the apex of the value system of central European war culture had been the concept of sacrifice: a voluntary surrender to loss, suffering or pain for a higher cause. German and Austro-Hungarian societies sacrificed men in staggering numbers in 1914–18: 2,036,897 German soldiers were killed.[29] Austro-Hungarian casualties were never properly calculated, but totalled between 1,100,000 and 1,200,000. Austrian Germans and Hungarians suffered most, followed closely by Slovenes and Moravian Czechs.[30] Habsburg defeat did not, at least officially, devalue the sacrifices of Czech, Polish or Yugoslav soldiers. The new states simply reinterpreted the men's deaths as in the cause of independence. There was no public space for alternative views.[31] For Germans, by contrast, defeat brought great cognitive dissonance. Ruth Höfner blurted out the dilemma immediately on learning of the armistice. 'For what have German mothers sacrificed their sons?' she asked.[32] For Anna Kohnstern, the Hamburg woman who for four years had devotedly sent letters and gifts of love to her soldier son Albert at the front, this question must have been accompanied by extraordinary pain. He was killed on 26 October 1918, barely two weeks before the fighting at last stopped.[33] With spite, the French government refused until 1925 to permit ordinary Germans to visit war graves on its soil, making the mourning of parents even more difficult, their lives even more empty.[34]

People across and beyond east-central Europe struggled to come to terms with the mass death of 1914–18. The dilemma of how to vindicate the sacrifices of beloved sons, brothers and fathers after a lost war gave the German interwar cult of the fallen soldier a unique character and intensity. The municipal, Church and local networks that had supported soldiers when they had lived, mobilized again to honour them in death. Many individuals took comfort from thinking of the fallen as Christ-like martyrs or as reposing in deep sleep. The idea too that the dead looked on, and that like Christ or a sleeper they must rise again, permeated national consciousness. The questions of what they had died for and what they desired divided Germans across the political spectrum, but even republicans imagined the dead admonishing the living to resurrect the Fatherland. The far right, which strove to establish itself as the voice of veterans and the guardians of the memory of fallen soldiers, would embrace a literal and militant understanding of this wish. For its adherents, the defeat of 1918 was in fact a betrayal to be avenged and overturned.[35]

The First World War was a catastrophe for central and eastern Europe. The new republics that replaced the old, discredited empires were themselves undermined by the war's bitter legacy. Impoverished, insecure and frequently with large, resentful minorities, most proved unstable. War had rent the fabric of their multi-ethnic societies and disastrously exacerbated racial divisions, bequeathing lasting antagonisms above all against older Jewish and new German minorities. Within a decade, there was little left of Wilson's new democratic order, for most of the east had fallen under the rule of autocratic strongmen. Germany too was ruined. The national unity of 1914 had through war collapsed in acrimony, and the divisions between the left and an anti-Semitic right widened and became more vicious in its aftermath. The struggle had been a people's war. The suffering and sacrifice had been immense. Those who survived the ordeal were left with the question of what it had all been for.

Notes

INTRODUCTION

1. Marshal Joffre, the Ex-Crown Prince of Germany, Marshal Foch and Marshal [*sic*] Ludendorff, *The Two Battles of the Marne* (London, 1927), p. 213.
2. G. F. Kennan, *The Decline of Bismarck's European Order: Franco-Russian Relations, 1875–1890* (Princeton, NY, 1979), p. 3.
3. R. Overmans, 'Kriegsverluste', in G. Hirschfeld, G. Krumeich, I. Renz and M. Pöhlmann (eds.), *Enzyklopädie Erster Weltkrieg*, 2nd edn (Paderborn, 2004), pp. 664–5.
4. Bethmann Hollweg, quoted in K. H. Jarausch, *The Enigmatic Chancellor: Bethmann Hollweg and the Hubris of Imperial Germany* (New Haven, CT, and London, 1973), p. 280.
5. See A. Watson, *Enduring the Great War: Combat, Morale and Collapse in the German and British Armies, 1914–1918* (Cambridge, 2008), p. 156, and G. Gratz and R. Schüller, *Der wirtschaftliche Zusammenbruch Österreich-Ungarns. Die Tragödie der Erschöpfung* (Vienna and New Haven, CT, 1930), pp. 150–51.
6. S. Broadberry and M. Harrison, 'The Economics of World War I: An Overview', in S. Broadberry and M. Harrison (eds.), *The Economics of World War I* (Cambridge, New York, Melbourne, Madrid, Cape Town, Singapore and São Paulo, 2005), p. 8.
7. M. Dydyński (Cracow), diary/memoir, p. 125, 15 March 1915. AN Cracow: 645–70.
8. C. Führ, *Das k.u.k. Armeeoberkommando und die Innenpolitik in Österreich, 1914–1917* (Graz, Vienna and Cologne, 1968), and W. Deist (ed.), *Militär und Innenpolitik im Weltkrieg, 1914–1918* (2 vols., Dusseldorf, 1970).
9. T. Nipperdey, *Deutsche Geschichte, 1866–1918. Machtstaat vor der Demokratie* (2 vols., Munich, 1998), ii, pp. 47, 51, 182–3 and 188–91, and R. A. Kann, *A History of the Habsburg Empire, 1526–1918* (Berkeley and Los Angeles, CA, and London, 1974), pp. 326–42.

10. For an introduction, see H. Lasswell's pioneering *Propaganda Technique in the World War* (London and New York, 1927).

I. DECISIONS FOR WAR

1. J. Redlich, *Schicksalsjahre Österreichs, 1908–1919. Das politische Tagebuch Josef Redlichs*, ed. F. Fellner (2 vols., Graz and Cologne, 1953), ii, p. 153 (entry for 3 November 1916).
2. J. Leslie, 'Österreich-Ungarn vor dem Kriegsausbruch. Der Ballhausplatz in Wien im Juli 1914 aus der Sicht eines österreichisch ungarischen Diplomaten', in R. Melville, C. Scharf, M. Vogt and U. Wengenroth (eds.), *Deutschland und Europa in der Neuzeit. Festschrift für Karl Otmar Freiherr von Aretin zum 65. Geburtstag. 2. Halbband* (Stuttgart, 1988), pp. 675 and 678–80.
3. C. Clark, *The Sleepwalkers: How Europe Went to War in 1914* (New York, 2013), pp. 396–7.
4. V. Dedijer, *The Road to Sarajevo* (London, Fakenham and Reading, 1967), pp. 175–80, 290–301 and 366–81. Also Clark, *Sleepwalkers*, pp. 48–9.
5. F. Fellner, 'Die "Mission Hoyos"', in W. Alff (ed.), *Deutschlands Sonderung von Europa, 1862–1945* (Frankfurt am Main, Bern and New York, 1984), pp. 294–5 and 309–11; Clark, *Sleepwalkers*, pp. 114–15 and 400–402.
6. Wilhelm II on a report from the German ambassador to Vienna, Baron Heinrich von Tschirschky und Bögendorff, to Bethmann Hollweg, 30 June 1914, in I. Geiss (ed.), *July 1914: The Outbreak of the First World War: Selected Documents* (London, 1967), p. 65.
7. Szögyényi to Berchtold, 5 July 1914, in Geiss (ed.), *July 1914*, pp. 76–7.
8. Szögyényi to Berchtold, 6 July 1914, in ibid., p. 79.
9. Fellner, 'Die "Mission Hoyos"', p. 311.
10. Falkenhayn to Moltke, 5 July 1914, in Geiss (ed.), *July 1914*, pp. 77–8, and Plessen, diary, 5 July 1914, in H. Afflerbach (ed.), *Kaiser Wilhelm II. als Oberster Kriegsherr im Ersten Weltkrieg. Quellen aus der militärischen Umgebung des Kaisers, 1914–1918* (Munich, 2005), p. 641.
11. Fellner, 'Die "Mission Hoyos"', pp. 312–13, and Jarausch, *The Enigmatic Chancellor*, pp. 155–6. For the contrary but unsustainable view that the Germans pushed Vienna to war during July, see F. Fischer, *Germany's Aims in the First World War* (London, 1967), esp. pp. 57–61.
12. Minutes of the Council of Ministers, 7 July 1914, in L. Bittner and H. Ueebersberger (eds.), *Österreich-Ungarns Aussenpolitik von der bosnischen Krise 1908 bis zum Kriegsausbruch 1914* (Vienna and Leipzig, 1930), pp. 343–51. The translations follow the abridged version in Geiss (ed.), *July 1914*, pp. 80–87. Also S. R. Williamson, Jr, *Austria-Hungary and the Origins of the First World War* (Basingstoke and London, 1991), pp. 197–200.

13. Tschirschky to Jagow, 10 July 1914, in Geiss (ed.), *July 1914*, p. 107, and M. Rauchensteiner, *Der Tod des Doppeladlers. Österreich-Ungarn und der Erste Weltkrieg* (Graz, Vienna and Cologne, 1993), p. 75.

14. Clark, *Sleepwalkers*, pp. 391–7.

15. Ibid., pp. 381–7 and 453–4.

16. D. G. Herrmann, *The Arming of Europe and the Making of the First World War* (Princeton, NJ, 1996), p. 234.

17. Berchtold to Franz Joseph, 14 July 1914, in Geiss (ed.), *July 1914*, p. 103.

18. F. Conrad von Hötzendorf, *Aus meiner Dienstzeit, 1906–1918. 24. Juni 1914 bis 30. September 1914. Die politischen und militärischen Vorgänge vom Fürstenmord in Sarajevo bis zum Abschluß der ersten und bis zum Beginn der zweiten Offensive gegen Serbien und Rußland* (4 vols., Vienna, 1923), iv, pp. 51 and 53–6.

19. S. Tisza, *Count Stephen Tisza, Prime Minister of Hungary: Letters (1914–1916)*, trans. C. de Bussy (New York, San Francisco, Bern, Frankfurt am Main, Paris and London, 1991), pp. 29–30 (letter of 26 August 1914).

20. Clark, *Sleepwalkers*, pp. 101–4 and 392.

21. Tschirschky to Bethmann, 14 July 1914, and Minutes of the Council of Ministers, 19 July 1914, in Geiss (ed.), *July 1914*, pp. 116 and 139.

22. Williamson, *Austria-Hungary*, pp. 200–202.

23. Berchtold to Giesl, 20 July 1914, in Geiss (ed.), *July 1914*, pp. 142–6. For the composition of the ultimatum, see Rauchensteiner, *Tod des Doppeladlers*, pp. 78–9.

24. Clark, *Sleepwalkers*, pp. 452–7.

25. Docs. 10396, 10399 and 10400 in Bittner and Uebersberger (eds.), *Österreich-Ungarns Aussenpolitik*, pp. 518–19 and 522–6.

26. Szápáry, telegram, 21 July 1914, in ibid., p. 568. See also the masterful account in Clark, *Sleepwalkers*, pp. 444–6.

27. Jagow to Lichnowsky, 18 July 1914, in Geiss (ed.), *July 1914*, p. 122.

28. Czernin to Berchtold, 22 June 1914, quoted in G. A. Tunstall, Jr, 'Austria-Hungary', in R. F. Hamilton and H. Herwig (eds.), *The Origins of World War I* (Cambridge, New York, Melbourne, Madrid and Cape Town, 2003), p. 128. For other foreigners' negative perceptions of the Habsburg Empire, see B. Jelavich, 'Clouded Image: Critical Perceptions of the Habsburg Empire in 1914', *Austrian History Yearbook* 23 (1992), pp. 23–35.

29. R. A. Kann, *A History of the Habsburg Empire, 1526–1918* (Berkeley and Los Angeles, CA, and London, 1974), pp. 331–4.

30. R. Okey, *Taming Balkan Nationalism* (Oxford, 2007), pp. vii–viii, 26 and 217–23.

31. C. A. Macartney, *The Habsburg Empire, 1790–1918* (London, 1968), pp. 693, 758–66, Kann, *History of the Habsburg Empire*, pp. 456–61, and F. T. Zsuppán, 'The Hungarian Political Scene', in M. Cornwall (ed.), *The*

Last Years of Austria-Hungary: A Multi-National Experiment in Early Twentieth-Century Europe (Exeter, 2002), pp. 100–103.

32. R. Okey, *The Habsburg Monarchy: From Enlightenment to Eclipse* (New York, 2001), pp. 305–8, and Macartney, *Habsburg Empire*, pp. 664–9.

33. Macartney, *Habsburg Empire*, p. 681.

34. M. Cattaruzza, 'Nationalitätenkonflikte in Triest im Rahmen der Nationalitätenfrage in der Habsburger Monarchie 1850–1914', in Melville, Scharf, Vogt and Wengenroth (eds.), *Deutschland und Europa in der Neuzeit*, pp. 722–3.

35. C. Albrecht, 'The Rhetoric of Economic Nationalism in the Boycott Campaigns of the Late Habsburg Monarchy', *Austrian History Yearbook* 32 (2001), pp. 56–61.

36. G. E. Rotheberg, *The Army of Francis Joseph* (West Lafayette, IN, 1976, 1998), p. 130, and G. Kronenbitter, 'Krieg im Frieden'. *Die Führung der k.u.k. Armee und die Großmachtpolitik Österreichs-Ungarns, 1906–1914* (Munich, 2003), pp. 215–16.

37. K. Bachmann, *'Ein Herd der Feindschaft gegen Rußland'. Galizien als Krisenherd in den Beziehungen der Donaumonarchie mit Rußland (1907–1914)* (Vienna and Munich, 2001), pp. 29–33.

38. Bachmann, *'Ein Herd der Feindschaft'*, pp. 132–8, 173–90 and 219–58, and I. L. Rudnytsky, 'The Ukrainians in Galicia under Austrian Rule', in A. S. Markovits and F. E. Sysyn (eds.), *Nationbuilding and the Politics of Nationalism: Essays on Austrian Galicia* (Cambridge, MA, 1982), pp. 60–67. Also Z. A. B. Zeman, *The Break-Up of the Habsburg Empire, 1914–1918: A Study in National and Social Revolution* (London, New York and Toronto, 1961), pp. 4–5, and J. Redlich, *Austrian War Government* (New Haven, CT, and London, 1929), pp. 32–3.

39. Clark, *Sleepwalkers*, pp. 88–9.

40. Kann, *History of the Habsburg Empire*, pp. 446–8, and Macartney, *Habsburg Empire*, pp. 767–70.

41. Minutes of Common Ministerial Council meeting, 7 July 1914, in Bittner and Uebersberger (eds.), *Österreich-Ungarns Aussenpolitik*, p. 347.

42. Okey, *Taming Balkan Nationalism*, pp. 195, 198 and 202–16, and Dedijer, *The Road to Sarajevo*, pp. 235–45. Also W. S. Vucinich, 'Mlada Bosna and the First World War', in R. A. Kann, B. K. Király and P. S. Fichtner (eds.), *The Habsburg Empire in World War I: Essays on the Intellectual, Military, Political and Economic Aspects of the Habsburg War Effort* (Boulder, CO, and New York, 1977), pp. 51–5.

43. Conrad, *Aus meiner Dienstzeit*, iv, p. 34.

44. J. Leslie, 'The Antecedents of Austria-Hungary's War Aims: Policies and Policy-Makers in Vienna and Budapest before and during 1914', *Wiener Beiträge zur Geschichte der Neuzeit* 20 (1993), p. 309.

45. Conrad, *Aus meiner Dienstzeit*, iv, pp. 37–8.

46. Ibid., p. 309. Also, Berchtold at the Common Ministerial Council, 7 July 1914, reproduced in Bittner and Uebersberger (eds.), *Österreich-Ungarns Aussenpolitik*, pp. 343–4.

47. S. Wank, *In the Twilight of Empire: Count Alois Lexa von Aehrenthal (1854–1912), Imperial Habsburg Patriot and Statesman. Volume 1: The Making of an Imperial Habsburg Patriot and Statesman* (2 vols., Vienna, Cologne and Weimar, 2009).

48. M. Twain, 'Stirring Times in Austria', *Harper's New Monthly Magazine* 96 (December 1897–May 1898), p. 530.

49. For Franz Joseph's image and symbolism see M. Healy, *Vienna and the Fall of the Habsburg Empire: Total War and Everyday Life in World War I* (Cambridge, 2004, 2007), pp. 216 and 281–2, and D. L. Unowsky, *The Pomp and Politics of Patriotism: Imperial Celebrations in Habsburg Austria, 1848–1916* (West Lafayette, IN, 2005).

50. Unowsky, *The Pomp and Politics of Patriotism*, esp. pp. 26, 94–101.

51. Kronenbitter, *'Krieg im Frieden'*, p. 223. Also L. Cole, 'Military Veterans and Popular Patriotism in Imperial Austria, 1870–1914', in L. Cole and D. L. Unowsky (eds.), *The Limits of Loyalty: Imperial Symbolism, Popular Allegiances, and State Patriotism in the Late Habsburg Monarchy* (New York and Oxford, 2007), pp. 36–61.

52. For the continued significance of historical borders, see R. J. W. Evans, 'Essay and Reflection: Frontiers and National Identities in Central Europe', *The International History Review* 14(3) (August 1992), pp. 480–502.

53. H. LeCaine Agnew, 'The Flyspecks on Palivec's Portrait: Franz Joseph, the Symbols of Monarchy, and Czech Popular Loyalty', in L. Cole and D. L. Unowsky (eds.), *The Limits of Loyalty: Imperial Symbolism, Popular Allegiances, and State Patriotism in the Late Habsburg Monarchy* (New York and Oxford, 2007), pp. 86–112.

54. Redlich, *Austrian War Government*, pp. 15–24 and 46–51. See also J. King, 'The Municipal and the National in the Bohemian Lands, 1848–1914', *Austrian History Yearbook* 42 (2011), pp. 89–109.

55. Macartney, *Habsburg Empire*, pp. 562–3 and 574, and Okey, *Habsburg Monarchy*, pp. 198–200.

56. G. B. Cohen, 'Nationalist Politics and the Dynamics of State and Civil Society in the Habsburg Monarchy, 1867–1914', *Central European History* 40(2) (June 2007), esp. p. 276.

57. Clark, *Sleepwalkers*, pp. 3–31.

58. P. W. Schroeder, 'Stealing Horses to Great Applause: Austria-Hungary's Decision in 1914 in Systematic Perspective', in H. Afflerbach and D. Stevenson (eds.), *An Improbable War: The Outbreak of World War I and European Political Culture Before 1914* (New York and Oxford, 2007), pp. 17–42.

For the influential, aggressive sections of Russian public opinion, see D. Lieven, *Russia and the Origins of the First World War* (London, 1983), pp. 128–33.

59. D. Stevenson, 'Militarization and Diplomacy in Europe before 1914', *International Security* 22(1) (summer 1997), pp. 133–5, Schroeder, 'Stealing Horses', pp. 35–8, and Clark, *Sleepwalkers*, pp. 83–7.

60. E. J. Erickson, *Defeat in Detail: The Ottoman Army in the Balkans, 1912–1913* (Westport, CT, and London, 2003).

61. D. Stevenson, *Armaments and the Coming of War: Europe, 1904–1914* (Oxford, 1996), pp. 232–9 and 253–65.

62. Clark, *Sleepwalkers*, pp. 281–92. For Serbian figures, see D. Stevenson, *1914–1918: The History of the First World War* (London, 2005), p. 12.

63. Leslie, 'Österreich-Ungarn', p. 675.

64. S. McMeekin, *The Russian Origins of the First World War* (Harvard, MA, and London, 2011), p. 22.

65. Minutes of the Council of Ministers, 7 July 1914, in Geiss (ed.), *July 1914*, p. 85.

66. S. Wank, 'Desperate Counsel in Vienna in July 1914: Berthold Molden's Unpublished Memorandum', *Central European History* 26(3) (September 1993), p. 308.

67. L. Bittner, 'Österreich-Ungarn und Serbien', *Historische Zeitschrift* 144(1) (1931), pp. 97–8.

68. Variants of this idea were expressed by Andrian, Hoyos, Molden, and also earlier (see below) Tisza. See Leslie, 'Österreich-Ungarn', p. 675, Fellner, '"Mission Hoyos"', p. 314, and Wank, 'Desperate Counsel', p. 300.

69. Tisza in March 1914, quoted in Herrmann, *Arming of Europe*, p. 211.

70. Conrad, *Aus meiner Dienstzeit*, iv, p. 55.

71. Fellner, '"Mission Hoyos"', p. 309.

72. Conrad, *Aus meiner Dienstzeit*, iv, pp. 36–7.

73. Kaiser Wilhelm II, 8 December 1912, quoted in J. C. G. Röhl, *The Kaiser and his Court: Wilhelm II and the Government of Germany* (Cambridge, 1994, 1999), p. 173.

74. H. Afflerbach, *Falkenhayn. Politisches Denken und Handeln im Kaiserreich* (Munich, 1994), esp. pp. 150–52 and 155.

75. Jarausch, *Enigmatic Chancellor*, pp. 148–51.

76. P. Bairoch, 'International Industrialization Levels from 1780 to 1980', *Journal of European Economic History* 11(2) (1982), p. 292.

77. Quotation from N. Ferguson, *The Pity of War* (London, 1998), p. 33. Figures from J. H. Clapham, *Economic Development of France and Germany, 1815–1914*, 4th edn (Cambridge, 1936, 1968), p. 5, and T. Nipperdey, *Deutsche Geschichte, 1866–1918. Arbeitswelt und Bürgergeist* (2 vols., Munich, 1998), i, pp. 9 and 234–7.

78. Clark, *Sleepwalkers*, pp. 92–3.

79. W. Mulligan, *The Origins of the First World War* (Cambridge, 2010), pp. 32–4.

80. Fischer, *Germany's Aims*, pp. 20–22, Mulligan, *Origins*, p. 54, and Clark, *Sleepwalkers*, pp. 150–52.

81. A point made by Paul W. Schroeder in 'World War I as Galloping Gertie: A Reply to Joachim Remak', *The Journal of Modern History* 44(3) (September 1972), pp. 322–3. For the military restraint of the Germans in comparison with other continental powers during international crises, see Stevenson, 'Militarization and Diplomacy', pp. 130–47.

82. Clark, *Sleepwalkers*, pp. 155–7, and Mulligan, *Origins*, pp. 54–8.

83. Schroeder, 'World War I as Galloping Gertie', pp. 324–5 and 328–9. Also Clark, *Sleepwalkers*, pp. 158–9.

84. H. H. Herwig, *'Luxury' Fleet: The Imperial German Navy, 1888–1918* (London, Boston and Sydney, 1980), pp. 33–92, and P. Kennedy, *The Rise of the Anglo-German Antagonism, 1860–1914* (London, 1980), pp. 444 and 451.

85. G. C. Peden, *Arms, Economics and British Strategy: From Dreadnoughts to Hydrogen Bombs* (Cambridge, 2009), p. 43. Royal Navy: twenty dreadnoughts and ten battlecruisers, including one Australian; twenty-six of these ships were in home waters, three battlecruisers were in the Mediterranean and one was in the Pacific. *Kriegsmarine*: thirteen dreadnoughts and five battlecruisers. All these ships were in home waters except for one battlecruiser in the Mediterranean.

86. See H. Strachan, *The First World War. Volume I: To Arms* (3 vols., Oxford, 2001), i, p. 27, and, for the French ambassador's appeal, Clark, *Sleepwalkers*, pp. 540–41.

87. Mulligan, *Origins*, pp. 129–30, and Stevenson, *Armaments*, pp. 291–8. For the 1911 intake, see M. Ingenlath, *Mentale Aufrüstung. Militarisierungstendenzen in Frankreich und Deutschland vor dem Ersten Weltkrieg* (Frankfurt and New York, 1998), p. 155, fn. 81.

88. Clark, *Sleepwalkers*, pp. 204–10, and Mulligan, *Origins*, pp. 71–4.

89. N. Stone, 'Army and Society in the Habsburg Monarchy, 1900–1914', *Past and Present* 33 (April 1966), p. 107, and Herrmann, *Arming of Europe*, pp. 234 and 237.

90. See Herrmann, *Arming of Europe*, pp. 183–91.

91. For the German political system, see T. Nipperdey, *Deutsche Geschichte, 1866–1918. Machtstaat vor der Demokratie* (Munich, 1998), pp. 85–109. For European franchises, see Ferguson, *Pity of War*, p. 29.

92. N. Ferguson, 'Public Finance and National Security: The Domestic Origins of the First World War Revisited', *Past & Present* 142 (February 1994), pp. 153–68, and Herrmann, *Arming of Europe*, pp. 190–91.

93. Ferguson, 'Public Finance and National Security', p. 149.

94. Herrmann, *Arming of Europe*, p. 183.

95. D. Stevenson, 'War by Timetable? The Railway Race before 1914', *Past & Present* 162 (February 1999), pp. 178 and 186.

96. Kaiser Wilhelm II to Prince Henry of Prussia, 12 December 1912, reproduced in J. C. G. Röhl, 'Die Generalprobe. Zur Geschichte und Bedeutung des "Kriegsrates" vom 8. Dezember 1912', in W. Alff (ed.), *Deutschlands Sonderung von Europa, 1862–1945* (Frankfurt am Main, Bern and New York, 1984), p. 184.

97. See J. C. G. Röhl, 'Admiral von Müller and the Approach of War, 1911–1914', *The Historical Journal* 12(4) (December 1969), pp. 661–2.

98. Ibid., p. 664.

99. For the meeting as a turning point for the Kaiser, see especially I. V. Hull, *The Entourage of Kaiser Wilhelm II, 1888–1918* (Cambridge, 1982), pp. 261–5. For its lack of concrete results, see Strachan, *First World War*, i, pp. 52–5.

100. Jarausch, *Enigmatic Chancellor*, pp. 132–9.

101. K. H. Jarausch, 'The Illusion of Limited War: Chancellor Bethmann Hollweg's Calculated Risk, July 1914', *Central European History* 2(1) (March 1969), p. 58.

102. For Russian fears about the consequences of the German military mission, see McMeekin, *Russian Origins*, pp. 31–3. For the newspaper articles, see Jarausch, *Enigmatic Chancellor*, p. 140.

103. Strachan, *First World War*, i, pp. 62–3.

104. Bethmann Hollweg, quoted in Jarausch, 'Illusion of Limited War', 48. For the military's pressure for preventative war, see A. Mombauer, *Helmuth von Moltke and the Origins of the First World War* (Cambridge, 2001), p. 172. For Falkenhayn's desire for a preventative war, see Afflerbach, *Falkenhayn*, pp. 101–2.

105. See esp. Mulligan, *Origins*, pp. 89–90, for the effect of the Anglo-Russian naval talks on German decision-making. Also Jarausch, *Enigmatic Chancellor*, p. 157, and Clark, *Sleepwalkers*, p. 422.

106. See, for example, Strachan, *First World War*, i, p. 63.

107. See Clark, *Sleepwalkers*, pp. 418–19.

108. Jarausch, 'Illusion of Limited War', pp. 58–61.

109. Grey, quoted in Z. S. Steiner, *Britain and the Origins of the First World War* (London and Basingstoke, 1977), pp. 221–2.

110. Geiss (ed.), *July 1914*, pp. 174–5. See also D. A. Rich, 'Russia', in R. F. Hamilton and H. Herwig (eds.), *The Origins of World War I* (Cambridge, New York, Melbourne, Madrid and Cape Town, 2003), p. 218.

111. F. Fellner, 'Der Krieg in Tagebüchern und Briefen. Überlegungen zu einer wenig genützten Quellenart', in K. Amann and H. Lengauer (eds.),

Österreich und der Große Krieg, 1914–1918. Die andere Seite der Geschichte (Vienna, 1989), p. 209.

112. Jarausch, *Enigmatic Chancellor*, p. 165.

113. Clark, *Sleepwalkers*, pp. 47–64 and 457–69.

114. Conversation between Berchtold and the Russian chargé d'affaires, 24 July 1914, in Geiss (ed.), *July 1914*, pp. 173–4.

115. Minutes of the Council of Ministers, 19 July 1914, in ibid., pp. 140–41. Also Williamson, *Austria-Hungary*, p. 212.

116. Fischer, *Germany's Aims*, pp. 62–71.

117. Wilhelm II to Jagow and Bethmann Hollweg to Tschirschky, both 28 July 1914, in Geiss (ed.), *July 1914*, pp. 256–7 and 259–60. Also Fischer, *Germany's Aims*, pp. 71–2, Clark, *Sleepwalkers*, p. 523, and H. Herwig, 'Germany', in Hamilton and Herwig (eds.), *Origins of World War I*, p. 178.

118. Strachan, *First World War*, i, pp. 78 and 80, and N. Stone, 'Die Mobilmachung der österreichisch-ungarischen Armee 1914', *Militärgeschichtliche Mitteilungen* 16(2) (1974), pp. 73–4 and 78. Fischer is especially clear on the problems caused to the German policy of localization by Austria-Hungary's slow move to military readiness. Fischer, *Germany's Aims*, p. 74.

119. Clark, *Sleepwalkers*, pp. 481–2.

120. S. R. Williamson and E. R. May, 'An Identity of Opinion: Historians and July 1914', *The Journal of Modern History* 79(2) (June 2007), p. 369.

121. Prince Troubetzkoi quoted in K. Wilson, 'Hamlet – With or Without the Prince: Terrorism at the Outbreak of the First World War', *The Journal of Conflict Studies* 27(2) (2007). Accessed at: http://journals.hil.unb.ca/index.php/jcs/article/view/10541/11751#no40 on 18 July 2013. For Troubetzkoi's acute understanding of broader Russian foreign policy, see Lieven, *Russia*, pp. 91–101.

122. Lieven, *Russia*, pp. 141–2.

123. Ibid., pp. 149–50.

124. McMeekin, *Russian Origins*, pp. 54–64. For details of the Period Preparatory to War and a more sympathetic interpretation, see also Lieven, *Russia*, p. 144.

125. U. Trumpener, 'War Premeditated? German Intelligence Operations in July 1914', *Central European History* 9(1) (March 1976), p. 64.

126. Afflerbach, *Falkenhayn*, pp. 151–3, and Mombauer, *Helmuth von Moltke*, pp. 190–96.

127. Trumpener, 'War Premeditated?', pp. 65–71. By questioning passengers arriving on trains from Russia, the Habsburg army was also learning about the extensive preparations. Large quantities of field artillery passing through Warsaw, strict censorship and rumours of the drafting of the youngest three

year groups of reservists in Russian Poland were among the pieces of information gathered. See AN Cracow: DPkr 96: fos. 1577–8.

128. See esp. Mombauer, *Helmuth von Moltke*, p. 202.

129. Moltke to Bethmann Hollweg, 29 July 1914 (composed on the previous day), in Geiss (ed.), *July 1914*, pp. 282–4.

130. Ibid., p. 284.

131. McMeekin, *Russian Origins*, p. 73.

132. Lieven, *Russia*, p. 146.

133. Trumpener, 'War Premeditated?', p. 80.

134. Afflerbach, *Falkenhayn*, pp. 155–7 and 159, fn 54. See also Mombauer, *Helmuth von Moltke*, pp. 202–4. While the Bavarian and Saxon military representatives in Berlin found Moltke publicly belligerent on 29 July, his private memorandum and advice to the Chancellor and Kaiser are far more significant and contradict Mombauer's claim that on this day he was 'adamant that Germany needed to announce general mobilization'.

135. Clark, *Sleepwalkers*, pp. 528–9.

136. See Goschen to Grey, 29 July 1914, in Geiss (ed.), *July 1914*, pp. 300–301.

137. Fischer, *Germany's Aims*, pp. 76–9.

138. Cabinet Council for Common Affairs, 31 July 1914, in Geiss (ed.), *July 1914*, pp. 318–22, and Conrad, *Aus meiner Dienstzeit*, iv, pp. 148–51.

139. Trumpener, 'War Premeditated?', pp. 79–80.

140. Afflerbach, *Falkenhayn*, pp. 158–9, and Fischer, *Germany's Aims*, pp. 80–81.

141. Moltke to Bethmann Hollweg, 29 July 1914, in Geiss (ed.), *July 1914*, p. 283.

142. Conrad, *Aus meiner Dienstzeit*, iv, p. 152.

143. Moltke's adjutant Major Hans von Haeften, quoted in A. Mombauer, 'A Reluctant Military Leader? Helmuth von Moltke and the July Crisis of 1914', *War in History* 6(4) (October 1999), p. 437. The view was reiterated by Moltke in his admittedly self-exculpatory 'Considerations and Reminiscences' of November 1914. See E. von Moltke (ed.), *Generaloberst Helmuth von Moltke. Erinnerungen – Briefe – Dokumente, 1877–1916. Ein Bild vom Kriegsausbruch, erster Kriegsführung und Persönlichkeit des ersten militärischen Führers des Krieges* (Stuttgart, 1922), p. 16.

144. Trumpener, 'War Premeditated?', pp. 80–82.

145. Hamilton and Herwig (eds.), *Origins of World War I*, pp. 516–18.

146. H. H. Herwig, *The First World War: Germany and Austria-Hungary, 1914–1918* (London, New York, Sydney and Auckland, 1997), pp. 31–2.

147. G. A. von Müller, *The Kaiser and his Court: The Diaries, Note Books and Letters of Admiral Georg Alexander von Müller, Chief of the Naval Cabinet, 1914–1918*, ed. W. Görlitz and trans. M. Savill (London, 1961), p. 11.

148. Moltke (ed.), *Generaloberst Helmuth von Moltke*, p. 20.

149. Mombauer, *Helmuth von Moltke*, p. 222.
150. Kennedy, *Rise of the Anglo-German Antagonism*, pp. 461–2, and Clark, Sleepwalkers, pp. 529–47.
151. Redlich, *Schicksalsjahre Österreichs*, i, p. 237 (entry for 15 July 1914).
152. Afflerbach, *Falkenhayn*, p. 161.
153. Bethmann, quoted in Jarausch, 'Illusion of Limited War', 59.

2. MOBILIZING THE PEOPLE

1. 'Die Ermordung des Thronfolgers und seiner Gemahlin', *Reichspost. XXI. Jahrgang. Nr. 298* (29 June 1914), p. 1.
2. 'Die Ermordung des Thronfolgerpaares', *Illustrirtes Wiener Extrablatt. 43. Jahrgang. Nr. 178* (29 June 1914), p. 1, and 'Der Thronfolger und seine Gemalin ermordet', *Christlich-soziale Arbeiter-Zeitung. XIX. Jahrgang. Nr. 27* (4 July 1914), p. 1.
3. 'Feuilleton', *Neue Freie Presse. Nr. 17904* (30 June 1914), p. 1.
4. A. J. May, *The Passing of the Habsburg Monarchy, 1914–1918* (2 vols., Philadelphia, PA, 1966), i, pp. 23–9.
5. *Reichspost. XXI. Jahrgang. Nr. 308* (4 July 1914), pp. 2–3.
6. M. M. Reiter, *Balkan Assault: The Diary of an Officer, 1914–1918*, trans. S. Granovetter (London, 1994), pp. 3–4 (entry for 3 July 1914).
7. Ibid., p. 2 (entry for June 1914).
8. *Wiener Bilder. Illustriertes Familienblatt. XIX. Jahrgang. Nr. 27* (5 July 1914), pp. 1 and 4–5.
9. 'Sarajevská tragedie', *Národní Listy* (30 June 1914).
10. *Wiener Bilder. Illustriertes Familienblatt. XIX. Jahrgang. Nr. 27* (12 July 1914), pp. 1 and 4–5. Also, for example, *Die Neue Zeitung. Illustrirtes unabhängiges Blatt. 7. Jahrgang. Nr. 180* (3 July 1914), p. 1, and *Sport & Salon. Illustrierte Zeitschrift für die vornehme Welt. 17. Jahrgang. Nr. 28* (11 July 1914), p. 1.
11. 'Ein offizieller Bericht über das Attentat in Sarajevo' and 'Volkskundgebungen in Wien', *Reichspost. XXI. Jahrgang. Nr. 300* (30 June 1914), p. 2, and *Nr. 302* (1 July 1914), p. 3.
12. See *Neue Freie Presse. Nr. 17906* (2 July 1914), p. 6, *Nr. 17907* (3 July 1914), pp. 4–5, and *Nr. 17908* (4 July 1914), pp. 9–10. Also, *Reichspost. XXI. Jahrgang. Nr. 306* (3 July 1914), p. 8, *Nowa Reforma. Wydanie Popołudniowe. Rok XXXIII. Nr. 260* (3 July 1914), p. 1, and *Kurjer Lwowski. Rok XXXII. Nr. 279* (4 July 1914), p. 1, and *Nr. 281* (5 July 1914), p. 3.
13. *Die Neue Zeitung. Illustrirtes unabhängiges Blatt. 7. Jahrgang. Nr. 181* (4 July 1914), p. 5.

14. For these numbers, see *Reichspost. XXI. Jahrgang. Nr. 308* (4 July 1914), p. 9, and *Neue Freie Presse. Nr. 17908* (4 July 1914), p. 9.

15. T. Raithel, *Das 'Wunder' der inneren Einheit. Studien zur deutschen und französischen Öffentlichkeit bei Beginn des Ersten Weltkrieges* (Bonn, 1996), pp. 157 and 161, fn 122.

16. L. L. Farrar, Jr, 'Reluctant Warriors: Public Opinion on War during the July Crisis 1914', *East European Quarterly* 16(4) (Winter 1982), pp. 419–20.

17. I. Daszyński, *Pamiętniki* (2 vols., Warsaw, 1957), ii, p. 145.

18. 'Zgon następcy tronu Arcyks. Franciszka Ferdynanda i Jego Małżonki', *Czas. Rocznik LXVII. Nr. 251* (29 June 1914).

19. *Kurjer Lwowski. Rok XXXII. Nr. 271* (29 June 1914), pp. 2–3. For Vienna's Prater park, see Redlich, *Schicksalsjahre Österreichs*, i, p. 235 (entry for 29 June 1914).

20. P. Bobič, *War and Faith: The Catholic Church in Slovenia, 1914–1918* (Leiden and Boston, MA, 2012), pp. 7 and 15–17.

21. J. Vit, *Wspomnienia z mojego pobytu w Przemyślu podczas rosyjskiego oblężenia 1914–1915*, trans. L. Hofbauer and J. Husar (Przemyśl, 1995), p. 31.

22. A. Czechówna, diary, 2 July 1914. AN Cracow: IT 428/38.

23. M. Schwestek, diary/memoir, 28 June 1914. KA Vienna: NL Schwestek, B/89.

24. *Neue Freie Presse. Nr. 17904* (30 June 1914), pp. 2–3, and *Nr. 17906* (2 July 1914), pp. 3 and 5.

25. Ibid., *Nr. 17909* (5 July 1914), p. 7, *Nr. 17910* (6 July 1914), pp. 3–4, and *Nr. 17913* (9 July 1914), p. 5. Also *Kurjer Lwowski. Rok XXXII. Nr. 275* (2 July 1914), p. 1.

26. *Neue Freie Presse. Nr. 17907* (3 July 1914), p. 3, and *Nr. 17912* (8 July 1914), p. 4.

27. M. Moll, '"Verräter und Spione überall". Vorkriegs- und Kriegshysterie in Graz im Sommer 1914', *Historisches Jahrbuch der Stadt Graz* 31 (2001), pp. 309–15.

28. K.u.k. Festungskommando in Trient to k.u.k. Korpskommando in Innsbruck, 8 August 1914. KA Vienna: Zentralstellen – KÜA 1914 (Aktenkartons): Karton 3: Nr. 1646.

29. O. C. Tăslăuanu, *With the Austrian Army in Galicia* (London, n.d.), p. 5.

30. M. Healy, *Vienna and the Fall of the Habsburg Empire: Total War and Everyday Life in World War I* (Cambridge, 2004, 2007), p. 238.

31. *Nowa Reforma. Wydanie Popołudniowe. Rok XXXIII. Nr. 296* (24 July 1914), p. 2. Also *Neue Freie Presse. Abendblatt. Nr. 17927* (23 July 1914), p. 4.

32. *Kurjer Lwowski. Rok XXXII. Nr. 272* (30 June 1914), p. 4, and *Nr. 282* (6 July 1914), p. 4, and *Nr. 297* (15 July 1914), p. 1; *Nowa Reforma. Wydanie Popołudniowe. Rok XXXIII. Nr. 276* (13 July 1914), p. 2.

33. Raithel, *Das 'Wunder'*, pp. 147–54 and 171–7.

34. A. Orzoff, 'The Empire Without Qualities: Austro-Hungarian Newspapers and the Outbreak of War in 1914', in T. R. E. Paddock (ed.), *A Call to Arms: Propaganda, Public Opinion and Newspapers in the Great War* (Westport, CT, 2004), p. 166.

35. 'Die Sitzung des Abgeordnetenhauses', *Pester Lloyd. Abendblatt. 61. Jahrgang. Nr. 167* (24 July 1914), p. 1; 'Wiener Stimmungsbild vom heutigen Abend', *Neue Freie Presse. Abendblatt. Nr. 17928* (24 July 1914), p. 6.

36. *Neue Freie Presse. Nr. 17930* (26 July 1914), p. 4, and *Die Neue Zeitung. Illustrirtes unabhängiges Blatt. 7. Jahrgang. Nr. 203* (26 July 1914), p. 4. Also B. de Quidt, journal, p. 2. IWM: 96/32/1.

37. J. Verhey, *The Spirit of 1914: Militarism, Myth, and Mobilization in Germany* (Cambridge, 2000), pp. 26-31, and Raithel, *Das 'Wunder'*, pp. 228-33.

38. Verhey, *Spirit*, pp. 35 and 65; Raithel, *Das 'Wunder'*, pp. 242-77.

39. See *Neue Freie Presse. Nr. 17931* (27 July 1914), p. 2, and *Nr. 17934* (30 July 1914), pp. 7-8.

40. 'Wenn sich der Doppeladler erhebt . . .', *Reichspost. Extraausgabe. XXI. Jahrgang. Nr. 347* (26 July 1914), p. 1.

41. *Neue Freie Presse. Nr. 17930* (26 July 1914), p. 4. Also, for larger figures, *Oesterreichische Volks-Zeitung. 60. Jahrgang. Nr. 204* (26 July 1914), pp. 4 and 21.

42. Baernreither, diary, 28 July 1914, quoted in Fellner, 'Krieg in Tagebüchern', p. 209. For Germany, see Verhey, *Spirit*, pp. 40-43.

43. A. Eisenmenger, *Blockade: The Diary of an Austrian Middle-Class Woman, 1914-1924* (London, 1932), p. 10.

44. T. Rohrkrämer, 'August 1914 – Kriegsmentalität und ihre Voraussetzungen', in W. Michalka (ed.), *Der Erste Weltkrieg. Wirkung, Wahrnehmung, Analyse* (Munich and Zurich, 1992), pp. 767-73. Also Raithel, *Das 'Wunder'*, pp. 235-7.

45. S. Levsen, *Elite, Männlichkeit und Krieg. Tübinger und Cambridger Studenten, 1900-1929* (Göttingen, 2006), pp. 125, 137-9, 171-4 and 177.

46. S. Kawczak, *Milknące Echa. Wspomnienia z wojny 1914-1920* (Warsaw, 1991), p. 6.

47. C. E. Wirth, diary, 11 August 1914. DTA, Emmendingen: 1798,6.

48. Raithel, *Das 'Wunder'*, pp. 178 and 242.

49. See decrees by the k.k. Statthaltereipräsidium in Böhmen, 30 July 1914. KA Vienna: Zentralstellen – KÜA 1914 (Aktenkartons): Karton 2: Nr. 624. For Germany, see Verhey, *Spirit*, pp. 47-8.

50. Conrad, *Aus meiner Dienstzeit*, iv, p. 34.

51. Statthalter Prag to Minister des Innern, 26 July 1914. KA Vienna: KÜA 1914 (Aktenkartons): Karton 1: Nr. 43.

52. Führ, *K.u.k. Armeeoberkommando*, pp. 17-19.

53. Quoted in S. Miller, *Burgfrieden und Klassenkampf. Die deutsche Sozialdemokratie im Ersten Weltkrieg* (Düsseldorf, 1974), p. 44.

54. Nipperdey, *Deutsche Geschichte*, ii, pp. 232 and 561. For Austrian figures, see Macartney, *Habsburg Empire*, p. 673.

55. W. Kruse, *Krieg und nationale Integration. Eine Neuinterpretation des sozialdemokratischen Burgfriedensschlusses, 1914/15* (Essen, 1993), pp. 18–29 and 40.

56. *Hamburger Echo*, 25 July 1914, quoted in Raithel, *Das 'Wunder'*, p. 175.

57. Quoted in Miller, *Burgfrieden*, p. 39.

58. Kruse, *Krieg und nationale Integration*, pp. 30–42. Also, Raithel, *Das 'Wunder'*, p. 185, and Verhey, *Spirit*, pp. 52–7.

59. See Nipperdey, *Deutsche Geschichte*, i, p. 269, and Okey, *Habsburg Monarchy*, p. 239.

60. H. Heiss, 'Andere Fronten. Volksstimmung und Volkserfahrung in Tirol während des Ersten Weltkrieges', in K. Eisterer and R. Steininger (eds.), *Tirol und der Erste Weltkrieg* (Innsbruck, 1995), p. 142.

61. M. Sperber, *God's Water Carriers*, trans. J. Neugroschel (New York and London, 1987), pp. 69–70.

62. D. Ściskała, *Z dziennika kapelana wojskowego, 1914–1918* (Cieszyn, 1926), p. 7.

63. R. Höfner, diary, 27 December 1914 (referring to war's outbreak). DTA, Emmendingen: 1280,1.

64. K. Małłek, *Z Mazur do Verdun. Wspomnienia, 1890–1919* (n.p., 1967), p. 176.

65. B. Ziemann, *Front und Heimat. Ländliche Kriegserfahrung im südlichen Bayern, 1914–1923* (Essen, 1997), pp. 40–43.

66. 'An meine Völker', printed in *Reichspost. Morgenblatt. XXI. Jahrgang. Nr. 352* (Vienna, 29 July 1914), p. 1.

67. See *Neue Freie Presse. Nr. 17932* (28 July 1914), pp. 2–4, and *Pester Lloyd. Morgenblatt. 61. Jahrgang. Nr. 177* (28 July 1914), pp. 3–4. Cf. Raithel, *Das 'Wunder'*, pp. 179–80.

68. 'Ministerpräsident Graf Stephen Tisza über den Zwischenfall bei Temeskubin', *Pester Lloyd. Morgenblatt. 61. Jahrgang. Nr. 177* (28 July 1914), p. 5.

69. N. Stone, 'Die Mobilmachung der österreichisch-ungarischen Armee 1914', *Militärgeschichtliche Mitteilungen* 16(2) (1974), pp. 70–71.

70. 'Weltkrieg oder Lokalerkrieg', *Neue Freie Presse. Abendblatt. Nr. 17933* (29 July 1914), p. 1.

71. G. Gruber to Cousine E. Hoch, 9 January 1915. DTA, Emmendingen: 138a.

72. W. Wagner, diary, 30 July 1914 (accessed at www.europeana1914-1918.eu on 19 September 2012).

73. *Frankfurter Zeitung und Handelsblatt. Abendblatt. 58. Jahrgang. Nr. 209* (30 July 1914). Also Raithel, *Das 'Wunder'*, pp. 188–90 and 253–5.

74. Kaiser Wilhelm II's speech of 31 July 1914, reproduced in R. H. Lutz (ed.), *Fall of the German Empire, 1914–18* (2 vols., Stanford, CA, London and Oxford, 1932), i, p. 4.

75. *Kölnische Zeitung*, quoted in Raithel, *Das 'Wunder'*, pp. 188–9 and 256–60.

76. G. Gruber to Cousine E. Hoch, 9 January 1915. DTA, Emmendingen: 138a. Cf. W. Wagner, diary, 31 July 1914 [*sic?*] (accessed at www.europeana 1914–1918.eu on 19 September 2012), and Raithel, *Das 'Wunder'*, p. 265.

77. E. Stempfle, diary, 1 August 1914. DTA, Emmendingen: 1654.

78. Kaiser Wilhelm, 1 August 1914, quoted in Verhey, *Spirit*, pp. 65–6. My description of the reaction to mobilization in Germany owes much to Raithel, *Das 'Wunder'*, pp. 263–8 and 276–7.

79. *Volksblatt*, quoted in L. James, 'War and Industry: A Study of the Industrial Relations in the Mining Regions of South Wales and the Ruhr During the Great War, 1914–1918', *Labour History Review* 68(2) (August 2003), p. 202.

80. See Heeres-Sanitätsinspektion des Reichskriegsministeriums (ed.), *Sanitätsbericht über das Deutsche Heer (Deutsches Feld- und Besatzungsheer) im Weltkriege 1914/1918 (Deutscher Kriegssanitätsbericht 1914/18). Die Krankenbewegung bei dem deutschen Feld- und Besatzungsheer im Weltkriege 1914/1918* (3 vols., Berlin, 1934), iii, p. 12; G. Gratz and R. Schüller, *Der wirtschaftliche Zusammenbruch Österreich-Ungarns. Die Tragödie der Erschopfung* (Vienna and New Haven, CT, 1930), p. 151; and Reichsarchiv, *Der Weltkrieg 1914 bis 1918. Die Grenzschlachten im Westen* (14 vols., Berlin, 1925), i, p. 38.

81. A. Hausner, diary, 27 July 1914. KA Vienna: NL Hausner, B/217.

82. Ściskała, *Z dziennika kapelana*, p. 8. Cf. Bobič, *War and Faith*, pp. 28–34, and Ziemann, *Front*, pp. 50–52.

83. Wilhelm Eildermann, quoted in Kruse, *Krieg und nationale Integration*, p. 59.

84. Tăslăuanu, *With the Austrian Army*, p. 9, and Kawczak, *Milknące Echa*, p. 9.

85. H. Götting, diary, 11 August 1914. DTA, Emmendingen: 700/I.

86. Verhey, *Spirit*, p. 93, and Rauchensteiner, *Tod des Doppeladlers*, p. 140.

87. See J. Kocka, *Facing Total War: German Society, 1914–1918* (Leamington Spa, 1984), p. 23.

88. J. Lawrence, 'The Transition to War in 1914', in J. Winter and J.-L. Robert (eds.), *Capital Cities at War: Paris, London, Berlin, 1914–1919* (Cambridge, New York and Melbourne, 1997), p. 143. Also G. Mai, *Kriegswirtschaft und Arbeiterbewegung in Württemberg, 1914–1918* (Stuttgart, 1983), pp. 65–7.

89. U. Daniel, *The War from Within: German Working-Class Women in the First World War* (Oxford and New York, 1997), p. 26.

90. Reports of Polizeipräsident in Berlin, 25 and 26 August 1914. BA Berlin Lichterfelde: R43/ 2398: fo. 109 and reverse of fos. 113–14.

91. 'Skutki okonomiczne wojny', 3 September 1914. AN Cracow: DPKr97: fo. 1063.

92. K.u.k. Kriegsüberwachungsamt, order, 8 August 1914. KA Vienna: Zentralstellen – KÜA 1914 (Aktenkartons): Karton 2: Nr. 743.

93. Raithel, Das 'Wunder', p. 449, also, more generally, pp. 447–54.

94. H. P. Hanssen, Diary of a Dying Empire, trans. O. Osburn, ed. R. H. Lutz, M. Schofield and O. O. Winther (Port Washington, NY, and London, 1955, 1973), pp. 22–3.

95. Kommandantur Posen, poster, 1 August 1914. AP Poznań: Polizei-Präsidium Posen: 8975.

96. 2. Polizei Revier, Telephonische Mitteilung, 3 August 1914. AP Poznań: Polizei-Präsidium Posen: 8976.

97. Letter from anonymous Unteroffizier der Reserve, 8 August 1914. AP Poznań: Polizei-Präsidium Posen: 8976.

98. Landrat at Montabaur to Regierungspräsident in Wiesbaden, 6 August 1914. HHStA Wiesbaden: Preußisches Regierungspräsidium Wiesbaden (405): Nr. 2739: fo. 53.

99. S. O. Müller, Die Nation als Waffe und Vorstellung. Nationalismus in Deutschland und Großbritannien im Ersten Weltkrieg (Göttingen, 2002), pp. 67–9. Also Verhey, Spirit, pp. 84–6.

100. For Germany, see Verhey, Spirit, pp. 85–6. For Austria, see the documentation of the Kriegsüberwachungsamt from August 1914 in KA Vienna: KÜA 1914 (Aktenkartons): Karton 1: Nr. 538; Karton 3, Nr. 1507; and Karton 4: Nrs. 2278 and 2581. Also telegrams in AN Cracow: DPKr 96: fos. 1087, 1099, 1105, 1113 and 1115.

101. Miller, Burgfrieden, p. 51.

102. SPD statement, 4 August 1914, reproduced in Lutz (ed.), Fall, i, p. 16.

103. Miller, Burgfrieden, pp. 41–3 and 50–51.

104. See doc. 77, preußischer Kriegsminister to preußische Generalkommandos, 25 July 1914, in W. Deist (ed.), Militär und Innenpolitik im Weltkrieg 1914–1918 (2 vols., Düsseldorf, 1970), i, pp. 188–92. Also pp. XLI–XLIV.

105. See the documentation in AP Gdańsk: Regierung Marienwerder (Regencja w Kwidzynie) (10): 10230: fos. 27–43, and Oberpräsident der Provinz Westpreußen to the Minister des Innern, GStA PK, Berlin: I. HA Rep 77, Tit. 863a, 17: fo. 2.

106. A. Majkowski, Pamiętnik z wojny europejskiej roku 1914, ed. T. Linkner (Pelplin and Wejherowo, 2000), p. 75 (entry for 7 August 1914). For the public mood and the military's measures in Germany's eastern borderlands, see the Landräte reports in AP Gdańsk: Rejencja w Kwidzenie (10): 10229: fos. 94–179, and AP Opole: Rejencja Opolska – Biuro Prezydialne: 141:

193–237, and Oberpräsident der Provinz Posen, report, 6 January 1915. GStA PK, Berlin: I. HA Rep 90A, 3748: fo. 100, reverse of fo. 103.

107. A. Kramer, 'Wackes at War: Alsace-Lorraine and the Failure of German National Mobilization, 1914–1918', in J. Horne (ed.), *State, Society and Mobilization in Europe during the First World War* (Cambridge, 1997), p. 108. Also Statthalter in Elsaß-Lothringen to Armee-Oberkommando der 7. Armee, 20 August 1914. GLA Karlsruhe: 465 F7 Nr. 165 and Chancellor to Prussian War Minister, 19 September 1914, and Bishop of Metz to Kaiser, 10 September 1914. BA Berlin Lichterfelde: R43/2465c: fos. 17 and 25–6.

108. C. Bundgård Christensen, *Danskere på Vestfronten, 1914–1918* (Copenhagen, 2009), p. 25.

109. Kruse, *Krieg und nationale Integration*, pp. 52–89. Also, Miller, *Burgfrieden*, pp. 46–6 and 51–74.

110. Bethmann's speech of 4 August 1914, reproduced in Lutz (ed.), *Fall*, i, pp. 9–13.

111. Kaempf's speech of 4 August 1914, reproduced in ibid., pp. 14–15.

112. SPD statement, 4 August 1914, reproduced in ibid., pp. 15–16.

113. Miller, *Burgfrieden*, pp. 39 and 65–8. Also, *Verhandlungen des Reichstags. XIII Legislaturperiode. II. Session. Band 306. Stenographische Berichte. Von der Eröffnungssitzung am 4. August 1914 bis zur 34. Sitzung am 16. März 1916* (Berlin, 1916), pp. 1–12, and Raithel, *Das 'Wunder'*, pp. 283–5.

114. Hanssen, *Diary of a Dying Empire*, p. 12 (entry of 2 August 1914).

115. Anonymous doctor, diary, 4 August 1914. DTA, Emmendingen: 1792.

116. H. Götting, diary, 7 August 1914. DTA, Emmendingen: 700/I. Cf. K. Wehrhan, *Gloria, Viktoria! Volkspoesie an Militärzügen* (Leipzig, 1915).

117. W. Schuhmacher, *Leben und Seele unseres Soldatenlieds im Weltkrieg* (Frankfurt am Main, 1928), pp. 150–51. See also A. Gregory, 'Railway Stations: Gateways and Termini', in Winter and Robert, *Capital Cities at War*, ii, p. 29.

118. W. Wagner, diary, 2–3 August 1914 (accessed at www.europeana1914–1918.eu on 19 September 2012).

119. E. Mortler, diary, 7 August 1914. DTA, Emmendingen: 260.

120. See K. Flasch, *Die geistige Mobilmachung. Die deutschen Intellektuellen und der Erste Weltkrieg* (Berlin, 2000), esp. pp. 43–4 and 79–80.

121. Polizeipräsident in Berlin to Unterstaatssekretär in der Reichskanzlei, 'Fünfter Stimmungsbericht', 5 September 1914. BA Berlin Lichterfelde: R43/ 2398: fo. 142.

122. This quotation is from F. Rubenbauer, 'Der Sturm auf Ypern, Freiwillige vor!', in F. Solledor (ed.), *Vier Jahre Westfront. Geschichte des Regiments List R.I.R. 16* (Munich, 1932), p. 4, but for newspaper reports giving the same message, see, for example, early August editions of the *Berliner Tageblatt*.

123. See, for example, the diary of an anonymous war volunteer. BA-MA Freiburg: Msg 2/65. For the volunteers in comparative context, see A. Watson, 'Voluntary Enlistment in the Great War: A European Phenomenon?', in C. Krüger and S. Levsen (eds.), *War Volunteering in Modern Times: From the French Revolution to the Second World War* (Basingstoke and New York, 2011), pp. 163–88.

124. Kruse, *Krieg und nationale Integration*, pp. 76–7.

125. A. Watson, '"For Kaiser and Reich": The Identity and Fate of the German Volunteers, 1914–1918', *War in History* 12(1) (January 2005), pp. 50–56.

126. See G. L. Mosse, *Fallen Soldiers: Reshaping the Memory of the World Wars* (New York and Oxford, 1990), pp. 17–28.

127. J. Segall, *Die deutschen Juden als Soldaten im Kriege 1914–1918* (Berlin, 1922), pp. 18–22. For motivations, see T. Grady, *The German-Jewish Soldiers of the First World War in History and Memory* (Liverpool, 2011), pp. 24–31.

128. A. Watson, 'Fighting for Another Fatherland: The Polish Minority in the German Army, 1914–1918', *The English Historical Review* 126(522) (October 2011), pp. 1142–3.

129. P. Plaut, 'Psychographie des Kriegers', in W. Stern and O. Lipmann (eds.), *Beihefte zur Zeitschrift für angewandte Psychologie. 21. Beiträge zur Psychologie des Krieges* (Leipzig, 1920), p. 13. Cf. also Watson, 'Identity and Fate', pp. 57–62.

130. C. Geinitz and U. Hinz, 'Das Augusterlebnis in Südbaden: Ambivalente Reaktionen der deutschen Öffentlichkeit auf den Kriegsbeginn 1914', in G. Hirschfeld, G. Krumeich, D. Langewiesche and H.-P. Ullmann (eds.), *Kriegserfahrungen. Studien zur Sozial- und Mentalitätsgeschichte des Ersten Weltkriegs* (Essen, 1997), pp. 29–30.

131. M. Bäckmann to the Kaiser, 6 August 1914. HHStA Wiesbaden (405): Nr. 2770: fo. 100. The appeal, which was refused, was not unique. See E. Buchner (ed.), *Kriegsdokumente. Der Weltkrieg 1914/15 in der Darstellung der zeitgenössischen Presse* (9 vols., Munich, 1914), ii, pp. 134–5, docs 193, 193b and 193c.

132. Kaiserin's appeal of 6 August 1914, reproduced in Lutz (ed.), *Fall*, i, pp. 21–2.

133. A. Süchtig-Hänger, *Das 'Gewissen der Nation'. Nationales Engagement und politisches Handeln konservativer Frauenorganisationen 1900 bis 1937* (Düsseldorf, 2002), p. 103.

134. E. Stempfle, diary, 26, 28 and 30 August and 4–8 September 1914. DTA, Emmendingen: 1654.

135. Süchtig-Hänger, *Das 'Gewissen der Nation'*, pp. 90–107 (quotation at p. 95), Daniel, *War from Within*, p. 73, Nipperdey, *Deutsche Geschichte*, i, pp. 73–94, and U. Planert, 'Zwischen Partizipation und Restriktion:

Frauenemanzipation und nationales Paradigma von der Aufklärung bis zum Ersten Weltkrieg', in D. Langewiesche and G. Schmidt (eds.), *Föderative Nation. Deutschlandkonzepte von der Reformation bis zum Ersten Weltkrieg* (Munich, 2000), p. 423.

136. Moltke, quoted in Mombauer, *Helmuth von Moltke*, p. 299.

137. See R. Chickering, *The Great War and Urban Life in Germany: Freiburg, 1914–1918* (Cambridge, 2007), pp. 70 and 371.

138. See E. Bruckmüller, 'Patriotic and National Myths: National Consciousness and Elementary School Education in Imperial Austria', in L. Cole and D. L. Unowsky (eds.), *The Limits of Loyalty: Imperial Symbolism, Popular Allegiances, and State Patriotism in the Late Habsburg Monarchy* (New York and Oxford, 2007), pp. 11–35.

139. T. Zahra, 'Imagined Noncommunities: National Indifference as a Category of Analysis', *Slavic Review* 69(1) (Spring 2010), pp. 93–119.

140. For the lack of a cross-Empire 'Habsburg society', see E. Bruckmüller, 'Was There a "Habsburg Society" in Austria-Hungary?', *Austrian History Yearbook* 37 (2006), pp. 1–16.

141. Suffragan Bishop of Salzburg, quoted in G. Barth-Scalmani, ' "Kriegsbriefe". Kommunikation zwischen Klerus und Kirchenvolk im ersten Kriegsherbst 1914 im Spannungsfeld von Patriotismus und Seelsorge', in K. Brandstätter and J. Hörmann (eds.), *Tirol – Österreich – Italien. Festschrift für Josef Riedmann zum 65. Geburtstag* (Innsbruck, 2005), p. 67.

142. J. Galántai, *Hungary in the First World War* (Budapest, 1989), pp. 72–9.

143. Führ, *K.u.k. Armeeoberkommando*, pp. 17–23, and J. Redlich, *Austrian War Government* (New Haven, CT, and London, 1929), pp. 77–86 and 149–50.

144. Redlich, *Schicksalsjahre Österreichs*, i, p. 252 (entry for 26 August 1914).

145. 'Allgemeine Mobilisierung, Stimmung der Bevölkerung', 2 August 1914: KA Vienna: KÜA 1914 (Aktenkartons): Karton 1: Nr. 443.

146. A. Hausner, diary, 1 August 1914. KA Vienna: NL Hausner, B/217. Also, Galántai, *Hungary*, p. 68.

147. K.k. Landespräsidium in Krain to Minister des Innern, 31 July 1914. KA Vienna: KÜA 1914 (Aktenkartons): Karton 1: Nr. 285/I.

148. K.u.k. Militärkommando in Prag to k.u.k. Kriegsüberwachungsamt, 'Stimmungsberichte', 19 October 1914. KA Vienna: KÜA 1914 (Aktenkartons): Karton 13: Nr. 7626.

149. 'Auszug aus mehreren Rapporten der Nordwestbahndirektion an das Eisenbahnministerium aus Anlaß der Mobilisierung'. KA Vienna: KÜA 1914 (Aktenkartons): Karton 1: Nr. 229.

150. Heiss, 'Andere Fronten', p. 142.

151. Order of k.k. Ldw. Inf. Trpen. Div. Kdo. in Zaleszczyki, 9 August 1914. Kriegsarchiv Vienna: NFA. 43. Sch. Division: Karton 2179 (Op. Akten v, August 1914): doc. 8.

152. Minister des Innern to k.k. Statthalter in Lemberg, 8 August 1914. AN Cracow: DPKr 96: 2959/14: fo. 495. Cf. W. Witos, *Moje Wspomnienia* (3 vols., Paris, 1964), ii, p. 12, and, generally for Austria-Hungary, Bundesministerium für Heereswesen und Kriegsarchiv, *Österreich-Ungarns letzter Krieg. Das Kriegsjahr 1914. Vom Kriegsausbruch bis zum Ausgang der Schlacht bei Limanowa-Lapanów* (7 vols., Vienna, 1930), i, p. 26.

153. 'Die Kriegsbegeisterung in Oesterreich', *Reichspost. Morgenblatt. XXI. Jahrgang. Nr. 359* (1 August 1914), p. 7. Also, 'Meldungen zum freiwilligen Kriegsdienst', *Reichspost. Morgenblatt. XXI. Jahrgang. Nr. 368* (6 August 1914), p. 7.

154. See minutes of Austrian Ministerrat meeting, 24 August 1914. AVA Vienna: MR-Prot. 1914-18. Karton 28: Nr. 43.

155. R. Hecht, 'Fragen zur Heeresergänzung der gesamten bewaffneten Macht Österreich-Ungarns während des Ersten Weltkrieges', unpublished PhD thesis, University of Vienna (1969), p. 159.

156. S. Sperber to Kriegsministerium, *c.* early August 1914. KA Vienna: KÜA 1914 (Aktenkartons): Karton 2: Nr. 864.

157. Galántai, *Hungary*, pp. 58 and 70.

158. Josef Redlich, an astute political commentator, certainly believed this to be true. See Redlich, *Austrian War Government*, pp. 98-9.

159. Stürgkh to Landeschefs, quoted in Führ, *K.u.k. Armeeoberkommando*, p. 27.

160. See, for example, *Neue Freie Presse. Nr. 17935* (31 July 1914), p. 9, and *Nr. 17936* (1 August 1914), p. 9.

161. E. Kwaśny, '*Krakowskie dzieci' (Trzynasty Pułk) na polu chwały, 1914-1915* (Cracow, 1917), p. 30.

162. Bobič, *War and Faith*, pp. 29-30.

163. See, e.g., *Nowa Reforma. Wydanie Popołudniowe. Rok XXXIII. Nr. 309* (30 July 1914), p. 2.

164. Kgl. Grenzpolizeihauptmannschaft in Sušak, 16 October 1916, and k.u.k. Militärkommando in Prague to k.u.k. Kriegsüberwachungsamt in Vienna, 19 October 1914. KA Vienna: KÜA 1914 (Aktenkartons): Karton 13: Nrs. 7594 and 7626; Bobič, *War and Faith*, pp. 28-9; J. Hupka, *Z czasów wielkiej wojny. Pamiętnik nie kombatanta* (Lwów, 1937), p. 12. For the medallions, see report to k.k. mährische Statthalterei-Praesidium, 13 October 1914. KA Vienna: KÜA 1914 (Aktenkartons): Karton 13: Nr. 7384.

165. M. L. Rozenblit, *Reconstructing National Identity: The Jews of Habsburg Austria during World War I* (Oxford and New York, 2001), pp. 28-31 and 43-54.

166. Poster, 10 August 1914, reproduced in J. J. Sosnowski, *Prawda dziejowa, 1914-1917* (Warsaw, 1925), p. 19.

167. K.u.k. Militärkommando in Zagreb to k.u.k. Stationskommandanten in Fiume, 17 September 1914; Kgl. Grenzpolizeihauptmannschaft in Sušak, 16 October 1916, and Kgl. kroat. slav. Gendarmeriekmdo, Lt. Dragatin Čanić,

15 October 1914. KA Vienna: KÜA 1914 (Aktenkartons): Karton 13: Nr. 7594.

168. W. Conze, *Polnische Nation und deutsche Politik im Ersten Weltkrieg* (Cologne and Graz, 1958), pp. 54 and 91.

169. Hecht, 'Fragen zur Heeresergänzung', pp. 99–111.

170. K. Bachmann, *'Ein Herd der Feindschaft gegen Rußland'. Galizien als Krisenherd in den Beziehungen der Donaumonarchie mit Rußland (1907–1914)* (Vienna and Munich, 2001), pp. 65–95 and 119–27. Also J. T. Nowak, 'Działania I Brygady Legionów Polskich, 1914–1915', in W. Milewska, J. T. Nowak and M. Zientara (eds.), *Legiony Polskie, 1914–1918. Zarys historii militarnej i politycznej* (Cracow, 1998), pp. 13–22.

171. J. M. Majchrowski, *Pierwsza Kompania Kadrowa. Portret Oddziału* (Cracow, 2004), pp. 18–22.

172. Quoted in Bachmann, *'Herd der Feindschaft'*, p. 127.

173. W. Sukiennicki, *East Central Europe during World War I: From Foreign Domination to National Independence* (2 vols., Boulder, CO, 1984), i, pp. 88–90; J. Mleczak, *Akcja werbunkowa Naczelnego Komitetu Narodowego w Galicji i Królestwie Polskim w latach 1914–1916* (Przemyśl, 1988), pp. 113–17, 125–8, 149–52 and 158–9. Also L. Dudek, 'Polish Military Formations in World War I', in B. K. Király and N. F. Dreisziger (eds.), *East Central European Society in World War I* (Boulder, CO, and Highland Lakes, 1985), pp. 454–60, and Nowak, 'Działania I Brygady Legionów Polskich', pp. 19–31.

174. Galántai, *Hungary*, pp. 95–8.

175. Stürgkh to Landeschefs, quoted in Führ, *K.u.k. Armeeoberkommando*, p. 27.

176. F. Exner, *Krieg und Kriminalität in Österreich. Mit einem Beitrag über die Kriminalität der Militärpersonen von Prof Dr G. Lelewer* (Vienna and New Haven, CT, 1927), p. 26.

177. M. Moll, 'Erster Weltkrieg und Ausnahmezustand, Zivilverwaltung und Armee: Eine Fallstudie zum innerstaatlichen Machtkampf 1914–1918 im steirischen Kontext', in S. Beer, E. Marko-Stöckl, M. Raffler and F. Schneider (eds.), *Focus Austria: vom Vielvölkerreich zum EU-Staat. Festschrift für Alfred Ableitinger zum 65. Geburtstag* (Graz, 2003), pp. 390 and 395.

178. 'Verzeichnis über Strafsachen betreffend serbo- und russophile Kundgebungen und Aeusserungen', appendix to k.k. mähr. schles. Oberstaatsanwalt in Brünn to k.k. Justizministerium, 12 August 1914. KA Vienna: KÜA 1914 (Aktenkartons): Karton 4: Nr. 2232.

179. M. Moll, 'Österreichische Militärgerichtsbarkeit im Ersten Weltkrieg – 'Schwert des Regimes'? Überlegungen am Beispiel des Landwehrdivisionsgerichtes Graz im Jahre 1914', *Mitteilungen des Steiermärkischen Landesarchivs* 50 (2001), pp. 314–43 and 352–3.

180. Bobič, *War and Faith*, pp. 137–9; Moll, 'Erster Weltkrieg und Ausnahme-zustand', pp. 387–8, 390 and 395.

181. Galántai, *Hungary*, pp. 95–6

182. M. Glettler, 'Die slowakische Gesellschaft unter der Einwirkung von Krieg und Militarisierung 1914–1918', in H. Mommsen, D. Kováč, J. Malíř and M. Marek (eds.), *Der Erste Weltkrieg und die Beziehungen zwischen Tschechen, Slowaken und Deutschen* (Essen, 2001), p. 100.

183. Conrad, quoted in I. Marin, 'World War I and Internal Repression: The Case of Major General Nikolaus Cena', *Austrian History Yearbook* 44 (2013), p. 195.

184. 'Verhaftung von politisch verdächtigen Personen in allen Teilen der Monar-chie', KA Vienna: MKSM (1914): 69–11/2.

185. Tisza to Franz Joseph, 27 July 1914; 'Bericht über die in Sudungarn, Kroatien und Slavonien gepflogenen Erhebungen', in, respectively, KA Vienna: MKSM (1914): 69–6/12 and 69–11/2–3.

186. Bolfras to Conrad, 24 August 1914; Conrad, *Aus meiner Dienstzeit*, iv, p. 549.

187. Kriegsminister to Franz Joseph, 16 September 1914; KA Vienna: MKSM (1914): 69–11/2.

188. Tisza to Franz Joseph, 27 July 1914; KA Vienna: MKSM (1914): 69–6/12; also Tisza, *Letters*, p. 49 (telegram to Archduke Friedrich, 19 September 1914).

189. A. Hausner, diary, 22 August 1914. KA Vienna: NL Hausner, B/217.

3. WAR OF ILLUSIONS

1. Reichsarchiv, *Weltkrieg*, i, pp. 38–9. These numbers refer only to Field Armies. Some mobilized troops (see ch. 2 for details) were for home and training duties.

2. S. Broadberry and M. Harrison, 'The Economics of World War I: An Over-view', in S. Broadberry and M. Harrison (eds.), *The Economics of World War I* (Cambridge, New York, Melbourne, Madrid, Cape Town, Singapore and São Paulo, 2005), pp. 7 and 10.

3. S. Förster, 'Der deutsche Generalstab und die Illusion des kurzen Krieges, 1871–1914. Metakritik eines Mythos', *Militärgeschichtliche Mitteilungen* 54(1) (1995), p. 79.

4. H. Herwig, 'Disjointed Allies: Coalition Warfare in Berlin and Vienna, 1914', *The Journal of Military History* 54(3) (July 1990), pp. 272–7.

5. G. Kronenbitter, 'Die militärische Planung der k.u.k. Armee und der Schlief-fenplan', in H. Ehlert, M. Epkenhans and G. P. Groß, *Der Schlieffenplan. Analysen und Dokumente* (Paderborn, Munich, Vienna and Zurich, 2006), pp. 216–20; M. Schmitz, 'Verrat am Waffenbruder? Die Siedlice-Kontroverse

im Spannungsfeld von Kriegsgeschichte und Geschichtspolitik', *Militär-geschichtliche Zeitschrift* 67(2) (2008), pp. 397–407.

6. Herwig, *First World War*, p. 45.

7. Historians' understanding of the 'Schlieffen Plan' has recently been radically revised. For a starting point, see T. Zuber's innovative 'The Schlieffen Plan Reconsidered', *War in History* 6(3) (July 1999), pp. 262–9. The interpretation of the plan put forward here follows the convincing critique of Zuber's ideas and impressive source analysis in T. M. Holmes, 'The Reluctant March on Paris: A Reply to Terence Zuber's "The Schlieffen Plan Reconsidered"', *War in History* 8(2) (April 2001), pp. 208–32, idem, 'The Real Thing: A Reply to Terence Zuber's "Terence Holmes Reinvents the Schlieffen Plan"', *War in History* 9(1) (January 2002), pp. 111–20, and idem, 'Asking Schlieffen: A Further Reply to Terence Zuber', *War in History* 10(4) (November 2003), pp. 464–79.

8. Moltke's plan for the campaign of 1914 is lost to us; still top secret in 1939, it was locked in the Prussian military archive and consumed by flames when British bombs hit the building at the end of the Second World War. Historians have carried out some impressive detective work in order to reconstruct his intentions. See, besides the literature in note 7, G. P. Groß, 'There was a Schlieffen Plan: Neue Quellen', in H. Ehlert, M. Epkenhans and G. P. Groß (eds.), *Der Schlieffenplan. Analysen und Dokumente* (Paderborn, Munich, Vienna and Zurich, 2006), pp. 117–60.

9. Förster, 'Der deutsche Generalstab', p. 84.

10. Holmes, 'Asking Schlieffen', pp. 476–9.

11. Reichsarchiv, *Weltkrieg*, i, pp. 22–3, 69 and 696, Strachan, *First World War*, i, pp. 228–9, R. A. Doughty, *Pyrrhic Victory: French Strategy and Operations in the Great War* (Cambridge, MA, and London, 2005), p. 29, Herwig, *First World War*, p. 59, and H. Jäger, *German Artillery of World War One* (Ramsbury, 2001), pp. 23–8.

12. Herrmann, *Arming of Europe*, pp. 200–4.

13. Moltke, 1911, quoted in Mombauer, *Helmuth von Moltke*, p. 229.

14. Ibid., pp. 34–41, and T. N. Dupuy, *Genius for War: The German Army and General Staff, 1807–1945* (London, 1977), esp. pp. 302–5. Also, for the Great General Staff's narrow focus, especially after 1890, see D. E. Showalter, 'From Deterrence to Doomsday Machine: The German Way of War, 1890–1914', *Journal of Military History* 64(3) (July 2000), pp. 679–710.

15. R. T. Foley, 'Preparing the German Army for the First World War: The Operational Ideas of Alfred von Schlieffen and Helmuth von Moltke the Younger', *War & Society* 22(2) (October 2004), pp. 1–25. Also, more generally, M. Samuels, *Command or Control? Command, Training and Tactics in the British and German Armies, 1888–1918* (London, 1995), esp. pp. 10–18, 31–3 and 283–4.

16. A. Watson, 'Junior Officership in the German Army during the Great War, 1914–1918', *War in History* 14(4) (November 2007), pp. 431–2, and H. Ostertag, *Bildung, Ausbildung und Erziehung des Offizierkorps im deutschen Kaiserreich, 1871–1918. Eliteideal, Anspruch und Wirklichkeit* (Frankfurt am Main, 1990), pp. 56–7. For the noble ethos of the peacetime corps and the change that it underwent during the war, see also W. Deist, 'Zur Geschichte des preussischen Offizierkorps, 1888–1918', in H. H. Hofmann (ed.), *Das deutsche Offizierkorps, 1860–1960* (Boppard am Rhein, 1980), pp. 39–57.

17. M. Hewitson, 'Images of the Enemy: German Depictions of the French Military, 1890–1914', *War in History* 11(1) (January 2004), pp. 13–16 and 21–3, and R. T. Foley, 'Easy Target or Invincible Enemy? German Intelligence Assessments of France before the Great War', *The Journal of Intelligence History* 5 (Winter 2005), pp. 11–12. These assessments did have some grounding in fact. See D. Porch, *The March to the Marne: The French Army, 1871–1914* (Cambridge, New York and Melbourne, 1981) pp. 78–9 and 196.

18. [Preußisches] Kriegsministerium, *Felddienst-Ordnung (F.O.)* (Berlin, 1908), p. 10.

19. Watson, 'Junior Officership', pp. 440 and 448. For Socialists' complaints in peacetime, see M. Kitchen, *The German Officer Corps, 1890–1914* (Oxford, 1968), pp. 182–5.

20. 'Zum Exerzier-Reglement. Kampfschule. Allgemeines', November 1916. BA-MA Freiburg: PH 3/28 and [Preußisches] Kriegsministerium, *Felddienst-Ordnung*, p. 12, Point 4. More generally, Watson, *Enduring the Great War*, pp. 115–20.

21. E. O. Volkmann, *Soziale Heeresmißstände als Mitursache des deutschen Zusammenbruches von 1918. Die Ursachen des deutschen Zusammenbruches im Jahre 1918. Zweite Abteilung. Der innere Zusammenbruch* (12 vols., Berlin, 1929), xi(2), p. 35.

22. *Sanitätsbericht*, iii, p. 12.

23. Samuels, *Command or Control?*, pp. 79–80 and 224, W. Schmidt-Richberg, 'Die Regierungszeit Wilhelms II', in Militärgeschichtliches Forschungsamt (ed.), *Handbuch zur deutschen Militärgeschichte, 1648–1939. Von der Entlassung Bismarcks bis zum Ende des Ersten Weltkrieges (1890–1918)* (10 vols., Frankfurt am Main, 1968), v, pp. 91–5; Herrmann, *Arming of Europe*, p. 203, and D. R. Jones, 'Imperial Russia's Forces at War', in A. R. Millett and W. Murray (eds.), *Military Effectiveness. Volume I: The First World War* (3 vols., Boston, MA, London, Sydney and Wellington, 1988), p. 281.

24. Hewitson, 'Images of the Enemy', pp. 8–10 and 24. For peacetime conscription, see Ingenlath, *Mentale Aufrüstung*, pp. 144–57.

25. See L. V. Smith, *Between Mutiny and Obedience: The Case of the French Fifth Infantry Division during World War I* (Princeton, NJ, 1994).

26. Hewitson, 'Images of the Enemy', pp. 16–18 and 23, and Foley, 'Easy Target', p. 9.

27. U. Frevert, *A Nation in Barracks: Modern Germany, Military Conscription and Civil Society* (Oxford and New York, 2004). Also G. A. Ritter and K. Tenfelde, *Arbeiter im deutschen Kaiserreich, 1871 bis 1914* (Bonn, 1992), pp. 730–46, and Ziemann, *Front*, pp. 47–8 and 70–71.

28. H. Strachan, 'Ausbildung, Kampfgeist und die zwei Weltkriege', in B. Thoß and H.-E. Volkmann (eds.), *Erster Weltkrieg, Zweiter Weltkrieg. Ein Vergleich* (Paderborn, 2002), p. 274.

29. T. Zuber, *The Battle of the Frontiers: Ardennes 1914* (Stroud, 2007, 2009), pp. 83–6, and, for more critical views, S. D. Jackman, 'Shoulder to Shoulder: Close Control and "Old Prussian Drill" in German Offensive Infantry Tactics, 1871–1914', *Journal of Military History* 68(1) (January 2004), pp. 73–104, and Strachan, *First World War*, i, pp. 206 and 237–9. For the French regulations of 1913, see Doughty, *Pyrrhic Victory*, pp. 26–8.

30. G. Kronenbitter, *'Krieg im Frieden'. Die Führung der k.u.k. Armee und die Großmachtpolitik Österreichs-Ungarns, 1906–1914* (Munich, 2003), pp. 115–16.

31. N. Stone, 'Die Mobilmachung der österreichisch-ungarischen Armee 1914', *Militärgeschichtliche Mitteilungen* 16(2) (1974), pp. 68–77 and 83, *ÖULK*, i, p. 87, and Stevenson, 'War by Timetable?', pp. 167–8. The largest Habsburg transports, with 49 wagons, had 100 axles and weighed 500 tons. German military trains had 110 axles and weighed 600 tons. French trains weighed 480–550 tons.

32. N. Golovin, 'The Russian War Plan: II. The Execution of the Plan', *The Slavonic and East European Review* 15(43) (July 1936), pp. 72 and 75.

33. Stone, 'Army and Society', 97–8, and G. E. Rothenberg, *The Army of Francis Joseph* (West Lafayette, IN, 1976, 1998), pp. 74–8.

34. *ÖULK*, i, p. 27.

35. Rothenberg, *Army of Francis Joseph*, pp. 81 and 110–11.

36. I. Deák, *Beyond Nationalism: A Social and Political History of the Habsburg Officer Corps, 1848–1918* (New York and Oxford, 1990), pp. 99–102, and *ÖULK*, i, pp. 38–40 and 52.

37. Deák, *Beyond Nationalism*, pp. 127–38, 161–3 and 169.

38. See ibid., pp. 178–85. Part of the problem is that it is unclear what question the Austro-Hungarian army asked its officers when compiling these figures. Officers may have given the language they most often used, rather than their mother tongue(s). Statistics collected for military schools indicate a much lower proportion of Germans.

39. Ibid., pp. 174–5. In Germany, only the Bavarian army was willing to commission Jews as reserve officers before the First World War. For German military policies towards Jews, see W. T. Angress, 'Das deutsche Militär und die Juden im Ersten Weltkrieg', *Militärgeschichtliche Mitteilungen* 19 (1976), pp. 77–146.

40. Rothenberg, *Army of Francis Joseph*, p. 83, and Deák, *Beyond Nationalism*, pp. 98 and 102–3. For the Habsburg force's shortage of career NCOs, see *ÖULK*, i, p. 49, and Jones, 'Imperial Russia's Forces', p. 281. For the miserable inter-rank relations in Russia's army, see J. Buschnell, 'The Tsarist Officer Corps, 1881–1914: Customs, Duties, Inefficiency', *The American Historical Review* 86(4) (October 1981), pp. 753–80.

41. *ÖULK*, i, p. 56.

42. Compare the ratios of Field Army strengths to trained manpower in Reichsarchiv, *Weltkrieg*, i, pp. 38–9.

43. C. Jahr, *Gewöhnliche Soldaten. Desertion und Deserteure im deutschen und britischen Heer, 1914–1918* (Göttingen, 1998).

44. C. Hämmerle, 'Die k. (u.) k. Armee als "Schule des Volkes"? Zur Geschichte der Allgemeinen Wehrpflicht in der multinationalen Habsburgermonarchie (1866–1914/18)', in C. Jansen (ed.), *Der Bürger als Soldat. Die Militärisierung europäischer Gesellschaften im langen 19. Jahrhundert: ein internationaler Vergleich* (Essen, 2004), pp. 202–3 and 213. For literacy in different parts of the Empire, see D. F. Good, *The Economic Rise of the Habsburg Empire, 1750–1914* (Berkeley and Los Angeles, CA, 1984), p. 156.

45. Kageneck to Moltke, 24 July 1914, quoted in G. Kronenbitter, 'Die Macht der Illusionen. Julikrise und Kriegsausbruch 1914 aus der Sicht des deutschen Militärattachés in Wien', *Militärgeschichtliche Mitteilung* 57(2) (1998), p. 537.

46. Rothenberg, *Army of Francis Joseph*, p. 174; J. M. B. Lyon, '"A Peasant Mob": The Serbian Army on the Eve of the Great War', *The Journal of Military History* 61(3) (July 1997), p. 491, and A. K. Wildman, *The End of the Russian Imperial Army: The Old Army and the Soldiers' Revolt (March–April 1917). Volume I* (2 vols., Princeton, NJ, and Guildford, 1980), i, p. 73. The Russian total comprises forty-eight field guns in divisions and half of the twenty-four light howitzers controlled by each corps. Habsburg corps each had eight 150 mm heavy howitzers. Russian and Serb heavy guns were pooled at army level.

47. Kronenbitter, 'Krieg im Frieden', pp. 189–94, Rothenberg, *Army of Francis Joseph*, pp. 126–7 and 174–5, and A. Krauß, *Die Ursachen unserer Niederlage. Erinnerungen und Urteile aus dem Weltkrieg*, 3rd edn (Munich, 1923), pp. 94–5; also Strachan, *First World War*, i, pp. 285 and 995–8.

48. Samuels, *Command or Control?*, p. 79, and Strachan, *First World War*, i, p. 206.

49. See the introduction by T. Cave in United States War Office, *Histories of Two Hundred and Fifty-One Divisions of the German Army which partici-pated in the War* (London, 1920, 1989), p. iii. Also A. Gat, *The Development of Military Thought: The Nineteenth Century* (Oxford, 1992), pp. 151–4.

50. *ÖULK*, i, pp. 28 and 32, and Krauß, *Ursachen unserer Niederlage*, pp. 90–94. For details of the march battalions' use in action, see G. A. Tunstall, *Blood on the Snow: The Carpathian Winter War of 1915* (Lawrence, KS, 2010), pp. 13, 88 and 90.

51. Kronenbitter, '*Krieg im Frieden*', pp. 82–99. For the French, see Doughty, *Pyrrhic Victory*, pp. 25–9.

52. Conrad, *Aus meiner Dienstzeit*, iv, pp. 290–94.

53. Wagner, 'K.(u.)k. Armee', p. 627.

54. T. Hadley, 'Military Diplomacy in the Dual Alliance: German Military Attaché Reporting from Vienna, 1906–1914', *War in History* 17(3) (July 2010), pp. 307–8.

55. Förster, 'Deutsche Generalstab', pp. 83–95.

56. W. Meyer, *Das Infanterie-Regiment von Grolman (1. Posensches) Nr. 18 im Weltkriege* (Oldenburg i. O. and Berlin, 1929), pp. 2–3.

57. Reichsarchiv, *Weltkrieg*, i, p. 142, and Strachan, *First World War*, i, p. 207. For a description of the seven phases of German mobilization, see Herwig, *First World War*, pp. 56–7 and 75.

58. This account follows Strachan, *First World War*, i, pp. 211–12, and Herwig, *First World War*, pp. 96–7.

59. K. von Einem, *Ein Armeeführer erlebt den Weltkrieg. Persönliche Aufzeich-nungen des Generalobersten v. Einem*, ed. J. Alter (Leipzig, 1938), p. 37 (diary entry for 11 August 1914).

60. Soldier's account published in *Kölnische Volkszeitung*, 13 August 1914, and reproduced in Buchner (ed.), *Kriegsdokumente*, i, p. 203 (doc. 312d).

61. Ibid., p. 35 (letter and diary entry for 8 August 1914).

62. J. Horne and A. Kramer, *German Atrocities, 1914: A History of Denial* (New Haven, CT, and London, 2001), pp. 10–23; here esp. pp. 14 and 23. For the *Garde Civique*, see ibid., pp. 125–9.

63. Doughty, *Pyrrhic Victory*, pp. 56–63, and Strachan, *First World War*, i, pp. 212–16.

64. *Sanitätsbericht*, iii, pp. 6*, 82*, 84* and 88* (shot, stab and other wounds).

65. See the Josephine and Clara B., 'Kriegschronik', 16 August–3 September 1914. DTA, Emmendingen: 898.

66. A. Spemann, diary, 17 August 1914. HStA Stuttgart: M660/041, nr. 1; Armee-Oberkommando Strasburg, telegram to Generalkommando, XIV Reservekorps, 14 August 1914, and Generalkommando, XIV Reservekorps

to Armee-Oberkommando, 6. Armee, 19 September 1914. GLA Karlsruhe: 456 F 7 nr. 165. Also more generally, C. J. Fischer, *Alsace to the Alsatians? Visions and Divisions of Alsatian Regionalism, 1870–1939* (New York and Oxford, 2010), pp. 102–3, and Horne and Kramer, *German Atrocities*, p. 22.

67. J.-J. Becker and G. Krumeich, *Der Grosse Krieg. Deutschland und Frankreich im Ersten Weltkrieg, 1914–1918* (Essen, 2010), pp. 178–9.

68. J.-C. Farcy, *Les Camps de concentration français de la première guerre mondiale (1914–1920)* (Paris, 1995), pp. 51–60. Also Armeeoberkommando VII to Generalkommando XIV Reservekorps, 31 August 1914. GLA Karlsruhe: 465 F7 nr. 165.

69. J. Bell (ed.), *Völkerrecht im Weltkrieg. Dritte Reihe im Werk des Untersuchungsausschusses* (5 vols., Berlin, 1927), i, pp. 161 and 167–9. See also T. Zahra, 'The "Minority Problem" and National Classification in the French and Czechoslovak Borderlands', *Contemporary European History* 17(2) (May 2008), esp. pp. 138–9 and 149–58.

70. Ruffey, quoted in Doughty, *Pyrrhic Victory*, p. 75.

71. Zuber, *Battle of the Frontiers*, esp. pp. 266 and 275–80; Strachan, *First World War*, i, pp. 218–19 and 230.

72. M. van Creveld, *Supplying War: Logistics from Wallenstein to Patton* (Cambridge, London, New York and Melbourne, 1977), p. 135.

73. Zuber, *Battle of the Frontiers*, p. 29.

74. *Sanitätsbericht*, iii, p. 136. For descriptions of the exhausted troops, see P. Münch, *Bürger in Uniform. Kriegserfahrungen von Hamburger Turnern 1914 bis 1918* (Freiburg i. Br., Berlin and Vienna, 2009), p. 88.

75. E. Baier, letter to parents, 22 August 1914. BA-MA Freiburg: PH10II/52.

76. Calculated from figures in *Sanitätsbericht*, iii, p. 36, Table 28.

77. Horne and Kramer, *German Atrocities*, pp. 74 and 76.

78. Becker and Krumeich, *Grosse Krieg*, p. 176.

79. Horne and Kramer, *German Atrocities*, pp. 38–42 and 217–18.

80. Ibid., pp. 24–32 and 42–52.

81. Ibid., esp. pp. 175–225 and 249–61. See also R. Harris, 'The "Child of the Barbarian": Rape, Race and Nationalism in France during the First World War', *Past & Present* 141 (November 1993), pp. 170–206.

82. J. Lipkes, *Rehearsals: The German Army in Belgium, August 1914* (Leuven, 2007), esp. pp. 563–74.

83. For anti-Catholicism and race (which they see as contributory rather than the sole factors behind the atrocities), see Horne and Kramer, *German Atrocities*, pp. 104–7 and 156–8. For Catholic German soldiers, see T. Weber, *Hitler's First War: Adolf Hitler, the Men of the List Regiment, and the First World War* (Oxford, 2010), p. 37, and for Kalisz, see L. Engelstein, '"A Belgium of Our Own": The Sack of Russian Kalisz, August 1914',

Kritika: Explorations in Russian and Eurasian History 10(3) (Summer 2009), pp. 441–73.

84. R. Browning, *Ordinary Men: Reserve Police Battalion 101 and the Final Solution in Poland* (New York, 1992). For the cognitive processes behind atrocities, see K. E. Taylor, 'Intergroup Atrocities in War: A Neuroscientific Perspective', *Medicine, Conflict and Survival* 22(3) (July–September 2006), pp. 230–44.

85. M. R. Stoneman, 'The Bavarian Army and French Civilians in the War of 1870–71: A Cultural Interpretation', *War in History* 8(3) (July 2001), p. 272, and Horne and Kramer, *German Atrocities*, pp. 141–2.

86. E. Baier, letter to parents, 10 August 1914. BA-MA Freiburg: PH10 – II/52. The word he used was 'Freischärler'. For similar comments, see W. Jacobson, *Z armią Klucka na Paryż* (Toruń, 1934), p. 14.

87. Newspaper extracts from 9–18 August 1914 in Buchner (ed.), *Kriegsdokumente*, i, p. 203 (docs. 312a, b, c, d and h).

88. E. Baier, letter to parents, 13 August 1914. BA-MA Freiburg: PH10 – II/52.

89. W. Schweiger, diary, 17 August 1914. DTA, Emmendingen: 1386.

90. Ibid., 20 August 1914.

91. I. V. Hull, *Absolute Destruction: Military Culture and the Practices of War in Imperial Germany* (Ithaca, NY, and London, 2005), pp. 119–26.

92. Article 2 of the Annex entitled 'Regulations Respecting the Laws and Customs of War on Land' to 'Convention Concerning the Laws and Customs of War on Land. 2d Peace Conference, The Hague, 18 Oct. 1907. IV', in *Conventions and Declarations between the Powers Concerning War, Arbitration and Neutrality (Declaration of Paris, 1856 – of St Petersburg, 1868 – of The Hague, 1899 – Convention of Geneva, 1906 – 2d Peace Conference, The Hague, 1907 – Declaration of London, 1909). English – French – German* (The Hague, 1915). Also G. Best, *Humanity in Warfare: The Modern History of the International Law of Armed Conflicts* (London, 1980), pp. 145–6, 180–81, 185 and 190–200, and Horne and Kramer, *German Atrocities*, pp. 144–5. The interpretation of the 1907 Hague Convention here follows A. Alexander, 'The Genesis of the Civilian', *Leiden Journal of International Law* 20(2) (June 2007), esp. pp. 360–65.

93. See Showalter, 'Deterrence to Doomsday Machine', esp. p. 690.

94. J. Horne and A. Kramer, 'German "Atrocities" and Franco-German Opinion, 1914: The Evidence of German Soldiers' Diaries', *The Journal of Modern History* 66(1) (March 1994), esp. p. 16, and Horne and Kramer, *German Atrocities*, p. 132.

95. Alexander, 'Genesis', p. 365.

96. See Article 50 of the Annex to 'Convention Concerning the Laws and Customs of War'.

97. Generalleutnant Kosch, postcard to wife, 20 August 1914. BA-MA Freiburg: N 754/1.

98. Horne and Kramer, *German Atrocities*, pp. 18 and 162–7.

99. S. de Schaepdrijver, 'Belgium', in J. Horne (ed.), *A Companion to World War I* (Malden, MA, Oxford and Chichester, 2010), p. 388.

100. An estimate for the population of the territories invaded in August and early September 1914 derived from figures in the Ministère de l'Intérieur, *Annuaire statistique de la Belgique et du Congo belge. Quarante-deuxième année – 1911. Tome XLII* (Brussels, 1912), p. 4, and M. Huber, *La Population de la France pendant la Guerre* (Paris and New Haven, CT, 1931), pp. 381, 390 and 394, and maps in Horne and Kramer, *German Atrocities*, pp. 10 and 182. For the quotation and a different interpretation, see also ibid., pp. 165 and 419–31.

101. For Napoleonic massacres, see P. G. Dwyer, '"It Still Makes Me Shudder": Memories of Massacres and Atrocities during the Revolutionary and Napoleonic Wars', *War in History* 16(4) (November 2009), pp. 381–405. Lipkes' *Rehearsals* attempts most explicitly to connect the atrocities of 1914 with Germans' genocidal violence thirty years later, but the implication is also present in Horne and Kramer's *German Atrocities* and Hull's *Absolute Destruction*. The literature on the Holocaust and atrocities on the Eastern Front in the Second World War is too extensive to be given here, but especially relevant to the above argument is O. Bartov, *Hitler's Army: Soldiers, Nazis and War in the Third Reich* (Oxford, 1992). For comparisons with other contemporary armies' violence, see the following sections and the next chapter.

102. See the chart and commentary in Horne and Kramer, *German Atrocities*, pp. 77–8.

103. See, for example, not only Einem's comments above but also Generalleutnant Kosch, letter to his wife, 25 August 1914. BA-MA Freiburg: N 754/1.

104. Generalleutnant Kosch, letter to his wife, 26 August 1914. BA-MA Freiburg: N 754/1. For 10th Division's atrocities, see Horne and Kramer, *German Atrocities*, pp. 58–60.

105. Strachan, First World War, i, pp. 224–31 and 242–50; Doughty, *Pyrrhic Victory*, pp. 76–82.

106. Van Creveld, *Supplying War*, pp. 113, 116–17, 126, 129–32 and 137.

107. E. Baier, letters to parents, 29 and 30 August 1914. BA-MA Freiburg: PH10 – II/52. For the distance covered by First Army units, see Münch, *Bürger in Uniform*, p. 88.

108. Strachan, *First World War*, pp. 248–61; Herwig, *First World War*, pp. 99–105, and Holmes, 'Asking Schlieffen', pp. 476–7.

109. E. Baier, letter to his parents, 8 September 1914. BA-MA Freiburg: PH10 – II/52.

110. J. Krüger-Franke, 'Über truppenärztliche Erfahrungen in der Schlacht', *Berliner klinische Wochenschrift* 1 (4 January 1915), p. 7.

111. E. Baier, letter to his parents, 8 September 1914. BA-MA Freiburg: PH10 – II/52.

112. G. A. Tunstall, Jr, 'The Habsburg Command Conspiracy: The Austrian Falsification of Historiography on the Outbreak of World War I', *Austrian History Yearbook* 27 (1996), pp. 181–98.

113. Conrad, *Aus meiner Dienstzeit*, iv, pp. 266 and 275.

114. See Clark, *Sleepwalkers*, pp. 102–5, and L. Sondhaus, *Franz Conrad von Hötzendorf: Architect of the Apocalypse* (Boston, MA, 2000), pp. 145–8.

115. Stone, 'Mobilmachung', pp. 79–80 and 86.

116. N. Stone, *The Eastern Front, 1914–1917* (London and New York, 1975, 1998), p. 76.

117. Tunstall, 'Habsburg Command Conspiracy', pp. 193–5.

118. Stone, 'Mobilmachung', pp. 79–80 and 86.

119. Stone, *Eastern Front*, p. 84.

120. R. Jeřábek, *Potiorek. General im Schatten von Sarajevo* (Graz, Vienna and Cologne, 1991), pp. 107, 111–12, 119–20 and 130. Also Stone, *Eastern Front*, p. 79.

121. Stone, 'Mobilmachung', pp. 90–92.

122. T. Snyder, *Bloodlands: Europe between Hitler and Stalin* (New York, 2010).

123. Jeřábek, *Potiorek*, pp. 9–15 and 27–32.

124. Ibid., pp. 115–16.

125. Ibid., pp. 113–14.

126. Ibid., pp. 104–5 and 108. Figures for Serbian strength from Lyon, '"A Peasant Mob"', p. 501.

127. A. Fiedler, diary, 13 August 1914. KA Vienna: NL Fiedler, B/240, nr. 1.

128. Jeřábek, *Potiorek*, pp. 118–22.

129. A. Fiedler, diary, 14 August 1914. KA Vienna: NL Fiedler, B/240, nr. 1.

130. For information on Reiss and his investigation, see B. M. Scianna, 'Reporting Atrocities: Archibald Reiss in Serbia, 1914–1918', *Journal of Slavic Military Studies* 25(4) (2012), pp. 597–607.

131. See Horne and Kramer, *German Atrocities*, pp. 200–204. For similar examples on the German side, see the testimony of Wehrmann August Schult, 24 January 1915, in AP Olsztyn: RP Allenstein: 179: fo. 465 and Auswärtiges Amt, Greueltaten russischer Truppen, esp. Anlagen 35, 39, 40, 41 and 74.

132. R. A. Reiss, *Report upon the Atrocities Committed by the Austro-Hungarian Army during the First Invasion of Serbia Submitted to the Serbian Government* (London, 1916), pp. 33, 42, 60, 103, 142 and 167.

133. See J. Gumz, *The Resurrection and Collapse of Empire in Habsburg Serbia, 1914–1918* (Cambridge and New York, 2009), esp. pp. 54–8, and A. Holzer, *Das Lächeln der Henker. Der unbekannte Krieg gegen die Zivilbevölkerung, 1914–1918* (Darmstadt, 2008), pp. 113–44.

134. A. Hausner, diary, 17 August 1914. KA Vienna: NL Hausner, B/217.

135. Reiss, *Report upon the Atrocities*, pp. 39–40, 45–51, 131–2 and 142. Gumz, *Resurrection and Collapse*, pp. 55–8, and Holzer, *Lächeln*, pp. 118–23.

136. This paragraph follows Gumz, *Resurrection and Collapse*, esp. pp. 29–30. For Hranilović and the intelligence report, see Holzer, *Lächeln*, p. 115.

137. J. R. Schneider, 'Defeating Balkan Insurgency: The Austro-Hungarian Army in Bosnia-Herzegovina, 1878–82', *The Journal of Strategic Studies* 27(3) (September 2004), esp. pp. 541–5 and 547–8.

138. For these traits, see Kronenbitter, *'Krieg im Frieden'*, pp. 522–3.

139. O. Jászi, *The Dissolution of the Habsburg Monarchy* (Chicago, IL, and London, 1929, 1966), p. 14.

140. Quoted in Gumz, *Resurrection and Collapse*, p. 39. Whether Habsburg Serbs did actually attack their army is unclear. When the Serb and Montenegrin forces invaded Bosnia at the end of August and in September, local civilian authorities reported that the Serb population did collaborate with their compatriots. The invaders killed and raped the Muslim population of the areas that they overran. When the Habsburg army retook the region, it executed more than 120 local Serbs. See report of the Landesregierung in Sarajevo, 18 October 1914, pp. 13–16. KA Vienna: KÜA (1914), Karton 15: Nr. 8389, and Z. A. B. Zeman, *The Break-Up of the Habsburg Empire, 1914–1918: A Study in National and Social Revolution* (London, New York and Toronto, 1961), p. 59.

141. Gumz, *Resurrection and Collapse*, pp. 41–2, and Holzer, *Lächeln*, p. 117.

142. 'Belagsziffern der Internierungs- und Unterbringungsorte am 18. September 1914', KA Vienna: MSKM (1914) 69–11/1.

143. Quoted in Gumz, *Resurrection and Collapse*, p. 33. These regulations dated from 1912.

144. Holzer, *Lächeln*, pp. 78–9.

145. Reiss, *Report upon the Atrocities*, pp. 181–3.

146. A. Fiedler, diary, 7 August 1914. KA Vienna: NL Fiedler, B/240, nr. 1.

147. Lyon, '"A Peasant Mob"', pp. 487–8 and 497–9.

148. Quoted in Jeřábek, *Potiorek*, p. 127.

149. A. Hausner, diary, 17 August 1914. KA Vienna: NL Hausner, B/217.

150. Krauß, *Ursachen unserer Niederlage*, pp. 148–9, fn. 1.

151. K.u.k. Ministerium des Äussern, *Sammlung von Nachweisen für die Verletzungen des Völkerrechts durch die mit Österreich-Ungarn Krieg führenden Staaten. Abgeschlossen mit 31. Jänner 1915* (Vienna, 1915), pp. 168–9, 176 (docs. 123–5, 134–6). For similar stories circulating at the front, see Reiss,

Report upon the Atrocities, pp. 174–5, and A. Hausner, diary, 17 August 1914. KA Vienna: NL Hausner, B/217.

152. Jeřábek, *Potiorek*, p. 132.

153. J. R. Schindler, 'Disaster on the Drina: The Austro-Hungarian Army in Serbia, 1914', *War in History* 9(2) (April 2002), pp. 171–4, and Jeřábek, *Potiorek*, pp. 118–32.

154. For a summary of the campaigns, if now a somewhat outdated analysis, see G. E. Rothenberg, 'The Austro-Hungarian Campaign against Serbia in 1914', *The Journal of Military History* 53(2) (April 1989), pp. 127–46.

155. A. Fiedler, diary, 26 August 1914. KA Vienna: NL Fiedler, B/240, nr. 1; A. Hausner, diary, 20 August 1914. KA Vienna: NL Hausner, B/217, and Schindler, 'Disaster on the Drina', pp. 175–7.

156. Rauchensteiner, *Tod des Doppeladlers*, p. 126.

157. 'Telephonischer chiffrierter Bericht der Statthalterei in Lemberg vom 1. August, 12 Uhr 45 früh'. KA Vienna: Zentralstellen – Kriegsüberwachungsamt (Aktenkartons) 1914: Karton 1: Nr. 252.

158. Bachmann, '*Ein Herd der Feindschaft*', pp. 227–33. See also chs. 1 and 2.

159. Prezydyum c.k. Namiestnictwa, Lwów to wszystkich c.k. Starostów i ... c.k. Dyrektorów Policyi we Lwowie i Krakowie, 8 August 1914. KA Vienna: Zentralstellen – Kriegsüberwachungsamt (Aktenkartons) 1914: Karton 1: Nr. 252.

160. Statthalterei-Präsidiums in Lemberg to Ministerium des Innern, minutes from a telephone call, 18 August 1914. KA Vienna: Zentralstellen – Kriegsüberwachungsamt (Aktenkartons) 1914: Karton 3: Nr. 1842.

161. See esp. Schmitz, 'Verrat am Waffenbruder?', pp. 385–407. More generally, Strachan, *First World War*, i, pp. 289–90; Herwig, *First World War*, p. 89.

162. Stone, *Eastern Front*, p. 80, and Rauchensteiner, *Tod des Doppeladlers*, pp. 126–7.

163. Stone, *Eastern Front*, pp. 85–9, and Strachan, *First World War*, i, pp. 350–54.

164. J. E. Romer, *Pamiętniki* (Warsaw, n.d.), p. 41. Cf. T. Ritter von Zeynek, *Ein Offizier im Generalstabskorps erinnert sich*, ed. P. Broucek (Vienna, Cologne and Weimar, 2009), p. 194.

165. K.u.k. Armeeoberkommando, 'Erfahrungen as den bisherigen Kämpfen', 28 September 1914. KA Vienna: NFA 43. Sch. D. 1914 (Op. Akt. Sept.–Okt.) (Karton 2180): Op. Nr. 2610 (in folder for 1 October 1914).

166. J. Gamst, diary, 29 August 1914. DTA, Emmendingen: 1719,2.

167. See Führ, *K.u.k. Armeeoberkommando*, p. 64. Conrad was unnerved when a Russian army pamphlet entitled 'Galicia and the Present' was captured which listed Russophile agents in Galicia. A translated copy of the pamphlet entitled 'Das Galizien der Gegenwart' is in KA Vienna: MKSM 1914: 69–8/9.

168. Drjur. Longin Cehelskzj, 'Die Wahrheit über den Verrat in Ostgalizien', p. 8, KA Vienna: MKSM (1915) 28-3/2.

169. See, for example, k.k. Statthalter von Galizien to Minister des Innern, 11 November 1915, p. 8. AVA Vienna: MdI Präsidiale (1916–17) 22/Galiz. Karton 2117: Nr. 4403.

170. K.u.k. Armeegruppenkmdo, GdI von Kövess to alle Kps, JTDionen, KTDionen, Lst. Brigaden u. Kps Trains der Armeegruppe, weiters an die exponierten Gend. Stabsoffz. von Lemberg, Stanislau u. Czernowitz, 19 August 1914. KA Vienna: NFA, 43. Sch. D. Karton 2179 (Op. Akten v. August 1914): doc. 80. Fourth Army also issued an order to its troops on 13 August 1914 to treat civilians harshly. See Stone, *Eastern Front*, pp. 82 and 312, endnote 12. Another similar order of 19 August 1914 to 3 Army Command and other units is cited in Holzer, *Lächeln*, p. 62.

171. K.u.k. Militärkommando in Krakau to k.k. Polizeidirektion Krakau, 11 September 1914. AN Cracow: DPKr 97: (1914) 3518/14: fo. 1867.

172. J. Słomka, *From Serfdom to Self-Government: Memoirs of a Polish Village Mayor, 1842–1927*, trans. W. J. Rose (London, 1941), pp. 221–6.

173. For composition, see M. Zgórniak, 'Polacy w Armii Austro-Węgierskiej w czasie I Wojny Światowej', *Studia i Materiały do Historii Wojskowości* 30 (1988), p. 237.

174. K.u.k. 1 Kpskmdo, Op. Nr. 408–18, 31 August 1914. KA Vienna: NFL 12 ID (1914 Op. Nr. v. 2.8–30.9) Karton 719. Also, for the belief in these stories across the army, see GdI von Dankl, diary, vol. 1, p. 105 (31 August 1914). KA Vienna: NL Dankl, B/3: 5/1.

175. K.u.k. 12 ITD Kmdo, Op. Nr. 70 to 23 Brig. Kmdo., 30 August 1914. KA Vienna: NFL 12 ID (1914 Op. Nr. v. 2.8–30.9) Karton 719.

176. K.u.k. 12 ITD Kmdo, Op. Nr. 70 to and from Jägerbaon 5, 3 September 1914. KA Vienna: NFL 12 ID (1914 Op. Nr. v. 2.8–30.9) Karton 719.

177. K.u.k. Traindivision No. 1 to k.u.k. 12 ITD on 'Informationsperson', 4 September 1914. KA Vienna: NFL 12 ID (1914 Op. Nr. v. 2.8–30.9) Karton 719.

178. P. Szlanta, '"Najgorsze bestie to są Honwedy". Ewolucja stosunku polskich mieszkańców Galicji do monarchii habsburkiej podczas I wojny światowej', in U. Jakubowska (ed.), *Galicyjskie spotkania 2011* (n.p., 2011), p. 166. For the widespread perception of Hungarians as exceptionally brutal, see W. Mentzel, 'Kriegsflüchtlinge in Cisleithanien im Ersten Weltkrieg', unpublished PhD thesis, Vienna University (1997), p. 105. For their similar reputation in Serbia, see Reiss, *Report upon the Atrocities*, pp. 36–7, 40–41, 60 and 76.

179. P. A. Hanebrink, *In Defense of Christian Hungary: Religion, Nationalism, and Antisemitism, 1890–1944* (Ithaca, NY, and London, 2006), pp. 28–46, and Okey, *Habsburg Monarchy*, pp. 325–30.

180. A. Hausner, diary, 22 October 1914. Cf. also entry for 20 October 1914. KA Vienna: NL Hausner, B/217.

181. See Taylor, 'Intergroup Atrocities', pp. 230–44.

182. For the use of German in particular in Galicia, see K. Baedeker, *Austria-Hungary with Excursions to Cetinje, Belgrade, and Bucharest: Handbook for Travellers by Karl Baedeker*, 11th edn (Leipzig, London and New York, 1911), p. 24.

183. Redlich, *Schicksalsjahre Österreichs*, i, p. 265 (entry for 2 Sept. 1914).

184. Dr. jur. Longin Cehelskzj, 'Die Wahrheit über den Verrat in Ostgalizien', p. 3. KA Vienna: MKSM (1915) 28–3/2.

185. Memorandum on alleged Russophiles in internment, 7 November 1914. KA Vienna: MKSM (1914) (Karton 1141) 69–11/5. Also, Mentzel, 'Kriegsflüchtlinge', pp. 86–91. For cases of whole Ruthenian communities being forcibly deported, see the army's request to remove the 1,200 Ruthenes from Solotwina and Manasterczany in March 1915. K.u.k. Armeeoberkommando. Etappenoberkommando, 'Evakuierung der Bevölkerung von Solotwina und Manasterczany wegen russophiler Gesinnung', 12 March 1915. KA Vienna: AOK-QU.-Abteilung (Karton 1493), Nr. 31187.

186. Ritter von Semaka, 14. Sitzung der XXII. Session am 4. Juli 1917 and Ritter von Singalewycz, 21. Sitzung der XXII. Session am 15. Juli 1917 in *Stenographische Protokolle über die Sitzungen des Hauses der Abgeordneten des österreichischen Reichsrates im Jahre 1917. XXII. Session. 1. (Eröffnungs-) bis 21. Sitzung. (S. 1 bis 1155)* (4 vols., Vienna, 1917), i, pp. 652 and 1103. Also, C. Mick, *Kriegserfahrungen in einer multiethnischen Stadt: Lemberg, 1914–1947* (Wiesbaden, 2010), p. 72.

187. See ch. 1. For Ruthenian parties in the Reichsrat, see L. Höbelt, '"Well-Tempered Discontent": Austrian Domestic Politics', in M. Cornwall (ed.), *The Last Years of Austria-Hungary* (Exeter, 1990), p. 58.

188. Tăslăuanu, *With the Austrian Army*, p. 37. Also, Mentzel, 'Kriegsflüchtlinge', pp. 96–7.

189. 'Bericht des Legationsrates Baron Andrian über seine Informationsreise nach Ostgalizien', 26 July 1915, p. 19. AVA Vienna: MdI Präsidiale (1914–15) 22/Galiz. Karton 2116: Nr. 19644. For other reports and for civilian authorities' role in drawing up the internment lists, see Mentzel, 'Kriegsflüchtlinge', pp. 97 and 104.

190. Dr. jur. Longin Cehelskzj, 'Die Wahrheit über den Verrat in Ostgalizien', pp. 1–2 and 8–10. KA Vienna: MKSM (1915) 28–3/2. Cf. Speech by Abgeordneter Ritter von Singalewycz in *Stenographische Protokolle*, i (XXII. Session. 21. Sitzung), esp. pp. 1103–4.

191. Strachan, *First World War*, i, pp. 353–6.

192. K. Lauer, diary, 26 and 29 August 1914. KA Vienna: NL Lauer, B/366: Nr. 1.

193. A. Hausner, diary, 2 September 1914. KA Vienna: NL Hausner, B/217.

194. Mentzel, 'Kriegsflüchtlinge', pp. 92–102 and esp. 104.

195. K.u.k. Kriegsministerium, order on 'Superarbitrierung von Offizieren des Armeestandes, des Ruhestandes und im Verhältnisse außer Dienst, behufs Einteilung bei den Feldformationen', KA Vienna: KÜA 1914 (Aktenkartons): Karton 13: Nr. 7377.

196. Herwig, First World War, p. 94.

197. See K. Lauer, diary, 24 September 1914. KA Vienna: NL Lauer, B/366: Nr. 1. Also E. Dietrich, 'Der andere Tod. Seuchen, Volkskrankheiten und Gesundheitswesen im Ersten Weltkrieg', in K. Eisterer and R. Steininger (eds.), Tirol und der Erste Weltkrieg (Innsbruck, 1995), pp. 258–9. Some 78,279 cholera sufferers were treated in the army during the war, of whom 16,266 died. Nearly all the cases were contracted before the summer of 1915.

198. K.u.k. 4. Korpskommando to kgl. ung. 42. LITD, 9 September 1914. KA Vienna: NFA 43. Sch. D. 1914 (Op. Akt. v. Sept.–Okt.) (Karton 2180): Op. Nr. 36.

199. See K. Lauer, diary, 11 September 1914. KA Vienna: NL Lauer B/366: Nr. 1 and A. Hausner, diary, 20 October 1914. KA Vienna: NL Hausner, B/217. Also A. Krasicki, Dziennik z kampanii rosyjskiej 1914–1916 (Warsaw, 1988), p. 42 (diary entry for 29 August 1914).

200. ÖULK, i, pp. 337–8.

201. K.u.k. 2 Armeekommando, order, 6 September 1914. KA Vienna: NFA 43. Sch. D. 1914 (Op. Akt. v. Sept.–Okt.) (Karton 2180): Op. Nr. 447.

202. See K. Lauer, diary, 12 September 1914. KA Vienna: NL Lauer, B/366: Nr. 1.

203. Falkenhayn, quoted in H. Afflerbach, 'Planning Total War? Falkenhayn and the Battle of Verdun, 1916', in R. Chickering and S. Förster (eds.), Great War, Total War: Combat and Mobilization on the Western Front, 1914–1918 (Washington, DC, and Cambridge, 2000), p. 118. Also, more generally, Afflerbach, Falkenhayn, pp. 187–210. For the shell shortage, see Strachan, First World War, i, pp. 993–4.

204. Führ, K.u.k. Armeeoberkommando, pp. 64–71. For Poles' reaction, see Szlanta, '"Najgorsze bestie to są Honwedy"', pp. 168–9, and for the rise in anti-Semitism, see Mick, Kriegserfahrungen, pp. 146–53.

205. Herwig, First World War, pp. 94 and 120.

206. R. A. Prete, 'French Military War Aims, 1914–1916', The Historical Journal 28(4) (December 1985), pp. 889–90, and D. Stevenson, 'French War Aims and the American Challenge, 1914–1918', The Historical Journal 22(4) (December 1979), p. 878.

207. A. Fontaine, French Industry during the War (New Haven, CT, and London, 1926), pp. 270–71 and 405.

208. M. Augé-Laribé and P. Pinot, *Agriculture and Food Supply in France during the War* (New Haven, CT, and London, 1927), p. 55.
209. *Sanitätsbericht*, iii, p. 140*.

4. THE WAR OF DEFENCE

1. *Berliner Tageblatt und Handels-Zeitung. Morgen-Ausgabe* 43, 387 (2 August 1914).
2. See W. J. Mommsen, 'The Topos of Inevitable War in Germany in the Decade before 1914', in V. R. Berghahn and M. Kitchen (eds.), *Germany in the Age of Total War* (London and Totowa, NJ, 1981), pp. 23–45. Also T. R. E. Paddock, *Creating the Russian Peril: Education, the Public Sphere, and National Identity in Imperial Germany, 1890–1914* (Rochester, NY, 2010). For Russian belligerence in Galicia before the First World War, see Bachmann, *'Herd der Feindschaft'*, ch. 3.
3. Tsar to French ambassador, quoted in N. Golovin, 'The Russian War Plan: II. The Execution of the Plan', *The Slavonic and East European Review* 15(43) (July 1936), p. 74. For Russian war plans, see J. Snyder, *The Ideology of the Offensive: Military Decision Making and the Disasters of 1914* (Ithaca, NY, and London, 1984), pp. 157–98, and Strachan, *First World War*, i, pp. 297–316.
4. See 'Bericht des Oberpräsidenten der Provinz Ostpreußen an den Minister des Innern', 20 March 1915, reproduced in Auswärtiges Amt, *Greueltaten russischer Truppen gegen deutsche Zivilpersonen und deutsche Kriegsgefangene* (Berlin, 1915), Anlage 1. A copy is held in BA-MA Freiburg: RM5/2514. For concern at the November attack, see Stellv. Generalkommando des V. Armeekorps to Erzbischof D. Likowski, 9 November 1914. AP Poznań: OA X 39. For the Galician campaign, see Stone, *Eastern Front*, ch. 4, and Strachan, *First World War*, i, pp. 347–67 and 371–3.
5. See M. von Hagen, *War in a European Borderland: Occupations and Occupation Plans in Galicia and Ukraine, 1914–1918* (Seattle, WA, 2007), pp. 19–42.
6. See A. Funk, *Geschichte der Stadt Allenstein von 1348 bis 1943* (Gelsenkirchen, 1955), pp. 216–34, and A. Kossert, *Ostpreußen. Geschichte und Mythos* (Munich, 2005), pp. 118–19.
7. P. Hirschberg, *Die Russen in Allenstein. Die Besetzung und Befreiung der Stadt am 27., 28. und 29. August 1914*, 2nd extended edn (Allenstein, 1918), pp. 3–4.
8. Much of the following account is based on a report by Polizeiinspektor Schroeder[?], 15 April 1915. AP Olsztyn: Akta Miasta Olsztyn 259/168: fos. 16–17.

9. Examples of the atrocity stories spread by refugees early in the war can be found in P. Kuhr, *There We'll Meet Again: The First World War Diary of a Young German Girl*, trans. W. Wright (n.p., 1998), esp. pp. 18–19 (entry for 9 August 1914) and p. 42 (entry for 10 September 1914).

10. Poster, 22 August 1914. AP Olsztyn: Akta Miasta Olsztyn 259/168: fo. 1.

11. Rittel, diary, 25 August 1914. AP Olsztyn: Akta Miasta Olsztyn 259/169.

12. *Allensteiner Zeitung, Extra-Ausgabe Nr. 59*, 25 August 1914.

13. 'Die Allensteiner Russentage', *Allensteiner Zeitung, 72. Jahrgang, Nr. 208*, 10 September 1914.

14. Polizeiinspektor Schroeder[?], report, 15 April 1915. AP Olsztyn: Akta Miasta Olsztyn 259/168: fo. 40. The local newspaper estimated that only 2,000 people remained in the city. See 'Die Allensteiner Russentage', *Allensteiner Zeitung, 72. Jahrgang, Nr. 208*, 10 September 1914.

15. The sources disagree about when exactly this looting took place. This account follows that of the teacher, Herr Rittel, who was tasked with assessing the damage to the pub caused by the plunderers. See Rittel, diary, 26 August 1914. AP Olsztyn: Akta Miasta Olsztyn 259/169.

16. Hirschberg, *Russen in Allenstein*, p. 9.

17. 'Die Allensteiner Russentage', *Allensteiner Zeitung, 72. Jahrgang, Nr. 208*, 10 September 1914.

18. Hirschberg, *Russen in Allenstein*, pp. 9–10.

19. Rittel, diary, 30 September 1916. AP Olsztyn: Akta Miasta Olsztyn 259/169.

20. Polizeiinspektor Schroeder[?], report, 15 April 1915. AP Olsztyn: Akta Miasta Olsztyn 259/168: fo. 40; 'Als die Russen in Allenstein waren', *Allensteiner Zeitung, 72. Jahrgang, Nr. 204*, 5 September 1914. Details about the clash between the Russian and German cavalry are in 'Die Allensteiner Russentage', *Allensteiner Zeitung, 72. Jahrgang, Nr. 208*, 10 September 1914.

21. Polizeiinspektor Schroeder[?], report, 15 April 1915. AP Olsztyn: Akta Miasta Olsztyn 259/168: fo. 40; Rittel, diary, 30 September 1916. AP Olsztyn: Akta Miasta Olsztyn 259/169.

22. Accounts of the Russians' entry into Allenstein are in broad agreement about the main events, although with some variation in the times that are given. The evidence for this passage comes from the *Allensteiner Zeitung, 72. Jahrgang, Nr. 211* and *213*, 13 and 16 September 1914; Rittel, diary, 27 August 1914. AP Olsztyn: Akta Miasta Olsztyn 259/169; Polizeiinspektor Schroeder[?], report, 15 April 1915. AP Olsztyn: Akta Miasta Olsztyn 259/168: fo. 40; Telegram from Oberbürgermeister Allenstein to Regierungspräsident Allenstein, 29 August 1914. GStA PK, Berlin: XX. HA Rep 2II, 3576: fo. 128.

23. 'Die Allensteiner Russentage', *Allensteiner Zeitung, 72. Jahrgang, Nr. 211*, 13 September 1914.

24. Hirschberg, *Russen in Allenstein*, pp. 11–12.

25. Ibid., pp. 15–16. Cf. 'Die Allensteiner Russentage', *Allensteiner Zeitung, 72. Jahrgang, Nr. 211* , 13 September 1914.

26. Telegram from Oberbürgermeister Allenstein to Regierungspräsident Allenstein, 29 August 1914. GStA PK, Berlin: XX. HA Rep 2II, 3576: fo. 128.

27. Rittel, diary, 30 September 1916, section entitled 'Unter russischer Herrschaft'. AP Olsztyn: Akta Miasta Olsztyn 259/169.

28. Hirschberg, *Russen in Allenstein*, pp. 19–21.

29. Rittel, diary, 27 August 1914, and also the section of his memoir entitled 'Das Brotbacken in der Russennacht'. AP Olsztyn: Akta Miasta Olsztyn 259/169.

30. 'Die Allensteiner Russentage', *Allensteiner Zeitung, 72. Jahrgang, Nr. 211, 13* September 1914.

31. Ibid., *Allensteiner Zeitung, 72. Jahrgang, Nr. 222, 26* September 1914, and Polizeiinspektor Schroeder[?], report, 15 April 1915. AP Olsztyn: Akta Miasta Olsztyn 259/168: fo. 40. Schroeder was present during these conversations.

32. 'Die Allensteiner Russentage', *Allensteiner Zeitung, 72. Jahrgang, Nr. 223,* 27 September 1914.

33. The troops who liberated Allenstein belonged to the 36th Reserve Division, a formation raised in West Prussia, the province neighbouring East Prussia. See D. E. Showalter, *Tannenberg: Clash of Empires* (Hamden, CT, 1991, p. 288.

34. 'Die Allensteiner Russentage', *Allensteiner Zeitung, 72. Jahrgang, Nr. 223,* 27 September 1914; Rittel, diary, 30 September 1916, section entitled 'Unsere Befreiung'. AP Olsztyn: Akta Miasta Olsztyn 259/169; Polizeiinspektor Schroeder[?], report, 15 April 1915. AP Olsztyn: Akta Miasta Olsztyn 259/168: fos. 39–40; Hirschberg, *Russen in Allenstein*, p. 24, and telegram from Oberbürgermeister Allenstein to Regierungspräsident Allenstein, 29 August 1914. GStA PK, Berlin: XX. HA Rep 2II, 3576: fo. 128.

35. Hirschberg, *Die Russen in Allenstein*, p. 29, 'Die Allensteiner Russentage', *Allensteiner Zeitung, 72. Jahrgang, Nr. 223,* 27 September 1914, and AP Olsztyn: Akta Miasta Olsztyn 259/169: Rittel, diary, 28 August 1914.

36. F. Gause, *Die Russen in Ostpreußen, 1914/15. Im Auftrage des Landeshauptmanns der Provinz Ostpreußen* (Königsberg Pr., 1931), pp. 191–2 and 218.

37. For Zülch's award, see Rittel, diary, 30 September 1916, section entitled 'Kleine Erlebnisse'. AP Olsztyn: Akta Miasta Olsztyn 259/169.

38. 'Die Allensteiner Russentage', *Allensteiner Zeitung, 72. Jahrgang, Nr. 213,* 16 September 1914.

39. Rittel, diary, 30 September 1916, section entitled 'Unsere Befreiung'. AP Olsztyn: Akta Miasta Olsztyn 259/169; Polizeiinspektor Schroeder[?], report, 15 April 1915. AP Olsztyn: Akta Miasta Olsztyn 259/168: fo. 41.

40. Hirschberg, *Russen in Allenstein*, p. 5.

41. See the daily 'War Reports' filed by the Regierungs-Präsident of Gumbinnen County, esp. 13, 15 and 17 August 1914 in GStA PK, Berlin: XX HA Rep 2II, 3559.

42. M. Hoffmann, *War Diaries and Other Papers* (2 vols., London, 1929), i, p. 40 (entry for 23 August 1914).

43. For fatalities and destruction, see Gause, *Russen in Ostpreußen*, esp. p. 229. Gause's figure is likely to be controversial, so it is worth stating here that it was the result of honest and impressively detailed research. As shown by surviving archival documentation, the East Prussian administration's wartime investigations concluded that 1,615 civilians were deliberately killed by the Russian army over both invasions (see the tables for Königsberg and Allenstein Counties in 'Besichtigung der durch die Russeneinfällen beschädigten Teile der Provinz Ostpreußen durch die Minister [Staatsministerium]', *c*. April 1915 and the Gumbinnen table of 4 June 1915 in, respectively, GStA PK, Berlin: I. HA Rep 90A, 1064 and AP Olsztyn: OP Ostpreußen: 3/529: fos. 72–4). Through close examination of local chronicles written shortly after the invasions, Gause eliminated double counting and accidental deaths to reach his total of 1,491 East Prussians killed. For a full discussion of the investigations and killed, see A. Watson, '"Unheard of Brutality": Russian Atrocities against Civilians in East Prussia, 1914–15', forthcoming in *The Journal of Modern History* 86(4) (December 2014).

44. See ibid., p. 57. For the East Prussian population's size and ethnic composition, see A. Hesse and H. Goeldel, *Grundlagen des Wirtschaftslebens von Ostpreußen. Denkschrift zum Wiederaufbau der Provinz. Die Bevölkerung von Ostpreußen* (6 vols., Jena, 1916), iii, p. 2, and L. Belzyt, *Sprachliche Minderheiten im preußischen Staat 1815–1914. Die preußische Sprachenstatistik in Bearbeitung und Kommentar* (Marburg, 1998), pp. 17 and 25.

45. 'Bekanntmachung allen Einwohneren Ost.Preussens [*sic*]', signed by Rennenkampf, 18 August 1914, in HHStA Wiesbaden: Plakate und Kriegsdocumente: Nr. 3012/3472.

46. Y. Danilov, *La Russie dans la Guerre Mondiale (1914–1917)*, trans. A. Kaznakov (Paris, 1927), p. 204. For the examples, see Watson, '"Unheard of Brutality"'.

47. Gause, *Russen in Ostpreußen*, pp. 200–11 and 229.

48. For Eydtkuhnen, see 'Die Besetzung des Postamts Eydtkuhnen durch die Russen', *Liegnitzer Tageblatt. 79. Jahrgang, Nr. 196, 1 Beilage* (22 August 1914). The other individuals were later given cash awards for their bravery. See the list compiled by the Geheimer Regierungsrat at the Landrat

in Memel on 19 October 1914. GStA PK, Berlin: XX. HA Rep 2II, 3670: fos. 28 and 32, and Landrat in Heydekrug to the Regierungspräsident of Gumbinnen, 20 November 1914. AP Olsztyn: RP Gumbinnen: 1576/14: fos. 83–4.

49. Gause, *Russen in Ostpreußen*, p. 175. This was a semi-official investigation carried out in the aftermath of the First World War. For its reliability see Watson, ' "Unheard of Brutality" '.

50. Gause, *Russen in Ostpreußen*, pp. 212–19.

51. Report of Königliches Konsistorium der Provinz Ostpreußen to Evangelischer Ober-Kirchenrat in Berlin-Charlottenburg, 23 October 1914. GStA PK, Berlin: I. HA Rep 90A, 1059: page 3 of report. Also, Gouvernement von Königsberg to Kriegsministerium, 25 Sept. 1914. GStA PK, Berlin: XX. HA Rep 2II, 3587: fo. 42. For the fear of Cossacks, see R. Traba, '*Wschodniopruskość'. Tożsamość regionalna i narodowa w kulturze politycznej Niemiec* (Poznań and Warsaw, 2005), pp. 252–5.

52. Gause, *Russen in Ostpreußen*, pp. 164–9.

53. Report by Fußgend. Wachtmeister Sahm I, 14 September, 1914. AP Olsztyn: Königlicher Regierungs-Präsident zu Allenstein (Rejencja Olsztyńskie) [hereafter RP Allenstein]: 179: fo. 105, and Gause, *Russen in Ostpreußen*, pp. 161–2.

54. A. V. Prusin, *Nationalizing a Borderland: War, Ethnicity, and Anti-Jewish Violence in East Galicia, 1914–1920* (Tuscaloosa, AL, 2005), p. 29.

55. Gause, *Russen in Ostpreußen*, pp. 152–4, and Oberwachtmeister Meyer, gendarmerie report, 17 September 1914. AP Olsztyn: RP Allenstein: 179: fos. 93–5. The accounts of what took place in Santoppen vary, although there is agreement over the number of fatalities. Gause's account suggests only one woman was killed, but he mentions another woman among the prisoners executed, so Meyer's report, which gives her name, is to be preferred.

56. Report by Fußgend. Wachtmeister Sahm I, 11 and 14 September, 1914. AP Olsztyn: RP Allenstein: 179: fos. 19 and 105–7, and Gause, *Russen in Ostpreußen*, pp. 177–8.

57. Gause, *Russen in Ostpreußen*, pp. 183–4.

58. Anna S., testimony (and supporting statements by others), 11 September 1914. AP Olsztyn: RP Allenstein: 178: fos. 3–4.

59. See, for example, the report of Oberwachtmeister Sadowski at Darkehmen on 4 March 1915 on the thorough investigations undertaken by the Russian army into a case of attempted rape and murder by one of their men. AP Olsztyn: OP Ostpreussen: 3/528: fos. 308–10.

60. See 'Besichtigung der durch die Russeneinfällen beschädigten Teile der Provinz Ostpreußen durch die Minister [Staatsministerium]', GStA PK, Berlin: I. HA Rep 90A, 1064.

61. Information on births resulting from rape is in a report on 'Fürsorge für die Russenkinder', accompanied by a letter from Oberpräsident to Minister des Innern, 24 November 1916, and also a letter from Oberpräsident to Regierungshauptkasse in Königsberg, 5 May 1917. AP Olsztyn: OP Ostpreußen: 3/530: fos. 290–93 and 391–4 and 399. For modern research, see M. M. Holmes, H. S. Resnick, D. G. Kilpatrick and C. L. Best, 'Rape-Related Pregnancy: Estimates and Descriptive Characteristics from a National Sample of Women', *American Journal of Obstetrics & Gynecology* 175(2) (August 1996), pp. 320–25.

62. Anna N., sworn court testimony, 26 January 1915. Cf. also her mother's testimony, following. AP Olsztyn: RP Allenstein: 184: fos. 81–3. Cf. with testimonies of French rape victims in R. Harris, 'The "Child of the Barbarian": Rape, Race and Nationalism in France during the First World War', *Past & Present* 141 (November 1993), pp. 176–9.

63. An estimate of 400, later corrected to 1,000, survives only for East Prussia's southern county, where Samsonov's army operated. Rennenkampf's army in the north and east of the province took 704 men and 10 women from the northern Königsberg County and probably even more military-aged men from the easterly Gumbinnen County when it withdrew. See the Allenstein and Gumbinnen County reports of 29 October and 25 September 1914 in AP Olsztyn: OP Ostpreußen: 3/528: fos. 38–62 and 64–79, and the table for Königsberg, c. April 1915, in GStA PK, Berlin: I. HA Rep 90A, 1064.

64. Letter of Bernard F. to Regierungspräsident in Allenstein, 29 September 1914. AP Olsztyn: RP Allenstein: 179: fos. 85–7.

65. E. Lohr, *Nationalizing the Russian Empire: The Campaign against Enemy Aliens during World War I* (Cambridge, MA, and London, 2003), pp. 17–18 and 124.

66. Gause, *Russen in Ostpreußen*, pp. 142–4. See also the lists of deported for the Königsberg, Allenstein and Gumbinnen Counties from c. 1916–17 in GStA PK, Berlin: XX. HA Rep 2II, 3578, 3579 and 3580.

67. Calculated from reports by Regierungspräsidenten in Allenstein and Gumbinnen, 16 February and 21 April 1915. GStA PK, Berlin: XX. HA Rep 2II, 3560: fo. 158 and I. HA Rep 90A, 1064: report pages 7–8; and Landräte reports for Johannisburg (15 February 1915), Lötzen (18 February 1915), Sensburg (19 February 1915) and Lyck (26 February 1915) districts. AP Olsztyn: RP Allenstein: 177: fos. 21–3, 27–8, 31–5 and 45–7. For the evacuation, see Gause, *Russen in Ostpreußen*, pp. 69–70.

68. See Lohr, *Nationalizing the Russian Empire*, p. 124, Auswärtiges Amt, *Greueltaten russischer Truppen*, annex 81, and Gause, *Russen in Ostpreußen*, pp. 242–3.

69. Report by Regierungspräsident in Gumbinnen to Unterstaatssekretär Heinrichs, 21 April 1915. GStA PK, Berlin: I. HA Rep 90A, 1064, pp. 7–8 of report. See also Gause, *Russen in Ostpreußen*, pp. 242–3.

70. Gause, *Russen in Ostpreußen*, p. 117.

71. For the deportation of Russia's enemy expatriates and ethnic Germans, see Lohr, *Nationalizing the Russian Empire*, pp. 122–37.

72. Gause, *Russen in Ostpreußen*, esp. pp. 253 and 282. Also, for conditions in internment, see the US ambassadorial reports reproduced in S. Tiepolato, 'Reports of the Delegates of the Embassy of the United States of America in St Petersburg on the Situation of the German Prisoners of War and Civil Persons in Russia', *DEP – Deportate, esuli, profughe. Rivista telematica di studi sulla memoria femminile* 4 (2006), pp. 185–92.

73. T. Wolff, *Tagebücher, 1914–1919. Der Erste Weltkrieg und die Entstehung der Weimarer Republik in Tagebüchern, Leitartikeln und Briefen des Chefredakteurs am 'Berliner Tageblatt' und Mitbegründers der 'Deutschen Demokratischen Partei'*, ed. B. Sösemann (2 vols., Boppard am Rhein, 1984), i, p. 96 (diary entry for 30 August 1914). For the period before, see the fourth 'Stimmungsbericht' of Polizeipräsident in Berlin, 2 September 1914. BA Berlin Lichterfelde: R43/2398: fo. 138.

74. See A. von der Goltz, *Hindenburg: Power, Myth, and the Rise of the Nazis* (Oxford, 2009), pp. 14 – 27. For the Kaiser's attempt to exploit the victories for his own personal standing, see G. A. von Müller, *The Kaiser and his Court: The Diaries, Notebooks and Letters of Admiral Georg Alexander von Müller, Chief of the Naval Cabinet, 1914–1918*, ed. W. Görlitz and trans. M. Savill (London, 1961), p. 65 (entry for 15 February 1915).

75. See A. Hausner, diary (vol. 2), 16 November 1914 (p. 18). KA Vienna: Nachläße: B/217 Hausner.

76. Deputy Stücklein in the Reichstag on 26 August 1915, quoted in J. M. Read, *Atrocity Propaganda, 1914–1919* (New York, 1941, 1972), pp. 113–14.

77. Oberbürgermeister of Munich, 4 March 1915, quoted in Münchner Ostpreußenhilfe, *Ostpreußennot und Bruderhilfe. Kriegsgedenkblätter* (Munich, 1915), p. 1.

78. Ostpreußisches Landesmuseum Lüneburg (ed.), *Die Ostpreußenhilfe im Ersten Weltkrieg. Zur Ausstellung 'Zum Besten der Ostpreußenhilfe' (23.9.2006–28.1.2007)* (Husum, 2006), p. 16. For further details see Watson, '"Unheard of Brutality"'.

79. Von Hagen, *War in a European Borderland*, p. 20.

80. See P. Holquist, 'The Role of Personality in the First 1914–1915 Russian Occupation of Galicia and Bukovina', in J. Dekel-Chen, D. Gaunt, N. M. Meir and I. Barton (eds.), *Anti-Jewish Violence: Rethinking the Pogrom in European History* (Bloomington and Indianapolis, IN, 2010) p. 57.

81. N. Davies, *God's Playground: A History of Poland. 1795 to the Present*, revised edn (2 vols., Oxford and New York, 2005), ii, pp. 282-3.

82. Słomka, *From Serfdom to Self-Government*, pp. 215-20.

83. S. Ansky, *The Enemy at his Pleasure: A Journey through the Jewish Pale of Settlement during World War I*, ed. and trans. J. Neugroschel (New York, 2002), p. 116.

84. Holquist, 'Role of Personality', p. 57.

85. Report of exponierter Stabsoffizier des Landesgendarmeriekommandos 5 in Lemberg, 13 December 1915, in k.u.k. Ministerium des Äussern, *Sammlung von Nachweisen für die Verletzungen des Völkerrechts durch die mit Österreich-Ungarn Krieg führenden Staaten. III. Nachtrag. Abgeschlossen mit 30. Juni 1916* (Vienna, 1916), pp. 53-4.

86. For the differences in the violence against East Prussians and Habsburg Jews, see Watson, '"Unheard of Brutality"'.

87. See the report on Brody by the Jewish aid worker Dr Bernard Hausner in CAHJP, Jerusalem: HM2-9177 (originals held in Tsentral'nyi derzhavnyi istorychnyi arkhiv Ukrainy, L'viv: fond 146 opis 4), fos. 23-6, and Ansky, *Enemy at his Pleasure*, pp. 68-70.

88. See the reports on Jaryczów Nowy, Zabłotów and Nadwórna by Hausner in CAHJP, Jerusalem: HM2-9177, fos. 110, 46-7 and 14, 59, and Holquist, 'Role of Personality', p. 54.

89. 'Kriegsschaden in Westgalizien – Gendarmerieberichte', 1 December 1914. AVA Vienna: MdI (1914) 19 in generl. Akte 45930.

90. Mick, *Kriegserfahrungen*, pp. 105-6. Also Ansky, *Enemy at his Pleasure*, p. 78.

91. See the complaints in the anonymous 'Denkschrift' sent to Minister President Stürgkh in the autumn of 1915 in AVA Vienna: MdI, allgemein 28 in gen. (1914-16) (Karton 2231): doc. 57652. Its complaints about Ruthene hostility towards the Jews are confirmed in k.k. Statthaltereipräsidium to Ministerium des Innern, 24 November 1915, p. 10. AVA Vienna: MdI, Präsidiale (1914-15): 22/Galiz. Karton 2116: doc. 25414, and also Hauser's reports, esp. those from Horodenka, Delatyn and Grodek. See CAHJP, Jerusalem: HM2-9177, fos. 4, 13 and 103. For Russian commanders' reactions to the pogroms, see Prusin, *Nationalizing a Borderland*, pp. 26-9.

92. J. Schoenfeld, *Shtetl Memories: Jewish Life in Galicia under the Austro-Hungarian Empire and in the Reborn Poland, 1898-1939* (Hoboken, NJ, 1985), p. 135. Hausner's report for Śniatyn notes that the civilian population did not take part in the Russians' robbing of the town. See CAHJP, Jerusalem: HM2-9177.1: fos. 49-50.

93. Reports by Dr Hausner and the local k.k. Gendarmeriepostenkommando, 3 May 1916. See CAHJP, Jerusalem: HM2-9177.1: fos. 31 and 34.

94. See Prusin, *Nationalizing a Borderland*, pp. 21-3, Mentzel, 'Kriegsflüchtlinge', pp. 31-2, and B. Hoffmann-Holter, *'Abreisendmachung'*.

Jüdische Kriegsflüchtlinge in Wien 1914 bis 1923 (Cologne and Weimar, 1995), p. 29.

95. G. Faust, *Kriegsnöte der deutschen Gemeinden in Galizien und der Bukowina* (Leipzig, 1915), pp. 7-10.

96. Sitzung des königlichen Staatsministeriums, 16 October 1914. BA Berlin Lichterfelde: R43/2466c: fos. 112 – reverse of 118. For a case of scandal, see the documentation from the local Amtsgericht and Landrat, 1 September 1914, dealing with the flight of the (West Prussian) Landrat of Strasburg in GStA PK, Berlin: XIV. HA Rep 181, 30307.

97. KA Vienna: KÜA 1914 (Aktenkartons): Karton 4: Nr. 2146.

98. Landesgerichtsrat A. Regius, diary, 4 September 1914. KA Vienna: NL Regius B/395.

99. F. Forstner, *Przemyśl. Österreich-Ungarns bedeutendste Festung*, 2nd edn (Vienna, 1997), pp. 149 and 160. For security aspects, see Mentzel, 'Kriegsflüchtlinge', pp. 75-7, and for population, see A. von Guttry, *Galizien. Land und Leute* (Munich and Leipzig, 1916), p. 56.

100. J. Bieniarzówna and J. M. Małecki, *Dzieje Krakowa. Kraków w latach, 1796-1918* (6 vols., Cracow, 1979), iii, pp. 360 and 379.

101. C.i.k. Komenda Twierdzy, 'Obwieszczenie', 13 Sept. 1914. AN Cracow: DPKr 104: fos. 847-8.

102. J. Dąbrowski, *Dziennik, 1914-1918*, ed. J. Zdrada (Cracow, 1977), pp. 38-9 (diary entries for 5, 16 and 21 September 1914).

103. C.k. Prezydium Dyrekcji policy w Krakowie, 'Informacya poufna', 18 September 1914. AVA Vienna: MdI (1914) 19 in generl. Karton 1921: Nr. 36570.

104. For the military actions, see *OÜLK*, i, pp. 370-72, 383-93, 487-8 and 501-17.

105. Dąbrowski, *Dziennik*, p. 46 (diary entry for 15 November 1914).

106. Mentzel, 'Kriegsflüchtlinge', p. 80.

107. Message to Kriegsüberwachungsamt, 5 November 1914. AVA Vienna: MdI (1914) 19 in generl.: Akte 45676.

108. K.u.k. Festungskommando in Krakau to k.k. Polizeidirektion in Krakau, 6 November 1914. AN Cracow: DPKr 99: 4624/14: fo. 1787.

109. J. Mikułowski Pomorski (ed.), *Kraków w naszej pamięci* (Nowy Wiśnicz, 1991), pp. 65-6.

110. Statthaltereipräsidium, telephone call to Ministerium des Innern, 4 November 1914. AVA Vienna: MdI (1914) 19 in generl.: Akte 45676.

111. K.u.k. Festungskommando in Krakau to k.k. Polizeidirektion in Krakau, 10 November 1914. AN Cracow: DPKr 100: 4669/14: fo. 21.

112. Minutes of discussion between Festungskommandant Krakau and Kriegsminister, 2 December 1914. AVA Vienna: MdI (1914) 19 in generl.: Akte 45676.

113. See Strachan, *First World War*, i, pp. 372-3 and, for a detailed account of the military operations, *ÖULK*, i, pp. 522-63.

114. Quoted in P. Szlanta, 'Der Erste Weltkrieg von 1914 bis 1915 als identitäts-stiftender Faktor für die moderne polnische Nation', in G. P. Groß (ed.), *Die vergessene Front. Der Osten 1914/15. Ereignis, Wirkung, Nackwirkung* (Paderborn, Munich, Vienna and Zurich, 2006), p. 160.

115. Bobrinskii, quoted in von Hagen, *War in a European Borderland*, p. 32. For Bobrinskii's regime, see Mick, *Kriegserfahrungen*, pp. 85–96.

116. Prusin, *Nationalizing a Borderland*, pp. 34–5; von Hagen, *War in a European Borderland*, pp. 27–8; and Holquist, 'Role of Personality', pp. 52–73.

117. Mick, *Kriegserfahrungen*, pp. 87–92, and von Hagen, *War in a European Borderland*, p. 25.

118. Von Hagen, *War in a European Borderland*, p. 25.

119. 'Bericht des Legationsrates Baron Andrian über seine Informationsreise nach Ostgalizien', 26 July 1915, pp. 4–13. AVA Vienna: MdI, Präsidiale (1914–15) 22/Galiz. Karton 2116: doc. 19644. Also, undated report headed 'Sekretarz Naczelnego Komitetu Narodowego', in AN Cracow: NKN 280: fos. 26–32.

120. For hostage-taking, see Mick, *Kriegserfahrungen*, p. 129. The activities and arrest of Sheptits'kyi are covered by von Hagen, *War in a European Borderland*, pp. 37–40.

121. For Russophiles, see Bachmann, *'Herd der Feindschaft'*, pp. 24–8 and ch. 3.

122. Mick, *Kriegserfahrungen*, pp. 98 and 111–12, and von Hagen, *War in a European Borderland*, p. 33.

123. 'Bericht des Legationsrates Baron Andrian', pp. 24–5.

124. Ibid., p. 17. Also report by k.k. Statthalter von Galizien, Hermann von Colard, 11 November 1915, pp. 9–10. AVA Vienna: MdI, Präsidiale (1916–17) 22/Galiz. Karton 2117: doc. 4403.

125. Evlogii, quoted in Mick, *Kriegserfahrungen*, p. 121.

126. Ansky, *Enemy at his Pleasure*, pp. 73–4.

127. These passages follow Mick, *Kriegserfahrungen*, pp. 111–27. Cf. also von Hagen, *War in a European Borderland*, pp. 37–42. For the murdered clergy, see 'Bericht des Legationsrates Baron Andrian', p. 22. For Galician parishes, see J. Springer, *Statistik des österreichischen Kaiserstaates* (2 vols., Vienna, 1840), i, p. 341.

128. 'Bericht des Legationsrates Baron Andrian', p. 14.

129. For hostages, see Mick, *Kriegserfahrungen*, p. 109, and Prusin, *Nationalizing a Borderland*, p. 49. For the eastern Galician population, see P. Wróbel, 'The Jews of Galicia under Austro-Polish Rule, 1869–1918', *Austrian History Yearbook* 25 (1994), pp. 110–11.

130. Prusin, *Nationalizing a Borderland*, p. 42.

131. Ansky, *Enemy at his Pleasure*, pp. 122-3. See also Prusin, *Nationalizing a Borderland*, pp. 41-2, and von Hagen, *War in a European Borderland*, pp. 27-8.

132. Jüdischer Nationalverein in Oesterreich to k.k. Ministerium des Innern, 3 September 1915. AVA Vienna: MdI, Präsidiale (1914-15) 22/Galiz. Karton 2116: doc. 19412. Cf. 'Bericht des Legationsrates Baron Andrian', p. 13.

133. See anonymous letter entitled 'Polnische Politik!', stamped 9 July 1915, and k.k. Bezirkshauptmannschaft in Przemyśl, Polizeiabteilung, report to Statthaltereipräsidium on 'Verhalten der Polen in Galizien gegenüber der jüdischen Bevölkerung', 27 September 1915. AVA Vienna: MdI, Präsidiale (1914-15) 22/Galiz. Karton 2116: doc. 15635, and Präsidiale (1916-17) 22/Galiz. Karton 2117: doc. 26250.

134. See *Sprawozdanie c.k. Namiestnictwa, Centrali krajowej dla gospodarczej odbudowy Galicyi za czas od czerwca 1916 do lutego 1917* (Cracow, 1917), p. 4.

135. Reports gathered on Jewish communities in eastern Galicia by Hausner in early 1916. See CAHJP, Jerusalem: HM2-9177.1: fos. 37, 14, 3-4, 107 and 110-12.

136. Sperber, *God's Water Carriers*, p. 83.

137. Holquist, 'Role of Personality', p. 59.

138. Prusin, *Nationalizing a Borderland*, pp. 37-44.

139. For the later, much bloodier dynamic under totalitarian regimes, see T. Snyder, *Bloodlands: Europe between Hitler and Stalin* (New York, 2010). For the development of Imperial Russia's wartime deportation policies, see above and also Lohr, *Nationalizing the Russian Empire*, pp. 121-65.

140. Holquist, 'Role of Personality', pp. 62-5.

141. Prusin, *Nationalizing a Borderland*, p. 27.

142. Gendarmerie reports from Mościska, 10 May 1916, and Tyśmienica, 14 May 1916, reports collected by Hausner on both places in early 1916 and the statement of a victim from Tyśmienica, 2 June 1916. See CAHJP, Jerusalem: HM2-9177.1: fos. 9, 51-2, 54 and 56-7.

143. Prusin, *Nationalizing a Borderland*, pp. 48-54, and Holquist, 'Role of Personality', pp. 66-7.

144. Ansky, *Enemy at his Pleasure*, pp. 134-63.

145. Słomka, *From Serfdom to Self-Government*, p. 234, Faust, *Kriegsnöte*, pp. 23-4, and 'Bericht des Legationsrates Baron Andrian', p. 13.

146. See Mick, *Kriegserfahrungen*, p. 130, Prusin, *Nationalizing a Borderland*, pp. 56 and 62, and Holquist, 'Role of Personality', p. 67.

147. Führ, *K.u.k. Armeeoberkommando*, pp. 63-70. For Polish elites' disapproval, see undated report marked 'Sekretarz Naczelnego Komitetu Narodowego' in AN Cracow: NKN 280: fo. 29.

148. Ansky, *Enemy at his Pleasure*, pp. 114–15. Cf. also p. 161. Estimates of how many Ruthenes fled with the Russians vary from thousands up to tens of thousands. See von Hagen, *War in a European Borderland*, p. 41, and 'Bericht des Legationsrates Baron Andrian', pp. 15–16.

149. See the extracts from two notes passed by the Ministerium des Äußern to the k.k. Ministerium des Innern, January 1916. AVA Vienna: Min. des Innern, Präsidiale 22. Galiz. (1916–17). Karton 2117: doc. 400.

150. Szlanta, '"Najgorsze bestie to są Honwedy"', p. 166, and Mick, *Kriegserfahrungen*, pp. 143–6.

151. 'Die Zustände in Lemberg', 23 December 1915, pp. 1–4. AVA Vienna: MdI, Präsidiale 22. Galiz. (1916–17). Karton 2117: doc. 400. Cf. also 'Bemerkungen ueber Lemberg nach der Befreiung von der russischen Invasion'. AN Cracow: NKN 280: fos. 33–40. This latter may have been a source for the former report.

152. For land, see M.-S. Schulze, 'Austria-Hungary's Economy in World War I', in Broadberry and Harrison (eds.), *The Economics of World War I*, p. 92, and for livestock, T. Kargol, 'Ziemiaństwo wobec sytuacji gospodarczej Galicji w czasie I wojny Światowej', in D. Grinberg, J. Snopko and G. Zackiewicz (eds.), *Lata wielkiej wojny. Dojrzewanie do niepodległości, 1914–1918* (Białystok, 2007), p. 222.

153. A. F. Frank, *Oil Empire: Visions of Prosperity in Austrian Galicia* (Cambridge, MA, and London, 2005), pp. 173 and 188–9.

154. The figure comprises 600,000 refugees without means registered in December 1914, between 300,000 and 400,000 people able to support themselves independently, and others residing illegally in the hinterland. See Mentzel, 'Kriegsflüchtlinge', p. 5.

155. Hoffmann-Holter, *'Abreisendmachung'*, p. 49.

156. K.k. Minister des Innern in Wien to k.k. Statthalter in Galizien, 5 October 1914, and k.u.k. Generalstabsabteilung der Festung Krakau to das Präsidium der k.k. Polizeidirektion in Krakau, 18 October 1914. AN Cracow: DPKr 104, fo. 339, and DPKr 99: 4333/14, fo. 971.

157. Ministerium des Innern in Wien to the k.k. Statthalterei in Galizien, 8 Oct. 1914. AN Cracow: DPKr 99: 4258/14, fo. 81.

158. Mentzel, 'Kriegsflüchtlinge', pp. 8–13.

159. 'Instruktion betreffend die Beförderung und Unterbringung von Flüchtlingen aus Galizien und der Bukowina'. AN Cracow: DPKr 122: doc. 3894/14. Also Mentzel, 'Kriegsflüchtlinge', pp. 236–7 and 242–7.

160. Anonymous complaint letter, November 1914. AVA Vienna: Ministerium des Innern (1914) 19 in generl.: 45827. For details of the refugees in Hungary, see Mentzel, 'Kriegsflüchtlinge', pp. 191–207.

161. Translated report from the Wiedeński Kuryer Polski, 11 January 1915. AVA Vienna: MdI (1914) 19 in generl.: doc. 46124. See also Mentzel,

'Kriegsflüchtlinge', p. 293, and Hoffmann-Holter, 'Abreisendmachung', p. 38, fn. 30.

162. D. Rechter, 'Galicia in Vienna: Jewish Refugees in the First World War', *Austrian History Yearbook* 28 (1997), p. 118.

163. H. J. W. Kuprian, 'Flüchtlinge, Evakuierte und die staatliche Fürsorge', in K. Eisterer and R. Steininger (eds.), *Tirol und der Erste Weltkrieg* (Innsbruck, 1995), p. 285.

164. Mentzel, 'Kriegsflüchtlinge', p. 272.

165. For an illustration of such views, see Kuprian, 'Flüchtlinge, Evakuierte und die staatliche Fürsorge', p. 295. For East Prussia and Galicia in contemporaries' imaginations, see Kossert, *Ostpreußen*, and L. Wolff, *The Idea of Galicia: History and Fantasy in Habsburg Political Culture* (Stanford, CA, 2010).

166. M. Schwestek, diary/memoir, 29 September 1914. KA Vienna: B89.

167. Statthalter of Vorarlberg, quoted in Kuprian, 'Flüchtlinge, Evakuierte und die staatliche Fürsorge', p. 293. Also Mentzel, 'Kriegsflüchtlinge', pp. 171-5.

168. Hoffmann-Holter, 'Abreisendmachung', pp. 35-6 and 40.

169. A. S. Lindemann, Esau's Tears: Modern Anti-Semitism and the Rise of the Jews (Cambridge, 1997), pp. 194-7.

170. Hoffmann-Holter, 'Abreisendmachung', pp. 47-51 and 79-81.

171. Rechter, 'Galicia in Vienna', pp. 116 and 120-24.

172. Rudolf Schwarz-Hiller, quoted in Hoffmann-Holter, 'Abreisendmachung', p. 74. For private relief efforts, see also Mentzel, 'Kriegsflüchtlinge', pp. 347-55.

5. ENCIRCLEMENT

1. A. Hausner, diary, 12 December 1914. KA Vienna: NL Hausner, B/217.

2. Broadberry and Harrison, 'The Economics of World War I', p. 9.

3. E. von Moltke (ed.), *Generaloberst Helmuth von Moltke. Erinnerungen – Briefe – Dokumente, 1877-1916. Ein Bild vom Kriegsausbruch, erster Kriegsführung und Persönlichkeit des ersten militärischen Führers des Krieges* (Stuttgart, 1922), p. 308 (letter to his wife, 29 January 1905).

4. Strachan, *First World War*, i, pp. 1014-25 and 1042-3. Also H. Pogge von Strandmann (ed.), *Walther Rathenau, Industrialist, Banker, Intellectual, and Politician: Notes and Diaries, 1907-1922*, trans. C. Pinder-Cracraft (Oxford, 1985), pp. 186-91.

5. Lawrence, 'Transition to War', pp. 156-7.

6. G. D. Feldman, *Army, Industry and Labor in Germany, 1914-1918* (Providence, RI, and Oxford, 1966, 1992), pp. 64-73; J. R. Wegs, 'Austrian

Economic Mobilization during World War I: With Particular Emphasis on Heavy Industry', unpublished PhD thesis, University of Illinois (1970), pp. 181–2.

7. B. J. Davis, *Home Fires Burning: Food, Politics, and Everyday Life in World War I Berlin* (Chapel Hill, NC, and London, 2000), pp. 24–7.

8. 'Amtliche Preislisten für den Landkreis Thorn: Höchster Verkaufspreis', in *Kreis-Blatt für den Land- und Stadtkreis Thorn*, 29 August and 5 December 1914. AP Toruń: Star. Pow. w Toruniu, 1818–1920: Nr. 1020. Cf. the prices in Karlsruhe published in R. Chickering, *Imperial Germany and the Great War, 1914–1918*, 2nd edn (Cambridge: Cambridge University Press, 2004), p. 43.

9. Davis, *Home Fires*, pp. 24–5 and 51; Healy, *Vienna*, p. 40, and H. Loewenfeld-Russ, *Die Regelung der Volksernährung im Kriege* (Vienna and New Haven, CT, 1926), pp. 47–51.

10. Herwig, *First World War*, pp. 119–20, and R. Bessel, *Germany After the First World War* (Oxford, 1993), p. 9.

11. On hatred, see S. Audoin-Rouzeau and A. Becker, *1914–1918: Understanding the Great War*, trans. C. Temerson (London, 2002), pp. 102–3.

12. On this topic, see also the pioneering work of C. Hämmerle, '"Zur Liebesarbeit sind wir hier, Soldatenstrümpfe stricken wir . . ." Zu Formen weiblicher *Kriegsfürsorge* im Ersten Weltkrieg', unpublished PhD thesis, University of Vienna (1996).

13. Emmy W., diary, 25 October 1914. DTA Emmendingen: 586/ I.

14. A. Watson and P. Porter, 'Bereaved and Aggrieved: Combat Motivation and the Ideology of Sacrifice in the First World War', *Historical Research* 83(219) (February 2010), pp. 146–54 and 160.

15. Kaiserin's appeal of 6 August 1914, reproduced in Lutz (ed.), *Fall*, i, pp. 21–2.

16. *Neckar-Zeitung*, Heilbronn, 5 August 1914, p. 4, quoted in E. Koch, '"Jeder tut, was er kann fürs Vaterland": Frauen und Männer an der Heilbronner "Heimatfront"', in G. Hirschfeld, G. Krumeich, D. Langewiesche and H.-P. Ullmann (eds.), *Kriegserfahrungen. Studien zur Sozial- und Mentalitätsgeschichte des Ersten Weltkriegs* (Tübingen, 1997), p. 41.

17. Hämmerle, '"Zur Liebesarbeit sind wir hier, Soldatenstrümpfe stricken wir . . ."', esp. pp. 104–29 and 159–83, and idem., (ed.), *Kindheit*, pp. 283–7.

18. Letters to A. Hartmuth; see esp. those from his mother, 27 January, 3 May (erroneously dated April) and 27 November 1915, and from his sister Trudi, 17 November 1916. Author's Collection.

19. Letter to A. Hartmuth from Direktion der Comerz- und Disconto-Bank, Hamburg, 27 November 1914. Author's Collection.

20. K. Meier, 'Evangelische Kirche und Erster Weltkrieg', in W. Michalka (ed.), *Der Erste Weltkrieg. Wirkung, Wahrnehmung, Analyse* (Munich and Zurich, 1994), pp. 708–9, and Bobič, *War and Faith*, pp. 142–5.

21. Letter to A. Hartmuth from his mother, 26 October 1914. Author's Collection. Cf. Chickering, *Great War and Urban Life*, pp. 111 and 368-9.

22. See the circular from the Kriegs-Ausschuß für warme Unterkleidung, 25 September 1914. AP Poznań: Polizei-Präsidium Posen 8979: fo. 5.

23. T. Zahra, *Kidnapped Souls: National Indifference and the Battle for Children in the Bohemian Lands, 1900-1948* (Ithaca, NY, and London, 2008), pp. 98-101.

24. Polizeipräsident in Berlin to Unterstaatssekretär in der Reichskanzlei, 'Zehnter Stimmungsbericht', 5 October 1914. BA Berlin Lichterfelde: R43/2398: fo. 202 and reverse.

25. Landes-Kriegshilfsbureau, Salzburg, to Kriegshilfsbureau des k.k. Ministerium des Innern, Vienna, 3 December 1914. AVA Vienna: MdI, Präsidiale (1914-15): 19/1. Box 1740: doc. 18224.

26. Hämmerle, '"Zur Liebesarbeit sind wir hier, Soldatenstrümpfe stricken wir..."', pp. 90-92.

27. Chickering, *Great War and Urban Life*, pp. 372-90.

28. E. Stempfle, diary, 18 October 1914. DTA, Emmendingen: 1654. Also G. Mai, '"Aufklärung der Bevölkerung" und "Vaterländischer Unterricht" in Württemberg, 1914-1918. Struktur, Durchführung und Inhalte der deutschen Inlandspropaganda im Ersten Weltkrieg', *Zeitschrift für Württembergische Landesgeschichte* 36 (1977), p. 202.

29. C. Nübel, *Die Mobilisierung der Kriegsgesellschaft. Propaganda und Alltag im Ersten Weltkrieg in Münster* (Münster, New York, Munich and Berlin, 2008), pp. 56-7.

30. M. Stibbe, *German Anglophobia and the Great War, 1914-1918* (Cambridge, 2001), p. 60.

31. J. Rüger, 'Laughter and War in Berlin', *History Workshop Journal* 67 (Spring 2009), pp. 33-5.

32. Kommandantur von Coblenz und Ehrenbreitstein, 'Bekanntmachung', 25 February 1916. HHStA Hessen: Preußisches Regierungspräsidium Wiesbaden (405): Nr. 2775: fo. 164.

33. K.k. Minister des Innern to k.k. Statthalter in Galizien, 14 July 1916. AN Cracow: DPKr 110: 267-8.

34. In this case, a public accusation against the Dunlop tyre company. See *Frankfurter Zeitung und Handelsblatt, Zweites Morgenblatt. 59. Jahrgang, Nummer 246* (5 September 1914), p. 6.

35. H. Rudolph, 'Kultureller Wandel und Krieg: Die Reaktion der Werbesprache auf die Erfahrung des Ersten Weltkriegs am Beispiel von Zeitungsanzeigen', in G. Hirschfeld, G. Krumeich, D. Langewiesche and H.-P. Ullmann (eds.), *Kriegserfahrungen. Studien zur Sozial- und Mentalitätsgeschichte des Ersten Weltkriegs* (Essen, 1997), pp. 294-300.

36. Advertisement in *Die Neue Zeitung. Illustriertes unabhängiges Tagblatt. 8. Jahrgang, Nr. 13* (13 January 1915), p. 8, and H. Berghoff, 'Patriotismus und Geschäftssinn im Krieg: Eine Fallstudie aus der Musikinstrumentenindustrie', in G. Hirschfeld, G. Krumeich, D. Langewiesche and H.-P. Ullmann (eds.), *Kriegserfahrungen. Studien zur Sozial- und Mentalitätsgeschichte des Ersten Weltkriegs* (Essen, 1997), p. 266.

37. Goltz, *Hindenburg*, p. 26.

38. See the wrapper from the Kryształ chocolate firm in Podgórze, in AN Cracow: Zb. KL 12.

39. H. Hoffmann, '"Schwarzer Peter im Weltkrieg": Die deutsche Spielwarenindustrie, 1914–1918', in G. Hirschfeld, G. Krumeich, D. Langewiesche and H.-P. Ullmann (eds.), *Kriegserfahrungen. Studien zur Sozial- und Mentalitätsgeschichte des Ersten Weltkriegs* (Essen, 1997), pp. 231–2.

40. Ferguson, *Pity of War*, p. 275.

41. Flyer (Merkblatt). See also the accompanying letter from Minister des Innern in Berlin to Regierungspräsidenten and den Polizeipräsidenten in Berlin, 17 November 1914. AP Toruń: Starostwo Powiatowe w Toruniu (Landratsamt Thorn), 1818–1920: Nr. 1021. Cf. Healy, *Vienna*, pp. 37–8.

42. Letter to A. Hartmuth from his mother, 27 January 1915. Author's Collection.

43. Feldman, *Army, Industry and Labor*, pp. 105 and 127. Also T. Loch, '"Aufklärung der Bevölkerung" in Hamburg. Zur deutschen Inlandspropaganda während des Ersten Weltkrieges', *Militärgeschichtliche Zeitschrift* 62(1) (2003), pp. 52–4.

44. See, for example, Memorandum from City of Thorn to Regierungs-Präsident in Marienwerder, 17 May 1915. AP Toruń: Akta Miasta Torunia: Nr. C9257, fos. 92–8. For Austria, see T. Dammelhart, 'Kleine Stadt im Großen Krieg. Kriegswirtschaft im 1. Weltkrieg, dargestellt am Beispiel der Stadt Retz', unpublished PhD thesis, University of Vienna (2001), pp. 283–4.

45. S. Brandt, 'Kriegskochbuch', in G. Hirschfeld, G. Krumeich, I. Renz and M. Pöhlmann (eds.), *Enzyklopädie Erster Weltkrieg* (Paderborn, Munich, Vienna and Zurich, 2003, 2004), p. 651.

46. *Fertige Kriegsküchenzettel für den einfachen Haushalt herausgegeben von der königliche Eisenbahndirektion Münster (Westf.). Praktische und verständliche Anleitung von Helene Range* (Münster i. W., n.d.), pp. 6–8.

47. Ibid., pp. 5, 37–9 and backcover.

48. Healy, *Vienna*, p. 117.

49. Cuttings from *Frankfurter Nachrichten und Intelligenz-Blatt. Nr. 273* (2 October 1914) and *Nr. 348*, 16 December 1914. HHStA Wiesbaden: Preußisches Polizeipräsidium Frankfurt a. M. (407): Nr. 248.

50. A. A. Donson, *Youth in the Fatherless Land: War Pedagogy, Nationalism, and Authority in Germany, 1914–1918* (Cambridge, MA, and London, 2010), pp. 108–9, and Hämmerle (ed.), *Kindheit*, p. 274.

51. K. Saul, 'Jugend im Schatten des Krieges. Vormilitärische Ausbildung – Kriegswirtschaftlicher Ersatz – Schulalltag in Deutschland, 1914–1918', *Militärgeschichtliche Mitteilungen* 34 (1983), p. 117.

52. Syndikus der Handelskammer zu Elbing to Handelskammer zu Thorn, 26 April 1918. AP Toruń: Akta Miasta Torunia: Nr. C8883, fo. 106.

53. M. Kronenberg, *Die Bedeutung der Schule für die 'Heimatfront' im Ersten Weltkrieg. Sammlungen, Hilfsdienste, Feiern und Nagelungen im deutschen Reich* (Norderstedt, 2010), pp. 35–6 and 43–4; Donson, *Youth in the Fatherless Land*, pp. 112–13. Also letter to A. Hartmuth from 'Lulu', 5 March 1915. Author's Collection.

54. Hämmerle (ed.), *Kindheit*, pp. 125 and 280.

55. Donson, *Youth in the Fatherless Land*, pp. 79–81 and 86–8, and Hämmerle (ed.), *Kindheit*, pp. 287–94.

56. Musketier A. Hartmuth. Letter from his sister, Lulu, 3 December 1915. Author's Collection.

57. Kuhr, *There We'll Meet Again*, pp. 112 and 155 (diary entries for 11 February and 10 August 1915).

58. M. Diers, *Schlagbilder. Zur politischen Ikonographie der Gegenwart* (Frankfurt am Main, 1997), pp. 78–84.

59. Goltz, *Hindenburg*, pp. 27–33, and S. Brandt, 'Nagelfiguren: Nailing Patriotism in Germany, 1914–1918', in N. J. Saunders (ed.), *Matters of Conflict: Material Culture, Memory and the First World War* (London and New York, 2004), pp. 64 and 69.

60. Brandt, 'Nagelfiguren', p. 66, Diers, *Schlagbilder*, pp. 84–8, and S. Goebel, 'Forging the Industrial Home Front: Iron-Nail Memorials in the Ruhr', in J. Macleod and P. Purseigle (eds.), *Uncovered Fields: Perspectives in First World War Studies* (Leiden and Boston, 2004), p. 160.

61. G. Schneider, 'Zur Mobilisierung der "Heimatfront": Das Nageln sogenannter Kriegswahrzeichen im Ersten Weltkrieg', *Zeitschrift für Volkskunde* 95 (1999), esp. pp. 38–42 and 55–62.

62. 'Die Enthüllungsfeier des "Eisernen Siegfried"', press cutting. HHStA Wiesbaden: 408: Nr. 121: fo. 159. For pricing, see the 'Invitation' to this event in ibid., fo. 157, and also Diers, *Schlagbilder*, p. 87.

63. Chickering, *Great War and Urban Life*, pp. 393–4.

64. Cutting from *Wiesbadener Neueste Nachrichten*, 25 October 1915. HHStA Wiesbaden: 405: Nr. 2778: fo. 167.

65. Schneider, 'Zur Mobilisierung', pp. 43–53.

66. J. Cisek, '"Kolumna Legionów" w Krakowie', *Krakowski Rocznik Archiwalny* 9 (2003), pp. 162–72. Also 'Uroczystość 16 sierpnia', *Nowa Reforma. Wydanie Popołudniowe. Rok XXXIV. Nr. 412* (16 August 1914), p. 1.

67. M. Zgórniak, 'Polacy w armii austro-węgierskiej w czasie I Wojny Światowej', *Studia i materiały do historii wojskowości* 30 (1988), pp. 236–8.

68. J. T. Nowak, *Tarcze Legionów Polskich, 1915–1917 w zbiorach Muzeum Historycznego Miasta Krakowa* (Cracow, 2006), pp. 36, 49, 54, 64, 67 and 76.

69. H. D. Lasswell, *Propaganda Technique in the World War* (London, 1927), p. 47.

70. 'Unser brutalster Gegner', *Frankfurter Zeitung und Handelsblatt 59. Jahrgang, Nr. 249, Zweites Morgenblatt* (8 September 1914), p. 1. See also Raithel, *Das 'Wunder'*, pp. 332–3.

71. Moltke, quoted in W. Nicolai, *Nachrichtendienst, Presse und Volksstimmung im Weltkrieg* (Berlin, 1920), p. 113.

72. K. Koszyk, *Deutsche Pressepolitik im Ersten Weltkrieg* (Düsseldorf, 1968), pp. 20–29, 46 and 186–8, and D. Welch, *Germany, Propaganda and Total War, 1914–1918: The Sins of Omission* (London, 2000), pp. 24–40.

73. See D. Geppert and R. Gerwarth (eds.), *Wilhelmine Germany and Edwardian Britain: Essays on Cultural Affinity* (Oxford and New York, 2008). Also K. Pryor, 'The Mobilization of Memory: The Battle of Waterloo in German and British Memory, 1815–1915', unpublished MA thesis, Southern Illinois University Carbondale (2010).

74. Haeckel and Eucken, 18 August 1914. Quoted in P. Hoeres, *Krieg der Philosophen: Die deutsche und britische Philosophie im Ersten Weltkrieg* (Paderborn, 2004), p. 122.

75. K. Schwalbe, *Wissenschaft und Kriegsmoral. Die deutschen Hochschullehrer und die politischen Grundfragen des Ersten Weltkrieges* (Göttingen, Zurich and Frankfurt am Main, 1969), pp. 22–3.

76. J. von Ungern-Sternberg and W. von Ungern-Sternberg, *Der Aufruf An die Kulturwelt!' Das Manifest der 93 und die Anfänge der Kriegspropaganda im Ersten Weltkrieg. Mit einer Dokumentation* (Stuttgart, 1996), pp. 163–4.

77. Schwalbe, *Wissenschaft und Kriegsmoral*, pp. 26–8.

78. Stibbe, *German Anglophobia*, pp. 49–79.

79. W. Sombart, *Händler und Helden. Patriotische Besinnungen* (Munich, 1915).

80. Buchner (ed.), *Kriegsdokumente*, iv, p. 188 (doc. 300).

81. Ibid., pp. 392–3 (doc. 486).

82. For the *Emden*, see P. G. Halpern, *A Naval History of World War I* (Annapolis, MD, 1994), pp. 72–7. Also E. Schwarz, diary, 28 October, 6 and 11 November 1914. DTA Emmendingen: 1654; A. Hartmuth, letter from 'Onkel Max', 2 November 1914. Author's Collection.

83. A. Offer, *The First World War: An Agrarian Interpretation* (Oxford, 1989), p. 25.

84. E. W. Osborne, *Britain's Economic Blockade of Germany, 1914–1919* (London and New York, 2004), pp. 63, 74 and 87–8.

85. Best, *Humanity in Warfare*, pp. 211-15 and 244-62.

86. Osborne, *Britain's Economic Blockade*, pp. 125-6 and 133.

87. P. Eltzbacher (ed.), *Die deutsche Volksernährung und der englische Aushungerungsplan* (Braunschweig, 1915), pp. 1-2.

88. U. Kröll, *Die internationale Buren-Agitation, 1899-1902* (Münster, 1973), esp. pp. 51-65 and 112-25. For death statistics, Hull, *Absolute Destruction*, p. 152.

89. Osborne, *Britain's Economic Blockade*, p. 95.

90. J. Lee, 'Administrators and Agriculture: Aspects of German Agricultural Policy in the First World War', in J. M. Winter (ed.), *War and Economic Development* (Cambridge, London, New York and Melbourne, 1975), pp. 229-36.

91. Offer, *The First World War*, pp. 25-8.

92. G. Hardach, *The First World War, 1914-1918* (London, 1977), pp. 115-18; Feldman, *Army, Industry and Labor*, pp. 100-102.

93. Davis, *Home Fires Burning*, pp. 28-32.

94. H. Götting, diary, 22 February 1915. DTA, Emmendingen: 700/ I.

95. Calculated using the available figures for February–December 1915 in *Sanitätsbericht*, iii, p. 132, and War Office (ed.), *Statistics of the Military Effort of the British Empire during the Great War, 1914-1920* (London, 1922), pp. 359-62.

96. See 'Die Dum-Dum Geschosse', *Frankfurter Zeitung und Handelsblatt 59. Jahrgang, Nr. 250, Zweites Morgenblatt* (9 September 1914), p. 1. For troops' belief in British dumdum bullets, see Watson, *Enduring the Great War*, p. 69.

97. Stibbe, *German Anglophobia*, pp. 38-44.

98. See Auswärtiges Amt, *Der Baralong-Fall* (Berlin, 1916), which contains the diplomatic exchange and copies of the American sailors' testimonies. BA-MA Freiburg: RM5/ 2971: fos. 76-110.

99. Copy of *Bremer Nachrichten* article, 16 October 1915. BA-MA Freiburg: RM3/5362: fos. 8-9. Cf. 'Die Ereignisse zur See', *Deutsche Kriegszeitung. Nr. 43* (24 October 1915), p. 7.

100. Staatssekretär des Reichs-Marine-Amts to Reichskanzler, 26 August 1914. BA Berlin Lichterfelde: R43/ 2398.

101. H. Götting, diary, 22 February 1915. DTA Emmendingen: 700/I.

102. Donson, *Youth in the Fatherless Land*, pp. 78-83 and 243-4.

103. Stibbe, *German Anglophobia*, p. 18, and Unteroffizier Groth, diary, 18 May 1915. DTA Emmendingen: 1613.

104. Stibbe, *German Anglophobia*, p. 22.

105. H. Jones, 'Encountering the "Enemy": Prisoner of War Transport and the Development of War Cultures in 1914', in P. Purseigle (ed.), *Warfare and Belligerence: Perspectives in First World War Studies* (Leiden and Boston, 2005), pp. 147-52.

106. Polizeipräsident in Berlin to Unterstaatssekretär in der Reichskanzlei, 'Zehnter Stimmungsbericht', 5 October 1914. BA Berlin Lichterfelde: R43/2398: fo. 202.

107. E. Stempfle, diary, 7 November 1914. DTA Emmendingen: 1654. For details of the raids, see Strachan, First World War, i, pp. 428–30.

108. Wolff, Tagebücher, i, p. 150 (entry for 21 January 1915).

109. Polizeipräsident in Berlin to Unterstaatssekretär in der Reichskanzlei, 'Neunter Stimmungsbericht', 28 September 1914. BA Berlin Lichterfelde: R43/2398: fo. 196.

110. Tirpitz, quoted in Jarausch, Enigmatic Chancellor, pp. 272–3.

111. J. Schröder, Die U-Boote des Kaisers. Die Geschichte des deutschen U-Boot-Krieges gegen Großbritannien im Ersten Weltkrieg (Lauf a. d. Pegnitz, 2000), pp. 90–91, and Halpern, Naval History, pp. 291–5.

112. Jarausch, Enigmatic Chancellor, pp. 271–80, and Halpern, Naval History, pp. 295–303.

113. Bethmann, quoted in Jarausch, Enigmatic Chancellor, p. 284.

114. See, for example, the newspaper cutting 'Amerikanische Kriegsmaterial-Lieferungen', in E. Stempfle, diary, 10 April 1915. DTA Emmendingen: 1654.

115. Jagow, quoted in Stibbe, German Anglophobia, p. 114.

116. ÖULK, i, p. 43.

117. Redlich, Schicksalsjahre Österreichs, i, p. 271 (9 September 1914).

118. Quoted in S. Beller, 'The Tragic Carnival: Austrian Culture in the First World War', in A. Roshwald and R. Stites (eds.), European Culture in the Great War: The Arts, Entertainment and Propaganda, 1914–1918 (Cambridge, 1999), p. 133.

119. J. D. Halliday, 'Censorship in Berlin and Vienna during the First World War: A Comparative View', The Modern Language Review 83(3) (July 1988), pp. 616–26, and M. Cornwall, 'News, Rumour and the Control of Information in Austria-Hungary, 1914–1918', History 77(249) (February 1992), pp. 52–3. Also Orzoff, 'Empire Without Qualities', pp. 166–9 and 194.

120. Kann, History of the Habsburg Empire, p. 606.

121. W. Achleitner, Gott im Krieg. Die Theologie der österreichischen Bischöfe in den Hirtenbriefen zum Ersten Weltkrieg (Vienna, Cologne and Weimar, 1997), p. 266.

122. Biskup Józef Sebastyan Pelczar, letter to the clergy of Przemyśl diocese, 17 February 1915, in Kronika Dyecezyi Przemyskiej. Rok 15, Zeszyt 1 (January–February 1915), p. 1. Cf. Bobič, War and Faith, p. 34.

123. Orzoff, 'Empire Without Qualities', pp. 162 and 175–8.

124. Loewenfeld-Russ, Regelung der Volksernährung, pp. 47–52.

125. Healy, *Vienna*, pp. 36–7 and 43–4.

126. E. S. Balogh, 'The Turning of the World: Hungarian Progressive Writers on the War', in R. A. Kann, B. K. Király and P. S. Fichtner (eds.), *The Habsburg Empire in World War I: Essays on the Intellectual, Military, Political and Economic Aspects of the Habsburg War Effort* (Boulder, CO, and New York, 1977), p. 193.

127. Hupka, *Z czasów wielkiej wojny*, p. 13 (entry for 17 August 1914).

128. P. M. Dabrowski, *Commemorations and the Shaping of Modern Poland* (Bloomington and Indianapolis, IN, 2004), pp. 191–8.

129. J. E. Romer, *Pamiętniki* (Warsaw, n.d.), p. 35.

130. A. Czechówna, diary, 5 August 1915. AN Cracow: IT 428/42. Also Hupka, *Z czasów wielkiej wojny*, pp. 105–6 (entry for 6 August 1915).

131. See S. Lambroza, 'The Pogroms of 1903–1906', in J. D. Klier and S. Lambroza (eds.), *Pogroms: Anti-Jewish Violence in Modern Russian History* (Cambridge, 1992), p. 200.

132. Deák, *Beyond Nationalism*, p. 174.

133. Generalmajor Demus-Moran, 'Heranziehung der Juden zur Milit. Dienstleistung', 29 March 1915. KA Vienna. NL Demus-Moran B/225–9. Also order from k.k. Statthaltereirat Galszewski, 22 June 1915. AVA Vienna: MdI, Präsidiale (1914–15): 22/Galiz.: Akte 19412.

134. M. L. Rozenblit, *Reconstructing a National Identity: The Jews of Habsburg Austria during World War I* (Oxford and New York, 2001), pp. 28–31 and 43–54.

135. A. J. May, *Passing of the Hapsburg Monarchy*, i, pp. 170–96.

136. *Neue Freie Presse. Morgenblatt. Nr. 18230* (25 May 1915), p. 2.

137. 'Wobec nowej fazy wojny', *Nowa Reforma. Wydanie poranne. Rok XXXIV, Nr. 259* (25 May 1915), p. 1.

138. See C. von Hartungen, 'Die Tiroler und Vorarlberger Standschützen – Mythos und Realität', in K. Eisterer and R. Steininger (eds.), *Tirol und der Erste Weltkrieg* (Innsbruck, 1995), pp. 64–5, and Bobič, War and Faith, pp. 45 and 56.

139. Quoted in Bobič, *War and Faith*, pp. 56 and 61.

140. Von Hartungen, 'Tiroler und Vorarlberger Standschützen', pp. 61–88, and W. Joly, *Standschützen. Die Tiroler und Vorarlberger k.k. Standschützen-Formationen im Ersten Weltkrieg. Organisation und Einsatz* (Innsbruck, 1998), pp. 15–49.

141. Von Hartungen, 'Tiroler und Vorarlberger Standschützen', pp. 85–8, Führ, *K.u.k. Armeeoberkommando*, p. 166, and k.u.k. 4. Armeekommando, order, 30 May 1916. KA Vienna: NFA 2 ID. Box 121: doc. 16000/40.

142. R. B. Spence, 'The Yugoslav Role in the Austro-Hungarian Army, 1914–18', in B. K. Király and N. F. Dreisziger (eds.), *East Central European Society in World War I* (Boulder, CO, and Highland Lakes, NJ, 1985), pp. 356–61.

143. Galántai, *Hungary*, p. 113.

144. Kriegsüberwachungsamt to AOK, 'Stimmungsbericht über Böhmen und Mähren', 20 February 1915. KA Vienna: AOK Op. Abteilung 18. Op. Akten 1915: Op. Nr. 7389.

145. Zeman, *Break-Up*, pp. 51–2.

146. K.k. Stationskommandant in Pisek to k.u.k. Militärkommando in Prague, 20 October 1914. KA Vienna: KÜA 1914 (Aktenkartons): Karton 13: Nr. 7659.

147. K.k. Bezirkshauptmannschaft in Ungarisch Brod, 23 October 1914. KA Vienna: KÜA 1914 (Aktenkartons): Karton 15: Nr. 8345.

148. R. Lein, *Pflichterfüllung oder Hochverrat? Die tschechischen Soldaten Österreich-Ungarns im Ersten Weltkrieg* (Vienna and Berlin, 2011), pp. 53–201.

149. K.u.k. Armeeoberkommando to Militärkommando Krakau and Minister des Innern in Vienna, 16 March 1915. KA Vienna: AOK Etappenoberkommando: Box 1943: Op. Nr. 31573.

150. A. Orzoff, *Battle for the Castle: The Myth of Czechoslovakia in Europe, 1914–1948* (Oxford and New York, 2009), pp. 25–33, and K. Pichlík, 'Europa nach dem Krieg in den Vorstellungen T. G. Masaryks im Exil', in H. Mommsen, D. Kováč, J. Malíř and M. Marek (eds.), *Der Erste Weltkrieg und die Beziehungen zwischen Tschechen, Slowaken und Deutschen* (Essen, 2001), pp. 67–8.

151. Zeman, *Break-Up*, pp. 73–6, and Orzoff, *Battle*, pp. 39–40.

152. Lein, *Pflichterfüllung oder Hochverrat?*, pp. 53–201.

153. Redlich, *Schicksalsjahre Österreichs*, ii, p. 34 (entry for 27 April 1915).

154. Führ, *K.u.k. Armeeoberkommando*, p. 30, and J. Křen, *Die Konfliktgemeinschaft. Tschechen und Deutsche 1780–1918*, trans. P. Heumos (Munich, 2000), p. 311.

155. Zahra, *Kidnapped Souls*, p. 88. Also H. Hautmann, 'Prozesse gegen Defätisten, Kriegsgegner, Linksradikale und streikende Arbeiter im Ersten Weltkrieg', in K. R. Stadler (ed.), *Sozialistenprozesse. Politische Justiz in Österreich, 1870–1936* (Vienna, Munich and Zurich, 1986), pp. 153–79.

156. 'Radnitz'. AVA Vienna: MdI Präsidium, Varia. Erster Weltkrieg. Box 33.

157. Redlich, *Austrian War Government*, p. 98.

158. K.k. Polizeidirektion in Prague to k.u.k. Kriegsüberwachungsamt in Vienna, 20 October 1914. Cf. k.u.k. Militärkommando in Prague to k.u.k. Kriegsüberwachungsamt in Vienna, 19 October 1914. KA Vienna: KÜA 1914 (Aktenkartons): Karton 13: Nrs. 7640 and 7626.

159. K.k. Stationskommando in Jičin to k.u.k. Militärkommando in Leitmeritz, 14 October 1914. KA Vienna: KÜA 1914 (Aktenkartons): Karton 13: Nr. 7345.

160. K.u.k. Militärkommando in Prague to Kriegsüberwachungsamt in Vienna, 21 October 1914. KA Vienna: KÜA 1914 (Aktenkartons): Karton 13: Nr. 7659.

161. J. Havránek, 'Politische Repression und Versorgungsengpässe in den böhmischen Ländern 1914 bis 1918', in Mommsen, Kováč, Malíř and Marek (eds.), *Der Erste Weltkrieg*, pp. 50–62.

162. Führ, *K.u.k. Armeeoberkommando*, pp. 31–47.

163. Excerpt from Kriegsministerium document, 26 November 1914. KA Vienna: MKSM 1914: 38–2/1.

164. Führ, *K.u.k. Armeeoberkommando*, ch. 6 and pp. 165–7.

165. Ibid., p. 171.

6. SECURITY FOR ALL TIME

1. Quotations from Franz Joseph's Manifesto 'To My People' (see ch. 2) and from Chancellor Bethmann Hollweg's speech in the Reichstag of 4 August in *New York Times Current History: The European War from the Beginning to March 1915. Who Began the War, and Why?*, Volume 1, No. 2 (New York, 1915), p. 222.

2. Wilhelm II in the Berlin Palace's White Room on 4 August 1914, reproduced in ibid., p. 210. Also Berchtold in ibid., p. 227.

3. Bethmann's Memorandum: 'Provisional Notes on the Direction of Our Policy on the Conclusion of Peace', 9 September 1914, in G. D. Feldman (ed.), *German Imperialism, 1914–1918: The Development of a Historical Debate* (London, Sydney and Toronto, 1972), pp. 125–6 (doc. 26).

4. P. Theiner, '"Mitteleuropa": Pläne in Wilhelminischen Deutschland', *Geschichte und Gesellschaft. Sonderheft* 10 (1984), pp. 128–36.

5. For pre-war ideas of a European customs union and the September programme, see D. Stevenson, 'The First World War and European Integration', *The International History Review* 34(4) (December 2012), pp. 842–6, and for its use against Britain see Jarausch, *Enigmatic Chancellor*, p. 196. Fischer exaggerates the continuity between pre-war and wartime German policy in general, including conceptions of a Mitteleuropa customs association. See his *Germany's Aims*, pp. 98–106 and 247–56. For Longwy-Briey, see ibid., pp. 257–9.

6. Stevenson, 'First World War and European Integration', p. 844.

7. Jarausch, *Enigmatic Chancellor*, p. 192.

8. 'Petition of the Six Economic Associations', 20 May 1915, in Feldman (ed.), *German Imperialism*, pp. 16–22 (doc. 4). For the annexationist pressure

groups, see esp. H. Hagenlücke, *Deutsche Vaterlandspartei. Die nationale Rechte am Ende des Kaiserreiches* (Düsseldorf, 1997), pp. 49–72.

9. S. Bruendel, *Volksgemeinschaft oder Volksstaat. Die 'Ideen von 1914' und die Neuordnung Deutschlands im Ersten Weltkrieg* (Berlin, 2003), pp. 77–8.

10. See Fischer, *Germany's Aims*, pp. 173–9.

11. Miller, *Burgfrieden*, pp. 75–132 and 190–239.

12. Afflerbach, *Falkenhayn*, pp. 198–210. For peace attempts in 1915, see Fischer, *Germany's Aims*, pp. 184–214.

13. Jarausch, *Enigmatic Chancellor*, pp. 209 and 216.

14. For Bethmann's minimum war aim as a customs union, see W. C. Thompson, 'The September Program: Reflections on the Evidence', *Central European History* 11(4) (December 1978), p. 353.

15. For this and the below, see Jarausch, *Enigmatic Chancellor*, pp. 204–21, and Fischer, *Germany's Aims*, pp. 247–56.

16. Stevenson, 'First World War and European Integration', pp. 847–8.

17. R. W. Kapp, 'Divided Loyalties: The German Reich and Austria-Hungary in Austro-German Discussions of War Aims, 1914–1916', *Central European History* 17(2/3) (June–September 1984), esp. pp. 124–6 and 133–5. Also Rauchensteiner, *Tod des Doppeladlers*, pp. 312–15.

18. R. W. Kapp, 'Bethmann-Hollweg, Austria-Hungary and Mitteleuropa, 1914–1915', *Austrian History Yearbook* 19 (1983), pp. 215–16 and 229–36.

19. Ibid., pp. 217–18 and 223.

20. A. Müller, *Zwischen Annäherung und Abgrenzung. Österreich-Ungarn und die Diskussion um Mitteleuropa im Ersten Weltkrieg* (Marburg, 2001), esp. pp. 195–6. Also Stevenson, 'First World War and European Integration', pp. 848–51. For the exchange of notes on Mitteleuropa, see S. Verosta, 'The German Concept of *Mitteleuropa*, 1916–1918, and its Contemporary Critics', in R. A. Kann, B. K. Király and P. S. Fichtner (eds.), *The Habsburg Empire in World War I: Essays on the Intellectual, Military, Political and Economic Aspects of the Habsburg War Effort* (Boulder, CO, and New York, 1977), pp. 209–14.

21. W. W. Hagen, *Germans, Poles, and Jews: The Nationality Conflict in the Prussian East, 1772–1914* (Chicago and London, 1980), pp. 180–94. Also, more broadly for pre-First World War German views of the east, see V. G. Liulevičius, *The German Myth of the East: 1800 to the Present* (Oxford, 2009), pp. 1–129.

22. Fischer, *Germany's Aims*, pp. 132–4 and 138–41.

23. See W. Conze, *Polnische Nation und deutsche Politik im Ersten Weltkrieg* (Cologne and Graz, 1958), pp. 60–67.

24. See, most recently, V. G. Liulevičius, *War Land on the Eastern Front: Culture, National Identity, and German Occupation in World War I* (Cambridge, New York and Melbourne, 2000), and A. H. Sammartino, *The Impossible Border: Germany and the East, 1914–1922* (Ithaca, NY, and London, 2010), ch. 1. The most extreme version of Fischer's argument is developed in his *War of Illusions: German Policies from 1911 to 1914* (London, 1975).

25. I. Geiss, *Der polnische Grenzstreifen, 1914–1918. Ein Beitrag zur deutschen Kriegszielpolitik im Ersten Weltkrieg* (Lübeck and Hamburg, 1960), pp. 43 and 70–74. Geiss deserves credit for being the first to explore these plans but is very misleading on the context in which they came about, suggesting erroneously that the German government consider a border strip after the Russians had 'once again for the most part been pushed out of East Prussia'. Fear, not aggression, in fact drove the Germans' interest in annexing this land.

26. K. Wicker, 'Der Weltkrieg in Zahlen. Verluste an Blut und Boden', in W. Jost (ed.), *Was wir vom Weltkrieg nicht wissen* (Leipzig, 1936), p. 521. Germany surrendered 50,730 square kilometres of territory in the east at the end of the war, including 46,150 square kilometres to Poland, 2,660 to Lithuania and 1,920 to the League of Nations enclave at Danzig.

27. Lohr, *Nationalizing the Russian Empire*, pp. 129–37.

28. Geiss, *Polnische Grenzstreifen*, pp. 74–8.

29. I. Ihnatowicz, 'Gospodarka na ziemiach polskich w okresie I Wojny Światowej', in B. Zientara, A. Mączak, I. Ihnatowicz and Z. Landau, *Dzieje Gospodarcze Polski do 1939 r.* (Warsaw, 1965), p. 457.

30. P. Gatrell, *A Whole Empire Walking: Refugees in Russia during World War I* (Bloomington and Indianapolis, IN, 1999), pp. 3 and 211–15. Also Liulevičius, *War Land*, p. 17. For good first-hand descriptions of the devastation caused by the Russians, see the letters of the German soldier Reinhold Sieglerschmidt, esp. those of 10, 14 and 15 August 1915 (accessed at www.europeana1914-1918.eu on 23 October 2013).

31. Kapp, 'Bethmann-Hollweg', p. 230.

32. L. Höbelt, '"Well-Tempered Discontent": Austrian Domestic Politics', in M. Cornwall (ed.), *The Last Years of Austria-Hungary: A Multi-National Experiment in Early Twentieth-Century Europe*, revised and expanded edn (Exeter, 2002), p. 48.

33. Leslie, 'Antecedents', pp. 311, 322, 358 and 371–3.

34. May, *Passing of the Hapsburg Monarchy*, i, pp. 175–6, 185–94 and 210.

35. M. Cornwall, 'The Habsburg Elite and the Southern Slav Question, 1914–1918', in L. Höbelt and T. G. Otte (eds.), *A Living Anachronism? European Diplomacy and the Habsburg Monarchy. Festschrift für Francis Roy Bridge zum 70. Geburtstag* (Vienna, Cologne and Weimar, 2010), pp. 249–53.

36. Liulevičius, *War Land*, p. 21.

37. Sammartino, *Impossible Border*, pp. 32–7. The quotation is from Bethmann Hollweg's speech in the Reichstag of 5 April 1916.

38. Fischer, *Germany's Aims*, pp. 273–9. For Sering and his plans, see R. L. Nelson, 'From Manitoba to the Memel: Max Sering, Inner Colonization and the German East', *Social History* 35(4) (2010), esp. pp. 442–53.

39. Liulevičius, *War Land*, p. 21.

40. E. Zechlin, 'Ludendorff im Jahre 1915. Unveröffentlichte Briefe', *Historische Zeitschrift* 211(2) (October 1970), pp. 335 and 338 (letter of 5 April 1915), 350 (letter of 10 October 1915) and 353 (letter of 29 December 1915). For exploitation as the primary purpose of Ober Ost, see Liulevičius, *War Land*, pp. 64–5.

41. Geiss, *Polnische Grenzstreifen*, pp. 78–107, and Liulevičius, *War Land*, pp. 95–6.

42. A. Tooze, *The Wages of Destruction: The Making and Breaking of the Nazi Economy* (London, 2006), pp. 466–76.

43. Geiss, *Polnische Grenzstreifen*, pp. 148–9. Also see 'Memorandum of the Supreme Command on the Polish Border Strip, July 5, 1918', in Feldman (ed.), *German Imperialism*, pp. 133–7.

44. For French wartime internments, see ch. 3. For the expulsions from Alsace-Lorraine in the war's aftermath, see Zahra, 'The "Minority Problem"', *Contemporary European History* 17(2) (May 2008), esp. pp. 138–9 and 149–58.

45. See ch. 4.

46. N. M. Naimark, *Fires of Hatred: Ethnic Cleansing in Twentieth-Century Europe* (Cambridge, MA, and London, 2001), pp. 22–41; D. Bloxham, 'The First World War and the Development of the Armenian Genocide', in R. G. Suny, F. M. Göçek and N. M. Naimark (eds.), *A Question of Genocide: Armenians and Turks at the End of the Ottoman Empire* (Oxford, 2011), pp. 260–75; U. Ü. Üngör, 'Orphans, Converts, and Prostitutes: Social Consequences of War and Persecution in the Ottoman Empire, 1914–1923', *War in History* 19(2) (April 2012), pp. 173–92.

47. Fischer, *War Aims*, pp. 189–97. For the central place of the Turkish Straits in Russia's aims, see McMeekin, *Russian Origins*, pp. 30–37.

48. Stevenson, 'French War Aims and the American Challenge', p. 881.

49. D. Larsen, 'War Pessimism and an American Peace in Early 1916', *The International History Review* 34(4) (December 2012), pp. 796 and 801–4.

50. Miller, *Burgfrieden*, pp. 123 and 183–4.

51. V. Klemperer, *Curriculum Vitae. Erinnerungen, 1881–1918*, ed. W. Nowojski (2 vols., Berlin, 1996), ii, pp. 410, 426 and 448. For the Czechs, see ch. 5.

7. CRISIS AT THE FRONT

1. A. A. Nofi, 'Comparative Divisional Strengths during World War I: East Central European Belligerents and Theaters', in B. K. Király and N. F. Dreisziger (eds.), *East European Society in World War I* (Boulder, CO, and Highland Lakes, NJ, 1985), pp. 268–9.

2. For the most recent account of the Chantilly meeting, see W. Philpott, *Bloody Victory: The Sacrifice on the Somme and the Making of the Twentieth Century* (London, 2009), pp. 56–61.

3. R. T. Foley, *German Strategy and the Path to Verdun: Erich von Falkenhayn and the Development of Attrition, 1870–1916* (Cambridge, 2005), pp. 181–2.

4. Doughty, *Pyrrhic Victory*, p. 172. For the French army's campaign in 1915, see ibid., pp. 153–202.

5. D. French, 'The Meaning of Attrition, 1914–1916', *English Historical Review* 103(407) (April 1988), pp. 397–404. See also J. M. Beach, 'British Intelligence and the German Army, 1914–1918', unpublished PhD thesis, University College London (2005), pp. 141–4.

6. Foley, *German Strategy*, pp. 154–5 and 187–90. Also Afflerbach, 'Planning Total War?', pp. 118–22.

7. *Sanitätsbericht*, iii, pp. 12 and 6–8* (figure for January 1916), and Gratz and Schüller, *Wirtschaftliche Zusammenbruch*, p. 151.

8. Philpott, *Bloody Victory*, pp. 52, 193 and 624–5.

9. *ÖULK*, i, p. 56, and E. O. Volkmann, *Soziale Heeresmißstände als Mitursache des deutschen Zusammenbruches von 1918. Die Ursachen des deutschen Zusammenbruches im Jahre 1918. Zweite Abteilung. Der innere Zusammenbruch* (12 vols., Berlin, 1929), xi(2), p. 34.

10. For the killed/wounded ratio, see C. von Altrock (ed.), *Vom Sterben des deutschen Offizierkorps* (Berlin, 1922), tables on pp. 68 and 74. Information on Austro-Hungarian prisoners is in R. Jeřábek, 'The Eastern Front', in M. Cornwall (ed.), *The Last Years of Austria-Hungary: A Multi-National Experiment in Early Twentieth-Century Europe*, revised and expanded edn (Exeter, 2002), p. 158. During the conflict, 61,100 Austro-Hungarian officers were held prisoner, as compared with 11,300 German officers. See A. Rachamimov, *POWs and the Great War: Captivity on the Eastern Front* (Oxford and New York, 2002), p. 39.

11. H. Cron, *The Imperial German Army, 1914–18: Organization, Structure, Orders of Battle*, trans. C. F. Colton (Solihull, 2002), pp. 101–2.

12. See L. Rüdt von Collenberg, *Die deutsche Armee von 1871 bis 1914* (Berlin, 1922), p. 118.

13. Watson, *Enduring the Great War*, pp. 120–22, Deák, *Beyond Nationalism*, pp. 193–5, and Rothenberg, *Army of Francis Joseph*, p. 193.

14. See W. Meteling, *Ehre, Einheit, Ordnung. Preußische und französische Städte und ihre Regimenter im Krieg, 1870/71 und 1914–19* (Baden-Baden, 2010), pp. 228–9. Also F. Altrichter, *Die seelischen Kräfte des deutschen Heeres im Frieden und im Weltkriege* (Berlin, 1933), pp. 236–7. NCOs with only limited education could at best be promoted to an inferior officer rank, the *Feldwebelleutnant*. Theoretically, the rules could be waived in cases of exceptional heroism, but this was done extremely rarely.

15. I. Deák, 'The Habsburg Army in the First and Last Days of World War I: A Comparative Analysis', in B. K. Király and N. F. Dreisziger (eds.), *East European Society in World War I* (Boulder, CO, and Highland Lakes, NJ, 1985), p. 305. For NCOs, see R. Jeřábek, 'Die Brussilowoffensive 1916. Ein Wendepunkt der Koalitionskriegführung der Mittelmächte', 2 vols., unpublished PhD thesis, University of Vienna (1982), ii, p. 576.

16. See *Sanitätsbericht*, iii, pp. 12 and 15, and *ÖULK*, i, pp. 28–31.

17. See *Sanitätsbericht*, iii, pp. 15–16, and Gratz and Schüller, *Wirtschaftliche Zusammenbruch*, p. 158.

18. K. Weiler, *Arbeit und Gesundheit. Sozialmedizinische Schriftenreihe aus dem Gebiete des Reichsministeriums. Heft 22. Nervöse und seelische Störungen bei Teilnehmern am Weltkriege, ihre ärztliche und rechtliche Beurteilung. Erster Teil: Nervöse und seelische Störungen psychogener und funktioneller Art* (Leipzig, 1933), pp. 124–5, 129 and 131. Also the essays by K. Bonhoeffer, R. Gaupp and G. Aschaffenburg, in K. Bonhoeffer (ed.), *Geistes- und Nervenkrankheiten* (2 vols., Leipzig, 1922), i, esp. pp. 26–7, 89 and 133.

19. Watson, *Enduring the Great War*, pp. 156–8 and 161–2.

20. See Schindler, 'Disaster on the Drina', 192, and Jeřábek, 'Brussilow offensive, pp. 528–9.

21. H. Kantorowicz, *Der Offiziershaß im deutschen Heer* (Freiburg, 1919), p. 11.

22. M. Hobohm, *Soziale Heeresmißstände als Teilursache des deutschen Zusammenbruches von 1918. Die Ursachen des deutschen Zusammenbruches im Jahre 1918. Zweite Abteilung. Der innere Zusammenbruch* (12 vols., Berlin, 1929), xi(1), p. 373. This flawed argument has also been repeated in modern literature. See, for example, Ziemann, *Front*, pp. 140–63.

23. Kantorowicz, *Offiziershaß*, p. 13, and G. Gothein, *Warum verloren wir den Krieg?* (Stuttgart and Berlin, 1919), pp. 83–6.

24. See the impressively supported, albeit in its interpretations highly politicized, study by Hobohm, *Soziale Heeresmißstände*, xi(1). For staff hatred in the French and British armies, see Meteling, *Ehre, Einheit, Ordnung*, pp. 271–2, and Watson, *Enduring the Great War*, p. 134.

25. Watson, *Enduring the Great War*, pp. 124–33.

26. Postüberwachung der 5. Armee, 12 July 1917, p. 20. BA-MA Freiburg: W-10/ 50794.

27. See the documents collected in Hobohm, *Soziale Heeresmißstände*, xi(1), pp. 13–79. The letter from the Deutscher Werkmeister-Verband of 12 August 1918 (doc. 27b) illustrates how widespread this resentment ultimately became, although it, like other sources, emphasizes the 'mature' age of the complainants. Younger troops who bore the burden of combat were much more likely to be satisfied with their commanders.

28. See Anlage 19, 'Hilfsgutachten des Oberarchivrates Cron', in Volkmann, *Soziale Heeresmißstände*, xi(2), pp. 135–7.

29. *ÖULK*, i, p. 54.

30. Krauß, *Ursachen unserer Niederlage*, p. 71.

31. H. Kollenz, diary, 5 April 1916. DTA, Emmendingen: 1844,1. More generally, *ÖULK*, i, p. 55.

32. Schuhmacher, *Leben und Seele unseres Soldatenlieds*, p. 169.

33. W. Ludwig, 'Beiträge zur Psychologie der Furcht im Kriege', in W. Stern and O. Lipmann (eds.), *Beihefte zur Zeitschrift für angewandte Psychologie. 21. Beiträge zur Psychologie des Krieges* (Leipzig, 1920), pp. 125–72.

34. Watson, *Enduring the Great War*, pp. 93–6.

35. P. J. Houlihan, 'Clergy in the Trenches: Catholic Military Chaplains of Germany and Austria-Hungary during the First World War', unpublished PhD thesis, University of Chicago (2011), pp. 75, 81 and 83, *ÖULK*, i, p. 39, and Bobič, *War and Faith*, pp. 100–102, 107 and 110–11.

36. Reservepionnier Ludwig Elšík of Sappeur-Bataillon Nr. 2, quoted in Kriegsüberwachungsamt to Armee-Oberkommando, 20 February 1915. Vienna: AOK – Op.-Abteilung 18 – Akten 1915: Op. Nr. 7389.

37. P. Göhre, *Tat-Flugschriften 22. Front und Heimat. Religiöses, Politisches, Sexuelles aus dem Schützengraben* (Jena, 1917), pp. 2–13, and Ziemann, *Front*, pp. 246–65.

38. P. Plaut, 'Psychographie des Kriegers', in W. Stern and O. Lipmann (eds.), *Beihefte zur Zeitschrift für angewandte Psychologie. 21. Beiträge zur Psychologie des Krieges* (Leipzig, 1920), p. 95.

39. Schuhmacher, *Leben und Seele unseres Soldatenlieds*, pp. 36–7. The first four stanzas only are reproduced here.

40. E. W. Küpper, letter to his wife, 25 March 1915. BA-MA Freiburg: MSg 2/5254.

41. G. Kirchner, letter to his sister, 21 October 1914. DTA, Emmendingen, 31 October 1914.

42. K. Reiter, diary, 20 June 1916. BA-MA Freiburg: MSg1/161. For the German Field Post, see B. Ulrich, *Die Augenzeugen. Deutsche Feldpostbriefe in Kriegs- und Nachkriegszeit, 1914–1933* (Essen, 1997), p. 40. For other

examples, see Watson, *Enduring the Great War*, p. 83, and for the import-ance of defending home for Habsburg troops, see ch. 5.

43. 'Allgemeiner Wegweiser für jede Familie' (Wochenschrift) Jg. 1917. Berlin, 1917, reproduced in E. Johann (ed.), *Innenansicht eines Krieges. Bilder, Briefe, Dokumente, 1914–1918* (Frankfurt am Main, 1968), pp. 287–8.

44. Letter to a soldier, copied out in H. Kollenz, diary, 1 September [erroneously dated August] 1916. DTA, Emmendingen: 1844,1.

45. O. Steinhilber, letter to his wife, 4 December 1915. Private Collection (Author) and H. McPhail, *The Long Silence: Civilian Life under the German Occupation of Northern France, 1914–1918* (London and New York, 1999, 2001), p. 203.

46. H. O. Henel, *Eros im Stacheldraht*, quoted in M. Hirschfeld and A. Gaspar (eds.), *Sittengeschichte des Ersten Weltkrieges* (Hanau am Main, n.d.), p. 248. For prostitution and sex in the war zone, see ibid., pp. 231–332.

47. *Sanitätsbericht*, iii, pp. 163–8, and S. Kirchenberger, 'Beiträge zur Sanitäts-statistik der österreichisch-ungarischen Armee im Kriege, 1914–1918', in C. Pirquet (ed.), *Volksgesundheit im Kriege* (2 vols., Vienna and New Haven, CT, 1926), i, pp. 47, 60 and 69.

48. Cron, *Imperial German Army*, pp. 122 and 145, Wegs, 'Austrian Economic Mobilization', p. 160, and Gratz and Schüller, *Wirtschaftliche Zusammen-bruch*, p. 114.

49. B. I. Gudmundsson, *Stormtroop Tactics: Innovation in the German Army, 1914–1918* (Westpoint, CT, 1989), pp. 43–53 and 77–88. Also C. Stachel-beck, *Militärische Effektivität im Ersten Weltkrieg. Die 11. Bayerische Infanteriedivision 1915 bis 1918* (Paderborn, Munich, Vienna and Zurich, 2010), p. 99. For Habsburg tactics in 1916, see k.u.k. Korpskommando Szurmay, 'Erfahrungen aus der Neujahrschlacht 1916 bei Toporucz-Rarancze'. KA Vienna: NFA 2 ID. Karton 121: Nr. 143/6.

50. A. Horne, *The Price of Glory: Verdun 1916* (London, 1962), pp. 46–50.

51. Afflerbach, *Falkenhayn*, pp. 363–4, and Foley, *German Strategy*, p. 190.

52. Reichsarchiv, *Der Weltkrieg. Die Operationen des Jahres 1916 bis zum Wechsel der Obersten Heeresleitung* (Berlin, 1936), x, pp. 61–4, and Gud-mundsson, *Stormtroop Tactics*, pp. 58–60.

53. Foley, *German Strategy*, pp. 194–7.

54. Ibid., pp. 204–5 and 215–17, Afflerbach, *Falkenhayn*, pp. 362 and 369, and Stachelbeck, *Militärische Effektivität*, p. 105.

55. H. von Obergassel, diary/memoir, p. 2 (21 February 1916).

56. Foley, *German Strategy*, pp. 194–7 and 204–5, and Afflerbach, *Falkenhayn*, p. 369.

57. The best account of Douaumont's capture is Horne, *Price of Glory*, pp. 105–24.

58. Foley, *German Strategy*, pp. 218–21 and 227, and Afflerbach, *Falkenhayn*, pp. 369–70.

59. Quoted in H. Afflerbach, '"Bis zum letzten Mann und letzten Groschen?" Die Wehrpflicht im deutschen Reich und ihre Auswirkungen auf das militärische Führungsdenken im Ersten Weltkrieg', in R. G. Foerster (ed.), *Die Wehrpflicht. Entstehung, Erscheinungsformen und politisch-militärische Wirkung* (Munich, 1994), p. 80.

60. *Sanitätsbericht*, ii, p. 655.

61. M. Wittmann, diary, 24–25 May 1916. DTA, Emmendingen: 926.

62. E. von Falkenhayn, *The German General Staff and its Decisions, 1914–1916* (New York, 1920), p. 270.

63. Foley, *German Strategy*, p. 259.

64. Reichsarchiv, *Der Weltkrieg 1914 bis 1918. Die Operationen des Jahres 1916 bis zum Wechsel in der Obersten Heeresleitung* (14 vols., Berlin, 1936), x, p. 406.

65. Foley, *German Strategy*, pp. 228–30 and 254–6.

66. See *Sanitätsbericht*, iii, p. 49, and, for French figures, Doughty, *Pyrrhic Victory*, p. 309.

67. Jeřábek, 'Brussilowoffensive', i, pp. 145–8, and Stone, *Eastern Front*, p. 227.

68. A good account of the preparations and attack can be found in Rauchensteiner, *Tod des Doppeladlers*, pp. 330–43.

69. M. Thompson, *The White War: Life and Death on the Italian Front, 1915–1919* (London, 2008), pp. 163–5, T. C. Dowling, *The Brusilov Offensive* (Bloomington and Indianapolis, IN, 2008), pp. 49–50, and Herwig, *First World War*, pp. 205–7.

70. Stone, *Eastern Front*, pp. 227–31.

71. Ibid., p. 239.

72. Jeřábek, 'Brussilowoffensive', i, pp. 209–28.

73. For Habsburg 'best practice' in trench building, see k.u.k. Korpskommando Szurmay, 'Erfahrungen aus der Neujahrschlacht 1916 bei Toporucz-Rarancze', esp. p. 4. KA Vienna: NFA (2. I.D). Karton 121: Nr. 143/6, and k.u.k. 4. Armeekommando, Nr. 1080, entitled 'Verschiedenes über Stellungskampf', May 1916. KA Vienna: NFA (2. I.D). Karton 121. For the defences in the Fourth Army's sector, see Jeřábek, 'Brussilowoffensive', pp. 175–8 and 199–200. Also Dowling, *Brusilov Offensive*, pp. 50–54.

74. K.u.k. 2.ITD, Op. Nr. 142/5, Reservat Abfertigung, 21 May 1916. KA Vienna: NFA (2. I.D). Karton 121.

75. Telegrams from 'Delta 70' at 4.10 nm, 'Kalif 10' at 6.48 nm and 'Delta 2' at 7.30 nm, 4 June 1916. KA Vienna: NFA (2. I.D.) Karton 121.

76. Oberstleutnant Max Schönowsky-Schönwies and Leutnant A. D. August Angenetter, quoted in Jeřábek, 'Brussilowoffensive', i, p. 259.

77. Ibid., pp. 259–63.

78. Ibid., pp. 264–85. For the advance's distance, see L. Sondhaus, *World War One: The Global Revolution* (Cambridge, 2011), p. 220.

79. T. Ritter von Zeynek, *Ein Offizier im Generalstabskorps erinnert sich*, ed. P. Broucek (Vienna, Cologne and Weimar, 2009), p. 246.

80. Stone, *Eastern Front*, pp. 252–4m and Jeřábek, 'Brussilowoffensive', i, p. 292 and ibid., ii, p. 522.

81. Dowling, *Brusilov Offensive*, p. 175.

82. Jeřábek, 'Brussilowoffensive', i, pp. 195–200, and Stone, *Eastern Front*, pp. 237–8.

83. Jeřábek, 'Brussilowoffensive', i, pp. 159–60 and 293, and Stone, *Eastern Front*, pp. 239, 242 and 251–2.

84. Zeynek, *Offizier im Generalstabskorps*, p. 242. The German officer alluded to was General Seekt. For his views, and for Habsburg General Staff officers' distance from their men, see Jeřábek, 'Brussilowoffensive', ii, pp. 560–61.

85. Jeřábek, 'Brussilowoffensive', i, pp. 211–18 and ibid., ii, p. 560. The minimal loss rate also bears out the inactivity of most Habsburg units in the months before the offensive. See Stone, *Eastern Front*, p. 240.

86. Redlich, *Schicksalsjahre Österreichs*, ii, p. 121 (14 June 1916).

87. Rauchensteiner, *Tod des Doppeladlers*, p. 348.

88. Evidenzbüro des k.u.k. Generalstabes to Generalstabsabteilung des Festungskommandos in Krakau, 23 July 1916. AN Cracow: DPKr 111: fos. 1735–6.

89. J. R. Schindler, 'Steamrollered in Galicia: The Austro-Hungarian Army and the Brusilov Offensive, 1916', *War in History* 10(1) (January 2003), pp. 46–7.

90. Rothenberg, *Army of Francis Joseph*, p. 195.

91. Jeřábek, 'Brussilowoffensive', i, pp. 230–38.

92. A. Klauser, diary, 6 July 1916. KA Vienna: B330.

93. Jeřábek, 'Brussilowoffensive', ii, pp. 523–5. Also Herwig, *First World War*, pp. 209–11.

94. Landesgerichtsrat A. Regius, diary, 6–18 June 1916 and 3 August 1917. KA Vienna: NL Regius B/395. For Russian conduct during the occupation, see the report of the k.k. Polizeidirektor in Czernowitz to k.k. Minister des Innern, 20 November 1917. AVA Vienna: MdI, Präsidiale 22/Bukowina (1900–18): Karton 2096: Nr. 23741.

95. Philpott, *Bloody Victory*, pp. 71–2, 77–83 and 121.

96. R. Prior and T. Wilson, *Command on the Western Front: The Military Career of Sir Henry Rawlinson, 1914–1918* (Barnsley, 1992, 2004), pp. 33, 77, 85 and 111.

97. R. Prior and T. Wilson, *The Somme* (New Haven, CT, and London, 2005), pp. 41–3.

98. Ibid., pp. 43, 47 and 50–51.

99. For the explosives estimate, see J. Keegan, *The Face of Battle: A Study of Agincourt, Waterloo and the Somme* (London, 1976, 1983), pp. 238–40.

100. 'Notes on German Dug-Outs Located North-West of Serre' (Annexe to G.H.Q. Summary, 26 November 1916). TNA: WO 157/15.

101. G. Hirschfeld, 'Die Somme-Schlacht von 1916', in G. Hirschfeld, G. Krumeich and I. Renz (eds.), *Die Deutschen an der Somme, 1914–1918* (Essen, 2006), p. 79.

102. Prior and Wilson, *Command on the Western Front*, p. 139.

103. Philpott, *Bloody Victory*, pp. 106–19.

104. For figures, see G. Sheffield, *Forgotten Victory: The First World War. Myths and Realities* (London, 2001), p. 95, P. Simkins, *Kitchener's Army: The Raising of the New Armies, 1914–1916* (Manchester, 1988), p. 17, and [British] War Office (ed.), *Statistics of the Military Effort of the British Empire during the Great War, 1914–1920* (London, 1922), table facing p. 64.

105. This follows Prior and Wilson, *Somme*, esp. pp. 114–16.

106. Keegan, *Face of Battle*, p. 226. Cf. also M. Middlebrook, *The First Day on the Somme, 1 July 1916* (London, 1971, 1984).

107. C. E. Carrington, 'Kitchener's Army: The Somme and After', *Journal of the Royal United Services Institution for Defence Studies* 123(1) (March 1978), p. 17.

108. 'Bericht des Reserve-Infanterie-Regiments 111 über die Kämpfe um Fricourt', GLA Karlsruhe: 456 F16 Nr. 123. Also, for the British New Armies' training, see Samuels, *Command or Control?*, p. 120, and for British divisions' arrival in France, I. F. W. Beckett and K. Simpson (eds.), *A Nation in Arms: A Social Study of the British Army in the First World War* (Manchester, 1985), Appendix I.

109. For the German Order of Battle, see Reichsarchiv, *Weltkrieg*, x, pp. 348–9. For a sense of the regiments' ethos, see their war histories, e.g. G. vom Holtz, *Das Württembergische Reserve-Inf.-Regiment Nr. 121 im Weltkrieg 1914–1918* (Stuttgart, 1922).

110. A. Spemann, diary, 24 June 1916. HStA Stuttgart: M660/041, Nr. 10.

111. Philpott, *Bloody Victory*, p. 167, Prior and Wilson, *Somme*, pp. 61–9, A. Tooze, 'The German National Economy in an Era of Crisis and War, 1917–1945', in H. Walser Smith (ed.), *The Oxford Handbook of Modern German History* (Oxford, 2011), p. 403, and 'Bericht des Reserve-Infanterie-Regiments No. 111 über die Kämpfe um Fricourt'. GLA Karlsruhe: 456 F16 Nr. 123.

112. 'Gefechtsbericht der 26. Reserve-Division für die Zeit vom 24.6. bis 30.6.1916. (einschl.)'. HStA Stuttgart: M43, Bü 60.

113. For Second Army's casualties, see *Sanitätsbericht*, iii, pp. 51–2.

114. Karl Eisler, report from August 1916, reproduced in G. Hirschfeld, G. Krumeich and I. Renz (eds.), *Die Deutschen an der Somme, 1914–1918. Krieg, Besatzung, Verbrannte Erde* (Essen, 2006), p. 101.

115. A. Spemann, diary, 24, 25, 26 and 27 June 1916. HStA Stuttgart: M660/041, Nr. 10.

116. See Spemann's entry in the regimental muster roll. HStA Stuttgart: M433/2, Bü 441.

117. A. Spemann, diary, 28 and 29 June 1916. HStA Stuttgart: M660/041, Nr. 10.

118. Copy of an order passed on by the division from XIV Res. Korps, 28 June 1916. HStA Stuttgart: M43, Bü 60. For troops eating more under bombardment, see 28 Reserve-Division, 'Gefechtsbericht für die Zeit vom 24.6. bis zum 6.7. 12° mittags', 20 August 1916, p. 14. GLA Karlsruhe: 456 F16 Nr. 64.

119. A. Spemann, diary, 28 June 1916. HStA Stuttgart: M660/041, Nr. 10.

120. 51. Res. Inf. Brig. (K. Württ), 'Gefechtsbericht. Die Schlacht an der Somme und der Ancre bei der 51. Res. Inf. Brig.', 21 July 1916, p. 3. HStA Stuttgart: M43, Bü 19.

121. Philpott, *Bloody Victory*, p. 175.

122. 51. Res. Inf. Brig. (K. Württ), 'Gefechtsbericht', p. 3. HStA Stuttgart: M43, Bü 19.

123. 'Gefechtsbericht des Resrve [sic] Infanterie Regiments Nr. 119 über die Zeit vom 24.6.–14.7.16', 24 July 1916, pp. 12–21. HStA Stuttgart: M43, Bü 19. For the attack from the British perspective, see Prior and Wilson, *Somme*, pp. 70–81.

124. See 51. Res. Inf. Brig. (K. Württ), 'Gefechtsbericht', p. 3. HStA Stuttgart: M43, Bü 19.

125. 'Bericht des Reserve-Infanterie-Regiments 111 über die Kämpfe um Fricourt', Battle Report of 28 Reserve Division, pp. 14 and 20–23, and 'Nachweisung der durchschnittlichen Mannschafts-Gefechtsstärken der Infanterie (ohne Radfahrer- und Maschinengewehr-Formationen) – Stand am 21. Juni 1916', GLA Karlsruhe: 456 F16, Nrs. 123 and 64, fos. 35, 61 and 65–6. For other information on the sector's defences, see Prior and Wilson, *Somme*, p. 103.

126. See Philpott, *Bloody Victory*, pp. 183–4 and 205.

127. Herwig, *First World War*, p. 199.

128. See Reichsarchiv, *Weltkrieg*, x, Anlage 2, 'Zum Angriff auf Verdun. Verzeichnis der vom 12. Februar bis zum 28. August auf dem Kampffelde von Avocourt bis zu den Côtes Lorraines (südöstlich von Verdun) eingesetzten Generalkommandos und Divisionen, ihrer Ablösungen, Verschiebungen und Verluste', pp. 6–7, and H. Cron, *Infanterie-Regiment Markgraf Karl (Nr. 60)* (Oldenburg i. O., 1926), pp. 130 and 132–47. For praise of the French, see Philpott, *Bloody Victory*, pp. 183–4 and 205.

129. Reichsarchiv, *Weltkrieg*, x, pp. 350–52. For losses in 121 Division, see ibid., Anlage 3, 'Zur Schlacht an der Somme 1916. Verzeichnis der vom 1. Juli bis Ende August auf dem Kampffelde eingesetzten Generalkommandos und Divisionen, ihrer Ablösungen, Verschiebungen und Verluste', pp. 2–3. Revealingly, after being relieved from the Somme, 121 Division was transferred to the less demanding Eastern Front.

130. Middlebrook, *First Day on the Somme*, pp. 263–4, and Philpott, *Bloody Victory*, p. 207. The German casualty figure is calculated on the basis of figures in Middlebrook added to the casualties of 121 Division (5,148 officers and men) south of the Somme.

131. Reichsarchiv, *Weltkrieg*, x, pp. 358–9.

132. A. Spemann, diary, 3 July 1916. HStA Stuttgart: M660/041, Nr. 11.

133. Reichsarchiv, *Weltkrieg*, x, pp. 363–4, and Sheffield, *Somme*, 79–86.

134. E. Klasen, letters to parents and siblings, 4 March, 30 and 31 July, and 9 and 27 August 1916. BA-MA Freiburg: PH 10II/42. For a British-orientated account of the fighting in this sector, see Prior and Wilson, *Somme*, pp. 141–51.

135. E. Klasen, letters to parents and siblings, 31 July and 9 and 27 August 1916. BA-MA Freiburg: PH 10II/42.

136. See Reichsarchiv, *Weltkrieg*, x, p. 384, and Reichsarchiv, *Der Weltkrieg 1914 bis 1918. Band 11. Die Kriegsführung im Herbst 1916 und im Winter 1916/17. Vom Wechsel in der Obersten Heeresleitung bis zum Entschluß zum Rückzug in die Siegfried Stellung* (14 vols., Berlin, 1938), xi, pp. 109–13.

137. M. von Gallwitz, *Erleben im Westen, 1916–1918* (Berlin, 1932), p. 115 (entry for 15–18 September 1916).

138. A judgement shown to be justified in Prior and Wilson, *Somme*, pp. 186–90.

139. J. H. Boraston (ed.), *Sir Douglas Haig's Despatches (December 1915–April 1919)* (London, Toronto and New York, 1919), pp. 19–20.

140. Reichsarchiv, *Weltkrieg*, xi, p. 103, and Sheffield, *Somme*, p. 151.

141. *Sanitätsbericht*, iii, pp. 50–51, 53 and 42*. Philpott's claim that the German army suffered 'probably more than 500,000 irreplaceable losses' is not borne out by any official figures and should be regarded as greatly exaggerated. See Philpott, *Bloody Victory*, p. 602.

142. *Sanitätsbericht*, iii, p. 7*.

143. See the Zentralnachweisamt figures reported in J. H. McRandle and J. Quirk, 'The Blood Test Revisited: A New Look at German Casualty Counts in World War I', *The Journal of Military History* 70(3) (July 2006), p. 688, Table 10. The figures almost certainly underestimate the total killed and other casualties but they reflect loss trends accurately.

144. All calculated from *Sanitätsbericht*, iii, pp. 52–3. Gas casualties on the Somme totalled 3,053 men. Nervous casualties totalled 9,354 men. See ibid., pp. 50 and 42*.

145. Quoted in R. Foley, 'Learning War's Lessons: The German Army and the Battle of the Somme, 1916', *The Journal of Military History* 75(2) (April 2011), p. 486.

146. Houlihan, 'Clergy in the Trenches', pp. 192–5, and Ziemann, *Front*, pp. 250–52, on the decline in religion in 1916. For the unusually extreme psychological demands of the Western Front fighting, and particularly 'battles of material' like the Somme, see Watson, *Enduring the Great War*, pp. 22–34.

147. Gallwitz, *Erleben*, pp. 115–16.

148. A. von Thaer, *Generalstabsdienst an der Front und in der O.H.L. Aus Briefen und Tagebuchaufzeichnungen, 1915–1919*, ed. S. A. Kaehler (Göttingen, 1958), p. 92 (entry for 13 October 1916).

149. Watson, *Enduring the Great War*, pp. 150–51. For the Somme, see A. Spemann, diary, 22 October 1916. HStA Stuttgart: M660/041, Nr. 12. For Douaumont, see Horne, *Price of Glory*, p. 314, and H. Fuchs, diary, 29 October 1916. BA-MA Freiburg, MSg 1/2966. For evidence of morale problems in both sectors, see 'Summary of Information. GHQ', 12 January 1917. TNA London: WO 157/17.

150. Gallwitz, *Erleben*, pp. 115–16. For confirmation, see also the railway military police report to stellvertrenden Generalstab des Armee IIIb, 1 September 1916. GLA Karlsruhe: 456 F8/260.

151. Von Thaer, *Generalstabsdienst*, p. 92 (entry for 13 October 1916). More generally, Schuhmacher, *Leben und Seele unseres Soldatenlieds*, p. 170.

152. For more on Italy and Romania, see respectively Thompson, *White War*, pp. 169–225, and Stone, *Eastern Front*, pp. 264–81.

153. Wegs, 'Austrian Economic Mobilization', pp. 99–101.

154. See Herwig, *First World War*, pp. 213–17, Jeřábek, 'Brussilowoffensive', ii, pp. 471–511, and von Zeynek, *Offizier im Generalstabskorps*, p. 257.

155. E. Ludendorff, *My War Memories, 1914–1918* (2 vols., Uckfield, 1919, 2005), i, p. 274.

156. Reichsarchiv, *Weltkrieg*, xi, pp. 11–12 and 62–3.

157. See M. Geyer, 'Rückzug und Zerstörung 1917', in G. Hirschfeld, G. Krumeich and I. Renz (eds.), *Die Deutschen an der Somme, 1914–1918* (Essen, 2006), pp. 163–79.

158. 'Erfahrungen der 1. Armee in der Sommeschlacht (24.6.–26.11.1916)'. GLA Karlsruhe: 456 F13, Nr. 10.

159. See M. Strohn, *The German Army and the Defence of the Reich: Military Doctrine and the Conduct of the Defensive Battle, 1918–1939* (Cambridge, 2011), pp. 49–54. See also esp. Foley, 'Learning War's Lessons', pp. 471–504. For the rise in desertions, see Jahr, *Gewöhnliche Soldaten*, p. 150.

8. DEPRIVATION

1. *Sanitätsbericht*, iii, pp. 6*–7* and 9*, Gratz and Schüller, *Wirtschaftliche Zusammenbruch*, p. 151, Bessel, *Germany*, p. 9, and M.-S. Schulze, 'Austria-Hungary's Economy in World War I', in S. Broadberry and M. Harrison (eds.), *The Economics of World War I* (Cambridge, New York, Melbourne, Madrid, Cape Town, Singapore and São Paulo, 2005), p. 81.

2. A. Hartmuth, letters from his mother, 13 March, 12 and 29 April, 15 November and 1 December 1916, and from his sister, Trudi, 17 November 1916. Author's Collection. Also, V. Ullrich, *Vom Augusterlebnis zur Novemberrevolution. Beiträge zur Sozialgeschichte Hamburgs und Norddeutschlands im Ersten Weltkrieg* (Bremen, 1999), pp. 58–60.

3. *Berliner Tageblatt*, 19 May 1916, cited abridged in A. Skalweit, *Die deutsche Kriegsernährungswirtschaft* (Stuttgart, Berlin and Leipzig, 1927), pp. 200–22.

4. Healy, *Vienna*, pp. 75–6 and 82.

5. Bessel, *Germany*, p. 32, and Schulze, 'Austria-Hungary's Economy', p. 100.

6. G. Bry, *Wages in Germany, 1871–1945* (Princeton, NJ: Princeton University Press, 1960), pp. 197–202 and 212.

7. M. Grandner, *Kooperative Gewerkschaftspolitik in der Kriegswirtschaft: Die freien Gewerkschaften Österreichs im ersten Weltkrieg* (Vienna, Cologne and Weimar, 1992), pp. 97–9 and 197; P. Heumos, '"Kartoffeln her oder es gibt eine Revolution". Hungerkrawalle, Streiks und Massenproteste in den böhmischen Ländern, 1914–1918', in H. Mommsen, D. Kováč, J. Malíř and M. Marek (eds.), *Der Erste Weltkrieg und die Beziehungen zwischen Tschechen, Slowaken und Deutschen* (Essen, 2001), p. 272.

8. Kocka, *Facing Total War*, pp. 84–90, and Mai, *Kriegswirtschaft*, pp. 396–7.

9. J. W. Boyer, 'Silent War and Bitter Peace: The Revolution of 1918 in Austria', *Austrian History Yearbook* 34 (2003), pp. 10–11.

10. A. Czechówna, diary, 14 September 1916. AN Cracow: IT 428/41. For civil servants' impoverishment, see Stellvertreter des k.u.k. Chefs des Generalstabes to Chef des Generalstabes, 12 November 1916 (p. 6). KA Vienna: NL Bolfras, B/75C.

11. Mikułowski Pomorski (ed.), *Kraków w naszej pamięci*, pp. 62–3. Cf. Chickering, *Great War and Urban Life*, pp. 266–7.

12. H. Hristov, *Revolutsionnata Kriza v Bulgaria prez 1918–1919* (Sofia, 1957), pp. 188–9. Also Davis, *Home Fires Burning*, p. 29; B. O'Driscoll, *Zmów Zdrowaśkę. Historia Marii i Jędrzeja Giertychów* (Radom, 2007), p. 28.

13. M. Franc, 'Bread from Wood: Natural Food Substitutes in the Czech Lands during the First World War', in I. Zweiniger-Bargielowska, R. Duffett and A. Drouard (eds.), *Food and War in Twentieth-Century Europe* (Farnham and Burlington, VT, 2011), pp. 76 and 80.

14. J. Tampke, *The Ruhr and Revolution: The Revolutionary Movement in the Rhenish-Westphalian Industrial Region, 1912–1919* (London: Croom Helm, 1979), p. 41.

15. Skalweit, *Deutsche Kriegsernährungswirtschaft*, pp. 53–61. Also Chickering, *Great War and Urban Life*, pp. 266–8, and Juni-Bericht des Gemeinsamen Zentralnachweisebureaus, Auskunftsstelle für Kriegsgefangene, Zensurabteilung über die Stimmung der österreichischen Bevölkerung im Hinterlande', p. 10. AVA Vienna: MdI, Präsidium (1917). 22/gen.: doc. 14234.

16. Daniel, *War from Within*, pp. 38–49 and 54–7, Grandner, *Kooperative Gewerkschaftspolitik*, pp. 147–8, and P. Pastor, 'The Home Front in Hungary, 1914–18', in B. K. Király and N. F. Dreisziger (eds.), *East European Society in World War I* (Boulder, CO, and Highland Lakes, NJ, 1985), p. 126.

17. A. Hartmuth, letters from his mother, 29 April, 16 and 26 May, and 24 October 1916. Author's Collection.

18. Donson, *Youth in the Fatherless Land*, pp. 146–52.

19. E. H. Tobin, 'War and the Working Class: The Case of Düsseldorf, 1914–1918', *Central European History* 18(3–4) (September 1985), pp. 275–98; Mai, *Kriegswirtschaft*, pp. 336 and 348; Grandner, *Kooperative Gewerkschaftspolitik*, p. 157.

20. K.-L. Ay, *Die Entstehung einer Revolution. Die Volksstimmung in Bayern während des Ersten Weltkrieges* (Berlin, 1968), pp. 162–8, and Chickering, *Great War and Urban Life*, pp. 246–9. For Austria, see Healy, *Vienna*, pp. 53–4.

21. Daniel, *War from Within*, p. 203.

22. J. M. Małecki, 'Życie gospodarcze Krakowa w czasie wielkiej wojny 1914–1918', in Towarzystwo Miłośników Historii i Zabytków Krakowa (ed.), *Kraków w czasie I wojny światowej. Materiały sesji naukowej z okazji dni Krakowa w roku 1988* (Cracow, 1990), p. 63. Also Ay, *Entstehung einer Revolution*, p. 166.

23. Davis, *Home Fires Burning*, pp. 216–17. For Austria, see Stellvertreter des k.u.k. Chefs des Generalstabes to Chef des Generalstabes, 12 November 1916, p. 14. KA Vienna: NL Bolfras, B/75C, and F. C. Weber, '"Wir wollen nicht hilflos zu Grunde gehen!" Zur Ernährungskrise der Steiermark im Ersten Weltkrieg und ihren politisch-sozialen Auswirkungen', *Blätter für Heimatkunde* 74(3) (2000), pp. 114–16.

24. Tampke, *Ruhr and Revolution*, p. 43.

25. Offer, *First World War*, p. 56.

26. R. Siedler, 'Behind the Lines: Working-Class Family Life in Wartime Vienna', in R. Wall and J. Winter (eds.), *The Upheaval of War: Family, Work and Welfare in Europe, 1914–1918* (Cambridge, 1988, 2005), pp. 126–7.

27. Chickering, *Great War and Urban Life*, pp. 185–6, and L. Grebler and W. Winkler, *The Cost of the World War to Germany and to Austria-Hungary* (New Haven, CT: Yale University Press, 1940), p. 83. Germany's goat population rose from 3,548,000 in 1913 to 4,321,000 in 1918.

28. Małecki, 'Życie gospodarcze Krakowa', p. 65, and J. Havránek, 'Politische Repression und Versorgungsengpässe in den böhmischen Ländern 1914 bis 1918', in H. Mommsen, D. Kováč, J. Malíř and M. Marek (eds.), *Der Erste Weltkrieg und die Beziehungen zwischen Tschechen, Slowaken und Deutschen* (Essen, 2001), p. 64.

29. A. Hartmuth, letter from his mother, 14 May 1917. Author's Collection.

30. Investigation of men in Ersatzbataillon, IR 46 in Jarotschin, end of 1916. BA-MA Freiburg: PH10II/73.

31. Donson, *Youth in the Fatherless Land*, p. 127. On civilian health more generally, see Offer, *First World War*, pp. 31–3.

32. C. Pirquet, 'Ernährungszustand der Kinder in Österreich während des Krieges und der Nachkriegszeit', in C. Pirquet (ed.), *Volksgesundheit im Kriege* (2 vols., Vienna and New Haven, CT, 1926), i, pp. 152–3.

33. Offer, *First World War*, pp. 34, 38 and 45–53, J. Roesle, 'Die Geburts- und Sterblichkeitsverhältnisse', in F. Bumm (ed.), *Deutschlands Gesundheitsverhältnisse unter dem Einfluss des Weltkrieges* (Stuttgart, Berlin and Leipzig, and New Haven, CT, 1928), pp. 54–9, and extract from a memorandum of the Reich Health Office, 16 December 1916, reproduced in H. Michaelis, E. Schraepler and G. Scheel (eds.), *Ursachen und Folgen. Vom deutschen Zusammenbruch 1918 und 1945 bis zur staatlichen Neuordnung Deutschlands in der Gegenwart. Eine Urkunden- und Dokumentensammlung zur Zeitgeschichte. Der Wende des ersten Weltkrieges und der Beginn der innerpolitischen Wandlung 1916/1917* (29 vols., Berlin, n.d.), i, pp. 283–8 (doc. 149).

34. Grebler and Winkler, *Cost of the World War*, p. 147.

35. See ch. 4. Also, for epidemics later in the war, Hoffmann-Holter, 'Abreisendmachung', p. 70.

36. Loewenfeld-Russ, *Regelung der Volksernährung*, pp. 7–10 and 147; Bobič, *War and Faith*, p. 243, and, for Croatia, the 'Oesterreich' morale reports in AVA Vienna: MdI, Präsidium. Erster Weltkrieg: Karton 33.

37. Gratz and Schüller, *Wirtschaftliche Zusammenbruch*, p. 81.

38. See K. Helly, 'Statistik der Gesundheitsverhältnisse der Bevölkerung der Republic Österreich in und nach dem Kriege', in Pirquet (ed.), *Volksgesundheit im Kriege*, i, p. 20, and Pirquet, 'Ernährungszustand der Kinder in Österreich', p. 153.

39. Healy, *Vienna*, p. 41.

40. Skalweit, *Deutsche Kriegsernährungswirtschaft*, pp. 10–12.

41. A. Ritschl, 'The Pity of Peace: Germany's Economy at War, 1914–1918 and Beyond', in S. Broadberry and M. Harrison (eds.), *The Economics of World War I* (Cambridge, New York, Melbourne, Madrid, Cape Town, Singapore and São Paulo, 2005), p. 46.

42. Grebler and Winkler, *Cost of the War*, pp. 83–4, and Ziemann, *Front*, pp. 292 and 308.

43. Quoted in R. G. Moeller, 'Dimensions of Social Conflict in the Great War: The View from the German Countryside', *Central European History* 14(2) (June 1981), p. 152.

44. Loewenfeld-Russ, *Regelung der Volksernährung*, pp. 7–9, 28–31 and 134–5.

45. Gratz and Schüller, *Wirtschaftliche Zusammenbruch*, p. 145, and Weber, '"Wir wollen nicht hilflos zu Grunde gehen!"', p. 100.

46. Loewenfeld-Russ, *Regelung der Volksernährung*, pp. 31–4.

47. C. F. Wargelin, 'The Economic Collapse of Austro-Hungarian Dualism, 1914–1918', *East European Quarterly* 34(3) (September 2000), pp. 268–72, and Loewenfeld-Russ, *Regelung der Volksernährung*, pp. 64–5.

48. Galántai, *Hungary*, pp. 119–21.

49. Gratz and Schüller, *Wirtschaftliche Zusammenbruch*, pp. 81, 247 (Stürgkh to Tisza, 17 December 1915) and 266 (Stürgkh to Tisza, 29 February 1916). Loewenfeld-Russ, *Regelung der Volksernährung*, pp. 48, 62, 64 and 110–12.

50. Osborne, *Britain's Economic Blockade*, pp. 120–32, and Skalweit, *Deutsche Kriegsernährungswirtschaft*, p. 23.

51. Skalweit, *Deutsche Kriegsernährungswirtschaft*, pp. 18–22, and Loewenfeld-Russ, *Regelung der Volksernährung*, pp. 363–7.

52. Davis, *Home Fires Burning*, pp. 115–17, and Feldman, *Army, Industry and Labor*, pp. 110–16.

53. Loewenfeld-Russ, *Regelung der Volksernährung*, pp. 289–307. Also Stellvertreter des k.u.k. Chefs des Generalstabes to Chef des Generalstabes, 12 November 1916 (p. 4). KA Vienna: NL Bolfras, B/75C.

54. Skalweit, *Deutsche Kriegsernährungswirtschaft*, p. 211, Davis, *Home Fires Burning*, pp. 47 and 163, Healy, *Vienna*, p. 43, Loewenfeld-Russ, *Regelung der Volksernährung*, p. 344, and Pastor, 'The Home Front in Hungary', p. 126.

55. Skalweit, *Deutsche Kriegsernährungswirtschaft*, p. 199.

56. Postcard entitled 'Bürgerliches Kochrezept', sent 13 October 1917. Author's Collection.

57. J. von Bókay and A. Juba, 'Ernährungszustand der Kinder in Ungarn', in C. Pirquet (ed.), *Volksgesundheit im Kriege* (2 vols., Vienna and New Haven, CT, 1926), i, p. 184.

58. Offer, *First World War*, p. 29, and Loewenfeld-Russ, *Regelung der Volksernährung*, p. 335.

59. Quoted in Daniel, *War from Within*, p. 205. See also Offer, *First World War*, p. 33.

60. Davis, *Home Fires Burning*, pp. 162–5.

61. Hämmerle (ed.), *Kindheit*, p. 52. Also Loewenfeld-Russ, *Regelung der Volksernährung*, p. 222, and Davis, *Home Fires Burning*, p. 41.

62. Skalweit, *Deutsche Kriegsernährungswirtschaft*, pp. 208–9, and Loewenfeld-Russ, *Regelung der Volksernährung*, p. 330.

63. Healy, *Vienna*, p. 44.

64. Loewenfeld-Russ, *Regelung der Volksernährung*, pp. 337 and 352, Davis, *Home Fires Burning*, pp. 170, 174, 187–8 and 195, and Tobin, 'War and the Working Class', p. 285.

65. Skalweit, *Deutsche Kriegsernährungswirtschaft*, pp. 40–43.

66. 'Eine Kriegsküche in Salzburg', *Neuigkeits-Welt-Blatt. Nr. 234* (12 October 1916), p. 23. Also Havránek, 'Politische Repression und Versorgungsengpässe', p. 63.

67. Davis, *Home Fires Burning*, pp. 138–46.

68. Loewenfeld-Russ, *Regelung der Volksernährung*, p. 354.

69. Mick, *Kriegserfahrungen*, p. 186. Also Davis, *Home Fires Burning*, pp. 138–57, and Chickering, *Great War and Urban Life*, p. 458. The statistic for participation in metropolises is calculated from figures in Skalweit, *Deutsche Kriegsernährungswirtschaft*, p. 51. A metropolis is defined here as a city with over half a million residents.

70. K. O. Nass (ed.), *Ein preußischer Landrat in Monarchie, Demokratie und Diktatur. Lebenserinnerungen des Walter zur Nieden* (Berlin, 2006), pp. 77–9.

71. Stellvertreter des k.u.k. Chefs des Generalstabes to Chef des Generalstabes, 12 November 1916, pp. 14–15. KA Vienna: NL Bolfras, B/75C. For an example of such localized obstruction, see G. Prassnigger, 'Hunger in Tirol', in K. Eisterer and R. Steininger (eds.), *Tirol und der Erste Weltkrieg* (Innsbruck, 1995), p. 186, and for similar conduct by municipalities in Germany, see K. Allen, 'Sharing Scarcity: Bread Rationing and the First World War in Berlin, 1914–1923', *Journal of Social History* 32(2) (Winter 1998), p. 377.

72. Mai, *Kriegswirtschaft*, pp. 414–15, Skalweit, *Deutsche Kriegsernährungswirtschaft*, pp. 221–2, Davis, *Home Fires Burning*, pp. 70 and 184, and Siedler, 'Behind the Lines', pp. 126–7.

73. Chickering, *Great War and Urban Life*, pp. 176–7, and Mick, *Kriegserfahrungen*, p. 183. Cf. Małecki, 'Życie gospodarcze Krakowa', p. 64, and W. von Schierbrand, 'The Food Situation in Austria-Hungary', *The North American Review* 205(734) (January 1917), p. 49.

74. See Thorner Magistrat to Königliches Gouvernement, 14 May 1915, and the memo of 26 May 1915 furloughing Landsturmmann Frisch. Only in

April 1916 did the army refuse to renew his furlough. AP Toruń: Akta Miasta Torunia: Nr. C9257, fos. 99, 101 and 155.

75. Hämmerle (ed.), *Kindheit*, pp. 328–33.

76. Saul, 'Jugend im Schatten des Krieges', pp. 114–15, Donson, *Youth in the Fatherless Land*, pp. 144–5, and Nass (ed.), *Ein preußischer Landrat in Monarchie*, p. 82.

77. Report of XIV Armeekorps, quoted in Kriegsministerium, 'Zusammenstellung der Monats-Berichte der stellv. Generalkommandos' for November 1916, 3 December 1916, p. 6. GStA PK, Berlin: I. HA Rep 90A, Nr. 2685. Cf. also Kriegsministerium, 'Zusammenstellung der Monats-Berichte der stellv. Generalkommandos vom 15.9.16', 26 September 1916, ibid. (p. 3 of report).

78. Moeller, 'Dimensions of Social Conflict', pp. 147–51, Offer, *First World War*, pp. 64–8, and Ziemann, *Front*, pp. 311–12.

79. Stellv. Generalkdo, XI Armeekorps, Cassel, 13 October 1916. HStA Hessen: 405: Nr. 2776: fo. 232.

80. Ministerium für Landwirtschaft, Domänen und Forsten to sämtliche Regierungspräsidenten, 22 February 1917. HStA Hessen: 405: Nr. 2777: fo. 174.

81. Nicolai, *Nachrichtendienst*, p. 128.

82. Skalweit, *Deutsche Kriegsernährungswirtschaft*, pp. 204–6.

83. Hämmerle (ed.), *Kindheit*, p. 46, Ziemann, *Front*, pp. 291–5, 314–18 and 341–4. Also Bobič, *War and Faith*, p. 159, and Healy, *Vienna*, pp. 54–5.

84. Kriegsministerium, 'Zusammenstellung der Monats-Berichte der stellv. Generalkommandos vom 3.12.16', GStA PK, Berlin: I. HA Rep 90A, Nr. 2685 (pp. 5–6 of report), and Healy, *Vienna*, p. 53.

85. Resolution of Vorstands- und Vertrauensmännersitzung der Mittelstandsvereinigung für Mitteldeutschland, Sitz Wiesbaden, 18 August 1916. HStA Hessen: 408: Nr. 121: fos. 143–5.

86. Davis, *Home Fires Burning*, pp. 185–9 and 195–6.

87. J. Baten and R. Schulz, 'Making Profits in Wartime: Corporate Profits, Inequality, and GDP in Germany during the First World War', *The Economic History Review*, New Series 58(1) (February 2005), esp. pp. 43–9 and 52–3. Also Ritschl, 'Pity of Peace', pp. 53–7. This new research contradicts and replaces Jürgen Kocka's classic thesis in *Facing Total War* that wealth redistribution in favour of the rich brought about revolution at war's end.

88. 'Der Kettenhandel', *Die Neue Zeitung. 9. Jahrgang, Nr. 274* (3 October 1916), p. 6.

89. Davis, *Home Fires Burning*, pp. 80–81, 85 and 89, and Healy, *Vienna*, pp. 65 and 68.

90. M. Liepmann, *Krieg und Kriminalität in Deutschland* (Stuttgart, Berlin, Leipzig and New Haven, CT, 1930), pp. 15, 56, 134, 136 and 139–43. For rationing fraud, see Skalweit, *Deutsche Kriegsernährungswirtschaft*, pp. 199–200. For the alleged relationship between women's sex drive and criminal tendencies, see F. Exner, *Krieg und Kriminalität in Österreich. Mit einem Beitrag über die Kriminalität der Militärpersonen von Prof Dr G. Lelewer* (Vienna and New Haven, CT, 1927), p. 147.

91. Liepmann, *Krieg und Kriminalität in Deutschland*, p. 98, and Exner, *Krieg und Kriminalität*, p. 171.

92. Donson, *Youth in the Fatherless Land*, pp. 126, 129, 137–41 and 166. For Austria, see Exner, *Krieg und Kriminalität*, pp. 172–87.

93. Donson, *Youth in the Fatherless Land*, pp. 149–52 and 166–70; Daniel, *War from Within*, pp. 160–70; Healy, *Vienna*, pp. 251–4. In backward Galicia, the fear of youth depravity appears only to have begun in the summer of 1917. See Prezydym c.k. Namiestnictwa, 6 August 1917, in AN Cracow: DPKr 117: 459.

94. Aleksandra Czechówna, diary (p. 69), 8 March 1917. AN Cracow: IT 428/41. Also Healy, *Vienna*, pp. 69–71.

95. 'Wie man an fleischlosen Tagen in Krakau lebt', *Neuigkeits-Welt-Blatt*. Nr. 234 (12 October 1916), p. 25.

96. Loch, '"Aufklärung der Bevölkerung"', p. 57, fn. 106; account of Vorstands- und Vertrauensmännersitzung der Mittelstandsvereinigung für Mitteldeutschland, Sitz Wiesbaden, 18 August 1916. HStA Hessen: 408: Nr. 121: fo. 143.

97. Skalweit, *Deutsche Kriegsernährungswirtschaft*, pp. 209 and 214, and Ay, *Entstehung einer Revolution*, pp. 137–48.

98. J. W. Boyer, *Culture and Political Crisis in Vienna: Christian Socialism in Power, 1897–1918* (Chicago, IL, and London, 1995), pp. 420–21.

99. Report on Rosental, politischer Bezirk Reichenberg, 1916. AVA Vienna: MdI, Präsidiale, Varia Erster Weltkrieg: Karton 33. Also Stürgkh to Tisza, 15 October 1916, reproduced in Gratz and Schüller, *Wirtschaftliche Zusammenbruch*, pp. 305–6.

100. Reports on Prague, 1916. AVA Vienna: MdI, Präsidiale, Varia Erster Weltkrieg: Karton 33.

101. Zahra, *Kidnapped Souls*, pp. 93–4. Also Loewenfeld-Russ, *Regelung der Volksernährung*, p. 333, and Prassnigger, 'Hunger in Tirol', p. 186.

102. E. Zechlin, *Die deutsche Politik und die Juden im Ersten Weltkrieg* (Göttingen, 1969), pp. 518–19, 524–7.

103. Major General Ernst von Wrisberg, the Director of the General War Department within the War Ministry, claimed after the war that the census was instituted in response to public complaints about Jewish shirking. He also

published its results. See E. von Wrisberg, *Heer und Heimat 1914–1918* (Leipzig, 1921), pp. 93–5. More generally on the notorious 'Jew Count', see Angress, 'Das deutsche Militär und die Juden im Ersten Weltkrieg', pp. 77–146, and Zechlin, *Deutsche Politik*, pp. 527–39.

104. For Bauer, see M. Kitchen, 'Militarism and the Development of Fascist Ideology: The Political Ideas of Colonel Max Bauer, 1916–1918', *Central European History* 8(3) (September 1975), pp. 199–220.

105. Segall, *Die deutschen Juden*, esp. pp. 9–17 and 35. These 2,022 Jews represented 9 per cent of around 220,000 officers commissioned during the war. Some Jews were commissioned by the armies of the southern German states before the war, but the overwhelming majority received their commission in the war years. It should be noted, however, that given the higher average level of education among German Jews than the rest of the German population, Jewish middle-class men may still have been under-represented in the officer corps, even at the war's end. For total officer figures, see Watson, *Enduring the Great War*, p. 121.

106. Kriegsministerium, 'Zusammenstellung der Monats-Berichte der stellv. Generalkommandos vom 3.12.16', GStA PK, Berlin: I. HA Rep 90A, Nr. 2685 (p. 10 of report).

107. For the much more active and successful political anti-Semitism in Austria compared with Germany, see Lindemann, *Esau's Tears*, pp. 334–54.

108. Rozenblit, *Reconstructing a National Identity*, p. 15.

109. Rechter, 'Galicia in Vienna', pp. 114–15 and 119.

110. Hoffmann-Holter, 'Abreisendmachung', pp. 91–2.

111. Mentzel, 'Kriegsflüchtlinge', pp. 172–3, and Hoffmann-Holter, 'Abreisendmachung', pp. 79 and 83–94. For Bohemia, see Zahra, *Kidnapped Souls*, p. 93. Also k.u.k. Militärkommando in Prag, 'Demonstration in Prag', 2 June 1917, p. 1, and k.u.k. Stationskommandant in Pilsen, 'Unruhen in Pilsen', 13 August 1917, p. 2. KA Vienna: MKSM 1917 (Karton 1305) 28–2/10–17.

112. Hämmerle (ed.), *Kindheit*, p. 304.

113. A. Hartmuth, letter from his sister, 19 January 1917. Author's Collection.

114. Morale reports, Bukovsko, pol. Bezirk Wittingau. AVA Vienna: MdI, Präsidium. Varia Erster Weltkrieg: Karton 33. More generally, see Healy, *Vienna*, pp. 64–8, and Davis, *Home Fires Burning*, esp. pp. 129–35.

115. Ferguson, *Pity of War*, p. 275.

116. Ullrich, *Vom Augusterlebnis zur Novemberrevolution*, pp. 58–60.

117. Heumos, '"Kartoffeln her oder es gibt eine Revolution"', pp. 256–7.

118. D. D. Alder, 'Friedrich Adler: Evolution of a Revolutionary', *German Studies Review* 1(3) (October 1978), p. 279.

119. For Adler and the assassination, see Alder, 'Friedrich Adler', pp. 270–84. For the public reception, see Healy, *Vienna*, p. 32, and for the student march, see

morale reports, Vienna. AVA Vienna: MdI, Präsidium. Varia Erster Welt-krieg: Karton 33.

120. Kriegsministerium, 'Zusammenstellung der Monats-Berichte der stellv. Generalkommandos vom 15.12.16'. GStA PK Berlin: I. HA Rep Nr. 90A, 2685 (p. 4 of report).

9. REMOBILIZATION

1. Ludendorff, *My War Memories*, ii, pp. 409–10.

2. W. Pyta, *Hindenburg. Herrschaft zwischen Hohenzollern und Hitler* (Munich, 2007, 2009), p. 246. For Hindenburg's public image, see also ibid., pp. 115–53, and for his political ambition, pp. 246–83. Also Goltz, *Hindenburg*, pp. 14–25 and 33–42.

3. M. Nebelin, *Ludendorff. Diktator im Ersten Weltkrieg* (Munich, 2010), pp. 35–6 and 81–97.

4. Ludendorff, *My War Memories*, esp. i, pp. 2–12.

5. Gudmundsson, *Stormtroop Tactics*, pp. 83–4. Foley, 'Learning War's Lessons', pp. 472–5 and 487–503.

6. E. von Wrisberg, *Wehr und Waffen, 1914–1918* (Leipzig, 1922), p. 96. More generally, see M. Geyer, *Deutsche Rüstungspolitik, 1860–1980* (Frankfurt am Main, 1984), pp. 98–103.

7. Quoted in Nebelin, *Ludendorff*, p. 246.

8. Feldman, *Army, Industry and Labor*, p. 169, and Kitchen, 'Militarism and the Development of Fascist Ideology', pp. 202–3.

9. Feldman, *Army, Industry and Labor*, pp. 180–96.

10. Ibid., pp. 194 and 291–300. See also Ludendorff, *My War Memories*, i, p. 342.

11. W. Groener, *Lebenserinnerungen. Jugend, Generalstab, Weltkrieg*, ed. F. Hiller von Gaertringen (Göttingen, 1957), p. 350; Ludendorff, *My War Memories*, i, pp. 339–40; Nicolai, *Nachrichtendienst*, p. 115.

12. See S. Gross, 'Confidence and Gold: German War Finance, 1914–1918', *Central European History* 42(2) (June 2009), pp. 242–3.

13. Feldman, *Army, Industry and Labor*, pp. 152–9, 255–6 and 262–73. Also von Wrisberg, *Wehr und Waffen*, pp. 94 and 285–8.

14. J. Thiel, *'Menschenbassin Belgien'. Anwerbung, Deportation und Zwangs-arbeit im Ersten Weltkrieg* (Essen, 2007), p. 80, and Feldman, *Army, Industry and Labor*, pp. 198–9.

15. Tampke, *Ruhr and Revolution*, p. 35.

16. E. Ludendorff (ed.), *The General Staff and its Problems: The History of the Relations Between the High Command and the German Imperial Government as Revealed by Official Documents*, trans. F. A. Holt (2 vols., London,

n.d.), i, pp. 76–9. For a good discussion, see Feldman, *Army, Industry and Labor*, pp. 172–3 and 301.

17. Rauchensteiner, *Tod des Doppeladlers*, pp. 404–5. For the 1912 War Law, see Wegs, 'Austrian Economic Mobilization', p. 11. For the extent of the decline, see the figures in Gratz and Schüller, *Wirtschaftliche Zusammen-bruch*, pp. 109–23. Only machine guns bucked the trend, but even here decline set in from early 1918.

18. Feldman, *Army, Industry and Labor*, pp. 174–8, 186–8 and 200. The Third OHL's calculations in insisting that the Reichstag must pass a law legitimizing the coercive measures are spelled out in Hindenburg's letter to the Chancellor of 1 November 1916, reproduced in Ludendorff (ed.), *The General Staff and its Problems*, i, pp. 98–9.

19. Feldman, *Army, Industry and Labor*, p. 209.

20. Ibid., pp. 190, 197–217. The draft bill of 10 November, which was the same as that put before the Reichstag Steering Committee except in the detail that the age of obligation for Patriotic Service was raised by ministers from sixteen to seventeen, is reproduced in W. Deist (ed.), *Militär und Innenpolitik im Weltkrieg, 1914–1918* (2 vols., Düsseldorf, 1970), i, pp. 515–19.

21. Ludendorff (ed.), *The General Staff and its Problems*, i, p. 103, footnote, and the extract from the minutes of the Prussian State Ministry meeting of 1 December 1916 reproduced in Deist (ed.), *Militär und Innenpolitik*, i, p. 527.

22. Feldman, *Army, Industry and Labor*, pp. 217–49.

23. Ludendorff, *My War Memories*, i, p. 333.

24. This follows Mai, *Kriegswirtschaft*, pp. 311–15. Feldman is more condemnatory but less convincing about the impact of the Auxiliary Service Law on the war effort. See his *Army, Industry and Labor*, pp. 308–16.

25. J. Oltmer, 'Zwangsmigration und Zwangsarbeit – Ausländische Arbeitskräfte und bäuerliche Ökonomie im Ersten Weltkrieg', *Tel Aviver Jahrbuch für deutsche Geschichte* 27 (1998), p. 142.

26. U. Herbert, *A History of Foreign Labor in Germany, 1880–1980: Seasonal Workers/Forced Laborers/Guest Workers* (Ann Arbor, MI, 1990), pp. 87, 90 and 94–5. Also E. M. Kulischer, *Europe on the Move: War and Population Changes, 1917–1947* (New York, 1948), p. 167, and, for an example of the controls, stellv. Gen Kdo. des XVIII. Armeekorps, order, 1 November 1915. AP Katowice: Oddział w Raciborzu: 18/237/4: 80: fo. 143.

27. M. Stibbe, *British Civilian Internees in Germany: The Ruhleben Camp, 1914–18* (Manchester and New York, 2008), esp. pp. 24–5.

28. Thiel, *'Menschenbassin Belgien'*, pp. 39 and 79–85. For Bissing's paternalistic instincts, see also Nebelin, *Ludendorff*, p. 253.

29. L. von Köhler, *Die Staatsverwaltung der besetzten Gebiete. Belgien* (Stuttgart, Berlin, Leipzig and New Haven, CT, 1927), pp. 151–2, and Thiel, '*Menschenbassin Belgien*', pp. 105–8, 123–4 and 136–7.

30. Thiel, '*Menschenbassin Belgien*', pp. 140–62, and M. Spoerer, 'The Mortality of Allied Prisoners of War and Belgian Civilian Deportees in German Custody during the First World War: A Reappraisal of the Effects of Forced Labour', *Population Studies* 60(2) (July 2006), p. 129.

31. Thiel, '*Menschenbassin Belgien*', pp. 202–6 and 220–37.

32. Ludendorff, *My War Memories*, i, p. 336.

33. R. Nachtigal, 'Zur Anzahl der Kriegsgefangenen im Ersten Weltkrieg', *Militärgeschichtliche Zeitschrift* 67(2) (2008), pp. 349–63, and H. Jones, *Violence against Prisoners of War in the First World War: Britain, France and Germany, 1914–1920* (Cambridge, 2011), p. 40.

34. See Jones, *Violence against Prisoners of War*, pp. 93–110.

35. Article 6 of the Annex entitled 'Regulations Respecting the Laws and Customs of War on Land' to 'Convention Concerning the Laws and Customs of War on Land. 2d Peace Conference, The Hague, 18 Oct. 1907. IV', in *Conventions and Declarations*.

36. K. Rawe, '. . . *wir werden sie schon zur Arbeit bringen!' Ausländerbeschäftigung und Zwangsarbeit im Ruhrkohlenbergbau während des Ersten Weltkrieges* (Essen, 2005), p. 75. Also Herbert, *History of Foreign Labor*, p. 90, Nachtigal, 'Zur Anzahl der Kriegsgefangenen', p. 352, and V. Moritz and H. Leidinger, *Zwischen Nutzen und Bedrohung. Die russischen Kriegsgefangenen in Österreich (1914–1921)* (Bonn, 2005), pp. 110–20.

37. Nachtigal, 'Zur Anzahl der Kriegsgefangenen', p. 352, and Moritz and Leidinger, *Zwischen Nutzen und Bedrohung*, p. 116.

38. Oltmer, 'Zwangsmigration und Zwangsarbeit', pp. 158–6.

39. For the death figures, see Nachtigal, 'Zur Anzahl der Kriegsgefangenen', pp. 356 and 360–61. For the conditions faced by prisoners in the Ruhr mines, see Rawe, '. . . *wir werden sie schon zur Arbeit bringen!*'. Jones, *Violence against Prisoners of War*, pp. 127–222, offers the best description of conditions in prisoner labour companies in the front area. The percentage of German prisoners in prisoner labour companies refers to August 1916.

40. Oltmer, 'Zwangsmigration und Zwangsarbeit', pp. 166–7.

41. Helene Grus to stellv. Gen Kdo., V, A. K., 5 April 1918. AP Poznań: Polizei-Präsidium Posen 8991: doc. 30.

42. L. M. Todd, '"The Soldier's Wife Who Ran Away with the Russian": Sexual Infidelities in World War I Germany', *Central European History* 44(2) (June 2011), pp. 257–78, and Daniel, *War from Within*, pp. 144–7.

43. Kriegsministerium, order to stellvertretende Generalkommandos entitled 'Anstiftung der Kriegsgefangenen zur Meuterei', 20 May 1917. GLA Karlsruhe: 456 F109: Nr. 1.

44. Stellv. Gen Kdo. des XVII. Armeekorps in Danzig to Landrat Thorn, 29 June 1917. AP Toruń: Starostwo Powiatowe w Toruniu (Landratsamt Thorn): Nr. 1025: fo. 129.

45. See C. von Roeder, 'Vom verhängnisvollen Einfluß der Sabotageakte auf die Kriegführung', in W. Jost (ed.), *Was wir vom Weltkrieg nicht wissen* (Leipzig, 1936), pp. 149–53. Roeder was the chief of the counter-espionage service ('Abwehrdienst') in Deputy Section IIIB of the German General Staff. While his account is exaggerated, he supplies interesting evidence, and much of what he claims is supported by contemporary documentation. For an example, see Order from Chef des Stellvertretenden Generalstab der Armee, Abteilung IIIb in Berlin, 8 April 1917. HHStA Wiesbaden: Preußisches Regierungspräsidium Wiesbaden (405): Nr. 2739: fo. 200.

46. The quotations are taken from a large, alarmingly orange poster issued by General Wagner of the stellv. Gen Kdo. des XVII. Armeekorps in Danzig, 4 May 1917. AP Toruń: Starostwo Powiatowe w Toruniu (Landratsamt Thorn): Nr. 1024: fo. 281. Cf. also Gouvernement der Festung Mainz to Territ. Komm. Mainz; Reg. Präsident Wiesbaden; Militär. Polizeistelle Mainz und Wiesbaden; Geh. Feldpolizei Bingen; Ic und F. G. A, 12 May 1917. HHStA Wiesbaden: Preußisches Regierungspräsidium Wiesbaden (405): Nr. 2739: fo. 207, and stellv. Gen Kdo. des V. Armeekorps to Erzbischof von Gnesen und Posen Dr. Dalbor, 18 June 1917. AA Poznań: OA X 76.

47. Regierungs-Präsident Wiesbaden, memo recounting a presentation by the stellvertretenden Generalstab der Armee, 27 January 1918. HHStA Wiesbaden: Preußisches Regierungspräsidium Wiesbaden (405): Nr. 2739: fo. 244.

48. Herbert, *History of Foreign Labor*, p. 99.

49. Figure from German propaganda poster 'Wer ist Sieger?', AP Poznań: Polizei-Präsidium Posen 5024: doc. 196.

50. Numbers from: B. Benvindo and B. Majerus, 'Belgien zwischen 1914 und 1918: ein Labor für den totalen Krieg?', A. Bauerkämper and E. Julien (eds.), *Durchhalten! Krieg und Gesellschaft im Vergleich, 1914–1918* (Göttingen, 2010), p. 136, T. Scheer, *Zwischen Front und Heimat. Österreich-Ungarns Militärverwaltungen im Ersten Weltkrieg* (Frankfurt am Main, 2009), p. 22, Gumz, *Resurrection and Collapse*, p. 6, and L. Mayerhofer, *Zwischen Freund und Feind – Deutsche Besatzung in Rumänien, 1916–1918* (Munich, 2010), pp. 40–41.

51. For figures, see M. Huber, *La Population de la France pendant la Guerre* (Paris and New Haven, CT, 1931), pp. 391–2.

52. Köhler, *Staatsverwaltung der besetzen Gebiete*, pp. 6–8, Mayerhofer, *Zwischen Freund und Feind*, pp. 46–52, and Scheer, *Zwischen Front und Heimat*, pp. 59–60.

53. Quoted in D. Hamlin, '"Dummes Geld": Money, Grain, and the Occupation of Romania in WWI', *Central European History* 42(3) (September 2009), p. 457.

54. Grebler and Winkler, *Cost of the World War*, pp. 76 and 97.

55. Ludendorff, *My War Memories*, i, pp. 354 and 287-8.

56. *Verhandlungen des Reichstags. XIII Legislaturperiode. II. Session. Band 306. Stenographische Berichte. Von der Eröffnungssitzung am 4. August 1914 bis zur 34. Sitzung am 16. März 1916* (Berlin, 1916), p. 660.

57. Stellvertreter des k.u.k. Chefs des Generalstabes to Chef des Generalstabes, 12 November 1916, pp. 18-19. KA Vienna: NL Bolfras, B/75C.

58. Von Zeynek, *Offizier im Generalstabskorps*, p. 276.

59. Skalweit, *Deutsche Kriegsernährungswirtschaft*, pp. 10-11; Grebler and Winkler, *Cost of the World War*, p. 83.

60. Ludendorff, *My War Memories*, i, p. 354.

61. Skalweit, *Deutsche Kriegsernährungswirtschaft*, p. 22.

62. Mayerhofer, *Zwischen Freund und Feind*, p. 214.

63. A. Arz von Straußenburg, *Zur Geschichte des Grossen Krieges, 1914-1918* (Vienna, Leipzig and Munich, 1924), pp. 189, 193 and 195-6. For the Habsburg officer corps' mentality and its struggle with civilians over food, see Gumz, *Resurrection and Collapse*, pp. 176-92.

64. Mayerhofer, *Zwischen Freund und Feind*, p. 212, and von Zeynek, *Offizier im Generalstabskorps*, p. 314.

65. A. Hartmuth, letter from his mother, 24 October 1916. Author's Collection.

66. See BN Warsaw: Microfilm 89065: Jaszczurowscy v. Jaszczórowscy herbu Rawicz: 'Wielka wojna światowa – Pamiętnik Tadeusza Alojzego Jaszczurowskiego', p. 105, Romer, *Pamiętniki*, p. 97, and Hamlin, '"Dummes Geld"', p. 464.

67. For a good introduction to the priorities of the Central Powers in the east, see S. Lehnstaedt, 'Imperiale Ordnungen statt Germanisierung. Die Mittelmächte in Kongresspolen, 1915-1918', *Osteuropa* 64(2-4) (2014), pp. 221-32.

68. Ludendorff, *My War Memories*, i, pp. 206 and 189.

69. Liulevičius, *War Land*, pp. 71-2, 96-9, 123-5 and 198, and C. Westerhoff, *Zwangsarbeit im Ersten Weltkrieg. Deutsche Arbeitskräftepolitik im besetzten Polen und Litauen, 1914-1918* (Paderborn, 2012), p. 171.

70. Quoted in Liulevičius, *War Land*, p. 66.

71. Ibid., pp. 65, 92-3, 100-103. Also Ludendorff, *My War Memories*, i, pp. 198 and 202.

72. Ludendorff, *My War Memories*, i, pp. 198-9. For recent historiography stressing similarities between Imperial German military and Nazi practices, see for example Hull, *Absolute Destruction*, esp. pp. 243-8.

73. Liulevičius, *War Land*, p. 72, and Ludendorff, *My War Memories*, i, pp. 197–8. For troop numbers, see *Sanitätsbericht*, III, p. 7*.

74. Westerhoff, *Zwangsarbeit*, pp. 143–77.

75. Ibid., pp. 191–6, 211–21 and 298–303, and Liulevičius, *War Land*, pp. 73–4.

76. A. Strazhas, *Deutsche Ostpolitik im Ersten Weltkrieg. Der Fall Ober Ost, 1915–1917* (Wiesbaden, 1993), p. 47.

77. Ibid., pp. 48–9. Also Liulevičius, *War Land*, pp. 75–6.

78. Liulevičius, *War Land*, pp. 200–15.

79. H. McPhail, *The Long Silence: Civilian Life under the German Occupation of Northern France, 1914–1918* (London and New York, 1999, 2001), pp. 45–8 and 51. Also Armee-Oberkommando 1, 'Armeebefehl betreffend Ueberwachung der Civilbevölkerung', 16 May 1917, reissued 10 January 1918. GLA Karlsruhe: 456 f6/250.

80. Schaepdrijver, 'Belgium', p. 391, and McPhail, *Long Silence*, pp. 137–9.

81. Thiel, 'Menschenbassin Belgien', pp. 127–9, and Hull, *Absolute Destruction*, pp. 252–3.

82. C. Gide and W. Ovalid, *Le Bilan de la Guerre pour la France* (Paris and New Haven, CT, 1931), pp. 175–7, and Fontaine, *French Industry*, pp. 16, 109–10 and 405.

83. Hull, *Absolute Destruction*, p. 252, and McPhail, *Long Silence*, pp. 48, 93 and 226.

84. For Bissing, see above. For factors moderating the conduct of his regime, see Hull, *Absolute Destruction*, p. 230, and for his economic policy, see Thiel, 'Menschenbassin Belgien', pp. 40–46.

85. H. Pirenne, *La Belgique et la Guerre Mondiale* (Paris and New Haven, CT, 1928), p. 127, and C. de Kerchove de Denterghem, *L'industrie belge pendant l'occupation Allemande, 1914–1918* (Paris and New Haven, CT, 1927), p. 28.

86. Thiel, 'Menschenbassin Belgien', pp. 88 and 247, and Herbert, *History of Foreign Labor*, p. 106.

87. B. Little, 'Humanitarian Relief in Europe and the Analogue of War, 1914–1918', in J. D. Keene and M. S. Neiberg (eds.), *Finding Common Ground: New Directions in First World War Studies* (Leiden and Boston, 2011), pp. 141–3 and 146–9, and McPhail, *Long Silence*, pp. 61–88.

88. A. Henry, *Études sur l'occupation allemande en Belgique* (Brussels, 1920), pp. 195–6 and 225.

89. A. Solanský, 'German Administration in Belgium', unpublished PhD thesis, Columbia University (1928), p. 115, and P. Liberman, *Does Conquest Pay? The Exploitation of Occupied Industrial Societies* (Princeton, NJ, 1996), p. 77.

90. Liberman, *Does Conquest Pay?*, pp. 73, 75 and 84. Also Thiel, 'Menschen-bassin Belgien', p. 42.

91. Conze, *Polnische Nation*, pp. 87–8 and 114–15.

92. Ibid., pp. 70–72 and 102–5.

93. See Westerhoff, *Zwangsarbeit*, pp. 203 and 233–4. Also, for documenta-tion on the 'Komittee den Notleidenden in den von deutschen Truppen besetzten Teilen Russisch-Polen', see AA Poznań: OA X 40, and the report of the Regierungspräsident in Marienwerder to Oberpräsident of West Prussia, 15 May 1915, in AP Gdańsk: Rejencja w Kwidzynie (10): 10229: fo. 309.

94. See, for the latest work on this state-building, J. C. Kauffman, 'Sovereignty and the Search for Order in German-Occupied Poland, 1915–1918', unpub-lished PhD thesis, Stanford University (2008).

95. Kries, quoted in Conze, *Polnische Nation*, p. 71.

96. Ihnatowicz, 'Gospodarka na ziemiach polskich', p. 457, and Conze, *Polnische Nation*, p. 132.

97. See the official response to an anonymous memorandum criticizing the occupation and sent to the Archbishop of Posen and Gnesen, p. 7, in AA Poznań: OA IX 204. Also M. Bemann, '". . . kann von einer schonenden Behandlung keine Rede sein". Zur forst- und landwirtschaftlichen Aus-nutzung des Generalgouvernements Warschau durch die deutsche Besatzungsmacht, 1915–1918', *Jahrbücher für Osteuropas, Neue Folge* 55(1) (2007), p. 9.

98. Conze, *Polnische Nation*, p. 129, and S. Czerep, 'Straty polskie podczas I wojny światowej', in D. Grinberg, J. Snopko and G. Zackiewicz (eds.), *Lata wielkiej wojny. Dojrzewanie do niepodległości, 1914–1918* (Białystok, 2007), p. 194. Also, the anonymous but informed and critical memorandum of 1917, pp. 13–18, in AA Poznań: OA IX 204.

99. K. Dunin-Wąsowicz, *Warszawa w czasie pierwszej wojny światowej* (War-saw, 1974), pp. 97, 170–75 and 180, and R. Blobaum, Jr, 'Going Barefoot in Warsaw during the First World War', *East European Politics and Societies and Cultures* 27(2) (May 2013), pp. 188–91. For a guide to German rations, see Offer, *First World War*, p. 30, fig. 1.1.

100. Anonymous critical memorandum on the occupation of Poland, 1917, pp. 7 and 20. AA Poznań: OA IX 204. This states that 3,381 people had been released by the GGW between September 1915 and February 1917 but that many thousands remained imprisoned.

101. Westerhoff, *Zwangsarbeit*, pp. 198–210.

102. Herbert, *History of Foreign Labor*, pp. 87 and 93–4. Also Westerhoff, *Zwangsarbeit*, p. 93.

103. Westerhoff, *Zwangsarbeit*, pp. 88–9, 114 and 252.

104. Ibid., pp. 201 and 206.

105. Ihnatowicz, 'Gospodarka na ziemiach polskich', p. 459.

106. Westerhoff, *Zwangsarbeit*, pp. 65–6, 115, 202, 260 and 332; anonymous critical memorandum on the occupation of Poland, 1917, pp. 21 and 31. AA Poznań: OA IX 204.

107. For Beseler's state-building activities, see Kauffman, 'Sovereignty and the Search for Order', chs. 2–4. For Warsaw University, see also J. Kauffman, 'Warsaw University under German Occupation: State Building and Nation *Bildung* in Poland during the Great War', *First World War Studies* 4(1) (March 2013), pp. 65–79.

108. Fischer, *Germany's Aims*, pp. 239–44.

109. Conze, *Polnische Nation*, pp. 177–91 and 211 for the quotation.

110. Conze, *Polnische Nation*, pp. 226–33, and W. Sukiennicki, *East Central Europe during World War I: From Foreign Domination to National Independence* (2 vols., Boulder, CO, 1984), i, pp. 266–71 and 289.

111. Reproduced in Ludendorff (ed.), *The General Staff and its Problems*, ii, pp. 379–80.

112. For the alienating effect of the economic and repressive measures in the GGW on Poles, as well as the naked desire for domination visible in the Central Powers' offer, see the letter of Graf von Hutten-Czapski to General von Chelius, 12 December 1916, reproduced in Michaelis, Schraepler and Scheel (eds.), *Ursachen und Folgen*, i, pp. 45–7 (doc. 27).

113. P. S. Wandycz, *The Lands of Partitioned Poland, 1795–1918* (Seattle, WA, and London, 1974), pp. 352–8, and Conze, *Polnische Nation*, pp. 242–306.

114. M. Przeniosło, 'Postawy chłopów Królestwa Polskiego wobec okupanta niemieckiego i austriackiego (1914–1918)', in D. Grinberg, J. Snopko and G. Zackiewicz (eds.), *Lata wielkiej wojny. Dojrzewanie do niepodległości 1914–1918* (Białystok, 2007), pp. 204 and 206, and S. Lehnstaedt, 'Fluctuating between "Utilization" and Exploitation: Occupied East Central Europe during the First World War', in J. Böhler, W. Borodziej and J. von Puttkamer (eds.), *Legacies of Violence: Eastern Europe's First World War* (Munich, 2014), p. 97.

115. Wegs, 'Austrian Economic Mobilization', p. 122.

10. U-BOATS

1. 'Entente Reply to the Peace Note of Germany and Her Allies, December 30, 1916', reproduced in Carnegie Endowment for International Peace (ed.), *Official Communications and Speeches Relating to Peace Proposals, 1916–1917* (Washington, DC, 1917), p. 40.

2. 'Aufzeichnung über die Besprechung zwischen Reichskanzler von Bethmann Hollweg, Generalfeldmarschall von Hindenburg und General Ludendorff in Pleß am 9. Januar 1917, 11.15 Uhr vorm', in Michaelis, Schraepler and Scheel (eds.), *Ursachen und Folgen*, i, p. 147 (doc. 84).

3. J. M. Cooper, Jr, 'The Command of Gold Reversed: American Loans to Britain, 1915–1917', *The Pacific Historical Review* 45(2) (May 1976), pp. 219–20.

4. Chef des Admiralstabes, Memorandum, 22 December 1916, p. 2. BA-MA Freiburg: RM 5/2971: fo. 281.

5. A. Offer, 'Economic Interpretations of War: The German Submarine Campaign, 1915–18', *Australian Economic History Review* 23(1) (March 1989), pp. 25–7, and H. H. Herwig, 'Total Rhetoric, Limited War: Germany's U-Boat Campaign, 1917–1918', in R. Chickering and S. Förster (eds.), *Great War, Total War: Combat and Mobilization on the Western Front, 1914–1918* (Washington, DC, and Cambridge, 2000), p. 194.

6. Holtzendorff, memorandum, 22 December 1916. BA-MA Freiburg: RM 5/2971: fos. 280–82.

7. Best, *Humanity in Warfare*, pp. 252–5.

8. Halpern, *Naval History*, p. 335.

9. Holtzendorff, memorandum, 22 December 1916. BA-MA Freiburg: RM 5/2971: fos. 280–82 and 295–9.

10. Offer, 'Economic Interpretations', pp. 28–31.

11. Holtzendorff, memorandum, 22 December 1916, p. 24. BA-MA Freiburg: RM 5/2971: fo. 294.

12. See Admiralstab der Marine, 'Die englische Wirtschaft und der U-Boot-Krieg', 12 February 1916, p. 21. BA-MA Freiburg: RM 5/2971: fo. 152.

13. Bethmann, quoted in Jarausch, *Enigmatic Chancellor*, p. 284.

14. 'Protokoll der Beratung über die Aufnahme des rücksichtslosen U-Boot-Krieges vom 31. August 1916', in Michaelis, Schraepler and Scheel (eds.), *Ursachen und Folgen*, i, pp. 123–7 (doc. 70).

15. Görlitz (ed.), *Kaiser and his Court*, p. 229 (entry for 8 January 1917).

16. G. Granier, 'Kriegführung und Politik am Beispiel des Handelskriegs mit U-Booten, 1915–1918', in K. Oldenhage, H. Schreyer and W. Werner (eds.), *Archiv und Geschichte. Festschrift für Friedrich P. Kahlenberg* (Düsseldorf, 2000), p. 621.

17. Nebelin, *Ludendorff*, pp. 289–9. Also Jarausch, *Enigmatic Chancellor*, pp. 296–7.

18. 'Aufzeichnung über die Besprechung zwischen Reichskanzler von Bethmann Hollweg', in Michaelis, Schraepler and Scheel (eds.), *Ursachen und Folgen*, i, p. 147 (doc. 84).

19. See 'President Wilson's Address of January 22, 1917', *The American Journal of International Law* 11(4) (October 1917), p. 318.

20. Ludendorff, *My War Memories*, ii, p. 415.
21. 'Aus den Aufzeichnungen des Chefs des Geheimen Zivilkabinetts v. Valentini über die Kronratssitzung vom 9. Januar 1917', in Michaelis, Schraepler and Scheel (eds.), *Ursachen und Folgen*, i, p. 148 (doc. 85).
22. J. M. Clark, *The Costs of the World War to the American People* (New Haven, CT, and London, 1931), p. 24.
23. The Kaiser to Houston Stewart Chamberlain, January 1917, quoted in Stibbe, *German Anglophobia*, p. 175.
24. For the pre-war German navy and Jutland, see Herwig, *'Luxury' Fleet*, esp. pp. 95–110 and 178–99. Also J. Rüger, *The Great Naval Game: Britain and Germany in the Age of Empire* (Cambridge, 2007).
25. Schröder, *U-Boote des Kaisers*, p. 319.
26. Kommando des Hochseestreitkräfte, order, 31 January 1917.
27. M. Schwarte, *Die Technik im Weltkriege* (Berlin, 1920), pp. 408–9, and E. Rössler, *The U-Boat: The Evolution and Technical History of German Submarines* (London, 1981, 2001), p. 67.
28. Leader of Submarines, 'Written record of the conference with captains of submarines on 17.1.1917', 27 January 1917. TNA London: ADM 137/3866.
29. Marine Generalkommando, memorandum, 10 March 1917. BA-MA Freiburg: RM 120/577.
30. Chef des Admiralstabes, intelligence report, 19 March 1917. BA-MA Freiburg: RM 86/226.
31. This follows Schröder, *U-Boote des Kaisers*, pp. 326–7.
32. Halpern, *Naval History*, p. 408.
33. 'Interrogation of Survivors' from *UC65* (November 1917), p. 17. TNA London: ADM 137/3060.
34. This description is based on details of *U97*, *U103*, *U104* and *U110* in 'Interrogation of Survivors'. TNA London: ADM 137/3872. For maximum torpedo stowage, see the list of 26 October 1917 in BA-MA Freiburg: RM 120/576.
35. G. G. von Forstner, *The Journal of Submarine Commander von Forstner*, trans. R. Codman (Boston and New York, 1917), p. 56.
36. M. Niemöller, *From U-Boat to Concentration Camp* (London, Edinburgh and Glasgow, 1939), pp. 19, 24–6 and 45. Also von Forstner, *Journal*, pp. 7–11.
37. 'Interrogation of Survivors' from *UC65* (November 1917), p. 17, *UC35* (May 1918), p. 10, and *UB85* (May 1918), p. 6. TNA London: ADM 137/3060. Also interrogation of survivors from *U64* (June 1918), p. 10. TNA London: ADM 137/3903.
38. E. von Spiegel, *Kriegstagebuch 'U202'* (Berlin, 1916), p. 27.
39. Schröder, *U-Boote des Kaisers*, pp. 398, 428–9 and 437.

40. 'Interrogation of Survivors' from *UB72* (June 1918), *U104* (May 1918), and *UC65* (November 1917). TNA London: ADM 137/3874, 3872 and 3060.

41. 'Interrogation of Survivors' from *UB81* (December 1917). TNA London: ADM 137/3060.

42. 'Information Obtained from Survivors of *U93*' (May 1917). TNA London: ADM 137/3872. The commander was Spiegel, whose book is cited above. See also the 'Interrogation of Survivors' from *U103* (May 1918), p. 6, in the same file and *UC65* (November 1917), p. 13, and *U58*, p. 6, in ADM 137/3060.

43. See 'Interrogation of Survivors' from *UB109* (September 1918), p. 9, and *UC65* (November 1917), p. 10, in TNA London: ADM 137/3874 and 3060.

44. 'Copy and Portion of a Further Statement by Captain Anthony Starkey of the SS "Torrington"' [c. 11 January 1919] and 'Interrogation of Machinist Alfred Berner' from *U48*, 26 November 1917. TNA London: ADM 137/4138 and 3902.

45. *UB124* (August 1918). TNA London: ADM 137/3901 and ADM 137/3874.

46. Von Forstner, *Journal*, pp. 69–70. Cf. 'A Conversation with the Crew of "*UB30*"', translated article from *De Telegraaf*, 2 March 1917. TNA London: ADM 137/3874.

47. Führer der Unterseeboote, order and appendix, 10 May 1917. BA-MA Freiburg: RM 86/226.

48. Kriegstagebuch *U93*, 1917. BA-MA Freiburg: RM 97/11034: fos. 7–23 and 92.

49. 'Report of Interrogation of Survivor' from *UC63* (November 1917), p. 3. TNA London: ADM 137/3060.

50. 'German Prize Crew from SS Older' [men from *U49* and *U50*], c. December 1916, pp. 24–5; 'Interrogation of Survivors' from *U48* (December 1917), p. 16; 'Interrogation of Survivors' from *UB72* (June 1918), pp. 10–15. TNA London: ADM 137/3902, 3872 and 3874.

51. 'Interrogation of Survivors' from *U103* (June 1918), p. 17. TNA London: ADM 137/3872.

52. 'Interrogation of Survivors' from *U48* (December 1917), p. 17, *UC63* (November 1917), p. 9, *UC65* (November 1917), p. 17, and *UC35* (May 1918), p. 9. TNA London: ADM 137/3872 and 3060.

53. 'Interrogation of Survivors' from *U58* (December 1917), p. 15. TNA London: ADM 137/3060. Cf. 'A Conversation with the Crew of "*UB30*"', 1 March 1917, pp. 1–2. TNA London: ADM 137/3874.

54. 'Aufstellung über den Stand der U-Boot-Spende', 28 July 1919. GStA PK, Berlin: I. HA Rep 191, 3643.

55. An extract from this film, *Der magische Gürtel*, is uploaded at: http://www. iwm.org.uk/collections/item/object/1060008290. Accessed on 25 April 2014.

56. 'Interrogation of Survivors' from *U104* (May 1918), p. 7, and *UB72* (June 1918), p. 7. TNA London: ADM 137/3872 and 3874.

57. 'Interrogation of Survivors' from *U103* (June 1918), p. 6, *U48* (December 1917), p. 8, *UB85* (May 1918), p. 5, and *UB109* (September 1918), p. 11. TNA London: ADM 137/3872, 3060 and 3874.

58. Draft memorandum, Marinekorps, Generalkommando to Chef des Admiralstabes der Marine, 28 April 1917.

59. Führer der Unterseeboote to I, II, III, IV Uflottille, 10 May 1917. BA-MA Freiburg: RM 86/226.

60. Hardach, *First World War*, pp. 50–51 and 125–30, and P. E. Dewey, 'Food Production and Policy in the United Kingdom, 1914–1918', *Transactions of the Royal Historical Society* 30 (December 1918), pp. 82–9.

61. 'Translation of Extract from Letter Written by Freiherr von Spiegel to his Wife', 7 May 1917. TNA London: ADM 137/3903.

62. Osborne, *Britain's Economic Blockade*, p. 155, and Halpern, *Naval History*, pp. 341–2.

63. D. Stevenson, *With Our Backs to the Wall: Victory and Defeat in 1918* (London, 2011), pp. 335–49. For British tonnage, see Hardach, *First World War*, pp. 44–6.

64. Schröder, *U-Boote des Kaisers*, p. 370.

65. Halpern, *Naval History*, pp. 351–60.

66. Ibid., pp. 362–5 and 394–5.

67. H. Herwig and D. F. Trask, 'The Failure of Imperial Germany's Undersea Offensive Against World Shipping, February 1917–October 1918', *The Historian* 33(4) (August 1971), pp. 628–32. Also Stevenson, *With Our Backs to the Wall*, pp. 315–16.

68. Stevenson, *With Our Backs to the Wall*, p. 364, and Schröder, *U-Boote des Kaisers*, p. 379.

69. Schröder, *U-Boote des Kaisers*, pp. 372–8 and 383–4, and Stevenson, *With Our Backs to the Wall*, pp. 313–15, 325 and 345–6.

70. Halpern, *Naval History*, pp. 343–4 and 366–8.

71. 'Interrogation of Survivors' from *UB52* (July 1918), p. 7. TNA London: ADM 137/3060.

72. 'Interrogation of Survivors' from *U48* (December 1917), pp. 8–12. TNA London: ADM 137/3872. Cf. also 'Interrogation of Survivors' from *U64* (June 1918), p. 9. TNA London: ADM 137/3903.

73. See Chef des Admiralstabes, order, 'O-Sache' to Hochseekommando, 3 June 1917. BA-MA Freiburg: RM 120/576. Also Halpern, *Naval History*, pp. 425–7.

74. Herwig, *'Luxury' Fleet*, p. 220, and Schröder, *U-Boote des Kaisers*, p. 436.

75. 'Interrogation of Survivors' from *UC65* (November 1917), p. 17. TNA London: ADM 137/3060. See also 'Interrogation of Survivors' from *U110* (April 1918), p. 16. TNA London: ADM 137/3872.

76. Halpern, *Naval History*, pp. 159–60, 349–50, 406–7 and 440–41.

77. Chef des Admiralstabes, memorandum to Kommando der Hochstreitseekräfte, 7 December 1917. BA-MA Freiburg: RM 120/576.

78. 'Interrogation of Survivors' from *U48* (December 1917), p. 17. TNA London: ADM 137/3872.

79. Herwig, 'Total Rhetoric', p. 205, and Schröder, *U-Boote des Kaisers*, p. 429.

80. 'Interrogation of Survivors' from *U110* (April 1918), p. 7. TNA London: ADM 137/3872.

81. Ibid., p. 17. Cf. also the 'Interrogation of Survivors' from *U103* (June 1918), p. 15 in TNA London: ADM 137/3872.

82. 'Interrogation of Survivors' from *UB81* (December 1917), p. 14, and *UB109* (September 1918), pp. 8–9. TNA London: ADM 137/3060 and 3874.

83. 'Interrogation of Survivors' from *U110* (April 1918), p. 7. TNA London: ADM 137/3872.

84. 'Interrogation of Survivors' from *UB85* (May 1918), pp. 3–5. TNA London: ADM 137/3060.

85. 'Interrogation of Survivors' from *U64* (June 1918), p. 8. TNA London: ADM 137/3903.

86. See A. Bucholz, *Hans Delbrück and the German Establishment: War Images in Conflict* (Iowa City, IA, 1985), pp. 98–101, and Redlich, *Schicksalsjahre Österreichs*, ii, pp. 188–9 (diary entry for 5 February 1917).

87. Wolff, *Tagebücher*, pp. 478–81 (entries for 5, 11 and 14 February 1917).

88. 'Zusammenstellung der Monatsberichte der stellv. Generalkommandos an das preußische Kriegsministerium betr. die allgemeine Stimmung im Volke' for February 1917 (3 March 1917), p. 3. GStA PK, Berlin: I. HA Rep 90A, Nr. 2685. See also P. Scheidemann, *Der Zusammenbruch* (Berlin, 1921), p. 54 (although he contradicted this on p. 50).

89. C. J. Child, 'German-American Attempts to Prevent the Exportation of Munitions of War, 1914–1915', *The Mississippi Valley Historical Review* 25(3) (December 1938), pp. 351–68. For propaganda on the US weapons trade, see, for example, K. L. Henning, *Die Wahrheit über Amerika* (Leipzig, 1915), pp. 20–25, and see Buchner (ed.), *Kriegsdokumente*. From volume 4 onwards, Buchner's books reproduce numerous press reports on the American supply of war equipment and munitions to the Entente.

90. F. Gygi, 'Shattered Experiences – Recycled Relics: Strategies of Representation and the Legacy of the Great War', in N. J. Saunders (ed.), *Matters of Conflict: Material Culture, Memory and the First World War* (London and New York, 2004), pp. 83 and 85. For an example of indignation in the

German public, see E. Stempfle, diary, 10 April 1915. DTA, Emmendingen: 1654. Next to a newspaper cutting listing the hundreds of thousands of rifles, millions of cartridges and multifarious other weapons ordered from the United States by Russia, France and Britain, she commented sardonically 'This is how America stays neutral!'

91. 'Zusammenstellung der Monatsberichte der stellv. Generalkommandos an das preußische Kriegsministerium betr. die allgemeine Stimmung im Volke' for February 1917 (3 March 1917), p. 3. GStA PK, Berlin: I. HA Rep 90A, Nr. 2685.

92. Reich Navy Office quoted in C. Brocks, '"Unser Schild muss rein bleiben". Deutsche Bildzensur und propaganda im Ersten Weltkrieg', *Militärgeschichtliche Zeitschrift* 67(1) (2008), p. 42.

93. See, e.g., 'Die Ereignisse zur See', *Deutsche Kriegszeitung 1917. Illustrierte Wochen-Ausgabe herausgegeben vom Berliner Lokal-Anzeiger. Nr. 12*, 25 March 1917, p. 6, and *Nr. 16*, 22 April 1917, p. 6. For the statistics given to allies, see 'Vertreter des Admiralstabes der Marine im Großen Hauptquartier to königlich bulgarischer Militärbevollmächtigten im Großen Hauptquartier', 1 July 1917. BA-MA Freiburg: RM 120/576.

94. Koszyk, *Deutsche Pressepolitik*, pp. 203–4.

95. M. L. Hadley, *Count Not the Dead: The Popular Image of the German Submarine* (Quebec City, 1995), pp. 18 and 36.

96. K. Roesler, *Die Finanzpolitik des deutschen Reiches im Ersten Weltkrieg* (Berlin, 1967), p. 207.

97. S. Bruendel, 'Vor-Bilder des Durchhaltens. Die deutsche Kriegsanleihe-Werbung, 1917/18', in A. Bauerkämper and E. Julien (eds.), *Durchhalten! Krieg und Gesellschaft im Vergleich, 1914–1918* (Göttingen, 2010), p. 87.

98. Poster, 6. Kriegsanleihe, 1917. Bibliothek für Zeitgeschichte: 2.5/72 a. Also Welch, *Germany, Propaganda and Total War*, pp. 130–31.

99. Wolff, *Tagebücher*, pp. 478–81 (entry for 2 and 5 March 1917).

100. H. Muhsal, diary, 9 March 1917. BA-MA Freiburg: MSg 1/3109.

101. R. Höfner, diary, 16 April 1917. DTA Emmendingen: 1280,1.

102. 'Entwicklung der Stimmung im Heere 1916/17'. Forschungsarbeit von Obkircher (1936), p. 37. BA-MA Freiburg: W-10/51507.

103. Feldman, *Army, Industry and Labor*, p. 337.

104. Kriegsministerium, 'Zusammenstellung der Monats-Berichte der Generalkommandos vom 3.4.17' (p. 3) and ibid., '3.5.17.' (pp. 5–6) GStA PK, Berlin: I. HA Rep 90A, 2685. Also, E. Stempfle, diary, 8 April 1917. DTA, Emmendingen: 1654.

105. A. Hartmuth, letter from his mother, 27 June 1917. Author's Collection. More generally, see also R. Fiebig von Hase, 'Der Anfang vom Ende des Krieges: Deutschland, die USA und die Hintergründe des amerikanischan Kriegseintritts am 6. April 1917', in W. Michalka (ed.), *Der Erste*

Weltkrieg. Wirkung, Wahrnehmung, Analyse (Munich and Zurich, 1994), p. 132.

106. 'Denkschrift der Vorstände der Sozialdemokratischen Partei Deutschlands und der Sozialdemokratischen Reichstagsfraktion', 28 June 1917, in Michaelis, Schraepler and Scheel (eds.), *Ursachen und Folgen*, i, pp. 211–16 (doc. 129).

107. 'Rede des Abgeordneten Erzberger im Hauptausschuß des Reichstags. 6. Juli 1917', in H. Michaelis, E. Schraepler and G. Scheel (eds.), *Ursachen und Folgen. Vom deutschen Zusammenbruch 1918 und 1945 bis zur staatlichen Neuordnung Deutschlands in der Gegenwart. Eine Urkunden- und Dokumentensammlung zur Zeitgeschichte. Der militärische Zusammenbruch und das Ende des Kaiserreichs* (29 vols., Berlin, n.d.), ii, pp. 3–7 (doc. 233). Cf. Erzberger's own account: M. Erzberger, *Erlebnisse im Weltkrieg* (Stuttgart and Berlin, 1920), pp. 251–69.

108. 'Die Friedensresolution des deutschen Reichstags vom 19. Juli 1917', in Michaelis, Schraepler and Scheel (eds.), *Ursachen und Folgen*, ii, pp. 37–8 (doc. 241).

109. Memorandum for Staatssekretär [des Reichsmarineamts], 8 October 1917. BA-MA Freiburg: RM 5/3818: fos. 2–3.

110. Koszyk, *Deutsche Pressepolitik*, p. 205.

111. Halpern, *Naval History*, pp. 356–7, and Herwig and Trask, 'Failure of Imperial Germany's Undersea Offensive', pp. 613, 618, 627 and 629.

112. Documentation from the Presseabteilung in the Admiralstab, late 1917. BA-MA Freiburg: RM 5/3818: fos. 101 and 103–4. For the destruction of troop transports, see Schröder, *U-Boote des Kaisers*, p. 383. Another four troop transports were sunk when sailing back empty across the Atlantic.

113. 'German Submarine Propaganda', p. 4, 23 April 1918. TNA London: ADM 137/3872.

114. Herwig, *'Luxury' Fleet*, p. 223, and Hardach, *First World War*, p. 48.

115. See Stevenson, *With Our Backs to the Wall*, pp. 247, 338–9, 345 and 351.

11. DANGEROUS IDEAS

1. E. Manela, *The Wilsonian Moment: Self-Determination and the International Origins of Anticolonial Nationalism* (Oxford and New York, 2007), p. 36.

2. Quoted in R. A. Wade, *The Russian Search for Peace, February–October 1917* (Stanford, CA, 1969), pp. 16 and 29.

3. 'President Wilson's Address of January 22, 1917', *The American Journal of International Law* 11(4) (October 1917), p. 323.

4. O. Figes, *A People's Tragedy: The Russian Revolution, 1891–1924* (London, 1996, 1997), p. 381.

5. *Vorwärts*, 6 November 1917, quoted in BA-MA Freiburg: RM3/11682b: fo. 49.

6. Quoted in M. Cornwall, 'Disintegration and Defeat: The Austro-Hungarian Revolution', in M. Cornwall (ed.), *The Last Years of Austria-Hungary: A Multi-National Experiment in Early Twentieth-Century Europe*, revised and expanded edn (Exeter, 2002), p. 169.

7. C. Brennan, 'Reforming Austria-Hungary: Beyond his Control or Beyond his Capacity? The Domestic Policies of Emperor Karl I, November 1916–May 1917', unpublished PhD thesis, London School of Economics (2012), pp. 16–19, 97–8 and 106–7.

8. Personnel changes are detailed in E. von Glaise-Horstenau, *The Collapse of the Austro-Hungarian Empire* (London and Toronto, 1930), pp. 14–17. Also Brennan, 'Reforming Austria-Hungary', pp. 143–4.

9. Brennan, 'Reforming Austria-Hungary', pp. 107–9.

10. Křen, *Konfliktgemeinschaft*, pp. 335–6, and H. L. Rees, *The Czechs during World War I: The Path to Independence* (Boulder, CO, 1992), pp. 27–9.

11. Kaiser Karl I to Kaiser Wilhelm II, 14 April 1917, in Michaelis, Schraepler and Scheel (eds.), *Ursachen und Folgen*, i, pp. 378–9 (doc. 201).

12. Galántai, *Hungary*, pp. 224–6 and 240–45, and G. Vermes, 'Leap into the Dark: The Issue of Suffrage in Hungary during World War I', in Robert A. Kann, Béla K. Király and Paula S. Fichtner (eds.), *The Habsburg Empire in World War I: Essays on the Intellectual, Military, Political and Economic Aspects of the Habsburg War Effort* (Boulder, CO, and New York, 1977), pp. 35–7.

13. Brennan, 'Reforming Austria-Hungary', pp. 153–229.

14. Jarausch, *Enigmatic Chancellor*, p. 310.

15. Wolff, *Tagebücher*, p. 495 (diary entry, 22 March 1917).

16. Müller, *Kaiser and his Court*, p. 249 (diary entry for 22 March 1917).

17. Scheidemann, *Zusammenbruch*, pp. 40–22. For the meeting, see Fischer, *Germany's Aims*, p. 328.

18. Miller, *Burgfrieden*, pp. 285–6. For the background to the party schism, see ibid., pp. 113–65.

19. Wilhelm II's 'Easter Message', trans. J. Verhey and R. Chickering at: http://germanhistorydocs.ghi-dc.org/pdf/eng/922_Wilhelm_Easter_Message_186.pdf. Accessed on 31 May 2013. For a description of the debates leading to the 'Easter Message', see Jarausch, *Enigmatic Chancellor*, pp. 327–35.

20. Miller, *Burgfrieden*, p. 286, and Fischer, *Germany's Aims*, pp. 397–9.

21. Pyta, *Hindenburg*, pp. 161–2 and 256–8.

22. Roesler, *Finanzpolitik*, p. 208.

23. A. J. Ryder, *The German Revolution of 1918: A Study of German Socialism in War and Revolt* (Cambridge, 1967), pp. 49–58 and 72–3.

24. Jarausch, *Enigmatic Chancellor*, p. 327.

25. Erzberger in the Reichstag Steering Committee, 6 July 1917, in Michaelis, Schraepler and Scheel (eds.), *Ursachen und Folgen*, ii, p. 6 (doc. 233).

26. Miller, *Burgfrieden*, p. 304.

27. Scheidemann, *Zusammenbruch*, pp. 80–81.

28. Haase on Chancellor Hertling, 29 November 1917, quoted in Miller, *Burgfrieden*, p. 331. For the crisis, see W. J. Mommsen, 'Die deutsche öffentliche Meinung und der Zusammenbruch des Regierungssystems Bethmann Hollweg im Juli 1917', *Geschichte in Wissenschaft und Unterricht* 19(11) (November 1968), esp. pp. 665–71.

29. Reichstag Peace Resolution, 19 July 1917, trans. J. Verhey and R. Chickering at: http://germanhistorydocs.ghi-dc.org/pdf/eng/1007_Reichstag%27s%20Peace%20Resolution_194.pdf. Accessed on 5 June 2013.

30. Fischer, *Germany's Aims*, pp. 401–4, Erzberger, *Erlebnisse*, pp. 266–8, and D. Stevenson, 'The Failure of Peace by Negotiations in 1917', *The Historical Journal* 34(1) (March 1991), p. 72. For Haase's criticism and the SPD, see Miller, *Burgfrieden*, pp. 288 and 311.

31. Ludendorff at the Crown Council of 14 September 1917, reproduced in Ludendorff (ed.), *General Staff and its Problems*, ii, p. 494.

32. Fischer, *Germany's Aims*, pp. 316–17 and 347.

33. Ibid., pp. 342–6.

34. Ibid., p. 347.

35. See the report of Legationssekretärs Freiherr von Lersner to the Foreign Secretary of 5 May 1917, reproduced in Deist (ed.), *Militär und Innenpolitik*, ii, pp. 744–6 (doc. 293).

36. Record of the Kreuznach Discussions, 23 April 1917, in Feldman (ed.), *German Imperialism*, pp. 32–3 (doc. 9). Also Fischer, *Germany's Aims*, pp. 346–51.

37. Fischer, *Germany's Aims*, pp. 365–9.

38. M. Cornwall, *The Undermining of Austria-Hungary: The Battle for Hearts and Minds* (Basingstoke and New York, 2000), pp. 40–59.

39. Kriegstagebuch, 12. Inf. Div., 'Übersicht über die Zeit vom 1. bis 11.4. 17' and entries for 12–15 and 23–30 April 1917. BA-MA Freiburg: PH8I/ 11.

40. Cornwall, *Undermining*, pp. 58–62.

41. D. Stevenson, *1914–1918: The History of the First World War* (London, 2004), p. 297.

42. Ludendorff (ed.), *General Staff and its Problems*, ii, pp. 712–21.

43. See D. A. Harvey, 'Lost Children or Enemy Aliens? Classifying the Population of Alsace after the First World War', *Journal of Contemporary History* 34(4) (October 1999), pp. 537–54, and L. Boswell, 'From Liberation to Purge Trials in the "Mythic Provinces": Recasting French Identities in Alsace and Lorraine, 1918–1920', *French Historical Studies* 23(1) (Winter 2000), pp. 129–62.

44. Stevenson, 'French War Aims', pp. 879–80 and 883, and D. Stevenson, 'French War Aims and Peace Planning', in M. F. Boemeke, G. D. Feldman and E. Glaser, *The Treaty of Versailles: A Reassessment after 75 Years* (Washington, DC, and Cambridge, 1998), pp. 93–101.

45. See 'Entente Reply to President Wilson's Peace Note, January 10, 1917', in Carnegie Endowment for International Peace (ed.), *Official Communications and Speeches Relating to Peace Proposals, 1916–1917* (Washington, DC, 1917), pp. 49–50.

46. For an analysis of the problems of making peace in 1917 stressing the existence of entrenched territorial disputes and alliance solidarity, see Stevenson, 'Failure of Peace by Negotiations', pp. 65–86.

47. For France at the 1919 Paris Peace Conference, see M. MacMillan, *Peacemakers: Six Months that Changed the World* (London, 2001), esp. pp. 176–86.

48. Ludendorff, *War Memories*, ii, p. 517.

49. Ludendorff (ed.), *General Staff and its Problems*, ii, pp. 494–7, Feldman (ed), *German Imperialism*, pp. 32–3 (doc. 9), and Ludendorff, *War Memories*, ii, pp. 517–20.

50. H. H. Herwig, 'Admirals *versus* Generals: The War Aims of the Imperial German Navy, 1914–1918', *Central European History* 5(3) (September 1972), pp. 214–20.

51. Ludendorff (ed.), *General Staff and its Problems*, ii, p. 494.

52. Adolf Hitler, 17 September 1941, quoted in J. Zimmerer, 'Holocaust und Kolonialismus. Beitrag zu einer Archäologie des genozidalen Gedankens', *Zeitschrift für Geschichtswissenschaft* 51(12) (2003), p. 1098.

53. Ludendorff, *War Memories*, ii, p. 520.

54. For the quotation, see Ludendorff, letter to Professor Hans Delbrück, 29 December 1915, reproduced in Zechlin, 'Ludendorff im Jahre 1915', p. 352. For other details, see Liulevičius, *War Land*, pp. 94–6, and Sammartino, *Impossible Border*, pp. 31–7.

55. Stevenson, 'Failure of Peace by Negotiations', pp. 67–9, Galántai, *Hungary*, pp. 234–5, and Rauchensteiner, *Tod des Doppeladlers*, pp. 419 and 553–4.

56. Galántai, *Hungary*, p. 234.

57. Rauchensteiner, *Tod des Doppeladlers*, p. 487, and Fischer, *Germany's Aims*, p. 344.

58. Stevenson, 'Failure of Peace by Negotiations', pp. 67–9, and May, *Passing of the Habsburg Monarchy*, i, pp. 486–91.

59. Bethmann Hollweg, 4 August 1914, reproduced in Lutz (ed.), *Fall*, i, p. 13.

60. Fischer, *Germany's Aims*, pp. 360, 374, and Chancellor Michaelis, 21 August 1917. Lutz (ed.), *Fall*, i, p. 367.

61. Czernin, quoted in Fischer, *Germany's Aims*, p. 351.

62. Aleksandra Czechówna, diary (p. 69), 8 March 1917. AN Cracow: IT 428/41.

63. Rees, *Czechs during World War I*, p. 37, and Davis, *Home Fires Burning*, p. 196. For strikes, see Schlegelmilch, 'Massenprotest', p. 293.

64. 'Juni-Bericht des Gemeinsamen Zentralnachweisebureaus, Auskunftsstelle für Kriegsgefangene, Zensurabteilung über die Stimmung der österreichischen Bevölkerung im Hinterlande', p. 1. AVA Vienna: MdI, Präsidium (1917). 22/gen. Nr. 14234.

65. For Germany, see the 'Zusammenstellung der Monatsberichte der stellv. Generalkommandos an das preußische Kriegsministerium betr. die allgemeine Stimmung im Volke', in GStA PK, Berlin: I. HA Rep 90A, Nr. 2685. For Austria, see 'Juni-Bericht des Gemeinsamen Zentralnachweisebureaus, Auskunftsstelle für Kriegsgefangene, Zensurabteilung über die Stimmung der österreichischen Bevölkerung im Hinterlande'. AVA Vienna: MdI, Präsidium (1917). 22/gen. Nr. 14234.

66. Quoted in Redlich, *Austrian War Government*, pp. 150–51, fn. 2.

67. Glaise-Horstenau, *Collapse*, p. 31.

68. Brennan, 'Reforming Austria-Hungary', esp. pp. 273–4 and 279.

69. V. S. Mamatey, 'The Union of Czech Political Parties in the *Reichsrat*, 1916–1918', in R. A. Kann, B. K. Király and P. S. Fichtner (eds.), *The Habsburg Empire in World War I: Essays on the Intellectual, Military, Political and Economic Aspects of the Habsburg War Effort* (Boulder, CO, and New York, 1977), p. 16.

70. Brennan provides the most detailed discussion of the debates surrounding the drawing up of the Czech Union's statement. See his 'Reforming Austria-Hungary', pp. 264–8, 276–9 and 289–93.

71. Zeman, *Break-Up*, pp. 127–9.

72. Glaise-Horstenau, *Collapse*, p. 37.

73. Zahra, *Kidnapped Souls*, pp. 81–2 and 94–5.

74. Redlich, *Austrian War Government*, pp. 150 and 156–7, and Cornwall, *Undermining*, p. 284.

75. Rauchensteiner, *Tod des Doppeladlers*, pp. 477–8, and Rees, *Czechs during World War I*, pp. 49–50. Also 'Stimmung in Prager Polizeirayon', 25 July 1917, in Prague (No. 163). AVA Vienna: MdI, Präsidium. Varia Erster Weltkrieg: Karton 33.

76. Brennan, 'Reforming Austria-Hungary', pp. 268–9, and Zeman, *Break-Up*, pp. 122–3.

77. P. Hanák, 'Die Volksmeinung während des letzten Kriegsjahres in Österreich-Ungarn', in R. G. Plaschka and K. Mack (eds.), *Die Auflösung des Habsburgerreiches. Zusammenbruch und Neuorientierung im Donauraum* (Vienna, 1970), pp. 60–61. There are a number of ways of interpreting Hanák's evidence, but the combination that he gives of over 75 per cent of

all correspondents wishing for 'Selbstständigkeit' and (from another sample) 13.5 per cent for 'Unabhängigkeit' favours the above interpretation.

78. Rees, *Czechs during World War I*, pp. 33–8.
79. K.u.k. Militärkommando in Prag, 'Stimmungsbericht', 15 February 1917, p. 3. KA Vienna: MKSM 1917 (Karton 1305), 28–2/10.
80. Poster in Aurinowes (Uhříněves), pol. Bezirk Zizkow, March 1917. AVA Vienna: MdI, Präsidium. Varia Erster Weltkrieg: Karton 33.
81. Mamatey, 'The Union of Czech Political Parties', p. 18, and k.u.k. Militärkommando in Prag, 'Demonstration in Prag', 31 May 1917, pp. 1–2. KA Vienna: MKSM 1917 (Karton 1305), 28–2/10–17. For the Czech vote (of 1911), see Höbelt, '"Well-Tempered Discontent"', p. 58.
82. Hupka, *Z czasów wielkiej wojny*, p. 335 (entry for 18 December 1917).
83. K.u.k. Militärkommando in Prag, 'Stimmungsbericht', 15 May 1917, pp. 1–3. KA Vienna: MKSM 1917 (Karton 1305), 28–2/10–3.
84. 'Juni-Bericht des Gemeinsamen Zentralnachweisebureaus, Auskunftsstelle für Kriegsgefangene, Zensurabteilung über die Stimmung der österreichischen Bevölkerung im Hinterlande', pp. 2 and 5; 'Stimmung und wirtschaftliche Lage des österreichischen Bevölkerung im Hinterland (Septemberbericht), p. 2. AVA Vienna: MdI, Präsidium (1917). 22/gen. Nr. 14234 and 21657. For the rumours about Kaiser Wilhelm, see k.u.k. Militärkommando in Prag, 'Stimmungsbericht', 15 May 1917, pp. 1–3. KA Vienna: MKSM 1917 (Karton 1305), 28–2/10–3.
85. J. R. Wegs, 'Transportation: The Achilles Heel of the Habsburg War Effort', in R. A. Kann, B. K. Király and P. S. Fichtner (eds.), *The Habsburg Empire in World War I: Essays on the Intellectual, Military, Political and Economic Aspects of the Habsburg War Effort* (Boulder, CO, and New York, 1977), p. 128.
86. Quoted in Křen, *Konfliktgemeinschaft*, p. 354.
87. K.u.k. Militärkommando in Prag, 'Stimmungsbericht', 15 December 1917, p. 2. KA Vienna: MKSM 1917 (Karton 1305), 28–2/10–17.
88. Hanák, 'Volksmeinung', pp. 63–5.
89. For the background, see Mamatey, 'The Union of Czech Political Parties', pp. 16–23. The text is cited in Rees, *Czechs during World War I*, pp. 80–81.
90. 'Denkschrift der Obersten Heeresleitung über die deutsche Volks- und Wehrkraft', pp. 17–18. BA-MA Freiburg: PH 3/446.
91. For food, see Offer, *First World War*, p. 29. For requisitions, see the posters in AP Toruń: Starostwo Powiatowe w Toruniu (Landratsamt Thorn) 1818–1920: Nr. 1023: Bl. 91, 180, 293, 295, 432, 450, 478, 479, and for the resistance to the removal of church bells, see the circular from Edmund, Archbishop of Gnesen und Posen, 6 August 1917. AA Poznań: OA X 76.

92. 'Zusammenstellung der Monatsberichte der stellv. Generalkommandos an das preußische Kriegsministerium betr. die allgemeine Stimmung im Volke' for June 1917 (3 July 1917), p. 1. GStA PK, Berlin: I. HA Rep 90A, Nr. 2685.

93. 'Zusammenstellung der Monatsberichte der stellv. Generalkommandos an das preußische Kriegsministerium betr. die allgemeine Stimmung im Volke' for May 1917 (3 June 1917), p. 22. GStA PK, Berlin: I. HA Rep 90A, Nr. 2685.

94. Miller, *Burgfrieden*, pp. 143–77, Ryder, *German Revolution*, pp. 76–83, and Tampke, *Ruhr and Revolution*, pp. 53–6.

95. Ryder, *German Revolution*, p. 99. For Müller and the revolutionary shop stewards, see R. Hoffrogge, 'Räteaktivisten in der USPD: Richard Müller und die Revolutionären Obleute in Berliner Betrieben', in U. Plener (ed.), *Die Novemberrevolution 1918/1919 in Deutschland. Für bürgerliche und sozialistische Demokratie. Allgemeine, regionale und biographische Aspekte. Beiträge zum 90. Jahrestag der Revolution* (Berlin, 2009), pp. 189–94.

96. Copy of revolutionary leaflet from the April strikes passed to Kommandantur Coblenz-Ehrenbreitstein by Kriegsministerium, 3 May 1917. HHStA Wiesbaden: Preußisches Regierungspräsidium Wiesbaden (405): Nr. 2777: fo. 152.

97. Feldman, *Army, Industry and Labor*, pp. 337–9, and Ryder, *German Revolution*, pp. 100–101.

98. In the context of the April strikes, see especially Magistrat in Frankfurt a.M., report to Reg. Präs. in Wiesbaden, 17 April 1917. HHStA Wiesbaden: Preußisches Regierungspräsidium Wiesbaden (405): Nr. 2777: fo. 349.

99. Feldman, *Army, Industry and Labor*, pp. 340–48. Hindenburg's appeal is reproduced in Michaelis, Schraepler and Scheel (eds.), *Ursachen und Folgen*, i, p. 202 (doc. 126).

100. Feldman, *Army, Industry and Labor*, pp. 362–404.

101. Minister des Innern, circular to all Regierungspräsidenten and the Polizeipräsident in Berlin, 12 July 1917. GStA PK, Berlin: XIV. HA Rep 181,31389.

102. Chef des Generalstabes des Feldheeres, memorandum, 15 November 1917. HHStA Wiesbaden: Preußisches Regierungspräsidium Wiesbaden (405): Nr. 2739: fos. 230–32.

103. Poster signed by Gouverneur der Festung Mainz, 2 May 1917. For the Mormons and Adventists, see Minister des Innern in Berlin to Regierungspräsidenten – mit Ausnahme von Koeslin – und Herrn Polizeipräsidenten [in Berlin], 4 October 1917, and Kriegsministerium, order, 19 March 1918. HHStA Wiesbaden: Preußisches Regierungspräsidium Wiesbaden (405): Nr. 2777: fo. 338, and AP Toruń: Star. Pow. Toruniu: Nr. 1009: fo. 921.

104. See Generalquartiermeister at Gr. HQ, order, 25 July 1917, and Chef des Stabes des Feldheeres, 'Einführung von Hetzschriften in das Heer', 24 May 1917. For the order against enemy pilots, see Chef des Feldheeres, telegram, 24 April 1917. GLA Karlsruhe: 456 F 109, Nr. 1, and 456 F 7, Nr. 91.

105. Jahr, *Gewöhnliche Soldaten*, p. 155, and Watson, *Enduring the Great War*, pp. 168–72.

106. German Fifth Army censorship report, 12 July 1917, p. 15. BA-MA Freiburg: W-10/50794.

107. Schuhmacher, *Leben und Seele unseres Soldatenlieds*, pp. 172–3.

108. Von Thaer, *Generalstabsdienst*, p. 122 (diary entry for 15 May 1917).

109. See Watson, *Enduring the Great War*, pp. 202–4. Also U. Kluge, *Soldatenräte und Revolution. Studien zur Militärpolitik in Deutschland 1918/19* (Göttingen, 1975), pp. 94–105.

110. D. Horn (ed.), *The Private War of Seaman Stumpf: The Unique Diaries of a Young German in the Great War* (London, 1969), p. 342.

111. D. Horn, *Mutiny on the High Seas: The Imperial German Naval Mutinies of World War One* (London, 1969), esp. chs. 3 and 4.

112. Hagenlücke, *Deutsche Vaterlandspartei*, ch. 3.

113. See B. Ulrich and B. Ziemann (eds.), *Frontalltag im Ersten Weltkrieg. Ein Historisches Lesebuch* (Essen, 2008), pp. 133–5, docs. 51a and 51d.

114. 'Schreiben des Chefs des Generalstabes des Feldheeres an die Chefs des Stabes der Heeresgruppen und Armeen über die Notwendigkeit der Aufklärungstätigkeit unter den Truppen', 31 July 1917, reproduced in Deist (ed.), *Militär und Innenpolitik*, ii, p. 847 (doc. 332).

115. A. Lipp, *Meinungslenkung im Krieg. Kriegserfahrungen deutscher Soldaten und ihre Deutung, 1914–1918* (Göttingen, 2003), pp. 70–88. Also A. K. Rice, 'Morale and Defeatism in the Bavarian "Heer und Heimat" in the First World War (1916–18)', unpublished MPhil thesis, University of Oxford (2004), pp. 53–64.

116. Mai, '"Aufklärung der Bevölkerung"', p. 215. Also, stellv. Generalkommando XI A.K., 'Aufklärung bei den Truppen'. HHStA Wiesbaden: 405: Nr. 2777: fo. 304.

117. 'Was der Feind will!', poster issued in early 1917. See HStA Stuttgart: M33/2: Bü 516.

118. BA-MA Freiburg, PH 5 IV/2: Leitsätze für den Vaterländischen Unterricht der Armee-Abteilung A, 15 November 1917, pp. 5–6. Older work by Wilhelm Deist and Benjamin Ziemann has been shown to have underestimated the effectiveness of Patriotic Instruction. See the more balanced and better supported assessments in Lipp, *Meinungslenkung*, pp. 62–90, and Rice, 'Morale and Defeatism'.

119. See letter of Chief of the General Staff to Chancellor, 17 December 1916, reproduced in Ludendorff (ed.), *General Staff and its Problems*, ii, pp. 401–3.

120. R. Wiehler, *Deutsche Wirtschaftspropaganda im Weltkrieg* (Berlin, 1922), pp. 17–18 and 21.

121. See Mai, '"Aufklärung der Bevölkerung"', pp. 206–13 and 216–29, and Loch, '"Aufklärung der Bevölkerung"', pp. 59–69.

122. Bruendel, 'Vor-Bilder des Durchhaltens', p. 87. More generally on the background to these campaigns, see Wiehler, *Deutsche Wirtschaftspropaganda*, pp. 35–43.

123. Roesler, *Finanzpolitik*, p. 207.

124. For one estimate of German wartime morale, see the US Military Intelligence graph reproduced in G. G. Bruntz, *Allied Propaganda and the Collapse of the German Empire in 1918* (Stanford, CA, London and Oxford, 1938), insert between pp. 192–3.

125. 'Die 7. Kriegsanleihe'. HStA Stuttgart: J150, Nr. 232/8. For Hindenburg, see Welch, *Germany, Propaganda and Total War*, 210.

126. 'Wie brennt der Wunde – brennt die Schmach!' HStA Stuttgart: J150, Nr. 232/8. More generally, cf. Koszyk, *Deutsche Pressepolitik*, p. 199.

127. 'Zukunft des deutschen Landwirtes im Falle eines englischen Sieges!' HStA Stuttgart: M77/1 Bü 497.

128. Ibid. and 'An das deutsche Volk!' HStA Stuttgart: M77/1 Bü 497 and J150, Nr. 232/8.

129. See the leaflets 'Zukunft des deutschen Landwirts im Falle eines englischen Sieges!' and 'Der Feind im Land!', and cf. 'Wie brennt die Wunde – brennt die Schmach!', all in Bibliothek für Zeitgeschichte: Flugblattsammlung 7. Kriegsanleihe (1917). Also the front page of the pamphlet 'Die 7. Kriegsanleihe' in HStA Stuttgart: J150, Nr. 232/8.

130. Staging directions for *Der Heimat-Schützengraben* (1916), reproduced in U. Oppelt, *Film und Propaganda im Ersten Weltkrieg. Propaganda als Medienrealität im Aktualitäten- und Dokumentarfilm* (Stuttgart, 2002), pp. 337–8. The film was shot as an advertisement for the Sixth War Loan but was reused in the Seventh War Loan Campaign. See J. Kilian, 'Propaganda für die deutschen Kriegsanleihen im Ersten Weltkrieg', in J. Wilke (ed.), *Massenmedien und Spenden-kampagnen. Vom 17. Jahrhundert bis in die Gegenwart* (Cologne, Weimar and Vienna, 2008), pp. 136–7.

12. THE BREAD PEACE

1. Bethmann's 'Provisional Notes on the Direction of Our Policy on the Conclusion of Peace', September 1914, reproduced in Feldman (ed.), *German Imperialism*, p. 125.

2. Kühlmann, quoted in Fischer, *Germany's Aims*, p. 479. See also pp. 456–69.

3. M. Kitchen, *The Silent Dictatorship: The Politics of the German High Command under Hindenburg and Ludendorff* (London, 1976), pp. 160–69.

4. For the strike in Berlin, see Feldman, *Army, Industry and Labor*, pp. 448–54. For strikes to the north, see Ullrich, *Vom Augusterlebnis*, pp. 109–57.

5. Fischer, *Germany's Aims*, pp. 505–6.

6. See Kitchen, *Silent Dictatorship*, p. 183.

7. Even Fischer, one of Imperial Germany's harshest critics, concedes this. See *Germany's Aims*, p. 508.

8. The Tsarist Empire's treatment of its minorities is covered in A. Kappeler, *The Russian Empire: A Multi-Ethnic History* (Harlow, 2001), ch. 7.

9. For a recent account of the horrors of Ukraine's interwar experience, see Snyder, *Bloodlands*, pp. 21–53.

10. Emperor Karl on 17 January 1918, quoted in May, *Passing of the Hapsburg Monarchy*, p. 617.

11. C. F. Wargelin, 'A High Price for Bread: The First Treaty of Brest-Litovsk and the Break-Up of Austria-Hungary, 1917–1918', *The International History Review* 19(4) (November 1997), quotation at p. 765. See also pp. 772–3. For the January strike and Cattaro mutiny, see R. G. Plaschka, H. Haselsteiner and A. Suppan, *Innere Front. Militärassistenz, Widerstand und Umsturz in der Donaumonarchie, 1918. Zwischen Streik und Meuterei* (2 vols., Munich, 1974), i, pp. 59–90 and 107–48.

12. Wargelin, 'High Price for Bread', pp. 765–7 and 773–4.

13. Memorandum, p. 1, probably from the German 224 Division, 10 June 1918, in BA-MA Freiburg: PH8I/58.

14. For the Ukrainian National Council, see A. Wilson, *The Ukrainians: Unexpected Nation*, 2nd edn (New Haven, CT, 2002), pp. 121–4, and A. Roshwald, *Ethnic Nationalism and the Fall of Empires: Central Europe, Russia and the Middle East, 1914–1923* (London and New York, 2001), pp. 95–8.

15. Wargelin, 'High Price for Bread', pp. 765–7, 773–4.

16. Loewenfeld-Russ, *Regelung der Volksernährung*, p. 402.

17. See the memorandum, probably from 224 Division, 10 June 1918, in BA-MA Freiburg: PH8I/58.

18. W. Dornik and P. Lieb, 'Misconceived *Realpolitik* in a Failing State: The Political and Economical Fiasco of the Central Powers in the Ukraine, 1918', *First World War Studies* 4(1) (March 2013), pp. 115–16. Also Loewenfeld-Russ, *Regelung der Volksernährung*, pp. 400–401.

19. C. F. Wargelin, 'The Austro-Polish Solution: Diplomacy, Politics and State Building in Wartime Austria-Hungary, 1914–1918', *East European Quarterly* 42(3) (September 2008), p. 268. Also Mick, *Kriegserfahrungen*, pp. 170–71.

20. See the Galician newspaper summaries ('Übersicht Nr. 14'), November 1916, pp. 19–23, in AP Poznań: Polizei Präsidium Posen 5062 and Präsidium der Polizeidirektion in Lwów to Statthaltereipräsidium in Biała, 3 March 1917, in AVA Vienna: MdI, Präsidium (1916–17) 22/Galiz: Karton 2117: Nr. 9438.

21. Conze, *Polnische Nation*, pp. 256, fn. 81, and 296–7.

22. W. L. Jaworski, *Diarusz, 1914–1918* (Warsaw, 1997), p. 208 (diary entry for 29 July 1917).

23. 'Stimmung und wirtschaftliche Lage des österreichischen Bevölkerung im Hinterland (Septemberbericht)', p. 2. AVA Vienna: MdI, Präsidium (1917). 22/gen. Nr. 21657. For the diversion of food, see Wargelin, 'High Price for Bread', p. 780.

24. H. Binder, *Galizien in Wien. Parteien, Wahlen, Fraktionen und Abgeordnete im Übergang zur Massenpolitik* (Vienna, 2005), pp. 499–501. Also Wargelin, 'High Price for Bread', pp. 784–5.

25. The Fourteen Points can be found at http://avalon.law.yale.edu/20th_century/wilson14.asp, accessed on 30 January 2014. See also M. B. Biskupski, 'Re-Creating Central Europe: The United States "Inquiry" into the Future of Poland in 1918', *The International History Review* 12(2) (May 1990), pp. 249–79.

26. A flyer published by the Komitet wspólny wszystkich stronnictw i grup w Nowym Sączu advertising the strike of 18 February 1918 (pasted into diary/memoir). KA Vienna: NL Schwestek, B/89. Cf. the similar flyers in AN Cracow: DPKr 552.

27. W. Witos, *Moje wspomnienia* (Warsaw, 1978), p. 520. Cf. also documents in AN Cracow: DPKr 551.

28. Mick, *Kriegserfahrungen*, pp. 173–4.

29. Statthalter in Galizia to Ministerium des Innern, 'Ausschreitungen in Galizien im Februar 1918'. AVA Vienna: MdI, Präsidium (1918) 22/Galiz: Karton 2118: Nr. 11226.

30. See the documentation dealing with this demonstration in AN Cracow: DPKr 117: fos. 1149–64.

31. C.k. Dyrekcya poczt i telegrafów we Wiedniu to k.k. Post- und Telegraphendirektion in Wien, 15 February 1918. AN Cracow: DPKr 187: fos. 1271–2; also 'Relacya', 23 February 1918 in ibid., fo. 1273.

32. See J. Buszko, 'Die polnischen Politiker über die Ereignisse des Jahres 1918 in Österreich-Ungarn', in R. G. Plaschka and K. Mack (eds.), *Die Auflösung des Habsburgerreiches. Zusammenbruch und Neuorientierung im Donauraum* (Vienna, 1970), pp. 181–2, and Plaschka, Haselsteiner and Suppan, *Innere Front*, i, pp. 97–101.

33. See Hupka, *Z czasów wielkiej wojny*, p. 343, and report, 16 May 1918; 'Anfrage der Abgeordneten Wolf, Pacher und Genossen', in Haus der Abgeordneten, 5 March 1918. AN Cracow: DPKr 119: fo. 165.

34. 'Wyciąg z reskr. Min. spraw. wewn', 16 May 1918; 'Anfrage der Abgeordneten Wolf, Pacher und Genossen', in Haus der Abgeordneten, 5 March 1918. AN Cracow: DPKr 119: fos. 147–8 and 165.

35. J. Bieniarzówna and J. M. Małecki, *Dzieje Krakowa. Kraków w latach, 1796–1918* (6 vols., Cracow, 1979), iii, pp. 318–19; C. Bąk-Koczarska, 'Władze miejskie Krakowa w latach wojny', in Towarzystwo Miłośników Historii i Zabytków Krakowa (ed.), *Kraków w czasie I wojny światowej. Materiały sesji naukowej z okazji dni Krakowa w roku 1988* (Cracow, 1990), p. 70, and M. Gałas and A. Polonsky, 'Introduction', in M. Gałas and A. Polonsky (eds.), *Polin: Studies in Polish Jewry, Volume 23. Jews in Kraków* (Oxford and Portland, OR, 2011), pp. 4, 12–15 and 41. For the riots in western Galicia, see D. L. Unowsky, 'Peasant Political Mobilization and the 1898 Anti-Jewish Riots in Western Galicia', *European History Quarterly* 40(3) (July 2010), pp. 412–35.

36. See chs. 2 and 5, and for Polish Legion recruitment see Mleczak, *Akcja werbunkowa*, pp. 162–3.

37. Wróbel, 'The Jews of Galicia', pp. 119 and 121.

38. K.k. Oberleutnant a.D. Dr Stanislaus v. Turowski, 'Bemerkungen über die letzten Unruhen in der Stadt', to k.u.k. Abteilungskommando in Kraków, 14 May 1917. AN Cracow: DPKr 112: fos. 2850–51.

39. K.k. Polizei-Direktor in Krakau, 'Tages-Rapport', 6 December 1917. AVA Vienna: MdI, Präsidiale (1916–17) 22/Galiz: Karton 2117: Nr. 24226.

40. Summary of damage caused by mid-January 1918 demonstrations. AN Cracow: DPKr 119: fo. 1639.

41. Denunciation, 19 March 1918. AN Cracow: DPKr 188: fo. 347.

42. 'Große Exzesse gegen die Juden in Krakau', Fremdenblatt. 72 Jahrgang, Nr. 102. Morgenausgabe (23 April 1918), p. 6.

43. For the attacks on Jews on 16 and 17 April 1918, see k.k. Polizei-Direktor in Krakau, 'Tages-Rapport', 16 and 17 April 1918. AVA Vienna: MdI, Präsidiale (1918) 22/Galiz: Karton 2118: Nr. 9180 and 9035, and the documentation in AN Cracow: DPKr 118: fos. 1659–93, 1727 and 1729–31. For 20 April, see 'Protokoll', 25 May 1918, and the accompanying reports. AN Cracow: DPKr 189: fos. 131–3, 135–6, 139–41.

44. For information on anti-Semitic riots in Wieliczka and Klasno in May, see AVA Vienna: MdI, Präsidiale (1918) 22/Galiz: Karton 2118: Nr. 1206. For later violence against Jews, see F. Golczewski, *Polnische-Jüdische Beziehungen, 1881–1922. Eine Studie zur Gechichte des Antisemitismus in Osteuropa* (Wiesbaden, 1981), pp. 169–75 and 181–213.

45. K.k. Polizei-Direktor in Krakau, 'Tages-Rapport', 19 April 1918. AVA Vienna: MdI, Präsidiale (1918) 22/Galiz: Karton 2118: Nr. 9226. Also 'Bericht über die Exzesse am 19./4.1918 am Tandelmarkte in der ul. Szeroka', 19 April 1918. AN Cracow: DPKr 118: fos. 1751–2.

46. Oblt. i.d. Res. Robert Steiner. 'Meldung über Misshandlung', 16 April 1918. AN Cracow: DPKr 118: fo. 1719.

47. K.k. Polizei-Direktor in Krakau, 'Tages-Rapport', 17 April 1918. AVA Vienna: MdI, Präsidiale (1918) 22/Galiz: Karton 2118: Nr. 9035.

48. See 'Bericht über die Exzesse am 19./4.1918 am Tandelmarkte in der ul. Szeroka', 19 April 1918. AN Cracow: DPKr 118: fos. 1751–2.

49. Nachrichtenstelle des k.u.k. Mil. Mdos, Krakau, 17 May 1918. AVA Vienna: MdI, Präsidiale (1918) 22/Galiz: Karton 2118: Nr. 14672.

50. K.k. Ministerium für Landesverteidigung to k.k. Ministerium des Innern, 'Galizien – Stimmung', 18 June 1918, and k.u.k. Militärkommando Przemyśl, 'Lagebericht', 21 June 1918. AVA Vienna: MdI, Präsidiale (1918) 22/Galiz: Karton 2118: Nr. 14297, and Karton 2119: Nr. 16443.

51. K.u.k. Militärkommando Przemyśl, 'Lagebericht', 21 June 1918. AVA Vienna: MdI, Präsidiale (1918) 22/Galiz: Karton 2118: Nr. 14297, and Karton 2119: Nr. 16443. Also K. Pichlík, 'Der militärische Zusammenbruch der Mittelmächte im Jahre 1918', in Plaschka and Mack (eds.), *Die Auflösung des Habsburgerreiches*, p. 258.

52. See F. Barac, *Croats and Slovenes, Friends of the Entente in the World War: A Few Official Documents Derived from the Archives of the Imperial and Royal Military Commands* (Paris, 1919), pp. 60–62 (doc. 26) and 88–90 (doc. 44). For background, see also J. P. Newman, 'Post-Imperial and Post-War Violence in the South Slav Lands, 1917–1923', *Contemporary European History* 19(3) (August 2010), esp. pp. 249–50 and 253–6, and, most importantly, Plaschka, Haselsteiner and Suppan, *Innere Front*, ii, pp. 70–89 and 94–101.

53. See the summary reports for Prague, 6. Bogen and 11. Bogen, entries 141 and 275 for end of April 1917 and 5 May 1918. Also the reports for Tabor (1917) and Plaschin. polit. Bezirk Plan (7 February 1918). AVA Vienna: MdI, Präsidiale. Varia Erster Weltkrieg: Karton 33.

54. Rechter, 'Galicia in Vienna', pp. 126–8.

55. 'Bericht des Gemeinsamen Zentralnachweisebureaus, Auskunftsstelle für Kriegsgefangene, Zensurabteilung in Wien für den Monat Dezember 1917 über die Stimmung der österreichischen Bevölkerung im Hinterlande', pp. 2 and 5. AVA Vienna: MdI, Präsidium (1918). 22/gen. Nr. 2358.

56. Herwig, *First World War*, p. 365, Rothenberg, *The Army of Francis Joseph*, p. 213, and Pichlík, 'Militärische Zusammenbruch', p. 253.

57. Plaschka, Haselsteiner and Suppan, *Innere Front*, i, pp. 33–4.

58. Cornwall, *Undermining*, pp. 272–7.

59. Romer, *Pamiętniki*, pp. 155–7.

60. Wegs, 'Austrian Economic Mobilization', pp. 165–6, 207 and 216.

61. Plaschka, Haselsteiner and Suppan, *Innere Front*, i, pp. 46–51.

62. G. Lelewer, 'Die Militärpersonen', in Exner, *Krieg und Kriminalität in Österreich*. For a comparison of execution rates in the First World War,

see A. Watson, 'Morale', in J. Winter (ed.), *The Cambridge History of the First World War: The State* (3 vols., Cambridge, 2014), ii, pp. 178–9.

63. AOK, 'Stellungsname zu Op.N 45286 betreffend die Ursachen von Desertion', 25 September 1917. KA Vienna: AOK-Op.-Abteilung: Karton 133: Nr. 45286.

64. K.u.k. Heeresgruppenkommando F. M. Freiherr von Conrad, 'Erhebungen über Desertion', 15 September 1917. KA Vienna: AOK-Op.-Abteilung: Karton 133: Nr. 45286.

65. Pichlík, 'Militärische Zusammenbruch', p. 263, endnote 11.

66. R. Nachtigal, 'Privilegiensystem und Zwangsrekrutierung. Russische Nationalitätenpolitik gegenüber Kriegsgefangenen aus Österreich-Ungarn', in J. Oltmer (ed.), *Kriegsgefangene im Europa des Ersten Weltkriegs* (Paderborn, Munich, Vienna and Zurich, 2006), pp. 174–5 and 182–90.

67. Lenin, quoted in I. Volgyes, 'Hungarian Prisoners of War in Russia, 1916–1919', *Cahiers du monde russe et soviétique* 14(1/2) (January–June 1973), p. 78.

68. Ibid., pp. 56–7, 63, 69, and, for the Kun quotation, 75.

69. Plaschka, Haselsteiner and Suppan, *Innere Front*, i, pp. 280–84.

70. A. Rachamimov, 'Imperial Loyalties and Private Concerns: Nation, Class and State in the Correspondence of Austro-Hungarian POWs in Russia, 1916–1918', *Austrian History Yearbook* 31 (2000), pp. 87–105.

71. The pioneering study is A. L. Vischer, *Barbed Wire Disease: A Psychological Study of the Prisoner of War* (London, 1919).

72. For details, see R. Nachtigal, *Die Murmanbahn, 1915–1919 – Kriegsnotwendigkeit und Wirtschaftsinteressen* (Remshalden, 2007), and G. Wurzer, 'Die Erfahrung der Extreme. Kriegsgefangene in Rußland, 1914–1918', in J. Oltmer (ed.), *Kriegsgefangene im Europa des Ersten Weltkriegs* (Paderborn, Munich, Vienna and Zurich, 2006), pp. 108–9, 112–13 and 118. The death rate on this railway was, incidentally, far worse than that on the much more famous Burma railway in the Second World War. Under Japanese oversight, 12,000 of the 62,000 Western prisoners who worked there died, a mortality rate of 19 per cent. At least 73,000 Asian civilian forced labourers also died, a rate of 27 per cent. See P. H. Kratoska (ed.), *The Thailand-Burma Railway, 1942–1946: Documents and Selected Writings* (6 vols., Abingdon and New York, 2006), i, p. 11.

73. Plaschka, Haselsteiner and Suppan, *Innere Front*, i, p. 281, fn. 12.

74. O. Wassermeier, 'Die Meutereien der Heimkehrer aus russischer Kriegsgefangenschaft bei den Ersatzkörpern der k.u.k. Armee im Jahre 1918', unpublished PhD thesis, University of Vienna (1968), p. 279.

75. Plaschka, Haselsteiner and Suppan, *Innere Front*, i, pp. 323–41.

76. O. Czernin, *In the World War* (New York and London, 1920), p. 31.

77. Fischer, *Germany's Aims*, pp. 527–9, and May, *Passing of the Hapsburg Monarchy*, ii, pp. 630–36 and 722–6.

78. Plaschka, Haselsteiner and Suppan, *Innere Front*, i, pp. 37–42.

13. COLLAPSE

1. Thaer, *Generalstabsdienst an der Front*, pp. 150–51 (diary entry for 31 December 1917).

2. Ludendorff, *My War Memories*, ii, p. 543.

3. See e.g. the Frankfurt Magistrat report on 'Stimmung der Zivilbevölkerung', 17 December 1917. HHStA Wiesbaden: 405: Nr. 6359: fo. 37. More generally, 'Zusammenstellung der Monatsberichte der stellv. Generalkommandos an das preußische Kriegsministerium betr. die allgemeine Stimmung im Volke', for November 1917 (3 December 1917), pp. 1, 39–40. GStA PK, Berlin: I. HA Rep 90A, Nr. 2685.

4. Scheidemann in the Reichstag Steering Committee, 24 January 1918, reproduced in Michaelis, Schraepler and Scheel (eds.), *Ursachen und Folgen*, ii, p. 245 (doc. 327).

5. Wetzell, quoted in Herwig, *First World War*, p. 394.

6. For German knowledge of the French mutinies, see Generalquartiermeister, memorandum, 27 July 1917. GLA Karlsruhe: 456 F 109, Nr. 1. For conditions on the home front, see Becker and Krumeich, *Grosse Krieg*, pp. 121 and 127–8.

7. Abteilung Fremde Heere, 'Mitteilung über die britische Armee Nr. 4', 1 January 1918. HStA Stuttgart: M33/2, Bü 536. For the planning of the Spring Offensive, see D. T. Zabecki, *The German 1918 Offensives: A Case Study in the Operational Level of War* (Abingdon and New York, 2006), pp. 93–112.

8. For command, see Samuels, *Command or Control?*, ch. 8, and T. Travers, *How the War was Won: Command and Technology in the British Army on the Western Front, 1917–1918* (London, 1992), ch. 3. For the troops, see Watson, *Enduring the Great War*, pp. 175–83.

9. Rawlinson to Wilson, 18 April 1918, quoted in I. M. Brown, *British Logistics on the Western Front, 1914–1919* (London, 1998), p. 191. For a full discussion, see D. T. Zabecki, 'Railroads and the Operational Level of War in the German 1918 Offensives', in J. D. Keene and M. S. Neiberg (eds.), *Finding Common Ground: New Directions in First World War Studies* (Leiden and Boston, MA, 2011), pp. 161–86.

10. Zabecki, *The German 1918 Offensives*, p. 109.

11. M. Middlebrook, *The Kaiser's Battle, 21 March 1918: The First Day of the German Spring Offensive* (London, 1978), pp. 70–74.

12. G. Fong, 'The Movement of German Divisions to the Western Front, Winter 1917–1918', *War in History* 7(2) (April 2000), pp. 229–30.

13. Zabecki, *The German 1918 Offensives*, pp. 126–33.

14. Ibid., pp. 125–6.

15. 'What are you fighting for?', propaganda leaflet, issued on 26 February 1918. HStA Stuttgart: M33/2 Bü 516.

16. Postüberwachung der 5. Armee, reports of 10 January and 24 February 1918. BA-MA Freiburg: W-10/50794: fos. 35 and 45.

17. L. Wernicke, diary, 21 March 1918. DTA, Emmendingen: 1040, II.

18. Von Heydekampf, diary extract, reproduced in Michaelis, Schraepler and Scheel (eds.), *Ursachen und Folgen*, ii, p. 251.

19. Middlebrook, *Kaiser's Battle*, pp. 322–3. Also Samuels, *Command or Control?*, pp. 214–21.

20. Müller, *Kaiser and his Court*, p. 344 (diary entry for 23 March 1918).

21. Leutnant B. to Oberarzt Travers, 30 March 1918. HHStA Wiesbaden: Feldpostbriefe – Paul Travers: 1073, Nr. 8.

22. Kitchen, *German Offensives*, p. 94.

23. Watson, *Enduring the Great War*, p. 181.

24. For a day-by-day analysis of the offensive, see Zabecki, *German 1918 Offensives*, pp. 139–73. For gains, see Stevenson, *With Our Backs to the Wall*, p. 67.

25. W. Deist, 'Verdeckter Militärstreik im Kriegsjahr 1918?', in W. Wette (ed.), *Der Krieg des kleinen Mannes: Eine Militärgeschichte von unten* (Munich and Zurich, 1992, 1995), pp. 149–50. For an example of heavy infantry casualties, see the account of the losses of 1st Guards Reserve Division in H. Fuchs, diary, 30 March 1918. BA-MA Freiburg: MSg 1/2968.

26. Zabecki, *German 1918 Offensives*, pp. 184–205.

27. R. Foley, 'From Victory to Defeat: The German Army in 1918', in A. Ekins (ed.), *1918: Year of Victory* (Auckland and Wollombi, 2010), p. 77.

28. Zabecki, *German 1918 Offensives*, p. 199.

29. R. Lechmann, letter to his sister, 28 April 1918. Private Collection (Author).

30. Kuhl's diary, quoted in Stevenson, *With Our Backs to the Wall*, p. 75.

31. Thaer, *Generalstabsdienst an der Front*, p. 182 (diary entry for *c.* 18 April 1918).

32. Zabecki, *German 1918 Offensives*, esp. p. 219.

33. Lutz (ed.), *Causes of the German Collapse*, p. 69. Cf. also Gallwitz, *Erleben im Westen*, p. 340, and Görlitz (ed.), *Kaiser and his Court*, p. 374 (entry for 23 July 1918).

34. Stevenson, *With Our Backs to the Wall*, pp. 112–69, and Griffith, *Battle Tactics*, p. 22.

35. Major Ludwig Beck, quoted in Deist, 'Verdeckter Militärstreik', p. 151.

36. For the state of front-line units in the last weeks, see the reports in A. Philipp (ed.), *Die Ursachen des Deutschen Zusammenbruches im Jahre 1918*.

Zweite Abteilung. Der innere Zusammenbruch (Berlin, 1928), vi, pp. 321–86. For machine-gunners, see Summaries of Information. Fourth Army, Report No. 287, 1 October 1918, p. 7. TNA London: WO 157/199.

37. For figures, see Deist, 'Military Collapse', p. 197, and *Sanitätsbericht*, iii, p. 143*.

38. L. P. Ayres, *The War with Germany: A Statistical Summary* (Washington, 1919), p. 104. For US transports, see Stevenson, *With Our Backs to the Wall*, p. 345.

39. Deist, 'Military Collapse', p. 190, and Kitchen, *German Offensives*, p. 14.

40. For tactics, see J. Boff, *Winning and Losing on the Western Front: The British Third Army and the Defeat of Germany in 1918* (Cambridge, 2012), chs. 5 and 6; Stachelbeck, *Militärische Effektivität*, pp. 236–45. For divisional strengths, see A.F.B.D., 'Some Military Causes of the German Collapse', *The United Service Magazine* 60 (October 1919–March 1920), p. 292, and Deist, 'Verdeckter Militärstreik', p. 159.

41. Ludendorff's speech of 23 October 1918, as reported by the Saxon *Militärbevollmächtigter* to the War Minister, 24 October 1918. HStA Dresden: Militärbevollmächtigter Nr. 4216: fos. 114–15.

42. Altrichter, *Die seelischen Kräfte*, pp. 134–6.

43. Watson, *Enduring the Great War*, pp. 196–7 and 205–6.

44. Ibid., p. 212.

45. Lutz (ed.), *Causes of the German Collapse*, pp. 142–5. See also the Prussian War Ministry's order entitled 'Disziplinlosigkeiten bei Ersatztransporten', 22 July 1918. HStA Stuttgart: M38/17 Bü 5: fo. 53.

46. W. Giffenig, quoted in Watson, *Enduring the Great War*, p. 212. For other examples of indiscipline, see ibid., p. 213.

47. Ludendorff, *My War Memories*, ii, pp. 586, 613 and 642, von Kuhl's report in Lutz (ed.), *Causes of the German Collapse*, pp. 84–5.

48. Thaer, *Generalstabsdienst*, p. 188 (diary entry for 26 and 27 April 1918).

49. Kitchen, *German Offensives*, p. 209, and Nachtigal, 'Repatriierung der Mittelmächte-Kriegsgefangenen', p. 246.

50. Report from the draft battalion of Reserve Infantry Regiment Nr. 111 in Donaueschingen, 1 September 1918. GLA Karlsruhe 456 F55, Nr. 76. For other examples, see Watson, *Enduring the Great War*, pp. 213–14.

51. Ludendorff, *My War Memories*, ii, p. 679.

52. Summaries of Information. Fourth Army, 'Weekly Appreciation: For Period from 10th to 16th August (inclusive)', 17 August 1918, pp. 3–4. TNA London: WO 157/197.

53. 41 Division, order of 14 August 1914, reproduced in Scheidemann, *Zusammenbruch*, pp. 185–6. For the number of prisoners, see United States War Office, *Histories of Two Hundred and Fifty-One Divisions of the German Army which Participated in the War* (London, 1920, 1989), p. 449.

54. Res. Feldartillerie Regt. 3, 'Erfahrungen aus den Kämpfen vom 18. bis 21.7.1918', 25 July 1918. BA-MA Freiburg: PH 8-II/4. Also, for the military's response, 'Bestimmungen über die Organisation zur Sammlung und Weiterleitung von Versprengten an der Westfront, 13 September 1918. GLA Karlsruhe: 456 Fr, Nr. 110.

55. Chef des Generalstabes, order, 1 August 1918. GLA Karlsruhe: 456 F6, Nr. 110. For other examples, see Deist, 'Military Collapse', p. 202.

56. Dr G., diary/memoir, 26 September 1918. BA-MA Freiburg: MSg 2/628. More generally on shirking and influenza, see H. Strachan, 'The Morale of the German Army, 1917–18', in H. Cecil and P. H. Liddle (eds.), Facing Armageddon: The First World War Experienced (London, 1996), pp. 394–5.

57. See Ulrich and Ziemann (eds.), Frontalltag, p. 140 (doc. 56c), and anon., Why Germany Capitulated, p. 60.

58. Volkmann, Soziale Heeresmißstände, xi(2), p. 66. For modern historians still echoing these claims see, most recently, B. Ziemann, Gewalt im Ersten Weltkrieg. Töten – Überleben – Verweigerung (Essen, 2013), chs. 6 and 7. Ziemann's arguments for a 'covert strike' rest on a mix of hyperbole and an uncritical reading of army orders. His work noticeably fails to explain adequately why neither contemporary desertion figures nor the records of straggler posts support his claim of a large exodus of soldiers from the line before October 1918. It is also disconcertingly credulous in its treatment of the highly politicized post-war estimates of shirking, and refuses to engage with research deconstructing these figures.

59. Stachelbeck, Militärische Effektivität, pp. 151, 297, fn 215 and 346–7, and Jahr, Gewöhnliche Soldaten, pp. 157 and 159, graphs 1 and 3. For further confirmation of the modest rate of desertion in the second half of 1918, see also the figures supplied for the Württemberg contingent in R. E. Zroka, 'If Only this War would End: German Soldiers in the Last Year of the First World War', unpublished PhD thesis, University of California, San Diego (2013), pp. 73–4.

60. See Jahr, Gewöhnliche Soldaten, pp. 166–7, and Watson, Enduring the Great War, p. 210.

61. For German military law, see Jahr, Gewöhnliche Soldaten, pp. 162, 195–7 and 232–5. For more detail on the German collapse and a revision of older arguments about desertion, see Watson, Enduring the Great War, ch. 6.

62. J. P. Harris and N. Barr, Amiens to the Armistice. The BEF in the Hundred Days' Campaign, 8 August–November 1918 (London, 1998), p. 291. For total German prisoners, see M. Huber (ed.), La Population de la France pendant la Guerre (Paris and New Haven, CT, 1931), p. 132.

63. Von Einem, Armeeführer, pp. 434–5 (letter of 14 September 1918).

64. Summaries of Information. Fourth Army: 'Weekly Appreciation: For Period from August 31st to 6th Sept., 1918 (Incl.)', 7 September 1918, pp. 3–4, and Report No. 266, 10 September 1918, p. 5. TNA London: WO 157/198.

65. Jahr, *Gewöhnliche Soldaten*, p. 165, and Lasswell, *Propaganda Technique*, p. 184.

66. G. G. Bruntz, *Allied Propaganda and the Collapse of the German Empire in 1918* (Stanford, CA, 1938), pp. 98, 111–12 and 124–5.

67. Denunciation by R. Peyke to the Saxon War Minister of an overheard conversation, 23 August 1918. HStA Dresden: 11352 Stellv. Gen-Kdo XIX AK KA(P) 24170, fo. 145.

68. See *Sanitätsbericht*, iii, p. 132*.

69. Letter of H. Schützinger to M. Hobohm, 30 March 1927, reproduced in Hobohm, *Soziale Heeresmißstände*, xi.i, p. 424.

70. Rupprecht von Bayern, *Kriegstagebuch*, ii, p. 443.

71. Censorship report of 6. Armee, 4 September 1918, in Michaelis, Schraepler and Scheel (eds.), *Ursachen und Folgen*, ii, p. 303 (doc. 356).

72. Mechow's account in file, p. 1517. BA-MA Freiburg: W-10/50677.

73. Rupprecht, *Kriegstagebuch*, iii, p. 28 (letter to his father, 14 October 1918).

74. The New York Times, *The New York Times Current History: The European War. July–August–September 1918* (20 vols., New York: The New York Times), xvi, p. 400.

75. This account follows Watson, *Enduring the Great War*, pp. 215–29. For the penalties for deserting to the enemy, see the order issued by Chef des Gen Stabes des Feldheeres, 25 June 1918, reproduced in Ulrich and Ziemann (eds.), *Frontalltag*, pp. 123–4 (doc. 47c).

76. R. Gaupp, 'Schreckneurosen und Neurasthenie', in K. Bonhoeffer (ed.), *Geistes- und Nervenkrankheiten* (2 vols., Leipzig, 1922), i, p. 91.

77. Nebelin, *Ludendorff*, pp. 423–4.

78. Thaer, *Generalstabsdienst*, p. 222 (diary entry for 15 August 1918).

79. Nebelin, *Ludendorff*, pp. 446–50 and 454–5. Also Kitchen, *Silent Dictatorship*, p. 252.

80. See the notes of Colonel Mertz von Quirnheim, reproduced in Michaelis, Schraepler and Scheel (eds.), *Ursachen und Folgen*, ii, p. 293 (doc. 353).

81. W. Foerster, *Der Feldherr Ludendorff im Unglück. Eine Studie über seine seelische Haltung in der Endphase des ersten Weltkrieges* (Wiesbaden, 1952), pp. 73–4.

82. Ibid., pp. 76–9.

83. Nebelin, *Ludendorff*, pp. 423–4.

84. Reichskanzlei, *Vorgeschichte des Waffenstillstandes. Amtliche Urkunden* (Berlin, 1919), p. 6.

85. Thaer, *Generalstabsdienst*, p. 234 (diary entry for 1 October 1918).

86. Ibid.

87. See von Hintze's notes on the meeting, reproduced in Michaelis, Schraepler and Scheel (eds.), *Ursachen und Folgen*, ii, pp. 319–20 (doc. 365).

88. R. Höfner, diary, 3 April 1918. DTA, Emmendingen: 1280,1.

89. For food, see Offer, *First World War*, pp. 48–50. For the influenza, see G. Kolata, *Flu: The Story of the Great Influenza Pandemic of 1918 and the Search for the Virus that Caused it* (New York, 2001), p. 7.

90. Kühlmann's speech in the Reichstag, 24 June 1918, reproduced in Michaelis, Schraepler and Scheel (eds.), *Ursachen und Folgen*, ii, p. 274 (doc. 340a).

91. Koszyk, *Deutsche Pressepolitik*, p. 192.

92. Landrat of St Goarshausen to Regierungspräsident, Wiesbaden, 16 September 1918. HHStA Wiesbaden: 405: Nr. 6360: fo. 117, and letter from a member of the public to Stellvertretendes Generalkommando Stuttgart, 20 September 1918. HStA Stuttgart: M77/1, Bü 786. For just one example of reports testifying to the sense of crisis in the German public, in large part as a result of events at the front, see N.O. des stellv. Generalkommandos XIII A.K. in Stuttgart, 'Die Gegenwärtigen Maßnahmen zur Hebung der Stimmung in Württemberg', 16 September 1918. HStA Stuttgart: M77/1 Bü 787: fo. 172.

93. F. Schlamp, letters, 4, 10 and 14 September and 16 October 1918. Author's Collection.

94. May, *Passing of the Hapsburg Monarchy*, ii, pp. 722–7 and 748–55.

95. Rothenberg, *Army of Francis Joseph*, pp. 212–13.

96. For statistics, see Herwig, *First World War*, p. 370, Thompson, *White War*, p. 342, and Gratz and Schüller, *Wirtschaftliche Zusammenbruch*, p. 151. Also Zeman, *Break-Up*, pp. 218–19.

97. Thompson, *White War*, pp. 344–6, and Herwig, *First World War*, pp. 370–71. For the poor state of the troops, see Cornwall, *Undermining*, pp. 287–99, and for an account of the battle, see Romer, *Pamiętniki*, pp. 161–4.

98. Glaise-Horstenau, *Collapse*, p. 175.

99. May, *Passing of the Hapsburg Monarchy*, ii, p. 723.

100. Healy, *Vienna*, pp. 187–8.

101. Rauchensteiner, *Tod des Doppeladlers*, p. 567.

102. Loewenfeld-Russ, *Regelung der Volksernährung*, p. 70.

103. See Glaise-Horstenau, *Collapse*, p. 155, and Loewenfeld-Russ, *Regelung der Volksernährung*, p. 71.

104. For summary reports giving a good overview of the plight of the Empire's cities, see AVA Vienna: MdI, Präsidium. Varia Erster Weltkrieg: Karton 33.

105. Plaschka, Haselsteiner and Suppan, *Innere Front*, i, pp. 39–42.

106. May, *Passing of the Hapsburg Monarchy*, ii, pp. 760–63.

107. Minutes of Common Ministerial Council, Vienna, 27 September 1918, reproduced in Cornwall (ed.), *Last Years of Austria-Hungary*, p. 198.

108. For the background to the manifesto, see Rauchensteiner, *Tod des Doppeladlers*, pp. 603–8, and Glaise-Horstenau, *Collapse*, pp. 207–9. A copy is posted online at: http://www.bl.uk/collection-items/to-faithful-austrian-people-emperor-karl# (accessed 11 April 2014).

109. See Křen, *Konfliktgemeinschaft*, pp. 371–2.

110. Macartney, *Habsburg Empire*, p. 831.

111. See the account in Redlich, *Schicksalsjahre Österreichs*, ii, p. 305 (diary entry for 21 October 1918).

112. Galántai, *Hungary*, pp. 315–22.

113. Plaschka, Haselsteiner and Suppan, *Innere Front*, ii, pp. 247–59.

114. Ibid., pp. 260–77. For Tisza's death, see May, *Passing of the Habsburg Monarchy*, ii, p. 789.

115. Rauchensteiner, *Tod des Doppeladlers*, pp. 614–15.

116. Plaschka, Haselsteiner and Suppan, *Innere Front*, ii, pp. 143–58, 184–5 and 217.

117. See Glaise-Horstenau, *Collapse*, pp. 260–61 and 264–7.

118. Redlich, *Schicksalsjahre Österreichs*, ii, p. 310 (diary entry for 30 October 1918).

119. A. Czechówna, diary, 1 November 1918. AN Cracow: IT 428/42.

120. Plaschka, Haselsteiner and Suppan, *Innere Front*, ii, pp. 289–301, and Bieniarzówna and Małecki, *Dzieje Krakowa*, iii, p. 394.

121. Plaschka, Haselsteiner and Suppan, *Innere Front*, ii, pp. 213 and 316, and Golczewski, *Polnische-Judische Beziehungen*, pp. 205–13.

122. Quoted in M. Mazower, 'Minorities and the League of Nations in Interwar Europe', *Daedalus* 126(2) (Spring 1997), p. 50. For the Polish-Ukrainian conflict and pogrom in the city, see Mick, *Kriegserfahrungen*, pp. 203–56.

123. H. R. Rudin, *Armistice 1918* (New Haven, CT, 1944), pp. 53–4.

124. M. von Baden, *Erinnerungen und Dokumente* (Hamburg, 1927, 2011), pp. 331 and 335. For the composition of the government, see Rudin, *Armistice*, p. 81.

125. Rudin, *Armistice 1918*, pp. 53 and 56–80.

126. M. Geyer, 'Insurrectionary Warfare: The German Debate about a Levée en Masse in October 1918', *The Journal of Contemporary History* 73(3) (September 2001), pp. 477–82.

127. Rudin, *Armistice 1918*, p. 80.

128. Ibid., pp. 104, 121–32.

129. Geyer, 'Insurrectionary Warfare', p. 494.

130. See the meeting's minutes in Ludendorff (ed.), *The General Staff and its Problems*, ii, esp. pp. 666, 674 and 686. Also Nebelin, *Ludendorff*, pp. 477–82.

131. Ibid., p. 668. For the unfeasibility of drafting these 600,000 men, see E. von Wrisberg, *Heer und Heimat 1914–1918* (Leipzig, 1921), p. 100. Groener

believed that those who could be drafted were already in the army: Groener, *Lebenserinnerungen*, p. 448.

132. See esp. Boff, *Winning and Losing*, p. 38.

133. Gallwitz, *Erleben im Westen*, p. 429 (diary entry for 21 October 1918).

134. Rupprecht von Bayern, *Kriegstagebuch*, ii, p. 459 (diary entry for 12 October 1918). Cf. Einem, *Armeeführer*, pp. 450–51 (letter of 15 October 1918), and Kriegsministerium to Reichskanzler, 31 October 1918. BA Berlin Lichterfelde: R43/2440: fo. 270.

135. See Max's statement at the 17 October meeting in Ludendorff (ed.), *The General Staff and its Problems*, ii, p. 686.

136. Quoted in Rudin, *Armistice 1918*, p. 173.

137. Vizepräsident des Staatsministeriums to Reichskanzler, 22 October 1918. BA Berlin Lichterfelde: R43/2440.

138. Nebelin, *Ludendorff*, p. 493.

139. Kaiser, quoted in Nebelin, *Ludendorff*, pp. 497–8.

140. Herwig, 'Luxury Fleet', p. 245.

141. W. Deist, 'Die Politik der Seekriegsleitung und die Rebellion der Flotte Ende Oktober 1918', *Vierteljahrshefte für Zeitgeschichte* 14(4) (October 1966), pp. 349 and 355. Also Herwig, 'Luxury Fleet', p. 245.

142. See esp. G. P. Groß, 'Eine Frage der Ehre? Die Marineführung und der letzte Flottenvorstoß 1918', in J. Duppler and G. P. Groß (eds.), *Kriegsende 1918. Ereignis, Wirkung, Nachwirkung. Beiträge zur Militärgeschichte. Herausgegeben vom Militärgeschichtlichen Forschungsamt. Band 53* (Munich, 1999), pp. 354–65.

143. Ibid., pp. 350–51, and Herwig, 'Luxury Fleet', pp. 247 and 250.

144. Deist, 'Politik der Seekriegsleitung', pp. 347–8.

145. This account is taken from ibid., pp. 361–4, Herwig, 'Luxury Fleet', p. 250.

146. H. Leidinger, 'Der Kieler Aufstand und die deutsche Revolution', in V. Moritz and H. Leidinger (eds.), *Die Nacht des Kirpitschnikow. Eine andere Geschichte des Ersten Weltkriegs* (Vienna, 2006), pp. 220–35, and Horn, *Mutiny on the High Seas*, pp. 234–46.

147. Kluge, *Soldatenräte*, pp. 48–56.

148. For Wilson's note, see Rudin, *Armistice 1918*, pp. 321–2.

149. Kluge, *Soldatenräte*, p. 65.

150. Rudin, *Armistice 1918*, pp. 327–9 and 349–51.

151. For this episode, see S. Stephenson, *The Final Battle: Soldiers of the Western Front and the German Revolution of 1918* (Cambridge, 2009), pp. 83–90.

152. Rudin, *Armistice 1918*, pp. 345–59, and Kluge, *Soldatenräte*, pp. 82–7.

153. M. Jessen-Klingenberg, 'Die Ausrufung der Republik durch Philipp Scheidemann am 9. November 1918', *Geschichte in Wissenschaft und Unterricht* 19(11) (November 1968), p. 653.

154. Rudin, *Armistice 1918*, pp. 333, 381–3 and 427–32.

155. For the German revolutions, see U. Kluge, *Die deutsche Revolution 1918/1919. Staat, Politik und Gesellschaft zwischen Weltkrieg und Kapp-Putsch* (Frankfurt am Main, 1985). For the turmoil in the eastern borderlands from December 1918, see A. Czubiński, *Powstanie Wielkopolskie 1918–1919. Geneza-charakter-znaczenie* (Poznań, 1988).

EPILOGUE

1. An engaging account of the deliberations in Paris is Margaret MacMillan's *Peacemakers*. However, see also for a summary of the independent military actions by new states in east-central Europe, J. Rothschild, *East Central Europe Between the Two World Wars* (Washington, DC, 1978).

2. S. Marks, '"My Name is Ozymandias": The Kaiser in Exile', *Central European History* 16(2) (June 1983), pp. 122–70.

3. May, *Passing of the Hapsburg Monarchy*, ii, pp. 806–8. For the beatification, see http://news.bbc.co.uk/1/hi/world/europe/3710810.stm, accessed on 26 April 2014.

4. Jarausch, *Enigmatic Chancellor*, pp. 1–3.

5. See the entry on Berchtold in S. C. Tucker (ed.), *The Encyclopedia of World War I: A Political, Social and Military History* (Santa Barbara, CA, 2005), pp. 200–201. Leon Biliński, *Wspomnienia i dokumenty* (2 vols., Warsaw, 1924 and 1925), see esp. i, pp. 274–94, and ii, pp. 200–312, for his experiences in July 1914 and as Polish Finance Minister respectively.

6. Sondhaus, *Franz Conrad von Hötzendorf*, pp. 225–7.

7. Nebelin, *Ludendorff*, p. 507, and R. Chickering, 'Sore Loser: Ludendorff's Total War', in R. Chickering and S. Förster (eds.), *The Shadows of Total War: Europe, East Asia, and the United States, 1919–1939* (Washington, DC, and Cambridge, 2003), pp. 151–78.

8. Pyta, *Hindenburg*, pp. 461ff.

9. See V. N. Dadrian and T. Akçam, *Judgement at Istanbul: The Armenian Genocide Trials* (New York and Oxford, 2011).

10. G. Hankel, *Die Leipziger Prozesse. Deutsche Kriegsverbrechen und ihre strafrechtliche Verfolgung nach dem Ersten Weltkrieg* (Hamburg, 2003), esp. pp. 97–104.

11. Naimark, *Fires of Hatred*, p. 57.

12. See R. J. W. Evans, 'The Successor States', in R. Gerwarth (ed.), *Twisted Paths: Europe 1914–1945* (Oxford, 2007), p. 212.

13. A. Sharp, 'The Genie that would not Go Back in the Bottle: National Self-Determination and the Legacy of the First World War and the Peace Settlement', in S. Dunn and T. G. Fraser, *Europe and Ethnicity: World*

War I and Contemporary Ethnic Conflict (London and New York, 1996), p. 25.

14. H. Batowski, 'Nationale Konflikte bei der Enstehung der Nachfolgestaaten', in R. G. Plaschka and K. Mack (eds.), *Die Auflösung des Habsburgerreiches. Zusammenbruch und Neuorientierung im Donauraum* (Vienna, 1970), p. 342.

15. MacMillan, *Peacemakers*, p. 475 (for quotation), and, more generally, pp. 475–81. For Wilson's note of 23 October 1918, see Rudin, *Armistice 1918*, p. 173.

16. Wicker, 'Weltkrieg in Zahlen', pp. 521–2, and R. Pearson, 'Hungary: A State Truncated, a Nation Dismembered', in S. Dunn and T. G. Fraser, *Europe and Ethnicity: World War I and Contemporary Ethnic Conflict* (London and New York, 1996), pp. 95–6.

17. D. Kirk, *Europe's Population in the Interwar Years* (New York, 1946), and Pearson, 'Hungary', pp. 98–9. The German figure excludes 3.3 million Swiss and 1.2 million Soviet Germans.

18. G. Rhode, 'Das Deutschtum in Posen und Pommerellen in der Zeit der Weimarer Republik', in Senatskommission für das Studium des Deutschtums im Osten an der Rheinischen Friedrich-Wilhelms-Universität Bonn (Cologne and Graz, 1966), p. 99. Other estimates are higher, see R. Blanke, *Orphans of Versailles: The Germans in Western Poland, 1918–1939* (Lexington, KY, 1993), pp. 32–4.

19. L. Boswell, 'From Liberation to Purge Trials in the "Mythic Provinces": Recasting French Identities in Alsace and Lorraine, 1918–1920', *French Historical Studies* 23(1) (Winter 2000), p. 141.

20. I. I. Mocsy, *The Effects of World War I. The Uprooted: Hungarian Refugees and their Impact on Hungary's Domestic Politics, 1918–1921* (New York, 1983), p. 10.

21. S. Marks, 'The Myths of Reparations', *Central European History* 11(3) (September 1978), pp. 231–9. Also Ferguson, *Pity of War*, pp. 399–432.

22. See Liberman, *Does Conquest Pay?*, ch. 5. For the French African troops, see K. L. Nelson, 'The "Black Horror on the Rhine": Race as a Factor in Post-World War I Diplomacy', *The Journal of Modern History* 42(4) (December 1970), pp. 606–27.

23. See esp. Mosse, *Fallen Soldiers*, pp. 11, 160–81, 219.

24. Bessel, *Germany*, pp. 77–81 and 88–90, and Stephenson, *Final Battle*, pp. 205–10. For paramilitary violence, see R. Gerwarth, 'The Central European Counter-Revolution: Paramilitary Violence in Germany, Austria and Hungary after the Great War', *Past and Present* 200 (August 2008), pp. 175–209.

25. R. W. Whalen, *Bitter Wounds: German Victims of the Great War, 1914–1939* (Ithaca, NY, and London, 1984), p. 95.

26. Grebler and Winkler, *Cost of the World War*, p. 136 (1923 figures).

27. M. Mann, *The Dark Side of Democracy: Explaining Ethnic Cleansing* (Cambridge, 2004, 2005), pp. 223-8. For an illustration of how the collapse of multi-ethnic communities in the Reich bore some similarity to the case of Cracow described in this book, see the documentation dealing with the riot at Culmsee in West Prussia in AP Toruń: Star. Pow. Toruniu 1818-1920, Nr. 1009: fos. 701-35.

28. Jászi, *Dissolution*, p. 455.

29. *Sanitätsbericht*, iii, p. 12.

30. Grebler and Winkler, *Cost of the War*, p. 144, and W. Winkler, *Die Totenverluste der öst.-ung. Monarchie nach Nationalitäten. Die Altersgliederung der Toten. Ausblicke in die Zukunft* (Vienna, 1919), pp. 6-8.

31. For an excellent illustration of how veterans reinterpreted their sacrifice in line with official narratives for political and material gain, see J. Eichenberg, *Kämpfen für Frieden und Fürsorge. Polnische Veteranen des Ersten Weltkriegs und ihre internationalen Kontakte, 1918-1939* (Munich, 2011).

32. R. Höfner, diary entry, 10 November 1918. DTA, Emmendingen: 1280,1.

33. Letter from Elisabeth Harmuth to Gertrud Kohnstern, 2 November 1918. Author's Collection.

34. Becker and Krumeich, *Grosse Krieg*, p. 310.

35. See S. Goebel, 'Re-Membered and Re-Mobilized: The "Sleeping Dead" in Interwar Germany and Britain', *Journal of Contemporary History* 39(4) (October 2004), pp. 487-501. C. Siebrecht, *The Aesthetics of Loss: German Women's Art of the First World War* (Oxford, 2013), esp. ch. 5, and the classic works on the dead and mourning after the First World War, Mosse, *Fallen Soldiers*, ch. 5, and J. Winter, *Sites of Memory, Sites of Mourning: The Great War in European Cultural History* (Cambridge, 1995).

Abbreviations

AOK	Armeeoberkommando (Habsburg Army High Command)
GGB	Generalgouvernement Belgien (General Government Belgium)
GGW	Generalgouvernement Warschau (General Government Warsaw)
HITD	Honvéd-Infanterietruppendivision (Habsburg *Honvéd* Division)
ITD	Infanterietruppendivision (Habsburg Infantry Division)
k.k.	Kaiserlich-königlich (Imperial-royal)
KÜA	Kriegsüberwachungsamt (War Supervision Office)
k.u.k.	Kaiserlich und königlich (Imperial and royal)
LITD	Landwehr-Infanterietruppendivision (Habsburg *Landwehr* Division)
OHL	Oberste Heeresleitung (German Army High Command)
ÖULK	Bundesministerium für Heereswesen und Kriegsarchiv, *Österreich-Ungarns letzter Krieg* (7 vols., Vienna: Verlag der Militärwissenschaftlichen Mitteilungen, 1930–38) (The official Austrian military history of the First World War)
Sanitätsbericht	Heeres-Sanitätsinspektion des Reichskriegsministeriums (ed.), *Sanitätsbericht über das deutsche Heer (Deutsches Feld- und Besatzungsheer) im Weltkriege 1914/1918 (Deutscher Kriegssanitätsbericht 1914/18)* (3 vols., Berlin: E. S. Mittler & Sohn, 1934–8) (The official German military medical history of the First World War)

SPD	Sozialdemokratische Partei Deutschlands (Social Democratic Party of Germany)
USPD	Unabhängige Sozialdemokratische Partei Deutschlands (Independent Social Democratic Party of Germany)
ZAB	Zivilarbeiterbataillon (Civil Worker Battalion)
AA	Archiwum Archidiecezjalne (Archiepiscopal Archive)
AN	Archiwum Narodowe (National Archive)
AP	Archiwum Państwowe (State Archive)
AVA	Allgemeines Verwaltungsarchiv (General Administration Archive)
BA	Bundesarchiv (Federal Archive)
BA-MA	Bundesarchiv Militärarchiv (Federal Military Archive)
BfZ	Bibliothek für Zeitgeschichte (Library of Contemporary History)
BN	Biblioteka Narodowa (National Library)
CAHJP	The Central Archives for the History of the Jewish People
DTA	Deutsches Tagebucharchiv (German Diary Archive)
GLA	Generallandesarchiv (General Regional Archive)
GStA PK	Geheimes Staatsarchiv Preußischer Kulturbesitz (Secret State Archives Prussian Cultural Heritage Foundation)
HHStA	Hessisches Hauptstaatsarchiv (Main State Archive of Hessen)
HStA	Hauptstaatsarchiv (Main State Archive)
IWM	Imperial War Museum
KA	Kriegsarchiv (War Archive)
TNA	The National Archives

Where personal papers held by the Bundesarchiv-Militärarchiv, Deutsches Tagebucharchiv and Bibliothek für Zeitgeschichte have been cited in the text or footnotes, pseudonyms have been used to protect their authors' identities.

Bibliography

ARCHIVES
Austria

Österreichisches Staatsarchiv
  Allgemeines Verwaltungsarchiv
  Kriegsarchiv

Germany

Bibliothek für Zeitgeschichte, Stuttgart
Bundesarchiv Berlin-Lichterfelde
Bundesarchiv-Militärarchiv Freiburg
Deutsches Tagebucharchiv, Emmendingen
Geheimes Staatsarchiv Preußischer Kulturbesitz, Berlin
Generallandesarchiv Karlsruhe
Hauptstaatsarchiv Dresden
Hauptstaatsarchiv Stuttgart
Hessisches Hauptstaatsarchiv, Wiesbaden

Israel

The Central Archives for the History of the Jewish People, Jerusalem

Poland

Archiwum Archidiecezjalne w Poznaniu
Archiwum Narodowe w Krakowie

Archiwum Państwowe w Katowicach: Oddział w Raciborzu
Archiwum Państwowe w Olsztynie
Archiwum Państwowe w Poznaniu
Archiwum Państwowe w Toruniu
Biblioteka Narodowa, Warsaw (Microfilm Collection)

United Kingdom

Imperial War Museum, London
The National Archives, London

PUBLISHED PRIMARY SOURCES
Newspapers

Berliner Tageblatt
Czas
Deutsche Kriegszeitung
Frankfurter Zeitung und Handelsblatt
Illustrierte Geschichte des Weltkrieges 1914/15. Allgemeine Kriegszeitung
Illustrierte Ostdeutsche Kriegs-Zeitung
Kurjer Lwowski
Liegnitzer Tageblatt
Nowa Reforma
Pester Lloyd
Reichspost
Wiener Bilder. Illustriertes Familienblatt
Zusammenbruch. Dezemberheft 1918 der Süddeutschen Monatshefte

Books

Afflerbach, H. (ed.), *Kaiser Wilhelm II. als Oberster Kriegsherr im Ersten Welt-krieg. Quellen aus der militärischen Umgebung des Kaisers 1914–1918* (Munich: R. Oldenbourg, 2005).
Altrichter, F., *Die seelischen Kräfte des deutschen Heeres im Frieden und im Welt-kriege* (Berlin: E. S. Mittler & Sohn, 1933).
Altrock, C. von (ed.), *Vom Sterben des deutschen Offizierkorps* (Berlin: E. S. Mittler & Sohn, 1922).

Ansky, S., *The Enemy at his Pleasure: A Journey through the Jewish Pale of Settlement during World War I*, ed. and trans. J. Neugroschel (New York: Metropolitan Books, 2002).

Antipa, G., *L'Occupation Ennemie de la Roumanie et ses Conséquences Économiques et Sociales* (Paris and New Haven, CT: Les Presses Universitaires de France and Yale University Press, 1929).

Arz von Straußenburg, A., *Zur Geschichte des Grossen Krieges 1914–1918* (Vienna, Leipzig and Munich: Rikola, 1924).

Augé-Laribé, M. and Pinot, P., *Agriculture and Food Supply in France during the War* (New Haven, CT, and London: Yale University Press and Humphrey Milford, Oxford University Press, 1927).

Ayres, L. P., *The War with Germany: A Statistical Summary* (Washington: G.P.O., 1919)

Bachelin, E. and Geiger, W., *Das Reserve-Infanterie-Regiment Nr. 111 im Weltkrieg 1914 bis 1918* (Karlsruhe: Südwestdeutsche Druck- und Verlagsgesellschaft, 1937).

Bächtold, H., *Deutscher Soldatenbrauch und Soldatenglaube* (Strassburg: Karl J. Trübner, 1917).

Baden, M. von, *Erinnerungen und Dokumente* (Hamburg: Severus, 1927, 2011).

Baedeker, K., *Austria-Hungary with Excursions to Cetinje, Belgrade, and Bucharest: Handbook for Travellers by Karl Baedeker*, 11th edn (Leipzig, London and New York: Karl Baedeker, T. Fischer Unwin and Charles Scribner's Sons, 1911).

Barac, F., *Croats and Slovenes, Friends of the Entente in the World War: A Few Official Documents Derived from the Archives of the Imperial and Royal Military Commands* (Paris: Lang, Blanchong & Co. Printing, 1919).

Baumgart, W. (ed.), *Von Brest-Litovsk zur deutschen Novemberrevolution. Aus den Tagebüchern, Briefen und Aufzeichnungen von Alfons Paquet, Wilhelm Groener und Albert Hopman März bis November 1918* (Göttingen: Vandenhoeck & Ruprecht, 1971).

Bayern, Kronprinz R. von, *In Treue fest. Mein Kriegstagebuch* (3 vols., Munich: Deutscher National Verlag A.-G., 1929).

Bell, J. (ed.), *Völkerrecht im Weltkrieg. Dritte Reihe im Werk des Untersuchungsausschusses* (5 vols., Berlin: Deutsche Verlagsgesellschaft für Politik und Geschichte, 1927).

Bethmann Hollweg, T. von, *Reflections on the World War*, trans. G. Young (London: Thornton Butterworth, 1920).

Biliński, L., *Wspomnienia i dokumenty* (2 vols., Warsaw: F. Hoesicka, 1924 and 1925).

Bittner, L., 'Österreich-Ungarn und Serbien', *Historische Zeitschrift* 144(1) (1931), pp. 78–104.

Blücher, Princess E., *An English Wife in Berlin: A Private Memoir of Events, Politics and Daily Life in Germany throughout the War and the Social Revolution of 1918* (New York: E. P. Dutton, 1920).

Bókay, J. von and Juba, A., 'Ernährungszustand der Kinder in Ungarn', in C. Pirquet (ed.), *Volksgesundheit im Kriege* (2 vols., Vienna and New Haven, CT: Hölder-Pichler-Tempsky and Yale University Press, 1926), i, pp. 180–224.

Bruntz, G. G., *Allied Propaganda and the Collapse of the German Empire in 1918* (Stanford, CA: Stanford University Press, 1938).

Brussilov, A. A., *A Soldier's Note-book, 1914–1918* (London: Macmillan, 1930).

Buchner, E. (ed.), *Kriegsdokumente. Der Weltkrieg 1914/15 in der Darstellung der zeitgenössischen Presse* (9 vols., Munich: Albert Langen, 1914–15).

Bundesministerium für Heereswesen und Kriegsarchiv, *Österreich-Ungarns letzter Krieg* (7 vols., Vienna: Verlag der Militärwissenschaftlichen Mitteilungen, 1930–38).

Carnegie Endowment for International Peace (ed.), *Official Communications and Speeches Relating to Peace Proposals, 1916–1917* (Washington, DC: Carnegie Endowment for International Peace, 1917).

Child, C. J., 'German-American Attempts to Prevent the Exportation of Munitions of War, 1914–1915', *The Mississippi Valley Historical Review* 25(3) (December 1938), pp. 351–68.

Clark, J. M., *The Costs of the World War to the American People* (New Haven, CT, and London: Yale University Press, Humphrey Milford and Oxford University Press, 1931).

Conrad von Hötzendorf, F., *Aus meiner Dienstzeit 1906–1918. Vierter Band: 24. Juni 1914 bis 30. September 1914. Die politischen und militärischen Vorgänge vom Fürstenmord in Sarajevo bis zum Abschluß der ersten und bis zum Beginn der zweiten Offensive gegen Serbien und Rußland* (4 vols., Vienna: Rikola, 1923).

Conventions and Declarations between the Powers Concerning War, Arbitration and Neutrality (Declaration of Paris, 1856 – of St Petersburg, 1868 – of The Hague, 1899 – Convention of Geneva, 1906 – 2d Peace Conference, The Hague, 1907 – Declaration of London, 1909). English – French – German (The Hague: Martinus Nijhoff, 1915).

Cron, H., *Die Organisation des deutschen Heeres im Weltkriege* (Berlin: E. S. Mittler & Sohn, 1923).

Czernin, O., *In the World War* (New York and London: Harper & Brothers, 1920).

Dąbrowski, J., *Dziennik 1914–1918*, ed. J. Zdrara (Kraków: Wydawnictwo Literackie, 1977).

Daszyński, I., *Pamiętniki* (2 vols., Warsaw: Książka i Wiedza, 1957).

Deist, W. (ed.), *Militär und Innenpolitik im Weltkrieg 1914–1918* (2 vols., Düsseldorf: Droste, 1970).

Deuerlein, E. (ed.), *Briefwechsel Hertling-Lerchenfeld 1912–1917. Dienstliche Privatkorrespondenz zwischen dem bayerischen Ministerpräsidenten Georg Graf von Hertling und dem bayerischen Gesandten in Berlin Hugo Graf von und zu Lerchenfeld* (2 vols., Boppard am Rhein: Harald Boldt, 1973).

Die Russenherrschaft in Ostpreußen und ihr Ende. Dargestellt in 275 Abbildun-gen, Bildnissen, Karten u. Urkunden (Munich: F. Bruckmann, 1915).

Einem, K. von, *Ein Armeeführer erlebt den Weltkrieg. Persönliche Aufzeichnun-gen des Generalobersten v. Einem*, ed. J. Alter (Leipzig: v. Hase/Koehler, 1938).

Eisenmenger, A., *Blockade: The Diary of an Austrian Middle-Class Woman, 1914–1924* (London: Constable & Co., 1932).

Eltzbacher, P. (ed.), *Die deutsche Volksernährung und der englische Aushun-gerungsplan* (Braunschweig: Friedr. Vieweg & Sohn, 1915).

Emin, A., *Turkey in the World War* (New Haven, CT, and London: Yale Univer-sity Press and Oxford University Press, 1930).

Erzberger, M., *Erlebnisse im Weltkrieg* (Stuttgart and Berlin: Deutsche Verlags-Anstalt, 1920).

Everth, E., *Tat-Flugschriften 10. Von der Seele des Soldaten im Felde. Bemerkun-gen eines Kriegsteilnehmers* (Jena: Eugen Diederich, 1915).

Exner, F., *Krieg und Kriminalität in Österreich. Mit einem Beitrag über die Krimi-nalität der Militärpersonen von Prof Dr G. Lelewer* (Vienna and New Haven, CT: Hölder-Pichler-Tempsky and Yale University Press, 1927).

Falkenhayn, E. von, *The German General Staff and Its Decisions, 1914–1916* (New York: Dodd, Mead & Company, 1920).

Faust, G., *Kriegsnöte der deutschen Gemeinden in Galizien und der Bukowina* (Leipzig: Paul Eger, 1915).

Felger, F., 'Frontpropaganda bei Feind und Freund', in W. Jost (ed.), *Was wir vom Weltkrieg nicht wissen* (Leipzig: H. Fikentscher, 1936), pp. 440–59.

Foerster, W., *Der Feldherr Ludendorff im Unglück. Eine Studie über seine see-lische Haltung in der Endphase des ersten Weltkrieges* (Wiesbaden: Limes, 1952).

Fontaine, A., *French Industry during the War* (New Haven, CT, and London: Yale University Press and Humphrey Milford, Oxford University Press, 1926).

Forstner, G. G. von, *The Journal of Submarine Commander von Forstner*, trans. R. Codman (Boston and New York: The Houghton River Side Press, 1917).

Gallwitz, M. von, *Meine Führertätigkeit im Weltkriege 1914/1916. Belgien – Osten – Balkan* (Berlin: E. S. Mittler & Sohn, 1929).

_____, *Erleben im Westen 1916–1918* (Berlin: E. S. Mittler & Sohn, 1932).

Gause, F., 'Die Quellen zur Geschichte des Russeneinfalls in Ostpreußen im Jahre 1914', *Altpreußische Forschungen* 7(1) (1930), pp. 82–106.

_____, *Die Russen in Ostpreußen 1914/15. Im Auftrage des Landeshauptmanns der Provinz Ostpreußen* (Königsberg Pr.: Gräfe und Unzer Verlag, 1931).

Geiss, I. (ed.), *July 1914: The Outbreak of the First World War: Selected Docu-ments* (London: B. T. Batsford, 1967).

Gide, C. and Ovalid, W., *Le Bilan de la Guerre pour la France* (Paris and New Haven, CT: Les Presses Universitaires de France and Yale University Press, 1931).

Glaise-Horstenau, E. von, *The Collapse of the Austro-Hungarian Empire*, trans. I. F. D. Morrow (London and Toronto: J. M. Dent and Sons, 1930).

Goeldel, H., *Grundlagen des Wirtschaftslebens von Ostpreußen. Denkschrift zum Wiederaufbau der Provinz. Fünfter Teil. Wohlstandsverhältnisse in Ostpreußen* (6 vols., Jena: Gustav Fischer, 1917).

Göhre, P., *Tat-Flugschriften* 22. *Front und Heimat. Religiöses, Politisches, Sexuelles aus dem Schützengraben* (Jena: Eugen Diederich, 1917).

Golovin, N., 'The Great Battle of Galicia (1914): A Study of Strategy', *The Slavonic Review* 5(13) (June 1926), pp. 25–47.

_____, 'The Russian War Plan of 1914', *The Slavonic and East European Review* 14(42) (April 1936), pp. 564–84.

_____, 'The Russian War Plan: II. The Execution of the Plan', *The Slavonic and East European Review* 15(43) (July 1936), pp. 70–90.

Gothein, G., *Warum verloren wir den Krieg?* (Stuttgart and Berlin: Deutsche Verlags-Anstalt, 1919).

Gourko, B., *War and Revolution in Russia, 1914–1917* (New York: Macmillan, 1919).

Gratz, G. and Schüller, R., *Der wirtschaftliche Zusammenbruch Österreich-Ungarns. Die Tragödie der Erschöpfung* (Vienna and New Haven, CT: Hölder-Pichler-Tempsky A.-G. and Yale University Press, 1930).

Grebler, L. and Winkler, W., *The Cost of the World War to Germany and to Austria-Hungary* (New Haven, CT: Yale University Press, 1940).

Groener, W., *Lebenserinnerungen. Jugend, Generalstab, Weltkrieg*, ed. F. F. Hiller von Gaertringen (Göttingen: Vandenhoeck & Ruprecht, 1957).

Guttry, A. von, *Galizien. Land und Leute* (Munich and Leipzig: Georg Müller, 1916).

Hämmerle, C. (ed.), *Kindheit im Ersten Weltkrieg* (Vienna, Cologne and Weimar: Böhlau, 1993).

Hansch, J. and Weidling, F., *Das Colbergsche Grenadier-Regiment Graf Gneisenau (2. Pommersches) Nr. 9 im Weltkriege 1914–1918* (Oldenburg i. O. and Berlin: Gerhard Stalling, 1929).

Hansen, J., *Grundlagen des Wirtschaftslebens von Ostpreußen. Denkschrift zum Wiederaufbau der Provinz. Zweiter Teil. Die Landwirtschaft in Ostpreußen* (6 vols., Jena: Gustav Fischer, 1916).

Hanssen, H. P., *Diary of a Dying Empire*, trans. O. Osburn, ed. R. H. Lutz, M. Schofield and O. O. Winther (Port Washington, NY, and London: Kennikat Press, 1955, 1973).

Heeres-Sanitätsinspektion des Reichskriegsministeriums (ed.), *Sanitätsbericht über das Deutsche Heer (Deutsches Feld- und Besatzungsheer) im Weltkriege 1914/1918 (Deutscher Kriegssanitätsbericht 1914/18). III. Band. Die Krankenbewegung bei dem deutschen Feld- und Besatzungsheer im Weltkriege 1914/1918* (3 vols., Berlin: E. S. Mittler & Sohn, 1934).

_____ (ed.), *Sanitätsbericht über das Deutsche Heer (Deutsches Feld- und Besatzungsheer) im Weltkriege 1914/1918 (Deutscher Kriegssanitätsbericht 1914/18). II. Band. Der Sanitätsdienst im Gefechts- und Schlachtenverlauf im Weltkriege 1914/1918* (3 vols., Berlin: E. S. Mittler & Sohn, 1938).

Henning, K. L., *Die Wahrheit über Amerika* (Leipzig: Julius Klinkhardt, 1915).

Henry, A., *Études sur l'occupation allemande en Belgique* (Brussels: Office de Publicité, Anciens établissements J. Lebègue & Cie, Éditeurs Société Coopérative, 1920).

Herzog, R., *Ritter, Tod und Teufel. Kriegsgedichte von Rudolf Herzog* (Leipzig: Quelle u. Meyer, 1915).

Hesse, A. and Goeldel, H., *Grundlagen des Wirtschaftslebens von Ostpreußen. Denkschrift zum Wiederaufbau der Provinz. Dritter Teil. Die Bevölkerung von Ostpreußen* (6 vols., Jena: Gustav Fischer, 1916).

Hirschberg, P., *Die Russen in Allenstein. Die Besetzung und Befreiung der Stadt am 27., 28. und 29. August 1914*, 2nd extended edn (Allenstein: Druck und Verlag der Volksblatt-Druckerei, 1918).

Hirschfeld, M. and Gaspar, A. (eds.), *Sittengeschichte des Ersten Weltkrieges* (Hanau am Main: Karl Schustek, n.d.).

Hobohm, M., *Soziale Heeresmißstände als Teilursache des deutschen Zusammenbruches von 1918. Die Ursachen des deutschen Zusammenbruches im Jahre 1918. Zweite Abteilung. Der innere Zusammenbruch. Elfter Band. Erster Halbband* (12 vols., Berlin: Deutsche Verlagsgesellschaft für Politik und Geschichte, 1929).

Hofmann, H., 'Die deutsche Nervenkraft im Stellungskrieg', in F. Seeßelberg, *Der Stellungskrieg 1914–18* (Berlin: E. S. Mittler & Sohn, 1926).

Hoffmann, M., *War Diaries and Other Papers* (2 vols., London: Martin Secker, 1929).

Holsten, H. (ed.), *Landwehr-Infanterie-Regiment 76 im Weltkriege* (Stade: n.p., 1938).

Horn, D. (ed.), *The Private War of Seaman Stumpf: The Unique Diaries of a Young German in the Great War* (London: Leslie Frewin, 1969).

Huber, M., *La Population de la France pendant la Guerre* (Paris and New Haven, CT: Les Presses Universitaires de France and Yale University Press, 1931).

Hupka, J., *Z czasów wielkiej wojny. Pamiętnik nie kombatanta* (Lwów: Księgarnia A. Krawczyński, 1937).

Jacobson, W., *Z armią Klucka na Paryż* (Toruń: Nakładem autora, 1934).

Jaworski, W. L., *Diarusz 1914–1918* (Warsaw: Oficyna Naukowa, 1997).

Joffre, M., the Ex-Crown Prince of Germany, Marshal Foch and Marshal [*sic*] Ludendorff, *The Two Battles of the Marne* (London: Thornton Butterworth, 1927).

Johann, E. (ed.), *Innenansicht eines Krieges. Bilder, Briefe, Dokumente 1914–1918* (Frankfurt am Main: Heinrich Scheffer, 1968).

Jürgensen, W., *Das Füsilier-Regiment 'Königin' Nr. 86 im Weltkriege* (Oldenburg i. O. and Berlin: Gerhard Stalling, 1925).

Kantorowicz, H., *Der Offiziershaß im deutschen Heer* (Freiburg im Breisgau: J. Bielefelds Verlag, 1919).

Kawczak, S., *Milknące echa. Wspomnienia z wojny 1914–1920* (Warsaw: Libra, 1991).

Keiser, J. von, *Geschichte des Inf.-Regts. v. d. Marwitz (8. Pomm.) Nr. 61 im Weltkriege 1914–1918* (Berlin: Offizierverein des früheren Inf.-Regts. v. d. Marwitz (8. Pomm.) Nr. 61 E.V., n.d.).

Kellen, T., 'Von der Unbekannten Materialnot. Was im Kriege alles gesammelt wurde', in W. Jost (ed.), *Was wir vom Weltkrieg nicht wissen* (Leipzig: H. Fikentscher, 1936), pp. 366–83.

Kerchnawe, H., *Der Zusammenbruch der Österr.-Ungar. Wehrmacht im Herbst 1918. Dargestellt nach Akten des Armee-Ober-Kommandos und andere amtlichen Quellen* (Munich: J. F. Lehmanns Verlag, 1921).

de Kerchove de Denterghem, C., *L'Industrie Belge pendant l'Occupation Allemande 1914–1918* (Paris and New Haven, CT: Les Presses Universitaires de France and Yale University Press, 1927).

Kirchenberger, S., 'Beiträge zur Sanitätsstatistik der österreichisch-ungarischen Armee im Kriege 1914–1918', in C. Pirquet (ed.), *Volksgesundheit im Kriege* (2 vols., Vienna and New Haven, CT: Hölder-Pichler-Tempsky and Yale University Press, 1926), i, pp. 47–77.

Klemperer, V., *Curriculum Vitae. Erinnerungen 1881–1918. Vol. II*, ed. W. Nowojski (2 vols., Berlin: Aufbau Taschenbuch Verlag, 1996).

Knox, A., *With the Russian Army, 1914–1917: Being Chiefly Extracts from the Diary of a Military Attaché* (London: Hutchinson, 1921).

Köhler, L. von, *Die Staatsverwaltung der besetzten Gebiete. Belgien* (Stuttgart, Berlin, Leipzig and New Haven, CT: Deutsche Verlags-Anstalt and Yale University Press, 1927).

Krauß, A., *Die Ursachen unserer Niederlage. Erinnerungen und Urteile aus dem Weltkrieg*, 3rd edn (Munich: J. F. Lehmanns Verlag, 1923).

Kreisler, F., *Four Weeks in the Trenches: The War Story of a Violinist* (Boston, MA, and New York: Houghton Mifflin Company, 1915).

Krüger-Franke, J., 'Über truppenärztliche Erfahrungen in der Schlacht', *Berliner klinische Wochenschrift* 1 (4 January 1915), pp. 7–9.

Kuhl, H. von, *Der Weltkrieg 1914–1918 dem deutschen Volke dargestellt* (2 vols., Berlin: Verlag Tradition Wilhelm Kolk, 1929).

Kuhn, A., *Die Schreckenstage von Neidenburg in Ostpreußen. Kriegserinnerungen aus dem Jahre 1914* (Minden: Wilhelm Köhler, n.d.).

Kuhr, P., *There We'll Meet Again: The First World War Diary of a Young German Girl*, trans. W. Wright (n.p.: Walter Wright, 1998).

K.u.k. Ministerium des Äussern, *Sammlung von Nachweisen für die Verletzungen des Völkerrechts durch die mit Österreich-Ungarn Krieg führenden Staaten. Abgeschlossen mit 31. Jänner 1915* (Vienna: K.k. Hof- und Staatsdruckerei, 1915).

K.u.k. Ministerium des Äussern, *Sammlung von Nachweisen für die Verletzungen des Völkerrechts durch die mit Österreich-Ungarn Krieg führenden Staaten. III. Nachtrag. Abgeschlossen mit 30. Juni 1916* (Vienna: K.k. Hof- und Staatsdruckerei, 1916).

Kwaśny, E., *'Krakowskie dzieci' (Trzynasty Pułk) na polu chwały 1914–1915* (Cracow: Nakład autora, 1917).

Laeger, A., *Das I. Westpreußische Fußartillerie-Regiment Nr. 11 im Weltkriege 1914/18* (Zeulenroda-Thüringen: Bernhard Sporn, 1934).

Langsdorff, W. von (ed.), *U-Boote am Feind. 45 deutsche U-Boot-Fahrer erzählen* (Gütersloh: C. Bertelsmann, 1937).

Lasswell, H. D., *Propaganda Technique in the World War* (London and New York: Kegan, Paul, Trench, Trubner & Co. and Alfred A. Knopf, 1927).

Lewin, K., 'Kriegslandschaft', *Zeitschrift für angewandte Psychologie* 12(5 and 6) (1917), pp. 440–47.

Liepmann, M., *Krieg und Kriminalität in Deutschland* (Stuttgart, Berlin, Leipzig and New Haven, CT: Deutsche Verlags-Anstalt and Yale University Press, 1930).

Loewenfeld-Russ, H., *Die Regelung der Volksernährung im Kriege* (Vienna and New Haven, CT: Hölder-Pichler-Tempsky A.-G. and Yale University Press, 1926).

Ludendorff, E., *My War Memories, 1914–1918* (2 vols., Uckfield: The Naval and Military Press, 1919, 2005).

_____ (ed.), *The General Staff and its Problems: The History of the Relations Between the High Command and the German Imperial Government as Revealed by Official Documents*, trans. F. A. Holt (2 vols., London: Hutchinson, n.d.).

Ludwig, W., 'Beiträge zur Psychologie der Furcht im Kriege', in W. Stern and O. Lipmann (eds.), *Beihefte zur Zeitschrift für angewandte Psychologie. 21. Beiträge zur Psychologie des Krieges* (Leipzig: Johann Ambrosius Barth, 1920), pp. 125–72.

Lutz, R. H. (ed.), *The Fall of the German Empire, 1914–1918* (2 vols., Stanford, CA, and London: Stanford University Press and Humphrey Milford, Oxford University Press, 1932).

_____ (ed.), *The Causes of the German Collapse in 1918: Sections of the Officially Authorized Report of the Commission of the German Constituent Assembly and of the German Reichstag, 1919–1928, the Selection and the Translation Officially Approved by the Commission*, trans. W. L. Campbell (n.p.: Archon Books, 1969).

Majkowski, A., *Pamiętnik z wojny europejskiej roku 1914*, ed. T. Linkner (Pelplin and Wejherowo: Bernardinum, 2000).

Meyer, W., *Das Infanterie-Regiment von Grolman (1. Posensches) Nr. 18 im Weltkriege* (Oldenburg i. O. and Berlin: Gerhard Stalling, 1929).

Michaelis, H., Schraepler, E. and Scheel, G. (eds.), *Ursachen und Folgen. Vom deutschen Zusammenbruch 1918 und 1945 bis zur staatlichen Neuordnung Deutschlands in der Gegenwart. Eine Urkunden- und Dokumentensammlung zur Zeitgeschichte. Erster Band. Der Wende des ersten Weltkrieges und der Beginn der innerpolitischen Wandlung 1916/1917* (29 vols., Berlin: Dokumenten-Verlag Dr Herbert Wendler & Co., n.d.).

———, *Ursachen und Folgen. Vom deutschen Zusammenbruch 1918 und 1945 bis zur staatlichen Neuordnung Deutschlands in der Gegenwart. Eine Urkunden- und Dokumentensammlung zur Zeitgeschichte. Zweiter Band. Der militärische Zusammenbruch und das Ende des Kaiserreichs* (29 vols., Berlin: Dokumenten-Verlag Dr Herbert Wendler & Co., n.d.).

Mikułowski Pomorski, J. (ed.), *Kraków w naszej pamięci* (Nowy Wiśnicz: Wydawnictwo i Drukarnia 'Secesja', 1991).

Ministère de l'Intérieur, *Annuaire statistique de la Belgique et du Congo belge. Quarante-deuxième année – 1911. Tome XLII* (Brussels: Imprimerie A. Lesigne, 1912).

Molnár, F., *Galicja 1914–1915. Zapiski korespondenta wojennego*, trans. Á. Engelmayer (Warsaw: Most, 2012).

Moltke, E. von (ed.), *Generaloberst Helmuth von Moltke. Erinnerungen – Briefe – Dokumente 1877–1916. Ein Bild vom Kriegsausbruch, erster Kriegsführung und Persönlichkeit des ersten militärischen Führers des Krieges* (Stuttgart: Der Kommende Tag A.-G., 1922).

Müller, G. A. von, *The Kaiser and his Court: The Diaries, Note Books and Letters of Admiral Georg Alexander von Müller, Chief of the Naval Cabinet, 1914–1918*, ed. W. Görlitz and trans. M. Savill (London: Macdonald, 1961).

Münchner Ostpreußenhilfe, *Ostpreußennot und Bruderhilfe. Kriegsgedenkblätter* (Munich: Knorr & Hirth, 1915).

Nass, K. O. (ed.), *Ein preußischer Landrat in Monarchie, Demokratie und Diktatur. Lebenserinnerungen des Walter zur Nieden* (Berlin: Berliner Wissenschafts-Verlag, 2006).

Neymann, C. A., 'Some Experiences in the German Red Cross', *Mental Hygiene* 1(3) (July 1917), pp. 392–6.

Nicolai, W., *Nachrichtendienst, Presse und Volksstimmung im Weltkrieg* (Berlin: Ernst Siegfried Mittler und Sohn, 1920).

Niemöller, M., *From U-Boat to Concentration Camp* (London, Edinburgh and Glasgow: William Hodge, 1939).

Nowak, K. F., *Der Sturz der Mittelmächte* (Munich: Georg D. W. Callwey, Verlag für Kulturpolitik, 1921).

Ostdeutsche Volkszeitung (ed.), *Beiträge zum Einfall der Russen in Ostpreußen 1914 aus der Russenzeit in Insterburg* (Insterburg: Ostdeutsche Zeitung, 1914).

Palmer, S. and Wallis, S. (eds.), *A War in Words: The First World War in Diaries and Letters* (London, Sydney, New York and Toronto: Pocket Books, 2003).

Pawlowski, E. (ed.), *Tilsit unter russischer Herrschaft. 26. August bis 12. September 1914* (Tilsit, Ostpr.: Eduard Pawlowski, 1915).

Pfeilschifter, G., 'Seelsorge und religiöses Leben im deutschen Heere', in G. Pfeilschifter (ed.), *Kultur Katholizismus und Weltkrieg. Eine Abwehr des Buches La Guerre Allemande et la Catholicisme* (Freiburg im Breisgau: Herdersche Verlagshandlung, 1916), pp. 235–68.

Pirenne, H., *La Belgique et la Guerre Mondiale* (Paris and New Haven, CT: Les Presses Universitaires de France and Yale University Press, 1928).

Pirenne, J. and Vauthier, M., *La Legislation et l'Administration Allemandes en Belgique* (Paris and New Haven, CT: Les Presses Universitaires de France and Yale University Press, 1925).

Pirquet, C., 'Ernährungszustand der Kinder in Österreich während des Krieges und der Nachkriegszeit', in C. Pirquet (ed.), *Volksgesundheit im Kriege* (2 vols., Vienna and New Haven, CT: Hölder-Pichler-Tempsky and Yale University Press, 1926), i, pp. 151–79.

Pirscher, F. von, *Das (rheinisch-westfälische) Infanterie-Regiment Nr. 459* (Oldenburg i. O.: Gerhard Stalling, 1926).

Plaut, P., 'Psychographie des Kriegers', in W. Stern and O. Lipmann (eds.), *Beihefte zur Zeitschrift für angewandte Psychologie. 21. Beiträge zur Psychologie des Krieges* (Leipzig: Johann Ambrosius Barth, 1920), pp. 1–123.

Pogge von Strandmann, H. (ed.), *Walther Rathenau, Industrialist, Banker, Intellectual, and Politician: Notes and Diaries, 1907–1922*, trans. C. Pinder-Cracraft (Oxford: Clarendon Press, 1985).

Redlich, J., *Austrian War Government* (New Haven, CT, and London: Yale University Press and Humphrey Milford, Oxford University Press, 1929).

——, *Schicksalsjahre Österreichs 1908–1919. Das politische Tagebuch Josef Redlichs*, ed. F. Fellner (2 vols., Graz and Cologne: Hermann Böhlau, 1953).

Reichsarchiv, *Der Weltkrieg 1914 bis 1918. Band 1. Die Grenzschlachten im Westen* (14 vols., Berlin: E. S. Mittler & Sohn, 1925).

——, *Der Weltkrieg 1914 bis 1918. Band 2. Die Befreiung Ostpreußens* (14 vols., Berlin: E. S. Mittler & Sohn, 1925).

——, *Der Weltkrieg 1914 bis 1918. Band 5. Der Herbst-Feldzug 1914. Im Westen bis zum Stellungskrieg. Im Osten bis zum Rückzug* (14 vols., Berlin: E. S. Mittler & Sohn, 1929).

——, *Der Weltkrieg 1914 bis 1918. Band 6. Der Herbst-Feldzug 1914. Der Abschluß der Operationen im Westen und Osten* (14 vols., Berlin: E. S. Mittler & Sohn, 1929).

_____, *Der Weltkrieg 1914 bis 1918. Band 7. Die Operationen des Jahres 1915. Die Ereignisse im Winter und Frühjahr* (14 vols., Berlin: E. S. Mittler & Sohn, 1931).

_____, *Der Weltkrieg 1914 bis 1918. Band 10. Die Operationen des Jahres 1916 bis zum Wechsel in der Obersten Heeresleitung* (14 vols., Berlin: E. S. Mittler & Sohn, 1936).

_____, *Der Weltkrieg 1914 bis 1918. Band 11. Die Kriegsführung im Herbst 1916 und im Winter 1916/17. Vom Wechsel in der Obersten Heeresleitung bis zum Entschluß zum Rückzug in die Siegfried Stellung* (14 vols., Berlin: E. S. Mittler & Sohn, 1938).

_____, *Der Weltkrieg 1914 bis 1918. Band 14. Die Kriegsführung an der Westfront im Jahre 1918* (14 vols., Berlin: E. S. Mittler & Sohn, 1944).

Reichskanzlei, *Vorgeschichte des Waffenstillstandes. Amtliche Urkunden* (Berlin: Reimar Hobbing, 1919).

Reiss, R. A., *Report upon the Atrocities Committed by the Austro-Hungarian Army during the First Invasion of Serbia Submitted to the Serbian Government* (London: Simpkin, Marshall, Hamilton, Kent & Co., 1916).

Reiter, M. M., *Balkan Assault: The Diary of an Officer, 1914–1918*, trans. S. Granovetter (London: The Historical Press, 1994).

Roeder, C. von, 'Vom verhängnisvollen Einfluß der Sabotageakte auf die Kriegführung', in W. Jost (ed.), *Was wir vom Weltkrieg nicht wissen* (Leipzig: H. Fikentscher, 1936), pp. 139–54.

Roesle, J., 'Die Geburts- und Sterblichkeitsverhältnisse', in F. Bumm (ed.), *Deutschlands Gesundheitsverhältnisse unter dem Einfluss des Weltkrieges* (Stuttgart, Berlin and Leipzig, and New Haven, CT: Deutsche Verlags-Anstalt and Yale University Press, 1928), pp. 3–61.

Romer, J. E., *Pamiętniki* (Warsaw: Muzeum Historii Polski and Bellona, n.d.).

Schauwecker, F., *Im Todesrachen. Die deutsche Seele im Weltkriege* (Halle: Heinrich Diekmann, 1921).

Scheidemann, P., *Der Zusammenbruch* (Berlin: Verlag für Sozialwissenschaft, 1921).

Schierbrand, W. von, 'The Food Situation in Austria-Hungary', *The North American Review* 205(734) (January 1917), pp. 46–52.

_____, *Austria-Hungary: The Polyglot Empire* (New York: Frederick A. Stokes, 1917).

Schlenther, P., *Zwischen Lindau und Memel während des Krieges* (Berlin: G. Fischer, 1915).

Schoenfeld, J., *Shtetl Memories: Jewish Life in Galicia under the Austro-Hungarian Empire and in the Reborn Poland, 1898–1939* (Hobeken, NJ: Ktav Publishing House, 1985).

Scholz, L., *Seelenleben des Soldaten an der Front. Hinterlassene Aufzeichnungen des im Kriege gefallenen Nervenarztes* (Tübingen: J. C. B. Mohr, 1920).

Schuhmacher, W., *Leben und Seele unseres Soldatenlieds im Weltkrieg* (Frankfurt am Main: Moritz Diesterweg, 1928).

Schulz, D., *Infanterie-Regiment Graf Bülow von Dennewitz (6. Westfälisches) Nr. 55 im Weltkriege* (Detmold: Verlag der Meyerischen Hofbuchhandlung [Max Staecke], 1928).

Schwarte, M., *Die Technik im Weltkriege* (Berlin: Ernst Siegfried Mittler und Sohn, 1920).

Ściskała, D., *Z dziennika kapelana wojskowego 1914–1918* (Cieszyn: Nakład autora, 1926).

Segall, J., *Die deutschen Juden als Soldaten im Kriege 1914–1918* (Berlin: Philo-Verlag, 1922).

Skalweit, A., *Die deutsche Kriegsernährungswirtschaft* (Stuttgart, Berlin and Leipzig: Deutsche Verlags-Anstalt, 1927).

Słomka, J., *From Serfdom to Self-Government: Memoirs of a Polish Village Mayor, 1842–1927*, trans. W. J. Rose (London: Minerva, 1941).

Sperber, M., *God's Water Carriers*, trans. J. Neugroschel (New York and London: Holmes & Meier, 1987).

Spiegel, E. von, *Kriegstagebuch 'U202'* (Berlin: August Scherl, 1916).

Sprawozdanie c.k. Namiestnictwa, Centrali krajowej dla gospodarczej odbudowy Galicyi za czas od czerwca 1916 do lutego 1917 (Cracow: Drukarnia Eug. i Dr Kaz. Koziańskich, 1917).

Stein, General von, *A War Minister and his Work: Reminiscences of 1914–1918* (London: Skeffington & Son, n.d.).

Stenographische Protokolle über die Sitzungen des Hauses der Abgeordneten des österreichischen Reichsrates im Jahre 1917. XXII. Session. 1. (Eröffnungs-) bis 21. Sitzung. (S. 1 bis 1155). I. Band (4 vols., Vienna: K.k. Hof- und Staatsdruckerei, 1917).

Strug, A., *Odznaka za wierną służbę* (n.p.: Czytelnik, 1957).

Tăslăuanu, O. C., *With the Austrian Army in Galicia* (London: Skeffington & Son, n.d.).

Thaer, A. von, *Generalstabsdienst an der Front und in der O.H.L. Aus Briefen und Tagebuchaufzeichnungen 1915–1919*, ed. S. A. Kaehler (Göttingen: Vandenhoeck & Rupprecht, 1958).

Tisza, S., *Count Stephen Tisza, Prime Minister of Hungary: Letters (1914–1916)*, trans. C. de Bussy (New York, San Francisco, Bern, Frankfurt am Main, Paris and London: Peter Lang, 1991).

Twain, M., 'Stirring Times in Austria', *Harper's New Monthly Magazine* 96 (December 1897–May 1898), pp. 530–40.

Ulrich, B. and Ziemann, B. (eds.), *Frontalltag im Ersten Weltkrieg. Wahn und Wirklichkeit* (Frankfurt am Main: Fischer Taschenbuch, 1994).

United States War Office, *Histories of Two Hundred and Fifty-One Divisions of the German Army which Participated in the War* (London: London Stamp Exchange, 1920, 1989).

Verhandlungen des Reichstags. XIII Legislaturperiode. II. Session. Band 306. Stenographische Berichte. Von der Eröffnungssitzung am 4. August 1914 bis zur 34. Sitzung am 16. März 1916 (Berlin: Druck und Verlag der Norddeutschen Buchdruckerei und Verlags-Anstalt, 1916).

Vischer, A. L., *Barbed Wire Disease: A Psychological Study of the Prisoner of War* (London: John Bale & Sons and Danielsson, 1919).

Vit, J., *Wspomnienia z mojego pobytu w Przemyślu podczas rosyjskiego oblężenia 1914–1915*, trans. L. Hofbauer and J. Husar (Przemyśl: Południowo Wschodni Instytut Naukowy, 1995).

Volkmann, E. O., *Soziale Heeresmißstände als Mitursache des deutschen Zusammenbruches von 1918. Die Ursachen des deutschen Zusammenbruches im Jahre 1918. Zweite Abteilung. Der innere Zusammenbruch. Elfter Band. Zweiter Halbband* (12 vols., Berlin: Deutsche Verlagsgesellschaft für Politik und Geschichte, 1929).

[British] War Office (ed.), *Statistics of the Military Effort of the British Empire during the Great War, 1914–1920* (London: HMSO, 1922).

Wehrhan, K., *Gloria, Viktoria! Volkspoesie an Militärzügen* (Leipzig: Wilhelm Heims, 1915).

Why Germany Capitulated on November 11, 1918: A Brief Study Based on Documents in the Possession of the French General Staff (London, New York and Toronto: Hodder and Stoughton, 1919).

Wicker, K., 'Der Weltkrieg in Zahlen. Verluste an Blut und Boden', in W. Jost (ed.), *Was wir vom Weltkrieg nicht wissen* (Leipzig: H. Fikentscher, 1936), pp. 515–24.

Wiehler, R., *Deutsche Wirtschaftspropaganda im Weltkrieg* (Berlin: E. S. Mittler und Sohn, 1922).

Wild von Hohenborn, A., *Briefe und Tagebuchaufzeichnungen des preußischen Generals als Kriegsminister und Truppenführer im Ersten Weltkrieg*, ed. H. Reichold (Boppard am Rhein: Harald Boldt, 1986).

Winkler, W., *Die Totenverluste der öst.-ung. Monarchie nach Nationalitäten. Die Altersgliederung der Toten. Ausblicke in die Zukunft* (Vienna: L. W. Seidl & Sohn, 1919).

Witkop, P. (ed.), *Kriegsbriefe gefallener Studenten* (Munich: Albert Langen/Georg Müller, 1928).

Witos, W., *Moje wspomnienia* (Warsaw: Ludowa Spółdzielnia Wydawnicza, 1978).

Wolff, T., *Tagebücher 1914–1919. Der Erste Weltkrieg und die Entstehung der Weimarer Republik in Tagebüchern, Leitartikeln und Briefen des Chefredakteurs am 'Berliner Tageblatt' und Mitbegründers der 'Deutschen Demokratischen Partei'*, ed. B. Sösemann (2 vols., Boppard am Rhein: Harald Boldt, 1984).

Wrisberg, E. von, *Heer und Heimat 1914–1918* (Leipzig: K. F. Koehler, 1921).

_____, *Wehr und Waffen 1914–1918* (Leipzig: K. F. Koehler, 1922).

Zache, H., 'Weshalb der schonungslose U-Boot-Krieg geführt wurde und weshalb er nicht zum Ziele führte', in W. Jost (ed.), *Was wir vom Weltkrieg nicht wissen* (Leipzig: H. Fikentscher, 1936), pp. 253–6.

Zeynek, T. Ritter. von, *Ein Offizier im Generalstabskorps erinnert sich*, ed. P. Broucek (Vienna, Cologne and Weimar: Böhlau, 2009).

PRINTED SECONDARY SOURCES

Achleitner, W., *Gott im Krieg. Die Theologie der österreichischen Bischöfe in den Hirtenbriefen zum Ersten Weltkrieg* (Vienna, Cologne and Weimar: Böhlau, 1997).

Afflerbach, H., ' "Bis zum letzten Mann und letzten Groschen?" Die Wehrpflicht im deutschen Reich und ihre Auswirkungen auf das militärische Führungsdenken im Ersten Weltkrieg', in R. G. Foerster (ed.), *Die Wehrpflicht. Entstehung, Erscheinungsformen und politisch-militärische Wirkung* (Munich: R. Oldenbourg, 1994), pp. 71–90.

——, *Falkenhayn. Politisches Denken und Handeln im Kaiserreich* (Munich: R. Oldenbourg, 1994).

——, 'Wilhelm II as Supreme Warlord in the First World War', *War in History* 5(4) (October 1998), pp. 427–49.

——, 'Planning Total War? Falkenhayn and the Battle of Verdun, 1916', in R. Chickering and S. Förster (eds.), *Great War, Total War: Combat and Mobilization on the Western Front, 1914–1918* (Washington, DC, and Cambridge: German Historical Institute and Cambridge University Press, 2000), pp. 113–31.

——, 'The Topos of Improbable War in Europe before 1914', in H. Afflerbach and D. Stevenson (eds.), *An Improbable War: The Outbreak of World War I and European Political Culture Before 1914* (New York and Oxford: Berghahn, 2007), pp. 161–82.

——, 'Das Wilhelminische Kaiserreich zwischen Nationalstaat und Imperium', in L. Höbelt and T. G. Otte (eds.), *A Living Anachronism? European Diplomacy and the Habsburg Monarchy: Festschrift für Francis Roy Bridge zum 70. Geburtstag* (Vienna, Cologne and Weimar: Böhlau, 2010), pp. 223–38.

Alder, D. D., 'Friedrich Adler: Evolution of a Revolutionary', *German Studies Review* 1(3) (October 1978), pp. 260–84.

Alexander, A., 'The Genesis of the Civilian', *Leiden Journal of International Law* 20(2) (June 2007), pp. 359–76.

Allen, K., 'Sharing Scarcity: Bread Rationing and the First World War in Berlin, 1914–1923', *Journal of Social History* 32(2) (Winter 1998), pp. 371–93.

Anderson, M. L., 'A German Way of War?', *German History* 22(2) (April 2004), pp. 254–8.

Angress, W. T., 'Das deutsche Militär und die Juden im Ersten Weltkrieg', *Militärgeschichtliche Mitteilungen* 19 (1976), pp. 77–146.

Ashworth, T., *Trench Warfare, 1914–1918: The Live and Let Live System* (London: Pan, 1980, 2000).

Audoin-Rouzeau, S. and Becker, A., *1914–1918: Understanding the Great War*, trans. C. Temerson (London: Profile Books, 2002).

Ay, K.-L., *Die Entstehung einer Revolution. Die Volksstimmung in Bayern während des Ersten Weltkrieges* (Berlin: Duncker & Humblot, 1968).

Bachmann, K., *'Ein Herd der Feindschaft gegen Rußland'. Galizien als Krisenherd in den Beziehungen der Donaumonarchie mit Rußland (1907–1914)* (Vienna and Munich: Verlag für Geschichte und Politik and R. Oldenbourg, 2001).

Bąk-Koczarska, C., 'Władze miejskie Krakowa w latach wojny', in Towarzystwo Miłośników Historii i Zabytków Krakowa (ed.), *Kraków w czasie I wojny światowej. Materiały sesji naukowej z okazji dni Krakowa w roku 1988* (Cracow: Towarzystwo Miłośników Historii i Zabytków Krakowa, 1990), pp. 69–96.

Balderston, T., 'War Finance and Inflation in Britain and Germany, 1914–1918', *Economic History Review* 42(2) (May 1989), pp. 222–44.

Balogh, E. S., 'The Turning of the World: Hungarian Progressive Writers on the War', in R. A. Kann, B. K. Király and P. S. Fichtner (eds.), *The Habsburg Empire in World War I: Essays on the Intellectual, Military, Political and Economic Aspects of the Habsburg War Effort* (Boulder, CO, and New York: East European Quarterly and Columbia University Press, 1977), pp. 185–201.

Barth-Scalmani, G., '"Kriegsbriefe". Kommunikation zwischen Klerus und Kirchenvolk im ersten Kriegsherbst 1914 im Spannungsfeld von Patriotismus und Seelsorge', in K. Brandstätter and J. Hörmann (eds.), *Tirol – Österreich – Italien. Festschrift für Josef Riedmann zum 65. Geburtstag* (Innsbruck: Universitätsverlag Wagner, 2005), pp. 67–76.

Bartov, O., *Hitler's Army: Soldiers, Nazis and War in the Third Reich* (Oxford: Oxford University Press, 1992).

Baten, J. and Schulz, R., 'Making Profits in Wartime: Corporate Profits, Inequality, and GDP in Germany during the First World War', *The Economic History Review*, New Series 58(1) (February 2005), pp. 34–56.

Batowski, H., 'Nationale Konflikte bei der Entstehung der Nachfolgestaaten', in R. G. Plaschka and K. Mack (eds.), *Die Auflösung des Habsburgerreiches. Zusammenbruch und Neuorientierung im Donauraum* (Vienna: Verlag für Geschichte und Politik, 1970), pp. 338–49.

Becker, J.-J. and Krumeich, G., *Der Grosse Krieg. Deutschland und Frankreich im Ersten Weltkrieg 1914–1918* (Essen: Klartext, 2010).

Beller, S., 'The Tragic Carnival: Austrian Culture in the First World War', in A. Roshwald and R. Stites (eds.), *European Culture in the Great War: The*

Arts, Entertainment and Propaganda, 1914–1918 (Cambridge: Cambridge University Press, 1999), p. 133.

Bemann, M., '". . . kann von einer schonenden Behandlung keine Rede sein". Zur forst- und landwirtschaftlichen Ausnutzung des Generalgouvernements Warschau durch die deutsche Besatzungsmacht, 1915–1918', *Jahrbücher für Osteuropas, Neue Folge* 55(1) (2007), pp. 1–33.

Benvindo, B. and Majerus, B., 'Belgien zwischen 1914 und 1918: ein Labor für den totalen Krieg?', in A. Bauerkämper and E. Julien (eds.), *Durchhalten! Krieg und Gesellschaft im Vergleich 1914–1918* (Göttingen: Vandenhoeck & Ruprecht, 2010), pp. 127–48.

Berger, S., 'Germany: Ethnic Nationalism par Excellence?', in T. Baycroft and M. Hewitson (eds.), *What is a Nation? Europe 1789–1914* (Oxford and New York: Oxford University Press, 2006), pp. 42–60.

_____, 'Germany', in R. Gerwarth (ed.), *Twisted Paths: Europe 1914–1945* (Oxford: Oxford University Press, 2007), pp. 184–209.

Berghoff, H., 'Patriotismus und Geschäftssinn im Krieg: Eine Fallstudie aus der Musikinstrumentenindustrie', in G. Hirschfeld, G. Krumeich, D. Langewiesche and H.-P. Ullmann (eds.), *Kriegserfahrungen. Studien zur Sozial- und Mentalitätsgeschichte des Ersten Weltkriegs* (Essen: Klartext, 1997), pp. 262–82.

Bergien, R., 'Paramilitary Volunteers for Weimar Germany's "*Wehrhaftmachung*": How Civilians were Attracted to Serve with Irregular Military Units', in C. G. Krüger and S. Levsen (eds.), *War Volunteering in Modern Times: From the French Revolution to the Second World War* (Basingstoke and New York: Palgrave Macmillan, 2011), pp. 189–210.

Bessel, R., *Germany After the First World War* (Oxford: Clarendon Press, 1993).

_____, 'Die Heimkehr der Soldaten: Das Bild der Frontsoldaten in der Offentlichkeit der Weimarer Republik', in G. Hirschfeld, G. Krumeich and I. Renz (eds.), *'Keiner fühlt sich hier mehr als Mensch . . .' Erlebnis und Wirkung des Ersten Weltkriegs* (Essen: Klartext, 1993), pp. 221–39.

_____, 'Mobilizing German Society for War', in R. Chickering and S. Förster (eds.), *Great War, Total War: Combat and Mobilization on the Western Front, 1914–1918* (Washington, DC, and Cambridge: German Historical Institute and Cambridge University Press, 2000), pp. 437–52.

Best, G., *Humanity in Warfare: The Modern History of the International Law of Armed Conflicts* (London: Weidenfeld and Nicolson, 1980).

Bieniarzówna, J. and Małecki, J. M., *Dzieje Krakowa. Tom 3. Kraków w latach 1796–1918* (4 vols., Cracow, Wydawnictwo Literackie, 1979).

Binder, H., 'Making and Defending a Polish Town: "Lwów" (Lemberg), 1848–1914', *Austrian History Yearbook* 34 (2003), pp. 57–81.

_____, *Galizien in Wien. Parteien, Wahlen, Fraktionen und Abgeordnete im Übergang zur Massenpolitik* (Vienna: Verlag der Österreichischen Akademie der Wissenschaften, 2005).

Biskupski, M. B., 'Re-Creating Central Europe: The United States "Inquiry" into the Future of Poland in 1918', *The International History Review* 12(2) (May 1990), pp. 249–79.

Blanke, R., *Orphans of Versailles: The Germans in Western Poland, 1918–1939* (Lexington, KY: University Press of Kentucky, 1993).

Blobaum, Jr, R., 'Going Barefoot in Warsaw during the First World War', *East European Politics and Societies and Cultures* 27(2) (May 2013), pp. 187–204.

Bobič, P., *War and Faith: The Catholic Church in Slovenia, 1914–1918* (Leiden and Boston, MA: Brill, 2012).

Boff, J., *Winning and Losing on the Western Front: The British Third Army and the Defeat of Germany in 1918* (Cambridge: Cambridge University Press, 2012).

Böhler, I., 'Ernährungskrise und Mangelwirtschaft im Ersten Weltkrieg am Beispiel der Textilstadt Dornbirn (Vorarlberg)', in H. J. W. Kuprian and O. Überegger (eds.), *Der Erste Weltkrieg im Alpenraum. Erfahrung, Deutung, Erinnerung. La Grande Guerra nell'arco alpino. Esperienze e memoria* (Innsbruck: Universitätsverlag Wagner, 2006), pp. 213–27.

Boswell, L., 'From Liberation to Purge Trials in the "Mythic Provinces": Recasting French Identities in Alsace and Lorraine, 1918–1920', *French Historical Studies* 23(1) (Winter 2000), pp. 129–62.

Boyer, J. W., *Culture and Political Crisis in Vienna: Christian Socialism in Power, 1897–1918* (Chicago, IL, and London: University of Chicago Press, 1995).

_____, 'Silent War and Bitter Peace: The Revolution of 1918 in Austria', *Austrian History Yearbook* 34 (2003), pp. 1–56.

Brandt, S., '*Nagelfiguren*: Nailing Patriotism in Germany, 1914–1918', in N. J. Saunders (ed.), *Matters of Conflict: Material Culture, Memory and the First World War* (London and New York: Routledge, 2004), pp. 62–71.

Broadberry, S. and Harrison, M., 'The Economics of World War I: An Overview', in S. Broadberry and M. Harrison (eds.), *The Economics of World War I* (Cambridge, New York, Melbourne, Madrid, Cape Town, Singapore and São Paulo: Cambridge University Press, 2005), pp. 3–40.

Brocks, C., '"Unser Schild muss rein bleiben". Deutsche Bildzensur und Propaganda im Ersten Weltkrieg', *Militärgeschichtliche Zeitschrift* 67(1) (2008), pp. 25–51.

Brown, I. M., *British Logistics on the Western Front, 1914–1919* (London: Praeger, 1998).

Bruckmüller, E., 'Was There a "Habsburg Society" in Austria-Hungary?', *Austrian History Yearbook* 37 (2006), pp. 1–16.

_____, 'Patriotic and National Myths: National Consciousness and Elementary School Education in Imperial Austria', in L. Cole and D. L. Unowsky (eds.),

The Limits of Loyalty: Imperial Symbolism, Popular Allegiances, and State Patriotism in the Late Habsburg Monarchy (New York and Oxford: Berghahn Books, 2007), pp. 11–35.

Bruendel, S., *Volksgemeinschaft oder Volksstaat. Die 'Ideen von 1914' und die Neuordnung Deutschlands im Ersten Weltkrieg* (Berlin: Akademie, 2003).

——, 'Vor-Bilder des Durchhaltens. Die deutsche Kriegsanleihe-Werbung 1917/18', in A. Bauerkämper and E. Julien (eds.), *Durchhalten! Krieg und Gesellschaft im Vergleich 1914–1918* (Göttingen: Vandenhoeck & Ruprecht, 2010), pp. 81–108.

Bry, G., *Wages in Germany, 1871–1945* (Princeton, NJ: Princeton University Press, 1960).

Bucholz, A., *Hans Delbrück and the German Establishment: War Images in Conflict* (Iowa City, IA: University of Iowa Press, 1985).

Bundgård Christensen, C., *Danskere på Vestfronten 1914–1918* (Copenhagen: Gyldendal, 2009).

Burk, K., *Britain, America and the Sinews of War, 1914–1918* (Boston, MA, London and Sydney: George Allen & Unwin, 1985).

Burleigh, M., 'Albert Brackmann (1871–1952) *Ostforscher*: The Years of Retirement', *Journal of Contemporary History* 23(4) (October 1988), pp. 573–88.

Buschnell, J., 'The Tsarist Officer Corps, 1881–1914: Customs, Duties, Inefficiency', *The American Historical Review* 86(4) (October 1981), pp. 753–80.

Cattaruzza, M., 'Nationalitätenkonflikte in Triest im Rahmen der Nationalitätenfrage in der Habsburger Monarchie 1850–1914', in R. Melville, C. Scharf, M. Vogt and U. Wengenroth (eds.), *Deutschland und Europa in der Neuzeit. Festschrift für Karl Otmar Freiherr von Aretin zum 65. Geburtstag. 2. Halbband* (Stuttgart: Franz Steiner Verlag Wiesbaden GMBH, 1988), pp. 709–26.

Chickering, R., 'Sore Loser: Ludendorff's Total War', in R. Chickering and S. Förster (eds.), *The Shadows of Total War: Europe, East Asia, and the United States, 1919–1939* (Washington, DC, and Cambridge: German Historical Institute and Cambridge University Press, 2003), pp. 151–78.

——, *Imperial Germany and the Great War, 1914–1918*, 2nd edn (Cambridge: Cambridge University Press, 2004).

—— and Förster, S., 'Are We There Yet? World War II and the Theory of Total War', in R. Chickering, S. Förster and B. Greiner (eds.), *A World at Total War: Global Conflict and the Politics of Destruction, 1937–1945* (Washington, DC, and Cambridge: German Historical Institute and Cambridge University Press, 2005), pp. 1–16.

——, *The Great War and Urban Life in Germany: Freiburg, 1914–1918* (Cambridge: Cambridge University Press, 2007).

Cisek, J., '"Kolumna Legionów" w Krakowie', *Krakowski Rocznik Archiwalny* 9 (2003), pp. 157–78.

Clark, C., *The Sleepwalkers: How Europe Went to War in 1914* (New York: Harper, 2013).

Cohen, G. B., 'Nationalist Politics and the Dynamics of State and Civil Society in the Habsburg Monarchy, 1867–1914', *Central European History* 40(2) (June 2007), pp. 241–78.

Cole, L., 'Military Veterans and Popular Patriotism in Imperial Austria, 1870–1914', in L. Cole and D. L. Unowsky (eds.), *The Limits of Loyalty: Imperial Symbolism, Popular Allegiances, and State Patriotism in the Late Habsburg Monarchy* (New York and Oxford: Berghahn Books, 2007), pp. 36–61.

Conze, V., 'Die Grenzen der Niederlage. Kriegsniederlagen und territoriale Verluste im Grenz-Diskurs in Deutschland (1918–1970)', in H. Carl, H.-H. Kortüm, D. Langewiesche and F. Lenger (eds.), *Kriegsniederlagen. Erfahrungen und Erinnerungen* (Berlin: Akademie, 2004), pp. 163–84.

Conze, W., *Polnische Nation und deutsche Politik im Ersten Weltkrieg* (Cologne and Graz: Böhau, 1958).

Cornwall, M., 'News, Rumour and the Control of Information in Austria-Hungary, 1914–1918', *History* 77(249) (February 1992), pp. 50–64.

———, 'Morale and Patriotism in the Austro-Hungarian Army, 1914–1918', in J. Horne (ed.), *State, Society and Mobilization in Europe during the First World War* (Cambridge, New York and Oakleigh: Cambridge University Press, 1997), pp. 173–91.

———, 'Austria-Hungary', in H. Cecil and P. H. Liddle (eds.), *At the Eleventh Hour: Reflections, Hopes and Anxieties at the Closing of the Great War, 1918* (Barnsley: Leo Cooper, 1998), pp. 285–300.

———, *The Undermining of Austria-Hungary: The Battle for Hearts and Minds* (Basingstoke and New York: Macmillan and St Martin's, 2000).

———, 'Disintegration and Defeat: The Austro-Hungarian Revolution', in M. Cornwall (ed.), *The Last Years of Austria-Hungary: A Multi-National Experiment in Early Twentieth-Century Europe*, revised and expanded edn (Exeter: University of Exeter Press, 2002), pp. 167–96.

———, 'The Habsburg Monarchy: "National Trinity" and the Elasticity of National Allegiance', in T. Baycroft and M. Hewitson (eds.), *What is a Nation? Europe 1789–1914* (Oxford and New York: Oxford University Press, 2006), pp. 171–91.

———, 'The Habsburg Elite and the Southern Slav Question, 1914–1918', in L. Höbelt and T. G. Otte (eds.), *A Living Anachronism? European Diplomacy and the Habsburg Monarchy: Festschrift für Francis Roy Bridge zum 70. Geburtstag* (Vienna, Cologne and Weimar: Böhlau, 2010), pp. 239–70.

Craig, G. A., 'The World War I Alliance of the Central Powers in Retrospect: The Military Cohesion of the Alliance', *The Journal of Modern History* 37(3) (September 1965), pp. 336–44.

Cramer, K., 'A World of Enemies: New Perspectives on German Military Culture and the Origins of the First World War', *Central European History* 39(2) (June 2006), pp. 270–98.

Crampton, R., *Bulgaria, 1878–1918: A History* (Boulder, CO, and New York: East European Monographs and Columbia University Press, 1983).

———, 'Deprivation, Desperation and Degradation: Bulgaria in Defeat', in H. Cecil and P. H. Liddle (eds.), *At the Eleventh Hour: Reflections, Hopes and Anxieties at the Closing of the Great War, 1918* (Barnsley: Leo Cooper, 1998), pp. 255–65.

———, 'The Balkans', in R. Gerwarth (ed.), *Twisted Paths: Europe 1914–1945* (Oxford: Oxford University Press, 2007), pp. 237–70.

Creutz, M., *Die Pressepolitik der kaiserlichen Regierung während des Ersten Weltkriegs. Die Exekutive, die Journalisten und der Teufelskries der Berichterstattung* (Frankfurt am Main: Peter Lang, 1994).

van Creveld, M., *Supplying War: Logistics from Wallenstein to Patton* (Cambridge, London, New York and Melbourne: Cambridge University Press, 1977).

Crim, B. E., '"Our Most Serious Enemy": The Specter of Judeo-Bolshevism in the German Military Community, 1914–1923', *Central European History* 44(4) (December 2011), pp. 624–41.

Czerep, S., 'Straty polskie podczas I wojny światowej', in D. Grinberg, J. Snopko and G. Zackiewicz (eds.), *Lata wielkiej wojny. Dojrzewanie do niepodległości 1914–1918* (Białystok: Wydawnictwo Uniwersytetu w Białymstoku, 2007), pp. 180–97.

Dabrowski, P. M., *Commemorations and the Shaping of the Polish Nation* (Bloomington and Indianapolis, IN: Indiana University Press, 2004).

Dadrian, V. N. and Akçam, T., *Judgement at Istanbul: The Armenian Genocide Trials* (New York and Oxford, 2011).

Damianov, S., 'Bulgaria's Decision to Enter the War: Diplomatic Negotiations, 1914–15', in B. K. Király and N. F. Dreisziger (eds.), *East Central European Society in World War I* (Boulder, CO, and Highland Lakes, NJ: Social Science Monographs and Atlantic Research and Publications, 1985), pp. 157–69.

Daniel, U., *The War from Within: German Working-Class Women in the First World War* (Oxford and New York: Berg, 1997).

Davies, N., *God's Playground: A History of Poland*, revised edn (2 vols., Oxford and New York: Oxford University Press, 2005).

Davis, B. J., *Home Fires Burning: Food, Politics and Everyday Life in World War I Berlin* (Chapel Hill, NC, and London: University of North Carolina Press, 2000).

Deák, I., 'The Habsburg Army in the First and Last Days of World War I: A Comparative Analysis', in B. K. Király and N. F. Dreisziger (eds.), *East Central*

European Society in World War I (Boulder, CO, and Highland Lakes, NJ: Social Science Monographs and Atlantic Research and Publications, 1985), pp. 301–12.

_____, *Beyond Nationalism: A Social and Political History of the Habsburg Officer Corps, 1848–1918* (New York and Oxford: Oxford University Press, 1990).

Dedijer, V., *The Road to Sarajevo* (London, Fakenham and Reading: MacGibbon & Kee, 1967).

Deist, W., 'Die Politik der Seekriegsleitung und die Rebellion der Flotte Ende Oktober 1918', *Vierteljahrshefte für Zeitgeschichte* 14(4) (October 1966), pp. 341–68.

_____, 'Zur Geschichte des preussischen Offizierkorps 1888–1918', in H. H. Hofmann (ed.), *Das deutsche Offizierkorps 1860–1960* (Boppard am Rhein: Harald Boldt, 1980), pp. 39–57.

_____, 'Der militärische Zusammenbruch des Kaiserreichs. Zur Realität der "Dolchstoßlegende"', in U. Büttner (ed.), *Das Unrechtsregime. Internationale Forschung über den Nationalsozialismus. Band I. Ideologie-Herrschaftssystem-Wirkung in Europa* (Hamburg: Christians, 1986), pp. 101–29.

_____, 'Verdeckter Militärstreik im Kriegsjahr 1918?', in W. Wette (ed.), *Der Krieg des kleinen Mannes: Eine Militärgeschichte von unten* (Munich and Zurich: Piper, 1992, 1995), pp. 146–67.

_____, 'The Military Collapse of the German Empire: The Reality Behind the Stab-in-the-Back Myth', *War in History* 3(2) (April 1996), pp. 186–207.

_____, 'The German Army, the Authoritarian Nation-State and Total War', in J. Horne (ed.), *State, Society and Mobilization in Europe during the First World War* (Cambridge: Cambridge University Press, 1997), pp. 160–72.

Diers, M., *Schlagbilder. Zur politischen Ikonographie der Gegenwart* (Frankfurt am Main: Fischer Taschenbuch, 1997).

Dietrich, E., 'Der andere Tod. Seuchen, Volkskrankheiten und Gesundheitswesen im Ersten Weltkrieg', in K. Eisterer and R. Steininger (eds.), *Tirol und der Erste Weltkrieg* (Innsbruck: Österreichischer Studien Verlag, 1995), pp. 255–75.

DiNardo, R. L. and Hughes, D. J., 'Germany and Coalition Warfare in the World Wars: A Comparative Study', *War in History* 8(2) (April 2001), pp. 166–90.

Donson, A., *Youth in the Fatherless Land: War Pedagogy, Nationalism, and Authority in Germany, 1914–1918* (Cambridge, MA, and London: Harvard University Press, 2010).

Dornik, W. and Lieb, P., 'Misconceived *Realpolitik* in a Failing State: The Political and Economical Fiasco of the Central Powers in the Ukraine, 1918', *First World War Studies* 4(1) (March 2013), pp. 111–24.

Doughty, R. A., 'French Strategy in 1914: Joffre's Own', *The Journal of Military History* 67(2) (April 2003), pp. 427–54.

_____, *Pyrrhic Victory: French Strategy and Operations in the Great War* (Cambridge, MA, and London: Harvard University Press, 2005).

Dudek, L., 'Polish Military Formations in World War I', in B. K. Király and N. F. Dreisziger (eds.), *East Central European Society in World War I* (Boulder, CO, and Highland Lakes, NJ: Social Science Monographs and Atlantic Research and Publications, 1985), pp. 454–70.

Dülffer, 'Kriegserwartung und Kriegsbild in Deutschland vor 1914', in W. Michalka (ed.), *Der Erste Weltkrieg. Wirkung, Wahrnehmung, Analyse* (Munich: Piper, 1992), pp. 778–98.

Dunin-Wąsowicz, K., *Warszawa w czasie pierwszej wojny światowej* (Warsaw: Państwowy Instytut Wydawniczy, 1974).

Dupuy, T. N., *Genius for War: The German Army and General Staff, 1807–1945* (London: MacDonald and Jane's, 1977).

Dwyer, P. G., '"It Still Makes Me Shudder": Memories of Massacres and Atrocities during the Revolutionary and Napoleonic Wars', *War in History* 16(4) (November 2009), pp. 381–405.

Eichenberg, J., 'The Dark Side of Independence: Paramilitary Violence in Ireland and Poland after the First World War', *Contemporary European History* 19(3) (August 2010), pp. 231–48.

_____, *Kämpfen für Frieden und Fürsorge. Polnische Veteranen des Ersten Weltkriegs und ihre inernationalen Kontakte, 1918–1939* (Munich: Oldenbourg, 2011).

_____ and Newman, J. P., 'Introduction: Aftershocks: Violence in Dissolving Empires after the First World War', *Contemporary European History* 19(3) (August 2010), pp. 183–94.

Eisterer, K., '"Der Heldentod muß würdig geschildert werden". Der Umgang der Vergangenheit am Beispiel Kaiserjäger und Kaiserjägertradition', in K. Eisterer and R. Steininger (eds.), *Tirol und der Erste Weltkrieg* (Innsbruck: Österreichischer Studien Verlag, 1995), pp. 105–37.

Engelstein, L., '"A Belgium of Our Own": The Sack of Russian Kalisz, August 1914', *Kritika: Explorations in Russian and Eurasian History* 10(3) (Summer 2009), pp. 441–73.

Erickson, E. J., *Ordered to Die: A History of the Ottoman Army in the First World War* (Westport, CT, and London: Greenwood Press, 2001).

Etschmann, W., 'Österreich-Ungarn zwischen Engagement und Zurückhaltung. K.u.k. Truppen an der Westfront', in J. Duppler and G. P. Groß (eds.), *Kriegsende 1918. Ereignis, Wirkung, Nachwirkung. Beiträge zur Militärgeschichte. Herausgegeben vom Militärgeschichtlichen Forschungsamt. Band 53* (Munich: R. Oldenbourg, 1999), pp. 97–105.

Evans, R. J. W., 'Essay and Reflection: Frontiers and National Identities in Central Europe', *The International History Review* 14(3) (August 1992), pp. 480–502.

_____, 'The Successor States', in R. Gerwarth (ed.), *Twisted Paths: Europe 1914–1945* (Oxford: Oxford University Press, 2007), pp. 210–36.

Farcy, J.-C., *Les Camps de concentration français de la première guerre mondiale (1914–1920)* (Paris: Anthropos, 1995).

Farrar, L. L., Jr, 'Separate Peace – General Peace – Total War: The Crisis in German Policy during the Spring of 1917', *Militärgeschichtliche Mitteilungen* 20 (1976), pp. 51–80.

_____, 'Reluctant Warriors: Public Opinion on War during the July Crisis 1914', *East European Quarterly* 16(4) (Winter 1982), pp. 417–46.

Feldman, G. D., *Army, Industry and Labor in Germany, 1914–1918* (Providence, RI, and Oxford: Berg, 1966, 1992).

_____, (ed.), *German Imperialism, 1914–1918: The Development of a Historical Debate* (New York, London, Sydney and Toronto: John Wiley & Sons, 1972).

Fellner, F., 'Die "Mission Hoyos"', in W. Alff (ed.), *Deutschlands Sonderung von Europa 1862–1945* (Frankfurt am Main, Bern and New York: Peter Lang, 1984), pp. 283–316.

_____, 'Der Krieg in Tagebüchern und Briefen. Überlegungen zu einer wenig genützten Quellenart', in K. Amann and H. Lengauer (eds.), *Österreich und der Große Krieg 1914–1918. Die andere Seite der Geschichte* (Vienna: Christian Brandstätter, 1989), pp. 205–13.

_____, 'Austria-Hungary', in K. Wilson (ed.), *Decisions for War* (London: UCL Press, 1995, 1998), pp. 9–25.

Feltman, B. K., 'Tolerance as a Crime? The British Treatment of German Prisoners of War on the Western Front, 1914–1918', *War in History* 17(4) (November 2010), pp. 435–58.

Ferguson, N., 'Public Finance and National Security: The Domestic Origins of the First World War Revisited', *Past & Present* 142 (February 1994), pp. 141–68.

_____, *Paper and Iron: Hamburg Business and German Politics in the Era of Inflation, 1897–1927* (Cambridge, New York and Oakleigh: Cambridge University Press, 1995).

_____, *The Pity of War* (London: Allen Lane/The Penguin Press, 1998).

_____, 'Prisoner Taking and Prisoner Killing in the Age of Total War: Towards a Political Economy of Military Defeat', *War in History* 11(2) (April 2004), pp. 148–92.

Fiebig von Hase, R., 'Der Anfang vom Ende des Krieges: Deutschland, die USA und die Hintergründe des amerikanischen Kriegseintritts am 6. April 1917', in W. Michalka (ed.), *Der Erste Weltkrieg. Wirkung, Wahrnehmung, Analyse* (Munich and Zurich: Piper, 1994), pp. 125–58.

Figes, O., *A People's Tragedy: The Russian Revolution, 1891–1924* (London: Pimlico, 1996, 1997).

Fischer, C. J., *Alsace to the Alsatians? Visions and Divisions of Alsatian Regionalism, 1870–1939* (New York and Oxford: Berghahn Books, 2010).

Fischer, F., *Germany's Aims in the First World War* (London: Chatto & Windus, 1967).

_____, *War of Illusions: German Policies from 1911 to 1914* (London: Chatto & Windus, 1975).

_____, 'German War Aims 1914–1918 and German Policy before the War', in Barry Hunt and Adrian Preston (eds.), *War Aims and Strategic Policy in the Great War* (London: Croom Helm, 1977), pp. 105–23.

Flasch, K., *Die geistige Mobilmachung. Die deutschen Intellektuellen und der Erste Weltkrieg* (Berlin: Alexander Fest, 2000).

Fletcher, R. (ed.), *Bernstein to Brandt: A Short History of German Social Democracy* (London, Victoria and Baltimore, MD: Edward Arnold, 1978).

Foley, R. T., 'The Origins of the Schlieffen Plan', *War in History* 10(2) (April 2003), pp. 222–32.

_____, 'Preparing the German Army for the First World War: The Operational Ideas of Alfred von Schlieffen and Helmuth von Moltke the Younger', *War & Society* 22(2) (October 2004), pp. 1–25.

_____, *German Strategy and the Path to Verdun: Erich von Falkenhayn and the Development of Attrition, 1870–1916* (Cambridge: Cambridge University Press, 2005).

_____, 'Easy Target or Invincible Enemy? German Intelligence Assessments of France Before the Great War', *The Journal of Intelligence History* 5 (Winter 2005), pp. 1–24.

_____, 'What's in a Name? The Development of Strategies of Attrition on the Western Front, 1914–1918', *The Historian* 68(4) (Winter 2006), pp. 722–46.

_____, 'Learning War's Lessons: The German Army and the Battle of the Somme 1916', *The Journal of Military History* 75(2) (April 2011), pp. 471–504.

Fong, G., 'The Movement of German Divisions to the Western Front, Winter 1917–1918', *War in History* 7(2) (April 2000), pp. 225–35.

Förster, J., 'Ludendorff and Hitler in Perspective: The Battle for the German Soldier's Mind, 1917–1944', *War in History* 10(3) (July 2003), pp. 321–34.

Förster, S., 'Der deutsche Generalstab und die Illusion des kurzen Krieges, 1871–1914. Metakritik eines Mythos', *Militärgeschichtliche Mitteilungen* 54(1) (1995), pp. 61–95.

Forstner, F., *Przemyśl. Österreich-Ungarns bedeutendste Festung*, 2nd edn (Vienna: ÖBV Pädagogischer Verlag, 1997).

Franc, M., 'Bread from Wood: Natural Food Substitutes in the Czech Lands during the First World War', in I. Zweiniger-Bargielowska, R. Duffett and A. Drouard (eds.), *Food and War in Twentieth-Century Europe* (Farnham and Burlington, VT: Ashgate, 2011), pp. 73–84.

Frank, A. F., *Oil Empire: Visions of Prosperity in Austrian Galicia* (Cambridge, MA, and London: Harvard University Press, 2005).

Freifeld, A., 'Empress Elisabeth as Hungarian Queen: The Uses of Celebrity Monarchism', in L. Cole and D. L. Unowsky (eds.), *The Limits of Loyalty: Imperial Symbolism, Popular Allegiances, and State Patriotism in the Late Habsburg Monarchy* (New York and Oxford: Berghahn Books, 2007), pp. 138–61.

French, D., 'The Meaning of Attrition, 1914–1916', *English Historical Review* 103(407) (April 1988), pp. 385–405.

Frevert, U., *A Nation in Barracks: Modern Germany, Military Conscription and Civil Society* (Oxford and New York: Berg, 2004).

Frey, M., 'Deutsche Finanzinteressen an den Vereinigten Staaten und den Niederlanden im Ersten Weltkrieg', *Militärgeschichtliche Mitteilung* 53(2) (1994), pp. 327–53.

Führ, C., *Das k.u.k. Armeeoberkommando und die Innenpolitik in Österreich 1914–1917* (Graz, Vienna and Cologne: Hermann Böhlaus Nachf., 1968).

Fuller, Jr, W. C., *Civil-Military Conflict in Imperial Russia, 1881–1914* (Princeton, NJ: Princeton University Press, 1985).

Funk, A., *Geschichte der Stadt Allenstein von 1348 bis 1943* (Leer: Gerhard Rautenberg, 1955).

Galántai, J., *Hungary in the First World War* (Budapest: Akadémiai Kiadó, 1989).

Gałas, M. and Polonsky, A., 'Introduction', in M. Gałas and A. Polonsky (eds.), *Polin: Studies in Polish Jewry. Vol. 23: Jews in Kraków* (Oxford and Portland, OR: The Littman Library of Jewish Civilization, 2011).

Gatrell, P., *A Whole Empire Walking: Refugees in Russia during World War I* (Bloomington and Indianapolis, IN: Indiana University Press, 1999).

———, 'Displacing and Re-Placing Population in the Two World Wars: Armenia and Poland Compared', *Contemporary European History* 16(4) (November 2007), pp. 511–27.

Geinitz, C. and Hinz, U., 'Das Augusterlebnis in Südbaden: Ambivalente Reaktionen der deutschen Öffentlichkeit auf den Kriegsbeginn 1914', in G. Hirschfeld, G. Krumeich, D. Langewiesche and H.-P. Ullmann (eds.), *Kriegserfahrungen. Studien zur Sozial- und Mentalitätsgeschichte des Ersten Weltkriegs* (Essen: Klartext, 1997), pp. 20–35.

Geiss, I., *Der polnische Grenzstreifen 1914–1918. Ein Beitrag zur deutschen Kriegszielpolitik im Ersten Weltkrieg* (Lübeck and Hamburg: Matthiesen, 1960).

———, 'The Outbreak of the First World War and German War Aims', *Journal of Contemporary History* 1(3) (July 1966), pp. 75–91.

———, *Das deutsche Reich und der Erste Weltkrieg* (Munich and Vienna: Carl Hanser, 1978).

Geppert, D. and Gerwarth, R. (eds.), *Wilhelmine Germany and Edwardian Britain: Essays on Cultural Affinity* (Oxford and New York: German Historical Institute and Oxford University Press, 2008).

Gersdorff, U. von, *Frauen im Kriegsdienst 1914–1945* (Stuttgart: Deutsche Verlags-Anstalt, 1969).

Gerwarth, R., 'The Central European Counter-Revolution: Paramilitary Violence in Germany, Austria and Hungary after the Great War', *Past and Present* 200 (August 2008), pp. 175–209.

_____ and Horne, J., 'The Great War and Paramilitarism in Europe, 1917–23', *Contemporary European History* 19(3) (August 2010), pp. 267–73.

_____ and Malinowski, S., 'Hannah Arendt's Ghosts: Reflections on the Disputable Path from Windhoek to Auschwitz', *Central European History* 42(2) (June 2009), pp. 279–300.

Geyer, M., *Deutsche Rüstungspolitik 1860–1980* (Frankfurt am Main: Suhrkamp, 1984).

_____, 'German Strategy in the Age of Machine Warfare, 1914–1945', in P. Paret (ed.), *Makers of Modern Strategy from Machiavelli to the Nuclear Age* (Oxford: Clarendon Press, 1986), pp. 527–97.

_____, 'Insurrectionary Warfare: The German Debate about a Levée en Masse in October 1918', *The Journal of Contemporary History* 73(3) (September 2001), pp. 459–527.

Glettler, M., 'Die slowakische Gesellschaft unter der Einwirkung von Krieg und Militarisierung 1914–1918', in H. Mommsen, D. Kováč, J. Malíř and M. Marek (eds.), *Der Erste Weltkrieg und die Beziehungen zwischen Tschechen, Slowaken und Deutschen* (Essen: Klartext, 2001), pp. 93–108.

Godsey, Jr, W. D., *Aristocratic Redoubt: The Austro-Hungarian Foreign Office on the Eve of the First World War* (West Lafayette, IN: Purdue University Press, 1999).

Goebel, S., 'Forging the Industrial Home Front: Iron-Nail Memorials in the Ruhr', in J. Macleod and P. Purseigle (eds.), *Uncovered Fields: Perspectives in First World War Studies* (Leiden and Boston, MA: Brill, 2004), pp. 159–78.

_____, 'Re-Membered and Re-Mobilized: The "Sleeping Dead" in Interwar Germany and Britain', *Journal of Contemporary History* 39(4) (October 2004), pp. 487–501.

_____, 'Schools', in J. Winter and J.-L. Robert (eds.), *Capital Cities at War: Paris, London, Berlin 1914–1919. Vol. 2: A Cultural History* (2 vols., Cambridge and New York: Cambridge University Press, 2007), pp. 188–234.

Golczewski, F., *Polnische-Jüdische Beziehungen 1881–1922. Eine Studie zur Geschichte des Antisemitismus in Osteuropa* (Wiesbaden: Franz Steiner, 1981).

Goltz, A. von der [published as Menge, A.], 'The *Iron Hindenburg*: A Popular Icon of Weimar Germany', *German History* 26(3) (July 2008), pp. 357–82.

_____, *Hindenburg: Power, Myth, and the Rise of the Nazis* (Oxford and New York: Oxford University Press, 2009).

Grady, T., *The German-Jewish Soldiers of the First World War in History and Memory* (Liverpool: Liverpool University Press, 2011).

Grandner, M., *Kooperative Gewerkschaftspolitik in der Kriegswirtschaft: Die freien Gewerkschaften Österreichs im ersten Weltkrieg* (Vienna, Cologne and Weimar: Böhlau, 1992).

Granier, G., 'Kriegführung und Politik am Beispiel des Handelskriegs mit U-Booten 1915–1918', in K. Oldenhage, H. Schreyer and W. Werner (eds.), *Archiv und Geschichte. Festschrift für Friedrich P. Kahlenberg* (Düsseldorf: Droste, 2000), pp. 595–640.

_____, 'Pirat oder Kriegsmann? Die active Teilnahme von Handelsschiffen am Seekrieg von 1914 bis 1918 und die Fälle der Kapitäne Fryatt und Blaikie', *Militärgeschichtliche Zeitschrift* 62(2) (2003), pp. 459–69.

Greenhalgh, E., *Foch in Command: The Forging of a First World War General* (Cambridge and New York: Cambridge University Press, 2011).

Gregory, A., 'Railway Stations: Gateways and Termini', in J. Winter and J.-L. Robert (eds.), *Capital Cities at War: Paris, London, Berlin, 1914–1919. Vol. 2: A Cultural History* (2 vols., Cambridge and New York: Cambridge University Press, 2007), pp. 23–56.

Groß, G. P., 'Eine Frage der Ehre? Die Marineführung und der letzte Flottenvorstoß 1918', in J. Duppler and G. P. Groß (eds.), *Kriegsende 1918. Ereignis, Wirkung, Nachwirkung. Beiträge zur Militärgeschichte. Herausgegeben vom Militärgeschichtlichen Forschungsamt. Band 53* (Munich: R. Oldenbourg, 1999), pp. 349–65.

_____, 'Im Schatten des Westens. Die deutsche Kriegführung an der Ostfront bis Ende 1915', in G. P. Groß (ed.), *Die vergessene Front. Der Osten 1914/15. Ereignis, Wirkung, Nachwirkung* (Paderborn, Munich, Vienna and Zurich: Ferdinand Schöningh, 2006), pp. 49–64.

_____, 'There was a Schlieffen Plan: Neue Quellen', in H. Ehlert, M. Epkenhans and G. P. Groß (eds.), *Der Schlieffenplan. Analysen und Dokumente* (Paderborn, Munich, Vienna and Zurich: Ferdinand Schöningh, 2006), pp. 117–60.

Gross, S., 'Confidence and Gold: German War Finance, 1914–1918', *Central European History* 42(2) (June 2009), pp. 223–52.

Groth, O., *Die Zeitung. Ein System der Zeitungskunde (Journalistik), I* (4 vols., Mannheim, Berlin and Leipzig: J. Bensheimer, 1928).

Gudmundsson, B. I., *Stormtroop Tactics: Innovation in the German Army, 1914–1918* (Westport, CT, and London: Praeger, 1989, 1995).

Gumz, J. E., *The Resurrection and Collapse of Empire in Habsburg Serbia, 1914–1918* (Cambridge and New York: Cambridge University Press, 2009).

Gygi, F., 'Shattered Experiences – Recycled Relics: Strategies of Representation and the Legacy of the Great War', in N. J. Saunders (ed.), *Matters of Conflict: Material Culture, Memory and the First World War* (London and New York: Routledge, 2004), pp. 72–89.

Hadley, M. L., *Count Not the Dead: The Popular Image of the German Submarine* (Quebec City: McGill-Queen's University Press, 1995).

Hadley, T., 'Military Diplomacy in the Dual Alliance: German Military Attaché Reporting from Vienna, 1906–1914', *War in History* 17(3) (July 2010), pp. 294–312.

Hagen, M. von, *War in a European Borderland: Occupations and Occupation Plans in Galicia and Ukraine, 1914–1918* (Seattle, WA: REECAS, University of Washington, 2007).

Hagen, W. W., *Germans, Poles, and Jews: The Nationality Conflict in the Prussian East, 1772–1914* (Chicago, IL, and London: University of Chicago Press, 1980).

Hagenlücke, H., *Deutsche Vaterlandspartei. Die nationale Rechte am Ende des Kaiserreiches* (Düsseldorf: Droste, 1997).

Hall, R. C., 'Bulgaria in the First World War', *The Historian* 73(2) (Summer 2011), pp. 300–15.

Halliday, J. D., 'Censorship in Berlin and Vienna during the First World War: A Comparative View', *The Modern Language Review* 83(3) (July 1988), pp. 612–26.

Halpern, P. G., *A Naval History of World War I* (Annapolis, MD: Naval Institute Press, 1994).

Hamilton, R. F. and Herwig, H. (eds.), *The Origins of World War I* (Cambridge, New York, Melbourne, Madrid and Cape Town: Cambridge University Press, 2003).

Hamlin, D., '"*Dummes Geld*": Money, Grain, and the Occupation of Romania in WWI', *Central European History* 42(3) (September 2009), pp. 451–71.

Hämmerle, C., 'Zur Liebesarbeit sind wir hier, Soldatenstrümpfe stricken wir … Anmerkungen zu einer besonderen Form weiblicher *Kriegsfürsorge* im Ersten Weltkrieg', *Austriaca. Cahiers Universitaires d'Information sur l'Autriche* 42 (June 1996), pp. 89–102.

—, 'Die k.(u.)k. Armee als "Schule des Volkes"? Zur Geschichte der Allgemeinen Wehrpflicht in der multinationalen Habsburgermonarchie (1866–1914/18)', in C. Jansen (ed.), *Der Bürger als Soldat. Die Militärisierung europäischer Gesellschaften im langen 19. Jahrhundert: ein internationaler Vergleich* (Essen: Klartext, 2004), pp. 175–213.

—, '"… dort wurden wir dressiert und sekiert und geschlagen …" Vom Drill, dem Disziplinarstrafrecht und Soldatenmisshandlungen im Heer (1868 bis 1914)', in L. Cole, C. Hämmerle and M. Scheutz (eds.), *Glanz – Gewalt – Gehorsam. Militär und Gesellschaft in der Habsburgermonarchie (1800 bis 1918)* (Essen: Klartext, 2011), pp. 31–54.

Hanák, P., 'Die Volksmeinung während des letzten Kriegsjahres in Österreich-Ungarn', in R. G. Plaschka and K. Mack (eds.), *Die Auflösung des*

Habsburgerreiches. Zusammenbruch und Neuorientierung im Donauraum (Vienna: Verlag für Geschichte und Politik, 1970), pp. 58–66.

Hanebrink, P. A., *In Defense of Christian Hungary: Religion, Nationalism, and Anti-Semitism, 1890–1944* (Ithaca, NY, and London: Cornell University Press, 2006).

Hankel, G., *Die Leipziger Prozesse. Deutsche Kriegsverbrechen und ihre strafrechtliche Verfolgung nach dem Ersten Weltkrieg* (Hamburg: Hamburger Edition, 2003).

Hardach, G., *The First World War, 1914–1918* (London: Allen Lane/The Penguin Press, 1977).

Harris, J. P., and Barr, N., *Amiens to the Armistice. The BEF in the Hundred Days' Campaign, 8 August–11 November 1918* (London: Brassey's, 1998)

Harris, R., 'The "Child of the Barbarian": Rape, Race and Nationalism in France during the First World War', *Past & Present* 141 (November 1993), pp. 170–206.

Hartungen, C. von, 'Die Tiroler und Vorarlberger Standschützen – Mythos und Realität', in K. Eisterer and R. Steininger (eds.), *Tirol und der Erste Weltkrieg* (Innsbruck: Österreichischer Studien Verlag, 1995), pp. 61–104.

Harvey, D. A., 'Lost Children or Enemy Aliens? Classifying the Population of Alsace after the First World War', *Journal of Contemporary History* 34(4) (October 1999), pp. 537–54.

Haselsteiner, H., 'The Habsburg Empire in World War I: Mobilization of Food Supplies', in B. K. Király and N. F. Dreisziger (eds.), *East Central European Society in World War I* (Boulder, CO, and Highland Lakes, NJ: Social Science Monographs and Atlantic Research and Publications, 1985), pp. 87–102.

Hautmann, H., 'Prozesse gegen Defätisten, Kriegsgegner, Linksradikale und streikende Arbeiter im Ersten Weltkrieg', in K. R. Stadler (ed.), *Sozialistenprozesse. Politische Justiz in Österreich 1870–1936* (Vienna, Munich and Zurich: Europaverlag, 1986), pp. 153–79.

Havránek, J., 'Politische Repression und Versorgungsengpässe in den böhmischen Ländern 1914 bis 1918', in H. Mommsen, D. Kováč, J. Malíř and M. Marek (eds.), *Der Erste Weltkrieg und die Beziehungen zwischen Tschechen, Slowaken und Deutschen* (Essen: Klartext, 2001), pp. 47–66.

Healy, M., *Vienna and the Fall of the Habsburg Empire: Total War and Everyday Life in World War I* (Cambridge: Cambridge University Press, 2004, 2007).

Heiss, H., 'Andere Fronten. Volksstimmung und Volkserfahrung in Tirol während des Ersten Weltkrieges', in K. Eisterer and R. Steininger (eds.), *Tirol und der Erste Weltkrieg* (Innsbruck: Österreichischer Studien Verlag, 1995), pp. 139–77.

Herbert, U., 'Zwangsarbeit als Lernprozeß. Zur Beschäftigung ausländischer Arbeiter in der westdeutschen Industrie im Ersten Weltkrieg', *Archiv für Sozialgeschichte* 24 (1984), pp. 285–304.

_____, *A History of Foreign Labor in Germany, 1880–1980: Seasonal Workers/ Forced Laborers/Guest Workers* (Ann Arbor, MI: The University of Michigan Press, 1990).

Herrmann, D. G., *The Arming of Europe and the Making of the First World War* (Princeton, NJ: Princeton University Press, 1996).

Herwig, H. H., 'Admirals *versus* Generals: The War Aims of the Imperial German Navy, 1914–1918', *Central European History* 5(3) (September 1972), pp. 208–33.

_____, *'Luxury' Fleet: The Imperial German Navy, 1888–1918* (London, Boston and Sydney: George Allen & Unwin, 1980).

_____, 'Tunes of Glory at the Twilight Stage: The Bad Homburg Crown Council and the Evolution of German Statecraft, 1917/1918', *German Studies Review* 6(3) (October 1983), pp. 475–94.

_____, 'The Dynamics of Military Necessity: German Military Policy during the First World War', in A. R. Millett and W. Murray (eds.), *Military Effectiveness. Vol. I: The First World War* (3 vols., Boston, MA, London, Sydney and Wellington, 1988), pp. 80–115.

_____, 'Disjointed Allies: Coalition Warfare in Berlin and Vienna, 1914', *The Journal of Military History* 54(3) (July 1990), pp. 265–80.

_____, *The First World War: Germany and Austria-Hungary, 1914–1918* (London, New York, Sydney and Auckland: Arnold, 1997).

_____, 'Total Rhetoric, Limited War: Germany's U-Boat Campaign, 1917–1918', in R. Chickering and S. Förster (eds.), *Great War, Total War: Combat and Mobilization on the Western Front, 1914–1918* (Washington, DC, and Cambridge: German Historical Institute and Cambridge University Press, 2000), pp. 189–206.

_____, 'Germany and the "Short-War" Illusion: Toward a New Interpretation?', *The Journal of Military History* 66(3) (July 2002), pp. 681–93.

_____, 'Germany', in R. F. Hamilton and H. Herwig (eds.), *The Origins of World War I* (Cambridge, New York, Melbourne, Madrid and Cape Town: Cambridge University Press, 2003), pp. 151–87.

_____, 'Why Did It Happen?', in R. F. Hamilton and H. Herwig (eds.), *The Origins of World War I* (Cambridge, New York, Melbourne, Madrid and Cape Town: Cambridge University Press, 2003), pp. 443–68.

_____ and Trask, D. F., 'The Failure of Imperial Germany's Undersea Offensive Against World Shipping, February 1917–October 1918', *The Historian* 33(4) (August 1971), pp. 611–36.

Heumos, P., '"Kartoffeln her oder es gibt eine Revolution". Hungerkrawalle, Streiks und Massenproteste in den böhmischen Ländern 1914–1918', in H. Mommsen, D. Kováč, J. Malíř and M. Marek (eds.), *Der Erste Weltkrieg und die Beziehungen zwischen Tschechen, Slowaken und Deutschen* (Essen: Klartext, 2001), pp. 255–86.

Hewitson, M., 'Images of the Enemy: German Depictions of the French Military, 1890–1914', *War in History* 11(1) (January 2004), pp. 4–33.

Hirschfeld, G., Krumeich, G., Renz, I. and Pöhlmann, M. (eds.), *Enzyklopädie Erster Weltkrieg* (Paderborn, Munich, Vienna and Zurich: Ferdinand Schöningh, 2003, 2004).

———, 'Die Somme-Schlacht von 1916', in G. Hirschfeld, G. Krumeich and I. Renz (eds.), *Die Deutschen an der Somme 1914–1918* (Essen: Klartext, 2006), pp. 79–89.

Höbelt, L., '"Well-Tempered Discontent": Austrian Domestic Politics', in M. Cornwall (ed.), *The Last Years of Austria-Hungary: A Multi-National Experiment in Early Twentieth-Century Europe*, revised and expanded edn (Exeter: University of Exeter Press, 2002), pp. 47–74.

Hoeres, P., *Krieg der Philosophen: Die deutsche und britische Philosophie im Ersten Weltkrieg* (Paderborn: Ferdinand Schöningh, 2004).

———, 'Die Slawen. Perzeptionen des Kriegsgegners bei den Mittelmächten. Selbst- und Feindbild', in G. P. Groß (ed.), *Die vergessene Front. Der Osten 1914/15. Ereignis, Wirkung, Nachwirkung* (Paderborn, Munich, Vienna and Zurich: Ferdinand Schöningh, 2006), pp. 179–200.

Hoffmann, C., 'Between Integration and Rejection: The Jewish Community in Germany, 1914–1918', in J. Horne (ed.), *State, Society and Mobilization in Europe during the First World War* (Cambridge: Cambridge University Press, 1997), pp. 89–104.

Hoffmann, H., '"Schwarzer Peter im Weltkrieg": Die deutsche Spielwarenindustrie 1914–1918', in G. Hirschfeld, G. Krumeich, D. Langewiesche and H.-P. Ullmann (eds.), *Kriegserfahrungen. Studien zur Sozial- und Mentalitätsgeschichte des Ersten Weltkriegs* (Essen: Klartext, 1997), pp. 323–35.

Hoffmann-Holter, B., *'Abreisendmachung'. Jüdische Kriegsflüchtlinge in Wien 1914 bis 1923* (Cologne and Weimar: Böhlau, 1995).

Hoffrogge, R., 'Räteaktivisten in der USPD: Richard Müller und die Revolutionären Obleute in Berliner Betrieben', in U. Plener (ed.), *Die Novemberrevolution 1918/1919 in Deutschland. Für bürgerliche und sozialistische Demokratie. Allgemeine, regionale und biographische Aspekte. Beiträge zum 90. Jahrestag der Revolution* (Berlin: Karl Dietz, 2009), pp. 189–99.

Holmes, T. M., 'The Reluctant March on Paris: A Reply to Terence Zuber's "The Schlieffen Plan Reconsidered"', *War in History* 8(2) (April 2001), pp. 208–32.

———, 'The Real Thing: A Reply to Terence Zuber's "Terence Holmes Reinvents the Schlieffen Plan"', *War in History* 9(1) (January 2002), pp. 111–20.

———, 'Asking Schlieffen: A Further Reply to Terence Zuber', *War in History* 10(4) (November 2003), pp. 464–79.

Holquist, P., 'To Count, to Extract, and to Exterminate: Population Statistics and Population Politics in Late Imperial and Soviet Russia', in R. G. Suny and

T. Martin (eds.), *A State of Nations: Empire and Nation-Making in the Age of Lenin and Stalin* (Oxford and New York: Oxford University Press, 2001), pp. 111–44.

_____, 'Les Violences de l'Armée Russe à l'Encontre des Juifs en 1915: Causes et Limites', in J. Horne (ed.), *Vers la Guerre Totale: Le Tournant de 1914–15* (Paris: Tallandier, 2010), pp. 191–219.

_____, 'The Role of Personality in the First (1914–1915) Russian Occupation of Galicia and Bukovina', in J. Dekel-Chen, D. Gaunt, N. M. Meir and I. Barton (eds.), *Anti-Jewish Violence: Rethinking the Pogrom in European History* (Bloomington and Indianapolis, IN: Indiana University Press, 2010), pp. 52–73.

Holzer, A., *Das Lächeln der Henker. Der unbekannte Krieg gegen die Zivilbevölkerung 1914–1918* (Darmstadt: Primus, 2008).

Horn, D., *Mutiny on the High Seas: The Imperial German Naval Mutinies of World War One* (London: Leslie Frewin, 1969).

Horne, A., *The Price of Glory: Verdun 1916* (London: Macmillan, 1962).

Horne, J. and Kramer, A., 'German "Atrocities" and Franco-German Opinion, 1914: The Evidence of German Soldiers' Diaries', *The Journal of Modern History* 66(1) (March 1994), pp. 1–33.

_____, *German Atrocities, 1914: A History of Denial* (New Haven, CT, and London: Yale University Press, 2001).

Houlihan, P. J., 'Was There an Austrian Stab-in-the-Back Myth? Interwar Military Interpretations of Defeat', in G. Bischof, F. Plasser, and P. Berger (eds.), *From Empire to Republic: Post-World War I Austria* (New Orleans, LA: University of New Orleans Press, 2010), pp. 67–89.

Howard, M., 'Men against Fire: Expectations of War in 1914', *International Security* 9(1) (Summer 1984), pp. 41–57.

Hristo, H., *Revolutsionnata Kriza v Bulgaria prez 1918–1919* (Sofia: Bulgarian Communist Party, 1957).

Hull, I. V., *The Entourage of Kaiser Wilhelm II, 1888–1918* (Cambridge: Cambridge University Press, 1982).

_____, *Absolute Destruction: Military Culture and the Practices of War in Imperial Germany* (Ithaca, NY, and London: Cornell University Press, 2005).

Hürten, H., 'Die katholische Kirche im Ersten Weltkrieg', in W. Michalka (ed.), *Der Erste Weltkrieg. Wirkung, Wahrnehmung, Analyse* (Munich and Zurich: Piper, 1994), pp. 725–35.

Ihnatowicz, I., 'Gospodarka na ziemiach polskich w okresie I Wojny Światowej', in B. Zientara, A. Mączak, I. Ihnatowicz and Z. Landau, *Dzieje Gospodarcze Polski do 1939 r.* (Warsaw: Wiedza Powszechna, 1965), pp. 455–65.

Ingenlath, M., *Mentale Aufrüstung. Militarisierungstendenzen in Frankreich und Deutschland vor dem Ersten Weltkrieg* (Frankfurt and New York: Campus, 1998).

Jackman, S. D., 'Shoulder to Shoulder: Close Control and "Old Prussian Drill" in German Offensive Infantry Tactics, 1871–1914', *Journal of Military History* 68(1) (January 2004), pp. 73–104.

Jahn, H., 'Die Germanen. Perzeptionen des Kriegsgegners in Russland zwischen Selbst- und Feindbild', in G. P. Groß (ed.), *Die vergessene Front. Der Osten 1914/15. Ereignis, Wirkung, Nachwirkung* (Paderborn, Munich, Vienna and Zurich: Ferdinand Schöningh, 2006), pp. 165–77.

Jahn, P., '"Zarendreck, Barbarendreck" – Die russische Besetzung Ostpreußens 1914 in der deutschen Öffentlichkeit', in K. Eimermacher and A. Volpert (eds.), *Verführungen der Gewalt. Russen und Deutsche im Ersten und Zweiten Weltkrieg* (Munich: Wilhelm Fink, 2005), pp. 223–41.

Jahr, C., *Gewöhnliche Soldaten. Desertion und Deserteure im deutschen und britischen Heer 1914–1918* (Göttingen: Vandenhoeck & Ruprecht, 1998).

James, L., 'War and Industry: A Study of the Industrial Relations in the Mining Regions of South Wales and the Ruhr during the Great War, 1914–1918', *Labour History Review* 68(2) (August 2003), pp. 195–215.

Jarausch, K. H., 'The Illusion of Limited War: Chancellor Bethmann Hollweg's Calculated Risk, July 1914', *Central European History* 2(1) (March 1969), pp. 48–76.

———, *The Enigmatic Chancellor: Bethmann Hollweg and the Hubris of Imperial Germany* (New Haven, CT, and London: Yale University Press, 1973).

Jászi, O., *The Dissolution of the Habsburg Monarchy* (Chicago, IL, and London: University of Chicago Press, 1929, 1966).

Jelavich, B., 'Clouded Image: Critical Perceptions of the Habsburg Empire in 1914', *Austrian History Yearbook* 23 (1992), pp. 23–35.

Jeřábek, R., *Potiorek. General im Schatten von Sarajevo* (Graz, Vienna and Cologne: Styria, 1991).

———, 'The Eastern Front', in M. Cornwall (ed.), *The Last Years of Austria-Hungary: A Multi-National Experiment in Early Twentieth-Century Europe*, revised and expanded edn (Exeter: University of Exeter Press, 2002), pp. 149–65.

Jessen-Klingenberg, M., 'Die Ausrufung der Republik durch Philipp Scheidemann am 9. November 1918', *Geschichte in Wissenschaft und Unterricht* 19(11) (November 1968), pp. 649–56.

Johnson, D., 'French War Aims and the Crisis of the Third Republic', in B. Hunt and A. Preston (eds.), *War Aims and Strategic Policy in the Great War* (London: Croom Helm, 1977), pp. 41–54.

Johr, B., 'Die Ereignisse in Zahlen', in H. Sander and B. Johr, *Befreier und Befreite. Krieg, Vergewaltigung, Kinder* (Frankfurt am Main: Fischer Taschenbuch, 2005), pp. 46–73.

Joll, J., *The Origins of the First World War*, 2nd edn (London and New York: Longman, 1984, 1992).

Joly, W., *Standschützen. Die Tiroler und Vorarlberger k.k. Standschützen-Formationen im Ersten Weltkrieg. Organisation und Einsatz* (Innsbruck: Universitätsverlag Wagner, 1998).

Jones, D. R., 'Imperial Russia's Forces at War', in A. R. Millett and W. Murray (eds.), *Military Effectiveness. Vol. I: The First World War* (3 vols., Boston, MA, London, Sydney and Wellington, 1988), pp. 249–328.

Jones, H., 'Encountering the "Enemy": Prisoner of War Transport and the Development of War Cultures in 1914', in P. Purseigle (ed.), *Warfare and Belligerence: Perspectives in First World War Studies* (Leiden and Boston, MA: Brill, 2005), pp. 133–62.

_____, 'The German Spring Reprisals of 1917: Prisoners of War and the Violence of the Western Front', *German History* 26(3) (July 2008), pp. 335–56.

_____, 'Imperial Captivities: Colonial Prisoners of War in Germany and the Ottoman Empire, 1914–1918', in S. Das (ed.), *Race, Empire and First World War Writing* (Cambridge and New York: Cambridge University Press, 2011), pp. 175–93.

_____, *Violence Against Prisoners of War in the First World War: Britain, France and Germany, 1914–1920* (Cambridge: Cambridge University Press, 2011).

Kann, R. A., *A History of the Habsburg Empire, 1526–1918* (Berkeley and Los Angeles, CA, and London: University of California Press, 1974).

_____, 'Trends in Austro-German Literature during World War I: War Hysteria and Patriotism', in R. A. Kann, B. K. Király and P. S. Fichtner (eds.), *The Habsburg Empire in World War I: Essays on the Intellectual, Military, Political and Economic Aspects of the Habsburg War Effort* (Boulder, CO, and New York: East European Quarterly and Columbia University Press, 1977), pp. 159–83.

Kapp, R. W., 'Bethmann-Hollweg, Austria-Hungary and Mitteleuropa, 1914–1915', *Austrian History Yearbook* 19 (1983), pp. 215–36.

_____, 'Divided Loyalties: The German Reich and Austria-Hungary in Austro-German Discussions of War Aims, 1914–1916', *Central European History* 17(2/3) (June–September 1984), pp. 120–39.

Kappeler, A., *The Russian Empire: A Multi-Ethnic History* (Harlow: Longman, 2001).

Kargol, T., 'Ziemiaństwo wobec sytuacji gospodarczej Galicji w czasie I wojny światowej', in D. Grinberg, J. Snopko and G. Zackiewicz (eds.), *Lata wielkiej wojny. Dojrzewanie do niepodległości 1914–1918* (Białystok: Wydawnictwo Uniwersytetu w Białymstoku, 2007), pp. 215–28.

_____, *Odbudowa Galicji ze zniszczeń wojennych w latach 1914–1918* (Cracow: Towarzystwo Wydawnicze 'Historia Iagellonica', 2012).

Kennedy, P., *The Rise of the Anglo-German Antagonism, 1860–1914* (London: Allen & Unwin, 1980).

King, J., 'The Municipal and the National in the Bohemian Lands, 1848–1914', *Austrian History Yearbook* 42 (2011), pp. 89–109.

Kirk, D., *Europe's Population in the Interwar Years* (New York: Gordon and Breach, Science Publishers, 1946).

Kitchen, M., *The German Officer Corps, 1890–1914* (Oxford: Clarendon Press, 1968).

———, 'Militarism and the Development of Fascist Ideology: The Political Ideas of Colonel Max Bauer, 1916–1918', *Central European History* 8(3) (September 1975), pp. 199–220.

———, *The Silent Dictatorship: The Politics of the German High Command under Hindenburg and Ludendorff* (London: Croom Helm, 1976).

———, *The German Offensives of 1918* (Stroud: Tempus, 2001).

Klein, H.-D., 'Zwischen Burgfrieden und Komintern. Die Unabhängige Sozialdemokratie in Halle-Merseburg 1917–1920', in H. Grebing, H. Mommsen and K. Rudolph (eds.), *Demokratie und Emanzipation zwischen Saale und Elbe. Beiträge zur Geschichte der sozialdemokratischen Arbeiterbewegung bis 1933* (Essen: Klartext, 1993), pp. 181–95.

Kluge, U., *Soldatenräte und Revolution. Studien zur Militärpolitik in Deutschland 1918/19* (Göttingen: Vandenhoeck & Ruprecht, 1975).

———, *Die deutsche Revolution 1918/1919. Staat, Politik und Gesellschaft Zwischen Weltkrieg und Kapp-Putsch* (Frankurt am Main: Suhrkamp, 1985).

Knoch, P., 'Kriegsalltag', in P. Knoch (ed.), *Kriegsalltag. Die Rekonstruktion des Kriegsalltags als Aufgabe der historischen Forschung und der Friedenserziehung* (Stuttgart: J. B. Metzlersche Versbuchhandlung, 1989), pp. 222–51.

———, 'Erleben und Nacherleben: Das Kriegserlebnis im Augenzeugenbericht und im Geschichtsunterricht', in G. Hirschfeld, G. Krumeich and I. Renz (eds.), *'Keiner fühlt sich hier mehr als Mensch . . .' Erlebnis und Wirkung des Ersten Weltkriegs* (Essen: Klartext, 1993), pp. 199–219.

Koch, E., '"Jeder tut, was er kann fürs Vaterland": Frauen und Männer an der Heilbronner "Heimatfront"', in G. Hirschfeld, G. Krumeich, D. Langewiesche and H.-P. Ullmann (eds.), *Kriegserfahrungen. Studien zur Sozial- und Mentalitätsgeschichte des Ersten Weltkriegs* (Essen: Klartext, 1997), pp. 36–52.

Kocka, J., *Facing Total War: German Society, 1914–1918* (Leamington Spa: Berg, 1984).

———, 'German History before Hitler: The Debate about the German *Sonderweg*', *Journal of Contemporary History* 23(1) (January 1988), pp. 3–16.

Kolata, G., *Flu: The Story of the Great Influenza Pandemic of 1918 and the Search for the Virus that Caused it* (New York: Touchstone, 2001).

Kossert, A., *Preußen, Deutsche oder Polen? Die Masuren im Spannungsfeld des ethnischen Nationalismus 1870–1956* (Wiesbaden: Harrassowitz, 2001).

———, *Ostpreußen. Geschichte und Mythos* (Munich: Siedler, 2005).

Koszyk, K., *Deutsche Pressepolitik im Ersten Weltkrieg* (Düsseldorf: Droste, 1968).

Kramer, A., 'Wackes at War: Alsace-Lorraine and the Failure of German National Mobilization, 1914–1918', in J. Horne (ed.), *State, Society and Mobilization in Europe during the First World War* (Cambridge: Cambridge University Press, 1997), pp. 105–21.

———, 'Italienische Kriegsgefangene im Ersten Weltkrieg', in H. J. W. Kuprian and O. Überegger (eds.), *Der Erste Weltkrieg im Alpenraum. Erfahrung, Deutung, Erinnerung. La Grande Guerra nell'arco alpino. Esperienze e memoria* (Innsbruck: Universitätsverlag Wagner, 2006), pp. 247–58.

———, *Dynamic of Destruction: Culture and Mass Killing in the First World War* (Oxford and New York: Oxford University Press, 2007).

———, 'Combatants and Noncombatants: Atrocities, Massacres, and War Crimes', in J. Horne (ed.), *A Companion to World War I* (Malden, MA, Oxford and Chichester: Wiley-Blackwell, 2010), pp. 188–201.

Kratoska, P. H. (ed.), *The Thailand-Burma Railway, 1942–1946: Documents and Selected Writings. Vol. 1: Summary Accounts* (6 vols., Abingdon and New York: Routledge, 2006).

Křen, J., *Die Konfliktgemeinschaft. Tschechen und Deutsche 1780–1918*, trans. P. Heumos (Munich: R. Oldenbourg, 2000).

Kronenberg, M., *Die Bedeutung der Schule für die 'Heimatfront' im Ersten Weltkrieg. Sammlungen, Hilfsdienste, Feiern und Nagelungen im deutschen Reich* (Norderstedt: GRIN, 2010).

Kronenbitter, G., 'Die Macht der Illusionen. Julikrise und Kriegsausbruch 1914 aus der Sicht des deutschen Militärattachés in Wien', *Militärgeschichtliche Mitteilung* 57(2) (1998), pp. 519–50.

———, *'Krieg im Frieden'. Die Führung der k.u.k. Armee und die Großmachtpolitik Österreichs-Ungarns 1906–1914* (Munich: R. Oldenbourg, 2003).

———, 'Die militärische Planung der k.u.k. Armee und der Schlieffenplan', in H. Ehlert, M. Epkenhans and G. P. Groß, *Der Schlieffenplan. Analysen und Dokumente* (Paderborn, Munich, Vienna and Zurich: Ferdinand Schöningh, 2006), pp. 205–20.

Kruse, W., 'Die Kriegsbegeisterung im deutschen Reich zu Beginn des Ersten Weltkrieges', in M. van der Linden and G. Mergner (eds.), *Kriegsbegeisterung und mentale Kriegsvorbereitung. Interdisziplinäre Studien* (Berlin: Duncker und Humblot, 1991), pp. 73–87.

———, *Krieg und nationale Integration. Eine Neuinterpretation des sozialdemokratischen Burgfriedensschlusses 1914/15* (Essen: Klartext, 1993).

———, 'Krieg und Klassenheer. Zur Revolutionierung der deutschen Armee im Ersten Weltkrieg', *Geschichte und Gesellschaft. Zeitschrift für Historische Sozialwissenschaft* 22(4) (1996), pp. 530–61.

——— (ed.), *Eine Welt von Feinden. Der Große Krieg 1914–1918* (Frankfurt am Main: Fischer Taschenbuch, 1997).

Kulischer, E. M., *Europe on the Move: War and Population Changes, 1917–1947* (New York: Columbia University Press, 1948).

Kundrus, B., 'Gender Wars: The First World War and the Construction of Gender Relations in the Weimar Republic', in K. Hagemann and S. Schüler-Springorum (eds.), *Home/Front: The Military, War and Gender in Twentieth-Century Germany* (Oxford and New York: Berg, 2002), pp. 159–79.

Kuprian, H. J. W., 'Flüchtlinge, Evakuierte und die staatliche Fürsorge', in K. Eisterer and R. Steininger (eds.), *Tirol und der Erste Weltkrieg* (Innsbruck: Österreichischer Studien Verlag, 1995), pp. 277–305.

Kwan, J., 'Nationalism and All That: Reassessing the Habsburg Monarchy and its Legacy', *European History Quarterly* 41(1) (January 2011), pp. 88–108.

Larsen, D., 'War Pessimism and an American Peace in Early 1916', *The International History Review* 34(4) (December 2012), pp. 795–817.

Latzel, K., *Deutsche Soldaten – nationalsozialistischer Krieg? Kriegserlebnis – Kriegserfahrung 1939–45* (Paderborn, Munich, Vienna and Zurich: Ferdinand Schöningh, 1998).

Lawrence, J., 'The Transition to War in 1914', in J. Winter and J.-L. Robert (eds.), *Capital Cities at War: Paris, London, Berlin, 1914–1919* (Cambridge, New York and Melbourne: Cambridge University Press, 1997), pp. 135–63.

Lee, J., 'Administrators and Agriculture: Aspects of German Agricultural Policy in the First World War', in J. M. Winter (ed.), *War and Economic Development* (Cambridge, London, New York and Melbourne: Cambridge University Press, 1975), pp. 229–38.

Lehnstaedt, S., 'Fluctuating between "Utilisation" and Exploitation: Occupied East Central Europe during the First World War', in J. Böhler, W. Borodziej and J. von Puttkamer (eds.), *Legacies of Violence: Eastern Europe's First World War* (Munich: Oldenbourg, 2014), pp. 89–112.

——, 'Imperiale Ordnungen statt Germanisierung. Die Mittelmächte in Kongresspolen, 1915–1918', *Osteuropa* 64(2–4) (2014), pp. 221–32.

Leidinger, H., 'Der Kieler Aufstand und die deutsche Revolution', in V. Moritz and H. Leidinger (eds.), *Die Nacht des Kirpitschnikow. Eine andere Geschichte des Ersten Weltkriegs* (Vienna: Deuticke, 2006), pp. 206–41.

——, 'Suizid und Militär. Debatten – Ursachenforschung – Reichsratsinterpellationen 1907–1914', in L. Cole, C. Hämmerle and M. Scheutz (eds.), *Glanz – Gewalt – Gehorsam. Militär und Gesellschaft in der Habsburgermonarchie (1800 bis 1918)* (Essen: Klartext, 2011), pp. 337–58.

Lein, R., *Pflichterfüllung oder Hochverrat? Die tschechischen Soldaten Österreich-Ungarns im Ersten Weltkrieg* (Vienna and Berlin: Lit, 2011).

Lerner, P., *Hysterical Men: War, Psychiatry, and the Politics of Trauma in Germany, 1890–1930* (Ithaca, NY, and London: Cornell University Press, 2003).

Leslie, J., 'Österreich-Ungarn vor dem Kriegsausbruch. Der Ballhausplatz in Wien im Juli 1914 aus der Sicht eines österreichisch-ungarischen Diplomaten', in

R. Melville, C. Scharf, M. Vogt and U. Wengenroth (eds.), *Deutschland und Europa in der Neuzeit. Festschrift für Karl Otmar Freiherr von Aretin zum 65. Geburtstag. 2. Halbband* (Stuttgart: Franz Steiner Verlag Wiesbaden GMBH, 1988), pp. 661–84.

_____, 'The Antecedents of Austria-Hungary's War Aims: Policies and Policy-Makers in Vienna and Budapest before and during 1914', *Wiener Beiträge zur Geschichte der Neuzeit* 20 (1993), pp. 307–94.

Levsen, S., *Elite, Männlichkeit und Krieg. Tübinger und Cambridger Studenten 1900–1929* (Göttingen: Vandenhoeck & Ruprecht, 2006).

Liberman, P., *Does Conquest Pay? The Exploitation of Occupied Industrial Societies* (Princeton, NJ: Princeton University Press, 1996).

Lieven, D. C. B., *Russia and the Origins of the First World War* (London: Macmillan, 1983).

Lindemann, A. S., *Esau's Tears: Modern Anti-Semitism and the Rise of the Jews* (Cambridge: Cambridge University Press, 1997).

Linke, H. G., 'Rußlands Weg in den Ersten Weltkrieg und seine Kriegsziele 1914–1917', *Militärgeschichtliche Mitteilung* 32(2) (1982), pp. 9–34.

Lipkes, J., *Rehearsals: The German Army in Belgium, August 1914* (Leuven: Leuven University Press, 2007).

Lipták, L., 'Soldatenrevolten und die Spaltung der Nationalitäten in Ungarn 1918', H. Mommsen, D. Kováč, J. Malíř and M. Marek (eds.), *Der Erste Weltkrieg und die Beziehungen zwischen Tschechen, Slowaken und Deutschen* (Essen: Klartext, 2001), pp. 287–92.

Little, B., 'Humanitarian Relief in Europe and the Analogue of War, 1914–1918', in J. D. Keene and M. S. Neiberg (eds.), *Finding Common Ground: New Directions in First World War Studies* (Leiden and Boston, MA: Brill, 2011), pp. 139–58.

Liulevičius, V. G., *War Land on the Eastern Front: Culture, National Identity, and German Occupation in World War I* (Cambridge, New York and Melbourne: Cambridge University Press, 2000).

_____, 'Precursors and Precedents: Forced Migration in Northeastern Europe during the First World War', *Nordost-Archiv. Zeitschrift für Regionalgeschichte. Neue Folge XIV* (2005), pp. 32–52.

Ljuben, B., 'The Bulgarian Economy during World War I', in B. K. Király and N. F. Dreisziger (eds.), *East Central European Society in World War I* (Boulder, CO, and Highland Lakes, NJ: Social Science Monographs and Atlantic Research and Publications, 1985), pp. 170–83.

Loch, T., '"Aufklärung der Bevölkerung" in Hamburg. Zur deutschen Inlandspropaganda während des Ersten Weltkrieges', *Militärgeschichtliche Zeitschrift* 62(1) (2003), pp. 41–70.

Lohr, E., 'The Russian Army and the Jews: Mass Deportation, Hostages, and Violence during World War I', *Russian Review* 60(3) (July 2001), pp. 404–19.

_____, *Nationalizing the Russian Empire: The Campaign against Enemy Aliens during World War I* (Cambridge, MA, and London: Harvard University Press, 2003).

_____, '1915 and the War Pogrom Paradigm in the Russian Empire', in J. Dekel-Chen, D. Gaunt, N. M. Meir and I. Barton (eds.), *Anti-Jewish Violence: Rethinking the Pogrom in European History* (Bloomington and Indianapolis, IN: Indiana University Press, 2010), pp. 41–51.

Loidl, T., *Andenken aus Eiserner Zeit. Patriotische Abzeichen der österreichisch-ungarischen Monarchie von 1914 bis 1918* (Vienna: Verlag Militaria, 2004).

Lowry, B., *Armistice 1918* (Kent, OH, and London: Kent State University Press, 1996).

Lyon, J. M. B., '"A Peasant Mob": The Serbian Army on the Eve of the Great War', *The Journal of Military History* 61(3) (July 1997), pp. 481–502.

Macartney, C. A., *The Habsburg Empire, 1790–1918* (London: Weidenfeld and Nicolson, 1968).

MacMillan, M., *Peacemakers: Six Months that Changed the World* (London: John Murray, 2001).

Mai, G., 'Burgfrieden und Sozialpolitik in Deutschland in der Anfangsphase des Ersten Weltkrieges (1914/15)', *Militärgeschichtliche Mitteilungen* 20 (1976), pp. 21–50.

_____, '"Aufklärung der Bevölkerung" und "Vaterländischer Unterricht" in Württemberg 1914–1918. Struktur, Durchführung und Inhalte der deutschen Inlandspropaganda im Ersten Weltkrieg', *Zeitschrift für Württembergische Landesgeschichte* 36 (1977), pp. 199–235.

_____, *Kriegswirtschaft und Arbeiterbewegung in Württemberg 1914–1918* (Stuttgart: Klett-Cotta, 1983).

Majchrowski, J. M., *Pierwsza Kompania Kadrowa. Portret Oddziału* (Cracow: Dundacja Centrum Dokumentacji Czynu Niepodległościowo, Księgarnia Akademicka, 2004).

Małecki, J. M., 'Życie gospodarcze Krakowa w czasie wielkiej wojny 1914–1918', in Towarzystwo Miłośników Historii i Zabytków Krakowa (ed.), *Kraków w czasie I wojny światowej. Materiały sesji naukowej z okazji dni Krakowa w roku 1988* (Cracow: Towarzystwo Miłośników Historii i Zabytków Krakowa, 1990), pp. 53–68.

_____, 'Cracow Jews in the 19th Century: Leaving the Ghetto', *Acta Poloniae Historica* 76 (1997), pp. 85–96.

Mamatey, V. S., 'The Union of Czech Political Parties in the *Reichsrat* 1916–1918', in R. A. Kann, B. K. Király and P. S. Fichtner (eds.), *The Habsburg Empire in World War I: Essays on the Intellectual, Military, Political and Economic Aspects of the Habsburg War Effort* (Boulder, CO, and New York: East European Quarterly and Columbia University Press, 1977), pp. 3–28.

Manela, E., *The Wilsonian Moment: Self-Determination and the International Origins of Anticolonial Nationalism* (Oxford and New York: Oxford University Press, 2007).

Mann, M., *The Dark Side of Democracy: Explaining Ethnic Cleansing* (Cambridge: Cambridge University Press, 2004, 2005).

Marin, I., 'World War I and Internal Repression: The Case of Major General Nikolaus Cena', *Austrian History Yearbook* 44 (2013), pp. 195–208.

Marks, S., 'The Myths of Reparations', *Central European History* 11(3) (September 1978), pp. 231–55.

———, '"My Name is Ozymandias": The Kaiser in Exile', *Central European History* 16(2) (June 1983), pp. 122–70.

Marquis, A. G., 'Words as Weapons: Propaganda in Britain and Germany during the First World War', *Journal of Contemporary History* 13(3) (July 1978), pp. 467–98.

Marshall, A., 'Russian Military Intelligence, 1905–1917: The Untold Story behind Tsarist Russia in the First World War', *War in History* 11(4) (October 2004), pp. 393–423.

May, A. J., *The Passing of the Hapsburg Monarchy, 1914–1918* (2 vols., Philadelphia, PA: University of Pennsylvania Press, 1966).

Mayerhofer, L., 'Making Friends and Foes: Occupiers and Occupied in First World War Romania, 1916–1918', in H. Jones, J. O'Brien and C. Schmidt-Supprian (eds.), *Untold War: New Perspectives in First World War Studies* (Leiden and Boston, MA: Brill, 2008), pp. 119–49.

———, *Zwischen Freund und Feind – Deutsche Besatzung in Rumänien 1916–1918* (Munich: Martin Meidenbauer, 2010).

Mazower, M., 'Minorities and the League of Nations in Interwar Europe', *Daedulus* 126(2) (Spring 1997), pp. 47–63.

McMeekin, S., *The Russian Origins of the First World War* (Cambridge, MA, and London: Belknap Press, 2011).

McNeal, R. H., *Tsar and Cossack, 1855–1914* (Basingstoke and London: Macmillan in association with St Antony's College, Oxford, 1987).

McPhail, H., *The Long Silence: Civilian Life under the German Occupation of Northern France, 1914–1918* (London and New York: I. B. Tauris, 1999, 2001).

McRandle, J. H. and Quirk, J., 'The Blood Test Revisited: A New Look at German Casualty Counts in World War I', *The Journal of Military History* 70(3) (July 2006), pp. 667–701.

Meier, K., 'Evangelische Kirche und Erster Weltkrieg', in W. Michalka (ed.), *Der Erste Weltkrieg. Wirkung, Wahrnehmung, Analyse* (Munich and Zurich: Piper, 1994), pp. 691–724.

Mende, R., 'Arbeiterschaft und Arbeiterbewegung in Halle im Ersten Weltkrieg', in H. Grebing, H. Mommsen and K. Rudolph (eds.), *Demokratie und*

Emanzipation zwischen Saale und Elbe. Beiträge zur Geschichte der sozialdemokratischen Arbeiterbewegung bis 1933 (Essen: Klartext, 1993), pp. 171–80.

Meteling, W., *Ehre, Einheit, Ordnung. Preußische und französische Städte und ihre Regimenter im Krieg, 1870/71 und 1914–19* (Baden-Baden: Nomos, 2010).

Mick, C., *Kriegserfahrungen in einer multiethnischen Stadt: Lemberg 1914–1947* (Wiesbaden: Harrowitz, 2010).

Middlebrook, M., *The First Day on the Somme, 1 July 1916* (London: Allen Lane/The Penguin Press, 1971, 1984).

_____, *The Kaiser's Battle, 21 March 1918: The First Day of the German Spring Offensive* (London: Allen Lane/The Penguin Press, 1978).

Milewska, W., Nowak, J. T. and Zientara, M., *Legiony Polskie 1914–1918. Zarys historii militarnej i politycznej* (Cracow: Księgarnia Akademicka Wydawnictwo Naukowe, 1998).

Miller, S., *Burgfrieden und Klassenkampf. Die deutsche Sozialdemokratie im Ersten Weltkrieg* (Düsseldorf: Droste, 1974).

Mleczak, J., *Akcja werbunkowa Naczelnego Komitetu Narodowego w Galicji i Królestwie Polskim w latach 1914–1916* (Pryemyśl: Polskie Towarzystwo Historyczne, 1988).

Mócsy, I. I., *The Effects of World War I. The Uprooted: Hungarian Refugees and their Impact on Hungary's Domestic Politics, 1918–1921* (New York: Brooklyn College Press, 1983).

Moeller, R. G., 'Dimensions of Social Conflict in the Great War: The View from the German Countryside', *Central European History* 14(2) (June 1981), pp. 142–68.

Molenda, J., 'Social Changes in Poland during World War I', in B. K. Király and N. F. Dreisziger (eds.), *East Central European Society in World War I* (Boulder, CO, and Highland Lakes, NJ: Social Science Monographs and Atlantic Research and Publications, 1985), pp. 187–201.

Moll, M., 'Österreichische Militärgerichtsbarkeit im Ersten Weltkrieg – "Schwert des Regimes"? Überlegungen am Beispiel des Landwehrdivisionsgerichtes Graz im Jahre 1914', *Mitteilungen des Steiermärkischen Landesarchivs* 50 (2001), pp. 301–55.

_____, ' "Verräter und Spione überall". Vorkriegs- und Kriegshysterie in Graz im Sommer 1914', *Historisches Jahrbuch der Stadt Graz* 31 (2001), pp. 309–30.

_____, 'Erster Weltkrieg und Ausnahmezustand, Zivilverwaltung und Armee: Eine Fallstudie zum innerstaatlichen Machtkampf 1914–1918 im steirischen Kontext', in S. Beer, E. Marko-Stöckl, M. Raffler and F. Schneider (eds.), *Focus Austria: vom Vielvölkerreich zum EU-Staat. Festschrift für Alfred Ableitinger zum 65. Geburtstag* (Graz: Institut für Geschichte der Karl-Franzens-Universität Graz, 2003), pp. 383–407.

_____, '"Heimatfront Steiermark". Ein gemischtsprachiges Kronland im ersten totalen Krieg', in H. J. W. Kuprian and O. Überegger (eds.), *Der Erste Weltkrieg im Alpenraum. Erfahrung, Deutung, Erinnerung. La Grande Guerra nell'arco alpino. Esperienze e memoria* (Innsbruck: Universitätsverlag Wagner, 2006), pp. 181–96.

Mombauer, A., 'A Reluctant Military Leader? Helmuth von Moltke and the July Crisis of 1914', *War in History* 6(4) (October 1999), pp. 417–46.

_____, *Helmuth von Moltke and the Origins of the First World War* (Cambridge: Cambridge University Press, 2001).

Mommsen, H., 'Militär und zivile Militarisierung in Deutschland 1914 bis 1938', in U. Frevert (ed.), *Militär und Gesellschaft im 19. und 20. Jahrhundert* (Stuttgart: Klett-Cotta, 1997), pp. 265–76.

Mommsen, W. J., 'Die deutsche öffentliche Meinung und der Zusammenbruch des Regierungssystems Bethmann Hollweg im Juli 1917', *Geschichte in Wissenschaft und Unterricht* 19(11) (November 1968), pp. 656–71.

_____, 'The German Revolution, 1918–1920: Political Revolution and Social Protest Movement', in R. Bessel and E. J. Feuchtwanger (eds.), *Social Change and Political Development in Weimar Germany* (London and Totowa, NJ: Croom Helm and Noble Books, 1981), pp. 21–54.

_____, 'The Topos of Inevitable War in Germany in the Decade before 1914', in V. R. Berghahn and M. Kitchen (eds.), *Germany in the Age of Total War* (London and Totowa, NJ: Croom Helm and Barnes & Noble, 1981), pp. 23–45.

_____, *Der autoritäre Nationalstaat. Verfassung, Gesellschaft und Kultur im deutschen Reich* (Frankfurt am Main: Fischer Taschenbuch, 1990).

_____, 'German Artists, Writers and Intellectuals and the Meaning of War, 1914–1918', in J. Horne (ed.), *State, Society and Mobilization in Europe during the First World War* (Cambridge: Cambridge University Press, 1997), pp. 21–38.

Morgan, D. W., 'Ernst Däumig and the German Revolution of 1918', *Central European History* 15(4) (December 1982), pp. 303–31.

Moritz, V. and Leidinger, H., *Zwischen Nutzen und Bedrohung. Die russischen Kriegsgefangenen in Österreich (1914–1921)* (Bonn: Bernard & Graefe, 2005).

Mosse, G. L., *Fallen Soldiers: Reshaping the Memory of the World Wars* (New York and Oxford: Oxford University Press, 1990).

Müller, A., *Zwischen Annäherung und Abgrenzung. Österreich-Ungarn und die Diskussion um Mitteleuropa im Ersten Weltkrieg* (Marburg: Tectum, 2001).

Müller, S., 'Toys, Games and Juvenile Literature in Germany and Britain during the First World War: A Comparison', in H. Jones, J. O'Brien and C. Schmidt-Supprian (eds.), *Untold War: New Perspectives in First World War Studies* (Leiden and Boston, MA: Brill, 2008), pp. 233–57.

Müller, S. O., *Die Nation als Waffe und Vorstellung. Nationalismus in Deutschland und Großbritannien im Ersten Weltkrieg* (Göttingen: Vandenhoeck & Ruprecht, 2002).

Mulligan, W., *The Origins of the First World War* (Cambridge: Cambridge University Press, 2010).

Münch, P., *Bürger in Uniform. Kriegserfahrungen von Hamburger Turnern 1914 bis 1918* (Freiburg i. Br., Berlin and Vienna: Rombach, 2009).

Nachtigal, R., 'Die Repatriierung der Mittelmächte-Kriegsgefangenen aus dem revolutionären Rußland. Heimkehr zwischen Agitation, Bürgerkrieg und Intervention 1918–1922', in J. Oltmer (ed.), *Kriegsgefangene im Europa des Ersten Weltkriegs* (Paderborn, Munich, Vienna and Zurich: Ferdinand Schöningh, 2006), pp. 239–66.

———, 'Privilegiensystem und Zwangsrekrutierung. Russische Nationalitätenpolitik gegenüber Kriegsgefangenen aus Österreich-Ungarn, in J. Oltmer (ed.), *Kriegsgefangene im Europa des Ersten Weltkriegs* (Paderborn, Munich, Vienna and Zurich: Ferdinand Schöningh, 2006), pp. 167–93.

———, 'Zur Anzahl der Kriegsgefangenen im Ersten Weltkrieg', *Militärgeschichtliche Zeitschrift* 67(2) (2008), pp. 345–84.

Naimark, N. M., *The Russians in Germany: A History of the Soviet Zone of Occupation, 1945–1949* (Cambridge, MA, and London: The Belknap Press, 1995).

Narskij, I., 'Kriegswirklichkeit und Kriegserfahrung russischer Soldaten an der russischen Westfront 1914/15', in G. P. Groß (ed.), *Die vergessene Front. Der Osten 1914/15. Ereignis, Wirkung, Nachwirkung* (Paderborn, Munich, Vienna and Zurich: Ferdinand Schöningh, 2006), pp. 249–61.

Nebelin, M., *Ludendorff. Diktator im Erstern Weltkrieg* (Munich: Siedler, 2010).

Nelson, K. L., 'The "Black Horror on the Rhine": Race as a Factor in Post-World War I Diplomacy', *The Journal of Modern History* 42(4) (December 1970), pp. 606–27.

———, 'German Comrades – Slavic Whores: Gender Images in the German Soldier Newspapers of the First World War', in K. Hagemann and S. Schüler-Springorum (eds.), *Home/Front: The Military, War and Gender in Twentieth-Century Germany* (Oxford and New York: Berg, 2002), pp. 69–85.

———, 'From Manitoba to the Memel: Max Sering, Inner Colonization and the German East', *Social History* 35(4) (2010), pp. 439–57.

Newman, J. P., 'War in the Balkans, 1914–1918', *War in History* 18(3) (July 2011), pp. 386–94.

Nipperdey, T., *Deutsche Geschichte 1866–1918* (2 vols., Munich: C. H. Beck, 1998).

Nofi, A. A., 'Comparative Divisional Strengths during World War I: East Central European Belligerents and Theaters', in B. K. Király and N. F. Dreisziger (eds.),

East Central European Society in World War I (Boulder, CO, and Highland Lakes, NJ: Social Science Monographs and Atlantic Research and Publications, 1985), pp. 263–70.

Nowak, J. T., 'Działania I Brygady Legionów Polskich 1914–1915', in W. Milewska, J. T. Nowak and M. Zientara (eds.), *Legiony Polskie 1914–1918. Zarys historii militarnej i politycznej* (Cracow: Księgarnia Akademicka Wydawnictwo Naukowe, 1998), pp. 13–78.

———, *Tarcze Legionów Polskich 1915–1917 w zbiorach Muzeum Historycznego Miasta Krakowa* (Cracow: Muzeum Historyczne Miasta Krakowa, 2006).

Nübel, C., *Die Mobilisierung der Kriegsgesellschaft. Propaganda und Alltag im Ersten Weltkrieg in Münster* (Münster, New York, Munich and Berlin: Waxmann, 2008).

Offer, A., *The First World War: An Agrarian Interpretation* (Oxford: Clarendon Press, 1989).

———, 'Economic Interpretation of War: The German Submarine Campaign, 1915–18', *Australian Economic History Review* 29(1) (March 1989), pp. 21–41.

Okey, R., *The Habsburg Monarchy c. 1765–1918: From Enlightenment to Eclipse* (Basingstoke and London: Macmillan, 2001).

———, *Taming Balkan Nationalism* (Oxford: Oxford University Press, 2007).

Olt, R., *Krieg und Sprache. Untersuchungen zu deutschen Soldatenliedern des Ersten Weltkriegs* (2 vols., Giessen: Wilhelm Schmitz, 1980 and 1981).

Oltmer, J., 'Zwangsmigration und Zwangsarbeit – Ausländische Arbeitskräfte und bäuerliche Ökonomie im Ersten Weltkrieg', *Tel Aviver Jahrbuch für deutsche Geschichte* 27 (1998), pp. 135–68.

Oppelt, U., *Film und Propaganda im Ersten Weltkrieg. Propaganda als Medienrealität im Aktualitäten- und Dokumentarfilm* (Stuttgart: Franz Steiner, 2002).

Orton, L. D., 'The Formation of Modern Cracow (1866–1914)', *Austrian History Yearbook* 19–20 (1983–4), pp. 105–17.

Orzoff, A., 'The Empire Without Qualities: Austro-Hungarian Newspapers and the Outbreak of War in 1914', in T. R. E. Paddock (ed.), *A Call to Arms: Propaganda, Public Opinion and Newspapers in the Great War* (Westport, CT: Praeger, 2004), pp. 161–99.

———, *Battle for the Castle: The Myth of Czechoslovakia in Europe, 1914–1948* (Oxford and New York: Oxford University Press, 2009).

Osborne, E. W., *Britain's Economic Blockade of Germany, 1914–1919* (London and New York: Frank Cass, 2004).

Ostertag, H., *Bildung, Ausbildung und Erziehung des Offizierkorps im deutschen Kaiserreich 1871–1918. Eliteideal, Anspruch und Wirklichkeit* (Frankfurt am Main: Peter Lang, 1990).

Ostpreußisches Landesmuseum Lüneburg (ed.), *Die Ostpreußenhilfe im Ersten Weltkrieg. Zur Ausstellung 'Zum Besten der Ostpreußenhilfe' (23.9.2006–28.1.2007)* (Husum: Husum Druck- und Verlagsgesellschaft, 2006).

Paddock, T. R. E., 'Still Stuck at Sevastopol: The Depiction of Russia during the Russo-Japanese War and the Beginning of the First World War in the German Press', *German History* 16(3) (July 1998), pp. 358–376.

———, 'German Propaganda: The Limits of *Gerechtigkeit*', in T. R. E. Paddock (ed.), *A Call to Arms: Propaganda, Public Opinion and Newspapers in the Great War* (Westport, CT: Praeger, 2004), pp. 115–60.

———, *Creating the Russian Peril: Education, the Public Sphere, and National Identity in Imperial Germany, 1890–1914* (Rochester, NY: Camden House, 2010).

Pamuk, Ş., 'The Ottoman Economy in World War I', in S. Broadberry and M. Harrison (eds.), *The Economics of World War I* (Cambridge, New York, Melbourne, Madrid, Cape Town, Singapore and São Paulo: Cambridge University Press, 2005), pp. 112–36.

Papp, T., 'Die Königlich Ungarische Landwehr (Honvéd) 1868 bis 1914', in A. Wandruszka and P. Urbanitsch (eds), *Die Habsburgermonarchie 1848–1918. Band V. Die Bewaffnete Macht* (5 vols., Vienna: Verlag der Österreichische Akademie der Wissenschaften, 1987), pp. 634–86.

Pastor, P., 'The Home Front in Hungary, 1914–18', in B. K. Király and N. F. Dreisziger (eds.), *East Central European Society in World War I* (Boulder, CO, and Highland Lakes, NJ: Social Science Monographs and Atlantic Research and Publications, 1985), pp. 124–34.

Pearson, R., 'Hungary: A State Truncated, a Nation Dismembered', in S. Dunn and T. G. Fraser (eds.), *Europe and Ethnicity: World War I and Contemporary Ethnic Conflict* (London and New York: Routledge, 1996).

Peball, K., 'Um das Erbe. Zur Nationalitätenpolitik des k.u.k. Armeeoberkommandos während der Jahre 1914 bis 1917', *Österreichische Militärische Zeitschrift Sonderheft* 2 (1967), pp. 28–39.

Penslar, D., 'The German-Jewish Soldier: From Participant to Victim', *German History* 29(3) (September 2011), pp. 423–44.

Pfalzer, S., 'Der "Butterkrawall" im Oktober 1915. Die erste größere Antikriegsbewegung in Chemnitz', in H. Grebing, H. Mommsen and K. Rudolph (eds.), *Demokratie und Emanzipation zwischen Saale und Elbe. Beiträge zur Geschichte der sozialdemokratischen Arbeiterbewegung bis 1933* (Essen: Klartext, 1993), pp. 196–201.

Philpott, W., *Bloody Victory: The Sacrifice on the Somme and the Making of the Twentieth Century* (London: Little, Brown, 2009).

Pichlík, K., 'Der militärische Zusammenbruch der Mittelmächte im Jahre 1918', in R. G. Plaschka and K. Mack (eds.), *Die Auflösung des Habsburgerreiches. Zusammenbruch und Neuorientierung im Donauraum* (Vienna: Verlag für Geschichte und Politik, 1970), pp. 249–65.

_____, 'Europa nach dem Krieg in den Vorstellungen T. G. Masaryks im Exil', in H. Mommsen, D. Kováč, J. Malíř and M. Marek (eds.), *Der Erste Weltkrieg und die Beziehungen zwischen Tschechen, Slowaken und Deutschen* (Essen: Klartext, 2001), pp. 67–80.

Planert, U., 'Zwischen Partizipation und Restriktion: Frauenemanzipation und nationales Paradigma von der Aufklärung bis zum Ersten Weltkrieg', in D. Langewiesche and G. Schmidt (eds.), *Föderative Nation. Deutschlandkonzepte von der Reformation bis zum Ersten Weltkrieg* (Munich: Oldenbourg, 2000), pp. 387–428.

Plaschka, R. G., 'Contradicting Ideologies: The Pressure of Ideological Conflicts in the Austro-Hungarian Army of World War I', in R. A. Kann, B. K. Király and P. S. Fichtner (eds.), *The Habsburg Empire in World War I: Essays on the Intellectual, Military, Political and Economic Aspects of the Habsburg War Effort* (Boulder, CO, and New York: East European Quarterly and Columbia University Press, 1977), pp. 105–19.

_____, 'The Army and Internal Conflict in the Austro-Hungarian Empire, 1918', in B. K. Király and N. F. Dreisziger (eds.), *East Central European Society in World War I* (Boulder, CO, and Highland Lakes, NJ: Social Science Monographs and Atlantic Research and Publications, 1985), pp. 338–53.

_____, Haselsteiner, Horst and Suppan, Arnold, *Innere Front. Militärassistenz, Widerstand und Umsturz in der Donaumonarchie 1918. Erster Band. Zwischen Streik und Meuterei* (2 vols., Munich: R. Oldenbourg, 1974).

_____, Haselsteiner, Horst and Suppan, Arnold, *Innere Front. Militärassistenz, Widerstand und Umsturz in der Donaumonarchie 1918. Zweiter Band. Umsturz* (2 vols., Munich: R. Oldenbourg, 1974).

Porch, D., *The March to the Marne: The French Army, 1871–1914* (Cambridge, New York and Melbourne: Cambridge University Press, 1981).

_____, 'The French Army in the First World War', in A. R. Millett and W. Murray (eds.), *Military Effectiveness. Vol. I: The First World War* (3 vols., Boston, MA, London, Sydney and Wellington, 1988), pp. 190–228.

Prassnigger, G., 'Hunger in Tirol', in K. Eisterer and R. Steininger (eds.), *Tirol und der Erste Weltkrieg* (Innsbruck: Österreichischer Studien Verlag, 1995), pp. 179–210.

Prete, R. A., 'French Military War Aims, 1914–1916', *The Historical Journal* 28(4) (December 1985), pp. 887–99.

Prior, R. and Wilson, T., *Command on the Western Front: The Military Career of Sir Henry Rawlinson, 1914–1918* (Barnsley: Pen & Sword, 1992, 2004).

_____, *The Somme* (New Haven, CT, and London: Yale University Press, 2005).

Prusin, A. V., 'The Russian Military and the Jews in Galicia, 1914–15', in E. Lohr and M. Poe (eds.), *The Military and Society in Russia, 1450–1917* (Leiden, Boston, MA, and Cologne: Brill, 2002), pp. 525–44.

_____, *Nationalizing a Borderland: War, Ethnicity, and Anti-Jewish Violence in East Galicia, 1914–1920* (Tuscaloosa, AL: University of Alabama Press, 2005).

Przenioslo, M., 'Postawy chłopów Królestwa Polskiego wobec okupanta niemieckiego i austriackiego (1914–1918)', in D Grinberg, J Snopko and G. Zackiewicz (eds.), *Lata wielkiej wojny. Dojrzewanie do niepodległości 1914–1918* (Białystok: Wydawnictwo Uniwersytetu w Białymstoku, 2007), pp. 198–214.

Pyta, W., *Hindenburg. Herrschaft zwischen Hohenzollern und Hitler* (Munich: Pantheon, 2007, 2009).

Rachamimov, A., 'Imperial Loyalties and Private Concerns: Nation, Class and State in the Correspondence of Austro-Hungarian POWs in Russia, 1916–1918', *Austrian History Yearbook* 31 (2000), pp. 87–105.

_____, *POWs and the Great War: Captivity on the Eastern Front* (Oxford and New York: Berg, 2002).

Raithel, T., *Das 'Wunder' der inneren Einheit. Studien zur deutschen und französischen Öffentlichkeit bei Beginn des Ersten Weltkrieges* (Bonn: Bouvier, 1996).

Rauchensteiner, M., *Der Tod des Doppeladlers. Österreich-Ungarn und der Erste Weltkrieg* (Graz, Vienna and Cologne: Styria, 1993).

Rawe, K., '. . . wir werden sie schon zur Arbeit bringen!' Ausländerbeschäftigung und Zwangsarbeit im Ruhrkohlenbergbau während des Ersten Weltkrieges* (Essen: Klartext, 2005).

Read, J. M., *Atrocity Propaganda, 1914–1919* (New York: Arno Press, 1941, 1972).

Rechter, D., 'Galicia in Vienna: Jewish Refugees in the First World War', *Austrian History Yearbook* 28 (1997), pp. 113–30.

Reed Winkler, J., 'Information Warfare in World War I', *The Journal of Military History* 73(3) (July 2009), pp. 845–67.

Rees, H. L., *The Czechs during World War I: The Path to Independence* (Boulder, CO: East European Monographs, 1992).

Reimann, A., *Der große Krieg der Sprachen. Untersuchungen zur historischen Semantik in Deutschland und England zur Zeit des Ersten Weltkriegs* (Essen: Klartext, 2000).

Remak, J., 'The Healthy Invalid: How Doomed the Habsburg Empire?', *The Journal of Modern History* 41(2) (June 1969), pp. 127–43.

_____, '1914 – The Third Balkan War: Origins Reconsidered', *The Journal of Modern History* 43(3) (September 1971), pp. 353–66.

Renzi, W. A., 'Who Composed "Sazonov's Thirteen Points"? A Re-Examination of Russia's War Aims of 1914', *The American Historical Review* 88(2) (April 1983), pp. 347–57.

Reynolds, M. A., *Shattered Empires: The Clash and Collapse of the Ottoman and Russian Empires, 1908–1918* (Cambridge and New York: Cambridge University Press, 2011).

Rich, D. A., 'Russia', in R. F. Hamilton and H. Herwig (eds.), *The Origins of World War I* (Cambridge, New York, Melbourne, Madrid and Cape Town: Cambridge University Press, 2003), pp. 188–226.

Ritschl, A., 'The Pity of Peace: Germany's Economy at War, 1914–1918 and Beyond', in S. Broadberry and M. Harrison (eds.), *The Economics of World War I* (Cambridge, New York, Melbourne, Madrid, Cape Town, Singapore and São Paulo: Cambridge University Press, 2005), pp. 41–76.

Ritter, G. A. and Tenfelde, K., *Arbeiter im deutschen Kaiserreich 1871 bis 1914* (Bonn: J. H. W. Dietz Nachf., 1992).

Roesler, K., *Die Finanzpolitik des deutschen Reiches im Ersten Weltkrieg* (Berlin: Dunker & Humblot, 1967).

Rohde, G., 'Das Deutschtum in Posen und Pomerellen in der Zeit der Weimarer Republik', in die Senatskommission für das Studium des Deutschtums im Osten an der Rheinischen Friedrich-Wilhelms-Universität Bonn (ed.), *Die deutschen Ostgebiete zur Zeit der Weimarer Republik. Studien zum Deutschen im Osten* (Cologne and Graz: Böhlau, 1966), pp. 88–132.

Rohkrämer, T., 'August 1914 – Kriegsmentalität und ihre Voraussetzungen', in W. Michalka (ed.), *Der Erste Weltkrieg. Wirkung, Wahrnehmung, Analyse* (Munich and Zurich: Piper, 1992), pp. 759–77.

———, 'Der Gesinnungsmilitarismus der "kleinen Leute" im deutschen Kaiserreich', in W. Wette (ed.), *Der Krieg des kleinen Mannes. Eine Militärgeschichte von unten* (Munich and Zurich: Piper, 1992), pp. 95–109.

Röhl, J. C. G., 'Admiral von Müller and the Approach of War, 1911–1914', *The Historical Journal* 12(4) (December 1969), pp. 651–73.

———, 'Die Generalprobe. Zur Geschichte und Bedeutung des "Kriegsrates" vom 8. Dezember 1912', in W. Alff (ed.), *Deutschlands Sonderung von Europa 1862–1945* (Frankfurt am Main, Bern and New York: Peter Lang, 1984), pp. 149–224.

———, *The Kaiser and his Court: Wilhelm II and the Government of Germany* (Cambridge: Cambridge University Press, 1994, 1999).

———, 'Germany', in K. Wilson (ed.), *Decisions for War* (London: UCL Press, 1995, 1998), pp. 27–54.

Rojahn, J., 'Arbeiterbewegung und Kriegsbegeisterung: Die deutsche Sozialdemokratie 1870–1914', in M. van der Linden and G. Mergner (eds.), *Kriegsbegeisterung und mentale Kriegsvorbereitung. Interdisziplinäre Studien* (Berlin: Duncker und Humblot, 1991), pp. 57–71.

Rollet, C., 'The Home and Family Life', in J. Winter and J.-L. Robert (eds.), *Capital Cities at War: Paris, London, Berlin, 1914–1919. Vol. 2: A Cultural History* (2 vols., Cambridge and New York: Cambridge University Press, 2007), pp. 315–53.

Roshwald, A., *Ethnic Nationalism and the Fall of Empires: Central Europe, Russia and the Middle East, 1914–1923* (London and New York: Routledge, 2001).

Rothenberg, G. E., 'The Habsburg Army and the Nationality Problem in the Nineteenth Century, 1815–1914', *Austrian History Yearbook* 3 (1967), pp. 70–87.

———, *The Army of Francis Joseph* (West Lafayette, IN: Purdue University Press, 1976, 1998).

———, 'The Austro-Hungarian Campaign against Serbia in 1914', *The Journal of Military History* 53(2) (April 1989), pp. 127–46.

Rothschild, J., *East Central Europe Between the Two World Wars* (Washington, DC: University of Washington Press, 1978).

Rozenblit, M. L., *Reconstructing a National Identity: The Jews of Habsburg Austria during World War I* (Oxford and New York: Oxford University Press, 2001).

———, 'Sustaining Austrian "National" Identity in Crisis: The Dilemma of the Jews in Habsburg Austria, 1914–1919', in P. M. Judson and M. L. Rozenblit (eds.), *Constructing Nationalities in East Central Europe* (New York and Oxford: Berghahn Books, 2005), pp. 178–91.

Rudin, H. R., *Armistice 1918* (New Haven, CT: Yale University Press, 1944).

Rudnytsky, I. L., 'The Ukrainians in Galicia under Austrian Rule', in A. S. Markovits and F. E. Sysyn (eds.), *Nationbuilding and the Politics of Nationalism: Essays on Austrian Galicia* (Cambridge, MA: Harvard, 1982), pp. 23–67.

Rudolph, H., 'Kultureller Wandel und Krieg: Die Reaktion der Werbesprache auf die Erfahrung des Ersten Weltkriegs am Beispiel von Zeitungsanzeigen', in G. Hirschfeld, G. Krumeich, D. Langewiesche and H.-P. Ullmann (eds.), *Kriegserfahrungen. Studien zur Sozial- und Mentalitätsgeschichte des Ersten Weltkriegs* (Essen: Klartext, 1997), pp. 283–301.

Rüger, J., 'Laughter and War in Berlin', *History Workshop Journal* 67 (Spring 2009), pp. 23–43.

Ryder, A. J., *The German Revolution of 1918: A Study of German Socialism in War and Revolt* (Cambridge: Cambridge University Press, 1967).

Sammartino, A. H., *The Impossible Border: Germany and the East, 1914–1922* (Ithaca, NY, and London: Cornell University Press, 2010).

Samuels, M., *Command or Control? Command, Training and Tactics in the British and German Armies, 1888–1918* (London: Frank Cass, 1995).

Saul, K., 'Jugend im Schatten des Krieges. Vormilitärische Ausbildung – Kriegswirtschaftlicher Ersatz – Schulalltag in Deutschland 1914–1918', *Militärgeschichtliche Mitteilungen* 34 (1983), pp. 91–184.

de Schaepdrijver, S., 'Belgium', in J. Horne (ed.), *A Companion to World War I* (Malden, MA, Oxford and Chichester: Wiley-Blackwell, 2010), pp. 386–402.

Scheck, R., 'Der Kampf des Tirpitz-Kreises für den uneingeschränkten U-Boot-Krieg und einen politischen Kurswechsel im deutschen Kaiserreich 1916–1917', *Militärgeschichtliche Mitteilung* 55(1) (1996), pp. 69–91.

Scheer, T., 'Typisch Polen: Facetten österreichisch-ungarischer Besatzungspolitik in Polen (1915–1918)', in Heeresgeschichtliches Museum (ed.), *Polnisch-österreichische Kontakte sowie Militärbündnisse 1618–1918. Symposium und Abendvortrag 11. und 12. September 2008* (Vienna: Bundesministerium für Landesverteidigung und Sport/Heeresdruckerei, 2009), pp. 233–55.

———, *Zwischen Front und Heimat. Österreich-Ungarns Militärverwaltungen im Ersten Weltkrieg* (Frankfurt am Main: Peter Lang, 2009).

Schindler, J. R., 'Disaster on the Drina: The Austro-Hungarian Army in Serbia, 1914', *War in History* 9(2) (April 2002), pp. 159–95.

———, 'Steamrollered in Galicia: The Austro-Hungarian Army and the Brusilov Offensive, 1916', *War in History* 10(1) (January 2003), pp. 27–59.

———, 'Defeating Balkan Insurgency: The Austro-Hungarian Army in Bosnia-Herzegovina, 1878–82', *The Journal of Strategic Studies* 27(3) (September 2004), pp. 528–52.

Schlegelmilch, A., 'Massenprotest in der Burgfriedengesellschaft. Deutschland 1914–1918', in H. Mommsen, D. Kováč, J. Malíř and M. Marek (eds.), *Der Erste Weltkrieg und die Beziehungen zwischen Tschechen, Slowaken und Deutschen* (Essen: Klartext, 2001), pp. 293–305.

Schmidt-Richberg, W., 'Die Regierungszeit Wilhelms II', in Militärgeschichtliches Forschungsamt (ed.), *Handbuch zur deutschen Militärgeschichte 1648–1939. Band V. Von der Entlassung Bismarcks bis zum Ende des Ersten Weltkrieges (1890–1918)* (10 vols., Frankfurt am Main: Bernard & Graefe, 1968), pp. 9–156.

Schmitz, M., 'Verrat am Waffenbruder? Die Siedlice-Kontroverse im Spannungsfeld von Kriegsgeschichte und Geschichtspolitik', *Militärgeschichtliche Zeitschrift* 67(2) (2008), pp. 385–407.

Schneider, G., 'Zur Mobilisierung der "Heimatfront": Das Nageln sogenannter Kriegswahrzeichen im Ersten Weltkrieg', *Zeitschrift für Volkskunde* 95 (1999), pp. 32–62.

Schönberger, B., 'Motherly Heroines and Adventurous Girls: Red Cross Nurses and Women Army Auxiliaries in the First World War', in K. Hagemann and S. Schüler-Springorum (eds.), *Home/Front: The Military, War and Gender in Twentieth-Century Germany* (Oxford and New York: Berg, 2002), pp. 87–113.

Schröder, J., *Die U-Boote des Kaisers. Die Geschichte des deutschen U-Boot-Krieges gegen Großbritannien im Ersten Weltkrieg* (Lauf a. d. Pegnitz: Europaforum-Verlag, 2000).

Schroeder, P. W., 'World War I as Galloping Gertie: A Reply to Joachim Remak', *The Journal of Modern History* 44(3) (September 1972), pp. 319–45.

———, 'Stealing Horses to Great Applause: Austria-Hungary's Decision in 1914 in Systematic Perspective', in H. Afflerbach and D. Stevenson (eds.), *An Improbable War: The Outbreak of World War I and European*

Political Culture Before 1914 (New York and Oxford: Berghahn, 2007), pp. 17–42.

Schulze, M.-S., 'Austria-Hungary's Economy in World War I', in S. Broadberry and M. Harrison (eds.), *The Economics of World War I* (Cambridge, New York, Melbourne, Madrid, Cape Town, Singapore and São Paulo: Cambridge University Press, 2005), pp. 77–111.

Schuster, F. M., *Zwischen allen Fronten. Osteuropäische Juden während des Ersten Weltkrieges (1914–1919)* (Cologne: Böhlau, 2004).

Schwalbe, K., *Wissenschaft und Kriegsmoral. Die deutschen Hochschullehrer und die politischen Grundfragen des Ersten Weltkrieges* (Göttingen, Zürich and Frankfurt: Musterschmidt, 1969).

Schwendinger, C., *Kriegspropaganda in der Habsburgermonarchie zur Zeit des Ersten Weltkriegs. Eine Analyse anhand fünf ausgewählter Zeitungen* (Hamburg: Diplomica, 2011).

Scianna, B. M., 'Reporting Atrocities: Archibald Reiss in Serbia, 1914–1918', *Journal of Slavic Military Studies* 25(4) (2012), pp. 596–617.

Seipp, A. R., *The Ordeal of Peace: Demobilization and the Urban Experience in Britain and Germany, 1917–21* (Farnham and Burlington, VT: Ashgate, 2009).

Sevela, M., 'Chaos versus Cruelty: Sakhalin as a Secondary Theater of Operations', in R. Kowner (ed.), *Rethinking the Russo-Japanese War, 1904–5. Vol. I: Centennial Perspectives* (2 vols., Folkestone: Global Oriental, 2007), pp. 93–108.

Sharp, A., 'The Genie that would not Go Back in the Bottle: National Self-Determination and the Legacy of the First World War and the Peace Settlement', in S. Dunn and T. G. Fraser (eds.), *Europe and Ethnicity: World War I and Contemporary Ethnic Conflict* (London and New York, 1996), pp. 10–29.

Sheldon, J., *The German Army on the Somme* (Barnsley: Pen & Sword, 2005).

Showalter, D. E., *Tannenberg: Clash of Empires* (Hamden, CT: Archon Books, 1991).

——, 'From Deterrence to Doomsday Machine: The German Way of War, 1890–1914', *Journal of Military History* 64(3) (July 2000), pp. 679–710.

Siebrecht, C., *The Aesthetics of Loss: German Women's Art of the First World War* (Oxford: Oxford University Press, 2013).

Siedler, R., 'Behind the Lines: Working-Class Family Life in Wartime Vienna', in R. Wall and J. Winter (eds.), *The Upheaval of War: Family, Work and Welfare in Europe, 1914–1918* (Cambridge: Cambridge University Press, 1988, 2005), pp. 109–38.

Silberstein, G. E., 'The High Command and Diplomacy in Austria-Hungary, 1914–1916', *The Journal of Modern History* 42(4) (December 1970), pp. 586–605.

Sked, A., *The Decline and Fall of the Habsburg Empire 1815–1918*, 2nd edn (Harlow and London: Pearson Education, 2001).

_____, 'Austria and the "Galician Massacres" of 1846: Schwarzenberg and the Propaganda War. An Unknown but Key Episode in the Career of the Austrian Statesman', in L. Höbelt and T. G. Otte (eds.), *A Living Anachronism? European Diplomacy and the Habsburg Monarchy: Festschrift für Francis Roy Bridge zum 70. Geburtstag* (Vienna, Cologne and Weimar: Böhlau, 2010), pp. 49–118.

Snyder, J., *The Ideology of the Offensive: Military Decision-Making and the Disasters of 1914* (Ithaca, NY, and London: Cornell University Press, 1984).

Snyder, T., *Bloodlands: Europe between Hitler and Stalin* (New York: Basic Books, 2010).

Sondhaus, L., *Franz Conrad von Hötzendorf: Architect of the Apocalypse* (Boston, MA: Humanities Press, 2000).

_____, *World War One. The Global Revolution* (Cambridge: Cambridge University Press, 2011).

Speckmann, T., 'Der Krieg im Alpenraum aus der Perspektive des "kleinen Mannes". Biographische Studien am Beispiel der Aufzeichnungen von Hugo Dornhofer', in H. J. W. Kuprian and Oswald Überegger (eds.), *Der Erste Weltkrieg im Alpenraum. Erfahrung, Deutung, Erinnerung. La Grande Guerra nell'arco alpino. Esperienze e memoria* (Innsbruck: Universitätsverlag Wagner, 2006), pp. 101–16.

Spence, R. B., 'The Yugoslav Role in the Austro-Hungarian Army, 1914–18', in B. K. Király and N. F. Dreisziger (eds.), *East Central European Society in World War I* (Boulder, CO, and Highland Lakes, NJ: Social Science Monographs and Atlantic Research and Publications, 1985), pp. 354–65.

Spoerer, M., 'The Mortality of Allied Prisoners of War and Belgian Civilian Deportees in German Custody during the First World War: A Reappraisal of the Effects of Forced Labour', *Population Studies* 60(2) (July 2006), pp. 121–36.

Stachelbeck, C., *Militärische Effektivität im Ersten Weltkrieg. Die 11. Bayerische Infanteriedivision 1915 bis 1918* (Paderborn, Munich, Vienna and Zurich: Ferdinand Schöningh, 2010).

Stambrook, F., 'National and Other Identities in Bukovina in Late Austrian Times', *Austrian History Yearbook* 35 (2004), pp. 185–203.

Steffen, D., 'The Holtzendorff Memorandum of 22 December 1916 and Germany's Declaration of Unrestricted U-boat Warfare', *The Journal of Military History* 68(1) (January 2004), pp. 215–24.

Steiner, Z. S., *Britain and the Origins of the First World War* (London and Basingstoke: Macmillan, 1977).

Stephenson, S., *The Final Battle: Soldiers of the Western Front and the German Revolution of 1918* (Cambridge: Cambridge University Press, 2009).

Stevenson, D., 'French War Aims and the American Challenge, 1914–1918', *The Historical Journal* 22(4) (December 1979), pp. 877–94.

———, *The First World War and International Politics* (Oxford: Oxford University Press, 1988).

———, 'The Failure of Peace by Negotiation in 1917', *The Historical Journal* 34(1) (March 1991), pp. 65–86.

———, *Armaments and the Coming of War: Europe 1904–1914* (Oxford: Clarendon Press, 1996).

———, 'French War Aims and Peace Planning', in M. F. Boemeke, G. D. Feldman and E. Glaser, *The Treaty of Versailles: A Reassessment after 75 Years* (Washington, DC, and Cambridge: German Historical Institute and Cambridge University Press, 1998), pp. 87–110.

———, 'War by Timetable? The Railway Race before 1914', *Past & Present* 162 (February 1999), pp. 163–94.

———, *1914–1918: The History of the First World War* (London: Allen Lane, 2004).

———, *With Our Backs to the Wall: Victory and Defeat in 1918* (London: Allen Lane, 2011).

———, 'The First World War and European Integration', *The International History Review* 34(4) (December 2012), pp. 841–63.

Stiasny, P., *Das Kino und der Krieg. Deutschland 1914–1929* (Munich: edition text + kritik, 2009).

Stibbe, M., *German Anglophobia and the Great War, 1914–1918* (Cambridge: Cambridge University Press, 2001).

———, *British Civilian Internees in Germany: The Ruhleben Camp, 1914–18* (Manchester and New York: Manchester University Press, 2008).

Stone, N., 'Army and Society in the Habsburg Monarchy, 1900–1914', *Past and Present* 33 (April 1966), pp. 95–111.

———, 'Die Mobilmachung der österreichisch-ungarischen Armee 1914', *Militärgeschichtliche Mitteilungen* 16(2) (1974), pp. 67–95.

———, *The Eastern Front, 1914–1917* (London and New York: Penguin, 1975, 1998).

Stoneman, M. R., 'The Bavarian Army and French Civilians in the War of 1870–71: A Cultural Interpretation', *War in History* 8(3) (July 2001), pp. 271–93.

Strachan, H., 'The Morale of the German Army, 1917–18', in H. Cecil and P. H. Liddle (eds.), *Facing Armageddon: The First World War Experienced* (London: Leo Cooper, 1996), pp. 383–98.

———, 'The Battle of the Somme and British Strategy', *The Journal of Strategic Studies* 21(1) (March 1998), pp. 79–95.

———, *The First World War. Vol. I: To Arms* (3 vols., Oxford: Oxford University Press, 2001).

———, 'Ausbildung, Kampfgeist und die zwei Weltkriege', in B. Thoß and H.-E. Volkmann (eds.), *Erster Weltkrieg, Zweiter Weltkrieg. Ein Vergleich* (Paderborn: Ferdinand Schöningh, 2002), pp. 265–86.

——, 'Training, Morale and Modern War', *Journal of Contemporary History* 41(2) (April 2006), pp. 211–27.

Strazhas, A., *Deutsche Ostpolitik im Ersten Weltkrieg. Der Fall Ober Ost, 1915–1917* (Wiesbaden: Harrassowitz, 1993).

Strohn, M., *The German Army and the Defence of the Reich: Military Doctrine and the Conduct of the Defensive Battle, 1918–1939* (Cambridge: Cambridge University Press, 2011).

Stubbs, K., *Race to the Front: The Material Foundations of Coalition Strategy in the Great War* (Westpoint, CT, and London: Praeger, 2002).

Süchtig-Hänger, A., *Das 'Gewissen der Nation'. Nationales Engagement und politisches Handeln konservativer Frauenorganisationen 1900 bis 1937* (Düsseldorf: Droste, 2002).

Sukiennicki, W., *East Central Europe during World War I: From Foreign Domination to National Independence* (2 vols., Boulder, CO: East European Monographs, 1984).

Szabó, D. I., 'The Social Basis of Opposition to the War in Hungary', in B. K. Király and N. F. Dreisziger (eds.), *East Central European Society in World War I* (Boulder, CO, and Highland Lakes, NJ: Social Science Monographs and Atlantic Research and Publications, 1985), pp. 135–44.

Szarkowa, J., 'Obchody rocznic narodowych w działalności propagandowej Naczelnego Komitetu Narodowego (1914–1917)', *Rocznik Biblioteki Polskiej Akademii Nauk w Krakowie* 39 (1994), pp. 181–95.

Szlanta, P., '"Najgorsze bestie to są Honwedy". Ewolucja stosunku polskich mieszkańców Galicji do monarchii habsburkiej podczas I wojny światowej', in U. Jakubowska (ed.), *Galicyjskie spotkania 2011* (n.p.: Instytut Badań Literackich PAN, 2011), pp. 161–79.

——, 'Der Erste Weltkrieg von 1914 bis 1915 als identitätsstiftender Faktor für die moderne polnische Nation', in G. P. Groß (ed.), *Die vergessene Front. Der Osten 1914/15. Ereignis, Wirkung, Nackwirkung* (Paderborn, Munich, Vienna and Zurich: Ferdinand Schöningh, 2006), pp. 153–64.

Szymczak, D., 'Die Rolle des "militärischen Faktors" im österreichisch-deutschen Konflikt in der polnischen Frage während des Ersten Weltkrieges', in Heeresgeschichtliches Museum Wien (ed.), *Österreichische-polnische militärische Beziehungen im 20. Jahrhundert. Symposium 6. November 2009* (Vienna: Bundesministerium für Landesverteidigung und Sport/Heeresdruckerei, 2010), pp. 51–66.

Tampke, J., *The Ruhr and Revolution: The Revolutionary Movement in the Rhenish-Westphalian Industrial Region, 1912–1919* (London: Croom Helm, 1979).

Taylor, K. E., 'Intergroup Atrocities in War: A Neuroscientific Perspective', *Medicine, Conflict and Survival* 22(3) (July–September 2006), pp. 230–44.

Theiner, P., '"Mitteleuropa": Pläne in Wilhelminischen Deutschland', *Geschichte und Gesellschaft. Sonderheft* 10 (1984), pp. 128–48.

Thiel, J., *'Menschenbassin Belgien'. Anwerbung, Deportation und Zwangsarbeit im Ersten Weltkrieg* (Essen: Klartext, 2007).

Thompson, M., *The White War: Life and Death on the Italian Front, 1915–1919* (London: Faber and Faber, 2008).

Thompson, W. C., 'The September Program: Reflections on the Evidence', *Central European History* 11(4) (December 1978), pp. 346–54.

Tobin, E. H., 'War and the Working Class: The Case of Düsseldorf, 1914–1918', *Central European History* 18(3–4) (September 1985), pp. 257–98.

Todd, L. M., '"The Soldier's Wife Who Ran Away with the Russian": Sexual Infidelities in World War I Germany', *Central European History* 44(2) (June 2011), pp. 257–78.

Tooze, A., 'The German National Economy in an Era of Crisis and War, 1917–1945', in H. Walser Smith (ed.), *The Oxford Handbook of Modern German History* (Oxford: Oxford University Press, 2011), pp. 400–22.

Traba, R., *'Wschodniopruskość'. Tożsamość regionalna i narodowa w kulturze politycznej Niemiec* (Poznań and Warsaw: Wydawnictwo Poznańskiego Towarzystwa Przyjaciół Nauk, 2005).

Travers, T., *How the War was Won: Command and Technology in the British Army on the Western Front, 1917–1918* (London: Routledge, 1992).

Trumpener, U., 'War Premeditated? German Intelligence Operations in July 1914', *Central European History* 9(1) (March 1976), pp. 58–85.

Tucker, S. C. (ed.), *The Encyclopedia of World War I: A Political, Social and Military History* (Santa Barbara, CA: ABC-CLIO, 2005).

Tunstall, Jr, G. A., 'The Habsburg Command Conspiracy: The Austrian Falsification of Historiography on the Outbreak of World War I', *Austrian History Yearbook* 27 (1996), pp. 181–98.

_____, 'Austria-Hungary', in R. F. Hamilton and H. Herwig (eds.), *The Origins of World War I* (Cambridge, New York, Melbourne, Madrid and Cape Town: Cambridge University Press, 2003), pp. 112–49.

_____, 'Austria-Hungary and the Brusilov Offensive of 1916', *The Historian* 70(1) (Spring 2008), pp. 30–53.

_____, *Blood on the Snow: The Carpathian Winter War of 1915* (Lawrence, KS: University Press of Kansas, 2010).

Turner, L. C. F., 'The Russian Mobilization in 1914', *Journal of Contemporary History* 3(1) (January 1968), pp. 65–88.

Überegger, O., 'Auf der Flucht vor dem Krieg. Trentiner und Tiroler Deserteure im Ersten Weltkrieg', *Militärgeschichtliche Zeitschrift* 62(2) (2003), pp. 355–93.

Ullrich, V., 'Entscheidung im Osten oder Sicherung der Dardanellen: das Ringen um den Serbienfeldzug 1915', *Militärgeschichtliche Mitteilung* 32(2) (1982), pp. 45–63.

_____, 'Kriegsalltag. Zur inneren Revolutionierung der Wilhelmischen Gesellschaft', in W. Michalka (ed.), *Der Erste Weltkrieg. Wirkung, Wahrnehmung, Analyse* (Munich and Zurich: Piper, 1994), pp. 603–21.

_____, *Vom Augusterlebnis zur Novemberrevolution. Beiträge zur Sozial-geschichte Hamburgs und Norddeutschlands im Ersten Weltkrieg* (Bremen: Donat, 1999).

Ulrich, B., 'Kriegsfreiwillige. Motivationen – Erfahrungen – Wirkungen', in Ber-liner Geschichtswerkstatt (ed.), *August 1914. Ein Volk zieht in den Krieg* (Berlin: Dirk Nishen, 1989), pp. 232–41.

_____, 'Feldpostbriefe im Ersten Weltkrieg – Bedeutung und Zensur', in P. Knoch (ed.), *Kriegsalltag. Die Rekonstruktion des Kriegsalltags als Aufgabe der his-torischen Forschung und der Friedenserziehung* (Stuttgart: J. B. Metzlersche Verlagsbuchhandlung, 1989), pp. 40–83.

_____, 'Die Desillusionierung der Kriegsfreiwilligen von 1914', in W. Wette (ed.), *Der Krieg des kleinen Mannes. Eine Militärgeschichte von unten* (Munich and Zurich: Piper, 1992), pp. 110–26.

_____, *Die Augenzeugen. Deutsche Feldpostbriefe in Kriegs- und Nachkriegszeit 1914–1933* (Essen: Klartext, 1997).

_____, 'Die umkämpfte Erinnerung. Überlegungen zur Wahrnehmung des Ersten Weltkrieges in der Weimarer Republik', in J. Duppler and G. P. Groß (eds.), *Kriegsende 1918. Ereignis, Wirkung, Nachwirkung. Beiträge zur Militärge-schichte. Herausgegeben vom Militärgeschichtlichen Forschungsamt. Band 53* (Munich: R. Oldenbourg, 1999), pp. 367–75.

Ungern-Sternberg, J. von, and Ungern-Sternberg, W. von, *Der Aufruf 'An die Kul-turwelt!' Das Manifest der 93 und die Anfänge der Kriegspropaganda im Ersten Weltkrieg. Mit einer Dokumentation* (Stuttgart: Franz Steiner Verlag, 1996).

Üngör, U. Ü., 'Orphans, Converts, and Prostitutes: Social Consequences of War and Persecution in the Ottoman Empire, 1914–1923', *War in History* 19(2) (April 2012), pp. 173–92.

Unowsky, D. L., *The Pomp and Politics of Patriotism: Imperial Celebrations in Hab-sburg Austria, 1848–1916* (West Lafayette, IN: Purdue University Press, 2005).

_____, 'Peasant Political Mobilization and the 1898 Anti-Jewish Riots in Western Galicia', *European History Quarterly* 40(3) (July 2010), pp. 412–35.

Unruh, K., *Langemarck. Legende und Wirklichkeit* (Koblenz: Bernard & Graefe, 1986).

Verhey, J., *The Spirit of 1914: Militarism, Myth, and Mobilization in Germany* (Cambridge: Cambridge University Press, 2000).

Vermes, G., 'Leap into the Dark: The Issue of Suffrage in Hungary during World War I', in R. A. Kann, B. K. Király and P. S. Fichtner (eds.), *The Habsburg Empire in World War I: Essays on the Intellectual, Military, Political and Eco-nomic Aspects of the Habsburg War Effort* (Boulder, CO, and New York: East European Quarterly and Columbia University Press, 1977), pp. 29–44.

Verosta, S., 'The German Concept of *Mitteleuropa*, 1916–1918, and its Contem-porary Critics', in R. A. Kann, B. K. Király and P. S. Fichtner (eds.), *The Habsburg Empire in World War I: Essays on the Intellectual, Military,*

Political and Economic Aspects of the Habsburg War Effort (Boulder, CO, and New York: East European Quarterly and Columbia University Press, 1977), pp. 203–20.

Volgyes, I., 'Hungarian Prisoners of War in Russia, 1916–1919', *Cahiers du Monde Russe et Soviétique* 14(1/2) (January–June 1973), pp. 54–85.

Volkmann, H.-E., 'Der Ostkrieg 1914/15 als Erlebnis- und Erfahrungswelt des deutschen Militärs', in G. P. Groß (ed.), *Die vergessene Front. Der Osten 1914/15. Ereignis, Wirkung, Nachwirkung* (Paderborn, Munich, Vienna and Zurich: Ferdinand Schöningh, 2006), pp. 263–93.

Vondung, K., 'Deutsche Apokalypse 1914', in K. Vondung (ed.), *Das wilhelminische Bildungsbürgertum. Zur Sozialgeschichte seiner Ideen* (Göttingen: Vandenhoeck und Ruprecht, 1976), pp. 153–71.

Vucinich, W. S., 'Mlada Bosna and the First World War', in R. A. Kann, B. K. Király and P. S. Fichtner (eds.), *The Habsburg Empire in World War I: Essays on the Intellectual, Military, Political and Economic Aspects of the Habsburg War Effort* (Boulder, CO, and New York: East European Quarterly and Columbia University Press, 1977), pp. 45–70.

Wade, R. A., *The Russian Search for Peace, February–October 1917* (Stanford, CA: Stanford University Press, 1969).

Wagner, W., 'Die k.(u.)k. Armee – Gliederung und Aufgabenstellung 1866 bis 1914', in A. Wandruszka and P. Urbanitsch (eds.), *Die Habsburgermonarchie 1848–1918. Band V. Die Bewaffnete Macht* (5 vols., Vienna: Verlag der Österreichische Akademie der Wissenschaften, 1987), pp. 142–633.

Wandruszka, A., and Urbanitsch, P. (eds.), *Die Habsburgermonarchie 1848–1918. Band III. 1. Teilband. Die Völker des Reiches* (Vienna: Verlag der Österreichischen Akademie der Wissenschaften, 1980).

Wandycz, P. S., *The Lands of Partitioned Poland, 1795–1918* (Seattle, WA, and London: University of Washington Press, 1974)

_____, 'The Poles in the Habsburg Monarchy', in A. S. Markovits and F. E. Sysyn (eds.), *Nationbuilding and the Politics of Nationalism: Essays on Austrian Galicia* (Cambridge, MA: Harvard University Press, 1982), pp. 68–93.

Wank, S., 'Some Reflections on Conrad von Hötzendorf and His Memoirs Based on Old and New Sources', *Austrian History Yearbook* 1 (1965), pp. 74–88.

_____, 'Foreign Policy and the Nationality Problem in Austria-Hungary, 1867–1914', *Austrian History Yearbook* 3 (1967), pp. 37–56.

_____, 'Desperate Counsel in Vienna in July 1914: Berthold Molden's Unpublished Memorandum', *Central European History* 26(3) (September 1993), pp. 281–310.

_____, 'Some Reflections on the Habsburg Empire and its Legacy in the Nationalities Question', *Austrian History Yearbook* 28 (1997), pp. 131–46.

_____, *In the Twilight of Empire: Count Alois Lexa von Aehrenthal (1854–1912), Imperial Habsburg Patriot and Statesman. Vol. 1: The Making of an Imperial*

Habsburg Patriot and Statesman (2 vols., Vienna, Cologne and Weimar: Böhlau, 2009).

Wargelin, C. F., 'A High Price for Bread: The First Treaty of Brest-Litovsk and the Break-Up of Austria-Hungary, 1917–1918', *The International History Review* 19(4) (November 1997), pp. 757–88.

——, 'The Economic Collapse of Austro-Hungarian Dualism, 1914–1918', *East European Quarterly* 34(3) (September 2000), pp. 261–88.

——, 'The Austro-Polish Solution: Diplomacy, Politics and State Building in Wartime Austria-Hungary, 1914–1918', *East European Quarterly* 42(3) (September 2008), pp. 253–73.

Watson, A., '"For Kaiser and Reich": The Identity and Fate of the German Volunteers, 1914–1918', *War in History* 12(1) (January 2005), pp. 44–74.

——, 'Self-Deception and Survival: Mental Coping Strategies on the Western Front, 1914–18', *Journal of Contemporary History* 41(2) (April 2006), pp. 247–68.

——, 'Junior Officership in the German Army during the Great War, 1914–1918', *War in History* 14(4) (November 2007), pp. 429–53.

——, 'Culture and Combat in the Western World, 1900–1945', *The Historical Journal* 51(2) (June 2008), pp. 529–46.

——, *Enduring the Great War: Combat, Morale and Collapse in the German and British Armies, 1914–1918* (Cambridge: Cambridge University Press, 2008).

——, 'Fighting for Another Fatherland: The Polish Minority in the German Army, 1914–1918', *The English Historical Review* 126(522) (October 2011), pp. 1137–66.

——, 'Voluntary Enlistment in the Great War: A European Phenomenon?', in C. Krüger and S. Levsen (eds.), *War Volunteering in Modern Times: From the French Revolution to the Second World War* (Basingstoke and New York: Palgrave Macmillan, 2011), pp. 163–88.

——, 'Morale', in J. Winter (ed.), *The Cambridge History of the First World War. Vol. II: The State* (3 vols., Cambridge: Cambridge University Press, 2014), pp. 174–95.

——, '"Unheard of Brutality": Russian Atrocities against Civilians in East Prussia, 1914–15', *The Journal of Modern History* 86(4) (December 2014), forthcoming.

—— and Porter, P., 'Bereaved and Aggrieved: Combat Motivation and the Ideology of Sacrifice in the First World War', *Historical Research* 83(219) (February 2010), pp. 146–64.

Wawro, G., 'Morale in the Austro-Hungarian Army: The Evidence of Habsburg Army Campaign Reports and Allied Intelligence Officers', in H. Cecil and P. H. Liddle (eds.), *Facing Armageddon: The First World War Experienced* (London: Leo Cooper, 1996), pp. 399–412.

Weber, F. C., '"Wir wollen nicht hilflos zu Grunde gehen!" Zur Ernährungskrise der Steiermark im Ersten Weltkrieg und ihren politisch-sozialen Auswirkungen', *Blätter für Heimatkunde* 74(3) (2000), pp. 96–131.

Weber, T., *Hitler's First War: Adolf Hitler, the Men of the List Regiment, and the First World War* (Oxford: Oxford University Press, 2010).

Wegs, J. R., 'Transportation: The Achilles Heel of the Habsburg War Effort', in R. A. Kann, B. K. Király and P. S. Fichtner (eds.), *The Habsburg Empire in World War I: Essays on the Intellectual, Military, Political and Economic Aspects of the Habsburg War Effort* (Boulder, CO, and New York: East European Quarterly and Columbia University Press, 1977), pp. 121–34.

Wehler, H.-U., *The German Empire, 1871–1918* (Leamington Spa and Dover, NH: Berg, 1985).

Welch, D., *Germany, Propaganda and Total War, 1914–1918: The Sins of Omission* (London: The Athlone Press, 2000).

Wendland, A. V., 'Post-Austrian Lemberg: War Commemoration, Interethnic Relations, and Urban Identity in L'viv, 1918–1939', *Austrian History Yearbook* 34 (2003), pp. 83–102.

Westerhoff, C., *Zwangsarbeit im Ersten Weltkrieg. Deutsche Arbeitskräftepolitik im besetzten Polen und Litauen 1914–1918* (Paderborn, Munich, Vienna and Zurich: Ferdinand Schöningh, 2012).

Wette, W., 'Die militärische Demobilmachung in Deutschland 1918/19 unter besonderer Berücksichtigung der revolutionären Ostseestadt Kiel', *Geschichte und Gesellschaft* 12(1) (1986), pp. 63–80.

Whalen, R. W., *Bitter Wounds: German Victims of the Great War, 1914–1939* (Ithaca, NY, and London: Cornell University Press, 1984).

Wieland, L., 'Der deutsche Englandhass im Ersten Weltkrieg und seine Vorgeschichte', in W. Alff (ed.), *Deutschlands Sonderung von Europa 1862–1945* (Frankfurt am Main, Bern and New York: Peter Lang, 1984), pp. 317–53.

Wilcox, V., 'Discipline in the Italian Army, 1915–1918', in P. Purseigle (ed.), *Warfare and Belligerence: Perspectives in First World War Studies* (Leiden and Boston, MA: Brill, 2005), pp. 73–100.

———, 'Generalship and Mass Surrender during the Italian Defeat at Caporetto', in I. F. Beckett (ed.), *1917: Beyond the Western Front* (Leiden and Boston, MA: Brill, 2009), pp. 25–46.

Wildman, A. K., *The End of the Russian Imperial Army: The Old Army and the Soldiers' Revolt (March–April 1917). Vol. I* (2 vols., Princeton, NJ, and Guildford: Princeton University Press, 1980).

Williamson, Jr, S. R., 'Influence, Power, and the Policy Process: The Case of Franz Ferdinand, 1906–1914', *The Historical Journal* 17(2) (June 1974), pp. 417–34.

———, *Austria-Hungary and the Origins of the First World War* (Basingstoke and London: Macmillan, 1991).

_____, 'Aggressive and Defensive Aims of Political Elites? Austro-Hungarian Policy in 1914', in H. Afflerbach and D. Stevenson (eds.), *An Improbable War: The Outbreak of World War I and European Political Culture Before 1914* (New York and Oxford: Berghahn, 2007), pp. 61–74.

_____ and May, E. R., 'An Identity of Opinion: Historians and July 1914', *The Journal of Modern History* 79(2) (June 2007), pp. 335–87.

Wilson, A., *The Ukrainians: Unexpected Nation*, 2nd edn (New Haven, CT: Yale Nota Bene, 2002).

Wilson. K. M., 'Understanding the "Misunderstanding" of 1 August 1914', *The Historical Journal* 37(4) (December 1994), pp. 885–9.

Winkle, R., *Der Dank des Vaterlandes. Eine Symbolgeschichte des Eisernen Kreuzes 1914 bis 1936* (Essen: Klartext, 2007).

Winter, J., *Sites of Memory, Sites of Mourning: The Great War in European Cultural History* (Cambridge: Cambridge University Press, 1995).

Wittmann, K., 'Firmenerfolg durch Vermarktung von Nationalbewußtsein? Die Werbestrategie des Markenartiklers Bleyle vor und im Ersten Weltkrieg', in G. Hirschfeld, G. Krumeich, D. Langewiesche and H.-P. Ullmann (eds.), *Kriegserfahrungen. Studien zur Sozial- und Mentalitätsgeschichte des Ersten Weltkriegs* (Essen: Klartext, 1997), pp. 302–22.

Wolff, L., *The Idea of Galicia: History and Fantasy in Habsburg Political Culture* (Stanford, CA: Stanford University Press, 2010).

Wood, N. D., 'Becoming a "Great City": Metropolitan Imaginations and Apprehensions in Cracow's Popular Press, 1900–1914', *Austrian History Yearbook* 33 (2002), pp. 105–29.

Wróbel, P., 'Przed Odzyskaniem Niepodległości', in J. Tomaszewski et al. (ed.), *Najnowsze Dzieje żydów w Polsce w zarysie (do 1950 roku)* (Warsaw: Wydawnictwo Naukowe PWN, 1993), pp. 13–39.

_____, 'The Jews of Galicia under Austro-Polish Rule, 1869–1918', *Austrian History Yearbook* 25 (1994), pp. 97–138.

Wurzer, G., 'Die Erfahrung der Extreme. Kriegsgefangene in Rußland 1914–1918', in J. Oltmer (ed.), *Kriegsgefangene im Europa des Ersten Weltkriegs* (Paderborn, Munich, Vienna and Zurich: Ferdinand Schöningh, 2006), pp. 97–125.

Xu, G., *Strangers on the Western Front: Chinese Workers in the Great War* (Cambridge, MA: Harvard University Press, 2011).

Yanikdağ, Y., 'Ottoman Prisoners of War in Russia, 1914–22', *Journal of Contemporary History* 34(1) (January 1999), pp. 69–85.

Zabecki, D. T., *The German 1918 Offensives: A Case Study in the Operational Level of War* (Abingdon and New York: Routledge, 2006).

_____, 'Railroads and the Operational Level of War in the German 1918 Offensives', in J. D. Keene and M. S. Neiberg (eds.), *Finding Common Ground: New Directions in First World War Studies* (Leiden and Boston, MA: Brill, 2011), pp. 161–86.

Zahra, T., *Kidnapped Souls: National Indifference and the Battle for Children in the Bohemian Lands, 1900–1948* (Ithaca, NY, and London: Cornell University Press, 2008).

———, 'The "Minority Problem" and National Classification in the French and Czechoslovak Borderlands', *Contemporary European History* 17(2) (May 2008), pp. 137–65.

———, 'Imagined Noncommunities: National Indifference as a Category of Analysis', *Slavic Review* 69(1) (Spring 2010), pp. 93–119.

Zechlin, E., *Die deutsche Politik und die Juden im Ersten Weltkrieg* (Göttingen: Vandenhoeck & Ruprecht, 1969).

———, 'Ludendorff im Jahre 1915. Unveröffentlichte Briefe', *Historische Zeitschrift* 211(2) (October 1970), pp. 316–53.

Zeman, Z. A. B., *The Break-Up of the Habsburg Empire, 1914–1918: A Study in National and Social Revolution* (London, New York and Toronto: Oxford University Press, 1961).

Zgórniak, M., 'Polacy w armii austro-węgierskiej w czasie I Wojny Światowej', *Studia i materiały do historii wojskowości* 30 (1988), pp. 227–46.

Ziemann, B., 'Fahnenflucht im deutschen Heer 1914–1918', *Militärgeschichtliche Mitteilungen* 55 (1996), pp. 93–130.

———, 'Verweigerungsformen von Frontsoldaten in der deutschen Armee 1914–1918', in A. Gestrich (ed.), *Gewalt im Krieg. Ausübung, Erfahrung und Verweigerung von Gewalt in Kriegen des 20. Jahrhunderts* (Münster: Lit, 1996), pp. 99–122.

———, *Front und Heimat. Ländliche Kriegserfahrung im südlichen Bayern 1914–1923* (Essen: Klartext, 1997).

———, 'Enttäuschte Erwartung und kollektive Erschöpfung. Die deutschen Soldaten an der Westfront 1918 auf dem Weg zur Revolution', in J. Duppler and G. P. Groß (eds.), *Kriegsende 1918. Ereignis, Wirkung, Nachwirkung. Beiträge zur Militärgeschichte. Herausgegeben vom Militärgeschichtlichen Forschungsamt. Band 53* (Munich: R. Oldenbourg, 1999), pp. 165–82.

———, 'Germany 1914–1918: Total War as a Catalyst of Change', in H. Walser Smith (ed.), *The Oxford Handbook of Modern German History* (Oxford: Oxford University Press, 2011), pp. 378–99.

———, *Gewalt im Ersten Weltkrieg. Töten – Überleben – Verweigerung* (Essen: Klartext, 2013).

Zimmerer, J., 'Holocaust und Kolonialismus. Beitrag zu einer Archäologie des genozidalen Gedankens', *Zeitschrift für Geschichtswissenschaft* 51(12) (2003), pp. 1098–1119.

———, 'War, Concentration Camps and Genocide in South-West Africa: The First German Genocide', in J. Zimmerer and J. Zeller (eds.), *Genocide in German South-West Africa: The Colonial War (1904–1908) in Namibia and its aftermath* (Monmouth: The Merlin Press, 2003), pp. 41–63.

Zuber, T., 'The Schlieffen Plan Reconsidered', *War in History* 6(3) (July 1999), pp. 262–305.

———, 'Der Mythos vom Schlieffenplan', in H. Ehlert, M. Epkenhans and G. P. Groß (eds.), *Der Schlieffenplan. Analysen und Dokumente* (Paderborn, Munich, Vienna and Zurich: Ferdinand Schöningh, 2006), pp. 45–78.

———, *The Battle of the Frontiers: Ardennes 1914* (Stroud: The History Press, 2007, 2009).

Zunkel, F., 'Die ausländischen Arbeiter in der deutschen Kriegswirtschaftspolitik des 1. Weltkrieges', in *Entstehung und Wandel der modernen Gesellschaft. Festschrift für Hans Rosenberg zum 65. Geburtstag*, ed. G. A. Ritter (Berlin: Walter de Gruyter & Co., 1970), pp. 280–311.

UNPUBLISHED DISSERTATIONS

Brennan, C., 'Reforming Austria-Hungary: Beyond his Control or Beyond his Capacity? The Domestic Policies of Emperor Karl I, November 1916–May 1917', unpublished PhD thesis, London School of Economics (2012).

Dammelhart, T., 'Kleine Stadt im Großen Krieg. Kriegswirtschaft im 1. Weltkrieg, dargestellt am Beispiel der Stadt Retz', unpublished PhD thesis, University of Vienna (2001).

Hämmerle, C., '"Zur Liebesarbeit sind wir hier, Soldatenstrümpfe stricken wir . . ." Zu Formen weiblicher *Kriegsfürsorge* im Ersten Weltkrieg', unpublished PhD thesis, University of Vienna (1996).

Hecht, R., 'Fragen zur Heeresergänzung der gesamten bewaffneten Macht Österreich-Ungarns während des Ersten Weltkrieges', unpublished PhD thesis, University of Vienna (1969).

Houlihan, P. J., 'Clergy in the Trenches: Catholic Military Chaplains of Germany and Austria-Hungary during the First World War', unpublished PhD thesis, University of Chicago (2011).

Jeřábek, R., 'Die Brussilowoffensive 1916. Ein Wendepunkt der Koalitionskriegführung der Mittelmächte', 2 vols., unpublished PhD thesis, University of Vienna (1982).

Kauffman, J. C., 'Sovereignty and the Search for Order in German-Occupied Poland, 1915–1918', unpublished PhD thesis, Stanford University (2008).

Mentzel, W., 'Kriegsflüchtlinge in Cisleithanien im Ersten Weltkrieg', unpublished PhD thesis, University of Vienna (1997).

Rice, A. K., 'Morale and Defeatism in the Bavarian "Heer und Heimat" in the First World War (1916–18)', unpublished MPhil thesis, University of Oxford (2004).

Solanský, A., 'German Administration in Belgium', unpublished PhD thesis, Columbia University (1928).

Teicht, A., 'Die Offiziersausbildung in Bayern während des I. Weltkriegs', unpublished Pädagogik Diplomarbeit, Hochschule der Bundeswehr Munich (1978).

Wassermeier, O., 'Die Meutereien der Heimkehrer aus russischer Kriegsgefangenschaft bei den Ersatzkörpern der k.u.k. Armee im Jahre 1918', unpublished PhD thesis, University of Vienna (1968).

Wegs, J. R., 'Austrian Economic Mobilization during World War I: With Particular Emphasis on Heavy Industry', unpublished PhD thesis, University of Illinois (1970).

Zroka, R. E., 'If Only this War would End: German Soldiers in the Last Year of the First World War', unpublished PhD thesis, University of California, San Diego (2013).

Index

Russia – *cont.*
  'Plan 19' 160
  and Poland 148, 182, 411
  Provisional Government 509
  and Reinsurance Treaty 30
  religion 90
  revolutions 5, 31, 403, 413, 417,
    450, 451, 454, 455, 458, 461,
    470, 474, 513, 544;
    consequences of 478, 479,
    483, 553
  and Serbia 8
  South-west Front 161
  SPD and 456
  spy network in Galicia 151
  Stavka (High Command) 161, 189,
    194, 196, 197, 302
  and Turkish straits 275
  and Ukraine 269
  Workers' and Soldiers' Council 460
  see also Soviet Union
Russian Orthodox Church 20, 90, 192–3
Russians
  in eastern territories 267, 399
  as prisoners of war 389–90
Russo-Japanese War 150
Russophilia 19–20, 149, 151–2, 155
Ruthenes 19, 155, 190–91, 203, 206,
    559 aspirations of 471
  in Austria 200, 273–4
  in Austro-Hungarian army
    115 (Table 4), 253, 286 (Table
    5), 308
  Conrad on 154, 197
  evicted by Habsburg army 186
  executions and military violence
    against 154–6, 158
  in Galicia 19–20, 154–5, 269,
    497, 499
  in Habsburg Empire 16 (Table 1)
  loyalty to Habsburg regime 151
  in Lwów 546
  as refugees 203
  religion 20, 191, 192
  Russians and 182, 184, 190–92,
    193, 197–8
  and security troops 540

  Ukrainian nationalists (Ukrainophiles)
    19, 97, 148–9, 181, 191, 197
Rutowski, Tadeusz 190

Saar district 107, 464
Šabac 142, 143, 145
sabotage, on farms 391
sacrifice, as concept 564–5
St Petersburg 12, 14, 191
Sakrau 69
Salandra, Antonio 246
Salonika (Thessaloniki) 25
Salzburg 91
  People's Kitchens 355
  refugees in 202
  War Assistance Bureau 214
Šámal, Přemysl 250
Sambre, river 126
Samsonov, General Aleksandr 166,
    171, 173
San, river 140, 149, 156
Santoppen 174
Sarajevo
  anti-Serb riots in 57–8, 60
  see also Franz Ferdinand, Archduke:
    assassination
Saxony 368, 379, 424
  Prussian 443
Sazonov, Sergei 38, 42–3, 46
Scandinavia 419, 435, 436
Scarborough 238
Scheer, Admiral Reinhard 425, 551, 552
Scheer Programme 551
Scheidemann, Philipp 81, 261, 456,
    459, 515, 555
Scheüch, General Heinrich 549
Schiller, Friedrich, *Wallenstein's Camp* 214
Schleswig 180
Schlieffen, Alfred Graf von 104–7
Schlieffen Plan 106–8, 122
schools 365
Schulenburg, Colonel Count von der
    515–6
Schweinemord 234
Schwerin, Friedrich von 272
Scotland 426, 441
Scutari (Shkodra) 26

ALLEN LANE
an imprint of
PENGUIN BOOKS

Recently Published

Dominic Lieven, *Towards the Flame: Empire, War and the End of Tsarist Russia*

Noel Malcolm, *Agents of Empire: Knights, Corsairs, Jesuits and Spies in the Sixteenth-Century Mediterranean World*

James Rebanks, *The Shepherd's Life: A Tale of the Lake District*

David Brooks, *The Road to Character*

Joseph Stiglitz, *The Great Divide*

Ken Robinson and Lou Aronica, *Creative Schools: Revolutionizing Education from the Ground Up*

Clotaire Rapaille and Andrés Roemer, *Move UP: Why Some Cultures Advances While Others Don't*

Jonathan Keates, *William III and Mary II: Partners in Revolution*

David Womersley, *James II: The Last Catholic King*

Richard Barber, *Henry II: A Prince Among Princes*

Jane Ridley, *Victoria: Queen, Matriarch, Empress*

John Gray, *The Soul of the Marionette: A Short Enquiry into Human Freedom*

Emily Wilson, *Seneca: A Life*

Michael Barber, *How to Run a Government: So That Citizens Benefit and Taxpayers Don't Go Crazy*

Dana Thomas, *Gods and Kings: The Rise and Fall of Alexander McQueen and John Galliano*

Steven Weinberg, *To Explain the World: The Discovery of Modern Science*

Jennifer Jacquet, *Is Shame Necessary?: New Uses for an Old Tool*

Eugene Rogan, *The Fall of the Ottomans: The Great War in the Middle East, 1914-1920*